# The Gospel of John

# The Gospel of John
## A Commentary

## VOLUME II

Craig S. Keener

HENDRICKSON
PUBLISHERS

Hendrickson Publishers, LLC
P. O. Box 3473
Peabody, Massachusetts 01961-3473

ISBN 978-1-59856-537-9

*Printed in the United States of America*

*First Printing Softcover Edition — March 2010*

**Library of Congress Cataloging-in-Publication Data**

Keener, Craig S., 1960–
      The Gospel of John : a commentary  /  Craig S. Keener.
         p. cm.
      Includes bibliographical references and index.
      ISBN 1-56563-378-4 (hardcover : alk. paper)
      1. Bible. N.T. John—Commentaries.  I. Title.
      BS2615.53.K44 2003
      226.5′07—dc22

                                                    2003016153

# 11:1–12:50

# INTRODUCING THE PASSION

Technically, the introduction to the passion stretches from 11:1 (or, more generally, from 1:19!) to the passion proper; but we have separated 13:1–17:26 (technically, perhaps 13:31–17:26) to mark off the last discourse, which constitutes a major component of the passion introduction. Some commentators view chs. 11 and 12 as an interlude between the two halves of the Gospel.[1]

---

[1] E.g., Burridge, *One Jesus,* 137.

# DYING TO LIVE

## 11:1–12:11

TO RAISE LAZARUS FROM THE DEAD, Jesus would have to go to Judea, the place of hostility, risking (and ultimately encountering) death (11:7–8, 14–16).[1] Lazarus was the "friend" of Jesus and the disciples (11:11),[2] and therefore it was appropriate to die for him (15:13–15). Yet once Lazarus receives life, he must likewise share Jesus' death (12:10–11).

### Raising Lazarus (11:1–44)

This climactic sign of Jesus' ministry joins the opening sign in framing Jesus' public ministry. The opening sign (2:1–11) recounts Jesus' benevolence at a wedding; the last involves it at a funeral. The joy of weddings and mourning of funerals could function as opposites in ancient literature.[3] While few of Jesus' signs in John's Gospel specifically parallel Moses' signs, his first and last signs may be exceptions.[4] In both cases, the signs may suggest contrasts: whereas Moses' first sign was transforming water to blood, Jesus benevolently transforms it into wine. Likewise, whereas the final plague against Egypt was the death of the firstborn sons, the climax of Jesus' signs is raising a dead brother-provider.

### 1. John's Account

Many are skeptical of pre-Johannine tradition in the narrative about Lazarus's raising, because the story seems too central to Jesus' ministry to have been unknown to the Synoptic writers and, if known, not mentioned by them. Some have even proposed that John composed the story by weaving together various elements of Lukan tradition.[5] To be sure,

---

[1] He would also go to Lazarus, who was dead (11:14–15), which Thomas ironically misinterprets—yet inadvertently correctly applies—as Jesus going to the realm of death and his disciples following him there (11:16).

[2] Since "friend" applies to all disciples (15:15), there is no reason to find in the cognate "beloved" (11:3) an allusion to the "beloved" disciple (*pace* Nepper-Christensen, "Discipel," and others; see our introduction, pp. 84–89) or to one of two such disciples in the Gospel (Vicent Cernuda, "Desvaído").

[3] Cf. Jer 7:34; Matt 11:17; *p. Ketub.* 1:1, §6; comments in Keener, *Matthew,* 300.

[4] There are other exodus parallels (e.g., 3:14), but paralleling the signs and plagues could work at best only at the level of general categories (contrast explicit parallels in Rev 8–9; 16): perhaps darkness for healing the blind (Exod 10:21–22; John 9:5), but then why does John mention darkness in 8:12 and 12:35, 46 but mention only "night" in 9:4? Crop-destroying locusts (Exod 10:13–14) could oppose the bread of life, but its exodus background is really manna; likewise, Jesus heals (4:50–53; 5:8–9; 9:7) but the object is not boils (Exod 9:9–11).

[5] Pearce, "Raising"; cf. the caution of Smith, *John* (1999), 217. A connection with Luke 10:38–39, while unlikely, is more plausible than the allusion to the parable of Lazarus (Luke 16:20;

the story has much symbolic significance for the author of the Fourth Gospel;[6] proposed external corroborations for the story are weak.[7]

Other scholars have responded that Mark tends to omit much of Jesus' Judean ministry anyway, partly due to a theological emphasis on Galilee.[8] Further, for the Synoptics Jesus' raisings of the dead were simply dramatic healings. Also, whereas John may emphasize Lazarus's restoration to prefigure Jesus' resurrection, Mark may not wish to risk diminishing the appearance of the uniqueness of Jesus' resurrection as an eschatological event.[9] It is even possible that Mark may have suppressed the story to protect Lazarus and his sisters, who still lived near Jerusalem.[10] If the story was originally part of the passion narrative, one might expect protective anonymity, as in the case of some other disciples who figured prominently in it (e.g., Mark 14:51–52);[11] but in this instance the story was well-known enough that drawing attention to it, even anonymously, could have caused trouble for the family (John 12:10–11). By contrast, if the story was not originally part of the passion narrative, Mark is no more obligated to report this event than the resuscitation at Nain (Luke 7:11–17; Q mentioned multiple raisings, Matt 11:5/Luke 7:22) or dramatic healings such as the centurion's servant (Matt 8:5–13/Luke 7:1–10). If the early passion narrative or, alternatively, Mark, suppressed or simply omitted the story, Matthew and Luke may not have known of it or may not have understood it as critical to the movement of the story in the way John does. John's community does seem to have already known of Mary's involvement in the final anointing of Jesus (see comment on 11:2).

A number of scholars have concluded that the story probably has a historical core.[12] As difficult as it is to distinguish tradition and redaction anywhere in this Gospel, including in this narrative,[13] Meier provides convincing evidence that the Lazarus story goes back to John's tradition, though it was originally a brief story unrelated to Jesus' passion. Hence he does not regard it as surprising that the Synoptics omit it.[14] By all critical approaches other than a philosophical predisposition against it, traditions indicate a popular belief that at least on some occasions Jesus raised the dead.[15] It may be significant that third-century rabbis acknowledged these raisings but attributed them to necromancy;[16]

---

the figure in the parable—who is not raised—could as easily derive from the event later reported in John; both stories are quite different, as noted by Streeter, *Gospels,* 389); Eleazar was a common name (see below).

[6] Nevertheless, even Gamble, "Philosophy," 55, denies that the narrative is allegorical, emphasizing the realism of the narrative.

[7] Smith, *John* (1999), 216–17, points to Jesus raising a young man in Bethany at his sisters' request in *Secret Gospel of Mark;* but this document is at worst spurious and at best post-Johannine (see Stanton, *Gospel Truth,* 93; Brown, *Death,* 297).

[8] Harris, "Dead," 312.

[9] Michaels, *Servant,* 197–98.

[10] Harris, "Dead," 312.

[11] See Theissen, *Gospels,* 186–88.

[12] Blomberg, *Reliability,* cites Sabourin, *Miracles;* Latourelle, *Miracles;* Hunter, "John 11:41b–42"; Harris, "Dead"; Twelftree, *Miracle Worker.* Not surprisingly, some of these studies reflect an apologetic tendency; equally unsurprisingly, some of the most skeptical writers on the passage reflect a thoroughgoing skeptical tendency.

[13] See rightly Harris, "Dead," 311.

[14] Meier, *Marginal Jew,* 2:798–832. On our view of authorship, which allows for the story to derive from an eyewitness account, the story has nevertheless been recast for its function in the whole Gospel narrative.

[15] Meier, *Marginal Jew,* 2:773–873.

[16] Stauffer, *Jesus,* 101, unconvincingly seeks to make Luke 16:31 an early response to that charge.

they may, however, well be responding to later Christian claims from the Gospels rather than to the traditions behind the Gospels. Although some ancients told resuscitation stories with a degree of skepticism, most of the ancient Mediterranean culture, including reports from the Hebrew Bible, accepted that raisings sometimes occurred.[17] They appear commonly enough in both Greek[18] and Jewish[19] sources, though the records follow the reported events by a much greater span of time than those in the Gospels.[20] Sorcerers might sometimes be thought to resuscitate corpses,[21] but (apart from lacking modern Western antisupernaturalist sentiments) such accounts have nothing in common with the Gospel reports: they include drilling holes to pour in hot blood, the moon's poison, the froth of dogs, and so forth.[22] They also worked at night when no one could see them,[23] for their works were considered impious and worthy of death.[24] If anything, John's account undercuts accusations of secretive, magical activity (cf. 18:20). The "resurrection" that became a familiar topic in ancient novels was most frequently only apparent resurrection from apparent death (so as not to strain credulity) and seems to have responded especially to the spread of the Christian story.[25]

Whatever its origins, this story is critical for John's plot development. This is the longest single sign account in the Fourth Gospel, and, apart from the Passion Narrative, the longest narrative without a substantial discourse section. In John's schema "it is the climactic and most miraculous episode in the series of signs he presents."[26] Whereas in Mark Jesus dies because he challenges the municipal aristocracy of Jerusalem by his prophetic act in the temple, in John Jesus dies most immediately because he has given life to a disciple (11:14–16, 50–52; 12:9–11).[27] That Jesus dies to give life fits, on a symbolic level, the very heart of John's soteriological message (3:16–17). Historically Jesus was already in trouble, even in the Fourth Gospel, which may have left the significance of the miracle ambiguous enough for some other writers to omit it;[28] but its significance is unmistakable for John.[29]

---

[17] Meier, *Marginal Jew*, 2:773. Some reports involve natural resuscitations (e.g., Valerius Maximus 1.8.12; 1.8.*ext*.1).

[18] E.g., with Asclepius (Grant, *Gods*, 66; Aeschylus *Agamemnon* 1022–1024; Euripides *Alc.* 124–130; Pausanias 2.26.5; 2.27.4; Apollodorus 3.10.3), Empedocles (Diogenes Laertius 8.2.59), and many others (Apollodorus 2.5.12; 2.6.2; 3.3.1; 3.5.3; Bultmann, *Tradition*, 233–34; Blackburn, "ΑΝΔΡΕΣ," 190, citing, e.g., Pliny *Nat.* 7.124; Apuleius *Florida* 19). Often deities proved unable to resuscitate the dead (Ovid *Metam.* 2.617–618; 4.247–249).

[19] Fairly rarely in the rabbis (*b. B. Qam.* 117a; *p. Šeb.* 9:1, §13, 38d) and more frequently in Jewish (*T. Ab.* 18:11A; 14:6B) and Christian (*Acts John* 47, 52, 73–80; *Acts of Peter* [8] 28) religious fiction. Cf. 1 Kgs 17:17–24; 2 Kgs 4:18–37.

[20] Cf., e.g., Harvey, *History*, 100, on the differences.

[21] E.g., Ovid *Amores* 1.8.17–18. In a Latin novel, an Egyptian magician could reportedly resuscitate a corpse (Apuleius *Metam.* 2.28), although the person might not wish to leave Hades (*Metam.* 2.29; cf. 1 Sam 28:15).

[22] Lucan *C.W.* 6.667–775.

[23] Ovid *Amores* 1.8.13–14.

[24] Heliodorus *Aeth.* 6.14–15.

[25] See Bowersock, *Fiction as History*, 99–113, though he connects the spread of this motif too closely with early Christian influence.

[26] Witherington, *Women*, 106; cf. Harris, "Dead," 313.

[27] See, e.g., Dodd, *More Studies*, 58.

[28] Dunkerley, "Lazarus," 326; Harris, "Dead," 313.

[29] Interestingly, later rabbis also relate Jesus' execution to his miracle-working, there called magic (*b. Sanh.* 43a), as Stauffer, *Jesus*, 103, points out; but the tradition is late and may well be secondary on this point.

## 2. The Request (11:1–6)

In this account Jesus does his Father's will, recognizing what such obedience will cost him; as in previous narratives (e.g., 4:4), Jesus' movements follow divine necessity, and thereby provide a model for the believer (cf. 3:8, though it explicitly refers only to the oirgin and destination). In 7:1–10 others close to Jesus sought to persuade him to go to Jerusalem, but Jesus objects. In 11:1–16, Jesus announces that he is going in spite of his disciples' objection; the contrast between the narratives stems from the fact that in 7:1–10, Jesus' time had not yet come (7:6); now his "hour" is arriving.[30]

Ancient writers sometimes assumed knowledge shared by their readers when recounting something commonly known; given the wide circulation of the Synoptics, undoubtedly the anointing at Bethany was such an incident (Mark 14:3, 9).[31] That Bethany is identified as the village of "Mary and her sister Martha" but that Lazarus's identity must be explained suggests that Mary and Martha are already known to the audience. Further, "Lazarus is wholly passive and silent," making his sisters the main characters of this narrative and their faith the primary issue.[32] Martha (11:1, 5; 12:2) was an uncommon but sufficiently attested Jewish name in this period,[33] including in the Diaspora;[34] Eleazar is a more common Jewish name, sometimes occurring in transliteration in Greek[35] and sometimes occurring in an alternative Greek form, Lazarus (11:1).[36] Because Mary, Martha, and Eleazar (sometimes "Lazarus" in Greek) appear together among names in a burial cave in Bethany, some suspect that these may be the friends of Jesus mentioned in this narrative.[37] John shows no clear knowledge of the story in Luke 10:38–42, which independently and earlier attests Mary and Martha as friends of Jesus in a village. John also writes about Mary's anointing of Jesus' feet (12:1–8) as if his audience already knows that a particular Mary anointed Jesus' feet (11:2), evidencing pre-Johannine tradition on this count even though that tradition is no longer extant outside this Gospel.[38]

Miracle stories often include messengers sent to request a miracle worker's coming.[39] It seems to have been customary to report to a rabbi if someone close to him, such as his

---

[30] Meeks, *Prophet-King*, 59.

[31] Xenophon *Cyr.* 7.2.15 assumes his audience's knowledge of the common story of Croesus and the Delphic oracle (cf. Herodotus 1.46–48; Xenophon does this elsewhere, cf. Brownson, "Introduction," x); 2 Chr 32:31 seems to assume knowledge of the story preserved in 2 Kgs 20:12–21.

[32] Grayston, *Gospel*, 89–90.

[33] On a Jerusalem ossuary, see *CIJ* 2:264, §1261; 2:265, §1263; 2:290, §1311. See also *Sipre Deut.* 281.1.2.

[34] E.g., *CPJ* 2:19, §147; 2:20–22, §148; *CIJ* 1:417, §566.

[35] In various forms, see, e.g., *CPJ* 3:175.

[36] E.g., *CIJ* 2:139, §935; 2:140, §938. Lazarus also appears in Hebrew (*CPJ* 3:183), but Λάζαρος explicitly translates אלעזר, Eleazar, in *CIJ* 2:123, §899 (undated, from Joppa in Palestine). Vermes, *Jesus the Jew*, 190–91, argues that "Lazarus" is a Galilean form because Galileans typically dropped the opening gutteral in Aramaic. By this period, however, the form was probably more widely distributed.

[37] Yamauchi, *Stones*, 121; cf. Finegan, *Archeology*, 240. For a more contemporary excavation report of a Second Temple period tomb from Bethany, see Loffreda, "Tombe" (also including Byzantine data); the *hospitium* of Martha and Mary in Bethany is Byzantine (Taylor, "Cave").

[38] Witherington, *Women*, 104; Haenchen, *John*, 2:57. There is no need to see the verse as a later addition to the text (cf. 1:40); it may point the reader forward to Jesus' passion (O'Day, "John," 685–86).

[39] Theissen, *Stories*, 49, cites, e.g., Acts 9:36; *b. Ber.* 34b; Lucian *Philops.* 11; Philostratus *Vit. Apoll.* 4.10.

teacher, was ill, so that the rabbi could visit him.[40] The message of Mary and Martha, however, is an implied request (11:3), as in 2:3; in both cases, Jesus fails to act immediately (2:4; 11:6). If Martha presses her request by her mention of "whatever" Jesus "asks" (11:22), she echoes Jesus' mother in 2:5.[41] Such polite forms of insistence would have been intelligible in an ancient Mediterranean milieu (see comment on 1:37–39). In John 2, Jesus does the sign secretly, so that only his disciples and the servants know (2:9, 11); in ch.11, however, he does his sign even in front of those who will respond negatively (11:46)—because now his hour has come (2:4).

The purpose of Lazarus's sickness was not "for death" (πρὸς θάνατον, 11:4; applied figuratvely in 1 John 5:16 for spiritual death). Instead, the purpose of the sickness is to provide opportunity for God to manifest his glory (11:4; cf. 11:40),[42] as in 9:3; John's teaching that suffering can provide the opportunity for divine intervention foreshadows the significance of Jesus' own death and resurrection. Lazarus's sickness and raising also lead to and prefigure Jesus' death and resurrection.[43] Of course, in John's theology physical death could also bring God glory (12:23–24; 13:31; 21:19), just as Jesus' signs would (2:11). To the informed, repeated reader of this Gospel, the promise of Jesus' glorification through Lazarus's death constitutes a double entendre: Jesus is glorified because Lazarus's raising leads directly to Jesus' arrest and passion, by which he is "glorified" (12:23–24).

Given the urgency of the request for a miracle worker, Jesus' delaying could appear to dishonor the family and trivialize its suffering;[44] even if Lazarus would have died before his arrival, the family was counting on his rapid arrival. Lest readers misunderstand the reason for Jesus' delay (11:6), John explicitly emphasizes Jesus' love for the family (11:5; cf. 11:36),[45] an emphasis that particularizes more general statements about divine love toward humanity or the disciples in the Gospel (3:16; 13:1, 34; 14:21). John's community, like other early Christian communities (cf. 1 Thess 4:13), not unlike Christian communities today, undoubtedly experienced untimely deaths and suffering that on the level of human understanding seemed to conflict with the assurance of God's love (cf. 11:21). Assurance that Jesus did care, that God did have long-range purposes in the suffering, even that Jesus joined in weeping with the bereaved as well as ultimately held power over life and death, would mean much to believers facing that universal human predicament of death, whether or not related to persecution (cf. 1 John 3:16; 2:10, 13). Jesus had been "remaining" in Perea (10:40) and now "remained" two additional days, as he had among the Samaritans (4:40), leaving to raise Lazarus on the third day.

Nevertheless, Jesus' delay (11:6) apparently did not prolong Lazarus's suffering. Bethany was only a single day's journey, so if Jesus delayed two days after receiving the message and arrived to find that Lazarus had been dead four days (11:39),[46] Lazarus may have been dead by the time the messengers reached Jesus, dying shortly after they left to

---

[40] E.g., *p. Ḥag.* 2:1, §10.

[41] For the parallel, see Barrett, *John*, 390; Witherington, *Women*, 106–7.

[42] On God's revealing his glory here, see Holwerda, *Spirit*, 5.

[43] E.g., Ellis, *Genius*, 9, 184.

[44] So Malina and Rohrbaugh, *John*, 195, noting that he also missed the funeral (though messengers would not have reached him in time to announce this).

[45] Haenchen, *John*, 2:57.

[46] Burial on the day of death was the Jewish custom (Watkins, *John*, 259; cf. 11:17, 39; Acts 5:6–10).

seek him.[47] That many members of John's audience would not know the area around Jerusalem suggests that this information is not central to John's point in the narrative; but the information is explicitly there is the text for anyone who did in fact remember Judean geography, which some of John's audience probably did (since some were probably Judeans who left Judea after the war with Rome, although on our dating these would be primarily the older nucleus rather than the majority of the community).

## 3. Going to Judea (11:7–16)

Jesus had had good reason to avoid Judea (cf. 7:1), where his life had been threatened recently (10:31, 39; 11:8). But now Jesus goes to Judea (11:7) at the Father's bidding, providing a model for disciples to walk in the light (11:9–10). The cost of such obedience may be death (11:8), for followers as well as for Jesus (11:16). Not stumbling because one walked in daylight (11:9) was natural wisdom (cf. 9:4; 12:35; 1 John 2:10);[48] but the metaphor would also be transparent. Thus the scribes of the Qumran community claimed that the children of righteousness, ruled by the hand of the Prince of Lights, walk in the ways of light, whereas those ruled by the hand of the Angel of Darkness walk in the ways of darkness (1QS 3.20–21).[49] Another early Jewish writer could warn that passions blind one's soul, so that one moves in the day as if it were night (ἐν ἡμέρᾳ ὡς ἐν νυκτὶ πορεύεται, T. Jud. 18:6).[50] Jesus' metaphor in 11:10, that the light is not "in him," refers to spiritual light, but may play on an image borrowed from some ancient views of science, that light resided in the eye.[51] The "light of this world" here is metaphorical (cf. 9:4), but throughout the Gospel refers to Jesus and his mission (1:9; 3:19; 8:12; 9:5; 12:46); perhaps it applies in Jesus' case to light from the Father (cf. 1 John 1:5).

Lazarus was the "friend" of Jesus and the disciples (11:11), and therefore it was appropriate to die for him (15:13–15). That Jesus speaks of Lazarus being asleep (11:11) need not have confused the disciples. "Sleep" usually meant literal sleep,[52] but the sleep of death was a common usage in the LXX,[53] Jewish tomb inscriptions in Greek[54] and Latin,[55] and

---

[47] Barrett, *John* 391; Morris, "Jesus," 42. The trip from the Jordan plain (10:40) to the hills around Bethany (11:1) would take longer than the downhill trip from Bethany to the plain; Bethany is nearly 2,700 feet above sea level, and the Jordan plain roughly 1,100 feet below it (LaSor, *Knew*, 51).

[48] Haenchen, *John*, 2:58, cites the "narrow, stone-strewn paths" in much of Palestine, apart from Roman roads. Having depended heavily on flashlights for traversing such paths in the dark in rural Nigeria, I can testify to the difficulties where lighting was unavailable.

[49] Outsiders to the community naturally walked in darkness, i.e., did evil (1QS 4.11). Tannaim could apply an expression such as "The fool walks in darkness" (Eccl 2:14) to the theologically foolish, e.g., those who did not consistently agree with one of the Pharisaic schools (t. ʿEd. 2:3).

[50] See also comments on 1:4–5.

[51] Brown, *John*, 1:423. Ancients debated whether light entered or came from the eye (cf. Aristotle *On Sense and Sensible Objects* 2, 438ab; Aulus Gellius 5:16; Diogenes Laertius 9.7.44; Plutarch *T.T.* 1.8.4, *Mor.* 626C; *Jos. Asen.* 6:6/3; cf. Allison, "Eye"; perhaps Matt 6:22–23).

[52] See Bernard, *John*, 2:378. Nevertheless, the claim that Lazarus was merely nearly dead (Bretherton, "Lazarus") violates the story line (11:39) and its theology (11:25).

[53] E.g., Dan 12:2; 2 Macc 12:45; most often in the phrase "slept with his fathers," e.g., 1 Kgs 1:21; 2:10; 11:21, 43; 1 Chr 17:11; 2 Chr 9:31; 16:13; 21:1; 26:2, 23; 27:9; 28:27; 32:33; 33:20; 36:8.

[54] Where it is one of the most frequent expressions: *CIJ* 1:8, §3; 1:12, §17; 1:17–19, §§16–20; 1:21, §24; 1:26, §35; 1:28, §37; 1:31, §44; 1:34, §50; 1:37, §55; 1:39, §§62–63; 1:41, §69; 1:56, §81; 1:59, §85; 1:60, §86; 1:62, §88; 1:63, §90; 1:65, §92; 1:66, §93; 1:67, §95; 1:70, §99; 1:71, §100; 1:72, §102; 1:73, §103; 1:74, §105; 1:75, §106; 1:76, §109; 1:78, §111; 1:81, §117; 1:84, §121; 1:90, §129; 1:92, §131; 1:92, §132; 1:95, §136; 1:96, §137; 1:97, §138; 1:102, §144; 1:103, §145; 1:104, §146; 1:105,

literature, both Jewish[56] and Gentile.[57] Indeed, because of their resemblance,[58] Sleep and Death were twin brothers in pagan myth (e.g., Homer *Il.* 14.231; Statius *Thebaid* 5.197–199). Yet often in literature recounting accurate revelations or prophecies, mortals could interpret a revelation too figuratively or vice versa;[59] this is the case with Jesus' words elsewhere in the gospel tradition (e.g., Mark 8:15–18) and regularly in John (e.g., 3:4; 6:52). The disciples, taking Jesus too literally (how would Jesus "awaken" Lazarus from *death?*), appeal to the common observation that sleep helps one recover (11:12).[60] That he "may recover" (11:12) employs terminology that in John usually indicates the world's "salvation" (3:17; 5:34; 10:9; 12:47); this language may be significant, even if simply to indicate the inadequacy of their soteriology and the depth of their misunderstanding.[61] Jesus corrects their misunderstanding by speaking "plainly" (11:14; cf. 16:29; comment on 7:4): he was glad[62] that he was not there because the sign would deepen their faith (11:15; cf. 2:11; 11:45); the delay would not cause Lazarus's death (see above) but would intensify the public effect of the sign.[63]

---

§147; 1:107, §149; 1:109, §151; 1:110, §152; 1:111, §154; 1:113, §§156–157; 1:114, §159; 1:118–19, §167; 1:121–22, §169; 1:121, §171; 1:124, §172; 1:130, §180; 1:131, §§184–185; 1:135, §192; 1:195, §277; 1:202, §286.

55 *CIJ* 1:144–45, §206; 1:149, §210; 1:150, §212; 1:160, §224; 1:162, §228; 1:187–88, §265; 1:338, §458; 1:473, §658; 1:473, §659 (with Hebrew also); 1:473, §660. But some Latin inscriptions have this stereotypical phrase in Greek (*CIJ* 1:163, §229; 1:166, §222; 1:338, §459; 1:342–43, §464; 1:384, §523).

56 1 Th 4:13; Acts 7:60; Rev 14:13; Sir 30:17; *Jub.* 23:1; 36:18; *1 En.* 89:38; *Pss. Sol.* 2:31; *L.A.B.* 3:10; *4 Ezra* 7:31–32; *2 Bar.* 11:4; 21:25; 36:11; *T. Mos.* 10:14; *L.A.E.* 48:2; *T. Dan* 7:1; *T. Iss.* 7:9; *T. Zeb.* 10:6; *Gen. Rab.* 62:2.

57 E.g., Sophocles *Oed. col.* 1578; Callimachus *Epigrams* 11, 18; Plutarch *Apoll.* 12, *Mor.* 107D; Propertius *Eleg.* 2.28.25; Diogenes Laertius 1.86; Ps.-Callisthenes *Alex.* 3.6. See also in unrelated societies (Mbiti, *Religions*, 204–5).

58 Cf. also *T. Reu.* 3:1.

59 E.g., Chariton 5.5.5–6; for such an announcement that one was dead, Plutarch *Cimon* 18.7. An orator sometimes intended an audience to take his words the opposite of the way he put them (Cicero *Or. Brut.* 40.137), but this was irony, not deliberate obscurity.

60 Sleep allows respite from pain (Sophocles *Trach.* 988–991); conversely, loss of sleep can hasten death (Livy 40.56.9) or illness (Livy 22.2.11); one could be tortured to death by lack of sleep (Aulus Gellius 7.4.4; Cicero *Pis.* 19.43; Valerius Maximus 9.2.*ext.*1). Lack of sleep could stem from self-discipline (Dionysius of Halicarnassus *R.A.* 9.64.2; Livy 23.18.12; Silius Italicus 9.4–5), devotion to Torah (Ps 119:55, 148; 1QS 6.7–8), or repentance (*Jos. Asen.* 18:4 MSS); sickness (Hippocrates *Regimen in Acute Diseases* 1–2; *Prorrhetic* 1.135–136; love-sickness (Achilles Tatius 1.6; PGM 101.5–7), jealousy (Plutarch *Themistocles* 3.3–4), fear (Publilius Syrus 359; Plutarch *Alex.* 31.4; Silius Italicus 13.256–257), anxiety caused by vice (Plutarch *Virt.* 2, *Mor.* 100F), or other anxiety (Homer *Il.* 2.2–3; Aristophanes *Lys.* 27; Livy 40.56.9; Plutarch *Cicero* 35.3); mourning (Homer *Il.* 24.4–6); idleness during the day (*m. ʾAbot* 3:4); or hardships (Arrian *Ind.* 34.7; Gen 31:40; perhaps 2 Cor 11:27; Chariton 1.2.3).

61 In 11:13 δοκέω (here the aorist ἔδοξαν) signifies misunderstanding, as it always does in John (5:39, 45; 13:29; 16:2; 20:15), including in this context (11:31, 56).

62 Bernard, *John*, 2:380, suggests that Jesus' joy relates to fulfilling his mission (cf. 4:36; 15:11; 17:13).

63 Some later traditions suggest the retention of the soul for three days after death (until the soul sees the body begin to decompose; *m. Yebam.* 16:3; *Gen. Rab.* 100:7; *Lev. Rab.* 18:1; though cf. Dola, "Interpretacja"), as in Persian beliefs of uncertain date (Vendidad 19.28; Yasht 22.2ff., in Bousset, *Kyrios Christos,* 59), or required three days of purgatory before preparation to appear before God (*3 En.* 28:10; cf. *Apoc. Zeph.* 4:7); some commentators note such traditions here (Strachan, *Gospel*, 153). (Cf. three days of heavy lamentation, Apollonius of Rhodes 1.1059.) This belief is not widely attested in the early period (Michaels, *John,* 190), but in any case, after three days the body would not be identifiable due to decomposition (*m. Yebam.* 16:3).

In v. 16 Thomas[64] ironically understands Jesus correctly: for Jesus to raise Lazarus will cost him his life, and Thomas and the other disciples should (though will not) follow him to the cross. The disciples recognized that Jesus had faced most of his opposition in Judea (11:7–8);[65] the recent stoning attempt to which they refer would be 10:31–32, with 8:59 not far behind, both in Jerusalem. "Going" (11:7–8, 11, 15–16) is often associated with Jesus' death in the Farewell Discourse (13:3, 33, 36; 14:2–5, 28, 31; 16:5); he calls his disciples to follow (14:31). Thomas is thus more courageous than Jesus' brothers (cf. the second person imperative in 7:3), who did not believe in Jesus (7:5). This is surely a positive illustration; some ancient ethicists debated whether one should obey an order when it seems in the better interests of the order's giver not to do so,[66] but Thomas, like some heroic characters in other works,[67] is determined to follow.

But Thomas's determination proves ironic in this Gospel and for any readers familiar with the gospel tradition: despite Thomas's apparent willingness to suffer death for the sake of Jesus, Jesus will die alone.[68] Casual oaths were common in the period,[69] and widely known Jesus tradition elsewhere indicates that the sense of loyalty faded in the face of the horror of arrest and execution (Mark 14:20). Not only was Thomas among those who fled (16:31–32), but he would initially fail to believe the apostolic testimony about Jesus' resurrection (20:25).

### 4. Martha Meets the Life (11:17–27)

John points out Bethany's proximity to Jerusalem (11:18) to underline the risk of hostility Jesus was embracing to serve Lazarus (10:39; 11:8), but also to identify the many "Judeans" who came to visit Martha and Mary as the theological equivalent of Jerusalemites, who will again (7:43; 9:16; 10:19) be divided by Jesus' ministry (11:46–47). Bethany may have been near the Mount of Olives (Luke 19:29; cf. Luke 24:50 with Acts 1:12).[70]

That many had come to console Martha and Mary (11:19) fits what we know of Judean custom. Because Lazarus has been in the tomb four days (11:17), the most intense mourning period of sitting *shiva* (i.e., seven days) remains in effect.[71] Palestinian Judaism required burial of the deceased on the day of death, but six days of mourning (for a total of seven) followed,[72] in which the bereaved family members would remain at home while

---

[64] The name appears in, e.g., *CIJ* 2:74, §825 (194 C.E., Dura Europos).

[65] Stauffer, *Jesus,* 172, thinks that Thomas has in view here Jerusalem's mass crucifixions over the past few centuries.

[66] Aulus Gellius 1.13. Some ancient rulers reacted with such hostility to bad news that their servants withheld it from them (Plutarch *Lucullus* 25.1; cf. 2 Sam 18:20–22, 29).

[67] E.g., Apollonius of Rhodes 2.638–639; Cornelius Nepos 23 (Hannibal), 8.3.

[68] See Duke, *Irony,* 59.

[69] See Derrett, *Audience,* 68, citing Tob 8:20; 9:3; 10:7; Sir 18:22–23; 23:9–11; on casual oaths, cf. Keener, *Matthew,* 192–95, 549.

[70] Josephus gives less than half the distance for Olivet (*Ant.* 20.169) that John gives for Bethany (Johnson, *Acts,* 33), but though both undoubtedly knew the place, it is unlikely that either measured the distance; and Luke 19:29 just requires proximity.

[71] The custom is ancient (Sir 22:12; Jdt 16:24; cf. *L.A.E.* 51:2; *Apoc. Mos.* 43:3). Later rabbis did not feel that the mourning period exempted one from most duties except tefillin (*b. Ber.* 11a), but popular custom may not have taken this into account.

[72] The seven days were probably originally related to the isolation period of corpse uncleanness (Num 19:13–20; Josephus *Ant.* 3.262); cf. also seven days of Roman mourning (for the emperor, Herodian 4.2.4; wealthy Romans kept the body for mourning seven days, Jeffers, *World,* 45).

others came to supply food and express sympathy.[73] Such intense mourning for at least a week after death is common to various traditional cultures.[74] (Probably it is so-called modern cultures, more lacking in grief rituals, that may be less adapted to the needs of the human psyche.)[75] Probably a significant number of people in Bethany were visiting or had visited the family. More distant relatives might also offer special comfort to the closest relatives.[76] Anyone who passes a funeral procession should join it and share its lamentation.[77] Visiting the bereaved was an important aspect of piety.[78]

Normally word would travel ahead of a famous teacher that he was arriving, and this could be the case here; people might know that Jesus had been invited (11:3).[79] Given the need for relative secrecy about his presence again in Judea, however, and the fact that those who had come to comfort the family seemed not to expect him (11:28, 30–31), Jesus may have sent a disciple ahead as a messenger to notify Martha of his arrival, while he waited outside the village (as in 11:30). In any case, she hears of his arrival (11:20). Although it was expected that during mourning Martha should stay in the house and let Jesus come to her, she paid him great respect by going out to meet him (cf. 12:13),[80] though leaving Mary behind to continue mourning and receive visitors (11:20). Perhaps, too, she knew of the danger Jesus might be in if word spread that he was back in Judea; Jesus delays entering the village as long as possible (11:28, 30). In any case her going forth at such a time shows him special honor. But in the following context Jesus will demand more than such expressions of honor: he will demand faith.

The brief dialogue between Jesus and Martha that ensues (11:21–27) emphasizes for John's audience the symbolic import of the narrative:[81] Christology realizes eschatology, so that Jesus brings resurrection life in the present era. Occasionally in narratives people appear unable to speak because of grief (e.g., Josephus *Ant.* 6.337; cf. Mark 9:6), but Martha articulates a degree of faith in Jesus' power: his presence could have healed Lazarus (11:21; cf. 11:32). Jesus demands greater faith: he is present now; is his power limited even by death itself (11:23)?[82]

When Martha indicates that she trusts that whatever he asks of God, God will give him (11:22), she is probably making an implied, oblique request as in 11:3 (cf. 2:3, 5). Her expression of confidence in Jesus—that God would grant whatever he asked (11:22; cf.

---

[73] E.g., Jeremias, *Theology*, 132; Sandmel, *Judaism*, 200–201. By the Amoraic period, rabbinic regulations were detailed (*b. Ketub.* 8b and sources in Sandmel, *Judaism*, 201); for reciting mourner's blessings in the synagogue, see, e.g., *p. Moʾed Qaṭ.* 1:5, §5.

[74] E.g., Mbiti, *Religions*, 197.

[75] One ancient proverb opined that one experienced a personal death whenever one lost loved ones (Publilius Syrus 252); some also believed that one could die from mourning too hard (*Jub.* 34:15).

[76] E.g., *Jub.* 36:22. Near relatives mourned deeply (*Jub.* 23:6).

[77] Josephus *Ag. Ap.* 2.205.

[78] E.g., Sir 7:34–35; *Sem.* 12; Bonsirven, *Judaism*, 151.

[79] Supporting this possibility, see Malina and Rohrbaugh, *John*, 199, on gossip networks.

[80] One would honor persons by meeting them and conducting them to their destination (e.g., 12:13; Dionysius of Halicarnassus *R.A.* 7.7.2; Chariton 4.7.6; Judg 4:18; 11:31, 34; 1 Sam 13:10; 16:4; 21:1; 25:32; cf. royal parousia contexts, e.g., 1 Thess 4:17; cf. 2 Sam 19:25; Jdt 5:4; 7:15; *Pesiq. Rab.* 51:8). Certainly cities treated visiting dignitaries in this manner, and the same is probably true for visiting scholars among those who respected them (cf. Acts 28:15). Yet at least by later custom, one should not greet a mourner (*p. Ber.* 2:6, §3).

[81] Dodd, *Interpretation*, 368.

[82] Cf. Ellis, *World*, 71.

3:35; 13:3)—thus would illustrate the sort of prayer God might hear in Jesus' name (16:24). While this could be a request for comfort, it is more likely a request that Jesus raise her brother. Some suggest that in 11:24 she forgets the request, hence allowing Jesus to articulate more Johannine theology;[83] misunderstanding motifs are common in miracle stories,[84] and it is not unlike John to narrate one of this nature (5:7).

But it is no less possible that she is continuing her insistence by seeking clarification; from the standpoint of Johannine theology, confession in a future resurrection was correct (5:28–29; 6:39) even if not Jesus' point here.[85] The wording of Jesus' response in 11:25–26 would not necessarily resolve any ambiguity in his words for Martha; most Jews believed in the soul's life after death before the resurrection anyway.[86] But the wording of Jesus' response (Jesus as the life, 11:25–26; cf. 1:4; 6:48; 14:6; 1 John 1:2; 5:11–12, 20)[87] would encourage John's audience, who might not expect to customarily face immediate physical resuscitations but believed that they possessed eternal life in the present (3:16, 36).[88] Temporary resuscitations of mortals in history could be understood to prefigure the ultimate future resurrection (e.g., 4:50 and comment),[89] so John could make explicit how Jesus' words to Martha applied to his own audience in his own generation.

Martha's confession (11:27) is as firm as Peter's (6:69); the confession of Christ, however, is not Peter's (6:69), but the Baptist's (3:28), Andrew's (1:41), the Samaritan woman's (4:25, 29), perhaps a healed man's (9:22, 35–38), and now Martha's (11:27). That Jesus was the one "coming into the world" (11:27) is Johannine christological language implying his incarnate status (e.g., 1:9, 27; 3:31), though we need not suppose that Martha understood this point (cf. 6:14; 12:13). Jesus offers private revelations of his identity to the Samaritan woman (4:25–26) and to Martha (11:25), and later reveals himself to Mary Magdalene (20:15–17) after Peter and the beloved disciple have departed (20:10). He seems to have favored women and/or those marginalized from the centers of structural power. Whether John, by the confessions of Martha and Peter, is intentionally balancing gender the way

---

[83] Haenchen, *John*, 2:61. Others regard her faith as inadequate; "any Pharisee could have said this" (Fenton, *John*, 122).

[84] Theissen, *Stories*, 55, citing Philostratus *Vit. Apoll.* 4.45; 2 Kgs 5:5–7; Mark 5:39; cf. Acts 3:5.

[85] One could also apply resurrection language figuratively to deliverance from danger, even when mentioning the grave (e.g., 4Q437 2 2.11; cf. Ps 9:13; 18:4–5).

[86] Cf. similarly Koester, *Symbolism*, 109. On the soul's immortality, see, e.g., Sir 9:12; Josephus *War* 1.84; 2.154–155, 163; 7.341–348; *Ant.* 17.354; 18.14, 18; Philo *Abraham* 258; *Moses* 2.288; *T. Ab.* 1:24–25A; 4:9; 9:8B; Ps.-Phoc. 108; *Apoc. Mos.* 13:6; 32:4; 33:2; *Jos. Asen.* 27:10; Wolfson, *Philo*, 395–413. For exceptions, see 1 Macc 2:63; Josephus *Ant.* 18.16.

[87] Malzoni, "La résurrection," prefers the shorter reading "I am the resurrection" (following some Old Syriac witnesses); the textual tradition would more likely be expansive here, and the omission has significant and early geographic range. The longer reading is more widely attested from the beginning, however (cf. Metzger, *Commentary*, 234). In either case, "life" is implicit in "resurrection" and "lives."

[88] "Not die" makes "live" more emphatic (e.g., *L.A.B.* 23:10; see comment on 8:51), but it deals with the question of eternal life, not the question of Lazarus's physical raising central to the narrative itself (unless to say that Lazarus's physical state was irrelevant to his eternal life; cf. Gamble, "Philosophy," 55; 1 Thess 4:13–14).

[89] Such foreshadowing made sense in a Jewish framework, e.g., *Pesiq. Rab Kah.* 9:4. John elsewhere uses "tomb" only for that of Jesus (19:41–20:11) or the dead he will raise (5:28). Derrett, "Lazarus," infers a connection, probably anachronistically, between Lazarus's resurrection and Moses bringing water from the rock (based on later Roman catacomb paintings). Pagans could also distinguish temporary resuscitations followed by death from perpetual life (Philostratus *Hrk.* 2.9–11, third century C.E.).

Luke seems to do[90] or (less likely) includes her confession without such considerations, her confession, the climactic confession preceding Jesus' passion, suggests a relatively high role for women's faith vis-à-vis the majority views of John's culture.[91]

## 5. Mourning with Mary and Others (11:28–37)

Jesus continues to remain outside the village (11:28, 30), probably for safety (11:8),[92] to prolong his "hour" until its appointed moment at the Passover (11:46–47). Martha takes over receiving visitors at the house while Mary slips out to meet with Jesus. That Martha speaks "secretly" (11:28) likely indicates her wish to protect Jesus; his hour had not yet come (7:4, 6, 10). But visitors, naturally supposing that she was going to mourn at the tomb outside the boundaries of Bethany proper,[93] followed Mary and found themselves facing Jesus (11:31). Falling to the ground (11:32) was a way to entreat those in authority,[94] but also a way to worship God himself (1 Esd 9:47; Rev 4:10; Esth 3:2), which may be significant on the Johannine level, in which the audience recognizes what Mary does not (20:28; see comment on 9:38).

Mary expresses her faith no less forcefully than Martha and in almost identical language (11:32; cf. 11:21). Although Martha is mentioned first in 11:19 and comes first in 11:20, Mary is mentioned first in the opening reference to the two sisters (11:1), as if she is better known to the community (cf. also her role in Luke 10:39, 42). Although sequence of names is not always significant,[95] it often was.[96] It may be that Mary's role in the narrative is second not because it is secondary, but because it is climactic. Then again, Martha's faith seems fundamental to the development of the narrative (11:39–40); each plays a decisive role, Martha perhaps as the elder and leader, Mary perhaps as the more forward and perhaps emotionally closer to Jesus (as in Luke 10:38–42). The faith of both women (11:21, 32) contrasts with the weaker faith of their comforters (11:37).[97]

Jesus' own spirit was grieved or troubled (11:33), as it would be by his own impending death (12:27; 13:21) but as he warned that his followers need not be (14:1, 27).[98] Another

---

[90] Cf. Maly, "Women"; Flanagan, "Women"; Tannehill, *Luke,* 132–39.

[91] This is not to suggest that women's religious activities were not prominent in many circles (see, e.g., Abrahamsen, "Reliefs"; idem, "Women"; Kraemer, "Ecstatics"; idem, "Ecstasy"; idem, *Maenads;* Brooten, *Leaders*) but that in public discourse most ancient circles featured it less dominantly than men's in comparison to Luke and John, as a firsthand survey of the ancient sources will reveal. Fehribach, *Bridegroom,* 83–113, finds community types in Jesus' relationships with the various women in this Gospel, including here; yet this argument seems less plausible here than at some other points.

[92] Brown, *John,* 1:425.

[93] Gravesites were to be outside residential areas (cf. Heb 13:11–12; *4 Bar.* 7:13; Wilkinson, *Jerusalem,* 146). For regularly visiting gravesites to mourn, see, e.g., Apoll. K. *Tyre* 30–31.

[94] In miracle stories, see Theissen, *Stories,* 53 (citing, e.g., Tacitus *Hist.* 4.81).

[95] E.g., *Mek. Pisha* 1.17–34.

[96] It is especially significant when a wife's name appears before a husband's (MacMullen, "Women," 209–10; Flory, "Women").

[97] See Barrett, *John,* 398.

[98] Ταράσσω was idiomatic for human inner turmoil (e.g., when meeting an angel, Tob 12:16; Luke 1:12) and was regularly associated in this sense with πνεῦμα, ψυχή, and καρδία, e.g., Gen 41:8; Ps 6:3 [6:4 LXX]; 38:10 [37:10 LXX]; 42:6 [41:7 LXX]; 55:4 [54:5 LXX]; 143:4 [142:4 LXX]; Prov 12:25; Isa 19:3; *T. Ab.* 13:6B; *T. Dan* 4:7; cf. 2 Sam 13:21 LXX. A goal of philosophy, by contrast, was to be ἀτάραχον (Epictetus *Diatr.* 2.5.2; 4.8.27; Diogenes Laertius 10.85; 10.144.17; cf. *T. Dan* 4:7; *T. Job* 36:3/4–5; ἀπαθείας in Crates *Ep.* 34, to Metrocles).

term here depicts his emotion in the strongest possible terms; he was "moved" (ἐμβρι-μάομαι, 11:33, 38), an unusually strong term, usually denoting anger, agitation, and typically some physical expression accompanying it (cf. Mark 1:43; 14:5).[99] Scholars debate whether he is angry with Mary and Martha for lack of faith (11:32, 40), at the crowds for their unbelief (11:37), or at death itself. On the one hand, the term might be qualified by a parallel expression in 13:21 (cf. 12:27; 14:1), suggesting that John figuratively stretches the sense to include emotional disturbance without anger per se; it may stem from observing Mary's grief and wailing (11:33).[100] Some think that "anger" overstates the case, though "troubled" is too weak.[101]

But 13:21 may refer to a similar yet different emotion, and the term employed here does indicate anger when applied to humans.[102] If Jesus is angry, one may think he is angry at sin, Satan, or death as a consequence of sin.[103] While that proposal may be good theology (and may also fit the experience of some subsequent healers and exorcists, and perhaps of Jesus as well, cf. Mark 1:25; 4:39; 9:25; Luke 4:39), it lacks direct support in this text. More likely, he is angry at the lack of faith on the part of those who should be exercising it,[104] as God was angry at Israel's unbelief despite his previous signs (e.g., Num 14:11) or Jesus was angry with the unbelief of disciples in Mark (e.g., Mark 4:40; cf. Mark 1:43; 3:5). In both cases (11:33, 38), it occurs immediately after statements that Jesus *could* have done something before Lazarus died (11:32, 37)—perhaps implying disbelief that he could do something now. Jesus is not, however, angry with their grief itself; he seems emotionally moved more by Mary's tears (11:33) than by Martha's words, and responds by weeping himself (11:35).[105] In any case, Jesus' internal disturbance over others' pain emphasizes his humanity "and/or the passionate nature of his divinity."[106] It reveals his character, which leads to his suffering on others' behalf (cf. 1:29; cf. Heb 4:15–5:8). By weeping, Jesus shows his solidarity with the mourners (11:35).

That Jesus asked where the burial site was (11:34) would have suggested to his hearers that he wanted to join in mourning at the burial site (cf. 11:31); their invitation to "Come and see" (11:34) is an invitation to join in the mourning.[107] Perhaps more significantly, his

---

[99] Michaels, *John*, 191; often used, e.g., for "the snorting of horses" (Morris, "Jesus," 48). Cf. ἐμβρίμημα in Lam 2:6 LXX.

[100] The term κλαίω (11:31, 33) may bear less than wholly negative connotations for a repeated reader, since joy follows such weeping in every other appearance of it in this Gospel (16:20; 20:11–16).

[101] Marsh, *John*, 433.

[102] E.g., Carson, *John*, 415; O'Day, "John," 690–91. Story, "Attitude," suggests that Jesus "rebuked" himself; but see Lindars, "Rebuking."

[103] Evans, *John*, 121–22; Bruce, *John*, 246; Sloyan, *John*, 143; Whitacre, *John*, 289. It was understood that one's pain could become anger and lead to lashing out (Plutarch *Cor.* 21.1–2). Carson, *John*, 416, suggests Jesus is angry at perhaps sin and death as well as their unbelief.

[104] Marsh, *John*, 433; Borchert, *John*, 359–60. Malina and Rohrbaugh, *John*, 200, suggest "indignation" at Mary's public challenge in 11:32, questioning whether he has acted like "a true friend." This would make sense, but can 11:32 really be a challenge? I think it more likely intended praise that proves inadequate, since Jesus calls for higher faith.

[105] Tears often moved authorities to action (e.g., Lysias *Or.* 32.10, §505; Cicero *Sest.* 11.26; Caesar *Gallic W.* 1.20). On male authorities being particularly moved by women's pleas in the ancient Mediterranean world, see Luke 18:2–5; 2 Sam 14:1–21; 20:16–22; 1 Kgs 1:11–16; 2:17; Matt 20:20; P.Sakaon 36; Lysias *Or.* 32.11–18, §§506–511; perhaps Valerius Maximus 8.3; comment on 2:4.

[106] Kysar, *John*, 181.

[107] "Come and see" is a familiar invitation formula (see comment on 1:39) but, apart from Johannine style, probably bears no other relation to 1:39, 46 and 4:29.

question, "Where have you laid him?" anticipates Mary Magdalene's question about where Jesus has been laid (20:15),[108] underlining the implicit contrast between Lazarus, who awaits Jesus to raise him, and Jesus whose body is already gone (as well as the contrast between Lazarus's burial by his family and Jesus' by two leaders of "the Jews" yet not the expected disciples).

Jesus' tears (11:35) would be considered pious as well as compassionate.[109] As noted above, Jewish people considered sharing in others' lamentation a religious duty. But showing lavish emotion at the appropriate time, especially grief over bereavement, was considered praiseworthy behavior throughout the ancient Mediterranean world[110] and could move an audience.[111] Ancient writers would describe a hero's tears for others' pain as part of his praiseworthy behavior,[112] or the tears of those who loved and sacrificed themselves for others.[113] (Many philosophers and moralists, who counseled against the value of grief, proved to be the exception;[114] some others shared their perspective,[115] though this was probably more often a stereotypical counsel than a genuine expectation.[116] Brave heroes might also hold out against tears, refusing to be deterred from a mission.)[117] One might weep out of sympathy for others' grief, though not grieving for the situation itself (e.g., Ps.-Callisthenes *Alex.* 2.21); thus Moses, initially not mourning over his own imminent

---

[108] See O'Day, *Word*, 92.

[109] Jesus presumably weeps in 11:35 because he "shares the sadness of his friends and their neighbors" (Smith, *John* [1999], 225). By ancient Mediterranean standards, mere tears were hardly wildly demonstrative (Virgil *Aen.* 11.148–150; cf. especially women, e.g., Homer *Il.* 18.30–31; Aeschylus *Cho.* 22–31, 423–428). Jewish mourners did not, however, participate in the more masochistic mourning rites of their pagan neighbors (e.g., Deut 14:1).

[110] Malina, *Windows*, 24–25, citing Plutarch *Caesar* 5.2; 11.3; 41.1; 48.2; *Cicero* 47.2; Acts 20:37; Lightfoot, *Gospel*, 229, cites Juvenal *Sat.* 15.132–133. Cf. also 2 Kgs 8:11–12; Homer *Il.* 1.348–349, 413; *Od.* 4.113–119; 16.190–191; 23.231–232; Sophocles *Ajax* 819–820; Philostratus *Hrk.* 45.6. Note amplification in Josephus's hellenized accounts: Moses' prayer with tears for God's vindication against Korah (Josephus *Ant.* 4.51); David's prayers with tears during Absalom's revolt (Josephus *Ant.* 7.203; 2 Sam 15:23, 30).

[111] E.g., Livy 1.26.12; 23.8.4; Dionysius of Halicarnassus *R.A.* 9.10.1; for rhetoric, see, e.g., Lysias *Or.* 32.10, §505; Cicero *Mil.* 38.105; *Rosc. Amer.* 9.24; *Rab. post.* 17.47; *Cael.* 24.60; *Sest.* 11.26; Seneca *Controv.* 4.pref.6; Menander Rhetor 2.13, 423.30; Philostratus *Vit. soph.* 1.19.512; 2.1.561; 2.5.574; 2.9.582; 2.10.586; Acts 20:19. Narrators used tears to stir pathos (e.g., Xenophon *Eph.* 1.11); Polybius 2.56.7 complains about historians who sensationalize with tragic scenes of women's tears invented to arouse pathos; John may deliberately evoke pathos here.

[112] E.g., Appian *R.H.* 8.19.132; on Alexander of Macedon, Diodorus Siculus 17.69.4 (it was meant to praise him; cf. 17.69.9); Arrian *Alex.* 7.11.5; 7.12.3.

[113] So the father and son in Diodorus Siculus 34/35.11.1.

[114] Seneca *Dial.* 11.4.1; *Ep. Lucil.* 116.1; Socratics *Ep.* 21; Plutarch *Apoll.* 33, *Mor.* 118E; Iamblichus *V.P.* 32.226; 33.234; *Let. Aris.* 268; *T. Zeb.* 10:1–2. Virtue supposedly protected from this malady (Epictetus *Diatr.* 1.9.7; *Let. Aris.* 232). More reasonably, on limits, cf. Plutarch *Consol.* 2, *Mor.* 608C; 4, *Mor.* 608F–609A; Pliny *Ep.* 2.1.10–11; 3.21.1–6; *Syr. Men.* 463–469; perhaps 1 Thess 4:13.

[115] Sophocles *Ajax* 852; *El.* 1171–1173; Theon *Progymn.* 8.55.

[116] On stereotypes in condolence letters, see, e.g., Theon *Progymn.* 8.53; Dio Chrysostom *Or.* 30, *On Charidemus* passim; Lewis, *Life*, 89–81; Stowers, *Letter Writing*, 142–46. Funerary inscriptions and rhetoric contain stereotypical expressions of mourning (Demosthenes *Or.* 60, *Funeral Speech* 1–37; *Greek Anth.* 7.339–340, 389); time is sorrow's best healer in Diodorus Siculus 34/35.17.1.

[117] Apollonius of Rhodes 1.292–305; Acts 21:13; cf. also the Roman attachment to duty (Ovid *Fasti* 4.845–848, though cf. 849–852; Dionysius of Halicarnassus *R.A.* 5.8.6; Appian *R.H.* 8.12.81–82, 86).

death, was said to have been moved to tears by his people weeping so much over it (Josephus *Ant.* 4.321).[118] That this tradition about Moses was widely known is not likely; that it reflects broader feelings in the milieu about the heroic protagonist's tears is virtually certain. It is thus not surprising that those who have come to mourn with Mary recognize that Jesus cared deeply for Lazarus (11:36; cf. 11:5).

That John contrasts some "others" (11:37) with those who praised his love (11:38) suggests that the latter group, while perhaps recognizing his love, doubted his power to have changed the situation. Some scholars suspect that this is the reason for Jesus' possible "anger" in 11:38 (see comment on 11:33).

## 6. The Miracle (11:38–44)

Lazarus's rescucitation prefigures Jesus' resurrection for the Fourth Gospel, and parallels of language between the two are more than fortuitous, such as the stone (11:38; 20:1), the essential role of a woman close to the deceased (11:39; 20:1–18), and the wrappings (11:44; 20:6–7). Nevertheless, the primary purpose of the parallels may be to draw attention to the equally explicit contrasts between the two. In Lazarus's case, people must remove the stone (11:39), but Jesus' resurrection produces an immortal body following a different order of existence (cf. 1 Cor 15:42–44; Phil 3:21); his resurrection may leave the grave clothes untouched (20:5, 7) and allows him to enter closed rooms (20:19, 26).[119]

Many private burials employed vertical shaft tombs, but this burial was in a cave, probably oriented horizontally (11:38).[120] The stone (11:38) would keep animals from the body.[121] Martha's objection about the stench (11:39) makes sense on natural human assumptions. Spices could cover the stench for a while,[122] but after four days the stench of decomposition would be intense.[123] Unlike ancient Egyptians, Jewish people did not embalm the dead to prevent decomposition[124] but in this period actually encouraged decomposition to allow for secondary burial a year later.[125] Yet Jesus challenges her to act in faith in his word, contrary to natural expectations. Although throughout the Gospel seeing signs often provokes the most basic level of faith, Jesus calls Martha, who already has confessed her faith (11:21–22, 27), to a deeper level of faith: if she believes, then she will see. Thus she would see God's glory (11:40) in Jesus' sign (2:11), like Israel in the exodus (Exod

---

[118] Likewise of the archangel Michael, provoked by Abraham's tears (*T. Ab.* 3:9–10A; 3:9–10B); and of Abraham, provoked by Isaac's tears over his impending death (*T. Ab.* 5:9–10A); tears were apparently contagious (Josephus *Ant.* 7.202–203; Josephus himself is moved by others' tears in *Life* 205–210). Not weeping over a matter not requiring mourning (cf. 11:25–26) differs from mourning only when others are looking, hence seeking praise but meriting ridicule (Martial *Epigr.* 1.33).

[119] Fenton, *John,* 124.

[120] Brown, *John,* 1:426; Barrett, *John,* 401. For more detail on tombs of this period, see Meyers and Strange, *Archeology,* 94–103.

[121] Lightfoot, *Gospel,* 229; Brown, *John,* 1:426.

[122] Meyers and Strange, *Archaeology,* 97–98; for spices at funerals, see, e.g., Josephus *Ant.* 17.199; *War* 1.673; *m. Ber.* 8:6; Herodian 4.2.8.

[123] Many felt the soul departed after three days and decomposition started (*m. Yebam.* 16:3); the fourth day thus underlines the miracle (Barkhuizen, "Lazarus"; cf. Whitacre, *John,* 283–84).

[124] Brown, *John,* 1:426.

[125] Cf., e.g., *m. Sanh.* 6:6; *Moʾed Qaṭ.* 1:5; *Pesaḥ.* 8:8; *b. Sanh.* 47b; *p. Moʾed Qaṭ.* 1:5, §§4–5; Hachlili and Killebrew, "Necropolis," 172. One year was also a traditional Greek period for mourning (Euripides *Alc.* 336; cf. 430–431; Roman women for a brother or father ten months, Plutarch *Cor.* 39.5; but cf. in unrelated cultures as well, e.g., Gelfand, "Disorders," 160).

16:7, 10). In this case, the glory was the divine purpose for which Lazarus had died: that Jesus might be glorified (11:4), ultimately by the cross (see comment on 1:14; 11:4).

The Gospel emphasizes Jesus' deity, which might be one reason that prayer preceded the miracles recorded to this point in only one case at most (cf. 6:11).[126] Nevertheless, Jesus' prayer (11:41–42) would not strike an ancient Jewish-Christian audience as too unexpected; prayers often appear in Israelite and early Jewish healing stories.[127] In earliest Christian literature public healings usually occurred by commands rather than by prayer (e.g., Mark 5:41; Acts 3:6), but prayer or a lifestyle of prayer often preceded such commands to be healed (Mark 9:29; Acts 3:1; 9:40; 28:8).[128] Lifting one's face toward heaven was a known posture for prayer (11:41; cf. 17:1),[129] and (especially given some charges that Jesus was a magician) many people in the ancient Mediterranean would have distrusted a silent prayer.[130]

More important for our consideration is the specific function of this prayer in its Johannine context. Although the Fourth Gospel emphasizes Jesus' deity, it also underlines his obedience to the Father's will and offers significant prayers of Jesus to the Father. Jesus prays in 11:41–42 that the sign may produce faith in his divine mission. Essentially he prays for the Father's glory (11:40), as he will soon offer prayers for the Father to be glorified by his own death and resurrection shortly to follow that prayer (12:27–28; 17:1–5). He expects the crowd to hear the prayer before God acts so that when God does act they may understand why he acted (cf. 14:29). In the same way, God speaks to Jesus in 12:29 for the sake of the crowds (12:30). John may want his audience to understand how important it is to their Lord "that the world may know" that Jesus is the Father's agent in part because, as he will soon inform them, they must share in that mission by their unity (17:23).

Jesus begins with thanks, as in the closest parallel to an earlier pre-miracle prayer in the Gospel (6:11). By emphasizing that the Father has heard him, Jesus reiterates his dependence on the Father, a frequent Johannine theme;[131] the Father "always" heard him because of his perfect obedience (8:29), a model for John's audience (14:12–15; 15:7). That signs provide an opportunity for faith (11:42)[132] is also a frequent Johannine motif (2:11), though this context illustrates the increased hostility invited by such signs from those who choose to continue in unbelief (11:45–47).

Jesus spoke loudly to Lazarus (11:43), presumably partly so the crowd could also hear (cf. 7:37; 11:42).[133] That he calls his name may recall 10:3: Jesus calls his own sheep by

---

126 According to R. Johanan (third century C.E.), even God says prayers (*b. Ber.* 7a); but such a view was not likely widespread in the first century.

127 Theissen, *Stories*, 65, citing, e.g., 1 Kgs 17:21; *b. Ber.* 34b; *Ḥag.* 3a. Like speeches, prayers could be inserted into preexisting historical narratives even if the narrator had no access to the actual speech (1 Macc 7:36–38). Opposition to petitionary prayer (cf. Van der Horst, "Maximus") must have been exceptional.

128 Healings in the setting of the believing community may have differed from apostolic and prophetic healings in this respect (Jas 5:14).

129 See Ezra 9:6; Job 22:26; Ps 123:1; *Jub.* 25:11. See comment on 17:1.

130 Cf. Van der Horst, "Prayer"; Croy, "Religion," 929; 1 Sam 1:13.

131 Dowd, "Theology," 322–23.

132 A corpse is resuscitated in *4 Bar.* 7:19–20 "in order that they might believe" (ἵνα πιστεύσωσιν). Other texts are more frivolous, e.g., raising a person one had earlier struck dead (*T. Ab.* 14:14A; *b. B. Qam.* 117a). Greco-Roman tradition also reported both speech (Xenophon *Cyr.* 6.3.10; Ps.-Callisthenes *Alex.* 2.21) and signs (Eunapius *Lives* 459) for the sake of bystanders.

133 For an emphasis on loud speech so the crowds could hear, see Josephus *Ant.* 4.40. One mortal's prayer could divinely constitute a sign to another (Homer *Od.* 20.111, 120).

name, and leads them forth;[134] that he raises him with his voice recalls 5:28–29, the future resurrection to which this points on a temporal, symbolic level (cf. 11:24–26).[135] Unlike in the Synoptics, there is no emphasis on Jesus touching the impure in John; even Lazarus is raised not by a touch (cf. Mark 5:41; Luke 7:14) but by a command.[136] John would, of course, agree with Mark's perspective that Jesus' signs sometimes challenge purity customs (2:6); but he illustrates the point differently.

Lazarus came forth in his graveclothes, a contrast with Jesus' greater resurrection that left such cloths behind (20:5, 7) made all the more obvious by the parallel description of Jesus' burial (19:40). Jewish sources frequently mention such shrouds for wrapping and binding the corpse.[137] To prevent premature distortion of tissue, those preparing the body would bind the cheeks to keep the mouth closed; they closed the body's orifices and sometimes placed the body on cold sand to inhibit swelling.[138] If our later sources approximate relevant conditions, as they probably would in this case, the head cloth was about one yard square.[139]

Some commentators suggest that Jews wrapped corpses less tightly than Greeks did, which would have allowed Lazarus at least to shuffle out under his own power;[140] yet such an activity would demand an extraordinary amount of patience from the bystanders, especially once it became evident that he was emerging. That Lazarus could not have physically come out of the tomb by his own power when so wrapped (as most of John's audience should have known) merely contributes to John's portrayal of the sign's magnitude.[141] But, as noted above, the grave wrappings also contribute to an implicit contrast between Lazarus's restoration to die again and Jesus' resurrection to immortality. Jesus left his garments behind in the tomb, never to need them again.[142]

## Responses to the Raising (11:45–12:11)

Not surprisingly, most of those present recognized Jesus' power, but even some of the witnesses became Jesus' betrayers (11:45–46). The Judean elite, already opposed to Jesus (5:18; 8:59; 10:31, 39), now solidify a plan to kill him (11:47–53); Jesus withdraws and the crowds wonder if he will show himself during the Passover (11:54–57). But John also focuses on the consequences of Lazarus's raising for Lazarus and his family, probably para-

---

[134] Fenton, *John*, 125. One might compare the sort of story in which witches would seek to summon a corpse by name (but could accidentally procure someone else of the same name lying nearby; Apuleius *Metam.* 2.30), but John does not seek to evoke magic (magical texts usually designate which person of a particular parentage, e.g., *PGM* 36.82–83), nor is recuscitation the same as stealing a corpse.

[135] Cf. also, e.g., McPolin, *John*, 161–62.

[136] For the severity of corpse uncleanness, see Num 19:13–20; Josephus *Ant.* 3.262; 4QMMT B lines 72–4. Some Greeks considered such corpse avoidance superstitious (Theophrastus *Char.* 16.9).

[137] Safrai, "Home," 777, citing *m. Kil.* 9:4; *Maʿaś. Š.* 5:12; *t. Ned.* 2:7; *Sem.* 12:10. Amoraim also understood *m. Naz.* 9:3 as requiring burials with limbs unbent (Safrai, "Home," 780–81).

[138] Safrai, "Home," 773, citing *m. Šabb.* 23:5; *Sem.* 1.

[139] Jeremias, *Parables*, 61 n. 51.

[140] E.g., Beasley-Murray, *John*, 195.

[141] "The skeptical question of how Lazarus got out of the tomb if his hands and feet were bound is really rather silly in an account which obviously presupposes the supernatural" (Brown, *John*, 1:427).

[142] Ibid.

digmatic in some way for the resurrection life experienced by believers (cf. 14:19). Mary lavishes her devotion on Jesus and provides a radical contrast with Judas (12:1–8); as the price of new life, Lazarus now faces the threat of death from the same people who want to kill Jesus (12:9–11).

## 1. Faith and Betrayal among Witnesses (11:45–46)

Many of the bystanders responded in faith (11:45; cf. 11:15, 40); the language suggests that the majority did so.[143] (On the significance of such signs-faith, see comment on 2:11 and related texts.) That John calls the bystanders "the Jews" indicates his continuing confidence that even among those who constitute the primary opposition (see introduction on "the Jews"), faith remains possible. Although it is not part of his purpose to emphasize it, John may even share the earlier Christian optimism in an eschatological repentance of his Jewish people (Rom 11:26).[144]

But the specter of rejection remains, for some of the bystanders took word to the authorities that Jesus was again in Judea and doing signs that were influencing others' opinions (John 11:46). In an analogous setting in the Fourth Gospel, a report about Jesus' signs directed toward the elite is intended not as witness (as in 7:46; 9:30–33) but as betrayal (5:15–16); given the equally immediate hostile response, such is probably in view here. New Testament miracle stories frequently include rejection, but nearly all other ancient miracle stories lack this element, although its converse, acclamation, is common.[145] The motif of rejection or persecution after miracles[146] undoubtedly stems from the ministry of Jesus and/or the experience of his earliest followers.

## 2. The Elite Plot Jesus' Death (11:47–53)

The plot of the leaders (11:47–53) fittingly follows the Lazarus narrative (11:1–44); Jesus is the resurrection and the life, but to give Lazarus life must set his own in danger (11:8, 16). In this epitome of Johannine irony, Jesus would die on behalf of others (11:50).[147]

### 2A. Historical Plausibility

Mark also draws on a tradition in an earlier passion narrative in which leaders plot against Jesus (Mark 14:1–2), very likely in response to his demonstration and teaching in the temple earlier that week (Mark 11:15–18). In John, the demonstration in the temple opens Jesus' public ministry, framing it with the ethos of the passion week and the Jerusalem leaders' hostility. In John, the immediate precedent and provocation for the final plotting is Lazarus's resuscitation. Because this was Jesus' climactic sign before the cross, it suggests a rejection of his whole public ministry (1:11).[148]

---

[143] But not "all," as rightly pointed out Brown, ibid., 1:438.

[144] Cf. also Matt 23:39 and comment in Keener, *Matthew*, 558–59; possibly also Rev 11:11–13 (Keener, *Revelation*, 296–97).

[145] Theissen, *Stories*, 72. The skepticism of some that a report directly to Jesus' enemies would injure him (Bernard, *John*, 2:402, citing 5:15, which further weakens his case) ignores both the indications in the context that it is known that the authorities wish to arrest Jesus (11:8, 16, 20, 28, 30; cf. 7:13, 25, 44; 8:59; 10:31) and the contrast with the more receptive "Jews" of 11:45.

[146] Outside the Gospels, see esp. Acts 4:2–3; 5:16–18; 6:8–11; 14:10–19; 16:18–19; 19:10–12, 26–28.

[147] Dodd, *More Studies*, 58.

[148] Pancaro, *Law*, 119.

John's account of the plot (11:47–53) fits what we know of the period. Plotting seems to have characterized Jewish as well as Roman aristocratic politics in the first century; thus John of Gischala's allies "took counsel" with him how to undo Josephus (Josephus *Life* 236).[149] Jerusalem's leaders were desperate to prevent actions which would provoke the Romans (Josephus *War* 2.237); Josephus reports that later aristocratic priests and Pharisees desired peace and only feigned to go along with the populace to save their lives (Josephus *Life* 21–22). Josephus's report of Antipas's reason for mistrusting and executing John the Baptist fits the reasoning of these leaders.[150]

Further, one would hardly expect Jesus' execution without the cooperation of a council of Jerusalem aristocrats (see comment on the Sanhedrin at the introduction to the Passion Narrative). Local municipal aristocracies normally brought persons to trial before the Romans;[151] indeed, the Roman legal system as a whole depended heavily on *delatores*, accusers.[152] Many are thus inclined to accept a substantial amount of prior tradition in this report.[153] Though John may add the Pharisees to preserve the unity of opposition in his Gospel,[154] the spokesman for the opposition is Caiaphas the high priest (11:49), and the high priesthood is the part of the opposition first named (11:47). The Synoptics and Acts suggest that the most brutal opposition came especially from the Sadducean aristocracy.[155]

Such considerations argue for early tradition, not necessarily historicity. A leak from the Jerusalem aristocracy is not at all implausible and happened on other occasions where the object of discussion had allies in the aristocracy (cf., e.g., Josephus *Life* 204).[156] If Joseph of Arimathea became an ally of the disciples at some point, his sharing of information with them is more probable than not. Although evidence suggests that the early Christians carefully guarded their traditions, one cannot be certain on purely historical grounds whether the tradition stems from sources like Joseph or from hearsay that a persecuted sect found believable without eyewitness verification.

---

[149] Cf. other corrupt leaders (from Josephus's perspective) in Josephus *Life* 216. Greek priesthoods also could engage in plots to deceive people politically (Plutarch *Lysander* 26.1–3, on some Delphic priests).

[150] Vermes, *Jesus the Jew*, 50, citing Josephus *Ant.* 18.117–118. Thus, whether or not Caiaphas spoke these words, it was the establishment's attitude (Vermes, *Jesus and Judaism*, 12).

[151] Brown notes the necessity of the Sanhedrin's conviction for execution in Josephus *Ant.* 14.167 (Brown, *Death*, 339); although this text reflects practice in the time of Herod the Great, Roman governors who had less reason to accommodate the people held less power than Herod and may have accommodated custom (cf. 18:39). Less convincing would be Stauffer's use of later evidence for the necessity of the Jerusalem Sanhedrin sentencing false prophets (*Jesus*, 207–8).

[152] E.g., Pliny *Ep.* 10.97; Herodian 7.3.2; Judge, *Pattern*, 71; cf. Harvey, *History*, 16; Sherwin-White, *Society*, 47.

[153] E.g., Winter, *Trial*, 37.

[154] Pharisees are elsewhere attested alongside high priests (see, e.g., Von Wahlde, "Terms," 233), and undoubtedly, aristocratic Pharisees participated in the municipal aristocracy; but John consistently heightens their pre-70 role; see their presence with the aristocratic priests in 7:32; 11:57.

[155] Sanders, *Jesus and Judaism*, 286. Some Pharisaic opposition remains likely; Paul was a Pharisee (Phil 3:5) and persecuted Christians (Phil 3:6), though he acted in connection with the high priest (Acts 9:1–2); but other Pharisees, perhaps especially Hillelites, were more consistent with their general stance of tolerance (Acts 5:34–35).

[156] Among other aristocracies, e.g., Cornelius Nepos 4 (Pausanias), 5.1; 14 (Datames), 5.3.

## 2B. Caiaphas, High Priest "That Year" (11:49)

Caiaphas's[157] involvement with Jesus' trial makes historical sense.[158] That Caiaphas held power as long as he did (nineteen years) reinforces the suspicion one gets from other nonpriestly sources concerning the character of the high priesthood in this period: he was a skilled but probably often ruthless politician. He kept the public peace in a manner that satisfied both Rome and the populace, and in so doing preserved his own position.[159] He was well-to-do,[160] part of the most hellenized elite,[161] and hence had much at stake personally in keeping the peace. Yet it is reasonable to suppose that, even given the purest of concern for their people's welfare—on which their own rose or fell—the priestly aristocracy would regard unrest, hence the popularity of Jesus, as a threat.[162]

The phrase "high priest for that year" (11:49; cf. 18:13) has produced considerable discussion. Greeks dated years by officials who held office in a particular year; chronological listings included lists of priests and priestesses as well as magistrates, victors in the games, and so forth.[163] Greeks usually changed priests annually, and in keeping with this custom, chief priests changed each year in Syria and Asia Minor.[164] Thus some suggest that John, writing in Asia Minor (or perhaps Syria), simply assumed that his local custom applied to pre-70 Jerusalem.[165] But it is not very likely that John, who reports so much tradition that presupposes a Palestinian Jewish context, would be unaware that high priests did not change annually. He knew the OT; his intimate knowledge of Jerusalem's pre-70 topography makes an ignorance of the more widely known longer-than-annual duration of high priests' offices unlikely.[166] Likewise it is possible, but not likely, that John simply accommodated the expectations of those familiar with local cults, for he has no apparent reason to mention an annual duration to conform practice with local custom. Further, even some (the minority of) Greek priesthoods were lifelong,[167] inviting Greeks to distinguish which were which.

More to the point, the Jerusalem high priest no longer held the office for life. Some have suggested that the text could allude "to a Roman insistence on an annual confirma-

---

[157] His Jewish name was Joseph, but his cognomen was Caiaphas, perhaps meaning "inquisitor" (Stauffer, *Jesus,* 122).

[158] Winter, *Trial,* 39, doubts that Caiaphas was much involved with the trial. But while Luke also knows of Caiaphas (Luke 3:2; Acts 4:6), only Matthew and John (Matt 26:3, 57; John 18:13–14, 24, 28) connect him with Jesus' trial, which strongly suggests (in view of John's very likely independence from Matthew) independent traditions attesting Caiaphas's role. On Annas and Caiaphas in John, see Brown, *Death,* 404–11.

[159] Stauffer, *Jesus,* 102. (Stauffer, p. 54, thinks that Caiaphas "held his peace" when Pilate introduced standards into Jerusalem; but Josephus *Ant.* 18.57–59 is unclear.)

[160] See the very debated, so-called Caiaphas family tomb (Riesner, "Familiengrab"; Reich, "Inscriptions"; idem, "Name"; Evans, "Caiaphas Ossuary"). Even if it did not belong to Caiaphas himself, it probably belonged to aristocratic priests (see Horbury, "Ossuaries") and so illustrates the point; for health advantages of Jerusalem's upper class, cf. Zias, "Remains."

[161] On pagan features of the tomb (see note above), see Greenhut, "Tomb"; idem, "Cave."

[162] E.g., Case, *Origins,* 56; cf. Winter, *Trial,* 43. The aristocracy undoubtedly considered their method of silencing Jesus successful; Rome regarded Palestine as quiet during Tiberius's reign (Judge, *Pattern,* 23, citing Tacitus *Hist.* 5.9).

[163] Aune, *Environment,* 85.

[164] Grundmann, "Decision," 304.

[165] E.g., Sandmel, *Judaism,* 133, 476 n. 39.

[166] Cf. also Schnackenburg, *John,* 2:348.

[167] Mylonas, *Eleusis,* 230. Cf. also Caesar as Pontifex Maximus, which appears in Greek as ἀρχιερεύς (P.Lond. 1912.14; Alexandria, 41 C.E.).

tion of the Jerusalem high priest," though this is unattested elsewhere.[168] Others suggest that it simply means, "the (memorable) year in which Jesus was executed"; this seems the most common position.[169] This view takes the genitive temporally ("in that year"), probably emphasizing especially ἐκείνου, "that."[170] One may compare "that day" (11:53),[171] John's words about Jesus' "hour" (e.g., 2:4; 7:30; 8:20) or "time" (7:6, 8), or John's mention of other special moments in revelation (e.g., 4:53). This view accounts for the emphatic, threefold mention of the priesthood "in that year" (11:49, 51; 18:18) better than do proposals that John simply made a mistake[172] or accommodated audience expectations here.

If, however, John can presuppose some knowledge of Jerusalem politics on the part of transplanted Judeans in his audience, he may strike a note of irony: Rome could depose priests at will; deposed high priests like Caiaphas's father-in-law Annas could still meddle in the city's affairs (cf. 18:13); and only a high priest who cooperated well with Rome could rule so long. Perhaps John even cynically presents the high priest as a Greek-type caretaker, an honorary office, rather than a divine appointment; he recognized that the high priesthood was an honor no one should take to oneself (Heb 5:4). Thus, for example, whereas Egyptians had hereditary priesthoods, Romans allowed Greek temples in Egypt to perpetuate Greek customs, but these temples "had no clergy, only officiators and administrators, a laity that the metropolites selected from their own class, in annual rotation, to see to the physical upkeep and cultic requirements of the shrines."[173] He also may link this ἀρχιερεύς with the other ἀρχιερεῖς of which he is a part;[174] he acts on behalf of the whole corrupt group. John's complaint against the Jerusalem elite, which he believes executed Jesus and prevented a wider acceptance of the Jesus movement among his people, is political as well as religious.[175]

## 2C. The Leaders' Reasoning (11:47–50)

The leaders fear that Jesus' signs (11:47) will produce faith among "all people" (11:48), ironically fulfilling the purpose of Jesus' coming into the world and John's witness (1:7–9), foreshadowing the Gentile mission (12:19–21). Their fear begins to come to pass in 12:18, where even Jerusalem's crowds begin to follow Jesus because of this sign (cf. also 12:11). (In John, unlike the Synoptics, the crowds do not later pass judgment against Jesus; the responsibility for persecution against Jewish Christians lay primarily at the feet of the nation's recognized leaders.) Ultimately, their very plan to have Jesus killed to prevent all from coming to him (11:48–50) will have the opposite result (12:32)—thereby confirming the widely recognized ancient view that even attempts to thwart fate (or God's plan) would

---

[168] Grundmann, "Decision," 304.

[169] Westcott, *John,* vi; Strachan, *Gospel,* 157; MacGregor, *John,* 256; Hoskyns, *Gospel,* 411; Lightfoot, *Gospel,* 230; Reicke, *Era,* 148 n. 17; Grundmann, "Decision," 304; O'Day, "John," 697, with Origen.

[170] Schnackenburg, *John,* 2:348; Brown, *John,* 1:439–40, citing Blass, Debrunner, and Funk, *Grammar,* 99–100, §186.

[171] Michaels, *John,* 196.

[172] Implied, e.g., in Sandmel, *Judaism,* 133.

[173] Lewis, *Life,* 90–91. Cf. *BGU* 4.1199 (Sherk, *Empire,* 30, §14).

[174] Such language was intelligible; cf., e.g., the chief of nine Athenian archons called the archon (Philo *Abraham* 10).

[175] For political more than religious critique here, see Umoh, *Plot to Kill Jesus* (who notes that these political leaders' leadership model conflicts with the kind proposed in the Gospel).

simply help fulfill it.[176] The authorities' frantic question, "What are we doing?" (11:47) is answered in the parallel context in 12:19, when the Pharisees complain that "We are not doing good" (literally, profiting nothing) and that the world is finally going after him (12:19). In a sense, John offers the hostility of such leaders as the reason that the world did not more quickly embrace Jesus.[177]

In a document addressing an audience after 70 C.E., the elite's fear that the Romans would take away their place and nation if they did not execute Jesus (11:48) is a striking irony.[178] If John's audience felt like many other Jewish Christians, they probably viewed Jerusalem's destruction as the direct consequence of Jesus' execution (Matt 23:31–39)! Such irony fits earlier biblical models; thus, for example, the very matter that Egypt feared (Israel's freedom because of their strength—Exod 1:10) the Egyptians provoked by oppressing them (Exod 2:23–25). (The "nation" may mean Judea's freedoms as a national entity in Syria-Palestine; the "place" may refer to Jerusalem but probably refers to the temple.)[179]

Caiaphas's claim that the priests "know nothing at all" (11:49) represents the epitome of Johannine irony, like the Pharisees' admission that they do nothing good (12:19). The informed readers of the Gospel by this point will read such statements on a much more literal level than their speakers in the story world intended them![180] (On unintended truth, see comment on 11:51.) But Paul Duke may be right to point out, perhaps tongue-in-cheek, that while it is true that they know nothing (underlined by three negatives), the high priest goes on to show that he knows even less.[181]

The high priest's claim that it is better for one to die for the people (11:50) is important enough to John to bear repetition; it is the chief declaration for which John remembers him (18:14). If the texts that report this claim do not simply develop a commonsense tenet based on a community perspective,[182] it might reflect a popular recognition in ancient Jewish ethics,[183] though the Tannaim clearly opposed it under some circumstances.[184] Using different wording, Josephus was willing to suffer more because the

---

[176] E.g., Apollodorus 3.12.5; Babrius 136; Sophocles *Oed. tyr.* passim; 1 Kgs 22:30; Josephus *Ant.* 8.419. On fate's inescapability in a more general sense, Homer *Il.* 1.5; Demosthenes *Crown* 289; Josephus *War* 6.84; Horsley, *Documents,* 4, §5, pp. 20–21; §6, p. 25; §9, pp. 33–34.

[177] That they dare not "let" Jesus "alone" (11:48) and that Jesus commands the woman's critics to "let" her "alone" (12:7) might reflect a contrast of leadership styles (although ἀφίημι appears fourteen times in the Gospel).

[178] See Duke, *Irony,* 26, on "irony of events" (citing Amos 5:19). This irony would be intelligible in ancient plausibility structures; e.g., some thought Socrates' execution the cause of Athens's (and Greece's) decline (Eunapius *Lives* 462).

[179] For the temple, see 4:20; Acts 6:13–14; 7:7; Michaels, *John,* 196.

[180] Ancients would readily grasp the double entendre; Cicero ridiculed a witness's claim to know nothing by taking it more generally (Plutarch *Cicero* 26.6).

[181] Duke, *Irony,* 87–88. This is "dramatic irony" (pp. 23–24).

[182] Employed at times in military strategies, e.g., Cornelius Nepos 15 (Epaminondas), 9.1; 1 Kgs 22:31; battles to eliminate potential tyrants (Cicero *Phil.* 3.8.19; 8.5.15); or the punishment of offenders to deter corporate suffering (*Apoll. K. Tyre* 46; cf. 2 Sam 20:21) or to establish deterrents (Aeschines *Timarchus* 192–193, 196).

[183] E.g., *Gen. Rab.* 91:10. See further citations in Haenchen, *John,* 2:79; Falk, *Jesus,* 130–31 (improbably stressing that it was a Shammaite view); Smith, *Parallels,* 139. Cf. also *Gk. Apoc. Ezra* 1:11 (συμφέρει γὰρ μίαν ψυχὴν; God rejects the proposed substitution here, perhaps as polemic against Christian doctrine).

[184] E.g., *m. Ter.* 8:12.

multitude of Galileans was so great (Josephus *Life* 212).[185] Josephus elsewhere assumes this principle of greater and lesser worth when he declares that Agrippa II admonished the crowds not to fight the numerous Romans and invite wholesale slaughter of their people for the sake of a single offender and a few who suffered unjustly (*War* 2.353, 399); if they do fight, the Romans will burn their city and destroy their nation (*War* 2.397). At least in the rabbinic stream of tradition, a guilty Israelite may suffer to atone for his own sins as well as to keep Israel from being led astray.[186] Later rabbis continued to debate whether an innocent Israelite should be sacrificed for the rest of Israel, and the view that he should apparently prevailed in the Amoraic period.[187]

Whether such views were current in the first century, however, Caiaphas's view, as portrayed in John, stems more from "expediency" than from moral principle.[188] At least sometimes Jerusalem aristocrats reasoned in this manner. For example, Jonathan's allies reportedly reason that four rulers from Jerusalem are better than one (Josephus); by contrast, the masses are unpersuaded, trusting Josephus (Josephus *Life* 278–279). "Expediency" was a standard tool of moral reasoning among Greek philosophers,[189] not surprising given the sort of education John's audience could expect such elite priests to have had. But ironically the priest is quite right: it is better for the people if Jesus dies (cf. 16:7); Jesus had to die "on behalf of" his sheep (ὑπέρ, 10:15; 11:51–52), the "scattered children of God" (10:16; 11:52).

2D. Unintended Truth (11:51–53)

John declares that the high priest inadvertently uttered truth that differed considerably from the message he intended as truth (11:51). Oracular utterances frequently proved notoriously ambiguous and misinterpreted until their fulfillment,[190] for instance, rulers sometimes understood prophecies as referring to the slaughter of enemies when it referred to their own defeat;[191] or a prophecy could be fulfilled by the very attempt to evade its fulfillment.[192] Ancients often believed that prophetic frenzy displaced

---

[185] Willingness to suffer or die on behalf of others accorded with Greek conceptions of heroism (e.g., Euripides *Iph. aul.* 1394–1397, 1420, 1553–1560; see comment on 15:13).

[186] *M. Sanh.* 6:2; *t. Ber.* 6:17; *Kip.* 4:8–9; *᾽Abot R. Nat.* 29; 39A; *b. Ber.* 60a, *bar.*; *Sanh.* 47b; *Šebu.* 13a; *p. Šebu.* 1:6, §5; *Num. Rab.* 8:5; *Eccl. Rab.* 4:1, §1; hence posthumous stoning (*b. Ber.* 19a; *p. Mo᾽ed Qaṭ.* 3:1, §9; cf. Christian material in *Sib. Or.* 7.161–162) or suffering (*Pesiq. Rab Kah.* 11:23). Cf. *L.A.B.* 25:6–7; 26:1; 27:15; on a corporate level, *Jub.* 30:14–17; 33:10–14; 41:26.

[187] Schnackenburg, *John*, 2:349.

[188] Ibid.; cf. Judg 9:2.

[189] Plato *Alc.* 1:115–127; *Greater Hippias* 295E; Aristotle *Rhet.* 1.7.1, 1363b; Seneca *Benef.* 4.5.1; 4.21.6; 7.8.2; Epictetus *Diatr.* 1.2.5–7; 1.6.6; 1.6.33; 1.18.2; 1.22.1; 1.28.5; 2.7.4; 2.8.1; 3.21.15; 4.7.9; 4.8.17; Marcus Aurelius 6.27; 9.1.1; *Phaedrus* 3.17.13; Diogenes Laertius 7.1.98–99; 10.150.31; 10.152.37; Sextus Empiricus *Eth.* 2.22; Theon *Progymn.* 8.45; Sir 37:28; 1 Cor 6:12.

[190] Retrospect provided the appropriate perspective on purported oracles (e.g., Aeschylus *Agamemnon* 1112–1113; Sophocles *Oed. tyr.* 439; *Trach.* 1169–1173; Plutarch *Alex.* 37.1; Lycophron *Alex.* 1–15; Apollodorus 2.8.2; 3.5.7; 3.15.6; Statius *Thebaid* 1.495–496; Virgil *Aen.* 6.98–101; Dio Cassius 62.18.4; Arrian *Alex.* 7.26.2–3; Xenophon *Eph.* 1.6–7; Philostratus *Hrk.* 15.2–3, 5; Josephus *War* 1.80). Misplaced political agendas could be held to distort the interpretations of oracles (Plutarch *Lysander* 22.5–6); for poetic license, cf. Ovid *Metam.* 15.823–824.

[191] E.g., Philip of Macedon (Diodorus Siculus 16.91.2–3); or the story of Croesus in Herodotus *Hist.* 1.46–48; 1.53.3; Maximus of Tyre *Or.* 5.2; Cyrus in Philostratus *Hrk.* 28.11–12; Hamilcar in Valerius Maximus 1.7.*ext.*8; cf. also Valerius Maximus 1.5.4; 1.8.10.

[192] E.g., Sophocles *Oed. tyr.* 717–725, 744–745, 788–797; Valerius Maximus 1.8.10; 1 Kgs 22:30, 34.

the prophet's mind,[193] which is not the case here;[194] but a key parallel is the concept that one who prophesied was not responsible for, or the originator of, his or her words.

Josephus, who was a priest and claimed to be a prophet, regarded the Jewish priesthood as particularly prophetically endowed;[195] whether or not John regards the priesthood as prophetically endowed,[196] he believed that God could arrange for them to speak truth. Perhaps borrowing the Greek conception of ecstatic loss of control in prophecy,[197] the rabbis referred to prophecies unintended and unrecognized by the speaker.[198] Other early Jewish sources[199] and Gentile sources, such as (reportedly) the Egyptians,[200] recognized the possibility of unintended prophetic insights. The principle sometimes applied to truth prevailing through speakers' unintended double entendres, even without reference to prophecy. Thus hearers laughed when a speaker said one thing on a literal level in which they heard an unintended play on the accused's behavior; they claimed that truth had prevailed over the speaker's intention.[201]

When Caiaphas speaks of the "people" (11:50; 18:14), he refers to the Jewish people.[202] But whereas the "children of God" scattered abroad (11:52) could refer to Diaspora Jews,[203] especially if we thought of how Caiaphas would have meant the phrase had he been the one to use it here, the prophetic, hence divine, perspective must agree with the omniscient narrator, and in the context of the Fourth Gospel it refers to believers in Jesus (1:12; 3:3–5).[204] That they would be "one" (11:52) reflects Jesus' mission for his followers (10:16; 17:22), after he delivers them from being "scattered" (10:12; 16:32). John might adapt the tenth petition of the *Amidah* for the regathering of the dispersed, applying it to believers, including Gentiles (cf. 12:20–23).[205]

---

[193] E.g., Lucan *C.W.* 1.673–695; Dionysius of Halicarnassus *R.A.* 1.31.1; Piñero, "Inspiration"; other sources in Keener, *Spirit,* 21–26.

[194] Cf. Burkhardt, "Inspirationslehre," who doubts that Philo's view of inspiration was ecstatic possession; but this thesis is open to question (cf. Keener, *Spirit,* 24–25).

[195] See Blenkinsopp, "Prophecy"; Hill, *Prophecy,* 30; Aune, *Prophecy,* 138–44; Grundmann, "Decision," 305. Cf. *Num. Rab.* 21:9; cf. also the idea of a hereditary prophetic gift in Arrian *Alex.* 2.3.3.

[196] Michaels, *John,* 196, finds it doubtful, pointing out that those who had the gift (Josephus *War* 1.68–69; *Ant.* 11.327, 333–334; 13.299–300) were exceptional. Cf. Josephus *Ant.* 10.80; but one might rather attribute it more prominently to the Essenes (e.g., Josephus *War* 1.78–80; 2.159; *Ant.* 17.346), whose priestly connection is less evident in Josephus.

[197] See Keener, *Spirit,* 24, and sources cited there.

[198] *ʾAbot R. Nat.* 43, §118B (biblical examples); *b. Soṭah* 12b (pagans). See further Aune, *Prophecy,* 139, following Billerbeck, *Kommentar,* 2:546. Grudem, *Prophecy,* 38, cites some later rabbinic references explaining biblical prophetesses as accurate predictors without divine authority.

[199] Jdt 6:2 (where προφήτευσας refers to truth spoken unwittingly).

[200] Egyptians reportedly looked for unintended prophecies through children (Plutarch *Isis* 14, *Mor.* 356E); cf. also Xenophon *Eph.* 5.4; Augustine *Confessions* 8.12.

[201] Aeschines *Timarchus* 84; cf. Pysche in Apuleius *Metam.* 5.6; Saul in 1 Sam 14:39. An accurate societal critic could also be dubbed "oracular" in a figurative sense because he spoke truth (Seneca *Controv.* 1.pref.9).

[202] E.g., *Liv. Pro.* 2:1 (*OTP* 2:386)/Jeremiah 2 (ed. Schermann 81); Matt 2:4, 6; 4:16, 23; 13:15; 15:8; 21:23; 27:64; Acts 2:47.

[203] So Robinson, "Destination," 127.

[204] Many commentators apply it to either Gentiles only (Hunter, *John,* 118) or (as we do) to both Jewish and Gentile Christians (Pancaro, "People," 126–27, 129). Freed, "Samaritan Influence," 583, suggests that it refers to the Samaritans.

[205] Grundmann, "Decision," 308–10. The biblical theme of the scattering of God's people as judgment appears in early Jewish texts, e.g., *1 En.* 89:75; *T. Ash.* 7:3 (though followed by a Christian interpolation); 7:6.

### 3. Danger during Passover Season (11:54–57)

Recognizing that the level of threat was no longer that of mob violence (8:59; 10:31, 39) but premeditated and planned violence (11:53), Jesus stopped the "public" ministry he had begun in 7:4–14 (11:54; see comment on παρρησία in 7:4).[206] God would protect Jesus until his hour (7:30; 8:20), but Jesus would also cooperate with his Father's plan to do so. In 11:54 Jesus continued to "remain" (cf. 10:40; 11:6; 12:24) in the wilderness (cf. the new exodus theme in 1:23; 3:14; 6:39, 49), again no longer walking in Judean territory because of his enemies (as in 7:1).

Some think that "Ephraim" (11:54) was in Samaritan territory, hence that Jesus took refuge there with his friends from Samaria (4:40).[207] This is possible, though probably only the former Palestinian Jewish Christians in the community would understand the geographical allusion.[208] That Jesus withdrew from "the Judeans" to find refuge in "Ephraim," often a name for the northern kingdom in the biblical prophets (especially Hosea), may have struck more of them.

That "the Jewish festival of Passover was near" (11:55) recalls the earlier Passovers in the Gospel, announced in almost identical words (2:13; 6:4). Both previous Passovers in the story became occasions for severe conflict (2:15–19; 6:66), and the earlier Gospel tradition reserves the paschal announcement for the passion week (Mark 14:1, 12; Matt 26:18). Most significantly, however, the reader knows from previous depictions of feasts that Jesus goes to Jerusalem for such feasts (e.g., 2:13; 5:1; 7:2, 10; 10:22); unless Jesus goes secretly (7:10), he is about to return to the place where Judeans have been wishing to kill him (5:18; 7:1; 8:59; 10:31; 11:8, 53). Even if one approached the Gospel unaware of the passion tradition (and most of John's original audience would not), one would recognize that, barring divine intervention (7:30; 8:20), his "hour" was soon at hand (12:23, 27; 13:1).

Many went to Jerusalem early to "purify themselves" before the festival (11:55; cf. 2:6; 3:25). Like other pilgrims, they probably joked and made merry on the way.[209] But Diaspora Jews in particular would want to arrive early to purify themselves ritually; many could do it nowhere else (cf. Acts 21:24, 26; 24:18).[210] Many, especially those with corpse impurity, would need to arrive at least a week early.[211] Jesus needed no further purification (cf. 10:36), but nevertheless is near Jerusalem several days before the festival (12:1).

Those who were seeking him in the temple (11:56) probably included these Jewish people from outside Jerusalem (11:55) who remembered hearing Jesus at earlier recent feasts (thus presumably they were mostly Galileans rather than distant foreigners, who could make pilgrimage only rarely); in contrast to the leaders mentioned in 11:57, they do not appear uniformly hostile to Jesus. They had good reason to wonder whether he would come to the feast (11:56); although it was considered pious behavior to come, they were also aware that the leaders wanted to kill Jesus (11:57; cf. 8:59; 10:31; 11:8). Thus John

---

[206] Meeks, Prophet-King, 60.

[207] Stauffer, Jesus, 104.

[208] The reference is usually taken as genuine historical information (e.g., Dunn, "John," 299); perhaps it was near a preexilic site with a similar name (2 Chr 13:19).

[209] Sanders, Judaism, 128, comparing pilgrims to Bubastis in Herodotus.

[210] Safrai, "Temple," 876–77, citing, e.g., Josephus War 1.229. Michaels, John, 201, thinks those living among Gentiles would have to purify themselves as well.

[211] DeSilva, Honor, 274–75; Sanders, Judaism, 134–35, thinks relevant in this connection Josephus War 6.290; Philo Spec. Laws 1.261. Cf. 2 Chr 30:17–20. For annual purifications among Greeks, see, e.g., Philostratus Hrk. 53.5.

again builds suspense as his narrative begins to climax in Jesus' final coming to, and suffering in, Jerusalem.

### 4. Mary's Lavish Devotion (12:1–8)

Even though Jesus' passion overshadows the entire body of the Gospel from ch. 2 on, fully one-third of the Gospel specifically occurs during the week of Jesus' execution, mostly in or near Jerusalem. This reflects and further augments the sort of emphasis on the passion that one finds in Mark. In contrast to most modern biographies, some ancient biographies devoted an extensive proportion of their space to events immediately preceding and surrounding their protagonists' deaths.[212]

R. Alan Culpepper points to structural parallels between John 12 and 13:

| Category | John 12 | John 13 |
|---|---|---|
| Time | Six days before Passover | Before Passover |
| Companion | Lazarus | Beloved disciple |
| Washing feet | Mary washed Jesus | Jesus washed disciples |
| Jesus' death | Day of my burial | Took off robe (implied) |
| Jesus' departure | You do not always have me | Hour to depart from the world |

As Culpepper notes, this repetition increases pathos.[213] The repetition also builds toward a climax, the discourse making Jesus' death and departure more explicit.

Most of ch. 12 is transitional, closing Jesus' public ministry and (with 11:45–57) leading into the Passion Narrative.[214]

Mary's anointing at Bethany contrasts starkly with the preceding scene of calculated plans to have Jesus killed: "a supreme act of ignorant unbelief and a supreme act of intelligent faith."[215] The smaller units (11:45–46, 54–57; 12:9–11) in this section underline the mixed response to Jesus; the two longest units, however, contrast the high priests (11:47–53) and Mary (12:1–8), while linking Judas with the attitude of the Judean elite (12:4–6).[216] After the leaders have plotted against Jesus' life (11:47–53), Mary lovingly anoints him for burial, Jesus is acclaimed king of Israel (12:13) as he will be at the cross (18:39; 19:3, 14–15, 19), and Jesus' brief discourse elaborates on his impending death (12:23–33), preparing the way for the Passion Narrative.[217]

### 4A. The Tradition

Different versions of the anointing story occur in the four canonical gospels. The differences in the accounts of the anointing among the Gospels may have arisen through oral traditions, which developed in different directions; different evangelists may have mixed

---

[212] Burridge, *Gospels,* 224–25, citing Tacitus *Agricola* (26 percent); Plutarch *Agesilaus* (37 percent); *Cato Minor* (17.3 percent); Philostratus *Vita Apollonii* (26.3 percent). John's passion and resurrection proper constitute only 15.7 percent.

[213] Culpepper, *John,* 202–3.

[214] Culpepper, *Anatomy,* 94.

[215] Hoskyns, *Gospel,* 408.

[216] Judas is, however, worse than the Judean elite; the moral reasoning of the latter may be incorrect, but at least it involves moral reasoning, whereas Judas is portrayed as completely morally debased.

[217] Dodd, *More Studies,* 58.

different strands of the tradition.[218] Similarities do, however, indicate common sources rather than free invention.[219] Origen improbably suggested three anointings to harmonize the accounts,[220] but conflations from two basic anointing stories (which represent either variants of one original incident or a second incident imitating the first) seem far more likely.

The particular mixture of different traits suggests that the various writers may have conflated two different anointing stories, with Luke's story being the most distinctive (and characteristically Lukan). Moule, for instance, provides a basic summary comparison of some key elements:[221]

| Mark | Matthew | Luke | John |
|------|---------|------|------|
| Bethany | Bethany | — | Bethany |
| Simon | Simon | Simon | (Lazarus [Eleazar]) |
| the leper | the leper | a Pharisee | — |
| a woman | a woman | a sinful woman | Mary |
| head[222] | head | feet | feet |
| anointing | anointing | gratitude for | anointing |
| for burial | for burial | forgiveness | for burial |

As E. P. Sanders notes, "These stories probably rest on memories, though details have been exchanged and possibly confused."[223] It would have been only natural that in the oral tradition some conflation between two anointing stories would occur; it would be equally natural that each evangelist, reporting only one incident, would employ the most suitable features of the anointings for his own account. Sanders thinks that John 12 may represent a composite between Luke 7 and the accounts in Matt 26/Mark 14, or the traditions associated with them.[224]

The two stories we propose would be either divergent traditions stemming from one event,[225] or a second event in which a second woman probably followed the example of the first. In view of the likely pre-Markan divergence (except in his programmatic scene at Nazareth, Luke rarely takes such liberties as to rewrite an entire Markan narrative from scratch, and the Johannine account probably confirms the independent antiquity of some of its details), and in view of what most often seems accurate preservation of tradition in the early period (though this pattern would not preclude exceptions transmitted in different circumstances), two distinct anointings eventually conflated in the tradition seem more likely.[226]

---

[218] Dodd, *Tradition,* 172; cf. Mack, *Myth,* 200. Sanders, *Figure,* 127, suggests that "details have been exchanged and possibly confused."

[219] See Michaels, *John,* 202, on the correspondence in very rare words between 12:3 and Mark 14:3. Otherwise, however, verbal agreements are not particularly close.

[220] Origen *Comm. Matt.* 77; Wiles, *Gospel,* 16.

[221] Moule, *Mark,* 112.

[222] Calvin, *John,* 2:11 (on John 12:2), harmonizes accounts by noting that ancients usually anointed the head, that those who anointed also the ankles indulged in excess luxury (following Pliny), and that Matthew, Mark, and John agree "that Mary did not anoint Christ sparingly."

[223] Sanders, *Figure,* 127.

[224] Ibid., 126–27. In any case, he thinks it "evident that Jesus attracted women who were not 'followers,' but who admired him."

[225] E.g., Mack, *Myth,* 200. For a survey of views as of 1976, see esp. Holst, "One Anointing."

[226] With Blomberg, *Reliability,* 176 (and numerous others, though it remains a minority position).

John probably reflects accurate and independent tradition here, not mere reliance on the Synoptics.[227] The specific association of the tradition with Mary sister of Martha almost certainly predates its appearance in the Fourth Gospel. We know of Mary and Martha from Luke 10:38–42, and they appear to be known to John's audience as well (John 11:1). Further, the manner in which Mary's anointing was introduced in 11:2 (see comment there) suggests that John's audience already knows a form of the tradition in which the person who anointed Jesus was Mary.

Because of the festival crowds (11:55),[228] many pilgrims found overnight accommodation in nearby villages such as Bethany, as here (12:1).[229] Some more well-to-do pilgrims may have brought their own tents to camp in during Passover,[230] but many people showed traveling teachers hospitality in return for teaching,[231] and Lazarus's family had been close to Jesus even before Lazarus's raising (11:3). The Synoptics also report his lodging in Bethany (Mark 11:11–12; Matt 21:17), but claim that it was in the house of one Simon the leper (Mark 14:3; Matt 26:6). One can debate whether Lazarus was a former leper also named Simon (double names were not uncommon);[232] Simon was the father of Lazarus, Mary and Martha; "leper" was a nickname (on nicknames see comment on 1:42) or a former state that Jesus had healed; or other possibilities. In any case, John has not likely simply transferred an earlier story to Lazarus and his sisters; as we have noted, his audience already seems to know about Mary as the one who anointed Jesus (11:2). The original source of that tradition may be inaccessible today, but is not simply a matter of John's theological interpretation.

### 4B. The Setting (12:1–2)

Six days before the Passover (12:1) Jerusalem would already be filling, both for purification (11:55) and for Diaspora Jews making pilgrimage who could neither calculate the exact time of their arrival nor risk arriving late. In John's story world (in which Passover begins Friday evening; see 18:28; 19:14), this timing apparently indicates Saturday evening after sundown, when Martha could serve at table.[233] Yet Mark strongly implies that the anointing occurred two days before Passover (Mark 14:1–3). Some think that John corrects Mark on the basis of independent tradition;[234] whether the difference involves a deliberate correction or not, it does emphasize the independence of the tradition. Mark may

---

[227] Cf. Coakley, "Anointing."

[228] Estimates range as high as 125,000, but today many think 10,000 more likely (Haenchen, *John*, 1:182, following Safrai, *Pilgrimage*, 71–75); yet would the estimate of 10,000 permit even the numerous Galileans who would make the journey? Josephus's guesses may be unreliable, but the priests might have some estimate of the number of lambs required.

[229] Freyne, *Galilee*, 181; Sanders, *Judaism*, 129. Bethany was walking distance from Jerusalem (11:18; Luke 24:50).

[230] Sanders, *Judaism*, 129; see Josephus *Ant.* 17.213, 217. People employed leather tents, but also linen *tabernacula* for shade and market stands (cf. Lampe, "Zeltmacher").

[231] Koenig, *Hospitality*, 17.

[232] E.g., P.Oxy. 494.32; 1273.3, 49; Appian *R.H.* pref.13; Acts 1:23; see further documentation under John 14:22. Most early Jewish interpreters would understand the same for instances such as Jethro/Reuel/Hobab (Exod 2:18; 3:1; 4:18; 18:1–12; Num 10:29; Judg 4:11, though the term for male in-law may include distinct persons).

[233] Brown, *John*, 1:447, allowing but not endorsing the possibility that it may represent the meal of the Habdalah service, which closed the Sabbath, though we know little about the Habdalah service in this period.

[234] Howard, *Gospel*, 151.

have moved the anointing closer to Passover to clarify the connection or increase suspense, or to recount it after the fateful meeting of authorities, which he places two days before Passover (Mark 14:1–2) but which John places earlier (John 11:47–53). John may wish to begin passion week with the anointing; having recounted Jesus' conflicts in Jerusalem as early as 2:14–18, he now must bring the passion to an end quickly once Jesus enters the holy city. It is also possible, in view of an early Christian tradition concerning the transfiguration (Mark 9:2; Matt 17:1), that John uses the six days to allude to the waiting period for the revelation of God's glory at Sinai (Exod 24:16); at the Passover Jesus would be "glorified" (12:23–24), and his disciples would behold his glory as Moses had (1:14).[235] Less likely (though reflecting the Pentateuch's most frequent use of "six days") it refers to the period of work preceding a Sabbath (cf. John 19:14, 31, 42). The six days might also allow a careful interpreter to note the transition to the next day (12:12) and thus to suggest that Jesus entered Jerusalem on the day the Passover lambs were set aside (Exod 12:3), four days before their offering (Exod 12:6); but the lack of explicit chronological indication at the time of Jesus' entrance, when it would be most helpful to convey this point, renders unlikely the suggestion that John sought to communicate this impression.

The meal setting is probably a banquet celebrating Lazarus's resuscitation,[236] but may also foreshadow the implied meal setting of Jesus' pre-passion washing of his disciples' feet in ch. 13. Martha's "serving" (12:2) apparently reflects an activity for which Martha was known in the gospel tradition (Luke 10:40). Although the matter is unclear, it might also provide a model for, or a contrast with, the kind of humble service to which Jesus calls his followers (12:26, the Gospel's only other use of διακονέω).[237] The ultimate symbolic expression of service before the cross, however, is Jesus washing his disciples' feet (13:5, 14); the one disciple to carry this act out in this Gospel, even in advance of Jesus, is emphatically Mary (11:2; 12:3).

### 4C. The Anointing (12:3)

The measure of ointment here is a λίτρα, a Roman pound, close to twelve U.S. ounces or 324 grams.[238] To have expended all this on Jesus' feet is an act of lavish devotion (though it contrasts for its simplicity with the sacrifice of a genuinely rich man in 19:39). That such ointment would have been "costly," as John emphasizes (12:3, 5), would have been obvious. A wealthy person might give perfume at a banquet, poetically boasting that it smells sweeter than love itself so that the recipient will want to consist entirely of nose.[239]

---

[235] Glasson, *Moses*, 72, who also compares (less persuasively) glory revealed on a seventh day in 2:11 (where chronology is not mentioned) and possibly 7:37 (which we believe may be the eighth)

[236] E.g., Bruce, *John*, 255. It may have been a meal in Jesus' honor; for the significance of this and status issues of seating, see Malina and Rohrbaugh, *John*, 207–8; and our comment on status and the foot washing in ch. 13.

[237] It occurs sixteen times in the Synoptics, including in a saying quite consonant with John 12:26 (Mark 10:45; Matt 20:28; Luke 22:26–27). Seven of its appearances are in Luke alone, including Luke 10:40; but it appears frequently enough elsewhere for one to doubt that John must simply reproduce Luke's style rather than earlier tradition here.

[238] Beare, *Matthew*, 505, complains that such a quantity would not fit in a usual alabaster flask; but even if this is the case, John omits mention of such a flask (a common container; see Witherington, *Women*, 55) present in the Synoptic accounts (Matt 26:7; Mark 14:3; Luke 7:37), reinforcing our picture that John is independent of them here.

[239] Catullus 13.9–14; by contrast, Seneca *Ep. Lucil.* 108.16 and others advocated avoiding perfumes *(unguento)*, preferring no scent.

The term for "myrrh" normally indicates a perfume or ointment of myrrh, whether as a dried powder or liquid, made "from the gummy resin that exudes from a low shrubby balsam tree which grows in west-central South Arabia and in northern Somaliland."[240] But like Mark (Mark 14:3), John uses the term more generically.[241] "Nard" refers to spikenard, a fragrant oil from the root of the nard plant of the mountains of northern India.[242] In the Mediterranean world, eastern nard remained the fare of the well-to-do.[243]

A countercultural Cynic might anoint his feet rather than his head, so he could better inhale the unguent;[244] people also anointed feet on some other occasions, rare as these reports are.[245] Normally, however, one anointed kings, guests, or others on their heads;[246] that Mary anoints Jesus' feet (12:3; cf. Luke 7:38, 44–46, 48) indicates an even greater respect for Jesus (cf. Luke 10:39); she takes the posture of a servant (1:27; 13:5). (One may compare a later story in which one who wished to greatly honor R. Jonathan kissed his feet.)[247] That she also wipes Jesus' feet with her hair (12:3) reinforces this portrait of humble servitude; a woman's hair was her "glory" (1 Cor 11:7).[248] Commentators often observe that it would have violated the Palestinian Jewish custom that required women to keep their heads covered.[249] This custom obtained only for married women, however, and it is unclear that either Mary or Martha is married; given the nature of ancient sources, one would expect them to report if either was married, but we instead get the impression (though it is never explicit) that Mary and Martha live in their brother's home, and that if either had been married, they were not married now. They appear to be Lazarus's closest relatives (11:19–20), suggesting that all were unmarried (which might suggest their youth, and *perhaps* that Simon the leper in Mark 14:3 was their deceased father); but John may simply omit extraneous characters and information, so we cannot say for certain.

Whether Mary was single or married, however, to use her prized feminine hair (see above) to wipe Jesus' feet, when normally only servants even touched the master's feet (see comment on 1:27), indicates the depth of her humble submission to and affection for Jesus.[250] Banqueters were known to wipe excess water or oil on the head or hair of servants;

---

[240] Brown, *John,* 1:448. Essentially the same population type lived on both sides of the Red Sea (Huntingford, "Axum," 28; Rashidi, "Africans," 22–23). On myrrh, see further Harrison, "Myrrh."

[241] Brown, *John,* 1:448.

[242] Ibid., also commenting that the rare πιστικός may translate overliteraly an Aramaic expression that can mean "genuine" nard or apply to "faith" (better than Hunter, *John,* 121).

[243] E.g., Horace *Carm.* 2.11.16 *(Assyriaque nardo).*

[244] Diogenes Laertius 6.2.39.

[245] See Witherington, *Women,* 113, citing Athenaeus *Deipn.* 12.553 and Billerbeck, *Kommentar,* 1:427–28, 986. Bruns, "Jn 12:3," cites the same Athenaeus reference and relates anointing to royalty by Polybius 26.1.12–14.

[246] Exod 29:7; Lev 8:12; 21:10; 1 Sam 10:1; 15:17; 26:11, 16; 2 Sam 1:16; 2 Kgs 9:3, 6; Ps 23:5; Matt 6:17; Luke 7:46; also Polybius 26.1.13–14 (which stresses the lavishness and enjoyment). One might anoint a guest at table (*b. Ḥul.* 94a); one would anoint the head first at a bath (*b. Šabb.* 41a; *Soṭah* 11b; in Lachs, *Commentary,* 400).

[247] *P. Peʾah* 1:1, §13.

[248] Cf. Artemidorus *Onir.* 1.18; see Keener, *Paul,* 38–39.

[249] Morris, *John,* 576–77; Witherington, *Women,* 55; on the eastern Mediterranean Jewish custom, see, e.g., *m. Ketub.* 7:6; *Soṭah* 1:5; *Sipre Num.* 11.2.3; *ʾAbot R. Nat.* 3; 17A; 14, §35B; cf. *Jos. Asen.* 15:1–2; 18:6; Belkin, *Philo,* 230; further sources in Keener, *Paul,* 19–69; idem, "Headcoverings."

[250] See Brant, "Husband Hunting," for comments on how Mary within the story world might view Jesus (though this narrative, in contrast to that of the Samaritan woman, turns to pathos).

Mary seeks this servant's role as an expression of devotion to Jesus.[251] And given the taboos of the very pious against even speaking with women,[252] and undoubtedly the suspicions of most people when too much cross-gender affection between nonrelatives appeared in public, her action would probably seem immoral to many bystanders if they were present.[253] That the fragrance of anointing "filled the house" might recall the biblical image of God's glory filling his house when it was consecrated (Exod 40:34–35; 1 Kgs 8:10–11; on Jesus' consecration as a new temple, cf. perhaps John 10:36).

4D. Judas's Protest (12:4–6)

That Judas was already intending to betray Jesus by this point (12:4; 13:2) in the story is not unlikely. In John's story world, the opposition to Jesus is clear by this point, the sides are drawn (11:8), and the price of following Jesus is becoming clear (11:16). Even Paul's passion narrative may recall the act of betrayal (1 Cor 11:23); nor is it a datum the early Christians are likely to have invented, shaming as it would be to Jesus in their cultural context.[254] That a betrayer was necessary suggests that it became difficult to locate Jesus when he was not teaching publicly.[255]

That the ointment would have been expensive, perhaps an heirloom, beyond the means of most people, would have been obvious.[256] With Mark 14:5, John reports that the ointment's cost would have been nearly a year's wages for an average worker (12:5); it would be more than most women would inherit, and may represent Mary's entire inheritance (though given the fact that it may indicate a well-to-do Bethany family, it may not). Mary's devotion makes sense against the backdrop of her brother's restoration (the cause is less obvious in Matthew and Mark). Tradition assumes that disciples were sometimes entrusted with a rabbi's funds.[257]

John's remark that Judas was not concerned for the poor (12:6) underlines Judas's evil character; he employs the same term for "unconcerned" here as he earlier employed for the hirelings who did not care for the shepherd's flock in 10:13[258]—a context in which false leaders of the flock also earn the title "thief" (10:1, 8, 10; 12:6). Whereas Mark contrasts the costly devotion of the woman (Mark 14:3–9) with Judas's betrayal for money (Mark 14:10–11) by narrating them in succession, John implies the same contrast simply by transferring the tradition's general distaste of bystanders for the woman's sacrifice (Mark 14:4–5; disciples in Matt 26:8–9) to Judas (John 12:5) and mentioning his plans for betrayal (12:4) and his past theft (12:6).[259] For Judas's retention of the money (12:6), which

---

[251] See Witherington, *Women*, 113, citing Petronius *Sat.* 27. Petronius likely assumes a more widespread custom, probably known to John's audience and plausibly to Mary as well.

[252] See comment on 4:27.

[253] Mack, *Myth*, 200–201. That ancient novelists often combined heroines' heroism with feminine modesty and decency (Wiersma, "Novel") may increase the shock value here.

[254] Abandonment was shameful (e.g., Cornelius Nepos 14 [Datames], 6.3) and hence fits the criterion of embarrassment; cf. Keener, *Matthew*, 642–43; Robbins, *Jesus*, 30. Still, ancients recognized the difficulty of trusting no one (Polybius 8.36.1–9).

[255] Stauffer, *Jesus*, 112.

[256] See Lachs, *Commentary*, 401.

[257] *Pesiq. Rab.* 25:2 (an apocryphal story about R. Tarfon and R. Akiba).

[258] Brown, *John*, 1:448. Imputing motives to historical figures was a common practice, though it could draw criticism (Plutarch *Malice of Herodotus* 25, *Mor.* 861DE).

[259] The contrast here between Mary and Judas is noted also by others, e.g., Blomberg, *Poverty*, 142.

some apparently thought was going to the poor (13:29), see comment on 6:5; teachers sometimes assigned their disciples such roles (e.g., 4:8; *Pesiq. Rab.* 25:2). By the criterion of embarrassment, it is likely that Judas's role as treasurer stems from genuine historical tradition; appointing someone who misadministrated funds could be scandalous, all the more if the one who made the appointment were now claimed to be omniscient.[260]

### 4E. Jesus' Response (12:7–8)

Jesus responds by defending Mary (12:7).[261] She may have intended the anointing as a royal anointing,[262] which fits the following context (12:13–15). But Jesus is enthroned king of the Jews on the cross (19:19), so a royal anointing is inseparable from an anointing for burial, to which Jesus somehow relates her act (12:7; see below).[263] People used perfumes to suppress a stench, including for corpses,[264] and often anointed corpses.[265] When executed criminals were buried, they usually would have been denied anointing; thus the anointing takes place in advance, by anticipation, in Matthew and Mark (Matt 26:12; Mark 14:8);[266] John's wording is more ambiguous because of a further anointing in 19:39–40.[267] The mention of Jesus' impending burial fits the suspense suggested by the hostility of the chief priests in the immediate context (11:57; 12:10).

After explicitly noting that Judas's own concern was nothing so pious as care for the poor (12:6), John cites the same tradition which also appears in Mark (Mark 14:7): they will always have opportunity to serve the poor, but not always to serve Jesus while he is with them in the flesh (12:8). Jewish society did not imagine that it could eliminate poverty, but did stress its relief;[268] Jesus here alludes to Deut 15:11, which in context promises that God will supply the needs of all the people if they cared for the poor; but the poor would never depart from the land.[269] The context does not permit neglect of

---

[260] Ancients recognized that some treasurers grew rich by abusing their office, embarrassing the official for whom they worked (Aeschines *Timarchus* 56); they respected statesmen who did not touch public revenues (Iamblichus *V.P.* 27.129). Wisdom warned against entrusting fiscal responsibilities to stingy or greedy persons (e.g., 4Q424 frg. 1, line 10; the issue remained among early Christians, e.g., Acts 6:1–3; 20:33; 1 Thess 2:5; 1 Tim 3:3; Tit 1:7).

[261] In Luke he defended the same Mary on different grounds in Luke 10:42; but Jesus also defends the woman in the other anointing accounts (Mark 14:6; Matt 26:10; Luke 7:40–50). For her continuing "memory" in the oral passion narrative (Mark 14:9), cf. analogous statements in Virgil *Aen.* 9.446–449; 11.846–847; Ovid *Metam.* 15.877–879.

[262] Stauffer, *Jesus*, 107. On the historical level, affection would be a closer motive; but on the theological level, a royal anointing may play a role.

[263] *Pace* some interpreters, the anointing here (with perfume, not oil) does not relate to the later practice of extreme unction; see Brown, *Essays*, 101–2.

[264] *T. Job.* 31:2; Herodian 4.2.8.

[265] Homer *Il.* 18.351; 24.582; Virgil *Aen.* 6.219; Martial *Epigr.* 3.12; *Apoll. K. Tyre* 26; *T. Ab.* 20:11A; *m. Šabb.* 23:5; cf. further Safrai, "Home," 776; Hagner, *Matthew*, 758.

[266] Daube, "Gospels," 342.

[267] The further anointing in Mark 16:1 is left unfulfilled. John may have preserved the earlier form of the language in the tradition also found in Mark 14:8, but probably creates the ambiguity to allow for the later anointing.

[268] Goodman, *State*, 39.

[269] Later rabbis literalistically understood this to include the messianic era (Lachs, *Commentary*, 401, citing *b. Šabb.* 63a). Whitacre, *John*, 302, notes that some acts, such as burial (hence 12:7), were regarded as greater than charity (citing *b. Sukkah* 49b); but here Christology is central. That some things would "always be" also fits Greco-Roman rhetorical usage (Seneca *Benef.* 1.10.4).

the poor, either in Deuteronomy or in John (13:29; cf. 1 John 3:17); but in the gospels which record the saying, the emphasis is on the priority of Jesus and/or the urgency of serving him while he remains with them, since he was soon to depart.

### 5. The Danger to Lazarus (12:9–11)

The narrative (12:10–11) rings with irony: Jesus went to Judea, risking his life to give life to Lazarus; now Lazarus's new life may cost him his life. The paradigm for disciples could not be clearer: those who would follow Jesus must be prepared to die (12:25, 27), for the world will hate them and wish to kill them (15:18; 16:2). But faith would not be decreased by such martyrdom-producing new life; the sign of Lazarus's new life brought others to faith (12:11; cf. 11:45, 48).

# JERUSALEM AND ITS KING

## 12:12–50

ONCE JESUS ARRIVES IN JERUSALEM (12:12–19), people respond to him in various ways. The Gentiles seek him (12:20–22), provoking his remark that the time for his death had come (12:23–33). His own people, however, whose king he is (12:13–15), remained blind (12:37–43; cf. 9:39–41), unable to see Jesus' glory which Isaiah saw, which is the light (Jesus' discussion of which frames the comment on their blindness—12:34–36, 44–50). Yet Jesus remained God's agent and standard for judgment (12:44–50).

## The Arrival of Zion's King (12:12–19)

Earlier passages had introduced Jesus as rightful king of Israel (1:49), but also warned that his "own" as a whole did not receive him (1:11; or that they misunderstood his kingship—6:15; cf. 18:36–37). Both themes are present here, but John is careful to emphasize that his people as a whole would have been more open to him (12:17–18), but that it was the leaders who were responsible for their people being led wrongly (12:19).

### 1. Authenticity of the Core Tradition

That someone would go out to meet with respect an important teacher (11:20), signs worker (12:18) or king (12:13) is not unlikely (see comment on 11:20); that crowds already present loudly welcomed many incoming pilgrims is virtually certain. Yet because Jesus' claim to kingship is often doubted, some are doubtful that the triumphal entry happened. If people hailed Jesus as king, why did the Romans not intervene suddenly?

But the Gospels present the grandness of the event in the light of their theology about Jesus' identity; most of the accounts do not require us to suppose an originally large-scale notice.[1] In the bustle of a city milling with pilgrims, more of whom were arriving throughout the day, the Romans need not have noticed this relatively obscure event.[2] The Roman garrison was concentrated on the Temple Mount, and Jesus was hardly the only Passover pilgrim welcomed by the crowds already present. More importantly, leaders of the municipal aristocracy, normally charged with keeping peace for the Romans, were also concentrated on the Temple Mount at this season (being mainly priests) and had they been notified of the entry in time to stop it—which assumes a much longer period of acclamation than is likely—they preferred not to act in front of the crowd anyway (Mark 11:32;

---

[1] Matthew's stirring of "the entire city" (Matt 21:10), however, may invite the reader to compare this event with an earlier disturbance of Jerusalem (Matt 2:3).

[2] Sanders, *Jesus and Judaism*, 306; Catchpole, "Entry." In favor of reliability, see also Losie, "Entry," 858–59.

14:2). In John the leaders, who are now Pharisees, continue to be concerned about the opinions of the crowd (12:19).

That many people would hail the "prophet" from Galilee is likely.[3] (For John, the welcomers surely include Galileans; cf. 11:55.)[4] But many people in first-century Judea wanted to acclaim prophetic figures as kings,[5] and both Markan and Johannine tradition suggest royal acclamation. Already in Mark the acclamation alludes to a psalm in the Hallel (Ps 118:26), employed at Passover, that would most suitably address a king (Mark 11:9–10); that Jesus himself is the king, the son of David, becomes clearer in Matthew (Matt 21:9) and Luke (Luke 19:38).[6] Reminiscences of the Passover Hallel are likely historical;[7] yet if Jesus were greeted simply the way all other Passover pilgrims were greeted, it is doubtful that the disciples would have preserved the account, given more significant events to report and that they must have received the same greetings themselves. Such considerations support the historicity of the event.

## 2. The Event and Its Significance (12:12–13)

To say that John depends on prior and likely authentic historical tradition here is not to deny that he draws theological capital from the wording; "the one who comes" has already functioned as a messianic title (1:15, 27; 3:31; 6:14; 11:27); Jesus had indeed come "in the name of the Lord," his Father (5:43; 10:25); and John makes "king of Israel" explicit, echoing 1:49.[8] The entry's primary significance is probably what the Gospels imply: Jesus intended to present himself as a king but—by means of the donkey (12:14–15)[9]—to define his kingship as one of peace (cf. 18:36–37).[10]

To be sure, the observers might not understand the entry in peaceful terms. Rulers were welcomed with similar fanfare.[11] The palm branches (12:13; only in John) suggest a

---

[3] In view of ancient patronal social patterns, Jesus' numerous "benefactions" would also produce an entourage, seeking favors, that could potentially double as a political support base, exacerbating his threat to the political elite (DeSilva, Honor, 135).

[4] Also for Matthew (Matt 21:10–11); in Luke those who hail him are disciples (Luke 19:37, 39); even in Mark, where "many" participate, those who go before and after him are probably those who knew of his ministry in Galilee (Mark 11:8–9). This may represent a very different crowd from the one that condemned him (Matt 27:20–25; Mark 15:11–14; Luke 23:13, 18, 21, 23)—certainly in John, where the condemning "Jews" are the "high priests" (19:6–7, 12–15).

[5] See introduction, pp. 271–72, 284–89; comment on 6:15.

[6] Pope, "Hosanna," suggests a Hebrew original addressed to the son of David in the vocative. The vocative does not seem clear, but its point (that Jesus is son of David) seems implied in any case.

[7] Stendahl, Matthew, 65, thinks early Christian liturgy adapted the language of the Hallel here; in any case, its paschal context suggests that such words were uttered in some form. The Hallel was even more dominant at Tabernacles (m. Sukkah 3:9–10; 4:1, 8) but used at Passover as well (m. Pesaḥ. 5:7; 9:3; 10:7).

[8] Michaels, John, 207. Because the disciples misunderstand (12:16), Painter, "Church," 362, thinks that for John Jesus is not "King of Israel," for his kingdom is not from this world (18:36); but the issue here is what kind of king (as Painter agrees), not whose king (1:49–50).

[9] One might expect the eschatological king instead to ride a splendid throne-chariot (cf., e.g., Pesiq. Rab. 36:1).

[10] See Borg, Vision, 174; Sanders, Jesus and Judaism, 308. Asses were of lower status than horses (Babrius 76.18–19).

[11] E.g., Herodian 4.1.3; for governors, see Menander Rhetor 2.3, 381.7–17. Van den Heever, "Socio-rhetorical Reading," plausibly suggests a challenge to the imperial cult here.

triumphal entry for a military triumph or a royal acclamation (1 Macc 13:51; 2 Macc 10:7; 14:4);[12] the carrying or waving of branches would also communicate triumph or royal welcome to ancient readers unfamiliar with the specific Maccabean associations known to Mediterranean Jews.[13] We should digress at this point to note that, because such palm branches would have to be brought from Jericho and were normally used at Tabernacles,[14] some have suggested that the original triumphal entry took place at the Feast of Tabernacles.[15] This suggestion is not likely; the abundant details matching Passover in the traditional passion narrative (as emphasized especially by Jeremias) were hardly added simply by later writers, for whose audiences many of the connections would seem meaningless. John could have added palm branches simply to augment the symbolism of messianic acclamation;[16] his probable audience seems familiar with palm branches to symbolize victory or triumphal entry (Rev 7:9). Otherwise his independent tradition probably focuses on and so magnifies the use of a smaller number of palm branches perhaps brought by pilgrims from the vicinity of Jericho (a region where Jesus also ministered), perhaps for constructing temporary shelters during the Passover.[17] Whether one judges the use of palm branches likely will depend on one's prior predisposition toward the historicity of Johannine tradition, but there is in fact nothing historically implausible about the presence of palm branches if Jesus' disciples may have anticipated a sort of triumphal entry, as some gospel tradition may suggest (Mark 10:37); according to both the gospel tradition (Mark 10:46) and a likely route for paschal pilgrims from Galilee, Jesus and his followers had just come from the vicinity of Jericho and his followers may have brought such branches for this very purpose.

The cry "Hosanna!" renders the Hebrew of Ps 118:25,[18] and similar Hebrew cries for salvation could address kings (2 Sam 14:4; 2 Kgs 6:26); coupled with the branches (see below), this suggests that the crowds hoped for him as a king or national deliverer.[19] Hence he is "king of Israel," as Nathanael recognized (1:49). In John's Gospel this royal expectation recalls 6:15, but on this occasion Jesus does not retreat, for his hour of enthronement on the cross is approaching. Ironically, the leaders of his people will claim no king but Caesar (19:15).

---

[12] As is regularly noted (Westcott, *John,* 179; Hoskyns, *Gospels,* 421; Meeks, *Prophet-King,* 86; Bruce, "Trial," 8; Bruce, *John,* 259; Stauffer, *Jesus,* 110; Witherington, *Christology,* 106 n. 279; Moloney, *Signs,* 184; see esp. Schnackenburg, *John,* 2:374). Hill, "Βαΐα," interestingly but improbably suggests that φοινίκων alludes to the Phoenix myth associated with resurrection.

[13] E.g., Herodian 8.6.5; 8.7.2; suppliants to deities also might hold fresh branches (Aeschylus *Suppl.* 333–334); or one might carry a branch simply for festivity (*p. Pe'ah* 1:1, §15). Some cultures used branches as symbols of alliance (Polybius 3.52). Inviting the treading on garments (Mark 11:8) indicated great honor (Aeschylus *Agamemnon* 906–913, 925, 946–949).

[14] E.g., *Gen. Rab.* 41:1; *Pesiq. Rab Kah.* 27:2; *Pesiq. Rab.* 51:8. For palm branches from Jericho, cf. Deut 34:3; Judg 1:16; 3:13; Josephus *Ant.* 9.7; 14.54; Pliny *Nat.* 5.15.70.

[15] Sanders, *John,* 287; cf. Pope, "Hosanna." Gemünden, "Palmensymbolik," suggests associations with Sukkoth and triumph over death.

[16] Schnackenburg, *John,* 2:374. He could have even sought to assimilate Passover with Tabernacles to reemphasize his earlier Tabernacles motifs.

[17] On the use of tents in general, see Josephus *Ant.* 17.213, 217.

[18] Noted, e.g., by Jerome *Homilies* 94. It may have come to function as a jubilant cry (as some words became in Gentile refrains, e.g., Callimachus *Hymns* 2 [to Apollo], 21, 25, 97, 103; Catullus 61.117–118, 137–138, 142–143; Menander Rhetor 2.7, 409.11–13); Augustine *Tr. Ev. Jo.* 51.2 explains it as an interjection.

[19] See Talbert, *John,* 185.

### 3. Scripture Fulfilled (12:14–16)

The disciples did not recognize the allusion to Zech 9:9[20] until after Jesus' death and resurrection (12:14–16),[21] obvious as it may seem in retrospect.[22] If extant later sources may reflect ideas circulating in the late first century, they suggest that this verse was understood messianically in early Judaism.[23] Most ancient Mediterranean hearers would honor the image of a ruler who was merciful and kind to his enemies.[24] John's special touch is evident even in the details. It was not an unusual practice to abbreviate a narrative by omitting intermediaries,[25] as Matthew seems to do on some occasions (Matt 8:5 // Luke 7:3–4; Matt 9:18 // Mark 5:35); thus no one will be alarmed that Jesus himself "finds" the donkey (12:14), in contrast to the fuller version in the probably more widely circulated version of the passion week (Mark 11:1–6).[26] After all, even in that version, Jesus was ultimately responsible for locating the donkey (Mark 11:2). But what is most theologically significant is that in John's language Jesus finds the donkey—just as he gives the sop (13:26) and in other ways shows himself sovereign over the details of the Passion Narrative.

That the disciples did not understand at first fits John's version of the Messianic Secret. After Jesus' glorification, the Spirit would come (7:39) and cause the disciples to remember Jesus' message (14:26); his glorification thus allowed the disciples to recall Jesus' action and understand it in light of Scripture here (12:16). John had earlier offered a similar comment about the disciples after the resurrection remembering Jesus' costly zeal for the temple (2:22). The repetition suggests a key hermeneutical point for John: the biblical record and Jesus' ministry and glorification should be read in light of one another, led by the Spirit who continues his presence.

### 4. Immediate Responses to Jesus' Entry (12:17–19)

The present description of the report of Lazarus's raising (12:17), like the account of Lazarus's raising itself, somewhat resembles the description of the future resurrection (5:28: μνημεῖον; φωνή/φωνέω), functioning as a public advance notification of that day.

---

[20] Of the extant gospels, only the two with the most Jewish audiences, Matthew and John, make the Zechariah allusion explicit (Longenecker, *Christology*, 112). All four gospels include the colt (for breaking a colt, see Xenophon *Horsemanship* 2.1–5; Maximus of Tyre *Or.* 1.8).

[21] On "glorification" as including Jesus' passion, see comment on 7:39.

[22] With modifications (cf., e.g., Schuchard, *Scripture*, 71–84): "Do not fear, Zion" may derive from Zeph 3:16 (cf. Isa 10:24; 40:9; Smith, *John* [1999], 236, adds especially Isa 35:4; 40:9), midrashically linked with "Rejoice, daughter of Zion" (Zech 9:9). Menken, "Redaktion," attributes some changes to Jewish traditions (cf. Gen 49:11). Later rabbis applied the messianic promise of salvation (here omitted) to the suffering Messiah (*Pesiq. Rab.* 34:2).

[23] *B. Sanh.* 99a; *Gen. Rab.* 75:6; *Eccl. Rab.* 1:9, §1. A second-century Tanna expected the messianic fulfillment at the time of the temple's rebuilding.

[24] E.g., Diodorus Siculus 27.16.2; Dionysius of Halicarnassus *R.A.* 3.54.2; Polybius 1.72.3; 3.99.7; 39.7.3–6; Arrian *Alex.* 1.17.12; 4.19.6; Appian *R.H.* 10.4.24; Cornelius Nepos 8 (Thrasybulus), 2.6; Herodian 1.2.4; cf. also Josephus *Life* 353; *Sipre Deut.* 323.4.1; despite Achilles' more commonly vengeful personality, Homer *Il.* 24.507–508, 665–670; see further Good, *King*, 47–49.

[25] E.g., Plutarch *Consol.* 1, *Mor.* 608B.

[26] The earlier account may emphasize Jesus' simplicity (he did not own the donkey), in contrast to traveling charlatans (cf. Mark 6:8–9; 2 Cor 2:17; 1 Thess 2:5; Malherbe, "Gentle," 206–7, 14); although "found" allows a contrast here with covetous Judas (John 12:6), John's narrative lacks elaboration of this emphasis here.

Those who had believed (11:44) now functioned as witnesses (12:17), which fits John's paradigm for discipleship. The interest of the crowds (12:18) again shows that John recognizes the diverse Jewish responses to Jesus; his "enemies" are not his fellow Jews, but the "Pharisees" (12:19).

That the Pharisees tell one another, "You are doing no good" (12:19), is vintage Johannine irony;[27] they mean, "We have proved ineffective in stopping Jesus" ("profit nothing," as in 6:63), but they actually comment on their own deficit of righteousness. Further, their complaint about "the world" is telling; they may mean "the rabble," but their words become an unintended prophecy (cf. 11:51) of Gentiles turning to Jesus (12:20; cf. 11:48),[28] which must have been compounding the offense of Christianity for the enemies of John's audience.[29] As in 11:48, their words are also exaggeration on a literal level even for John; every member of the world follows Jesus no more than every individual already honors the Father (5:23); John is not a universalist. But the word becomes widespread and crosses all boundaries of culture and geography.

## Gentiles and the Cross (12:20–36)

The rest of the chapter (12:20–50) moves directly into the passion.[30] The Pharisees had unwittingly prophesied the coming of Gentiles to Jesus (12:19); proleptically this coming begins in 12:20–21. The coming of Gentiles (12:20–21) marks the final prerequisite for the "hour" of Jesus' glorification (12:23).[31]

### 1. The Coming of Gentiles? (12:20–22)

John could intend Diaspora Jews here,[32] perhaps as representatives of the Gentiles.[33] More likely, however, John has Gentile Greeks in view (see comment on 7:35);[34] as Brown points out, nothing less dramatic than "the understanding that the first Gentiles have come to Jesus explains his exclamation that the hour has come" (12:23).[35] Many Diaspora

---

[27] "Dramatic" irony, employing speakers whose irony is unintentional (Duke, *Irony*, 23–24).

[28] E.g., Hunter, *John*, 123. The world going "after" him may reflect the language of discipleship (Mark 1:17, 20; 8:34).

[29] Yet in Exodus the wisest of Egypt recognized their state while Pharaoh remained hardened (Exod 10:7); in view of the one greater than Moses, such a comparison portrays the Pharisees as harder than the pagans.

[30] Dahl, "History," 187, sees 12:20–50 as the transition between John 1–12 and John 13–20. Goulder, "Ministry," curiously finds this section dependent on the language of Luke 9–10.

[31] Contrast the reportedly Tannaitic tradition that glory did not dwell in the second temple because Cyrus was responsible for its rebuilding (*Pesiq. Rab.* 35:1). On appointed times, see comment on 2:4; 7:6.

[32] Robinson, *Trust*, 88; Strachan, *Gospel*, 159. Strachan, *Gospel*, 159, also allows the possibility of proselytes; proselytes clearly went up (Safrai, "Relations," 199–200; Acts 2:10), but "Greeks" would be an unusual term for them here.

[33] Kossen, "Greeks," 108, citing Isa 49; Haenchen, *John*, 2:96; Smith, *John* (1999), 237–38.

[34] So, e.g., Bernard, *John*, 2:430; Schnackenburg, *John*, 2:381; Michaels, *John*, 214; cf. Regopoulos, "Ἕλληνες," who finds most likely hellenized pagans. Bernard wrongly supposes, however, that this fact supports a Gentile audience (*John*, 2:429). Yet Matthew, with a clearly Jewish audience, stresses the Gentile mission far more heavily than John does!

[35] Brown, *John*, 1:466. In the context of "lifting up" and "glorified" (Isa 52:13 LXX in John 12:23, 32), an allusion to Isa 52:15 LXX is not impossible (cf. Beutler, "Greeks"), but it remains unclear.

Jews did come to the feasts (Josephus *War* 5.199), though probably not frequently.[36] But many interested Gentiles would also attend;[37] most of these would have been "God-fearers," a widely attested class of Gentiles interested in Judaism.[38] Probably a fairly large percentage of the visiting Greeks would be from the region, especially from Syria and the Decapolis.[39]

Philip had elsewhere introduced a person to Jesus (1:44–46), but the text does not provide an explicit reason why the Greeks approached Philip first, if not at random (12:21). Unlike the names of many of the disciples, Philip was a popular Greek name (especially after the father of Alexander of Macedon).[40] But more critically if true, some from the Decapolis may have known of Philip. Philip's Bethsaida (12:21) was technically not in Antipas's "Galilee" but, until 34 C.E., in the tetrarchy of Philip; but people on both sides of the artificial border ignored the regularly changing boundaries.[41] John's explicit Bethsaida "of Galilee" reinforces the connection between Galilee and others distant from the Judean elite.

Like Philip, Andrew (12:22) had introduced someone to Jesus (1:40); he was also from the same town as Philip with possibly the same kinds of connections (1:44). Andrew may have even known the lad in 6:7 because of contacts on the lake of Galilee.

These Greeks' "desire" to see Jesus (12:21) is not explicitly granted in this text, but the results are clear in light of the whole of John's Gospel; those who "want" to do God's will ultimately recognize the truth of Jesus' teachings (7:17), and no one who comes to Jesus will be cast out (6:37).

## 2. The Cross and Divine Glory (12:23–34)

The coming of the Greeks (12:20–22) signals the arrival of Jesus' hour (2:4; 13:1; 17:1), when he will glorify God by the cross (12:23–24, 27–34); those who follow him must follow the same pattern of glorifying God (12:25–26). Meanwhile, the crowds failed to understand most of Jesus' point (12:29, 34), because they could not believe (12:37–43).

### 2A. Jesus' Hour of Glory (12:23–24)

When Jesus speaks of his glorification, it is not a matter of ignoring the Greeks nor necessarily a direct refusal;[42] it does not appear that he spoke to them, but whether he did so or not remains unclarified because it is irrelevant to John's point.[43] The event pro-

---

[36] Sanders, *Judaism*, 130, arguing that in Josephus only Palestinian Jews were required to come annually (Josephus *Ant.* 4.203).

[37] E.g., Josephus *War* 6.427; probably *Ant.* 3.318–319.

[38] See, e.g., Levinskaya, "Aphrodisias"; *pace* Kraabel, "Disappearance"; see in greater detail the documentation on John 9:31. Ridderbos, *John*, 427, suggests Gentiles here.

[39] Morris, *Gospel*, 591. Given ethnic tensions there, most of those in Alexandria were probably less likely to have been disposed toward Judaism.

[40] Morris suggests (ibid.) that it was because of Philip's Greek name; Andrew (12:22) also had one. Greek names were fairly common (cf. Cohen, "Names"; but *Let. Aris.* 47–50 probably reflects an Egyptian rather than Palestinian milieu; Williams, "Personal Names," 109, limits them mainly to the more hellenized urban elite), but far more common among Diaspora Jews (Leon, *Jews*, 107–8; Acts 6:5; *p. Git.* 1:1, §3), though the cultural interchange of names in the East was ancient (Astour, "Names").

[41] Theissen, *Gospels*, 50.

[42] Schnackenburg, *John*, 2:382, believes it "a direct refusal" until Jesus undergoes death (12:24).

[43] Haenchen, *John*, 2:96.

vokes another of the Johannine discourses, many of which do not end a narrative with any explicit narrative conclusions (e.g., 3:21–22; 3:36–4:1; 5:47–6:1), though John does include other narrative interruptions here, emphasizing the unbelief of his own people (12:28–29, 34). Rather than replying to them directly in the text, however, Jesus interprets their presence.[44]

This passage clarifies some motifs in the Gospel that would otherwise remain ambiguous until this point for the first-time reader. Jesus' glorification (12:23) includes the cross (12:24; see note on 7:39); along with the double entendre involved in Jesus being "lifted up" on the cross (12:32–33), this image of "glory" and "lifting up" together hark back to the LXX rendering of Isa 52:13 (ὁ παῖς μου καὶ ὑψωθήσεται καὶ δοξασθήσεται σφόδρα), the beginning of the Servant Song that includes Isa 53.[45] On the one hand Jesus is exalted to a position of honor; on the other hand, he is exalted by way of the cross, there crowned "king of the Jews."[46] The cross was the epitome of shame in the Roman world; in light of Isaiah, however, this worldly shame becomes Jesus' honor, his "glorification."[47] God's honor and that of the world prove mutually exclusive (12:43).

The image in various early Christian sources of a grain dying to produce fruit (esp. 1 Cor 15:36–38) may draw on a catechetical tradition,[48] but need not do so; it was a commonplace image (12:24; cf. Mark 4:27–29).[49] Presumably Jesus refers to the seed's "dying" in a nontechnical sense, especially on the level of John's probably urban audience: its death probably is a graphic metaphor for when it falls to the ground or (for any farmers listening) when the shoots begin to sprout from the body of the fallen seed.[50] In the first instance, it refers to Jesus (12:23, 27, 32–33);[51] but the principle must also apply to Jesus' followers (12:25–26). Between Jesus' death and the expansion of early Christianity lay his resurrection, but the saying follows the familiar Semitic format of encompassing a whole by mentioning its beginning and ending.[52] "Fruit" can refer to the produce of a believer's life (15:8) but here refers to the harvest of other lives (4:36).

## 2B. The Price of Following Jesus (12:25–26)

Ironically, Lazarus had died that Jesus might raise him (11:4), but his new life might paradoxically cost him his death at the hands of the world personified in the Judean authorities (12:10–11). When Jesus speaks here of dying to live (12:25),[53] he sounds like he is

---

[44] Schnackenburg, *John*, 2:382. Shedd, "Meanings," 251, argues that their desire to "see" Jesus (12:21) is fulfilled in Jesus' glorification (12:23).

[45] E.g., Price, "Qumran," 34; Griffiths, "Deutero-Isaiah," 360; Lindars, *Apologetic*, 83, 234; Barrett, *John*, 214.

[46] Cf. Bruce, *Message*, 107.

[47] See Neyrey, "Shame of Cross," 118–19; on its shame, cf., e.g., Cicero *Rab. perd.* 5.15–16.

[48] See Riesenfeld, *Tradition*, 176–81, noting 1 Cor 15:36 and citing secondarily Mark 4; 1 Cor 9:11; 2 Cor 9:10; Gal 6:8; 1 Pet 1:23. Jeremias, *Parables*, 148, cites also *b. Sanh.* 90b; *1 Clem.* 24:4–5.

[49] Seed must be buried and hidden to produce fruit (Epictetus *Diatr.* 4.8.36); teachers widely used grains as illustrations (Lucretius *Nat.* 2.371–373; Epictetus *Diatr.* 2.6.11). Cf. also the image of dying (albeit metaphorically) to live in *b. Tamid* 32a. Bury, *Logos-Doctrine*, 56, improbably appeals to the ear of corn in the Eleusinian Mysteries.

[50] Riley, *Fruits*, 29, notes that an embryo is already growing in the wheat seed as it falls; usually after two days in moist soil, it breaks through the seed coating.

[51] Barrett, *John*, 423, suggests that though the article is generic, it might allude to Christ as the specific grain; but this grammatical explanation is not likely.

[52] Jeremias, *Parables*, 220 n. 58.

[53] Cf. ἀντεισαγωγή, the rhetorical figure of contrasting thoughts (Anderson, *Glossary*, 20).

speaking Johannine theology; but though the saying is transposed into Johannine idiom, 12:25–26 represents a pre-Johannine saying that appears in the Synoptic tradition.[54] This suggests that Johannine idiom need not indicate that John creates material without the use of sources; rather, he rewrites his sources so thoroughly that we can discern them only where they plainly overlap with Synoptic materials.

Losing one's life in this age would be a small price to preserve it in the eternal age to come, a notion not unfamiliar to Jesus' Jewish contemporaries.[55] Philosophers talked about being ready to face death,[56] as did military historians[57] and an oath of loyalty to the divine emperor.[58] Biographers could praise statesmen who sacrificed their lives for their people.[59] Generals typically warned troops before battle that those who risked their lives ultimately were more apt to preserve them.[60] Some felt that prayer for one's life would demean that person's heroic character (Longinus *Subl.* 9.10, on Ajax). Despite similarities in wording, the Fourth Gospel's Jewish audience and sources would probably understand Jesus' words more in line with the biblical tradition of preparedness to suffer for God's honor. Moses, Elijah, Jeremiah, and David suffered for God's honor, but none of them suffered gladly; Jesus likewise suffers, but not because he desires to suffer (12:27). First-century texts frequently portray Jewish people prepared to die for the honor of their ancestral customs,[61] and early Jewish texts speak of loving eternal life more than life in the present world, so enduring the world's hostility (*1 En.* 108:10).[62]

Jesus here provides such a choice between two ways.[63] Johannine literature elsewhere speaks of loving not the world (3:19; 1 John 2:15), its honor (12:43), or one's life even to the point of death (Rev 12:11). Serving Jesus (12:26) demanded seeking humility rather than honor (cf. 12:2) and required following Jesus' model of servanthood, which shortly follows in the narrative (13:5, 14–16).[64] Yet those who shared Jesus' suffering would also share his glory: wherever Jesus would be,[65] there his servants would be as well (12:26),

---

[54] Cf. likewise Schnackenburg, *John,* 2:384. For a detailed comparison, see Morgen, "Perdre."

[55] Cf. *1 En.* 108:10; *2 Bar.* 51:15–16; *m. ʾAbot* 4:17; ʾ*Abot R. Nat.* 32, §71B; *b. Tamid* 32a; *Lev. Rab.* 3:1; *Deut. Rab.* 11:10; *Eccl. Rab.* 4:6, §1; Daube, *Judaism,* 137. Boring et al., *Commentary,* 106, suggest that the summons of the analogous Matt 16:25 resembles the typical prebattle speech of generals: risking life in battle more often than not yields its preservation (Tyrtaeus frg. 8.11–13).

[56] Cf., e.g., Seneca *Ep. Lucil.* 12.9, quoting Virgil *Aen.* 4.653.

[57] E.g., Livy 5.46.2–3.

[58] E.g., the oath to Augustus and his descendants, 3 B.C.E., in *IGRR* 3.137; *OGIS* 532; *ILS* 8781 (Sherk, *Empire,* 31); or to Gaius, 37 C.E., in *CIL* 2.172; *ILS* 190 (Sherk, *Empire,* 78).

[59] Lucan *C.W.* 2.380–383.

[60] Xenophon *Anab.* 3.2.39; also Boring et al, *Commentary,* 106, citing Tyrtaeus frg. 8.11–13 (seventh century C.E.) and Ps.-Menander. See Publilius Syrus 242.

[61] E.g., Josephus *Ag. Ap.* 1.212; 1.191; 2.218–219, 233–235. Sanders, *Judaism,* 239, cites Josephus *War* 2.169–174; *Ant.* 15.248; 18.262; *Ag. Ap.* 2.227–228; Philo *Embassy* 192; cf. Dio Cassius 66.6.3.

[62] Cf. also *Deut. Rab.* 11:10; *Eccl. Rab.* 4:6, §1.

[63] On the two ways in ancient literature, Seneca *Ep. Lucil.* 8.3; 27.4; Diogenes *Ep.* 30; Plutarch *Demosthenes* 26.5; Deut 30:15; Ps 1:1; 4Q473 frg. 1 (developing Deut 11:26–28; probably also 4Q185 frg. 1–2, col. 2, lines 1–4); *m. ʾAbot* 2:9; *T. Ash.* 1:3, 5; *Eccl. Rab.* 1:14, §1; *Lev. Rab.* 30:2; *Deut. Rab.* 4:3; *Song Rab.* 1:9, §2; Matt 7:13–14; Luke 13:24; *Did.* 1.1–6.2; *Barn.* 18.1–21.9; cf. the two roads after death in Virgil *Aen.* 6.540–543; Cicero *Tusc.* 1.30.72; *4 Ezra* 7:3–16, 60–61; 8:1–3; *T. Ab.* 11:2–11A; 8:4–16B; ʾ*Abot R. Nat.* 25A; *b. Ber.* 28b; *Pesiq. Rab Kah.* 27:2; *Gen. Rab.* 100:2.

[64] Coulot, "Quelqu'un," provides arguments that 12:26a probably stems from Jesus. On serving as following, persevering, and discipleship here, see Cachia, "Servant."

[65] John may place the εἰμί before the ἐγώ to avoid inadvertently introducing christological connotations from other contexts (such as 8:58) where they are not the issue (Bernard, *John,* 2:435).

both in death and in the Father's presence (14:3). Those who suffered for Jesus should seek only God's honor (5:23), and themselves would be honored by the Father (12:26) rather than by mortals (5:41, 44; 12:43).

### 2C. Glorifying God by Suffering (12:27–30)

Jesus was "troubled" (12:27) to face death, and prayed accordingly. Throughout the Mediterranean world people considered praiseworthy those heroes who faced suffering bravely, often without tears or signs of sorrow,[66] though stories could also underline the humanity of their heroes by showing them distraught by hostile odds.[67] In other cases one might face death bravely simply because she knew it was fated, hence inevitable.[68] Philosophers exhorted people to "pray simply for the Good and leave the decision to the god," though the vast majority of people continued to pray simply for what they wanted.[69] The Gospels do not fit such philosophic or sometimes heroic expectations;[70] Jesus would go to the cross to obey his Father's will, but not as if death were not a trauma for him. This is true of John as of the Synoptics.

Those familiar with the passion tradition would now understand the source of John's "hour" (e.g., 2:4; 7:30; 8:20) if they had not recognized it previously: in the passion tradition, Jesus had prayed for his "hour" to pass (Mark 14:35). John here likely echoes—and adapts—the same tradition that independently appears in the Synoptic account of Gethsemane.[71] Whereas the Markan line of tradition, probably dependent on an earlier passion narrative, emphasizes Jesus' trauma at Gethsemane (Mark 14:32–42; Matt 26:36–46; Luke 22:39–46), John brings it forward to 12:27 and turns the prayer into a question ("*Shall* I say, '*Save* me from this hour?'"). ("My soul is troubled" likely reflects Ps 41:7 LXX [42:6]; some argue that the immediate context of that verse may also inform the background of Jesus' Gethsemane prayer in Mark.)[72] John thereby tones down the intensity of Jesus' agony before the cross yet hardly brings Jesus' character into line with Greco-Roman expectations for heroism. In idiomatic language,[73] John emphasizes that Jesus' soul is "troubled" in the face of death (which is shortly to follow; "now" signifies the imminence of Jesus' hour, e.g., 13:1, 31); as in 11:33, this statement contradicts philosophers' demands.[74] In contrast to some of his second- and third-century readers, most of John's initial audience were not philosophers or aristocrats and might resonate better with this portrait of one who shared their humanity (1:14).[75]

---

[66] E.g., Dionysius of Halicarnassus *R.A.* 7.68.2–3; Josephus *Ant.* 3.208; 4.322; 6.126–127; Xenophon *Mem.* 4.8.2; Lysias *Or.* 2.25, §193; 2.78–79, §198; Epameinondas 2 in Plutarch *S.K., Mor.* 192C; cf. Dionysius of Halicarnassus *Isoc.* 5.

[67] Apollonius of Rhodes 2.623.

[68] Cassandra in Aeschylus *Agamemnon* 1295–1301.

[69] Burkert, *Religion,* 75.

[70] Neither, however, are they antiheroic, like Abraham's unwillingness to die in *T. Ab.* passim.

[71] See Brown, *Essays,* 250–51.

[72] Dodd, *Tradition,* 71 (cf. also Beasley-Murray, *John,* 207), traces the form in John 12:27 and Mark 14:36 to Ps 41 and argues for authenticity on the grounds of multiple attestation (cf. Heb 5:7).

[73] One's spirit or soul being troubled is idiomatic language (ἐταράχθη ψυχή in Gen 41:8; Ps 6:3 [6:4 LXX]; 42:6 [41:7 LXX]); see comment on 11:33. Jesus' heart was troubled (12:27; 13:21) so those of his disciples need not be (14:1; Carson, *Discourse,* 43).

[74] From Epicurus (ἀταραξίαν in Diogenes Laertius 10.85; cf. 10.144.17) to Stoics (ἀτάραχος in Epictetus *Diatr.* 4.8.27).

[75] Such language was not, however, incompatible with deity; see God in Gen 6:6, who was grieved to his heart over humanity (ויתעצב אל־לבו, MT).

Jesus then prays for the Father's "glory" (12:28), a characteristically Johannine equivalent for the earlier passion tradition's "your will be done" (Mark 14:36). The context has already reminded the reader that Jesus had come in the Father's name (e.g., 12:13) and that the hour had come for Jesus' glory (12:23), which was inseparable from the Father's glory (13:32). This prayer may represent the nucleus which is continued and developed more fully in Jesus' next and final Johannine prayer in ch. 17, which begins with a prayer for God's glory (17:1–5).

Prayers for God to glorify his name were common[76]—for example, the petition for the sanctification of God's name in the Kaddish, after which the Lord's Prayer is probably patterned.[77] In the context of the Fourth Gospel, however, this prayer for "glory" is a prayer for the hastening of the cross (7:39; 12:23–24); as in Mark 14:36, Jesus dislikes his impending death (John 12:27) but he nevertheless submits to his Father's plan (12:28). Responding to Jesus' prayer, a "heavenly voice," an earlier oracular form the rabbis later called a *bat qol*, publicly confirms Jesus' mission in 12:28.[78] This heavenly voice appears frequently in later rabbinic texts,[79] but its antiquity seems assured in view of sufficient analogues in a wider range of early Jewish and Mediterranean literature (cf. Dan 4:31).[80] Later rabbis considered the *bat kol* subordinate to Scripture and prophecy, but its appearance in conjunction with such other revelatory testimonies in the Fourth Gospel provides a corroborating function (as in Mark 1:3–11).[81]

Having omitted an audible heavenly voice at Jesus' baptism and transfiguration (because he has omitted both events, making Jesus' whole public ministry a transfiguration of sorts), John may feel free to introduce a heavenly voice here. But if John has an independent tradition, one cannot argue against authenticity simply on the grounds that "this oracular response conforms to no known type of oracle."[82] One could as easily argue the opposite; whereas the *bat qol* did not always conform to oracular form, or God might not be expected to conform only to Greco-Roman oracular forms, one would expect a rhetorically polished writer to conform newly composed oracles to accepted oracular form. In the final analysis, neither direction of argument carries much weight; if John rewords Jesus' teachings and other tradition in his own style, one would expect the same for this *bat qol*. Ironically, it is rejection by his opponents (12:19, 33, 37) that provides the context for Jesus' ultimate glorification in this Gospel.[83]

---

[76] E.g., Tob 3:11; 8:5, 15; 11:14.

[77] With, e.g., Jeremias, *Prayers*, 98; Smith, *Parallels*, 136; Vermes, *Jesus and Judaism*, 43; Davies and Allison, *Matthew*, 1:595; Luz, *Matthew*, 371; *pace*, e.g., Meier, *Marginal Jew*, 1:361–62 n. 36.

[78] With, e.g., Strachan, *Gospel*, 160–61.

[79] E.g., *m. ʾAbot* 6:2; *b. B. Bat.* 73b; 85b; *Mak.* 23b; *ʿErub.* 54b; *Šabb.* 33b; 88a; *Soṭah* 33a; *p. Ber.* 1:3, §4; *Peʾah* 1:1, §15; *Soṭah* 7:5, §5; *Pesiq. Rab Kah.* 15:5; *Lev. Rab.* 19:5–6; *Lam. Rab.* proem 2, 23; *Lam. Rab.* 1:16,§50; *Ruth Rab.* 6:4; *Eccl. Rab.* 7:12, §1; *Song Rab.* 8:9, §3; *Pesiq. Rab Kah.* 11:16; *Tg. Neof.* 1 on Gen 22:10; 27:33; 38:25; Num 21:6; *Tg. Ps.-J.* on Gen 38:26; Num 21:6; Deut 28:15; 34:5.

[80] Josephus *Ant.* 13.282–283; Artapanus in Eusebius *Praep. ev.* 9.27.36; *Sib. Or.* 1.127, 267, 275; outside early Judaism, Plutarch *Isis* 12, *Mor.* 355E; *Mart. Pol.* 9.1; from terrestrial locations in Dionysius of Halicarnassus *R.A.* 1.56.3; 5.16.2–3; 8.56.2–3; Valerius Maximus 1.8.5; 2.4.5; 7.1.2; Lucan *C.W.* 1.569–570; Plutarch *Camillus* 6.1; 14.2; Philostratus *Hrk.* 18.4; cf. talking serpents in Arrian *Alex.* 3.3.5. Cf. Johnson, *Prayer*, 62–63.

[81] See Keener, *Matthew*, 133–34, on Matt 3:17.

[82] Aune, *Prophecy*, 272.

[83] So also Whitacre, *Polemic*, 117.

Because God's voice is often identified with thunder,[84] and other heavenly voices could come as thunder (Rev 6:1; 10:3–4;14:2; 19:6), it is not surprising that some bystanders would mistake the heavenly voice for thunder. Pagans also often associated thunder with the supreme deity[85] and believed that the supreme deity sometimes thundered to strike terror into an enemy army,[86] or to encourage a favored mortal or to confirm his prayer.[87] (If an allusion to Sinai were intended,[88] God's confirmation of Jesus' mission of the cross would constitute the new Sinai revelation; but cf. comment on 1:14–18.) On the theological level, however, this merely testifies to the depth of their incomprehension; even when God speaks from heaven, they cannot understand or believe.

Some thought the voice was thunder; others, illustrating the continuing division in the multitude (7:12; 9:16), thought that an angel spoke to him (12:29).[89] Because early Judaism often expected that God responded to prayers through angels,[90] it is also not surprising that some would think that an angel had spoken to him; but while this conclusion represents more insight than assuming mere thunder, it underestimates the direct intimacy between the Father and the Son (8:29; 11:42) and again misunderstands Jesus' identity. By their misinterpretations "they confirm the assertions of Jesus that the 'Jews' know neither him nor his Father (5:37; 8:19, 55; 15:21; 16:3; 17:25) and that they have never heard the voice of the Father (5:37)."[91]

One could argue that they thought that Jesus' "Father" (12:28) was an angel, but Jewish prayers typically invoked God as "father" and sought his glory. For that matter, readers would have assumed that even Gentiles should have understood Jesus' point; educated Jews knew that Greeks called Zeus "father" (Josephus *Ag. Ap.* 2.241). Greek references to the chief deity as "father" are abundant, including in the widely recited literature of the classical past.[92] Greek religion from the earliest written period and Roman religion from

---

[84] 2 Sam 22:14; Job 37:2, 5; 40:9; Ps 18:13; 29:3–7; *Sib. Or.* 1.219, 323; 2.239; 5.62–63, 344–345. God ruled thunder (e.g., Exod 9:23, 28–29; Josephus *Ant.* 3.184) and sometimes used it in theophanies (e.g., Exod 19:16; 20:18; Josephus *Ant.* 3.80; *L.A.B.* 11:4–5; 19:16; Rev 4:5; 10:3); for delegation to angels, cf., e.g., *1 En.* 6:7; *Jub.* 2:2; Rev 6:1.

[85] As Baal was the thunderer of Canaanite faith, Zeus was "the high-thunderer" (ὑψιβρεμέτης) of the Greek pantheon (e.g., Homer *Od.* 5.4; Pausanias 10.9.11; Pindar *Ol.* 8.44), who produced thunder and lightning (Homer *Il.* 7.443, 454; 8.2–3, 75–77, 133; 9.236–237; 10.5; 13.624; Aristophanes *Lys.* 773; Apollonius of Rhodes 1.510–511, 730–731; Pausanias 5.22.5; 5.24.9; Apollodorus 1.2.1; Pindar *Pyth.* 4.23; 6.24; *Ol.* 4.1; 9.7; 13.77; Plutarch *Alex.* 28.2; Silius Italicus 17.474–478; differently, Pausanias 8.29.1; Pliny *Nat.* 2.18.82). Greeks and Romans shared with Jews the conception of the highest deity ruling storms (Brown, "Elements"); but for naturalistic explanations, cf., e.g., Pliny *Nat.* 2.18.82; Plutarch *Nat. Q.* 4, *Mor.* 912F–913A.

[86] E.g., Homer *Il.* 8.75–77, 133, 145–150, 167–171; 15.377, 379; 17.594–596; Valerius Maximus 1.6.12; Silius Italicus 12.623–625; cf. Pindar *Nem.* 9.25; armies facing lightning sometimes persuaded themselves, however, that it was not an omen (e.g., Silius Italicus 12.627–629; Plutarch *Alex.* 60.2). In Israel, see 1 Sam 2:10; 7:10; Isa 29:6; perhaps Judg 5:20; cf. judgment in *Sib. Or.* 4.113; 5.302–303.

[87] E.g., Homer *Od.* 20.101, 103; 21.413; Virgil *Aen.* 7.141–142; 8.523–526; 9.630–631; Pindar *Pyth.* 4.197–200; Silius Italicus 15.143–145; Ovid *Fasti* 3.369; Cicero *Cat.* 3.8.18; cf. Parthenius *L.R.* 6.6; Catullus 64.202–206; in Jewish tradition, see Exod 19:19; 1 Sam 12:17–18; Sir 46:16–17; cf. 1 Kgs 18:36–38, 44. In heavenly visions, cf. *1En.* 14:8; 17:3; 69:23; *3 En.* 29:2; *PGM* 4.694–696.

[88] Cf., e.g., thunder's role in Exod 19:16; 20:18; *L.A.B.* 11:4–5.

[89] Cf. the later tradition enshrined in 5:4.

[90] Johnson, *Prayer,* 63–65.

[91] Nicholson, *Death,* 130.

[92] E.g., Homer *Il.* 3.276, 320, 350, 365; 10.154; 11.56, 80, 182, 201, 544; 16.253; 17.46; *Od.* 14.440; 15.341; 16.260; 24.518; Hesiod *Op.* 169; Euripides *Medea* 1352; Aristophanes *Clouds* 1468–1469.

an early period recognized Zeus or Jupiter as "father of gods and men,"[93] "father of gods and king of men";[94] "father of gods";[95] humanity's father by virtue of creation;[96] "father" of all creation as its maker;[97] "omnipotent father";[98] or simply "the father" or "Zeus father."[99] Thus both the Olympian deities[100] and mortals[101] frequently addressed him as "father." In these images, the chief deity is the supreme patriarch and ruler of the cosmos, in the same way as the emperor could be hailed as "father" of the Roman state (Herodian 2.2.9; 2.6.2), "father" on earth as Jupiter was in heaven (Ovid *Fasti* 2.131).

By Jesus' day, however, a nearer context for a Galilean teacher was certainly early Judaism, and whatever the measure of Greek influence on its preference for the language, its most direct source was the Hebrew Bible. The Hebrew Bible recognized God as Israel's father by adoption in redemption[102] and Jewish literature in general continued this tradition (e.g., Wis 2:16; 3 Macc 5:7; 7:6). Jewish literature regularly calls God Israel's (occasionally in Diaspora Judaism, humanity's) "father."[103] Jewish tradition also employed this biblical image in prayer, though in a relatively restrained manner (3 Macc 6:8).[104] The form of synagogue Judaism we know from later rabbinic literature commonly calls God "our Father in heaven,"[105] as scholars conversant in the material regularly point out.[106] But even Jewish texts not in-

---

[93] Homer *Il.* 1.544; 4.68; 5.426; 8.49, 132; 12.445; 15.12, 47; 16.458; 20.56; 22.167; *Od.* 1.28; Hesiod *Theog.* 457, 468, 542; *Scut.* 27; *Op.* 59; Diodorus Siculus 1.12.1 (following Homer); Ovid *Metam.* 2.848; 14.807; Epictetus *Diatr.* 1.19.12; Phaedrus 3.17.10.

[94] Virgil *Aen.* 1.65; 2.648; 10.2.

[95] Homer *Il.* 1.503, 534, 578–579; Virgil *Aen.* 9.495; Ovid *Metam.* 9.245; Phaedrus 1.2.13.

[96] E.g., Epictetus *Diatr.* 1.6.40; 1.9.4–7; 1.13.3–4; 3.22.82; Diogenes Laertius 7.147; Acts 17:28.

[97] Plutarch *Plat. Q.* 2.1, *Mor.* 1000E; Alexander 15 in Plutarch *S.K., Mor.* 180D; *T.T.* 8.1.3, *Mor.* 718A; Babrius 142.3; *Orphic Hymns* 15.7; *PGM* 22b.1–5 (Jewish); other deities in Martial *Epigr.* 10.28; *Orphic Hymns* 4.1; 12.6. "Adonai" is "Father of the World" in *PGM* 1.305 (apparently as Apollo, 1.298). For the common usage in Philo, see documentation in comment on John 1:12.

[98] Virgil *Aen.* 1.60; 3.251; 4.25; 6.592; 7.141, 770; 8.398; 10.100; 12.178; Ovid *Metam.* 1.154; 2.304, 401; 3.336; 9.271.

[99] Homer *Il.* 8.69, 245, 397; 14.352; 15.637; 16.250; 22.60, 209; *Od.* 12.63; 13.51; Virgil *Aen.* 2.691; *Georg.* 1.121, 283, 328, 353; 2.325; *Orphic Hymns* 19.1. The deity is in a number of cases "father" as "creator" or progenitor (e.g., Sophocles *Ajax* 387; Epictetus *Diatr.* 1.3.1; Marcus Aurelius 10.1; see further documentation in comment on John 3:3); most of the Latin references above are to *pater*, but Jupiter is also called *genitor*, e.g., Virgil *Aen.* 12.843. No henotheism is in view; sometimes "father Zeus" is listed alongside Athene and Apollo (e.g., Homer *Od.* 4.340; 7.311; 17.132; 18.235; 24.376).

[100] Homer *Il.* 8.31; 22.178; 24.473; *Od.* 1.45, 81; 5.7; 8.306; 12.377; Aristophanes *Wasps* 652; even those not descended from him, such as his siblings (Homer *Il.* 5.757, 762; 19.121; *Od.* 13.128).

[101] Homer *Il.* 2.371; 7.179, 202, 446; 8.236; 12.164; 13.631; 15.372; 17.19, 645; 19.270; 21.273; 24.461; *Od.* 12.371; Cleanthes *Hymn to Zeus* in Stobaeus *Ecl.* 1.1.12; Sophocles *Oed. tyr.* 202; Aristophanes *Ach.* 223–225; Apollonius of Rhodes 4.1673; Plutarch *R.Q.* 40, *Mor.* 274B; Longinus *Subl.* 9.10.

[102] Jeremias, *Prayers*, 12.

[103] *Jub.* 1:25, 28; Wis 11:10; Tob 13:4; later, *Jos. Asen.* 12:14 MSS; *T. Job* 33:3 MSS, 9; *T. Ab.* 16:3; 20:13A; cf. *Pr. Jos.* 1.

[104] Jeremias, *Prayers*, 15–16; idem, *Message*, 14. Chilton, *Approaches*, 59, cites "Father" as a prayer invocation in *T. Job* and (probably later) the Targumim. Greeks and Romans may have employed the title less pervasively than Judaism and in contrast to Judaism applied the image to the deity's power rather than to his intimacy with Israel (cf. Johnson, *Prayer*, 61).

[105] *M. Soṭah* 9:15; *t. Ber.* 3:14; *B. Qam.* 7:6; *Ḥag.* 2:1; *Peʾah* 4:21; *Sipra Qed. pq.* 9.207.2.13; *Behuq. pq.* 8.269.2.15; *Sipre Deut.* 352.1.2; *b. Ber.* 30a, *bar.; p. Sanh.* 10:2, §8; *Pesiq. Rab Kah.* 24:9; *Lev. Rab.* 1:3; 7:1; 35:10; *Song Rab.* 7:11, §1.

[106] Marmorstein, *Names*, 56–60; Moore, *Judaism*, 2:204–9; McNamara, *Targum*, 116–18. Jeremias contends that "Father" is rarely attributed to first-century sages (*Prayers*, 16–17); but this ob-

tended for corporate use only rarely designate God as personally "my Father,"[107] whereas Jesus nearly always did.[108] Matthew and John, the most explicitly Jewish of the extant gospels, also emphasize Jesus' use of "Father" most frequently. But while "Father" should be clear to John's primarily Jewish audience and its peripheral Gentile adherents, the title's significance should have been lost on anyone in the story world. For John, their failure to understand emphasizes their denseness, and appears to stem from a failure to believe.

The voice came for their sakes (12:30; cf. 11:42); Jesus did not doubt his own identity (11:42), but they needed testimony and signs to believe (5:34; 10:38). Now the climactic time of Jesus' glorification had come; at the very point where the world system would seem to crush Jesus (12:32–33), the spiritual ruler of the world would be convicted and cast out (12:31).

## 2D. Judgment on the World's Ruler (12:31)

Jesus came not to judge the world (3:17; 12:47), but the moment of judgment nevertheless arrived in him. The world's judgment was at hand: the context is Jesus going to the cross (12:32–33); that judgment was coming "now" (12:31) revealed the eschatological significance of the cross in history (cf. 12:27; 13:31, 36; 16:5, 22; 17:5, 13). Jesus' death signaled defeat for the "prince of the world" (12:31; cf. 14:30; 16:11). Another document probably circulating in the same circle of believers as this Gospel depicts Satan being "cast out" from heaven in strikingly similar language, at the time of Jesus' exaltation (possibly on the cross; Rev 12:4, 9).

In most Jewish texts God is the ruler of the world.[109] Nevertheless, angels could function as "princes" with delegated authority under God,[110] and a third-century C.E. text could refer to a (good) angel as "the prince of the world."[111] Much earlier, the Dead Sea Scrolls contrast the Prince of Lights (שׂר האורים)[112] with Belial, prince of the wicked realm.[113] The Scrolls also present Belial as ruler of the army of the Kittim.[114] Although their date is uncertain, in some texts Beliar is also the angel of sin who rules the world.[115] Pagans applied titles such as "ruler of the world" to prominent deities[116] as well as the

---

servation omits some evidence (Vermes, *Jesus and Judaism,* 40) and fails to take into account the sparseness of rabbinic attributions in general in the earlier period.

[107] Sir 23:1, 4; Wis 2:16; cf. Jeremias, *Prayers,* 26, homiletically overstating the case.

[108] Jeremias, *Message,* 17; cf. idem, *Prayers,* 29–31.

[109] E.g., *Sipre Deut.* 27.2.1; *'Abot R. Nat.* 24, §51B; cf. *Jub.* 25:23 ("Lord of the age"). Satan assumes this role *(kosmokratōr)* only in some later texts (e.g., Hoskyns, *Gospel,* 426, cites *Exod. Rab.* on 24:7, following Billerbeck). Some gnostics later argued that the Jewish God was the lord of the world, whom they identified with Satan, inviting apologetic (Marmorstein, *Names,* 64, 99).

[110] E.g., *3 En.* 1:4. Michael regularly appears as ἀρχιστράτηγος or similar titles (Dan 10:13, 21; 12:1; *2 En.* 22:6J; 33:10; *3 Bar.* 11:4, 6–8; *T. Ab.* 1:13; 2:1A; 14:7B; *Jos. Asen.* 14:7; *Gk. Apoc. Ezra* 4:24; cf. Raphael in *Gk. Apoc. Ezra* 1:4).

[111] *3 En.* 30:2. Cf. Alexander, "3 Enoch," 243; Segal, "Ruler," 248.

[112] CD 5.18; "the prince of light" in 1QM 13.10 (Israel's helper).

[113] 1QM 17.5–6; Perkins, "John," 972, cites 1QM 1.1, 5, 13; 4.2; 11.8; 1QS 1.18; 2.19; 3.20–21. Brown, *John,* 1:468, rightly compares John and the Scrolls here. Cf. repeatedly "Prince Mastema" *(Jub.* 17:16; 18:9, 12; 48:2, 9, 12, 15; though elsewhere sometimes simply "Mastema," e.g., 49:2); the "Prince of Darkness" *(Pesiq. Rab.* 20:2; 53:2).

[114] 1QM 15.2–3.

[115] *Ascen. Isa.* 2:4 (Knibb thinks *Ascen. Isa.* 1–3 pre-Christian, but I am more skeptical).

[116] E.g., Lucan *C.W.* 6.742–743; Segal, "Ruler," 248–49; the Demiurge in Irenaeus *Haer.* 1.5.4. Pagans did not scruple to speak of even a chthonic deity as "ruler of the earth" (Smith, *Magician,* 52,

emperor.[117] Clearly, early Christians adopted the apocalyptic worldview in which God allowed the devil and his forces considerable activity among the nations in the present age (2 Cor 4:4; Eph 2:2; cf. Mark 3:22).[118] Although some later gnostic traditions portrayed Israel's God as an evil "ruler of this world,"[119] nothing analogous provides the background of this passage;[120] whereas the Fourth Gospel denies that the Pharisees know Israel's God, it never distinguishes Jesus' Father from Israel's true God.

At least in some later traditions, opposing the higher courts' right to pronounce sentence constituted a criminal offense;[121] many believed that the earthly court ruled on the authority of heaven.[122] Whatever the antiquity and pervasiveness of such particular traditions, they may reflect a longstanding respect for earthly courts in mainstream Jewish society. Yet here Jesus pronounces sentence not merely against the earthly courts that oppose him, but against the evil prince that stands behind them. "Casting out" the ruler moves the Johannine Jesus far beyond the level of merely individual earthly exorcisms (as in the Synoptics) to the defeat of Satan in the heavenly realm (Rev 12:9–10).[123]

Some Jewish texts that hail God as the world's ultimate ruler contrast his rule with that of earthly kings who seek to usurp such a role (2 Macc 7:9). Given the context, this "ruler of the world" may well be seen as the evil prince who ruled the angels of the nations, in this case at work not only through the political leaders of the world system as a whole but specifically through the leaders ("rulers") of Israel (12:42; cf. 7:48). The rulers feared lest they be "cast out" from the synagogue (12:42); the ruler of the world, however, was now being "cast out" from his position for opposing Christ, stripping the opposition of its power in heaven (12:31).

Again the text is laden with John's irony: Satan would be defeated and dislodged from his place of authority (12:31) and Jesus glorified and exalted (12:32) through the cross (12:33).[124] Satan's activity (13:2, 27) would undermine the devil himself.

## 2E. Jesus' Exaltation by the Cross (12:32–34)

God could accomplish his purposes even through acts of human rebellion or folly.[125] It was not through an act of brutal force but through submission to such force, through his

---

citing Lucian *Pharsalia* 6.697). See demonic "world-rulers" in Eph 6:12; *T. Sol.* 8:2–7 (third century C.E.); in the magical papyri, see Arnold, *Ephesians,* 65; later astrological powers in MacGregor, "Principalities"; Lee, "Powers," 60.

[117] Ovid *Metam.* 15.758–759, 859–860; cf. other rulers in *p. ᶜAbod. Zar.* 3:1, §3; *Exod. Rab.* 5:14. One might think of a coalescence of imperial and antichrist images if John's emphasis lay here.

[118] On the apocalyptic image, see, e.g., Segal, "Ruler," 247.

[119] Smith, *Magician,* 52, citing Hippolytus *Haer.* 10.14, 15, 19, 20, 21.

[120] *Pace* Segal, "Ruler," 246, 258–59, 262–63,

[121] *M. Sanh.* 11:1–2; sources cited in Stauffer, *Jesus,* 206.

[122] *T. Roš Haš.* 1:18; *ʾAbot R. Nat.* 2A; *Pesiq. Rab Kah.* 5:13; 23:4; *p. Roš Haš.* 1:3, §28; cf. *m. Roš Haš.* 3:1; *p. Roš Haš.* 3:1, §17. When earthly courts could not execute a requisite death sentence, the heavenly court would do so (*t. Sanh.* 14:16; *Sanh. Mak.* 5:16; *ʾAbot R. Nat.* 25A; *p. Ketub.* 3:1, §8; *Deut. Rab.* 5:5; *Midr. Pss.* 72, §3).

[123] Cf. similar language for the expulsion of Cronus by Zeus at the fall of the Titans (e.g., Cornutus 7.p.7, 20, in Van der Horst, "Cornutus," 171).

[124] John derives the terms "glorified" and "lifted up" from Isa 52:13 LXX (e.g., Lightfoot, *Gospel,* 252; see comment on 3:14). The potentially relevant *Targum Isaiah,* to which some would like to appeal, however, does not predate the NT (Chilton, "John xii34").

[125] Intelligible also to Greeks, e.g., Homer *Il.* 1.1–2, 5.

death on the cross, that Jesus would "draw" all humanity (12:32).[126] His language refers not to the salvation of all individuals (cf. 3:36), but representatives among all peoples (cf. Rev 5:9; 13:7); the context is the Pharisaic complaint that "the world" was now following him (12:19), and Gentiles were now ready to approach Jesus (12:20). Only the cross could make Jesus available to all by means of the Spirit (7:39; 15:26–27; 16:7; 17:20). This is truly Johannine paradox: "exaltation" and "glorification" in their positive sense hardly fit the shame of the cross, even the thought of which typically evoked horror.[127] An ancient audience would readily grasp the wordplay involved; writers could speak of raising one up on a cross.[128] A writer could also tell that Alexander promised that whoever had killed Darius would be rewarded by being "lifted up"; when the murderers came forward, he fulfilled his words literally by crucifying them.[129] More importantly, the Hebrew Bible already played on the double meaning of exalted or hanged (Gen 40:13, 19–22). On "lifting up," see comments on 3:14; 8:28; on "drawing," see comment on 6:43–44.

Jesus used this "lifting up" to "signify" (σημαίνων, function as a sign; cf. 2:18–19) the kind of death which he was going to die (12:33; also 18:32); this language could apply to prophetic or apocalyptic symbolism (Rev 1:1; Acts 11:28),[130] but in the Fourth Gospel (if one accepts our argument that John 21 is part of the Gospel) it applies especially to indicating the manner of impending death, Peter's as well as Jesus' (21:19).

Ironically, the crowds seem to understand in 12:34 that "lifting up" refers to death (12:33; cf. 8:22) and the Son of Man of whom Jesus speaks is the Messiah, but they do not understand who the Son of Man is. Perhaps John intends them to echo Jesus' own promise that the "son" remains forever (8:35), but this makes their demand that Jesus make explicit his identity all the less excusable. That the Messiah could die in some Jewish traditions may increase the irony,[131] but their view of an eternal Messiah does indeed derive from Scripture[132] (e.g., Isa 9:6;[133] Ps 110:4) and was probably widespread.[134] Thus they are right that the Christ will "remain forever"; they are right to finally recognize that "lifting up" means death; but they cannot comprehend the resurrection.

What makes their claim most ironic is that in this immediate context Jesus had not said that the "Son of Man" would be lifted up, but that he himself would be lifted up (12:32). In applying Jesus' plain self-claim to another figure, they appear to miss what is explicit in Jesus' words, as they had missed what was explicit in the Father's words when they thought that an angel had spoken to him (12:28–29). It is possible that they want him

---

[126] E.g., Hunter, *John*, 128. "Drawing" evokes the language of Jer 31:3; Hos 11:4.

[127] E.g., Cicero *Rab. perd.* 5.15–16 (Boring et al., *Commentary*, 157).

[128] Cicero *Verr.* 2.4.10.24 (*sustulit*). Despite allegorizing some other matters, ancient commentators typically understood that 12:32 refers in context to the cross (Augustine *Tr. Ev. Jo.* 52.11.3).

[129] Callisthenes *Alex.* 2.21.7–11 (Boring et al., *Commentary*, 260–61). Because crucifixion involved "exaltation," a dream about it signified good for a poor man (Artemidorus *Onir.* 2.53; Malina and Rohrbaugh, *John*, 212–13).

[130] Xenophon *Mem.* 1.1.4 (divine direction); Boring et al., *Commentary*, 292–93, cites Plutarch *Oracles at Delphi* 21.

[131] E.g., *4 Ezra* 7:29 (the Messiah dies along with everyone else).

[132] For all Scripture as the "law," see comment on 10:34. For an eternal reign of the "Son of Man," see Dan 7:13–14 (also Hoskyns, *Gospel*, 427). Bampfylde, "Light," cites Ps 61:6–7, which seems less likely a candidate (not a regular messianic testimonium of early Christians).

[133] McNeil, "Quotation," and Whitacre, *John*, 318, also cite Targumic support for a use of Isa 9:5 relevant to this passage, but cf. Chilton, "John xii34."

[134] E.g., *1 En.* 41:1; *2 Bar.* 40:3; *Midr. Pss.* 72:17; cf. *Pss. Sol.* 17:4; see introduction to Christology; Keener, *Matthew*, 487–88 and sources cited there.

to make explicit what they already believe he is implying (as perhaps in 8:25), having heard him speak earlier about the "Son of Man," but in this case this solution makes little sense of their substitution of a term he did not at that point say for one that he did. The ill-fitting dialogue may suggest sloppy redaction of John's sources or careless paraphrase (cf. 13:10–11), but given John's penchant for emphasizing the obduracy of mortals confronted by divine reality in Jesus, obduracy might be closer to the point (12:35–36).

### 3. Inviting Faith in the Light (12:35–36)

Jesus warns his hearers that the light will be among them only "a little while" longer (12:35; cf. 13:33; 16:16), and they should take advantage of his physical presence while it remained available (as in 12:8). As he himself had walked in the light to avoid stumbling (9:4–5; 11:9–10), now he summons others to do the same. He employs language familiar to readers of the Gospel, about walking in light (8:12; cf. 1 John 1:7; Eph 5:8; eschatologically, Rev 21:24) and about darkness proving unable to overtake those who were of the light (1:5). The conflict between the forces of light and darkness envisioned here fits the language of sectarian Palestinian Judaism, which also spoke of the "children of light" (בני אור; cf. 12:36; Luke 16:8; Eph 5:8; 1 Thess 5:5) versus the "children of darkness."[135]

Again it appears that Jesus does not trust the crowds (cf. 2:23–25), for their misunderstandings (12:29, 34) have proved them unreliable; by continuing to walk in darkness, becoming ignorant of where they are going (12:35; 1 John 2:11), they show that they have rejected the light of the world (12:46; cf. 8:12; 1 John 1:6). (By contrast, those who are of the light do know their origin and destination; see 3:8; 8:14.) Hence Jesus hides himself (12:36), just as he did when others sought to kill him (8:59).[136] They had failed to believe the light while he was among them (12:36); now where he was going they could not come (8:21–23; 13:33). Nevertheless, his final words to them remained an invitation: they could still become children (cf. 1:12) of light through faith (12:36).

## Israel's Unbelief (12:37–43)

In 12:37–50 John concludes the sign section of his Gospel;[137] this passage may provide a "rhetorical 'brake'" preparing the reader for the more detailed depiction of Jesus' passion—the hour of his glorification.[138] Many find in 12:37–43 a theological summary of people's responses to Jesus' public ministry, as many find in 12:44–50 an anthology of representative sayings.[139]

---

[135] E.g., 1QS 2.16; 3.13, 24, 25; 1QM 1.1, 9, 11, 13; 3.6; 13.14–15; 4Q176 frg. 12, 13, col. 1, lines 12, 16; frg. 10–11, 7–9, 20, 26, line 7 (Wise, Scrolls, 235); 4Q298 frg. 1, col. 1, line 1; 4Q548 lines 10–15. The parallel between Qumran and NT usage (also Luke 16:8; 1 Thess 5:5) is often noted, e.g., Charlesworth, "Comparison," 414; Vellanickal, Sonship, 36; Wilcox, "Dualism," 95. The stereotypical expression "sons of light" is the only point at which the Gospel and the Johannine Epistles fail to observe the distinction between Jesus as God's "son" (υἱός) and others as his "children" (τέκνα, τεκνία, παιδία; see Snodgrass, "ΠΝΕΥΜΑ," 197 n. 54).

[136] On the hiding, see comment on 8:59.

[137] Dodd, Interpretation, 379.

[138] Culpepper, Anatomy, 71.

[139] E.g., Evans, John, 139; McPolin, John, 175.

If Jesus proved unable to trust the crowds (12:36), 12:37–43 show why: they habitually misunderstood (12:29, 34) because they were blind by nature (12:38–40). The signs (12:37) and revelations of glory made sense only to those with eyes to see, like Isaiah the prophet (12:41). Some did believe, but were unwilling to confess him openly (12:42), because in contrast to Isaiah who proclaimed the glory of God that he witnessed (12:41), they loved human glory for themselves rather than God's (12:43).

## 1. Isaiah's Revelation (12:37–41)

Jesus' rejection by his own (1:11) is detailed in 1:19–12:36 and explained in 12:37–43.[140] Although John elsewhere sometimes may prefer eclectic texts, here he follows the LXX of Isa 53:1 (which represents the Hebrew fairly accurately), perhaps in deference to what had become early Christian tradition (John 12:38).[141] The appeal to this Servant Song confirms John's source of imagery for being "lifted up" and "glorified" earlier in the context (12:23, 32; Isa 52:13 LXX).[142]

By contrast, John appears to blend Greek and Hebrew versions of Isa 6:9–10 in 12:40,[143] though his quote appears closer to the Hebrew.[144] This text was central to the Jesus tradition and some early Christian missionary preaching, often employed to explain the unbelief of Israel (Mark 4:12; Matt 13:13–15; Acts 28:27).[145] Later rabbis emphasized the note of repentance and consequent restoration in the Isaiah text.[146] John points out that Israel's unbelief was promised in Scripture (12:38; cf. Rom 10:16). Significantly, for John such events related to the passion happen that Scripture might be fulfilled (12:38; cf. 13:18; 15:25); Israel's Scripture remains as authoritative for John as for his audience's opponents. John omits Isaiah's use of the "deafness" image to focus on blindness, which recalls the reader to his earlier explanation in 9:39–41.[147] If John uses literal blindness to teach principles about spiritual blindness (9:39–41), it is likely that he also uses healing the same way in his Gospel, although here he speaks of those who refuse to be "healed" (12:40) and uses the same term elsewhere only in 4:47 and 5:13.[148]

Other sources also recognized that sin caused spiritual blindness[149] (12:39–40; see comment on 9:39; introduction, ch. 6, on vision). Texts also spoke of God blinding peo-

---

140 Moloney, *Signs*, 195.

141 Cf. Rom 10:16; Lightfoot, *Gospel*, 253; Barrett, *John*, 431. Brown, *John*, 1:483 interprets the ἵνα of 12:38 as suggesting that the prophecy produced the unbelief (12:38–39).

142 With Michaels, *John*, 218. See comment on 3:14. *Tg. Isa.* 52:13—53:4, however, speaks of the Messiah's strength (52:13) and of only Israel's sufferings (53:3–4).

143 Lightfoot, *Gospel*, 253; Menken, "Zitates."

144 Barrett, *John*, 431, suggesting, probably rightly, that John may quote loosely from memory.

145 See Lindars, *Apologetic*, 159. Other, analogous prophetic texts likewise appear in early Christian apologetic (cf., e.g., in Rom 11:8).

146 Evans, "Isaiah 6:9–10," also noting that church fathers found in it a predestinarian emphasis. Hollenbach, "Irony," suggests that the language is ironic because Isaiah's Judah and John's "Jews" do not wish to turn or see.

147 Also Beasley-Murray, *John*, 216.

148 In the NT as a whole, it appears 26 times, especially in Luke-Acts (15 times); and 61 times in the LXX.

149 E.g., *T. Dan* 2:2, 4; *T. Jos.* 7:5; *T. Levi* 13:7 (associated with hardness, as here); Seneca *Ep. Lucil.* 50.3; *Benef.* 5.25.5–6; Epictetus *Diatr.* 1.18.4; 2.20.37; 2.24.19; 4.6.18; Marcus Aurelius 4.29. For classical parallels, see Renehan, "Quotations," 20 (though noting that the NT source is the OT—"Quotations," 21).

ple's hearts to punish their willful transgression.[150] The Qumran sectarians felt that only the true remnant of Israel could hear the voice of the glorious God and see his angels (1QM 10.10–11).[151] Others probably representing related circles felt that idolaters lacked eyes to see (e.g., *Jub.* 22:18), echoing earlier biblical teachings (Ps 115:4–6; 135:15–18; Isa 46:6–7). Those with faith to see could behold God's glory in Jesus' signs (2:11; 11:40); those who did not demanded signs that they might believe (4:48; 20:25), and sometimes did not develop faith despite the signs (6:30, 66). Ironically, whereas Israel as a whole failed to "see" (12:40), the Gentiles came to "see" Jesus (12:21).

Some later Jewish texts expressed Isaiah's vision in the language of respectful circumlocution, noting that Isaiah witnessed God's "glory," as here.[152] Isaiah was one of the chief prophets after Moses,[153] and in the context of the Fourth Gospel, Isaiah becomes a link between Moses and the apostles, who also witnessed Jesus' glory (1:14–18, alluding to Exod 33–34), as did Abraham (8:56).[154] By contrast, those without spiritual eyes to see could not recognize the glory among them (3:3; 6:30; 9:39–41). The glory revealed to both Moses and Isaiah was rejected by many of their contemporaries; early Christians applied this pattern to many of Jesus' "own" (1:11) rejecting him (cf. Matt 23:31; Luke 11:50; Acts 7:39, 52; 28:25–27; 2 Cor 3:13–15; 1 Thess 2:15), though some had seen his glory (1:14–18).[155]

Jewish tradition naturally expanded on Isaiah's revelations,[156] and the mystic stream of tradition undoubtedly interpreted Isaiah's vision as including "a visionary ascent to heaven."[157] Some early Hellenistic Jewish texts adapted Hellenistic motifs concerning visionary ascents; thus, for example, a throne-vision may have in some sense deified Moses or at least made him God's second in command over creation.[158] Yet Jesus is greater than Moses; as the one who descended from heaven to begin with, he is the supreme revealer (3:11–13). In any case, most of John's audience would know the biblical accounts to which John has alluded, whereas a smaller part of his audience might know these other traditions. (It is difficult to say how early, popular, or geographically widespread such traditions were, but safe to say that the biblical stories themselves would be most accessible to the broadest range of people.) As in other biblical theophanies, not the visionary but the one beheld is the object of worship. In Isaiah the glory belongs to God; here it belongs to Jesus (12:41 in context).[159] As Isa 52:13 is contextually implied in the citation of 53:1, Isa 6 relates to Christ's "glory."[160]

---

[150] Isa 29:9–10; 44:18; Plato *Laws* 5.728B; Cicero *Tusc.* 1.30.72; Epictetus *Diatr.* 1.12.21f.; *Jub.* 21:22; Wis 2:21; Josephus *War* 5.343; Rom 1:24; 2 Thess 2:11–12.

[151] Perhaps referring to Sinai. In *2 En.* 65:2, eyes to see and ears to hear constituted part of the divine image in humanity.

[152] In the Targumim (Westcott, *John*, 185; Dahl, "History," 131; Schnackenburg, *John*, 2:416; McNamara, *Targum*, 100; Boring et al., *Commentary*, 294; Kirchhevel, "Children"). On early Jewish premises concerning God's glory, this would be a natural inference from Isa 6:3–4.

[153] Young, "Isaiah," 221, even more forcefully.

[154] Lightfoot, *Gospel*, 253.

[155] Isaiah had predicted a new revelation of glory at the new exodus (Isa 40:5; cf. 40:3, cited in John 1:23; Isa 24:23; 35:2; 44:23; 46:13; 49:3; 58:8; 59:19; 60:1–2; 66:18–19; 4Q176 frg. 1–2, col. 1, lines 4–9).

[156] See Young, "Isaiah," 216–18.

[157] Dahl, "History," 131.

[158] Van der Horst, "Vision."

[159] E.g., Tenney, "Keys," 303; Schnackenburg, *John*, 2:416; Boice, *Witness*, 105.

[160] Hence the implicit midrashic link between the two texts (Doeve, *Hermeneutics*, 163).

In 12:41, John attributes to Isaiah's revelation of Christ's glory both Isaiah quotations (ancients did not speak of two or more Isaiahs), one about a scene of glory in the temple (12:39–40; Isa 6:1–10) and the other about the servant being glorified and lifted in suffering (12:38; Isa 52:13–53:1). Early Christians would have undoubtedly linked Isa 6:1 with 52:13, because both texts use "exalted and lifted up," as does 57:15. If so, they would have noticed that 6:1 and 57:15 spoke of God, and may have concluded that it was actually Jesus' lifting up by crucifixion that revealed his identity as deity (cf. 8:28).[161] This fits 12:23–24 and the place of 1:14–18 in the context of John's whole Gospel: Jesus' death is the ultimate theophany.

## 2. Preferring Their Own Glory (12:42–43)

But not everyone loved the divine glory that Isaiah saw (12:41); some preferred their own (12:43; cf. 5:41, 44; 7:18), hence feared to confess Jesus openly, though as rulers they could have influenced many people and so brought Jesus glory. Their failure to confess Jesus openly resembles the healed man's parents in 9:22 but contrasts starkly with the boldness of the witness, John the Baptist, in 1:20. "Loving" one's own honor, like loving the world (1 John 2:15) or one's life (John 12:25), demonstrated inadequate love for God and his agent.

The sample "ruler" John has in mind is Nicodemus (3:1), but he would ultimately come out into the open as a disciple of Jesus (19:39); this fact indicates that John still has hope even for some of the leaders of the people who were persecuting the believers. But the price of coming out could be severe, including some sort of excommunication, as here (9:22; 16:2), and potentially death, perhaps from Roman governors (cf. 12:24–26; 16:2). One would clearly have to love God's honor more than one's own. The specific mention of rulers recalls Nicodemus, but may also respond to and refute the implicit assurance behind the Pharisees earlier question: "Surely none of the rulers or Pharisees has believed in him!" (7:48). (John's use of "ruler" is interesting; some aristocrats may favor Jesus, but the Pharisees on the whole oppose him. This emphasis may reflect elements of John's audience's milieu, appearing opposite of the pre-70 situation depicted in Acts.)[162]

Greek δόξα often meant honor. Thus δόξα, reputation, could provide a basis for praise in an encomium (Theon *Progymn.* 9.18).[163] Yet many thinkers warned that such reputation depended on people's whims and was not worth expending much effort.[164] Although some thought the pursuit of honor would lead to noble exploits (in contrast to passions),[165] many thinkers regarded φιλοδοξία, love of glory, as something to be

---

[161] So Bauckham, *God Crucified*, 49–51, citing the interpretive principle *gezerâ shevâ*. He also suggests (p. 51) that exaltation to divine glory may have recalled Ps 110:1 (cf. Acts 2:33; 5:31; combined with Isa 57:15 in Heb 1:3).

[162] See esp. Acts 4:1–2; 5:34–35; 15:5; 21:20; 23:6–8; 26:5. "Rulers" work together with "Pharisees" in 7:26, 48; the world "ruler" who may stand behind earthly rulers is evil in 12:31; 14:30; 16:11; but 12:42, like 3:1, allows for more nuancing. For such nuancing with the Pharisees as well, see 9:16.

[163] Cf. Plutarch *Themistocles* 1.1; *Demosthenes* 12.1; Eunapius *Lives* 465. Alexander reportedly craved praise (Arrian *Alex.* 7.28.1). Some appreciated reputation but warned that it invited trouble (Babrius 4.7).

[164] Dio Chrysostom *Or.* 66, *On Reputation* (LCL 5:86–115); Seneca *Ep. Lucil.* 123.16; cf. also Porphyry *Marc.* 15.253 (where, however, the term bears the common nuance of "opinion," as in, e.g., 17.284). Human mortality also relativized the value of glory (Diogenes Laertius 5.40, citing Theophrastus), and reputation invited trouble (Babrius 4.6–8).

[165] E.g., Xenophon *Hiero* 7.3 (φιλοτιμία); Philostratus *Hrk.* 23.23; 45.8; see comment on 5:41 for the appropriate seeking of glory in antiquity.

avoided.[166] Cynics, of course, went so far as to refuse human commendations altogether.[167] Stoics could ridicule those concerned with what others thought.[168] In many Jewish texts the righteous who did exploits could be "honored," sometimes literally "glorified";[169] they could seek to bring honor to their nation.[170] Other Jewish texts praised those who would not concern themselves with human glory (cf. John 5:41, 44),[171] and noted that God would shame those presently honored.[172] Early Christian writers also adopted this virtue of seeking only divine commendation (Rom 2:29; 1 Cor 4:3; 2 Cor 3:1; 1 Thess 2:6).

Thus Jewish thinkers, like some Greek and Roman thinkers, emphasized the importance of transcending concern for honor. At the same time, honor was a dominant social value in the ancient Mediterranean, strongest among the elite. Pressures for conformity could be great, especially conformity in the name of public religion (e.g., Josephus *Life* 291).[173] The situation Jesus promised (16:2) and which confronted John's audience was also more severe than mere loss of reputation; unless confessors of Christ within the synagogue achieved sufficient numbers critical mass, they, too, could be expelled with potentially disastrous consequences (see introduction). These who loved human honor more than God's honor acted from fear rather than from courage (cf. 3:2); this behavior merited only shame, not honor, before the one who knows all hearts (2:23–25). Meanwhile, Jesus himself is about to become an example of relinquishing one's own honor (13:1–11), following the example of Mary (12:3–8) and setting an example for his disciples (13:14–17).

## Jesus as God's Standard of Judgment (12:44–50)

The closing paragraph of this section, 12:44–50, suggests that, on the story level, Jesus has come out of hiding for one remaining public discourse. This passage is extremely significant, but not because it introduces many new conceptions. Essentially it repeats in typically Johannine language Jesus' teachings from previous discourses, summarizing and epitomizing the message of Jesus in the Gospel to that point.[174] Although some scholars

---

[166] E.g., Diogenes Laertius 6.1.8 (Socrates); Diogenes *Ep.* 4; Socrates *Ep.* 6; cf. Epictetus *Diatr.* 3.9; Marcus Aurelius 7.34; Philo *Spec. Laws* 1.281. Diogenes the Cynic reportedly attacked all those who were bound by reputation (ἐνδοξολογοῦντας, Diogenes Laertius 6.2.47). Cf. condemnations (albeit sometimes qualified) of "self-love" in Epictetus *Diatr.* 1.19.11; Plutarch *Flatterer* 1, *Mor.* 49A; *Praising* 19, *Mor.* 546F; Sextus Empiricus *Pyr.* 1.90; Philo *Confusion* 128; *Worse* 32; 2 Tim 3:2; *Sent. Sext.* 138; more favorable in Aristotle *N.E.* 9.8.1–5, 1168ab; cf. also discussion in Grant, *Paul,* 41.

[167] E.g., Diogenes *Ep.* 9.

[168] Musonius Rufus 10, p. 76.30. Epictetus *Diatr.* 2.21.12–14. The diminutive δοξάριον in Marcus Aurelius 4.2; 8.8 may also suggest a sort of ridicule.

[169] E.g., 1 Macc 11:51 (ἐδοξάσθησαν); Wis 8:10. The verb could also refer to adorning or beautifying a sanctuary (1 Macc 14:15).

[170] E.g., 1 Macc 14:35.

[171] E.g., *T. Benj.* 6:4 (δόξης ἀνθρώπων). Competing social groups in the ancient Mediterranean world demanded that one seeking honor determine in which group(s) one should seek it (see DeSilva, "Honor and Shame," 520).

[172] 1QM 14.11–12 (ולנכבדיהם); 4QpNah 2.9 (also mentioning "rulers," ומושנלים); cf. 4QpNah 3.9; 4.4; *Gen. Rab.* 1:5.

[173] It was also not uncommon to charge others with covering unjust personal motives with a veneer of religion (e.g., Josephus *Life* 75).

[174] On epitomization, see, e.g., Epictetus *Enchiridion; Syriac Menander Epitome;* and the Qumran *Temple Scroll.*

dissent, applying 12:44–50 only to the triumphal entry,[175] most see it as a summary of Jesus' preceding discourses.[176] Whitacre suggests that 12:44–50 emphasizes his words as 12:37–41 emphasized his deeds.[177] Although the summary suits John's theological purposes, he likely draws from traditional materials.[178]

Positioned at the end of the narratives that precede the passion and immediately preceding the prologue to the farewell disourse, this unit recapitulates the themes that have preceded and prepares the reader for their fulfillment in the Passion Narrative which follows. Ancient writers frequently recapitulated or summarized themes at the conclusion of a work or, in many cases, a section.[179] This strategic location before the Paraclete sayings and passion may also suggest that the historic elements of Jesus' mission noted in this pericope are continued in the present by the Paraclete, who continues to mediate Jesus' presence (14:16–17, 26; 15:26–27; 16:7–15).

First, Jesus is God's agent (see introduction); believing in him is believing in the Father and is essential to genuine faith in the Father (12:44; cf. 14:1).[180] In this context, the link between believing in Jesus and believing in the Father (again in 14:1) functions as a summons to secret "believers" in the synagogue (12:42): just as one dare not be ashamed to confess God in the Shema, one dare not be ashamed to confess Jesus. The kind of belief Jesus demands pleases God who sent him rather than humans (12:43), hence is not the inoffensive private faith of those unwilling to suffer expulsion from the synagogue or the possibly comcomitant trouble with Roman authorities. Thus, playing on the different levels of faith in his Gospel, John asks of Israel in the language of Isaiah, "Who has [genuinely] *believed* our report?" (12:38).

Beholding Jesus is beholding the one who sent him (12:45); both John (1:14, 18) and Jesus (14:7, 9; cf. 6:36, 40, 46) elsewhere imply this (see also pp. 310–17, on agency). Thus Jesus is not only the Father's agent but also his image (like divine Wisdom in Jewish tradition). In this context, Isaiah beheld the glory of both and confessed them (12:41), in contrast to the rulers who would not confess him (12:42). Most of Israel did *not* behold Jesus' glory, however, because they were blinded and could not see (12:40), like the elite who expelled the man whose sight had been restored (9:39–41). The context explains the connection between the claims in 12:44 and 12:45—one could not believe in Jesus (12:38–39) if blinded to his glory (12:40); much of Israel, being blinded, proved incapable of faith (cf. 6:44; 12:32). This passage explains the obduracy of Jesus' "own"

---

[175] Feuillet, *Studies*, 145–46.

[176] Odeberg, *Gospel*, 336; McPolin, *John*, 177; Grayston, *Gospel*, 101; Kysar, *John*, 203; Bruce, *John*, 273, 276; Quast, *Reading*, 92; Carson, *John*, 451; Pryor, *John*, 54; Moloney, *Signs*, 198; Smith, *John* (1999), 245.

[177] Whitacre, *John*, 326, also suggesting a possible allusion to Moses' summary words in Deut 32:45–47 at the end of his public ministry.

[178] See Sloyan, *John*, 162–63 (compare 12:44 with Matt 10:40; 12:47 with Matt 7:24–27/Luke 6:47–49 and Mark 8:38; 12:48 with Luke 10:16); Blomberg, *Reliability*, 185. Some think this section was added to the Gospel before its circulation (MacRae, *Invitation*, 18).

[179] See, e.g., *Rhet. Alex.* 22, 1434b.11–18; Anderson, *Glossary*, 85 (s.v. παλιλλογία; cf. also recapitulative techniques, pp. 22, 24, 39, 51); in Paul, e.g., Anderson, *Rhetorical Theory*, 181–82; for decorative maxims, see *Rhet. Alex.* 35, 1441.20; 1441b.10–11; Anderson, *Glossary*, 55; further discussion under John 20:30–31.

[180] Not only Jewish texts concerning agency but also Greco-Roman letters of recommendation typically identified the sender with the one recommended (see Malherbe, *Aspects*, 102–3); the rhetorical pattern "Whoever does A does not only A but also B" appears elsewhere (e.g., Musonius Rufus 14, p. 93.35–36), including in the Jesus tradition (Mark 9:37).

(1:11)—undoubtedly an apologetic problem—as a result of God's sovereign purpose (the quote in 12:40 functions more or less the same way it does in Mark 4:12). Paul develops the same idea in Rom 11, but there is more explicit about the eschatological significance of the Gentile mission as a purpose for the hardness (Rom 11:11–14); John 12:20–23 may imply a connection but John is not explicit about it. These early Christian writers seem to have spoken of their own people being "blinded" (cf. 2 Cor 3:14–15; 4:4) because they could fathom no other reason for their people's lack of response to a message whose truth appeared obvious to the believers.

The language of revelation here recalls the Moses allusion of the prologue (1:14–18). If Moses, who saw God's glory and was renewed into the same image to a finite degree, could reflect God's glory, how much more the "Son" who bears his Father's likeness, who continually beholds his glory (1:1b; 3:11; 6:46; 8:38)? Disciples would especially "behold" Jesus after the resurrection (14:19; 16:16–17), when he would abide in them (14:23; 17:24). But spiritual vision (1:50–51; 6:40; 9:39–41; 11:40) must exceed merely "signs vision" (cf. 4:48; 6:30, 36; 15:24; 20:25–31), just as discipleship faith must exceed signs-faith. Unbelievers, even some studious in Torah, might fail to genuinely behold God (5:37).

In 12:46, discussion about beholding (12:45) may recall Jesus' previous declaration that he is the light (12:35–36), another motif in this Gospel (1:4–9; 3:19–21; 5:35; 8:12; 9:5; 11:9–10);[181] his "coming into the world" reinforces the Gospel's testimony to Jesus' incarnation to save the world (cf. 12:47; 1:9; 3:19; 6:14; 9:39; 11:27; 16:28; 18:37; 1 Tim 1:15). Jesus is the light who, when seen and believed, delivers his followers from darkness. In this context, John's emphasis on light suggests that those who are not blinded (12:40) can see the light (12:45) of his glory as Isaiah did (12:41), and those who respond in faith will be saved (12:46).

In 12:47 another Johannine motif emerges; though Jesus did not come to condemn (3:17; cf. 8:15), his coming itself constitutes a dividing line of judgment (3:19; 9:39; cf. 12:31), and he will act as God's agent at the judgment (5:22, 24, 27, 29–30; cf. 8:16, 26), whereas his opponents judge inaccurately (7:24, 51; 8:15; 18:31). The image in 12:47 shifts from "seeing" Jesus (12:45) to "hearing" his words (which in this case applies to hearing with or without obeying).[182] Those who reject the light do not require additional judgment from Jesus; they have simply rejected the salvation that would deliver them from the judgment already otherwise theirs (see esp. 3:17–21). Eschatologically, however, they would be judged by his word they had heard; their very opportunity to respond raised the standard of judgment.[183]

On the judgment at the last day according to Jesus' word (12:48), see comment on 5:24;[184] they would also be accused by the Father's previous word in the Torah delivered

---

[181] For ancient views relating light to vision, see Aristotle *On Sense and Sensible Objects* 2, 438ab; Plutarch *T.T.* 1.8.4, *Mor.* 626C; Aulus Gellius 5:16; Diogenes Laertius 9.7.44; *Jos. Asen.* 6:6/3. Here faith constitutes a prerequisite for true vision (cf. 3:3; 12:44).

[182] Texts often combined their metaphoric use (Aeschylus *Prom.* 447–448), but the usage in the prophets is especially relevant, most of all in Isa 6:9–10; though omitting the "hearing" part of the quotation in 12:40, he includes it here.

[183] Cf. early Jewish teachings that those who knew most were most accountable; e.g., Amos 3:2; *2 Bar.* 15:5–6; *b. Šabb.* 68ab; Luke 12:47–48; Rom 2:12.

[184] Human judges also appear in both Greek (Homer *Od.* 11.568–571; Euripides *Cycl.* 273; Virgil *Aen.* 6.431–433, 566–569; Lucian *Downward Journey* 13, 18, 23–28) and Jewish (*T. Ab.* 12–13A, esp. 13:4; 11:1–4B; *3 En.* 16:1) traditions. In various traditions one could be judged by one's own words or deeds (Cicero *Verr.* 1.1.2; *Num. Rab.* 16:21; Matt 12:37; Luke 19:22; 22:71).

through Moses, which testified to Jesus (5:39, 45). Jesus' word (12:48) is in fact the same as the Father's word (cf. 3:34; 5:47; 17:8), for all that he spoke he spoke in obedience to the Father (12:49–50). Jesus' teaching that those who reject him as God's agent reject God himself (12:48) fits Johannine theology (13:20; 14:6; cf. 1 John 2:23) but is plainly earlier Jesus tradition (Mark 9:37; Matt 10:40; Luke 9:48).[185] This word would serve as the criterion for judgment on the "last day" (12:48), a common Johannine expression for the time of the resurrection (6:39, 40, 44, 54; 11:24) of both righteous and unrighteous (5:29).[186]

Like the rest of the Fourth Gospel, John here insists that Jewish believers remain faithful to the God of Israel through fidelity to Jesus, not through satisfying the synagogue leadership (12:42–43). This is because Jesus is God's faithful agent; he neither spoke (14:10; cf. 16:13) nor acted (5:30; 8:28, 42) on his own (12:49), but only at the Father's command (12:49; see comment on 5:19).[187] By again reinforcing the portrait of Jesus as God's faithful agent, John reminds his hearers that their opponents who in the name of piety opposed a high view of Jesus were actually opposing the God who appointed him to that role.

"The Father's commandment is eternal life" (12:50) is presumably elliptical for "obedience to the Father's command produces eternal life," but also fits the identification of the word (1:4), Jesus' words (6:68), and knowing God (17:3) with life. For John, the concept of "command" should not be incompatible with believing in Jesus (6:27; cf. 8:12; 12:25), which is the basis for eternal life (3:15–16; 6:40, 47; 11:25; 20:31); faith involves obedience (3:36; cf. Acts 5:32; Rom 1:5; 2:8; 6:16–17; 15:18; 16:19, 26; 2 Thess 1:8; 1 Pet 1:22; 4:17). Jesus always obeys his Father's commands (8:29), including the command to face death (10:18; 14:31); his disciples must follow his model of obedience to his commandments by loving one another sacrificially (13:34; 14:15, 21; 15:10, 12).

---

[185] Some could distinguish between the messengers and the one who sent them, holding the latter responsible (Homer *Il.* 1.334–336).

[186] The author makes no allusion to the sort of temporal separation of the resurrections of righteous and unrighteous in Rev 20:4–6, whether that represents an apocalyptic literary device or is intended literally (interim periods appear elsewhere, e.g., *4 Ezra* 7:28; *2 Bar.* 40:3; *Sib. Or.* 3.741–759, 767–795; *T. Ab.* 13A; *Sifre Deut.* 34.4.3; 310.5.1; *b. Sanh.* 97ab; cf. *1 En.* 91:8–17).

[187] Smith, *John* (1999), 246, emphasizes John's "subordinationist" Christology here (yet combining it with the incarnation on p. 247).

# 13:1–17:26

# FAREWELL DISCOURSE

The discourse section is difficult to outline because it is more concerned with developing repetitive themes than with following a precise arrangement.[1] The discourse proper starts in 13:12 or 13:31[2] (some even start it in 14:1,[3] but this is too late; questions intervene not only in 13:36 but throughout, as in 14:5, 8, 22). But while the discourse starts well after 13:1, the first part of the discourse interprets Jesus' act of foot washing and so cannot be separated from that act in our outline; we regard the foot washing as the narrative introduction to the Farewell Discourse that prefigures the passion.[4]

---

[1] With others, e.g., Whitacre, *John,* 340. On the pervasive repetition of several themes, see also Kennedy, *Interpretation,* 85.

[2] Segovia, *Farewell,* 61–62, prefers 13:31, probably correctly.

[3] Cf. Lombard and Oliver, "Supper."

[4] For patristic exegesis of the discourse, see Bammel, "Discourse."

# INTRODUCTORY ISSUES

## 13:1–17:26

J UST AS MARK 13 INTERPRETS the imminent passion of Mark 14–15 for the disciples in
terms of their future tribulation, so Jesus' final discourse in John's Gospel interprets the
meaning of Jesus' passion for his disciples: they will share both his sufferings and his resurrection life.[1]

### Unity of the Discourse

Source critics have detected a variety of clues, especially alleged changes of focus and
editorial seams, that indicate divergent sources in the discourse.[2] Most commonly, scholars divide ch. 14 from chs. 15 and 16, suggesting that they are either alternative versions
(perhaps both hallowed by time, or one perhaps older than the other),[3] or a reworked version in addition to an original version (the original is more often thought to be John 14).[4]
Talbert suggests that John varies these discourses, since ancient critics recognized that repeating words exactly wearies the hearer.[5] Some scholars have challenged the thesis of du-
plicate discourses,[6] others have argued for distinct discourses offered by Jesus himself on
different nights of the Passover week,[7] and a minority of scholars have argued for the
discourse's unity.[8]

Some relatively recent source-critical work takes a chronological approach to the development of the discourse: thus Painter thinks that John composed three versions of the
Farewell Discourse, the first before conflict with the synagogue (13:31–14:31), the second
during rejection by the synagogue (15:1–16:4a) and the third (16:4b–33) in opposition to
the synagogue.[9] Berg largely concurs but adapts this position slightly,[10] thinking that
15:1–17 is probably "an independent unit" from the time of that conflict.[11] Such a detailed

---

[1] Paul seems to predicate the same goal on Jesus' accomplished mission (Phil 3:9–11).

[2] E.g., Becker, "Abschiedsreden." For a thorough summary of views on composition and
redactional questions, see Segovia, *Farewell*, 20–47.

[3] Berg, "Pneumatology," 99, cites C. K. Barrett, Porsch, and R. Brown.

[4] Berg (ibid.) cites Wellhausen, Becker, Schnackenburg, and Painter (holding John 14 as original); and Sasse (holding John 14 as a revision). Borig, *Weinstock*, sees John 15–17 as an alternative of
13:31–14:31, but both as stemming from the evangelist (Segovia, *Relationships*, 87).

[5] Talbert, *John*, 211, citing *Rhet. Ad Herenn.* 4.42.54.

[6] Reese, "Structure," accepting the composite character of the material but arguing, from the six
question-answer exchanges, that John 14 and 16 are not discourses in any case.

[7] Witherington, *Wisdom*, 244.

[8] Berg, "Pneumatology," 98, citing especially Dodd and Wilckens.

[9] Painter, "Glimpses"; idem, "Discourses."

[10] See Berg, "Pneumatology," 85–89.

[11] Ibid., 87–88.

reconstruction requires so much dependence on hypothetical reconstructions, and assumes John's lack of creative revision of his sources to such a degree, that it is not likely to commend much assent today despite its brilliance. More speculatively, some, especially earlier source critics, also have suggested displacements in parts of the discourse,[12] or alterations made in the the use of the discourse in various recensions of the Fourth Gospel.[13]

Most such source-critical theories remain speculative, although at least one editorial seam (14:31) appears convincing enough to allow the possibility (albeit not the certainty) that John 14 and John 15–16 represent two versions, or two sections, of an original discourse now bound together. This seam in 14:31 may be disputed (see our comment), but it is the strongest argument for the composite nature of the current discourse.[14] Apparent inconsistencies such as 13:36 and 16:5 are also possible indicators,[15] though they may simply reflect John's deliberately ambiguous use of language.

Others have argued in greater detail that authentic sayings of Jesus stand behind the Farewell Discourse(s).[16] John's last discourse, dominated more by realized than by future eschatology, replaces the Synoptic eschatological discourse, but Synoptic tradition also indicates that Jesus provided more general directions for the future (Luke 22:21–38).[17] The vision of form and source criticism naturally gave way to redaction criticism, however, so that one could acknowledge historical tradition in the discourse(s) yet prove more interested in how it (they) fit the community John is addressing.[18]

Today scholarship, more shaped by contemporary narrative criticism, would emphasize still more how the discourse fits together and fits the perspective of the Gospel as a whole. As Gail R. O'Day notes, the claim for two Farewell Discourses (14:1–31; 16:4–33) based on parallels between them "tends to discount the role of repetition as a literary technique throughout the Fourth Gospel."[19] Fernando Segovia, who authored one of the leading redaction-critical studies of the Farewell Discourse(s), now affirms much more unity and coherence in the text.[20] He notes that different stages of composition remain feasible,[21] but that repetition was standard in ancient literature[22] and that the farewell speech functions "as a self-contained artistic whole that is highly unified and carefully developed from beginning to end."[23] Repetition may indicate recycling of a source, but this is unclear. Whatever its origins, the discourse's final form, presumably the form in which it first ap-

---

[12] Strachan, *Gospel*, 174, places John 15–16 between 13:31a and 13:31b, following Moffatt; more recently, see Lattke, *Einheit*.

[13] Bacon, "Displacement," thinks John 14 was not originally a part of the Gospel. Boyd, "Ascension," thinks that the original edition of the Gospel included the teachings of John 14–17 after the resurrection but that the final edition displaced them to their present setting.

[14] See Segovia, *Relationships*, 82; Witherington, *Wisdom*, 244.

[15] Boyle, "Discourse," 210.

[16] For various sayings of Jesus in this Gospel, see Dodd, *Tradition*, 315–420.

[17] Burge, *Community*, 116 n. 9, who also compares Luke 22:39 and John 17.

[18] Johnston, *Spirit-Paraclete*, 127. First John has more in common with this discourse than with the rest of the Gospel (perhaps because this discourse focuses on Jesus' message to disciples), though this need not imply the Epistle's author redacting this discourse (Smalley, *Epistles*, xxix).

[19] O'Day, "John," 770; see further 736–37. Similarly Witherington, *Wisdom*, 248, who attributes the repetition to sapiential style and "successive discourses given in a short span of time."

[20] See Segovia, "Tradition History."

[21] Segovia, *Farewell*, 320–27; also Smith, *John*, 263, following Segovia's argument for stages.

[22] Segovia, *Farewell*, 51

[23] Ibid., 288; cf. also 320, 328.

peared in the finished Gospel, is the form the final author presented as a finished product, and is available to our analysis without speculation.

In keeping with this trend to understand the finished Gospel as a whole, we speak of "discourse" in the singular. We are not fully persuaded by repetition or "seams" that two discourses stand behind the present one, but even if they do, they provide one unified discourse in the context of the finished Gospel.[24] Thus one can point to interpretive clues that bind together the beginning and end of the section, for example, the coming of Jesus' hour (13:1; 16:32), his coming from God (13:3; 16:30), and his leaving the world to go to the Father (13:1; 16:28).[25] Fréderic Manns elucidates the structure of 14:1–31 as a threefold parallelism:[26]

| John 14:1–17 | John 14:18–26 | John 14:27–31 |
|---|---|---|
| 1 Be not troubled | 18 Not as orphans | 27b Be not troubled |
| 3 I will come | 18 I will come | 28 I will come |
| 10 I am in the Father | 20 I am in the Father | 28 The Father is greater |
| 12 Go to the Father | | 28 I go to the Father |
| Believes in me | 21 Keeps my commands | |
| 15 If you love me, | 21 One who loves me | 31 I love the Father, |
| keep commands | keeps commands | let us go |
| 16 The Paraclete | 26 The Paraclete | 30 Prince of the world |

Although he must omit material to make the pattern fit (and some items do not fit), he at least demonstrates the repetition of ideas, some following clear patterns.

It is also possible that most of the unified Farewell Discourse as a whole yields a chiastic structure as follows:

A Jesus' departure, glory, love in community (13:31–38 or –14:1)
   B Jesus' coming and abiding presence (14:1 or 14:2–15:17)
      C The World (15:18–16:12)
         a The world's hatred (15:18–25)
            b The Spirit's testimony to the world (15:26–27)
         a' The world's hatred (16:1–4)
            b' The Spirit's testimony to the world (16:5–12)
   B' Jesus' Coming and Abiding Presence (16:13–33)
A' Jesus' departure, glory, and unity of community (17:1–26)

If this basic structure is correct, unity (17:21–23) and love (13:34–35) are essentially synonymous images; secession from the community, as in 1 John, would thus prove equivalent to hatred and death.

The discourse provides an interpretive crux, corresponding to the narrator's perspective, though the narrator has often remained silent in this Gospel.[27] Even before current literary-critical emphases, however, commentators could recognize that the discourse in John 13–17 clarifies the significance of the passion events of John 18–20.[28]

---

[24] See Boyle, "Discourse," 210–11, 221–22.
[25] Manns, "Paraclet," 104, reporting this "triple inclusion."
[26] Ibid., 105.
[27] Culpepper, *Anatomy,* 38.
[28] Lightfoot, *Gospel,* 319.

# A Testament of Jesus?

Scholars have offered various proposals concerning the specific genre or generic associations of this discourse. Given the pervasiveness of the Last Supper tradition in early Christianity (1 Cor 11:23), a meal setting for the discourse (mentioned in passing in John 13:2, 4) may be presupposed even if John is conspicuous by his lack of emphasis on it;[29] in this case, ancient Mediterranean readers might view the discourse as taking place in a symposium setting.[30] This was in fact a common literary setting for important discourses and dialogues.[31] Most traditional Jews would have continued to discuss Passover among themselves for a few hours after the meal,[32] providing an opportunity for a discourse such as this one after the Last Supper. Some even understand the passage as Jesus' commentary on his Passover meal with his disciples—albeit before John redacted the Passover to the cross (19:36).[33] Because little dialogue occurs, however, the observation of a general symposium setting exercises little influence on interpretation.

Speeches before battle also included exhortations to endure hardship and are standard in ancient literature.[34] Exhortations to face what is coming (14:31) or be encouraged (16:33) could fit this genre, but because Jesus' passion is not a military encounter per se, this genre sheds only peripheral light on John's discourse.

With or without an allusion to the Last Supper, the background of the discourse includes traditional elements of the covenant form probably reminiscent of Deuteronomy, where Moses also gives his final discourses:[35] in the context of the whole Fourth Gospel, the one greater than Moses is providing his testament for the future. The death of a sage frequently became the occasion for paraenesis.[36] Many people thought that shortly before death some people exercised keen prophetic insight, an idea possibly related to those testaments which offer predictions for the future.[37] As in many cultures,[38] a person might leave

---

[29] The lack of emphasis may, however, speak against a eucharistic interpretation (*pace* Moloney, "Reading").

[30] E.g., Witherington, *Wisdom*, 232–34.

[31] E.g., Plato *Symp.*; Xenophon *Symp.*; Cicero *Tusc.*; Plutarch *Dinner*; *T.T.*; Athenaeus *Deipn.*; Aulus Gellius 7.13. For elements of a mock symposium, see Trimalchio's dinner in Petronius *Sat.* In a Diaspora Jewish setting, see *Letter of Aristaeus* (specifically, Hadas, *Aristeas*, 42–43), which may draw on 1 Esd 3–4 (the latter is not, however, a dinner setting); in the Gospels, Luke 7:36–50; 11:37–54; 14:1–24 (Aune, *Environment*, 122).

[32] Stauffer, *Jesus*, 118. Even after a main meal (perhaps occurring here in 13:2) had been finished, people could drink more (Xenophon *Cyr.* 8.4.9).

[33] Cf. Laufer, "Commentary."

[34] E.g., Homer *Il.* 13.95–124; *Battle of Frogs and Mice* 110–112, 132–159; Polybius 15.10; Dionysius of Halicarnassus *R.A.* 6.6.1–6.9.6; Appian *R.H.* 8.7.42; 8.17.116; *C.W.* 4.16.126; Arrian *Alex.* 3.9.5–7. Such exhortations, however, also occur outside military contexts (e.g., P.Tebt. 703.40–43).

[35] See esp. Lacomara, "Deuteronomy," 66–67, 82; also Smith, *John* (1999), 265. This may suggest that early readers educated enough to contemplate such distinctions may have viewed the discourse as deliberative rhetoric, though Kennedy, *Interpretation*, 73–85 (see esp. 77), makes a case for epideictic rhetoric; and one could identify even elements of forensic rhetoric (questioned by Burridge, "Gospels and Acts," 519, because it "is not a single speech"). But John 13–17 does not fit expected patterns for any "rhetorical" speech (rightly Stamps, "Johannine Writings," 618).

[36] Perdue, "Sage."

[37] Cf., e.g., Xenophon *Apol.* 30; Aune, *Prophecy*, 178; many references in Malina and Rhorbaugh, *John*, 221–22. People also believed that deities sometimes warned people in advance of their own death (e.g., Plutarch *Alc.* 39.1–2; but contrast Xenophon *Symp.* 4.5).

[38] E.g., 1 Kgs 2:1–9; Mbiti, *Religions*, 109.

special instructions before dying; sometimes the same format could be employed for a departure speech not necessarily indicating imminent death.[39] Farewell or departure speeches were a standard biblical[40] and early Jewish literary form;[41] they also appear elsewhere in Greco-Roman works[42] and the NT.[43] Testaments often included, as here, warnings to keep the stipulations of the covenant, mention of a successor,[44] and a prayer.[45] Thus many find a "testament of Jesus" in John's Farewell Discourse.[46]

Jesus' "testament" differs from typical testaments in some regards. Often those who delivered such testaments were aged, summoned listeners to hear, recounted much of the future (Jesus tells some about the future, e.g., 16:2–4, but mainly leaves such information to the Paraclete, 16:12–13). Such testaments also often include a blessing, burial instructions, an oath, descriptions of sad parting, and the person's death. But a testament need not (and most testaments did not) include all these characteristics to fit the general context of the genre; thus many NT scholars place Mark 13 and 2 Peter in this category, despite their having only some of these characteristics.[47] John 14 may fit the typical format of a farewell discourse better than John 15–16, but, given the attested variations within the format, there is no reason to doubt that this discourse could be distinctive in some respects.[48] The very fact that Jesus rises as well as dies within the Fourth Gospel requires major modifications in the typical testamentary format in any case.[49] Later rabbis also adapted the earlier testamentary genre to fit their characteristic emphases.[50] Segovia, after surveying dominant patterns in testaments and farewell scenes,[51] finds seven of nine major categories of farewell speech motifs in John 13–17, and notes that those missing would be out of place here.[52]

---

[39] Cf. Paul's Miletus speech (Acts 20:18–35; Michel, *Abschiedsrede*).

[40] E.g., Gen 47:29–49:33; Deut 31:1–33:29; Josh 23:1–24:30; 1 Kgs 2:1–10; cf. 1 Sam 12. On Genesis, cf. Endres, *Interpretation*, 199–201.

[41] *Jub.* 36:1–11; 4Q542 (on which see Falk, "4Q542"); Tob 4:3–21; 14:3–11; 1 Macc 2:49–69; *Testament of the Twelve Patriarchs*; *2 En.* 2:2; *p. Ketub.* 12:3, §§12–13; *Taʿan.* 4:2, §8; *Tg. Onq., Tg. Neof.* 1, and *Tg. Ps.-J.* on Gen 49 (in each case the most expansive part of the Targum); Bauckham, *Jude,* 131–35; in conjunction with deathbed visions, e.g., *p. ʿAbod . Zar.* 3:1, §2; *Soṭah* 9:16, §2; *Tg. Neof.* on Gen 49:1; *Tg. Ps.-J.* on Gen 49:1. On testaments, see further McNamara, *Judaism,* 89–92; Kolenkow, "Testament"; Collins, "Testamentary Literature"; in the rabbis, cf. Saldarini, "Deathbed Scenes." *T. Ab.* may be a nontestament because of Abraham's refusal to die, hence failure to prepare (see Kolenkow, "Role"; cf. *T. Ab.* 15:7–10).

[42] E.g., Plato *Phaedo;* Xenophon *Cyr.* 8.7.6–28; Babrius 47; cf. Menander Rhetor 2.15, 430.9–434.9. These differ from the farewell speech genre *(propemptikon)* in which one wishes farewell to a traveler (Menander Rhetor 395.4–30; Stowers, *Letter Writing,* 55–56).

[43] E.g., Luke 22:14–38 (Kurz, "Luke 22:14–38"); Acts 20 (Michel, *Abschiedsrede*); Mark 13 (Robbins, *Jesus,* 174–75); 2 Peter (Bauckham, *Jude,* 131–35).

[44] Testaments typically sought to provide for those left behind, which Jesus does especially through the Paraclete; see Müller, "Parakletenvorstellung."

[45] See Robbins, *Jesus,* 174–75.

[46] E.g., Käsemann, *Testament,* 4; O'Day, "John," 737–38.

[47] Robbins, *Jesus,* 174–75; Bauckham, *Jude,* 131–35.

[48] E.g., Burge, *Community,* 27–28, critiquing Müller, "Parakletenvorstellung."

[49] Neusner, "Death-Scenes," rightly notes the similarity of structure but divergence in other respects between Jesus' and rabbinic farewell scenes.

[50] See Goshen Gottstein, "Testaments."

[51] Segovia, *Farewell,* 5–20.

[52] Ibid., 308–9; although there are thirteen farewell motif categories, only nine appear in speeches.

Theologically, the discourse underlines the theme of Jesus' continuing presence with his people.[53] In place of an eschatological discourse preceding the passion, as in the Synoptic traditions and probably traditions known to the Johannine community (which was, however, also capable of eschatological interpretation; cf. Rev), John treats his audience to an emphasis on the present experience of Jesus' presence through his past return to them.[54]

---

[53] Woll, *Conflict,* 33 (on the "first" discourse); cf. pp. 48, 79–80 on the Paraclete as Jesus' successor. Jonge, *Jesus,* 172, finds the emphasis on "the life of the community in the interim," summarized especially in 13:31–38 and 17:20–26, which together frame the discourse.

[54] Future eschatology thus becomes not primarily anthropology (cf. Becker, "Abscheidsreden," 219–28; see 228 on 14:3, 19) but Christology and pneumatology, in which eschatology's focus is realized (cf. also 1 Cor 2:9–10; 2 Cor 1:22; 5:5; Eph 1:13–14; Heb 6:4–5).

# THE ULTIMATE MODEL FOR LOVE AND SERVICE

## 13:1–38

THE FOOT WASHING IN JOHN is the narrative introduction for the final discourse, part of the lengthy prolegomena to the Passion Narrative. Jesus' impending death dominates this scene. It intersperses Jesus' words and example of service (13:1, 3–10, 12–17, 31–35) with foreshadowings of his betrayal (13:2, 10–11, 18–30), then opens directly into discussion about Jesus' departure by way of the cross (13:36–38; 14:3–6).[1] This scene therefore paves the way for the Farewell Discourse (13:31–17:26).[2]

By the foot washing Jesus prefigures his impending glorification, which is the theological subject of most of the context (12:16, 23, 28, 41; 13:31–32). This act identifies Jesus as the Suffering Servant and defines his passion as an act of loving service. At the same time, however, it also summons Jesus' followers to imitate his model, serving and loving another to the extent of laying down their lives for one another (13:14–16, 34–35).

## The Setting (13:1–3)

John again links Jesus' imminent "hour" with the Passover season (13:1). (On the "hour," see comment on 2:4; cf. 12:23.) In contrast to the Synoptic picture of the Last Supper, however, Jesus' closing hours before his arrest in this Gospel are "before" Passover (13:1). This detail fits John's chronology (13:29; 18:28; 19:14, 31, 42),[3] which ultimately supports his portrayal of Jesus as the paschal lamb (1:29, 36; 19:36). At this point, however, John underlines a different aspect of the chronology: Jesus loved his own "to the end" (13:1). This is Johannine double entendre: it can imply "to the utmost," "fully," as well as "to the point of his death."[4] Such a double entendre reinforces the measure of God's love in the Fourth Gospel (3:16) and early Christianity (Rom 5:5–9): Jesus' death. The preceding context also illustrates Jesus' love (11:5) that would cost him his life (11:7–16), but here the specific objects of his love in the Lazarus story give way to all of "his own" (cf. 10:3) who would be remaining in the world (17:11).

John also emphasizes the role of Judas in the beginning of this scene (13:2), framing the scene immediately preceding the Farewell Discourse with the report of Jesus' betrayal

---

[1] Jesus' "going" to the Father includes his death (e.g., Holwerda, *Spirit,* 17–24).

[2] Noted by others, e.g., ibid., 18. Some source-critical theories have divided 13:1–20 into two independent earlier narratives (Georg Richter, summarized in Segovia, *Relationships,* 88), but this is unnecessary.

[3] E.g., Oesterley, *Liturgy,* 158–59.

[4] Brown, *John,* 2:550; Michaels, *John,* 231; O'Day, "John," 721; to display a virtue even to the point of death was viewed as praiseworthy (Valerius Maximus 4.5.6). The Targum (*Tg. Yer.* 1 and 2 on Deut 32) describes Moses' impending death similarly (Glasson, *Moses,* 74). Cf. the eschatological "last day" (6:39, 40, 44, 54; 8:24, 48; 11:24; 12:48; cf. 7:37; 8:56).

(13:21–30) as well as Satan's activity (13:2, 27; see comment on 13:27).[5] Finally, John prefaces the scene by emphasizing Jesus' authority, source, and destination, which heightens the significance of his service to the disciples that immediately follows (13:3).[6] The connection between 13:1 and 13:3 may suggest that Jesus takes his position as Lord of all things[7] (13:3; see comment on 3:35) only after enduring the death of the cross (13:1). In this light it appears all the more striking that the all-powerful Word became flesh and served disciples who consistently misunderstood and sometimes failed him. This perspective, more widespread in early Christianity (see Phil 2:6–11),[8] seems distinctive of early Christianity.

Who might be present at the banquet? Unless they met in a home of inordinate size, and especially if they met in an upper room as in the tradition (Mark 14:15; Luke 22:12; Acts 1:13), probably only a small number of disciples could be present (though cf. Acts 1:15, if it assumes the same location as 1:13). It is reasonable to identify these roughly with the Twelve (6:71). In much of the Hellenistic world, women typically attended drinking parties only if they were courtesans or part of the entertainment.[9] By contrast, a Passover meal such as depicted in the Synoptics would be more of a family setting;[10] but this does not settle who may have been present. If the meal involved a group of mostly male disciples (unlike most Passover meals), it may have been segregated by gender, unlike the Lord's Supper in the churches at a later time.[11] From John's own narrative, however, we can gather only that it was an intimate group of his closest disciples which included the beloved disciple, Peter, Philip, Thomas, and both disciples named Judas.

That Jesus and his disciples "reclined" (13:12, 23) indicates the nature of their seating. From the East, Greeks had adopted the practice of reclining on a couch during the main meal; because one propped oneself up by the left elbow, diners had only one free hand, so attendants cut up the food in advance and diners ate most often with their hands.[12] Thus a later Jewish report suggests that guests gathered on benches or chairs; when all the guests had arrived, they would each wash one hand, have appetizers, recline, and wash both hands before the main meal.[13] Tables were placed beside couches so that diners could readily reach their food.[14]

Although Jewish people in Palestine usually sat on chairs when available,[15] they had adopted the Hellenistic custom of reclining for banquets,[16] including the Passover,[17] a set-

---

[5] Cf. Grayston, *Epistles,* 81–82, who thinks Judas may represent the Johannine Epistles' dissidents.

[6] Lightfoot, *Gospel,* 273.

[7] All things in Jesus' "hands" in 13:3 is significant; tradition said that all things were in *God's* hands (4Q266 frg. 18, col. 5, lines 9–10; but for delegation, cf. Matt 11:27; Luke 10:22).

[8] See Nicol, "Washing."

[9] Isaeus *Estate of Pyrrus* 13–14; Plutarch *Alex.* 38.1; cf. Isaeus *Estate of Philoctemon* 21.

[10] E.g., *t. Pesaḥ.* 10:4.

[11] If the meal was gender-segregated, it is not likely the women would be doing much serving (in contrast to 12:2), since they would also be partaking somewhere.

[12] Cary and Haarhoff, *Life,* 96; Dupont, *Life,* 98–99; Haenchen, *John,* 2:110; Anderson, *Mark,* 104 (the position was not limited to banquets; cf. Valerius Maximus 5.1.ext.1b). For reclining at banquets, see, e.g., Plato *Rep.* 2.372D; Xenophon *Anab.* 6.1.4; Seneca *Ep. Lucil.* 47.5; Martial *Epigr.* 3.30.1 *(recumbis);* Ps.-Callisthenes *Alex.* 2.14; Athenaeus *Deipn.* 1.18ab; *Let. Aris.* 181, 183; *t. Ber.* 4:20; *Sipre Deut.* 41.2.5; *Pesiq. Rab Kah.* 6:3; *b. Ber.* 37a, 42b–43a; *Eccl. Rab.* 9:8, §1; this may have pertained only to adult males (Xenophon *Symp.* 1.8, where a boy sits beside his father).

[13] *P. Ber.* 6:6, §1, following *t. Ber.* 4:8.

[14] Safrai, "Home," 738. The common Passover bowl (cf. Stauffer, *Jesus,* 115) would be circulated.

[15] Safrai, "Home," 736–37.

[16] The Greek custom also spread into Egypt in the Hellenistic period (Horsley, *Documents,* 1:9, §1).

[17] Because reclining was the appropriate banquet posture for free persons in the Greek world, it proved especially appropriate for remembering the Passover (e.g., Daube, *Pattern,* 45; Lachs,

ting that the Fourth Gospel and its first audience might assume from the Gospel tradition despite the Fourth Gospel's symbolic shift of the Passover to one day later.[18] It probably implies that John has, after all, revised an earlier Passover tradition. (One would not expect John to harmonize all his traditions,[19] though his narrative may be more consistent in its portrayal of Jesus than that of Matthew or Luke is.)

## Authenticity and Significance of the Foot Washing

Although we will offer brief comment on specific verses below, many of the critical issues surround the passage as a whole.

### 1. The Question of Historical Authenticity

Against the tendency to suppose that whatever event is reported only in John is likely fictitious, it should be remembered that Matthew and Luke felt free to supplement Mark's outline with other material, much of which they share in common but much of which they do not. Given the small quantity of extant data to work with, multiple attestation works as a much more valid criterion when applied positively than when applied negatively. Manson thinks that Jesus may have washed the disciples' feet at the Last Supper, citing Luke 22:27.[20] Certainly Jesus there uses himself as an example of one who serves (Luke 22:27), while exhorting his disciples to serve one another (Luke 22:26).[21] Normally foot washing would precede a meal (cf. Luke 7:44), but the foot washing here follows most of the meal (13:2–4); the logic of the narrative prevents any further eating, for Jesus soon departs.[22] Given John's different date for Passover,[23] however, he may deliberately omit discussion of the meal to keep the emphasis on the cross itself.

### 2. The Message of the Foot Washing

The theology of the foot washing is, however, of greater importance to us here. Most scholars recognize the image of self-sacrifice in the foot washing.[24] By humbly serving his

---

*Commentary*, 406). The rabbinic form of Passover Seder reflects the Greco-Roman *symposium* (Levine, *Hellenism*, 119–24, debating whether its elements predate Yavneh).

[18] Sitting was the customary posture in daily life (e.g., *T. Ab.* 3:5A), but reclining (following a broader Mediterranean custom—Plato *Rep.* 2.372D; Seneca *Ep. Lucil.* 47.5; Martial *Epigr.* 3.30.1; Athenaeus *Deipn.* 1.18ab; *Let. Aris.* 183) for special occasions and banquets (e.g., *T. Ab.* 4:1–2, 4A; *Sipre Deut.* 41.2.5; *t. Ber.* 4:20; *b. Ber.* 37a, 42b–43a), including Pesach (*m. Pesaḥ.* 10:1; *b. Ḥag.* 14b; *Pesaḥ.* 108a; *Exod. Rab.* 20:18; cf. Daube, *Pattern*, 45).

[19] Ancient readers could similarly deconstruct the eastern Mediterranean's favorite work, Homer's *Iliad*, where, e.g., one could leap directly from Olympus (*Il.* 1.532; 4.78; cf. 5.885) or take a day to fall (*Il.* 1.592); where sweet sleep came on Zeus (*Il.* 1.610–611) but he alone could not sleep that night (*Il.* 2.2); or compare *Il.* 13.658 with 5.576; 13.365–366 with 3.124. Such variation appears permissible; cf., e.g., Cornelius Nepos 8 (Thrasybulus), 1.3, with Cornelius Nepos 7 (Alcibiades), passim, esp. 5.4; 6.3; 7.1; Plutarch *Cimon* 1.5–6.

[20] Manson, *Paul and John*, 87.

[21] With Ridderbos, *John*, 453–54, who notes a slave "at table" girding himself in Luke 12:37; 17:8 (though the purpose of girding differs in John 13:4).

[22] Bernard, *John*, 2:459. Thomas, *Footwashing*, 184, thinks that foot washing normally preceded the Lord's Supper in the Johannine community.

[23] On the difference between the Johannine and Synoptic calendars, and the probable preference for the Synoptic, see Keener, *Matthew*, 622–23.

[24] E.g., Levine, "Symbolism"; Smith, *John* (1999), 252.

disciples (13:4–16), Jesus takes the role of the Suffering Servant (cf. Isa 52:13–53:12) that John has just mentioned (12:38), epitomizing christological motifs from his Gospel and some other early Christian sources.[25] Because biblical and early Jewish customs use foot washing in welcoming guests, some see it as an act of eschatological hospitality.[26]

More critically, Jesus' act in this passage prefigures the passion.[27] The interspersing of the foot washing and its significance (13:3–10) with the betrayal (13:2, 10–11) clearly indicates Jesus' impending death. Other clues in the narrative support this thesis; "lay aside" and "take up" (13:4, 12) are not specifically sacrificial language, but a careful reader might recognize that the terms elsewhere appear together in John only in 10:17–18, perhaps also investing "rise" (13:4) with its usual significance in this Gospel.[28]

The more widespread early Christian chronology attested in the Synoptics makes the context of Jesus' final teaching to the disciples a Passover meal commemorating his death; John reserves the Passover for Jesus' actual death and makes the context of Jesus' final teaching a prefiguring of his death and the teaching focusing on Jesus' continuing presence with his disciples through the Spirit. Whereas the Synoptics agree with Paul (1 Cor 11:23), and presumably most of early Christianity, in instituting the Lord's Supper commemoration on the betrayal night, John includes a summons to foot washing (whether symbolically or literally), by which believers are called to exemplify the same pattern of self-sacrificial service to the death.

It seems natural to connect the image of water with its function earlier in the Gospel. It is true that the focus of the passage is on the sign of foot washing, not on the water itself;[29] in fact, however, most earlier passages where the water motif occurs also emphasize the sign rather than the water (2:6; 4:17–19; 5:8–9). Water earlier serves a salvific function (e.g., 3:5; 4:14; 7:37–38); this comports well with Jesus' suffering servanthood here. By prefiguring his death in his act of service to his disciples, he indicates the cost he is ready to pay to save them. By washing one another's feet, disciples would prefigure their service and love for one another after Jesus' model (13:14–17, 34–35); that is, they would declare their readiness to die for one another.[30]

Did the Johannine community practice, or did the Johannine Jesus expect them to practice, literal foot washing to represent his teachings about serving one another? Because foot washing was common in the culture (albeit not of social peers or superiors washing others' feet), and because concrete symbolism can reinforce social commitment, it is very likely that John would approve, and even possible that he did intend, his audience to practice such a symbol.[31] Greeks and Romans practiced ritual foot washing,[32] and foot washing

---

[25] See Nicol, "Washing."

[26] Hultgren, "Footwashing." Hospitality with hands and feet could prove salvific (R. Jannai in *Gen. Rab.* 81:4, MSS).

[27] So, e.g., Culpepper, "*Hypodeigma.*"

[28] Thus many commentators, including Hoskyns, *Gospel,* 376; Hunter, *John,* 105; Sanders, *John,* 306; Brown, *John,* 2:551; Fenton, *John,* 141, 142; *pace* Schnackenburg, *John,* 2:510, n. 108.

[29] Dunn, *Baptism,* 188. One may contrast interpretations in which the foot washing prefigures Christian baptism (Robinson, *Studies,* 166; cf. Sylvia Mary, *Mysticism,* 126–27; Moloney, "Reading").

[30] Weiss, "Foot Washing," thinks John's community used foot washing to prepare for martyrdom.

[31] Thomas, *Footwashing,* 126–85, argues that the Johannine community probably employed it as a religious rite. Early Christians retained it as part of baptism, and it persists among some German Pietists and some Anabaptists and Pentecostals today (Martin, "Footsteps," 43), as well as in Catholic Holy Thursday rites (I owe this observation to Joseph Carey).

[32] Thomas, *Footwashing,* 42–44 (citing Homer *Il.* 16.235; *Od.* 22.454–480; Strabo *Geog.* 7.328; Fabius Pictor *De jure sacerdotis* 16; Pliny *Nat.* 24.102).

appears in cultic settings in early Jewish sources.[33] John might not have expected it as a ritual, but in a culture where the practice was common, he at least would have expected the practice to be performed in a manner that challenged traditional social stratification.

## 3. The Practice of Foot Washing

Many ancient Eastern streets must have been "unpaved, narrow, badly crowded," and some "would have been choked with refuse and frequented" by dogs and other sources of excrement.[34] Hellenistic cities required proper sanitation in their main streets, prohibiting discarding refuse there,[35] but it would have been widely known that such sanitation was more available in some locations than others. In Rome running water was available only for the ground floors of buildings, so that poorer tenants who lived higher in the building often allowed filth to accumulate; wealthier persons on ground floors built latrines that emptied into cess trenches managed by manure merchants.[36] One would expect upper-city Jerusalem, which included private *mikvaot* in most of its wealthy homes and would have preserved the highest of Hellenistic-Roman standards, to have been much cleaner; any home large enough to house Jesus' disciples as guests, especially if an upper room is envisioned (Mark 14:15; Luke 22:12; Acts 1:13), would probably lie in a more well-to-do and sanitary part of town.[37] Nevertheless, the common practice and image would be clear enough. If nothing else, dust would rapidly accumulate on feet.[38]

Thus people often washed their feet when returning home;[39] washing one's feet was common enough that "unwashed feet" became proverbial in some places for "without preparation."[40] The face, hands, and feet seem to have been the most critical parts of the body to wash.[41] Hospitality included providing water for guests to wash their feet (Gen 18:4; 19:2; 24:32; Luke 7:44) or providing servants to wash their feet;[42] wives (1 Sam 25:41) or children might also adopt this servile posture toward the *pater familias*.[43] Only a document honoring a host's extreme humility might portray that host honoring an esteemed visitor by washing his feet himself.[44] John C. Thomas provides abundant evidence for the hospitality function of foot washing, both in early Judaism[45] and in the broader

---

[33] Thomas, *Footwashing*, 27–31.

[34] Rohrbaugh, "City," 135; cf. also Jeffers, *World*, 61.

[35] Avi-Yonah, *Hellenism*, 124.

[36] Carcopino, *Life*, 39–40. The saying in Lucian *Demonax* 4 also may correlate unwashed feet with ignorance (hence perhaps with lower-class status).

[37] The tradition that Jerusalem's streets were swept daily (*b. Pesaḥ.* 7a) may nostalgically exalt old Jerusalem (cf. tamer epideictic representations of cities such as Isocrates *Panathenaicus; Panegyricus;* Aelius Aristides *Oration to Rome*); Jerusalem is idealized as early as utopian imagery in *Let. Aris.* 116 and, eschatologically, Tob 13:9–18; 5Q15 (see Licht, "Town Plan").

[38] E.g., Stambaugh and Balch, *Environment*, 107.

[39] *Pesiq. Rab.* 23/24:2.

[40] Aulus Gellius 1.9.8. On Greco-Roman foot washing for hygiene, see Thomas, *Footwashing*, 44–46; on Jewish foot washing for comfort, see 31–35.

[41] Cf. *b. Šabb.* 39b, *bar.* On handwashing, see Keener, *Matthew*, 409.

[42] E.g., a triclinium wall mural in Carcopino, *Life*, 274; *Jos. Asen.* 7:1.

[43] Children in Hierocles *Parents* 4.25.53 (Malherbe, *Exhortation*, 92–93).

[44] *T. Ab.* 3:7, 9A; 3:6–8B (Abraham to Michael).

[45] Thomas, *Footwashing*, 35–40.

Mediterranean context.[46] Thus some emphasize Jesus' loving hospitality in this text;[47] Jesus as the host of the meal provides foot washing for his guests.

But whereas well-to-do hosts provided water and sometimes servants to wash a guest's feet, they rarely engaged in the foot washing themselves. Washing feet was a menial task,[48] and one who sought to wash another's feet normally took the posture of a servant or dependent.[49] From an early period Greek literature depicted servants washing the feet of strangers as an act of hospitality,[50] as well as washing their masters' feet.[51] Foot washing could also be performed by free women (1 Tim 5:10), who might compare their role with that of servants (1 Sam 25:41; *Jos. Asen.* 13:15/12; 20:4). In both early Jewish[52] and Greco-Roman[53] texts, foot washing frequently connotes servitude. After examining all the relevant literature, Thomas concludes that Jesus' act represents "the most menial task" and was "unrivalled in antiquity."[54]

## 4. The Model of Humility

It was honorable for a hero leader to motivate followers by his own example.[55] The servile nature of foot washing would not have put off but attracted those whose conceptions of virtue were shaped by the emphasis on humility in traditional Judaism.[56] Although religious practice often differs considerably from theory, in Christianity as well as other religious systems, Jewish literature affords us considerable insight into Jewish teachers' emphasis on humility. This is best recognized, however, against the backdrop of normal social expectations. Scholars often thought that others should serve scholars.[57] For one probably hyperbolic example, those who did not serve scholars, including serving them food, could deserve death![58] Likewise, any student who was so presumptuous as to offer a legal decision in front of his teacher might be struck dead.[59] Many also saw limits to their humility; thus R. Judah ha-Nasi, head of the rabbinic academy at the beginning of the third century, was so modest that he would do whatever anyone asked of him—*except* relinquish his position to place another above him.[60] R. Judah also felt that one should ob-

---

[46] Ibid., 46–50.

[47] See Niemand, "Fusswaschung"; Hultgren, "Footwashing."

[48] *Gen. Rab.* 60:8. A donkey owner had to wash a donkey's feet (Epictetus *Diatr.* 1.19.5). Cf. Hierocles, p. 58.27–30 = Stobaeus *Ecl.* 4.25.53 (Van der Horst, "Hierocles," 157).

[49] Barrett, *John,* 440, cites *Mek. Nez.* 1 on Exod 21:2 to argue that Jewish, unlike Gentile, slaves were exempted from such labor (also Beasley-Murray, *John,* 233); but cf. also comment on 1:27.

[50] Homer *Od.* 19.344–348, 353–360, 376, 505.

[51] Homer *Od.* 19.388–393; for compulsory servitude, e.g., Apollodorus *Epitome* 1.2.

[52] See Thomas, *Footwashing,* 40–41. This may have been limited by some to Gentile slaves only (see note 48).

[53] See Thomas, *Footwashing,* 50–55.

[54] Ibid., 115.

[55] E.g., Apollonius of Rhodes 1.363–364.

[56] It was less common in Greco-Roman thought, though not absent even there (see Lincoln, *Ephesians,* 235, citing Josephus *War* 4.494; Epictetus *Diatr.* 1.9.10; 3.24.56; see esp. Good, *King*).

[57] E.g., ʾ*Abot R. Nat.* 25A; see considerably more documentation in Keener, *Matthew,* 542–45, on Matt 23:7–11.

[58] ʾ*Abot R. Nat.* 27, §56B.

[59] E.g., *Sipra Sh. M.D.* 99.5.6; *Pesiq. Rab Kah.* 26:6/7.

[60] *P. Ketub.* 12:3, §6; *Gen. Rab.* 33:3.

serve honor distinctions, starting with the greatest when bestowing greatness and from the least when bestowing humiliation.[61]

Ancient Mediterranean etiquette required a leader to observe rank carefully when bestowing honor or gifts,[62] and many viewed it an honorable ambition to become great and famous.[63] Palestinian Jewish society included a heavy emphasis on honor and even hierarchy,[64] which Essenes characteristically seem to have taken to an extreme.[65] Later reports testify the special rank accorded esteemed sages.[66] Seating by rank was important in Greco-Roman banquets,[67] public assemblies,[68] and other events,[69] as it is even in much of the Middle East today.[70] Among Jewish teachers, others stood when more learned sages would enter;[71] seating was according to honor, often according to age.[72] As in the broader Mediterranean culture,[73] Jewish tradition emphasized respect for the aged.[74] In the ancient Mediterranean, formal settings might require the eldest to speak first;[75] young men should rise before elders to offer their seats.[76] Such practices probably permeated Jewish circles as well; seniority (by age or tenure in the community) generally dictated seating in Jewish circles as well.[77] The Therapeutae reportedly sat in order of their tenure in the community (Philo *Contempl. Life* 66–69); those in the Sanhedrin were reportedly seated by rank (*m. Sanh.* 4:4). Although one could argue for seating by some sort of rank on the basis of 13:23, Jesus' example in this passage repudiates the idea of rank among disciples.[78]

---

[61] *Sipra Sh. M.D.* 99.6.1

[62] E.g., Arrian *Alex.* 7.5.4.

[63] Xenophon *Anab.* 6.1.20–21.

[64] E.g., Ahiqar 142–144, sayings 54–55; Ps.-Phoc. 220–222.

[65] Sometimes praised by outsiders (Josephus *War* 2.150; Philo *Good Person* 87).

[66] *T. Sanh.* 7:8; *b. Hor.* 13b, bar; *p. Sanh.* 1:2, §13; *Taʿan.* 4:2, §§8–9. This widespread practice of rank probably also prevailed in first-century Pharisaic circles (e.g., Bowker, *Pharisees,* 35).

[67] E.g., Plutarch *T.T.* 1.2.3, *Mor.* 616E; Xenophon *Cyr.* 8.4.3–5; Luke 14:7–11; *p. Taʿan.* 4:2, §§9, 12; *Ter.* 8:7.

[68] Apuleius *Metam.* 10.7; among the deities, see Homer *Il.* 1.535; see further Garnsey and Saller, *Empire,* 117, and sources cited there (including Suetonius *Aug.* 44). In Jewish sources, see Gen 43:33; *t. Sanh.* 8:1; *p. Taʿan.* 4:2, §12; *b. Hor.* 13b, *bar.*

[69] Apuleius *Metam.* 10.7; Valerius Maximus 4.5.ext.2; Plutarch *Cicero* 13.2; 1QS 2.19–23; 1QSa 2.11–17; *p. Ketub.* 12:3, §6; *Roš Haš.* 2:6, §9; cf. *m. ʾAbot* 5:15; on the order in speaking out, cf. 1 Cor 14:29–30; Josephus *War* 2.132; 1QS 6.9–10.

[70] Eickelman, *Middle East,* 234.

[71] *T. Sanh.* 7:8.

[72] *T. Sanh.* 8:1; *p. Taʿan.* 4:2, §12; *p. Ter.* 8:7; cf. Gen 43:33.

[73] E.g., Aeschines *Timarchus* 25; Xenophon *Cyr.* 8.7.10; Aristotle *Pol.* 2.7.5, 1272a; Diodorus Siculus 21.18.1; Dionysius of Halicarnassus *R.A.* 8.15.1. Roman society also demanded giving way to one's elder (Cato *Coll. dist.* 10; Dionysius of Halicarnassus *R.A.* 7.47.1).

[74] Josephus *Ag. Ap.* 2.206; *Ant.* 3.47 (applied to the sages in *Sipra Qed. pq.* 7.204.3.1; *p. ʿAbod. Zar.* 3:1, §2; *Hor.* 3:5, §3; *Lev. Rab.* 11:8). Prominent local leaders tended to be those who were aged, as both literary texts (Josephus *Life* 266; *Let. Aris.* 32:39; Acts 14:23) and inscriptions (*CIJ* 1:294, §378; 1:426, §581; 1:432, §595; 1:433, §597; 2:9, §739; 2:45, §790; 2:46, §792; 2:53, §801; 2:76–77, §828a; 2:77, §828b; 2:79, §829; 2:137, §931; cf. *CIJ* 1:lxxxvi–lxxxvii) testify, as does the LXX (e.g., Josh 24:1; Judg 8:14, 16; 11:5–11; 21:16; Ruth 4:2–11; 2 Chr 34:29; Jer 26:17; Jdt 6:16; 7:23–24; 13:12; 1 Macc 1:26; 7:33; 11:23; 12:35; 13:36; 14:20, 28; 2 Macc 13:13; 14:37).

[75] Dionysius of Halicarnassus *R.A.* 7.47.1; Aeschines *Timarchus* 23–24.

[76] Lycurgus 14 in Plutarch *S.S., Mor.* 227F; Xenophon *Mem.* 2.3.16.

[77] Appropriate etiquette for rising before elders is discussed in *p. Bik.* 3:3, §§4–6.

[78] Cross, *Library,* 236.

The hortatory emphasis directed toward leaders, as toward all hearers,[79] was humility. Thus writers might amplify the biblical report of Moses' meekness (Num 12:3); under normal circumstances he acted like one of the multitude and sought not to be exalted above them.[80] He also declined any honor the people tried to confer on him,[81] perhaps like some statesmen from the Roman Republic who thought or pretended to think only in terms of their duty to the state. (Ancient sources often praised generals' or rulers' benevolence and mercy,[82] if not usually their humility in our modern sense of that phrase.)[83] Likewise through various stories rabbis extolled Hillel's humility and patience.[84] The literature regularly employs both God and rabbis as examples of humility.[85] Rabbis told of one teacher who, when his ass-driver answered more wisely than he, switched places with him.[86] They claimed that R. Meir endured spit in his eye to reconcile a wife and husband, following God's example of humility.[87] Some accounts of humble rabbis illustrated that it was meritorious to seek another's advancement above one's own,[88] even in matters of seating.[89] Rabbinic literature highly praises rabbis who served their guests with humility.[90] Another teacher faced death because he had been proud when he lectured the host of Israel.[91] Although rabbis emphasized humility far more than their contemporaries (compare the strife of Roman party politics), to some degree such patterns reflected broader Mediterranean ideals for great leaders. "Dictator" was a negative term, and power was noble only when used nobly.[92]

Perhaps reflecting the broader Mediterranean distaste for boasting,[93] a second-century teacher exhorted that one "should recount what is to his credit in a low voice and what is to his discredit in a loud voice."[94] Some said that Samuel "the small" was so known because he belittled himself.[95] A later rabbi claimed that when a sage boasted his wisdom departed.[96]

---

[79] E.g., *b. ʿAbod. Zar.* 20b; *Soṭah* 4b–5a. Lincoln, *Ephesians,* 236, cites Qumran texts extolling gentleness or meekness (1QS 2.24; 3.8; 5.3, 25; 11.1).

[80] Josephus *Ant.* 3.212. Cf. imperial propaganda, originally intended to preserve a veneer of Rome's republic, in which the emperor was merely the *princeps,* the first among many.

[81] Josephus *Ant.* 3.212. On his humility, cf., e.g., Sirat and Woog, "Maître."

[82] E.g., of Alexander (Arrian *Alex.* 1.17.12; Valerius Maximus 5.1.*ext.*1a) or others (Appian *R.H.* 10.4.24; Cornelius Nepos 1 [Miltiades], 8.4; 8 [Thrasybulus], 2.6; Herodian 1.2.4; Valerius Maximus 5.1, passim). Though Achilles slays many suppliants, the gods require his mercy toward Priam near the *Iliad*'s end (Homer *Il.* 24.507–508, 665–670; though even here cf. his limits in 24.559–570).

[83] One could praise a "meek" ruler, i.e., a "gentle" one (Babrius 102.3; Valerius Maximus 5.1.ext.1a; Menander Rhetor 2.4, 389.8); see further Good, *King,* 47–49.

[84] *ʾAbot R. Nat.* 15A; 29, §§60–62B. Rabbis also praised the humility of Simeon b. Shetah (*p. Sanh.* 6:6, §2) and others.

[85] See Maher, "Humble." On God's service, see also Bonsirven, *Judaism,* 13. God promised to exalt the humble (cf. Isa 2:11–12; 5:15–16; Ezek 21:26; Sir 11:5–6; *b. ʾAbot* 6:4, *bar.; ʾAbot R. Nat.* 11A; 22B; Matt 23:12; Xenophon *Anab.* 6.3.18).

[86] E.g., *Deut. Rab.* 3:6.

[87] *Num. Rab.* 9:20.

[88] *P. Taʿan.* 4:2, §8.

[89] *P. Taʿan.* 4:2, §9.

[90] Dalman, *Jesus-Jeshua,* 117.

[91] *ʾAbot R. Nat.* 38A; 41, §111B. Whoever exalted himself at the expense of another's humiliation would not inherit the coming world (an early Amora in *Gen. Rab.* 1:5).

[92] Dionysius of Halicarnassus *R.A.* 5.77.6.

[93] E.g., Quintilian 11.1.17–19; Phaedrus 1.11; Prov 27:2; 2 Cor 12:5–6; Lyons, *Autobiography,* 44–45, 53–59; see further comment in our introduction to 5:31–47.

[94] *B. Soṭah* 32b, *bar.* (R. Simeon b. Yoḥai; Soncino trans.)

[95] *P. Soṭah* 9:13, §2.

[96] *B. Pesaḥ.* 66b.

Such humility was often expressed toward those in positions of greater power. One should be quick to serve a "head," one in authority over oneself.[97] Two third-century teachers attributed their longevity partly to never having walked in front of someone greater than themselves.[98] But those in power dare never become too arrogant themselves. The aristocrat R. Gamaliel II insulted the dignity of R. Joshua, and was deposed from his position as head of the rabbinic academy until he went around and apologized.[99] As one Tanna, perhaps Akiba, put it, "Power buries those who possess it."[100] In what may be the most relevant parallel to our passage in John, Rabban Gamaliel mixed wine for R. Eliezer, who was unwilling to accept it. But R. Joshua and R. Zadok responded that Abraham and God himself serve others' needs; therefore it was appropriate for Gamaliel as the most honored to serve his colleagues.[101]

Gestures of humility must have been common among the pious, but adopting postures of slavery must have been rare. The most progressive aristocrats of Greco-Roman antiquity, such as Seneca and Pliny the Younger, could advocate dining with freedpersons or even slaves, but never serving them at table.[102] For a person of status, particularly a patron host, to wash his guests' feet as if a servant would be unthinkable! Although Jewish teachers may not have shared standard Roman aristocratic views of rank, in which most slaves and slaveborn could never acquire genuinely high status in aristocratic eyes,[103] some, especially the many whose family means would have allowed their pursuit of advanced study, did retain such views.[104] Some Jewish texts suggest that a Gentile slave consummated his entrance into servitude for a Jewish slaveholder by performing an act of menial service; perhaps Jesus demonstrates his servitude in such a manner here.[105]

## The Foot Washing and Its First Interpretation (13:4–20)

This section explains the salvific necessity of being washed by Jesus (13:6–11) and how it functions as a model for believers serving one another (13:12–20). Because an announcement of Jesus' departure immediately (13:1–3) as well as more distantly (12:8, 35–36) precedes this material, it seems clear that John invites us to read the foot washing in view of the cross. In the context of the betrayal (13:21–30) and another comment on the imminence of the passion (13:31–33), however, the following material grows even more explicit: loving and serving as Jesus did demands sacrifice for one another, potentially to the point of death (13:34–35). Sadly, however, the most prominent disciple would fall short of such sacrifice even directly for Jesus (13:36–38).

---

[97] *M. ʾAbot* 3:12 (R. Ishmael).

[98] *B. Meg.* 28a; *Taʿan.* 20b.

[99] E.g., *p. Taʿan.* 4:1, §14.

[100] *ʾAbot R. Nat.* 39A.

[101] *Sipre Deut.* 38.1.4.

[102] Buckwalter, "Saviour," 121, citing Seneca *Ep.* 47.5–8, 13–16; see also Pliny *Ep.* 2.6.3–4.

[103] Cf., e.g., Demosthenes *Against Leptines* 132; Chariton 1.11.3. Freedpersons often gained wealth (Petronius *Sat.* 38; cf. López Barja de Quiroga, "Mobility"), but advancement of rank normally occurred only with their children (MacMullen, *Relations*, 105; Finley, *Economy*, 72), and freedpersons retained responsibilities to former holders (*ILS* 7558, 7580; cf. Horsley, *Documents*, 4, §24, pp. 102–3; Dupont, *Life*, 65–66).

[104] See, e.g., *m. Hor.* 3:8; *Qidd.* 4:1; *Num. Rab.* 6:1; cf. Jeremias, *Jerusalem*, 272.

[105] See Derrett, "Domine."

## 1. The Act of Washing (13:4–5)

Other texts suggest that one might pour cold water into a basin, then add the hot, to prepare to wash feet.[106] Νιπτῆρα (13:5) can refer to a basin or laver; while it may be a pitcher for the meal used to pour water the way one typically washed (2 Kgs 3:11),[107] Jesus undoubtedly also uses a basin here (this would be necessary out of regard for the host's floor, all the more if an upper room is presupposed, although that detail remains unclear without recourse to the Synoptics).[108] That Jesus would have actually touched the feet reinforces the image of his service here.

The towel (13:4–5) may have been used for drying hands after the meal;[109] Jesus probably "girds" himself with it (13:4) so that he can use both hands in the washing.[110] Aside from the possible allusions to Jesus' death and resurrection in the description of Jesus "taking up" and "laying down" the towel (above), his posture is significant. Whereas masters and banqueters would sit or recline, servants might stand to serve them; Jesus "rises" (13:4) to wash their feet.[111] That the disciples reclined (13:12, 23, 28) sheds light on the posture of the washing (13:5). Couches were arranged so people's feet pointed away from the center of the banquet (see comment on reclining, 13:12, 23); thus Jesus comes away from the normal focus of gaiety to wash their feet.[112]

## 2. The Necessity of the Washing (13:6–11)

Peter, speaking for the disciples, again misunderstands (13:6), as do other disciples in this section (13:28; 14:5, 8, 22), reinforcing the Gospel's emphasis on their inability to understand fully.[113] Interactions in ancient Mediterranean culture proceeded according to status differences, so that one might expect the disciples to staunchly protest Jesus' taking the role of their servant.[114] Later rabbis told a story, perhaps parabolic, of R. Ishmael's vehement protest when his mother insisted on washing his feet (and drinking the water!).[115] The language of his protest is emphatic: by placing "Lord" at the beginning and "feet" at the end, the most emphatic points of a Greek sentence, he underlines the dramatic incon-

---

[106] Homer Od. 19.386–389. Ancients sometimes used warm water to relax weary limbs (Pindar Nem. 4.4).

[107] Brown, John, 2:551.

[108] Jesus probably poured more water from a pitcher over the feet into the basin, as was practiced in traditional Mediterranean handwashing, sometimes by servants (Homer Il. 9.174; Od. 1.136–138, 146; 2.260–261; 3.338; 4.52–54, 216; 12.336; 21.270; Apollodorus 2.7.6; Athenaeus Deipn. 9.408CD; 2 Kgs 3:11).

[109] Pesce and Destro, "Lavanda," cite slaves washing guests' feet with a linen cloth (λέντιον, as in 13:4–5) in Aesop's Romance.

[110] Some suggest that the image provides a deliberate contrast to the ancient image of a wrestling belt (Levine, "Symbolism"); a servant does not vie for power but relinquishes it. Beasley-Murray, John, 233, following Billerbeck 2:557, cites evidence for this as a slave posture (Abraham tying Hagar's shawl around her loins in Genesis Rabbah); more evidence, however, is necessary.

[111] Neyrey, "Shame of Cross," 117, citing Luke 17:7–8; Rev 4:10.

[112] Brown, John, 2:551; Cary and Haarhoff, Life, 96; cf. Luke 7:38, 44.

[113] Jonge, Jesus, 16.

[114] Malina, Windows, 40; cf. Sipre Deut. 38.1.4.

[115] The sages insisted that, to honor her, he must accommodate her desire (p. Pe'ah 1:1, §8).

gruity of the action;[116] the placing of the two pronouns together (an emphatic "you" preceding "my") probably reinforces the grammatical point further.[117]

Jesus responds that unless Peter submits to this washing, he has no part with Jesus (13:8), that is, no share in eternal fellowship with him;[118] in this discourse, having no part with Jesus is a serious situation (14:30; 15:6). This indicates that the washing symbolizes allowing Jesus to serve his followers by embracing his death for them. Social inferiors expected help from patrons, but not service from them; such a reversal of roles created discomfort. Yet true dependents on Christ cannot have his gift without his sacrifice and must acknowledge their dependence.[119] The seriousness of the matter is evident from the context: Judas protested Mary washing Jesus' feet (12:4–5); Peter, also misunderstanding Jesus' mission, protests Jesus washing his own (13:8). Mary and Jesus embody sacrifice and servanthood; Judas and Peter, impending betrayal and denial![120] Peter's emphatic reversal in 13:9 suggests a continued misunderstanding.[121] His misunderstanding is, however, momentarily mitigated by his loyalty: he is willing to accept whatever necessary to have a share with Jesus. Like other misunderstanding disciples (11:16), he felt that he was even ready to die with Jesus (13:37). When the time to do so would come, however, he, like the others, would prove unprepared (13:38; 18:25–27).

Although responding to Peter, Jesus employs the plural pronoun to include all his disciples as clean.[122] That the disciples were already "washed" (13:10)[123] may allude physically to the ritual purification preceding the eating of Passover.[124] (This might appear clearer in the earliest form of John's tradition than in the finished Gospel, where the events take place the day before Passover; but cf. 11:55.) Some Jews required handwashing before regular meals (Mark 7:1–5), but the Passover meal required a higher level of ritual purity.[125] Even after this cleansing, however, they would require ritual washing of hands and perhaps feet;[126] one who had bathed at home but walked to a banquet would likewise need to wash

---

[116] Haenchen, *John*, 2:107. One does expect the vocative address first, so it is its conjunction with "feet" at the end that makes these positions emphatic.

[117] Michaels, *John*, 231. Also Whitacre, *John*, 329, who comments (with John Chrysostom *Hom. Jo.* 70.2) that Peter's response reveals love, yet "defective love...[that] lacks humility."

[118] Michaels, *John*, 231. Deities gave humanity a "portion" of themselves (μέρος, Epictetus *Diatr.* 1.12; cf. 1.12.26; Marcus Aurelius 4.14; 7.13). But such potential parallels are too distant from the point of this text for relevance.

[119] Alexander, considered benevolent, was angrier with those who refused his gifts (so dishonoring him) than with those who asked for them (Plutarch *Alex.* 39.3); but mere benevolence is not humble service, as here.

[120] Cf. Beattie, "Discipleship of Love," who contrasts Mary in ch. 12 with Peter in ch. 13.

[121] E.g., Haenchen, *John*, 2:107–8.

[122] Suggit, "Nicodemus," 91, finds in the plural a typifying of Peter for all disciples.

[123] One might compare the "initial purification" for initiation into a mystery cult (e.g., Mylonas, *Eleusis*, 238), though this is especially καθαρμός (cf. Zuntz, *Persephone*, 307, for an early possible use of καθαρός for ritual purification). But the Jewish baptismal image would be nearer at hand (see comment on 1:25–26, 31).

[124] Jeremias, *Eucharistic Words*, 49; see also Kieffer, "L'arrière-fond juif"; idem, "Fottvagningens." Bowman, *Gospel*, 271, less persuasively finds an allusion to priests' morning bathing.

[125] Jaubert, "Calendar," 70, citing Num 9:6–11; 2 Chr 30:17–19; Ezra 6:20.

[126] On the former, see *m. Yad.* 1:1–2:4; *b. Bek.* 30b, *bar.; Ber.* 11b; 15a; 60b; *Sib. Or.* 3.591–594; Keener, *Matthew*, 409; for the feet as well, cf. Exod 40:31–32. Although "except the feet" is missing in א, it remains the more likely reading (Thomas, *Footwashing*, 19–25).

the feet.[127] On the symbolic level, however, they had been washed by his word which he had spoken (15:3); they no longer needed outward purifications not explicitly commanded in the Torah (2:6–11). Jewish people spoke of purifying the land from Gentile contamination (perhaps idolatry, 4 Macc 17:21);[128] some expected the greatest purifying in the time of the Messiah (*Pss. Sol.* 17:30). But Greek and Roman philosophers[129] and Greek-speaking Jewish writers[130] also spoke of purifying one's mind and soul from impure thoughts.

After declaring that all were clean, Jesus qualifies his statement by warning of an exception (13:10); ancients sometimes made general statements that they (or others) then qualified.[131] Perhaps for emphasis, John repeats Jesus' statement of 13:10 in slightly different words in 13:11, as he does various statements elsewhere (1:48, 50; 9:21, 23);[132] no one would trifle over divergences in such inexact quotes during repetition (e.g., Gen 39:17–19; 1 Sam 15:3, 18). Variation was standard rhetorical practice.[133] "Nowhere throughout ancient literature . . . did the authors feel the need to reproduce a text with verbal exactness."[134] Some modern interpreters of more literalist bent have objected to the writer's apparent practice of paraphrase reflected in its pervasive Johannine idiom; if they are persuaded by nothing else, this passage should be sufficient testimony that modern literalism would never have crossed the author's mind.

### 3. The Interpretation of the Washing (13:12–20)

On the reclining (13:12), see our comment on the setting (13:1–3). By opening with a statement of his superior rank (13:13), Jesus focuses his following words on the inversion of status and power among his followers, a theme elsewhere known from the Jesus tradition (e.g., Mark 9:36–37; 10:15, 42–45; Matt 18:3–4, 10; Luke 22:24–27). Whoever instructed a disciple in Torah was his master,[135] and Jesus certainly was the teacher of his disciples.[136] While disciples might call their teachers both "teacher" and "lord" ("sir"), on the Johannine level of meaning the latter term implies christological authority (13:13).[137]

---

[127] Thomas, *Footwashing,* 106; Whitacre, *John,* 330. On the historical level, a meal in a large upper room might be in the upper city and hence have ritual baths available (Stanton, *Gospel Truth,* 116; Avigad, *Jerusalem,* 139, 142).

[128] Cf. also *T. Job* 3:7. Greeks also spoke of purifying (καθαίρων) the land from injustice and lawlessness (Heracles in Epictetus *Diatr.* 2.16.44).

[129] Plato *Sophist* 227D (the Eleatic stranger, adapting ritual language, καθαρμός; cf. 230D); Epictetus *Diatr.* 4.1.112; 4.11.3, 5, 8; *Ench.* 33.6, 8; Marcus Aurelius 3.12. For postmortem purgatory of the soul, cf., e.g., Virgil *Aen.* 6.735–742.

[130] E.g., *T. Reu.* 4:8; 6:1.

[131] E.g., Appian *R.H.* 4.11; cf. 1 Cor 1:14–16; Keener, *Marries,* 22–27.

[132] Cf., e.g., Xenophon *Cyr.* 3.1.36, 41, who repeats a statement using a synonym for servitude. Orators sometimes repeated themselves as a rhetorical technique, but Demetrius considered this unsuitable for written works (226, as cited in Anderson, *Glossary,* 77, s.v. μιμητικόν).

[133] E.g., *Rhet. ad Herenn.* 4.28.38; Aulus Gellius 1.4; 2.5.1; cf. Robbins, "Plutarch and Gospels," 146–55.

[134] Gordon, *East,* 107.

[135] See *t. B. Meṣiʿa* 2:30, where rabbis seek to define the matter more specifically.

[136] The "articular nominative" (not an accusative) here functions as a vocative (Barrett, *John,* 443).

[137] With Barrett, *John,* 443. "Teacher" could also be an exalted title, depending on who was taught ("heaven and earth" in *T. Ab.* 11:3B). "Call" (13:13) could bear an exalted function (e.g., Acts 2:21; *Gen. Rab.* 39:16) but is not required by the term itself.

Following Jesus' example by washing one another's feet (13:14) evidences following the example of his love (13:34) but also evokes the image of the water motif (see comment on 2:6; 3:5), implying involvement in Christ's salvific work.[138] (For imitation of teachers and of God, see comment on 13:34–35.) If Jesus sacrifices his life to serve his followers, then his followers must also be ready to pay such a price to guard one another's perseverance in the faith. That they "ought" to wash one another's feet may reflect the moralist use of the language of obligation,[139] but is certainly acceptable vocabulary in the Johannine circle of believers (cf. 1 John 2:6; 3:16; 4:11; cf. 3 John 8).

When Jesus takes the role of a servant, he plainly inverts the roles of himself and the disciples in that society.[140] John utilizes in 13:16 a saying also attested in the Q tradition, which in its original form applied to disciples as well as slaves (Matt 10:24–25; Luke 6:40).[141] A disciple normally would not claim to be greater than his teacher;[142] if a master suffered, how much more should his servant be willing to endure it.[143] That a servant or disciple was like the master may have been a proverb and was probably at least a commonplace.[144]

Disciples would do for their teachers almost anything a slave would do except deal with their feet, which was considered too demeaning for a free person (see comment on 1:27).[145] By the late second century, a sage could exercise much of the authority over a disciple that a master could over a slave; he was even permitted to beat pupils.[146] Disciples of the sages should attend on the sages;[147] studying under rabbis involved serving them.[148] This passage in some sense repudiates the conception of servant-disciples prevalent in the rabbinic movement and probably the larger culture.[149] Its ideas are certainly consistent with other extant Jesus tradition (Mark 10:43–45). Jesus' disciples were servants (15:20); ultimately servants in the exalted sense of the biblical prophets (cf. Rev 1:1) yet servants of Jesus as well as of God (12:26). But they were also friends (15:15), invited into fellowship by a love that burst the bounds of social propriety (cf. 3:16).

---

138 Cf. Fenton, *John,* 143, citing 13:20; 14:12; 20:21, 23. Culpepper, *John,* 206, regarding the language of 13:14–15, points to parallels for "exemplary" deaths (2 Macc 6:27–28, 31; 4 Macc 17:22–23; Sir 44:16); see our comment on 13:34.

139 E.g., 4 Macc 16:18–19; Rom 1:14; 13:8; 15:1; Eph 5:28.

140 Pesce and Destro, "Lavanda," compare the inversion at the Saturnalia festival where masters temporarily served slaves.

141 Riesenfeld, *Tradition,* 13, also finds an echo of the saying of 13:17 in Jas 1:25.

142 Cf. Epictetus *Diatr.* 1.2.36, who seeks not to be better than, but at least not worse than, Socrates.

143 *Pesiq. Rab.* 36:2, concerning God and the Messiah; Alexander's exhortations in Arrian *Alex.* 5.26.7; 7.10.1–2.

144 See, e.g., Dalman, *Jesus-Jeshua,* 229. Certainly the servant's role to obey the master was a commonplace (e.g., Aelius Aristides *Defense of Oratory* 128, §40D).

145 Sanders, *John,* 309, following Billerbeck, *Kommentar,* 2:557, claims that a disciple would even wash the master's feet.

146 Goodman, *State,* 78; *t. B. Qam.* 9:11 (comparing rabbis to fathers and implicitly to slaveholders). Later texts also assume that rabbis held higher status than disciples and should never take a lesser position (e.g., *Lev. Rab.* 22:6).

147 R. Eliezer b. Hyrcanus in *ʾAbot R. Nat.* 25A. Serving a teacher might prove more important than studying with him (Tannaitic tradition in *b. Ber.* 7b).

148 *Gen. Rab.* 100:10, albeit also noting that teaching Israel was serving Israel; *Gen. Rab.* 22:2 (Akiba with Nahum of Gimzo).

149 Davies, *Sermon,* 135. For the exaltation of sages in the broader culture, see, e.g., Tiede, *Figure,* 55 (citing especially Seneca *On Providence* 6.6; *Ep. Lucil.* 31.11; 41.1; 73.14–16; 115.3ff.)

"One who is sent" (13:16) represents an agent, a familiar concept in this Gospel (see introduction; on the interchangeability of πέμπω and ἀποστέλλω, see 20:21). That those who received an agent received the sender (13:20) fits this motif and is attested elsewhere in extant Jesus tradition (Mark 9:37; Matt 10:40–41).

Jesus' promised blessing to those who serve one another takes the form of a beatitude (13:17), which appears on only one other occasion in this Gospel (20:29), although it is frequent in Revelation (Rev 1:3; 14:13; 16:15; 19:9; 20:6; 22:7, 14). That the form occurs in this Gospel only twice need not link these two passages together; the form was common in early Christian texts,[150] in the early Christians' Bible,[151] in early Judaism,[152] and appeared in non-Jewish Greek sources as well.[153] If the two passages are to be compared, however, it appears significant that 20:29 is a strategic verse which casts its theological shadow over the signs-faith of the entire Gospel. The beatitude here may similarly function to underline the importance of mutual service. Verse17 also echoes a familiar line of Jewish and other ancient ethics, namely, that behavior should correspond to knowledge (cf. Jas 1:22; 4:17; 1 John 3:18).[154]

Although John will address the betrayal in more detail (13:21–30), he introduces the matter here (13:18–19), framing it with the warning that Jesus' disciples will share his experience of betrayal and suffering (13:15–16, 20; cf. 15:18–20). Judas lifting his heel in betrayal at a meal (cf. 13:2) appears in striking contrast to Mary's washing Jesus' feet in service at another meal (12:2–3); Judas lifting his heel likewise contrasts with Jesus washing his disciples' (including Judas's) feet in this immediate context. The mention of the "heel" therefore serves an immediate literary function in the narrative in addition to its presence in a biblical quotation and its general cultural significance. The specific image in the psalm that Jesus quotes (Ps 41:9) might be that of a horse or mule kicking the person feeding it;[155] probably more likely here, showing another the bottom of one's foot is an expression of contempt (cf. Mark 6:11).[156]

Although it sometimes occurred,[157] people in ancient Mediterranean society considered betrayal by a friend (13:18) far more heinous than any insult by an enemy.[158] The deeper the

---

[150] The term μακάριος appears 40 times in the NT literature outside John and Rev, including 13 times in Matthew and 16 times in Luke-Acts, usually in sayings of Jesus.

[151] The term μακάριος appears 66 times in the LXX, including 25 times in the Psalms (including 1:1; 2:12; 31:1–2 [32:1–2 MT]), 11 times in Sirach (14:1–2, 20; 25:8–9; 26:1; 28:19; 31:8; 34:15; 48:11; 50:28), and 4 times in Proverbs (3:13; 8:34; 20:7; 28:14).

[152] Pss. Sol. 4:23; 5:16; 6:1; 10:1; Jos. Asen. 16:14/7; 1 En. 99:10; 2 En. 42.6–14; 44:5; Sipra VDDeho. par. 5.44.1.1; b. Ber. 61b; Ḥag. 14b; Hor. 10b, bar.; cf. 4Q525 (see Brooke, "Beatitudes"; Viviano, "Beatitudes"; idem, "Qumran"; idem, "Publication"; de Roo, "4Q525").

[153] Hom. Hymn 25.4–5; Contest of Homer and Hesiod 322; Pindar Threnoi frg. 137 (in Clement of Alexandria Strom. 3.3.17, using ὄλβιος); Polybius 26.1.13; Babrius 103.20–21; Musonius Rufus frg. 35, p. 134; Philostratus Hrk. 4.11; Porphyry Marc. 16.276–277. For μακάριος in Stoic and Christian literature, see Vorster, "Blessedness."

[154] Demosthenes 3 Olynthiac 14; 2 Philippic 1; Diodorus Siculus 9.9.1; Dionysius of Halicarnassus R.A. 7.33.3; 9.10.3; 9.47.4; 11.1.4; 11.58.3; Diogenes Laertius 6.2.64; Epictetus Diatr. 1.25.11; 2.9.13; Seneca Ep. Lucil. 20.2; Aulus Gellius 17.19; Herodian 1.2.4; Cornelius Nepos frg. 3.1; Josephus Ag. Ap. 2.169, 292.

[155] Hunter, John, 136; cf. Ps 32:9.

[156] Brown, John, 2:554, following observations about Near Eastern customs in Bishop, "Bread," 332–32, and rejecting dependence on Gen 3:15 LXX. Turning one's back may have functioned as an insult (Jer 2:27; 18:17; 32:33). If Judas holds the position to Jesus' right here, as seems likely, his heel would literally be far from Jesus.

[157] Some models of treachery (cf. Homer Il. 10.383, 446–459) may have been understood favorably (though Odysseus offered no oath). Even betrayal of friendship occurred in the hostile world of Roman partisan politics (e.g., in Stowers, Letter Writing, 63).

level of intimacy, the more that trust was a duty, and the more terrible its betrayal.[159] Breach of covenant such as treaties was regarded as terrible;[160] Judas's discipleship and its long-standing implicit covenant of friendship make his betrayal a heinous act of treachery,[161] but the meal context makes the betrayal even more heinous. For many, sharing food and drink represented the most important bond of kindness.[162] Although relatives were the most trustworthy of all, those who ate together shared a common bond and were normally assumed to be trustworthy.[163] Hospitality established friendly ties even with strangers and was mandatory in the ancient Mediterranean.[164] Guest friendships were politically binding,[165] and could effect reconciliation between political partisans at enmity.[166] Injuring or slaying those who had eaten at one's table was a terrible offense from which all but the most wicked would normally shrink;[167] such behavior was held to incur divine wrath.[168] Those who eat together at a table should not even betray friendship by slandering one another.[169] Though rarer due to the normal distribution of power, betraying or slaying one's host, as here, was equally terrible[170]—especially a host who had set aside his own honor to perform the most menial act of service for his guests (see comments on hospitality and foot washing above).

Just as the loyalty of one's adherents proved a matter for praise (e.g., Josephus *Life* 84), their disloyalty would prove a matter of a teacher's shame.[171] Earlier Jesus had announced

---

[158] E.g., Lysias *Or.* 6.23, §105; 8.5–6, §112; Chariton 5.6.2 (φίλος); Cornelius Nepos 14 (Datames), 6.3; 11.5; Sir 22:21–22; *T. Jud.* 23:3; cf. Derrett, *Audience,* 69. This remained true even if one's life were at stake (Babrius 138.7–8); refusing to betray a friend or husband was honorable (Athenaeus *Deipn.* 15.965F, item 25; Seneca *Controv.* 2.5.intro.). Treachery and betrayal warranted death (Valerius Maximus 9.6).

[159] Cicero *Rosc. Amer.* 40.116.

[160] E.g., Appian *R.H.* 6.8.43; 6.9.52; 6.10.60.

[161] Cf., e.g., disgust for traitors against their peoples in Xenophon *Hell.* 1.7.22; Cicero *Fin.* 3.9.32; Virgil *Aen.* 6.621; Livy 1.11.6–7; 5.27.6–10 (though cf. Livy 4.61.8–10); Valerius Maximus 1.1.13; Seneca *Controv.* 7.7.intro.; such behavior invited the hatred of even one's family (Livy 2.5.7–8; Cornelius Nepos 4 [Pausanias], 5.3). Loyalty to country might take precedence even over hospitality friendship (Xenophon *Hell.* 4.1.34; Cornelius Nepos 13 [Timotheus], 4.4), but disloyalty to friends remained despicable (e.g., *Rhet. Alex.* 36, 1442.13–14).

[162] Xenophon *Cyr.* 8.2.2–3.

[163] Xenophon *Cyr.* 8.7.14.

[164] Euripides *Cycl.* 125. See more detailed comment on John 4:40.

[165] E.g., Lysias *Or.* 12.14, §121; 18.10, §150; Plutarch *Cor.* 10.3; Cicero *Fam.* 13.19.1; 13.25.1; 13.36.1; Cornelius Nepos 5 (Cimon), 3.3; *Exod. Rab.* 28:1. This was true even over several generations (Homer *Il.* 6.212–231; Cicero *Fam.* 13.34.1) and could require the guest-friend to avenge his host (Philostratus *Hrk.* 46.2–3). Still, though it could be inherited, it could shift along with political interests (Marshall, *Enmity,* 18–21, 39–42).

[166] E.g., Plutarch *Cicero* 26.1.

[167] E.g., Homer *Il.* 21.76; *Od.* 4.534–535; 11.414–420; 14.404–495; Hesiod *Op.* 327; Euripides *Cycl.* 126–128; *Hec.* 25–26, 710–720, 850–856; Apollonius of Rhodes 3.377–380; Ovid *Metam.* 1.144; 10.225–228; Livy 25.16.6. This principle included providing protection from other enemies (Ovid *Metam.* 5.44–45; Cornelius Nepos 2 [Themistocles], 8.3).

[168] Homer *Od.* 21.26–28; Livy 39.51.12. Nevertheless, some warned that too much trust even of friends could prove dangerous (Hesiod *Op.* 370–372).

[169] Aeschines *False Embassy* 22, 55. For a guest to act unkindly was deceptive treachery (Catullus 64.176).

[170] Euripides *Heracl.* 1034–1036 (even by descendents in subsequent generations!); Cicero *Pis.* 34.83; betrayal by seeking the host's wife, Ovid *Her.* 17.3–4. On kindness due a host, see Cicero *Verr.* 2.2.47.117.

[171] Betrayed trust reflected badly only on the betrayer, however, if the betrayed had taken appropriate precautions (Polybius 8.36.4).

himself the bread of life after many had eaten with him, but warned even then that one would betray him (6:64). Yet Jesus made no mistake in choosing Judas (6:70); he was chosen precisely because his character would lead him to fulfill the role of betrayer prophesied in Scripture (Ps 41:9 [40:10 LXX]).[172] The language of Scripture could provide meaning for the shame of betrayal; Qumran's Teacher of Righteousness apparently alluded to this same text from Psalms to complain of his own suffering (1QH 5.22–24).[173]

Jesus tells his disciples about the betrayal beforehand so that, rather than doubting his foresight in choosing Judas, they will recognize him as a prophet and that he controls the situation (13:19; cf. 14:29).[174] The fulfillment of a prophet's words attests the prophet's accuracy (Deut 18:22).[175] But Jesus' wording in several passages suggests an allusion to the promises of God in the biblical prophets: he foretold the future so that they might recognize his identity as YHWH (Isa 43:9–10). Similarly here, Jesus speaks so that the disciples might realize that "I am,"[176] alluding to Isaiah's "I am" formula, which perhaps by this period already appeared in the Passover haggadah.[177] Likewise, Jesus had "chosen" them (13:18; 6:70; 15:16, 19) and "knew" those he chose. Rabbis rarely chose their own disciples (see comments on 1:38–43), yet in this context "chosen" suggests more than simply an unusually radical rabbi; it suggests that John again portrays Jesus in biblical language traditionally applied to God's relationship with Israel (see comment on 15:16).

Jesus then sounds an ominous warning in 13:20: Jesus is the Father's agent (see introduction; cf. Matt 10:40); the disciples as Jesus' agents will face the same sort of suffering and betrayal Jesus faced (13:16, 18, 21). Whereas brokers of patrons could build their own power base in Roman society, the context promises Jesus' agents suffering and the status of servants.[178]

## Interpreting the Washing in Light of the Cross (13:21–38)

In the context of the betrayal (13:21–30) and another comment on the imminence of the passion (13:31–33), loving and serving as Jesus did demands sacrifice for one another, potentially to the point of death (13:34–35). On the narrative level, however, John emphasizes that such commitment is more easily offered than demonstrated: the most prominent disciple would fall short of even such sacrifice directly for Jesus (13:36–38).

---

[172] Menken, "Translation," contends for John's free translation from the Hebrew, with slight influence from 2 Sam 18:28.

[173] Thus, though rabbis applied the passage to Ahithophel's betrayal of David, a specifically messianic use is only one possible use (cf. Brown, *John,* 2:554–55, who sees the absolute use of "I am" in 13:19).

[174] Sanders, *Jesus and Judaism,* 309, thinks the betrayal involved Judas's revealing the secret of Jesus' royal claim. The Gospels are clear, however, that he revealed Jesus' whereabouts to hand him over secretly.

[175] Meeks, *Prophet-King,* 46.

[176] This is John's absolute use (Brown, *John,* 2:554–55).

[177] Stauffer, *Jesus,* 116. For skepticism that any of the Pesach Haggadah predates 70, however, see Stemberger, "Pesachhaggada."

[178] See DeSilva, *Honor,* 138.

[179] Cf., e.g., Epictetus *Diatr.* 2.5.2; 4.8.27; Diogenes Laertius 10.85; 10.144.17; see comment on 11:33.

## 1. The Betrayal Announced (13:21–30)

The intimacy of the gathering implied by the seating arrangements (13:23) and perhaps by Jesus' expression of emotion (13:21) provides a model for believers' relationship with Jesus (14:23) and in the immediate context particularly underlines the heinousness of the betrayal (13:18).

Although John emphasizes Jesus' foresight (13:19) and determination to suffer for others (12:27–28; 13:33), he also underlines Jesus' emotion (13:21), even though some of his contemporaries would have viewed it as a mark of weakness.[179] He is "troubled in spirit" (13:21), as he was when facing the mourning of friends in 11:33 and 12:27.[180] Jesus' emotional suffering here and in 12:27 may correspond with his suffering in Gethsemane in the Passion Narrative that stands behind the Synoptic accounts.[181] That the disciples reacted to the announcement of the betrayal by wondering among themselves who would do it (13:22–24) fits other extant Jesus tradition (Mark 14:19; Luke 22:23).

One might surround oneself with one's most intimate friends during the later hours of a banquet (13:23); thus Josephus dismissed other banqueters after a few hours, retaining near him only his four closest friends, during a time of great distress.[182] At banquets disciples sat near their sages.[183] Participants were seated according to their status (see comment on status and the foot washing, earlier in the chapter). Many banquet settings assigned three participants to each table, arranging diners in such a manner that in this scene one to the right of Jesus would need only have leaned his head back to find himself near Jesus' chest.[184] Although we should not expect that Jerusalem could accommodate formal banquet settings for all the Passover pilgrims, a home large enough to accommodate all Jesus' disciples (presumably the Twelve, 6:70) might be better furnished than many, and traditional banquet arrangements may remain informative. The first of the three couches around a table included the three persons of highest rank; the middle position on each couch represented the highest rank on that couch.[185] Jeffers describes the Roman style of banqueting:

> Romans ate while reclining on couches, usually situated in a U shape (called a *triclinium*) around a low table. The triclinium had places of honor (Luke 14:8–10). Diners supported themselves on their left elbows and ate with their right hands. The ancients did not have forks, only knives and spoons. In any event, seated in this position it was more convenient to eat with one's fingers.[186]

If twelve disciples are present with Jesus and if specifically three couches were available (rather than simply a number of mats on the floor), three people (Jesus, the beloved

---

180 Against Ferraro, "Pneuma," πνεῦμα here refers to Jesus' spirit (cf. "soul" in 12:27), not to the activity of the Holy Spirit.

181 On the Gethsemane scene, see, e.g., Keener, *Matthew*, 633–40, and sources cited there.

182 Josephus *Life* 223.

183 *T. Sanh.* 7:9.

184 Haenchen, *John*, 2:110. One might also lay one's head on another's bosom, which in that culture, far more tactile than our own, had no necessary sexual connotations (Diogenes Laertius 1.84; cf. the seating in Plato *Symp.* 222E–223A; Malina, *World*, 22–23).

185 Malina and Rohrbaugh, *John*, 220. A genuine triclinium would be downstairs, not in the upper room depicted in Mark's tradition (Mark 14:15; might any of John's audience assume this setting here?); but one might still emulate the banquet practices as much as possible.

186 Jeffers, *World*, 39–40; see further our comments on "setting" at 13:1–2.

disciple, and apparently Judas) would be seated at the head couch, leaving a more crowded five to the other two.[187] That John could expect his implied audience to envision such an arrangement is evident from their assumed familiarity with the arrangement of a triclinium, suggested in his use of ἀρχιτρίκλινος for the governor of the banquet in 2:8.

Given seating etiquette in later rabbinic texts, some argue that the position to the left, rather than (as in this disciple's case) the position to the right, was the most honored.[188] According to an ancient tradition, one showed greater honor to the person seated to one's left because one's left side was more vulnerable to assault, hence one showed greater trust.[189] Sharing the same table or couch would have certainly been an honored position in any case (cf. Mark 10:37; Matt 8:11), but if the beloved disciple held the position to Jesus' right, the position to the left most likely went to the other person to whom Jesus could easily hand the food—Judas (13:26).[190] (Luke 22:21 also suggests that Judas and Jesus shared the same table, though Luke 22:23 suggests that Jesus' companions did not take his words in 22:21 literally.) This underlines favorably the intimacy of the beloved disciple, while further underlining the treachery of Judas's betrayal. Qumran texts illustrate the importance of speaking in proper order at a communal meal (1QS 6.10; cf. Josephus *War* 2.130); thus the beloved disciple, seated closer to Jesus and perhaps (from the standpoint of the Johannine story world) of higher rank than Peter, may prove the appropriate one to raise a question for Peter (13:25).[191] John's language might allude to Deut 33:12,[192] though without the use of κόλπος the comparison seems tenuous; probably both texts simply reflect an ancient portrait of special intimacy.

The beloved disciple and Judas apparently share Jesus' highest couch, whereas Peter does not! Nevertheless, the passage presents Peter and the beloved disciple as on friendly terms (13:24–25). Ancient speakers and writers could use comparison to show themselves more qualified than others for a particular task,[193] or to exalt or demean other persons.[194] But biographic (and other genres') comparison did not always demean one character at another's expense, although it sometimes did so.[195] Even when comparisons implied

---

[187] Whitacre, *John*, 335.

[188] Haenchen, *John*, 2:110, following Billerbeck; Malina and Rohrbaugh, *John*, 220; Whitacre, *John*, 335 (citing *t. Ber.* 5:5).

[189] Xenophon *Cyr.* 8.4.3.

[190] Brown, *John*, 2:574; Whitacre, *John*, 335. Jesus' two closest associates would normally be on either side (*b. Ber.* 46b; Blomberg, *Reliability*, 192–93).

[191] Fritsch, *Community*, 123, following K. G. Kuhn; Malina and Rohrbaugh, *John*, 226. Others suggest that John simply emphasizes the beloved disciple's paradigmatic discipleship function against Peter's pastoral one (cf. Hartin, "Peter").

[192] Charlesworth, *Disciple*, 257, suggesting thereby an allusion to Benjamin.

[193] Cicero *Div. Caec.* 12.37; *Brutus* 93.321–322; in rhetoric, cf. Demosthenes *On the Embassy* 174; Anderson, *Glossary*, 110–11 and ὑπεξαίρεσις ("removal" of another's claims), p. 121.

[194] E.g., Cicero *Verr.* 2.4.54.121; *Phil.* 3.6.15; *Rhet. Alex.* 3, 1426a.27–32; Valerius Maximus 5.2; sometimes using oneself, e.g., Cicero *Pis.* 22.51; also noted by Marshall, *Enmity*, 52–55, 348–53. On comparing characters, see Theon *Progymn.* 10.3–4; cf. Aphthonius 42.31R comment on the Spirit as "successor" in John 14:16.

[195] Explicit in Menander Rhetor 2.1–2, 376.31–377.2; 2.3, 378.18–26; 2.3, 380.30–31; 2.6, 402.26–29; 2.6, 403.26–32; 2.6, 404.5–8 (402–404 concern praise of bride and groom); 2.10, 417.5–17; Philostratus *Hrk.* 27.4; 37.2; 38.1. One could even contrast a single writer's best and worst passages (Dionysius of Halicarnassus *Thucyd.* 35, end). For *synkrisis* in biography, see Shuler, *Genre*, 50; Stanton, *New People*, 77–80, 83.

competition, those competing were sometimes friends.[196] Biographers could also compare characters they wanted to parallel; while this sometimes encouraged rhetoricians to invent some details,[197] it did not normally require a major distortion of basic facts. Thus, while stressing parallels (hyperbolically Plutarch declares Aristides so much like Marcus Cato that it is hard to discern the differences),[198] they still recognize the differences.[199] Rather than fabricate parallels, they might try to select carefully those whose lives offered sufficient parallels for the comparison.[200] The comparison, and at worst friendly competition, between Peter and the beloved disciple as dialoguing coworkers continues in 20:3–8; 21:20–24. Perhaps (and this is speculation at this remove) the comparison helps to secure recognition for the beloved disciple's tradition in circles where the Markan, Petrine tradition already held sway; but this Gospel is hardly anti-Petrine, even if it appears more egalitarian.[201]

Greek teachers sometimes selected a particular pupil to whom to give special love, sometimes related to the general Greek concept of "love of boys";[202] such a disciple might be a teacher's designated successor.[203] Some compare this role with the beloved disciple's special role in the story world of the Fourth Gospel, though pointing out that the beloved disciple acts differently with Jesus than the Greek teachers' "favorite" disciples did with their teachers.[204] The context for the analogy, however, is more distant than one might hope. Given John's Jewish context, any implied sexual relationship would be impossible without the Gospel somewhere indicating a lifting of Jewish sexual taboos, and without the sexual component the comparison loses at least some (and possibly much more) of its force. Rabbis also had favorite disciples whom they praised (e.g., *m. ᵓAbot* 2:8), and such praiseworthy disciples could become successors without any sexual overtones.

That one disciple would be particularly "beloved" does not contradict the Synoptic tradition, where some disciples were closer to Jesus than others. Given the tradition in Mark 10:37, it is possible that John son of Zebedee often reclined near Jesus in historical reality.[205] Brown contends that the beloved disciple represents a real person,[206] but not

---

[196] E.g., Philostratus *Hrk.* 13.3–4; 27.4. Some philosophers did wish to minimize competition among friends, while conceding that in practice this might be possible only toward social superiors (Iamblichus *V.P.* 22.101; 33.230).

[197] Cicero *Brutus* 11.42.

[198] Plutarch *Comparison of Aristides with Marcus Cato* 1.1.

[199] E.g., Plutarch *Comparison of Aristides with Marcus Cato* 5.1, 3–4; 6.1. Plutarch *Comparison of Alcibiades and Coriolanus* could still include contrasts (e.g., 3.1; cf. likewise *Comparison of Lysander and Sulla* 5.5), and Plutarch also told distinctive stories about each (in Plutarch *Alc.* passim, and *Cor.* passim). After his respective biographies of Aristides and Marcus Cato, he provides *Comparison of Aristides with Marcus Cato;* likewise, *Comparison of Lucullus and Cimon;* and so forth.

[200] Plutarch *Cimon* 3.1–3; Plutarch claimed that he sometimes merely observed similarities that God had created (Plutarch *Demosthenes* 3.2). Historical comparisons predate Plutarch as a technique of Greek historiography (e.g., Polybius 10.2.8–13).

[201] Cf. Hengel, *Mark,* 52, who argues that the comparison exalts the guarantor of the Johannine tradition over "the guarantor of the Markan-Synoptic tradition." For Mark's dependence on Peter, see Hengel, "Problems," 238–43; for possible qualified egalitarian sentiments also in Petrine tradition, see, e.g., 1 Pet 5:1–6.

[202] See Tilborg, *Love,* 77–81, 85–86, for evidence, though it appears more limited than he claims.

[203] Ibid., 246.

[204] Ibid., 81 (contrasting even Alcibiades, where Socrates, in exemplary manner, does not become aroused—Plato *Symp.* 217–218); Tilborg, *Ephesus,* 149.

[205] Michaels, *John,* xvii.

[206] Brown, *Community,* 31–32.

John son of Zebedee,[207] a community hero in whom the community is idealized.[208] We have argued earlier that, against the consensus of modern scholarship, the ancient view that the beloved disciple is indeed John son of Zebedee has strong support;[209] further, the third-person description cannot be weighed against it. Although participants in accounts often described themselves in the first person, they also often chose the third person, particularly if their identity was already known to their audience.[210] Of course, it was also not unusual to name the eyewitness who supplied one the information,[211] sometimes even with consistent reminders that the writer is conveying another's report.[212]

It is more essential here to note that the beloved disciple also serves an idealized literary function. As Jesus resided in the Father's bosom (1:18), so the beloved disciple rested in Jesus' bosom (13:23);[213] yet, by implication, the same is true of believers (cf. 14:23; Luke 16:22). So also believers, like the "beloved" disciple (13:23; 19:26; 20:2; 21:20), were special objects of Jesus' affection (14:21; 15:9, 12; cf. 3:16; 11:5, 36), including in the immediate context (13:1, 34). Other disciples such as Martha, Mary, and Lazarus also receive the same title of affection (11:5); rather than meaning "favorite" to the exclusion of others, it may be the voice of one marveling that he is the object of such love (cf. Gal 2:20; 1 Tim 1:12–16; 1 John 4:10–11). When Paul speaks of Christ loving him and dying for him (Gal 2:20; perhaps even showing him special mercy,1 Cor 15:10), he invites reader identification. Noting that God loved Moses very much, some could designate Moses as God's "favorite";[214] but in the context of the whole Fourth Gospel, the beloved disciple here probably does allude in some sense to Jesus' favor toward all his followers (as all of them function as a new Moses, 1:14; 14:8). One could even name one's child "beloved by God" without implying that such love was exclusive to the child (cf. the common compounding of θεο- and φιλ- roots with each other in antiquity).[215]

Jesus apparently extends an offer of love even to Judas (13:26); in traditional Middle Eastern societies "it is a mark of special favour for the host to dip a piece of bread in the common sauce-dish and hand it to a guest."[216] But what may be more striking to those fa-

---

[207] Ibid., 33–34, noting especially the competition between this disciple and Peter against the notion that the disciple was among the Twelve. Yet who but one of the Twelve could be laid most effectively against Peter?

[208] Ibid., 89. Note also the view that the Johannine "school," while respecting the author's anonymity, wove reports about the beloved disciple into the narrative to honor him (Michaels, *John*, xxi–xxii). Bruns, "Ananda," improbably seeks to derive John's role from that of Gotama's disciple in Indian Buddhism.

[209] See our introduction, pp. 81–139.

[210] So, e.g., Thucydides 1.1.1; 2.103.2; 5.26.1; Xenophon *Anab.* 2.5.41; 3.1.4–6; and passim; Caesar *Gall. W.* 1.7; 2.1; 3.28; 4.13; 5.9; 6.4; 7.17; and passim (despite occasional phrases such as "our" in 2.9; cf. John 1:14); *C.W.* 1.1 and passim; Polybius 31.23.1–31.24.12; 38.19.1; 38.21.1; 38.22.3.

[211] E.g., Xenophon *Apol.* 2; *Mem.* 4.8.4 (Hermogenes in both cases); Demosthenes *Ep.* 5 (to Heracleodorus), §1; Seneca *Ep. Lucil.* 47.1; 1 Cor 1:11 (but not always, e.g., Diogenes *Ep.* 20).

[212] So, e.g., Xenophon *Apol.* 10, 14, 27.

[213] Also Culpepper, *School*, 266. Westcott, *John*, 194, contrasts "bosom" as "the full fold of the robe" (13:23) with "breast," Jesus' "actual body," after John leans back.

[214] *L.A.B.* 19:16. Thus texts also spoke, e.g., of a "favorite" maid (Chariton 1.4.1, πρὸ πάντων φίλην; cf. *Jos. Asen.* 2:6/11; 10:4/6).

[215] E.g., Musonius Rufus 11, p. 80.26 (title); *Let. Aris.* 49; *I. Eph.* 1944; *CPJ* 1.xix; *CIJ* 1:lxvii.

[216] Hunter, *John*, 137; for Jesus seeking to win Judas back, see Whitacre, *John*, 335 (citing John Chrysostom *Hom. Jo.* 72.2). By contrast, Stauffer, *Jesus*, 116, connects the bitter herbs in which the bread was dipped with a curse (citing Deut 29:18–19), thereby prefiguring Judas's betrayal. The

miliar with the Markan line of tradition is that Jesus does not identify the betrayer by the betrayer's choice but by his own. In the Synoptics, Judas stretches out his own hand "with" Jesus, perhaps indicating a deliberate violation of rank, hence rebellion (Mark 14:20).[217] Given how widespread the pre-Markan passion narrative that Mark used probably was (1 Cor 11:23), this tradition was probably known to John's audience. Here, however, Jesus, rather than Judas, appears in full control of the betrayal (cf. 10:17–18),[218] just as in 1 John those who left the community were never really of it to begin with (1 John 2:19). It is possible that the beloved disciple did not understand the symbol (cf. 13:28), perhaps because Jesus would also offer the dipped bread to himself and others;[219] but if so, the narrative merely reinforces its portrait of the disciples' lack of comprehension, for it suggests that Jesus handed the sop to Judas immediately after speaking to the beloved disciple (13:26).

The mention of Satan (13:27) is significant. In contrast to the Synoptics,[220] John, who also omits Jesus' exorcisms, speaks only once of "Satan" (13:27) and three times of the "devil" (6:70; 8:44; 13:2).[221] The devil's role in this Gospel particularly surrounds the betrayal; Judas the betrayer was a "devil" (6:70), replacing Peter's function in the Markan tradition (Mark 8:33).[222] The writer of Revelation similarly associates "Satan" most frequently with persecution, both Roman and in the synagogues (Rev 2:9–10, 13; 3:9; 12:9–12; cf. 1 Pet 5:8), though Johannine literature outside the Gospel also associates him with false teaching (Rev 2:24; cf. 1 John 4:3) and sin (1 John 3:8, 10). The devil was a murderer (8:44), which is why his children wish to kill Jesus (8:40–41).

The devil had already put it into Judas's heart to betray Jesus (13:2), and once Judas prepares to execute his mission, Satan enters him to enable him to carry it out (13:27).[223] The entrance of spirits into individuals to empower them for a task, good or evil, was already familiar in the Mediterranean world.[224] More important, Satan's entrance into Judas contrasts starkly with the promise of God's Spirit entering the other disciples (14:20, 23).[225] Yet, as in the OT and general early Jewish perspective in which God is sovereign over the devil, Jesus here remains in control, so that the devil, like Judas, essentially (even if perhaps unwittingly) executes Jesus' will concerning the passion (13:26–27).[226]

Despite probable traditions to the contrary (such as reclining, 13:23, 28; or bread dipped in a dish of bitter herbs, 13:26), in John's story world it is not yet Passover (13:1;

---

*charosheth,* "or sauce in which the herbs, bread and meat were dipped," may be a Passover meal allusion from the tradition (Mark 14:20; Watkins, *John,* 307).

[217] If we read "with me" temporally, on the analogy of the Essene custom of dipping by rank (1QS 6.4–5; 1QSa [1Q28a] 2.20–21; Josephus *War* 2.130–131), as do Fensham, "Hand"; Albright and Mann, *Matthew,* 321; but this reading does not explain well why the disciples did not recognize the betrayer (Mark 14:19).

[218] Others also contrast the respective emphasis, in the Markan and Johannine portraits, of the passion (e.g., Boring et al., *Commentary,* 151, comparing Philostratus *Vit. Apoll.* 7.14).

[219] Edersheim, *Life,* 566.

[220] Matthew mentions "Satan" three times, Mark five (in four contexts), and Luke five times. The devil appears six times (in three contexts) in Matthew and five times (in two contexts) in Luke.

[221] Various titles of the devil were synonymous (on the term, see, e.g., Bruce, *Acts: Greek,* 132; Elgvin, "Devil"). Thus "Satan" is Sammael or Beliar (e.g., *Ascen. Isa.* 2:2).

[222] Peter's confession appears in both contexts (Mark 8:29; John 6:69).

[223] The image of Satan's inspiration or filling an agent's heart appears in Acts 5:3; *T. Job* 41:5/7; cf. the late *Apoc. Sedr.* 5:4–5; Boring et al., *Commentary,* 296, cite *T. Sim.* 2:7, where the prince of error moves Satan against Joseph.

[224] Homer *Il.* 17.210–211; Philostratus *Hrk.* 27.2.

[225] With Duke, *Irony,* 99.

[226] Cf. also Fenton, *John,* 146.

19:14). Thus Judas can be thought to be buying something for the feast (13:29), even though after sundown, once the Passover had begun, the bazaars would be closed.[227] Their other guess, that Judas was giving to the poor (13:29), is not incompatible with Passover. It was pious to share one's resources during a feast (e.g., Pentecost in Tob 2:2), and Passover was likely no exception.[228] That Judas had the money box (13:29; cf. 12:6) is not unlikely; Jesus and his disciples probably accepted support from others while traveling,[229] a particular disciple probably carried the money,[230] and it is not likely that the early Christians would have invented the treasurer being a thief. Yet Judas's role in carrying the money underlines his treachery by contrast with the group's trust. Their expectation that he was giving to the poor, consonant with that emphasis in the Jesus tradition (e.g., Matt 6:2–4, 19–24; Mark 10:21; Luke 12:33; 19:8; cf. 1 John 3:17), deepens the irony: Judas was stealing the money rightly allotted for the poor (12:5–6).[231]

That it was "night" when Judas went out (13:30) probably reflects John's assumption of historical tradition about Jesus' betrayal (1 Cor 11:23; Mark 14:17),[232] but John undoubtedly invests it with symbolic import (3:2; 9:4; 11:10; cf. Luke 22:53; Rev 21:25),[233] a symbolism emphasized at least as early as Origen.[234] Once Judas has gone out, Jesus reiterates that the time of his glorification has come; the betrayal sets the other events in motion.

## 2. The Passion Again Announced (13:31–33)

By linking the glory of Jesus' cross with the expectation that disciples love one another as Jesus loved them, John calls disciples to lay down their lives (13:31–35). He further warns that the cross may prove more difficult than disciples may suppose (13:36–38); but Christ's presence, made available at his coming after the resurrection (20:19–23), would empower disciples to follow him even to that extent (14:1–7). God will provide his nature and works for the disciples (14:8–12; cf. love and the commandments in 14:15), and full provision for what they must face as they carry on Jesus' work (14:13–27)—especially the Spirit (14:16–17, 25–26) and Jesus' presence available through obedience (14:18–24). (In this context, prayer and obedience are part of asking in Jesus' name, 14:13–16; and there appears to be an association between the Spirit's coming and peace, 14:1, 27; 16:33.)

The hour of Jesus' "glorification" (13:31–32) in this context can point only to the passion (12:23–24; cf. 7:39; 12:16);[235] 17:1–5 further develops the thoughts of 13:31–32.[236] God had promised to glorify his own name (12:28), but his glory is inseparable from the glory of

---

[227] Reicke, *Era*, 182.

[228] Jeremias, *Eucharistic Words*, 54, though *m. Pesaḥ.* 9:11, his primary text, is ambiguous.

[229] Cf., e.g., Sanders, *Figure*, 108.

[230] E.g., *Pesiq. Rab.* 25:2. A common purse was one sign of organization as a group (Livy 39.18.9).

[231] With Michaels, *John*, 237. One who was trusted could excuse oneself and then go elsewhere than where one's companions assumed, especially at night (Xenophon *Eph.* 3.10; cf. Iamblichus *V.P.* 2.11).

[232] The Passover meal was after nightfall (*m. Pesaḥ.* 10:1; *t. Pisha* 5:2; 10:9; *b. Ber.* 9a; *Pesaḥ.* 107b; cf. Lachs, *Commentary*, 405).

[233] With Bultmann, *John*, 482–83; Schnackenburg, *John*, 3:32; Lee, *Thought*, 35. Night symbolized evil in other sources as well (e.g., 4Q299 frg. 5, lines 1–4; cf. Aeschylus *Eumenides* 745).

[234] Wiles, *Gospel*, 23.

[235] With, e.g., Käsemann, *Testament*, 19; Caird, "Glory," 269; Dunn, *Baptism*, 173–74.

[236] See Schnackenburg, *John*, 3:167. Thus "now" in 13:31 may involve Judas's departure (Holwerda, *Spirit*, 13), but only because it foreshadows the cross (17:5; cf. "now" in 12:27; 13:1).

his Son (13:31–32; cf. 11:4, 40; 12:41; 14:13; 17:1, 5, 22, 24). The aorists of the context fit the perspective of completion from John's time, but also make sense within the story world; an aorist could depict an event immediately to follow, resembling the predictive language recognized by early Christians in some biblical prophets (e.g., Isa 53:5 LXX, ἐτραυματίσθη).

God would be glorified in Jesus, hence would glorify Jesus, and would do so "immediately" (13:32). The mutual glory of Father and Son (cf. 17:10) makes sense; the Father delighted to grant the Son's requests because the Son always pleased the Father (8:29; 11:42). The "immediately," however, appears less clear. In contrast to Mark, who uses εὐθύς almost as decoration (41 of 58, or roughly 71 percent, of NT uses), John uses εὐθύς only three times: 13:30, 32; 19:34. Thus it is possible that he intends "immediately" as a reference to 13:30, connecting Jesus' glorification with Judas's betrayal. Then again, the proximity of the two uses may suggest no more than that the particular term was fresh on the writer's mind; it probably functions as a rough equivalent of "now" in 13:31, emphasizing the imminence of the events. Then again, it may suggest a temporal connection between the glory of the Father and of the Son: once Jesus has glorified the Father by submitting to the cross, the Father will turn Jesus' death into a glorification of the Son by exalting him right away.[237]

Jesus addresses his disciples as "children" in 13:33 (cf. παιδία in 21:5), which figures in the Jesus tradition[238] as well as being a standard title for disciples in John's circle (1 John 2:1, 12, 28; 3:7, 18; 4:4; 5:21; παιδία in 2:14, 18). This title should not be thought to betray a confusion between the roles of Father and Son; apart from its application to Jesus, one would not even need to assume divine implications in Jesus being their implied "father" here.[239] Fictive kinship terminology based on active rather than genetic relationship was common (e.g., Phaedrus 3.15.18), and "father" was a title of great respect.[240] Ancients employed such fictive kinship terminology in an honorary manner, sometimes in direct address (e.g., 2 Kgs 5:13; 13:14; Diodorus Siculus 21.12.5); for example, they employed titles such as "father of the Jews" (2 Macc 14:37), "fathers of the world" for the first-century schools of Hillel and Shammai (*Gen. Rab.* 12:14),[241] "father of his country" or of the state for the emperor,[242] "fathers" for Roman senators,[243] for

---

[237] Thus Barrett, *John,* 450–51, reads the announcement as Jesus' sharing the Father's precreation glory (17:5), in contrast with those who expect this glory only eschatologically.

[238] In the cognate form τέκνον (Mark 10:24; sing. in Mark 2:5; perhaps Luke 15:31; 16:25; cf. Heb 2:13); cf. also "daughter" (Mark 5:34); Paul also uses τέκνα for believers (Gal 4:19; cf. sing. τέκνον for a disciple in 1 Tim 1:18; 2 Tim 2:1). Only Johannine literature in the NT employs the vocative of τεκνίον (this vocative never appears in the LXX as opposed to that of τέκνον, forty-eight times), but the diminutive had lost most of its force by this period, hence the difference between τέκνον and τεκνίον is insubstantial.

[239] Nor is it necessarily demeaning to them, though such a comparison could be so used (Aristophanes *Clouds* 821, where the diminutive retains its force).

[240] E.g., Homer *Il.* 24.507; Virgil *Aen.* 8.115; 9.735; 11.184, 904; 12.697. Greco-Roman society employed an analogy between benefactors and fathers (Stevenson, "Benefactor").

[241] "Father of the world" also came to be a title for the patriarchs (*Tg. Neof.* 1 on Gen 40:12; *Tg. Ps.-J.* on Gen 40:12; Deut 28:15).

[242] Ovid *Tristia* 4.4.13; *Fasti* 2.130–132, 637; Herodian 2.2.9; 2.6.2; or simply "parent" or "father" (Ovid *Ex Ponto* 4.9.134); so also for other kings (the fictitious Ethiopian king in Heliodorus *Aeth.* 10.17).

[243] Plutarch *R.Q.* 58, *Mor.* 278D; Lucan *C.W.* 3.109; Cornelius Nepos 23 (Hannibal), 12.2; Cicero *Cat.* 1.4.9; 1.2.4; 1.11.27; 1.12.29; 1.13.31–32; 2.6.12; 4.1.1, 2; 4.2.3, 4; 4.3.6; 4.5.9; 4.6.11; 4.8.16, 18; *Prov. cons.* 1.1; 2.3; 4.8; 5.11; 8.18; 9.23; 10.25; 12.30; 13.32; 16.38, 39; *Pis.* 20.46; 22.52; 24.56; 33.81; *Pro Marcello* 1.1, 2; 5.13; *Phil.* 1.1.1; 1.3.7; 1.4.11; *Fam.* 10.35.1, 2; *Invective against Sallustius Crispus* 1.1, 2, 3; 2.5; 4.12; 5.14; 6.16; 8.22; Silius Italicus 1.610, 675; Valerius Maximus

triumphant generals,[244] for other societal leaders or benefactors,[245] for rescuers in battle (Polybius 6.39.6–7), and for older mentors.[246] "Father" could apply to any respected elders;[247] thus, for example, the honorary title "father of a synagogue."[248] Age by itself was grounds for respect,[249] so from the earliest period younger persons could address older men respectfully as fathers,[250] and older men could address younger men as sons,[251] as could leaders their followers (e.g., Virgil *Aen.* 1.157). One could address even an older stranger as "father" (cf. 1 Tim 5:1–2).[252]

Of more immediate import to the present text, various texts apply father/son language to teachers and their disciples;[253] disciples were called "children" of their teachers,[254] and their teachers were their "fathers."[255] Wisdom discourses, which employ the sort of rhetoric one would expect among the early sages, were often addressed to sons (even in Proverbs, following models of the Egyptian royal courts).[256] Relevant to Jesus' final discourse, such wisdom language often occurs in the testamentary genre and hence requires

---

1.5.1; 2.2.1a; 2.7.ext.1; 2.8.4; 3.8.1; 4.1.4; 4.1.6b; 4.4.10; 4.5.1; 5.2.1; 5.8.3; 5.9.3; 6.1.10; 6.2.1; 6.6.3; 8.13.4; 8.15.1; Livy 1.8.7; 1.26.5; 2.1.10–11; 2.23.14; 2.24.2; 2.27.3; 2.32.12; 2.34.12; 2.35.3; 2.41.4; 2.48.8; 2.60.3; 3.13.7; 3.16.1; 3.21.1, 3, 4; 3.51.11; 3.52.6; 3.63.8; 4.1.4; 4.2.13; 4.60.1, 3; Sallust *Catil.* 6.6; 31.7; 51.1, 4, 7, 12, 15, 37, 41; 52.2.7, 35; *Jug.* 14.1, 3, 12, 13, 18, 25; 24.2; *Speech of Philippus* 1, 17; *Letter of Gnaeus Pompeius* 1, 6; *Letter to Caesar* 11.1; *Invective against Marcus Tullius* 1.

[244] Silius Italicus 7.734–735; 8.2; 17.651.

[245] Dionysius of Halicarnassus *R.A.* 12.1.8; Pausanias 8.48.5–6; 8.51.7; Cicero in Plutarch *Cicero* 23.3; for Rome's founding elders (Ovid *Fasti* 5.71); honorary title "father of the Greeks" (Philostratus *Vit. soph.* 2.27.617); a kind master (Xenophon *Cyr.* 8.1.44) ); an ideal ruler (Musonius Rufus 8, p. 64.14, claiming that this imitates Zeus's role). Cf., for leaders in the Mithraic cult, Burkert, *Cults,* 42.

[246] Homer *Il.* 9.607, employing a different term; *Od.* 1.308.

[247] Acts 7:2; 22:1; 1 Tim 5:1; 1 John 2:13; *4 Bar.* 5:28; Homer *Il.* 24.507.

[248] *CIJ* 1:xcv–xcvi; 1:66, §93; 1:250–51, §319; 1:360, §494; 1:372, §§508–509; 1:373, §510; 1:393, §533; 1:397, §535; 1:398, §537; 1:462, §645; 1:463, §646; 1:505, §694; 1:520, §720; 2:9, §739. The title was probably usually "purely an honorary one, probably involving no active duties" (Leon, *Jews,* 186).

[249] E.g., 1 Pet. 5:5; *t. Meg.* 3:24; *ᶜAbod . Zar.* 1:19; *4 Bar.* 5:20; Ps.-Phoc. 220–222; *Syr. Men.* 11–14, 76–93 (but cf. 170–172); Homer *Il.* 1.259; 23.616–623; Aulus Gellius 2.15; Diodorus Siculus 1.1.4; 2.58.6; Pythagoras in Diogenes Laertius 8.1.22–23.

[250] E.g., 1 Tim 5:1–2; Homer *Il.* 9.607 (different term); *Od.* 21.369 (a servant, addressed as ἄττα); P.Paris 47.1 (an elder brother, ca. 152 B.C.E.); Plutarch *Cicero* 45.1 (young Octavian to Cicero).

[251] E.g., Homer *Il.* 24.373; *Od.* 1.308; *4 Bar.* 5:28; cf. Homer *Od.* 7.22.

[252] E.g., Homer *Il.* 24.362, 371; *Od.* 7.28, 48; 8.145, 408; 17.553; 18.122; 20.199.

[253] Among philosophers, cf. Epicurus (Culpepper, *School,* 107, cites Lucretius *Nat.* 3.9); Epictetus *Diatr.* 3.22.82; Nock, *Christianity,* 30.

[254] E.g., Porphyry *Marc.* 1.6–8; Eunapius *Lives* 486, 493; 1 Cor 4:14–15; 1 Tim 1:2; Phlm 10; 3 John 4; *4 Bar.* 7:24; *Sipre Deut.* 34.3.1–3, 5; 305.3.4; *b. Pesaḥ.* 112a; *Šabb.* 25b; 31a (Hillel); *Pesiq. Rab.* 21:6 (Moses to Israel); 51:1. Other texts make analogues between fathers and teachers (e.g., *t. B. Qam.* 9:11). Some have suggested the same analogy for mystagogues and mystery initiates (Lohse, *Colossians,* 200).

[255] E.g., Philostratus *Vit. soph.* 1.490; 1.25.536, 537; Iamblichus *V.P.* 35.250; 2 Kgs 2:12; *4 Bar.* 2:4, 6, 8; 5:5; *t. Sanh.* 7:9; Matt 23:9; cf. *Gen. Rab.* 12:14 (Simeon b. Yohai of the sages of Beth Hillel and Shammai); for Christian usage from the second to fifth centuries, see Hall, *Scripture,* 50.

[256] E.g., *Ahiqar* 96 (saying 14A); Sir 2:1; *Did.* 5.2; 1 John 2:1; cf. Babrius prol.2; Babrius 18.15. This included astronomical and other revelatory wisdom (*1 En.* 79:1 [esp. MS B]; 81:5; 82:1–2; 83:1; 85:2; 91:3–4; 92:1).

such language.[257] Because rabbis sometimes claimed greater respect than parents,[258] it is not surprising that some early sages used the paternal title "abba" in the same way that most came to use "rabbi."[259] Thus Jesus' use of the title "children" for his disciples is more the language of a teacher and mentor than of a surrogate for the Father (cf. 16:27); the author of 1 John employs the same language (1 John 2:1, 12–13, 18, 28; 3:7, 18; 4:4; 5:21; 3 John 4), and presumably elders in his community would do the same (1 John 2:13–14; 2 John 1, 4, 13).

Jesus would remain with them just "a little while" (13:33; cf. the first "little while" of 16:16); as he has been saying (cf. aorists, plus "now" in 13:31 and perhaps "immediately" in 13:32), his departure is imminent. These are the same words he had offered the crowds in 7:33. Further, like "the Jews," the disciples could not yet follow Jesus where he was going (13:33), that is, to the Father by way of the cross (13:3; 14:5–6). "The Jews" (representing the elite Jewish opponents of John's Jewish audience; see introduction, ch. 5) could not follow Jesus where he was going (7:34–36) because they would die in their sin rather than lay down their lives for God's will (8:21–22). The disciples could not yet follow Jesus because they are not yet prepared to die; but they would follow him in death later (13:36–38; cf. 21:18–19). Jesus had been "with" them for a time (12:8, 35; 14:9; 16:4); in contrast to his enemies, however, who would never find him, his disciples would find him in a new way when he returned—that is, he would be with them in a new way.

Sandwiched between Jesus' comments about following him is a commandment. This commandment is relevant to the context, for it includes readiness to die: to love as he did would require laying down their lives for one another (13:34). The foot washing (13:3–10) illustrated this love, because it foreshadowed the salvific work of the Suffering Servant (13:1–2, 31–38). The commandment also articulated how believers could represent the most vital aspect of Jesus' presence among themselves after his departure: by loving one another, they would continue to experience his love.

### 3. Following Jesus' Model (13:34–35)

The exhortation to "love one another" (13:34–35) implied unity in the face of diversity (17:21–23), such as Jewish, Gentile, and Samaritan believers in Jesus might experience (4:39; 10:16). Representatives of various social groups now constituted together a new "in-group," and frequent early Christian exhortations to mutual service seem directed toward blending such diversity.[260] In the Johannine community, love is partly cohesiveness to the community; secessionists lack such love (1 John 2:19; 3:14).[261] Ethnic and other forms of reconciliation within the Christian community are essential to its identity as a Christian community; without such evidences the world cannot see the character of Jesus (13:35).

---

[257] E.g., *Jub.* 21:21; Tob 4:3, 4, 5, 12; 1 Macc 2:50, 64; *1 En.* 92:1; *T. Job* 1:6; 5:1; 6:1; *T. Jud.* 17:1; *T. Reu.* 1:3; *T. Naph.* 4:1; *Pesiq. Rab.* 21:6.

[258] E.g., *m. B. Meṣiʿa* 2:11; *Ker.* 6:9; *Sipre Deut.* 32.5.12; *p. Ḥag.* 2:1, §10; among Gentiles, Theon *Progymn.* 3. 93–97.

[259] Cf. Sandmel, *Judaism*, 106; Manson, *Sayings*, 232.

[260] Malina, *Windows*, 55. One may compare the frequent topic of unity in Greek speeches (e.g., Dionysius of Halicarnassus *R.A.* 7.53.1; Livy 24.22.17). Some characterized loving one another (φιλαλλήλους) as more naturally a rural phenomenon that could include sharing resources (Alciphron *Farmers* 29 [Comarchides to Euchaetes], 3.73, par. 2).

[261] Though Segovia, *Relationships*, 179, is correct that the Gospel, unlike 1 John, is involved in polemic with the synagogue rather than "intra-church."

The following section will speak of believers keeping Jesus' commandments (14:15, 21; 15:10), as God's people had kept his commandments in the Torah. Jesus had obeyed the Father's command in all that he spoke (12:49) and in laying down his life (10:18; 14:31); disciples now would share this obedience (14:31: ἄγωμεν, plural subjunctive). But the only specific duty spelled out for believers as a "commandment" in this Gospel is the first (13:34) and last (15:12) in the section: loving one another as he had loved them.[262] Given the measure of comparison, this was sufficient love to cover every other obligation to fellow believers (cf. Rom 13:8–10; 1 Pet 1:22)!

Love itself was hardly a new commandment (Lev 19:18), as the Johannine tradition itself recognized (1 John 2:7; 2 John 1:5);[263] Jewish tradition continued the emphasis on love of neighbor.[264] Still, loving one's neighbor as oneself was such a radical demand that biblical tradition might depict its actual occurrence only in the most intimate relationships (1 Sam 18:1, 3; 20:17).[265] In fact, Jesus' commands to love God and one another in the Farewell Discourse (13:34–35; 14:15–16, 21) echo the language of the essential substance of the law of Moses, as in Mark 12:29–34.[266]

What is new here is the standard for this love: "as I have loved you" (13:34; cf. 1 John 2:8). By laying down his life for others, Jesus loved the disciples more than his own life (11:5; 13:1).[267] John's terms of personal comparison, particularly καθώς,[268] underline the force of the demand; it applies both to Jesus' relationship with his Father (5:23; 12:50) and to that of his disciples with himself (15:12; 17:14), the latter often modeled after Jesus' relationship with his Father (6:57; 10:15; 15:9–10; 17:18, 21, 23; 20:21). Ancient writers regularly invoked positive models that invited imitation (as well as warning against negative examples);[269] sometimes this included attention to examples of brave death.[270] Students often would imitate their teachers in various respects (as noted below on 13:35). In the context of the Fourth Gospel, however, it is more significant that biblical ethics had long involved imitation of God's own character (Lev 11:44–45; 19:2; 20:26; 21:8).[271] Now imitation of God includes imitation of Jesus the servant (13:14), specifically of his mortal self-sacrifice.

---

[262] "Commandment(s)" appears frequently in the Johannine Epistles (1 John 2:3–4, 7–8; 3:22–24; 4:21; 5:2–3; 2 John 4–6; cf. also Rev 12:17; 14:12); the commandment specifically concerns love (1 John 3:23; 4:21) and accurate faith (1 John 3:23).

[263] It was new in the sense of realized eschatology (1 John 2:8). The Johannine Epistles may employ "from the beginning" meaning "from the beginning of the gospel tradition," however (1 John 2:24; 3:11; 2 John 6), perhaps as a double entendre with the beginning of creation (1 John 1:1; 2:13–14; 3:8).

[264] See, e.g., Söding, "Feindeshass"; Neudecker, "Neighbor."

[265] A Greek proverb also regarded a friend as a second self (Diodorus Siculus 17.37.6; cf. Cicero *Fam.* 13.1.5; *Fin.* 1.20.70; Seneca *Ep. Lucil.* 95.63). Bultmann, *Word,* 115–16, following Kierkegaard, emphasizes that such love ultimately overpowers self-love.

[266] Lacomara, "Deuteronomy," 75. John consolidates love for God and neighbor in 15:10–17 (see Grayston, *Epistles,* 67).

[267] Hoskyns, *Gospel,* 451. Segovia, *Relationships,* 124–25, rightly notes that love is christologically conditioned in 13:34–35 and 15:1–17, but probably reads too much into the situation when he finds antidocetic polemic here.

[268] Cf. also ὁμοίως in 5:19 and ὥσπερ in 5:21.

[269] E.g., Aeschines *False Embassy* 75; Lysias *Or.* 2.61, §196; Theophrastus *Char.* proem 3; Cicero *Sest.* 48.102; 68.143; see also examples in our introduction concerning the moral functions of biographical genre; Kurz, "Models," 176–85 on narrative models in antiquity (especially history and biography, pp. 177–83).

[270] Thucydides 2.43.4.

[271] Lacomara, "Deuteronomy," 76–77, citing texts about "walking" in God's "ways" (Deut 8:6; 10:12; 11:22; 19:9; 26:17; 28:9; 30:16). For the imitation of God, see further Cicero *Tusc.* 5.25.70;

The centrality of this commandment as the one specifically given by Jesus in this context is also distinctively Christian. Other Jewish sources make love of neighbor a central teaching,[272] but other corpora of early Jewish sources do not speak with the same sort of consensus found in earliest Christian texts.[273] The Ten Commandments, for example, remained prominent in early Jewish exhortation,[274] but Jesus does not appeal to them here. Instead, he gives one commandment that will define his community.[275]

John's report of Jesus' teaching here is distinctive among extant gospels not only in defining love according to Jesus' example and in its centrality, but in its community focus. Mark reports Jesus' teaching about loving everyone (Mark 12:31), a thesis adopted by early Christians in general (Rom 13:8–10; Gal 5:14);[276] the Q tradition also reports Jesus' teaching about loving enemies (Matt 5:44; Luke 6:27, 35). Some early Christian sources claim that Jesus applied love of neighbor cross-culturally (Luke 10:27–37), which makes sense of the broader context of Lev 19:18[277] (Lev 19:34, regarding sojourners),[278] though the nearer context specifically emphasizes one's own people (Lev 19:15–18).[279] By contrast, John's tradition focuses on internal community cohesion, as do references to loving one's fellow as oneself in the Dead Sea Scrolls.[280]

Nevertheless, it should be noted that John, while more focused, does not contradict here the Jesus tradition that we have in the Synoptics; his purely positive statement contrasts with the explicit Qumran exhortations to love members of the community but *hate* those outside.[281] Ancient writers were perfectly capable of exhorting members of a group to live in harmony with each other, without implying hostility toward

---

Seneca *Dial.* 1.1.5; Epictetus *Diatr.* 2.14.12–13; Heraclitus *Ep.* 5; Plutarch *Borr.* 7, *Mor.* 830B; *Let. Aris.* 188, 190, 192, 208–210, 254, 281; Philo *Creation* 139; Eph 5:1; *T. Ash.* 4:3; *Mek. Šir.* 3.43–44; *Sipra Qed. par.* 1.195.1.3; *Sent. Sext.* 44–45; Keener, *Matthew*, 205; Rutenber, "Imitation," chs. 2–3.

[272] E.g., tradition attributed to R. Akiba (e.g., *Sipra Qed. pq.* 4.200.3.7; *Gen. Rab.* 24:7); cf. the emphasis on love of neighbor in *m. ʾAbot* 1:12, attributed to Hillel; *Jub.* 36:4, 8.

[273] E.g., among the great diversity of views among early Jewish teachers, many felt that honoring parents was the greatest commandment (*Let. Aris.* 228; Josephus *Ag. Ap.* 2.206; Ps.-Phoc. 8; Moore, *Judaism*, 2:132); by contrast, early Christians were more united around a single primary teacher and his views. See Keener, *Matthew*, 530–31; cf. 248–49.

[274] Deut 5:1–27 appears in Qumran phylacteries and may have appeared on other early Jewish phylacteries before the second century (Vermes, "Worship").

[275] Cf 4 Ezra 3:7: God gave Adam one commandment, through the violation of which Adam incurred death.

[276] Smith, *John* (1999), 260, thinks Paul, like John, usually applies the commandment especially to believers; this is true in Gal 5:13–15 but less likely in the context of Rom 13:8–10 (cf. Rom 13:1–7).

[277] Probably the direct source for most Jewish teachings on love of neighbor (Barrett, *John*, 452).

[278] Cf. Hillel's exhortation to love humanity in *m. ʾAbot* 1:12; others in *T. Iss.* 7:6 (text B); cf. rabbinic examples in Dutheil, "Aimeras." Despite the ethnic perspective of *Jubilees*, love of neighbors appears to cross ethnic lines at least among nations descended from Abraham in *Jub.* 20:2; 36:4. Boer, *Morality*, 62–72, argues (against some) that Greek sources reveal little evidence of universal love of neighbor.

[279] One Tannaitic tradition may harmonize these emphases: love him if he acts like your people (*ʾAbot R. Nat.* 16 A).

[280] E.g., CD 6.20–21 (though also advising help of strangers); cf. 1QS 8.4, 13; 9.21–22. Boismard, "Epistle," 159, also notes this characteristic of community cohesion in Josephus (Josephus *War* 2.119) and Philo (in Eusebius *Praep. ev.* 8.11.2).

[281] Flusser, *Judaism*, 27–28, contrasting the Scrolls and early Christianity. Flusser (p. 483) sees the Essene doctrine as a reaction against the trend toward love of humanity attested in later rabbinic sources.

outsiders.[282] The claim that John here is "violently" exclusionary,[283] while reflecting some historical uses of the Gospel, ignores the centrality of Jesus as model, who is nowhere violent (including after being struck, 18:23) but accepts rejection and death at others' hands. This worldview is that of a marginalized rather than a privileged community; even the harshness of the public discourses better represents the protest of a marginalized community against elite controllers of public discourse.

Like the Qumran community, John's outlook is sectarian and dualistic;[284] "the world" is arrayed against the community (15:18–25), demanding internal cohesion (15:12–17). But the comparison even here should not be overdrawn; it is highly unlikely that the Johannine community had withdrawn from the world physically (17:11, 15, 18, 21), certainly not into a wilderness enclave as the Qumran community had. As Painter notes, John in no way negates love for those outside the community: first, the stated purpose for loving one another is as a witness to the world (13:35); second, they are not said to hate unbelievers as at Qumran (as noted above); third, God's love for Jesus (17:23, 26) and the world of humanity (3:16) should be active in disciples (17:26); fourth, the Father's love for Jesus (15:9) is the basis for his special love for disciples (15:12).[285]

That the world would see the truth through disciples' love for one another (13:35) is significant. Just as Moses' signs of judgment become signs of mercy in John (2:11), so the signs of judgment through which the Gentiles might know God's identity (Exod 6:7; 7:5, 17; 8:10, 22; 9:29; 10:2; 14:4, 18) become such signs of mercy in John, and ultimately this sign of the way believers treat one another (13:35; 17:21–23). "By this" (ἐν τούτῳ) elsewhere in this discourse applies to revealing God to the world (15:8);[286] it is an essential part of witnesses' testimony to πάντες (13:35), humanity as in 1:7 and the "world" as in 3:16.

To this point in the book, disciples have followed Jesus (2:12; 3:22; 11:7–16, 54; cf. 1:37; 18:15–16), believed in Jesus (2:11; cf. 4:27; 9:27–28), and done Jesus' work (4:2; 6:12; cf. 19:26–27); perseverance also is a criterion for true discipleship (8:31; cf. 2:17, 22; 12:16), and some disciples, by failing to persevere, have failed the test (6:60–61, 66; 12:4; cf. 8:31; 18:2, 17, 25). But here the mark of discipleship is following their master's example (13:34–35); pupils imitated their teachers.[287] The misbehavior of a disciple might require other disciples to provide apologetic: it was the disciple's failure to imitate the teacher's ways that led to this misbehavior; such a practice could prove relevant for John's response to Judas's betrayal (13:11, 21).[288] The behavior of disciples also was held to reflect, posi-

---

[282] Cf., e.g., Menander Rhetor 2.3, 384.23–25, which advocates both internal community cohesion and like treatment of strangers.

[283] Kelber, "Metaphysics," 152–53. His claim that the Gospel is anti-Jewish is addressed in our introduction, ch. 5, under "The Jews," pp. 214–28.

[284] See Flusser, *Judaism,* 198.

[285] Painter, *John,* 94.

[286] Less relevant are 9:30; 16:30; this is a matter of Johannine style, though often significant (fourteen times in 1 John, including 1 John 2:3–5; 3:10, 16; 4:2, 9–10); in 1 John it is often a criterion by which believers may test themselves (1 John 2:3, 5; 3:19, 24; 4:13, 17; 5:2; cf. 3:10).

[287] Xenophon *Mem.* 1.2.3; Quintilian 1.2.26; Philostratus *Vit. Apoll.* 5.21; Josephus *Life* 11; Kirschner, "Imitatio"; for an extreme example, see Seneca *Controv.* 9.3.12–13. Rabbis' behavior might even function as legal precedent (*t. Piska* 2:15–16; *Sipre Deut.* 221.1.1; *p. B. Meṣiᶜa* 2:11, §1; *Nid.* 1:4, §2; *Sanh.* 7:2, §4; *Yebam.* 4:11, §8), and in an entertaining illustration one later rabbi hid under his master's bed to learn from his private ways (*b. Ber.* 62a).

[288] Cf. Aelius Aristides *Defense of Oratory* 336, §111D; especially Alcibiades' behavior, which differed from Socrates (Xenophon *Apol.* 19; *Mem.* 1.2.12–18, 26; Plutarch *Alc.* 7.3). Not all disciples prove to be true disciples (John 8:30–31).

tively or negatively, on the reputation of their teachers.[289] Fruitful branches would prove to be his disciples (15:8), and unfruitful ones be cast away from him (15:6); in context, the fruit involves the command to love (15:9–12). The presence of the Spirit (14:16, 26) continues Jesus' presence for the disciples, who by the fruit of that presence (15:4–5) continue Jesus' activity in the world, experiencing his love through one another, so revealing what Jesus is like. From the standpoint of Johannine theology, one cannot persevere as a true disciple of Jesus without learning to love other true disciples. Given the First Epistle's polemic against the secessionists, persevering in love includes remaining part of the community of faith (1 John 2:9–11; 3:10, 14; 4:20).

### 4. Devotion to the Death? (13:36–38)

Following Jesus (13:36) must involve following his example of loving self-sacrifice (13:33–35). Yet Peter changes the subject back to the question of where Jesus is going (13:36a), as will another disciple shortly thereafter (14:5). On the level of the story world, Peter may prefer the discussion about Jesus' destination to contemplation of a difficult commandment (although the full intensity of "as I have loved you" would not yet be obvious to him).[290] On the level of John's literary artistry, however, the resumption of the theme of 13:31–33 allows John to frame the new commandment in the context of the passion; loving one another and following Jesus to the death are one and the same.[291]

When Jesus tells Peter that Peter cannot "follow" Jesus at this point (13:36), he refers to death.[292] Earlier he told his enemies that they cannot go where he is going (7:34; 8:22); instead they will die "in sin" (8:21). Despite their initial misunderstanding (7:35), they recognize the second time that Jesus' going involves dying, yet not in sin (8:22). In this context, Jesus is going to the Father by way of the cross (13:3; 14:28; 16:5); disciples can come to the Father through him (14:4–6), but eventually following him will involve their sharing his cross, as he has already warned them (12:25–26). Peter will not follow Jesus now, but he will follow him in martyrdom later (21:18–19).

Like Jesus' enemies in 8:21–22, Peter does not fully understand Jesus, but does understand in some sense that where Jesus is going involves death. When he protests that he can follow now, because he is willing to die with Jesus (13:37), the reader will likely approach this brash promise in the light of prior statements of devotion, such as Thomas's willingness to follow to the death in 11:16. A true disciple, after all, must follow Jesus to the death (12:25–26), must persevere to the end (8:31). This is, however, precisely what Peter will fail to do (13:38)! If Peter's promise of courage reflects an epic tradition of heroism,[293] Peter

---

[289] E.g., Aeschines *Timarchus* 171–173; *t.* ʿ*Ed.* 3:4; ʾ*Abot R. Nat.* 27A; 34, §76B; Mark 2:18, 24; perhaps Acts 4:13; Alciphron *Courtesans* 7 (Thaïs to Euthydemus), 1.34, par. 6–7.

[290] Cf. Barrett, *John*, 453.

[291] Digressions were a frequent literary device (Sallust *Catil.* 5.9–13.5; Livy 9.17.1–9.19.17, though he apologizes for it in 9.17.1; Arrian *Ind.* 6.1; Cornelius Nepos 16 (Pelopidas), 3.1; Josephus *Ag. Ap.* 1.57; *Life* 336–367).

[292] This is true also in *T. Ab.* 7:12; 8:2, 12; 15:10, 13; 19:4A, but there context qualifies rather than redefines the sense of ἀκολουθέω. Perhaps more relevant is the use of the philosophical martyr tradition (particularly epitomized in Socrates) as a moralist model in Greco-Roman sources (Tiede, *Figure*, 56).

[293] Cf. Job's courageous promise in *T. Job* 4:2/3 (followed by warning of the cost and, in 5:1, reaffirmation, followed by success); but *T. Job* 4:2/3 may echo the language of Israel's failed promise in Exod 19:8.

becomes here an antihero, a foil for Jesus' true heroism. Ancient literature was replete with images of flatterers who merely pretended friendship,[294] and provides an occasional parallel with the notion that one might swear loyalty to the death yet betray one to death.[295] But such pretense is the domain of Judas alone in this narrative (13:2); like some other ancient protagonists who proved weaker in character than in rhetoric,[296] Peter has noble intentions but proves too weak to fulfill them (cf. Mark 14:38).

Interestingly, if Peter's two comments count as one exchange, then the disciples ask questions four times (13:36–37; 14:5, 8, 22), the number of questions one would expect from children (cf. 13:33) to the *paterfamilias* or host on the night of the Passover. If these traditional questions were secure and widely used in a Passover haggadah tradition by John's day—and this is by no means certain[297]—readers accustomed to thinking of Jesus' final conversation with his disciples in the context of a Passover meal might take notice, even though for John the Passover begins the following day (18:28). Finding an exact correspondence between the disciples' questions and the specific four in the traditional Passover haggadah, however, is difficult. More generally, teachers often provided lectures in response to questions.[298]

Jesus' announcement of Peter's betrayal is early tradition, attested in other contexts in Mark 14:30 and Luke 22:31–34.[299] Especially based on the criteria of multiple attestation (in both Markan and Johannine tradition)[300] and embarrassment (probability is against early Christians inventing such a negative story about Peter),[301] the tradition of Peter's denials is very likely historical.[302] The criterion of embarrassment is most telling here; because the loyalty of one's followers reflected positively on one (e.g., Josephus *Life* 84) and early Christian storytellers would seek to provide a positive moral example (ancient historians sought to elucidate edifying morals in their writings; see introduction, pp. 14–16, 19, 46), the account's survival most likely testifies to its historical verity. Three denials might fit a storytelling pattern, particularly that of the pre-Markan passion narrative,[303] but even this detail is probably historical.[304]

More critical for understanding John's point, however, is how he employs this earlier tradition. In this context its emphasis becomes a warning to all disciples: following Jesus to the death, sometimes to avoid betraying one's fellow believers, is a necessary part of discipleship when the circumstances present themselves; but it proves more difficult than a disciple might expect. Granted, Peter had devotion to Jesus; he simply did not have

---

[294] See documentation under comment on John 7:4.

[295] See Lucian *Downward Journey* 11.

[296] Lucan *C.W.* 2.517–518 claimed that noble Romans preferred an honorable death to surrender, but when tested, Lucan himself vainly betrayed others, including his own mother, to try to save himself from Nero.

[297] Finkelstein, "Documents," 8–18, argues for roots in the Hasmonean period, though thinking (p. 17) that the current practice stems from much closer to 70 C.E. than 175 B.C.E. His arguments, unfortunately, do not seem strong.

[298] See, e.g., Musonius Rufus 3, p. 38.25–26; 4, p. 42.34–35; 16, p. 101.20–21; 17, p. 106.20–21. A teacher might also lecture in response to a comment: 14 p. 90.24–25; 14, p. 96.4.

[299] Dewey, "Curse," 106.

[300] See Brown, *Death*, 611–13.

[301] See ibid., 615.

[302] See more fully ibid., 614–21.

[303] See the discussion ibid., 11–12; Brown also acknowledges that basic historical fact could be retold in an imaginative manner (pp. 620–21).

[304] See the discussion ibid., 613–14.

enough. The Fourth Gospel repeatedly emphasizes the need for a deeper level of faith (e.g., 2:23–25; 8:30–32); disciples should prepare for the future times of testing by deepening their devotion insofar as possible. But the narrative also qualifies the sayings: following to the cross is necessary (12:24–26), but those who fail yet return and persevere will remain disciples—and may well be given another opportunity to demonstrate the depth of their faithfulness (21:15–17). The passage also provides Jesus a prophecy fulfilled in 18:25–27, thereby confirming for John's audience Jesus' role as a true prophet and guaranteeing the reliability of his other statements.[305]

Scholars debate the exact time of the cockcrow (13:38; 18:27); some point to the 3 A.M. trumpet call, called the *gallicinium,* or "cockcrow," of the Roman guard in the Fortress Antonia.[306] Various other periods for Palestinian cockcrow have been noted.[307] This is not, however, the most obvious allusion either for Galilean disciples or for Diaspora readers of the Gospel. Most people were not sufficiently awake during the nocturnal crowings to notice them; the most common use of cockcrow in ancient texts was to herald the dawn or a period immediately preceding it.[308] In any case, Brown may well be right in citing Cicero: "Is there any time, night or day, that cocks do not crow?"[309] The important point for the narrative is that, despite Peter's vehement protestations, his denial is quite imminent!

---

[305] Reinharz, "Prophet."

[306] E.g., Mounce, *Matthew,* 259.

[307] See the summary of views in Brown, *Death,* 607.

[308] E.g., Alciphron *Courtesans* 13 (courtesan to lady friend), frg. 6, par. 18; *Farmers* 2 (Iophon to Eraston), 3.10, par. 1, 3; [Virgil] *Moretum* 1–2; Babrius 124.12–18; Apuleius *Metam.* 2.26; Heliodorus *Aeth.* 1.18; Philostratus *Vit. soph.* 2.11.591; Polybius 12.26.1; 3 Macc 5:23; *b. Ber.* 60b; *p. Kil.* 9:3, §3; *Pesaḥ.* 10:6; cf. *p. Ber.* 9:1, §17 (God gave cocks wisdom when to crow). In particular, Mark's "second" cockcrow may refer to dawn, as in various other texts (Heliodorus *Aeth.* 5.3; Brown, *Death,* 137, cites Aristophanes *Ecclesiazusae* 30–31, 390–391; Juvenal *Sat.* 9.107–108; Ammianus Marcellinus *Res gestae* 22.14.4).

[309] Brown, *Death,* 607, citing Cicero *Div.* 2.26.56. Babrius 124.16–18 indicates that the cock signals other times in addition to dawn.

# JESUS' RETURN AND PRESENCE

## 14:1–31

A NY MODERN OUTLINE of the last discourse will be somewhat arbitrary; a flow chart would diagram the flow of thought much more accurately than an outline. The second-person verbs in 14:1 are plural and hence address all the disciples; yet the topic of 13:36–38 remains. An outline heading that coincides closely with a traditional chapter, as ours does, naturally warrants some suspicion; chapter breaks were added long after the writing of the NT. A section from 13:31–14:31 would work better in some respects but would equally arbitrarily separate 13:31–38 from its essential preceding context. Any outline will thus prove arbitrary; nevertheless, if one outlines this material, collecting 14:1–31 around a common theme can at least underline the basic unity of this section.

## Going to the Father (14:1–6)

The disciples want to know where Jesus is going so they can follow (13:36–38); Jesus informs them that they can follow him only after he has gone to the Father to prepare a place for them (14:1–6). The disciples cannot follow Jesus now, but they will follow him eventually (13:36); by his death, Jesus is going to prepare them a place in the Father's presence and will return after the resurrection as their way to the Father's presence. The prerequisite for their entrance here is not martyrdom but faith (14:10–12); yet true faith must ultimately be ready to meet the test of martyrdom (13:36–38). There is no real break between these verses and those that follow: that Jesus is the way to the Father (14:6) also means that he is the Father's revelation (14:7–10).

### 1. Trusting the Father and Jesus (14:1)

Shifting from addressing Peter alone to addressing all the disciples (evident in the shift to plural pronouns and verbs), Jesus encourages them not to be disturbed.[1] ("Heart" is singular here and in 14:27 and 16:6, 22, perhaps intended as analogous to most passages applying to corporate Israel in the law.)[2] The cause of anxiety in the context is clearly his indication that he is going away and that they cannot follow him yet (13:36–38); the following verses indicate how the disciples may follow Jesus' way to the Father when he returns to them after his resurrection (14:2–7). Some argue that Jesus'

---

[1] For "disturbed," see, e.g., Tob 12:16; Diogenes Laertius 10.85; 10.144.17; see more fully the comment on 11:33.

[2] E.g., Deut 5:29; 6:5–6; 7:17; 8:2, 5, 14, 17; 9:4–5; 10:12; 11:13, 18; 13:13. John follows the Semitic preference for a distributive singular (Brown, *John,* 2:618), probably in Septuagintal idiom.

reassurance in 14:1 and 27 bracket off the intervening section,[3] but it is more likely that 16:33 rather than 14:27 closes the bracket; 14:27 merely reiterates and develops the point.

It is likely that both uses of the verb πιστεύω in 14:1 should be taken in the same mood; probably either both are indicative or both are imperative; in either case, taking both the same way links Jesus with the Father as the supreme object of faith. In the context of their anxiety, the imperative is more likely: "Believe in God; believe also in me."[4] ("Believe in" could be idiomatic for "Trust," e.g., Gen 15:6 MT.) Such words of encouragement were common to those in distress,[5] such as the "Have courage" of 16:33;[6] Scripture was also replete with "Do not fear" oracles.[7] Glasson claims that this was a recurrent theme of Deuteronomy, and may be right that the fuller "Do not be troubled or afraid" of 14:27 reflects the double exhortation of Deut 31:8 (cf. Deut 1:21, 29; 7:18; Josh 1:9).[8]

These words do not allude to Jesus' deity per se, though in the light of the whole context of John's Christology these associations are certainly present as well. (Carson is right that first-century Jews did not exhort others to believe in them as they believed in God.)[9] The words themselves allude to the role of Moses, an object of faith (as God's agent) alongside God: when Israel "saw" how God destroyed the Egyptians, they feared the Lord and believed in both the Lord and his servant Moses (Exod 14:31 MT).[10] (The language, by extension, then applied to the prophets in general.)[11] As Israel at least temporarily believed Moses' sign (Exod 14:8), Jesus would invite trust on the basis of his works if necessary (John 14:11).[12] In context they do not constitute so much a summons to proceed beyond signs-faith to enduring faith (as in 20:31)[13] as an encouragement to continue persevering in the face of opposition. The difference between these alternatives is less one of substance than one of delivery style: both are deliberative, but the exhortation to deeper faith may constitute firmer rhetoric potentially evoking the epideictic rhetoric of blame, whereas this passage is closer to pure encouragement or consolation.[14]

---

[3] E.g., Berg, "Pneumatology," 105, following Bultmann, *John,* 599.

[4] So also, e.g., Bernard, *John,* 2:531; Michaels, *John,* 252.

[5] E.g., *1 En.* 92:2 ("Do not let your spirit be troubled from the times").

[6] Cf., e.g., Diogenes Laertius 1.113 (θάρρει).

[7] E.g., Gen 15:1; 26:24; Jer 1:8; in early Christian oracles, Act 18:9. "Do not fear" was the assurance one in power would supply a dependent (Gen 50:21).

[8] Glasson, *Moses,* 75. Given the Hebrew penchant for parallelism, the idiom is frequent, especially with the Chronicler (1 Chr 22:13; 28:20; 2 Chr 20:15,17; 32:7) and the later prophets (Jer 46:27; Ezek 2:6; 3:9; cf. Ps 6:10; 83:17; Isa 37:27; Jer 17:18), but the Pentateuch would provide the most obvious foundational text.

[9] Carson, *Discourse,* 18.

[10] *Mek. Beš.* 7.124–130 on Exod 14:31 emphasizes a *qal vaomer* here; how much more they believed in the Lord whose servant Moses was (see Smith, *Parallels,* 154). This link also became part of the Samaritan liturgy (MacDonald, *Samaritans,* 51, 180–81).

[11] 2 Chr 20:20; 1 Sam 12:18 (although in 1 Sam 12:24 Samuel exhorted them to fear specifically the Lord).

[12] With Glasson, *Moses,* 78.

[13] As in Berg, "Pneumatology," 113, who rightly doubts polemic against the unbelieving synagogue (Segovia) and especially against future eschatology (Becker).

[14] For "letters of consolation," see, e.g., Plutarch *Consol.* passim, *Mor.* 608B–612B; *Apoll.* passim, *Mor.* 101F–122A; Theon *Progymn.* 8.53; 1 Thess 4:13–18; P.Oxy. 1874.12–21; Stowers, *Letter Writing,* 142–46; Lewis, *Life,* 80–81.

## 2. Dwelling in the Father's House (14:2–3)

Modern interpreters frequently understand 14:2–3 as future eschatology, as one might expect in a Synoptic eschatological discourse. But the words by themselves here are ambiguous, and the following context plainly applies them to realized eschatology (although future eschatology does appear elsewhere in this Gospel). The apparently eschatological wording may be coincidence, or (perhaps more likely) John may consciously reapply the language of future eschatology to emphasize the eschatological presence of Jesus. In the latter case, future eschatology might provide a model for John's realized eschatology, which in turn provided a foretaste for his community's future expectations (which I believe are suggested most fully in Revelation). In either case, however, the emphasis on present dwelling is clear (cf. 14:23).

### 2A. The Father's House (14:2)

On the historical level, the large house prepared for the disciples (probably known in the oral tradition; cf. Mark 14:15) may have furnished Jesus an illustration for his disciples.[15] But the Gospel and early Judaism in general supplied rich associations for the imagery that would probably spring more quickly to the minds of John's first audience. A Torah scroll that was burnt was said to have returned to heaven, to "its Father's house."[16]

Holwerda thinks that the Father's house in John 14:2 refers to heaven,[17] but most scholars see it as an allusion to the temple.[18] The Father's house elsewhere in John is the temple of Jesus' body (2:16–19, using a cognate term) or the household in which the son but not the slave has a permanent part (8:35, employing the same term).[19] The temple is spoken of as a "house" in postbiblical as well as biblical Judaism; the Tannaim could call it "the Eternal House,"[20] and a Roman Jewish inscription calls it the οἶκος εἰρη(νη)ς, the house of peace.[21] (This house had more "rooms"—a possible sense of μοναί—than any other known to most Jewish people, even aside from the fact that the text speaks of the *Father's* house.)[22] This may be Johannine double entendre: a place in the Father's house could mean dwelling in Christ God's temple or entering God's family through Christ the Son. Some ancient commentators also noticed some of these Johannine motifs, although possibly because of their philosophic training: Augustine suggested that in 14:2 Jesus is talking about preparing the dwellers, for Christians are God's house, his temple.[23] This is not to deny that John plays on the language of future eschatology, however.

---

[15] Hunter, *John,* 141.

[16] Smith, *Parallels,* 158–59, citing *Sipre Deut.* 32:4.

[17] Holwerda, *Spirit,* 20 n. 52; also Calvin, *John,* 2:81 (on John 14:2), though denying the "degrees" interpretation prevalent in his day. Bury, *Logos-Doctrine,* 60, appeals to Philo to make this a symbol of the Logos.

[18] Pass, *Glory,* 66–68; MacGregor, *John,* 305 (as a metaphor for "God's immediate presence"); cf. Sanders, *John,* 321 (a king's palace). Michaels, *John,* 252, thinks the allusion is to the temple but that it is used as a metaphor for heaven.

[19] Kangus, "Father's House," applies the image here to Christ's body, the church.

[20] *T. Zebah.* 13:6. Cf. *t. Sukkah* 4:3/*b. Sukkah* 53b, attributed to Hillel, in which God says to Israel, "If you come to My house, I come to your house" (Urbach, *Sages,* 1:577; Sandmel, *Judaism,* 240). Cf. also Buchanan, *Hebrews,* 161.

[21] *CIJ* 1:378, §515.

[22] Blomberg, *Reliability,* 198, following esp. McCaffrey, *House.*

[23] Augustine *Tr. Ev. Jo.* 68.2.1; he suggested that God's people and kingdom is even now being built (68.2.2).

## 2B. Dwelling and Deity

The language of "dwelling" in relation to the worship of the divine may be significant. Philo can speak of dwelling (οἰκεῖν) in God's Word as in a fatherland (πατρίδα).[24] Plutarch stresses that the divine νόμος should always dwell with (συνοικῶν) the good ruler, indeed, within (ἐντός) him.[25] A Neoplatonist speaks of a wise person's mind as a temple and shrine for God.[26] Epictetus wants to dwell (οἰκεῖν) where no one can hinder him any longer, that is, in death,[27] and speaks of the presence of the deity in all people:

> Wherefore, when you close your doors and make darkness within, remember never to say that you are alone, for you are not alone; nay, God is within [ὁ θεὸς ἔνδον ἐστί], and your own genius is within [ὁ ὑμέτερος δαίμων ἐστί].[28]

> . . . you are a fragment of God; you have within you a part of Him [μέρη θεῶν . . . ἐν σεαυτῷ μέρος ἐκείνου]. Why, then, are you ignorant of your own kinship?[29]

Thus "God Himself is present within you [παρόντος ἔσωθεν]."[30] The Roman Stoic Seneca likewise insists that God comes near people, indeed, comes into them *(in homines venit)*, divine seeds being sown *(semina . . . dispersa)* in people.[31]

More to the point are Diaspora Jewish references to the Spirit dwelling in or upon those inspired by the prophetic Spirit.[32] In *L.A.B.* 28:6:

> And when they had sat down, a holy spirit came upon Kenaz and dwelled [lit., "dwelling"] in him and put him in ecstasy, and he began to prophesy, saying . . . [Et dum sederent, insiliit spiritus sanctus habitans in Cenez, et extulit sensum eius, et cepit prophetare dicens . . . ][33]

In *T. Sim.* 4:4, Joseph had the Spirit in him (ἔχων πνεῦμα θεοῦ ἐν αὐτῷ) and consequently did good. In the eschatological time, according to *T. Zeb.* 8:2, God would dwell in (or with) any compassionate person he found (ἐν αὐτῷ κατοικεῖ). *Testament of Dan* 5:1 admonishes,

> Avoid wrath, and hate lying, in order that the Lord may dwell among you [κατοικήσει ἐν ὑμῖν], and Beliar may flee [φεύξεται] from you.[34]

---

[24] *Flight* 76; in 77, it is "eternal life" to take refuge with him, but death to flee from him.

[25] Plutarch *Uned. R.* 3, *Mor.* 780CD.

[26] Porphyry *Marc.* 11.191–193, 196–198; 19.318–319 (νεώς is Attic for ναός); cf. also his neoplatonist alternative in which either the divine or an evil δαιμόνιον dwell in (ἐνοικέω) the soul (*Marc.* 21.333–336; cf. 19.321–322; 21.331–332, 336–339).

[27] Epictetus *Diatr.* 1.25.20–21.

[28] Epictetus *Diatr.* 1.14.13–14 (LCL 1:104–5).

[29] Epictetus *Diatr.* 2.8.10–11 (LCL 1:260–61).

[30] Epictetus *Diatr.* 2.8.14. The Loeb translator (1:262–63) translates temporally, "when" he is present, but the participle can as easily be taken as "since." One could beseech Mithras to "dwell" in one's ψυχή (*PGM* 4.709–710), an entreaty that might have erotic overtones (so Betz, *Papyri,* 52) or may even reflect Christian influence. Cf. 1 John 3:9.

[31] Seneca *Ep. Lucil.* 73.16 (after arguing that good people are divine, 73.12–16). In a different vein, Ovid *Fasti* 6.5–6 claimed that a god was in mortals, leaving them seeds *(semina)* of inspiration; cf. divinizing intimacy and union in Iamblichus *V.P.* 33.240.

[32] If Aune, *Prophecy,* 33–34, is correct that pre-Christian Greek literature has barely any real examples associating Pythian prophecy with possession, the OT background may be prominent here.

[33] *OTP* 2:341; Latin, p. 195.

[34] *OTP* 1:809 (Greek: ed. Charles, 136).

*Testament of Joseph* 10:2 promises:

> if you pursue self-control and purity . . . the Lord will dwell [κατοικήσει] among you [ἐν ὑμῖν], because he loves self-control.[35]

If the question of date renders the testimony of *Liber antiquitatum biblicarum* or the Testaments problematic, the same is not true with similar language in Paul, although John's language takes its own direction.[36] The testimony of Septuagintal texts regarding the indwelling of divine Wisdom is of still more direct import:

> And abiding (μένουσα) in her[self] makes all things new;
> and in all generations into holy souls entering she makes
> (them) friends of God and prophets.[37]

## 2C. A Dwelling Place (14:2)

Most scholars recognize that the μονή of 14:23 plays on the μονή of 14:2;[38] the movement between these verses is not polemical correction[39] but is developing 14:2–3 in Johannine terms.[40] One could argue for various allusions in John's use of μονή here. For instance, if this "dwelling" is related to Sukkoth, it emphasizes that the sukkah, or dwelling place, is the disciple's regular abode during the time of the feast[41] symbolizing the wilderness, the time between redemptive events. Such an allusion is possible, though it should be recalled that this passage appears in the context of Passover (11:55; 13:1), not Tabernacles (7:2).

Others have suggested that an eschatological "dwelling" is in view here. The idea of a future "dwelling" is not foreign to Judaism. Answering Peter's apparent willingness to follow him to the death (13:37), Jesus may be using the Jewish tradition of an abode after death. Tobit, for instance, notes that he is ready to die, and prays that he may go εἰς τὸν αἰώνιον τόπον (Tob 3:6). Similar sentiments may be expressed in Diaspora Jewish funerary inscriptions, in which the deceased have entered an eternal house (οἶκος αἰώνιος; בית עולם; *domi [a]eternae*).[42] This may ultimately reflect a reading of "eternal home" in Ecclesiastes (12:5, εἰς οἶκον αἰῶνος αὐτοῦ) that harmonized it with the rest of the canon; but both may simply reflect the popular Greek view that tombs were "eternal houses."[43] In *4 Ezra* 7:80, 85, 101, the righteous enter "habitations" shortly after their decease.[44]

One may compare some Greek texts about the abode of the soul after death, such as one of the *Cynic Epistles* attributed to Heraclitus:

---

[35] OTP 1:821 (ed. Charles, 196). In 10:3, where God dwells, God will rescue the person and exalt him.

[36] Cf. Sylvia Mary, *Mysticism*, 72.

[37] Wis 7:27; see also Wis 1:4; 10:16; thus the righteous would also abide with wisdom (Wis 7:28, συνοικοῦντα) and with God (3:9, προσμενοῦσιν), and wisdom would live with them (8:9, 16).

[38] Berg, "Pneumatology," 109.

[39] Ibid., 107–10.

[40] Ibid., 110.

[41] *M. Sukkah* 2:9; cf. *p. Sukkah* 2:10, §1.

[42] *CIJ* 1:264–65, §337; 1:384, §523; 1:387, §527; cf. 2:68, §820 (עלמא [ת] ב רנה קברא, "Ce tombeau, demeure éternelle"); the first of these references is also cited by Leon, *Jews*, 127.

[43] Cf. Ferguson, *Backgrounds*, 196; Epictetus *Diatr.* 1.25.21. Cf. the "dwellings of Hades" in Euripides *Alc.* 25, 73, 436–437.

[44] Cf. *2 En.* 61:2–3 (both A and J).

Yet my soul will not sink, but, since it is a thing immortal, it will fly on high into heaven [εἰς οὐρανόν]. The ethereal dwellings [αἰθέριοι δόμοι] will receive me.[45]

Some texts may refer to an eternal dwelling in the world to come, rather than one entered immediately at death. *Second Enoch* 65:10J parallels eternal dwelling places (A has the singular) and paradise,[46] and in *2 En.* 36:3A (not J), an eternal "place" is "prepared" for Enoch before God's face; in both recensions of 9:1, paradise "has been prepared" for the righteous (as Gehenna is for the wicked, 10:4; cf. Matt. 25:34, 41).

These references may all be too late to accurately reflect any Jewish eschatology in the Johannine period, but they may also act as commentary on *1 En.* 91:13, in which the righteous in the final time receive "houses" as rewards,[47] and some passages in the Similitudes (39:5, 41:2, 45:1). In *T. Ab.* 20:14 A, the σκηναί of the righteous ones and the μοναί of the holy ones, Isaac and Jacob, are in paradise.[48] Some also suggest an early eschatological reading of Ps 42:3, although the LXX (42:3) has σκηνώματα.[49]

A rabbinic tradition, apparently established by the early Amoraic period, promises a sukkah in the world to come to those who keep the commandment of dwelling in sukkoth in this world;[50] if such a tradition were substantiated as early, it could suggest that John develops a motif related to Jesus' fulfillment of the Feast of Tabernacles (chs. 7–9). In a tradition attributed to the Tanna R. Meir, the abode of the righteous "on high" is contrasted with that of the wicked in Gehenna;[51] some Amoraim spoke of ranks of canopies in the world to come, according to one's merit.[52]

But the term used here, μονή, is rare in Greek and occurs only twice in John—here and in v. 23, where the present reference is explained;[53] it is related to its verbal cognate μένω, which assumes prominence in the first paragraph of ch. 15 and is a theologically loaded term throughout the Gospel.[54] Both v. 23 and the use of the verb in ch. 15 indicate

---

[45] Heraclitus *Ep.* 5, to Amphidamas (*Cyn. Ep.* 194–95). Philo regarded air, the lowest of heavens, as the οἶκος of bodiless souls (*Dreams* 1.135).

[46] This is late, as may be the "rooms" of God's heavenly palaces in the Merkabah traditions, cited by P. Alexander on *3 En.* 1:1 (*OTP* 1:247).

[47] Texts B and C, followed by Knibb, ed., 219, against A, which E. Isaac, trans., 73, renders "great things." Edersheim, *Life,* 570, cites rabbinic support for eschatological abodes assigned by rank.

[48] In 7.15–16B, Abraham's soul was in heaven, but his body would μένει (rendering as if it were μενεῖ) on earth till the resurrection of all flesh.

[49] Hanson, *Gospel,* 177.

[50] *Pesiq. Rab Kah.* Sup. 2:3. The tradition attributed to R. Akiba in *Mek. Pisḥa* 14.15–21; *Beš.* 1.173–177 on Exod 12:37; 13:20 (in Bonsirven, *Judaism,* 204; Daube, *Judaism,* 30) may imply future sukkoth in the new exodus (cf. Lacomara, "Deuteronomy," 78). The Temple Scroll implies that ideally booths were erected in the temple itself during Sukkoth (Pfeiffer, *Scrolls,* 90), an image that might fit well the temple as the Father's house of 14:2; but most erected them elsewhere (e.g., atop other houses, Neh 8:16).

[51] *Lev. Rab.* 27:1.

[52] *B. B. Bat.* 75a; *Ruth Rab.* 3:4; *Pesiq. Rab.* 31:6. Bernard, *John,* 2:531, cites *2 En.* 62:2 and *1 En.* 39:4 as saying something like this; McNamara, *Judaism,* 239, also cites *2 En.* 62:2 and *1 En.* 41:2; but Barrett, *John,* 457, is probably correct that these passages are not relevant to the interpretation of John 14:2. Cf. the source attempts of Bacon, "House."

[53] Lightfoot, *Commentary,* 275.

[54] Davies, *Land,* 324–25. For uses of the term, see 1:32, 33, 38–39; 3:36; 4:40; 5:38; 6:56; 7:9; 8:31, 35; 9:41; 10:40 (cf. v. 38); (11:10); 11:54; 12:24, 46; (14:10, 11 [ἐν]); 14:17, (20 [ἐν]), 23, 25; (15:2 [ἐν]); 15:4, 5, 6, 7, 9, 10, 16; (17:21, 23, 26 [ἐν]); 21:22, 23. The idea of the new covenant (Jer 31:31–34; Ezek 36:24–28) and OT imagery for God's indwelling (though, more commonly, his resting upon) are probably also relevant; for a complete discussion, see Malatesta, *Interiority,* 42–77.

that the present experience of believers in God's presence is the point of "dwelling place" in John 14:2.[55] The idea is that the Shekinah will always be among them (cf. Matt 1:23; 18:20; 28:20) and the community ought always to recognize this.[56]

2D. A Place Prepared (14:2)

If, as we have argued above, "the Father's house" alludes to the temple, some might draw a connection between that house and the "place prepared." The temple was sometimes spoken of as a place that had been prepared, as the building "which will be revealed, with me, that was already prepared from the moment I decided to create Paradise."[57] Whether or not we accept McNamara's contention that "preparing a resting place" for God was a regular expression for God's sanctuary in this period,[58] the idea of preparing a place for the disciples in God's house might connote the places the priests would have in the eschatological temple (Ezek 45:4–5; cf. 40:45–46; 42:13; 44:16); and in the Fourth Gospel, the eschatological temple is clearly in Jesus himself.[59] Since the temple would naturally be viewed as a dwelling of the deity[60] and the hope of Israel was God's covenant-dwelling among them (Rev 21:3, 22),[61] the point of the text would not have been difficult to grasp. In Scripture, God had promised to dwell among his covenant people (Lev 26:12; Ezek 37:26–28); in the new covenant, God would put his laws in their hearts (Jer 31:33).

Nevertheless, it remains uncertain whether John intends a deliberate allusion to the temple with "prepared." Other texts speak of eschatological places God prepared for his people (Matt 20:23; 25:34; Heb 11:16), and most significantly, Revelation employs John's language for the present period of suffering and divine protection between the first and second coming, without reference to the temple (Rev 12:6).[62] The language of "preparing" was also appropriate for "preparing a house"—for instance, getting things there in order

---

[55] The shift between God being their dwelling place and them being his is not particularly significant, since both communicate the idea of presence and relationship (though cf. also *Pesiq. Rab.* 21:10).

[56] *B. Sanh.* 22a, attributed to Simon the Pious, says that this is the proper attitude for prayer (in Montefiore and Loewe, *Anthology,* 345, §907). See Abelson, *Immanence,* 377–79, for connections between the Holy Spirit and the Shekinah in rabbinic literature.

[57] *2 Bar.* 4:3.

[58] McNamara, "Resting-Place"; cf. idem, *Targum,* 142–43. Glasson, *Moses,* 75, comments reservedly on the view that a paschal tradition is in view (Exod 23:30 has a "place prepared," but Oesterley's connections to the paschal liturgy are not particularly convincing); but the woman in the "place prepared" in Rev 12 evokes more of the imagery of Sukkoth.

[59] Cf. the common use of *makom,* "place," as a divine title in later rabbinic circles, signifying God's omnipresence (*3 En.* 18:24; *m. ʾAbot* 2:9, 13; 3:14; *Sipra VDDen. pq.* 2.2.4.2; 4.6.4.1; *Sipra Sav M.D par.* 98.7.7; *Sh. M.D.* 99.1.4, 5, 7; 99.2.2, 3; 99.3.9, 11; 99.5.13; *Sipra Qed. par.* 1.195.2.3; *pq.* 7.204.1.4; *Sipra Emor pq.* 9.227.1.5; *Behuq. pq.* 5.266.1.1; *Sipre Deut.* 1.8.3; 1.9.2; 1.10.4; 2.1.1; 11.1.1; 21.1.1; 24.3.1; 26.4.1; 28.1.1; 32.3.2; 32.5.8; 33.1.1; 37.1.1, 3; 38.1.1, 3; Keener, *Marries,* 150 n. 27). Patte, *Hermeneutic,* 25, points out that Torah is a "place" of God's dwelling, a surrogate for God's presence in the temple; but this view may have arisen only gradually after 70 C.E. and is less common than the more common use as a title for God.

[60] For the localization of inspiration (albeit not the Spirit; see Keener, *Spirit,* 7–8) in Greek sanctuaries, see Aune, *Prophecy,* 31.

[61] For the Spirit indwelling the covenant community in the Scrolls, see 11QT 51.7–8; Bruce, "Spirit," 54; idem, *Corinthians,* 45; the Shekinah is inseparably connected with the community in *b. Sanh.* 58b; *B. Qam.* 83a; *Yebam.* 64a; cf. *Gen. Rab.* 86:6. For bibliography, see esp. Malatesta, *Interiority,* 345–48.

[62] For the connection with Rev 12:6, see also Beale, *Revelation,* 649 (interpreting John 14:2–3 as I do).

or meeting someone important (Tob 11:3); it so functions in the passion tradition familiar from Mark (Mark 14:15).

One may read 14:2, with many versions, as a question: "If it were not so, would I have told you that I am going to prepare a place for you?" Reading the line as a question allows one to take the ὅτι into account.[63] Others read the line as a statement rather than a question because Jesus had nowhere promised to prepare a place for them earlier in this Gospel and John is too thorough in foreshadowing to have likely omitted the explicit source for a reference here.[64] If Jesus' "going" to prepare a place for them (14:2–3) meant going to the Father by death (13:33, 36; 14:12, 28; 16:5, 7, 10, 17, 28), then presumably the preparation was completed on the cross, probably when Jesus declared, "It is finished" (19:30).

### 2E. Future or Realized Eschatology? (14:2–3)

Many have taken Jesus' words here as a promise of his future coming. Irenaeus read John 14:2 as a promise of future mansions: those who had performed the greatest works would have the largest mansions; those who produced fruit one hundredfold would live in the heavens; those who produced sixtyfold, in paradise; and those who produced thirtyfold, in the city.[65] Thus some scholars read this text as a promise of Jesus' future coming.[66] Holwerda argues this because Jesus will take the disciples to be with him where he is;[67] his argument falters, however, if "where Jesus is" means simply "in the Father's presence" (cf. 12:26; 16:28; 17:24; Rev 14:4), the only meaning one would need to derive from the context. He argues that "if His coming is fulfilled in the resurrection appearances, the disciples would again be orphans after the ascension,"[68] but this assumes that the impartation of the Spirit does not continue Jesus' presence in the same measure as it was experienced in the resurrection appearances, a position John appears to refute (14:16, 23; 20:19–23). Ridderbos suggests that scholars find realized eschatology here only because they deny future eschatology in John's Gospel.[69] This objection cannot apply to all scholars. I do recognize some future eschatology in John's Gospel (5:28; 6:39–40, 44, 54; 12:48), but there is also much realized eschatology (4:23; 5:25; 11:24–26); the question must thus be decided by the immediate context.

Others think that the language was originally eschatological but has here been adjusted toward the later Johannine perspective;[70] others feel that this is a Johannine double entendre, retaining an eschatological sense while emphasizing the present;[71] still others believe Jesus is going to the cross and the point is entirely personal communion with Jesus in the present age.[72]

---

[63] E.g., Michaels, *John*, 252 (but the ὅτι can be explained either way—cf. Smith, *John* [1999], 267).

[64] MacGregor, *John*, 305.

[65] Irenaeus *Haer.* 5.36.2. "Mansions" enters the AV and RV from Tyndale's use of the Vulgate and Old Latin, "where the word bears its proper meaning, 'places where a traveller halts and rests upon his journey'" (Swete, *Discourse*, 6; cf. also Whitacre, *John*, 348).

[66] E.g., Ellis, *Genius*, 220; Whitacre, *John*, 348. Cf. Luther, *Sermon on John 14*, contrasting the abodes with the earthly homes Christ's followers surrender for him (Matt 19:29).

[67] Holwerda, *Spirit*, 84.

[68] Ibid., 67. Akiba could say a generation was left fatherless when R. Eliezer died, since rabbis could be called "father" (*'Abot R. Nat.* 25 A).

[69] Ridderbos, *John*, 490–91.

[70] Burge, *Community*, 145.

[71] Gundry, "House," 69–70; cf. idem, *Tribulation*, 154–55. Cf. Légasse, "Retour."

[72] Ensley, "Eternity."

Given the context, one of the two latter views must be correct. Dodd[73] and Bultmann[74] are probably right that John here treats Jesus' death and resurrection as eschatological events, in which case the eschatological language that may be present should be construed in this instance (not everywhere in John) as focusing on Jesus' coming after the resurrection[75] to impart the Spirit who will continue his presence.[76] Jesus' return to the Father is how the place is prepared;[77] the "place prepared" may be connected to Rev 12:8,[78] developing the Johannine new-exodus motif in which the present age is portrayed as the wilderness (John 1:23; 3:14; 6:31; 11:54).

Some writers find a future "coming" in 14:3,[79] as in 21:22, but unless 14:2–3 includes a double entendre, their conclusion ignores the context, which develops the language of these more ambiguous lines, lines that of themselves need not have pointed to Parousia expectation unless assumed to belong to the context of early Christian future eschatology. Jesus makes it plain exactly where he is going in vv. 4–6—to the Father—and in the same verses says that they will end up in the same place by coming through Jesus. After his glorification is complete, he will come to them, manifest[80] himself to them, and impart the Spirit to them so that they may continue in his presence (vv. 7–26). This is the only coming (v. 18, 23, 28) and dwelling place (v. 23) of which the chapter as a whole speaks, and whatever sources John may or may not have incorporated into his text, this is the only way to make sense of the text as it now stands.

The emphasis in v. 17, then, that the Spirit of truth, the Spirit of Jesus, will abide with them, indicates that they will together constitute a new temple, the place where God and Jesus dwell and manifest their presence. This fits Qumran and early Christian imagery of the community as God's temple (cf. Ezek 36:27; 37:14, 27–28).

Jesus' words in 14:2–3, isolated from their context, are ambiguous enough to lend themselves to either an eschatological or an immediate postresurrection interpretation. Thus it is hardly surprising that the Johannine context proceeds to qualify the meaning of the promise for John's audience. (John structures the material for his purposes but very

---

[73] Dodd, *Interpretation,* 395.

[74] Bultmann, *Theology,* 2:57.

[75] As Berg, "Pneumatology," 144, points out, following other scholars, there is no inherent contradiction between referring this to the resurrection appearances and referring it to the Paraclete's coming, "which is associated with and yet distinct from those appearances."

[76] Cf. Bartlett, "Coming," 73 (John 14–16 points toward ch. 20, since John identifies Easter and Pentecost). This need not exclude future eschatology as foreign to John's thought, as Dodd, Bultmann, and Robinson, *Coming,* 176, may believe; but it does suggest that it is not here in view. It need not be a response to the delay of the Parousia (against Kysar, *Maverick Gospel,* 96).

[77] Barrett, *John,* 457; Carson, *Discourse,* 24 (although Carson reads the passage as referring to the end of the age).

[78] So also Brown, *John,* 2:620, although he speaks of it as "a place in heaven."

[79] Holwerda, *Spirit,* 84; Blomberg, *Reliability,* 198, and Talbert, *John,* 204 (comparing being "with the Lord" in 1 Thess 4:17, which admittedly does reflect traditional language). Traditional dispensational writers, among others, often hold this view; cf. Strombeck, *Rapture,* 24. Others may see a reference to Christ's coming for the believer at death, e.g., Strachan, *Gospel,* 194; Boettner, "Postmillenialism," 206; Payne, *Appearing,* 74, which at least could appeal to some contextual support (13:36–38), unlike the futuristic Parousia interpretation.

[80] Although such language had broad religious associations (Sir 6:22; Wis 1:2; *Let. Aris.* 264; Philo *Alleg. Interp.* 3.100–101; *Posterity* 16), this may reflect the Sinai motif in John, in which the disciples function as a new Moses (e.g., 1:14, cf. 2 Cor 3; Bernard, *John,* 2:540).

probably depends on earlier tradition.)[81] Like the first-time reader of the Gospel, Jesus' disciples do not grasp his import; Thomas insists that they do not know where Jesus is going, and still less (arguing *qal vaomer*) do they know the way (14:5).

Jesus responds that he himself is the way for them to follow where he is going, that is, to the Father (14:6), and they come to the Father by embracing Jesus as the full embodiment of the Father's revelation (14:7–11), which results in doing Jesus' "works" (14:12) and an intimate relationship with God (14:13). Jesus' "coming" in this context can represent only his postresurrection coming to impart to them the Spirit (14:16–18), and the "dwelling places" in the Father's presence can refer only to God dwelling in believers (14:23). Although both John (e.g., 5:28–29; 6:39–40, 44, 54; 11:24; 12:48) and his audience (cf., e.g., 1 John 2:28–3:3; Rev 1:7) accept future eschatology,[82] the emphasis of this passage is clearly realized rather than future eschatology.

The context develops more naturally as a flow chart than as an outline of points and subpoints, but some motifs recur throughout the context, especially as responses from disciples invite further development or explanation.[83] Sometimes a teacher would prepare disciples for the teacher's impending absence, such as in Socrates' encouragement of his disciples "in the wise pursuit of independent skills."[84] By contrast, Jesus here prepares his disciples for his absence by promising his continued presence (14:16–27; cf. Matt 28:20) and empowers them by inviting their dependence on him (15:4).

### 3. Jesus as the Way (14:4–6)

When Jesus tells the disciples that they "know" the way he is going, he alludes to his previous announcements of his impending death (12:23–25, 32–33), announcements that, however, they have not understood and hence do not now understand (14:5).[85] He is going by way of the cross,[86] and those who would follow him must go the same way (12:25–26); the road to experiencing such hostility from this world begins with embracing Jesus' identity (14:8–11) and thus sharing in his rejection by the world (15:18–16:4).

For the disciples, the "way" (14:6) means the way leading to the Father's presence.[87] Jesus goes to the Father by virtue of his identity and character; the disciples will come to the Father by means of Jesus and their participation in him.[88] The disciples "know the way" (14:4) precisely because they know Jesus, who is the way (14:6), whether or not they

---

[81] Thus the artificial similarity of the three questions (14:5, 8, 22) need not require pure invention, which might not well explain the citation of the obscure Judas (Brown, *John,* 2:641).

[82] Those who deny this acceptance (e.g., Bultmann) must employ a standard of consistency not applicable to other ancient sources, then impose their exegesis of some texts on the whole of John's theology by resorting to excising as interpolations passages for the removal of which there is no evidence.

[83] Segovia, "Structure," 482–84, followed by Berg, "Pneumatology," 111, suggest three elements in 14:4–14: (1) an opening christological statement (14:4, 7, 10); (2) the state of the disciples' belief (14:5, 8, 11); and (3) expansion of the opening christological statement (14:6, 9, 12–14), climaxing in 14:12–14.

[84] Robbins, *Jesus,* 172, comparing Xenophon *Mem.* 4.7.1–10 with Mark 13.

[85] For the misunderstanding motif here and elsewhere, see, e.g., Jonge, *Jesus,* 16.

[86] Recognized, e.g., by Carson, *Discourse,* 26, though he believes that 14:3 refers to a future coming.

[87] E.g., Gundry, "House," 70.

[88] Swete, *Discourse,* 14–15.

understand the implications of that fact; in the same way, the expected Spirit was already with them and known by them (14:17) because he was present in Jesus (1:33).

A cupbearer or some other high official could control access to a king's presence, but out of affection the king might waive this obstacle for his young son or grandson (cf. 8:35).[89] In turn, this child might receive whatever gifts he requested for his friends (cf. 14:13–14).[90] The idea here includes access (though it involves more, namely, remaining in his presence, 14:23), but also the access becomes direct in Jesus, no longer mediated through him at one remove (14:17; 16:26–27).

### 3A. Background of "the Way"

One suggestion is that the passage uses visionary literature's title "the way" as the route for heavenly ascents.[91] This suggestion is plausible but can be presumed as what John's ideal audience would have understood only if one reconstructs vision mysticism as central to their setting. This reconstruction, too, is plausible, but a preponderance of the evidence probably points in a different direction (below).

Another possible background for the "way" in 14:6 is Isaiah's "highway to Zion."[92] This explanation is reasonable, for the only prior reference to the "way" in the Fourth Gospel is the Isaiah citation in 1:23, in which John prepares Jesus' mission. In its Isaian context, the text proclaims a new exodus, by which God would return his people to the land; the "way" is the highway on which God's people will return to the Holy Land (Isa 35:8; 40:3; 42:16; 43:16, 19; 49:11; 57:14; 62:10; cf. 19:23). The image evokes the exodus of old (Isa 51:10).[93]

Yet an allusion to this single text would probably impress itself on John's intended audience less forcefully than a more common metaphoric use of "way."[94] The LXX of Isaiah (30:11, 21; 33:15; 40:14; 42:24; 48:17; 58:2; 63:17; 64:5) and other biblical tradition (e.g., Exod 18:20; 32:8; Deut 8:6; 9:16; 10:12; 11:22, 28), especially the wisdom tradition,[95] also apply the image of the "way" to the way of righteousness and wisdom. In both biblical (e.g., Isa 55:7–9; 56:11; 59:8; 66:3) and early Jewish sources,[96] "ways" refer to behavior, as in the rabbinic use of *halakot*.[97] "Ways" as behavior represents a usage that would be understood in John's circle of believers (Rev 15:3).

---

[89] Xenophon *Cyr.* 1.3.14. For the early Christian idea of divine access, see, e.g., Rom 5:2; Eph 2:18; Heb 4:16.

[90] Xenophon *Cyr.* 1.4.1; cf. *Apoll. K. Tyre* 17.

[91] DeConick, *Mystics*, 69–73 (citing Philo *Migration* 168–175, plus the later *Odes of Solomon* and Hermetica); cf. also Porphyry *Marc.* 6.105; 8.136. She also suggests that the way's localization in Jesus is meant to counter the *Gospel of Thomas* (the traditions of which are echoed in Thomas's ignorance in 14:5).

[92] Keener, *Background Commentary,* 299; Bell, *I Am,* 259.

[93] Cf. Exod 13:21; Deut 1:31; Josephus *Ant.* 3.18.

[94] See, e.g., O'Day, "John," 742.

[95] One may compare over seventy references to "ways" as behavior (e.g., the ways of righteousness or wickedness) in Proverbs LXX alone.

[96] E.g., Tob 1:3; *Jub.* 20:2; 23:20–21; 4Q400 frg. 1, col. 1 line 14; *Sib. Or.* 3.233. Cf. the use of "way" in Islamic Arabic (Bishop, *Apostles,* 107–8); and various pedagogic approaches in Iamblichus *V.P.* 19 (on which see Dillon and Hershbell, "Introduction," 28).

[97] Cf. also behavioral "walking" in *1 En.* 91:19; 94:1; *Jub.* 21:2; 25:10; 1QS 3.9, 18; 4.6, 12; 5.10; 6.2; 9.8, 19; CD 2.15–16; 7.4, 6–7; 8.9; 1 Cor 7:17; Gal 5:16, 25; 6:16; Phil 3:17–18; Col 1:10; 2:6; 1 Thess 2:12; 4:1.

Thus Philo can declare that Moses will guide the seeker on the way (ἡγεμόνα τῆς ὁδοῦ) and they will see the place that is the Word;[98] the way of discipline is the way of wisdom and is safe.[99] Tannaim spoke of Torah as the "way" (*m. ʾAbot* 6:4), hence the path for walking, for halakah; later rabbis spoke of the Torah as the "path of life."[100] More significantly (and perhaps allowing that John might allude to the new exodus anyway), the Dead Sea Scrolls present the "way" of Isaiah 40 as study of the law (1QS 8.15–16).[101] "The way" could also occasionally apply to hermeneutical method in Greek thought.[102] After Socrates notes the road (ὁδός) he has followed, others press him to discover what road he means, and like Jesus in this passage, he only gradually reveals to them what he means; Socrates means his method of investigating the truth.[103] Epictetus praises Chrysippus because his philosophical reasoning "shows the way" (δεικνύοντος τὴν ὁδόν) to correct thinking,[104] that is, to "truth."[105] Those who do not think properly have wandered astray and "do not know the road" (τὴν ὁδὸν ἀγνοοῦντα).[106]

## 3B. The Claim's Exclusivism

Because John envisions Jesus as the embodiment of divine Wisdom (1:1–18) and because the moral use of "way" was the predominant figurative use of the term, it is highly probable that this image constitutes the primary background for "way" in 14:6. In this case the "way" is no longer purely ethical but christological. This image also sharpens the claim of christocentric exclusivism, for the Jewish wisdom tradition portrayed morality in binary terms: one walked in ways of righteousness or in wickedness (e.g., Prov 4:18–19; 10:9, 17; 12:15). Jesus is the sole adequate revealer of God, for he alone knows God fully (3:13; 6:46). The image of a new exodus, if in view, would also point in the same direction.[107] Other evidence from the Jesus tradition suggests that Jesus did in fact adopt the binary image of the "two ways" from the broader religious milieu (Q material in Matt 7:13–14; Luke 13:23–27)[108] and believed that his teaching constituted a dividing line equivalent to wisdom in wisdom tradition and Torah in early rabbinic tradition (Matt 7:24–27; Luke 6:46–49; cf. Matt 7:22–23).[109] Just as Judaism as a whole drew boundaries around the claim of one God, Johannine Christians (and apparently most other early Christians as

---

[98] Philo *Confusion* 95–96; τόπον here invites some comparison with the later rabbinic use of *makom* for God's omnipresence (for Torah as a surrogate for God's presence, cf. Patte, *Hermeneutic,* 25). The Logos is God's house in Philo *Migration* 5–6.

[99] Philo *Flight* 203.

[100] E.g., *Lev. Rab.* 29:5 (fifth century C.E., citing Prov 3:18; 15:24); *Exod. Rab.* 30:12; Dodd, "Background," 335, cites a late midrash on Ps 25:10. Rabbis also spoke of a gate of right behavior leading to life (*Lev. Rab.* 30:2); see also comment on the two ways in Keener, *Matthew,* 250–51, on Matt 7:13–14.

[101] Cf. also Pryke, "Eschatology," 49. The Qumran sect's depiction of themselves as the "way" (1QS 9.17) probably also stems from Isa 40 (1QS 8.14; note also the allusion in 1QS 9.19–20).

[102] Older commentators cited the literal path through which mystery initiates discovered esoteric lore (Ramsay, *Teaching,* 302).

[103] Plato *Philebus* 16BC.

[104] Epictetus *Diatr.* 1.4.29.

[105] Epictetus *Diatr.* 1.4.31.

[106] Marcus Aurelius 6.22.

[107] Bell, *I Am,* 273.

[108] Cf., e.g., Seneca *Ep. Lucil.* 8.3; Deut 30:15; Ps 1:1; *m. ʾAbot* 2:9; Bricker, "Ways"; Thom, "*Akousmata,*" 106. See fuller documentation in comment on 12:25–26.

[109] For the parallel with Torah in an early rabbinic parable (*ʾAbot R. Nat.* 24A), see comments in Keener, *Matthew,* 255; Gundry, *Matthew,* 135. Others also cite various Synoptic sayings (e.g., Matt

well, e.g., Acts 4:12) drew boundaries around the claim that Jesus was the only fully adequate way to the one God.

Some prefer to reinterpret the exclusivism of texts such as 14:6 in light of a particular reading of cosmic-Christ texts such as 1:9.[110] Some others argue that the claim of 14:6a is legitimate but that this claim in 14:6b is redactional, hence not authoritative.[111] But whatever contemporary theology may do with the text, this was hardly what would appear to have been the point of the text for its ideal audience.[112] In whatever other sense John may or may not have been sectarian, he was certainly sectarian at least in believing that of his fellow Jews only those who followed Jesus became receptacles for the Spirit's regenerative activity (cf. 3:1–8), and if so, the rest of "the world" could have fared no better. Jesus was the "way" in the sense in which he was the "door"—only robbers tried to enter the sheepfold by other means (10:1, 7, 9)—a claim this Gospel directed specifically against members of the Judean religious elite.[113]

One cannot argue, as some have,[114] that the claim of 14:6 addresses merely Gentiles; both John's audience and Jesus' audience in the story world are Jewish, and the Fourth Gospel employs the claim particularly in its polemic against the "Jews," that is, the Jewish political and religious elite.[115] Early Christians were ethnically universalist but proved "much less willing to recognize the possibility of salvation for nonbelievers, be they Jews or Gentiles," than some other early Jewish groups.[116]

They were more like the highly sectarian Essenes, who regarded their "way" as normative, including for Israel. God would judge the nations in battle by "the perfect of way" (1QM 14.7); the Jews saved in the end time would be those who joined their ranks, for other Jews would prove apostate and suffer judgment with the nations.[117] Yet whereas the Qumran community viewed itself and its lifestyle as the "way" (e.g., 1QS 9.17; 10.21; 4Q403 1 1.22),[118] a general idea adopted by early Christians (Acts 9:2; 18:25–26; 19:9, 23;

---

10:32–33) in which one's public confession of Jesus determines one's status before God at the judgment (McKnight, "Jesus," 67).

[110] E.g., Kazui Yagi, "Theology," followed (or entertained) by Culpepper, "Culture," 122–23. White, "No One Comes," thinks that the text does not limit genuine spiritual experience to Jesus' followers, but does claim that such experiences of the divine are mediated by Christ alone.

[111] Charlesworth, "Exclusivism," 510. As we have noted, however, distinguishing redaction from tradition is not easy in John; further, different communities would differ on which elements are authoritative (e.g., some would reject even tradition and others accept even redaction), a question beyond the pale of exegesis per se.

[112] Although it is true that John also speaks from the perspective of a minority religious community concerned with self-definition and might therefore have articulated his views differently in a different context (O'Day, "John," 744–45; cf. also Charlesworth, "Exclusivism," comparing Qumran), it does not follow that he would have therefore abandoned his exclusivism, which seems entrenched in the essentially sectarian apostolic preaching of early Christianity; but beyond this observation this question is, in any case, a hermeneutical and pastoral rather than historical one and hence should not detain us extensively in a commentary focused on social-historical questions.

[113] Cf. Bell, *I Am*, 273.

[114] E.g., Falk, *Jesus*, 86.

[115] See introduction, pp. 214–28. Cf. Bell, *I Am*, 273–74, 282–83.

[116] Boccaccini, *Judaism*, 265.

[117] Cf. 4QpNah 4.3. Other Jews also could acknowledge some of their compatriots as apostate (1 Macc 1:51–53) or even expect apostasy of most in the end time (*T. Iss.* 6:1), but the Essenes were more sectarian, usually identifying their own community with the true remnant of Israel (Flusser, *Judaism*, 49).

[118] On the "way" in the Scrolls, cf., e.g., McCasland, "Way"; Zon, "Droga"; Fitzmyer, "Christianity," 240. "Ways" (דרכי) is common in an ethical and communal sense in the Scrolls (e.g., CD 1.13;

22:4; 24:14, 22; cf. Matt 21:32), this passage identifies Jesus himself as the way. Jesus as the "way" is the only "door" (10:7, 9) through which his sheep may find safety within the fold (10:1).[119] Given John's polemic, however, we should note that his exclusivity is not a claim that other ways to the Father existed and Jesus closed them off. The claim is more universal than that: given the world's alienation from God, there was no way to the Father, and Jesus provided one (3:18–19; cf. 1:10; 1 John 5:19).[120]

3C. Truth and Life (14:6)

"Truth" and "life" merely clarify the "way" in this passage;[121] as in Jewish wisdom tradition, God's ways were truth and life (e.g., Prov 2:19; 3:2, 16, 18; 4:10, 13, 22). Truth included moral integrity (cf. John 3:21). Later rabbis use "Truth" as a title for God because God's character was truth; they remarked that "truth" (אמת) used the first, last, and middle letters of the Hebrew alphabet, and God as the first and the last was therefore to be called the "truth."[122] Israel's God also appears as the "truth" in some popular circles, including magical texts.[123] Rabbis sometimes also felt that Scripture designated Torah as "truth."[124] Truth is central to John's theology because of his focus on revelation, but for John this is not the more Hellenistic conception of reality (see comment on 1:14) but truth in Christ.[125] John probably has in view primarily God's character revealed in Jesus (1:14–18; 8:31–32); only in truth could God be worshiped, through Jesus and, after his earthly ministry, through the Spirit of truth (4:23–24; 14:17).

On "life," see especially the comment on 1:4. The term is appropriate for a "way" of behavior but also appropriate to the one who brings them life (11:25; 14:19; 1 John 1:2; cf. Deut 30:20), the very source of their ability to walk in God's way (John 15:4–5).

# Revealing the Father (14:7–14)

Jesus is the way to the Father (14:4–6) because he reveals the Father's very character (14:7–9), just as did God's revelation of glory to Moses in Exod 33:19; 34:6–7. Jesus is here the revelation of the Father's glory (1:14–18). Those disinclined to believe otherwise

---

2.3; 4Q405 frg. 23, col.1.11; 4Q185 frg. 1–2, col. 2.1–2; 4Q400 frg. 1, col. 1.14; 4Q473 frg. 1); cf. also "paths" of righteousness (נתיבות, CD 1.16; cf. Matt 21:32; Charles, *Jubilees*, lxxxiv, may be right to suppose *Jub.* 23:20–21 relevant).

[119] Some associate "door" with the tabernacle (see comment on the fold in John 10), and "way" also makes sense here (Heb 9:8) but both are too specific a usage to be likely without other clues supporting them.

[120] See Smith, *John* (1999), 269.

[121] Brown, *John*, 2:621; Leal, "Via"; cf. the grammar of 1 Cor 1:30. The first καί "may be epexegetical or explanatory" (Brown, *John*, 2:621, following Blass, Debrunner, and Funk, *Grammar*, 228).

[122] E.g., *p. Sanh.* 1:1, §4; *Gen. Rab.* 81:2. See further Marmorstein, *Names*, 73, 179–81; Urbach, *Sages*, 1:181; cf. the "God of truth" in 4Q416 frg. 1, line 14 (with a moral emphasis). The personification of "truth" in occasional Greek texts (Maximus of Tyre *Or.* 10.1; Philostratus *Hrk.* 33.37) appears to be no more than a rhetorical device, though polytheism would have allowed for more.

[123] See *PGM* 5.145–147 (referring to Israel's God in 5.98–99; cf. Deissmann, *Light*, 142). This may, however, reflect a pagan pattern; Thoth appears as the master and embodiment of truth in *PDM* 61.74–75.

[124] B. ʿAbod. Zar. 4b, citing Prov 23:23. Painter, *John*, 46, believes that John plays on the Jewish idea of Torah as truth; cf. also Longenecker, *Christology*, 40.

[125] Potterie, "Truth," 63–64.

should believe because of his works, which testify of him (14:10–11); indeed, those who do believe would perform the same works (14:12–14).

Because one thought flows freely into another, clear breaks in this section are impossible. Jesus speaks of revealing the Father in 14:7 but is continuing a thought begun in 14:6; the "works" of 14:12–14 may include in some sense the "commandments" of 14:15, but the occurrence of commandments here parallels 14:21, 23–24 and in all these instances obeying the commandments may function as a prerequisite for receiving or maintaining the activity of the Spirit.

### 1. Seeing the Father in Jesus (14:7–9)

So thoroughly is Jesus the way to the Father that he is the Father's exact representation (14:9; cf. 12:45; Heb 1:3); rejecting the Father's image meant rejecting the Father as well (15:24). Although one might cite a few late sources suggesting that approaching a scholar full of Torah was analogous to approaching God,[126] the image evokes more common, hence more probable, sources. Moses reflected God's glory, but in the Fourth Gospel it is more often the disciples than Jesus who parallel Moses seeing God's glory (1:14; 14:8; cf. 2 Cor 3:7–18; though cf. John 6:46). Most clearly, wisdom was the exact representation of God's glory,[127] and Jesus fulfills this place in the Fourth Gospel (1:1–18, esp. 1:18). No one, including Moses, beheld God's full glory until Jesus (1:18); in Jesus, however, God had come unveiled. "From now on" (14:7) suggests that the climactic revelation of God in Jesus comes in his "glorification," beginning with the cross (13:31).[128]

Philip's question, like questions and objections in Socratic dialogues, provides the foil for advancing the explanation. John reports the words of several disciples in this section, including some featured much less in the Synoptic line of tradition: Thomas (14:5; cf. 11:16; 20:24–28; 21:2), Philip (14:8–9; cf. 1:43–46; 6:5–7; 12:21–22), and Judas not Iscariot (14:22). Writers and haggadists sometimes added names to traditions to make them more vivid;[129] but the consistent details of names in this section could also suggest a tradition based on recollections by an eyewitness. Thus Xenophon reports the names of troops who died when these were members of his own command, details not characteristic of the parts of his narrative where he was less likely to know the names of the soldiers.[130]

Philip's request that Jesus "show" them the Father (14:8) might echo the typical language of a rhetorical challenge seeking a demonstration.[131] More likely, however, he seeks a theophany, probably evoking Moses' request to see God's glory (δεῖξόν μοι τὴν σεαυτοῦ

---

[126] Marmorstein, *Anthropomorphism*, 104, citing *Tanḥuma*, ed. Buber, 2.115; for Cleanthes as the very "image" of his teacher Zeno, see Seneca *Ep.* 6. In 1397, Profiat Duran (Isaac ben Moses Halevi) claimed that this verse in John indicated intimacy with God but not divinity (Lapide, *Hebrew*, 40).

[127] Cf. Wis 7:24–27; Philo *Confusion* 97, 147; *Dreams* 1.239; 2.45; *Drunkenness* 133; *Eternity* 15; *Flight* 101; *Heir* 230; *Planting* 18; *Spec. Laws* 1.81; Col 1:15; Heb 1:3; see further comment on the prologue.

[128] Interestingly, in one strand of extant passion material, Jesus announced with such language that the world would see his glory at the Parousia (Matt 26:64; Luke 22:69; omitted in Mark 14:62); this illustrates John's emphasis on realized eschatology (cf. Rev 14:13) and the disciples.

[129] *Jub.* 11:14–15; *Liv. Pro.* 19 (Joad) (§30 in Schermann's Greek text); Josephus *Ant.* 8.231; *L.A.B.* 40:1. This may be the implication of Plutarch *Alex.* 20.4–5.

[130] Xenophon *Anab.* 4.1.18. Similarly he recalls the name of a hoplite who defended him (4.2.21) and a soldier who opposed him (3.4.47–49).

[131] Δεῖξον in Epictetus *Diatr.* 1.4.13; 1.11.8; 3.24.75; perhaps Jas 2:18; John 2:18.

δόξαν, Exod 33:18 LXX).[132] (The wording differs in Philo, who also emphasizes the event.)[133] One could also speak of God "manifesting" himself to others;[134] thus, according to Philo, God only became manifest (ἐμφανής) to Abraham when he gained true understanding.[135] But a specific allusion to Moses fits John's theology (1:14). Philo declares that Moses, as God's son, sought to see God as his father (i.e., creator) but could see only God's glory;[136] also that Moses was not satisfied with any reflection of God in his creation but became the supreme illustration of a mind pursuing full vision and knowledge of God.[137] John's circle of believers probably understood such revelation at least sometimes in apocalyptic, visionary terms (Rev 1:1; 4:1; 17:1; 21:9–10; 22:1, 6).[138] The model for receiving such revelation was Jesus himself, to whom the Father "showed" his works; Jesus then followed his Father's example by showing these works to others (2:18; 10:32; 20:20).

Philip's request not only evokes the account of Moses but also reflects the assumption that Jesus had access to God's glory, which he could in turn reveal to others, a true premise in Johannine theology (3:13, 32; cf. Q material in Matt 11:27; Luke 10:22). Viewing Jesus as the mediator of divine revelation was true Christology, but by itself it was inadequate; other recipients of revelations also showed the contents of their revelation to their circles (e.g., *1 En.* 83:1, 10).

## 2. Doing the Father's Works (14:10–11)

To see Jesus is to see the Father not as if Father and Son are the same person (see 1:1b) but because they are one (10:30), and here because they dwell in one another so thoroughly, and Jesus remains so utterly dependent on the Father's will,[139] that their character is indistinguishable, as his works demonstrate (14:10). To a lesser extent, Jesus' followers will also reflect his glory by reflecting the divine character of unity produced by Jesus' indwelling presence (17:23; cf. 14:20). The way to develop that intimacy is to keep his commandments (15:10; cf. 8:29; 11:42; 1 John 3:22).

As in the exodus tradition, divine signs attest the identity of the true Lord.[140] Jesus summons them to believe even if initially only because of the works (14:11). Early Judaism would have grasped the principle of pursuing a goal even if not for its own sake, recognizing that one would ultimately end up pursuing it for its own sake.[141] Indeed, within a

---

[132] E.g., Bernard, *John,* 2:540; Hanson, *Gospel,* 179. The eight uses of δείκνυμι in Revelation are apocalyptic, but many of the seven uses in John are visible to the eye (5:20; 10:32; 20:20), suggesting a request for a visible theophany (Boice, *Witness,* 33–34). Cf. pagan petitions for the invisible supreme deity to make himself manifest (Plutarch *Isis* 9, *Mor.* 354D).

[133] In Philo *Spec. Laws* 1.41 and *Posterity* 16, Moses' request becomes, ἐμφάνισόν μοι σαυτόν; Philo may have also viewed Moses' prophetic ecstasy as milder than Abraham's or Balaam's (Levison, "Prophecy in Philo"). For Israel's desire to see God at the giving of the law, see, e.g., *Exod. Rab.* 41:3.

[134] For Philo, one could see God only if God manifested himself (*Abraham* 80; cf. *Posterity* 16); cf. Wis 1:2 (God ἐμφανίζεται himself to those who do not disbelieve him).

[135] Philo *Abraham* 77.

[136] Philo *Spec. Laws* 1.41, 45.

[137] Philo *Alleg. Interp.* 3.100–101.

[138] DeConick, *Mystics,* 69–73, thinks that John 14:3–7 polemicizes against vision mysticism; she argues the same for John 14:20–23 on pp. 73–77.

[139] For the Son acting only at the Father's will, see further comment on 5:19, 30. "The words I speak to you" reflects consistent Johannine idiom (6:63).

[140] Lacomara, "Deuteronomy," 68–70.

[141] E.g., R. Huna, on study of Torah (*p. Ḥag.* 1:7, §3; *Pesiq. Rab Kah.* 15:5).

century after the Fourth Gospel's completion, some teachers felt that God told Israel in the wilderness that even if they would not believe God's promises concerning the future, they should at least believe what he had already accomplished for them.[142] See further the comments on 10:25, 38; cf. 15:24.

### 3. Disciples Doing the Same Works (14:12–14)

Comparison was a standard rhetorical technique,[143] but scholars debate the meaning of "greater works" in 14:12. (All are agreed that Jesus does not imply that the disciples themselves will be greater than Jesus; see 13:16.) Various options must be considered. Some suggest, for example, that it indicates the Gentile mission.[144] Others apply it to Jesus' ministry—for instance, continuing his ministry of healing and salvation through the church's sacraments.[145] One can make a particularly strong case for miraculous signs; certainly the early Christians believed that miraculous gifts continued in their day,[146] and as late as the fifth century, Theodore of Mopsuestia, not given to credulity, attests continuing miracles.[147] Because healings in this Gospel function as "signs" glorifying Jesus, it is natural to expect that John intended the reports of Jesus' signs as paradigmatic for his own audience doing signs to reveal Jesus' authority.[148] Which meaning of "greater works" best fits this context?

### 3A. The Meaning of "Works" (14:12)

A survey of Jesus' "works" in the Fourth Gospel will indicate that these may include miraculous signs (5:20, 36; 7:3; 9:3–4; 10:25, 32–33, 37–38; 15:24) but also his mission as a whole (4:34; 17:4). One might also apply the term to Jesus' ethical deeds (3:19–21; 7:7; 8:39, 41).[149] Thus Jesus might refer to his followers multiplying his righteous acts because there would be more of them to do them;[150] thus "keeping commandments" in 14:15 may include doing the Father's "works," because "works" in this Gospel includes doing God's will.

But the ethical nuances, while probably present, are probably not primary here. The "commandments" of 14:15 match more properly the line of thought in 14:21, 23–24, where they function as prerequisites for more fully acquiring or maintaining Jesus' presence, suggesting that 14:15 has more to do with 14:16–17 than with 14:12–14. In John most ethical uses of the term apply to others besides Jesus, who "works" in this context, and the immediate context is probably one of miraculous works (14:10–11), for it echoes 10:32, 37–38, which probably reflects Jesus' recent healing of a man born blind (9:3–4). Jesus had done many signs (20:30), and the world itself could not contain them all (21:25), but somehow his followers could do more works, whether by virtue of their numbers or the new state in salvation history.

---

[142] *Sipre Deut.* 25.6.1.

[143] E.g., Aristotle *Rhet.* 2.20.4, 1393b; see further Anderson, *Glossary,* 110–11, and sources there (esp. Quintilian 9.2.100–101).

[144] Jeremias, *Promise,* 38.

[145] Richardson, *Theology,* 360.

[146] See, e.g., Kydd, *Gifts;* Irvin and Sunquist, *Movement,* 145–47; Shogren, "Prophecy"; sources in Schatzmann, *Theology,* 82 n. 40.

[147] Swete, *Discourse,* 29.

[148] With Hays, *Vision,* 143.

[149] Some texts provide a bridge from miraculous to ethical works (6:28–29).

[150] Cf. Swete, *Discourse,* 29.

Thus disciples should do miraculous works through faith (though such signs by themselves cannot produce adequate faith and must be supplemented with proclamation, which remains central; cf. 20:29) as well as continue Jesus' ministry in other respects. This idea is consonant with the disciples joining the Spirit as witnesses (15:26–27) and the Spirit presenting the living Christ through their word (16:7–11); in short, disciples would reflect the life of Jesus present in them the way branches revealed the life of the vine (15:1–8). The reason for "greater" works may be debated. Some contend that the works are greater because Jesus worked in only one land whereas his followers work everywhere;[151] or that the work would be multiplied because no longer confined to one person's ministry;[152] or because the disciples participate in the newer and greater phase of redemptive history after the completion of Jesus' earthly work ("because I go to the Father").[153] In any case, "greater" works imply greater magnitude than one has seen in Jesus' earthly ministry (for this sense of "greater magnitude," see the parallel language of 1:50 and 5:20). The promise of "greater works" calls John's audience to look not only backward but also to the present, where Christ continues to remain active through his presence by the Paraclete and his proclaimed word.[154]

More miracles are reported of Elisha than of Elijah, which may supply part of the paradigm for Jesus' going in this context (cf., on the Paraclete as Jesus' successor, the comment on 14:16);[155] this is more explicit in Acts 1:8–11, which recalls the clearest OT ascension narrative as well as the impartation of the prophetic spirit in 2 Kgs 2. In view of John 14:13–14 and its possible invitation to ask for the Spirit (14:16), it is significant that in 2 Kgs 2:9 Elijah invites Elisha to "ask what he wills," and he requests Elijah's "spirit."

### 3B. Prayer in Jesus' Name (14:13–14)

The meaning of prayer "in Jesus' name" here (14:13; 15:16; 16:23–24) requires comment.[156] Practitioners of magic often employed name invocation,[157] and magical papyri attest the special proficiency of Jewish magicians who claimed access to the hidden name of God (cf. Acts 19:13–20).[158] Once one acquired an "angel's" name, one could offer sacrifice and become his friend,[159] and then the angel would do all sorts of magic for the person.[160] But the magical use is hardly in view here, where Jesus invites disciples to ask

---

151 Bernard, *John*, 2:543; cf. Luther, *Sermon on John 14.*

152 Thus Socrates multiplied his influence through disciples, Xenophon *Mem.* 1.6.15; cf. 2 Tim 2:2.

153 Carson, *Discourse,* 42; cf. Augustine *Tr. Ev. Jo.* 72.3.2.

154 Dietzfelbinger, "Werke." On Jesus' activity as a broker or mediator, see more extended comment on 15:15.

155 Ancients might attribute miracles to disciples of miracle workers, though usually somewhat less dramatically (Iamblichus *V.P.* 28.135; *p. Taʿan.* 3:8, §2).

156 Cf. Gabriel praying in God's name (*1 En.* 40:6).

157 *PGM* 1.160–161, 167, 216–217; 12.316; Lucan *C.W.* 6.732–734; Apuleius *Metam.* 2.28; 3.29. Pulleyn, "Names," however, doubts that Greek religion attached magical efficacy to name invocation of its gods.

158 For the sacred name of Israel's God, Incant. Text 20.11–12; 69.6–7; *CIJ* 1:485, §673; 1:486, §674; 1:490, §679; 1:517, §717; 1:523, §724; 2:62–65, §819; 2:90–91, §849; 2:92, §851; 2:217, §1168; *T. Sol.* 18:15–16; *Pr. Jos.* 9; *b. Giṭ.* 68ab; *Num. Rab.* 16:24; also revelatory texts in Scholem, *Gnosticism,* 32–33. For Jewish support of, and opposition to, magic, see sources in Keener, *Spirit,* 29–30 n. 21.

159 *PGM* 1.168–172. Contrast the emphasis on obedience in John's context.

160 *PGM* 1.172–190.

both himself and his Father in his name; early Christians in fact repudiated that use of Jesus' name (Acts 19:13–20).[161]

Aside from magic, one might compare this passage with various strands of Greek and Roman prayer practices.[162] In many cases pagans piled up multiple names of the deity they were entreating,[163] apparently hoping that at least one would prove effective.[164] Roman magistrates read prayers exactly as they had been handed down through tradition; "if one syllable or one ritual gesture was performed incorrectly, the prayer might well be invalid."[165] If during a sacrifice a priest's hat fell off, this disqualified him from the priesthood (Valerius Maximus 1.1.5), and if games were marred, deities could demand the games be done over (Valerius Maximus 1.7.4). Pagans also reminded a deity of favors owed, seeking an answer on contractual grounds, as many classical texts attest.[166] Israel's God was more apt to respond to moral obedience than to sacrifice, however, and it is obedience that this context emphasizes (14:15).

More likely, praying "in one's name" might evoke praying "on the merits of" or because of another's status before the one entreated. Thus the patriarchs had earned Israel favor before God, and they could seek God's favor on account of their ancestors' favor (Exod 32:13; Deut 9:27; 2 Chr 6:16–17).[167] Biblical tradition was clear that God answered the prayers of the righteous (e.g., Ps 34:15–18; Prov 15:8, 29; 21:27; 28:9)[168] and the repentant (2 Chr 7:14; Neh 1:6); but God in his mercy often showed favor to the descendants of the righteous (Deut 9:5), and prayer "in Jesus' name" could mean prayer predicated on his merit alone. (Some also find the background for "in his name" in the biblical tabernacle traditions; one praying in or toward God's house would secure an answer to prayer.)[169]

A related proposal draws on the ancient Mediterranean role of a broker;[170] patrons could write letters of recommendation to procure for their clients favors from other members of the elite, and others could use their favor as agents to secure favor for others as well. For example, a prince in the king's special favor might secure whatever he asked for

---

[161] Though in a later period, Christian magical syncretism also appeared (see, e.g., Gitler, "Amulets").

[162] Some were against petitionary prayer (Van der Horst, "Maximus"), but this was surely the exception.

[163] E.g., Homer *Il.* 1.37–38, 451–452; 2.412; *PGM* 4.2916–2927; Cleanthes' *Hymn to Zeus;* more restrained, *ILS* 190; cf. *Apoc. Zeph.* 6:7; *Apoc. Ab.* 17:8, 13. Garland, *Matthew,* 79 notes that after Catullus piles up titles of Diana, he concludes, "whatever name you prefer" (*Poems* 34).

[164] Burkert, *Religion,* 74.

[165] Stambaugh and Balch, *Environment,* 129; cf. also Plutarch *Cor.* 25.3; *Camillus* 5.7 (concerning Roman rituals); Jeffers, *World,* 90; Aune, "Religion," 919–20, 923; in the rabbis, cf. *p. Ber.* 1:5, §5.

[166] E.g., Homer *Il.* 1.39–41; 10.291–294; *Od.* 1.61–62, 66–67; 4.762–764; 17.240–242; Apollonius of Rhodes 1.417–419; Virgil *Aen.* 12.778; cf. also Maximus of Tyre, who reports the first *Iliad* example (*Or.* 5.2) but rejects its literal plausibility (5.3). When sacrifices did not achieve their effect, people might complain they were in vain (Alciphron *Farmers* 33 [Thalliscus to Petraeus], 3.35, par. 1); Zeus was too busy elsewhere (par. 2).

[167] See comments on John 8:33–39; for the efficacy of Abraham's intercessory prayer, see *T. Ab.* 14:8; 18:10–11A; 1QapGen 20:16, 28–29, though many religious figures shared this power (Harrington, "Abraham Traditions," 171).

[168] Also in early Judaism, e.g., *Let. Aris.* 192; *Pesiq. Rab.* 23:9; cf. John 9:31.

[169] E.g., Lacomara, "Deuteronomy," 80; Dowd, "Theology," 333, because believers are "in the Father and the Son." Compare "in the name" with being "in" Jesus (Westcott, *John,* 204, citing 6:56; 14:20; 15:4–7; 16:33; 1 John 5:20).

[170] See Malina and Rohrbaugh, *John,* 235 (on 15:12–17); DeSilva, *Honor,* 97–98, 137.

his friends.[171] Given the loving intimacy between the Father and the Son in this Gospel, the reader is secure that with Jesus as the agent or the one in whose name disciples ask, their request will be answered. This assumes, however, that they, too, have a close relationship with the Son.

In earlier biblical usage, "name" often connoted reputation, so that when God acted "on account of his name," he defended his honor, a matter readily understood in the ancient Mediterranean with its emphasis on honor and shame. "In God's name" could signify a representative acting on God's behalf (Exod 5:23; Deut 18:19–22; Jer 14:14–15), according to his command (Deut 18:5, 7), by his help (Ps 118:10–11; Prov 18:10), or using his name for a miraculous act (2 Kgs 2:24). In prayer, which might suit this context (John 14:13), calling on the deity's name meant addressing him (1 Kgs 18:24–26, 32; 2 Kgs 5:11; Ps 9:2; 18:49); similarly, in 1 Chr 16:2, when David blessed the people in the Lord's name, he apparently was calling on the Lord to bless them. That various early Jewish circles could employ "name" as a polite surrogate for pronouncing the divine name also fits this usage.[172] Which of these usages (or what combination of them) is in view here, given John's general usage?

Most likely, asking "in his name" signifies asking "as his representative, while about his business," just as Jesus came in his Father's name (5:43; 10:25).[173] It involves prayer "in keeping with his character and concerns and, indeed, in union with him."[174] This usage ("in the name of" meaning "as one's representative") was common[175] and fits the context (14:26; 15:21; cf. 15:26–27). (Later rabbis also spoke of passing on traditions in another's name, i.e., on another's authority, e.g., *m. ʾAbot* 2:8.)[176] Jesus' promise, "I will do it" (14:13), may well echo God's word to Moses in Exod 33:17;[177] this epitomizes the apparent paradox of Johannine Christology: like the Father, Jesus answers prayer (14:13–14), but the Father's rank remains superior, so that the Father is glorified in the Son (14:13).[178] Such prayer naturally implied desiring the sort of thing that Jesus would desire—hence praying, as best as one knows, according to God's will (cf. 1 John 5:14).

Some other thinkers in antiquity also recognized that people often prayed for what was not best from the divine perspective;[179] they regarded prayer as conversation with the

---

[171] Xenophon *Cyr.* 1.4.1; cf. *Apoll. K. Tyre* 17; a member of the household normally had special access (John 8:35). Alexander reportedly encouraged people to ask boldly, depending on his generosity (Plutarch *Alex.* 39.3–4; cf. Ps.-Callisthenes *Alex.* 2.21; 3.6). Objects of such favor were always selective; e.g., people might grant any special requests to heroes (Hermogenes *Issues* 81.5–23; Libanius *Declamation* 36.13); one ruler invited his teacher to request whatever he wished (Musonius Rufus 8, p. 66.28–29).

[172] *1 En.* 6:3 (if Semyaza means "he sees the Name"); perhaps 1 Chr 13:6 LXX; Jeremias, *Theology,* 10; Longenecker, *Christology,* 43; Bietenhard, "ὄνομα," 268–69. Bonsirven, *Judaism,* 7, cites *m. Ber.* 4:4; *Yoma* 3:8.

[173] Sanders, *John,* 324, comparing also Acts 3:6, 16; 4:10; 16:18; also Schnackenburg, *John,* 3:73; Malina and Rohrbaugh, *John,* 247–48.

[174] Whitacre, *John,* 355, citing Augustine *Tr. Ev. Jo.* 73.3. Augustine also notes that one receives what one asks only if one does not ask wrongly (*Tr. Ev. Jo.* 73.1.1, citing Jas 4:3).

[175] E.g., as a messenger of God (Deut 18:19–20; *1 En.* 10:2) or another (1 Sam 25:9).

[176] To speak "in God's name" could, however, simply mean to speak as one loyal to him (*Jos. Asen.* 9:1 in light of ch. 8; cf. Acts 4:17).

[177] Dowd, "Theology," 334.

[178] Berg, "Pneumatology," 152. By contrast, Lee, *Thought,* 256, suggests that "in the name" represents a Hebraism for prayer addressed to Jesus; but the texts themselves also speak of prayer to the Father in Jesus' name (16:23, 26).

[179] Valerius Maximus 7.2.ext.1a; Maximus of Tyre *Or.* 5 passim (e.g., 5.1, Midas's prayers); Diogenes Laertius 2.136; 6.2.42; *Sent. Sext.* 88.

gods rather than petition[180] and opined that deities would reward the deserving whether or not they prayed.[181] An analogous emphasis on intimacy with God did not lead early Christians, however, to avoid praying for themselves as it led some ancient thinkers to do.[182] Nor did Christians likely expect, as in some myths,[183] that their deity would grant destructive gifts for which they wrongly asked in their ignorance. As in early Judaism, right motives in prayer mattered.[184]

That anything believers ask in Jesus' name would be granted far exceeds the more specialized guarantees attached to most magical charms.[185] Such guarantees of answered prayer appear in early Jewish texts but are unusual.[186] For the most part, such broad expectations of answered prayer apply to special pietists such as Honi the Circle-Drawer or Hanina ben Dosa, with their Elijah-like faith; but the Jesus tradition invites all believers to that level of bold faith (Mark 11:23–24; Matt 7:7–11; Luke 11:8–13), a confidence continued in early Christianity (Jas 5:16–18; cf. Heb 4:16).[187] The Johannine circle of believers is no exception (15:16; 1 John 3:22); for them, the Gospel provides models of prayers through the confident example of Jesus (11:41–42; 17:1–26). Perhaps the primary object of asking, under which other enablements are subsumed, is the Holy Spirit, which Jesus will request for them (14:16, admittedly with a different term for asking) as in Luke 11:13's adaptation of Q (a more traditional form of which appears in Matt 7:11).[188]

The intimacy in prayer implied in this image would have appealed to many people in the ancient Mediterranean world on a popular level. As major cults became more formal during the first three centuries of the common era, many people turned toward noncultic religious expressions, such as oracles, for emotional attachment, with a corresponding shift from primarily communal to primarily individual spirituality.[189] The Fourth Gospel, more than the Synoptics, emphasizes an individual's relationship with God rather than solely a corporate perspective.[190]

---

[180] Maximus of Tyre *Or.* 5.8. For Maximus's similarity to (though stronger rejection of petition than) the Neoplatonists in 5.9, see Trapp, *Maximus,* 41.

[181] Maximus of Tyre *Or.* 5.3.

[182] Contrast Pythagoras in Diogenes Laertius 8.1.9; Iamblichus *V.P.* 28.145 (though supporting prayer, see *V.P.* 28.137; *Myst.* 1.12, 15; 5.26); also Seneca *Nat.* 4.6.2–3; 4.7.1; asking simply for "good things" generally in Xenophon *Mem.* 1.3.2; but cf. Rom 8:26.

[183] E.g., Ovid *Metam.* 2.44–102; 3.287–298, 308–309; 11.100–105; 14.129–153; Apollodorus 3.4.3; cf. Seneca *Ep. Lucil.* 95.2, who cites as a familiar saying, "Do not ask for what you will wish you had not gotten."

[184] E.g., *Let. Aris.* 18.

[185] Goodenough, *Symbols,* 2:160.

[186] E.g., *Lev. Rab.* 16:9. One guarantee of answered prayer apparently rests on its timing (*T. Adam* 1:10, probably redacted third century C.E.).

[187] Echoes of such promises abound into second-century tradition, though sometimes offering explanations for delays (e.g., Herm. *Mand.* 9, echoing Jas 1:6–8).

[188] Cf. Porphyry *Marc.* 13.226–227 (cf. 13.227–229) on asking for God himself, and 12.209–218, on asking only for what is eternal and divine. One with secret knowledge assures his guest that he may ask whatever information he wants (Philostratus *Hrk.* 6.1) concerning the secrets of Protesilaos (5.5–6). The request here could be revelatory, but see John 14:8–9.

[189] See Lewis, *Life,* 98. Despite some perceived decline in oracular interest (Plutarch *Obsol.* passim; Parke, *Oracle,* 381), they were still widely consulted (see Collins, *Oracles,* 5; Nilsson, *Piety,* 166; Aune, *Prophecy,* 51).

[190] See Moule, "Individualism."

## Jesus' Coming and Presence by the Spirit (14:15–26)

The dwelling place in the Father's presence (14:2–3) was achieved by approaching the Father through Christ (14:4–6), who had revealed what the Father was like (14:7–9). Believers would experience the continuing presence of the Father and the Son through the Spirit, whom Jesus would impart to believers when he came to them after his resurrection. As Gordon Fee emphasizes for Pauline Christianity, so among Johannine Christians the Spirit was an experiential and not merely theoretical matter.[191]

### 1. Preliminary Questions

The structure of the passage is debatable; the major theological themes, however, appear fairly clear.

### 1A. Structure

The structure of this section is open to much debate; it is not clear that John intended any particularly discernible structure. One might propose a minor chiastic structure in 14:16–26:

> A  Another Helper with them (14:16–17)
>   B  Jesus' coming and presence (14:18–20)
>     C  Revelation to the obedient (14:21–24)
>   B′  Jesus' current presence (14:25)
> A′  The Helper will reinforce Jesus' word (14:26)

The assymetry in the length of the units makes a conscious chiasm less likely, but not impossible. But if 14:15 belongs in this section, the emphasis on obedience occurs in 14:15, 21, 23–24, which undercuts the likelihood of an intentional chiasm here.

Segovia found in 14:15–27 a cyclical repetition of three major motifs: the meaning of love for Jesus (14:15, 21a, 23ab, 24), promises to those who love Jesus (14:16–17, 21b, 23cd, 25–26), and contrasts between lovers of Jesus and the world (14:17bd, 18–20, 22, 27ac), arranged in the sequence abc, cab, cab, and abc.[192] The amount of material available may remain too small to test Segovia's proposed pattern, however. Whether his proposal represents the precise structure of the passage or not, it is clear that the basic motifs he mentions recur throughout the passage. Jewish tradition also emphasized God's reward to those who love him more than worldly treasure or life.[193] The sort of cumulative argument by repetition rather than linear development possibly found here and in 1 John also characterized some other ancient writings.[194]

---

[191] Cf., e.g., Fee, *Spirit*, 95.

[192] Segovia, "Structure," 485, followed for the most part by Berg, "Pneumatology," 117–18.

[193] E.g., *1 En.* 108:8; Sir 1:10; 31:16; *Pss. Sol.* 4:25; 1 Macc 4:33; *T. Ab.* 3:3; 17:7A; Rom 8:28; 1 Cor 2:9; cf. for the "righteous" (*1 En.* 25:7; 103:3; cf. Isa 64:4).

[194] See Trapp, *Maximus*, 237 (though sometimes repetition stems from treating a topic under various headings; cf. Dillon and Hershbell, "Introduction," 3). On the rhetorical prominence of John's repetitions in this discourse, see Kennedy, *Interpretation*, 85.

## 1B. Theology

The section heavily emphasizes love for Jesus and the association of love for him with keeping his commandments. Keeping the commandments (in the context, especially love—13:34–35) seems a prerequisite for acquiring or continuing in the activity of the Spirit. God's blessings also were often conditional on keeping his commandments, as in 14:15[195] (e.g., Exod 15:26). Early Judaism generally believed in the renewal rather than the abrogation of Torah in the end time.[196] Faith and love, the central requirements of the covenant in Deuteronomy, also appear as the basic requirements here;[197] in biblical covenant tradition, those who love God will keep his commandments (Exod 20:6; Deut 5:10; 7:9; 11:1, 13; 30:16).[198] Thus, for John as for the law, love is not mere sentiment but defined by specific content through God's commandments.[199]

Does this imply that for John the Spirit can be earned? Evidence suggests that many Jewish people thought in terms of meriting the Spirit,[200] prophecy,[201] or (sometimes interchangeably in the accounts) the divine presence;[202] Christian tradition could certainly speak of God giving the Spirit only to the people who obey him (Acts 5:32).[203] Yet by contrast, early Christian tradition, which viewed the Spirit as more widely available than did most contemporaries, often viewed it simply as an eschatological gift (Rom 5:5; Gal 3:2; cf. Ezek 36:24–27). Clearly for John the Spirit is not simply merited; apart from Jesus' presence, the disciples can do nothing (15:5), and the Spirit is received through faith (7:39). At the same time, the Spirit comes only to the disciples, to those committed to Jesus (14:17); those who obey (14:15) receive greater power for obedience (14:16–17), moving in a cycle of ever deeper spiritual maturation. For John, an initial "experience" without continuing perseverance is not ultimately salvific (15:6; 8:30–31); the Spirit comes to believers and forms them into stronger believers (on the inadequacy of initial signs-faith, see introduction) who in turn become more obedient to the life of the Spirit. God's answers to Israel were conditional on obedience (e.g., Deut 7:12), but both promise and commandments were given only to a people already redeemed by God's covenant mercy (Exod 20:2).[204]

---

[195] Windisch, *Spirit-Paraclete*, 4, thinks 14:15–17 and 14:23 are doublets and that the condition in 14:15 may represent the same saying as in 15:10. Such observations are possible, though impossible to prove or disprove at our remove.

[196] E.g., *1 En.* 108:1; see our comments on pp. 358–59.

[197] Lacomara, "Deuteronomy," 75. Some Jewish farewell discourses (e.g., *Jub.* 36) included exhortations to obey the law (see Burge, *Community*, 26, summarizing U. B. Müller). On keeping the commandments, see further Pancaro, *Law*, 431–51.

[198] Also Sir 3:15–17. Love is the highest motivation for obedience (*Sipre Deut.* 32.1.1). Cf. also "lover of the law" (φιλόνομος) or "of the commandment" (φιλέντολος) in *CIJ* 1:78, §111; 1:92, §132; 1:372, §509; cf. 1:372, §508.

[199] Barrett, *John*, 461.

[200] *M. Soṭah* 9:15; *Mek. Beš.* 7.135–137; *Sipre Deut.* 173.1.3; *ʾAbot R. Nat.* 11, §28; *b. Sukkah* 28a, bar.; *p. ʿAbod. Zar.* 3:1, §2; *Hor.* 3:5, §3; *Soṭah* 9:16, §2; *Exod. Rab.* 5:20; *Lev. Rab.* 35:7; *Song Rab.* 1:1, §9; 8:9, §3; other references in Davies, "Mekilta," 98; idem, *Paul*, 207. For the Spirit or wisdom as a gift, see, e.g., Wis 8:21; 9:17; Sir 1:10; Rom 5:5; Gal 3:2; perhaps *Sib. Or.* 4.46.

[201] Josephus *Ant.* 3.192; *b. Sanh.* 39b; see also *L.A.B.* 42:5 (God's message); *Sipre Deut.* 176.1.1 (prophets); *t. Sanh.* 4:7 (gift of Torah).

[202] E.g., *3 En.* 2:4; *ʾAbot R. Nat.* 14A; 28, §57B; *b. B. Bat.* 10a; *Soṭah* 48b; *Num. Rab.* 12:21; *Deut. Rab.* 6:14.

[203] Cf. also the Greek principle that the gods listen to whoever obeys (Homer *Il.* 1.218).

[204] God first loved his people (Deut 7:6–8) and would keep covenant with them if they obeyed (7:9–10); thus, they should obey him (7:11). For a broader Mediterranean perspective, cf. also pa-

No less striking, commentators point out, is the section's Christology, repeatedly comparing Jesus with the Father's role in earlier biblical and postbiblical Jewish tradition; the disciple follows *Jesus'* commandments (14:15, 23; 15:10);[205] they expect an eschatological, life-giving vision of him (14:19); his presence will indwell his people alongside the Father's (14:23);[206] the Spirit also appears as Jesus' gift.[207] The role of Jesus in this passage (14:12–15), while expressly distinguished from that of the Father (14:12–13), is a role attributed to God in early Jewish texts: believing in Jesus, praying to him, Jesus answering for his name's sake, and them keeping his commandments because they love him.[208] But Jesus continues to subordinate himself to the Father as well (14:24, 28).

## 1C. The Paraclete Passages in Context

The Paraclete passages fulfill a strategic function for the Gospel and therefore merit more extended comment than some others. These passages essentially reveal the Jesus of gospel history to be leading his followers in the present through his agent, the Spirit; they provide a key to understanding John's emphasis on the situation of his audience as well as how he wants his audience to apply the rest of the Gospel in their own setting.

We will endeavor to interpret the Paraclete passages (14:16–17, 26; 15:26–27; 16:7–11) in their final, Johannine context,[209] although it has often been supposed that they derived from a source different from their context and that some of them fit this context only awkwardly.[210] The figure of the Paraclete, after all, appears only in the Johannine corpus,[211] with roughly the same function throughout.[212] The unity of the first two sayings with their context is generally accepted,[213] and the Paraclete sayings use Johannine language and style.[214]

Various purposes have been proposed for John's use or composition of these pericopes. Many argue that they function to validate the Johannine tradition against heretical or persecuting opposition.[215] Gottfried Locher suggests that the "Spirit of truth" protects the

---

trons' free gifts to clients, the continuance of which depended on clients' displays of gratitude (DeSilva, *Honor,* 148).

[205] Jesus speaks of keeping his commandments, but John's verb often appears in conjunction with observing God's commandments (Brown, *John,* 2:638).

[206] The primary function of the Paraclete promise is to stress Jesus' continuing presence (Berg, "Pneumatology," 123).

[207] For the Spirit as Jesus' gift in John, see Büchsel, *Geist,* 490–98. For links between 14:13 and 14:16, see Becker, *Evangelium,* 2:464.

[208] Smith, *Parallels,* 153.

[209] As Berg, "Pneumatology," 72, points out, scholars have increasingly "recognized that the understanding of the paraclete must be centered upon the presentation in G [John] itself."

[210] E.g., Müller, "Parakletenvorstellung." Becker, *Evangelium,* 2:470–75, compares the sayings in the John 14 level with those in John 15–16.

[211] Noted, e.g., by Becker, *Evangelium,* 2:471.

[212] *Pace* Michaelis, "Herkunft," 147 (contrasting the Gospel and 1 John). Grayston, *Epistles,* 13–14, thinks John 13–17 was written in response to issues raised by 1 John; Johnston, *Spirit-Paraclete,* 61–67, finds stylistic parallels with 1 John, and (pp. 75–78) thinks that 1 John may have been drawn upon in the Gospel's composition.

[213] Berg, "Pneumatology," 100.

[214] Mussner, "Parakletsprüche," 56–59. This does not mean that they cannot derive from sources; they may even have roots in the Synoptic tradition (Dodd and Brown, in Burge, *Community,* 205–6; Sasse, "Paraklet," 276). But all extant evidence suggests that they were part of the final, circulated edition of the Fourth Gospel.

[215] This essentially follows the line of ante-Nicene interpretation, in which the Paraclete establishes the true Catholic faith; see Casurella, *Paraclete,* 3–26.

disciples from error in the metaphorically forensic situation experienced subsequent to Jesus' departure.[216] Mussner believes that the pericopes are to verify the Jesus tradition, tying the Spirit to the historical Jesus, against the challenges of the Docetists.[217] Brown writes,

> John uses the concept of the Paraclete to justify the audacity of the Johannine proclamation. If there are insights in the Fourth Gospel that go beyond the ministry, Jesus foretold this and sent the Paraclete, the Spirit of Truth, to guide the community precisely in this direction (16:12–13). Yet the Paraclete is portrayed not as speaking anything new but as simply interpreting what came from Jesus (16:13–15; 14:26).[218]

Johnston proposes to extend the insights of Barrett, Bultmann, Schweizer, and Mowinckel, who apply the Paraclete's work to apostolic preaching, "to other aspects of the life of the Johannine church in a time of danger and crisis near the end of the first century: namely, teaching, interpreting what Jesus had said, prophesying, witnessing, and doing battle with the 'world' in the law-courts of Rome or the *beth din* of the synagogues."[219]

Undoubtedly all these activities were attributed to the work of the Spirit of God, but what is significant is that these functions of the Spirit relate to the general category of the prophetic Spirit in Judaism, who speaks the truth of God. The particular characteristics attributed to the Spirit must be examined passage by passage, however (below, on each passage).

## 2. Background of the Paraclete Image

The immediate background of the Paraclete image is widely debated. Because scholars are trained to establish themselves by demonstrating the unique value of their own contributions, many of the proposals offered contradict one another less than their proponents have claimed:[220] for instance, an understanding of how early Jewish readers would have generally understood supernatural intercessors is hardly in conflict with the view that the intercessor in this case is personified Wisdom. (Nevertheless, it remains unlikely that John was specifically alluding to, say, Michael, Metatron, and Wisdom all at once.) Our discussion will draw attention to useful perspectives even where we will not conclude that the data on which these perspectives are based provide the immediate antecedents for the Johannine Paraclete.

One proposed background that we will not investigate here is that of the protognostic and Mandean "helper."[221] The suggestion of a protognostic background for the Paraclete has been severely critiqued as deficient, as an inadequate parallel offered when much better parallels could be adduced;[222] it may be added to the variety of anachronistic

---

[216] Locher, "Geist."

[217] Mussner, "Parakletsprüche," 64–70.

[218] Brown, *Community,* 28–29. Johnston, *Spirit-Paraclete,* 123–25, critiques Brown's reconstruction of the *Sitz* (uneasiness caused by the eyewitnesses' deaths and the delay of the Parousia).

[219] Johnston, *Spirit-Paraclete,* 123.

[220] O'Day, "John," 747, thinks John probably draws on all meanings, including comforter, helper, and "one who makes appeal on one's behalf."

[221] This view was proposed by W. Bauer and argued particularly by Bultmann, but even Bultmann later backed off somewhat from his identification with the Mandean "helper" Yawar; see the summary in Burge, *Community,* 10–11.

[222] Michaelis, "Herkunft," 150–62, followed by Holwerda, *Spirit,* 30–32; Barrett, "Spirit in Gospel," 11; Shafaat, "Geber," 268–69. The Jawar of Mandean myth may actually have been modeled on the Johannine Paraclete (Sanders, *John,* 330).

interpretations given to the Paraclete, such as those applied to Montanus, Mani, or Muhammad.[223] The tendency today is to seek the background for the Paraclete in Jewish sources.[224]

## 2A. Senses Related to Παρακαλέω

The relationship of the term, which frequently bears a forensic usage, to the function of the Paraclete in John has been a subject of much academic discussion. On the analogy of one sense of the cognate verb παρακαλέω and the context as a farewell discourse,[225] some scholars read the Paraclete as the "Consoler." This view is at least as old as Origen[226] and has often been held by modern commentators in opposition to the forensic sense often inferred from the term.[227] J. G. Davies argued in 1953 that since παρακαλέω in the LXX normally means "console" and replicates much of the semantic range of נחם, παράκλητος, despite the passive form, referred to an active consoler.[228]

But the passive form should not be so easily ignored, and the fact remains that the noun is used quite differently than its verbal cognate—particularly since Johannine literature nowhere employs the verb.[229] The term "comforter" in the English Bible dates from Wycliffe's translation, based on the Latin *con* + *fortis, comfortare* (one who strengthens);[230] but this is simply not the standard use of the Greek noun, which typically connotes an intercessory function. None of the functions of the Johannine Paraclete specifically refer to comfort, and the context of Jesus' departure need not imply the meaning of comfort (cf. 14:28). More significantly, 16:7 suggests that Jesus is departing in order to send the Paraclete (as Shafaat points out, would he depart to send him to console the disciples over that departure?); and finally, this reading of "Paraclete" makes no sense of the "other comforter" in 14:16: concerning whose departure had Jesus been comforting them? We may conclude that there is no evidence for taking the Johannine παράκλητος in this sense.

In 1945–1946, an article of Norman Snaith argued that "Paraclete" meant a "convincer," based on the term's etymology.[231] Although such a sense would not be unrelated to the more common forensic usage suggested below, this sense cannot be regarded as established as the most natural reading of the term, since etymology is inadequate to establish meaning (as is now generally recognized).

Others have applied the cognate παρακαλέω in such a way as to establish a connection with παράκλησις, preaching and teaching.[232] To be sure, the Spirit in this context empowers

---

[223] Bammel, "Paraklet," 214, pointing out that John was actually attempting to limit the meaning by this specific term.

[224] Brown, *John,* 2:1137–39; see, e.g., Leaney, "Paraclete."

[225] On the sense this makes in the context of a farewell discourse, see Müller, "Parakletenvorstellung," 61–62.

[226] Casurella, *Paraclete,* 3–4, noting that Origen is the first extant witness to this interpretation. Cf. "comfort [or encouragement] of the Spirit" in Acts 9:31.

[227] Scott, *Spirit,* 199–200; Riesenfeld, "Paraclete," 273. Cf. the occasional use of "Comforter" for the Messiah in Amoraic texts (*Num. Rab.* 13:5; *Lam. Rab.* 1:16, §51), probably related to the restorationist comfort language of Second Isaiah (Isa 40:1; 51:3; 61:2; 66:13; cf. Isa 12:1; 22:4; similarly Luke 2:25).

[228] Davies, "Parakleitos," 35–38, esp. 37.

[229] As noted by Sanders, *John,* 327.

[230] Stevens, *Theology,* 190.

[231] Snaith, "Paraclete," 50.

[232] Barrett, "Spirit in Gospel," 14. Franck, *Revelation,* 30–36, argues for this as a part of the sense;

the church for proclamation. Johnston argues (probably rightly) that John 14:12 shows that the Paraclete's function is to be fulfilled through (rather than independently from) the ministers of the word.[233] Although these functions are attributed to the Johannine Paraclete, they are never expressed in terms of παράκλησις, and one is again left to draw an inference from a verbal cognate while ignoring the normal sense of the noun.[234]

Several other proposals have been offered that look for functional parallels to the Paraclete concept without seeking a linguistic parallel per se. Ahmad Shafaat argues for the *Geber* ("man") of the Qumran *Thanksgiving Hymns* and *Rule of the Community* as background for the Johannine Paraclete.[235]

Eskil Franck, in a learned study, suggests that the background for the Paraclete figure, who functions as a teacher, is the meturgeman in the synagogue.[236] Although this could be part of the context for understanding the conceptual range of teaching, it fails to cover most of the functions ascribed to the Paraclete in the Farewell Discourses. It also presupposes that the meturgeman was found in the average Palestinian synagogue of the first century C.E. or perhaps even in the Greek-speaking Diaspora, a premise open to challenge.

## 2B. Forensic Interpretation of the Paraclete

Although the proposed forensic background is not the only background for the Johannine Paraclete (perhaps the most essential is, of course, the Spirit in early Judaism and Christianity), it is likely an important one.

Παράκλητος in both classical and rabbinic usage refers to an advocate, frequently[237] in a forensic context.[238] As a loanword in rabbinic texts, פרקליט appears, as Mowinckel says, "als Zeuge, Fürsprecher und Ankläger," witness, intercessor, and prosecutor.[239] It is a

---

[233] Johnston, *Spirit-Paraclete,* 136. All of this would support the contention of Schnackenburg, "Gemeinde," that the Gospel's final form advocates a function of the Spirit fitting the whole framework of early Christianity, not a theologically marginal ecstatic experience.

[234] Cf. also Holwerda, *Spirit,* 35–36; Shafaat, "Geber," 267.

[235] Shafaat, "Geber," 263–69, on 1QH 3:8–10; 1QS 4:20–23. One may note how this interpretation would sound in an Islamic context (Shafaat authored this article from Saudi Arabia).

[236] Franck, *Revelation,* 132–44.

[237] Grayston, "ΠΑΡΑΚΛΗΤΟΣ," argues that the term only means "sponsor" or "patron" and that this was sometimes used in legal contexts; cf. Johnston, *Spirit-Paraclete,* 120, who advocates the translation "representative" because of its semantic breadth. Arndt and Gingrich, *Lexicon,* 618, also says that the technical meaning of "lawyer" or "attorney" is much rarer than "mediator, intercessor, or helper"; but this may simply mean that a legal image was naturally applied to other forms of intercession. Patristic literature often uses the term for the Holy Spirit, but also simply as "*advocate, intercessor, spokesman on someone's behalf*" (Lampe, *Lexicon,* 1018–19). Liddell and Scott, *Lexicon,* 1313, gives for the classical period first the forensic and then the intercessory sense. But the line between the two senses is not easily drawn once one allows metaphorical extensions, and Holwerda, *Spirit,* 27, naturally says that Paraclete nearly "always bears the forensic meaning of advocate or intercessor"; cf. similarly Quispel, "Qumran," 146; Hunt, "Paraclete," 25, 29; Le Déaut, "L'intercession," 48–49.

[238] With, e.g., Wotherspoon, "Paraclete"; Sanders, *John,* 327; Strachan, *Gospel,* 185; Swete, *Discourse,* 38; MacGregor, *John,* 293; Hunter, *John,* 145–46; Ladd, *Theology,* 293–94; Carson, *Discourse,* 51; Potterie, "Paraklet," 85; Trites, *Witness,* 117; cf. Kobelski, "Melchizedek," 184–211; Bacon, "Comforter," 275; Hunt, "Paraclete," 25, 29. In the papyri, e.g., a second-century mime in Deissmann, *Light,* 336 n. 5; in Philo, *Joseph* 239; cf. other, often nonforensic uses by Philo in Bernard, *John,* 2:496; Hoskyns, *Gospel,* 466; for the Logos as Paraclete in Philo, see Philo *Heir* 205; Howard, *Gospel,* 161 (with no reference); Hadidian, "Philonism," 219 n. 9.

[239] Mowinckel, "Geist," 129.

synonym for סניגור, συνήγορος, which appears as the opposite of κατήγωρ, "accuser."[240] Although some Mediterranean cultures omitted that office,[241] both the official and the more common unofficial use of the role would remain widely known.[242] Rhetors could function as advocates for their friends;[243] while the image is not so specific as a friend-advocate here, the idea is consistent with the context (15:15; 16:13).

Mowinckel was apparently the first to link this Paraclete to the מליץ of Job and thus to an angelic intercessor[244] but has been followed by Johnston[245] and others.[246] This suggestion is not without its problems—including the fact that this Hebrew term is not usually rendered by παράκλητος.[247] But it has at least pointed discussion in the fruitful direction of trying to explain the combination of personal, supernatural, and intercessory/legal features of the Johannine Paraclete image.

## 2C. Angelic Advocates and Accusers

Roman law provided no public prosecutor, depending instead on *delatores,* private accusers.[248] If rabbinic texts provide a sufficient window here, Palestinian Jewish practice probably presupposes both an advocate and a prosecutor,[249] but as with the Romans, witnesses against a person constituted de facto prosecutors, and witnesses for a person constituted de facto advocates.[250] An accuser (normally κατήγωρ, as in Rev 12:10)[251] was the opposite of an advocate,[252] and on the supernatural level, Michael[253] (the most popular

---

[240] Ibid., 101–2; Glasson, *Moses,* 104–5 (citing John 5:45); Windisch, *Spirit-Paraclete,* 15 (following Billerbeck); Manns, "Paraclet," 127–31; cf. Bernard, *John,* 2:496 (following Wetstein); Lee, *Thought,* 214 (following Schlatter); Westcott, *John,* 212; Sandmel, *Beginnings,* 384; in Greek texts, e.g., Aeschines *Ctesiphon* 37 (taking the laws figuratively as advocates).

[241] Reportedly the Egyptians, lest rhetoric sway judges from the laws' severity (Diodorus Siculus 1.76.1–2). For examples of forensic rhetoric, cf. Cicero's famous defenses or the trial speeches of Isaeus, Lysias, Aeschines, or Demosthenes.

[242] E.g., P.Thead. 15.3, 19 (280–281 C.E.); Chariton 3.4.15; *Nin. Rom.* frg. 1.A.4; Plutarch *Flatterer* 20, *Mor.* 61D; *Publicola* 2.1 (συνηγορίας); *Cicero* 5.2 (συνηγορεῖν); 39.5 (βοηθοῦντος); *CPJ* 2:84, §157; cf. Epictetus *Diatr.* 1.27.15; cf. also σύμβουλος (Plutarch *Mor.* 61D; 4 Macc 15:25; cf. Moses in 4 Macc 9:2, contrasted with Antiochus in 9:3; Mattathias's successor Simeon as a military ἀνὴρ βουλῆς in 1 Macc 2:65). In Philostratus's *Heroikos* a deceased hero can become a σύμβουλος, or advisor, counselor, to his mortal clients (4.7; 14.4; 23.18; 35.1; cf. 16.2; Maclean and Aitken, *Heroikos,* xxix); in Porphyry *Marc.* 10.189 it is (figuratively) his teachings.

[243] E.g., Isaeus *Estate of Nicostratus* 1.

[244] Mowinckel, "Geist," passim.

[245] Johnston, *Spirit-Paraclete,* 99–100, 120.

[246] Ladd, *Theology,* 293; Leaney, "Paraclete," 61. Cf. the qualifications of Ross, "Lament," 45–46.

[247] Forestell, "Paraclete," 182–83.

[248] Ferguson, *Backgrounds,* 51.

[249] *Exod. Rab.* 15:29; *Num. Rab.* 10:4; *Ruth Rab.* proem 1; Blinzler, *Trial,* 135.

[250] Pancaro, *Law,* 254.

[251] A loanword in rabbinic texts, and appearing in some papyri (Deissmann, *Light,* 93); cf. 2 Macc 4:5.

[252] *B. Ḥag.* 13b; *p. Roš Haš.* 3:2, §6; *Lev. Rab.* 5:6; 21:10; 30:6. Although none of these references has an attribution before the third century, this may parallel the Greco-Roman dependence on private rather than public prosecutors (Chariton 5.4.9; *CPJ* 2:64–65, §155; Josephus *War* 1.637–638; cf. Stambaugh and Balch, *Environment,* 34; for a relevant social depiction of second-century B.C.E. Roman prosecution, see David, "Eloquentia").

[253] *B. Yoma* 77a; *Exod. Rab.* 18:5; cf. *Apoc. Sedr.* 14:1; in *2 En.* 33:10 (rec. A), Michael will be an "intercessor" for Enoch (in rec. J, a "mediator"). He may also be "the Prince of the World" (contrast

angel in early Jewish literature),[254] as Israel's defending counsel, was opposed to Samma'el, Israel's accuser.[255]

Although the degree of angelic mediation or intercession varies in ancient Jewish texts,[256] the tradition of angels in God's court helping decide cases became widespread in rabbinic circles.[257] Satan,[258] or Mastema,[259] regularly appears as Israel's accuser in early Jewish texts; by the Amoraic period, he accuses Israel continually except on Yom Kippur[260] (cf. Rev 12:10). Satan's role as prosecuting attorney, of course, is as old as the book of Job, where *ha-Satan* is a title designating the accuser.[261] This is illustrated in many Jewish texts, some of them associated with the angels of the nations that opposed Israel in the heavenly

John 12:31; 14:30; 16:11), who defends the world before the Holy One (*3 En.* 30:2), and the angel who intercedes for Israel (*T. Levi* 5:6; he struggled with Jacob in *Tg. Ps.-J.* on Gen 32:25). Cf. Betz, *Paraklet,* 149–58, for one study on Michael as intercessor.

[254] From his role in Daniel, it was clear that he was among the chief angels (*1 En.* 9:1; 54:6; *3 En.* 17:1–3; *3 Bar.* 11:2; 1QM 8.15–16; *Sib. Or.* 2:214–220; *Gen. Rab.* 78:1; *Lam. Rab.* 3:23, §8; *Pesiq. Rab.* 46:3; cf. *1 En.* 40:9; *b. B. Meṣiᶜa* 86b; *Deut. Rab.* 5:12; *Song Rab.* 2:4, §1; 6:10, §1; *Pesiq. Rab.* 21:9; Coptic charm in Goodenough, *Symbols,* 2:174–88), sometimes *the* chief angel (*2 En.* 22:6; 33:10; probably *T. Ab.* 1:13A, 2:1, 13–14 and passim A; 4:6; 14:7B), perhaps even the angel of the Lord (*Exod. Rab.* 2:5; *Pesiq. Rab.* 40:6; cf. *L.A.E.* 25:2), and in some texts he was Israel's guardian angel (*3 En.* 44:10; 1QM 17.6–7 [see further Delcor, "Guerre," 374]; cf. *1 En.* 20:5 [ed. Knibb, 107; but contrast Isaac, trans., 24]).

[255] *Exod. Rab.* 18:5; cf. *T. Sol.* 1:7; Michael vs. the wicked prince in 1QM 17.6; Michael vs. Samma'el on Moses' death, *Deut. Rab.* 11:10; Jude 9 (against Philo *Sacrifices* 8; *b. Soṭah* 13b, etc.). In the Similitudes of Enoch (*1 En.* 40:7, 9), it is Phanuel who drives away the satans (plural). In *3 En.* 14:2, it is Enoch who is the exalted one appointed against Samma'el, the Prince of the Accusers greater than all the heavenly princes; in *Esth. Rab.* 7:13 (in Montefiore and Loewe, *Anthology,* 98–99), Moses in heaven and Mordecai on earth interceded for Israel against Satan the accuser; in *Exod. Rab.* 43:1, Moses and Satan oppose one another before God's court; in 2 Macc 15:12–14 Onias the deceased high priest and Jeremiah the prophet intercede for the people. God could also appear as an accuser (Marmorstein, *Names,* 78), but not of Israel.

[256] Angelic intercession appears in Tob 12:12, 15; *1 En.* 9:2–11; 40:6, 9; 99:3; 104:1; Rev 5:8; 8:3; *3 Bar.* 14:2; *Apoc. Mos.* 33:5; *T. Levi* 5:6; Dan 6:2 (if not interpolation); cf. *1 En.* 15:2; *T. Ab.* 9:3, 7A; Russell, *Apocalyptic,* 242; Montefiore, *Hebrews,* 39–40. Montefiore, "Judaism," 47, thinks they rarely functioned as mediators in rabbinic Judaism (cf. *Midr. Pss.* 4, §3), and Moore, "Life," 249, shows how this contrasted with Platonic Hellenism; but less "orthodox" texts show the popularity of angelic invocations (Smith, "Note"; Deissmann, *Light,* 455–57; Goodenough, *Symbols,* 2:174–88; *CIJ* 2:90–91 [sixth century C.E.]; 2:91, §850 [no date]; 2:109, §876; 2:373–374, §1448 [amulet, late third century]; cf. *JE* 1:588, 595); the divergent data is balanced well in Longenecker, *Christology,* 29–30; Bonsirven, *Judaism,* 37.

[257] E.g., *p. Roš Haš.* 1:3, §28; *Qidd.* 1:9, §2 (Tannaitic attribution); *Exod. Rab.* 31:14; *Pesiq. Rab.* 10:9 ("according to our Masters"); see Moore, *Judaism,* 1:406–7. Cf. *3 En.* 28:8–9; for accusing angels opposing the wicked, *t. Šabb.* 17:3; *ᶜAbod . Zar.* 1:18 (attributed to the same rabbi); *Apoc. Zeph.* 3:8; 6:17. These could be the same as the ministering angels, as in *3 En.* passim; *b. Ber.* 20b; *p. Sanh.* 10:2, §7; *Gen. Rab.* 55:4; *Pesiq. Rab Kah.* 24:11. In *3 En.* 4:6–7, three accusing angels come against Enoch, but in 4:8–10 Enoch is exalted over them by God's favor. Later Jewish Christianity portrayed the Paraclete in an angelic role; see Daniélou, *Theology,* 130.

[258] *Gen. Rab.* 38:7; 84:2; *Lev. Rab.* 21:10; *Eccl. Rab.* 3:2, §2. In *b. Sukkah* 52b, the evil *yetzer* tempts in this world, and in the world to come testifies against those he has seduced.

[259] *Jub.* 48:15–16. He appears as Beliar in *Jub.* 1:20; cf. Driver, *Scrolls,* 488, for parallels in the Scrolls. Prince Mastema in *Jub.* 17:15–18 acts just like Satan in Job.

[260] *B. Yoma* 20a; *Lev. Rab.* 21:4; *Num. Rab.* 18:21; *Pesiq. Rab.* 45:2; 47:4. This is predicated particularly on the numerical value of *ha-Satan:* 364.

[261] Cf., e.g., Trites, *Witness,* 171; Kelly, *Peter,* 209; Selwyn, *Peter,* 236; Ladd, *Theology,* 49 n. 15.

court: "Every day Satan sits with Samma'el, Prince of Rome, and with Dubbi'el, Prince of Persia, and they write down the sins of Israel on tablets and give them to the seraphim to bring them before the Holy One, blessed be he, so that he should destroy Israel from the world." But because the seraphim know God's will, they burn the tablets.[262] Commentators frequently see such a legal opposition between Michael as advocate and Satan as accuser in Rev 12:10–11 and context.[263]

Other intercessors besides Michael existed, although this is more prominent in our later texts. The Torah could serve as an intercessor against Satan (in some late texts),[264] although, like the Attribute of Justice,[265] it could also accuse Israel when she sinned.[266] Merits of the patriarchs also served an intercessory function in Amoraic texts.[267] A good deed (e.g., a lulab cluster) could testify on one's behalf at the Judgment; but if one had gotten it by robbery, this advocate would instead become an accuser.[268] One may compare the oft cited[269] phrase in ʾAbot 4:11:[270] "He who does one precept gains for himself one advocate [*peraqlit*]; and he who commits one transgression gains for himself one accuser."

In *m. ʾAbot* 4:22 God is judge, witness, and accuser at the Judgment;[271] redemption (Lam 3:58) and vindication by the prosecution of one's adversaries (Jer 51:10, 36) are related concepts, and the Spirit-Paraclete is not the first figure in Jewish texts to collapse these roles, which we would regard as distinct in our own culture.[272] In Job 16:19–21, God is Job's witness who can defend him before himself.[273] Amoraim could observe, "In human courts, two stand before the king, one acting as prosecutor and the other as defender; he who acts as an accuser does not act for the defence, while he that defends does not prosecute. Not so, however, is it in the case of God. He Himself both defends and accuses."[274] R. Hiyya bar Abba said that when Moses had finished defending Israel, the Holy Spirit pleaded on their behalf;[275] R. Aibu claimed that Israel's "advocate among the nations" was

---

[262] *3 En.* 26:12, *OTP* 1:281. The nations prosecute Israel in *Ruth Rab.* proem 1.

[263] Caird, *Revelation*, 154; Ford, *Revelation*, 206.

[264] *Exod. Rab.* (Yithro) 29:4–5; 31:2.

[265] E.g., *b. Meg.* 15b; cf. *Lev. Rab.* 23:2; *Pesiq. Rab.* 15:17; it is frequently opposed to the Attribute of Mercy, both of which regularly argue their case before the Throne (*b. ʿAbod. Zar.* 3b; *Gen. Rab.* 39:6; *Pesiq. Rab Kah.* 16:4; 19:3; cf. *Sipra VDDeho. par.* 12.65.2.4; *Sipre Num.* 8.8.2; *Sipre Deut.* 26.5.1; 323.4.1; *b. Ber.* 7a; *p. Taʿan.* 2:1, §1 (Tannaitic attribution); *Gen. Rab.* 12:15; 21:7; 26:6; 33:3; 73:3; 78:8; *Exod. Rab.* 3:7; 6:1, 3; 45:6; *Lev. Rab.* 29:4; *Num. Rab.* 9:18; 19:4; *Deut. Rab.* 4:3; *Eccl. Rab.* 4:1, §1; 8:1, §1; *Song Rab.* 2:17, §1; *Pesiq. Rab Kah.* 25:2; *Pesiq. Rab.* 39:1; 40:2; *3 En.* 31:1). The case of Dahl and Segal, "Name," that Philo's reversal of the rabbinic connection of divine names with judgment and mercy is earlier than the rabbis, would also suggest that the tradition of two such attributes is earlier.

[266] *B. Meg.* 15b; *Lam. Rab.* proem 24; cf. *Exod. Rab.* 31:14 (via angels).

[267] *Lev. Rab.* 29:7; *Pesiq. Rab Kah.* 23:7; 25:4. Cf. Le Déaut, "L'intercession," 49–50. This image is of course natural, given the prominence of patriarchal merit in these texts.

[268] *Pesiq. Rab Kah.* 27:6.

[269] E.g., Boice, *Witness*, 154, who cites it as 4:13.

[270] Also in *ʾAbot R. Nat.* 35, §80.

[271] Elsewhere God bears witness on behalf of the righteous (*4 Ezra* 7:94). Cf. the common image of God also as "helper" (βοηθός) more generally, e.g., Jdt 9:11.

[272] Trites, *Witness*, 118, points out that in Isa 40–55 and Job the same person could function as both witness and advocate.

[273] See esp. Hanson, *Gospel*, 177.

[274] *Exod. Rab.* 15:29, with citations from Isaianic texts that suggest that such a combination would have been perfectly natural in the biblical period as well. Cf. also R. Johanan (early third century) in *Ruth Rab.* proem 1.

[275] *Deut. Rab.* 3:11. The Holy Spirit appears as a "helper" in the sense of one that upholds (*samak*) the righteous in the Qumran hymns (Bruce, "Spirit," 52), but this is a much broader usage

the *bat qol*.[276] Despite the lateness of these texts in relation to the Johannine period, they may illustrate that the image of God or His Spirit defending Israel before his own court probably would not have sounded strange even to Judean immigrants in John's audience.

Johansson goes beyond Mowinckel's work to compare all kinds of intercessory roles in the OT[277] and Jewish tradition.[278] This broadening provides a healthy perspective and comparative control on parallels derived solely from angelic intercessors; but Johansson also has been critiqued for drawing conclusions from parallels far too distant in themselves to carry his case.[279]

Betz, on the other hand, narrows down the background of the Paraclete too much. Arguing for the role of *Fürsprecher* (intercessor) at Qumran, he believes John blends the spirit of truth known in Qumran literature with Michael the intercessor.[280] But although Michael does appear as an intercessor in early Jewish literature and probably in Rev 12, the intercessory function was nowhere limited to him, and we cannot suppose that the first readers of the Fourth Gospel must have known the Paraclete figure to allude to him.[281] The appeal to Rev 12 and thus to John 12:31[282] may falter on another point: in this passage in Revelation, Michael's heavenly correspondence is to Christ,[283] not directly to the second Paraclete. Nor need John have been the first to combine the two images; Satan the prosecutor versus the Angel of the Lord as advocate was probably already often understood in terms of Qumran's dualism of two spirits, although not necessarily always.[284] God appointed "the Prince of Light" as Israel's "helper" [עוזרנו], and "all the spirits of truth [רוחי אמת] are in his dominion" (1QM 13.10).

Greco-Roman ideas of patronal intercession, presupposed as a matter of common knowledge in Jewish sources by the third century,[285] may have also played a part in the development of intercessory figures, particularly given the patronal roles played by guardian angels of the nations in early Judaism. The patronal idea could be, although probably is not, present in John 15:15's language of friendship, as discussed below.

---

than we are considering here. Johansson, *Parakletoi*, 84–95, seeks evidence for the Spirit as intercessor in early Judaism, but his evidence is less than impressive here, and we may wonder whether early Christianity did not develop its Spirit intercession (e.g., Rom 8:26) from its image of Christ intercession (Rom 8:34) and its experience of the Spirit.

[276] *Song Rab.* 8:9, §3.

[277] Men of God and prophets, Johansson, *Parakletoi*, 3–21; angels (in Job and Zechariah), 22–40; the intercessor as witness, way-leader, and mediator *(Mittler)*, 41–48; concept of intercessor and the servant of YHWH as a leader, 49–62.

[278] In the Apocrypha and Pseudepigrapha excluding *1 Enoch*, Johansson, *Parakletoi*, 65–95; in *1 Enoch*, 96–119; in *3 Enoch*, Midrash, and Talmud, 120–78. Le Déaut, "L'intercession," 38–45, shows how the group of intercessors was enlarged, with divergences in kind; this includes prophets, 41ff., esp. 43–44; cf. also Bamberger, "Prophet," 305.

[279] Holwerda, *Spirit*, 32–35.

[280] See Betz, *Paraklet*, 36–116; for the identification, esp. 114.

[281] See Dion, "Paraclet," 148 (review of Betz). For the breadth of the figures, besides Johansson, see Le Déaut, "L'intercession," 35–57. It is also true, as Brown notes ("Paraclete," 126), that "there is not the slightest evidence in John's picture of the Paraclete that these remote angelic origins have remained influential."

[282] Betz, *Paraklet*, 152.

[283] This image also occurs elsewhere in early Christian literature; cf. Longenecker, *Christology*, 26ff.

[284] See Cross, *Library*, 214–15.

[285] Cf. Katzoff, "*Suffragium*," 235–40.

Torah would intercede for God's people.[286] More significant may be Moses' role as advocate in some Tannaitic parables,[287] a natural image in view of Exod 32:11–14; 33:12–13; 34:9; Jer 15:1. Because Jesus is the advocate of his people before the Father (1 John 2:1; cf. John 14:16), he may assume a role some sectors of Judaism ascribed to Moses, including perhaps among the adversaries of his community (5:45).[288] The Spirit who carries on Jesus' work among humanity naturally also is an advocate (same term as 1 John 2:1, and similar meaning).

## 2D. An Advocate in John 14–16?

A forensic reading of these passages fits the trial motif throughout the Fourth Gospel[289] and is becoming increasingly popular.[290] This is, as noted above, a quite natural way to read the term "Paraclete"; the problem is that some scholars[291] find difficulty relating this as a forensic term to what appear to be nonforensic functions in the Paraclete passages.[292] Shafaat admits the forensic connection of 15:18–16:7, which is inescapable once one recognizes that synagogues (16:2) also functioned as judicial assemblies (cf. Matt. 10:17); but he does not think the Spirit is said to provide forensic help for such a situation.[293] Pancaro objects that "among the functions of the Paraclete all are found attributed to the second Paraclete *except that of intercession*" and does not see an intercessory background to the Spirit-Paraclete at all.[294]

But the imagery of the Paraclete prosecuting the disciples' persecutors—who act particularly through the synagogue courts and possibly through Roman officials—seems to me clearly present in 16:7–11, as will be articulated in more detail below. The motifs of witness and God's agent standing against the religious establishment on behalf of his true followers appear throughout the Fourth Gospel, often in the context of dispute with the Jewish authorities charging Jesus and his disciples with breaches of the Law. This is especially clear in the excommunication narrative of John 9–10, where Jesus defends his followers by prosecuting the opponents for their breach of covenant with God. The other Paraclete continues this defending activity of Jesus.

## 2E. Divine Wisdom

As early as J. Rendel Harris, it was suggested that the personality of the Spirit in the Fourth Gospel has its roots in Jewish wisdom tradition, which provides the backdrop both for the personification of the Word and for the personification of the Spirit.[295] Marie

---

[286] Harvey, "Torah," 1239 (citing *Exod. Rab.* 29:4). For the Logos, cf. Philo *Heir* 205.

[287] Johnston, *Parables*, 592. In Amoraic texts, see, e.g., *Deut. Rab.* 3:11; in the Apocrypha and Pseudepigrapha, see Hafemann, "Moses."

[288] See Pancaro, *Law*, 256–57.

[289] Burge, *Community*, 141.

[290] Holwerda, *Spirit*, i, 64; Price, "Light," 23; Hasitschka, "Parakletworte"; Turner, *Spirit*, 85–87; cf. Porsch, *Wort*, 324 (the revelation is "in einer forensischen Situation").

[291] E.g., Forestell, "Paraclete," 155.

[292] Franck, *Revelation*, 9–10, who argues (17–21) that the macrostructure context is what provides the forensic meaning.

[293] Shafaat, "Geber," 267. Isaacs, *Spirit*, 95, sees the Paraclete not as an advocate before God but as a helper to the disciples.

[294] Pancaro, *Law*, 257–58.

[295] Harris, *Prologue*, 38, especially dealing with the Pleroma of sapiential traditions, though he does not develop it sufficiently in pre-Christian texts.

Isaacs has developed this thesis in arguing for a relationship between Hellenistic Jewish Wisdom language and the Johannine Paraclete,[296] and she is not alone in her view.[297] Burge even suggests that John transfers the common Jewish image of water for wisdom or the Law to the Spirit,[298] but given the OT precedent for water as the Spirit, the contrast with ritual purification in the Fourth Gospel is sufficient explanation for the Spirit-as-water symbolism of this Gospel, as we have argued above.

What makes this thesis so appealing is that it can be demonstrated without much difficulty that personified Wisdom imagery does indeed play an important role in the Fourth Gospel and, assuming that the prologue belongs to the same Gospel in which the Paraclete sayings were written or inserted, contributes to the most basic image of Jesus as the descending divine agent. We must begin with a brief survey of modern perspectives on the personality of the Spirit and, under that heading, return to the image of the Spirit as divine Wisdom.

## 3. The Personality of the Spirit in the Fourth Gospel (14:16–17, 26)

Although many scholars have argued that John's Spirit is a power rather than a person,[299] other scholars have argued that the Spirit is a person in the Fourth Gospel.[300] Some have based their position on the masculine pronouns, which once appear, in 16:13, even where the masculine antecedent is not immediately in view.[301] But this particular argument is open to some question. It is unlikely that John is trying to refute a later, more common gnostic view that the Spirit is feminine[302] (which could blend into the notion of a female divinity);[303] given the focus of the rest of the Gospel, such a polemic is unlikely here, and the Hebrew for "spirit" is feminine in any case.[304] At the same time, it is also not clear that a masculine pronoun would need to indicate personality. Further, the indications of the Spirit's personality in earlier Jewish and biblical traditions[305] are inadequate to

---

[296] Isaacs, *Spirit*, 20–21, 52–53, 136–37.

[297] Riesenfeld, "Paraclete," 272. Franck, *Revelation*, 130–31, accepts it as part of the background, but not the whole.

[298] Burge, *Community*, 103.

[299] Scott, *Spirit*, 194; Johnston, *Spirit-Paraclete*, 122–23.

[300] See Büchsel, *Geist*, 503–4 (on the Spirit as God's nature, 504–6).

[301] Burge, *Community*, 142; Quispel, "Qumran," 147; Barrett, *John*, 91; so also Crane, *Spirit*. Berg, "Pneumatology," 214, thinks that the masculine in 16:13 may presume that the fourth Paraclete saying originally immediately preceded the fifth; but this assumes an editorial ineptness not characteristic of John's relatively consistent style. For ἐκεῖνος as "he" in John, even when referred back to an immediate antecedent, see Arndt and Gingrich, *Lexicon*, 239.

[302] In Gnosticism, see Irenaeus *Haer.* 1.2.5; *Gospel of Philip* 70–71 (*NHL* 136); Wilson, "Spirit," 352; Pagels, *Gospels*, 52–53; Daniélou, *Theology*, 81. In Mandean texts, Wilson, "Spirit," 355; in Elkesite tradition, see Hippolytus *Haer.* 9.8; Daniélou, *Theology*, 140 (despite the gnostic formulation in Hippolytus, however, a feminine interpretation of the Spirit is natural from a Hebrew reading).

[303] On a female divinity in some gnostic texts, see Kraemer, *Maenads*, 371–85.

[304] There are some indications of feminine imagery for God already in the biblical tradition (De Boer, *Fatherhood*, passim), developed further in the second-century Christian text *Odes Sol.* 19:1–7, and Jesus could be portrayed in feminine terms in *Odes Sol.* 8:14 (though cf. similarly 1 Cor 3:2 for Paul; Homer *Il.* 8.271–272; *Od.* 20.14–16), and perhaps less self-consciously in Matt 23:37; Luke 13:34. A late Amora observes that "the Holy Spirit . . . is sometimes used as masculine and sometimes as feminine" (*Eccl. Rab.* 7:27, §1).

[305] Some cite Qumran angelology (Kobelski, *Melchizedek*, 184–211; cf. Betz, *Paraklet*, 114: "Geistige Kräfte," spiritual powers, came to be treated as "himmlischer Personen," such as Belial and Michael); or, as a literary device, in rabbinic literature (Abelson, *Immanence*, 199–200, 207, 224–37;

make the case, usually failing to distinguish the Spirit from God (in Johannine language, from the Father).[306] But given the possible Christian antecedents to a personalized Spirit[307] and particularly the parallels with the personal work of Jesus,[308] the case should weigh in favor of a personal Paraclete in the Fourth Gospel despite the weakness of earlier Jewish evidence supporting this view.

Some have suggested that Wisdom may also have formed the background for John's (and probably his tradition's) personification of the Spirit.[309] To this suggestion we now turn.

### 3A. Wisdom and the Personal Character of the Paraclete

If John could draw upon Wisdom as background for his portrayal of Jesus (see our full treatment on 1:1–18), he certainly could do so also for his portrayal of the Paraclete. As in the case of Jesus, the Paraclete is portrayed as a person because the Paraclete was (or should have been) experienced personally by the Johannine community. But the personal imagery upon which John can freely draw is the imagery of divine Wisdom, which his readers may recognize because of the parallel with Jesus, who is Wisdom/Torah incarnate.

Our investigation of this motif in the background of the Paraclete will not provide the same fertile ground we found in the prologue; here there is no concerted parallelism between John's subject and divine Wisdom, and also no development in rabbinic sources from Wisdom to the Spirit to provide material from that massive body of literature for analysis. But the parallels are at least suggestive, as Harris, Isaacs, and others have already noted.

In addressing the Pleroma of sapiential tradition, Harris argued early in the twentieth century that "the Holy Spirit came into the Christian Theology through the bifurcation of the doctrine of the Divine Wisdom, which, on the one side, became the Logos, and on the other the Holy Ghost."[310] While he failed to develop any "bifurcation" adequately in pre-Christian texts, his observations concerning the relationship of the Spirit and Wisdom derive sufficient support from the LXX wisdom traditions to warrant serious consideration as important background for the personality of the Spirit where this occurs in the NT. Regarding especially the Fourth Gospel, Isaacs observes that "it is an over-simplification to talk of a 'bifurcation'":

> Whatever was to take place in later theology, no such development has taken place in the Fourth Gospel. We have already seen [pp. 122–23] that John keeps Jesus and the spirit-paraclete in the closest possible relationship. In fact it could be argued that, far from reflecting any division, John drew upon wisdom concepts precisely in order to emphasize a continuity between the ministry of Jesus and that of the spirit.[311]

---

cf. 377–79). Other scholars derive the personality from nonpneumatic (or not necessarily pneumatic) images, whether the mythical intercessor (cf. Johansson, *Parakletoi*, 305) or the Word (Forestell, "Paraclete," 194).

[306] On the weakness of this evidence, cf. Isaacs, *Spirit*, 14; the Spirit is God in Josephus and Philo (p. 25; cf. 56–57). See Hawthorne, *Presence*, 14–15, 21–22, for the Spirit as God working actively in the OT.

[307] Hahn, "Verständnis," 144; Malatesta, "Spirit/Paraclete," 540 (though not all his references demonstrate his position); Stählin, "Πνεῦμα," 242–45.

[308] Schlier, "Begriff," 265; cf. 265–68.

[309] God's Word and Spirit could coalesce in their hypostatic functions; in Jdt 16:14, God created by speaking, and by his πνεῦμα (cf. similarly Word and Wisdom in Wis 9:1–3).

[310] Harris, *Prologue*, 38. For the Spirit's relation to Wisdom, see also Witherington, *Sage*, 99–103; in the DSS, see Menzies, *Pneumatology*, 84–87; Isaacs, *Spirit*, 136–37.

[311] Isaacs, *Spirit*, 136.

Wisdom and the Spirit are paralleled in Wis 9:17:

> And who has known your counsel,
> Unless you have given [ἔδωκας] wisdom [σοφίαν],
> And sent [ἔπεμψας] his holy Spirit from above [ἀπὸ ὑψίστων]?

Thus men of earth below were taught (Wis 9:18). Wisdom will not enter a sinful person (Wis 1:4), for the ἅγιον πνεῦμα of παιδεία will flee from sin and not let it enter (1:5).

> For Wisdom is a spirit who cares for men [Φιλάνθρωπον γὰρ πνεῦμα σοφία]; . . .

> For the Spirit of the Lord fills the world [ὅτι πνεῦμα Κυρίου πεπλήρωκεν τὴν οἰκουμένην].[312]

In Wisdom is an understanding πνεῦμα, which is ἅγιον, μονογενές, and so forth (7:22), and Wisdom is the ἀτμίς, breath or vapor, of God's power (δυνάμεως) (7:25), a σύμβουλος, or counselor (8:9).

Word and Spirit are often associated in the OT and later Jewish texts,[313] perhaps reflecting the ancient Near Eastern pattern of "word" as "a power effecting what it signifies."[314] Philo identifies λόγος (and hence probably Wisdom) and πνεῦμα in many ways; there are differences in usage, so that the Spirit is what is given rather than also the agency through which it is given.[315]

There is, however, a serious weakness in the argument that John draws his imagery of the Spirit primarily from Jewish wisdom traditions. The problem with the connection is not that it occurs too rarely in early Jewish literature; given the rarity of discussions about the Spirit in this literature, this is to be expected. The problem is rather that the connection is rarely demonstrable outside Wisdom of Solomon. While John unquestionably could have drawn directly upon Wisdom of Solomon rather than upon a common portrayal of the Spirit in the milieu, one might have expected that he would have made clearer allusions to that book here (as he does, e.g., in 3:12–13) if he intended his readers to recognize this dependence. He could, for instance, have replaced his Παράκλητος with Σύμβουλος. On the other hand, he perhaps substituted the former term for the latter as more clearly connoting a forensic context (though even this term is not necessarily forensic). Nevertheless Wisdom of Solomon was both early and widespread, and may constitute a primary source for John's image here. The evidence that wisdom tradition ultimately stands behind the personhood of the Spirit in John, whether mediated through Christian tradition or (more likely) modeled after Jesus' personhood, is sufficient for one to say that it is an entirely reasonable hypothesis; it is not sufficient, on the basis of currently extant sources, to demonstrate it beyond doubt. This is especially the case if, as is likely, the parallels with Jesus are the primary direct influence on John's personalization of the Spirit. (Because John's Jesus is divine Wisdom, the Spirit would then follow some characteristics of Wisdom by virtue of the Spirit's parallel with Jesus; Wisdom of Solomon might then prove useful to John in supporting such a connection.)

3B. The Spirit's Personality and Jesus

Some scholars have rightly pointed out that most of the personal functions of the Spirit are found in parallels with Jesus' functions and that the community may have seen

---

312 Wis 1:6–7.
313 Forestell, "Paraclete," 186–87; for connections, see 186–92.
314 Ibid., 187.
315 Isaacs, *Spirit*, 54–55

the Spirit as personal primarily because they experienced the Spirit as the personal presence of Jesus or the mediator of that presence.[316] The Spirit's activity in this Gospel is especially supportive, helping the Father, the Son, John the Baptist, and others fulfill their stated functions.[317] Early Christian teachings that supplied the basis for later formulations of the Trinity[318] might also lend themselves to a development that would parallel Jesus and the Spirit.

Burge summarizes the parallels:

| Paraclete | | Christ |
|---|---|---|
| 14:16 | given by the father | 3:16 |
| 14:16–17 | with, in, by the disciples | 3:22; 13:33; 14:20 |
| 14:17 | not received by the world | 1:11; 5:53 [sic:43]; (12:48) |
| 14:17 | not known by world (only believers) | 16:3; 8:19; 10:14 |
| 14:17 | not seen by world (only believers) | 14:19; 16:16–17 |
| 14:26 | sent by the Father | cf. chs. 5, 7, 8, 12 |
| 14:26 | teaches | 7:14–15; 8:20; 18:19 |
| 15:26; 16:7, 13 | he comes (from the Father into world) | 5:43; 16:28; 18:37 |
| 15:26 | gives testimony | 5:31ff.; 8:13ff.; 7:7 |
| 16:8 | convicts the world | (3:19f.; 9:41; 15:22) |
| 16:13 | speaks not from self but from what is heard | 7:17; 8:26ff.; 14:10 |
| 16:14 | glorifies his sender | 12:28; 17:1, 4 |
| 16:13ff. | reveals, discloses, proclaims | 4:25; (16:25) |
| 16:13 | leads into fulness of truth | 18:37; 14:6 |
| 15:26; 14:17; 16:13 | is Spirit of truth/is truth | 14:6 |
| 14:16 (etc.) | a Paraclete | (14:16); 1 John 2:1 |

Admittedly, several of the references in the Jesus column are directly to the glorified Christ, but most are to Jesus' identity and mission before his glorification. The discourses are clear that the Spirit, above all else, carries on Jesus' mission and mediates his presence, as will be noted further below. The personal functions of the Spirit are also the functions of Jesus in the rest of the book, and the sensitive reader cannot miss the connection.

Although it is easy enough to show that Jesus is a witness of the Father and convicts (ἐλέγχει) his accusers in the Fourth Gospel, where is the parallel to the Paraclete's probable forensic advocacy of his people in times of trial before the world? The best parallel is probably also the most significant indicator of the *Sitz im Leben* of the finished Gospel: John 9–10.

In preceding chapters, the law of witnesses is cited in Jesus' debates with the religious authorities (chs. 5, 8), setting those debates into the context of preliminary accusations that prefigure his final trial. In John 9, the synagogue authorities exercise their judicial authority to remove a supposed apostate from the community, directly anticipating the situation of the Johannine community spelled out in 16:2. The context would clearly be understood as forensic, for even in the Diaspora the Jewish community normally had its own synagogue courts to address internal religious issues.

---

[316] E.g., Berg, "Pneumatology," 70–71; Franck, *Revelation*, 38, 83–84; Burge, *Community*, 30, 49, 142. This was also my conclusion from the primary sources before locating this view in the secondary literature.

[317] Harner, *Analysis*, 31–43, esp. 43.

[318] See, e.g., 2 Cor 13:14; Matt 28:19; Fee, *Presence*, 839–42; for the Trinity in this Gospel, see, e.g., Gruenler, *Trinity*.

Because the Spirit continues Jesus' role as advocate, we can look to earlier passages in the Fourth Gospel that exemplify Jesus' advocacy in ways the Johannine community can expect to continue in their own day. Toward the end of John 9 and through the first paragraphs of John 10, Jesus acts as an advocate: he defends the formerly blind man, representing the true sheep of Israel, and in so doing prosecutes his persecutors who claim to see (9:40–41), showing them to be thieves and robbers.[319] He thus brings both help and judgment (cf. 9:39).[320] Jesus appears as the true advocate of his people in times of oppression, and the Spirit stands in for Jesus in the time of the Johannine community, representing the risen Christ through the community to their opponents in all his prophetic force.[321] Just as Jesus brings judgment while defending his own (9:39), so the Paraclete will prosecute as well as defend (16:8–11).

Earlier in the Fourth Gospel, the writer alludes to Moses' function as advocate/accuser of Israel (5:45); but in the following chapter it is Jesus who is the agent of the Father who sends the true bread from heaven, and who is greater than Moses (ch. 6). Moses as a teacher, witness, and mediator of God's glorious revelation in Torah, and the prophet par excellence, is perhaps the most natural single OT figure whose functions are performed by the Paraclete; but these functions all derive from the character of the Johannine Jesus, who himself parallels both Moses and the Law.

### 3C. The Spirit as Jesus' Successor

The Spirit could be viewed as a successor to Jesus, as some scholars have pointed out.[322] Müller has shown the importance of a departing religious figure leaving behind documents to mediate his continued word in Jewish farewell discourses,[323] and this parallel may help provide an apology for the Fourth Gospel itself. But succession texts provide closer parallels than this between the Johannine Jesus, on the one hand, and his dual successors (the Spirit and the believing community), on the other. Designation of a successor was essential; if a leader did not designate a successor, a power struggle usually quickly filled the void of ambiguity.[324]

---

[319] Curiously, the temple pericope omits the robbers in the temple of the Jesus tradition. Perhaps the tradition was not available to John, though this is improbable; but Judas provides another model of "thief."

[320] Dodd, *Interpretation,* 414, also sees 9:35–41 as an example of Christ "prosecuting" the world as the Advocate will, although he does not develop it.

[321] "Prophetic" force or inspired speech in a forensic context need not imply the usual early Christian prophetic form, attributing direct speech to the Spirit (Acts 21:11; Rev 2:7). Some members of the audience may have known that among classical Greek aristocrats (as opposed to Romans), speechwriters often provided speeches written for the plaintiff or defendant to deliver in the first person (e.g., Demosthenes or Isaeus passim).

[322] Particularly Brown, summarized by Kysar, *Evangelist,* 128; Müller, "Parakletenvorstellung," 57–60, both citing such relationships as Moses-Joshua (cf. also Glasson, *Moses,* 85); Woll, *Conflict,* 48, 79–80; Windisch, *Spirit-Paraclete,* 5. For the continuance of Jesus' work here, cf., e.g., Carson, *Discourse,* 50; Holwerda, *Spirit,* 26–27; Mielgo, "Presencia"; Gryglewicz, "Geist"; Martyn, *History,* 148; Bornkamm, "Paraklet," 12; Isaacs, "Spirit," 402–4; Hunt, "Paraclete," 21. The presence of two paracletes in 14:16 is difficult to miss and is generally recognized (e.g., Becker, *Evangelium,* 2:471); and Bacon, "Comforter," 277 (cf. Windisch, *Spirit-Paraclete,* 22), remarks that the doctrine of heavenly and earthly paracletes is also found in Rom 8.

[323] Müller, "Parakletenvorstellung," 55.

[324] The classical example was Alexander (e.g., Arrian *Alex.* 7.26.3).

In an early-second-century tradition, the disciples of the prophets (מתלמידי הנביאים) succeeded them: Joshua and Moses, and Elisha and Elijah, though Baruch proved an exception.[325] Jacob could replace Abraham as God's seed on the earth.[326] Such paradigms, probably already implied in the OT texts, had certainly become explicit by the time in which John was writing.

Acts 1:8–11 may also imply a succession narrative, in which the Spirit succeeds the ascending Jesus as Elisha did Elijah. The parallels between Luke and Acts indicate a planned parallel between Jesus and the church moved by the Spirit who had anointed Jesus,[327] just as Peter and Paul (perhaps as representatives of the predominantly Jewish and Gentile missions) are paralleled in Acts.[328]

Plutarch's *Parallel Lives* may provide an illuminating example of Greco-Roman literary technique applied to biography to create architectonic patterns useful to teach moral lessons.[329] Plutarch did not, of course, feel that he was contriving such parallels artificially; he felt he was discovering connections already present in the fabric of nature.[330] He nevertheless admitted that he drew the parallels between figures intentionally;[331] comparisons of different figures were a natural part of rhetorical technique,[332] and although few writers made such an art of it as Plutarch, such parallels were common enough to have been recognizable to the ancient reader trained in rhetoric.[333] Jewish writers also often felt that Jewish history was perpetually being reenacted.[334] Luke's use of architectonic parallels would thus likely not have been lost on his readers.

Although John is a very different sort of work than Luke-Acts, reflecting a much more traditional Jewish world of thought and less advanced Greco-Roman rhetorical training, it is probable that his readers would have grasped the connections between the figures of

---

[325] *Mek. Pisha* 1.150–153; cf. *'Abot R. Nat.* 1 A; *'Abot R. Nat.* 1, §2 B; the *baraita* in *Pesiq. Rab.* 51:2. Joshua appears as Moses' successor also in Sir 46:1 (διάδοχος); *T. Mos.* 1:7; 10:15; and Elisha as Elijah's apparently in Sir 48:12. Some late sources imply diminution of authority (*Pesiq. Rab Kah.* 24:18).

[326] *Jub.* 19:17.

[327] Foakes Jackson and Lake, "Evidence," 182; Ehrhardt, *Acts,* 12–13; Goulder, *Acts,* 54, 61–62; cf. Gibert, "L'invention." Tannehill, *Luke,* and idem, *Acts,* points out abundant connections between and within the works. Cf. similarly the martyrdom accounts of Acts 7 and Luke 23, and *Mart. Pol.* 6–8, 19, with Jesus' triumphal entry and execution.

[328] Brawley, *Jews,* 43; he cites a German work from 1841 that had already noted many of these parallels.

[329] E.g., Pericles and Fabius Maximus, Nicias and Crassus, Demosthenes and Cicero, Alexander and Caesar, etc. On his use of sources and compositional methods, see Pelling, "Plutarch's Method." Kee, *Miracle,* 190, also compares Luke's historiography to Greco-Roman practice on this point; cf. Aune, *Environment,* 119.

[330] Plutarch *Sertorius* 1.1. Greco-Roman historians examined parallels in history as signs of a divine plan (e.g., Appian *R.H.* 7.8.53; Plutarch *Demosthenes* 3.2); see further comments on 13:23–24.

[331] Plutarch *Theseus* 1.2. The essay *Greek and Roman Parallel Stories* (*Mor.* 305A–316B), may not be genuinely from Plutarch's hand but at least demonstrates that attention was given to his method.

[332] Theon *Progymn.* 2.86–88, remarking on this in Demosthenes (cf., e.g., Plato *Sophist* 221D); on comparison (σύγκρισις) of characters, Theon *Progymn.* 10.3–4; subjects, because they can compare characters on the basis of their deeds, can be compared in the same way (10.4–7). See further comment on 13:23.

[333] E.g., Quintilian 10.1.85, comparing the Greek Homer with the Roman Virgil; Appian *C.W.* 2.21.149, comparing Julius Caesar with Alexander.

[334] Jacobson, "Visions," though contrasting Greek historiography. Examples abound in the biblical tradition, e.g., Daniel's use of Joseph motifs, and the parallel of Jeremiah's reticence at his call to Moses'.

Jesus and his successors, the Spirit and the community empowered by the Spirit. Jesus' successor in the Fourth Gospel derives some of his literary characteristics from his association with Jesus in the Gospel.

The figure of the Johannine Jesus as personified Wisdom, the Law, and a successor to Moses subsumes under itself the most likely backgrounds for the particular images of the Paraclete in the Fourth Gospel, suggesting a close connection that would be useful in combating both synagogue authorities who rejected Jesus' messiahship and false prophets who claimed to have the Spirit but held inadequate Christologies.

If John or his community drew on the Jesus tradition and various Jewish motifs to portray the Spirit of Jesus in a personal way because that is how they experienced him, this may suggest that one important model of spiritual experience in this community, perhaps through or alongside the more ecstatic model, or perhaps often instead of it,[335] was the intimate experience of a relationship between persons (see comments on knowledge of God in the introduction, ch. 6). That the "Trinitarian" or proto-Trinitarian distinction of the Spirit from the Father and Jesus occurs elsewhere in early Christianity (e.g., 2 Cor 13:14; Matt 28:19; *Didache*) suggests that such an experience was not limited to the Johannine community alone.[336] That the community's continuing experience of Jesus was understood in terms of interpersonal communication is also suggested by many passages in the Fourth Gospel (esp. 10:3–4, 14–15; 15:15; 16:13–15).

Jesus appears as a prophet in the Fourth Gospel, though John's greater emphasis is that Jesus is the word himself;[337] Jesus is the pneumatic par excellence, the model Spirit bearer.[338] Some argue that John portrays Jesus along the model of later Christian prophets;[339] it seems more likely that the later prophets of John's audience would take as their model Jesus the pneumatic as they encountered him in the Johannine tradition.[340] But in any case, the Paraclete serves a sort of prophetic function,[341] and parallels among the Paraclete, Jesus,[342] and the disciples suggest the continuance of prophetic ministry in the Johannine community.[343] Parallels between the "other" Paraclete and Jesus[344] also suggest that the Spirit continues Jesus' presence in the Johannine community.[345]

---

[335] Boring, *Sayings*, 85–86, suggests that the lack of enthusiastic frenzy may characterize Johannine prophetism; cf. also Isaacs, "Spirit," 406. Berg, "Pneumatology," 142, could be right that this is mainly a modern distinction, but Herm. *Mand.* 11.2–9 (in Boring, *Sayings*, 85–86) suggests that it was at least considered in the early second century, and the Montanists (Aune, *Prophecy*, 313) were certainly ready to lay claim to the Fourth Gospel.

[336] As noted above, see most fully Fee, *Presence*, 839–42.

[337] Burge, *Community*, 107–10.

[338] Büchsel, *Geist*, 489–90.

[339] Boring, "Prophecy," 120.

[340] Burge, *Community*, 39.

[341] Betz, *Paraklet*, 128–30, argues for the Spirit's function as prophet in John and early Judaism (as the teacher, 130–33; the witness, 133–34; and protector of righteousness, 134–36); see also Bornkamm, "Paraklet," 18–20; Hill, *Prophecy*, 150; Boring, "Prophecy"; Isaacs, "Spirit," 392–99; Vawter, "Ezekiel," 455–58. Prophets' intercessory role in early Judaism (Glatzer, "Prophecy," 133–35) may also fit the Paraclete's activity.

[342] Comparing Jesus' and the Spirit's prophetic functions in John, see Isaacs, "Spirit," 399–402; cf. Vawter, "Ezekiel," 455–58. Compare even the hostility toward Jesus in John 7:20; 8:48 with Josephus *War* 6.303.

[343] Isaacs, "Spirit."

[344] See further, e.g., Gryglewicz, "Geist."

[345] So Dunn, *Jesus and Spirit*, 350–51.

Successor images could be graphic. A speaker could beseech a governor to be like another (ἄλλος) Alexander.[346] Romans could speak of Claudius as another Germanicus, or Tiberius as another Augustus, or of the spirit of previous leaders in new ones.[347] John the Baptist could be a new Elijah (Matt 17:12–13; Luke 1:17); Jesus, a greater Moses (Acts 3:22); and among Johannine Christians the beast, probably a new Nero (Rev 13:3, 18; 17:10–11), and the church, a new Moses and Elijah (Rev 11:5–6).[348] The Spirit is Jesus' successor in stronger ways than these (being more than his successor), but such examples still provide a context for how early Christians would have heard the passage.

## 3D. Spirit of Truth (14:17; 15:26; 16:13)

The phrase "spirit of truth" is not limited to Johannine literature (John 14:17; 15:26; 16:13; 1 John 4:6; cf. 5:6; also p. 618). It appears in *Jub.* 25:14 as an equivalent of the Spirit of prophecy: "And at that time, when a spirit of truth[349] descended upon her mouth, she placed her two hands upon the head of Jacob" and blessed him.[350] Qumran's *Rule of the Community* 4.21 equates the קוד רוח (spirit of holiness, "the holy spirit") with the אמת רוח (spirit of truth).[351] Of course, 1QS 4.3 can speak of "the spirit of humility, patience, love, goodness, wisdom, . . . understanding, purity," and so forth;[352] but the writer(s) of this document give(s) the אמת aspect of the Spirit special prominence. The spirit of truth seems to be identified with the prince of the host of angels from Dan 8:11.[353]

In some manuscripts of *Jos. Asen.* 19:11, Joseph's kiss imparts the spirit of truth.[354] The *Testament of Judah,* if a pre-Christian work, has at least Christian interpolations, but 20:5 may reflect the possible Jewish *Grundschrift;* either way, it sets the spirit of truth in a forensic context:

> And the spirit of truth testifies to all things and brings all accusations. He who has sinned is consumed in his heart and cannot raise his head to face the judge. [Καὶ τὸ πνεῦμα τῆς ἀληθείας κατηγορεῖ πάντων καὶ ἐμπεπύρισται ὁ ἁμαρτωλὸς ἐκ τῆς ἰδίας καρδίας. καὶ ἆραι πρόσωπον πρὸς τὸν κριτὴν οὐ δύναται.][355]

The early-second-century Christian work *Shepherd of Hermas* commands Hermas to love the truth and avoid all falsehood and lies, to walk in truth "and not to have joined

---

[346] Menander Rhetor 2.14, 426.23–24.

[347] See, e.g., Livy 5.49.7; Lucan *C.W.* 9.15–18; Suetonius *Titus* 7.

[348] For Rev 13, see, e.g., Kraybill, *Cult,* 161–65; Bauckham, *Climax,* 423–31; Keener, *Revelation,* 337–39, 355–56, 409–10; for Rev 11, see ibid., 290–93.

[349] One Ethiopian MS has "holy spirit."

[350] *OTP* 2:105.

[351] For the two spirits in the Scrolls, see Brown, *Essays,* 147–49 (for the struggle between them, 149–50).

[352] This too has probable early Christian parallels; cf., e.g., Eph 1:17; Gal 5:22–6:1; see also the Spirit of (or related to) wisdom in 1QS 2.3; *1 En.* 49:3; *4 Ezra* 5:22; *Jos. Asen.* 19:11 (some MSS); LXX Exod 28:3; 31:3; 35:31; Deut 34:9; Isa 11:2.

[353] Cf. Bampfylde, "Prince" (rejecting the identification with Michael). Brown, "Paraclete," 126, thinks that the spirit of truth is angelic in the Scrolls but that there is no evidence "that these remote angelic origins have remained influential" in the Fourth Gospel. See our discussion of the views on an angelic background in section 2, above.

[354] Of uncertain date; cf. sufflation in John 20:22.

[355] English, *OTP* 1:800 (Greek: ed. Charles, 96).

an evil conscience with the spirit of truth, nor to have caused sadness to the holy and true Spirit."[356]

Some texts indicate a contrast between the Prince of Light (the spirit of truth) and the Prince of Darkness (the spirit of error);[357] perhaps John intends an allusion to this in his opposition between Jesus and the "prince of this world" (or this age) in 12:31, 14:30, and 16:11.

*Testament of Judah* 20:1 employs this imagery:

> So understand, my children, that two spirits await an opportunity with humanity: the spirit of truth and the spirit of error [. . . δύο πνεύματα . . . τῷ ἀνθρώπῳ, τὸ τῆς ἀληθείας καὶ τὸ τῆς πλάνης].[358]

*Testament of Judah* 14:8 also speaks of the πνεῦμα τῆς πλάνης, which gets control of one's mind by much wine and can lead to sexual and other sins. *Testament of Reuben* 2:1, however (which may reflect a different hand), does not refer to a single spirit of deception but to seven πνευμάτων τῆς πλάνης, to match the seven good spirits with which people are created in 2:3–4. *Testament of Issachar* 4:4 similarly associates the plural τὰ πνεύματα τῆς πλάνης with lusting after women. Since the *Testament of Judah* and the *Testament of Levi* are most often suspected of being from a Christian hand or containing Christian interpolations (the latter is certainly true, the former possible), we might think that the earliest form of the Testaments speaks only of spirits of error in the plural, were it not for *T. Sim.* 3:1, where the hearer is admonished, "Beware of the spirit of deceit and envy [τοῦ πνεύματος τῆς πλάνης καὶ τοῦ φθόνου]."[359]

By the third century C.E., or whenever the *Testament of Solomon* was completed, ἡ Πλάνη was the name of a demon, the fifth of the seven astrological demons, the στοιχεῖα/ κοσμοκράτορες τοὺς σκότους (8:3); Error claimed to have been deceiving Solomon for some time (8:9). But the demonological developments between the first and third century, evident in rabbinic texts and possibly indicated by the magical papyri, render this evidence too tenuous to be read back into pre-Christian literature without other corroboration.

The Dead Sea Scrolls provide our strongest base of evidence for an early contrasting of two specific spirits, the spirit of truth and the spirit of error. One could speak of spirits of truth and of evil in 1QS 3.18–19, but the context indicates that one of each is intended (4.21–23). Charlesworth has shown parallels with the Fourth Gospel's language on the Spirit of truth.[360]

---

356 Herm. *Mand.* 3.4 (*ANF* 2:21).

357 McNamara, *Targum*, 105, thinks that most light/darkness texts in John bear more affinities to the developing Jewish liturgy than to the Qumran texts, but that is not possible here. Hahn, "Verständnis," 134, is more to the point in thinking that some OT ideas were developed according to the dualistic, exclusivistic outlook of Qumran; John either draws on such ideas current in the milieu or develops them in a manner parallel to the Qumran community.

358 *OTP* 1:800 (Greek: ed. Charles, 95). *T. Jud.* 20:2 says that the conscience is between these two. This parallel with NT language (1 John 4:6) was noted before Qumran (cf. Mowinckel, "Vorstellung," 98–99).

359 *OTP* 1:786 (Greek: ed. Charles, 18).

360 Charlesworth, "Comparison," 418. Sanders, *John*, 354, thinks the parallels in the Testaments are closer, but Grayston, *Epistles*, 119, notes that the two spirits of *T. Jud.* 20:1 are equivalent to the two inclinations (*T. Ash.* 1:5) whereas the Scrolls use the spirits to divide humanity into two groups. Other commentators have also pointed out the parallels between 1QS, and/or *T. Jud.* 20:1, and John, e.g., Houlden, *Epistles*, 106; Albright, "Discoveries," 168.

Betz thought that John identified the Spirit of God with Michael, the angelic spirit of truth; Johnston, conversely, thinks that the identification is pre-Johannine and that John combats this view as a heresy.[361] While Johnston may be right to challenge Betz's view that John made the identification, he offers little direct evidence to support his own position.[362] The use in the Scrolls is probably fluid enough that one could identify the spirit of truth either with an angelic power or with the holy Spirit of God; a Philonist might have seen little difference between the two. But John could easily enough have taken one identification available to him without knowing of, or necessarily polemicizing against, the other.

John may have adopted a variety of possible nuances available to him in the term. That Michael may appear as a heavenly advocate representing Christ (not the Spirit) in Rev 12 does not indicate that the Johannine community would have identified Michael and the Spirit of truth. But the fluid imagery in which the seven spirits could be identified with the Spirit of God (cf. Rev 1:4–5) or the seven archangels (compare 5:6 with Zech 3:9; 4:10, in light of Zech 1:10; 6:7) or the guardian angels of the churches (1:20) may warn us against excluding or including possible nuances every time the term appears; the Johannine community may have tolerated a degree of pneumatological ambiguity unthinkable to most theologically nuanced post-Nicene Christians.

By identifying what could have been the angelic spirit of truth, or the divine Spirit of truth (or both), with the Holy Spirit (14:26) and writing of him indwelling the disciples and fulfilling the functions of the Spirit of prophecy, the writer of the Fourth Gospel clearly points more in the direction of the divine Spirit than toward the angelic idea. Paralleling the Spirit with Jesus, whom the Gospel also presents as divine and distinct from the Father, further tends toward this position. The spirits of truth and error that correspond to true and false prophets in 1 John 4:1–6 can be understood in one of two ways: as angelic messengers who bring revelations[363] or as specific manifestations of the basic opposing forces: the Spirit of truth (the Spirit of God, v. 2) and the spirit of deception (the spirit of the antichrist, v. 3). Given the Epistle's dualism, emphasis on the divine indwelling, and lack of emphasis on angelology or demonology, we may suppose that the latter is more likely.

The title "Spirit of truth" is undoubtedly particularly relevant to the Farewell Discourses because of the earlier identification of Jesus as the truth (14:6).[364] This again binds the Spirit to Jesus.

## 4. Coming and Staying (John 14:15–20)

If the disciples keep Jesus' commandments (14:15), especially loving one another to the death (13:34–35), he will send them another Advocate to minister for them in his stead (14:16–17). Thus, when Jesus comes to them after the resurrection to give them

---

[361] Johnston, *Spirit-Paraclete,* 121–22. On p. 118 he suggests that John omits the name Michael through polemical intention; the Paraclete is not like the warrior Michael of the Apocalypse.

[362] A critique offered by Kysar, *Evangelist,* 239, and others.

[363] This is attested not only in magical papyri but in biblical tradition (e.g., 1 Kgs 22:20–23; 2 Chr 18:18–22), although in the latter it is not the primary form of prophecy by any means. For this as an issue of contention, see Gal 1:8 and Col 2:18; 1 Cor 12:10 may mean it in the generic sense of judging prophets (14:29) and thus may be read however one reads 1 John 4; 1 Cor 14:32 in context must refer to the human spirit (14:2, 14–16), against some interpreters (Ellis, "Christ and Spirit," 275; Bruce, *Corinthians,* 134–35).

[364] E.g., Berg, "Pneumatology," 135; Barrett, "Spirit," 8.

resurrection life (14:18–19), he will in some sense remain with them—indeed, *in* them (14:20). Although John presupposes that his audience knows of Jesus' ascension (20:17), like Matthew he does not narrate it because, as in Matthew, Jesus in some sense remains among his people (Matt 28:20).

Those who love Jesus keep his commandments (14:15, 21; cf. 21:15); those who keep his commandments will abide more securely in his love (14:21; 15:10). What Jesus describes here is not a formula—it is far too circular for that—but the pattern for a developing relationship. For discussion of the significance of the commandments of 14:15, see comment on 14:21–25.

### 4A. The Paraclete Brings Jesus' Presence (14:16–17)

For discussion of the "Paraclete," the "Spirit of truth," and possible legal implications of the image, see the lengthy introductory sections above, pp. 953–71. Of primary significance in these verses is the relation of the Spirit to Jesus; he is "another Paraclete," Jesus' "successor" (see discussion above). Further, like Jesus, the Spirit may be related in some manner to the image of divine Wisdom in early Jewish sources (see discussion above); if this connection is likely, then just as Jesus' opponents attacked the very divine Word they claimed to uphold, so do the opponents of John's audience attack what they purport to defend.

Later, after Jesus returned and the disciples were empowered, disciples would be able to ask what they wished in Jesus' name (16:26), but until that time they remained dependent on Jesus, who would secure the other Paraclete for them (14:16). Clearly, the Father must authorize the Spirit's sending (cf. Acts 5:32; 1 Pet 1:12), but Jesus also plays a direct role in it (15:26; 16:7; cf. 3:34; Luke 24:49). Further, as the Father dwelled in the Son (14:10), so would the Spirit dwell in the disciples (14:17). The remaining of the Spirit with them "forever" (14:16) reflects language familiar in the Johannine circle (cf. 2 John 2; perhaps John 8:35); just as the Spirit "remained" on Jesus (1:32), the Spirit would remain with the disciples (cf. 1 John 2:27). The disciples, ready to lament Jesus' departure, would in fact obtain his continuing presence by the Spirit once he was glorified!

While 14:16 designates the Spirit as "another Advocate," so relating the Spirit to Jesus (see comments on the Paraclete as Jesus' successor, above; 1 John 2:1), 14:17 assigns the Spirit's presence wholly to believers in Jesus, excluding "the world." In the context of the Fourth Gospel, "the world" is all those outside Jesus' following and is exemplified particularly by the Judean religious authorities who probably stand for the opposition in John's day. This passage fits its context by explaining Jesus' return and abiding presence among believers.[365]

The Spirit of truth, foreign to a world that could not know the truth or perceive the risen Christ (14:17, 19; cf. 1 John 3:1), would come to the disciples (14:17–18). As John puts it, assuming the more widely accepted reading:[366] ὑμεῖς γινώσκετε αὐτό, ὅτι παρ' ὑμῖν μένει καὶ ἐν ὑμῖν ἔσται. Although the "with" and the "in" may be equivalent,[367] if the μένει be read as a present and the ἔσται as a future, the present presumably refers to God's Spirit as present in Jesus and the future to the time when

---

[365] Forestell, "Paraclete," 157, doubts that the Paraclete saying is an interpolation, but believes that 14:12–17 as a whole interrupts the context.

[366] Metzger, *Commentary,* 245; Berg, "Pneumatology," 131; Morgan-Wynne, "Note." Michaels, *John,* 253, and Hunter, *John,* 146, take the second verb as present but read both verbs in a future sense.

[367] Michaels, *John,* 253; contrast Johnstone, "Paraclete."

the Spirit would indwell the believers directly.[368] This would fit the Johannine temporal perspective on pneumatology: although the availability of the Spirit could be proleptically implied as early as Nicodemus (3:5), the Spirit would be fully available only after Jesus' glorification (7:39, 20:19–23). (On the background of the dwelling image, see comment on 14:2–3.)

### 4B. Jesus Comes to Them (14:18)

Jesus promises to "come" to the disciples (14:18); in this context (14:16–17), the coming must refer to his coming in 20:19–23 to impart the Spirit to them (cf. 14:3, 23).[369] At the same time, that he will not leave them bereaved as "orphans" suggests that his presence will continue with them through the Spirit. "Orphan" language was sometimes applied figuratively to the loss of important figures in people's lives, certainly applicable to Jesus for the disciples (13:33).[370] Although "orphan" technically referred to the fatherless, it could also apply to other sorts of bereavement,[371] such as a proselyte rejected by her family on account of her destruction of their gods.[372] But the "fatherless" image is likely here. Because teachers could be compared with fathers, great teachers who died could be said to leave a generation "fatherless";[373] this fits Jesus' own portrayal of his relationship with them (see comment on 13:33).[374] In a general sense, the image fits the context of the Paraclete as Jesus' successor; in a pre-Christian testament, Mattathias, nearing death, exhorted his sons that their brother Simeon, a man of counsel (ἀνὴρ βουλῆς), would be a father to them (1 Macc 2:65).[375] But more specifically, because Jesus will overcome death and bring his eternal presence to them, they will not be fatherless in this manner.

There is a further sense in which the image of "orphans" may relate to the context of the Paraclete as a forensic intercessor. In light of biblical tradition, "orphans" were a class of people most susceptible to being oppressed;[376] Jesus and the Spirit would prove to be their advocates (see comment above on the meaning of the Paraclete), defending them against the oppression of the world.

---

[368] Berg, "Pneumatology," 140.

[369] This is acknowledged even by most who emphasize futurist eschatology in the Gospel (e.g., Holwerda, *Spirit*, 65, 76).

[370] Cicero *Fam.* 12.30.4 speaks of the Senate "bereft of relatives" *(orbus)* by the loss of its consuls (whom Cicero would have regarded as "fathers" to the state); murdering one's benefactor could be seen as parricide (Valerius Maximus 1.5.7; 1.6.13; 1.7.2; 1.8.8).

[371] E.g., Isa 47:8 LXX; 1 Thess 2:17; perhaps *Pss. Sol.* 4:10; cf. Bernard, *John*, 2:546. Achilles' mere absence from his (living) parents is described as ὀρφανιζομένῳ in Pindar *Pyth.* 6.22–23. No one else could fully replace a deceased father (Homer *Il.* 22.490–505); nevertheless, the KJV's "comfortless" is untenable (Bernard, *John*, 2:547).

[372] *Jos. Asen.* 11:3, 13; 12:5/7, 12–13; she claims she is an orphan because of her sin in 11:16.

[373] R. Akiba for R. Eliezer in *ʾAbot R. Nat.* 25A. Commentators frequently follow Billerbeck, *Kommentar*, 2:562 here (e.g., Holwerda, *Spirit*, 41–42; O'Day, "John," 748); Brown, *John*, 2:640 also cites Plato *Phaedo* 116A.

[374] Also, e.g., Brown, *John*, 2:640; Ellis, *Genius*, 222.

[375] Some texts compare Israel with an orphan suffering among the nations (Philo *Spec. Laws* 4.179) or adopted by God (*Deut. Rab.* 3:4; Vellanickal, *Sonship*, 33, cites 1QH 9.35–36; cf. Hos 11:1–4; 14:3).

[376] Holwerda, *Spirit*, 38–45. In later tradition "orphan" could be mildly derogatory (*b. Ḥul.* 111b), perhaps alluding to a father's death as punishment (e.g., allegedly Ben Azzai in *p. Meg.* 1:9, §19), but it was not necessarily a figure of shame (Tob 1:8). As children they remained legally defenseless (*p. Ketub.* 3:1, §4), although only as minors (*p. Ter.* 1:1).

### 4C. Resurrection Life at Jesus' Coming (14:19–20)

Here Jesus' "little while" refers to the second "little while" of 16:16 (or the sum of both "little whiles"); after his glorification, the world will remain unable to behold him, just as the disciples could not immediately after his death. The time would come when it would be too late for outsiders to hear Jesus (12:36); after that he remained hidden (cf. 12:36) except through the witness of his followers and the unity of their community of faith (1:7; 13:35; 17:21–23).

It is the risen Christ who comes to bring them the Spirit and breathe new life into them (20:22); thus, when Jesus comes to them (14:18) to impart the Spirit (14:16–17), the disciples receive resurrection life (14:19).[377] This newness of their life is predicated on his own (14:19; cf. 1 John 4:9; Rev 1:18) and is "eternal life" (see comment on 3:16), the product of a new birth (see comment on 3:3, 5). Probably many early Christians believed that Jesus' new life had created new life in those united with him by faith (Rom 6:4–5; 8:2, 11; 1 Cor 15:2, 20; 2 Cor 5:5; 13:4; 1 John 5:12).

"In that day" (14:20; cf. 16:23) can bear eschatological connotations[378] but, in keeping with John's emphasis in this context on realized eschatology, refers to the time beginning from Jesus imparting the Spirit. John 14:20–23 refers to Jesus' presence with his disciples by the Spirit after the resurrection.[379] For the mutual indwelling of Father and Son in 14:20, see also 14:11.

### 5. Revelation to the Obedient (14:21–25)

Jesus again emphasizes that keeping his commandments shows love for him (14:21, 23–24; cf. also 21:15–17; for more on "commandments," see comment on 13:34). The most striking feature here is the contrast between Jesus' teaching here and its narrative illustration: the disciples in fact fail to obey him, failing to love him or one another enough to lay down their lives (13:34–35), as Jesus himself predicted (13:36–38). Nevertheless Jesus gives them the Spirit (20:22)! But the text may imply some partial obedience on their part. Their only sign of mutual love is their group cohesion, their failure to scatter from one another (20:19); thus those present receive the Spirit, but Thomas, who was not among them, was not yet able to receive the Spirit (20:24). This might suggest that the Spirit is received by individuals primarily in the context of the believing community and that those who withdraw from that community (cf. 1 John 2:19) also withdraw from the true Spirit—that is, they exchange the Spirit of truth for the spirit of error (1 John 4:6).

When Jesus connects obedience with love, biblically literate Jewish hearers would immediately think of the associations between obeying God's commandments and loving God (Exod 20:6; Deut 5:10; 7:9; 10:12; 11:1, 13, 22; 19:9; 30:16; Neh 1:5; Dan 9:4; Sir 2:15; 4Q176 frg. 16, line 4). Some might also recall wisdom tradition: love (ἀγάπη) is the keeping (τήρησις) of Wisdom's laws (νόμων; Wis 6:18).[380] Jesus speaks of "having" and

---

[377] On the connection between the impartation of the Spirit and the resurrection, see also Schlier, "Begriff," 265.

[378] E.g., Isa 2:11, 17, 20; 3:18; 4:2; 24:21; Zech 14:4–13. Such prophecies were not always eschatological, however (e.g., 1 Sam 3:12; 8:18; Isa 22:20; 23:15).

[379] Holwerda, *Spirit*, 71.

[380] Also noted in DeSilva, "Wisdom of Solomon," 1275. On "keeping the word" in the Fourth Gospel, see Pancaro, *Law*, 403–30.

"keeping" the commandments. Jewish teachers debated whether knowing or doing Torah took precedence, but all agreed that both were necessary (see comment on 7:17).

Given the abundance of ancient literature, it is not difficult to find other examples of selective revelation (14:21; cf. Acts 10:41). Thus, for example, Odysseus and the dogs witnessed Athene, but Telemachus could not (Homer *Od.* 16.159–163); perhaps more relevant, Apollo appears only to the good (who must also be great, not lowly; Callimachus *Hymns* 2 [to Apollo], 9–10); likewise, on his people's behalf, God reveals his glory to all except his people (3 Macc 6:18). Some teachers also warned that their most special teachings were only for a select group, like initiates in the Mysteries.[381] Nevertheless, Jesus' selective revelation (14:21) has roots in the historical Jesus tradition (e.g., Acts 10:41; cf. Mark 8:11–12; Matt 16:1, 21). The world is skeptical because Jesus does not manifest himself or his Father to the world (7:4) but only to his own (17:6); this takes the idea of a messianic or kingdom secret to a new (and more chronologically extended) level. But on the theological level, Jesus' selective revelation especially conforms to his identity in this Gospel; Wisdom was not manifest (φανερά) to the masses (Wis 6:22); likewise, in wisdom tradition, God becomes manifest (ἐμφανίζεται) to those who do not disbelieve in her (Wis 1:2).[382] Another allusion might have impressed itself more quickly on John's first audience, however; as 14:8 echoed Moses' request to be shown the Father, so might Judas's desire to understand how only the disciples would receive the revelation in 14:22.[383]

Yet whereas the first eyewitnesses alone received the first postresurrection revelation (20:19–20) like Moses (1:14), here all believers are privileged to experience the same revelation by Jesus' continuing presence among his community (14:23). Jesus is not manifest to the world (14:22) because he is revealed only to those who love and obey him (14:23), not to those who do not (14:23). (The disciples' opponents, who claim to obey Torah yet do not obey Jesus, are not truly obedient to the Father's law; 5:45–47.) Narrative sequences such as 1:37–39 (and the presence of Jesus' disciples through the Gospel) may suggest that in practice a person can start with some revelation of Jesus, grow to love him more, and thus secure more revelation.

John writes not from purely historical interest concerning the first generation but also from theological and apologetic interest for his own. Subsequent generations continue to experience the glory greater than what Moses experienced, sharing with those who knew Jesus in the flesh (1:14–18, on the revelation of his character), because now the Spirit lives in them and reveals Jesus to them. They continue to embrace his glory (1:14) because, after his full glorification (7:39), the Spirit continues to glorify Jesus to the disciples (16:14).[384] Direct physical sight and hearing like Moses' are significant (Deut 34:10), as are visions and revelations (2 Cor 12:1; Acts 2:17), but for John the greatest revelation seems to be

---

[381] Dionysius of Halicarnassus *Lit. Comp.* 25; cf. Wis 2:22; 1QH 2.13–14; 9.23–24; see Keener, *Matthew,* 378–79. Gnostics may have developed their "secret tradition" to explain their lack of earlier attestation; but some authentic traditions actually were probably initially "secret."

[382] Similarly, God reveals himself (ἐπιφάνεια γίνεται) to the royal counselors (συμβούλοις) who are worthy (*Let. Aris.* 264). For angelic revelation (ἐμφανισθῆναι), cf., e.g., *T. Ab.* 4:10B.

[383] Glasson, *Moses,* 77; cf. Beasley-Murray, *John,* 259. In contrast to 14:8, however, 14:22 does not echo the language of the LXX here. Likewise, an appeal to the occasional selective vision of Greek deities (Homer *Il.* 1.194–200) would miss culturally nearer Jewish parallels (1 Sam 16:7; Ezek 1:1; cf. Acts 9:7), and parallels in magical papyri (*PGM* 1.186–187) are too distant from John's focus; he certainly does not desire to present Jesus as a magician (7:20; 8:48–49).

[384] Cf. 2 Cor 3:8–18; 4:7, which suggests that the glory is revealed especially in the midst of believers' sufferings (2 Cor 4:7–18).

recognizing Jesus' character and walking in the light of his character and presence continually (manifested in love, which provides general direction, and probably also specific prophetic long-range direction in 16:13d). Jesus continually saw (5:19–20) and heard (8:38) the Father, and the Father was continually with him (8:29), though his public activities make it doubtful that he continually experienced visions.

The name Judas and its distinction from Iscariot (14:22) probably represents simply a historical reminiscence. Just as many people bore multiple names,[385] ancient writers often listed others who shared the same name as a person about whom they were writing (sometimes in the same generation), to distinguish them,[386] and Judas (Judah) was a common Jewish name in the ancient Mediterranean.[387] If two people with the same name were present, one had to identify by a distinct title the lesser known (e.g., Polybius 9.24.5, using a nickname).

Through the Spirit (14:16–17, 26), Jesus and the Father would come (cf. 14:3, 18) and make their "dwelling place" within the believer (14:23; 15:4; for much more detail, see comment on 14:2; for the joint dwelling of Father and Son, cf., e.g., 1 John 2:24). In a figurative sense, God was already a "dwelling place" and refuge for his people (Deut 33:27; Ps 90:1; 91:2);[388] here Jesus may play more fully on the image of a new temple or the eschatological promise of God dwelling among his people (Ezek 37:26–28; Rev 21:3, 22).[389] But whereas most of the biblical promises and early Jewish images about the Shekinah applied to Israel as a whole, Jesus' promise applies to the experience of individual believers.[390] Effectively, Jesus' hearers may have envisioned the Jerusalem temple—one of the largest and most spectacular structures in the ancient world until a little over two decades before the composition of this Gospel[391]—dwelling in the believer.[392] (Similarly, Paul can apply the image of believers as a corporate temple [1 Cor 3:16] on a more personal level [1 Cor 6:19].) As Stephen S. Smalley points out, both Paul and John involve the whole Trinity in indwelling the believer, but John does so more fully:

---

[385] E.g., P.Oxy. 494.32; 1273.3, 49; *CPJ* 2:143, §261; 2:145, §§269–270; 2:146, §274; 2:147, §275; 2:147, §276; 2:151, §298; 2:153, §304; 2:154, §311; 2:156, §321; 3:9, §453; *CIJ* 1:24, §30; 2:111, §879; Acts 1:23; Eusebius *Hist. eccl.* 3.39; Leon, *Jews,* 107–13. On the history of the Roman practice, see Appian *R.H.* pref.13.

[386] E.g., Diogenes Laertius 6.2.81; Xenophon *Hell.* 1.2.13; Dionysius of Halicarnassus *Dinarchus* 1; Philostratus *Vit. soph.* 1.483; 2.20.600; cf. Horace *Sat.* 2.3.11; Plutarch *Themistocles* 32.1, 5. Sometimes the distinctions do, however, represent improbable harmonizations of widely divergent legendary sources (e.g., Arrian *Alex.* 2.16.1–4; 4.28.2; 5.13; Appian *R.H.* 6.1.2).

[387] E.g., *CIJ* 1:15, §12; 1:26, §33; 1:84, §121; 1:85, §122; 1:270–71, §345; 1:271, §346; 1:272, §347; 1:272, §348; 1:273, §349; 1:274, §350; 1:274–75, §351; 1:455, §636; 1:479, §668; 2:46, §791 (from Spain, Cilicia, but especially Rome).

[388] For rabbinic development of this theme (מעון ("abode," as a divine name), see Marmorstein, *Names,* 91.

[389] For the new-temple image in John 14:2–3, 23, see Coloe, *Temple Symbolism,* 157–78.

[390] For the Shekinah here, see Kugelman, "Pentecost," 261. On the Shekinah, see esp. comment on 1:14. Cf. later Greek portraits of deities "being with" or spending time with initiates (e.g., Philostratus *Hrk.* 2.8; 4.10; 5.1; 7.1, 3; 9.7).

[391] See Sanders, *Judaism,* 55–69; Josephus *War* 5.184–227; Cornfeld, *Josephus,* 346–61. It was renowned for its beauty (Josephus *War* 6.267; *ʾAbot R. Nat.* 28A; 48, §132B) and known throughout the Roman world (2 Macc 2:22; *Let. Aris.* 84–91; *CIJ* 1:378, §515).

[392] God was also the "Place," the omnipresent one who fills the universe; see *m. ʾAbot* 2:9, 13; 3:14; *t. Peʾah* 1:4; 3:8; *Šabb.* 7:22, 25; 13:5; *Roš Haš.* 1:18; *Taʿan.* 2:13; *B. Qam.* 7:7; *Sanh.* 1:2; 13:1, 6; 14:3, 10; *Sipre Num.* 11.2.3; 11.3.1; 42.1.2; 42.2.3; 76.2.2; 78.1.1; 78.5.1; 80.1.1; 82.3.1; 84.1.1; 84.5.1; 85.3.1; 85.4.1; 85.5.1. But his presence could dwell among his people in a special way (see comment on 1:14).

| You in God        | Col 3:3    | John 17:21               |
| You in Christ     | 2 Cor 5:17 | John 15:4–5              |
| You in the Spirit | Rom 8:9    | John 4:23–24             |
| God in you        | Phil 2:13  | John 14:23               |
| Christ in you     | Col 1:27   | John 14:18–20            |
| Spirit in you     | 1 Cor 3:16 | John 14:16–17[393]       |

Like most Jewish sages, John teaches through much repetition of his key themes; loving the Father requires loving the Son (8:42), which in turn requires keeping his commandments (14:24). When Jesus says he has spoken these things (14:25), he refers to the whole of his teaching in the discourse, for "These things I have spoken to you" becomes a familiar refrain concerning their activity in the world (15:11; 16:1, 33). But further revelation would come with the Spirit (16:6–7, 12–13), who would supplement and interpret Jesus' historical teaching for new situations (14:26).

## 6. Teaching Jesus Tradition (14:26)

The commandments and words Jesus had already given them (14:21–25) were incomplete; but rather than depending on midrashic techniques to apply Jesus' meaning to more specific situations, believers would have the Spirit to explain all these matters to them (14:26). That the Spirit comes "in Jesus' name" probably means "in his place," "as his representative" (see also comment on 14:13).[394]

### 6A. The Spirit as Teacher and Recaller (14:26)

The Spirit is here the "Holy Spirit," as elsewhere in John only in the Gospel's first and last references to the Spirit (1:33; 20:22); the full title may help draw attention to the statement. As in the Dead Sea Scrolls, the Holy Spirit could appear as a teacher (e.g., 1QS 2.3).[395] Given the difficulty of distinguishing between the Spirit as provider of inspired wisdom or insights[396] and the Spirit as inspirer of prophecy, I have elsewhere treated these categories together.[397]

The Paraclete had been sent not only to continue Jesus' presence in the experience of the community but also to expound the teachings of Jesus within the proper confines set by those teachings. Such teaching, like haggadic midrash,[398] could no doubt be

---

[393] Smalley, "Relationship," 98. Some of the senses may be more instrumental than locative (e.g., John 4:23–24) or corporate than personal (e.g., Col 1:27; but cf. Col 1:29), but the basic correctness of Smalley's proposal stands.

[394] See, e.g., Windisch, *Spirit-Paraclete*, 6 (hence the Spirit can complete as well as recall Jesus' teaching); Sanders, *John*, 333; cf. Turner, *Spirit*, 83.

[395] See esp. Bruce, "Spirit," 51–52. The Spirit could teach through the prophets (4Q381 frg. 69, line 4) and also empowered members morally and to seek God (4Q444 frg. 1, 1.1; 4Q509, 5.15–16).

[396] The clearest references for viewing revealed knowledge as a sort of prophecy in Grudem, *Prophecy*, 38–39 are mainly Amoraic, but a perusal of our material in Keener, *Spirit*, 12–13, will also show the difficulty of drawing a clear distinction between the two in the teachings of the sages.

[397] Keener, *Spirit*, 10–13; idem, "Pneumatology," 69–77.

[398] I use this term advisedly, in a generic sense; the earlier expansions of biblical narratives do not easily fit the later rabbinic categories from which the standard terms derive; see Harrington, "Bible," 242. I refer to such expansions as *Liber antiquitatum biblicarum* (which only rarely adds entire stories, though it often adds details); *Jubilees* and parts of *1 Enoch*; 4QAmram (see Kobelski, "Melchizedek," 46–72); material in Gen 49 (Yadin, "Commentaries," 66–68); *Genesis Apocryphon;*

expansive;[399] but it would have to remain faithful to the Johannine Jesus tradition held by the community.[400] The Fourth Gospel itself might be seen as such a valid articulation of the Jesus tradition.[401] This, too, is closely connected with the context,[402] which concerns keeping Jesus' commandments (14:15–25); the Johannine community's equivalent of traditional halakah was the guidance of the Spirit.

The Spirit was going to teach (διδάξει) them πάντα (a familiar term with more limited nuances than the term itself need suggest; cf. 16:13 [πάσῃ, with v. 15]; 1 John 2:20, 27) and bring to their remembrance πάντα that Jesus had spoken. Probably the phrase "which Jesus had spoken" should delimit both uses of πάντα here, so that the Spirit's teaching is neither wholly innovative nor simply repetitive (for the latter, "bring to remembrance" would have sufficed) but explanatory and applicational, like the exposition of Jewish sages.[403] The idea that the Spirit is "sent"[404] subordinates the Spirit to the sender's purpose as his agent, just as Jesus is also the Father's agent;[405] that he is sent "in Jesus' name" guarantees fidelity to the original message in the same way.[406]

The Spirit's "teaching" activity probably stems from authentic Jesus tradition (Luke 12:12)[407] and also draws on a function of the Spirit and Wisdom in Wisdom texts. In Wis 7:21, Wisdom ἐδίδαξε Solomon; in Wis 8:7, Wisdom ἐκδιδάσκει φρόνησιν; in 9:17–18, God sent (ἔπεμψας) his Holy Spirit from above and thus they were taught (ἐδιδάχθησαν).[408] For John, teaching must stem from God (6:45) and not merely fleshly

---

*History of Joseph; Testaments of the Twelve Patriarchs, Testament of Job*, and *Life of Adam and Eve* (very expansive, even novelistic). Although the genre (Harrington, "Bible," 242–43, argues that they do not comprise a distinct genre, but this appraisal depends on a narrower definition of "genre" than necessary) is common in the Scrolls, but this is not limited to them (Milik, "Ecrits"). Midrash could exercise a creative function (Goulder, *Midrash*, 30), but the use of exegetical and haggadic traditions in these texts should not be underestimated (Harrington, "Bible," 245–46; Fallon, "Theodotus," 786).

[399] Both expansion (cf., e.g., Theon *Progym.* 1.172–175; 2.115–123; 3.224–240) and abridgement (2 Macc 2:24–28) were standard practices; see our comments on pp. 18–19, 27–28. Post-Easter embellishment becomes far more common in the apocryphal gospels than in the Synoptics (see Carmignac, "Pré-pascal"); Hill, *Prophecy,* 169, thus is right to observe that the Johannine discourses "may indeed be homilies composed around sayings of Jesus," without being from Christian prophets.

[400] Many scholars emphasize the centrality of the Word and the Jesus tradition here; see Burge, *Community,* 213; Dietzfelbinger, "Paraklet," 395–402; for the reason for this emphasis, Dietzfelbinger, "Paraklet," 402–8. Cf. the importance of authentic memory of the right Teacher in the Scrolls (Stuhlmacher, "Theme," 13; cf. Roloff, "Lieblingsjünger," whom he cites).

[401] Contrast the (possibly protognosticizing?) opponents in 1 John whose prophecies may not have emphasized the tradition of the historical Jesus (at least to 1 John's satisfaction), although they employed traditions of the Johannine community (cf. 1 John 4:1–3; 5:6; 2 John 7).

[402] Against Forestell, "Paraclete," 164, and others.

[403] The priesthood had been engaged to teach the commandments in earlier Wisdom literature (Sir 46:17), but in later times this job fell to the rabbinic successors of those the Synoptics called scribes.

[404] Cf. also Wis 9:17–18; Gal 4:6 for the Spirit being sent. *T. Ab.* 18:11A (ἀπέστειλε) probably does not refer to the divine Spirit; the πνεῦμα ζωῆς here probably alludes to Gen 2:7.

[405] Isaacs, "Prophetic Spirit," 393; cf. Witherington, *Wisdom,* 251.

[406] Berg, "Pneumatology," 149–50. This is likely however one interprets the phrase. On acting in one's name, see discussion at 14:13.

[407] The wording may be Luke's, but the idea is earlier (Mark 13:11).

[408] Franck, *Revelation,* 44, points out that in Philo it is normally God or his Word or Moses who "teaches." Wegenast, "Teach," 760, observes that the term is normally used in the LXX for instruction in how to live the Torah, not for prophetic preaching.

human intellect (3:10). The Spirit's teaching role also appears as the "anointing" in 1 John 2:27, where the anointing teaches discernment between truth and error (2:26).

"Remembering," of course, was key to the learning process not only in Jewish education[409] but throughout the Greco-Roman world.[410] Greeks thought that deities could bring matters to one's remembrance,[411] and sometimes associated this with special inspiration (Homer *Il.* 2.492). Jewish sources also emphasize divine help for memory.[412] A closer and more specifically relevant parallel here may be Wis 12:2, where God both reproves (ἐλέγχεις) those who sin (cf. John 16:8–11) and reminds (ὑπομιμνῄσκων) them of what they have done; although the disciples are not accused of sin here, the verse may recall the tradition of God as the reminder in Wisdom of Solomon, a popular and widely read work. In this context of the Paraclete, 14:26 probably means that the Spirit will give wisdom in the hour of testing before the court of "the world," bringing to remembrance the polemic of the Fourth Gospel for use in debates with the hostile synagogue leaders and those influenced by them.[413] After Jesus was glorified, the Spirit would bring to remembrance his teachings and works and help believers understand them in light of Scripture (2:22; cf. Luke 22:61) and know how to apply them (16:4; cf. Rev 2:5).

## 6B. Implications for the Fourth Gospel

The Fourth Gospel is often thought to imply its own inspiration.[414] The parallels drawn by some scholars between the Paraclete and the implied author, the beloved disciple,[415] however, do not give enough attention to the fact that the whole community shares these parallels with the Paraclete and Jesus, as agents of the Father and/or Jesus.[416] But the case does not depend only on parallels between the Paraclete and the Fourth Gospel's implied author.

---

[409] E.g., *m. ʾAbot* 3:8; *Mek. Pisha* 1:135–136; *Sipre Deut.* 4.2.1; 48.1.1, 4; 306.19.1–3; *p. Meg.* 4:1, §4; cf. *Let. Aris.* 154 (Hadas, *Aristeas,* 161, also compares Philo *Spec. Laws* 4.106ff.). See comments on memory in our introduction; cf. in pre-Christian sapiential testaments, such as Tob 4:19 (perhaps Tob 1:11–12).

[410] *Rhet. ad Herenn.* 3.16.28; Plutarch *Educ.* 13, *Mor.* 9E; Diogenes Laertius 6.2.31; 10.1.12; Theon *Progym.* 2.5–8; Quintilian 1.3.1; 2.4.15; 11.2.1–51; probably Seneca *Dial.* 7.10.3; Culpepper, *School,* 50, 106, 193; Anderson, *Glossary,* 126–27; Kennedy, *Classical Rhetoric,* 98; Gerhardsson, *Memory,* 124–25. Understanding and remembering profitable sayings were *both* vital (Isocrates *Demon.* 18, *Or.* 1), and reminder was common enough in moral exhortation (Isocrates *Demon.* 21, *Or.* 1; Epictetus *Diatr.* 4.4.29; Phil 3:1; 2 Pet 1:12; cf. Cicero *Amic.* 22.85; Rom 15:15). Note taking was, of course, practiced; cf. Diogenes Laertius 2.48; Epictetus *Diatr.* 1.pref.; Quintilian 1.pref.7–8; introduction to Plutarch *Stoic Cont.* 13:369–603, in LCL 398–99.

[411] Homer *Od.* 12.38 (though cf. 12.226–227).

[412] In *Jub.* 32:25–26, Jacob receives divine help to "remember" an inspired dream (Charles, *Jubilees,* lxxxiii, also notes the parallel); *PGM* 4.726–731 likewise promises Mithras's help to recall a lengthy revelation.

[413] This can be argued on analogy with Matt 28:19, which probably invites the disciple makers to use the teaching blocs in Matthew catechetically.

[414] This is often argued; e.g., Dietzfelbinger, "Paraklet," 389–408. Franck, *Revelation,* 96, suggests that the connection between Paraclete and beloved disciple guarantees that disciple as an inspired transmitter of tradition. See introduction, ch. 3, esp. pp. 111–22.

[415] Sasse, "Paraklet," 260–77; Culpepper, *School,* 266–69; Boring, *Sayings,* 49; Kragerund, *Lieblingsjünger,* 113–29 and passim. Boismard, "Review," critiques Kragerund's identification of the beloved disciple with the Paraclete instead of with an idealized disciple figure. Much more cautious is Wilckens, "Paraclete," 203; they are not identical, but the beloved disciple represents the community that the Paraclete has founded.

[416] Cf. Hill, *Prophecy,* 151, against Sasse; cf. Burge, *Community,* 211.

D. Moody Smith is among many scholars who contends that the sayings tradition of the Fourth Gospel may have been heavily permeated by Christian prophecy: "If sectarian Judaism was the germinal ground of the Johannine tradition, spirit-inspired prophecy may well have provided the specific occasion for the emergence of Johannine Christian affirmation in the form of words of Jesus."[417] If one accepts this premise, however, one must ask whether the sayings were composed in the Johannine community and then transposed into Johannine idiom for the Gospel, as a collection of oracles,[418] or whether they were composed spontaneously by the author under prophetic inspiration. If the former proposal is accepted, we must question how the discourses fit so thoroughly well[419] into the themes of a Gospel whose fabric is so complexly interwoven that tradition (whether historical or prophetic) and redaction are virtually indistinguishable.[420]

Probably the author envisioned the inspiration of his Gospel as a whole. Narratives[421] and literary works[422] could also lay claim to inspiration; even extant oracular responses may have been edited, such as the Pythian utterances transposed into Homeric hexameter.[423] *Odes of Solomon* lays claim to inspiration for the process of its writing, not to prior stages of oral tradition.[424] Given the emphasis on inspiration of Christian witness in the Fourth Gospel, it is likely that the author conceived of his own work as reflecting at least a substantial measure of the Spirit's guidance. At the same time, claims to inspiration need not rule out dependence on genuine earlier tradition, as Smith also points out (citing 12:25; 13:34).[425]

But need such inspiration have functioned prophetically in the narrowest sense of that term (oracular utterances)? John's use of an omniscient narrator[426] and foreshadowing[427]

---

[417] Smith, *Johannine Christianity,* 30. This view is shared by Aune, *Eschatology,* 101; Boring, *Sayings,* 8 (on Dibelius), 49 (with a list of other scholars), 76, 85, 106–7, 127; Hays, *Vision,* 151. Boring sees this as something of a charismatic exegesis of Jesus as well as of the OT (p. 102).

[418] Oracle collections did indeed exist in antiquity, e.g., the *Sibylline Oracles.* See Collins, *Sibylline Oracles,* 6–7; Aune, *Prophecy,* 44. An oracle (χρησμός) was sometimes circulated (e.g., Achilles Tatius 2.14.1) by itself, although the scantiness of the evidence for this suggests that it was not a common practice.

[419] Even though skillful writers knew how to join sayings with narrative (Theon *Progym.* 5.388–425; cf. 4.73–79; 5.427–441) and both premeditation (Quintilian 10.6.1–2, 5) and a rough draft (Aune, *Environment,* 128) would permit the writer to prepare and relate material carefully. Arrian seems to impose more of his own grid on the Epictetus material in his more highly organized *Enchiridion* than in his *Diatribai,* but writers had a greater degree of freedom then than we would normally permit in biography today (Theon *Progym.* 1.93–171), as attested by tradition variants (cf. the tortures in 2 and 4 Macc [*OTP* 2:555; but probably 4 Maccabees diverged more from its antecedents]; Epictetus *Diatr.* 1.9.23–25 vs. Plato *Apol.* 29C, 28E), although some of these could have arisen from conflation of similar sayings or events (e.g., *p. B. Qam.* 2:6, §3).

[420] Against some of the source critics, such as Bultmann and Fortna.

[421] Grant, *Gods,* 38–39, on an inscription from Delos ca. 200 B.C.E.; Hill, *Prophecy,* 27, and Braun, "Prophet," on Josephus; for histories in general, see Hall, *Revealed Histories.* On didactic oracles, see Aune, *Prophecy,* 63.

[422] Artemidorus *Onir.* 4.pref. (δαίμονα). Further, written prophecy (e.g., Baruch read Jeremiah's scrolls) could be analogous to written prayers (cf. Tob 13:1, ἔγραψεν).

[423] Collins, *Oracles,* 5. Cf. Aune, *Prophecy,* 87–88, on the redaction of some OT oracles to fit narratives.

[424] Aune, *Prophecy,* 296, demonstrates this.

[425] Smith, *John* (1999), 299. On ancient inspiration, see also Forbes, *Prophecy.*

[426] E.g., Chariton 1.12.2–4 (though cf. 8.4.6; 8.8.4–6); Achilles Tatius 6.17; 1 Macc 6:10–13; 2 Macc 3:37–39. This often functions ironically with the characters, as in John; e.g., Tob 5:16. On narrative asides, see Stanton, *Jesus,* 122; for digressions in Greco-Roman literature, Aune, *Environ-*

are common literary techniques that need not imply prophecy; there are also other models that can explain how the Johannine Jesus tradition could have been adapted for publication addressing the current needs of the Johannine community.

> Were Christian prophets . . . the only preachers or homilists in the first-century Christian communities? Is it not every bit as likely, if not more so, that the discourses in the Fourth Gospel emanate from inspired *teachers,* able to discern the profound theological significance of traditional material concerning the earthly Jesus?[428]

Franck argues that since "teaching" can include midrashic exposition, John may use midrashic hermeneutics to interpret Jesus and that one thus cannot draw the line between old and new revelations.[429]

This would not rule out the presence of a prophetic element altogether; those who articulated the pesharim of Qumran no doubt felt that their expansive, currently oriented interpretations of the Word were insights into God's mysteries guided by his prophetic Spirit. The Fourth Gospel is very different from the apocalyptic/prophetic genre of Revelation, but both haggadic midrash and apocalyptic texts existed side by side in the Qumran community, and the Johannine community may have been no different.

It is difficult to demonstrate that writers of haggadic midrash would have always considered their writing inspired, but what is relevant is that John purports to report the postresurrection perspective of the Spirit and uses language implying that his work is a witness to divine revelation (20:30–31), perhaps analogous to the prophet-historians who were believed to have authored the OT narratives. If John's emphasis on the Spirit's enabling to speak may be compared with prophetic revelation, then it is also likely that his own text is to be understood as prophetically inspired. John may not have drawn the sort of distinction between prophetic and didactic genres we are more apt to draw today (cf. 6:45; 1 Cor 14:31).

But this ministry of the Spirit cannot be limited to the apostolic witness nor to the Fourth Gospel itself (cf. 1 John 2:20–27). The presence of the Spirit with them "forever" indicates that this exposition is expected to continue in the community, not to end with the death of the apostles;[430] the Paraclete would equip the community to confront ever new situations posed by the hostile world's charges. It is also possible that 14:27's promise of "peace" applies to the gift of the Spirit in a hostile world situation (cf. 20:19).

Most important, ancients sometimes believed that a text or tradition that was divinely inspired might require divine inspiration to understand (Iamblichus *V.P.* 1.1; cf. 1 Cor 2:12–16). Thus those who would misunderstand the Johannine tradition would be those lacking the genuine guidance of the Paraclete (1 John 2:20, 27; 4:2, 6).

---

*ment,* 93–95. In earlier Jewish tradition, prophecy sometimes was implied as the source of the narration, e.g., 2 Kgs 6:12.

[427] Cf. pictorial myths functioning as narrative omens, e.g., Achilles Tatius 5.3.

[428] Hill, *Prophecy,* 149. Cf. p. 151: "That the author of the Gospel, or parts of it, was himself a Christian prophet, must remain very hypothetical."

[429] Franck, *Revelation,* 99–124, ch. 5. This is similar to the position of Brown, "Paraclete," 129, who compares biblical ἀνάμνησις, a reenactment or re-presentation in a living manner; but Franck has developed this case in considerably more detail.

[430] Kugelman, "Pentecost," 268. Naturally, such a position has led to a variety of interpretations and responses, both Catholic and Protestant (see, e.g., Toon, *Doctrine*), but the point is that the Spirit's application of truth would remain faithful to apostolic tradition, not that any given community would perpetually remain the normative arbiter of that tradition.

The Spirit is thus given to the community not only to keep them aware of the continuing presence of Jesus among them but to enable them to continually reapply the teaching of Jesus to ever new situations without becoming dependent upon a system of communal halakah. The Spirit thus was also equipping the Johannine community for the situation that lay before them, enabling them to witness in the context of grave opposition.

## Encouragement for the Disciples (14:27–31)

Jesus leaves peace with the disciples (14:27), again encouraging them not to be afraid (14:27; see 14:1); he assures them that his departure will be better for him, not a cause of grief to them (14:28); he gives them advance warning, not to grieve them but so they may have confidence that this is part of God's plan (14:29); and he must go because it is the Father's commandment (14:31).

### 1. Peace in Jesus' Departure (14:27–29)

In an assurance oracle, Jesus provides a promise of peace after his departure (14:27). Jesus reiterates his earlier command not to be afraid (14:1), a theme that also closes his direct discourse to the disciples along with another assurance of peace (16:33). This promise relates to a central motif in Jesus' last discourse, recognizing that after Jesus departed, the disciples would have to confront a hostile world (15:18–16:4). The promise begins to be fulfilled in 20:19, 21.[431]

The language of assurance is standard (e.g., Jdt 11:1; *T. Ab.* 9:4B). "Peace" applies particularly to war[432] or human relationships,[433] but also (for Stoic thinkers especially) to tranquility in the midst of hardship[434] or to the bliss of the righteous after death;[435] it is also an eschatological hope for Israel.[436] The pacifist Pharisaic tradition that survived in rabbinic literature[437] highly extolled the value of peace.[438] While the emphasis on "peace"

---

[431] On internal referents in the fulfillment of many Johannine prophecies, see Reinhartz, "Prophet."

[432] Isocrates *Peace, Or.* 8; Cicero *Phil.* 1.1.1; *Sib. Or.* 3:751–755. Cf. especially the use in Roman political propaganda (see Sherk, *Empire*, 40; Grummond, "Pax Augusta"; also Bowley, "Pax Romana," 774, who contrasts 14:27 with the Roman political system).

[433] *T. Sanh.* 1:2; *ʾAbot R. Nat.* 40A; usually in Paul (with fellow believers, Rom 14:19; Eph 2:14–15; 4:3; Col 3:15; 1 Thess 5:13; with outsiders, Rom 12:18; 1 Cor 7:15; perhaps 2 Thess 3:16; with God, Rom 5:1; Eph 6:15).

[434] Epictetus *Diatr.* 3.13.9–11; probably *Let. Aris.* 273; cf. Epictetus *Diatr.* 2.2.3; Seneca *Dial.* 7.8.6.

[435] Wis 3:3.

[436] Tob 13:14; *1 En.* 1:6–8; 5:7–10; 71:17; 105:2 (contrast 98:11, 15; 99:13; 101:3; 103:8 for the wicked); *Jub.* 1:15; 23:29–30; 31:20; 1QM 1.9; 12.3 (after the battle); *Sib. Or.* 2.29; 3.367–380, 751–755, 780–782; 5.384–385; *T. Jud.* 22:2; *Lev. Rab.* 9:9, *bar.*; Christian material in *T. Dan* 5:11. Ford, "Shalom," compares the quietistic pacifism/Divine Warrior picture of Revelation with the Gospel's picture of Jesus submitting to suffering, in defining Johannine "peace" (cf. 16:33; 20:19, 21, 26).

[437] This wing of Pharisaism was probably a minority in the first century; see, e.g., Sanders, *Jesus to Mishnah*, 86, 324.

[438] Cf. the standard rabbinic "Great is peace, for . . ." (*Sipre Num.* 42.2.3; *Sipre Deut.* 199.3.1; *Gen. Rab.* 38:6 (Tannaitic attribution); 48:18; 100:8 (Tannaitic attribution); cf. *Sipra Behuq. pq.* 1.261.1.14). It is associated with keeping the commandments (*Sipra VDDen. pq.* 16.28.1.1, 3) and is a fruit of righteousness (*m. ʾAbot* 2:7, attributed to Hillel). Cf. *ʾAbot R. Nat.* 48, §134B; *Num. Rab.* 21:1.

is not unusual, Jesus' statement that he "leaves" it with them (ἀφίημι) may sound like a legacy from one departing (cf. 14:18).[439]

Their situation would be peace, and Jesus' situation would be better than it was while he was talking with them; he would be with the Father (14:28), as he had been explaining to his disciples earlier (14:2–6). Love for Jesus was earlier expressed by keeping his commandments (14:15), undoubtedly especially loving one another (13:34–35); here it is expressed by rejoicing for his joy once he returns to the Father. Unselfish joy for the bridegroom's exaltation also characterizes John the Baptist (3:29), though John's hearers rejoiced in him (5:35). The Fourth Gospel especially associates joy with Jesus' resurrection (16:20–22, 24; 20:20), hence with the new life believers experience in fellowship with him and with one another (15:11; 17:13).[440]

Jesus would be in a more pleasant state with his Father, he says, "because the Father is greater than I" (14:28). Elsewhere he speaks of the Father's greatness (5:36; 10:29); as Jesus is greater than those he sends (13:16; 15:20), so is the Father greater than Jesus as his sender. Ancient Mediterranean culture regarded fathers as greater in rank than sons,[441] and dependence on the abundance of a benevolent father or patron was a far superior state to dependence merely on one's own lesser means. Those who suggest, on the basis of texts such as 14:28, that John denies Jesus' deity[442] read them outside the broader context of John's theological framework. In the whole of his Gospel, John plainly affirms Jesus' deity (1:1; 8:58; 20:28) but distinguishes Jesus from the Father (1:1b, 2), a perspective that confuses modern logic (and not a few ancient thinkers, considering the christological arguments of early centuries) unless one proposes some sort of construct like the more explicit later Trinitarian thought.[443] The issue is not Jesus' nondeity, or even his distinction from the Father (which is assumed), but his subordination to the Father,[444] which portrays Jesus as the Father's obedient agent and therefore appeals to those who honor the Father to honor him.

By announcing his departure before it happens, Jesus guards his disciples against their faith being caught totally unprepared (14:29; cf. 16:4; Mark 13:23; Matt 24:25). Jews recognized that God normally declared his purposes in advance, through his servants the prophets;[445] the fulfillment of such prophecies would also vindicate the prophetic spokespersons who declared them (e.g., *Sib. Or.* 3.816–818).[446] Early Jewish sources echo

---

[439] The other expression, "give peace," is more natural (Lev 26:6; Num 6:26; 25:12; Hag 2:9; Isa 26:12; Jer 14:13; Luke 12:51; 2 Thess 3:16). John 18:22 ("gave Jesus a blow") might illustrate by contrast the world's "giving," though the connection is weak and the term frequent.

[440] This joy likewise characterizes the harvest of new believers (4:36; cf. Luke 15:6–7, 9–10, 23–24); cf. the realized eschatology in Abraham's foretaste of Jesus' day (8:56). In context, 15:11 includes love toward one another.

[441] E.g., Derrett, *Audience*, 35; Keener, "Family," 357–58.

[442] Trudinger, "Non-deity."

[443] Many philosophers regarded perfection as superlative (e.g., Seneca *Ep. Lucil.* 66.8–12) and hence would have to regard Jesus' character, if true deity, as nonsubordinate; but perfection of identity can be easily confused with identity of all that is perfect. For some historic interpretations of 14:28, see, e.g., Whitacre, *John*, 366–68. For more ontological rankings among pagan philosophers, cf., e.g., Porphyry *Marc.* 16.269–270 (only God is greater than virtue)

[444] On this theme in the Gospel, see, e.g., Barrett, *Essays*, 19–36; cf. Keener, "Subordination."

[445] Amos 3:7–8; Josephus *Ant.* 11.277–278; 4Q268 frg. 1, lines 3, 8. God's foreknowledge was a basic staple of Jewish teaching, e.g., Gen 15:13–14; *2 Bar.* 21:8; earlier tradition in *Deut. Rab.* 2:22; see more fully references on predestination in comment on John 3:19–21.

[446] Pagans also regarded fulfilments as confirmations, though they were sometimes deceptive (e.g., Ps.-Callisthenes *Alex.* 1.9, depending on magic).

the biblical perspective that the fulfillment of such warnings would prove that God was with his people (*Jub.* 1:6), but because the Bible was the most widely shared theological source for early Judaism, John's wording here probably suggests a specific allusion to God's advance warning in Isaiah, also given so that people might believe (Isa 41:26; 48:5–7).

## 2. The Coming Prince of the World (14:30)

The "prince of this world" probably corresponds to the early Jewish sectarian title "spirit of error." Some early Jewish sources recognized in the world both the "spirit of truth" and the "spirit of error" (cf. 1 John 4:6; see comment on 14:16). As Jesus announces the coming Spirit of truth (14:16–17), the Holy Spirit (14:26), he also announces "the prince of this world" (on this title, see more fully the comment on 12:31; cf. 16:11), apparently an eschatological figure (cf. 1 John 2:18; 4:3).[447] Although it is less clear that they were written before John than Qumran references to a spirit ruling the children of darkness, some other early Jewish texts could likewise speak of Beliar as ruling the world[448] or Satan as "the ruler of deception" (ὁ ἄρχων τῆς πλάνης)[449] or the "prince" of even Jews who followed him.[450] The rabbinic tradition and some other Jewish traditions normally reserve the title "prince of the world" for God,[451] defining the world as the created order; but once one defines the "world" in terms of the peoples hostile toward God, as John does, it is relevant that the rabbis also acknowledged that evil angels ruled nations hostile toward God's people.[452] In this instance the rabbis reflected views held much more widely in early Judaism (Deut 32:8 LXX; Dan 10:13, 20–21).[453]

Some suggest that Satan would come "in the person of Judas Iscariot," comparing the devil's work through him in 13:27 and Judas's impending coming in 18:2–3.[454] Certainly Judas is linked with Satan in John and acts as the devil's agent (6:70; 13:2); but "prince of the world" is hardly an appropriate title for Judas, who follows, rather than leads, the world's agenda. The Johannine community was familiar with the tradition of a com-

---

[447] This prince's "coming" (14:30) may also contrast with his own "coming" back to them after the resurrection (14:3, 28); the antichrist figure of Revelation often parodies God's Messiah (Rev 13:3–4, 18; 17:8).

[448] *Ascen. Isa.* 2:4 (although this text, with much or all of *Ascen. Isa.* 1–3, may be Christian material).

[449] *T. Jud.* 19:4 (in context, this ruler is the tempter). This figure "blinded" Simeon's mind in *T. Sim.* 2:7 (perhaps borrowing language from 2 Cor 4:4).

[450] *T. Dan* 5:6 (Satan as Dan's "prince"). Early Amoraim could also speak of a demon as "prince" over other spirits (*Lev. Rab.* 5:1). See much fuller documentation in comment on John 12:31; cf. commentaries on Eph 2:2; 2 Cor 4:4; Mark 3:22.

[451] E.g., *Gen. Rab.* 20:2 (the Shekinah); 2 Macc 7:9; cf. Michael in *b. Yebam.* 16b (Blau and Kohler, "Angelology," 588) and an angel in *Exod. Rab.* 17:4. Applications of the title to Satan (e.g., in Hoskyns, *Gospel*, 426) appear exceptional.

[452] 3 En. 29:1; 30:1–2; *Mek. Šir.* 2.112–115; *b. Ber.* 16b–17a; *Yoma* 77a; *Pesiq. Rab Kah.* 23:2; *Exod. Rab.* 32:3; *Lev. Rab.* 29:2; *Ruth Rab.* proem 1; *Pesiq. Rab.* 17:4. For their opposition to Israel, see *3 En.* 26:12; *Sipre Deut.* 315.2.1; *Gen. Rab.* 77:3; *Exod. Rab.* 21:5; *Lev. Rab.* 21:4; *Deut. Rab.* 1:22–23; *Song Rab.* 2:1, §3; 8:8, §1; for their eschatological judgment, see 1QM 15.13–14; *Pesiq. Rab Kah.* 4:9; 27:2; *Song Rab.* 8:14, §1.

[453] *Jub.* 15:31–32; 35:17; 49:2–4; cf. 1QM 14.15–16; 15.13–14; 17.5–8; *T. Sol.* 6:4; 8:10. This image probably develops the OT demythologization of national deities as angels in YHWH's court (in 11QMelch, see Kobelski, "Melchizedek," 123); cf. a δαίμων or guardian spirit of a nation in pagan thought (Plutarch *Fort. Rom.* 11, *Mor.* 324B).

[454] Fenton, *John*, 156; cf. Michaels, *John*, 254.

ing "antichrist," whose spirit the author of 1 John argues was already in the world (1 John 2:18, 22). As "son of destruction" (17:12), Judas may have embodied this impulse (cf. 2 Thess 2:3). Yet the allusion looks beyond Judas as the devil's agent. The "ruler of the world" appears in 12:31, 14:30, and 16:11; because the "ruler" is "cast out" by Jesus' realized-eschatological glorification in 12:31, it is likely that at least one segment of the Johannine community would have understood that the casting out refers to an end to Satan's rights in heaven (Rev 12:8–10).

The prince is likely the devil, but the devil is associated with those who carry out the devil's will (cf. 8:44). Interestingly, the language of "ruler" or "rulers" (ἄρχων) appears elsewhere in John only in regard to Jerusalem's elite (3:1; 7:26, 48; 12:42). A connection is not necessary but certainly possible; Paul and his contemporaries spoke of angelic "rulers" because they thought of the celestial rulers whose movements stood behind the earthly ones (Rom 8:38; Eph 1:21; 6:12; Col 1:16; 2:15; 1 Pet 3:19–22).[455] It is these hostile Judean authorities and their socially powerful allies in John's day (see 16:2) who specifically typify the broader community of "the world" in 15:18–25.

Jesus spoke about disciples being "in him" and the reverse, unless they refused to accept his sacrificial service for them (13:8), but is adamant that Satan has no place whatsoever in him (14:30).[456] That the prince has "nothing in" Jesus echoes a Semitic idiom indicating he has "no claim" on him.[457] Popular Jewish tradition already recognized that those who are of the devil's portion (μερίδος) would reap death (Wis 2:24). In one Jewish story, Sammael as the Angel of Death could not lay hold of Moses because he had no claim on him, so Moses died directly by God's agency.[458] Despite widely circulated traditions about the archangel Michael as Israel's guardian in apocalyptic circles, in one Jewish tradition God appointed rulers over the nations but dealt with Israel directly (Sir 17:17). The devil has no claim against Jesus because he is sinless (8:46);[459] Jesus dies exclusively at his Father's command (14:31).[460] Against those who attributed Jesus' activity to demons (7:20; 8:48), it is Jesus' opponents who are children of the devil and act accordingly (8:44).

### 3. Going to the Cross (14:31)

Many find in 14:31 a conclusion to a discourse, suggesting a seam between John's sources; the words can anticipate 18:1, so that an uninformed reader would not notice if chs. 15–17 had been excised.[461] A smaller number of scholars have argued that it is more

---

[455] See notes above on angels of nations in early Jewish thought.

[456] Cf. the language of Sammael dwelling in, and clinging to, Manasseh in *Ascen. Isa.* 2:1 (of uncertain date); more relevant, no place remains for Satan in heaven (Rev 12:8).

[457] Carson, *Discourse*, 83.

[458] Glasson, *Moses*, 77–78, comparing *Assumption of Moses* with John 14:30. Ben Azzai also claimed that one who died while obeying a commandment, as opposed to being engaged in some more frivolous matter, would be rewarded (*ʾAbot R. Nat.* 25A; cf. Akiba's martyrdom in *p. Soṭah* 5:5, §4).

[459] The devil often appears as accuser before God's throne; see, e.g., Rev 12:10; *Jub.* 1:20; 48:15, 18; *3 En.* 14:2; 26:12; *Gen. Rab.* 38:7; 84:2; *Exod. Rab.* 18:5; 31:2; *Lev. Rab.* 21:2; *Eccl. Rab.* 3:2, §2; with other angels *1 En.* 40:17; *3 En.* 4:8–10; *Apoc. Zeph.* 3:8; 6:17; and the very sense of "Satan" in Hebrew (cf. 1 Chr 21:1; Job 1:6–2:7; Zech 3:1–2). The exception, in later tradition, was the Day of Atonement (*b. Yoma* 20a; *Lev. Rab.* 21:4; *Num. Rab.* 18:21; *Pesiq. Rab.* 45:2; 47:4).

[460] Carson, *Discourse*, 83.

[461] Woll, *Conflict*, 9; Berg, "Pneumatology," 103; Smith, "Learned," 227; idem, *John* (1999), 28. Seams could stem from loose weaving of oral sources rather than redaction (Blomberg, *Reliability*,

likely that a single author would transpose his own sheets (attested, yet more likely, in Ps.-Asconius than in John); 14:25–31, then, should conclude after 16:33.[462] The problem with this proposal is that it presupposes a kind of book coming into widespread use only in the early second century.[463] The earliest manuscripts of John were probably scrolls, but even if they had been codices, if pages were misplaced in the manuscripts (after the author's time), why is this not reflected in the manuscript tradition? Further, why do the "misplaced pages" always end with clean sentence breaks rather than in midsentence? (It would be easier to propose that his *notes* were disordered or that he added later something he meant to add earlier; but this would not explain why he or his disciples failed to reedit their edition before publication.) Some others suggest that the words merely add realism, suggesting that the disciples left the room and they continued conversation as they walked toward the Mount of Olives;[464] this proposal is possible, though one would expect some narrative indicators to confirm this choreography.

John probably reflects the earlier passion narrative here: when Judas brought Jesus' earthly enemies, Jesus summoned his disciples with "Rise, let us go; the betrayer is at hand" (Mark 14:41–42); here the ruler of the world has provoked the similar moment of crisis for the disciples.[465] Certainly the parallel in wording is exact: ἐγείρεσθε, ἄγωμεν (Mark 14:42; John 14:31); but assuming that these words are from John's source in the Passion Narrative, perhaps known to his audience, could his emphasis on literary symbolism (e.g., 13:30) allow another reading here?

Dodd suggests that "let us go" connotes the rousing call to meet an enemy;[466] some others regard this reading as "strained."[467] The context, however, determines that we should hear the sense similarly, removing the need to view these words as representing an editorial seam. (Whether or not it is an editorial seam, the final author allowed the words to stand because they suited his overall point; ancient writers did not have as much opportunity as moderns to make word-processing errors that would interpolate lines at the wrong point.) In this case, Jesus is saying, "I am going to the Father, and I am the way for you to go to the Father" (14:3–6, 28, 31); thus, "Rise, let us go there" (14:31).[468] He then informs the disciples that they cannot do anything unless they participate in him; in life or in death, their life depends on his life (15:1–7; cf. 14:19). In obedience to his Father (14:31; cf. 10:18; 12:49–50), Jesus is going to his death (8:21; 13:3, 33; 14:2–3, 12; 16:5, 7, 10, 15, 28; esp. in context 14:28),[469] and as the plural subjunctive im-

---

45, citing Lindars, "Traditions"; Lindars, "Discourse and Tradition"); some even suggest that it represents a deliberate element of rhetorical obscurity (Stamps, "Johannine Writings," 620).

[462] So Streeter, *Gospels*, 380–81.

[463] Even if it did circulate among Christians particularly early in its history; see Ferguson, *Backgrounds*, 93–94.

[464] E.g., Westcott, *John*, 211; Hunter, *John*, 146; Carson, *Discourse*, 86.

[465] Dodd, *Interpretation*, 408.

[466] Ibid., 406–7; Gundry, *Matthew*, 536.

[467] Berg, "Pneumatology," 103–4. We may note in passing the rhetorical "come" or "go" in both Greek (e.g., Xenophon *Cyr.* 5.3.34; Epictetus *Diatr.* 1.2.29; 1.7.10; Plutarch *Mus.* 2, *Mor.* 1131E; Athenaeus *Deipn.* 11.459–460; *Sib. Or.* 3.562) and Latin (Horace *Sat.* 1.10.51; 2.3.152; Cicero *Tusc.* 3.20.49; Virgil *Georg.* 4.149; Martial *Epigr.* 1.42); but the conjunction of "arise" with a first plural subjunctive of "go" demands more than a merely rhetorical use here.

[468] Going "from here" (ἐντεῦθεν) may mean going "from the world" to the realm above (cf. 18:36).

[469] We are taking ὑπάγω and πορεύομαι as interchangeable in these texts, and in this case functionally interchangeable with ἄγω (14:31). It is possible that the invitation to join Jesus in

plies, the disciples are to follow (although at this point they will ultimately prove unprepared to do so, 13:36–38).

John's informed reader may already be equipped to understand the point here; in 11:11 Jesus goes to expose himself to death that Lazarus may live; in 11:16 the disciples are to accompany him. Jesus' obedience in all matters (14:31, emphasized by καθώς and οὕτως; cf. 8:29) would be praiseworthy;[470] contrary to the accusations of the opponents of John's audience, it is not Jesus but his opponents who undermine obedience to God.

---

"going" reflects a sacrificial Johannine application of Jesus' proclamation commission (20:17; Matt 10:7; 28:19); but more likely it simply reverses the "coming" of the incarnation (16:28), a sort of ascent (short of 20:17; perhaps 6:62) paralleling the descent (3:13).

[470] Cf. Moses, who did "just as he had also been commanded" (καθὼς αὐτῷ καὶ προείρητο, Josephus *Ant.* 2.349).

# RELATION TO JESUS AND THE WORLD

## 15:1–16:4

ESUS HAS BEEN TALKING ABOUT disciples "dwelling" in him after his return from the
Father to give them the Spirit (14:23); now he expands this "dwelling place" image by
emphasizing how branches must continue to depend on the vine or perish (15:1–7).
Branches that remain attached to and dependent on the vine "dwell" with or "remain" in it.
In this case the fruit that truly dependent branches bear is love for one another (15:8–17);
this suggests that secessionists from the community (who may join the synagogue leaders
in betraying some fellow Christians to local authorities) have also seceded from the vine
(1 John 2:9–11, 19; 3:11–18; 4:7–8).

## The Vine and Its Fruitful Branches (15:1–7)

In 15:1–17, Jesus reminds the disciples to "continue" (8:31) or "dwell" (14:17, 23)
in him like branches dependent for their life on the vine to which they are attached (15:1–7). Thus they will bear the fruit of love, which is also a commandment
(15:8–17). The whole section (15:1–17) functions as a unit contrasted with the world's
hatred (15:18–25), but because 15:1–7 and 15:8–17 are roughly distinguishable paragraphs (the distinction is more gradual than sudden; cf. 15:8) we have separated them in
our outline.

Some think that 15:1–17 reflects the same *Sitz im Leben* as 1 John, differentiating
this from the body of the Fourth Gospel.[1] But this passage is far too small to differentiate its milieu from that of the rest of the Fourth Gospel merely on the basis of motifs it
omits or includes. Some suggest a chiastic structure for all of 15:18–25, contrasting the
true vine in 15:1–6 with the synagogue in 15:18–25,[2] but the world's epitomization in
hostile synagogue authorities becomes explicit only in 16:2, and the structure is not
persuasive.

### 1. The Vine Image (15:1)

Like some of Jesus' Synoptic parables, this picture of the vine, vinedresser, and
branches is an allegory.[3] That Jesus would appeal to a vine image is not surprising. Aside
from evidence that Jesus used Isaiah's comparison of Israel with a vineyard (Mark 12:1),
vineyards and vines were so much a part of ancient Mediterranean life that they presented

---

[1] See Segovia, *Relationships,* 100–101, 179; Berg, "Pneumatology," 160.

[2] Ellis, *Genius,* 225. Cf. Israel's "vine" as the "vine of Sodom" in Deut 32:32.

[3] That Jewish parables often included allegorical elements is now clear, against earlier Aristote-
lian models; see Johnston, *Parables;* Keener, *Matthew,* 381–84; on "parables" (in the broader ancient
sense) in John, see comment on 10:6.

themselves naturally for comparisons.[4] The only fruit trees widely planted were the fig, olive, and vine,[5] which could resist drought; the last two received the most attention.[6] In the time and location probably most relevant to John's audience, Asia Minor, for instance, suffered under Domitian's policy restricting land for vineyards.[7] Viticulture thus was widely practiced and known in the ancient Mediterranean.[8] Archaeological as well as literary sources confirm the importance of wine and viticulture from an early period in ancient Israel;[9] some Jewish farmers in Egypt were also vinedressers.[10] Many Galilean farmers raised their own grapes, olives, and other supplies rather than merely specializing;[11] throughout the Mediterranean, small farms often planted vines and fig and olive trees close together;[12] some even recommended intertwining various kinds of vines and plants.[13] Some terrains proved more useful for particular crops than others did, however, and specialized vineyards were common (cf. Matt 21:33).

Jesus' parable does not need to be specific about the size of the vineyard here; although the title γεωργός (15:1)[14] could include a farmer who owns a vineyard,[15] it could just as easily imply a small holder who works other ground in addition to his vineyard.[16] Because agricultural writers recommended specialization on large estates, such as distinguishing slave vinedressers from other kinds of slave farmers,[17] the farmer so broadly titled in John 15 is probably envisioned as a smallholder or tenant farmer. Nor is the parable specific about the sort of vine, of which rural people seem to have known a considerable variety.[18]

---

[4] For moralists' various botanical illustrations, e.g., Seneca *Ep. Lucil.* 112.2; Plutarch *Demosthenes* 1.3; *Marcus Cato* 3.3 (and Jewish images, below); Eunapius *Lives* 461. John's circle of believers may have also compared the "world" with a vine in contrast to the community of believers (Rev 14:18), but the pervasiveness of vine imagery renders this judgment at most possible.

[5] E.g., Aristophanes *Ach.* 995–999.

[6] Cary and Haarhoff, *Life*, 111.

[7] Hemer, *Letters*, 158. Asia was particularly hard hit by the economic troubles of Domitian's reign (Koester, *Introduction*, 2:251).

[8] For procedures regarding vines, see Theophrastus *Caus. plant.* 3.11.1–3.16.4.

[9] Cohen, "Viticulture." For an example from the third century B.C.E. to the first century C.E., see Magen, "Q'l'ndyh"; for more information on viticulure in biblical texts, see Schwank, "Weinstock."

[10] *CPJ* 1:15, on both the Ptolemaic and the Roman periods.

[11] Horsley, *Galilee*, 203–4.

[12] Aelian *Farmers* 4 (Anthemion to Draces). Even five- or ten-acre plots could be sufficient for tenant farmers (Jeffers, *World*, 20), but a "small" vineyard could be even smaller (*m. Kil.* 4:5; *p. Kil.* 4:1, §4; 4:3/5).

[13] Theophrastus *Caus. plant.* 5.5.1–2. Rabbis, however, tried to prevent mixing of "diverse kinds," hence ultimately regulating even vine posts (*p. Kil.* 4:2).

[14] General for "cultivator," as distinguished from the more specific ἀμπελουργός ("vinedresser"; P.Thead. 17.11, 332 C.E.).

[15] Babrius 2.1; cf. the massive vineyard plantations of Hellenistic Egypt (P.Cair.Zen. 59736, ca. 250 B.C.E.). A noble Roman could be a husbandman (*agricola;* e.g., Cornelius Nepos 24 [Cato], 3.1) but would just own, not till.

[16] E.g., *Rev. Laws* 41.11 in *Sel. Pap.* 2:14–15 (259 B.C.E.). In the LXX, the term predominates in Prov (6:7; 9:12; 24:5, 30; 31:16; elsewhere only Gen 26:14; Sir 27:6; Jer 51:23; cf. Robertson and Plummer, *Corinthians*, 59).

[17] Columella *Rust.* 1.9.5–6. Columella *Rust.* 1.6.1 describes the ideal villa, but this would be relevant only to the rich; for ideal sites for vineyards, see Columella *Arb.* 4.1–5.

[18] See Pliny *Nat.* 14.4.20–14.5.52; 14.23.119; for different kinds of grapes, see Athenaeus *Deipn.* 14.653B–654A. On planting vines, see Pliny *Nat.* 17.35.156–187.

## 1A. Various Proposed Backgrounds to the Image

Thus vine imagery was common enough without necessary specific allusions to standard symbolisms.[19] Jewish engravers adopted the Roman association of doves and grapes in their artwork.[20] Further, whatever particular backgrounds may have been in mind, the primary image of branches dependent on the vine simply communicates that disciples are dependent on Jesus for their very life and can do nothing, produce no fruit genuinely pleasing to God, by themselves (15:4–5; cf. 3:6; Rev 22:2).[21]

Many scholars nevertheless suspect that this passage alludes to more than merely the standard function implied in the image of vines and branches. Some connect the vine here with the wine of the Lord's Supper.[22] That the Fourth Gospel omits the Lord's Supper, however, makes it difficult for us to connect the vine with the Lord's Supper unless we can safely assume that the audience would have caught the allusion despite its absence from the context. Granted, the audience very probably knew the Last Supper tradition and may have approached this section of John with such a setting in mind, but it asks too much to suppose that John wished the reader to catch the allusion yet omits any mention of the supper, which he could have included, when other associations are otherwise more obvious. Indeed, despite the expression for wine common in Jewish prayers ("fruit of the vine"), the image of cultivated vines did not always demand the image of its perfected product.[23] Jesus could replace the source of paschal wine easily enough;[24] in the context of an earlier Passover, only those who "drank his blood" would experience life (6:53, 55). But for John, this is the day preceding the Passover (18:28), diminishing the force of any proposed paschal allusion. A connection with the use of vines in the walls of sukkoth would be even less likely than allusions to Passover;[25] although the Gospel earlier alludes to Tabernacles (7:2, 37–39) and the motif of "dwelling" (μένω) in the narrative could support such an allusion, Passover rather than Tabernacles dominates the Passion Narrative.

The Targum to Ps 80:14–15 can identify the vine (as the Branch) with the Messiah, probably based on exegesis of that text rather than on a prior tradition; more important, *2 Bar.* 39:7 uses the "vine" as a symbol for the Messiah.[26] One might have also made the inference midrashically from the relation of a "son of man" to the vine in Ps 80:17,[27] although it is nowhere clear that John 15 has Ps 80 (one among many biblical vine

---

[19] E.g., on the goblets in *Let. Aris.* 79; or the ornamental grapevine on a "Nazirite" Herodian stone coffin (Avigad, *Jerusalem*, 166).

[20] Goodenough, *Symbols*, 1:156–57.

[21] That everything brings forth according to its own kind (cf. Gen 1:11) was a commonplace (see comment on John 3:6), also applicable to moral fruits (Seneca *Ep. Lucil.* 87.25; Matt 7:16–18; Gal 5:22; Jas 3:12).

[22] Bernard, *John,* 2:477–78; Brown, *Essays,* 102–3; Richardson, *Theology,* 377; Brodie, *Gospel,* 482; cf. Hoskyns, *Gospel,* 474, and Barrett, *John,* 472, who combine the immediate background in the Last Supper tradition with the biblical image of Israel as a vine. This tradition is likely early; *Did.* 9.2 uses Jesus as the vine as part of the eucharistic thanksgiving.

[23] Some even believed that sprinkling a vine with wine derived from it would wither the vine (Plutarch *Nat. Q.* 31, *Mor.* 919C).

[24] Oesterley, *Liturgy,* 185, connects the vine with Pesach wine.

[25] If later tradition is relevant, the vine's usefulness in a sukkah was quite limited (cf. *b. Sukkah* 11a, 22b).

[26] Cadman, *Heaven,* 175. More pervasive are connections with the "branch"; see, e.g., Isa 11:1; cf. Isa 4:2; Jer 23:5; 33:15; Zech 3:8; 6:12; 1QH 6.15; 7.19; 8.6, 8, 10; 4Q174, 3.12; cf. *T. Jud.* 24:4, if not an interpolation.

[27] E.g., Dodd, *Interpretation,* 411; Painter, *John,* 48.

references) in view. But these comparisons seem isolated and perhaps coincidental in view of much more pervasive uses of vine imagery; the same passage of *2 Bar.* 39, for example, compares the Messiah with a fountain.

Perhaps more important in view of John's Christology, personified Wisdom at least once appears as a vine.[28] Because the comparison is in Sirach (24:17), it may well have been known to John's audience in ways that less obvious allusions would not be; in the final analysis, however, the significance of the Sirach passage for John appears weakened by its incidental character. Sirach compares Wisdom to a variety of trees (24:13–17), of which the vine is only one; further, the person invited (in language John elsewhere employs, of coming, eating, and drinking) is invited to eat Wisdom's fruits (24:19–21), not bear them.

Most possible Hellenistic associations appear distant from the point of the passage. The vine was sacred to Heracles on a particular island named for him (Aelian 6.40); wine and the vine were sometimes associated with various figures,[29] but most frequently they were associated with Dionysus (Virgil *Ecl.* 7.61; Martial *Epigr.* 3.24.1; 8.26). Dionysus allegedly taught people how to use vines and wine,[30] and the vine was his special gift to the world.[31] Some have argued that the vine represents the good things of earth and that the vine represents Jesus in the Platonic sense of shadows depicting heavenly reality;[32] the narrow basis for comparison straitjackets the multiple possible uses of ancient metaphor.[33] But whereas Greek readers would have recognized the image of God as a farmer who cultivates the world, the vine figure undoubtedly stems from the Bible.[34]

## 1B. Israel as a Vine

Commentators most frequently point to the biblical image of Israel as a vine (Ps 80:8–16; Isa 27:2–6; Jer 2:21; Ezek 15:2–6; 17:5–10; 19:10–14) or vineyard (Isa 5:1–7);[35] the latter image appears elsewhere in the Jesus tradition (Mark 12:1–9).[36] (Most draw from this the implication that John believes that those grafted into Christ, rather than merely into ethnic Israel, are in salvific covenant with God.)[37] Early Jewish traditions also portray

---

[28] Painter, *John*, 48; Feuillet, *Studies*, 88–89; Culpepper, *John*, 214; Wisdom is identified with the law in 24:23.

[29] Samian Hera had a vine branch in her hair (Callimachus *Aetia* 4.101; the *Diegesis* associates this with her conflicts with Dionysus). Perhaps Philo allegorized Ganymede, Zeus's wine pourer, as God's forth-flowing Logos (Dillon, "Ganymede"; idem, "Logos").

[30] Diodorus Siculus 1.15.8, who also reports, however, that the Egyptians (who link him with Osiris) believe that he prefers ivy (Diodorus Siculus 1.17.5).

[31] Otto, *Dionysus*, 49, 147. For Dionysus as its discoverer, see, e.g., Apollodorus 3.5.1.

[32] Gamble, "Philosophy," 56.

[33] For the vine in Mandean texts, see Borig, *Weinstock*, 135–94 (comparing John 15 and other texts in pp. 177–94).

[34] Dodd, *Interpretation*, 411.

[35] Caragounis, "Vineyard," argues that ἄμπελος became "vineyard" and κλήματα "vines" in pre-Christian Koine. Given the description of pruning, "vine" is a better translation in John 15 than "vineyard," but the semantic overlap illustrates the importance of both vine and vineyard data.

[36] On the Qumran interpretation of Isa 5:1–7, see 4Q500, in Baumgarten, "Vineyard." The vine image is also consistent with the Jesus tradition's use of "fruit"; see comment below.

[37] E.g., Augustine *Tract. Ev. Jo.* 80.1.2 (citing Jer 2:21 and Isa 5:4); Köstenberger, *John*, 159; Strachan, *Gospel*, 176; Hunter, *Message*, 78; idem, *John*, 148; Barrett, "Old Testament," 164; idem, *John*, 472; Hoskyns, *Gospel*, 474; Sanders, *John*, 337; Richardson, *Israel*, 187; Fenton, *John*, 158; Morris, *John*, 668; van der Waal, "Gospel," 36; Hickling, "Attitudes," 353; Ellis, *Genius*, 225; Painter, *John*, 48; Carson, *Discourse*, 91.

Israel as a vineyard[38] or a vine.[39] Such images are not surprising given the prevalence of vineyards in the Mediterranean and the frequency of diverse images by which Israel is portrayed in early Jewish literature;[40] but their commonness is nevertheless significant. In general, Israel frequently appears as a plant;[41] some congregations also may have been called by the names of trees.[42] Some doubt that the vine can allude to Israel here, objecting that the church, rather than Christ, "replaces" Israel.[43] The objection is, however, wide of the mark; it is through identifying with Christ that believers both Jewish and Gentile are grafted into the historic people of God (e.g., Gal 3:16).[44]

The Herodian temple sported a massive (and annually augmented) golden vine,[45] and it is likely that it also was meant to evoke Israel. Some suspect that Jesus, who had led the disciples out of the upper room in the upper city in 14:31, now points to the golden vine in the temple, which they are passing;[46] after all, the temple doors were reportedly left open at night during the Passover season.[47] But such allusions are unlikely; the transition of 14:31 is not clearly physical (though the geographic marker of 18:1 could allow that they had started walking), and the vine lay in front of the doors that divided the porch and the holy place, not easily visible unless one actually entered the temple enclosure.[48] More likely, the temple's golden vine merely presents us another sample of the pervasive use of vine symbolism in early Jewish art. Probably adapting some pagan symbolism,[49] the vine and wine

---

[38] E.g., *3 Bar.* 1:2; *Exod. Rab.* 30:17; 34:3; *Song Rab.* 2:16, §1; 7:13, §1; *Pesiq. Rab Kah.* 16:9. Some texts explicitly conjoin this image with God's flock as well (e.g., *Mek. Pisha* 1.162; *Sipre Deut.* 15.1.1; cf. John 10:1).

[39] *4 Ezra* 5:23; *2 Bar.* 39:7; *L.A.B.* 12:8–9; 23:12; 28:4; *b. Ḥul.* 92a; *Gen. Rab.* 88:5; 98:9; *Exod. Rab.* 44:1; *Num. Rab.* 8:9; *Esth. Rab.* 9:2; either Israel or the elect in 4QHodayot-like frg. 2, line 3 (Wise, *Scrolls*, 447). This could also be conjoined with the image of God's flock (*4 Ezra* 5:23–24; cf. John 10).

[40] E.g., some of the same texts also compare Israel with a lily (*4 Ezra* 5:23) or various trees (*Esth. Rab.* 9:2); some also used the vine to symbolize Torah or Jerusalem (*b. Ḥul.* 92a) or Sarah (*Gen. Rab.* 53:3; cf. *Pesiq. Rab Kah.* 27:9), or its branches to symbolize Moses and others (*Gen. Rab.* 88:5). R. Meir reportedly thought the tree of knowledge was a vine, but others disagreed (*b. Ber.* 40a).

[41] Cf., e.g., Jer 1:10; 24:6; 31:28; 42:10; *Jub.* 1:16; 7:34; 16:26; 21:24; 36:6; 1QS 8.5; 11.8; CD 1.7; 1QapGen 1.1 (reconstructed); *2 Bar.* 51:3; Fujita, "Plant"; Mussner, "Gleichnis"; Wirgin, *Jubilees,* 22–26; perhaps *1 En.* 10:16; 84:6. See also Matt 15:13; Rom 6:5; 11:16–24; 1 Cor 3:6–9; Herm. *Sim.* 8. For the patriarchs, see, e.g., *1 En.* 93:2, 5, 10; *b. Yebam.* 63a (were the image more common, one could argue that John portrays Jesus as the greater foundation for God's people). The moralistic uses (cf. 1 Macc 1:10; *T. Ash.* 1:7) may be a Hellenistic borrowing (Plutarch *Educ.* 7, *Mor.* 4C) but may actually undergird the early image (e.g., "uprooting" in judgment in 2 Chr 7:20; Prov 2:22; Jer 12:14–15; *Jub.* 6:12; 15:26, 28, 34; 16:9; 20:4; 21:22; 22:20; 24:29, 31, 33; 26:34; 30:7, 10, 22; 31:17, 20; 33:13, 17, 19; 35:14; 36:9; 37:23; 49:9).

[42] For a Roman congregation possibly named for the olive tree and one in Sepphoris for a vine, see Leon, *Jews,* 146; for common Greco-Roman tree symbolism in Diaspora Jewish art from the second to the fifth centuries, see Goodenough, *Symbols,* 7:87–134.

[43] Bernard, *John,* 2:477–78.

[44] The "vineyard" in Yavneh (e.g., *b. Ber.* 63b) is also understood figuratively as the disciples there (*p. Taʿan.* 4:1, §14).

[45] E.g., Josephus *War* 5.210; pagan views of this were negative (cf. Cicero *Pro Flacco* 28.66–67; Tacitus *Hist.* 5.5).

[46] Pass, *Glory,* 165; he suggests, as an unproved but useful working hypothesis, that Jesus delivered this discourse in the temple (Pass, *Glory,* 174). Cf. Hunter, *John,* 148, though he emphasizes especially the connection with Israel.

[47] Pass, *Glory,* 172.

[48] Josephus *War* 5.207–210.

[49] Goodenough, *Symbols,* vols. 5–6; see esp. 6:125.

cup may constitute the most common symbols for "Jewish life and hope" on later Jewish coins.[50] Others suggest that the sight of vineyards en route to Gethsemane may have suggested the image,[51] which is possible but not provable nor, if correct, incompatible with other options.

The vine image could thus imply a sense of community[52] the Jewish believers inherited from early Judaism in general. Whereas the Eleusinian cult of Demeter, for example, met only annually and did not lead initiates to associate with one another, early Judaism and Christianity were exclusivistic and carried a strong sense of community.[53] Nevertheless, early Christian literature provides no examples of early Christian communities with the sort of rigid hierarchical structure expected of Qumran Covenanters (e.g., 1QS 5.23–24; 6.2). Most early Jews and Christians associated for common worship and need; formal structures were less rigid than Qumran, but sufficient.

If the vine alludes to Israel, the designation "true" (15:1) may forcefully contrast Jesus with Israel.[54] One should not overstate the contrast; whereas "true" can exclude any others (17:3), it can also simply contrast with "mere." "True bread" does not contrast Jesus with Torah but does contrast him with mere manna (6:32, 55); "true light" contrasts him with an inferior though accurate witness (1:9). Such passages may respond to opponents of the Johannine community's witness who claim that Jesus' way is not "true" (cf. 5:31–32; 7:18; 8:13–17; 19:35; 21:24). John's "vine" image may function in the same way that Paul's "olive tree" image does; in both cases, disobedient branches are broken off (John 15:2, 6; Rom 11:17), though John, most of whose audience probably already regards itself as Jewish, does not emphasize any grafting on of foreign branches. Here as elsewhere (cf. comment on 3:3–5), for John, "becoming a true Jew and becoming a Christian are one and the same thing."[55]

## 2. The Vinedresser's Pruning (15:1–3)

The figure of God as the vinedresser (15:1) is not completely unexpected. Gardeners often belonged to the poorest class (Apuleius *Metam.* 9.31), such as those who might lease rather than own a vineyard (P.Oxy. 1631.9–13).[56] Yet not all farmers (γεωργοί) were poor,[57] and in any case, this fact is less significant than other backgrounds for the image;

---

[50] Ibid., 1:276; 2:3. Porton, "Grape-Cluster," notes that the symbol becomes most prominent on these coins only in the Bar Kokhba period; but for other probable plant symbolism as early as Maccabean coins, see Wirgin, *Jubilees*, 22–26.

[51] Blomberg, *Reliability*, 205 (noting that teachers often lectured as they walked).

[52] Cf. O'Grady, "Shepherd," who suggests an individual relation to Christ in collectivity, as in the shepherd image of John 10.

[53] Gager, *Kingdom*, 131–32.

[54] The comparison with Greek philosophy's contrast between spiritual reality and mere appearance (e.g., Scott, *Gospel*, 253) is strained.

[55] Robinson, "Destination," 121–22; also see Painter, *John*, 97–98, likewise emphasizing the Jewishness of John's community.

[56] Neighbors of other occupations might help during the harvest or vintage (Longus 2.1; Matt 20:2–4) or at least lend baskets for gathering (Alciphron *Farmers* 12 [Cotinus to Trygodorus], 3.15). The designation might reflect low status from an urban or mercantile perspective (Philostratus *Hrk.* 4.11), but not to rural people (4.12).

[57] Some had others working under them (Ptolemy *Tetr.* 4.4.179; Philostratus *Hrk.* 1.6). Socrates considered γεωργία an honorable occupation (Xenophon *Oec.* 6.11), but vinedressing could be arduous (cf. Sir 7:15).

Jesus himself appears as a sort of gardener in 20:15.[58] Naturally, Greek texts could sometimes portray Dionysus as the ultimate vinedresser (Achilles Tatius 2.3.2).[59] Far more important, OT images of Israel as God's vine imply God or his workers as tenders of that vine; Paul speaks of God's church as his field, his γεώργιον (1 Cor 3:9).

## 2A. A Vinedresser's Attention

The state of a tree's fruit (καρπός) was said to attest how well its farmer (γεώργιον) had cared for it (Sir 27:6), reinforcing the importance of a gardener's care for it.[60] Evidence from ancient literature shows that, in the West at least, large-scale vine cultivation could yield substantial profits;[61] nevertheless, less expensive wines could flood the market and be sold at low prices.[62] One could never take adequate productivity and profit for granted. Pruning (15:2) was essential to provide long-range, healthy fruit, and those leasing a vineyard were responsible for cutting away the useless wood.[63]

Of all fruit plants, the vine requires the most attention,[64] starting with tying the vines to their supports (sometimes trees, but usually wooden posts) in the spring.[65] In Italy during the summer, farmers would break up the soil around the roots and selectively prune the tendrils (the shoots that could coil around other objects); further work continued into October.[66] Pliny the Elder observed that his contemporaries practiced spring trimming no longer than ten days after May 15, before the vine began to blossom; his contemporaries varied on whether the later trimming should occur after the blossoms disappear or when the grapes are beginning to ripen.[67] He observes that vinedressers undertook pruning right after the grape vintage but while it was still warm; this was because late winter cold could harm vines weakened by recent pruning.[68] The earlier one pruned vines, the better wood they supplied; the later one pruned them—provided it was not too cold—the better for the fruit; thus one might prune weak vines earlier and stronger ones later.[69]

---

[58] Though it remains possible, that 20:15 does not reapply the wording of this text decreases the likelihood of an intentional allusion that would parallel Jesus and the Father there.

[59] For the gardener image from Greco-Roman philosophy onward, see Thurn, "Gartner"; cf. a semidivine hero as a vinedresser in Philostratus *Hrk.* 17.2; and another's mortal advocate in *Hrk.* 1.1 and passim (cf. Maclean and Aitken, *Heroikos,* xxviii, xxxvii–xxxviii).

[60] On care for vines, see, e.g., Virgil *Georg.* 2.273–419. Vineyards had to be guarded from animals such as foxes (Song 2:15; Alciphron *Farmers* 19 [Polyalsus to Eustaphylus], 3.22, par. 1) and thieves (*CPJ* §21, 1:157–58).

[61] Friedländer, *Life,* 1:189.

[62] Cary and Haarhoff, *Life,* 111. The most expensive wines came especially from Campania and some Aegean islands.

[63] P.Oxy. 1631.9 (ξυλοτομία).

[64] In contrast to vines, olives require no tending, including no pruning (Virgil *Georg.* 2.420–422).

[65] Cary and Haarhoff, *Life,* 111.

[66] Ibid. For preparing soil for new trees, see Theophrastus *Caus. plant.* 3.4.1; for planting vines, see 3.11.5–3.12.3; for manuring trees, 3.6.1–2; 3.9.1–5; for pruning vines, 3.7.5; 3.11.1–3.16.4; for pruning other kinds of trees, 3.7.6–12 (root pruning in 3.8.1–2).

[67] Pliny *Nat.* 17.35.190. Theophrastus advocates cutting a young vine's sprouts in spring if it is not too cold (*Caus. plant.* 3.13.1), and cutting the fruit in autumn (3.13.2). For mature vines, see 3.14.1; thinning the shoots is like a second dressing, as soon as the promise of fruit appears (3.16.1–4).

[68] Pliny *Nat.* 17.35.191.

[69] Pliny *Nat.* 17.35.192.

Pliny's comments probably reflect conditions more characteristic of the northern Mediterranean, but milder winters presumably permitted a somewhat different schedule in the southern Mediterranean.[70] In Egypt, farmers pruned vines in January and February, preparing well in advance for the vintage of August and September.[71] One botanist observes on conditions in Palestine:

> Pruning of the vines takes place during winter dormancy, and, except for side shoots, not at the height of development (Isa 18:5). The previous season's growth is cut back and the long leafless twigs are used for fuel (John 15:6). Pruning helps to ensure that the fruit is of good quality, for otherwise during the following season there would be too many clusters of fruit to be nourished by the roots, resulting in only poor grapes.[72]

Pruning had long been known in Israel; the Hebrew Bible provides numerous references to the practice (Lev 25:3–4; Song 2:12; Isa 2:4; 5:6; 18:5; Joel 3:10; Mic 4:3). If the vine is weak, one prunes it more, leaving less fruit, and the next year the vine will be stronger and there will be more grapes.[73]

Useless growths on fruitful branches are pruned back in the spring to augment the branches' eventual yield; before this, unfruitful branches are removed in the winter to prevent them from sapping strength better reserved for fruit-bearing branches.[74] Columella advised that one prune a weak vine on dry land before midwinter and finish pruning about February 1; one should not use a knife on any vine between December 13 and January 13.[75] Virgil likewise advises that one spare the vines when they were just budding, because they were young and weak;[76] one should pick here and there with one's fingers,[77] clip them only later, when they became sturdy,[78] and finally apply the pruning knife.[79] Regardless of divergence of geography and opinion on details, the earlier vine trimming was a stripping of useless twigs and leaves—anything that will not bear grapes—by hand shortly before the vine begins to blossom *(pampinatio)*,[80] distinct from, and perhaps more important than, the later pruning with a knife *(putatio)* when the vine was stronger.[81] Because

---

[70] Theophrastus *Caus. plant.* 14.2–3 advocates sensitivity to local conditions and in 3.15.1–5 offers seasons for pruning based on region.

[71] Lewis, *Life*, 125.

[72] Hepper, *Plants*, 98.

[73] Ibid. The exception was the sabbatic year, when (as on the weekly Sabbath) pruning would be prohibited (cf. *p. Kil.* 8:1, §5). Grapes were also subject to tithe (4Q266 frg. 12), like olives (4Q270 frg. 6).

[74] Swete, *Discourse*, 73; Schnackenburg, *John*, 3:97. Those leasing a vineyard were responsible for collecting and removing the wood (P.Oxy. 1631.10).

[75] Columella *Arb.* 10.2. Using a mattock (Babrius 2.1–2), one should begin trenching around October 15 and finish by midwinter (Columella *Arb.* 5.3; cf. breaking up ground around vines in P.Oxy. 1631.9–13); one can cut back the vine's roots during winter provided one leaves at least an inch so as not to damage the vine (Columella *Arb.* 5.3–4), and one should not cut back the old vine (6.1).

[76] Virgil *Georg.* 2.362–363.

[77] Virgil *Georg.* 2.364–366.

[78] Virgil *Georg.* 2.367–370.

[79] Virgil *Georg.* 2.416–419.

[80] Columella *Rust.* 4.27.1–2; *Arb.* 11.1–2. Columella's advice that one should trim and not just prune (11.1) might suggest that some did only the latter.

[81] Columella *Rust.* 3.10.1–8 proposes parts of the vine from which to take cuttings (against the practice of many actual vinedressers); on the length of cuttings, see 3.19.1–3.

the fruitlessness is obvious here, however (15:2), the parable may envision the spring pruning with the knife (cf. Song 2:11–12).[82]

Immediately after the autumn vintage, one would prune again with the sharpest instruments to cut smoothly.[83] Some agriculturalists advised that one should draw the pruning knife toward oneself rather than hack lest one miss and wound the stock of the vine.[84] It was understood that if one did not remove the shoots properly, one could damage the vine.[85] Columella advises, "Cut away all shoots which are too broad, or old, or badly grown, or twisted; but allow those to grow which are young and fruitful and sometimes a suitable off-shoot. . . . Finish the pruning as quickly as possible. Shoots which are old and dry cannot be cut away with a pruning-knife," so one should employ a sharp axe.[86]

These practices naturally lent themselves to moral analogies at times. Thus Statius notes that many squander their youth like a tree, never pruned by the knife, that "luxuriates in growth and wastes its fuitfulness in leaf."[87]

## 2B. "Cleansing" (15:2–3)

Although καθαίρει (lit., "cleanses") clearly means "prunes" in this analogy (15:2), it is not the most common expression from viticulture,[88] instead infusing the analogy with an image from Johannine theology (cf. the related καθαρίζω in 1 John 1:7–9; elsewhere 2 Cor 7:1; Tit 2:14; Heb 9:14, 22–23; 10:2). When Jesus speaks of the continued "cleansing" of the branches (15:2) after they have already become "clean" (καθαροί, 15:3), the disciples in the story world and John's ideal audience might recall 13:10, which implies that the disciples are mostly clean but their feet must still be washed.

Greek philosophers could use related expressions for the purity of the heavenly deities and the soul;[89] they could also apply this language to moral matters.[90] Jewish tradition emphasized cleansing one's heart (καθάρισον καρδίαν) from all sin (Sir 38:10). Appealing to his Hellenistic-educated audience, Josephus includes in the Essene initiation oath the promise to keep one's soul pure (ψυχὴν . . . καθαράν) from desiring unholy gain (Josephus War 2.141). The image could involve judgment or difficulty; early Jewish texts also could describe the flood as a "cleansing" of the earth (1 En. 106:17) or speak of the Messiah purging (καθαριεῖ) Jerusalem to restore it in holiness (ἐν ἁγιασμῷ, Pss. Sol. 17:30).[91]

---

[82] Jesus' analogy does not cover all possible points; e.g., a vinedresser might remove even fruitful branches if they are too many (Columella Rust. 4.27.4) lest the vine have too much fruit to carry to maturity (4.27.5).

[83] Columella Arb. 10.1.

[84] Columella Rust. 4.25.2–3; on the knife, see 4.25.1.

[85] P.Cair.Zen. 59736.27–29 (ca. 250 B.C.E.).

[86] Columella Arb. 10.2 (LCL 3:374–75).

[87] Statius Silvae 5.2.69–70 (LCL 1:294–95).

[88] See, e.g., Morris, John, 669; Barrett, John, 473; Brown, John, 2:660; Ridderbos, John, 516 n. 115. The most frequently cited agricultural parallels (Xenophon Oec. 18.6; 20.11; Philo Dreams 2.64) do not imply pruning without further specification; in a rural setting, one might purify other things (e.g., fountains, Longus 4.1).

[89] E.g., Epictetus Diatr. 4.11.3, 5; Iamblichus V.P. 16.70; Philostratus Hrk. 7.3; Porphyry Marc. 11.204; 15.255–56 (cf. also 23.368; 24.374–76; 26.402–3).

[90] E.g., Musonius Rufus 3, p. 40.17, 28; 4, p. 44.25; 16, p. 104.35; 18B, p. 118.4–5; Epictetus Diatr. 4.11.8; Ench. 33.6, 8; Menander Rhetor 2.10, 416.7–8; Acts 15:9; 1 Cor 6:11; 2 Cor 7:1; 2 Tim 2:21; Heb 9:14; 10:22; 2 Pet 1:9).

[91] In Rev 15:6 purity accompanies the image of angelic linen; see 19:40; 20:7, 12 and our comment for the significance of linen and white as purity images.

John may use the term in contrast with merely outward rituals of purification (2:6; 3:25). Jesus had cleansed them through his "word," his entire message (14:23–24), which in the context of the Gospel as a whole communicated Christ's very person (16:8–15; cf. 1:1–18).

## 3. Fruit Bearing (15:2, 4–5, 7–8)

At least in the northern Mediterranean, the region probably most familiar to most of John's audience, the vintage arrived in autumn,[92] at which time the gathered grapes would be trodden to yield their juice.[93] In Palestine, the grapes ripen in late summer as the shoots stop growing and the bark changes from green to darker shortly before the vintage of August or September.[94]

Yet John writes figuratively; of what sort of fruit does the passage speak? In John's larger usage, one might suppose the fruit of Christian witness (4:36; 12:24), but the immediate context, which bears more weight than John's usage elsewhere when the usage is so rare (two texts), suggests moral fruit.[95] This is the most common sense of the metaphor in other traditions about Jesus and John the Baptist with which this Gospel's first audience may have been familiar (Matt 3:8, 10; 7:16–20; 12:33; Luke 3:8–9; 6:43–44; 13:6–9; probably Mark 11:14; 12:2); other early Christian writers also develop it (Gal 5:22; Phil 1:11; Eph 5:9; Col 1:10; Heb 12:11; Jas 3:18; Jude 12).[96]

In an agrarian society such as ancient Israel's, the image of fruit bearing naturally proved recurrent, albeit less frequently in the sense of its usage in this passage than one might expect. In Hosea, Israel thought God's gifts were from other lovers (Hos 2:5, 8–9), and Israel the vine yielded fruit for idolatry (10:1), a fruit of poisonous weeds (10:4). Though his people had sown and reaped sin (10:13), God would make them sow and reap righteousness (10:11–12); God would be the dew and cause Israel to blossom and bear fruit (14:5–7), and he would be the source of their fruit (14:8). One early Jewish text could speak of God's law bearing fruit in the hearts of the righteous (*4 Ezra* 3:20).[97] Greeks also offered such comparisons, although again, perhaps because of the urban setting of much literature preserved for us, moral uses of fruit are less common than one might expect.[98] Plutarch reports that Socrates wanted to cultivate Alcibiades as a plant so that his "fruit" would not be destroyed.[99] Given their emphases, it is not surprising that philosophers used the metaphor especially in an intellectual sense. Thus, for example, Epictetus compares figs with "the fruit (καρπόν) of human intelligence,"[100] and Marcus Aurelius expounds on

---

[92] Longus 1.28; 2.1.

[93] Ovid *Metam.* 2.29. For drying grapes in the hot sun, see Aelian *Farmers* 1 (Euthycomides to Blepaeus).

[94] Hepper, *Plants,* 99.

[95] See Borig, *Weinstock,* 238–39.

[96] That Gal 5 contrasts the Spirit's fruit with law-works (cf. Gal 5:4–5, 14, 18, 23; 6:1–2) suggests a contrast with traditional Jewish understanding of means of obedience; such a contrast would naturally fit John's polemic, though abundant other early Christian uses of the image do not require us to limit the image to this purpose.

[97] In one of several interpretations of a text, some Amoraim interpreted a tree's fruitfulness as good deeds (*Num. Rab.* 3:1); in a natural parallel, the results of learning Torah could be compared with fruit (*Num. Rab.* 21:15).

[98] *Apoc. Sedr.* 12:5 has ποιήσῃ καρπὸν δικαιοσύνης, but this is late.

[99] Plutarch *Alc.* 4.1.

[100] Epictetus *Diatr.* 1.15.8. Epictetus *Diatr.* 1.17.9 may suggest "fruitfulness" as a broader cultural metaphor for utility; certainly it could mean "profit" (cf. e.g., Musonius Rufus 14, p. 92.23).

the fruit of reason;[101] Philo felt that the best fruit of the soul is unforgetful remembering.[102] On the whole, however, the accepted setting of the vine and the normal agrarian image probably exercised more effect than specific extrabiblical precedent for using fruit as a moral image.

For John, Jesus is the source of fruit; without him the disciples can do nothing, that is, bear no fruit (15:5); that Jesus himself remains utterly dependent on the Father, "able to do nothing from himself" (5:19; cf. 8:28), underlines the point still more starkly for disciples. (The image may develop the biblical picture of God requiring fruit from Israel; Hos 14:8 emphasizes that Israel's fruit comes only from the Lord.) "Without him" (15:5) probably signifies "without remaining, abiding, in him."[103] Some later teachers claimed that Israel could do nothing without its leaders,[104] usually referring to its scholars who handle Scripture, God's Word.[105] But for John, Jesus' activity in the present era is mediated through the indwelling of the Spirit (14:16–17, 26); this image nicely complements Paul's emphasis on the fruit of the Spirit in Galatians 5:22–23[106] (although Paul also uses other moral fruit images, e.g., Phil 1:11; cf. Eph 5:9). Paul also acknowledged that he had no adequacy apart from God's enablement (2 Cor 3:5; cf. 2:16), which he attributed to the Spirit (2 Cor 3:6). John's line in 15:5 neatly summarizes a good bit of Johannine thought: new birth, new life, and religion genuinely pleasing to God all must come from above, from the Spirit, from Jesus, who is from above (see comment on 3:3–6); the best of human effort apart from God's own enablement is worthless.

The promise of answered prayer in 15:7 suggests a connection with, or interpretation of, prayer "in Jesus' name" (14:13–14; 16:23–26), which is related to loving and believing Jesus (16:27) and keeping his commandments (14:15). "Abiding" in Jesus and allowing his words to abide in one (which is roughly equivalent in practice)[107] entail continuing to love and trust in Jesus, with the assurance that the lover of Jesus, whose desires are ultimately for Jesus' agendas, will receive answered prayer. (See more fully the comment on 14:13–14.)

### 4. Perseverance or Apostasy (15:6)

The condition for fruit bearing, hence for perseverance, is "abiding" (μείνατε) in Jesus (15:4). This term (μένω and cognates) appears eleven times in 15:4–16, dominating the theology just as the vine and fruit dominate the image.[108] Those who truly "abide" will bear fruit (cf. 1 John 2:6) because they have the Spirit (1 John 3:24; 4:13). In view of possible internal community problems (1 John 2:18–27)[109] and particularly the world's hostility emphasized in the context (15:18–25), the call to perseverance here is not surprising.

---

[101] Marcus Aurelius 9.10.

[102] Philo *Migration* 205.

[103] Cf. Michaels, *John*, 257, arguing for a minor chiastic pattern here.

[104] E.g., *Song Rab.* 4:1, §2; 1:15, §2.

[105] See Bonsirven, *Judaism*, 54–55, and citations there. Boring et al., *Commentary*, 301, cite, as an example of the "hymnic topos" of dependence on a deity, Aelius Aristides *Or.* 37.10: people will never "do anything useful without Athena."

[106] Cf. Smalley, "Relationship," 98.

[107] Bruce, *John*, 309, rightly notes in this connection that Jesus "is the living embodiment of all his teaching."

[108] With, e.g., Fenton, *John*, 159.

[109] Cf. Segovia, *Farewell*, 302.

### 4A. The Johannine Meaning of "Abiding"

Others in the Gospel had already experienced a foretaste of this life by staying or being with him during his ministry (1:38–39; 4:40; 7:33; 11:54; 13:33; 14:17, 25; 16:4). Now through the Spirit the disciples would dwell with him and he with them in a more intimate manner (6:56; 14:17; 15:4–10); in contrast to the religious-political elite (5:38), they themselves would become his dwelling places (14:23); this is the intimacy Jesus shared with the Father (14:10).

Glasson thinks that "abide" reflects the Deuteronomic emphasis on "cleaving" to the Lord but in a greater sense of union.[110] The Greek term and its cognates, however, function broadly, applying, for example, to qualities remaining in a person.[111] Most likely it develops here the prior image of believers as the dwelling place of the Father, Son, and Paraclete and that believers also would have dwellings in the Father's presence (14:2–3, 23; cf. the verb in 14:17). In connection with the vine, the image connotes complete and continued dependence[112] for the Christian life on the indwelling Christ,[113] which recalls an emphasis in Pauline theology (e.g., Gal 2:20; Col 1:29),[114] though it is not attested much elsewhere in early Judaism.[115] The image is not simply symbolic (Jesus supplanting Israel's vine) but is also organic, like Paul's adaptation of the ancient "body" image for the church (Rom 12:4–6; 1 Cor 10:16; 12:12; Eph 4:12–16; cf. *1 Clem.* 37.5).[116]

The image of organic union works well for (and goes even beyond) the idea of intimate relationship.[117] The Spirit abiding with them would teach them (14:16–17), hence Jesus' words would remain in them (15:7).[118] As they continued in this union, they would know Jesus better (15:15; 16:13–15) and hence begin to reflect the "fruit" of his character (15:8–9).[119] One who kept the commandments (especially love, 13:34–35; 15:12–13) would make one's permanent dwelling in God's love (14:23; 15:9–10), internalizing the principle of love. To rebel against the love way is to endanger the health of other branches,

---

[110] Glasson, *Moses,* 76, citing Deut 10:20; 11:22; 13:4; 30:20; Josh 22:5; 23:8–11.

[111] *Let. Aris.* 226 (διαμένη).

[112] For vine grafting, see Columella *Rust.* 3.9.6–7; 4.29.1–9; *Arb.* 8.1–5; also Seneca *Ep. Lucil.* 112.2, who applies it as a moral illustration. Vines could be transplanted in February or as late as the end of March (Seneca *Ep. Lucil.* 86.20–21).

[113] For its spiritual significance in this Gospel, see, e.g., Potterie, "Demeurer" (stressing "mystic" interiority).

[114] For sharing Christ's death and resurrection, and his risen life active in the believer or special agents, see further Rom 6:3–11; 8:2–14; 15:18; 1 Cor 6:15–19; 12:11–13; 2 Cor 5:17; 12:9; 13:3–4; Gal 5:16–25; 6:14–15; Phil 2:13; Col 2:10–13, 20; 3:1–5; 2 Tim 2:11; probably Phlm 6. In Eph 3:20 God's power works in Christians according to the greatest example of his power, Jesus' resurrection, the beginning of the new creation (Eph 1:20; cf. Phil 3:21; 1 Cor 15:43–44); cf. Ezek 36:27 and, for devotional expressions of dependence on God as the strength for life, e.g., Ps 18:1; 27:1; 28:7–8; 31:2, 4; 37:39; 73:26; 118:14; 138:3; 140:7.

[115] See Keener, *Spirit,* 215–16.

[116] Stoics and others applied it most frequently to the cosmos (e.g., Epictetus *Diatr.* 1.12.26; Marcus Aurelius 7.13; Diodorus Siculus 1.11.6; Long, "Soul") and to the state (e.g., Cicero *Resp.* 3.25.37; Sallust *Letter to Caesar* 10.6; originally from Menenius Agrippa, Dionysius of Halicarnassus *R.A.* 6.83.2–6.86.5; Livy 2.32.9–12; Dio Cassius 4.17.10–13).

[117] The encounter aspect of the relationship might be experienced in worship by the Spirit (John 4:24).

[118] Cf. the Stoic notion of allowing reason (λόγον) to remain (ἐμμένοντα) in one's soul (Musonius Rufus frg. 36, p. 134.11).

[119] The idea of transformation through knowledge appears in Christian tradition as early as 2 Cor 3:18 (building on the same Moses analogy as in John 1:14–18).

requiring removal from the loving community. While disciples might be accepted provisionally on a basic level of faith (such as signs faith), it was those who were progressing to discipleship who would actualize their relationship.[120]

The present tense of the verb in 15:5–6 suggests that John refers not simply to the moment of entering God's presence in Christ (14:6) but continued dependence on him, as one might continue to dwell in a shelter or tabernacle, or as the branch continues to depend on the vine. To continue to dwell is to persevere in keeping Jesus' commandments (14:21–23; 1 John 3:24), especially to love one another (13:34–35; 15:10–12). John's use of "abide" sometimes (e.g., 6:27; 8:31, 35; cf. 19:31), including in this context (15:16), can demand continuance, perseverance.

The demand for perseverance plays a central role in this pericope. In this context, μένω signifies not only "dwell" (as in 14:10, 17) but "remain" (both are legitimate components of the term's semantic range functioning in this context). John 8:31 warns initial believers that they must "abide" in his "word" so that they may be his "disciples" in truth. The present passage alludes back to all the major concepts of 8:31, expanding them in connection with the image of the vine: they must "abide" (15:4–7); his "word" has cleansed them (15:3) and his "words" should abide in them (15:7);[121] those who abide bear fruit and hence prove to be his "disciples" (15:8).[122] Those who do not persevere in their dependence on Jesus are ultimately destroyed (15:6). That only some who initially embrace Jesus' message would persevere in fruitfulness to salvation (Mark 4:7–8) and that the unfruitful will perish (Matt 3:10, 12; 7:19; Luke 3:9, 17; 13:7–9) is consistent with the Synoptic tradition[123] (more than with the usual Johannine use of καρπός, 4:36; 12:24).[124] But—instructive for those who overemphasize the Gospel's harshness toward Israel—the Gospel's closest image to "hell" is reserved for unfaithful Christians. Whereas in some Synoptic passages it is unfruitful leaders or members of Israel who are burned (like vine cuttings in Ezek 15:2–6), here it is unfruitful alleged disciples.

### 4B. Burning Unfruitful Branches

Though never destroying his people as a whole, God had earlier executed judgment against unfaithful vine branches among his people (Jer 5:10). Because αἴρει in 15:2 apparently comes from αἴρω, "to lift," rather than from αἱρέω, "to take away," some commentators suggest that the operation in 15:2 is not the destruction of the branch but its salvage; a vinedresser would lift a fallen vine from the ground, where it was easily damaged, back into place to heal.[125] While by itself such a position might seem

---

[120] For one model of "being in" yet also accommodating concrete "progress," cf. Engberg-Pedersen's depiction of Stoic conversion ideology in *Paul and Stoics,* passim; a Jewish boy's maturation in Torah might be comparable.

[121] In 15:7 John employs ῥήματα rather than λόγος, but he is almost invariably consistent in simply employing λόγος for the singular and ῥήματα for the plural. For "what one heard" abiding in one (cf. 1 John 1:10) and for one also abiding in the Son and Father, see 1 John 2:24.

[122] It is also possible, though far less likely, that the ἀληθινή vine (15:1) alludes back to those who were disciples ἀληθῶς (8:31).

[123] Niemand, "Taüferpredigt," thinks the image may stem from tradition brought by John the Baptist's disciples when they became Christians; but it is a natural image (though Jesus could have drawn directly from the Baptist).

[124] Interpreting this passage by comparison with the partial burning of saved ministers' works in 1 Cor 3:15 is thus inappropriate here; while branches might need to be pruned, those which do not abide in the vine are not saved but consumed (cf. Heb 6:4–8).

[125] Harrison, "Vine," 986.

insightful, it falters on four points: first, it is not the vine but a "branch" that is lifted. Second, "lifting" can refer to removal no less than "taking away" does (cf. 1:29; 2:16; 5:8–12; 10:18; 11:39, 41, 48; 16:22); John never employs αἱρέω.[126] Third, Palestinian farmers may have often done without supports,[127] marring the image of "lifting" the vine back into place; admittedly this knowledge was probably foreign to much of John's audience. Finally, and most significantly, the branch is lifted away because it bears no fruit, the result in this context of failing to "abide" (15:4–5), a condition that 15:5 explicitly claims results in being cast away and eventually burned. Thus it is probable that the image of 15:2, like the image of 15:6, addresses apostate branches who have failed to persevere.[128]

The vinedresser wields his pruning-knife (see comment on 15:2–3) against both fruitful and unfruitful branches, but to different ends. The purpose of the vine is to bear fruit, and fruitless plants are useless (cf. Luke 13:7).[129] The cutting (15:2) and burning (15:6) of unfruitful branches repeats the vital Johannine warning against falling away (2:23–25; 8:30–31). Such an image would have made sense in an ancient Mediterranean context; applying the figure to the human rather than a covenant community, a Stoic philosopher warns that as a branch (κλάδος) cut off (ἀποκοπείς) from a neighboring branch is necessarily disconnected from the entire plant, so a person who cuts himself off from another person has severed himself from the circle of humanity.[130]

Because most biblical passages in which the vine represents Israel conclude with the vine's corruption, some scholars find also an implied reference to Judas's apostasy. Certainly the burning of bad branches does appear (Ps 80:16; Ezek 15:6; 19:12), as here (John 15:6),[131] and Judas is John's supreme illustration of apostasy (6:70–71),[132] but this may point to a more general warning about apostasy within God's people.[133] In a probably third-century parable probably based partly on Isa 5, God accepts as his own the vineyard when it produces good wine, but rejects it as that of his tenants when it produces bad wine. But at the end of the parable, Moses pleads for God to accept Israel regardless of whether they sin (produce bad wine) or not.[134] Even early Jewish views of the covenant, however, acknowledged

---

[126] To the extent the distinctions are clear, Koine apparently preferred αἴρω (261 times in the LXX; 97 times in the NT, including 23 in John); the term αἱρέω appears clearly in the LXX only 12 times, in NT only 3 times, none of them in John, and often without the clear sense "take away." Writers could, however, play on words sharing the same spelling (Rowe, "Style," 132).

[127] Hepper, *Plants*, 98.

[128] Derickson, "Viticulture," assigns all of 15:2 to the spring pruning of fruitful branches and 15:6 to the postharvest removal of dead branches in autumn. His distinction between seasons is helpful, but the activities of 15:2 need not all occur at the same season; the metaphor of "unfruitful branches" probably bears the same meaning throughout the parable (15:2, 4, 6).

[129] Cf. *Tg. Neof.* 1 on Num 21:34, where Og mocked Abraham and Sarah as fruitless trees before Isaac's birth; or Musonius Rufus 21, p. 128.2–4, comparing something with pruning a vine "to remove what is useless" (trans. Lutz).

[130] Marcus Aurelius 11.8. John's κλῆμα is more appropriate with, though not exclusively used for, branches of vines (Liddell and Scott).

[131] Hoskyns, *Gospel*, 474. Seneca *Ep. Lucil.* 112.2 uses the vine image to illustrate that only some people can receive philosophy (as branches can be grafted only onto some kinds of vines).

[132] Thus the text may include an implied comparison with Judas (cf. Hunter, *John*, 150); one could read the τις as a "certain one." But Judas is, in any case, a negative model and warning for others (cf. 1 Cor 10:11).

[133] E.g., Barrett, "Old Testament," 164; Carson, *Discourse*, 91.

[134] *Pesiq. Rab Kah.* 16:9.

that individual Jews could be lost through apostasy.[135] John certainly affirms that many of his people had forsaken the covenant by rejecting Jesus;[136] but he also wishes to warn those who have begun to believe in Jesus but have not progressed to the full faith of discipleship, that is, of perseverance with an unpopularly high Christology (8:30–31).[137]

Dressings of vineyards useful for nothing else would be burned,[138] though it is unlikely that the disciples would have actually witnessed these while walking with Jesus to the Mount of Olives that night.[139] Nevertheless, the image of burning is an apt early Jewish description of the fate of the wicked,[140] especially in Gehenna.[141] Early Judaism was not unanimous on the punishment of the wicked in Gehenna or its eternal duration; many believed that it was eternal for at least the worst sinners,[142] but in the most common early Jewish view, most sinners endure hell only temporarily and are then destroyed[143] or released.[144] By contrast, the gospel tradition preserved in the Synoptics settles unanimously on the harshest view (Matt 3:10–12; 18:8; 25:41, 46; Mark 9:43, 48).[145] Likewise, the image of being "cast forth" (15:6) provides an apt figure of banishment from God's presence (Matt 3:10; 5:13, 29; 7:19; 18:8–9; 22:13; 25:30; Mark 9:42, 45, 47; Luke 3:9; 12:5; 13:28; 14:35; 17:2).[146]

## The Love Commandment (15:8–17)

Love is both the fruit of remaining in Jesus (15:8) and the commandment that functions as the condition for remaining in Jesus (15:10, 12). The close connection between the

---

[135] The classic text is *m. Sanh.* 10:1. Despite some detractors (*b. Sanh.* 103a), most later teachers continued to follow its tradition that very wicked rulers such as Manasseh and Jeroboam would be lost (*b. Ḥag.* 15b; *Num. Rab.* 14:1; *Song Rab.* 1:1, §5; *Pesiq. Rab.* 1:5; see also *2 Bar.* 64:7–9).

[136] Painter, *John*, 48, even sees Israel's apostasy in the vine image here.

[137] Calvin, *John*, 2:110 (on John 15:6) also allows that this text refers to destruction of apostates, though he emphasizes that these are hypocrites who merely appear to be saved, not the true elect.

[138] See Westcott, *John*, 218. More substantial branches might be used for construction wood, but small vine branches provided fuel.

[139] Brown, *John*, 2:662, against Westcott, *John*, 216. Even notwithstanding the present or approaching Passover, the time of year was wrong.

[140] E.g., *L.A.B.* 25:5–6; *1 En.* 48:9; for fire as future judgment, see, e.g., Isa 26:11; 66:15–16, 24; CD 2.4–6; *1 En.* 103:8; *Sib. Or.* 4.43, 161, 176–178; *2 Thess* 1:6–7; *Exod. Rab.* 15:27. Cf. Heb 6:8; Herm. *Vis.* 3.2.

[141] Many Jewish storytellers conflated Gehenna with the Greek Tartarus (e.g., *Sib. Or.* 1.10, 101–103, 119; 4.186; 5.178; 11.138; cf. *Gk. Apoc. Ezra* 4:22; *b. Giṭ.* 56b–57a; *p. Ḥag.* 2:2, §5; *Sanh.* 6:6, §2; *Apoc. Pet.* 5–12); for the burning of the wicked in Tartarus's river Phlegethon in pagan mythology, see Virgil *Aen.* 6.551–559 (though cf. also purgatorial fire in 6.735–742).

[142] *4 Macc* 9:9; 12:12; *t. Sanh.* 13:5; probably *1 En.* 108:5–6; *L.A.B.* 38:4; *Ascen. Isa.* 1:2; *3 En.* 44:3; *t. Ber.* 5:31; *b. Roš Haš.* 17a; *p. Ḥag.* 2:2, §5; *Sanh.* 6:6, §2; cf. Diodorus Siculus 4.69.5; Plutarch *D.V.* 31, *Mor.* 567DE. For Gehenna's vast size, note *b. Pesaḥ.* 94a; *Taʿan.* 10a; *Song Rab.* 6:9, §3; cf. Virgil *Aen.* 6.577–579).

[143] Cf. 1QS 4.13–14; *Gen. Rab.* 6:6; most sinners in *t. Sanh.* 13:3, 4; *Pesiq. Rab Kah.* 10:4; *Pesiq. Rab.* 11:5; cf. 2 Macc 12:43–45.

[144] *Num. Rab.* 18:20. Other texts are unclear, e.g., Sir 7:16; *Sipre Num.* 40.1.9; *Sipre Deut.* 311.3.1; 357.6.7; *ʾAbot R. Nat.* 16 A; 32, §69B; 37, §95B. Twelve months is a familiar duration (*b. Šabb.* 33b; *Lam. Rab.* 1:11–12, §40).

[145] Also Jude 7; *Mart. Pol.* 11.2. Although Luke does not reject future eschatology in his effort to contextualize for Greek readers (Acts 17:31–32; 23:6; 24:15), as do some Jewish sources (e.g., Josephus *Ant.* 18.14, 18; *War* 2.163; Philo *Sacrifices* 5, 8), Matthew's emphases retain more of their original Jewish flavor (cf. Milikowsky, "Gehenna").

[146] Philo *Cherubim* 1 finds eternal banishment in Gen 3:24.

fruit and the commandment suggests that in Johannine as well as Pauline theology, essential works for "staying in" are simply the fruit of genuinely being in and continuing to depend ("believe") as one did to "get in" (cf. Gal 5:22–23).

As Jesus concludes his words about believers' love for one another and God's love for them (15:9–17), and before he begins his words concerning the world's hatred for them (15:18–25), he illustrates the intimate love relationship between himself and believers in one more way. The contrasts between love and hatred, friendship and enmity intensify the portrait of friendship here; ancient Mediterranean social wisdom recognized that having friends meant sharing one's friends' enemies and so one could not have friendships without also having enemies (cf. 15:18, 20).[147]

## 1. God Loves Those Who Keep His Commandments (15:8–11)

These verses require less background because they repeat ideas already emphasized earlier in the discourse. Some important emphases emerge here, however. In 15:8, the Father is glorified not only by Jesus' fruit-bearing sacrifice (12:23–24) but also by disciples bearing the fruit of love (13:35); they might "bear much fruit" through laying down their lives in love as Jesus did (cf. 12:24).

Further, it becomes clear that the sort of intimate union Jesus promises the disciples is not merely a mystical experience but a relational encounter, for he gives it content with the term "love" (15:9–10).[148] Disciples demonstrate this love concretely by obeying Jesus' commandments (15:10; cf. 14:15, 21; 15:14),[149] just as Jesus obeyed the Father's command to lay down his life (10:18; 14:31). Jesus likewise demonstrated his love for the Father by keeping the Father's commands (14:31) and so also merited the Father's love (10:17). Protestant scholars may feel uncomfortable with the condition of obedience for God's love in this passage, but throughout John the initiative comes from God, who then provides more love in response to human obedience and perseverance; what is portrayed is, as mentioned above, not a formula but a developing relationship. In the Synoptics as well, one's continuance in grace depends on one's granting grace to others (Matt 6:12, 14–15; 18:35; Mark 11:25; Luke 11:4). This may also fit ancient Mediterranean perspectives on benefactors' relationships with their dependents.[150] But whereas the tradition followed by Mark and the other Synoptics links love toward God and neighbor as parallel commands, John's reports link them more directly:[151] those who keep God's or Jesus' commands (most important, to love one another) thus remain in God's or Jesus' love (13:34–35; 15:10).[152]

"These things I have spoken to you" (15:11) is a refrain throughout this discourse (14:25; 16:1, 33), perhaps explaining to the disciples why he must tell them what they do

---

[147] Plutarch *Many Friends* 6–7, *Mor.* 96AB.

[148] See Dodd, *Interpretation*, 199–200; Bruce, *Message*, 108–9.

[149] A disciple would normally follow a teacher's wisdom (e.g., Xenophon *Anab.* 3.1.5–7), but in view of his Christology, John would undoubtedly expect his informed audience to think of more than this (cf. comment on John 1:27).

[150] See DeSilva, *Honor*, 148.

[151] Because μένω predominates in 13:31–15:10 (thirteen of its fourteen occurrences in the discourse), Boyle ("Discourse," 211) makes 15:10 the pivotal verse, with 15:12–16:33 treating exterior relations (p. 213). But love (concerning God and one another) unites 15:1–17, so the new section (focusing on hate and relations with the world) begins with 15:18.

[152] See Grayston, *Epistles*, 67. Lacomara, "Deuteronomy," 77, finds in the καθώς of 13:34 and 15:12 a parallel with Pentateuchal commands to imitate God's ways.

not yet understand.[153] Joy (15:11) related well to love and friendship;[154] later Jewish teachers also associated it heavily with keeping God's commandments,[155] as here (15:10–12). "Filled with joy" or "joy made full" (15:11; 16:24; 17:13; 1 John 1:4; 2 John 12) was a familiar enough expression[156] (on joy, see further the comment on 3:29). Earlier Christian tradition had also linked joy with love as a fruit of God's presence (Gal 5:22) and recognized it as a sign of God's present reign (Rom 14:17).

## 2. The Love of Friends (15:12–17)

The commandment to love (15:12, 17) frames the section, but the closing mention of it abbreviates the formula; 15:12, which includes the whole formula, is emphatic that believers must love one another in the same way that Jesus loved them (15:12; cf. 13:34), which means dying for their friends, as Jesus would die for them (15:13–14).[157]

### 2A. Dying for Friends (15:13)

If believers love one another as he has loved them (15:12), they must lay down their lives for one another (see comment on 13:34). This principle was illustrated earlier when Jesus spoke of going to Lazarus because Lazarus was their "friend" (φίλος, 11:11), whom Jesus "loved" (φιλέω, 11:3) and for whose life Jesus laid down his own (11:8–16).[158] Thus Jesus digresses to illustrate his love for them by speaking of how he would lay down his life for them as his friends (15:13–15).[159] Early Jewish sources prohibit sacrificing another to spare one's own life but still allowed that one's life takes precedence over another's life.[160] Nevertheless, though one was not required to love one's neighbor more than oneself, Judaism did praise as heroic the rare persons who would sacrifice their lives on behalf of their friends.[161]

---

[153] In the Gospels, λελάληκα, the first-person perfect active indicative of λαλέω, appears only in Jesus' speech in John (6:63; 8:40; 14:25; 15:3, 11; 16:1, 4, 6, 25, 33; 18:20), underlining the significance of his words.

[154] Aristotle *N.E.* 8–9 (a fifth of the work) addresses friendship, relating it to the goal of a happy life (Engberg-Pedersen, *Paul and Stoics*, 74; cf. 77). On enjoying friendship, see Seneca *Ep. Lucil.* 63.

[155] E.g., *b. Yoma* 4b; *Lev. Rab.* 16:4 (purportedly from Ben Azzai); *Pesiq. Rab.* 21:2/3; 51:4; Urbach, *Sages,* 1:390–92; Bonsirven, *Judaism,* 95; see especially the Tannaitic sources in Urbach, *Sages,* 1:390; most fully, Anderson, "Joy." In *Song Rab.* 4:11, §1, public teaching of Torah should generate as much joy as wedding guests experience from beholding a bride (cf. John 3:29).

[156] E.g., *Let. Aris.* 294; Acts 13:52; Phil 2:2.

[157] For classicists' discussion of friendship, see Fitzgerald, "Introduction," 7–10. In pre-Aristotelian Greek literature, see Fitzgerald, "Aristotle"; in Jewish sources, see Manns, "Amis." I treated ancient friendship elsewhere, overlapping with some material here, in "Pneumatology," 350–63; more fully, "Friendship"; see more on the topic in Fitzgerald, *Friendship* (very favorably reviewed in Keener, "Fitzgerald").

[158] John is also Jesus' "friend" (3:29); but Jesus' death for him is unstated, and John's own execution is at most implied (3:24), whether because assumed from tradition or because his witness continues to speak.

[159] The relation between φίλοι and ἀγαπάω reinforces a comparison of the uses of φιλέω and ἀγαπάω in the Gospel: in the final analysis, they are more or less interchangeable semantically.

[160] Jacobs, "Love," 42–44 (on Akiba). One should not interpret this as cowardice; the sages reported Akiba's own devotion in martyr accounts; cf., e.g., Urbach, *Sages,* 1:416–17, 443.

[161] Jacobs, "Love," 47. Leaders of the community had to act with the benefit of the community in mind (*Exod. Rab.* 27:9, citing R. Nehemiah, late second century).

Courageous, heroic, and honorable death was an ancient Mediterranean virtue,[162] a virtue soon to be illustrated in John's Passion Narrative. Josephus, for example, portrays those desiring to die nobly for their nation or for fame (e.g., Josephus *War* 1.43–44, 58); rabbis praised a Roman senator (probably fictitious) who died to spare the Jews.[163] Because the Greek world highly regarded laying down one's life for another[164] or for one's nation[165] and also recognized its occasional value as "an expiatory sacrifice to assuage the anger of the gods,"[166] Greeks or Romans would readily grasp the early Christian concept that Jesus died "on their behalf," with or without the benefit of understanding atonement in the Levitical system.

Perhaps especially because great dangers normally obliterated the closest ties, even those of friendship,[167] true friends were viewed as those who would share in one's hardships,[168] who would do whatever necessary for one,[169] and the greatest expression of devoted friendship was regarded as willingness to die together[170] or die for one another.[171] For example, one might pretend to be a condemned friend to try to rescue him.[172] Yet such signs of devotion were not commonplace; Epicurus reportedly noted that the wise person would sometimes (ποτέ) die on a friend's behalf (ὑπὲρ φίλου).[173] Such self-sacrifice was truly the "greatest" act of love one could bestow (15:13). See further the comment on friendship ideals below (especially concerning loyalty).

---

[162] Epameinondas 2 in Plutarch *S.K., Mor.* 192C; see other references in the comment on 12:27. Roman military oaths also demanded willingness to die on behalf of the state (*IGRR* 3.137; *OGIS* 532; *ILS* 8781, in Sherk, *Empire,* 31; cf. praises of Gaius Caesar in *CIL* 11.1421; *ILS* 140, in Sherk, *Empire,* 34); Iphigeneia is prepared to die to save (σῶσαι) Greece (Euripides *Iph. aul.* 1420).

[163] *Deut. Rab.* 2:24 (probably late, though citing early Tannaim).

[164] Hengel, *Atonement,* 9; cf. DeSilva, *Honor,* 136–37. See, e.g., Euripides *Alc.* 12–18; *Heracl.* 547–601; *Andr.* 413–415; cf. Seneca *Nat.* 4.pref.15; but such self-sacrifice is voluntary and not expected (Euripides *Alc.* 689–690; some writers, such as Lucian, seem to have rejected it—see Pervo, "Friends"). On slaves for masters, e.g., Appian *C.W.* 4.4.26; one man also offered his life for a boy with whom he was infatuated (Xenophon *Anab.* 7.4.7–10); some similarly died because of love for spouses (cf. Valerius Maximus 4.6.2–5; 4.6.ext.1–3); Cicero would have preferred his own death to his daughter's (*Fam.* 9.11.1).

[165] E.g., Livy 10.28.12–18; 10.29.1; Lucan *C.W.* 2.380–383.

[166] Hengel, *Atonement,* 19; cf. 27. Cf. Euripides *Iph. aul.* 1394–1397, 1553–1560; Livy 22.57.6; Plutarch *G.R.P.S.* 35, *Mor.* 314C–D; Lightfoot, *Notes,* 201.

[167] Achilles Tatius 3.3.5. In a summons to war, some people scrambled to get others to fight (and hence die) in their places (Xenophon *Agesilaus* 1.24).

[168] Isocrates *Demon.* 25, *Or.* 1; Valerius Maximus 4.7.pref.

[169] Euripides *Orest.* 652 (Orestes, in war); Aulus Gellius 1.3.4–8 (law court); Maximus of Tyre *Or.* 15.9; Philostratus *Hrk.* 51.12; P.Oxy. 32.5, 8–14 (second century C.E.).

[170] E.g., Euripides *Orest.* 1069–1074, 1155; *Iph. taur.* 674–686; Chariton 4.3.5; 7.1.7. Cf. *Syr. Men.* 406–407; *Syr. Men. Epit.* 22–23. Romances also emphasized this for lovers (e.g., Xenophon *Eph.* 1.11; 2.1, 7; 3.5; 4.5; 5.4).

[171] E.g., Diodorus Siculus 10.4.4–6; Epictetus *Diatr.* 2.7.3; Musonius Rufus 7, p. 58.23; Valerius Maximus 2.6.11; 4.7 passim (e.g., 4.7.2); cf. Iamblichus *V.P.* 33.235–236. Schnackenburg, *John,* 3:108, finds many parallels to 15:13; Boring et al., *Commentary,* 121–22, cite Demetrius Lacon the Epicurean *Life of Philonides;* Diogenes Laertius 10.121; Seneca *Ep. Lucil.* 1.9.10; Philostratus *Vit. Apoll.* 7.11; others in Anderson, *Rhetorical Theory,* 225.

[172] Valerius Maximus 4.7.6 (cf. wives doing this for husbands in Valerius Maximus 4.6.ext.3; a slave for a master, 6.8.6).

[173] Diogenes Laertius 10.120; cf. Rom 5:7. Aristotle defines as a friend any who seeks to do for another what he believes to be to the other's benefit (*Rhet.* 1.5.16, 1361b).

Jesus had already announced in this Gospel that he would lay down his life (10:17) and that his model of love was the standard for those who would follow him (13:34), which 1 John explicitly interprets as laying down one's life for fellow believers (1 John 3:16; in contrast to unwillingness to sacrifice for their needs, 1 John 3:17).[174]

### 2B. Kinds of Friendship in Antiquity

"Friendship" was a regular ancient topic of discourse,[175] the subject of numerous essays.[176] There were, however, a variety of different perspectives on, and kinds of, friendship, not only in the philosophers but throughout Greco-Roman and Jewish society. "Friendship" could signify a relationship of dependence or of equality, of impersonal alliances or of personal bonds of affection. Although some of these divisions can be expressed by opposing Roman and Greek conceptions, there was sufficient interpenetration of the two by the early empire that a hard-and-fast categorization along these lines is not useful for our purposes.[177]

One of the most common usages of "friendship" in our literary sources refers to political dependence on a royal patron.[178] This applies to tyrants of the classical period,[179] to the intimate circle of Alexander of Macedon,[180] to a high office in Hellenistic Syria,[181] to friendship with Caesar in the Roman imperial period,[182] and to other rulers.[183] Some insisted that true friends of a ruler ought to have freedom to speak frankly, as opposed to the flatterers with which tyrants surrounded themselves.[184] The fact that John 19:12 probably refers to this position of honor[185] may suggest that John 15:15 presents friendship with

---

[174] For application of the ancient motif of dying for a friend here, see, e.g., Keener, "Pneumatology," 350–51; Mitchell, "Friends," 258.

[175] E.g., Epictetus *Diatr.* 2.22; Musonius Rufus 15, p. 96.28–29; Iamblichus *V.P.* 16.69–70; 33.229–236. On types of friendships, see Marshall, *Enmity,* 24–32; Keener, "Pneumatology," 351–55.

[176] E.g., Aristotle *E.E.* 7.1234b–1246a; *N.E.* Books 8–9; Plutarch *Many Friends, Mor.* 93A–97B; Dio Chrysostom *Or.* 3, *On Kingship 3,* §§99–100; Cicero *Amic.*; Seneca *Ep. Lucil.* 3 ("On True and False Friendships"), 9 ("On Philosophy and Friendship"); Theophrastus (according to Aulus Gellius 1.3.10–11). See Malherbe, *Exhortation,* 85, 144; Sevenster, *Seneca,* 172–77.

[177] Plutarch, e.g., weaves together both Greek and Roman traditions of friendship (see O'Neil, "Plutarch on Friendship").

[178] In ancient Israel, see, e.g., 2 Sam 15:37; 16:16–17; 1 Kgs 4:5; 1 Chr 27:33; perhaps 13:3.

[179] Diogenes Laertius 1.54 (Pisistratus, offering a position to Solon).

[180] Diodorus Siculus 17.31.6; 17.39.2; 17.100.1. For friends of Cassander, see Diodorus Siculus 18.55.1.

[181] Diodorus Siculus 33.4.4a.

[182] Epictetus *Diatr.* 4.1.45–50; Martial *Epigr.* 5.19.15–16; Herodian 4.3.5; inscriptions in Deissmann, *Light,* 378; cf. Friedländer, *Life,* 1:70–82, 4:58–74. Of Jewish tetrarchs and rulers, only King Agrippa I adopted this title in his coins; see Meyshan, "Coins." The probably late and fabricated evidence of *CPJ* 2:71–72, §156a, and 2:76, §156b, nevertheless reflect earlier custom.

[183] 1 Macc 10:20; 15:28, 32; 2 Macc 7:24; *Let. Aris.* 40–41, 44, 190, 208, 225, 228, 318; Josephus *Ant.* 12.366 (though cf. 12.391); 13.146, 225; *Life* 131; Cornelius Nepos 9 (Conon), 2.2; 18 (Eumenes), 1.6; Chariton 8.8.10; cf. *Sipre Deut.* 53.1.3; *Gen. Rab.* 34:9. Cf. perhaps *Sib. Or.* 3.756 (probably second-century B.C.E. Alexandria); Deissmann, *Studies,* 167–68. The Roman title "Friends of the People" reflects an office advocating for the people but of less rank than being a leader in the Senate (Cicero *Sest.* 49.105; *Prov. cons.* 16.38).

[184] Maximus of Tyre *Or.* 14.7.

[185] See Sherwin-White, *Society,* 47; also many commentators (Brown, *John,* 2:879; Barrett, *John,* 543; Michaels, *John,* 309; Stauffer, *Jesus,* 133). By contrast, Westcott, *John,* 271, thinks that in 19:12 the phrase is "used in a general and not in a technical sense."

Jesus as friendship with a king.[186] This is more likely than the proposal that John 15:13–15 looks back to the "friend of the bridegroom" in 3:29.[187]

In one of its most common usages in ancient literature, "friendship" (φιλία) could similarly apply to alliances, cooperation, or nonaggression treaties among peoples; this usage appears in classics[188] and other rhetoric and literature[189] and naturally predominates in military biographers[190] and historians.[191] It could likewise apply to personal and familial relationships undertaken for political expediency.[192] Stowers observes that the Roman ideal of *amicitia* differed from the Greek idea of friendship:

> Traditionally, the concept of *amicitia* did not emphasize sentiment and male affection as the Greek concept did. Amicitia was also firmly anchored in the Roman family and alliance of families. It was often an alliance of utility between social equals and was sometimes equated with "political party" *(factio)*.[193]

To say that Romans "were rather incapable of a heartfelt friendship"[194] might be an exaggeration based on the one-sided portrayal of the literature of the social elite.[195] There are plenty of political elements in Cicero's letters of friendship, including implicit negotiations with other political figures and letters of recommendation;[196] but one cannot escape the clear impression of affection that pervades much of his correspondence. Nevertheless, the generalization does reflect the recognition of the importance of political connections in the urban Roman conception of friendship.

---

[186] Cf. Strachan, *Fourth Gospel*, 179. That a contrast between closeness to Caesar and closeness to God's agent could be intended is not impossible; cf. Epictetus *Diatr.* 1.9.7.

[187] Lee, "Friends," although he does not exclude other associations.

[188] E.g., Homer *Il.* 3.93, 256; 4.17; 16.282; Virgil *Aen.* 11.321.

[189] E.g., Lysias *Or.* 2.2, §192; Aeschines *False Embassy* 30, 39; Demosthenes *On the Navy-Boards* 5; *On the Embassy* 62; *Ep.* 3.27; Strabo *Geog.* 8.5.5; Josephus *Ag. Ap.* 1.109 (but cf. similar interests in 1.111); 2.83; cf. *Rhet. ad Herenn.* 3.3.4 *(societates atque amicitias);* Maximus of Tyre *Or.* 35.7–8; Philostratus *Hrk.* 35.4 (for individuals).

[190] E.g., Xenophon *Cyr.* 3.2.23; Arrian *Alex.* 1.28.1; 4.15.2, 5; 4.21.8; 7.15.4; Plutarch *Comparison of Lycurgus and Numa* 4.6; Plutarch *Pelopidas* 5.1, 29.4; Epameinondas 17 in Plutarch *S.K., Mor.* 193DE; Cornelius Nepos 7 (Alcibiades), 4.7; 5.3; 7.5; 14 (Datames), 8.5; 23 (Hannibal), 10.2; Josephus *Life* 30, 124.

[191] E.g., Polybius 1.62.8; 14.1; Dionysius of Halicarnassus *R.A.* 3.28.7; 3.51.1; 5.26.4; 5.50.3; 6.21.2; 6.95.1; 8.9.3; 8.36.3; 15.7.2; Diodorus Siculus 14.30.4; 14.56.2; 17.39.1; 17.54.2; 19.66.6; 19.67.1; 21.12.6; 31.5.3; 32.16.1; 33.28b.4; 40.1.2; Livy 6.2.3; 27.4.6; 43.6.9; 45.12.6; Sallust *Jug.* 14.17; 102.6; Herodian 4.7.3; 4.15.8; 1 Macc 12:1, 3, 8; 14:40; cf. 1 Kgs 5:1; 2 Macc 11:14. For further discussion in Dionysius of Halicarnassus, see Balch, "Friendship."

[192] Often in Plutarch (e.g., *Agesilaus* 23.6; *Pompey* 70.4; *Statecraft* 13, *Mor.* 806F–809B; *Philosophers and Men in Power* 1, *Mor.* 776AB; *O.M.P.A.* 6, *Mor.* 787B); but also elsewhere (e.g., Achilles Tatius 4.6.1–3). Contrast the older Stoic values of Chrysippus in Diogenes Laertius 7.7.189; but cf. Engberg-Pedersen, *Paul and Stoics,* 74. Even among Greeks, whereas Aristotle notes friendships based on goodness, pleasure, or utility (*E.E.* 7.2.9–13, 1236a; 7.10.10, 1242b; *N.E.* 8.13.1, 1162ab), he assigns most to utility (*E.E.* 7.2.14, 1236a).

[193] Stowers, *Letter Writing,* 29, going on to note the use for clients.

[194] Friedländer, *Life,* 1:225. Cf. Judge, *Pattern,* 33–34 (in the context of imperial friendships): "not simply a spontaneous relationship of mutual affection. It was a status of intimacy conferred on trusted companions."

[195] Cf. Stowers, *Letter Writing,* 29: "It is doubtful that any but those with some wealth and leisure could attain either the Greek or the Roman ideal of friendship."

[196] Also Cicero *Verr.* 1.7.18 (one must be careful what one says about friends of rank); on friendship in his letters, see Fiore, "Theory."

Especially in, but not limited to, the Roman sphere, "friendship" did not always imply social equality of the parties involved, a fact that may be significant for the relationship of Jesus and the disciples in John 15:15. Both the royal and the nonroyal political images of friendship are probably related to the use of the word for patron-client relationships. Patrons were called the clients' friends, [197] and clients were called friends of their patron.[198] Romans might categorize friendships according to greater, equal, or lesser friends and (lesser still) clients, according to their available resources.[199] (Clients sometimes exploited their understanding of this "friendship" to challenge some inequities in the patronal understanding of the relationship.)[200] This usage may have influenced the usage of "friendship" as the relationship between philosopher and disciple.[201] Friendship was in general conditional, often including "obligations and expectations,"[202] whether formally or informally.

But not all ancient Mediterranean conceptions of friendship reflected this hierarchical sort of relationship, even where reciprocity was anticipated. In the eastern Mediterranean, societies of friends could include fellow members of one's guild[203] or toward one's age-peers.[204] Although age-group societies may have declined in the Hellenistic and Roman periods,[205] the classical Greek wealthy image of friendship tended to be companionship based on groupings of the same sex and age, which constituted political parties.[206] One may perhaps compare the relationship of associates in the Jewish chabûrah.[207] Among the Greek schools, the Epicureans in particular emphasized friendship,[208] regarding it as a source of pleasure.[209] Although Roman patronal friendship made only the vaguest pretense to equality, if any pretense at all, this Greek image of friendship, even when related to benefaction, demanded equality, as in Plato:

> Friendship is the name we give to the affection of like for like, in point of goodness, and of equal for equal; and also to that of the needy for the rich, which is of the opposite kind; and when either of these feelings is intense we call it "love."[210]

---

[197] E.g., Dionysius of Halicarnassus *Lit. Comp.* 1; Valerius Maximus 7.8.7; Philostratus *Hrk.* 4.3; 10.2; Acts 19:31; cf. *AE* 1912.171 (in Sherk, *Empire*, 235). Iamblichus *V.P.* 22.101; 33.230, admonishes respect for benefactors in a friendship.

[198] Martial *Epigr.* 3.36.1–3; 3 Macc 5:26; probably P.Oxy. 2861 (in Stowers, *Letter Writing*, 63); cf. Musonius Rufus 15, p. 98.5–6; DeSilva, *Honor*, 99. See also, e.g., a magician dependent on a spirit (*PGM* 1.172, 190–191).

[199] Garnsey and Saller, *Empire*, 149, citing Pliny *Ep.* 2.6.2; 7.3.2; Seneca *Ep.* 94.14.

[200] See Konstan, "Patrons."

[201] Diogenes Laertius 6.2.36; Iamblichus *V.P.* 31.187; Stowers, *Letter Writing*, 39.

[202] Meeks, *Christians*, 30; cf. Aune, *Environment*, 166–67; esp. and most fully, Marshall, *Enmity*, 1–24. See, e.g., Alciphron *Farmers* 12 (Cotinus to Trygodorus), 3.15; *Fishermen* 7 (Thalassus to Pontius), 1.7; most fully and helpfully Evans, "Friendship," 202, on mutual obligation in private letters.

[203] See Horsley, *Documents*, 4:17–18, §3 (from Saittai, close to Ephesus).

[204] Iamblichus *V.P.* 31.188.

[205] See Stowers, *Letter Writing*, 30.

[206] See ibid., 28–30, 39, 60; cf. Gould, *Love*, 143–45; perhaps Cicero *Amic.* 5.18. Plutarch *T.T.* 4.intr., *Mor.* 660A, advocates befriending only the good while showing goodwill toward all. Age group associations appear in other cultures as well (cf. the Maasai; Mbiti, *Religions*, 165–66).

[207] Cf. Oesterley, *Liturgy*, 172.

[208] Culpepper, *School*, 101; Stowers, *Letter Writing*, 66; Meeks, *World*, 57; Stambach and Balch, *Environment*, 143.

[209] Diogenes Laertius 10.120; 148.27–28; Cicero *Fin.* 1.20.65–70. The view of the Epicurean Lucretius in *Nat.* 5.1019–1023 sounds like later social-contract theories. Stoics, by contrast, valued friendship for its own sake (Cicero *Fin.* 3.21.70).

[210] Plato *Laws* 8, 837AB (LCL 9:152–53).

Aristotle cited an earlier saying, "Friendship is equality" (ἰσότης ἡ φιλότης),[211] and is said to have

> defined friendship as an equality [ἰσότητα] of reciprocal good-will, including under the term as one species the friendship of kinsmen, as another that of lovers, and as a third that of host and guest.[212]

The motif of friendship as equality also prevailed in the neo-Pythagorean writings.[213] As early as Homer, a leader could honor a special friend above his other companions, regarding him as "equal" (ἴσος) to himself.[214] Alexandrian Jewish writers also picked up on this; in Aristeas 228, the highest honor is to be shown to parents, but the next honor to one's friends, for a friend is the "equal of one's own soul."[215] Thus one letter recommends a friend *(amicum)* by exhorting the receiver to view him "as if he were me."[216] In Greek thought, a friend was like a "second self,"[217] meaning that one would care about one's friend the way one would care for oneself.[218] Implications of such a conception for the Johannine concept of agency are evident.

2C. Ancient Ideals of Friendship

Hellenistic ideals of friendship include a strong emphasis on loyalty. Isocrates argues that good men love (ἀγαπῶσι) their friends always, even when far away, but base men honor friends only when they are present;[219] others carried on the criticism of those who were merely friends in name and the lamentation that faithfulness in friends was rare.[220] *Sentences of the Syriac Menander* stresses loyalty to friends.[221] In narratives, the loyalty of a good friend adds to the delight of the story; for instance, in Chariton's novel, Polycharmus leaves his parents to face danger with his friend (ἑταῖρος) Chaereas[222] because he was his φίλος;[223] the idea would also be construed from the relationship between David and Jonathan in the OT. The Jewish writer in Sir 6:7–10, 14–16, and 12:8 also argues that one really knows one's friends only in the hard times, when friends' loyalty is tested. True friends were known in time of trouble, when they were most needed.[224] Ideally, one could trust

---

[211] Aristotle *E.E.* 7.9.1, 1241b. Nevertheless, Aristotle treats friendship in especially political terms (for relations in a classical polis); see Schroeder, "Friendship," 56 (for the Peripatetic tradition, cf. 45–56).

[212] Diogenes Laertius 5.31 (LCL 1:478–79; cf. Aristotle *Rhet.* 2.4.28, 1381b 33, from LCL note). Any kind of friendship could exist either between equals or with one as a superior (Aristotle *E.E.* 7.3.2, 1238b; 7.10.10, 1242b; *N.E.* 8.7.1, 1158b; 8.13.1, 1162ab); Aristotle further defined "equality" more proportionately than quantitatively (*N.E.* 8.7.2–3, 1158b).

[213] See Thom, "Equality"; Iamblichus, *V.P.* 29.162; 30.167.

[214] Homer *Il.* 18.81–82.

[215] Quoted from Hadas's translation, p. 189.

[216] P.Oxy. 32.5–6 (second century C.E.); cf. Phlm 17–19.

[217] E.g., Diodorus Siculus 17.37.6; Cicero *Fam.* 7.5.1; 13.1.5.

[218] E.g., Cicero *Fin.* 1.20.70; Seneca *Ep. Lucil.* 95.63.

[219] Isocrates *Demon.* 1, *Or.* 1 (LCL 1:4–5).

[220] Phaedrus 3.9.1; cf. Prov 20:6. Socrates reportedly emphasized valuing friends and choosing good ones (Xenophon *Mem.* 2.4.1–2.6.39).

[221] *Syr. Men.* 25.

[222] Chariton 3.5.7–8; cf. other examples in Valerius Maximus 4.7 passim; audiences would regard such behavior as praiseworthy (*Rhet. Alex.* 36, 1442a.13–14).

[223] Chariton 3.3.1. At the end of the book, Polycharmus receives Chaereas's sister in marriage as a reward for his faithful friendship (8.8.12–13). On this friendship, see further Hock, "Friend," 147–57.

[224] Valerius Maximus 4.7.pref.

one's friends with one's life, rejecting false accusations about them;[225] they would not abandon one even in exile.[226]

Friends were also recipients of one's confidence and intimacy, as noted above in Philo's portrayal of Abraham.[227] One difference between servant-master relationships and those between friends is that servants withhold secrets from the master but friends do not withhold them from each other.[228] Isocrates advises a careful testing of friends, to see if they are worthy of confidence with secrets;[229] and it is a moralist commonplace that true friends are those who can speak openly (παρρησία) instead of praising a person only to his face,[230] as Plutarch particularly emphasizes:

> The great difference between flatterer and friend may be most clearly perceived by his disposition towards one's other friends. For a friend finds it most pleasant to love and be loved along with many others, and he is always constant in his endeavours that his friend shall have many friends and be much in honour; believing that "friends own everything in common" he thinks that no possession ought to be held in common as friends.[231]

Aristotle notes that true friendship requires confidence (πίστις) in one's friend, which requires standing the test of time.[232] Josephus, writing about Judaism for a Greco-Roman readership, is eager to point out the similar emphasis in Jewish ethics: the Law

> allows us to conceal nothing from our friends, for there is no friendship without absolute confidence; in the event of subsequent estrangement, it forbids the disclosure of secrets.[233]

Friends were especially supposed to be able to maintain confidences.[234] This kind of intimacy and equality could carry over into talk about God, as in the case of Abraham, with whom God "no longer talked . . . as God with man but as a friend with a familiar."[235] An ideal friend would share one's joys and sorrows.[236]

As Plutarch notes in the passage above, friends share not only secrets but, ideally, everything they possess. The maxim that friends share all things in common is attested in Aristotle but by this period had become a commonplace.[237] Diogenes Laertius describes the Stoic view of friendship:

---

[225] Valerius Maximus 3.8.ext.5–6; for refusing to abandon their honor, see Valerius Maximus 4.7.1, 4.

[226] Musonius Rufus 9, p. 68.13–15.

[227] Philo *Sobriety* 55. Perhaps the remark in Diogenes Laertius 7.1.23 is related to this concept: a friend is "another I" (ἄλλος . . . ἐγώ). But this could relate to loyalty. See the intimacy in Theocritus work 12, *The Beloved*. See Philodemus frg. 42 for friends sharing secrets.

[228] Mitchell, "Friends," 259, citing Cicero *Amic.* 6.22. Masters also should avoid confiding in servants (Theophrastus *Char.* 4.2).

[229] Isocrates *Demon.* 24–25, *Or.* 1.

[230] Isocrates *Ad Nic.* 28, *Or.* 2; Seneca *Dial.* 10.15.2; Maximus of Tyre *Or.* 14.6.

[231] Plutarch *Flatterer* 24, *Mor.* 65AB (LCL 1:344–45); cf. *Flatterer* 17, *Mor.* 59A; *Educ.* 17, *Mor.* 13B. Cf. Stowers, *Letter Writing*, 39.

[232] Aristotle *E.E.* 7.2.40, 1237b; Iamblichus *V.P.* 33.232.

[233] Josephus *Ag. Ap.* 2.207 (LCL 1:376–77).

[234] Sir 6:9; 22:22; 27:17; cf. 42:1.

[235] Philo *Abraham* 273.

[236] Philostratus *Hrk.* 49.1; Menander Rhetor 2.7, 407.26–29.

[237] Aristotle *N.E.* 9.8.2, 1168b, cited in Stowers, *Letter Writing*, 58; Witherington, *Acts,* 205 (on Acts 4:32). Cf. Arius Didymus 11C.

And by friendship they mean a common use of all that has to do with life, wherein we treat our friends as we should ourselves. They argue that a friend is worth having for his own sake and that it is a good thing to have many friends.[238]

That friends shared all things in common becomes a frequent phrase in the literature of Greco-Roman antiquity, not limited to the Stoics.[239] The view seems to have become pervasive enough that even in rural areas it could be used to justify the traditional code of reciprocity or sharing among friends.[240] From an early period, rulers might at times place their resources at their allies' disposal, claiming all that belonged to themselves belonged to their allies.[241] But the Cynics and the Stoics particularly propagated the syllogism that the wise man was a friend of the gods, the gods owned everything, and therefore everything belongs to the wise man. Diogenes the Cynic purportedly reasoned,

All things belong to the gods. The wise are friends of the gods, and friends hold all things in common. Therefore all things belong to the wise.[242]

The Stoics held the same view.[243] Being a friend of the gods therefore entitled one to sharing in whatever was theirs. This may account for the sharing of Jesus' things with the disciples through the Spirit of truth, just as Jesus had shared the Father's things (16:14–15), although in the context this probably means specifically revealing his truths (16:13; 15:15).

## 2D. Friends of God

The supreme example of patronal friendship in ancient sources might be thought to be discovered in passages referring to friendship with God.[244] In many of these texts, however, it is not the patronal but the voluntary, reciprocal elements of the relationship that come to the fore.[245] Thus a later rhetorician could praise those who love the gods and are friends (φιλεῖν) with them.[246] Being a "friend of God" sometimes meant virtuous perspectives and behavior.[247] Some references are too brief for this to be determined, as in some Cynic epistles:

---

[238] Diogenes Laertius 7.1.124 (LCL 2:228–29). Also Seneca *Benef.* 7.4.1.

[239] Martial *Epigr.* 2.43.1–16; Herodian 3.6.1–2; Cornelius Nepos 15 (Epaminondas), 3.4; Iamblichus V.P. 19.92 (cf. 29.162; 30.167–168; 33.237–240); cf. 1 Macc 12:23 and perhaps Ps.-Phoc. 30; Euripides *Andr.* 585 (but cf. 632–635); Plutarch *Bride* 19, *Mor.* 140D; Longus 1.10; Martial *Epigr.* 8.18.9–10.

[240] E.g., Alciphron *Farmers* 27 (Ampelion to Euergus), 3.30, par. 3; 29 (Comarchides to Euchaetes), 3.73, par. 2; *Fishermen* 7 (Thlassus to Pontius), 1.7.

[241] E.g., Xenophon *Cyr.* 5.4.29; 1 Kgs 22:4.

[242] Diogenes Laertius 6.2.37 (LCL 2:38–39); also 6.2.72; cf. Antisthenes in 6.1.11.

[243] Diogenes Laertius 7.1.125; Plutarch *Cicero* 25.4. On friendship between good men and the gods, cf., e.g., Seneca *Dial.* 1.1.5; on all things belonging to them, Seneca *Benef.* 7.4.6, cf. Philo *Cherubim* 84. The maxim is especially cited in works on 1 Corinthians (Willis, *Meat*, 169; Conzelmann, *Corinthians*, 80; cf. also Fitzgerald, *Cracks*, 200–201; Grant, *Christianity*, 102–3).

[244] E.g., people invoked divinities as φίλοι to help them in battle (Aeschylus *Sept.* 174); cf. a mortal as a "friend" who honors his patron demigod in Philostratus *Hrk.* 58.1 (the hero is also his friend in 10.2); cf. perhaps Iamblichus *V.P.* 10.53 (where the friendship is demonstrated by deities' past favors).

[245] This observation (in contrast to some other observations above) may run counter to the suggestion of Judge (*Pattern*, 38) that vv. 13–15 of John 15 "reveal the peculiar combination of intimacy and subordination" characteristic of the patronal relationship.

[246] Menander Rhetor 1.3, 361.24–25.

[247] Maximus of Tyre *Or.* 19.4; Iamblichus *V.P.* 33.229. This might involve sharing the divine character (Iamblichus *V.P.* 33.240).

only the wise man [τὸν σπουδαῖον] is a friend of God [φίλον τῷ θεῷ μόνον].[248]

But Epictetus addresses the subject rather frequently. Heracles had few friends—indeed, no friend "dearer than God" (φίλτερον τοῦ θεοῦ);

> That is why he was believed to be a son of God, and was. It was therefore in obedience to His will that he went about clearing away wickedness and lawlessness.[249]

One who does not care about circumstances is like a free man and can "look up to heaven as a friend of God."[250]

> Did not Socrates love his own children? But in a free spirit [ὡς ἐλεύθερος], as one who re-members that it was his first duty to be a friend to the gods [θεοῖς εἶναι φίλον] . . . [251]

> for I am a free man [ἐλεύθερος] and a friend of God [φίλος τοῦ θεοῦ], so as to obey Him of my own free will [πείθωμαι αὐτῷ].[252]

Diaspora Jewish literature seems to use the phrase in a manner similar to Epictetus. In Wisdom of Solomon, Wisdom enters the righteous, making them God's friends and prophets;[253] in Philo, Virtue makes God a friend of the righteous.[254] The second-century Tanna Rabbi Meir, whose image of friendship may have been affected by Greco-Roman conceptions to a lesser degree, observed that whoever occupies himself with the Torah for its own sake is called God's friend.[255] In rabbinic parables, Israel is sometimes portrayed as a friend of God the king.[256] The image of God speaking with Israel as friend appears as early as 4Q377 (frg. 2, col. 2, lines 6–7), though this text draws its language from comments about Moses in Exod 33:11 (on which see below).

Following the OT designation of Abraham as God's friend (Isa 41:8; 2 Chr 20:7), early Jewish literature especially applies the title to Abraham.[257] This is especially because of his

---

[248] Crates Ep. 26, to the Athenians (Cyn. Ep. 76–77); cf. likewise Diog. Ep. 10, to Metrocles (Cyn. Ep. 104–5). Cf. Plato Leg. 4.716D (cited in Mayor, James, cxxv); fellowship between mortals and dei-ties in the golden age (Babrius prol.13).

[249] Epictetus Diatr. 2.16.44 (LCL 1:334–35).

[250] Epictetus Diatr. 2.17.29 (LCL 1:344–45).

[251] Epictetus Diatr. 3.24.60 (LCL 2:204–5).

[252] Epictetus Diatr. 4.3.9 (LCL 2:310–11). In the Loeb introduction, 1:vii, an epigram attributed by Macrobius to Epictetus also calls him God's friend.

[253] Wis 7:27; cf. 7:14, 8:18; see the theme of Ringe, Wisdom's Friends.

[254] Philo Contempl. Life 90, although there is a textual variant for "God's." God is a friend to Virtue in Philo Creation 81 and to Wisdom in Sobriety 55. Philo develops some Stoic friendship ide-als; on Philo's friendship ideals in general, see Sterling, "Bond."

[255] M. ʾAbot 6:1. Cf. similarly Justin Dial. 28: God's friend is whoever knows and obeys him; Sent. Sext. 86ab: self-discipline produces piety, which seeks friendship with God.

[256] Sipre Deut. 53.1.3; b. Sukkah 55b; this is much less frequent than Israel as God's son in such parables. Cf. other, later references, in Deut. Rab. 3:11; Pesiq. Rab. 5:5, 11; and Marmorstein, Names, 57; on God as friend to the world, Marmorstein, Names, 72–73, 86. God also befriends proselytes (Num. Rab. 8:4).

[257] Jub. 19:9; 4Q176 frg. 1–2, col. 1, line 10 (quoting Isa 41:8–9); Philo Abraham 89 (θεοφι-λοῦς), 273; Sobriety 55; T. Ab. 1:7; 2:3, 6; 8:2; 9:7; 15:12–14; 16:3A; Apoc. Ab. 10:5 (no earlier than second century C.E.); Apoc. Zeph. 9:4–5 (possibly a second-century Ebionite work); Mek. Pisḥa 18.8 (literally "beloved"); Šir. 10.54–55; Gen. Rab. 65:10; Exod. Rab. 27:1; Lev. Rab. 11:7; also Jas 2:23; 1 Clem. 10.1, 17.2. The title is applied to Jacob in some MSS of Jos. Asen. 23:10; cf. perhaps Gen. Rab. 69:2 (where the Shekinah may be a friend to Jacob, apparently in third-century tradition). The title

intimate relationship with God, so that God could take Abraham into his confidence, not treating him as a servant (cf. John 15:15):

> For wisdom is rather God's friend than His servant. And therefore He says plainly of Abraham, "shall I hide anything from Abraham my friend?" (Gen. xviii.17).[258]

Or it is because of his obedience to God instead of his own spirit's will (cf. John 15:14)?[259] It would not at all be unnatural, therefore, if John 15:13–15 were making an allusion to Abraham,[260] particularly given the emphasis on election in 15:16.

But another OT allusion is also possible, one that perhaps was more prominent to early readers of the OT because it was in the Torah proper. In Exod 33:11, Moses is the friend of God; this becomes the basis on which he can appeal to God for a revelation of his glory. This designation also appears in early Jewish texts;[261] it is the most common usage in Tannaitic parables (though not by a large margin).[262] This allusion becomes likely in John 15:15 because in 1:14–18 the disciples are compared to a new Moses to whom God revealed his glory in Jesus, the embodiment of Torah in flesh (cf. 2 Cor 3).[263]

Although Jesus fills the role of God here, friendship with Jesus would also bring one into a welcome relationship with the Father. Individuals' friendships provided ties, whenever feasible, between households.[264]

## 2E. Friends, Not Servants (15:15)

The earlier contrast between servants and children (John 8:33–35; cf. Gal 4:7) is here supplemented with a contrast between friends and servants. The contrast was familiar enough in Mediterranean antiquity; a Roman, for example, could describe conquered people as "slaves" but allies as "friends" (Sallust *Jug.* 102.6). Under Jewish law, a slave could not inherit, no matter how many goods were left to him, unless the will freed the slave or granted him "all" his master's goods (including himself; *m. Peʾah* 3:8). There would be no point in Jesus promising to share his words or goods with the disciples unless they were friends and not slaves. The image especially involves what Jesus entrusts the disciples with, as he states in 15:15; as noted above, one difference between servant-master relationships and those between friends is that servants withhold secrets from the master but friends do not withhold them from each other.[265]

---

is only rarely applied to postbiblical characters (R. Ishmael in *3 En.* 1:8) or biblical characters other than Abraham or Moses (Levi in *Jub.* 30:20–21; Cambridge Genizah Text C lines 8–9).

258 Philo *Sobriety* 55. In *T. Ab.* 9:2A, Michael told Abraham "everything which he had heard from the Most High" (εἶπεν αὐτῷ πάντα ὅσα ἤκουσεν παρὰ τοῦ ὑψίστου) (ed. Stone, 20–21).

259 CD 3.2. Similarly, Isaac and Jacob kept God's word and came to be inscribed as friends for God (אוהבים לאל) (3.3–4).

260 Schnackenburg, *John,* 3:111.

261 Philo *Sacrifices* 130 and the texts in Barrett, *John,* 477; *L.A.B.* 23:9, 24:3, 25:5 *(amicus Domini); Sipre Num.* 78.1.1; *Exod. Rab.* 45:2. Moses' special closeness to God also appears in Diaspora magical texts; see Gager, *Moses,* 140–45. *Sib. Or.* 2.245 is probably a Christian interpolation.

262 Moses (four times); Israel (three times); sometimes Aaron, once each for Joshua, Noah, Abraham, and the three patriarchs (Johnston, "Parables," 591).

263 See comment on 1:14–18.

264 See Malina and Rohrbaugh, *John,* 236; in ancient texts, Homer *Il.* 6.212–231; Cicero *Fam.* 13.34.1.

265 Mitchell, "Friends," 259, citing Cicero *Amic.* 6.22; Aristotle *N.E.* 8.11.6, 1161a. Xenophon *Cyr.* 1.6.45 warns that those who treat potential friends as "slaves" will suffer justly. Slaves could not be friends in Aristotle *N.E.* 8.11.6–7, 1161b.

John is not alone in drawing a contrast between servants and friends of God—Philo does the same:

> indeed, it is folly to imagine that the servants [τοὺς δούλους] of God take precedence of His friends [τῶν φίλων τοῦ θεοῦ] in receiving their portion in the land of virtue.[266]

Abraham, like Wisdom, is God's friend and not his servant, and those who are his friends are also his only son (μόνος υἱός).[267]

By saying that he no longer calls his disciples slaves, Jesus could be alluding back to 13:16 and suggesting that they need no longer assume the role of subordinates but rather of equals. Against this proposal is the fact that Jesus cites the same saying in 15:20, *after* he has promised to call them servants no longer,[268] and the fact that their friendship is predicated on obedience to Jesus' command to love (15:14). As Carson has pointed out,

> The distinction Jesus draws between a servant and a friend is not the distinction between obeying and not obeying, but the distinction between not understanding and understanding.[269]

When Jesus declares that he "no longer" (οὐκέτι) calls them slaves (15:15), he signals a new era in salvation history,[270] the transition point being Jesus' departure to, and return from, the Father in chs. 18–20 (16:16; cf. 14:19, 30; 16:10, 16, 21, 25; 17:11). In communicating to them what he has heard from the Father (15:15), Jesus acts the role of a faithful disciple who passes on the teachings of the Father,[271] thus providing a model for the Spirit and the disciples (15:26–27). Even more to the point, just as Wisdom possesses all the special, secret knowledge of God (Wis 8:4)[272] and is thus the truest source of insight about God, Jesus is the truest revealer of the Father. The eschatological king would be "taught by God" (διδακτὸς ὑπὸ θεοῦ, *Pss. Sol.* 17:32; cf. John 6:45).

## 2F. Concluding Observations on Friendship

Although an allusion to patronal friendship is possible in this passage, the Greco-Roman ideals of loyalty, intimacy, and sharing are more likely in view. The subordination of the disciples in obedience is probably more an expression of covenant loyalty, qualified by their continuing role as servant-disciples, than the subordination of a client to a patron. The disciples are clearly dependent on Jesus in 15:1–7, and that dependence might have been read by clients patronally; but it need not have been so understood (cf., e.g., Hos 14:8d).

Jesus intimately shares the secrets of his heart with his disciples, treating them as friends, as God treated Abraham and Moses by revealing himself to them. The parallels with John 16:13–15 indicate that the Spirit of truth would continue passing down the revelations from the Father and Jesus to the disciples. Jesus passed on what he heard from the Father

---

[266] Philo *Migration* 45; cf. Seneca *Dial.* 1.5.6. The contrast between the image of "friends" and "slaves" in general is common, e.g., Sallust *Jug.* 102.6–7 (allies vs. subjects).

[267] Philo *Sobriety* 55, also cited above. Bernard, *John*, 2:487, on John 15 cites this passage in Philo. God shared "secrets" with Abraham (Gen 18:17; cf. the righteous in Ps 25:14).

[268] Contrast Bousset's overemphasis, which misses the context, on the "not servants" paradigm as a possibly anti-Pauline Christ mysticism (*Kyrios Christos*, 211–12).

[269] Carson, *Discourse*, 105–6.

[270] With Schnackenburg, *John*, 3:111.

[271] Cf., e.g., Socrates' disciples in Socrates *Ep.* 20.

[272] Wis 8:4 describes her as a μύστις, an initiate into Mysteries; this is related to God's special love for her and her living with him (8:3).

(5:20; 8:26); the Spirit would pass on to disciples what he heard from Jesus (16:13). Just as Jesus heard and saw the Father (5:19–20; 8:38), his disciples would see and hear him. (It is doubtful that the Fourth Gospel restricts this relationship to the literal level of visionary experience, but at least in the Pauline apostolic circle, visions were probably part of such experience—2 Cor 12:1; cf. Acts 2:17.)[273] John therefore portrays friendship with Jesus as an intimate relationship with God and his agent, one that John believed was continuing in his own community, and one that no doubt set them apart from the synagogue, which had a much more limited understanding of continuing pneumatic revelation.

They are his friends, and therefore objects of his self-sacrifice (15:13), if they do what he commands them (15:14). The paradoxical image of "friends-not-slaves" who "obey" Jesus' commandments is meant to jar the hearer to attention; friendship means not freedom to disobey but an intimate relationship that continues to recognize distinctions in authority. (Authority distinctions remained in patron-client relationships; at the same time, Jesus' complete sharing with his disciples resembles the Greek notion of "equality" in friendships.)[274] By obeying, they continue to make themselves more open recipients of God's love, "abiding" and persevering in ever deeper intimacy with God. Disciples as Jesus' "friends" might stem from Jesus tradition[275] and may have become a title for believers (3 John 15) as in some philosophical groups.

## 2G. Chosen and Appointed (15:16)

Jesus several times refers to the chosenness of his disciples (6:70; 13:18; 15:16, 19). It may be relevant that the choosing of apostles or other special groups of ministers appears elsewhere in early Christian tradition;[276] normally disciples chose their own teachers, but according to the Synoptic tradition, Jesus had chosen these disciples.[277] Yet John probably invites deeper theological reflection than that observation alone entails, fitting his theme elsewhere of Jesus' foreknowledge (e.g., 1:51; 2:19; 6:70–71). If one argued for an Abraham allusion in 15:15 (I think a Moses allusion more likely), one might also see an Abraham allusion in the "chosen" of 15:16. Jewish teachers commented frequently on Israel's "chosenness."[278] But both in the Bible (Gen 18:19; Neh 9:7; Ps 105:6; Isa 41:8) and in some later Jewish traditions,[279] this chosenness stemmed from God's initial choice of Abraham. Nor could it be neglected that God had chosen Abraham and the other patriarchs because of grace (Deut 26:5; cf. Deut 7:7–8).[280]

But our text may, without specific reference to Abraham, simply allude to the chosenness of God's people as a whole (cf. 2 John 1, 13; Rev 17:14; Mark 13:20, 22, 27; Acts

---

[273] Some third-century C.E. paganism portrays personal knowledge of a deceased hero by conversation rather than dependence on dreams and visions, but this might reflect the spreading influence of early Christian spirituality (cf. Maclean and Aitken, *Heroikos*, lxi–lxii, lxxvi).

[274] Hays, *Vision*, 154, comments on the remarkably egalitarian language here and its implications for the meaning of leadership in John's community.

[275] It is a title in Luke 12:4 (though stylistically a Lukan preference); cf. the charge in Matt 11:19; Luke 7:34.

[276] Esp. in Luke-Acts (Luke 6:13; Acts 1:2, 24; 6:5; 15:7); of the poor in Jas 2:5.

[277] Morris, *John*, 676.

[278] On predestination, see comment on 3:19–21.

[279] E.g., *T. Ab.* 2:3A. See fuller comment on 8:39–40. Abraham could share this chosen status with others, such as Jacob and Moses (*Num. Rab.* 3:2).

[280] Also rehearsed annually in the Passover haggadah, if these details were in wide use by the end of the first century (*m. Pesaḥ.* 10:4).

13:17; Eph 1:4; 1 Pet 1:1), here applied to the branches on the true vine, in contrast to Jewish pictures of Israel as God's vine (see the introduction to 15:1–7). Deuteronomy frequently recalled the chosenness of God's people (4:37; 7:6–7; 10:15; 14:2); chosen "out of the world" (15:19) may even reflect Deuteronomy's chosen "out of all peoples" (Deut 7:6; 10:15; 14:2).[281]

That Jesus "appointed" (ἔθηκα) them (15:16) suggests that he not only exercised a purpose concerning them but "established" that purpose. Some connect the verb to its recent use in 15:13 and 10:11–18, for laying down one's life; their commission would thus follow Jesus' model of love.[282] This interpretation, while plausible, is not secure; τίθημι is a frequent term (seventeen times in John, albeit most commonly surrounding Jesus' death) with a broad semantic range (cf., e.g., the thirty-nine uses in Isaiah LXX). That the term is not the usual one for God's call or commission lends credence to an allusion back to 15:13; at the same time, it can apply to God establishing his covenant with Abraham and establishing Abraham in his purposes (Gen 17:2, 5).[283]

If the disciples are bearing fruit, they may ask "in Jesus' name" (15:16), probably meaning as his representatives carrying out his work (cf. 14:12–14).[284] Alternatively, one may connect "in Jesus' name" with "he may give," as possibly in 16:23, probably connoting "because of Jesus."[285] In either case, whether because they act as his representatives or bear favor on his account, disciples have this blessing because they depend on Jesus' act on their behalf.[286] John concludes again with the command to love, thus framing the section (15:17; cf. 15:12, 14).

## The World's Hatred (15:18–16:4)

If 15:8–17 discusses the love of God and believers, 15:18–16:4 discusses the world's hatred. While we often describe John's thought here as sectarian, John might object that whereas his community represented the minority, the intolerance for difference stemmed also from the outside: the world would hate those who did not belong to its way of thinking and behaving (7:7; 17:14; 1 John 3:13; cf. Jas 4:4).

### 1. Introductory Matters

Farewell speeches often included warnings (e.g., Josephus *Ant.* 4.177–193), but like some other early Christian examples of this genre (e.g., Mark 13; Acts 20:28–31), the words of warning in 15:18–25 reflect the traditional apocalyptic perspective of suffering before the end. The Gospel's emphasis on realized eschatology underlines the immediacy of the eschatological situation of tribulation; one may also compare the similar result of imminent eschatology in the book of Revelation.

---

[281] Glasson, *Moses*, 75; cf. Lacomara, "Deuteronomy," 72; Lee, *Thought*, 169.

[282] Lightfoot, *Gospel*, 292; Brown, *John*, 2:664–65. Barrett, *John*, 478, suggests a Semitizing construction.

[283] It can describe "the assignment of a special post" (Westcott, *John*, 221). Neither of the LXX texts using both τίθημι and καρπός (Ps 132:11; Jer 2:7) proves relevant.

[284] Sanders, *John*, 342.

[285] Lee, *Thought*, 254.

[286] Dowd, "Theology," 325, believes that both 15:7 and 15:16 equate fruit bearing "with receiving answers to petitionary prayer."

## 1A. Part of the Context

Some argue that the focus of 15:18–16:15 is quite different from ch. 14;[287] certainly the focus moves from the relationship of believers with God and one another (13:31–15:17) to the relationship of believers to hostile society. Yet one need not view 15:18–16:4 as an independent discourse formed under circumstances distinct from the rest of the Gospel;[288] the Gospel as a whole is basically consistent in its dualism (see introduction).

## 1B. The Worldview of the Passage

The worldview presupposed in 15:18–25 is one common to sectarian groups, in which apocalyptic ideologies (in the modern sense of that expression) often prevail. Some early Christian writers, such as Luke, seem to represent a socioeconomic stratum and social conditions that provide more optimism for engaging the broader culture from a Christian perspective. Thus Acts includes eschatology (1:11; 3:19–21; 10:42; 17:31; 24:15; 26:6–8) but focuses more on the current mission (1:6–8); one finds favorable and just officials (5:34; 10:4; 13:7; 18:12–16; 19:31; 22:29; 23:9, 23–24; 25:25; 26:31–32; 27:43) and others (e.g., 28:2, 10, 21). John, however, expects his audience to view the world as hostile, with a perspective comparable to other Johannine literature (1 John 2:15–17; 4:4–5; 5:19; Rev 13:7–17).[289] This admittedly characterized also those who, while working within society, shared an apocalyptic worldview (Rom 12:2; 13:11–12; 1 Cor 10:11; Gal 1:4; 2 Thess 2:1–13).[290] Such hostility from the out-group would also help define the boundaries and strengthen cohesiveness of the in-group.[291]

Still, John's emphasis on the world's hatred, relevant to his own situation and outlook, probably stems from authentic Jesus tradition. Both Jesus' teachings (cf., e.g., Mark 13:12; Matt 5:10–11; 10:21, 25, 35–39; cf. Luke 6:40; 14:26–27) and his sacrificial death (cf., e.g., Mark 8:34–38) provide ample material for addressing the world's hostility. Parallels with the Synoptic eschatological discourse[292] probably indicate authentic Jesus tradition behind this passage. Further, we should not exaggerate John's difference from other early Christian sources but should distinguish degrees of "sectarian" outlook. There are certainly differences among models, such as wholesale withdrawal from the world (e.g., the Qumran Essenes), individual protest in urban culture (e.g., the Cynics), and a politically disenfranchised (or in this case unenfranchised) movement that could remain within the society yet view it as hostile. Presumably, first-century Pharisees experienced some degree

---

[287] Becker, "Abschiedsreden," 236–41, esp. 239, noting that it emphasizes ecclesiology more than Christology.

[288] Argued by Segovia, "Addition."

[289] One may compare the sectarian fundamentalism of some early-twentieth-century groups in the United States (some amillennial, but largely dispensational) who felt cut off from previous access to society and hence felt the need to form an alternative and defensive subculture (see briefly Noll, *History,* 373–86; Marsden, *Fundamentalism;* Gaustad, *History,* 395–99), or pockets of marginalized minority religious subcultures in various parts of the world today. Early Christian literature provides not a single unified model of Christian relations to society but divergent models representing divergent social settings.

[290] Among fully sectarian groups, see, e.g., 1QS 1.18; 2.19; 3.22; 4.20; 1QM 1.6; 14.9; CD 1.5; 6.10; 1QpHab 5.7–8; among others, e.g., *t. Taʿan.* 3:14; *Gen. Rab.* 98:7; probably also those represented in Ferch, "Aeons"; Bowman, *Documents,* ii. Even philosophers distinguished themselves (not for apocalyptic reasons) from the masses (e.g., Philo *Abraham* 38).

[291] Cf. Malina and Rohrbaugh, *John,* 237–39, on in-groups and out-groups.

[292] See Brown, *John,* 2:694; Evans, *John,* 166.

of political marginalization from Sadducean aristocrats, and Palestinian Jewish revolutionaries found the system entirely unworkable; Johannine Christians fall somewhere in between.

Interestingly, however, the discussion of the world's opposition (John 15:18–25; 16:1–4) frames an announcement of the Paraclete's and disciples' role to bear witness against the world (15:26–27). Shortly after this, one learns that the Paraclete prosecutes the world (16:8–11), presumably through the witness of believers (16:7) who themselves know Jesus intimately (16:12–15). The worldview is not merely defensive, waiting till the end as in some apocalyptic treatises; it remains offensive and evangelistic (cf. the combination of these elements in Revelation 11–13).

The worldview of this passage is also as pervaded by moral dualism as Revelation or Qumran's *Rule of the Community*. The Spirit thus confronts the world (16:7–11) with the truth that one falls on either one side or the other: "Die nur noch christliche oder antichristlich sein kann."[293] The rigidity of boundaries created by the world's hostility undoubtedly strengthens the community's internal cohesiveness, so that persecution intensifies the attention of community members to loving one another. The same social setting provides a faith committed to and expecting probable martyrdom, as in Revelation. Israeli scholar David Flusser argues, "Christianity surpasses Judaism, at least theoretically, in its approach of love to all men, but its only genuine answer to the powerful wicked forces of this world is, as it seems, martyrdom."[294] If John is less concerned with the question of loving those outside the community than the Synoptics are, he is more consumed by martyrdom; he seems to believe this the likely price of those who submit to the high Christology he proclaims and to a consequently likely expulsion from the synagogue community.

## 1C. The Opposition

The "world" bears wider implications than Jesus' elite Jerusalem accusers or John's audience's accusers, but John's immediate concern is particularly his audience's opposition. "The Jews" embody "the world" in the Fourth Gospel in general[295] and this context in particular, for it is the same "world" that opposed Jesus (15:20, 24); they claim biblical law (15:25), and they will expel Jesus' followers from the synagogues (16:2). Whereas "the Jews" form a prism for "the world," they are not, however, its only representatives in this Gospel; they collaborate with Pilate, who defends a worldly kingdom (18:36). It is also important to note the greater but often neglected nuancing in John's narratives; the "world" epitomized in Jerusalem is divided, not uniformly hostile (7:43; 9:16; 10:19).

The explicitness of the connection between Jesus' sufferings and his followers' impending sufferings indicates that John intends his followers to understand their current (or imminent) situation in light of Jesus' sufferings in this Gospel.[296] We have no evidence that Jewish opponents were killing Jewish followers of Jesus in the real world of John; what is more likely is that they were "delivering" them, that is, acting as *delatores* to accuse them, to Roman officials, who themselves carried out the harshest acts of persecution (see comment on 16:2).

---

[293] Schlier, "Geist," 106.
[294] Flusser, *Judaism*, 489.
[295] See, e.g., Baum, *Jews*, 124; Hickling, "Attitudes," 353–54.
[296] See Whitacre, *Polemic*, 6.

## 2. Hating Father, Son, and Followers (15:18–25)

15:18–21 connects disciples' suffering with that of Jesus. Berg summarizes the structure basically as follows, with D in the center:[297]

> A  If the world hates you, it hated me first (15:18).
> > B  If you were of the world, they would love you (but you are not) (15:19ab).
> > > C  Because I chose you, the world hates you (15:19cd).
> > > > D  The servant is no greater than the master (15:20ab).
> > > A′  If they persecuted me, they will persecute you (15:20c).
> > B′  If they kept my word, they will keep yours (15:20d).
> C′  They will persecute you for Jesus' and the Father's sake (15:21).

A and A′ might well be substituted for C and C′, providing an A-B-A-D-A-B-A pattern, but in any case the point Berg designates as D remains central and significant. If "the servant is not greater than the master,"[298] as Jesus has already told them in another context (13:16), they can expect to suffer no less than what he suffered (15:20).[299]

The world's hatred (15:18) for those not belonging to it, both Jesus (7:7) and his followers (17:14), had been amply demonstrated in its response to Lazarus's testimony (12:10).[300] Just as Jesus loved his "own" (cf. 10:3), the world loved its "own," but the meaning of that love requires some consideration. Presumably this does not imply solidarity of thought in the world system on any but the most theoretical level, a solidarity that would contradict John's narrative expositions (e.g., 7:43; 9:16; 10:19; 12:42, although these divisions were created by Jesus' entrance). Perhaps it means something like the logion about sinners loving those close to them (Matt 5:46; Luke 6:32); probably it means that the world as a whole shares the same values (cf. 1 John 4:5), united at least in its opposition to the alien values "from above." Those in the world could understand one another (7:7), but those born from above were incomprehensible (3:8). As many Gentiles hated Jews for their "hatred of humanity," that is, their uncompromisingly different customs, so would the world as a whole hate true followers of Christ.[301]

The thought of 15:18–19 follows naturally from the preceding context. In the system of political alliances found in at least many Mediterranean cities, if one was friends with another's enemy, one became the other's enemy as well.[302] Thus, if Christ's followers are friends of Jesus (15:15), the world who hated him would also hate them. As Jewish people experienced the world's hatred as a chosen people,[303] Jesus' disciples experienced the

---

[297] Berg, "Pneumatology," 164–65.

[298] Apparently a popular proverb (Dalman, *Jesus-Jeshua*, 229; see comment on 13:16).

[299] Blomberg, *Reliability*, 209, points out that the sense in 15:20 is very similar to its use in Synoptic contexts (Matt 10:24; Luke 6:40).

[300] Hanson, *Gospel*, 185–86, finds an allusion to Isa 66:5 in 15:18–19; although this is plausible (especially if connected with John 16:2), it is by itself unclear, especially since John's explicit citation (15:25) points elsewhere.

[301] E.g., Bruce, *John*, 313 (citing Tacitus *Ann.* 15.44.5 on the Christians).

[302] E.g., (Ps.-)Lysias *Or.* 9.13, §115; this could lead to prosecution in a court (9.10, §115) or at least denunciation (e.g., Aeschines *Timarchus* 193–195; Cicero *Pro Scauro* 17.38); see further Marshall, *Enmity*, 67–69. Cf. the contrast between political rivalry and friendship in Valerius Maximus 2.9.6a (though friends could also be rivals, Philostratus *Hrk.* 27.4).

[303] For Gentile anti-Judaism, see, e.g., Josephus *Ag. Ap.* 2; Philo *Flaccus* 1, 47, 85; *CPJ* 1:24–25; 2:36–55, §153; 3:119–21, §520; *Sib. Or.* 3.271–272; Horace *Sat.* 1.5.100–101; Juvenal *Sat.* 14.96–106; Quintilian 3.7.21; Tacitus *Hist.* 5.1–5.

world's hatred because Jesus had "chosen" them out of that world (15:16, 19). Enmity, regularly accompanied by public invective, was a typical feature of ancient Mediterranean urban culture in general.[304]

The general description of the world's hatred in 15:18–19 becomes more concrete and specific in 15:20–21: the disciples would face severe persecution.[305] The "persecution" that Jesus endured and in which believers followed (15:20) could easily escalate into the threat of death (5:16, 18; cf. Rev 12:13). That Jesus promises persecution for his own "name's" sake (15:21) probably connects him with the Father, again underscoring his divinity. Jewish people spoke of persecution for the sake of God's commandments (Ps 119:23, 157, 161)[306] and God or his name (Ps 44:22);[307] the hope of resurrection should encourage one not to fear sinners' abuse (1 En. 103:4). "On account of my name" could represent a Semitic expression meaning simply "on my account," and Mark also reports that disciples would suffer for Jesus' name (Mark 13:13); but in the context of the Fourth Gospel, it more likely recalls that Jesus bears the divine name.[308]

If Jesus suffered, disciples must suffer for his name (15:20–22). Jesus would die for his friends (15:13), those who kept his commandments (15:14); but keeping his commandments involved especially loving as he loved, that is, dying on one another's behalf (13:34). Betraying others in the face of persecution may be a common response to persecution (cf. Mark 13:12),[309] but true followers of Jesus dare not respond in this manner (cf. 1 John 3:16). If dying for friends was a rare but praiseworthy practice, the same may be said of dying for a master.[310] That Jesus' disciples must be prepared to die for his name reflects earlier Jesus tradition (cf., e.g., Matt 10:22; 5:11).[311] Through the Spirit, disciples carry on Jesus' mission (15:26–27; 16:7–11) and hence experience the same opposition as he did.[312]

Jesus' coming unveiled the "world's" sin (15:22, 24); this claim fits both his earlier exposures of his enemies' sin (8:21, 34) and the claim that those who try to conceal their sin are those who cannot be rid of it (3:20; 9:41).[313] Moralists sometimes opined that wrongdoers could not keep their sins concealed indefinitely.[314] In Jewish tradition, the law could

---

[304] See esp. Marshall, *Enmity*, 35–69 (for invective and shaming enemies, see 46–69). Even Pythagoras reportedly permitted repudiating friendships in the case of a serious vice (Iamblichus *V.P.* 22.102; 33.232).

[305] Segovia, *Farewell*, 179. As Malina and Rohrbaugh, *John*, 87, note, "hatred" was not primarily an internal feeling, as it is understood in modern Western thought.

[306] Also, e.g., *Pesiq. Rab.* 21:2/3.

[307] Also, e.g., Ps 69:7; Isa 51:7; *2 En.* 50:3–4.

[308] Brown, *John*, 2:687. Cf. Rev 2:3, 13; 3:8.

[309] Sometimes a person could, on the condition of securing immunity, denounce others and let them be executed—whether or not the confession was true (Thucydides 6.60.2–5; Plutarch *Alc.* 21.2–4; without immunity, cf. Josephus *War* 1.498).

[310] E.g., Appian *C.W.* 4.4.26; Valerius Maximus 3.3.ext.7; cf. also claims about the Iberians (Strabo *Geog.* 3.4.18; Valerius Maximus 2.6.11). For other instances of slaves' loyalty, e.g., Appian *R.H.* 7.1.2; 8.3.17; slaves who defended their master's life deserved freedom and great reward (Cicero *Mil.* 22.58). DeSilva, *Honor*, 115, 144, compares the honorable behavior of sharing a patron-friend's suffering (Seneca *Ep. Lucil.* 81.27; *Benef.* 4.20.2; 4.24.2).

[311] With, e.g., Swete, *Discourse*, 99; Blomberg, *Reliability*, 209.

[312] Berg, "Pneumatology," 270.

[313] This text does not exonerate those who did not see or hear him, as if negating the Gospel's earlier statements that the world stands condemned before his coming (3:17–18) or that Jesus is the only way to the Father (14:6); πρόφασις simply means "pretext" (Whitacre, *John*, 382–83, note).

[314] Prov 26:26; Sir 11:27–28; Isocrates *Demon.* 17, *Or.* 1; Diodorus Siculus 14.1.1–2; Livy 3.36.1; Aulus Gellius 12.11; cf. 1 Tim 5:24–25; Matt 10:26–27; *b. Soṭah* 22b; *Exod. Rab.* 8:2; *Num. Rab.* 9:12;

expose sin and leave sinners without excuse.[315] Philo declares that God's angel and priest, reproof (ἔλεγχος), exposes such impure thoughts (*Unchangeable* 135) and those who do not listen will face destruction (*Unchangeable* 182–183); this image reinforces the sense that the Paraclete continues Jesus' mission in this Gospel (ἐλέγξει in 16:8–11).

Applying his motif of agency, John reports that just as those who opposed the disciples opposed Jesus (15:18–21), so those who oppose Jesus oppose his Father, who sent him (15:21, 23). The world's hatred (15:19, 24–25; 17:14) will not surprise a reader by this point; Jesus had already warned that those who did evil were those who hated the light (3:20) and that the world hates one who reveals its sin (7:7). Jesus' "signs" and other works revealed enough of his identity and sender that those who hated him could be said to have beheld both him and his Father (15:24; cf. 14:7).[316] Those who rejected him were without excuse; as Jesus has repeatedly emphasized, his works revealed his identity and sender, and hence rejection of him exposed the true state of his opponents' hearts (14:11; see comment on 10:32, 37–38).

Jesus cites their own law against them (15:25). Because Jewish literature reports pagans speaking to Israel of "your law,"[317] one could argue that the Fourth Gospel here preserves a non-Jewish perspective. But John repeatedly enlists the support of the law, which he accepts as authoritative (e.g., 2:17, 22; 5:45–47; 19:36–37). Jesus applies to Scripture the formula "in order that [the word] might be fulfilled" (15:25; 13:18; 17:12), which elsewhere in this Gospel refers to Jesus' own teaching (18:9, 32) as well as to Scripture (12:38; 19:24, 36); it is difficult to think of a more authoritative claim for Scripture than that the events of the passion had to occur to fulfill it. The use of "your" or "their" law means "the law which even they profess to accept" (10:34)[318] and probably implies irony (see our introduction, pp. 214–28).[319] "They hated me without cause" reflects the language of various psalms (Ps 35:19; 69:4; 109:3; cf. 35:7);[320] because Ps 69:4 comes from the same context as Ps 69:9, quoted in John 2:17, commentators generally prefer this reference if a specific text is in view.[321]

## 3. Witnesses against the World (15:26–27)

In the context (15:18–25; 16:1–4), the passage about witness refers not to some timid words (cf. 20:19) but to a bold counteroffensive; the "world" far outnumbers believers, but believers depend on God, whose power can at any time overrule the purposes of the world

---

cf. delayed judgment in Babrius 127; *Sib. Or.* 3.258–260; *ʾAbot R. Nat.* 39A; 44, §123B; *Num. Rab.* 19:6; *2 Clem.* 16.3.

[315] E.g., *Exod. Rab.* 41:3. Epp, "Wisdom," 141, cites Rom 7:7–9.

[316] Lacomara, "Deuteronomy," 68–70, compares God's signs in ancient Israel; in view of their absence in this Gospel, Richardson's finding the sacraments in 15:24 (*Theology,* 378) is improbable.

[317] *M. ʿAbod. Zar.* 3:4; see further the comment on 10:34. Torah was one of two or three divisions of Scripture (e.g., 4 Macc 18:10; *Pesiq. Rab Kah.* 12:13; see more fully the comment on John 1:45) but in the general sense included the whole (e.g., *3 En.* 48D:4; *Sipre Deut.* 32.5.12) and even extrapolations (e.g., *t. Ber.* 6:19).

[318] Cf., e.g., Carson, *Discourse,* 125.

[319] Appeals to defend the law against other Jews who would betray it in collaboration with the Romans stir nationalistic sentiments (Josephus *Life* 135).

[320] E.g., Grayston, *Gospel,* 134.

[321] Beasley-Murray, *John,* 276; Hanson, *Gospel,* 187. Comparing also Matt 27:34 and Rom 15:3, Blomberg, *Reliability,* 210, suggests that "a dominical origin" helps account for Ps 69's widespread early Christian use.

(cf. 18:9; 19:11). That the world's hostility frames these comments on witness does not imply that they are simply a later insertion into a foreign context: both 15:18–25 and 16:1–4 are constructed distinctively. The previous pericope (15:18–25) includes two quotations, one from Jesus himself (15:20) and one from Scripture (15:25). The following pericope (16:1–4) is carefully constructed and set apart from 15:18–25 by its *inclusio,* suggesting an intended break between 15:18–25 and 16:1–4.

John further emphasizes here the inseparable relationship between the Father and the Son, repeatedly emphasized and clarified throughout the Gospel (e.g., 1:1–2). The Spirit "proceeds" from the Father (cf. Rev 22:1)[322] but is sent by the Son (15:26; 16:7; cf. Luke 24:49) as well as by the Father (14:16, 26); yet even in sending the Spirit, Jesus first receives the Spirit from the Father (15:26; Acts 2:33; cf. Rom 8:11). John attempts no precise disinction between the roles of the Father and the Son here except in acknowledging the Father's superior rank; the Father often delegates his own roles to the Son in the Gospel (5:20–29). Various other early Christian texts likewise appear unconcerned to make stark differentiations between the roles of Father and Son here; some portray the Spirit as from the Father (e.g., Acts 2:17; 5:32; cf. Eph 1:17; Phil 3:3; 1 Pet 1:12), others perhaps from the Son (cf. Rom 8:2, 9; Phil 1:19; 1 Pet 1:11). Early Christians probably regarded the alternatives as complementary rather than contradictory (see esp. Gal 4:6). On the title "Spirit of truth," see comment on 14:17.

### 3A. The Spirit Testifies against the World

Certainly the Spirit's witness is not limited to prosecuting the world as in 16:8–11; the Spirit can witness to believers to confirm their relationship with God, as both the Johannine tradition (1 John 5:6–8, 10) and other early Christian tradition (Rom 8:16; cf. 9:1; Acts 15:8) concurs. But in this context the emphasis lies on prophetic witness to the world (cf. Rev 19:10). Certainly "witness" appears in a forensic sense in some Jesus tradition reported in Mark 13: believers will be brought before authorities for a witness to (or against) them (Mark 13:9), which will be empowered by the Holy Spirit (Mark 13:11).

Although the world could not receive the Spirit (14:26), the Spirit could witness to it (15:26–16:11), just as Jesus testifies but no one receives his witness (3:11, 32; 1:10–11). The Spirit of truth and the disciples would both testify concerning Jesus. It is possible that this Paraclete saying is a general statement that summarizes the next two: when the Spirit comes, he will bear witness both to the world (16:8–11) and to the community (16:13–15); both of these sayings are introduced in a manner similar to the ὅταν ἔλθῃ of 15:26, and in each instance the Spirit comes to believers (15:26; 16:7, 12–13).[323]

But in the context of the preceding and following pericopes, the Spirit and the disciples together carry on Jesus' witness to a hostile world characterized as a judicial body thinking it was passing judgment on them, as it thought it had passed judgment

---

[322] Philo may portray the Logos as flowing from God like wine (Dillon, "Logos," citing *Unchangeable* 155–158; *Dreams* 2.249); but if a fluid image is intended here (not demanded by the verb but possible on analogy with Rev 22:1), the sense may follow from the frequent OT image of the Spirit being poured like water (e.g., Prov 1:23; Isa 32:15; Ezek 39:29; Joel 2:28). In any case, the image in context may address the Spirit's mission (cf. 8:42; 13:3; 16:27; Barrett, *John,* 482), not the ontology of the Trinity, and hence may prove textually irrelevant to the *filioque* controversy that officially divided the Eastern and Western churches in later centuries.

[323] "When he comes" further underlines the connection between the Spirit and Jesus (4:25), who also "announces" (ἀναγγελεῖ) things to his people (4:25; cf. 16:13–15).

on Jesus.[324] Like the remnant of "Deutero-Isaiah," the righteous martyrs in the day of judgment in Wis 5:1, or the righteous from among the nations in later Jewish tradition,[325] Jesus' followers in this context bear witness against the world before God's court. The disciples here act as witnesses, but prosecuting witnesses were *delatores,* accusers; they pronounce judgment as well as forgiveness (20:23).[326]

"Witness" is not always a judicial image, of course, however the term may have originally been used.[327] But in the Fourth Gospel, it probably has forensic significance,[328] as the term often does in secular Greek[329] and early Jewish literature.[330] Burge even considers the judicial context for witness throughout the Gospel "one of the assured results of Johannine scholarship in recent years."[331] The present text is no exception to the forensic context of this Johannine motif. The forensic context continues in the ἀποσυναγώγους of 16:2.

## 3B. The Forensic Context

The ἀποσυναγώγους of 16:2 (more than the ἀποκτείνας of the same verse) presupposes the sort of judicial context found in 9:13–34, in which synagogue authorities gather witnesses and seek to ascertain whether or not the person tried should be disciplined or put out of the community. The following chapters show this same "world" trying Jesus and condemning him, and 15:20 shows that the same treatment is to be regarded as normative for disciples of Jesus; yet as his words convicted his opponents (15:20, 22), so would theirs. This is the Johannine context of "witness" in 15:26–27; as Berg notes, Bultmann denied a connection between this passage and Mark 13:11[332]

> because the paraclete saying was not related to witness before an earthly court. . . . The placement of the saying, which must play a central role in its interpretation, suggests, however, that the writer *did* have in mind the testimony borne in the midst of hatred and persecution.[333]

---

[324] Boice, *Witness,* 153, argues that the Spirit does not plead the cause of the disciples with God or the world but is Christ's advocate, "pleading Christ's cause with the disciples and, in a different but closely related sense, with unbelievers."

[325] E.g., *Pesiq. Rab.* 35:3; Matt. 12:41–42; cf. the same principle in *Mek. Pisha* 1:81–82; *3 En.* 4:3; *'Abot R. Nat.* 6A; *'Abot R. Nat.* 12, §30B (later tradition transferred this from Akiba to Hillel, *b. Yoma* 36b). Cf. Enoch in *Jub.* 4:18, 19, 22; 10:17.

[326] Isaacs, "Spirit," 405. Athenian juries were to execute judgment "in place of the gods" as well as on their own behalf (speaker in Demosthenes *Or.* 59, *Against Neaera* 126).

[327] Plutarch *Apoll.* 14, *Mor.* 108E (of the deity); *Oracles at Delphi* 22, *Mor.* 405A; *Nicias* 6.3; 2 Macc 3:36; *1 En.* 104:11, 105:1; *T. Ab.* 11:2B (perhaps late use as "martyr").

[328] Widely held, e.g., Meeks, *Prophet-King,* 65 (relating μαρτυρία and κρίσις in Johannine texts); Trites, *Witness,* 78–127; cf. Caird, *Revelation,* 18; Harvey, *Trial.*

[329] Trites, *Witness,* 4–15

[330] On the LXX, see Trites, *Witness,* 20–47, esp. 35–47 on Isa 40–55; in rabbinic literature, 231–39; on other Jewish texts, 48–65. In *Pesiq. Rab Kah.* 24:15, God himself witnesses against evildoers and on behalf of the righteous; the attribution is to R. Eliezer ben R. Jose the Galilean.

[331] Burge, *Community,* 204–5. Franck, *Revelation,* 52, thinks the usage in 15:26 is too broad to be forensic, although he earlier acknowledged a forensic context for the Paraclete.

[332] Contrast, e.g., Berrouard, "Paraclet," 388. The earthly tribunals become an all-encompassing theological motif in John, however; cf. Zerwick, "Wirken," 226.

[333] Berg, "Pneumatology," 181, although he admits (p. 170) that the saying may not originally derive from the same material as its context. Forestell, "Paraclete," 165, and others are right that this saying could be removed from its context "without disturbing the sequence of thought between 15:18 and 16:4"; this is not the same, however, as supposing that the saying does not make good sense in this context, purposely bracketed with material about the world's hostility, at whatever

Synagogues functioned as judicial assemblies even in the Diaspora; Roman laws usually permitted them to exercise internal discipline over their own communities. In many rabbinic texts, the OT image of God's angelic court is developed and applied either to angels or to sages in heaven, and it is possible that this image was in wide enough circulation by the end of the first century for readers of the Fourth Gospel to have caught an allusion to it. But here the verdict of the earthly courts is contrasted with that of the heavenly court, in contrast to usual rabbinic teaching (cf. also Matt 16:19, 18:15–20); typical Johannine irony makes the accusers of Jesus and his community the ones really on trial before God. (An ancient Mediterranean audience may not have found such irony foreign; for example, a king might unwittingly condemn a deity, only to learn in the end that it is he himself who would suffer.)[334] The Paraclete, who defends the disciples brought before worldly courts (cf. Mark 13:11; Matt 10:19–20), is also the one who will charge the world with its sins (16:8–11).[335]

### 3C. Prophetic Witness

Prophets in the OT also functioned as witnesses to God's righteousness, particularly when they declared his covenant lawsuits against Israel. Lukan pneumatology (which emphasizes the Spirit of prophecy more than that of any other extant early Christian writer) also connects prophetic empowerment to declare the risen Christ with Luke's witness motif (Acts 1:8; 2:32–33; 4:33; 5:32), although Luke probably limits the immediate use of "witness" to eyewitnesses more strictly than John does.[336]

Thus the Paraclete not only continues the presence of Jesus in a general way and expounds Jesus' teachings but also enables the believers to boldly testify for Jesus, recognizing that it is the world, and not the believers, that is really on trial before God.[337] This image naturally leads to the next Paraclete passage, in which the Spirit acts as prosecutor (John 16:8–11).

The disciples who would bear witness in this passage were those with him from "the beginning" (15:27), undoubtedly the beginning of his ministry (2:11; 8:25; 16:4; cf. 6:64; Acts 1:21–22; Phil 4:15),[338] perhaps intended to evoke the era of the new creation (cf. 1:1–2; 8:44; 9:32; 17:24; 1 John 1:1; 2:13–14; 3:8).[339] But for the Johannine community,

---

stage it came to be there. The contention that the Paraclete sayings in John 15–16 are substantially different from those in ch. 14 and are thus secondary (e.g., Müller, "Parakletenvorstellung," 65–75) is not persuasive, basing itself on a small sampling of material and variations that are common enough in Johannine rhetoric (cf. Chevallier, "Filioque,"; also the scholars cited in Berg, "Pneumatology," 175). (Jesus is, of course, the Spirit sender in John; see, e.g., Schulze-Kadelbach, "Pneumatologie," 279; God sends his Holy Spirit in Wis 9:17.)

334 Euripides *Bacch.* 500–508, 515–518.

335 Cf. Josephus *Ant.* 4.46, where God acts on Moses' behalf (against Korah), as both judge and witness.

336 Lofthouse, "Spirit," 336, uses the conceptual parallels between the two documents to suggest that their source here is Jesus' teaching.

337 "Witness" in 15:27 is undoubtedly indicative, based on the parallel with 15:26 (somewhat less securely, Westcott, *John*, 225, cites 3 John 12).

338 Thus Diodorus Siculus 4.8.5 seeks to recount Heracles' acts "from the beginning" (ἀπ' ἀρχῆς), i.e., starting with the first act. The phrase often signifies the beginning of the period in question (*T. Ab.* 15:14A; 4:13B). Socrates insisted that leaders receive training (Xenophon *Mem.* 4.2.6).

339 While this discourse probably does date from the circles that produced 1 John, the ἀπ' ἀρχῆς is of itself inadequate to suggest the connection (*pace* the suggestion in Berg, "Pneumatology," 171 n. 26).

perhaps all believers could count their first experience of the gospel analogously (1 John 2:24; 3:11; 2 John 6).

## 4. Coming Persecution (16:1–4)

The heart of the new material in 16:1–4 is the specific prediction of 16:2, which fits the audience's experience (expulsion from their synagogues) and anticipation (martyrdom); 16:3 reiterates 15:21, and 16:1, 4 frames the section by explaining the necessity for this advance warning (cf. 13:19; 14:29).

Jesus' assurance that he had spoken to them (on λελάληκα, see 14:25; 16:4, 6; and comment on 15:11) in advance that they might not "stumble" or fall away (16:1)[340] recalls earlier statements that Jesus was giving advance warning that they might believe (see comment on 13:19; 14:29). That it was to prevent them from "stumbling," or falling away (cf. 6:61), most directly recalls the immediately preceding context: they would have to endure the world's hatred after Jesus' departure (15:18–25) and be inspired witnesses to the world and against the world before the divine court (15:26–27).[341]

With 16:4 (when these matters come to pass, they may remember that he had forewarned them), 16:1 forms an *inclusio* around Jesus' most specific warning about impending trials in 16:2–3: the world's hatred (15:18–25) will be expressed by expulsion from the synagogues and by death at the hands of those who think they are serving God (16:2). The Spirit's work in causing disciples to "remember" Jesus' teaching (14:26) suggests that their memory here (16:4) will also be supplemented by the Spirit's interpretative work (16:12–13), such as is perhaps found in works like the book of Revelation.

### 4A. Expulsion from Synagogues

Most contemporary commentators find in the expulsion of the Jewish Christians the experience of the Johannine community.[342] To claim relevance to this situation is not to deny the influence of prior tradition;[343] yet at the very least, regardless of prior tradition, John would have little reason to emphasize this expulsion as he does (not only here but in 9:22; 12:42; nowhere explicitly in the Synoptics) unless it were a recent or imminent threat to his audience. Some earlier interpreters recognized the influence of a Jewish-Christian schism here;[344] in the wake of Martyn's thesis, some associated the schism very specifically with the Birkath Ha-minim; the prevalent tendency today is to recognize Johannine Christians' recent rejection but not to connect it exclusively or necessarily primarily with the Birkath Ha-minim (see introduction, pp. 207–14). The warning that the synagogue community would seek to "kill" disciples as an act of worship to God appears more problematic.

### 4B. Martyrs

By announcing that an "hour" was coming for their persecution, the text announces two points. First, the disciples will ultimately share Jesus' "hour," his suffering and death;

---

[340] "Stumbling" refers to apostasy (see comment on 6:61). It is most frequent in Matthew and Mark but rare in Luke and John (probably not because of his Judean focus, as Swete, *Discourse*, 109, thinks).

[341] Apart from the conflict implied in 15:26–27, it appears to fit its context loosely; see comments above on the Paraclete sayings fitting their context.

[342] E.g., Martyn, *Theology*, 66–67; Pancaro, *Law*, 247ff.; Berrouard, "Paraclet," 361.

[343] See Dodd, *Tradition*, 410; Beasley-Murray, *John*, 277–78.

[344] Bultmann, *John*, 555, on 16:2.

the Gospel describes Jesus' appointed hour as either "not yet come" or as having "come" (e.g., 7:30; 8:20; 12:23; see comment on 2:4). Second, the full phrase "an hour is coming" may represent future eschatology in the Gospel (or present eschatology when accompanied by the phrase "and now is"; 4:23; 5:25), as in 5:28 (and probably 4:21; but cf. 16:25; apart from 16:2, each instance of "an hour is coming" is quickly followed by the longer expression including "and has come"); the immediate context does not require this interpretation but may be interpreted consistently with it: Jesus' death and glorification inaugurates the eschatological hour (see 16:25), the wilderness period of the new exodus in which the people of God must carry on Jesus' war against the devil (cf. Rev 12:1–6). The disciples would suffer in Jesus' "hour" (16:25, 32); but as his followers, they would also have their own hour that would flow from it (12:25–26; 13:16; 15:20). Within John's narrative, the story of Lazarus provides a telling illustration of the kind of death Jesus' followers must be willing to expect (12:10). (That Lazarus's death is not narrated probably suggests that the narrator did not believe that the authorities actually succeeded in carrying out their intentions, at least not within a time frame that could be reasonably reported within his Gospel.)

Rome did not grant the *ius gladii,* the right of the sword, freely to all its subjects; if worshipers of God in the synagogues (16:2) directly killed disciples, it would not be legally sanctioned by Rome. Yet Hare, who doubts that much lynching actually was taking place, suggests that 16:2 may reflect anxiety concerning "Jewish declarations that Christians *ought* to be lynched."[345] He notes that Philo advocates the execution of Jewish idolaters without trial, that one Tanna supported executing idolaters, and that 3 Maccabees praises the slaughter of apostate Jews;[346] but given the successful career of the Alexandrian apostate Tiberius Alexander, he doubts that lynching was common.[347] Even in Revelation, we read of only one explicit martyr to date (Rev 2:13), although the writer clearly anticipates others to follow quickly.

Yet John and Revelation hardly would have stressed these warnings unless severe tensions with the synagogue or other reasons led them to believe that such conflicts were on the rise. Conditions may have changed somewhat in the second century; Justin claims that "Jews" kill Christians whenever they are able, specifically noting that Bar Kokhba had ordered the execution of Christians and only Christians (*1 Apol.* 31.6).[348] But atrocity reports were often exaggerated in the course of circulation;[349] hyperbole was a regular feature of polemic and invective (generally from both sides).[350] Some non-Christian Jews actually protected Christians during Roman persecutions;[351] and in any case, lynchings would have been far less prevalent among Jews under Roman rule than during the Bar Kokhba revolt, when Roman scruples about executions without Roman supervision would have been dismissed.

---

[345] Hare, *Persecution,* 41.

[346] Philo *Spec. Laws* 1.54–55 (the interpretation is debatable); *t. Sanh.* 11:11 (although R. Eleazar ben Zadok's view was a minority position; see *m. Sanh.* 8:7); 3 Macc 7.

[347] Hare, *Persecution,* 41.

[348] Amoraic traditions speak of executing Jesus' disciples (e.g., *b. Sanh.* 43a, in Herford, *Christianity,* 90–95), but this may reflect rabbinic wish rather than fact. Martyn, *Theology,* 80–81, suggests that Ben Stada, said to be executed in rabbinic literature, was a Jewish-Christian rabbi rather than Jesus; but his evidence does not seem compelling.

[349] Cf. Bailey, *Peasant Eyes,* 75. On Justin, see also Flannery, *Anguish,* 28.

[350] See Marshall, *Enmity,* 56–61.

[351] See Flannery, *Anguish,* 28.

More likely is the proposal that the Jewish Christians felt that their Jewish opponents, by expelling them from synagogues (see introduction), were deliberately delivering them over to the sword of the Roman governor.[352] Surely in time Christians, once portrayed as apostates no longer welcome in the synagogue community, would face death for their unwillingness to worship Caesar (Rev 13:15). Indeed, early-second-century sources testify that some Christians had been executed for such an offense (Pliny *Ep.* 10.96). Roman prosecution also depended on *delatores*, private accusers,[353] as Pliny's correspondence with Trajan likewise indicates;[354] at a later stage of mutual antagonism, the second-century *Martyrdom of Polycarp* reproaches the Jewish community in Smyrna not for merely expelling the Jewish Christians (cf. Rev 2:9) but for actively supplying the accusers of the Christians (*Mart. Pol.* 17.2).[355]

## 4C. Johannine Irony

Nevertheless, the context supplies the warning with abundant Johannine irony. Believers would be on trial before the world, personified in local synagogue courts (16:2; cf. Mark 13:9),[356] just as Jesus would be on trial before the world (the Pharisees and the Roman governor) in succeeding chapters (18–19). But in the end, the believers joined the Advocate as witnesses (15:26–27), and became vehicles for the Advocate as he prosecuted the world (16:7–11).[357] The world, not believers, was on trial before the highest court![358] Some other thinkers in the ancient world also opined that the justice of judges' sentences reflected on themselves no less than on the accused.[359]

The behavior of the believers' enemies itself condemns them. The believers' opponents believe that the death of Christians offers priestly sacrifice to God (16:2), no doubt pleasing to God the way Phinehas's execution of an Israelite idolater had been.[360] In fact, however, they think in this manner precisely because they have never genuinely known God or his agent (16:3). Jewish Christians were not the only minority group in Judaism to respond with hostility to what they regarded as the broader hostility of Israel. Qumran interpreters concluded that Belial caught Israel in nets by presenting them as

---

[352] See, e.g., the discussion in Setzer, *Responses,* 172, including Justin's claim that other peoples carried out the synagogue curses (*Dial.* 96.2).

[353] See O'Neal, "Delation"; corrupt leaders cultivated abuse of informers (e.g., Herodian 7.3.2; 7.6.4).

[354] Pliny *Ep.* 10.96–97; cf. Hemer, *Letters,* 67. Johnson, "*Delatorum,*" suspects political reasons for the accusations, rooted in intraurban factionalism and city rivalries.

[355] Setzer, *Responses,* 114, doubts the specific claims of *Mart. Pol.* 17.2; 18.1. But such claims at the least reflect some early Christians' expectations concerning some leaders in the synagogue community.

[356] On such courts, see sources in Keener, *Matthew,* 322–23, on Matt 10:17.

[357] Derrett, "Cursing," compares 1 Cor 12:3 with the Spirit's help in confessing Christ during excommunication; but this may be an anachronistic reading of 1 Cor 12.

[358] On the heavenly court, see, e.g., Keener, "Court"; it became dominant in Amoraic texts (*ʾAbot R. Nat.* 32A; *b.* ʿ*Abod. Zar.* 36a; *B. Meṣiʿa* 75a; 85b; 86a; *Giṭ.* 68a; *Mak.* 13b; *Pesaḥ.* 53b; *Šabb.* 129b; *p. Sanh.* 1:1, §4; 11:5, §1; *Gen. Rab.* 49:2; 64:4; *Exod. Rab.* 12:4; 30:18; *Lev. Rab.* 11:8; 24:2; 29:1, 4; *Num. Rab.* 3:4; 18:4; 19:3; *Ruth Rab.* 4:3, 5; *Eccl. Rab.* 1:11, §1; 2:12, §1; 5:11, §5; *Song Rab.* 3:11, §2; *Pesiq. Rab Kah.* 23:4; 24:11; *Pesiq. Rab.* 15:19).

[359] Publilius Syrus 698 (*tam de se iudex iudicat quam de reo*).

[360] Ps 106:30–31; cf. 1 Macc 2:24–26, 54; Philo *Confusion* 57; *Moses* 1.304; *m. Sanh.* 9:6 (by allusion); *b. Sanh.* 82b; *Num. Rab.* 21:3; see comment on John 2:17. Cf. here similarly Culpepper, *John,* 217; Talbert, *John,* 218; Whitacre, *John,* 386.

forms of righteousness (CD 4.15–17; cf. comment on John 16:10 below).[361] A further note of irony appears in the persecutors' conviction that their acts offer worship to God. In fact, those whom they martyr do "glorify" God by their deaths (21:19),[362] as Jesus had (12:23–24; 13:31–33).

Because Jesus' hearers in this passage had been with him from the "beginning," they were qualified to witness (15:27), but now he was providing warnings they had not needed at the "beginning" (16:4). His presence had been enough for them (16:4), but now that he was leaving (16:5),[363] they would need to be warned of what was coming (16:2–3). Other hardships awaited them, but Jesus could not explain them at this point (16:12); they were already weighed down with sorrow (16:6).[364] When, however, Jesus' successor, the Spirit of truth, would come, he would reveal the rest of Jesus' secrets (16:13–15), including the things to come (16:13). Undoubtedly this included a revelation of future sufferings, beyond Jesus' own summary in this context (15:18–16:3), such as one finds in the book of Revelation.

---

[361] Because shame was corporate (e.g., Derrett, *Audience*, 40), the misbehavior of some members of the group reflected on the entire group.

[362] Fenton, *John*, 164.

[363] His language for returning to God, who sent him, would be familiar (Raphael in Tob 12:20, though using ἀναβαίνω and ἀποστείλαντα). None of them asked where he was going because his previous answers had been so emphatic—even if they continued to appear obscure (14:4–9; cf. 16:28–29).

[364] This could be a case of paralipsis, in which one goes on to precisely what one claims to avoid saying (*Rhet. ad Herenn.* 4.27.37), but Jesus' words become no harsher than the earlier 16:2.

# REVELATION OF JESUS

## 16:5–33

A LTHOUGH A GRADUAL SHIFT takes place from the emphasis on persecution in 16:1–4, there is no decisive break here with the preceding context. When Jesus was with the disciples, they did not need warning about future sufferings (16:5), presumably because he would protect them (18:8–9). But now that he was going and their hearts were burdened with sorrow (16:6), he had to assure them that the Paraclete would continue to reveal him to them and through them (16:7–15). He had warned them of coming sufferings (15:18–16:4), but they could not bear further revelation of such matters now (16:12); when the Paraclete would come, however, he would prepare them for the rest, telling them more things to come (16:13), presumably including events such as those narrated in the book of Revelation (if, as we have argued, John and Revelation reflect the same community).

The coming of the Paraclete would enable the disciples to go on the offensive (15:26–27) because through him Jesus would remain among them (16:13–15). In him they would have victory over the world, despite their tribulation (16:33).

### His Departure for Their Good (16:5–7)

In the context of the disciples' discouragement due to the world's hostility (16:1–6), the Paraclete would come to prosecute the world (16:8–11). The disciples could be strong in the face of persecution, despite Jesus' absence, because the Paraclete would be with them (v. 7); this suggests that the Paraclete's prosecution of the world is on their behalf and through their testimony.[1] They grieved that Jesus was "going" (16:5–6), but resurrection joy would soon swallow their grief concerning the cross (16:22; cf. 1 Pet 1:6).[2] Jesus' return would provide them the Spirit, who would continue Jesus' presence with them.

Because of their grief (16:6), Jesus assures them emphatically ("I tell you the truth")[3] that they will be better off with him departing to send them the other advocate he has mentioned (14:16).[4] The Paraclete is better for them than Jesus in the flesh would have

---

[1] Tribble, "Work," 278; Hunt, "Paraclete," 94; Sanders, *John*, 350; Holwerda, *Spirit*, 52; cf. Schlier, "Geist," 106–7; Boring, *Sayings*, 62. Carson, "Paraclete," 564, thinks the conviction is partly through the disciples.

[2] The lack of questions about his departure does not contradict 13:36 and 14:5; it is present tense, and in the story world the disciples have not been asking questions since 14:22 (Barrett, *John*, 485; Blomberg, *Reliability*, 213).

[3] Perhaps roughly equivalent to a Johannine statement prefaced with ἀμὴν, ἀμὴν, λέγω, "I tell you the truth" was a strenuous statement (Luke 4:25; Rom 9:1; 1 Tim 2:7); but it also could be said of Jesus' other teaching (8:45–46).

[4] On the technical use of συμφέρει in moral texts, see comment on 11:50; but the moralistic usage exercises little influence on this passage.

been (16:7) because he re-presents Jesus dynamically to the world in each hostile situation. Jesus had also challenged the world concerning sin, righteousness, and judgment, and the prophetic Spirit, proclaiming the same Jesus through his community, would continue the challenge.[5] This continuity between the two should not be understood as identity, as in the docetic reading of John,[6] nor even to imply that the Spirit cannot bring new teachings;[7] the Spirit will say some new things (16:12–13) but in continuity with Jesus' revelation.[8] But it does mean that Jesus himself is present in the Spirit, though only those in his community recognize his presence.[9]

## The World's Prosecutor (16:8–11)

In view of 16:7 ("send him to *you*"), it appears clear that the Spirit's work in 16:8–11 is through the disciples.[10] Jesus sends the Spirit to the disciples (16:7), but through the disciples the Spirit-Paraclete continues Jesus' ministry to the world (16:8–11). Thus, as Jesus prosecuted the world (3:20; cf. 8:46), the Paraclete continues to prosecute the world (16:8–11) through the apostolic preaching of Jesus (cf. 16:7). The image of a speaker in court might follow naturally the context of Jesus' friends (15:13–15) and enemies (15:18–25): at least in Hellenistic Greek practice, one who spoke for another in a court might claim that he acted on behalf of friendship (φιλίαν) with one party or enmity (ἔχθραν) with the other.[11] The introductory statement of 16:8 is explicated by a specification of the charges in 16:9–11; the outlining of headings that would then be expanded was a common rhetorical technique.[12]

### 1. *Prosecuting the World*

The verb ἐλέγξει can simply mean to reprove[13] or to prove,[14] whether by one's conscience,[15] by the behavior of the righteous,[16] by the Lord,[17] or from other sources.[18] Thus it

---

[5] For parallels between Jesus and the Spirit, see, e.g., Brown, "Paraclete," 126; Bornkamm, "Paraklet," 12; Schlier, "Geist," 107–8. On the Spirit's relation to the kerygma, see, e.g., Boice, *Witness*, 120–22, 143–45.

[6] Argued by Colwell and Titus, *Spirit*, 121, 138.

[7] Cf. Bammel, "Paraclet," 214–16; Zerwick, "Wirken," 230; Hegstad, "Hellige"; Bultmann, *John*, 575 (though Bultmann is correct that the Spirit does restate Jesus' word). Haenchen, *John*, 2:144, argues that the Spirit will go beyond the earthly Jesus as John goes beyond his sources' traditions.

[8] Burge, *Community*, 215.

[9] Schlier, "Begriff," 271. Cf. McNaugher, "Spirit" (Christ is the substance of the Spirit's revelation).

[10] Cf. Efferin, "Paraclete"; earlier, Luther, *Sermon on John 16*.

[11] *Rhet. Alex.* 36, 1442b.12–14.

[12] For an example, see Porphyry *Marc.* 24.376–384; see esp. Anderson, *Glossary*, 32–33; Rowe, "Style," 134.

[13] Dio Chrysostom *Or.* 8, *On Virtue*, §5; Sir 35:17 (ἐλεγμόν).

[14] Marcus Aurelius 1.17.1; 6.21; to "refute" in Musonius Rufus 8, p. 62.39–40; in rhetoric, "refutation" (see Anderson, *Glossary*, 40).

[15] Philo *Worse* 146; cf. *Unchangeable* 125.

[16] Dio Chrysostom *Or.* 8, *On Virtue*, §5; Wis 2:14.

[17] *Pss. Sol.* 10:1; Sir 21:6; Wis 1:3, 5. It stands for judgment in Sir 16:12 (see 16:6–14); for instructive reproof (with παιδεύων and διδάσκων) in 18:13. In Wis 1:8 Justice, or Vengeance, will "reprove" (convict?) the wicked.

[18] A friend in Sir 19:13–15, fitting the Hellenistic motif of a friend's παρρησία.

is natural that some scholars should think a juridical significance too limiting here.[19] But given the forensic context—a Paraclete's witness and defense in the context of synagogue trials (16:2)—the frequent forensic significance of the term[20] is probably to be preferred here.[21] Anyone could bring a charge, but under law a Roman governor could not try a case and convict someone without an accuser offering a charge.[22] Barrett suggests that the Paraclete's act of ἐλέγξει "is the activity of a judge and a prosecuting counsel in one."[23] Although roles such as prosecutor and advocate were not to be confused,[24] witnesses "against" functioned as prosecutors (albeit sometimes very skilled rhetoricians),[25] and God was free to assume all the roles of advocate, prosecutor, and judge.[26] If the Synoptic promises of the Spirit's help when one is on trial[27] stand behind or are related to this passage, "John has characteristically (cf. chs. 9, 18f.) pressed home this idea so that the Spirit, not content with defending the believers, takes the offensive against the world."[28]

Thus part of the Paraclete's defense of the disciples is to turn the tables, bringing charges against their accusers,[29] just as Jesus usually managed to turn the tables on his accusers in the Fourth Gospel (e.g., 5:16, 45–47; 8:46; 9:39–41).[30] (It was standard judicial rhetorical practice to invert opponents' claims about right and wrong, wisdom and folly.)[31] In ancient courts, a persuasive accuser could generally demolish defendants of lower status; a persuasive patronal advocate with ties to the judge would also be difficult to defeat. In fact, in many ancient judicial proceedings, social inferiors could not even bring suit against social superiors;[32] before God's court, the Christians' accusers would have no

---

[19] Lutkemeyer, "Paraclete," 222, maintains this on the basis of an opposition between a social religious Hebraic sense (after citing Isa 11:4!) and a forensic judicial Greco-Roman sense. Cf. Forestell, "Paraclete," 168–69 (presenting evidence for both positions); Swete, *Discourse,* 116–17 (convinces understanding and convicts conscience); Hatch, "Meaning," 104 (confute or convict).

[20] Smith, "John 16," 60; Carson, *Discourse,* 138; Trites, *Witness,* 118–19; Johnston, *Spirit-Paraclete,* 144; Sanders, *John,* 350; Witherington, *Wisdom,* 264; cf. Porsch, *Pneuma,* 275–89; Potterie, "Paraclet," 101–5, though Baum, *Jews,* 129–30, overstates the consensus when he says that "all commentators are agreed that there is a question here of a trial before God, where the world is the accused party and the Spirit the prosecutor." This is more than just convincing the world that it is wrong (cf. Stevens, *Theology,* 211; Carson, "Paraclete," 558).

[21] Cf. Wis 4:20, where the very sins of the wicked will convict (ἐλέγξει) them on the Day of Judgment.

[22] E.g., Cicero *Verr.* 2.2.38.94.

[23] Barrett, *John,* 90. Many see the Paraclete here as prosecutor, e.g., O'Day, "John," 771.

[24] E.g., *b. Ḥag.* 13b; *Exod. Rab.* 15:29; *Lev. Rab.* 5:6; 21:10. Technically, judges were not to be witnesses (Aeschines *Timarchus* 89).

[25] Pancaro, *Law,* 254; Stambaugh and Balch, *Environment,* 34; cf. Chariton 5.4.9; *CPJ* 2.64–66, §155; Josephus *War* 1.637–638; David, "Eloquentia."

[26] E.g., Josephus *Ant.* 4.46; *Exod. Rab.* 15:29. For God as witness and advocate for the righteous, see, e.g., *4 Ezra* 7:94.

[27] Kennedy, *Classical Rhetoric,* 127, compares this promise in Mark 13:9–13 with Moses being equipped in the Hebrew Bible.

[28] Barrett, *John,* 487.

[29] Cf., e.g., Reese, "Paraclete." Witness, judge, and prosecutor were not then the mutually exclusive functions they are today; see Harvey, *History,* 31.

[30] Cf. Dodd, *Interpretation,* 414; Holwerda, *Spirit,* 49–50, for the Paraclete's work here as a continuance of Jesus' forensic conflicts with the religious authorities.

[31] E.g., *Rhet. ad Herenn.* 3.3.6. See fuller examples in the comment on 8:37–51.

[32] On rank, status, and lawcourts, see, e.g., Gaius *Inst.* 4.183; Petronius *Sat.* 14; P.Hal. 1.124–127; Meeks, *Moral World,* 32; Stambaugh and Balch, *Environment,* 113; also divisions of penalty by rank in ancient Near Eastern legal collections.

case.) As Jesus proclaims God and refutes his adversaries' charges in the Fourth Gospel, so the Paraclete equips the Johannine community for witness and apologetic in the setting of conflict.[33] Likewise, as Jesus is the intercessor before God's throne, the Spirit is "another advocate" aiding the disciples before an earthly tribunal.[34] Whereas the "world" personified in the community's opponents trusts in Moses, Moses will accuse them (5:45; cf. ἐλέγχω in Jas 2:9); the Spirit who inspired the law of Moses and continues the work of Jesus will continue the prosecuting work of each.

## 2. Background in the Biblical Prophets

The Paraclete here is thus both intercessor and prosecutor of those who bring a charge against God's servants. The idea of God pleading the case of the afflicted against their adversaries appears in an eschatological context[35] in Jer 50:34; 51:36 (RSV):

> Their Redeemer is strong; the LORD of hosts is his name. He will surely plead their cause, that he may give rest to the earth, but unrest to the inhabitants of Babylon.

> Therefore thus says the LORD:
> "Behold, I will plead your cause and take vengeance for you . . .
> and Babylon shall become a heap of ruins . . . "

The work of prosecution, or accusation, was regarded as primarily the work of Satan if directed against God's people.[36] Satan,[37] or Mastema,[38] regularly appears as Israel's accuser in early Jewish texts; by the Amoraic period, he accuses Israel continually except on Yom Kippur[39] (cf. Rev 12:10; see further the note on John 14:16). But God himself was perfectly able to prosecute his people or the nations for breach of covenant faithfulness (e.g., Ps. 50:8–21); later teachers could envision the law accusing God's people when they disobeyed it.[40] More to the point in the context of this Gospel, it was really the accusers who were on trial in the accusations and trial of Jesus (3:19–20). As Schnackenburg observes:

> Having been counsel for the disciples' defence in human lawsuits, the Paraclete now becomes the plaintiff in God's judgment against the world. This is a function that was not originally

---

[33] Cf. Johnston, *Spirit-Paraclete,* 123, on the Spirit's proclamation function in a late-first-century context.

[34] E.g., Dion, "Paraclet," 148; see at much greater length the comment on 14:16.

[35] Johnston, *Spirit-Paraclete,* 125, thinks that "the End is very much in the background" and that John 16:8–11 is not a foretaste of the Last Judgment. In my thinking, associations between God's judgments in history and the final judgment are naturally connected, though the connection would not be universally grasped; that John intends to unite the two is, I think, clear in his Gospel (3:17; 5:21–28).

[36] On the transfer of Satan's usual role, see Windisch, *Spirit-Paraclete,* 11, while also noting that this characterizes the "prophetic and apostolic preaching of judgment."

[37] A biblical title also frequent in Amoraic texts, e.g., *Gen. Rab.* 38:7; 84:2; *Exod. Rab.* 18:5; *Lev. Rab.* 21:10; *Eccl. Rab.* 3:2, §2; *3 En.* 26:12. In *b. Sukkah* 52b, the evil yetzer tempts in this world, and in the world to come testifies against those he has seduced.

[38] *Jub.* 48:15–16. For other accusing angels, see *3 En.* 28:8–9; *t. ʿAbod. Zar.* 1:18; *Šabb.* 17:3; *Gen. Rab.* 55:4; angels of nations in *3 En.* 26:12; *Lev. Rab.* 21:4; *Song Rab.* 2:1, §3; 8:8, §1; cf. accusations from good angels in *p. Sanh.* 10:2, §7; *Pesiq. Rab Kah.* 24:11.

[39] *B. Yoma* 20a; *Lev. Rab.* 21:4; *Num. Rab.* 18:21; *Pesiq. Rab.* 45:2 (on the Day of Atonement); 47:4.

[40] E.g., *Lam. Rab.* proem 24 (the twenty-two letters of the alphabet, used in the law). Cf. also God's angel "Conviction" (ἔλεγχος), the priest (Philo *Unchangeable* 135, 182–183).

present in the concept of a Paraclete—in Judaism, the *parqlit* (= *s'negor*) is simply the counterpart to the plaintiff or accuser *(kategor)*. In the Johannine thinking about the "crisis," however, this interchange between the two functions is already established and given a firm foundation in that the accused is really accuser in Jesus' trial.[41]

Such an image would have been grasped easily enough by Greco-Roman readers, whether or not they would have all taken natural comfort in the idea; for example, Cicero presented evidence for Verres' guilt so thoroughly that he declared it was really the jury that was on trial before the rest of the world.[42] Later writers also charged that (before the bar of history) it was not Socrates but his supposed judges, the people of Athens, who were on trial.[43] One may likewise compare Epictetus's friend Heracleitus, who

> had an unimportant lawsuit about a small piece of land in Rhodes; after he had pointed out the justice of his claim he went on to the peroration in which he said, "But neither will I entreat you, nor do I care what your decision is going to be, and it is you who are on trial rather than I. And so he ruined his case.

He should rather have either made no entreaties at all, Epictetus concludes, or not provoked his judges before the appropriate time (unlike Socrates, who waited for the proper time).[44] Yet Epictetus accepted this kind of thinking if the issue and timing warranted it: "You imply, then, that Socrates did not fare badly?—He did not; it was his judges [οἱ δικασταί] and accusers [οἱ κατήγοροι] who fared badly."[45]

This prosecution is part of the forensic activity of the biblical prophets, who were Israel's accusers perhaps more often than her intercessors.[46] To miss this function of the prophets is to read them (from the standpoint of Greco-Roman categories) as only deliberative rather than also judicial rhetoric,[47] but this is far too narrow. The *rîb*, or covenant lawsuit, is a standard Israelite prophetic form,[48] undoubtedly rooted in the picture of Yahweh's divine (angelic) assembly as a court.[49]

It was still imitated in the early Christian period,[50] probably including the most explicit examples we have of the Johannine community's prophetism, the letters of Rev

---

[41] Schnackenburg, *John,* 3:143. Cf. also Johnston, *Spirit-Paraclete,* 144. For this lawsuit as merely the culmination of the Johannine trial motif, see Dahl, "History," 139. Such reversal provided irony (cf. Aeschines *Timarchus* 117–118; Xenophon *Mem.* 4.8.9–10; Seneca *Controv.* 6.5; also Keener, *Background Commentary,* 342–43, on Acts 7:54–56, 58, 60).

[42] Cicero *Verr.* 2.5.69.177.

[43] Maximus of Tyre *Or.* 3.2, 8 (echoing Plato *Apol.* 39cd; he also emphasizes that they were not qualified to evaluate him, 3.1, 5, 7; cf. 1 Cor 2:15); cf. similarly Xenophon *Apol.* 29.

[44] Epictetus *Diatr.* 2.2.17–18.

[45] Epictetus *Diatr.* 4.1.123.

[46] Also Isaacs, "Spirit," 395–96.

[47] As Kennedy, *Classical Rhetoric,* 124, does. Aune, *Prophecy,* 97, recognizes the Israelite judicial speech.

[48] See, e.g., Blenkinsopp, "Reproach"; Boyle, "Lawsuit"; Gemser, "Controversy-Pattern"; Weinfeld, "Patterns," 187–88 (comparing ancient Near Eastern legal practice and treaty language); Ramsey, "Speech-Forms" (probable on secular use, although I do not believe he has established the cultic use).

[49] Cross, *Myth,* 188–89; cf. Rabe, "Prophecy," 127. Derrett, "Advocacy," finds a background in Daniel's defense of Susanna and in Isa 11:4–5; a Jewish audience might have recalled such passages as part of the larger forensic background (cf. Isa 11:1–2).

[50] CD 1.1–2 (ריב). In Pauline thought, see Barth, *Justification,* 15–21, 26, who sees the OT covenant lawsuit language as part of the background for Pauline justification.

2–3,[51] in which the term ἐλέγχω appears in Rev 3:19; the term also describes other early Christian prophecies (1 Cor 14:24; cf. Luke 3:19).

### 3. The Charges

If ἐλέγχω means here "to prosecute," then the three parallel περί clauses represent the charges leveled against the opponents of the community. As Holwerda notes, "In a judicial process it would seem proper that when conviction occurs the grounds for conviction would also be presented."[52]

The ὅτι clauses probably explain the shorter, single-word charges; Carson's objection to the ὅτι explicative is predicated on his improbable view that v. 10 refers to the *world's* (pseudo-)righteousness.[53] The conclusion of my exegetical analysis is virtually the same as that of W. H. P. Hatch:

> First, that it has sinned because it has not believed in Christ; second, that believers are justified or acquitted because Christ has gone to the Father to act as their advocate (παράκλητος); and third, that evil has been condemned because the ruler of this world (the devil) has been condemned. The whole context is forensic.[54]

The Paraclete would convict the world of sin, righteousness, and judgment:[55] the sin is[56] the world's unbelief in the Son, the one provision for salvation (v. 8; cf. 1:29, 8:24);[57] the righteousness is that of God and his people, established by the vindicated, exalted Jesus as heavenly advocate against all the accusations of the world (v. 9; cf. 8:46);[58] the judgment (condemnation) is that the ruler of the world, the accuser of God's true people, has been judged in Jesus' glorification and shown to be wrong (v. 11; cf. comment on 12:31–32, 14:30–31).

---

[51] Shea, "Form," correctly observes parallels to Israelite and ancient Near Eastern covenant formulas (cf. Aune, *Environment,* 159, 242, for the thesis, probably also correct, of parallels with "ancient royal and imperial edicts"); but although most of these letters include praise as well as blame (Stowers, *Letter Writing,* 80–81, noting that this was standard; cf. p. 173), the judgment oracles in this covenant context may well be reminiscent of the *rîb* controversy speech of earlier prophets. The listings of cities and nations in oracles of judgment had been standard since biblical times and continues in many of the (Diaspora Jewish) *Sibylline Oracles.*

[52] Holwerda, *Spirit,* 56.

[53] Carson, "Paraclete," 549, 561. This view has not gained much support (cf. Burge, *Community,* 209–10), and the more traditional view that the righteousness is that of Christ (e.g., Tribble, "Work," 275) or his people is to be preferred.

[54] Hatch, "Meaning," 105.

[55] Bammel, "Paraklet," 203, contends that this triad is comparable to similar triads summing up the law's meaning in Judaism or that of secret knowledge in gnosticism but offers no compelling evidence for the case. Stanton, "Convince," thinks that the last two clauses are less clear because John has compressed more expanded material, but the partial parallelism suggests that if the parallelism existed in John's source at all, it was not more expansive than John has it here.

[56] Reading ὅτι as "in that," rather than "because," against Burge, *Community,* 209; Holwerda, *Spirit,* 56.

[57] Similarly, Haenchen, *John,* 2:143.

[58] Against Carson, "Paraclete," 559–60; Carson, *Discourse,* 141; Hunt, "Paraclete," 109 (although the idea of counterfeit righteousness is not unknown; cf. CD 4.15–17 and the Amoraim in *Gen. Rab.* 49:9). Carson's main argument insists on parallel form, but as Berg, "Pneumatology," points out, "the subjects of the subsidiary clauses are quite un-parallel" (p. 206). The revelation of the rightness of the divine agent exposes the sin of the accusers, 9:41; 15:24.

The Paraclete continues Jesus' ministry of exposing the world's sin (3:20; 7:7; 15:22). Christ's own δικαιοσύνη—justification, or vindication—is established by the Father's witness in enthroning him;[59] the disciples' δικαιοσύνη is established because they are bound together with him in the Spirit and his exaltation is their vindication as well (cf. 1 John 2:1).[60] But just as the believers are justified with Christ, so also is the world condemned[61] in its ruler (16:11).[62]

It is not difficult to see how the Paraclete, acting as their defender, would encourage the Johannine community in their conflict with the synagogue.[63] As in the Synoptic tradition (Mark 13:9–11), even when the disciples would be brought before synagogue tribunals and other literal courts, their testimony was only a necessary prelude to the world's judgment, and their own vindication was soon at hand. Like the prophets of old, the disciples were to concern themselves more with laying God's charges against the disobedient than with any persecution they might face for doing so; and against the backdrop of early Jewish pneumatology, these Spirit-moved disciples would most readily be understood as prophets.

## Revealing Jesus to the Disciples (16:13–15)

Since the world could not be confronted with its sin apart from the Paraclete's work in the disciples (16:7), it is quite natural for John to turn next to the illumination of the disciples.[64] The Spirit's primary task here is christological, revealing the message of Jesus.[65]

### 1. Function in Context

As in v. 6, the weakness of the disciples in the face of what is to come calls for Jesus' reassuring response: they could not bear[66] any more of his predictions of future hardship (cf. 14:28–29) now, but the Paraclete would continue to show them what they needed to know in the face of the world's hostility (16:12–13). This is not to say that the revelation was wholly new; Bultmann is at least partly right in saying that it would simply be newly

---

[59] Cf. Dahl, "History," 139: "The vindication of Jesus by his ascension." Stenger, "*Dikaiosyne*," thinks δικαιοσύνη here refers to Jesus' righteousness even before the incarnation (cf. 1 John 2:1, 29, 3:7). But while the clause no doubt assumes the eternal rightness of God's side, it is Jesus' glorification that establishes this fact. Conversely, Porsch, *Pneuma*, 286; Potterie, "Paraclet," 104, and others (cf. Tribble, "Work," 275) are probably too narrow to limit this even to Jesus' righteousness; his exaltation establishes the rightness of his disciples before God's court as well (1 John 2:1).

[60] Hatch, "Meaning," 105, also defines it as the believers' justification, due to the Johannine Advocate with the Father.

[61] In this forensic context, κρίσις must bear the sense of condemnation (see Hatch, "Meaning," 105, and John's typical usage).

[62] For more detailed comment on the "ruler of this world," see comment on 12:31; 14:30.

[63] See Berrouard, "Paraclet," 361; it applies to the opponents of the community as well as to Jesus' first opponents (pp. 365–66).

[64] Cadman, *Heaven*, 193.

[65] Potterie, "Parole," 201.

[66] John might allude to "bearing" the cross (19:17), but he omits the most explicit saying to that effect (Mark 8:34; though cf. John 12:25 // Mark 8:35), and the figurative use of βαστάζω is common (e.g., *T. Ab.* 17A; 11:5; 13:7B); see Bauer, Gingrich, and Danker, *Lexicon*, 137; Bultmann, *John*, 573 n. 1.

understood.[67] But the same Jesus could clearly continue to speak new strategies to new situations, whether or not they had been directly addressed in any manual of his teachings.

Those who have thus regarded 16:13–15 as a promise addressed only to the apostles[68] are thus wide of the mark.[69] The analogy with 1 John 2:20, 27, addressed to the community during a crisis of epistemological authority, supports a direct application to the community, which probably identified more with the beloved disciple than with the apostles led by Peter anyway.[70]

## 2. Guiding Believers in Truth (16:13)

The Paraclete here ὁδηγήσει, leads or guides, the community with regard to the truth. Ὁδηγέω is often used literally for leading, for example, the blind,[71] but it has a variety of metaphorical extensions. Greco-Roman philosophers and moralists could speak of God[72] or reason[73] as a guide (ὁδηγός or ἡγεμών); scholars have pointed to a Philonic passage in which the Spirit guided Moses' mind to truth.[74] In Wisdom of Solomon, Wisdom could lead (ὁδηγήσει) the righteous;[75] God as the "way of wisdom" leads the wise to wisdom.[76] (Qumran scrolls also could speak of knowing God's "ways" because of the gift of his Spirit.)[77] In Diaspora Jewish texts, the term could be used negatively, as when wine "leads [ὁδηγεῖ] the eyes into the path of error [lust]" in *T. Jud.* 14:1,[78] or positively, as when "the angel of peace guides" the life of the righteous in *T. Benj.* 6:1.[79] In CD 1.11, God "raised up for them a teacher of righteousness [or a righteous teacher] to lead [way-make] them in the way of his heart [להדריכם בדרך לבו]"; and in *Pss. Sol.* 17:40–41, Messiah will

---

67 Bultmann, *John*, 573 n. 2; cf. Zerwick, "Wirken," 230.

68 Some conservative scholars have even seen it as a specific promise of the NT writings (e.g., Godet, *Gospel*, 182; cf. Bruce, *Parchments*, 105). Other conservative scholars, while agreeing that inspired records of the apostolic witness to Christ are included in the promise, see a broader intention in this text (e.g., Ladd, *Theology*, 220, 268, 296; Boice, *Witness*, 143–44; Horton, *Spirit*, 120–21).

69 Cf. the argument against apostolic succession in the Fourth Gospel in Grant, "Church," 116. Cf. Smith, "John 16," 60 (the plural "you" is read as the community).

70 This is not to concur with the scholars who view the beloved disciple as if he were in opposition to Peter (cf. Brown, *Community*, 31–32, 34, 82–84, 90, 162, 189–91); the beloved disciple may be superior to Peter, but Peter is not presented in a worse light than in the Synoptics, and all the Twelve except Judas appear in a generally positive light (even if they typically misunderstand Jesus); indeed, no one would have questioned that this text's address at least included them. This is true regardless of the authenticity of the original saying (disputed by Kremer, "Verheissung," 272; but everything in the Fourth Gospel is in Johannine idiom, even where we recognize the tradition [e.g., John 12:25]).

71 Bauer, Gingrich, and Danker, *Lexicon*, 553; Rom 2:19.

72 Epictetus *Diatr.* 2.7.11; 3.21.12, respectively; Xenophon *Cyr.* 7.1.10; cf. the δαίμων in Marcus Aurelius 5.26–27; gods in Iamblichus *V.P.* 1.2.

73 Plutarch *Lect.* 1, *Mor.* 37E (reason is the divine guide of life; this is the same as following God). Cf. education (παιδείαν) as parallel to getting a guide (ὑφηγησόμενον) in Socrates *Ep.* 4 (*Cyn. Ep.* 228–29); Musonius Rufus's teaching in 1, p. 32.12 (ἐπάγων).

74 MacGregor, *John*, 298; Sanders, *John*, 353, on *Moses* 2.265.

75 Wis 9:11.

76 Wis 7:15. Cf. Crates *Ep.* 31 (to Hipparchia): "Reason [λόγος] is a guide [ἡγεμών] for the soul."

77 4Q504 frg. 4, line 5.

78 *OTP* 1:799; Greek, p. 88.

79 *OTP* 1:826; Greek, p. 222.

shepherd God's flock and lead (ἄξει) them in his way (in John's circle of early Christianity, cf. the similar ὀδηγήσει in Rev 7:17).[80] Here the guiding in(to) truth probably relates to Jesus being the truth in 14:6.[81]

It is possible that this is the language of a new exodus; in the first exodus, God or Moses ὀδεύσει the Israelites.[82] In the context of other new-exodus language, Paul describes the believers in Jesus as being led (ἄγονται) by God's Spirit (Rom. 8:14; cf. also Gal. 5:18), and this could imply a broader early Christian tradition in which the community of the new exodus was led by the Spirit in the present time.

But while new-exodus language may be in the background of this passage, it is probably not in the foreground.[83] More to the point are passages in which the psalmist prays for God to guide his ways "in truth,"[84] that is, in accordance with his covenant faithfulness. Dodd cites the most obvious text, Ps. 24(25):5, but argues,

> Here אמת is that fundamental trustworthiness or rectitude which is an attribute of God, and to which by his help his servants may attain. This however is clearly not the sense of ἀλήθεια in John xvi.13. The context speaks of things to be spoken, announced, and heard. . . . The content of these words is concisely summed up in the word ἀλήθεια, which is therefore not אמת, "faithfulness," but "truth."[85]

Dodd thus maintains his view that the Johannine conception of "truth" is essentially the Hellenistic meaning, "reality."[86] It is true that ἀλήθεια can mean intellectual truth,[87] for example, about the gods[88] or about the nature of reality,[89] but a Greek-speaking or any other Diaspora Jewish reader could understand moral truth,[90] as in the law.[91] And in John 14:6, "truth" presumably has more to do with the character of God in his faithfulness to his

---

[80] MSS vary between "in holiness" and "in equality."

[81] Brown, *John*, 2:707; Hunt, "Paraclete," 83; Swete, *Discourse*, 125.

[82] *Sib. Or.* 3.248, 251, probably second-century B.C.E. material. Wisdom διήγαγεν them through the waters in Wis 10:18; for many other LXX texts, see Forestell, "Paraclete," 171–72.

[83] Except to the extent that the "Way" of 14:6 might be compared, for LXX-steeped readers, with the highway of the new exodus of Deutero-Isaiah. In *Lev. Rab.* 11:9 God leads his people in the world to come, but this is isolated (based on a unique exegesis of a text) and late.

[84] E.g., Forestell, "Paraclete," 171–72; Sanders, *John*, 353.

[85] Dodd, *Interpretation*, 174.

[86] Ibid., 170–78; also Cadman, *Heaven*, 24. Contrast Barrett, *John*, 167; Boice, *Witness*, 62; Ladd, *Theology*, 264–65; van der Waal, "Gospel," 28–33; Schnackenburg, *John*, 2:225–37; Albright, "Discoveries," 169.

[87] Parmenides (ca. 500 B.C.E.) is said to have been the first to have contrasted truth and opinion (Diogenes Laertius 9.22). Perhaps Marcus Aurelius 1.14. For a discussion of the Stoic conception, see Mates, *Logic*, 33–36: truth is especially "'in' or 'about' propositions" (pp. 33–34). Irenaeus (*Haer.* 1.1.1) reports the gnostic pairing of "Truth" with "Mind"; cf. the discussion of Justin Martyr and the *Gospel of Truth* in Storey, *Truth*, 220.

[88] Plutarch *Isis* 2, *Mor.* 351E, although Plutarch no doubt affirms a suprarational element in its pursuit.

[89] Marcus Aurelius 9.1.2.

[90] *T. Jud.* 14:1; as a standard of justice, 1 Esd 4:38–39. Virtue calls for truth in Marcus Aurelius 3.11.2. In *Let. Aris.* 206, one practices the truth by not lying.

[91] *T. Ash.* 6:1; *2 Bar.* 44:14. *Exod. Rab.* 30:12 (purportedly Hadrianic but surely later) associates law and truth; also in *Num. Rab.* 12:3 (R. Simeon b. Lakish, third-century Palestine); cf. Dodd, "Background," 335 (citing a late midrash). Philo relates it to the Logos (*Alleg. Interp.* 3.45) (one should note, however, that he relates most positive things to the Logos). Barrett, "Spirit," 8, suggests "theological truth" in Jesus.

people, his covenant integrity,[92] and this is certainly the sense in 1:14.[93] Although it must be admitted that the first readers would have found other nuances of the Greek term even in its LXX occurrences, it did not lose its covenantal flavor: in Wis 15:1, God is χρηστός (kind) and ἀληθής (true), long-suffering and merciful; Exod 34:6, which is probably adapted in John 1:14 (as is widely noted, despite the departure from LXX language),[94] continued to be read as stressing God's mercy.[95] Roughly 90 percent of the uses of ἀλήθεια in the LXX have אמת or cognates behind them.[96]

If "truth" here retains some of its Semitic flavoring, it is also quite possible that the reading "in truth" should be preferred to the reading "into truth." The latter could have easily arisen through a scribe who did not grasp the LXX construction but, preferring the more idiomatic Greek, thought to do John a favor by polishing his rhetoric. Ἐν has wider geographical distribution, and the patristic support for εἰς may be due to dogmatic reasons. As Metzger observes, the εἰς and the accusative may "have been introduced by copyists who regarded it as more idiomatic after ὁδηγήσει than the construction of ἐν and the dative."[97] Ἐν matches some LXX constructions after which these words are modeled. The idea is thus more "the whole truth,"[98] the full revelation of God's character in Christ (14:6), than "all possible knowledge on any subject."[99]

## 3. The Paraclete Speaks for Jesus (16:13)

The Paraclete, like Jesus (e.g., 5:19, 30; see comment on 5:19), will not speak "from himself," or on his own (16:13);[100] rather, again like Jesus with regard to the Father (15:15), the Paraclete speaks whatever he hears (16:13). As surely as the community can trust that Jesus speaks for the Father, they can trust that the Spirit Jesus sent speaks for Jesus.[101] This would imply that disciples of later generations could experience the same relationship with Jesus his first disciples did, an intimacy modeled by Jesus in his relationship with the Father (1:2, 18; 10:14–15). This band of continuity may serve the same function as the tying of the true Spirit to the historical Jesus, the Jesus who came in flesh and was known

---

[92] As in 1QS 11.4; 1QM 13.9–10. The rabbis saw truth as characterizing the nature of God so much that it became one of his names; see Marmorstein, *Names*, 180.

[93] E.g., Kuyper, "Grace," 15–19. Harrison, "John 1:14," 33, argues that either the Hebraic or the Hellenistic concept is a priori possible, since John knew both. The contrast made between Hebraic and Hellenistic would not be regarded as nuanced today, but the point is that readers of the LXX would be accustomed to some nuances in the term that other Greek speakers would be less likely to catch.

[94] Kuyper, "Grace," 3–13; Dahl, "History," 132; Epp, "Wisdom," 138; Westcott, *John*, 13; Stuart, "Examination," 316; Dodd, *Studies*, 141–42; Dodd, *Bible*, 75; Dodd, *Interpretation*, 82; Boismard, *Prologue*, 54–56; Barrett, *John*, 167; Hoskyns, *Gospel*, 150; Lee, *Thought*, 40; Schnackenburg, *John*, 1:272; Gaston, *Stone*, 209; Ladd, *Theology*, 230.

[95] Cf. *b. Roš Haš.* 17b; Urbach, *Sages*, 1:450.

[96] Epp, "Wisdom," 138–39.

[97] Metzger, *Textual Commentary*, 247. Contrast Bammel, "Paraklet," 205–6, who regards ἐν as a clarification or explanation of εἰς.

[98] Cf. Bar 3:36, where God knows πᾶσαν ὁδὸν ἐπιστήμης (the law that dwelt among people, 3:37–4:1).

[99] Cf. Bultmann, *John*, 574–75, and notes by some of the older commentators, such as Westcott, *John*, 230; Tholuck, *John*, 377–78. Contrast Harrison, "Ministry," 194.

[100] That is, not "on his own authority" (*T. Ab.* 15:8; 19:4A; Philostratus *Hrk.* 8.2). This is also characteristic of the role of prophets (2 Pet 1:21; cf. *Num. Rab.* 18:12); disciples should also speak what they hear (Socrates *Ep.* 20). See comment on 8:28.

by the witness who stands behind the Fourth Gospel, in 1 John: John may be showing that the true Spirit is the one who represents Jesus in accordance with the Johannine tradition, as opposed to any spirit that conflicts with this tradition.[102] Some think this may respond "to a belief that the Spirit is the mediator of the experience of God independent of Jesus,"[103] but while this is certainly possible,[104] it is more easily argued that the schismatics simply felt free to create new constructs about Jesus and his teaching that the rest of the community felt departed from the Jesus tradition as they had received it.

Such a proposal makes good sense in light of 1 John, but the Gospel context suggests a different emphasis. Since Jesus as the agent of the Father is wholly to be trusted and to repudiate Jesus is to repudiate the one who sent him, to repudiate the Spirit's representation of Jesus is to repudiate Jesus himself. In other words, the Spirit is viewed as the agent of Jesus active in and through the community; if the synagogue or false prophets reject the message of Jesus through his community (a message preserved for us particularly in the Fourth Gospel), they are rejecting Jesus and thus God.

It also suggests a kind of charismatic intimacy that characterizes the true community, perhaps comparable to the Pauline "Abba" cry experience (Rom 8:15; Gal 4:6). Jesus' disciples while he was in the world heard from him whatever he had heard from the Father and so were his friends (15:15); since the Spirit enables the believers in John's day to hear whatever Jesus was still saying, the relationship should be as intimate as it had been when Jesus was in the world, and true disciples should learn to hear his voice just as accurately.[105] Jesus' disciples know his voice (10:3–4) and indeed know him—in terms of an established, complete covenant relationship—as intimately as he knew his Father (10:14–15). This must include the continuing sense of his presence and intimate communication through the Spirit in the community. Such an experience would certainly mark off the Johannine community from the synagogue and could arguably serve as evidence that the eschatological, messianic reign had been initiated in the true community, identifying which group was really in communion with God.

## 4. Announcing the Coming Matters (16:13)

Just as Jesus announces (ἀναγγελεῖ) everything regarding true worship of God in the Spirit ("when he [the Messiah] comes," 4:25; cf. the other Paraclete in 16:8, 13) and announces the Father himself (16:25), so the Spirit will announce what is to come (16:13), all the matters of Jesus (16:14–15).[106] This may lead to the question whether "the things to

---

[101] For a similar apologetic (albeit not experiential) chain, cf. Josh 11:15, where God commanded Moses, who commanded Joshua; or Rev 1:1.

[102] See Berg, "Pneumatology," 219–22, 255; Smith, "John 16," 61. Although the emphasis here lies with believers hearing the Spirit afresh (cf. 1 John 2:20, 27; Rev 2:7), it also applies to the Spirit-inspired Johannine witness (1 John 1:5; 4:6).

[103] Berg, "Pneumatology," 235; cf. 276–77.

[104] If the false prophets of Rev 2–3 advocate compromise with the imperial cult or with non-Christian Judaism and took John the Baptist as one of their models (as suggested above in comment on John 1:6–8), ecstatic experience could have been substituted for the objectivity of the Jesus tradition. The Paraclete passages lack any indications of ecstatic activity (Boring, *Sayings*, 85–86, citing as an analogy of nonecstatic inspiration Herm. *Mand.* 11.2–9).

[105] See comment on 15:13–15. Wisdom had access to secret divine knowledge (Wis 8:4).

[106] Potterie, "Paraklet," 95, denies that this is simply "une proclamation kérygmatique" and associates it rather with a nuance found in apocalyptic literature, "révéler, dévoiler," often in Daniel. On p. 96 he observes that this is not always a new revelation but, as in Daniel and elsewhere, it can

come" (v. 13) are equivalent in content to the "things of Jesus" (vv. 14–15) or refer to something else.[107]

There are various interpretations of τὰ ἐρχόμενα. Some apply the phrase τὰ ἐρχόμενα to the present, which may suit John's realized eschatology. Some of these scholars, reading it as parallel with "my things" in vv. 14–15, take it as an eschatological interpretation of the passion events[108] or the new order inaugurated in Jesus.[109] As in Pauline theology (Rom 8:23; 1 Cor 2:9–10; 2 Cor 1:22; Eph 1:13–14), the Spirit provides a foretaste of the future era.[110] Bultmann, who holds this view, believes that it is the old word of Jesus unfolded in ever new power.[111] Other scholars, who also take a nonfuturistic interpretation of the phrase, see it as a promise that the Spirit will superintend doctrinal developments in the later community[112] or that the Paraclete will help them to address their new situations in light of Jesus.[113] These two very different interpretations stress a nonfuturistic reading of τὰ ἐρχόμενα, which could be consistent with John's frequently realized eschatology.

Other scholars read this as predictive prophecy, given to the disciples to enable them to endure what would come (cf. 13:19, 14:28; Isa. 48:5).[114] One could also think of God's good promises for his people (see Isa 45:11 LXX). In favor of the future interpretation is the clear indication of the context that the disciples will share Jesus' "hour" of suffering but they could not bear further details until the coming of the Paraclete (v. 12). This also fits Jesus' foreknowledge of "things coming" to him (τὰ ἐρχόμενα, 18:4). It could prove intelligible to a Jewish sectarian audience; the Qumran community believed they had some advance knowledge of future things coming on the world.[115] In this interpretation, the book

---

mean "to give the interpretation of earlier revelation that is obscure and mysterious." Young, "Isaiah," 224, roots the term in Isaiah LXX (where it appears fifty-seven times).

[107] Godet, *Commentary*, 184, argues for their equivalence through the asyndeton between 16:13 and 16:14.

[108] Bultmann, *John*, 575; Tasker, *John*, 181; Isaacs, "Spirit," 398; Holwerda, *Spirit*, 62. For a critique of Bultmann's total exclusion of eschatology from the Fourth Gospel, see, e.g., Brown, "Paraclete," 130–31.

[109] Hunter, *John*, 155. Westcott, *John*, 231, sees it as the church. "Coming One" also functioned as a title for the Messiah in the Johannine community (e.g., 6:14, 11:27; cf. 2 John 2). Berg, "Pneumatology," 217–18, shows the weaknesses of the view that the text here means Jesus as the one to come, or the new reality or age initiated in Jesus, but nonetheless concludes (p. 236) that "the things of Jesus," rather than apocalyptic secrets of the end, are in view.

[110] On this view of the Spirit, see, e.g., Dunn, "Spirit," 701.

[111] Bultmann, *John*, 576.

[112] Lutkemeyer, "Paraclete," 228; cf. Swete, *Discourse*, 123; the Roman Catholic position of Gabriel Moran in Toon, *Development*, 99–103.

[113] Forestell, "Paraclete," 173–74. Cody, "Paraclete," 174, suggests that the Spirit indicates which things of the present will be of ultimate significance in the future.

[114] Johnston, *Spirit-Paraclete*, 137–41; Boring, *Sayings*, 102; Burge, *Community*, 215. The phrase is normally futuristic (Bauer, Gingrich, and Danker, *Lexicon*, 311; Black, *Approach*, 132, finds here an Aramaism), but cf. 14:2–3. Cf. Berg, "Pneumatology," 216–18, 235–36, who suggests that John is correcting this eschatological interpretation by placing it in a different sort of context; and Hamilton, *Spirit*, 38, who speaks of the future benefits revealed in the present in the exalted Lord Jesus. In Wis 8:8, Wisdom knows both ancient things and τὰ μέλλοντα (cf. the same phrase for things in the near future signified by an omen, in Philostratus *Hrk.* 33.5).

[115] 4Q268 frg. 1, lines 3, 8. Many ancient writings spoke of divine knowledge of what was, is, and is coming, the last naturally being the most difficult (Homer *Il.* 1.70; Plutarch *E at Delphi* 6, *Mor.* 387B; Egyptian *Book of the Dead* spell 172.S-3; *Jub.* 1:4; *Sib. Or.* 1.3–4; 11.319–320; *Barn.* 1.7; see Keener, *Revelation*, 98, on Rev 1:19).

of Revelation (in which Jesus' voice is also the central voice of prophecy in the book)[116] could almost be read as a sequel work of the Paraclete in the Johannine community.[117]

Both the nonfuturistic and the futuristic interpretations can derive some plausibility from the context. The Spirit will reveal the difficult situations that the community will confront, or the Spirit will reveal the solution to those situations. But if John's eschatology may include futuristic elements—and there is evidence that it does, provided one does not edit out these passages as inconsistent redaction—the futurist interpretation seems more probable. Some might even see in it authorization for John's application of his Jesus traditions to the situation of his community in conflict with the synagogues. A Johannine ἀποκάλυψις of Jesus Christ can include specific details about what the community must suffer, details not included in the Johannine reports of Jesus' teachings. As Jesus warned of the impending events of his passion in advance (13:19; 14:29; cf. 14:2), so the Spirit would continue to prepare Jesus' followers for testing in coming times (cf. Amos 3:7) or for their future inheritance. Whether futuristic or exhortative prophecy is in view, the association of the Spirit of God and announcing may suggest the prophetic function of the Spirit.[118]

## 5. Sharing What Belongs to Jesus (16:14–15)

But vv. 14–15 tie the Spirit as inseparably to Jesus as the rest of the Fourth Gospel ties Jesus to the Father. For John, not all the Spirit's words will have been reported in the Fourth Gospel, but all of them will be consistent with it (cf. 1 John 4:1–3), just as all Jesus' words in the Fourth Gospel are consistent with the Jesus of history known to the witness behind the Johannine tradition.

The glorification of Jesus by the Spirit (16:14) may relate to a continuing exposition of his character,[119] as suggested in 1:14. John 1:14–18 alludes to Exod 33–34, as argued earlier, where God's glory, revealed to Moses, includes an exposition of God's gracious and faithful character; throughout the Fourth Gospel, Jesus' signs reveal his identity,[120] but the ultimate revelation/glorification comes in the cross and exaltation of Jesus (see esp. 12:23–24; 17:1–5).[121] The disciples could not understand Jesus until after Jesus' glorification (2:22, 12:16, 13:7) because only then was the Spirit given (7:39) to continue to confront the community with the reality of Jesus. Their fresh revelation of Jesus stands in continuity with, rather than of being of a quality inferior to, the disciples' experience of Jesus during his earthly ministry.[122]

This passage indicates that as Jesus passed on the Father's message, so the Spirit would continue to mediate Jesus' message (16:14–15). The idea of intermediary passing on of revelation is familiar enough in Jewish circles, whether regarding apocalypses through

---

[116] Hill, *Prophecy,* 151 (citing Rev 1:12–16; cf. 2:1).

[117] Bengel, *Gnomen,* 2:454; Lenski, *John,* 1092. Cf. Johnston, *Spirit-Paraclete,* 139; Boring, *Sayings,* 102. Later writers could also take prophecies unfulfilled in earlier works' accounts as points of departure for their own (compare, e.g., Troy's Aeneas in Virgil *Aeneid* with Homer *Il.* 20.303–308).

[118] Cf. Smith, "John 16," 61.

[119] Cf. Schlier, "Begriff," 269, who says that the Spirit illuminates the work of Jesus in his glory. In Wis 8:3, Wisdom δοξάζει, but the object is her own nobility.

[120] John Chrysostom believed that the Spirit would glorify Jesus by performing greater miracles, as in 14:12 (*Hom. Jo.* 78).

[121] For connections with John 17, see Schnackenburg, *John,* 3:136.

[122] Cf., e.g., Titus, *Message,* 204.

angelic mediators[123] or regarding the Torah through Moses[124] or angels.[125] Of course, the whole Jewish concept of pneumatic inspiration is seen as intermediary if one views the Spirit personally or hypostatically.

What is passed on? The phrase "my things" means "my possessions" or "whatever belongs to me," the specific delimiting factor being only context.[126] The logic of shared resources, or here of shared truth, may reflect the Greek communal ideal espoused by Diogenes the Cynic and others:

> He used also to reason thus: "All things belong to the gods. The wise are friends of the gods, and friends hold things in common. Therefore all things belong to the wise."[127]

(See further the comment on 15:15.) Such sharing of all resources also can reflect members of a family (Luke 15:31), an illustration appropriate for the relationship between Father, Son, and other children. As Athanasius later articulated more explicitly, the Spirit joins believers in Jesus to the divine communion of the Father and the Son.[128] This sharing of resources, implied in the first line of 16:15, appears to be central to the case; "for this reason I said" (διὰ τοῦτο εἶπον) later in 16:15 probably signifies clarification of an earlier statement, as elsewhere in the Gospel (6:65; 9:23; 13:11).[129] The question of particular items shared is unclear from the vocabulary itself; thus an oracle of Orpheus told Cyrus, "What is mine [τὰ ἐμά] is yours [σά]"—which sounded positive but turned out to mean that Cyrus would die the same way Orpheus had.[130] But context clarifies, and here as in 15:15, the shared resources are especially the words of the Father. Jesus received "all things," particularly in terms of revelation of the Father (5:20; 17:7), and passed them on to his followers (4:25; 15:15); the Spirit would continue this work.[131]

In this passage, the prophetic Spirit enables the Johannine community to continue the first disciples' experience with Jesus and so provides them with an epistemological framework not available to their opponents. This affirmation, as much as the Spirit's prosecution of their opponents, serves the agendas of Johannine polemic.

Given this context about the coming of the Spirit, the passage into which 16:13–15 flows speaks of Jesus' historical departure and his presence by the Spirit from the point of

---

[123] E.g., *1 En.* 1:2; 72:1; 74:2; 75:3; *Jub.* 32:21; *3 Bar.* 1:8; 5:1; 6:1; *4 Ezra* 4:1; Rev 1:1; *b. Ber.* 51a; *Ned.* 20ab; cf. gnostic traditions in *Paraphrase of Shem* (*NHL* 308–28) and *Hypsiphrone* (*NHL* 453). It also appears in negative polemic (Gal 1:8; Col 2:18), some of which reflects the Prometheus myth (*b. Šabb.* 88a; *Gen. Rab.* 50:9; 68:12; 78:2).

[124] *T. Mos.* 1:14; 3:12; *Sipra Behuq. pq.* 8.269.2.15; *b. Ned.* 38a; Acts 7:38; cf. Isaacs, *Spirit,* 130. Aelius Aristides claimed that Athena passed on what she received from her Father (37.4–7, in Van der Horst, "Acts," 57).

[125] *Jub.* 1:27, 29; 2:1; Josephus *Ant.* 15.136; Acts 7:53; Gal 3:19; Heb 2:2; cf. VanderKam, "Author." For polemic against this view, see *'Abot R. Nat.* 1, §2; for other angels at Sinai, see, e.g., Deut 33:2; Ps 68:17; *Pesiq. Rab Kah.* 12:22; 16:3.

[126] Cf., e.g., Diogenes Laertius 6.1.11 (Antisthenes); Achilles Tatius 3.10.4; 1 Macc 12:23; *T. Job* 18:8 (*OTP* 1:847)/18:7 (ed. Kraft, 40).

[127] Diogenes Laertius 6.2.37 (LCL); cf., e.g., Crates *Ep.* 26–27 (to the Athenians); Anacharsis *Ep.* 9:12–14 (to Croesus). In early Christian literature, see, e.g., *Sent. Sext.* 228. See further the comment on 15:15.

[128] Pollard, *Christology,* 232.

[129] Berg, "Pneumatology," 231–32.

[130] Philostratus *Hrk.* 28.11–12.

[131] In the Q tradition cf. Matt 11:27; Luke 10:22; for Jesus passing to the disciples what he received from the Father, cf., e.g., Luke 22:29.

his final historical encounter with the disciples (16:16–24).[132] Although it is reasonable to begin a new paragraph with 16:16,[133] it refers to the same event in 20:19–23 as provides the disciples with the experience of the Spirit in 16:13–15. Jesus would return to them after the resurrection, and they would "see" him (16:16; 20:20);[134] the physical sight of 20:20 would give way to permanent spiritual sight on the part of disciples (17:24).[135] This experience and the new relationship with the Father that it entailed would bring them "joy" (16:20, 22, 24; 20:20). In the context of John 16:16, this eschatological foretaste of the resurrection becomes a continuing experience of Jesus' presence in the community through the Spirit (16:13–15; 20:22).[136]

## Meeting Jesus Again (16:16–22)

As with most other paragraphs in John's discourse sections, particularly those in the final discourse, the boundaries of this paragraph are fluid. Because Jesus imparts his permanent presence through the Spirit at the same time that he "returns" to them (20:19–23), the Spirit revealing Jesus (16:13–15) essentially enables disciples to experience afresh the encounter of 16:16–24, including generations subsequent to the first, such as John's own. More important, the travail (16:21–22) gives way immediately to requests to the Father on the day Jesus returns (16:24–28); but one could break that paragraph just as easily by starting a new paragraph with Jesus announcing that he no longer speaks figuratively (16:25; cf. 16:29).

### 1. A Little While (16:16–19)

The Gospel repeatedly uses the familiar[137] phrase "a little while" for the remaining days before Jesus' hour of glorification, which begins with the cross (7:33; 12:35). In 16:16, the first "a little while" (μικρόν) refers to the hours remaining before the crucifixion (13:33); the second "a little while" refers to the brief interval between the crucifixion and the resurrection appearances (14:19; 16:19–20).[138]

Within the story world, however, the disciples understand his meaning no more than they understood the passion predictions in the Synoptic Gospels. They wished to ask him the meaning of his words (16:17–18) but did not, presumably because their

---

[132] Cf., e.g., Holwerda, *Spirit*, 132. Brown (*John*, 2:728) divides 16:16–33 into a chiasmus: prediction of a test and subsequent consolation (16:16, 31–33); intervening remarks of disciples (16:17–19, 29–30); and promise of blessings to be enjoyed by disciples (16:20–23a, 23b–28). But the structure is too general to be clear, and remarks about a test and consolation appear elsewhere in the section (16:20–21).

[133] E.g., Nestle-Aland; UBS; NIV; Lightfoot, *Gospel*, 288.

[134] Pass, *Glory*, 233 (cf. also Westcott, *John*, 231–32; Phillips, "Faith," 89; Derrett, "Seeing"), tentatively suggests a distinction between the two terms here "behold" (for bodily sight) and "see" (for spiritual vision); in view of Johannine usage, however, the terminological distinction cannot hold (see "vision" in our introduction; also Sánchez Navarro, "Acerca").

[135] Cf. 9:39–41; 11:40; 12:40; 14:17, 19; 17:24; 1 John 3:6; Tholuck, *John*, 378–79; Lenski, *John*, 1098; Lightfoot, *Gospel*, 277, 293. On spiritual vision, see our introduction, pp. 247–51.

[136] On the Spirit and eschatological experience in John, see esp. Kysar, *Evangelist*, 235–40.

[137] Sometimes it appears in eschatological settings (Heb 10:37; Rev 6:11) probably rooted in the vernacular of Israelite prophecy about impending judgment (LXX Hos 1:4; Isa 10:25; Jer 28:33 [= 51:33]).

[138] E.g., Michaels, *John*, 271–72; Witherington, *Wisdom*, 266; Titus, *Message*, 204; Bernard, *John*, 2:513.

previous inquiries had merely exposed their ignorance (13:36–38; 14:5–7, 8–9; cf. perhaps 14:22–23).[139] Although disciples of teachers were supposed to learn partly by asking questions,[140] novices were supposed to learn quietly.[141] John portrays the disciples as a foil for Jesus, hence novices in his presence (cf. comment on 3:4). Jesus knows what they want to ask him about, fitting John's portrayal of Jesus' divine knowledge in this Gospel (see comment on 2:23–25).

## 2. Messianic Travail (16:20–22)

Jesus' "hour" of death (2:4) would finally come (16:21), though it would also become an hour of revelation to his followers (16:25). Although tears were appropriate to farewells in general (e.g., Josephus *Ant.* 4.194; Acts 20:37–38), "weeping" (16:20) appears in this Gospel only in conjunction with death, whether that of Lazarus (11:31, 33) or that of Jesus (20:11, 13, 15); the death of the latter is specifically in view here. The term λύπη in 16:20–22 probably includes another wordplay: it can include "sorrow," as in 16:6, or "pain," as in childbirth.[142]

Just as grief was particularly appropriate at the time of a loved one's death, the transformation of sorrow into joy (16:20, 22) fits the image of eschatological joy at the resurrection of the righteous (cf. 20:20).[143] In early Christian belief, Jesus' resurrection was the first installment of the resurrection of the righteous (1 Cor 15:23; Phil 3:21); in John's theology, it introduces the believers immediately into the experience of resurrection life (14:19; cf. 3:16). In one Jewish work of uncertain date, God tells Adam that though those who lured Adam into sin are rejoicing, God would turn their joy into sorrow (χαράν . . . λύπην) and Adam's sorrow into joy;[144] it is possible, however, that this work here reflects the language of the Fourth Gospel.

The comparison between their anguish and that of a birthing mother (16:21) is not incidental.[145] Some considered any mother's labor in birth as bringing her close to death.[146] Even on the Sabbath, Jewish pietists expected midwives and others to proceed to whatever lengths possible to insure a mother's comfort during childbirth.[147] Nevertheless, ancient childbearing lacked the benefits of modern means to reduce pain, and a mother's pain became proverbial for great travail.[148] Although joy following birth pangs

---

[139] Cf. similarly Mark 9:32, following a previous rebuke (Mark 8:32–33).

[140] Plutarch *Lect.* 11, *Mor.* 43BC; Aulus Gellius 1.26.2; 12.5.4; 20.10.1–6; *t. Sanh.* 7:10; *ʾAbot R. Nat.* 6A; see also Goodman, *State,* 79.

[141] Cf. Isocrates *Demon.* 41, *Or.* 1; Plutarch *Lect.* 18, *Mor.* 48A. Pythagoreans carried this further than others (Seneca *Ep. Lucil.* 52.10; Aulus Gellius 1.9.4; Diogenes Laertius 8.1.10).

[142] Cf. Smith, *John* (1999), 301.

[143] Cf. also 8:56; 17:13. For the association of joy with the resurrection of the righteous, see *T. Jud.* 25:4. See further the comment on 3:29.

[144] *Apoc. Mos.* 39:1–2.

[145] Dodd, *Tradition,* 370, compares the formal structure of 16:21 to 12:24 and Luke 11:21–22.

[146] *Syr. Men.* 97–98; Xenophon *Mem.* 2.2.5. Often mothers did die in childbirth (Safrai, "Home," 765, noting texts that blame such deaths on disobedience to the law; see Keener, *Paul,* 118–19), albeit not frequently enough to produce a decline in the Jewish population.

[147] Safrai, "Home," 765, citing *m. Šabb.* 18:3; *Roš Haš.* 2:5; *ʾOhal.* 7:4; also among Gentiles, e.g., Maximus of Tyre *Or.* 10.4. On the importance of midwives, see, e.g., Aristophanes *Lys.* 746–747; Galen *N.F.* 3.3.151–152; on the urgency, Seneca *Ep. Lucil.* 117.30.

[148] Descriptions of it nearly always focus on pain (e.g., Ovid *Metam.* 9.292–304; Phaedrus 1.18.2–3).

was expected,[149] this did not reduce the intensity of the pain involved; the epitome of igno-rance, in fact, might be a fool who publicly asked his mother how her pangs were at his birth and then lectured her that nobody can have pleasure without having some pain mixed in as well.[150] Some had compared the unspeakable grief of losing those close to one-self,[151] or the experience of being violently repressed for one's piety,[152] with birth pangs. Such birth pangs were said to strengthen the mother's sympathy and love for her children (4 Macc 15:7).

The common eschatological associations of this image are critical here, as commenta-tors often recognize.[153] The biblical prophets employed birth pangs as an image of extreme anguish.[154] In Jewish literature, these birth pangs came to illustrate the period of intense suffering immediately preceding the end,[155] as the final sufferings giving birth to a new world.[156] Here, too, the birth pangs are eschatological, except that they relate to the real-ized eschatology inaugurated among believers through Jesus' resurrection.

The image may most directly reflect Isa 26:16–21, which uses "little while," labor pains, and resurrection.[157] An equally valid or perhaps better candidate is Isa 66:8–14, in which Zion travails to bring forth the restored people of God (66:8), and when God's people "see" (ὄψεσθε), they become "glad" (χαρήσεται, 66:14).[158] Revelation (which we argued in the introduction, pp. 126–39, derives from a Johannine community) employs this same image to mark Jesus' glorification (Rev 12:2) at the time that the dragon is "cast out" (Rev 12:8–10; John 12:31; cf. 16:11) and the beginning of the interim period of suffer-ing and divine provision for the rest of the woman's seed (Rev 12:6, 14–17). Revelation em-ploys the image in a manner analogous with John; in contrast with the Synoptics, the messianic woes begin not after Jesus' death (Mark 13:8) but in it (John 16:20–22).[159] Thus the woman experiences "tribulation" (16:21), which the disciples also must anticipate (16:33; Rev 1:9; 7:14).[160]

Though the birth pangs apply especially to Jesus, they apply also to the whole of the people of God (cf. Isa 66:8; Rev 12:17). Jesus' followers can be "born from above" (3:3–5) because of the birth pangs in the cross. Just as birth pangs are temporary and normally yield a longer joy, so here they receive a joy that no one can take from them (16:22; cf.

---

[149] Cf., e.g., Menander Rhetor 2.8, 412.20–22 (though the point resembles that in Luke 11:27).

[150] Theophrastus *Char.* 20.7–8.

[151] *T. Job* 18:4 *(OTP)*/18:5 (ed. Kraft).

[152] 1QH 3.7–12.

[153] E.g., Lightfoot, *Gospel,* 294; Morris, *John,* 706; Cadman, *Heaven,* 196; Fenton, *John,* 169; Robinson, *Coming,* 174; Carson, *Discourse,* 162.

[154] See, e.g., Ps 48:6; Isa 13:8; 21:3; 26:17; 42:14; Jer 4:31; 6:24; 13:21; 22:23; 30:6; 31:8; 48:41; 49:22, 24; 50:43; Hos 13:13; Matt 24:8; 1 Thess 5:3. Not surprisingly, the pain of childbirth was a wide-spread image (Sir 7:27; 19:11; *L.A.B.* 12:5; Plutarch *Plat. Q.* 1.4, *Mor.* 1000E; Phaedrus 1.18.2–3).

[155] Cf. 1QH 3.3–18; *1 En.* 62:4; *b. Sanh.* 98b; *Šabb.* 118a.

[156] Cf. realized eschatology in Rev 12:2, 5; Rom 8:22. Many spoke of the final turmoil without the specific metaphor of "birth pangs" (e.g., *Jub.* 23:13; 36:1; 1QM 15.1; *Sib. Or.* 3.213–215; *4 Ezra* 8:63–9:8; 13:30; *2 Bar.* 26:1–27:13; 69:3–5; *T. Mos.* 7–8; *m. Soṭah* 9:15; *b. Sanh.* 97a; *Pesiq. Rab Kah.* 5:9).

[157] Beasley-Murray, *John,* 285–86.

[158] Cf. Hoskyns, *Gospel,* 487–88. The distributive singular for "heart" (14:1; 16:22; Brown, *John,* 2:618) might also reflect Isa 66:14 LXX here.

[159] Robinson, *Coming,* 174 (on John 16).

[160] The term for "tribulation" here (16:21, 33, θλῖψις) also could refer to the final period of suffering for the righteous (Dan 12:1; Mark 13:24; Rev 7:14) or to the day of God's vengeance (Zeph 1:15; Rom 2:9; 2 Thess 1:6), although it did not always point to them (cf. Whitacre, *John,* 395).

10:28).[161] Their permanent joy (16:22) will include a new relationship with the Father, inaugurated by Jesus' continuing presence among them through the Spirit (16:13–16); whatever they would now ask in Jesus' name, God would provide (cf. 14:13–14; 15:7, 16).[162]

## Clearer Understanding (16:23–33)

The boundaries between paragraphs are ambiguous in this discourse and could be divided in various ways; the continuity of thought is more essential than specific divisions, and therefore if one holds too tightly to an outline, it can obscure the flow of thought rather than reveal it. The travail of 16:21–22 yields immediately to requests to the Father on the day Jesus returns (16:24–28). One could break up 16:24–28 by introducing a new paragraph with Jesus announcing that he no longer speaks figuratively (16:25; cf. 16:29).

### 1. Asking in Jesus' Name (16:23–28)

By going to the Father and returning with the Spirit, Jesus would bring the disciples directly to God: the Father would give their requests directly if they asked as Jesus' representatives instead of depending on Jesus to ask for them. This "directness" does not imply lack of mediation in all senses; rather, disciples come to the Father through Jesus (14:6), but as long as they remain in Jesus (14:20, 21–24), they remain in the Father's presence, with direct access to him in prayer. When he returns with the Spirit, Jesus will no longer need to speak of heavenly matters in earthly parables (3:12; 15:1); Jesus will reveal the Father more directly to them (16:25).

"In that day" (16:23, 26) is frequently eschatological language, which would fit John's emphasis on realized eschatology: Jesus returns in the resurrection to impart eschatological life through the Spirit (cf. 14:20).[163] In classical usage and often in the first century, ἐρωτάω (16:23) means "ask a question."[164] But by the first century, it could also mean "request" (e.g., Matt 15:23; Mark 7:26), as it commonly does for Paul (Phil 4:3; 1 Thess 4:1; 5:12; 2 Thess 2:1), Luke (Luke 4:38; 5:3; 7:3, 36; 8:37; 11:37; 14:18–19, 32; 16:27; Acts 3:3; 10:48; 16:39; 18:20; 23:18), and John (4:31, 40, 47; 12:21; 14:16; 17:9, 15, 20; 19:31, 38; cf. 1 John 5:16; 2 John 5).

The most immediate context suggests "request," given the remainder of 16:23–24 and the typical usage in prayer (16:26; 17:9, 15, 20); but the context also speaks of asking questions (16:5, 19, 30). If it refers to asking questions,[165] perhaps Jesus is saying that the Paraclete will teach them all they need to know (16:12–13),[166] or that their lack of understanding of God's plan will be met by the fulfillment of that plan (16:19–20), or that God

---

[161] It may have been a commonplace that, even if one was robbed of possessions, others could not seize one's abilities or identity (cf. Cicero *Att.* 3.5; Philostratus *Vit. soph.* 2.26.614); but the childbirth analogy remains central here.

[162] Dowd, "Theology," 334, compares Moses' relationship with God in Exodus.

[163] Barrett, *John,* 494, cites many early Christian eschatological uses in the NT. The prophets often used it eschatologically (e.g., Isa 2:11, 17, 20; 4:2; 24:21; 27:1; Hos 2:16, 18, 21; Joel 3:18; Amos 8:9; 9:11; Zeph 3:16; Zech 14:4), though in the broad sense of any future prophecy (e.g., Isa 7:18, 20–21; 10:27; 23:15; Jer 4:9).

[164] E.g., Matt 16:13; 19:17; 21:24; Mark 4:10; 8:5; Luke 9:45; 19:31; 20:3; 22:68; 23:3; Acts 1:6; John 1:19, 21, 25; 5:12; 8:7; 9:2, 15, 19, 21; 16:5, 19, 26, 30; 18:19, 21.

[165] E.g., Holwerda, *John,* 75; Michaels, *John,* 276.

[166] So Sanders, *John,* 360.

will guide them even before they need to ask (16:30). Perhaps he refers to the fulness of eschatological knowledge (Jer 31:34; 1 Cor 13:12), which obviates the need for questions.[167] Probably he is telling the disciples that instead of depending on Jesus to request the Father for them, they can approach the Father immediately as Jesus' representatives (16:26–27), which nevertheless implies Jesus' continued mediation (14:6). Jesus' previous use of obscure speech (16:25; cf. 6:60) will give way to the open speech others had long wanted from him (16:25; 10:24; 11:14; see comment on 7:4).[168] Previously he had shown them the Father (14:7–9), but now he would explain openly about the Father (16:25; cf. 4:25), and the Spirit would continue this work (16:13–15). Perhaps, given the semantic range of ἐρωτάω, John and his first audience would have felt less concern to distinguish these nuances. John is, in any case, a master of double entendre.[169]

The second part of 16:23, however, clearly concerns requesting in Jesus' name.[170] They can make their requests directly to the Father (16:26) because the Father loves them on Jesus' behalf (16:27; cf. 15:9–10; 17:23).[171] We have discussed this motif more fully under 14:13–14; cf. 15:7, 16. This Gospel elsewhere stresses God's gracious benevolence (e.g., 1:12; 3:16; 4:10; 6:32), and even oblique requests may receive answers (2:3; 11:21) The fulness of joy (16:24) reflects not only Jesus' resurrection (16:20–22; 17:13) but its consequences for their continuing life with him (15:10–11; 16:24).

Jesus is from the Father and returning to the Father (16:28), and so can bring them direct access to, and relationship with, the Father in his name (14:6). Now Jesus, who had "come into the world" (cf. 1:9; 3:17; 18:37), was "leaving the world" (16:28), and the disciples finally understand what he means by "going" from them (13:33, 36; 14:2–4, 12, 28; 16:5, 7, 10); although still potentially ambiguous (cf. 1 Cor 5:10), "leaving the world" was more explicit from their perspective than going to the Father.[172]

## 2. Limited Faith (16:29–33)

Now that Jesus has finally answered his disciples' question and they understand that he is going to the Father and returning, they affirm their faith in him (16:29–30). But like signs-faith elsewhere in the Gospel, this initial profession of faith will prove inadequate to withstand the coming testing unless it proceeds to full discipleship—which it will do only later. As in 13:36–38, Jesus warns his disciples that they will indeed grow weak in faith and

---

[167] Cf. Bultmann, *John*, 583.

[168] Teachers sometimes answered obscurely until students became true adherents (Xenophon *Mem.* 4.2.8–39, completed in 4.2.40; Iamblichus *V.P.* 23.103; 34.245); Keener, *Matthew*, 378–79. Maximus of Tyre *Or.* 38.4 opines that old poets spoke myths as allegories but philosophers use understandable language. Brakke, "Plain Speech," compares 16:25 with the later *Ap. Jas.* 7.1–6, though noting that the former stems from a sect within Judaism, the latter within Christianity.

[169] Note that the two terms for "ask" in 16:23–24, 26 appear to remain interchangeable, in contrast to late Greek (Smith, *John* [1999], 302).

[170] "In his name" may signify "as his representatives" (5:43; 10:25; 14:26; Sanders, *John*, 361); see comment on 14:13–14; 15:16. Bernard, *John*, 2:518, suggests taking "in my name" with "ask the Father" rather than "give you" (cf. 15:16).

[171] A patron might write a letter of recommendation on his client's behalf, asking that the client be so treated that he recognizes "that I love him and that you love me" (Cicero *Fam.* 13.47.1 [LCL 3:120–21]), i.e., so as to prove that the patron urged the letter recipient on the client's behalf and has influence with the recipient.

[172] Cf. Josephus *Ant.* 4.179, 189, of Moses.

abandon him (16:31–32); yet Jesus is not totally abandoned, for, as the Fourth Gospel repeatedly emphasizes, he is inseparable from the Father's presence (16:33).

Jesus' power demonstrated his divine origin, recognized even by Nicodemus from the start (3:2); the recognition that he knew "all things" (16:30; 18:4; 21:17),[173] however, should have pointed the disciples not only to Jesus' origin but to his deity (see 1 John 3:20; comment on 2:23–25).

Jesus further demonstrates this superhuman knowledge by predicting their betrayals (16:31–32).[174] That an "hour was coming and already had come" may reflect Johannine language for realized eschatology (4:23; 5:25); the hour of suffering about to come upon them was of a piece with the eschatological tribulation they would suffer. They would be scattered; this was the usual fate of troops whose leader had fallen,[175] but in biblical tradition, it was especially the fate of sheep without a shepherd, the condition of Israel when lacking faithful shepherds (1 Kgs 22:17; 2 Chr 18:16; Ezek 34:5; Zech 11:16; 13:7; 1 Macc 12:53) or scattered in the exile (Jer 31:10; Bar 2:13; *1 En.* 89:75). (On scattering, see more fully the comment on 10:12.) The saying in this case probably reflects the saying from the passion tradition also cited in Mark 14:27–28, based on Zech 13:7.[176] Being abandoned, left "alone," was normally viewed as a great hardship;[177] to be abandoned by one's disciples was a mark of great shame.[178] (Each returning "to his own home"[179] may recall biblical language for defeated soldiers fleeing the battle after losing their leader—1 Kgs 22:17.)

But Jewish piety recognized that God might help those who were otherwise alone,[180] and in this Gospel, Jesus has affirmed that he is not alone (8:16) because the Father is with him (8:29; 16:32).[181] This affirmation might reflect the consistent portrayal of Jesus as triumphant in John's Passion Narrative, as opposed to the tradition in the Synoptics, or might even answer theological questions raised by Mark. Whereas, in Mark, Jesus' cries in anguish can be interpreted as a sign of the Father's temporary abandonment (Mark 15:34), here Jesus affirms that the Father is with him without interruption (John 16:32; cf. Luke 23:46).

Finally, Jesus encourages his followers with a summary: great hardship awaits them, but in going to the Father through his death and consequent resurrection, Jesus has overcome the world (16:33).[182] In the context of John's Gospel and early Christian eschatology, this note of triumph is not merely the Stoic notion of being unconquered no matter what

---

[173] Some see this as antignostic polemic (e.g., Fenton, *John*, 170). Such a reconstruction of the Fourth Gospel's *Sitz im Leben* is improbable (see our introduction, esp. pp. 168–69), but polemical usage is possible (see 1 John 2:20–27).

[174] Michaels takes 16:31 as a statement (*John*, 276), but it is probably a question; in any case, it reveals Jesus' skepticism (cf. 2:24; 13:38).

[175] E.g., Arrian *Alex.* 4.27.2; 4.24.4–5; Silius Italicus 15.807–808.

[176] Cf. also Lightfoot, *Gospel*, 294.

[177] The exception was Stoic philosophy, e.g., Epictetus *Diatr.* 3.13.4 (who claims that even Zeus was alone at the periodic conflagration of the cosmos); but the Stoic Musonius Rufus notes that true friends will not abandon one on account of exile (9, p. 68.13–15).

[178] Malina, *Windows*, 17–18; Cornelius Nepos 14 (Datames), 6.3. Betrayal by one's troops appears tragic in Cornelius Nepos 18 (Eumenes), 10.2.

[179] On this sense, see Brown, *John*, 2:727.

[180] *T. Jos.* 1:6 (μόνος).

[181] Because the Gospel also proclaims the "oneness" of God with the same adjective (μόνος, 5:44; 17:3), the Son "not being alone" might also respond to synagogue polemic against Jesus' deity; but this is not necessary.

[182] Proposed translation errors from Aramaic here (Schwarz, "Welt") are very speculative.

the suffering[183] but a promise that evil and suffering do not ultimately prevail for Christ's followers. Jesus had spoken to them the words of this final discourse (cf. "spoken these things" in 14:25; 15:11; 16:1, 4, 6; 17:1) to bring them encouragement. Even so, the "peace" he promises here (16:33; cf. 14:27) would become more fully theirs only at Jesus' resurrection appearances; this "peace" (16:33) would come through Jesus' defeat in the eyes of the world, through which God brings victory in the resurrection (20:19, 21, 26).[184] The summons to be of good courage, θαρσεῖτε, was a general exhortation and comfort,[185] appropriate, for instance, to wish-prayers,[186] exhortations before battle,[187] promises of God's faithfulness to his people,[188] and burial epitaphs.[189] The disciples would face tribulation in Jesus' death (16:21) and in sharing his sufferings afterwards (Rev 1:9), but this did not mean defeat.

In the theology of the canonical Johannine corpus, believers overcome the evil one and the world by faithful obedience (1 John 2:13–14; 4:4), trusting in the accomplished victory of Christ (1 John 5:4–5). Such overcoming also demands persevering (Rev 2:7, 11, 17, 26; 3:5, 12, 21; 21:7), especially achieved through martyrdom (Rev 5:5; 12:11; 15:2).[190] Ironically—quite in contrast with the world's view of victory[191]—it is accomplished even when the forces of the world "overcome" the saints in a worldly sense (Rev 11:7; 13:7), in view of Christ's future defeat of the world's forces (Rev 17:14).

---

183 E.g., Seneca *Ep. Lucil.* 67.16 *(invictus; vincit)*.

184 Cf. comments in Ford, "Shalom."

185 E.g., Homer *Il.* 24.171; *Od.* 2.372; 4.825; 19.546; 24.357; Sophocles *El.* 916; *Phil.* 810; Diogenes Laertius 1.113.

186 Tob 7:18.

187 Homer *Il.* 15.254 (Apollo to Hector); Dionysius of Halicarnassus *R.A.* 6.92.4. Cf. John 14:31.

188 Bar 4:5; cf. 1 Esd 4:59.

189 Jewish as well as pagan and Christian (Leon, *Jews,* 126); e.g., *CIJ* 1:86, §123; 1:263, §335; 1:295, §380; 1:309, §401; 1:334, §450; 2:118, §891; 2:190, §1039; 2:193, §1051; 2:205, §1125; 2:244, §1209.

190 Rhetoricians could praise those slain in battle as "undefeated" (Demosthenes *Or.* 60, *Funeral Speech* 19); likewise Stoics could speak of overcoming *(vincit)* by being unmoved by hardships (Seneca *Dial.* 1.2.2). But John refers to an unseen eschatological triumph here (cf. Rev 12:11).

191 Romans celebrated victories by producing coins bearing the image of Nike, goddess of victory, including one commemorating the defeat of Judea by Titus (Carmon, *Inscriptions,* 101, 216, §213).

# JESUS' PRAYER FOR DISCIPLES

## 17:1–26

Here Jesus shifts from addressing the disciples to addressing the Father (17:1–26); after he returns to bestow the Spirit in 20:19–23, the disciples will pray directly to the Father for themselves (16:23–26) because he will have given them a new relationship with the Father (16:27) based on his own (16:28). Nevertheless, this prayer undoubtedly provides a model for their own; disciples concerned with their Lord's agendas ought to place a high priority on unity with other disciples. Just as such unity would have helped them through the crisis imminent during Jesus' prayer (cf. 16:31–32), it would give believers victory in their continuing conflict with the world (16:33; cf. 13:35; 15:18–27). For comments on ancient prayer and believers praying as Jesus' representatives, see 14:13–14; cf. also comment on Jesus' prayer in 11:41–42.

### Introductory Issues

Käsemann emphasizes the testamentary character of ch. 17,[1] but as we have remarked earlier, the testament as a whole begins in ch. 13. Where the testamentary genre is most relevant to ch. 17 is the frequency of blessings and wish-prayers in testaments (e.g., Gen 49; Deut 32—33).[2] That John closes the previous section of the last discourse before opening this prayer (ταῦτα ἐλάλησεν, 17:1) suggests the prayer's special significance for John's audience.[3] Käsemann rightly notes that much of the Gospel's theology climaxes in this concluding section of Jesus' final discourse in the Gospel,[4] though one should note that many other passages also provide prisms that refract larger cross sections of Johannine theology. As Minear points out, this prayer represents "the decisive turning point between ministry and passion," viewing the hour of Jesus' glorification "both proleptically and retrospectively."[5]

The chapter also reflects standard Jewish motifs, such as the unity of God's people, their love for God, God's glory, obedience to God's message, the election and setting apart of God's people, and the importance of obeying God's agent (Moses in Jewish tradition). One writer links such motifs specifically to the Cairo Geniza manuscript of the Palestinian Targum to Exod 19–20,[6] another points to parallels with a hymn from Qumran;[7] in short,

---

[1] Käsemann, *Testament,* 4.

[2] Cf. Smith, *John* (1999), 309; Blomberg, *Reliability,* 218. Käsemann, *Testament,* 5, regards it as a proclamation to the Father so the disciples can hear (cf. 11:42), rather than as a prayer; but this claim reflects a modern dichotomy (see, e.g., Ps 22:22, 25; 35:18; 40:9–10; 107:32; 111:1; 149:1).

[3] Cf. Carson, *Discourse,* 175.

[4] Käsemann, *Testament,* 3.

[5] Minear, "Audience," 343.

[6] Marzotto, "Targum."

[7] Hanson, "Comparison."

most of the motifs reflect common Judaism, yet reinterpreted in a christocentric manner and reapplied to the christologically defined community.

Further, to whatever degree John has adapted the discourse and prayer to encourage his audience in their particular situation,[8] it is clear that a prayer of Jesus before his passion already stands in the passion tradition (Mark 14:36).[9] But whereas, in Mark, Jesus prays for the Father to spare him from the passion if possible (Mark 14:36), here he recognizes and accedes to the Father's purpose, requesting the hour of glorification (17:1).[10] John does not deny Jesus' reluctance to face the cross (12:27) but places heavier emphasis on Jesus' obedience.[11]

Traditionally some have viewed Jesus' intercession in this passage in terms of the OT role of high priest[12] (Jesus' role in some early Christian traditions; Heb 2:17; 3:1; 4:14–15; 5:10; 6:20; 7:26; 8:1; 9:11); the chapter title "Jesus' High-Priestly Prayer" has circulated since the theologian David Chyträus (1531–1600).[13] But Jewish tradition also emphasized the intercessory role of prophets;[14] more significantly, the probably testamentary character of the final discourse might point to patriarchal blessings,[15] particularly the prayer and blessing of Moses (Deut 32–33),[16] as background. But because the content of these blessings does not parallel John 17 very closely,[17] one may need to look to the experience of John's audience for more of the content. A variety of backgrounds are possible, but most important within the context of the Fourth Gospel is that Jesus becomes, before his exaltation, the first Paraclete, or intercessor (Rom 8:26; 1 John 2:1; see extended comment on 14:16).[18] This suggests that John 17 models part of the ministry of the Paraclete who would come after Jesus' departure (14:16) and of those who share his ministry (15:26–27).[19] The Fourth Gospel presents the Paraclete especially as an advocate or prosecutor in the

---

[8] Even generally conservative commentators usually will not claim that the chapter was intended as a verbatim recollection (Ridderbos, *John*, 546–47).

[9] E.g., Smalley, *John*, 189; Burge, *Community*, 116 n. 9. On the antiquity of the tradition, see, e.g., Keener, *Matthew*, 633; Witherington, *Christology*, 219. Supposed parallels between John 17 and Matt 6:9–13 (Walker, "Prayer"; cf. Dodd, *Tradition*, 333) are possible but not impressive. Motifs such as "Father," "Name," "glorify" or "hallow," "keep" from "testing," and "deliver" or "protect" from "the evil one" (Carson, *Discourse*, 174) were relatively standard fare in early Jewish prayers (Jeremias, *Prayers*, 104–5; *b. Ber.* 60b; *Sanh.* 64a). At most, the sequential parallels may suggest coherence with extant Jesus tradition (Blomberg, *Reliability*, 219), which adapts many elements of contemporary Jewish prayer (Keener, *Matthew*, 215–16).

[10] The aorist implies the perspective of completion, although this need not require the speaker in the story world to speak after the events (Blass, Debrunner, and Funk, *Grammar*, 171–72). The καὶ νῦν of 17:5 may reflect a temporal transition (cf. Laurentin, "*We'attah*," on the OT and Lukan usage for reversal) but need not do so (e.g., 1 John 2:28).

[11] As Smith notes (*John* [1999], 327), John may know the Gethsemane tradition (12:27; Heb 5:7–8), but John emphasizes Jesus dying intentionally (10:17–18). For distinctives of various early Christian writers on the final prayer, see more fully Dodd, *Tradition*, 71.

[12] cf. Gordon, "Prayer" (consecrating disciples as priests).

[13] Schulz, *Evangelium*, 213.

[14] See Aune, *Prophecy*, 124, citing 2 Macc 15:14; cf. 1 Sam 7:8; 12:23; 15:11; Jer 7:16; 11:14; 14:11; 15:1; 37:3; 42:2, 4, 20.

[15] Schnackenburg, *John*, 3:198, cites the use of parting prayers in Gen 49; Deut 32; *Jub.* 1:19–21; 10:3–6, 20–22; 36:17; cf. *1 En.* 91; *4 Ezra* 8:20–36, 45; *2 Bar.* 48:1–24; 84–85.

[16] See Minear, "Audience," 343.

[17] See Schnackenburg, *John*, 3:198, on their "form and function."

[18] Also Painter, *John*, 59.

[19] Appold, *Motif*, 199, suggests connections "with the worship experiences of the Johannine church" (cf. 4:23–24); but the hymns in Revelation, which differ considerably from this prayer, may be more revealing.

disciples' conflict with the world, but Jesus has also been promising them more direct access to the Father in prayer once he goes to the Father (14:13–14; 15:7, 16; 16:26–27).

The setting of the prayer is essentially the same as that of the last discourse, excepting the specific mention of a change in Jesus' posture. "Lifting up" one's "eyes" was a common posture of prayer (11:41; cf. Mark 6:41; 7:34) in early Judaism (1 Esd 4:58; 4 Macc 6:6, 26)[20] and appeared among Gentiles.[21] Because God was envisioned as being in heaven,[22] both Jews[23] and Gentiles[24] regularly lifted their hands in prayer, supplication, or worship.

## Reciprocal Glory of Father and Son (17:1–5)

John 17:1–5 alludes back to previous declarations that the hour of glory had come, through which the Father and Son would glorify one another in the cross (12:23–24, 28; 13:31–32).[25] In the context of the entire Gospel, Jesus' return to glory here includes his exaltation but takes place by way of the cross.[26] The reader of the Fourth Gospel is by now prepared for such a statement, but we should not miss the striking offensiveness of the language: glory was partly honor, whereas the cross was one of the greatest humiliations conceivable to the ancient Mediterranean mind.[27] Jesus "looks for glory in the last place" the world would expect it.[28] In this passage as in others, a complex of associations cluster together, including Jesus' glory and love, God's name, and the revealing of God's word;[29] this is the natural outworking of the analogy with Moses introduced in 1:14–18 (see comment

---

[20] Also Tob 3:11–12; 4Q213 frg. 1, col. 1, line 8; *4 Bar.* 6:5; *Jos. Asen.* 11:19/12:1; *t. Ber.* 3:14; *Pesiq. Rab.* 3:5; *p. Ber.* 4:6; Carson, *Discourse,* 175; see comment on 4:35. Prayer toward Jerusalem was, however, normative as well: 1 Kgs 8:44; Dan 6:10; 1 Esd 4:58; *m. Ber.* 4:5–6; *t. Ber.* 3:14; for standing in prayer, see, e.g., Matt 6:5; Luke 18:11; *p. Ber.* 1:1, §8; Lachs, *Commentary,* 210.

[21] Homer *Il.* 7.178, 201; Xenophon *Cyr.* 6.4.9; Virgil *Aen.* 2.405–406 (because she could not lift her hands); 12.195; Silius Italicus 1.508; Chariton 8.7.2; cf. some (albeit only some) traditional cultures in Mbiti, *Religions,* 84. *PGM* 4.585 reports closing eyes for prayer, but some parts require the eyes to be open (*PGM* 4.625; cf. Iamblichus *V.P.* 28.156); the magical papyri require many different magical gestures.

[22] E.g., Judaism frequently associates God with "heaven" (e.g. 1 Esd 4:58; Tob 10:13; Jdt 6:19; 1 Macc 3:18, 50, 60; 4:24; 3 Macc 7:6; *1 En.* 83:9; 91:7). Greeks also sometimes located Zeus in heaven (Achilles Tatius 5.2.2; cf. Seneca *Dial.* 12.8.5). As a circumlocution for God, see comment on John 3:3.

[23] Ezra 9:5; Lam 2:19; 3:41; Isa 1:15; *1 En.* 84:1; *Jub.* 25:11; Ps 155:2; 1 Esd 9:47; 2 Macc 3:20; 14:34; 15:12, 21; 3 Macc 5:25; 4 Macc 4:11; *Sib. Or.* 3.559–560, 591–593; 4.162–170; Josephus *Ant.* 3.26, 53; 4.40; *Ag. Ap.* 1.209; 3.26; *T. Mos.* 4:1; *Mek. Pisha* 1.38; *t. Moʾed Qaṭ.* 2:17. Cf. also 1 Tim 2:8; *1 Clem.* 29.1; *Acts John* 43.

[24] E.g., Homer *Il.* 1.450; 3.275, 318; 5.174; 6.257; 7.130; 8.347; 15.368–372; 19.254; *Od.* 9.294, 527; 17.239; 20.97; Euripides *El.* 592–593; Apollonius of Rhodes 1.248; 4.593, 1702; Virgil *Aen.* 1.93; 4.205; 9.16; 12.195; Ovid *Metam.* 2.477, 580; 6.261–262; 9.702–703; 11.131; 13.410–411; Diodorus Siculus 14.29.4; Dionysius of Halicarnassus *R.A.* 3.17.5; 15.9.2; Appian *C.W.* 2.12.85; *R.H.* 2.5.5; Livy 7.6.4; Suetonius *Nero* 41; Arrian *Alex.* 4.20.3 (a Persian); Epictetus *Diatr.* 4.10.14; Plutarch *Cleverness* 17, *Mor.* 972B; Chariton 3.1.8.

[25] For parallels, see, e.g., Lightfoot, *Gospel,* 300; Schnackenburg, *John,* 3:167; Brown, *John,* 2:740.

[26] E.g., Holwerda, *Spirit,* 15–16; Käsemann, *Testament,* 19; comment on 12:23; 13:31–32. Both the emphasis on the cross and and that on preexistent glory refute Smith's comparison with a magical text (*PGM* 7.504; *Magician,* 132).

[27] E.g., Diodorus Siculus 34/35.12.1; Epictetus *Diatr.* 3.26.22; sources in Brown, *Death,* 946–47; Davies, *Paul,* 284.

[28] Morris, *John,* 721.

[29] Käsemann, *Testament,* 50.

there). Thus Jesus' crucifixion and exaltation to the Father is the theophany that will reveal the divine name to the disciples.

Jesus and the narrator had been declaring that his "hour" would "come" from 2:4 onward (7:30; 8:20); from 12:23 they have been declaring that it had finally arrived (12:27; 13:1; 16:32; cf. Mark 14:41). The request that the Father glorify the Son so that the Son might glorify the Father was in effect a request that the Father now hasten the cross (12:23–24; 13:31–32), revealing the Son's love for, and devotion to, the Father.[30] This prayer is strikingly different from Jesus' Gethsemane prayer in the Markan passion tradition, but John undoubtedly intends this prayer to complement Jesus' revulsion to the cross, not to contradict it. It continues the Johannine "Gethsemane" prayer of 12:27–28[31] and fits "Your will be done" at the close of Mark 14:36. Jewish literature often declared the eschatological sanctification[32] or glorification of God's name. Jewish literature also recognized that God must be praised or glorified in the present.[33] Because one's "name" involved one's "honor," it is not surprising that some texts link name and glory.[34]

Perhaps lest the accusers of John's audience complain that glorifying Jesus detracted from God's glory, John is at pains to demonstrate that it is the Father himself who glorifies Jesus and that Jesus' costly glory glorifies the Father (7:18; 8:50, 54; cf. 1 John 2:23). Jesus is exalted on the basis of his prior submission to suffering for the Father's honor.[35] In Isaiah, God glorified himself in glorifying Israel (Isa 44:23; 46:13; 49:3; 55:5; 60:1–2, 7, 9, 19, 21; 61:3); thus an Amora could remark, for example, that God told Moses to glorify Israel, for Israel's glorification would glorify God.[36]

That Jesus rules "all flesh" (17:2) simply means that he rules "all humanity."[37] This was a role normally attributed to God alone,[38] but the Fourth Gospel reveals that the Father has repeatedly delegated his authority to the Son (3:35; 5:22, 26–27; 13:3);[39] the Father's gifts to the Son (especially disciples; also glory, revelation, and authority) and the Son's gifts to disciples in fact make the present context the Gospel's greatest concentration of δίδωμι (17:2, 4, 6–9, 11–12, 14, 22, 24). That Jesus was authorized to give eternal life to his own would encourage those whose faith was challenged by opponents who claimed to speak for God apart from Jesus (cf. 6:37–40; 10:28–29).

---

[30] Writers could employ prayers in response to oracles, like oracles themselves, to foreshadow a narrative's direction (e.g., Xenophon *Eph.* 5.1).

[31] Cf. Beasley-Murray, *John,* 294.

[32] Isa 5:16; 29:23; Ezek 38:23; 39:7, 27; 1QM 11.15; 4Q176 frg. 12–13, col. 1, line 15 (Wise, *Scrolls,* 234); see also the Kaddish.

[33] *Jub.* 25:11.

[34] E.g., *2 Bar.* 5:2.

[35] See Carson, *Discourse,* 178–79.

[36] *Pesiq. Rab Kah.* 2:7 (R. Judah bar R. Simon). For God "glorifying" Israel, cf. also *Tg. Isa.* 1:2; he both "sanctified" and "glorified" them in *Tg. Isa.* 5:2 (cf. John 17:17, 19).

[37] E.g., Gen 6:3, 12–13; Num 16:22; Ps 78:39; 145:21; Isa 40:5–6; 49:26; Jer 25:31; 45:5; Ezek 20:48; 21:4–5; Rom 3:20; *Jub.* 25:22; 1QS 11.9; CD 1.2; 2.20; 1QH 13.13, 16; 1QM 12.12; 4Q511 frg. 35, line 1 (probably); Sir 28:5; *T. Jud.* 19:4; *T. Zeb.* 9:7; *T. Ab.* 7:16B; *T. Job* 27:2/3. It also can include animals (e.g., Gen 9:16; Num 18:15; Ps 136:25; *Jub.* 5:2). Smith suggests an Isaian allusion, such as to Isa 40:5 (*John* [1999], 310), though "all flesh" is also common in Gen 6–9 and somewhat in Ezekiel.

[38] E.g., Bel and the Dragon 5.

[39] The Father also delegates some authority to others (see 19:11), but no such statement is comparable to the kinds of authority the Gospel attributes to Jesus. Reigning under God (Gen 1:26; Dan 7:14) is qualitatively different from the reign depicted for Jesus here; on the early Christian portrait of Jesus sharing God's sovereignty in a way granted to not even the highest angels, see Bauckham, *God Crucified,* 28–29.

John 17:3 continues the connection between the Father and the Son; eternal life, eschatological life, involves an intimate relationship with the Father and the Son (see discussion of "knowledge" in the introduction, ch. 6).[40] The connection between Jesus and the Father in 17:3 is very close. It is even grammatically possible to construe the dual object as a hendiadys, identifying Jesus Christ with "the only true God," but this construction is impossible both logically and from the standpoint of Johannine theology.[41] In John's theology, the Son is not the Father, and it is hardly coherent for Jesus to identify himself as the Father he was addressing. The close association, however, places Jesus in the role reserved for the Father (or at least divine Wisdom) in standard Jewish teaching. Besides 1:17, "a legitimate anachronism," 17:3 is the only instance in the Gospel in which "Christ" appears as part of a proper name and not simply a title.[42]

If any ambiguity remains concerning Jesus' identity in 17:3, it vanishes in 17:5, which affirms Jesus' preexistence with the Father in glory.[43] Jesus is not paralleled here primarily with Moses but with God's own revelation, presumably with Wisdom and Torah in early Jewish thought. Greek philosophers could speak of one's spirit returning to its prenatal existence at the body's death,[44] but such an image fits neither the language of this passage nor the worldview of the Gospel as a whole; likewise isolated Jewish examples of God keeping the names of his chosen ones with him[45] do not match the exalted image of this passage nor relate to the Christology of this Gospel.

The "glory" harks back to its first mention in the Gospel, in 1:14, where Jesus' disciples, like Moses, saw God's glory in Jesus; like Moses with respect to God, they will reveal Jesus' character as they reflect his glory (13:35; 15:8; cf. 2 Cor 3–4, esp. 4:6). Jesus' glory in the flesh expands the theology implicit in the Synoptic transfiguration tradition (Mark 9:2–8; Matt 17:1–8; Luke 9:28–36) or perhaps Paul's experience as reported in Acts (Acts 9:3; 22:6; 26:13). Both the transfiguration narratives and Paul's encounter as depicted in Acts reflect the tradition of God's glory revealed to Moses on Mount Sinai.[46]

This makes all the more likely that Jesus is here God's word or wisdom, with the disciples taking the place of Moses.

Although the relation between knowledge of God and eternal life (17:3; cf. 1 John 5:20) makes passable sense in a Hellenistic framework,[47] it also fits the covenantal use of "knowing God" in the biblical tradition (Jer 31:34; Hos 2:20).[48] Hellenistic Jewish wisdom had already identified knowing (ἐπίστασθαί, εἰδέναι) God and his power with righteousness and immortality (Wis 15:3). More may hinge on the ἵνα in 17:3; if one takes it in

---

[40] The identification of knowing God with immortality also appears in Wis 15:3 (DeSilva, "Wisdom of Solomon," 1274).

[41] On the possibility but unlikelihood, see also Harris, *Jesus as God*, 258–59.

[42] Ladd, *Theology*, 242–43. Some argue that v. 3, which interrupts the thought between the preceding and following verses, may reflect the author's parenthetical "targumic" commentary on eternal life in 17:2 (Blomberg, *Reliability*, 219). That it addresses the Father, however, may leave it unclear whether it is any more "targumic" than its context.

[43] As normally recognized, e.g., Stevens, *Theology*, 118.

[44] Epictetus *Diatr.* 2.1.17.

[45] 1QM 12.1 (in his כבודכה, "glorious," dwelling).

[46] On the transfiguration, see Keener, *Matthew*, 437; Moses, *Transfiguration Story*, 84–85.

[47] Philo also identifies eternal life with knowing God (Dodd, *Interpretation*, 65), albeit in a somewhat different sense.

[48] E.g., Ellis, *John*, 241–42. Hos 6:2–3 LXX probably even associates knowing God with the time of the resurrection (Dodd, *Interpretation*, 163); Driver, *Scrolls*, 545, compares 1QS 2.3.

its most frequent (and classical) sense as "in order that," knowing God would be the result of eternal life. This could be taken as corresponding to the more radical second-century gnostic ideologies, such as Valentinianism, where knowledge "is not only an instrument of salvation but itself the very form in which the goal of salvation, i.e., ultimate perfection, is possessed."[49] Such a view might, however, still equate knowledge with eternal life, which reading the grammatical construction in this manner would not. Further, a grammatical argument based on the classical force of ἵνα would be misleading; this construction in 17:3 may simply represent a Semitism[50] or, more likely, an example of the broadened use of conjunctions in Koine.[51] In this case it means "that" (e.g., 4:34; 6:29), which is how translators usually take it. Knowing God includes embracing his revelation in Christ, sharing his "things" (16:13–15; 17:14, 17), particularly an intimate relationship of love with him (17:25–26).[52]

That Jesus glorified the Father "on the earth" (17:4) refers to the whole of his earthly ministry. Jesus was not "of the earth" (3:31) but spoke in earthly analogies (3:12) and, in a sense, provided, to some degree, an earthly analogy in his incarnate life to explain the character of God in humanly comprehensible form; finally, he would be lifted up from the earth into glory (12:32).[53] In the cross, he finished the work the Father called him to do (cf. 4:34; 19:30), though his followers still need to be "completed" or perfected in unity (17:23).

His request for glorification in 17:5 repeats the thought of 17:1, except that it adds the notion of Jesus' precreation glory. This is no Jewish-Christian adaptation of the Hellenistic concept of apotheosis for heroes;[54] Jesus is not becoming God but returning to the glory he shared with the Father before creation. His preincarnate glory appears in 12:41, but his precreation glory harks back to the very opening of the Gospel (1:1–2), manifested in a way obscure to the people among whom he lived in the Gospel (1:10–11, 14).

## Prayer for the Disciples (17:6–24)

The prayer is arranged chronologically; after Jesus prays for himself in 17:1–5, he turns to prayer for his disciples.[55] Jesus' prayer for the disciples falls into two primary sections: his prayer for his current disciples (17:6–19, esp. 17:11–19) and his prayer for his future disciples (17:20–24; cf. this concern in 20:29–31). The first prayer primarily concerns protection from the evil one who works in the world into which they are sent but of which they are not a part (17:15); their separation from the world recalls Jesus' own, as in 15:18–25. The second prayer focuses on another issue apparently still paramount in John's day: the unity of believers, that the world might recognize Jesus' activity among them (17:21–23).

---

[49] Jonas, *Religion*, 35.

[50] Burney, *Origin*, 69; Black, *Approach*, 76–79.

[51] Bruce, *Books*, 66–67.

[52] Countryman, *Crossing*, 128–32, thinks the goal is to pass beyond mere believing (20:30–31) to knowing (17:3) to union with God. By contrast, the Gospel presents believing as a way to know, and faith as the Gospel's explicit purpose (20:30–31).

[53] That he died "on the earth" (12:24) may be relevant if John intends a double entendre, but this is not clear.

[54] One may compare Josephus's adaptation of apotheosis language (cf. Tabor, "Divinity"; Begg, "Disappearance").

[55] E.g., Carson, *John*, 557.

## 1. What Belongs to Jesus and the Father (17:6–10)

Jesus gives the Father's message to the disciples because he has the Father's message (17:6–8); likewise, Jesus has the disciples precisely because they, too, belong to the Father (presumably through divine ordination) and hence have been entrusted to the Son (17:9–10). This paragraph continues the emphasis on the solidarity and (still more so) the mutual sharing of the Father and the Son that is introduced in 17:1–5.

Jesus revealed to the disciples God's "name" (17:6), partly meaning his honor[56] but very probably also implying his character and identity (14:9; 17:26).[57] Acting by God's name could represent dependence on God (e.g., 1QM 11.3). When God acted in history, he often did so for the sanctifying of his name,[58] as he would do also at the final day.[59] God expected his people to sanctify his name (*kiddush haShem* was central to Jewish ethics), especially by righteous deeds.[60] Some rabbis opined that God's name was hidden in the present age but would be revealed in the coming age;[61] Jesus' revelation of the Father's name is thus consonant with John's emphasis on realized eschatology. Moses sought to know God's "name" to reveal God to the people (Exod 3:13; cf. 33:18; 34:6–7); here Jesus provides his disciples, who are like Moses, with the same privilege.[62] This experience would continue more fully after Jesus' glorification (14:21).

That Jesus' disciples kept the word he gave them (17:6; cf. 8:51; 14:23; 15:20), as Jesus kept the Father's (8:55), may recall the obedience of Moses but probably reflects more generally the obedience of Israel or a faithful remnant within Israel (Deut 33:3, 9).[63] Yet in giving them the Father's word (17:6, 8), Jesus is again greater than Moses, who gave the word to Israel; in John's language, the law was given "through" Moses, but the actual giver of the law was God himself (1:17; cf. 6:32); thus the passage again portrays Jesus in a divine role. At the same time, Jesus remains subordinate to the Father, emphasizing that whatever he gave the disciples was from the Father (17:7). Perhaps, in the language of Exodus, Jesus is the "angel of YHWH" (Exod 3:2), but in the language of John (1:1–18) and of the early Jewish context he reflects, Jesus is divine Wisdom, which imparts God's teachings to Moses and all those who will hear (e.g., Wis 7:27; 10:16; 11:1).

The disciples realized that all that the Father had given Jesus was genuinely from the Father (17:7), in this case referring especially to Jesus' message (17:8; cf. 12:47–50; 16:15). That the Father had "given" disciples to Jesus (17:9; also 17:24) reiterates a striking image in the Fourth Gospel. Early Judaism taught that Israel as a whole was predestined (see comment on 6:43–44), but like some other early Jewish Christian writers (e.g., Rom 9:6–32; Eph 1:4–5), John emphasizes the predestination of individuals in Christ through their faith in Christ. Jesus prays on behalf of the disciples (17:9) in a way

---

[56] People praised God's "name" (e.g., Tob 3:11; 11:14; Rev 15:4).

[57] Cf. Sanders, *John,* 369; Malina and Rohrbaugh, *John,* 247–48 (the name representing the person himself); *Did.* 10.

[58] E.g., 1QM 17.2; *Num. Rab.* 4:5.

[59] 1QM 11.14.

[60] E.g., *Num. Rab.* 4:6; 8:4; 12:21; *Ruth Rab.* proem 7; *Song Rab.* 2:7, §1; cf., e.g., *Sipre Deut.* 221.6.1; *b. Šabb.* 89b; *p. Sanh.* 3:5, §2. See further Urbach, *Sages,* 1:357–60, 444, 507, 2:283–84; Moore, *Judaism,* 2:101; Siegal, "Israel," 107.

[61] Dodd, *Interpretation,* 96.

[62] Cf. Enz, "Exodus," 213; Dowd, "Theology," 334 (comparing Moses and Jesus). Moses declares God's name, glorifying it, in Deut 32:3 (Glasson, *Moses,* 77).

[63] Glasson, *Moses,* 77.

that provides a model for how disciples will soon be authorized to pray for themselves in his name (16:26–27).

When Jesus says that "all things" (πάντα, neuter) that are his are also the Father's (17:10), underlining the point of 17:7, he merely repeats the general wisdom of 16:15; the Father and Son are so intimate that they share everything in common. Likewise, the Son by inheritance is a lord over the Father's house (cf. 8:35). In this context, he states this general principle to reinforce the more specific point of 17:9: the disciples for whom Jesus prays already belong to the Father as well as to himself (10:14, 28–29), and hence the Father will surely answer Jesus' prayer. Jesus is glorified in his followers (17:10; cf. 2 Thess 1:12) the same way the Father is: by their fruitfulness (15:8), especially by their love for one another (13:35) expressed in unity (17:21–23). Although the idea is less central to this chapter, he may also be glorified in their sufferings (21:19) and in their triumph following such sufferings (11:4; cf. 9:3).

## 2. Guarding His Own in the World (17:11–19)

Though Jesus was leaving the world (17:11), he was sending the disciples into the world just as the Father had sent him into the world (17:18). Nevertheless, because they had his message, they were not of the world (17:14) but were being set apart by that message (17:17) as Jesus was set apart (17:19). Those whom the Father gave Jesus (17:9–10) now are again in the Father's hands (17:11), except for the one destined to be lost (17:12).

### 2A. Separation from the World (17:11, 14–19)

Although Jesus was leaving, his disciples would remain "in the world" (17:11; cf. 13:1), which carried with it the attendant challenge to be "in the world" yet not "of it" (17:14–18)—a task Israel usually proved unable to fulfill when confronted by pagan practices around it. The address "Holy Father" (17:11) is not unexpected in an early Jewish milieu[64] but specifically fits this context: Jesus has been keeping the disciples separate from the world (17:12), and now the Father will continue to keep them set apart (17:11).[65] God is the measure of holiness (cf. Rev 4:8), and whatever is "holy" is "separated" to him (e.g., Exod 28:36; 30:10, 32, 36–37; 31:14–15; 39:30; Lev 21:6–8). The goal of their being kept from the world is that they may be "one" (17:11; cf. 10:16; see comment on 17:21–23). Separation from the world naturally produces internal community cohesion (see comment on 15:18–25), but here the idea seems to be that the common unity with the Father and the Son, apart from the world's quite contrary interests, yields unity among Jesus' followers (cf. 17:21–23).

Jesus "kept" the disciples from the world by God's name (17:11). The ἐν here is probably both locative and instrumental:[66] on the one hand, if the disciples are "in the world," they must be protected "in God's name";[67] on the other hand, God protects his people by

---

[64] Cf. "holy Lord" (*1 En.* 91:7); "holy God" (*Sib. Or.* 3.478). "Holy Father" became more popular in early Christian circles (*Did.* 10.2; *Odes Sol.* 31:5).

[65] Westcott, *John*, 243. On Jesus' holiness, see 6:69; 10:36; 17:19.

[66] With, e.g., Brown, *John*, 2:759.

[67] Robinson, "Destination," 122, suggests that John parallels Jesus with Jerusalem, where God's name would dwell (Deut 12:11). While such an observation might fit Johannine theology had one put the question to the author (cf. Rev 21:22), there is no direct indication of such a specific allusion in this text.

means of his name. As in Revelation, believers can remain faithful to God's name (e.g., Rev 2:3, 13; 3:8) and are marked off from the world by God's name, his symbol of authority over them (Rev 3:12; 14:1; 22:4; cf. 7:3; 13:17). In the Fourth Gospel, "keeping" (τηρεῖν) usually refers to God's commandments[68] but in 17:11, 12, 15 (cf. 1 John 5:18) refers to God keeping those who obey him, perhaps playing on the language of God keeping those who keep his word (cf. Rev 3:10). He keeps them in the face of the world's hostility (John 15:18–25).[69]

### 2B. The Apostate (17:12)

That Jesus lost none of his own in the first generation except one foreknown for apostasy (17:12) might encourage persecuted believers whose community had already experienced some defections (cf. 1 John 2:19); the point is important enough for John to reiterate it for his audience (18:9; cf. 6:37). Jesus protected them in part by laying down his life to prevent their death (explicitly in 18:8–9; cf. 10:15); given the weakness of the disciples (13:38; 18:25), preventing their arrest at this point may also have prevented their terminal apostasy. That John elsewhere emphasizes that Jesus had lost no sheep (10:11–12) and that, in fact, no one could seize them from his or his Father's hand (10:28–29) suggest that this was a matter of encouragement John felt his audience needed.

If the reconstruction of the Johannine community most commonly held today is correct in its basic contours, John may here encourage Jewish believers whose faith has been rendered less stable through the polemic of respected leaders in their synagogue communities. They had never considered that following Jesus might separate them from Israel, the people of God, and their opponents' claims that they had been separated from God's people may have shaken them. Throughout the Gospel, John therefore reminds them of Jesus' union with the Father, whom their opponents do not personally know; by union with Jesus, his followers are united with the Father and remain the people of God regardless of the views of some hostile synagogue officials (cf. Rev 3:8–9).

John's audience could be assured that neither those who left the community in John's day (1 John 2:29) nor Judas (6:64) took Jesus by surprise. As "son of destruction,"[70] the betrayer was destined or foreknown for his role (17:12). Jewish wisdom texts could call wicked Sodom "people of destruction" (ἔθνος ἀπωλείας), that is, "people for destruction" (Sir 16:9). The Dead Sea Scrolls speak of the wicked as "children of the pit" (השחת), that is, those destined for destruction (CD 6.15; 8.14); Jubilees also calls the wicked of past eras "children of destruction."[71] Perhaps most strikingly, at least one extant witness to early Christian tradition suggests that some Christians had already designated the anticipated "man of lawlessness"[72] as a "son of destruction" (2 Thess 2:3; cf. Rev 17:8). Just as many "antichrists" who opposed the true teaching about Christ could reflect the character of a future anticipated antichrist (1 John 2:18) and just as the Fourth Gospel emphasizes the eschatological condition of the present more frequently than future eschatology, Judas

---

[68] See comments in Vellanickal, *Sonship*, 280–81.

[69] Kysar, *John*, 258–59.

[70] Rhetoricians classified such substitution of descriptive titles as antonomasia (Rowe, "Style," 128, citing Cicero *Consil.* 4.9; Porter, "Paul and Letters," 579, citing Rom 5:14; Anderson, *Glossary*, 23, citing Quintilian 8.6.29–30).

[71] *Jub.* 10:3; 15:26. Greeks and Romans recognized that some offenses, including betrayal (here, of one's people), could merit punishment in the afterlife (Sallust *Speech of Gaius Cotta* 3).

[72] For discussion of this figure, see, e.g., Keener, *Matthew*, 573–75.

functions as a paradigm for human evil.[73] Because Judas probably also provides a model for apostate members of the community (cf. 6:66–71; as does the antichrist, 1 John 2:18–19), this association casts apostates in a very negative light (cf. 15:6).

Opponents of John's audience may have complained about what appeared to them an inconsistency in the gospel tradition: Jesus is omniscient, yet he chose a disciple who ultimately betrayed him. John is at pains to point out that Jesus foreknew the betrayer, whose role was part of God's plan (6:64, 71; 13:21, 26, 27); in support of such a thesis is the point that the only disciple whom Jesus lost was, in fact, the betrayer himself. John reinforces this point by informing his audience that the loss of the betrayer fulfilled Scripture (17:12) and hence was necessary because, as even their opponents recognized, Scripture cannot be broken (10:35). The necessity of a betrayer might be inferred simply from Scripture concerning Jesus' suffering (cf., e.g., 19:24, 28, 36–37; 20:9), but "Scripture" here probably alludes to the passage already cited in 13:18 about the betrayer. It is not necessary to find a text that directly mentions a "son of destruction."[74] When John later refers back to this text, however, it is not only that Scripture (the Hebrew Bible or its Greek translations) might be fulfilled but also that the "word" of Jesus might be fulfilled (18:9); for John, both are God's message.

### 2C. Their Joy May Be Full (17:13)

As Jesus prepares to leave, he speaks "these things" that their joy might be full (17:13), implying that his words (coupled with the second Paraclete, 14:16–17, 26) function as a surrogate for his bodily presence as the Word among them. At first, one might think that he refers solely to the words of the immediate context, namely, the prayer.[75] But ταῦτα consistently refers to the whole message he has been giving his disciples (13:17, 21; 14:24; 15:17; 16:1, 4, 6, 25, 33),[76] including in the immediate context (17:1; probably 18:1). Most important, the words that bring fulness of joy (17:13) must include his earlier words to them (15:11).

### 2D. God Preserves Believers from the Evil One (17:14–17)

Because they, like Jesus, are not from the world (e.g., 8:23), the disciples share with Jesus in being objects of the world's hatred (17:14; 15:18). Because of this, Jesus prays further for the Father to "keep" them, that is, to preserve them, from the evil one (17:15).[77] Such preservation does not involve removal from the world and its hatred (17:15) but protection from succumbing to the designs of the evil one (cf. Matt 6:13).[78] (The substantive use of "evil" often points to Satan.)[79] Other Jewish pietists praised God for "keeping" or

---

[73] Many commentators suspect that John adapted this figure to realized eschatology (e.g., Lightfoot, *Gospel*, 301; Glasson, *Moses*, 109; Freed, *Quotations*, 97; Best, *Thessalonians*, 285), though cf. the correct caution of Quast, *Reading*, 115.

[74] *Pace* Freed, *Quotations*, 97, who therefore cites Prov 24:22a, though (p. 96) he thinks an allusion back to Jesus' own words in 6:70–71 is more likely (despite ἡ γραφή).

[75] E.g., Carson, *Discourse*, 192, favors this position, but only very tentatively.

[76] We leave aside uses of ταῦτα in the discourse that refer to others (15:21; 16:3).

[77] Cf. similarly 1 John 5:18; Rev 3:10. Prayers for protection from demons (e.g., *Tg. Ps.-J.* on Num 6:24) became common, especially as popular demonological speculation grew.

[78] This could echo the close of the Lord's Prayer (e.g., Bury, *Logos-Doctrine*, 69) but need not do so. On similar Jewish prayers for deliverance in testing, see Jeremias, *Prayers*, 105.

[79] *Jub.* 50:5; Matt 13:19, 38; Eph 6:16; 2 Thess 3:3; for rhetorical use of antonomasia, see comment on 17:12. The other Johannine texts (1 John 2:13–14; 3:12; 5:18–19) are particularly relevant.

"guarding" them from those who would destroy them.[80] Wisdom, too, was said to "keep" or "guard" God's servants (e.g., various forms of φυλάσσω, τηρέω, and their cognates in Wis 9:11; 10:1, 5).

Believers must be "kept" because they are "in the world" (17:11, 16), yet they are not "of" the world (17:14).[81] They reflect the character of Jesus rather than that of the world (15:1–17) and hence are in conflict with the world (15:18–25). This is a separation of values, not of geography. Whereas the Qumran community was to remain physically separate from outsiders (1QS 5.18; 9.8–9; CD 13.14–15)—especially practical for the wilderness Essenes—the separation of Johannine believers is an internal rather than a geographical one.[82]

That God's "truth" was also his word or law fits early Jewish thought about the law (cf. Ps 119:142, 151, 160).[83] Jewish tradition recognized that God had sanctified Israel, that is, set Israel apart for himself;[84] some early texts associate this setting apart with God's commandments.[85] Jewish blessings regularly praised God for sanctifying his people through the commandments he had given them; these blessings usually included a reaffirmation of the particular commandment the person was fulfilling.[86] Priests were consecrated to God in a special way, not given land to till (Deut 18:1–5) that they might devote themselves undistracted to God's work. Most of all, disciples would be set apart like Jesus, who was consecrated wholly for the Father's purposes (10:36), pursuing wholly the agendas from above alien to the world. Jesus' word had set his disciples apart (17:17) and cleansed them (15:3) if they, like those who offered these blessings for God's commandments, obeyed the word in practice (13:17).[87] John may allude to Jesus himself (cf. 1:1–18) as well as his spoken words as the message through which God would set them apart more fully;[88] his own presence was mediated through his words (12:47–48) and his disciples' witness for him (16:7–15).

This text presupposes that God's word is already set apart.[89] In 10:36, Jesus declares that the Father set him apart before sending him into the world; in 17:19, he consecrates himself again so they may be consecrated in truth—perhaps meaning in himself (14:6).[90] For God to make his people holy was to make them like himself (17:11; cf. Lev 11:44–45; 1 Pet 1:16).[91] John's idea of holiness is not, however, physical separation from the world so

---

[80] E.g., 1QM 14.10 (שׁמרתה).

[81] *Diogn.* 6 echoes John 17:14 but interprets it in a platonizing direction.

[82] It appears symbolic even in Rev 12:6, where it alludes to the exodus.

[83] E.g., *2 Bar.* 44:14; cf. *1 En.* 99:2.

[84] E.g., *Jub.* 22:29; 30:8; 1QS 8.21; 9.6; 1QM 14.12; Wis 18:9; 3 Macc 6:3; *Exod. Rab.* 15:24; cf. 1QM 9.8–10; 1 Cor 1:2; *1 Clem.* 1.1.

[85] E.g., *Jub.* 2:19, 21; 15:27. Among later texts, see, e.g., *b. Ber.* 33b.

[86] E.g., *t. Ber.* 5:22; 6:9, 10, 13, 14; *b. Ber.* 51a, *bar.;* 60b; *Pesaḥ.* 7b; *Šabb.* 137b; *p. Sukkah* 3:4, §3; *Pesiq. Rab.* 3:2; also noted by many commentators (e.g., Hoskyns, *Gospel,* 502). Some think "sanctify" here is a verbal link with the Lord's Prayer (e.g., Fenton, *John,* 176), but it seems to have been a frequent motif in early Jewish prayers.

[87] The sanctification is "worked out in their doing of the truth" (Morris, *John,* 730).

[88] As Smith, *John* (1999), 315, notes, the prologue sets the stage for the rest of the Gospel, including 17:17. Suggit, "LOGOS," finds a title for Jesus here, citing in support also various early Christian texts.

[89] A later blessing recited before reading Torah praised God for sanctifying Torah (R. Eleazar reports earlier tradition in *Pesiq. Rab Kah.* Sup. 1:2; cf. *Deut. Rab.* 11:6); or one praised God again for sanctifying his people by his commandments (*b. Ber.* 11b). God sanctifies the law and delights in those who obey it.

[90] Brown, *John,* 2:762, parallels Jesus' holiness with the Father (17:11).

[91] Thus Brown, *John,* 2:761, finds an echo in 17:17 of "holy" Father in 17:11.

much as it is separation from the world's values; like Jesus, the disciples were "sent into the world" (17:18; cf. 20:21).[92]

### 3. Prayer for Unity of Later Disciples (17:20–24)

As Jesus had prayed for his first disciples rather than the world (17:9), now he prayed for his future disciples (17:20)—generations like John's own (cf. 16:2). Others would believe through the first witnesses' message (17:20) and be sanctified through that message (17:17). These subsequent believers should remain united with other believers, particularly the apostolic founders (17:21), so the world might believe (17:21, 23). Jesus' mission was to glorify the Father by the cross (17:1–5); he yearned for his disciples to display God's glory through unity (17:22–24).

The evangelist especially wishes his audience to overhear 17:20: the prayer for unity concerns not merely the first generation but their own generation as well, just as their generation's faith will be rewarded even more than that of the first generation (20:29–31).[93] Subsequent generations would believe through the first generation's "word" (17:20), thus sanctifying them as well (17:17); their "word" was God's own word, Jesus himself mediated through the witness of the disciples (see comment on 16:7–11).[94] The witnesses in the Fourth Gospel, from John the Baptist to the disciples to the Samaritan woman, thus become a bridge to, as well as a paradigm for, the faith of John's audience.

This renders all the more relevant for John's audience Jesus' specific prayer on their behalf: unity for the sake of their witness. Just as the unity of Father and Son was central to John's apologetic (one thus dare not oppose the Son while claiming loyalty to the Father, 10:30), the unity of believers is at the heart of John's vision for believers (10:16; 11:52; 17:11, 21–23). The Fourth Gospel equipped John's audience with an apologetic approach from Scripture but most of all summoned them to invite the open-minded to "come and see" (1:39, 46; 4:29, 39–42), which in their day must have included the questioning to experience the presence of Jesus living among his followers by the Spirit. This presence of Jesus would be experienced through prophetic proclamation (16:7–11) but also through the mutual love of the disciples, who thus revealed Jesus' character (13:34–35; 15:8–12). The way believers treat one another is an essential component of proclaiming Jesus to the world.[95] Indeed, if one compares this prayer with Jesus' earlier prayer in 11:42, one finds that the unity of believers provides the same kind of witness concerning Jesus' origin as Jesus' raising of Lazarus (ὅτι σύ με ἀπέστειλας, 11:42; 17:23).

It is noteworthy that when the prayer turns to generations after those of the first disciples, the mention of unity (17:11) becomes a central emphasis (17:21–23). Whereas the "world" was divided (e.g., 7:43; 9:16; 10:19; 12:42–43), Jesus' followers were to be cohesive (13:34–35; 17:21–23).[96] Disunity characterized the broader culture as a whole.[97] Intercity

---

[92] As Ridderbos, *John,* 557, suggests, John's primary dualism is a moral dualism created by the world's alienation from God; yet even then it remains the object of God's saving love.

[93] The emphasis throughout this prayer on the unity of believers probably points to a need for unity among believers in, and in the proximity of, John's audience (cf. Käsemann, *Testament,* 57).

[94] Cf. Minear, "Audience," 345, 348.

[95] Robinson, *Coming,* 179, thinks this the Johannine equivalent of worldwide evangelism in Mark 13:10; Matt 24:14.

[96] Sectarian groups tend to be cohesive; for comparison and contrast between unity here and that in the Qumran Scrolls, see de Wet, "Unity."

[97] This is not to attribute to Greeks an individualistic concept that transcended group loyalties; see Martin, "Ideology."

rivalries, for example, were common.[98] Writers and speakers emphasized the need for unity for the state,[99] for armies,[100] for families,[101] and so forth, and the dangers of disunity;[102] they might praise those who made peace.[103] Personal enmity was standard in partisan politics[104] but also extended to matters such as favored teachers[105] and literary competition.[106] Sometimes, however, enemies could be reconciled.[107]

Although a unity rooted in love would address other issues as well, one matter of unity the Gospel surely addresses is ethnic unity. The emphasis on the Samaritans' ready acceptance of Jesus points in this direction (4:39–42), as does Jesus' objective of "one flock," probably referring to the influx of Gentile Christians to follow (10:16; cf. 11:52). Unity also challenges the secessionists of 1 John.

John 17:22–23 repeats and amplifies the basic thoughts of 17:21: Jesus wants the disciples to be one as he and the Father are one that the world may recognize the divine origin of both Jesus and his disciples.[108] Beasley-Murray notes that the Qumran community "called themselves the unity" but sought unity between themselves and angelic saints above, whereas in John the unity is rooted in God's work in Christ.[109] The church has already "achieved in Christ" the miracle of unity, as in Gal 3:28, though in practice the early church clearly continued to experience divisions (Acts 6:1; 3 John 9–12);[110] believers must work to keep the unity of the Spirit that Christ established. But in any case, the loving unity between the Father and the Son provides a model for believers, not necessarily a metaphysical, mystical ground for it.[111] Jesus and the Father mutually indwell each other (17:21; also 10:38; 14:10); by Jesus dwelling in them and with the Father dwelling in him (cf. also 14:23), Jesus' followers would experience God's presence in such a way that unity would be the necessary result (17:23). John would probably view the inability of believers to walk in accord with one another as, first of all, a failure to accede to the demands of the divine presence both share.

---

[98] Heraclitus *Ep.* 9; Babrius 15.5–9; Herodian 3.2.7–8; Yamauchi, *Archaeology,* 164–65; Ramsay, *Cities,* 115; cf. Dionysius of Halicarnassus *R.A.* 1.36.2–3; *Rhet. ad Herenn.* 3.3.4; *Gen. Rab.* 34:15.

[99] E.g., Dionysius of Halicarnassus *R.A.* 7.53.1; Livy 2.33.1; 5.7.10; 24.22.1, 13, 17; Seneca *Ep. Lucil.* 94.46; Musonius Rufus 8, p. 64.13; Maximus of Tyre *Or.* 16.3; Menander Rhetor 2.3, 384.23–25; some thinkers even applied this globally (cf. Whitacre, *John,* 417; Keener, *Revelation,* 341). In early Christianity, cf. 1 Cor 1:10; 11:18–19; Phil 2:1–2; 4:2.

[100] Babrius 85.

[101] Valerius Maximus 2.6.8 (spoken to children and grandchildren by one about to die, as in testaments).

[102] E.g., Homer *Il.* 1.255–258; Livy 2.60.4; 3.66.4; Sallust *Jug.* 73.5; Herodian 8.8.5; Babrius 44.7–8; 47.

[103] E.g., Homer *Od.* 1.369–371; Iamblichus *V.P.* 7.34; 9.45.

[104] E.g., Sallust *Jug.* 73.5; Plutarch *Sulla* 4.4; 7.1; Aulus Gellius 6.19.6; Cornelius Nepos 7 (Alcibiades), 4.1; 25 (Atticus), 7.1–11.6.

[105] See esp. Winter, *Philo and Paul,* passim.

[106] E.g., Aulus Gellius 17.4.3–6; Plutarch *Cimon* 8.7. Note the need for self-defense in most of Terence's prologues (e.g., *Lady of Andros* 1–27; *Self-Tormentor* 16–52; *Eunuch* 1–45; *Phormio* 1–23; *Mother-in-Law* 1–57; *Brothers* 1–25) and in Phaedrus 2.9.7–11; 3.prol.23; 4.prol.15–16.

[107] See Valerius Maximus 4.2 passim.

[108] For the parallelism, see, e.g., Brown, *John,* 2:769; Appold, *Motif,* 157, though the alleged parallel between 17:20 and 17:22a is unconvincing.

[109] Beasley-Murray, *John,* 302.

[110] Ibid., 307.

[111] Pamment, "17:20–23." Contrast the oneness *(unum)* of Stoic writers, who tended toward pantheism (Seneca *Ep. Lucil.* 95.52).

Jesus receives glory (17:22, 24) and gives it to believers (17:22) that they may glorify God (cf. 17:21, 23; 15:8);[112] if they are to glorify God as Jesus does, however (17:4), they must love him and one another to the extent that he did, to the point of death (21:19 with 12:32–33). As in Paul's theology, believers who would share Jesus' glory must first share his suffering (Rom 8:18; 2 Cor 4:17; cf. Eph 3:13; 2 Thess 1:5–6, 10). Jesus shared with them teaching (17:14) and everything he had received from the Father (15:15), as the Spirit continues to mediate to believers (16:13–15). Now Jesus says that he has shared with his disciples God's "glory" (17:22); this statement directly fulfills 1:14, for the glory that Moses could see only in part the disciples now witness in full (see comment on 1:14–18). The law was given through Moses, but the full revelation of God's character is given to the disciples in Jesus Christ (1:17).[113] Believers who walk in this revelation of God's character cannot divide from one another (17:22).

The great love of the Father and the Son for believers is a staple of early Christianity in general (Rom 8:37) and of the Johannine tradition in particular (e.g., 14:21; 16:27; cf. 1 John 3:1; Rev 3:9). Nevertheless, that the Father loved Jesus' disciples "even as" (καθώς) he loved Jesus (17:23) is one of the most remarkable statements of the Gospel, given the enormity of God's love for his uniquely obedient Son (3:35; 5:20; 10:17).[114] Yet this depiction of the measure of God's love toward believers is consonant with the emphasis that God demonstrated his love for the world by sending his Son to die for it (3:16). Jewish tradition celebrated God's love for Israel, but some Tannaim found inconceivable the notion that God would love Israel more than the first patriarchs.[115] God's love for Jesus' followers is of the same character as his love for his unique Son, Jesus—so that in the end, *all* of Jesus' true disciples become "beloved disciples."[116] One might think that "completed" in unity suggests that such unity is a goal rather than a presupposition for believers (cf. 4:34; 17:4); but one might conversely take the perfect tense of the participle to suggest an established reality stemming from the divine indwelling (17:23), so that believers need merely guard a unity already accomplished by Christ (as in Eph 4:3). In either case, the sense would be the same in practice: Christ's indwelling produces the unity among his followers, and believers must therefore walk accordingly.

Jesus wants the disciples to dwell with him where he is (17:24), that is, in the Father's presence (14:3–6).[117] The Father had given Jesus both the disciples and Jesus' own glory (17:24), and Jesus wanted the disciples to dwell in his presence, beholding his glory. The image is eschatological (e.g., Rev 21:11, 23) but, in John's emphasis on realized eschatology and especially in light of 14:1–3, emphasizes disciples beholding Jesus' glory in the present. They beheld his preexistent glory (12:41; 17:5)[118] during his earthly ministry (1:14; 2:11;

---

[112] Cf. Kysar, *Maverick Gospel*, 100.

[113] See esp. Epp, "Wisdom," 144.

[114] The Father's love for the Son before the "foundation of the world" (17:24) is equivalent to "in the beginning" (1:1–2; cf. 9:32; καταβολή in Matt 13:35; Luke 11:50; Heb 4:3; 9:26; it often appears in the NT in predestinarian contexts, such as Rev 13:8; 17:8; Matt 25:34; Eph 1:4; 1 Pet 1:20); they shared glory before the world began (17:5).

[115] *Sipre Deut.* 97.2, on Deut 14:2.

[116] With Beck, *Paradigm*, 132 (following Kurz, "Disciple," 102), which he rightly takes (pp. 133–36) as evidence for reader identification with the beloved disciple.

[117] This refers to the experience of the Spirit, not merely to heaven after death (*pace*, e.g., Witherington, *Wisdom*, 271).

[118] Even Glasson's moderately worded connection with Moses' preexistent mission in *As. Mos.* 1:14 (*Moses*, 77; cf. Bernard, *John*, 2:580, based on a few words) is too far from the mark; the

8:54; 11:4) and would continue to do so through the Spirit (16:14; cf. 7:39). Undoubtedly this means that they would continue to experience his glory through the Spirit's testimony as they continued to recite his acts of glory in the gospel tradition (14:26); it also implies continuing revelation of Jesus to the disciples through the Spirit (16:13–15).[119]

## Conclusion: Making God Known (17:25–26)

The world had not known God though knowing him was eternal life (17:3); but because Jesus knew the Father and the disciples knew that Jesus represented the Father (17:25), Jesus would make the Father known to the disciples that God might enjoy an intimate, loving relationship with them by Jesus dwelling in them (17:25; cf. 10:14–15).

The "holy" Father (17:11) is also the "righteous" Father (17:25; cf. 1 John 1:9),[120] perfectly just (7:24; 16:8, 10; cf. Rev 15:3), and the one who can put his own people in the right.[121] John climaxes on a summation (17:25–26): Jesus had revealed the Father to them[122] to provide them an intimate, loving relationship with him and one another. As Carson puts it:

> Jesus' departure does not have as its goal the abandonment of the disciples to solitary isolation. Far from it: his goal is to sweep up those the Father has given him into the richness of the love that exists among the persons of the triune God.[123]

Disciples' intimacy with the Father is mediated through Jesus (14:6), but because of their immediacy with Jesus, they also have immediate contact with the Father (16:26–27). Because their direct relationship with the Father and the Son is a central theme of the final discourse, its centrality for the Gospel as a whole cannot be overestimated. John encourages his community that their very relationship with the God of their ancestors testifies that they, and not their accusers, are heirs of Israel's covenant promises.

---

preexistence here is divine (Barrett, *John*, 514), the sort of preexistent glory attributed to Wisdom and Torah (see comment on 1:1–2).

[119] The long discourse of chs. 13–17 concludes with a note that Jesus had "said these things" (18:1), a familiar way for a narrator to close a discourse (*Jub.* 32:20; 50:13; Musonius Rufus 8, p. 66.26; Acts 20:36; it becomes standard in Matthew—7:28; 11:1; 13:53; 19:1; 26:1; cf. Keener, *Matthew*, 256).

[120] Cf. *1 En.* 90:40 ("Lord of righteousness," which could be rendered "righteous Lord"). This was appropriate for a ruler (cf. Prov 20:28; 25:5); cf. the address to Ptolemy (βασιλεῦ δίκαιε) in *Let. Aris.* 46.

[121] See Painter, *John*, 61. Cf. Isa 1:27; 56:1; 58:8; 1QS 10.11; 11.2, 5, 9, 12–14; 1QH 4.29–32, 36–37; Przybylski, *Righteousness*, 37–38; in the LXX and elsewhere, see Stendahl, *Paul*, 31; Dahl, *Paul*, 99; Piper, *Justification*, 90–96; in the rabbis, e.g., *Gen. Rab.* 33:1; *Ruth Rab.* proem 1.

[122] Barrett, *John and Judaism*, 73, notes that "knowledge and the sending of the heavenly emissary," which appear in 17:25, are "the most significant Gnostic themes"; but they are too common (and the gnostic redeemer too late) for this observation to prove relevant (see our introduction).

[123] Carson, *Discourse*, 206

# 18:1–20:31

# THE PASSION AND RESURRECTION

Here the Fourth Gospel's conflict theme climaxes, and the narrative concretely illustrates Jesus' teaching about his glorification and the world's hostility and its being on trial before God (cf. 16:1–12; 17:1–5).[1] This part of the Gospel reveals most plainly Jesus' glory (1:14; 12:23–24), the narrative fulfillment of the theme of God's sacrificial love in 3:16–18, and the meaning of the world's rejection (1:10–11; 3:19–21). The Passion Narrative likewise invites Jesus' disciples to join in his sufferings. John presents Jesus' sacrifice immediately after its interpretation in terms of his obedience to the Father and his experience of the world's hatred as a model for disciples.

---

[1] On the real trial being that of Pilate and the Jerusalem aristocracy, see, e.g., Reid, "Trial"; Van der Watt and Voges, "Elemente." Cf. Euripides *Bacch.* 500–508, 515–518, cited earlier.

# THE PASSION

## 18:1–19:42

T
HE "HOUR" JESUS ANNOUNCED as early as 2:4 has arrived; Jesus is the paschal lamb that
John announced in 1:29. Peter Ellis suggests that John's Passion Narrative fits a chiastic
structure, as follows:[1]

A   Arrested *in a garden, bound* and led to trial (18:1–12)
    B   *True high priest* tried; *beloved disciple* present (18:13–27)
        C   Jesus, king of Israel, judged by Pilate, rejected by his people (18:28–19:16)
    B'  *True high priest* carries wood of his own sacrifice (like Isaac); *beloved disciple* present
        (19:17–30)
A'  *Bound* with burial clothes, buried *in a garden* (19:31–42)

Because many of the features on which he focuses to achieve this structure are so secondary and because the units may be adapted to suit the proposed structure, the suggested chiasmus ultimately proves less than persuasive. It does, however, evidence some patterns that
point to the narrative artistry of their designer.

More persuasive is the observation by Ellis and others that irony pervades the narrative. Thus Judas who went forth into "the night" in 13:30 now returns in darkness to arrest
the light of the world; Pilate the governor questions if Jesus is a king when the readers
know that he is; Pilate demands, "What is truth?" when the readers know that Jesus is
(14:6); the soldiers hail Jesus as "king of the Jews" in mockery, unaware that Jesus truly is
the king of Israel (1:49), whose lifting up on the cross must introduce his reign.[2]

## Historical Tradition in the Passion Narrative

We must address some preliminary issues concerning John's narratives and the history
behind them (especially as preserved in the Synoptics) before examining the specific texts in
John 18–19.[3] Where John diverges from the traditions reported in the Synoptics, we do think
likely that John adapts rather than contradicts the passion sequence on which they are based,
probably at least sometimes on the basis of other traditions and probably at least sometimes
for a measure of theological symbolism. Although, on the whole, we think John essentially
independent from the Synoptics, the Passion Narrative is different; John's audience probably
already knows the basic passion story from other sources (cf. 1 Cor 11:23–25). Their prior
knowledge would not render John's version of the story any less intriguing to his audience,
however: stories were told repeatedly in the ancient Mediterranean, and a good story could

---

[1] Ellis, *Genius*, 247. For the garden *inclusio*, see also Malina and Rohrbaugh, *John*, 249.
[2] Ibid., 248.
[3] Most of this section has been adapted from Keener, *Matthew*, 607–11.

build suspense even if one knew the final outcome.[4] John's very adaptations, at least wherever they might diverge from the traditions commonly known among his ideal audience, invite his audience's special attention. Where theological symbolism guides his adaptations, it is generally in the service of Christology: Jesus is the Passover lamb (cf. 1:29), who lays down his life freely (10:17–18).

## 1. The Genre of the Passion Narratives

First we should address the genre ancient readers may have recognized in the Passion Narrative. Naturally, in the Gospels readers would approach it as a common part of ancient biographies, but we must also ask about the independent passion narrative (or, perhaps more likely, various passion narrations) that stands behind this portion of the Gospels.

Because both address the unjust death of the righteous, the passion narratives repeat some themes also appearing in martyr stories (e.g., 2 Macc 6–7; Wis 2:12–20),[5] as many scholars have properly emphasized.[6] Ancient moralists and historians praised honorable and heroic deaths, whether within or beyond martyr stories.[7] Writers may have also drawn on a stock arsenal of motifs when expanding martyr stories for dramatic purposes.[8] At the same time, analogous story lines illustrate the nuances with which an ancient audience would have heard the story, but need not demonstrate dependence or genetic relationship. Those who stood against the establishment regularly invited repression.

Important as comparisons with martyr stories are for analysis of the texts, the comparisons contain some limitations. Apart from the fact that both martyr stories and Gospel passion narratives involve a righteous person's unjust death, the parallels may be inadequate to place the Gospel passion stories fully in this genre, especially given the differences.[9] Some features characteristic of martyr stories, such as betrayal, refusal to compromise, and sentencing,[10] reflect the common pattern of ancient law and Jewish resilience rather than the borrowing of motifs. This is not to deny that the *recording* of such details augments the hortatory value of the narratives. For example, prior Greek thought readily supplied for Greeks intelligibility to an atoning-martyr tradition,[11] widespread

---

[4] For the use of climax in rhetoric, see *Rhet. ad Herenn.* 4.34–35.

[5] Cf. Sisti, "Figura"; *Acts of the Alexandrian Martyrs*, in *CPJ* 2:55–107, §§154–159.

[6] E.g., Dibelius, *Tradition*, 201; Donahue, "Temple," 65–66; Weeden, *Mark*, 66; Nickelsburg, "Genre"; Aune, *Environment*, 52–53; Robbins, *Jesus*, 173, 188). The tradition places Jesus especially within the rejected-prophet tradition (cf. Robbins, *Jesus*, 186).

[7] Epameinondas 2 in Plutarch *S.K., Mor.* 192C; cf. accounts of Socrates' brave end (Xenophon *Apol.* 1).

[8] Compare, e.g., the mother in Maccabean accounts with the Spartan mother Argileonis in Plutarch *S.S.W., Mor.* 240C. Cf. Robbins, *Jesus*, 185, following Nickelsburg, "Genre," 156, on the tradition of a righteous sufferer vindicated by God.

[9] Boring et al., *Commentary*, 156, lists contrasts with the Maccabean martyr accounts: the Gospels avoid sensationalistic details, interpretive speeches by Jesus, a Stoic lesson contrasting reason with emotions (Plutarch *W.V.S.C.U.* 2; 4 Macc 8:15; though this feature says more about the social context of the Maccabean audience than about any larger genre per se), and "vengeful threats."

[10] Boring et al., *Commentary*, 152. On the diversity of Jewish martyr stories, see van Henten, "Prolegomena."

[11] Cf. Robbins, *Jesus*, 187, following Williams, *Death*, 137–254. The concept of atonement in general appears in the Hebrew Bible and the ancient Near East (e.g., Gurney, *Aspects*, 48) and is widespread in apparently unrelated cultures.

among first-century Jews as well.[12] To a lesser degree, the ancient Mediterranean champion tradition might also provide a context for the concept.[13] More specifically, early Jewish Christians probably drew on the Isaian Servant Songs, which came to be widely applied to Jesus (e.g., Matt 12:17–21; Acts 8:32–35).[14]

Of the other motifs both share, many are no more distinctively characteristic of martyr stories than of other ancient literature. For example, where possible, Diogenes Laertius ends his discussions of the lives of eminent philosophers with their death.[15] Martyr stories, of course, could vindicate their protagonist's devotion and so packed more impact than other death accounts; a legendary figure might even receive a legendary martyrdom.[16]

Nevertheless, barely anyone would suggest that Jesus' execution was merely fabricated to fit this genre; early Christians had every reason to avoid fabricating a story that would bring them into repeated conflict with Roman authorities and their own Jewish elite. Further, most biographies that reported their subjects' death did not conclude with martyrdom, and nearly all scholars concur, with good reason, that the basic kerygma arose shortly after Jesus' execution. Jewish accounts stress martyrdom as an example of commitment, but despite the use of Jesus' death as a model in the Gospel narratives (12:23–33), summaries of the earliest gospel (e.g., 1 Cor 15:3–4) suggest their very early kerygmatic function as well. In other words, martyr stories may explain the form in which some cohesive passion narrative or narratives circulated, but would not indicate their composition as fiction.

Theissen thus concludes his own analysis: "There is no analogy to the Passion narrative in all of ancient literature. Elements of Hellenistic acts of the martyrs and Jewish tales of martyrdom have been melded into something quite new."[17] If he overstates their uniqueness from a formal standpoint, he nevertheless corrects an overemphasis on parallels that explain less than some other scholars would claim. The vast majority of ancient biographies concluded with the subject's death, funeral, and related events.[18] Many biographies focused a significant amount of space on the conclusion of their subjects' lives, especially if the end was central to the subject's achievements.[19]

If the Passion Narrative is not simply a martyr story, neither is it a typical Greek apotheosis story; the focus in the Synoptic Gospels is on Jesus' mortal suffering, not a

---

[12] See 4 Macc 6:27–30; 9:7, 24; 17:21–22; cf. 1 Macc 2:50; 2 Macc 7:9, 37; 1QS 8.3–4; *T. Mos.* 9; *Mek. Pisha* 1.105–113; *b. Ber.* 62b; *Gen. Rab.* 44:5; *Lev. Rab.* 20:12; *Song Rab.* 1:15, §2; 4:1, §2. On vicarious atonement through other humans' judgment, e.g., *Sipre Deut.* 333.5.2; without human bloodshed, cf., e.g., Lev 1:4; 4:20, 26, 31, 35, and passim; *Mek. Bah.* 7.18–22; *Sipre Deut.* 1.10.2; *p. Hor.* 2:7, §1; 3:2, §10; *Šebu.* 1:6, §6; *Pesiq. Rab Kah.* 24:17; *Eccl. Rab.* 9:7, §1; without mention of any bloodshed, e.g., Prov 16:6; Sir 3:14–15; *Pss. Sol.* 3:8–10; 1QS 9.4; *b. Ber.* 17a; *Num. Rab.* 14:10; *Deut. Rab.* 3:5.

[13] E.g., Homer *Il.* 3.69–70, 86–94, 253–255; 7.66–91, 244–273; Apollonius of Rhodes 2.20–21; Dionysius of Halicarnassus *R.A.* 3.12.3–4; Virgil *Aen.* 10.439–509; 11.115–118, 217–221; 12.723–952; Livy 1.24.1–1.25.14; 7.9.8–7.10.14; Aulus Gellius 9.13.10; also in the Hebrew Bible (1 Sam 17; 2 Sam 2:14–16; cf. Gordon, *Civilizations*, 262).

[14] Cf., e.g., Jeremias, *Theology*, 292–93; Davies and Allison, *Matthew*, 3:95–97; other references in Keener, *Matthew*, 487, on 20:28.

[15] E.g., with Cleanthes in 7.5.176.

[16] Cf. the end of *Life of Aesop*, in Drury, *Design*, 29.

[17] Theissen, *Gospels*, 123.

[18] Burridge, *Gospels*, 146–47, 179–80. The rest of the Gospels foreshadow this climax, and this is also the case in some contemporary biographies (p. 199).

[19] Ibid., 198, has 26 percent for Philostratus; Mons Graupius consumes 26 percent of Tacitus *Agricola*, and the Persian campaign 37 percent of Plutarch *Agesilaus* (p. 199).

promotion to divinity.[20] In the Fourth Gospel, however, one may come closer to apotheosis (except for the claim that Jesus was already deity!) than in the Synoptics; his Passion Narrative underlines Jesus' control of the situation (18:4–9; cf. 10:18; 13:26–27). Mark 15:38–39 probably implies a sort of hidden theophany, and Matt 27:51–54 a more explicit one. Jesus suffers, but the focus of his mortality in John is more explicitly theophanic; in his death he is glorified (12:23–24). One might symbolically summarize the difference between Mark's passion and John's in Jesus' closing recorded words in each, whether "My God, my God, why have you forsaken me?" (Mark 15:34) or a triumphant "It has been completed!" (John 19:30; cf. Mark 15:37). Yet John hardly presents an apotheosis in the Greek sense even though the latter category includes deification in the midst of mortal suffering (as with Heracles). In contrast to Greek heroes becoming divine, Jesus is returning to his preexistent glory with the Father; here is not a mere hero among many but the image of divine Wisdom returning home (cf. *1 En.* 42:2).

## 2. The Historical Foundation for the Passion Narratives

The extreme skepticism expressed by the most radical scholars is surely unwarranted. Burton Mack, for instance, suggests that scholars have simply gone easy on the passion narratives from faith prejudice.[21] Nevertheless, he shows little familiarity with the evidence cited by such "prejudicial" scholarship[22] and, in dismissing previous scholarship on the passion narratives as uncritical, seems unaware of his predecessors who have focused critical attention on the passion narratives.[23] In contrast to Mack's position, we have no record of any Christianity where the basic structure of the kerygma was missing, whether or not Christians had yet constructed full passion narratives.[24] Other narratives may have figured frequently in early Christian ethical preaching, but it is likely that early Christians would have told and retold the passion story, which lay at the heart of their kerygma, and that the Gospel writers would have here a variety of oral and perhaps written traditions from which to draw.[25] Paul has a sequence similar to Mark's (1 Cor 11:23; 15:3–5; cf. Jewish and Roman responsibility in 1 Thess 2:14–15; 1 Cor 1:23), and if, as is probable, John represents an independent tradition,[26] it is significant that his Passion Narrative again confirms the outline Mark follows, suggesting a pre-Markan passion narrative.[27] In preaching, one could flesh out the full sequence or omit some of the stories, but the basic outline remained the same.[28]

---

[20] Boring, *Commentary*, 151, contrasting the Markan passion with Philostratus *Vit. Apoll.* 7.14.

[28] Mack, *Myth*, 249; for his arguments, see 249–68. For a critique of Crossan's approach to the Passion Narrative (depending on the late *Gospel of Peter*), see Evans, "Passion," especially analogies with Justin *1 Apol.* 16.9–13 and Mark 16:9–20 (pp. 163–65).

[22] Mack cites Jeremias (a "conservative" scholar, *Myth*, 254) only three times, and never Blinzler, Hengel, or other more conservative Continental scholars.

[23] Perry, *Sources*, published as early as 1920; cf. Lietzmann's skepticism on some points in 1931 ("Prozess").

[24] Dibelius, *Tradition*, 178–217, thinks that "the Passion story is the only piece of Gospel tradition which in early times gave events in their larger connection."

[25] Thus Jewish scholars with no faith commitment to the narratives may also suggest that other gospels draw on pre-Markan passion material (e.g., Flusser, *Judaism*, 575–87, though he may presuppose Lukan priority here).

[26] E.g., Kollmann, *Kreuzigung*, sees John 's Passion Narrative as independent from the Synoptics, though using a tradition.

[27] Brown, *Death*, 53–55, 77–80.

[28] Ibid., 54.

But more specific evidence than this favors the substantial reliability of the passion narratives. Theissen argues for the most part (and sufficiently) persuasively that the pre-Markan passion narrative as a whole was in use by 40 C.E. in Jerusalem and Judea.[29] Thus, for example, Mark preserves names (such as those of the sons who identify the second Mary and Simon, Mark 15:21, 40, 47; 16:1) that serve no recognizable function in his own narrative—but that may well have been recognizable to those who passed on the traditions behind his early Jerusalem source (Mark 15:40, 43).[30] Place names such as Nazareth, Magdala, and Arimathea would mean nothing to audiences outside Palestine[31] (we should add here that the Galilean names may have meant little to most of the Jerusalem church as well, who may have preserved them for the same reasons that Mark did). Although one normally identifies local persons through their father's name, most persons in the Passion Narrative (which identifies more people "than elsewhere in the synoptic tradition") are identified by their place of origin instead. This practice makes the most sense in the church's first generation in Jerusalem, when (and where) it consisted of people from elsewhere.[32] Mark presumes his audience's prior knowledge of Pilate and (more significantly) Barabbas and other insurrectionists. That Barabbas's name is preserved when Pilate had numerous confrontations with such revolutionaries whose names are lost to us suggests that this particular insurrectionist's name was preserved in connection with the Passion Narrative.[33] Finally, some central characters in the account remain anonymous, probably to protect living persons who could face criminal charges in Jerusalem, fitting other ancient examples of protective anonymity.[34] Taken together, these arguments seem persuasive.[35]

Evidence does suggest that Mark edited his Passion Narrative,[36] but this no more denies the authenticity of the prior tradition than frequent rewriting of sources by any other ancient author, including other writers of the Gospels; thus, for example, the Passion Narrative in Matthew and Luke may agree against Mark at points (e.g., Mark 14:72).[37] Independent tradition drawn on by Matthew, Luke, and John preserves the name of the high priest, but Mark may follow the oldest passion account in omitting his name for political prudence, though Pilate, now deposed and despised, could easily be named in this period.[38] Brown suspects that Mark may have acquired some of his style from frequent

---

[29] Theissen, *Gospels*, 166–99. Pesch, "Jerusalem," argues that the passion narrative was the oldest tradition in the Jerusalem church; Hengel is right, however, that Pesch is too optimistic in his ability to reconstruct sources ("Problems," 209–10).

[30] Theissen, *Gospels*, 176–77.

[31] Ibid., 179. For excavations at Magdala, see Reich, "H'rh."

[32] Theissen, *Gospels*, 180. When a narrative introduces someone foreign, it often gives the place of birth (e.g., Appian *C.W.* 1.14.116); lists of names from disparate places typically list the places (e.g., Apollonius of Rhodes 1.40, 49, 57, 77, 95, 105–106, 115, 118, 139–140, 146–147, 151–152, 161, 177, 207).

[33] Theissen, *Gospels*, 171, 182–83. Livy occasionally cites a name as if familiar despite lack of previous mention (e.g., 40.55.2), perhaps incompletely following a source. Dodd, *Tradition*, 120, thinks the question of treason relevant in Palestine only before 70 C.E., but this argument is questionable; granted, the issue fits Tiberius's time very well, but it would remain relevant after 70.

[34] Theissen, *Gospels*, 186–88. Some view the fleeing young man of Mark 14:51–52 only in terms of his symbolic significance in the narrative (Crossan, "Tomb," 147–48; Fleddermann, "Flight"; Kelber, *Story*, 77), but Theissen is probably right to find genuine tradition from the early Palestinian church here (*Gospels*, 186; cf. Dibelius, *Tradition*, 182–83; Stauffer, *Jesus*, 121).

[35] Some of Theissen's other arguments (*Gospels*, 189–97) are weaker.

[36] For Markan structuring, see, e.g., Beavis, "Trial."

[37] Dewey, "Curse," 102–3.

[38] Theissen, *Gospels*, 172–74; cf. Philo *Embassy* 299–304.

recitation of the passion narrative;[39] further, Mark may have rephrased the narrative in his own words, especially where his sources were oral. One should see most fully the 1994 essay by Marion Soards,[40] who makes a strong case both that Mark uses a source and that we probably cannot separate the tradition from the redaction.

Another line of evidence also supports the substantial reliability of the picture of Jesus' execution found in the Passion Narrative: it fits what we know of the period in question. Thus Craig Evans[41] compares the Synoptic version of the passion narrative with Josephus's account of Jesus ben Ananias, who similarly entered the temple area during a festival (Josephus *War* 6.300–301). Like Jesus, he spoke of doom for Jerusalem, the sanctuary, and the people, even referring (again like Jesus) to the context of Jeremiah's prophecy of judgment against the temple (Jer 7:34 in *War* 6.301; cf. Jer 7:11 in Mark 11:17).[42] The Jewish leaders arrested and beat Jesus ben Ananias (*War* 6.302) and handed him over to the Roman governor (6.303), who interrogated him (6.305). He refused to answer the governor (6.305), was scourged (6.304), and—in this case unlike Jesus (though cf. Mark 15:9)—released (6.305). The different outcome is not difficult to account for: unlike Jesus ben Ananias, Jesus of Nazareth was not viewed as insane and already had a band of followers plus a growing reputation that could support messianic claims.[43] Jesus ben Ananias could be simply punished; Jesus of Nazareth had to be executed.

Where John's Passion Narrative diverges from the Synoptics, it sometimes displays special Johannine interests. At the same time, D. Moody Smith argues that some of its divergences, such as Jesus carrying his own cross or the legs of the crucified men being broken, appear more historically likely than the Synoptics.[44] Thus one should not rule out historical tradition in John's Passion Narrative.

Neyrey argues plausibly that John's Passion Narrative demonstrates the sort of techniques by which honor challenges were reversed. Although mocking, beating, and execution by crucifixion were public experiences of shame, the way Jesus endures them brings him honor with the informed readers whose perspective is larger than that of a bystander inside the story world. Enduring suffering silently was a sign of honor and courage (Cicero *Verr.* 2.5.162; Josephus *War* 6.304).[45] The Synoptic Gospels provide the same reversal, however, and even leave Jesus more silent (though John portrays him as even more in con-

---

[39] Brown, *Death*, 56 (citing the way some twentieth-century evangelists acquired their style from the KJV).

[40] Soards, "Passion Narrative." Brown, *Death*, 554 also emphatically challenges some earlier redaction-critical studies on the trial narrative in Mark 14:55–64 (cf. perhaps Donahue, "Temple"), complaining that though "Mark used earlier material . . . *our best methods do not give us the ability to isolate confidently that material in its exact wording, assigning preMarkan verses and half-verses* from the existing, thoroughly Markan account" (emphasis his).

[41] Evans, "Jesus," 108; idem, "Jesus ben Ananias."

[42] On the opposition Jeremiah faced for his "unpatriotic" prophecies, cf., e.g., Jer 26:6–24; Josephus *Ant.* 10.89–90; angry crowds could also vent their rage on any they felt brought them misfortune (Josephus *Life* 149). A man inside Tyre likewise reportedly prophesied its judgment and faced the charge of being a traitor (Diodorus Siculus 17.41.7–8, which may be legendary or repeat Alexander's propaganda).

[43] Cf. Sanders, *Figure*, 267. A number of followers would be deemed necessary to provide a substantial threat (Xenophon *Mem.* 1.2.10).

[44] Smith, "Problem," 263–65.

[45] Neyrey, "Shame of Cross," 113–14; Malina and Rohrbaugh, *John*, 264. This is not to say that the shame of the cross was eliminated for observers in the story world; Paul may have behaved honorably in Philippi, but he still felt he had been publicly humiliated there (1 Thess 2:2; see comment

trol of the action; for example, he bears his own cross).[46] Especially it is noteworthy that, for all his emphasis on Jesus' honor, John mostly reinterprets rather than removes symbols of shame in the tradition.

### 3. The High Priests and Jerusalem's Elite

Even in the Fourth Gospel, adapted in many ways to the post-70 situation, the high priests provide part of Jesus' opposition (18:3), albeit conjoined with the "Pharisees" (7:32). It is possible that various representatives of the aristocracy, and not well-to-do Pharisaic survivors alone, found temporary influence at Yavneh; nevertheless, it would be difficult for John to omit the high priests from the traditional passion narrative or the events leading up to it. Whatever the reason, John, who focuses on the Pharisees, does not eliminate altogether the high-priestly opposition in the Jesus tradition (though he omits explicit mention of the Sadducees, the group to which most of the high priests adhered).[47]

A few comments on the high priesthood, and what John's audience might know about them, are therefore in order.[48] Elsewhere in the Roman Empire, the title did not always bear the prestige it held in Palestine.[49] Perhaps under foreign influence, Jewish writers came to speak of the priestly aristocracy or high-priestly family as high priests, rather than merely the ruling chief priest, the *kohen hagadol* of the OT.[50]

Even Pharisaic tradition respected the office of high priest,[51] though Sadducees dominated it. The priesthood as a whole reportedly included both those committed to extrabiblically stringent purity rules (probably Pharisees or their sympathizers) and those who were not (*p. Ter.* 6:1). Jewish high priests held considerable political authority,[52] recognized even among Gentiles (Diodorus Siculus 40.3.5–6). Contrary to Israelite law, however, Roman officials freely gave and revoked the office of high priests; thus Quirinius installed Annas (Josephus *Ant.* 18.26), and Vitellius retired Caiaphas after Pilate's recall to Rome (Josephus *Ant.* 18.95).

Josephus experienced the opposition of high priests he considered corrupt (*Life* 216). He especially regards the chief priests as corrupt during the period of Agrippa II (59–65 C.E.),[53] but this specification may reflect his own uncomfortable experiences and may suggest a broader corruption within the aristocratic ranks from which such priests were

---

in Bruce, *Thessalonians,* 25); the term implies no mild insult (e.g., Euripides *Tro.* 69; Dionysius of Halicarnassus *R.A.* 10.35.3; P.Hal. 1.210–213).

[46] It is perhaps noteworthy that Porphyry (or whoever wrote *Apocrit.* 3.1–6) complained that Jesus' failure to reveal himself during the passion contradicts his divinity (the opposite of the early Christian perspective).

[47] On the Sadducees, see esp. Meier, *Marginal Jew,* 3:389–411 (most relevantly here, 393–99). Some, however, believe Saducean dominance of the priestly aristocracy is generally overstated (e.g., Porton, "Sadducees," 1052).

[48] I have taken these comments largely from Keener, *Matthew,* 613–16; cf. also comments in Basser, "Priests"; Reid, "Sacrifice," 1048–49.

[49] Cf. Lewis, *Life,* 47; Reicke, *Era,* 147.

[50] E.g., 1QM 2:1; Josephus *War* 2.243, 316, 320, 342; 410–411; 4.151, 315; *Life* 197; Mark 2:26; Acts 4:6; Stern, "Aspects," 601, 603; Sanders, *Figure,* 327–32; Jeremias, *Sayings,* 51.

[51] E.g., *m. Hor.* 3:1; *p. Sanh.* 2:1, §2; Acts 23:5–6.

[52] See Smallwood, "Priests."

[53] Sanders, *Figure,* 324; see, e.g., Josephus *Ant.* 20.206–207. For Josephus's negative view of the Sadducees, see Baumbach, "Sadducees"; of some high priests (but not their office), Thoma, "Priesthood" (attributing it to Josephus's pro-Hasmonean tendencies).

drawn.[54] Qumran and others opposed the priestly aristocracy that controlled the temple. "For many marginalized groups in this period the problem, in short, was the local leaders and politicians in Roman Palestine."[55]

The Fourth Gospel speaks of a συνέδριον only once (11:47), and there the term seems to refer to an ad hoc council, albeit gathered from among the elite and chaired by the high priest.[56] The leading players in John's account at this point are simply Pharisees and chief priests. Because the historical figures behind John's Pharisees and chief priests were Jerusalem aristocrats, however, some comments about Jerusalem's municipal aristocracy may be in order.[57] The comments shed more light on 11:47, but because John's Passion Narrative invites comparison with those of the Synoptics, we include discussion of the Sanhedrin here.

A συνέδριον was a ruling council, equivalent to a βουλή, or a senate.[58] Cities such as Tiberias had their own ruling senates composed of the leading citizens (Josephus *Life* 64, 69, 169, 313, 381); such assemblies were distinguishable from the larger citizen assembly (*Life* 300).[59] Municipal senates consisted of aristocrats the Romans called *decuriones,* and in the eastern Mediterranean "varied in size from thirty to five hundred members."[60] The Jerusalem Sanhedrin was in a sense the municipal aristocracy of Jerusalem; but just as the Roman senate wielded power far beyond Rome because of Rome's power, Jerusalem's Sanhedrin wielded some influence in national affairs, to the degree that Roman prefects and Herodian princes allowed.[61]

The Sanhedrin may well have held seventy-one members, as tradition indicates;[62] yet if it simply represented a body of ruling elders from the municipal aristocracy, this may have

---

[54] Perhaps in part because I find myself skeptical that religion regularly changes human nature, especially when it is coupled with power, I am less sympathetic to their piety than is Sanders, *Figure,* 336. They probably acted in their own self-interest, as well as for the peace, in relations with the Romans (Horsley, "High Priests"). The charges may be stylized, sectarian polemic, as Sanders suggests (and against the priesthood in general he may be right [*Judaism,* 182–89]), but one should not dismiss too readily the reasons for the polemic (cf. 1QpHab. 9.4–5; *T. Levi* 14:1; *2 Bar.* 10:18; *t. Menaḥ.* 13.21, in Avigad, *Jerusalem,* 130; Avigad, "Burnt House," 71; Hengel, *Property,* 23); corrupt priesthoods were common targets of polemic in the ancient Near East through the first century (Crocker, "Priests"; cf. Plutarch *Lysander* 26.1–3; Libanius *Declamation* 44.43). Cf., e.g., the servants of the later Ananias who beat poorer priests to seize their tithes (Josephus *Ant.* 20.181, 206).

[55] Overman, *Community,* 329.

[56] Key leaders might gather quickly when summoned (cf. Valerius Maximus 2.2.6 on old Rome).

[57] We have borrowed these comments largely from Keener, *Matthew,* 614–16.

[58] "Sanhedrin" is a broad rather than restrictive term, applicable also to Greek texts to an informal assembly of advisors (Diodorus Siculus 13.111.1) or frequently to Rome's "senate" (e.g., Diodorus Siculus 40.1.1; Dionysius of Halicarnassus *R.A.* 5.70.5; 6.30.2; 6.81.1; 6.85.2; 8.69.2; 9.32.5; 10.2.6; 12.1.14; 12.6.2 [4]; in these texts it appears interchangeably with βουλή, a more common term, e.g., Dionysius of Halicarnassus *R.A.* 5.71.1; 6.1.1; 6.21.1; 6.81.4). Usage was broad; a βουλή traditionally could constitute a local council (Aristophanes *Knights* 475, 653) but also a leader's war council (Homer *Il.* 2.84).

[59] Officials could also assemble their own administrative "councils" from among their friends (e.g., Josephus *Life* 368).

[60] Jeffers, *World,* 186.

[61] Overman, *Community,* 372–73, 385, regards the Sanhedrin as a Roman political institution, although conceding that "some of the local Jewish elite may have been involved." Yet the dominance of the Jewish elite is clear; in cities like Jerusalem, Rome ruled through municipal aristocracies—here, pro-Roman Jewish aristocrats.

[62] *M. Sanh.* 1:6; cf. later *Tg. Neof.* 1 on Exod 15:27. Cf. also Josephus's Galilean council of 70 in *War* 2.570 and *Life* 79, and that of the Zealots in *War* 4.336, both undoubtedly following the stan-

been simply an average figure. It is, in any case, doubtful that all members were expected to be present on all occasions (especially an emergency meeting on the night when people had eaten—or in John's story world would the next evening eat—the Passover).[63] The Sanhedrin included the high priest, who according to tradition could break ties.[64] Again according to tradition, they met in the Chamber of Hewn Stone on the Temple Mount;[65] otherwise they met close to the Temple Mount (cf. Josephus *War* 5.144).[66] Our first-century sources, the NT and Josephus, include Sadducees and other groups in the Sanhedrin, under high-priestly control; later rabbis portray the Sanhedrin as an assembly of rabbis.[67] The later portrayals should not surprise us; rabbinic portraits of the Sanhedrin include more striking anachronisms than this, depicting leaders of the Sanhedrin in biblical times.[68]

According to rabbinic (and probably Pharisaic) ideals, judges who proved themselves locally could be promoted to the Sanhedrin (*t. Šeqal.* 3:27), but in actuality the Sanhedrin in Jesus' day probably consisted largely of members of the Jerusalem aristocracy and wealthy landowners in the vicinity. Rulers could use sanhedrins, or assemblies, the way some politicians today use committees: to secure the end one wants without taking full responsibility for that decision. In Josephus, rulers such as Herod appointed the Sanhedrin members they wished and obtained the results they wished.[69] Before Herod came to power, the Jerusalem Sanhedrin exercised significant authority (Josephus *Ant.* 14.177). In Pilate's time, without Herod the Great's interference and with the Romans expecting local aristocracies to administer the business they could (cf. Josephus *War* 2.331, 405; *Ant.* 20.11), we should not be surprised that chief priests would convene a Sanhedrin (Josephus *Ant.* 20.200), especially since the priestly aristocracy constituted a large portion of it.[70] We should also not be surprised if the Sanhedrin sought to please Rome.[71]

Less than four decades after the events the Gospels describe, Jerusalem's aristocracy continued to act as a body. When the high priest and the leading Pharisee allegedly acted

---

dard contemporary model; the models probably ultimately derive from Mosaic tradition (Exod 24:9; Num 11:16, 24; cf. Ezek 8:11). Josephus also assumed a council of seven judges as a lower court in every city (*War* 2.571; *Ant.* 4.214). An odd number to break a tie made sense; as in Roman law (Dionysius of Halicarnassus *R.A.* 7.64.6), a tie vote would yield acquittal.

[63] Brown, *Death*, 348–49, doubts that an exact list of seventy-one members existed in the first century, suggesting that it merely included elders from distinguished families alongside chief priests, representatives of whom were expected to appear.

[64] Cf. Ferguson, *Backgrounds*, 453.

[65] *T. Šeqal.* 3:27; *b. Yoma* 25a; *Gen. Rab.* 70:8; *Num. Rab.* 19:26; *Eccl. Rab.* 1:1, §1. A location near the temple is not surprising; at times other peoples' leaders could use temples (the senate in Cicero *Fam.* 8.4.4).

[66] For bibliography on the Sanhedrin, see Safrai, "Self-Government," 418 (the section on the Sanhedrin is pp. 379–400). Josephus generally prefers the term συνέδριον, "sanhedrin," "assembly," in the *Jewish Antiquities,* and βουλή, "council," in the *Jewish War.* The rabbis believed that God supported the decrees of the rabbinic *Beth din hagadol*, great assembly (*Exod. Rab.* 15:20), on which Israel rightly depended (*Song Rab.* 7:3, §1; *Lam. Rab.* 2:4, §8).

[67] Cohen, *Maccabees*, 156.

[68] E.g., *b. Ber.* 3b; *Gen. Rab.* 74:15; *Exod. Rab.* 1:13; *Pesiq. Rab.* 11:3. Some of the "scribes" may have been Pharisees, but Pharisees were not dominant in the Sanhedrin (Brown, *Death*, 350–52), despite Josephus's possible favoritism toward them (Josephus *Ant.* 18.15, 17; cf. *Life* 1, 12 and *Ant.* passim; Brown, *Death*, 353–56).

[69] See Sanders, *Figure*, 482–83; cf. Josephus *Ant.* 15.173; 20.216–218.

[70] Cf. Sanders, *Figure*, 484–87; Josephus *War* 2.331, 336; *Ant.* 17.160, 164; 20.216–217; probably the municipal aristocracy in *Ant.* 14.91, 163, 167, 180; *Life* 62.

[71] Cf. Kennard, "Assembly."

without the approval of the rest of the assembly, they provoked that assembly's anger (Josephus *Life* 309).

A small minority of scholars, wishing to preserve both the later rabbinic portrait of the Sanhedrin and the one found in Josephus and early Christian sources, have opted for two Sanhedrins—the religious Sanhedrin of the rabbis and the political Sanhedrin attested in first-century sources. Some of these scholars came to argue that the political Sanhedrin tried Jesus, thereby exonerating the religious Sanhedrin of the rabbis. One scholar favoring the rabbinic picture has even argued that the Gospels and Acts are late sources on this matter, with changes into the fourth century.[72] Nevertheless, even apart from textual evidence to the contrary, evidence within the early Christian texts refutes this theory: later writers fail to clear up conflicts and to impose later theology.[73] In the final analysis, it is simply anachronistic to reject all our first-century portraits on the basis of later, idealized rabbinic accounts, although reliable tradition may remain in them at points. Few scholars have therefore accepted the double-Sanhedrin thesis.[74]

After examining Josephus's three mentions of "Sanhedrin" and five of βουλή (Josephus *War* 2.331, 336; 5.142–144, 532; *Ant.* 20.11, 200–201, 216–217; *Life* 62), Brown concludes that Josephus's portrait of the Sanhedrin is quite close to that of the Gospels and Acts. They judge, consist of "chief priests, scribes, and rulers or influential citizens (= elders)," sentence those found guilty of crimes, and constitute the leading Jewish body with which Roman rulers would deal. Clearly they "played a major administrative and judicial role in Jewish self-governance in Judea."[75]

## Betrayal and Arrest (18:1–11)

Although the temple police had earlier refused to arrest Jesus, recognizing that no one had ever spoken like him (7:45–46), one of his own disciples now aids in his arrest. The tradition of the betrayal is certainly historical but, in the context of the whole Gospel, strikes a note of Johannine irony: after building a flat portrait of the Judean elite that is almost entirely negative (excepting the secret believers and sympathizers among them), John now reminds his audience that the most severe betrayals may come from those once considered disciples. The emphatic warnings against apostasy in the Fourth Gospel (e.g., 8:30–32, 59; 15:6) suggest that it was a genuine threat to his audience (cf. 1 John 2:19).

### 1. The Setting and Betrayer (18:1–2)

If Jesus and his disciples feasted in upper-city Jerusalem, they may have taken a staircase that descends from the Temple Mount to the Kidron Valley (18:1);[76] despite some changes in the terrain, the Kidron Valley remains known[77] and might have been known to older members of John's audience who had emigrated from Judea or who had made pil-

---

[72] Mantel, *Sanhedrin.*

[73] Sutcliffe, "Review."

[74] See Blinzler, *Trial,* 15, 140; Brown, *Death,* 343–48.

[75] Brown, *Death,* 342–43. Levine, *Hellenism,* 88–90, argues that the Jerusalem Sanhedrin was probably simply an ad hoc group in some texts.

[76] Yamauchi, *Stones,* 106. Stauffer, *Jesus,* 118, overestimates their sense of threat at this point when he proposes that the disciples may have gone by different roads to prevent notice (Luke 22:39).

[77] See, e.g., Wilkinson, *Jerusalem,* 127.

grimage before the temple's destruction. The Kidron flowed only in the rainy winter season (hence χειμάρρου here)[78] and so would not have been hard to cross at Passover in April. An allusion to David's withdrawal from Jerusalem in the time of opposition and betrayal (cf. 2 Sam 15:23) is also possible[79] though—given the topography around Jerusalem, to begin with—not necessarily clear.[80] If an allusion is intended, it is not beyond the realm of possibility that Jesus himself offered it by choosing the site; the earliest Gospel writers may not have recognized (and hence would not have invented) the allusion to the site (Mark 14:26), but it is possible that Jesus also did not (cf. Luke 22:39; John 18:2).

Only John mentions the "garden" (18:1, 26; 19:41); gardens often were walled enclosures.[81] Perhaps John alludes to the reversal of the fall (cf. Rom 5:12–21) in the garden of Eden (Gen 2:8–16);[82] but John nowhere else uses an explicit Adam Christology, and the LXX uses κῆπος for the Hebrew's garden of Eden only in Ezek 36:35 (and there omits mention of Eden, normally preferring παράδεισος), rendering the parallel less likely. (John could offer his own free translation, but the proposed allusion, in any case, lacks adequate additional support to be clear.) The Markan line of tradition suggests that perhaps olive trees grew nearby; its name, Gethsemane, suggests an olive press and hence was probably the name for an olive orchard at the base of Mount Olivet.[83] In the LXX, a κῆπος appears as an agricultural unit alongside olive groves and vineyards (e.g., 1 Kgs 21:2; 2 Kgs 5:26; Song 6:11; Amos 4:9; 9:14). If the garden has symbolic import (which it might not), it may connect Jesus' arrest with his tomb and the site of his resurrection (19:41) or perhaps allude to the seed that must die (12:24) or to the Father's pruning (15:1).

Some scholars doubt the participation of a betrayer in Jesus' arrest,[84] but Romans normally did work through local informers, including in their dealings with Christians less than a century later.[85] Further, given the shame involved, early Christians would surely not have invented the betrayal. Judas's betrayal may also be attested in pre-Pauline tradition in 1 Cor 11:23, though the phrase could (less probably) refer to Jesus' betrayal by the elite to the Romans. As elsewhere, John sometimes anticipates questions the answer to which may have been assumed in the earliest passion traditions: that Judas knew the place because Jesus gathered his disciples there on other occasions (18:2) comports with other gospel tradition (Mark 13:3; Luke 21:37; 22:39), and this is a plausible explanation of how the authorities found Jesus.[86] By contrast, John does not dwell on disciples sleeping instead of "watching" as in Mark's line of tradition (Mark 14:34–41). This is not due to a higher opinion of the disciples' fidelity than in Mark (cf. 12:38; 16:32, though this is less John's emphasis than Mark's); perhaps John omits the

---

[78] Brown, *John*, 2:806. Many rivers and wadis in the East fill or overflow during the rainy winter or (sometimes) when winter snows melt in spring (Homer *Il.* 5.87–88; 13.137; *Od.* 19.205–207; Apollonius of Rhodes 1.9; Appian *R.H.* 12.11.76; Livy 44.8.6–7; Herodian 3.3.7; 8.4.2–3; Arrian *Alex.* 7.21.2).

[79] E.g., Davies and Allison, *Matthew*, 3:565.

[80] Cf. 1 Kgs 2:37; 15:13; 2 Kgs 23:4, 6, 12; 2 Chr 15:16; 29:16; 30:14; Jer 31:40.

[81] Harrison, "Garden," 400.

[82] See Manns, "Symbolisme"; cf. Suggit, "Gardener," and Wyatt, "Gardener" (on 20:15).

[83] Lane, *Mark*, 515. If the press originally belonged to an individual estate rather than a local village, the estate must have been sizeable (cf. Lewis, *Life*, 127). On the question of the Gethsemane tradition's historicity, see Green, "Gethsemane," 268.

[84] Cohn, *Trial*, 83, though citing a rabbinic tradition that "high priests were wont to engage in undercover activity."

[85] Pliny *Ep.* 10.96–97; cf. further the comment on 11:47–53.

[86] Cf., e.g., Appian *C.W.* 4.4.18 on the betrayal of Annalis.

"watching" because it was closely connected with the Passover, which he has apparently rescheduled (18:28).[87]

### 2. The Troops (18:3)

That those who came to arrest Jesus brought not only weapons[88] but lanterns and torches (18:3) may be significant. Not only Roman soldiers but also the temple police on their night watch would carry lanterns, and especially if they expected Jesus to flee into dark corners of the olive grove, they would hardly depend solely on the light of the Passover's full moon.[89] That John, alone of the Gospels, mentions this historically likely touch, however, may suggest that he also derives symbolic, ironic import from it: the agents of darkness prove completely unaware that they are approaching the light of the world.[90]

#### 2A. Roman Participation in the Tradition?

John, like the Synoptics, may assume a Jewish force coming to arrest Jesus; this certainly makes the most sense historically and probably represents what happened. Although they were not always efficient (except in Roman colonies such as Antioch and Philippi), local aristocracies used local watchmen to constitute their police force, and Jerusalem's temple guard (cf. Luke 22:52; Acts 4:1) fits this pattern.[91] Yet many scholars see here a Roman cohort[92] and think that John correctly preserves the tradition (against the Synoptics) that only Romans[93] or, more commonly, Romans in addition to the temple police[94] were involved in the arrest. Because of John's polemic against the Jewish authorities elsewhere, such information could appear unexpected and might well betray prior historical tradition.[95]

This inference is no more necessary from John, however, than from the Synoptics, to which these interpreters oppose him on this point. Although some military terms in 18:3 are Roman, Greek and Roman military terms had long before been transferred to Jewish soldiers (e.g., Josephus *Life* 242).[96] Both σπεῖρα (18:3, 12)[97] and χιλίαρχος

---

[87] Passover was a night "watch" (שמור; προφυλακὴ) for the Lord (Exod 12:42); cf. *t. Ketub.* 5:5; Lane, *Mark,* 509; Keener, *Matthew,* 637.

[88] Stauffer, *Jesus,* 120, thinks that clubs (Mark 14:43), in contrast to weapons that some would consider ornamental (*m. Šabb.* 6:4), violated the Sabbath. He counts this a reason against the Synoptic dating of the Last Supper, but if correct, his observation may simply imply an early Christian charge of priestly impiety or the priests' exploitation of exemption for defensive warfare in the case of what might appear a dangerous police action.

[89] MacGregor, *John,* 324; Brown, *John,* 2:809. Moonlight could help night vision, of course (Virgil *Aen.* 7.9; Ovid *Fasti* 2.697; Silius Italicus 15.616; Polybius 7.16.3; 9.15.12; cf. Plutarch *Alc.* 20.5; Plutarch's contention that tracks are harder to follow at full moon seems less persuasive, *Nat. Q.* 24, *Mor.* 917F).

[90] Ellis, *Genius,* 248; cf. Luke 22:53.

[91] Stambaugh and Balch, *Environment,* 34. Many scholars see the temple police instead of Romans here (e.g., Ridderbos, *John,* 575).

[92] E.g., Rensberger, *Faith,* 90; O'Day, "John," 801–2; Kaufman, "Anti-Semitism."

[93] E.g., Cohn, *Trial,* 78.

[94] E.g., Anderson, *Mark,* 327; Stauffer, *Jesus,* 119.

[95] E.g., Winter, *Trial,* 44; Bruce, "Trial," 9.

[96] See further Catchpole, *Trial,* 149; Blinzler, *Trial,* 64–65; Bammel, "Trial," 439–40; cf. Wilkinson, *Jerusalem,* 126–27.

[97] Catchpole, *Trial,* 149, cites here Jdt 14:11; 2 Macc 8:23; 12:20, 22; Josephus *Ant.* 17.215.

(18:12)[98] appear frequently enough for Jewish soldiers. The claim that the Jewish use of such language applies only to local or rebel leaders rather than to any soldiers the priestly aristocracy would have had at their disposal could qualify the case,[99] except that it demands a far more technical use of language than is likely in John's case. When one's initial pool of evidence is limited, one can usually divide it into smaller categories that exclude the case in question; but the Jewish uses of the term would be too familiar from widely read Jewish sources such as Judith and Maccabees for John's audience to be sure of Roman involvement without further qualification.[100]

Some are skeptical that Jewish officials such as the high priests or their agents would have participated,[101] but as we have argued, these were the same politically astute leaders responsible to the Romans for keeping peace; they were the ones most directly scandalized by Jesus' act in the temple; and a diversity of ancient sources testify to their abuse of power against competitors among their own people.

One could argue that the Romans lent the chief priests some troops, as they might to the temple police in quelling public disorders,[102] but this suggestion does not square with the evidence. The Roman garrison in the Antonia would have sided with the Levite police in the case of a riot, but they were not simply at the municipal aristocracy's disposal.[103] Further, even if the municipal aristocracy could have commandeered Roman troops at other times, it is unlikely that they would do so during the festival. Pilate, ready to greet petitioners early in the morning, was undoubtedly already in town (albeit asleep),[104] and it is unlikely that the high priests would have secured troops for such a mission without informing him; yet even John (see esp. 18:29) reads as if Pilate has insufficient acquaintance with the case at this point to have dispatched the troops. Indeed, Pilate explicitly assigns responsibility for the arrest to Jesus' own nation and its chief priests (18:35); Jesus likewise spoke of the lack of resistance his followers had offered to "the Jews" (18:36). The proposal of Roman involvement interprets selectively even the Gospel to which its appeal is made.

The silence of the Synoptics about Roman involvement in the arrest seems striking, especially given Luke's knowledge of the Roman military and the widespread knowledge of a garrison in Jerusalem.[105] One could argue that the pre-Markan passion narrative followed in the Synoptics suppressed Roman involvement beyond the reluctant sentence of Pilate, given the political realities of their day; but the same political realities might have

---

98 In the LXX, twenty to thirty times (e.g., Exod 18:21, 25; Num 1:16; 31:14, 48–54; Deut 1:15; Josh 22:14, 21; 1 Chr 13:1; 15:25). Catchpole, *Trial,* 149, cites here 1 Macc 3:55; Josephus *War* 2.578; *Ant.* 17.215; Mark 6:21. Cf. also Bammel, "Trial," 439–40. Not only Greek terminology but Western culture (including Roman artwork) was widespread in Herodian Judea (see Ovadiah, "Pavements").

99 See, e.g., Rensberger, *Faith,* 102 n. 15.

100 Even when Josephus refers to a Roman σπεῖρα on the temple roof—the sense of which ought to be obvious—he must limit it with Ρωμαική (*War* 2.224; 5.244; Catchpole, *Trial,* 149).

101 Cohn, *Trial,* 75 doubts that any but people of the "lower strata" would have joined this mission; but we suspect that the temple police would have followed the orders of the *sagan,* a member of the priestly aristocracy.

102 Cf., e.g., Hunter, *John,* 166; Hurtado, *Mark,* 233.

103 *Pace,* e.g., Bernard, *John,* 2:584.

104 The governor normally arrived with extra troops to control the Passover crowds if necessary (cf. Josephus *War* 2.224–226; *Ant.* 20.109–110); the crowds grew most restless at the pilgrimage festivals (*War* 1.88; cf. *War* 2.42, 254–256). That locals often invited governors to their festivals (Menander Rhetor 2.14, 424.3–430.8) seems less relevant.

105 Blinzler, *Trial,* 64–65.

invited them, albeit to a lesser extent, to have exonerated the priestly aristocracy, too, especially if the passion narrative stems from Jerusalem as Theissen has argued.[106]

Catchpole provides further evidence against the Roman interpretation of 18:3 and 18:12. First, he argues, Jesus would not appeal to what he had told *Romans* in the temple (18:20); this argument, however, is certainly weakened by the fact that Jesus makes this statement after being brought before the high priest (the officers of 18:22 are ὑπηρετῶν, who are certainly Jewish, as in 7:32; 18:12; 19:6). Second, he doubts that Judas would have been cooperating with the Romans. Third, would the Romans have taken Jesus to Annas, whom the Romans had deposed? Fourth, given Rome's commitment to suppressing nationalists, Romans would undoubtedly have sought to arrest Peter after his action with the sword. (This presupposes that they would have caught him.) Finally, retreat before the divine name (18:4–11) may suggest a Jewish reaction.[107] None of these arguments is completely compelling, but cumulatively they bear some weight.

2B. Roman Participation and John's Theology?

Then again, one could argue that even though the Roman involvement in the arrest is unlikely historically, John may have portrayed genuine Roman involvement in his narrative for theological reasons. Or if John had no tradition of Roman involvement, he may have used ambiguous language that would permit Roman involvement (for theological reasons) without requiring it (for historical ones). Because a σπεῖρα usually represents a cohort of roughly six hundred troops (although occasionally a *manipulus* of two hundred)[108] and because 18:12 mentions a χιλίαρχος, the *tribunus militum* in charge of a cohort,[109] John may envision hundreds of troops arriving to arrest Jesus in the garden. But this scenario is historically probable neither of a Jewish nor of a Roman force;[110] John may well refer loosely to a mere detachment from the cohort,[111] but the presence of a commander suggests that John deliberately employs language that permits a larger interpretation—perhaps Johannine hyperbole to underline the greatness of Jesus' power (18:6; cf. Matt 26:53). John does distinguish these troops from other Jewish officers in 18:3 and 18:12,[112] though this distinction need not make them Gentiles.

John may be making a theological statement: both Romans and Jews bore responsibility for Jesus' arrest;[113] here, as in the rest of the Passion Narrative, "the Jews," that is, the Jewish leaders, have shown their character as part of the "world." This also fits the Gospel's setting. Yet even within the story world of John, it remains unclear that Pilate was involved at this point,[114] and hence Roman participation seems unlikely (unless the logic of the narrative, as understood within a framework intelligible to its likely first-century audience, deconstructs at this point).

---

[106] On a putative Jerusalem origin for the passion narrative, see comments above.

[107] Catchpole, *Trial*, 149–50.

[108] The numbers did vary; cf. 505 troops in *BGU* 696.11–15 (156 C.E.), later reinforced.

[109] Brown, *Death*, 248.

[110] Contrast Stauffer, *Jesus*, 119, who believes that the Jewish leaders had denounced Jesus to the Romans as commanding a large and dangerous following.

[111] Bruce, "Trial," 8–9.

[112] Brown, *Death*, 248.

[113] Cf. ibid., 250. Cullmann, *State*, 43–44, assigns legal responsibility to the Romans but moral responsibility (perhaps too much) to the Jerusalem authorities.

[114] Brown, *Death*, 250–51.

## 2C. Judas's Responsibility

Judas "receives" the cohort in 18:3. John may allow his language to do double duty here: first, on the historical level, Judas led the police to Jesus. Second, while John's wording does not demand that Judas himself commanded the cohort,[115] it does allow that interpretation. Such an interpretation would seem absurdly implausible to anyone familiar even exclusively with John's own narrative, whether the cohort is Jewish or Roman, if pressed literally. But the strength of John's expression makes more sense as graphic Johannine irony: those who betray God's servants are as responsible for their executions as if they had killed them themselves (16:2).

John nowhere mentions Judas's kiss, so striking in the Synoptics.[116] Instead, although Judas remains the betrayer, Jesus identifies himself for those who came to arrest him, in order to protect his followers (18:4–9); John reminds his audience that Jesus died on their behalf, and did so purposely (10:18), a theme prominent in most of John's adaptations of the traditional passion narrative.

## 3. Jesus' Self-Revelation (18:4–9)

Jesus is aware of all things that are coming on him (18:4);[117] he knows "all things" (16:30; 21:17), including the "coming things" such as those the Paraclete will reveal (16:13; on implications for John's Christology, see comment on 2:24–25). John's depiction also illustrates that Jesus remained in control of the events; no one takes his life from him, but he lays it down freely (10:18). Even in the Synoptics, Jesus' responses to the Sanhedrin and to Pilate are calculated to secure his execution; here, however, Jesus theologizes on the matter (18:4–8, 36–37). This picture of Jesus' confidence in his Father's mission pervades the Fourth Gospel; thus, for example, instead of pointing out that one dipped with him in the dish (Mark 14:20), Jesus himself gives Judas the sop (John 13:26).

That Jesus reminds the guards that they have come to arrest him rather than the disciples (18:8) provides a vivid illustration of his mission to offer himself on their behalf (10:11, 15). Though Jesus' disciples may betray, deny, or abandon him, he remains faithful to them.[118] (It also provides an example for believers to lay down their lives for one another, 15:13; 1 John 3:16.) That guards working for the chief priests or even Rome would allow Jesus' followers to escape is not surprising; Romans normally did prefer to execute ringleaders rather than all those involved in a revolt.[119]

Jesus' self-revelation, "I am" (ἐγώ εἰμι, 18:5, 6, 8), can mean simply "I am (he)," that is, "I am the one you are seeking." But the reader of the Gospel by this point understands

---

[115] *Pace* Winter, *Trial,* 45, who thus proposes that the name here is an interpolation.

[116] Smith, *John* (1999), 330, suggests that this omission is to preserve the Johannine portrait of Jesus' dignity: the betrayer "does not touch—much less kiss—him." On the significance of the kiss in heightening the betrayal's heinousness, see Keener, *Matthew,* 641–42; cf. Valerius Maximus 7.8.9.

[117] Perhaps Jesus' divine knowledge in 18:4 contrasts with Judas's limited knowledge in 18:2, but the proximity of terms may be coincidental; it is difficult to see how else John would have explained Judas's knowledge of the site. Neyrey, "Shame of Cross," 119, emphasizes that Jesus in 18:4 takes the role of questioner, "the challenging or commanding position." Their falling also signals Jesus' vindication (ibid.; cf. Rev 3:9).

[118] Ancients regarded loyalty to friends as highly praiseworthy (e.g., *Rhet. Alex.* 36, 1442a.11–12; see further comment on John 15:13–15), as also the preference to suffer in the stead of those one loved (e.g., Valerius Maximus 2.4.5; Rom 9:3).

[119] E.g., Dionysius of Halicarnassus *R.A.* 3.40.3; 5.43.2. This would exclude the sword wielder (18:10).

that the Jesus of this Gospel means more than this; he is declaring his divine identity (see comment on 8:58).[120] Lest anyone fail to grasp this point, the response even of Jesus' opponents in the story world confirms it (as in 8:59; 10:31, 33, 39): the divine name causes their involuntary prostration (18:6).

That this passage is Johannine theology does not render incredible the possibility that it also reflects tradition. Those familiar with the history of revivalism are aware of the frequency of involuntary motor responses to sublime encounters;[121] such phenomena also appeared in ancient Israel (1 Sam 19:24). It is also possible that, given their suspicion that Jesus was a magician (7:20; 8:48, 52; 10:20), they might have fallen back in terror when he pronounced the divine name.[122] Indeed, within the story world, some of these officers (18:3) may have already been fearful of apprehending Jesus (7:45–46). But because we lack external corroboration, the historical accuracy of this report is beyond verification on purely historical grounds; what remains open to investigation is the significance John may wish his audience to find in the event.

Other ancient texts report falling backward in terror—for instance, fearing that one has dishonored God.[123] More important, if Eusebius correctly records his words, a Hellenistic Jewish writer roughly three centuries before John reports a significant and perhaps widely known tradition about the divine name. When Moses pronounced the name of his God in Pharaoh's ear, Pharaoh fell to the ground, unable to speak until raised by Moses; a priest who ridiculed the divine name was then struck dead.[124] Thus it is likely that John provides still another hint of Jesus' deity in his narration. Likewise, that Jesus' word (referring to 17:12) had to be "fulfilled" (18:9; cf. 18:32) functionally places it on a par with Scripture; John employs the same fulfillment formula for both (12:38;13:18; 15:25; 17:12; 19:24, 28, 36).[125]

## 4. Peter's Resistance (18:10–11)

The passion narrative followed by the Synoptics testifies that a disciple of Jesus cut off the ear of one of the high priest's servants (Mark 14:47), probably the more important right ear (Luke 22:50). Whereas the Synoptic Gospels leave the aggressor disciple anonymous, however, John reports that it was Peter (18:10). Such a description fits what we would know of Peter,[126] and the disciple's anonymity in the earliest passion narrative is not

---

[120] With most commentators, e.g., Lightfoot, *Gospel,* 135; Haenchen, *John,* 2:165; Longenecker, *Wine,* 121. Bauckham, *God Crucified,* 55, notes that John has seven absolute "I am" statements, with the seventh repeated twice more (18:5–8), matching the seven MT uses of *ani hu* plus two more emphatic forms (Isa 43:25; 51:12). But even if someone might have counted the uses in Isaianic material (six), would they have really counted through the entire MT (hence the Deuteronomy reference) without a modern concordance?

[121] For early U.S. history, see, e.g., Synan, *Tradition,* 12–14; Noll, *History,* 167; for extreme anxiety-induced motor symptoms, see, e.g., Goldenson, *Behavior,* 262.

[122] Sanders, *John,* 385.

[123] *Sipra Sh. M.D.* 99.5.12; cf. perhaps 1 Sam 4:18.

[124] Artapanus in Eusebius *Praep. ev.* 9.27.24–26 (*OTP* 2:901). Talbert, *John,* 233, adds later traditions in which priests fell on their faces when hearing the divine name (*b. Qidd.* 71a; *Eccl. Rab.* 3:11, §3) and Egyptians fell forward when they heard Simeon, whom they were to arrest (*Gen. Rab.* 91:6).

[125] E.g., Meeks, *Prophet-King,* 289. Biblical tradition applied such language to any prophetic words (e.g., 1 Kgs 8:15, 20, 24; Dan 4:33), but those extant in the first century were read as part of Scripture.

[126] One can thus argue for historical verity on the basis of consistency with other tradition here, but the case is not helpful without an eyewitness tradition that could clarify the earlier protective anonymity; where information was lacking, historians sometimes filled in what seemed historically plausible, as they practiced writing "speeches-in-character."

surprising if he were still alive and still in Jerusalem.[127] But the specific identification of Peter is especially striking in view of Peter's impending denial.[128] Peter's zeal proves a positive contrast to Judas's betrayal (18:10), but his own denial will prove a negative contrast with the commitment of Jesus (18:17–27).[129] Loyalty with a weapon in one's hand and hope of messianic help is not the same as loyalty when self-defense is impossible, and in John's account Peter's act soon comes back to haunt him (18:26). The narrative leaves no doubt that for Johannine Christians Jesus must be the only real hero; even the beloved disciple who follows Jesus to the cross does not take up his own cross to die with him (12:25–26; 19:26–27).[130]

The addition of names (Peter and Malchus) does not necessarily imply lateness of tradition,[131] nor should one suppose a symbolic meaning for the name Malchus.[132] Malchus was a common enough name in the Semitic East, both for Gentiles[133] and Jews;[134] if the early church had any contacts with the priesthood at all (Acts 6:7) and if this act of violence became a matter of common report, it is not implausible that the name of a highly placed person such as Malchus might be reported. Scholars have offered varied proposals for why Peter struck the ear. Daube suggests that disfigurement such as the removal of an ear rendered a member of the priestly class ceremonially unfit for service.[135] The servant of a high priest could wield considerable power and probably was wielding a prominent role in this expedition;[136] high priests often had great affection for their servants.[137] One wonders, however, whether the servant was himself necessarily a born Levite permitted to perform Levitical duties.

One might also assault the ear if it were the only organ available, as when Zeno of Elea pretended to lean toward a tyrant's ear to speak in it but bit it off instead.[138] Most likely, therefore, Peter removed Malchus's ear only because Malchus moved to avoid being hit in the neck. That Peter could intentionally remove only an ear requires us to believe either that Peter was very precise with his sword or that Malchus stood still while

---

[127] On the latter point, see Theissen, *Gospels,* 184–89 (who doubts John's identification with Peter).

[128] Droge, "Peter," argues that the identification fits John's negative characterization of Peter throughout the Gospel.

[129] Cf., e.g., Suggit, "Nicodemus," 91.

[130] Neyrey, "Shame of Cross," 120, argues that a disciple's militant defense of a teacher's honor (or life!) would normally be honorable in Mediterranean antiquity; but Jesus says nonresistance is honorable because he does the Father's will.

[131] Bruce, "Trial," 19 n. 10, with Sanders, *Tendencies,* 10, 24–25. Names often were added (e.g., Plutarch *Alex.* 20.4–5), but writers could also draw on more than one tradition.

[132] Bruce, "Trial," 10, against Guilding, *Worship,* 165–66 (who attributes it to Zech 11:6).

[133] E.g., Josephus *Ant.* 13.132; 14.370–375; *War* 1.276 (Malichus); Eunapius *Lives* 456 (a Syrian whose name means "king"). Some thus suggest that Malchus was a Nabatean Arab or a Syrian (Lane, *Mark,* 526), though this surmise goes beyond the evidence.

[134] E.g., Malichus in Josephus *Ant.* 14.84, 273; *War* 1.162, 223–235.

[135] Daube, "Notes," 59–60 (citing *t. Parah* 3:8). Cf. Derrett, "Sword," whose allegorizing here is mostly uncontrolled.

[136] Cf., e.g., the managerial roles of some household servants (Epictetus *Diatr.* 3.22.3; Chariton 1.12.8; 2.2.1; 1 Cor 4:1); servants of prominent individuals often wielded more social influence than free persons of some rank, so that some even married into slavery to improve their station (cf. comment on 1:27).

[137] Cf. Josephus *Ant.* 20.210; for more on high priests' servants (cf. also 18:18, 26), see data in Fiensy, "Composition," 224.

[138] Diogenes Laertius 9.5.26.

Peter swung. It seems unlikely that ancient readers accustomed to battle stories would readily jump to either conclusion; even in accounts of ancient epic heroes, as in the *Iliad,* warriors often missed their targets, killing or wounding a different person than the one for whom they aimed.

Whereas the passion narrative preserved in Mark emphasizes Jesus' reluctance for (albeit submission to) the cup his Father had given him (Mark 14:36), John, consistent with his portrayal of Jesus' willingness to lay down his life (John 10:18), emphasizes his commitment to drink it (18:11; cf. Mark 10:39; 14:36).[139] One may compare Socrates' willingness to drink his cup of hemlock,[140] but the most likely comparison stems from the cup as a symbol of judgment in the biblical prophets.[141] This is not to imply that 18:11 is purely a Johannine invention; John betrays no clear indication of dependence on Matthew in his Gospel, yet Matthew 26:52 also reports Jesus' command to sheath the sword.[142] But the particular traditions John reports and the manner in which he arranges and presents them provide a different portrait of Jesus' approach to his death than the Markan stream of tradition emphasizes.

## Priestly Interrogation and Peter's Denial (18:12–27)

That Jesus' enemies now have him in their power and his own most prominent disciple simultaneously denies him provides a forceful comparison for John's audience: do not join Jesus' enemies by compromising with their position, even when they hold all the political power. From what we know of John's audience, this is probably a summons to continue to confess a full Christology despite opposition from local synagogue leaders. Although Mark confirms that John follows historical tradition in linking an interrogation by the Jerusalem elite with the time of Peter's betrayal, what John records as part of his Gospel he intends to have more than merely historical significance (20:30–31).

### 1. Who Was Responsible for Jesus' Condemnation?

Because of the anti-Semitic use to which the account of Jesus' trial has been put, many Jewish and sensitive Gentile scholars are reluctant to suspect the Sanhedrin of condemning Jesus, especially in the unethical manner depicted in the Gospels. Thus in 1866 Rabbi Ludwig Philippson first argued that Romans but not Jews had condemned Jesus, and many subsequent Jewish scholars have agreed.[143] In examining this issue from a historical standpoint today, it is important to recall that those who tried Jesus were not the sum total of ethnic Jewry in Jesus' day; there were select members of Jerusalem's municipal aristocracy in league with the high priests and acting to keep peace between Rome and the people. Like most political elites, they gained and held power at the expense of

---

[139] Cf., e.g., Wilkinson, *Jerusalem,* 126.

[140] It had become proverbial; e.g., Seneca *Dial.* 1.3.12; Maximus of Tyre *Or.* 25.7.

[141] Ps 11:6; 60:3; 75:8; Isa 29:9–10; 51:17, 21–23; 63:6; Jer 25:15–29; Lam 4:21; Zech 12:2; cf. 4Q176 frg. 6, 7, line 2 (quoting Isa 51:22–23); *Pss. Sol.* 8:14–15; Rev 14:10; in the ancient Near East, Albright and Mann, *Matthew,* 327. For a fuller treatment of the "cup," see Keener, *Matthew,* 637–38, cf. 486.

[142] Brown, *Death,* 86. Likewise, only John and Luke note that it was the servant's right ear (18:10; Luke 22:50).

[143] Blinzler, *Trial,* 9. See, e.g., Zeitlin, "Trial"; Flusser, *Judaism,* 588–92.

some other people and were resented by various groups they had suppressed or marginalized. Challenges to the historical reliability of the trial segment of the Gospels' passion narrative are addressed below.[144]

Some have overemphasized the Jewish leaders' responsibility.[145] One scholar even points to Jewish evidence for crucifixion on the charge of treason[146] though this was clearly normally a Roman penalty in this period[147] and Rome normally prevented its subjects from executing a person without a Roman hearing (18:31); mob lynchings occurred, but crucifixion was too slow for a secure lynching!

But neither does a total denial of involvement on the part of the Jewish officials make historical sense. What most supports the Gospel's basic description is that things were usually done as the Gospels describe. The local municipal elite would bring charges to the Roman governor, who depended on them for investigation and prosecution. As Overman notes, "That Jesus should come to the attention of [Roman officials] at all is owed, most likely, to local notables who found his group too annoying or dangerous."[148] Workers of miracles would naturally draw crowds, inviting the concern of those the Romans had left guardians of national stability.[149] Overturning tables in the temple (2:14–16) was certain to bring Jesus into collision with the priestly aristocracy.[150] Even Winter, while skeptical of some details of the narrative—doubtful that Jewish officers participated in Jesus' arrest and doubtful of a genuine Jewish trial—admits that, as in the Fourth Gospel, Jesus may have been "interrogated by a Jewish official before he was handed back to the Romans for trial."[151] The narratives make the most sense if both Jewish leaders and Romans were involved.[152]

But the Fourth Gospel, despite its generally pervasive polemic against the Jewish leaders, emphasizes a Jewish trial far less than the Synoptics do, and in the Fourth Gospel the issue is political (11:48) rather than religious (Mark 14:64).[153] Moroever, in contrast to Mark and Matthew, John "gives no indication of participation by the people"; one could read John's narrative as if the priestly elite alone were guilty of Jesus' condemnation.[154]

## 2. Historicity of the Trial Narrative

Some have assailed the historicity of the "trial" that occurs here;[155] others have shown that the arguments against authenticity are at best inconclusive and at worst fallacious.[156] Some evidence that could be adduced on the issue is questionable. Rabbinic sources

---

[144] For a full summary of views until the past quarter century, see Blinzler, *Trial*, 3–21; Rabello, "Conditions," 735–36 n. 295; and esp. Catchpole, *Trial*.

[145] Probably, e.g., Bammel, "Trial," 445.

[146] Betz, "Trial," citing 11QT 64:6–13.

[147] Most Jewish texts portray it as a Roman method of execution (Overman, *Community*, 380).

[148] Overman, *Community*, 381.

[149] Cf. Smith, *Magician*, 16.

[150] E.g., Vermes, *Religion*, ix–x.

[151] Winter, *Trial*, 30.

[152] So also Brown, *Death*, 250, though basing this partly on the involvement of Roman troops in the arrest; see comment above on 18:3.

[153] See Townsend, "Jews," 77.

[154] E.g., Kaufman, *Disciple*, 12.

[155] E.g., Winter, *Trial*; idem, "Trial"; Cohn, *Trial*, 98; Zeitlin, "Trial."

[156] Goppelt, *Jesus, Paul, and Judaism*, 84ff.; Sherwin-White, *Society*, 34ff.; cf. Sherwin-White, "Trial"; Catchpole, *Trial*, 271; Blinzler, *Trial*, 117–21; Corley, "Trial."

acknowledge the Jewish trial of Jesus yet not the Roman trial;[157] but the former record probably derives from a response to Jewish Christian polemic whereas the latter silence may derive from embarrassment for the need for Roman intervention[158] or from the same polemic.

## 2A. Violation of Legal Procedures?

Most often writers have cited against the Gospel account its incompatibility with rabbinic sources concerning proper legal procedures,[159] but this argument is difficult to defend today.[160] Although elements of the later Mishnaic code of legal conduct are probably early,[161] it is tenuous to dispute the historicity of the earlier Gospel accounts of the trials (which include traditions more contemporary than those on which the Mishnah is based) on the basis of conflicts with those rules.

First, the Mishnah reports Pharisaic idealizations of the law in its own day, at a period over a century later than Jesus' trial,[162] and the ruling council in Jesus' day was hardly dominated by Pharisees.[163] Second, rabbinic sources themselves indicate that the aristocratic priests did not always play by the rules;[164] in fact, because elements of proper legal procedure were standard throughout Mediterranean antiquity, the Gospel writers may expect us to notice significant breaches of procedure. Unless one presupposes that the aristocratic priests (like later rabbis) would follow careful procedure even in explosive political situations—which is unlikely—an argument from Mishnaic technicalities does not work against the Gospel narrative.[165] Sanders puts the matter best:

> The gospel accounts do present problems, but disagreement with the Mishnah is not one of them. . . . The system *as the gospels describe it* corresponds to the system that we see in Josephus. The trial of Jesus agrees very well with his stories of how things happened.[166]

Further, the "trial" account of Matthew and Mark probably represents what was more technically a preliminary inquiry, in which Jesus' interrogators would be even less likely to regard the rules as constraining;[167] the hearing is certainly not a technical trial in John (John 18:19–24, 28; cf. Luke 22:66). At this point John's account is actually easier to envision historically without corroborative evidence than Mark's;[168] thus Sanders opines, "There is nothing intrinsically improbable about the account in John,"[169] and one specialist in the trial narrative suggests that John's account of the trial "deserves the greatest respect from the point of view of historical reconstruction."[170] John's portrait fits his story

---

[157] Stauffer, *Jesus,* 225.

[158] So ibid., 225.

[159] E.g., Grant, "Review"; Cohn, *Trial,* 98, 105.

[160] For surveys of views concerning the legality of Jesus' trial, see, e.g., Brown, *Death,* 330–31.

[161] Abrahams, *Studies,* 2:129.

[162] Brown, *Death,* 357–63; Blinzler, *Trial,* 138–43.

[163] Cf. Anderson, *Mark,* 326; *pace* Cohn, *Trial,* 105.

[164] Cf. Klausner, *Jesus,* 337.

[165] Those with power (Roman governors, Herod, Agrippa I) usually executed whom they chose (Sanders, *Jesus and Judaism,* 317); others with more limited power undoubtedly exercised what they could.

[166] Sanders, *Judaism,* 487.

[167] See, e.g., Cullmann, *State,* 42, 46; Argyle, *Matthew,* 206; Reicke, *Era,* 146; Hagner, *Matthew,* 797.

[168] See Sanders, *Jesus and Judaism,* 318; also, e.g., Meier, *Matthew,* 330.

[169] Sanders, *Jesus and Judaism,* 317.

[170] Catchpole, *Trial,* 271.

world as well as the historical data; the Jerusalem elite had been wanting Jesus' death for some time.[171]

In John, Annas and then Joseph Caiaphas privately interrogated Jesus without a mention of witnesses or charge (although some leading local citizens may be assumed to have been present to provide support for the charge to Pilate the following morning, 18:31, 35).[172] The Synoptic traditions also confirm that Jesus was first at the house of the high priest (Mark 14:53–54, 66; Luke 22:54).[173] Josephus shows us that such informal trials could suffice for some high priests, who then made recommendations to the Roman governor.[174]

Finally, the Gospel writers probably intended to convey breach of procedure, not to pretend that the mock trial and abuse they depict were standard Jewish custom.[175] At this point we should pause to mention possible breaches of procedure (if the laws were early and the Gospel writers or their traditions seek to portray them as breaches of procedure). To the extent that the later sources provide a reliable picture of legal ethics that the Sanhedrin would have respected (and broader Mediterranean legal ethics suggest that they would have at least regarded many of the principles later preserved in rabbinic literature as ideal), probable breaches of legal ethics indicated in the Gospel trial narratives include the following.

First, judges must conduct and conclude capital trials during daylight (*m. Sanh.* 4:1);[176] this may explain a late, brief, more official meeting around 5:30 a.m., before conducting Jesus to Pilate (cf. Luke 22:66–71; cf. John 18:24), but the high priests probably were unconcerned with such details. Further, trials should not occur on the eve of a Sabbath or festival day,[177] as this day is (18:28); but officials may have regarded this as an emergency situation.[178] Even Pharisaic interpretation supported executing an extraordinary offender on a pilgrimage festival to warn others not to repeat the crime;[179] the offenders included those regarded as false prophets, among others.[180]

---

[171] See Michaels, "Trial."

[172] Stauffer, *Jesus*, 122, thinks the cognomen Caiaphas betrays skill as an inquisitor; but would he not have born this cognomen before his interrogatory activity?

[173] For the sort of palatial homes on the eastern slope of upper-city Jerusalem owned by many members of the priestly aristocracy, see Rupprecht, "House."

[174] Sanders, *Figure*, 67. Romans regarded it a crime to try and condemn one in a private rather than a public setting, especially the judge's home rather than his tribunal (Cicero *Verr.* 2.3.23.56; Seneca *Controv.* 9.2.4).

[175] Cf. Hooker, *Message*, 86; Rhoads and Michie, *Mark*, 120–21; Keener, "Mistrial." Brown, *Death*, 433 observes that "ancient literary accounts of famous trials" usually include polemic or bias. Trial scenes can also provide suspense in a plot, e.g., in Chariton, toward the beginning and later before the king of Persia.

[176] Cf. Pompey's interpretation of Roman law in Aulus Gellius 14.7.8.

[177] Cf. *m. Sanh.* 4:1; *Beṣah* 5:2; *t. Beṣah* 4:4; Philo *Migration* 91. Blinzler, *Trial*, 143–44, thinks rules against meeting on the eve of a holy day are later. Some Roman laws opposed certain kinds of trials on holidays (*Lex irnitana* tablet 10 A, ch. 92; Metzger, *Civil Trial*, 16–17) and may have required advance notice as well (*Lex irnitana* tablet 10 A, ch. 90; though Metzger, *Civil Trial*, 60, thinks this applies to postponements).

[178] A festival was also the one sort of occasion when one could gather more of the Sanhedrin if members came from outside Jerusalem (Reicke, *Era*, 145); but as we argued above, the Sanhedrin was largely drawn from the municipal aristocracy; and the point is moot, in any case, in the Fourth Gospel's account.

[179] Commentators (e.g., Dalman, *Jesus-Jeshua*, 98; Lane, *Mark*, 529–30; Stauffer, *Jesus*, 209) cite *m. Sanh.* 11:4; *t. Sanh.* 11:7. This differs from the Roman practice (Cicero *Cael.* 1.1; Seneca *Controv.* 5.4; Suetonius *Tib.* 61; cf. Acts 12:3–4).

[180] Hill, *Prophecy*, 52.

Other possible breaches of judicial ethics occur. If the Mishnah provides any indication of their view, Pharisaic scruples also required a day to pass before issuing a verdict of condemnation (*m. Sanh.* 4:1). But the Sadducees, disinclined to share power more than necessary, may have generally preferred speedier executions than the Pharisees thought appropriate.[181] Further, the Sanhedrin should not meet in the high priest's palace;[182] their normal meeting place (what rabbinic sources call "the chamber of hewn stone") was on or near the Temple Mount (*m. Mid.* 5:5; *Sanh.* 11:2; Josephus *War* 5.144).[183]

Most obviously, Jewish law opposed false witnesses, reported in the Synoptic passion narratives. The biblical penalty for false witnesses in a capital case was execution (Deut 19:16–21), and later Jewish ideals, at least, continued to regard this penalty as appropriate,[184] as did Roman law.[185] Cross-examination of witnesses was standard in Jewish law,[186] and apparently the examiners did their job well enough here to produce contradictions they did not expect. In the end, these witnesses could provide only a garbled account of Jesus' proclamation of judgment against the temple (cf. John 2:19; Acts 6:14), which could have seemed to the Sanhedrin political reason enough to convict him.[187] John reports no witnesses during the passion itself except Jesus (18:37), who challenges his opponents to bear witness of any wrong he has done (18:23; cf. 8:46).

## 2B. Other Evidence

While one cannot prove the veracity of the contents of the trial narrative at this remove, skepticism that the first followers of Jesus would have had access to such information[188] also assumes too much. Sources for the trial narrative may derive from Joseph of Arimathea (Mark 15:43), from connections within the high priest's household (John 18:15–16), from others who later became disciples or sympathizers (John 19:39; cf. perhaps Acts 6:7), or Jesus himself (cf. Acts 1:3); it is unthinkable at least that the early Palestinian tradition would have neglected the witness of anyone, such as Joseph, who could have had contacts present at the trial. That leaks from within the Jerusalem council occurred on other occasions in the first century (Josephus *Life* 204) does not prove that such a leak occurred in Jesus' case, but it does challenge the claims of those who suppose such a leak implausible.[189]

---

181 Cf. *m. Mak.* 1:6; the Sadducees did prefer stricter punishments (Josephus *Ant.* 20.199). Later rabbis preferred longer deliberation in capital cases (cf., e.g., *Tg. Neof.* 1 on Lev 24:12; Num 9:8; 15:34; 27:5; *Tg. Ps.-J.* on Lev 24:12; Num 9:8; 15:34; 27:5).

182 Cohn, *Trial*, 98, cites *b. ʿAbod. Zar.* 8b; *Sanh.* 41b; *Šabb.* 15a.

183 See Wilkinson, *Jerusalem*, 86–87; Brown, *Death*, 350.

184 Josephus *Ant.* 4.219; 11QT 61.7–11; *m. Mak.* 1:7; *t. Sanh.* 6:6; *Sipre Deut.* 190.5.1.

185 Ferguson, *Backgrounds*, 51; cf. the penalty in Seneca *Controv.* 5.4, if genuine. So also reportedly Egyptian custom (Diodorus Siculus 1.77.2). Diodorus Siculus 12.12.2 thus considers particularly merciful a law that merely shames false witnesses so much that they flee a city.

186 E.g., Sus 48–62; *m. ʾAbot* 1:9; *Sanh.* 5:1–4; *t. Sanh.* 6:3, 6; *Sipre Deut.* 93.2.1; 149.1.1–2; 189.1.3.

187 Brown, *Death*, 458; Stanton, *Gospel Truth*, 180–83. Greek rhetoric often preferred arguments from probability and internal consistency (which were frequent, e.g., Demosthenes *On the Embassy* 120; *Against Pantaenetus* 23; Aristotle *Rhet.* 1.15.17, 1376a; Dionysius of Halicarnassus *R.A.* 3.35.5–6; 11.34.1–6; Josephus *Ag. Ap.* 1.219–220, 267, 286; 2.8–27, 82, 148; *Life* 342, 350; Acts 26:8) to witnesses (see Kennedy, *Classical Rhetoric*, 20–21), but the effective testimony of witnesses was nevertheless adequate to convict (Dionysius of Halicarnassus *R.A.* 8.78.3). Any proofs were, however, better than mere assertions (Josephus *Ant.* 17.131).

188 E.g., Sanders, *Jesus and Judaism*, 299.

189 Those of rank, such as Joseph, would often have had friends aware of plots even if they themselves were not present (cf., e.g., Cornelius Nepos 4 [Pausanias], 5.1; 14 [Datames], 5.3). Even

Together the cleansing of the temple (which would offend the Sadducean aristocracy) and crucifixion by the Romans suggest the intermediary step of arrest by the priestly authorities; as Sanders observes, conflict with the Romans, crowds, or Pharisees would not explain subsequent events, but the continuing enmity of the chief priests against Jesus' followers (e.g., Acts 4:1–7; 5:17–18; 9:1–2) points to the priestly aristocracy as the main source of opposition.[190] Given high-priestly involvement, the Gospel writers are not so generous as to have alleged even the pretense of a hearing if in fact they had no tradition that one occurred. Like most modern preachers, the Gospel writers were more interested in applying their text than in creating a wholly new source to be applied.

## 3. Annas and Caiaphas (18:12–14)

Some writers have charged that John's use of the name Annas reflects Jewish-Christian tradition but lacks historical foundation, since Annas had long since retired from office.[191] Yet this approach reads too much into Annas's "retirement"; it is likely that he continued to exert power within his household (especially if they privately recognized the biblical tradition concerning the lifelong character of a high priest's calling), including through his son-in-law Caiaphas, until his death in 35 C.E. After Vitellius, legate of Syria, deposed Caiaphas in 36 C.E., he replaced him with Jonathan son of Annas;[192] in time all five sons of Annas followed in office, suggesting that Annas had in fact exercised considerable influence.[193] In any case, even though it was customary to refer to the entire high-priestly family by John's day as "high priests,"[194] John labels only Caiaphas here as "high priest," not Annas (contrast Acts 4:6).

John's report about Annas may well reflect historical tradition; it is independent from the Synoptics and not derived from John's theology.[195] John has no specific reason to preserve the names of high priests,[196] but if he would preserve any, Caiaphas, who actually was high priest at the time of the hearing, would make most sense; his audience already anticipates Jesus confronting Caiaphas (11:49). Quirinius installed Annas as high priest in 6 C.E.,[197] but Valerius Gratus deposed him in 15 C.E.[198] Because Jewish law mandated the high priesthood

---

the Roman senate's inner secrets often leaked out, in contrast to the earliest times (Valerius Maximus 2.2.1a).

[190] Sanders, *Jesus and Judaism*, 286. Rabbinic attestation of a religious trial of Jesus (Stauffer, *Jesus*, 225; cf. Herford, *Christianity*, 78–83) is late and probably derivative, and hence we do not admit it as independent evidence; but a Jewish hearing is essential. Even Winter, who emphasizes an arrest and agenda set by Romans (*Trial*, 30, 147), recognizes that Pilate would have expected the high priest's aides to prepare the case (p. 29).

[191] Winter, *Trial*, 33.

[192] Josephus *Ant.* 18.95.

[193] Josephus *Ant.* 20.198; on his power, see further Reicke, *Era*, 142–43.

[194] E.g., 1QM 2:1; Josephus *War* 2.243, 316, 320, 342; 410–411; 4.151, 315; *Life* 197; Mark 2:26; 11:27; 14:1; John 7:32; Acts 4:23; 5:24; 9:14, 21.

[195] See Blinzler, *Trial*, 88–89; Dodd, *Tradition*, 93–94.

[196] Matt 26:3, 57 and Luke 3:2 mention Caiaphas; Luke 3:2 briefly mentions Annas; neither name appears in Mark. John may mention both because the Synoptics attest two inquiries (Barrett, *John*, 529), but this is less probable given John's independence on the inquiries themselves.

[197] Josephus *Ant.* 18.26. Ananus is a variant Greek rendering of Annas; one may survey the frequent names, both masculine and feminine, cognate to Annas in antiquity (e.g., *CIJ* 1:62, §88; 1:228, §290; 1:244, §310; 1:314–15, §411; 2:127, §907; 2:155, §967; 2:186, §§1013, 1014; 2:195, §1066; *CPJ* 1:165–66, §24; Acts 9:10; see more fully *CPJ* 3:169).

[198] Josephus *Ant.* 18.34.

for life, many Jews may have still considered Annas the appropriate official to decide important cases like this one.[199] A second hearing before Caiaphas may correspond to the second, early-morning hearing in Mark 15:1.[200] The nature of Jesus' encounter with Annas fits the Johannine perspective on conflict with the authorities, but preservation of Annas's name and relation to Caiaphas probably suggests that the event itself, while capable of serving John's purposes, also reflects historical tradition.

Pharisaic tradition prohibited a single individual from acting as judge (*m. ʾAbot* 4:8),[201] but Annas would have cared little for Pharisaic scruples, would have enough colleagues present to provide a semblance of communal assent (18:31, 35), and could have asserted that he was conducting an informal rather than an official interrogation;[202] moreover, John is not necessarily inclined to portray Annas in a pious light, in any case. Because Annas was not officially high priest and was in no legal position to try Jesus, he was required to get the official verdict from his son-in-law Caiaphas (18:14); the behind-the-scenes maneuvering provides John with another polemical image with which to challenge the legitimacy of the Judean elite who prosecuted Jesus—and those whom he viewed as their Judean successors, who he believed were repressing his own generation of Jewish Christians.

That Caiaphas was priest "that year" (18:13) distinguishes his tenure from that of Annas, who lacked legal right to interrogate Jesus. The expression may imply "in that fateful year of Jesus' execution" and may also point to the instability of the priestly office and its perceived associations with Roman power. (See more fully the comment on the expression in 11:49, 51.) John recalls Caiaphas for his audience particularly by words that John interpreted as prophetically significant (18:14; 11:50).

## 4. Peter's First Denial (18:15–18)

An anonymous disciple introduced Peter into the high priest's household. Is the "other disciple" who was known to the high priest (18:15–16) the "beloved disciple"?[203] This was the assumption of most early Christian commentators.[204] The designation "known" could imply only a casual acquaintance, enough to get past the porter through knowledge of some of the servants.[205] Conversely, it may imply a member of the high priest's circle, perhaps a kinsman, rather than a mere acquaintance.[206] If so, it might be counted either for or against an identification with the beloved disciple, though much more *likely* against. In favor of the beloved disciple, this picture would fit the author's re-

---

[199] Ellis, *Genius*, 255.

[200] Ibid.

[201] The saying probably reflects mistrust for human fairness (cf. Vermes, *Religion*, 159).

[202] Blinzler, *Trial*, 136.

[203] So, e.g., Collins, *Written*, 42.

[204] Wiles, *Gospel*, 9, citing Theodore of Mopsuestia 233.23; John Chrysostom *Hom. Jo.* 83.2; Cyril of Alexandria 3.29.26–27 on John 18:15. Interestingly, Chrysostom (2.1) nevertheless thought that John must have been very poor or his father would not have allowed him to leave fishing to follow Jesus (Wiles, *Gospel*, 10). Fishermen could make more income if they sold directly to the rich rather than through middlemen (Alciphron *Fishermen* 9 [Aegialeus to Struthion], 1.9).

[205] Ridderbos, *John*, 581.

[206] Dodd, *Tradition*, 86–87. Dodd (p. 88) thus suggests that the Fourth Gospel provides information from a Judean disciple's source comparatively neglected by the Synoptics (though they also, he believes, show some Judean supporters of Jesus).

peated comparison of Peter and the beloved disciple, which favors the latter (13:23–24; 20:4–8)[207]—here in terms of status though being "known to" Jesus is far more important (cf. 10:14). But the nearly uniform opposition of Judeans, especially those of the Jerusalem elite, earlier in the Gospel makes an identification with one of Jesus' Galilean followers more difficult to conceive, and members of John's audience with much understanding of the Gospel's geographical politics might be skeptical of it.[208] Moreover, other disciples in the Gospel are anonymous (6:9; 21:2; perhaps 1:37), and at this point in the narrative, John would probably more plainly identify this disciple as the "disciple Jesus loved" if he intended for that identification to be clear.[209]

Doorkeepers were standard in any households of means.[210] In households of moderate means, a servant might fill this role among others,[211] but larger estates might employ a full-time porter. A doorkeeper's responsibility was to ask a visitor's identity, especially when one came at night,[212] and to observe who entered and exited the premises.[213] Indeed, even after entrance, anyone found in the house and not recognized as one of the servants might be asked to identify himself or herself.[214] Even if the woman trusted the first, unnamed disciple (exceptions might be made for acquaintances), her question whether this man was also (καί) one of Jesus' disciples is not likely a friendly one. Whether she discerned his Galilean accent (Mark 14:70), recalled having noticed him with Jesus in the nearby temple courts in recent days, or simply guessed on the basis of the man who introduced him to her is unclear and immaterial to the story's point.

Some suggest that Peter's denial of Jesus (18:17) would have appeared an appropriate way to maintain honor had he not thereby violated his earlier word of honor to follow Jesus even to the death (13:37–38).[215] In view of the greater potential threat to Peter (his life, not merely his honor), it would not be surprising if many of his contemporaries would have been tempted to follow the same course as Peter. But in view of the Passion Narrative's contrast between Peter's denials and Jesus' faithful confession on behalf of his followers (18:8; cf. 8:19–20),[216] Peter's denial appears shameful even had he not offered Jesus his

[207] For this disciple's favorable comparison with Peter here, see also Haenchen, *John,* 2:168; see comment on 13:23–24.
[208] Vicent Cernuda, "Desvaído," suggests Lazarus, which could be plausible if 12:10 is fictitious, but again, why not name him this late if John knows his identity?
[209] See also Charlesworth, *Disciple,* 336–59, but his proposal that the disciple was Judas (pp. 342–59) seems unlikely though Judas was probably from Judea and handled Jesus' money (343). John would probably name Judas if he implied him, though it is possible (as ibid., 359) that Judas played this role in John's tradition but John wished not to name him.
[210] E.g., Ovid *Amores* 1.6.1–2; Plutarch *Cicero* 15.1; 36.3; Seneca *Ep. Lucil.* 19.11; implied in Seneca *Controv.* 10.4.22. Householders who had porters had no reason to answer the door themselves (Theophrastus *Char.* 4.9 considers it ignorant behavior); a household member sneaking to answer the door might be suspected of mischief (Tibullus 1.2.7, 15–24, 41, 55–56). Undoubtedly porters screened unwelcome guests, provided safety, and moved the sometimes heavy doors.
[211] E.g., Aelius Aristides *Defense of Oratory* 380, §127; Acts 12:13.
[212] Cicero *Phil.* 2.31.77.
[213] E.g., Ovid *Fasti* 1.138, where this summarizes their job.
[214] Plutarch *Cicero* 28.2.
[215] Malina and Rohrbaugh, *Commentary,* 160–61.
[216] For the contrast between Jesus and Peter in the Synoptic account, cf. Theissen, *Gospels,* 196, though his reconstruction of the *Sitz im Leben* is dubious here. Ancient readers could grasp such a contrast; leaders who charged into battle sometimes thereby shamed their retreating troops into joining them (e.g., Appian *R.H.* 10.4.20). For a contrast between Peter's denial and the beloved disciple's testimony in the Gospel, see Beck, *Paradigm,* 141 (though cf. also 6:68–69).

word. Given the values of honor toward one's teacher, the view may have been widespread that the honor of a person's teacher or disciple should be as dear to one as one's own.[217] Falsely denying one's relationship with another was shameful.[218] The slave demanded whether Peter was one of Jesus' disciples, and he denied it (18:17)—just as the elite did when confronted with the same question from the formerly blind man (9:27–29), though some had been more open in private (cf. 9:16). Peter thus aligns himself with the enemies of Jesus here.

Only those willing to follow to the death were full disciples (12:25–26); Jesus demanded not mere signs-faith or profession that failed to persevere (8:30–31; 15:6) but open confession (12:42–43). Peter denies being Jesus' disciple, like the Pharisees who oppressed Jesus' followers but in contrast to the formerly blind man who became a paradigm for Christian discipleship (9:27–28; cf. also 1:20); intimidated by the brute force of the Judean elite (cf. 9:20–22), Peter proved a lover of their approval more than of the Lord for whom he claimed to be ready to die (12:42–43).[219] The text strikes a note of severe warning to John's audience: regardless of the opposition, they must maintain their faith (20:31).

At the same time, Peter's later restoration (21:7, 11, 15–17) provides an opportunity of hope for those who have proved weak but wish to return. Of the Gospels, John alone specifies that the fire by which Peter warmed himself was a charcoal fire (ἀνθρακιάν, only here and in 21:9 in the NT);[220] the term probably connects the scene of his denial with his later restoration, for it recurs in 21:9 as part of the setting of Peter's restoration. (Some take the cold weather as symbolic in 18:18, 25, but it fits an April night in Jerusalem and probably simply elucidates the commitment of Peter—favorably to at least this extent—and the suffering of Jesus or explains why Peter is near those who question him; see Mark 14:54, 67.)

## 5. Jesus and the High Priest (18:19–24)

The scene cuts between Peter, in the process of denying Jesus (18:15–18), and Jesus' courage (18:19–24), including in protecting his disciples (18:19). In this instance the parallel with the similar Markan digression and resumption need not indicate either dependence on Mark or an independent tradition shared by both; it might simply represent a standard literary device for building suspense.[221] Immediately following the first report of Peter's denial (18:17), Jesus evades a question about his disciples (18:19–20)[222] and suffers for it (18:22), as he earlier embraced arrest to preserve his disciples (18:8).

The teachings about which they wished to question him (18:19) may have included his public apparent threat against the temple, which had engendered some hostility (2:19–20); meanwhile the faction represented by Nicodemus, who thought Jesus' teaching was from God, has fallen silent (3:2; cf. 12:42). It is possible that Annas's line of question-

---

[217] E.g., ʾAbot R. Nat. 27A (R. Eleazar ben Shammua).

[218] E.g., Terence Phormio 392–394.

[219] Cf. Daube, "Limitations": Peter's denials in Mark begin with evasion, which later rabbis considered acceptable, but escalated into open, direct renunciation although sanctifying the divine name held precedence over protecting one's life.

[220] Presumably these servants and temple police, involved in Jesus' arrest, had not yet been dismissed because they would still need to escort Jesus elsewhere (18:24, 28).

[221] Evans, "Warming," noting parallel structure in, e.g., Greek romances.

[222] Interrogation about one's disciples fits the procedure in Deut 13 as later understood by the rabbis (b. Sanh. 43b, bar., in Dodd, Tradition, 95); for the charge of Jesus as a "seducer" in view of Deut 13 and 17, see, e.g., Hill, "Sanhedrin"; Schneider, "Charge," 414.

ing (18:19) is unethical; certainly striking a prisoner on trial was unethical (18:22). Yet apart from the well-to-do, few in the ancient world could expect justice when in conflict with the well-to-do; even ancient laws were slanted to favor the powerful,[223] and the powerful in some cases simply circumvented normal legal procedures[224] (e.g., Roman soldiers impressing animals belonging to local residents).[225] Other early Jewish reports about members of Jerusalem's priestly aristocracy (see above) suggest that others besides Jesus experienced this municipal aristocracy in a harsh way. Of course, John could have good polemical reasons for portraying Jesus' oppressors as abusing power; presenting one's opponents as at an advantage even though they have less to lose in the conflict was a useful form of argument.[226] But arguments did not have to be false to be effective. John hardly creates this charge of abuse of power from thin air; miscarriages of justice occurred frequently, and unless we think Jesus was historically a revolutionary (a thesis that does little to address the radically apolitical movement that preserved his teachings), the Romans and any elite Jewish allies they had committed such an act in Jesus' case.

## 5A. Interrogation and Response (18:19–21)

Some think that the high priest's line of interrogation (18:19) could have appeared unethical to some of John's audience.[227] Although Jewish law did not explicitly prohibit condemning a prisoner on his own testimony in a capital case before Maimonides, opposition to this practice, based on inference from the biblical text, may have been more ancient.[228] Others argue, building from forensic language earlier in John and from Jewish law, that Jesus, already publicly vindicated, recognizes that he cannot be legally tried again here.[229] Either proposal might answer why Jesus refuses to answer directly (18:20–21). But perhaps both proposals require more knowledge of Jewish law, especially Pharisaic law, than most of John's audience would recognize. John's audience would, however, have been familiar with the powerful's ability to pervert justice. As already mentioned, law codes themselves favored those of higher status,[230] and municipal aristocracies acting in secret might not even answer to such law codes.[231] Given the submissive cringing expected by those who appeared before the municipal authorities (e.g., Josephus *Ant.* 14.172–173), Jesus' lack of fear would also strike the audience as noteworthy.[232]

---

[223] Gaius *Inst.* 4.183; P.Hal. 1.124–127; Theissen, *Setting,* 97; ancient Mesopotamian legal collections such as Hammurabi, Lipit-Ishtar, and Eshnunna. Israelite and, for the most part, rabbinic law were exceptional in this regard (cf. *t. Sanh.* 1:8; 'Abot R. Nat. 20, §43; 33, §73B), but Jerusalem's aristocracy might interpret laws as needed for the public interest (cf. Josephus *Life* 189–195; *t. B. Qam.* 9:12; *Sanh.* 1:7).

[224] Lamented, e.g., in Petronius *Sat.* 14.

[225] For requisitioning, see, e.g., *Dig.* 50.4.18.4; 50.5.10.2–3; 50.5.11; *Cod. theod.* 8 passim, in Rapske, "Travel," 14; Sallust *Jug.* 75.4; for abuse of this right, see, e.g., Livy 43.7.11; 43.8.1–10; Apuleius *Metam.* 9.39; Herodian 2.3.4; 2.5.1; P.Lond. 3.1171, *IGLS* 5.1998 (= SEG 17.755), in Sherk, *Empire,* 89, 136; *P.S.I.* 446; Jones, *History,* 197; *p. Ḥag.* 2:1, §8; cf. P.Hal. 1.166–185.

[226] E.g., Dionysius of Halicarnassus *Lysias* 17.

[227] The rules may be Pharisaic and later, but we should note at least in passing the later procedure that would prevent a high priest from biasing his social inferiors by giving his view first (*m. Sanh.* 4:2; Blinzler, *Trial,* 135). Annas and Caiaphas here just seek a conviction.

[228] Barrett, *John,* 528; Ellis, *Genius,* 257.

[229] Thom, "Joodse." One might recount one's irreproachable life instead of stooping so low as to answer critics' charges (Appian *R.H.* 11.7.40–41).

[230] E.g., Gaius *Inst.* 4.183; Theissen, *Setting,* 97.

[231] Cf. the lack of due process in Apuleius *Metam.* 9.42.

[232] With Whitacre, *John,* 433.

Jesus' response makes good sense in this context (18:20–21).[233] Many teachers offered only private teachings,[234] some sectarian Jews believed they had special insight into mysteries hidden from others,[235] and some later rabbis offered particular esoteric teachings only in private settings;[236] Jesus has in fact provided some intimate teaching for his disciples privately in this Gospel (13:31–16:33). At the same time, Jesus in this Gospel has stated his identity much more openly than is recorded in the Synoptics (e.g., 8:58–59). Challenges that Jesus' teaching was private may have been important in John's setting (cf. 7:3–4), demanding a response.[237] If our reconstruction of the situation under Domitian is correct, some Roman officials were undoubtedly increasingly harsh with unregistered, secret religious associations.[238] Even in general, those who acted secretly were often thought to have much to hide.[239] Some later Jewish teachers also criticized false prophets as teaching secretly whereas teachers of Torah work publicly.[240] Perhaps some opponents of John's audience challenged the frequent high Christology of early Christians, especially Johannine Christians, in view of Jesus' less exalted claims in many of Jesus' public sayings—although it is admittedly unlikely that many of the opponents would have invested the time in learning much of the Jesus tradition.[241]

Jesus' appeal to the public nature of his teaching (cf. 7:14, 37; 8:20) also implicitly appeals to their failure to arrest him in public (cf. 7:26, 30, 32, 44–46; 8:20, 59; Luke 22:53)[242]—hence contrasting their secretive behavior with his own public behavior. In general, appeals to public knowledge strengthened one's case rhetorically (e.g., Josephus *Ag. Ap.* 2.107).[243] Rather than merely appealing to two or three witnesses, Josephus points to the support of the Galilean masses as witnesses on his behalf (*Life* 257), noting that they

---

[233] For somewhat evasive answers, cf. also Luke 22:67–68. Jesus talks more in John than in Mark, but cf. the variant Socratic tradition in which Socrates remained silent instead of answering his accusers (Maximus of Tyre *Or.* 3.4, 7; cf. Xenophon *Mem.* 4.8.4).

[234] Diogenes Laertius 3.63; 8.1.15; Aulus Gellius 13.5.5–12; even some rhetorical teachings were inappropriate for the general public or novices (Dionysius of Halicarnassus *Lit. Comp.* 25). Unwritten teachings provided "insiders" a superior status (see Botha, "Voice").

[235] E.g., 1QpHab 7.4–5, 13–14; 1QH 2.13–14; 9:23–24; 11:9–10, 16–17; 12:11–13; 1QS 8.1–2, 12; 9:13, 17–19; cf. 1QS 5.11–12; 11.3–5; 1QM 3:9; 17.9; *4 Ezra* 14:45–47.

[236] E.g., *b. Pesaḥ.* 119a; *Pesiq. Rab.* 22:2; especially regarding the throne-chariot (*t. Ḥag.* 2:1; *b. Ḥag.* 13a, bar; 14b, bar; *Šabb.* 80b; *p. Ḥag.* 2:1, §§3–4; cf. 4Qs140) and creation mysticism (*m. Ḥag.* 2:1; *t. Ḥag.* 2:1, 7; *ʾAbot R. Nat.* 39A; *b. Ḥag.* 15a, bar.; *p. Ḥag.* 2:1, §15; *Gen. Rab.* 1:5, 10; 2:4; *Pesiq. Rab Kah.* 21:5; *2 En.* 24:3).

[237] Sandmel, *Judaism,* 476 n. 48, suggests a polemic against Gnosticism here, but this is improbable; see our introduction, pp. 168–69. More persuasive would be the possibility of apologetic against the charges of political subversion, as in Acts 26:26 (see Malherbe, "Corner," 203).

[238] See our introduction; in other periods Romans also expressed concern over associations (e.g., Livy 39.15.11; *Dig.* 47.22.1; Judge, *Pattern,* 47–48), and even some earlier Greeks mistrusted the morality of some cult associations (Foucart, *Associations religieuses,* 153–77). Stauffer, *Jesus,* 122, reads distrust of secret associations into the high priest's interrogation.

[239] E.g., Dionysius of Halicarnassus *R.A.* 8.78.3; Livy 3.36.2; see comment on 3:2.

[240] *Sipre Deut.* 87.2.2.

[241] Cf. the alleged danger of contamination from even excess exposure to *minuth* a few decades after John (see, e.g., Herford, *Christianity,* 137–45, 388; Moore, *Judaism,* 2:250; Dalman, *Jesus,* 36–37).

[242] "Hour" and "darkness" in Luke 22:53 would have fit John's usage but perhaps not his Christology (with Jesus controlling the passion). In some cases, "Why did you not take me then?" could suggest a rhetorical appeal to a statute of limitations (Hermogenes *Issues* 44.10–12) but here refers simply to their secretive behavior.

[243] See also Demosthenes *Against Meidias* 1, 80; Euripides *Heracl.* 219; Plato *Apol.* 32E; Dionysius of Halicarnassus *R.A.* 7.43.2; Sallust *Speech of Gaius Cotta* 4; Josephus *Life* 361; Acts 26:4–5, 26.

can testify how he has lived (*Life* 258). Some Diaspora readers with a Hellenistic education might recall Socrates' reported claim before his judges never to have taught anything in private that he had not also spoken openly to the world.[244] An appeal to the public character of one's teaching, and lack of opposition at that point, would count as a strong argument against the subversiveness of one's speech—as well as an indictment of those now requiring a hasty, secret hearing (cf. John 18:13; Luke 22:53).

That Jesus spoke before the "world" in the synagogues and temple (18:20) continues John's identification of the Jewish authorities with the world.[245] The Fourth Gospel only once records Jesus' teaching in synagogues (6:59), but John's audience may presuppose them from more widely circulated gospel traditions (cf. Mark 1:39). The one example in John, however, certainly testifies that Jesus did not withhold potentially offensive information from prospective disciples (6:52, 66), just as his teaching in the temple did not (e.g., 8:59). The other mentions of synagogues in this Gospel all portray them as the ground of conflict between the synagogue authorities and Jesus' Jewish followers (9:22; 12:42; 16:2). Ironically, while Jesus ultimately offered some of his offensive teachings publicly, some who secretly suspected he was from God remained unwilling to say so "openly" for "fear of the Jews" (7:13; cf. 12:42).

## 5B. Abuse of the Prisoner (18:22–24)

One of the Jewish officers present struck Jesus for his response (18:22), just as Roman representatives of the world would (19:3). The officers, or at least those present at this point, have become more hostile since their first appearance in 7:32, 45–46 (cf. 18:3, 12, 18; 19:6). The indignation against Jesus' response may derive in part from the biblical prohibition against cursing a ruler of the people (Exod 22:28; cf. Acts 23:3),[246] but Jesus has not cursed the high priest. By contrast, whatever else may have violated Jewish law, striking a prisoner[247] during an informal hearing (18:22; cf. Acts 23:2) certainly would, as biblically versed prisoners seem to have understood (18:23; Acts 23:3). (Public corporal discipline after a sentence was a different matter; but that is not what this text describes.)[248] This detail continues the image of exploitation of power by the religious-political elite; such practices are attested elsewhere.[249] The detail is not a Johannine invention; the Synoptic tradition also reports abuse by Jewish captors, and the Synoptics do not simply attempt to convey Jewish responsibility, for they portray the Gentile mockers no less severely (cf. 19:2).[250] But John reports the Jewish abuse in less detail than the Synoptic line of tradition does (Mark 14:65).

---

[244] Plato *Apol.* 33, in MacGregor, *John*, 331. Secretive action is hostile (Philodemus frg. 41.2–3).

[245] E.g., Michaels, *John*, 296–97.

[246] Brown, *Death*, 585; for unofficial blows for reviling leaders in another ancient Mediterranean tradition, cf. Homer *Il.* 2.265; on honor accruing to even a disobedient priest, e.g., Acts 23:5; *p. Sanh.* 2:1, §2. On the requisite formality with social superiors, see, e.g., Malina, *Windows*, 37–38.

[247] Even those in authority who struck soldiers for discipline (Xenophon *Anab.* 5.8.12–13) might afterwards need to justify it (5.8.18). One might interpret "giving" a blow (also 19:3) as a worldly parody of the "giving" motif in John (cf. comment on 3:16), though here it may be simply idiomatic (cf. *Gen. Rab.* 78:11). For ῥάπισμα, see Isa 50:6 LXX.

[248] Deut 25:2–3; Josephus *Ant.* 4.238, 248; *m. Ḥul.* 5:2; *Kil.* 8:3; *Mak.* passim, e.g., 1:1–3; 3:3–5, 10–11; *Naz.* 4:3; *Pesaḥ.* 7:11; *Tem.* 1:1; *Sipra Qed. pq.* 4.200.3.3; *Sipre Deut.* 286.4.1; 5.1; *b. B. Meṣiʿa* 115b; *Ker.* 15a; *Ketub.* 33b; *Pesaḥ.* 24ab; *p. Bešah* 5:2, §11; *Naz.* 4:3, §1; *Ter.* 7:1; *Yoma* 77a; *Pesiq. Rab Kah.* 4:3.

[249] Cf. Brown, *John*, 2:827; Morris, *John*, 757 (citing the assault by the attendant in *b. Šebu.* 30b).

[250] Brown, *Death*, 877.

Jesus' response may allude to Exod 22:28, denying that he has cursed the authorities and inviting those present to function as witnesses.[251] (Witty retorts to such violence also appear as praiseworthy in the Greek school tradition.)[252] Jesus appears more careful to observe Jewish legal procedure than his interrogators do.[253] Lacking another advocate,[254] Jesus functions as his own παράκλητος (see comment on 14:16; 16:7–11).[255] Yet Jesus offers little defense for himself here; rather, he challenges the legal procedures of his accusers, for before God's court, it is his opposition, not himself, who stands on trial, and he exposes their sin (15:22). Likewise his followers would need to be prepared to face the world's hostility and to join their Paraclete in testifying against the world (16:7–11). Despite their inability to testify to any evil he has spoken (κακῶς ἐλάλησα, 18:23), his opposition will accuse him to Pilate as an "evildoer" (κακὸν ποιῶν, 18:30).

## 6. Peter's Final Denials (18:25–27)

Whereas Jesus proves bold, Peter's denials (18:25–27) appear shameful. In Jewish martyr stories, the protagonists refuse to renounce their ancestral faith even under the most terrible tortures and executions.[256] The third accusation against Peter came from a relative of Malchus, probably another important servant of the high priest (see comment on 18:10). The accusation of one of such high status would undoubtedly carry significant weight;[257] further, if he genuinely recognized Peter from the garden, he probably also recognized or would soon recall that Peter was the active aggressor with a sword. Whereas Jesus could not be justly convicted for a crime, Peter could be. The high priest's earlier inquiry about Jesus' disciples (18:19) may have partly indicated concern about such violent and possibly revolutionary sentiments as had been directed against his own servant Malchus; the charge against Jesus was sedition (18:33–35), and if anything, Peter's act had only helped to make that charge more credible.

Whereas Jesus suffers for Peter, Peter disowns Jesus and his own responsibility. If Peter is one Johannine paradigm for discipleship (albeit less secure than the beloved disciple), it is only because the good shepherd lays down his life for the sheep to restore them to the right way (10:11–15). Yet as Ridderbos points out, in this Gospel Peter's denial constitutes "the dramatic climax of Peter's recurrent . . . resistance to Jesus' self-humiliation (13:6ff.) and self-offering in death (13:24, 36f.; 18:10)."[258]

The denial scene closes with Peter's conviction by the crowing of the cock (18:27), signaling the fulfillment of Jesus' warning that Peter would in fact deny him (13:38).

---

[251] Brown, *John*, 2:827.

[252] Diogenes the Cynic, once accosted, allegedly complained that he forgot to don his helmet that morning (Diogenes Laertius 6.2.41–42). Jesus' answer with dignity here contravenes an inappropriately literalist reading of Matt 5:39 (Vermes, *Religion*, 36; cf. idem, *Jesus and Judaism*, 53).

[253] Stauffer, *Jesus*, 122, thinks 18:22–23 portrays Jesus as skilled in Jewish legal argument.

[254] Blinzler, *Trial*, 135, suggests that proper public trials required an advocate, which Jesus appears to have lacked; but he also concedes (pp. 142–43) that the Mishnaic rules are late.

[255] Cf. Leaney, "Paraclete," 38.

[256] Josephus *Ag. Ap.* 1.191, citing Hecateus of Abdera; 2.218–219, 233–235. They also would die rather than disobey their laws (1.212) and wanted to kill those they thought brought harm to the nation (Josephus *Life* 149).

[257] The testimony of those of higher status normally carried more weight (cf. comment on 18:19–22); in most cities, judges were chosen from among the well-to-do and respectable (MacMullen, *Relations*, 117).

[258] Ridderbos, *John*, 584–85.

Cockcrowing was a negative omen to the superstititious in some parts of the empire,[259] but more critically here, the cockcrowing also signaled early morning,[260] when leading representatives of the municipal aristocracy could bring Jesus before Pilate (18:28). Clients could approach their patrons for legal advice at "cockcrow" (Horace *Sat.* 1.1.9–10).

## Pilate's Inquiry (18:28–38a)

Pilate's inquiry (18:28–38a) constitutes part of a larger scene (18:28–19:16) in which Pilate plays a lead character; as a foil to Jesus, his character dominates 18:28–19:16. Pilate taunts Jewish nationalism with claims of Jesus' innocence and kingship,[261] but while not friendly to the Jewish aristocracy—the world remains divided (cf. 7:43; 9:16)—he remains a representative of the "world," essentially hostile toward Jesus because not one of his followers.[262]

A The Jewish leaders demand Jesus' execution (18:29–32)
  B Jesus and Pilate talk (18:33–38a)
    C Pilate finds no reason to condemn Jesus (18:38b–40)
      D The scourging and crowning with thorns (19:1–3)
    C' Pilate finds no reason to condemn Jesus (19:4–8)
  B' Jesus and Pilate talk (19:9–11)
A' The Jewish leaders are granted Jesus' execution (19:12–16)[263]

Although the immediate opposition of John's audience seems to be the synagogue leadership, as most Johannine scholars have argued, the power of Rome stands not far in the background. The mortal threat of synagogue leadership to John's urban audience is probably their role as accusers to the Romans (see introduction; comment on 16:2). The gospel tradition makes clear that Jerusalem's aristocracy and the Roman governor cooperated on Jesus' execution even if the Jerusalem aristocracy had taken the initiative. John undoubtedly has reason to continue to highlight this emphasis, although he, too, emphasizes the initiative of the leaders of his own people because it is they who, he believes, should have known better.

### 1. The Setting (18:28)

The brief transition between Jesus' detention at the hands of the high priest and his betrayal to Pilate provides important chronological markers. Some of these are of primarily

---

[259] Petronius *Sat.* 74, mocking Trimalchio's superstition. Peter and the disciples were not above superstition (Mark 6:49), but that is not likely the point here.

[260] E.g., Apuleius *Metam.* 2.26; see comment on 13:38. Some (Hunter, *John,* 169) think the crowing refers to the "rooster" trumpeting, the *gallicinium,* from the Antonia at ca. 3 a.m.; for various views, see Brown, *John,* 2:828.

[261] Rensberger, *Faith,* 93–94.

[262] Ibid., 92.

[263] Boismard, *Prologue,* 79. Ellis, *Genius,* 258, adds location to this arrangement: (a) request for and granting executing, outside (18:28–32; 19:12–16a); (b) Pilate questions Jesus about his kingship and power, inside (18:33–38a; 19:9–11); (c) Pilate finds no crime in him, outside (18:38b–40; 19:4–8); and (d) Jesus is scourged and mocked as "King of Jews," inside (19:1–3; he suggests, pp. 260–61, that John moves the scourging from the end [Mark 15:15] to the middle of the trial). Others also note the alternation (Brown, *John,* 859; Whitacre, *John,* 435); cf. also Neyrey, "Shame of Cross," 122 ("outside" representing a public honor contest), though he denies that any of the scenes are private (soldiers were present).

historical interest ("early"), but the most critical are of theological import (reinforcing the Johannine portrait of Jesus' crucifixion on Passover). The former markers might have been assumed by John's audience without much comment; the latter probably challenge their expectations and, for those familiar with the Jewish reckoning of Passover chronologies (as most of his audience would be), would strike them immediately.

## 1A. They Came "Early"

Some scholars complain that the Gospels report too many events between Jesus' arrest and crucifixion for a short period,[264] but if some Jerusalem aristocrats met during the night, as the Gospels imply, and the hearing before Pilate took place "early" (18:28), the chronology makes sense. Indeed, πρωΐ could signify the final watch of the night, from 3 a.m. to 6 a.m.;[265] they probably brought Jesus to Pilate ca. 6 a.m. (On some other matters John's chronology differs from that of the Synoptics; see comments on John's dating of the Passover in 18:28 and on 19:14.)

Clients approached their patrons early in the morning, those in front of the line receiving attention beginning around dawn, ca. 6 a.m.[266] For Romans, "late morning" in summer was before 8 or 9 a.m.;[267] most upper-class Romans ended their transaction of public business around noon.[268] Romans normally only slept in if they were drunkards who had partied too late and had to "sleep off their overnight excesses."[269] Jewish people were well aware of officials' early schedule; "friends" or clients of officials could visit them even before the sunlight was widely viewed (3 Macc 5:26).[270]

Naturally, Roman governors followed the same pattern of early-morning meetings.[271] Like other Romans of rank, they would normally keep part of their day for leisure,[272] though Pilate would undoubtedly have less of this when he visited Jerusalem. When a Roman official came to town, he was often swamped with legal requests. In Roman Egypt a prefect came to local municipalities for only a few days each year, and fielded 700–750 petitions a day. Because regulations allowed the prefect's office to remain open only ten hours in a day, more than one petitioner would have presented a case each minute, suggesting that clerks and aides processed the less important ones.[273] In urban Jerusalem, elders from the municipal aristocracy undoubtedly judged most cases themselves, reducing the number of petitions that would be brought before the governor. But regardless of the

---

[264] E.g., Winter, *Trial*, 7.

[265] Brown, *John*, 2:844.

[266] E.g., Horace *Sat.* 1.1.9–10; *Ep.* 2.1.103–105; Martial *Epigr.* 3.36.1–3; see further Friedländer, *Life*, 1:86–93; Clarke, "Italy," 475; receiving guest-clients was important to civic-minded nobles (e.g., Plutarch *Cicero* 8.3–4). Senators also could assemble at daybreak (Cicero *Fam.* 1.2.4; Plutarch *Cicero* 15.3; 19.1); even schools started then (Watson, "Education," 311–12).

[267] Carcopino, *Life*, 152.

[268] Plutarch *R.Q.* 84, *Mor.* 284D. Friedländer, *Life*, 1:207, ends the business day in the afternoon "at the principal meal." Isaeus reportedly prepared his orations from dawn till noon (Philostratus *Vit. soph.* 1.20.514).

[269] Carcopino, *Life*, 151; see esp. Seneca *Ep. Lucil.* 122.1–4.

[270] Jewish schools also started early (Safrai, "Education," 954); one offered morning prayers before work at sunrise (*m. Ber.* 1:2).

[271] E.g., Cicero *Verr.* 2.4.66.147 (despite the exceptional circumstances—allowing one to come only at daybreak may reflect arrogance, as it does in Theophrastus *Char.* 24.7); Plutarch *Cicero* 36.3.

[272] Seneca *Nat.* 4A.pref.1.

[273] Lewis, *Life*, 190.

length of line waiting to see Pilate that morning, the urgencies of the municipal aristocracy would take precedence and summon his immediate attention, especially if a prolonged detention held the potential to arouse unrest. The claim that the high priests could not have access to Pilate early in the morning unless he had earlier been apprised of Jesus' arrest and the charge against him[274] is therefore unfounded.

Historical tradition supports the correctness of John's chronological marker here (cf. Mark 15:1). It is also possible—though by no means certain—that John also emphasizes "early" either here or (more likely) in 20:1 to connect the two passages together, stressing the urgency of the priestly aristocrats to be rid of Jesus and the urgency of Mary to find him; these are John's only two uses of πρωΐ (cf. also πρωΐα in 21:4). Still, it is possible to read too much into the perceived connection; πρωΐ is a common enough adverb (over 180 occurrences in the LXX) and appears at the same place in the Markan passion tradition (Mark 15:1; 16:2; cf. Mark 16:9).

## 1B. The Praetorium and Uncleanness

When the priestly leaders bring Jesus before Pilate, John declares that they avoided entering the "praetorium" lest they be defiled (18:28). Some earlier commentators identified the praetorium with the Fortress Antonia, adjoining the temple courts,[275] where a Roman garrison remained on the Temple Mount year-round. Some earlier and most current commentators, however, prefer the old palace of Herod the Great.[276] This palace is somewhat farther from the temple but remained in the wealthy upper city not far from the temple;[277] its lavishness suited it as a temporary residence for the governor (who would undoubtedly take the best quarters available),[278] and it better fits the direct ancient sources concerning where the governor stayed when in Jerusalem.[279] Provincial governors generally chose "for their official residence the home of the former native ruler,"[280] and Herod's old palace at Caesarea Maritima was also the Roman governor's residence there.[281]

Houses of non-Jews were ritually impure;[282] by entering this residence, scrupulous Jews could contract Gentile impurity and hence prove unable to participate fully in the Passover (Num 9:6).[283] Such sensitivities would not have been unusual for the priestly aristocracy,[284] most of whom had *mikvaot* in their own homes;[285] John Hyrcanus had earlier

---

274 Winter, *Trial*, 29.

275 E.g., Yamauchi, *Stones*, 106; cf. Josephus *War* 2.328–331. On the Antonia, see, e.g., Wightman, "*Baris*."

276 E.g., Brown, *Death*, 705–10; Strachan, *Gospel*, 212; Blinzler, *Trial*, 173–76; Reicke, *Era*, 140; Benoit, *Jesus*, 1:167–88; idem, "Reconstitution"; Gundry, *Matthew*, 552; Carson, "Matthew," 567; Schürer, *History*, 181; Lane, *Mark*, 548; Wilkinson, *Jerusalem*, 140.

277 Josephus *War* 1.401.

278 On this palace, with much archaeological commentary, see Josephus *War* 5.176–183; Cornfeld, *Josephus*, 340–43 (including comment on adjoining towers, Josephus *War* 5.156–175).

279 Pilate in Philo *Embassy* 299; Florus in Josephus *War* 2.301 (ἐν τοῖς βασιλείοις), 328.

280 Blinzler, *Trial*, 173.

281 Burrell, Gleason, and Netzer, "Palace."

282 *M. ʾOhal.* 18:7 (the custom is known by at least the time of R. Eliezer, ca. 90 C.E.; Pancaro, *Law*, 309); Acts 10:28; 11:3; see further Safrai, "Religion," 829.

283 Dalman, *Jesus-Jeshua*, 86, argues that John means only exclusion from the remainder of the Feast of Unleavened Bread.

284 Among Pharisees, stricter rules about Passover and Gentiles may have obtained among Shammaites (*b. Pesaḥ.* 21a, *bar.*), whose views probably often prevailed before 70 C.E. (see comment on 9:13–17).

285 E.g., Stanton, *Gospel Truth*, 116.

wanted to avoid Herod bringing non-Jews among the people during the purification before a festival (Josephus *War* 1.229). Roman officials generally sought to accommodate Jewish religious sensitivities;[286] though Pilate initially proved unsympathetic toward their customs (Josephus *Ant.* 18.55), here he is now more inclined to work with the aristocracy (perhaps due to their past threats)[287] and hence comes out to them.

John's point, however, is hardly Pilate's generosity; it is the hypocrisy of the Judean elite, who, after they have spent the night ignoring legal ethics to secure the quick execution of an innocent man, now are concerned with ritual purity. Such ritual purity was not high on John's list of virtues (2:6–10). This blatant contrast between scrupulous observance of ritual purity and ignoring the law's ethical demands epitomizes Johannine irony,[288] though not unique to the Fourth Gospel.[289] They wanted to "eat the Passover" but did not understand that, in having Jesus killed, they were slaying the new Passover lamb to be consumed (cf. 2:17; 6:51; 19:31).

## 1C. John's Passover Chronology

Some have used Passovers to reconstruct John's chronology[290] and have claimed conflicts with the Synoptics, but it seems better to read John's final Passover chronology symbolically.[291] Passover began at sundown with the Passover meal. Whereas in the Fourth Gospel Jesus is executed on the day of the Passover sacrifice preceding the evening meal (18:28; 19:14), the Synoptics present the Last Supper as a Passover meal, presupposing that the lamb has already been offered in the temple.[292] Both traditions—a paschal Last Supper and a paschal crucifixion—are theologically pregnant,[293] but we suspect that Jesus, followed by the earliest tradition, may have intended the symbolism for the Last Supper whereas John has applied the symbolism more directly to the referent to which the Last Supper itself symbolically pointed.

Many scholars have argued that John is historically correct,[294] noting that the Last Supper narrative does not explicitly mention a lamb[295] and that an execution on the first day of the feast was inconceivable and suggesting that the disciples could have celebrated Passover

---

[286] See Blinzler, *Trial,* 187 n. 2.

[287] He backed down in Josephus *Ant.* 18.59; he later suffered politically from Judean and Samaritan accusations (18.88–89)

[288] E.g., Barrett, "Old Testament," 159; Bruce, "Trial," 13; Ellis, *Genius,* 261.

[289] E.g., 2 Sam 11:4; Matt 27:4–7; Philo *Embassy* 30. Juvenal also satirizes religious hypocrisy (Stewart, "Domitian"); showing one's opponents' claims to piety to be hypocrisy was good rhetorical technique (*Rhet. ad Herenn.* 3.3.6).

[290] Estimates for the year of crucifixion usually settle on 30 or 33 C.E., with preference for the former (Blinzler, *Trial,* 72–80; Brown, *Death,* 1373–76; Meier, *Marginal Jew,* 1:402), including by me. Still, because of potential early Jewish observational mistakes, the astronomical evidence for any date remains indeterminate (Sanders, *Figure,* 284).

[291] With Borchert, "Passover," 316; Yee, *Feasts,* 68. Much of what follows is adapted from Keener, *Matthew,* 622–23.

[292] This makes harmonization difficult (though Story, "Chronology," thinks John agreed with Synoptic chronology here).

[293] Cf., e.g., Byron, "Passover"; Boring et al., *Commentary,* 147.

[294] E.g., Oesterley, *Liturgy,*158–67; Stauffer, *Jesus,* 143; Grappe, "Essai"; Wilkinson, *Jerusalem,* 125; Meier, *Marginal Jew,* 1:395–401; Brown, *Death,* 1351–73.

[295] Later tradition also permits apostates to partake of the meal except the lamb (Stauffer, *Jesus,* 210), but this prohibition is probably irrelevant here.

early, according to a sectarian calendar,[296] or that Mark inserted Passover references for theological reasons.[297] One could argue more reasonably that Jesus and the temple authorities followed separate calendars;[298] but our evidence for these calendars is relatively scant, and even if such separate calendars existed, why would John prefer that of the temple authorities? Other details of the passion narrative behind Mark, such as the Sanhedrin originally wishing to kill Jesus before the feast (Mark 14:1–2), Simon coming from the fields (15:21, which some take as coming from work), or burial on a "preparation day" (which in Mark 15:42 is preparation for the Sabbath but which some take as preparation for Passover),[299] can support the Johannine chronology. The rabbis also spoke of Jesus' execution on the eve of Passover,[300] although this is a late tradition probably deriving its information from early Christian sources that may reflect John's Gospel or its tradition.

The priestly aristocracy might act, however, even on Passover to preserve public order; Pilate would care little for calendrical matters; and an execution on the day on which the lamb had been eaten would deter crowds no less than the day on which they were being slaughtered if the site of execution were not far outside Jerusalem's walls. The minor details "behind" Mark's Passion Narrative could also be explained in other ways that fit the narrative equally well. Mark could simply be correct that the preparation was for the Sabbath;[301] Simon could come "from the fields" because he has spent the night in a suburb like Bethphage.[302]

The main argument against the Johannine chronology in a conflict between John and the Synoptics is that on most points Mark's narrative seems more dependable for historical detail, John's more expository (although many hold John's chronology to be an exception, especially regarding the duration of Jesus' ministry). Thus many scholars suggest that the Synoptics are correct; the Synoptics certainly portray the Last Supper as a Passover meal, even on details that their audiences would no longer have recognized as relevant.[303]

Those favoring the Johannine dating respond that whereas the Synoptics regard the meal as a Passover meal (this is "challenged by no one"), this does not decide the *historical* question.[304] But then how do Mark and Paul, writing for Gentile audiences, conform the narrative so closely to Passover traditions? And if the Synoptics report the disciples actually keeping the Passover but on a "sectarian" date, would sectarians have observed so many other paschal customs as the text suggests? Jeremias admittedly depends on later Passover traditions for his parallels with the Last Supper, but what evidence we do have fits the Gospel narratives and Jewish traditions can hardly have derived from the Gospels. As scholars commonly note,[305] John certainly had theological reasons to place the death of God's lamb (John 1:29) on Passover (19:36).

---

[296] Reicke, *Era*, 179–82; Meier, *Marginal Jew*, 1:396; see our fuller discussion of Jaubert's thesis below.

[297] Jewett, *Chronology*, 27; cf. Meier, *Matthew*, 316.

[298] E.g., Morris, *John*, 785.

[299] Theissen, *Gospels*, 167.

[300] *B. Sanh.* 43a, *bar.* ("on the eve of Passover").

[301] Despite disagreement on the relation to the festival, most commentators agree that the crucifixion occurred on a Friday (Brown, *Death*, 1350–51). Even by the third century, rabbis were not unanimous about trying and executing someone on a Sabbath (*p. Sanh.* 4:6, §2; starting Friday sundown).

[302] On the Sanhedrin wishing to kill Jesus before the feast, see comment on Matt 26:1–2, in Keener, *Matthew*, 617.

[303] Jeremias, *Eucharistic Words*, 20–23, 62–84; Hagner, *Matthew*, 772–73; cf. Hill, *Matthew*, 336–37.

[304] Bornkamm, *Experience*, 132.

[305] E.g., Higgins, "Eucharist," 208–9.

One attempt to harmonize the Johannine and Synoptic dating, originally associated with a proposal of Annie Jaubert in 1957,[306] has commended itelf to a number of scholars. According to this proposal, Jesus followed a solar calendar like the one used at Qumran, but Jerusalem's official Passover and the one followed by John occur afterward. Given sectarian calendars (cf. *Jub.* 49:10, 14)[307] and even calendrical differences among rabbis due to different witnesses regarding the new moon (*m. Roš Haš.* 2:9), it is not impossible that Jesus' disciples followed an Essene, sectarian date for the Passover.[308]

But scholars have raised important objections against this thesis.[309] For one, would such an important disagreement with the temple authorities have gone unnoted in the tradition? After all, calendrical matters constituted a major debate in early Judaism, and had they been central to Jesus' conflict with the authorities, one might expect mention of this point. (The exception would be if this information were suppressed by the later church, which had reverted to the common practice. But probability is against its siding with the authorities against its own teacher; other sects would not have done so.) Further, if Jesus followed a sectarian calendar at this Passover, why do John's narratives imply that he did not do so at other festivals (2:13; 7:2; 10:22)?[310] It is also possible that John followed a Palestinian, and the Synoptics the Diaspora, reckoning of Passover,[311] but this proposal fails to explain the paschal character of the Last Supper tradition, the accommodation of Diaspora pilgrims at the festival, and again the inadequacy of supporting evidence in the tradition. Calendrical differences may allow us to harmonize John and the Synoptics, but most likely, John has simply provided a theological interpretation of Jesus' death, the way he opens Jesus' ministry with the temple cleansing so that the shadow of passion week may cover the whole period.

If the two accounts must be harmonized, however, the simplest, Ockham's razor solution would be the best; one such possibility is that "Jesus, knowing that he would be dead before the regular time for the meal, deliberately held it in secret one day early."[312] Another

---

[306] Jaubert, *Date.* (The French original of this work was published in 1957.)

[307] Herr, "Calendar." The calendar of *Jubilees* may have had some impact on public policy in the second century B.C.E. (Wirgin, *Jubilees,* 12–17, 42–43) and has some parallels with later rabbinic calendrical halakah (Grintz, "Jubilees," 325), but, in contrast to what became mainstream Judaism, preserves the older solar calendar (Morgenstern, "Calendar"; cf. Marcus, "Scrolls," 12), for which some even (probably wrongly) label it pre-Hasmonean (Zeitlin, "Jubilees," 224; cf. idem, "Character," 8–16). Opposition to the lunar calendar is implied even in its creation narrative (*Jub.* 2:9–10; cf. 6:36). This places *Jubilees* much closer to Qumran thought than to Pharisaism (e.g., Brownlee, "Jubilees," 32; Baumgarten, "Beginning"; Grintz, "Jubilees," 324); Rivkin, "Jubilees," even thinks that *Jubilees* writes polemically against the Pharisaic calendar.

[308] Cf. Driver, *Scrolls,* 330, 335; Simon, *Sects,* 151; Stauffer, *Jesus,* 115; Bruce, *Documents,* 57; Bruce, "Jesus," 78; Morris, *John,* 785; cf. Svensson, "Qumrankalendern" (John tried to harmonize Qumran's with the dominant lunar calendar). One carefully researched approach too recent for discussion here is Busada, "Calendar."

[309] E.g., Benoit, *Jesus,* 1:87–93; Abegg, "Calendars," 183.

[310] Brown, *Essays,* 207–17, arguing that John reports the real date whereas the Synoptics report Jesus' Last Supper a day early.

[311] Shepherd, "Date." Carson, "Matthew," 529 also mentions other proposals, e.g., that Pharisees and Sadducees followed divergent calendars (Strack-Billerbeck) or that the Galileans followed the Pharisaic (and Synoptic) one and Judeans the Sadducean (and Johannine) one (though Josephus places most Pharisees in Jerusalem). But I suspect that a major difference in observance in the temple would have left more trace in extant first-century sources concerning feasts (such as Josephus).

[312] France, *Matthew,* 365. One cannot argue this, however, from the lack of mention of purification or lamb; these would be taken for granted (everyone in the Roman Empire expected animal

plausible suggestion is that 18:28 refers to them eating the *rest* of the Feast of Unleavened Bread,[313] a solution that is linguistically defensible (though not the text's most obvious sense) but does not seem to match the other clues in John's narrative; at the very least, John retains enough ambiguity to allow the reading (and, if we lacked the Synoptic passion tradition, to *assume* the reading) that Jesus was crucified on Passover. John probably does know the same tradition as Mark. Whatever the traditions behind the Gospels, however, Mark's and John's approaches at least imply (perhaps for theological reasons) the Passover on different days, yet derive from it the same theology: Jesus' death is a new passover, a new act of redemption (cf. also 1 Cor 5:7).

## 2. Pilate and the Chief Priests (18:29–32)

John focuses on the responsibility of the Judean elite; Jewish Christians in his own day felt repressed by a Jewish elite whom they viewed as analogous, and would view this elite as more culpable than the Romans precisely because they claimed to speak for Israel's God and for Judaism. While this is John's emphasis, however, he does not deny the Roman involvement; a public crucifixion in a Roman province demanded a Roman sentence.

### 2A. Pilate's Historical Involvement

Few historians would dispute that Jesus in fact appeared before Pilate (outside the Gospels and Acts, e.g., 1 Tim 6:13; Tacitus *Ann.* 15.44);[314] only the governor could order a person crucified. Further, if Pilate wished some semblance of order, he would provide at least a brief hearing. True, Pilate was known for his brutality (e.g., Josephus *Ant.* 18.85)[315] and sometimes had reportedly executed Jews without trial (Philo *Embassy* 299, 302). But that Pilate executed Jesus without some form of hearing is improbable, for this is the very sort of breach of normal procedure the earliest Christian sources would be most likely to report; yet they mention nothing of the kind.[316] Likewise, Jesus' own countrymen would normally perform the function of *delatores,* or accusers, to charge him with sedition.[317] The substance of the events in John's account match historical expectations: "It begins with a formal delation . . . and ends with a formal condemnation *pro tribunali*" (18:29; 19:13).[318] (The "governor" in Judea in this period was technically a "prefect," rather than

---

sacrifices and purifications for festivals), and it would be their omission that would have required comment (Sanders, *Figure,* 251).

[313] See Blomberg, *Reliability,* 238, 254 (citing esp. Smith, "Chronology of Supper"; Carson, *John,* 589–90, 622; Geldenhuys, *Luke,* 649–70; and linguistic data in Billerbeck, *Kommentar,* 837–38), taking the "high" Sabbath as a Sabbath that falls on a festival (19:31), and John's "preparation" (19:14) as for the Sabbath (cf. Mark 15:42) and merely during Passover (John 19:14). If we did not have the Synoptic tradition, however, no one would pursue such expedients; the language more naturally suggests the preparation was for Passover as well as the Sabbath. This is not to deny that John may depend on historical tradition (with this as the most workable suggestion) but to suggest that he at least exploits the ambiguity to present Jesus as the Passover lamb (1:29; 19:36).

[314] Accepted even by Crossan, *Jesus,* 372, as unlikely to have been invented.

[315] Much of the following section is adapted from Keener, *Matthew,* 662–67.

[316] With Harvey, *History,* 17.

[317] Ibid., 16, citing, e.g., Pliny *Ep.* 10.97; cf. Ferguson, *Backgrounds,* 51. On *delatores,* see, e.g., O'Neal, "Delation."

[318] Sherwin-White, *Society,* 47. More fully, the Roman trial scheme may be summarized as arrest (18:4–11); charges (18:29–32); exam (18:33–37); verdict (18:38–40); warning (19:1–3); charges (19:4–8); exam (19:9–12); verdict (19:13–15); sentence (19:16; see Malina and Rohrbaugh, *John,* 249).

the later term "procurator" as in Tacitus *Ann.* 15.44; the Gospels simply use the general title "governor," which could have covered either.)[319]

That Jesus was crucified by the Romans is likewise inevitably historical;[320] Christians would hardly have invented execution at all, but certainly not Roman execution, which would have painted them thereafter as subversives in the Roman world.[321] Pilate often went to great lengths to quell so much as public complaints, including violent suppression of a crowd, leading to many deaths (Josephus *War* 2.176–177; *Ant.* 18.60–62). Romans had borrowed an earlier custom of hanging people,[322] and the victims of the punishment were disproportionately slaves[323] and the provincial poor.[324] Roman citizens could not be crucified legally, but slaves and provincials could be.[325] Although dangerous criminals (Suetonius *Julius* 4), like slaves, were regularly crucified, crucifixions of free persons in Palestine usually involved the charge of rebellion against Rome.[326]

## 2B. Provincial Politics and Law (18:29–31a)

Pilate's request for a charge (18:29) reflects the standard procedure of Roman officials, who relied on local subordinates as *delatores,* or accusers.[327] John's informed audience may have experienced the same sort of accusations (see introduction, ch. 5); they may also, however, find it ironic that the accusers bring a κατηγορίαν against Jesus (18:29) yet encounter Moses' law, which they are violating (*pace* their claim in 19:7), as their own κατηγορῶν (5:45).

The leaders' attempt to secure Pilate's cooperation without further investigation (18:30) fits the known "tendency to turn the legal situation to one's maximal advantage," as illustrated by Josephus's application of imperial edicts and other defenses of Jewish freedoms.[328] (Contrast their complaint that he is an "evildoer" here with their inability to convict him of even speaking evil in 18:23; cf. 8:46; Mark 15:14.) The Romans usually allowed internal religious matters to be handled by Jewish courts,[329] hence Pilate's reticence to ac-

---

[319] Literary sources employ the later term "procurator," but an inscription supports the earlier title (see Brown, *Death*, 336–37; Evans, "Pilate Inscription," 804). For the responsibilities of a governor, see, e.g., Justinian *Dig.* 1.16.4–13, in Jones, *History,* 180–83.

[320] Against the docetic idea of Jesus merely appearing to die, see comment on 19:25.

[321] Although the severest form of execution Pharisaic law acknowledged on the basis of the Hebrew Bible was stoning (*b. Sanh.* 49b–50a), Jewish rulers had used crucifixion before the Roman period. Under Roman rule, however, all official, public executions belonged to the Romans. Even the Essenes toned down capital sentences from Moses' law (CD 12.2–5), while also detesting Gentile executions in the Holy Land (CD 9.1). The apparently Jewish execution in *b. Sanh.* 43a depends on Christian tradition, though preserving the crucifixion's association with the Passover season.

[322] E.g., Arrian *Alex.* 6.30.2.

[323] Livy 22.33.1–2; Suetonius *Dom.* 10; Cicero *Verr.* 2.5.66.169; Seneca *Controv.* 3.9 excerpts.

[324] E.g., Phaedrus 3.5.10 (for throwing a stone at a rich man).

[325] Stauffer, *Jesus,* 131. For the outrage at scourging, executing, and (worst of all) crucifying Roman citizens, see Cicero *Verr.* 1.5.13; 2.1.3.7–9; 2.3.3.6; 2.3.24.59; 2.4.11.26; 2.5.66.169).

[326] Harvey, *History,* 12; Overman, *Community,* 380–81, 387; e.g., Josephus *War* 2.75, 241, 253, 306; 3.321; 5.449; *Ant.* 20.102. It also appears as a fitting end for other military enemies (e.g., Diodorus Siculus 2.1.10; 25.5.2; Josephus *Ant.* 12.256; 13.380) and for the most horrid crimes (Apuleius *Metam.* 3.9); it was the epitome of a horrible way to die (Seneca *Ep. Lucil.* 101.10–12).

[327] See comment on 18:29–32.

[328] Bammel, "Trial," 419; cf. Malina and Rohrbaugh, *John,* 249. Throughout the Roman world, social superiors could win most prosecutions against social inferiors.

[329] See Josephus *Ant.* 14.235, 260–261; cf. Josephus *Ag. Ap.* 2.73; Acts 18:13–15; Judge, *Pattern,* 68.

cept the case at first (18:31a). (As the rest of the verse shows, he is not literally permitting them to simply execute Jesus themselves, though Roman officials occasionally handed even Romans over for execution to prevent unrest; cf. 19:6.)[330] While Pilate in the story world intends his rebuff as a refusal to enter Jewish religious disputes (cf. Acts 18:15), "Judge him according to your own law" serves an ironic function on the level that John's informed audience may catch: the leaders neither judge rightly (7:24) nor could convict him from their own law (e.g., 10:34).

But the local leaders responded that they needed Rome's approval to secure capital punishment (18:31b; cf. 19:15), implying that because of limitations Rome had placed on them, they needed Rome's cooperation to keep order in such cases. On the theological level, the leaders not only misunderstand God's word but also accommodate Rome's definition of what is lawful; they could not rightly execute him on their own (cf. ἔξεστιν in 5:10).

The narrative portrays those who brought the charge as quite insistent that Jesus be executed, and this behavior is hardly surprising given the situation portrayed. What is instead striking is Pilate's reticence to pronounce sentence; if no Roman citizens were involved, one would expect most governors to act quickly at the local aristocracy's request.[331] The Gospels show that Pilate did indeed act relatively quickly, but they also report his reluctance to do so. Thus some scholars question whether the Pilate of the Gospels is "in character" with the Pilate known to us from other sources.[332] Pilate executed people without trial; excessive use of capital punishment ultimately cost him his office (Philo *Embassy* 302; Josephus *Ant.* 18.88–89).[333] His earlier plundering of the temple treasury to support an aqueduct[334] and particularly his recent issue of coins bearing an insignia of the divine emperor[335] blatantly demonstrated his insensitivity to local Jewish concerns. (Pilate was an ethnocentric colonialist governor, but both the republic and the empire reveal even harsher cases of provincial exploitation and maladministration.)[336] From what Philo and especially Josephus show us of Pilate's character, any reticence to accept the local leaders' recommendation would be more out of spite for them than out of concern for justice.[337]

---

[330] Cf. Bammel, "Trial," 437–38.

[331] Cf. Harvey, *History,* 17; Sanders, *Figure,* 274; for an impoverished provincial condemned to death without trial, cf., e.g., Apuleius *Metam.* 9.42.

[332] Winter, *Trial,* 54–55, 60; Borg, *Vision,* 179.

[333] Sanders, *Figure,* 274. On governors being tried for abusing power, especially executing innocent people (particularly Roman citizens), see Pliny *Ep.* 2.11, in Jones, *History,* 192–95.

[334] Others viewed this act as misappropriation of funds (Josephus *War* 2.175–176; cf. *Ant.* 18.60; *The Suda,* Korbanas, in Sherk, *Empire,* 75); Pilate, however, probably assumed that he followed safe Roman precedent: Augustus and others paid for workmen on aqueducts from public and imperial treasuries (Frontinus *De aquis* 2.89–101, 116–118, in Jones, *History,* 207), and the use of public money would have been expected (Josephus *Life* 199) had it not been from the *temple* treasury. Romans themselves complained when designated funds in a public treasury were redirected (Appian *C.W.* 2.6.41; Lysias *Or.* 25.19, §173; 27.7, §178; 27.16, §179; Plutarch *Cicero* 17.2; *Caesar* 35.2–4; worse, despoiling temple treasuries, e.g., Valerius Maximus 1.1.21; see further Keener, *Matthew,* 557 n. 72); they would have been angriest had he profited himself, which sometimes happened (Catullus 10.7–13; cf. Jeffers, *World,* 111–12).

[335] Stauffer, *Jesus,* 72; Thompson, *Archaeology,* 308–9.

[336] E.g., Cicero *Verr.* 1.1.2; 1.4.12; 2.3.22.55; 2.3.28.69; *Sest.* 25.55; many Judean governors as presented by Josephus, e.g., *Ant.* 20.106–117, 162–163, 215, 253–257; *War* 2.223–245, 272–279.

[337] Cf. Benoit, *Jesus,* 1:141–42. Some first-century writers complained about societal injustice (e.g., Seneca *Ep. Lucil.* 95.30).

Yet this reticence need not be unhistorical.[338] As corrupt as the later governor Albinus was, he dismissed Jesus ben Hananiah from further punishment (after a scourging reportedly bared his bones) once he took him to be insane and hence harmless (Josephus *War* 6.305). Philo and especially Josephus are ill disposed to report good of Pilate;[339] they seem to have felt that the unrest in Judea is better blamed on deceased prefects such as Pilate (once supported by the corrupt Sejanus)[340] than left with the Judeans themselves. Even when governor, Pilate seems to have been quite unpopular.[341]

Still, the narratives go to great lengths to emphasize that Pilate cooperated with Jesus' execution against his own preference, and this emphasis is understandable for apologetic reasons. Minority sects often validate themselves through reports of praises by those respected among their oppressors; those writing in socially delicate situations also must show proper deference to officials. Thus, for example, Josephus repeatedly excuses Roman rulers' motives; for instance, Titus wished to spare the temple, but some soldiers failed to cooperate (*War* 6.254, 258, 260–266), or Titus allowed his soldiers to torture Jews only for good·reason (*War* 5.449–451). The *Letter of Aristeas* likewise defends the Ptolemaic ruler's motives against the Jews (*Let. Aris.* 14), and Josephus claims that Ptolemy Philadelphus praised the Jewish law (*Ag. Ap.* 2.45–47). In the same manner, early Christians commending themselves to an audience in the broader Roman world might wish to exonerate the Roman prefect[342] or even cite in their own defense Roman officials' reticence to condemn them (e.g., Acts 13:12; 18:14–15). John probably writes for a largely Jewish Christian rather than Gentile audience and probably depends on early Palestinian Jewish tradition; nevertheless he has ample reason to focus on the guilt of those of his own people who betray his Jewish Christian colleagues to the Romans, rather than on the Roman officials who execute sentences.

But while the Gospels have reason to emphasize Jewish rather than Roman responsibility, Pilate's hesitance may have historical foundation, as we have noted above. Pilate may have had good reason for political concern if he erred in judgment.[343] Philo notes the anti-Jewishness of Pilate's patron, Sejanus (Philo *Flaccus* 1). If Sejanus was executed on October 19, 31 C.E.,[344] some premonitions of his impending weakness might have been felt a year and a half earlier at the more likely time of Jesus' trial near Passover of 30 C.E. (This is admittedly at best a guess, rather than a direct inference from our sources, which, unanimously hostile to Sejanus, suggest that most of those who disagreed with him in Rome would have been more circumspect than to say so.) If one dates the crucifixion to 33 C.E., the second most accepted date, Pilate's position had certainly become much less secure. More clearly, Pilate, like most provincial officials,[345] was probably politically ambitious

---

[338] On the consistency of Pilate's behavior, cf., e.g., Hoehner, "Significance," 121–25.

[339] Cf. Brown, *Death,* 697. Smallwood, "Historians," concludes that Philo is even more accurate than Josephus when reporting the same historical events (in this case, concerning Caligula).

[340] Still despised in a later period, e.g., in Juvenal *Sat.* 10.66, 76, 89–90, 104; Phaedrus 3.prol.41–44; cf. also Brown, *Death,* 694, on Philo *Flaccus* 1; *Embassy* 160–161.

[341] Cf. rumors circulating in Luke 13:1 and Bailey, *Peasant Eyes,* 75. Brown, *Death,* 695–705, ultimately concludes, as we do, that most of the Gospel portrait fits what we know of Pilate from the other sources once all has been taken into account.

[342] Cf. Sanders, *Jesus and Judaism,* 298; Cohn, *Trial,* 326–27.

[343] The *baraita* in *b. Sanh.* 43a suggesting special caution regarding Jesus' conviction "because he was close to the kingdom" would be a Jewish deterrent but could have actually aggravated Roman hostility; it is, however, probably derived from later debate with Jewish Christians.

[344] Stauffer, *Jesus,* 132; Lane, *Mark,* 556–57 n. 34; Baum, *Jews,* 72; cf. Sherk, *Empire,* 75–77.

[345] See Reicke, *Era,* 138, 175.

and hence could ill afford too many bad reports about himself.[346] In contrast with many of his peers in office, being only an equestrian left him especially vulnerable apart from Sejanus's patronage.[347] More to the point, Pilate had already incurred the hatred of the Jewish people (e.g., Josephus *War* 2.169–177; *Ant.* 18.55–62) and on some other occasions had backed down to pacify them (Philo *Embassy* 301–302; Josephus *War* 2.171–174; *Ant.* 18.59), especially if threatened with appeal to the emperor (Philo *Embassy* 304–305; cf. John 19:12). Thus Pilate was not only cruel but, like many bullies, fearful of exposure to those in authority over him.[348]

If anything, this situation would probably require Pilate in time to become more, rather than less, cooperative with the more powerful of his subjects (cf. John 19:12–13); to fail to prosecute a potential revolutionary, accused by the leaders of his own people, could lay Pilate himself open to the charge of *maiestas.*[349] Even the suspicion of treason could be fatal under Tiberius, especially under Sejanus's influence, and despite Sejanus's patronage, he likely would not risk it.[350] Further, although Jesus may have proved politically innocuous,[351] cooperation with the local aristocracy would be politically more advantageous; that he survived as governor until 36 C.E.,[352] long after his patron's demise, suggests that he had belatedly acquired some political savvy. Even a better governor might have executed a potential troublemaker without much evidence, especially under pressure.[353] This was, after all, the provinces, not Rome.

In any case, the hearing before Pilate is brief, and the execution swift (a few hours later). Though less explicitly than Matthew, John employs the catchword παραδίδωμι to portray a whole web of guilt implicating Judas (6:64, 71; 12:4; 13:2, 11, 21; 18:2, 5, 36), the Jerusalem aristocrats (18:30, 35; 19:11), and Pilate (19:16).[354] Yet in the end it is Jesus himself who hands his life over to the Father (παρέδωκεν, 19:30), as he had previously announced (10:17–18).

2C. Capital Jurisdiction (18:31b–32)

When the Judean leaders respond that they are not permitted to put anyone to death—at least not legally (18:31)—they state accurately the situation not only in John's day but probably also in that of Jesus as well. The local aristocracy would prepare the charges and suggest action, but Pilate had to pronounce sentence. The governor held the

---

[346] Cf. Malina, *Windows,* 115–16.

[347] On the equestrian order, see, e.g., Jones, *History,* 134–40.

[348] Winter, *Trial,* 53–54.

[349] Blinzler, *Trial,* 236; Smallwood, *Jews,* 169.

[350] Although Tiberius was not the only paranoid emperor (e.g., Herodian 1.13.7), he reportedly viewed even negative remarks as *maiestas* (e.g., Dio Cassius *R.H.* 57.9.2; 57.19.1; 57.23.1–2; cf. Caligula—59.11.6), leading to many false accusations (57.4.5–6). Among Romans treason was the greatest crime (Dionysius of Halicarnassus *R.A.* 8.80.1).

[351] Cullmann, *State,* 46–47.

[352] Josephus *Ant.* 18.89 (though Krieger, "Problematik," doubts Josephus's reasons for Pilate's dismissal).

[353] Harvey, *History,* 17. Historically and socially, one who challenged the status quo of either Jerusalem's priestly elite or the Romans would likely face such consequences (Hanson and Oakman, *Palestine,* 94–95).

[354] Haenchen, *John,* 2:178, observes that the repetition of this catchword "has the effect of a clock sounding the death knell." The term is suitable for being handed over to an executioner (παρεδόθην, Chariton 4.2.7).

power of life and death in a province (Josephus *War* 2.117; cf. *b. Šabb.* 108a). Some scholars think that the Sanhedrin could execute capital sentences,[355] but this proposal does not fit what we know of the way Romans administered their provinces. Against Winter,[356] Acts 23:1–10 constitutes a preliminary inquiry to formulate a charge (22:30; 23:28–29), not evidence for capital authority, even though profanation of the temple (cf. 21:28–29) was the one charge for which the Romans permitted local executions.[357]

Although Theissen recognizes that the Sanhedrin lacked capital authority in Jesus' time,[358] he thinks that the Passion Narrative presupposes this jurisdiction and thus that it reads its own milieu's circumstances of 41–44 C.E., under Agrippa I, into the narrative.[359] Others might employ this approach to deny the Passion Narrative's own evidence that some of the high priests tried Jesus, but such a denial faces two major obstacles: First, the logic of the Passion Narrative actually presupposes that the Sanhedrin lacks capital authority; why else would they hand Jesus over to Pilate?[360] Second, Agrippa I, like Herod the Great, was a client king and had been on personal terms with an emperor—he was not merely the municipal aristocracy. In the last decade of the first century, Johannine tradition still preserves the Sanhedrin's lack of authority (John 18:31–32). An intermediate position is that Romans rarely delegated capital authority but Roman governors were authorized to do so;[361] but whatever governors of some provinces may have wished to do, it is inconceivable that Pilate would have shared this authority with the local aristocracy.[362]

Later rabbis discussed appropriate grounds[363] and means[364] for execution, but rabbinic literature itself shows that these discussions were primarily theoretical.[365] Some rabbinic tradition traces the loss of Jewish courts' capital authority to 70 C.E.,[366] other tradition to no later than 30 C.E.[367] Although Josephus naturally does not report any precedents unfavorable toward Jewish autonomy, this loss of sovereignty (for so it would be viewed—Ep. Jer. 14) must have begun much earlier. Although Rome delegated the right of the sword to Herod and other client rulers and although even Diaspora Jewish communi-

---

[355] Winter, *Trial*, 10–15; Smallwood, *Jews*, 150.

[356] Winter, *Trial*, 75–90.

[357] Cf. O'Rourke, "Law," 174; Sanders, *Judaism*, 61. Paul's Roman citizenship could shield him under normal circumstances (Rabello, "Condition," 738), but not for profaning a temple (Josephus *War* 2.224; Hesiod *Astron.* frg. 3).

[358] Theissen, *Gospels*, 191.

[359] Ibid., *Gospels*, 189–93. The execution R. Eliezer ben Zadok allegedly witnessed in his childhood (*m. Sanh.* 7:2; *t. Sanh.* 9:11) probably would have stemmed from the reign of Agrippa I (Bruce, "Trial," 12; cf. Acts 12:1–3).

[360] Cf. also Catchpole, *Trial*, 247.

[361] O'Rourke, "Law," 174–75.

[362] Brown, *Death*, 339 correctly observes that executions required ratification by the Sanhedrin in Josephus *Ant.* 14.167; while this datum is undoubtedly relevant, we should note that it describes the time of Herod the Great, not direct Roman rule.

[363] E.g., *Sipre Deut.* 154.2.1.

[364] E.g., *b. Sanh.* 49b–50a.

[365] Unless secret executions (cf. Winter, *Trial*, 70–73) were practiced; but Pharisaic requirements for evidence were so strict that even capital convictions must have remained very rare under their own rules.

[366] *Sipre Deut.* 154.1.1; *b. Sanh.* 37b. The date appears indeterminate in *Sipra Qed. par.* 4.206.2.9.

[367] E.g., *p. Sanh.* 1:1, §3; 7:2, §3. Safrai, "Self-Government," 398, cites also *b. Šabb.* 15a; ʿ*Abod . Zar.* 8b. This was the widespread view at the turn of the twentieth century (Abrahams, *Studies,* 1:73; Sanday, *Criticism,* 127; Edersheim, *Life,* 583).

ties could enforce corporal penalties on their own members,[368] Rome withheld capital jurisdiction from municipal aristocracies, who could employ it against citizens loyal to Rome, as we have noted.[369] For this, local rulers needed at least Roman ratification.

Some precedent existed for Romans overlooking past executions, or even human sacrifices, that could be justified by local custom, but they expected such practices to be discontinued,[370] so provable extrajudicial executions were not in the political interests of the priestly aristocracy. Although councils of subject territories could pronounce a death sentence, they had to bring their sentence before the governor for ratification.[371] Most scholars thus currently recognize that the Sanhedrin lacked the legal authority to execute prisoners in this period (Josephus *Ant.* 20.200).[372] As Roman legal scholar A. N. Sherwin-White notes,[373]

> When we find that capital power was the most jealously guarded of all the attributes of government, nor even entrusted to the principal assistants of the governors, and specifically withdrawn, in the instance of Cyrene, from the competence of local courts, it becomes very questionable indeed for the Sanhedrin.

The Sanhedrin could sentence offenders and recommend them for execution, but apart from violating the temple, few Jewish religious charges would receive an automatic capital sentence from the Romans (e.g., the case of Jesus ben Ananias).[374] It is not impossible that Roman officials might look the other way in the case of lynchings, but even these would be problematic if they could generate complaints to Rome.[375]

Jesus' mastery over those who engineer his execution is evident in 18:31–32. Local leaders lacked capital jurisdiction and depended on Pilate for a legal execution (18:31); this, however, was not a mark of their power but a matter of Jesus' own plan. The Romans normally executed by crucifixion those accused of treason.[376] Jesus had announced that he would be executed by being lifted up (12:32–33); now he was handed over to the Romans so that his purpose could be fulfilled (cf. 19:11). Perhaps some opponents of John's audience ridiculed Christians for worshiping one whose life had ended so shamefully at the hands of others, even if Christians claimed he was innocent; John is emphatic that Jesus' death was no tragic accident but part of the divine plan (cf., e.g., 3:14; 4:4; 19:30).[377]

## 3. The Kingdom of Truth (18:33–38a)

After Pilate speaks with the chief priests (18:29–31), he must make some inquiry from the prisoner himself (at least if he wishes to follow some semblance of Roman

---

[368] Blinzler, *Trial,* 164; Winter, *Trial,* 12–13.

[369] E.g., Morris, *Luke,* 319.

[370] Plutarch *R.Q.* 83, *Mor.* 283F (although he notes that Romans had themselves offered such sacrifices).

[371] Blinzler, *Trial,* 164–68; Ramsay, *Church,* 293.

[372] Benoit, *Jesus,* 1:135; Lane, *Mark,* 530; Stewart, "Procedure"; Sanders, *Jesus to Mishnah,* 17; Bruce, "Trial," 12–13.

[373] Sherwin-White, *Society,* 36; see more fully 32–43.

[374] Brown, *Death,* 363–72.

[375] Sanders, *Jesus to Mishnah,* 17.

[376] Blinzler, *Trial,* 238.

[377] Cf. Polycarp's manner of death fulfilling what God had said in *Mart. Pol.* 5, 12 (the stabbing of *Mart. Pol.* 16 may be an interpolation).

order, which had withheld capital jurisdiction for Roman officials precisely to prevent abuses by local muncipal aristocracies). What he finds, however, does not sit well with Roman justice for a conviction. Undoubtedly, John's audience would wish to make use of this apologetic line already figuring prominently in Acts and some other early Christian documents: despite their lack of welcome in some synagogues, Jewish Christians remained committed to their Jewish heritage; the issues of dispute between themselves and their accusers remained Jewish; and hence they should not be prosecuted in Roman lawcourts (see introduction, ch. 5).

3A. Questioning Jesus (18:33–34)

In normal judicial procedure, the accusers would speak first (18:29); Pilate is thus acquainted with the charge of treason (18:33) before he interrogates Jesus.[378] Pilate's initial interrogation of Jesus clarifies the charge the Sanhedrin has brought to Pilate, that Jesus claims to be a king; Rome, like the priestly aristocracy, would understand this claim in revolutionary terms (18:33). Whatever the possible religious motivations behind the charge, the charge against Jesus is political: by claiming to be a king, Jesus implied a worldly kingdom that would challenge Rome.[379] The political charge in Luke 23:2 accurately summarizes the gist of the charge in Mark and Matthew: Jesus was a revolutionary.[380] This is also the most natural way to take the Johannine charge.[381] The charge is technically that of *lese majesty*,[382] for which the normal punishment in the provinces was crucifixion.[383] Because Pilate had authority to conduct his inquiry without a jury or dependence even on the Roman *ordo,* the hearing was merely a *cognitio* to determine the facts and inform his decision.[384] Jesus' only answer in the Markan account (Mark 15:2) affirms the charge;[385] although the Johannine Jesus clarifies the faulty basis for the charge (18:36–37), he never denies it (18:34–37).

Pilate interrogates Jesus in 18:33; a hearing could consist of a *cognitio,* an inquiry to determine the truth of the charges.[386] In such an inquiry, the official could consult his *consilium,* composed of his "*accessores* (junior barristers) and *comites* (attendants)" who functioned as knowledgeable legal aides (cf. Acts 25:12); but the final decision was his own.[387] Roman judges should attend to imperial edicts, statutes, and custom (*moribus,* Justinian *Inst.* 4.17), but provincial officials were free to follow or disregard prior customs.[388]

---

[378] E.g., Chariton 5.4.9; Apuleius *Metam.* 10.7; *t. Sanh.* 6:3. Later rabbinic rules allowed the defendant to speak first in a capital case (*t. Sanh.* 7:2), but even if some Jewish teachers held this view in Jesus' day, Pilate would have operated under Roman procedure.

[379] E.g., Bruce, *History,* 199.

[380] Schneider, "Charge." Synoptic tradition suggests that Jesus' enemies had been planning this charge; with Luke 23:2 compare Mark 12:14.

[381] Robinson, "Witness."

[382] Blinzler, *Trial,* 213, citing *Dig.* 48.4.1, 3–4; cf. Bammel, "*Titulus,*" 357.

[383] Blinzler, *Trial,* 238.

[384] Bruce, "Trial," 13; Ferguson, *Backgrounds,* 50. Neyrey, "Shame of Cross," 123, finds in the *cognitio* challenges to Jesus' honor.

[385] Wrede, *Secret,* 47.

[386] Bruce, "Trial," 13.

[387] Brown, *Death,* 716; Bruce, "Trial," 13; O'Rourke, "Law," 174–75; see further Livy 44.34.2; Josephus *Ag. Ap.* 2.177; Acts 25:12.

[388] Ferguson, *Backgrounds,* 50.

3B. Jesus as King of the Jews (18:33–35)

Although Pilate repeats the Jewish authorities' charge (18:35), it appears fitting that he, as a representative of the Roman Empire, is the first voice in the trial narrative to announce Jesus as "king of the Jews" (18:33), a title to which the Jewish leaders object (19:21) and which they themselves never offer to Jesus.[389] On the level of the story world, Pilate's presentation of Jesus to "the Jews" as "king of the Jews" (18:39) may be ridicule (cf. 19:3);[390] the Gospel's ideal audience, however, will catch the irony (cf. 1:49). Probably the Johannine Christians find most Roman officials more tolerant of their claims to fidelity to their ancestral faith than the synagogue leaders are (cf. 4:9; 18:35). But as in many other cases in the Gospel, John is preaching from genuine tradition rather than creating it wholesale for his purposes. The charge, "king of the Jews" (18:33), is undoubtedly historical.[391] Jesus' triumphal entry (12:13) marked him as a royal aspirant; the priestly aristocracy would arrest, and the Romans execute, anyone who offered the slightest grounds for suspicion of treason against Rome. The title is not a traditional Christian confession; Jesus' "you say" in the tradition (Mark 15:2) suggests that it is not the title Jesus or the tradition would have emphasized, and Romans crucified many self-proclaimed kings and their followers under the *Lex Iulia de maiestate* (Josephus *Ant.* 17.285, 295).[392] Other Jewish rebels apparently hoped for kingship (Josephus *War* 2.443–444; *Ant.* 17.285),[393] but unless they desired repression, Christians would have hardly invented the claim that Jesus was crucified on these grounds (cf. Acts 17:7).[394] As broadly as "treason" could be defined in Roman law[395] and especially in Sejanus's Rome,[396] the charge of claiming to be a king on the part of an otherwise unimportant provincial might require little investigation to secure condemnation.

When Jesus asks whether Pilate says (cf. Mark 15:2, σὺ λέγεις) Jesus is king of the Jews "from himself" (18:34), on the story level he asks whether Pilate has received this title from Jesus' accusers;[397] on the ironic level, however, Jesus might imply that Pilate's charge was divinely guided, even contrary to his own knowledge (11:51; cf. 19:11). Pilate's role is essential to the functioning of the plot (18:31–32), but he remains "a complete outsider to the world within which the drama moves" (18:35).[398] Pilate protests that he himself is not a "Jew" (18:35), yet, in the narrative's irony, "is forced step by step to carry out the will of 'the Jews.'"[399] "Your own nation" employs the term ἔθνος, which elsewhere appears in this Gospel only in the leaders' decision to hand Jesus over to Pilate for the preservation of their nation, precisely because they thought the Romans would be angry if they did not (11:48,

---

[389] Cf. Jonge, *Jesus*, 67; Collins, "Speaking of Jews," 299–300.

[390] Michaels, *John*, 303.

[391] So even Winter, *Trial*, 108–9.

[392] Brown, *Death*, 968. As Fredriksen, *Christ*, 123, puts it, whether or not Jesus claimed a messianic title, "he certainly died as if he had."

[393] Harvey, *History*, 13 n. 12.

[394] Ibid., 13–14; Stanton, *Gospel Truth*, 173. Surely the largely apolitical Markan community would have been an unlikely source for the invention (cf. Kee, *Origins*, 120–21)

[395] Blinzler, *Trial*, 213, citing *Dig.* 48.4.1–4.

[396] E.g., Dio Cassius 57.4.5–6; 57.9.2; 57.19.1; 57.23.1–2.

[397] Some suggest that Jesus responds evasively in 18:34–36 because good Jews should avoid denouncing their own people (Witherington, *Wisdom*, 291; Blomberg, *Reliability*, 241); it appears unclear whether this ideology is in view here, but the ideology did exist (as in, e.g., Acts 28:19).

[398] Robinson, "Destination," 119.

[399] Meeks, "Jew," 161.

50–52). Most paradoxical and important of all, the two characters in this Gospel who comment on Jesus' own Jewishness are a Samaritan woman (4:9) and Pilate (18:35). In John's irony, "his own" did not receive him (1:11). This observation may mirror also the suffering of Johannine Christians, whose fidelity to their heritage is in question primarily from their own ethnic and religious siblings.

### 3C. The Nature of Jesus' Kingship (18:36–37a)

Pilate repeats the question about Jesus' kingship (18:37a), following basic trial procedure: if a defendant failed to offer a defense, the judge would normally ask about the charge three times before the defendant would be convicted by default.[400] Once Jesus admits to kingship (18:37), Pilate would normally be duty-bound to have him executed; thus one Jewish scholar argues that whereas Jesus was innocent, he pleaded guilty to secure martyrdom.[401] This proposal may be correct in some sense; nevertheless, in all our extant gospels, while Jesus is a king, he is not the sort of king whose kingship would constitute high treason.

Whereas, in other extant gospel tradition, Jesus reluctantly accepts the charge "king of the Jews" with the words "That is what you are saying" (Mark 15:2; Matt 27:11; Luke 23:3), here John transposes Jesus' response into John's own idiom, allowing him to explain the sense in which he is and the sense in which he is not "king of the Jews."[402] In a sense, Jesus rejects the title "king of the Jews" (18:33)—in the sense in which the Fourth Gospel uses the title "Jews" (see introduction, pp. 214–28)—preferring "king of Israel" (12:13), which appears in a very different light (see introduction, pp. 280–320). Jesus' kingship may be rejected by many of the leaders of his own people, but he is king over all who embrace his truth (18:36–37).[403] Only those born from above by God's Spirit can recognize or enter his kingdom (3:3, 5).

Jesus declares that his servants would not fight to protect him (18:36). Roman officials would have punished soldiers who did not risk their lives to protect their commander;[404] but Jesus shows Pilate that he and his followers are a different sort of kingdom. One of Jesus' servants had sought to fight the high priest's servant (18:10), but Jesus had stopped him (18:11); Jesus' way called on even his servants to die (12:26; 13:16; 15:20). If Romans had accompanied those who originally detained Jesus, Pilate may have heard of Jesus' command not to resist (18:11),[405] but as we noted above, Roman participation is unclear before the priestly delegation approaches Pilate in 18:28. In any case, Jesus mentions the matter now.

Rome's acknowledgement of Jesus' Jewishness through the character of Pilate and the acceptance by some Gentiles that Jesus was Israel's rightful king contrasted starkly with the hostile response of synagogue leaders to this claim, allowing John's audience to identify

---

[400] Brown, *John,* 2:853, following Sherwin-White, "Trial," 105.

[401] Cohn, *Trial,* 328.

[402] Bruce, "Trial," 14; cf. Bammel, "Trial," 420.

[403] Pancaro, *Law,* 298.

[404] Valerius Maximus 2.7.15d (15e: the senate declared that Romans should die honorably in battle rather than be captured).

[405] Stauffer, *Jesus,* 129; cf. Socrates' insistence on nonviolent persuasion (Xenophon *Mem.* 1.2.10). Smith, *John* (1999), 342–43, compares Jesus' pacifism in the Q tradition (Matt 5:38–42; Luke 6:29–31). The "servants" (ὑπηρέται) of Jesus (18:36) may contrast with the more militant officers (ὑπηρέται) of the opposition (7:32, 45–46; 18:3, 12, 18, 22; 19:6).

with Jesus' situation. Jesus' definition of his kingdom in terms of fidelity to his truth rather than of ethnic allegiances or military power (18:36) also fits the Johannine portrait of the revealer.[406] Yet the theology behind this pericope is not only Johannine but also goes back to the earliest sources of Christian faith. Sanders accepts as two "firm facts" Jesus' execution by the Romans as a professed "king of the Jews" and a messianic movement of Jesus' followers who entertained no anticipation of military triumph. "Thus not only was Jesus executed as would-be king even though he had no secular ambitions, his disciples also combined the same two points: Jesus was Messiah, but his kingdom was 'not of this world.'"[407] Allegiance to such a kingdom inevitably produced conflict with excessive claims of worldly kingdoms, inviting the martyrdom of those who remained loyal to it.[408]

### 3D. The Kingdom and Truth (18:37b–38a)

Jesus' claim that his "kingdom" had to do with "truth" would sound very different to purely hellenized ears and to those more steeped in ancient Jewish traditions although the semantic range of the word in Greek and Hebrew overlapped. (Presumably Jesus and Pilate converse in Greek, the *lingua franca* of the Eastern empire, known to all educated Romans.) Greek philosophy could speak of ἀλήθεια in terms of a true perspective on reality;[409] Romans could speak of *veritas* as accurate, factual representation of events (Cicero *Inv.* 2.53.161).[410] In light of the Hebrew Bible and many uses in the LXX, "truth" included "God's faithfulness to His covenant of redemption,"[411] hardly a politically innocuous concept in the hands of Jewish patriots such as those involved in the recent war of 66–70 C.E. At the same time, the Christian reader of the Gospel understands that Jesus means the term neither in the sense of Greek philosophers nor with connotations that Jewish patriots may have added to it, but in terms of God's revelation of his covenant character. God had revealed this character to Moses on Mount Sinai (Exod 34:6) and had fleshed it out fully in Jesus' own life and ministry (1:14; 14:6).

Just as the ultimate expression of God's glory (1:14) would be in the cross (12:23–24), so would be the ultimate expression of God's truth, God's covenant faithfulness; thus Jesus' mission to bear witness to the truth (18:37) would require his death. Pilate had to convict him; this was the plan of the Father and the Son, not of Pilate. Those who were of the truth, like the formerly blind man, heard Jesus' voice (18:37; 10:3);[412] Pilate would not hear, but he would nevertheless carry out God's purposes. If, when facing the truth in person (14:6), Pilate asks what truth is, he is clearly not of the truth, not one of "those whom 'the Father has given to Jesus'" (10:29).[413]

---

[406] Cf. De Maria, "Regno," for patristic views here. One might speak of one "coming into the world" (cf. comment on 1:9; cf. 16:21) or being born for a particular purpose (Seneca *Ep. Lucil.* 90.46, humans for virtue; Gal 1:15–16) with only missiological significance; but in view of the entire Gospel, these words have intense christological significance (3:19; 6:14; 9:39; 11:27; 12:46–47; 16:28).

[407] Sanders, *Jesus and Judaism*, 294; the entire sentence is italicized in the original. A messianic claim could only be indictable if construed as treason (Sanders, *Jesus and Judaism*, 55).

[408] Justin *1 Apol.* 11.

[409] Cf. comments on 1:14.

[410] Truth may be unattainable in its perfect form, but for Cicero it remains the object of inquiry rather than simply being persuasive (Cicero *Or. Brut.* 71.237; *Fin.* 1.5.13).

[411] Kuyper, "Grace," 17–19. Cf. Turner, "Thoughts," 46.

[412] Brown, *John*, 2:854, stresses the parallel with 10:3, noting that in the OT kings were "shepherds" of their people.

[413] Haenchen, *John*, 2:180.

Jesus' nonresistance (18:36) was a striking contrast to expected models of treason. What would have been clear from Pilate's perspective was the political harmlessness of a sage whose "kingdom" consisted of truth (18:37). As Diaspora readers would readily recognize, a Gentile hearing about a "kingdom of truth" would think not of political kingship but of a kingship of philosophers (cf. Epictetus *Diatr.* 3.22.49; Plutarch *Flatterer* 16, *Mor* 58E). From Plato on, philosophers claimed that they were the citizens best suited to rule the state,[414] wrote essays on appropriate forms of rulership,[415] and sometimes (especially among the Cynics) spoke of themselves as ruling.[416] No one took such claims as a threat to the security of the state because such philosophers rarely if ever challenged that security. True, Cynics often criticized rulers who fell short of their ideal of true kingship, and this criticism invited suspicion of wandering preachers;[417] but Pilate could readily discern the difference between such a political troublemaker and the more common form of apolitical visionary. To a pragmatic Roman governor, Jesus was nothing more than a harmless Cynic philosopher; a nuisance, perhaps, but surely no threat. Ironically, whereas Pilate views Jesus as a harmless sage, the Jerusalem aristocracy views him as a threat to Rome's interests (19:12, 15; cf. 11:49–50). From their respective inadequate conceptual frameworks, both misconstrue his identity.

Pilate's tone may be undecipherable, but as Duke notes, John's dramatic irony here is clear: Pilate asks, "What is truth?" of the very one who is the truth (14:6).[418] The meaning of "truth" might be debatable, but Pilate was hardly interested in what appeared to him to be philosophical matters (18:38a); he was interested in politics, and from that vantage point, Jesus was "not guilty" (18:38b). Pilate thus took the matter back to Jesus' accusers (18:38b–19:16).

## Pilate and the People (18:38b–19:16)

This section develops Pilate's encounter with Jesus, augmenting the (in a worldly sense) apolitical character of his kingdom stressed in 18:36–37; Jesus is no threat to Roman security (19:8–12). But the people provide Pilate other political realities to deal with, and become increasingly insistent that Jesus be handed over.

The people here are essentially the leaders of the people who bear primary responsibility for leading them to oppose Jesus: hence "the Jews" (18:38; 19:7, 12, 14) are the "leading priests and officers" (19:6, 15). A flat, composite character, they speak with one voice like a chorus in a Greek tragedy.[419]

---

[414] E.g., Quintilian 2.17.28; Diogenes Laertius 7.1.122; Seneca *Ep. Lucil.* 108.13; on Musonius Rufus, see Klassen, "Law." In Jewish circles, cf. CD 6.6; ʾ*Abot R. Nat.* 44, §124B; *Gen. Rab.* 93:2; *Deut. Rab.* 2:33. On the need for educated rulers, see, e.g., Plutarch *S.K., Cyrus* 2, *Mor.* 172E; *Uned. R.* passim, *Mor.* 779D–782F.

[415] E.g., Dio Chrysostom *On Kingship;* the symposium section of *Letter of Aristeas.* Cf. also smaller sections on the topic of kingship, e.g., Plato *Rep.* 5.472; Isocrates *Ad Nic.* 10–11, 29, *Or.* 2; Plutarch *S.R., Cato the Elder* 8, *Mor.* 198F; cf. Prov 8:15; *Sipre Deut.* 161.2.1.

[416] E.g., Horace *Sat.* 1.3.125; Plutarch *Dinner* 12, *Mor.* 155A; sources in Conzelmann, *Corinthians,* 87; perhaps 1 Cor 4:8.

[417] Liefeld, "Preacher," 162.

[418] Duke, *Irony,* 130. It is unlikely that we are to think of Pilate as a parody of Socrates who cross-examines people to achieve truth (Maximus of Tyre *Or.* 10.8); that is closer to Jesus' role (18:4, 7, 21, 23, 34).

[419] For "speaking with one voice," see also Virgil *Aen.* 11.122–131; Apuleius *Metam.* 11.13; Exod 24:3; 2 Chr 5:13; *1 En.* 61:11–13; Josephus *Life* 259; Acts 4:24; Rom 15:6.

## 1. Preferring a Terrorist (18:38b–40)

Pilate's first presentation of Jesus leads to repudiation; the chief priests, who supposedly hand over Jesus for a treason charge (18:33–35) and will claim no king but Caesar (19:15), yet want freedom for an insurgent instead (18:40).[420] Their real objections to Jesus' claim to be "son of God" may lie elsewhere (19:7; cf. 5:18; 10:33–36), but John's Asian audience will undoubtedly hear in their claim a support for the emperor cult (19:15), for lack of allegiance to which the Jewish Christians are being betrayed to the Roman authorities.

### 1A. Pilate's Attempt to Free Jesus (18:38b–39)

The conflict between Pilate and the Jewish leaders continues to unfold, emphasizing the responsibility of the leaders of Jesus' own people without denying that of Pilate.[421] Luke shares with John Pilate's threefold claim to find no guilt in Jesus (Luke 23:4, 14, 22; John 18:38; 19:4, 6); if John's source is not ultimately Luke, then both draw on a common passion tradition here.

If Jesus was no threat, Pilate would naturally be inclined to release him (18:39), just as an equally unscrupulous governor a few decades later would release another harmless prophet the chief priests wanted silenced (Josephus *War* 6.305).[422] The negative response of the priestly aristocracy is predictable, and one familiar only with this Gospel and not the rest of the gospel tradition (e.g., Mark 15:6–15)[423] might assume that the "Jews" who protest here (18:40) represent the elite with whom Pilate has been dealing (18:28, 35). But the elite often spoke for the masses who trusted and followed them, and John's audience probably already knows the basic passion story from other sources (cf. 1 Cor 11:23–25).

If the Jewish officials want Jesus executed but Pilate does not, it makes some sense that he would push the responsibility off onto the people; perhaps he thought that Jesus was popular enough with the masses for them to want to release him. But in the Fourth Gospel, the "Jews" and the authorities overlap at most points, so, in the logic of the story world, Pilate's attempt to release Jesus by appealing to the "Jews" reveals only his inadequate, foreigner's understanding of the ferment taking place within the Jewish community (7:43; 9:16; 10:19).[424]

### 1B. The Paschal Amnesty Custom (18:39)

Pilate's offer may suggest that he thought himself indulgent on special occasions; his otherwise brutal disposition, however, colors all the other brief Jewish reports of his activity that remain extant.[425] What is the historical likelihood that he might have followed an existing amnesty custom in Judea?

---

[420] For the irony, see also Duke, *Irony*, 131, who also contrasts the "robber" and good shepherd in 10:1, 8, 11.

[421] Nicholson, *Death*, 54, suggests this chiasm: Jesus as King (19:1–3, 17–22); Pilate and the "Jews" (19:4–7, 12–16); Pilate and Jesus (19:8–11).

[422] One could draw good examples from some behavior of even generally negative characters (see, e.g., Valerius Maximus 4.7.1; 4.2.7).

[423] Sanders, *Jesus and Judaism*, 298, sees the condemnation by the crowds as an example of the Gospels' slant "to incriminate the Jews and exculpate the Romans," on which see above.

[424] On Pilate's lack of wisdom on the historical level here, see Blinzler, *Trial*, 209.

[425] On the rhetorical bias of such accounts, see, e.g., Krieger, "Judenfeind"; Thatcher, "Pilate."

Although all four gospels attest the paschal amnesty custom,[426] most scholars remain skeptical of the custom because the proposed analogies from other locations appear inadequate.[427] Yet an argument against the custom from silence (in a narrative that can be confirmed at many other points) may not take adequate account of the burden of proof in favor of the Gospels' usual authenticity (see introduction, ch. 1).[428] One could argue that John follows a literary practice of his day in creating customs to suit his narrative,[429] but if John is independent of the Markan tradition (less likely in the Passion Narrative than elsewhere), it would testify to the pre-Johannine character of John's primary point here.

Like most customs of the Roman administration in Palestine, this one is currently unattested (a not surprising situation given the freedom of governors to ignore and supersede earlier customs),[430] but if the Gospels usually correctly report events, especially when they multiply attest them (as possibly here), the assumption should begin in favor of, rather than against, their claims if no hard evidence to the contrary is available. If the particular custom is unattested outside the Gospels, analogies suggest its general consistency with Roman policy. In tentative support of the custom, one can adduce parallels from other Roman administrations and the Gospel writers' assumption that their audiences were familiar with this practice in the gospel tradition.

Although Roman law dictated that judges should not ignore laws, decrees, or custom (Justinian *Inst.* 4.17), Roman provincial officials often followed, but were not bound by, "precedents of their predecessors or local customs."[431] Prefects were, in any case, free to issue amnesties.[432] Pilate's offer of amnesty thus could be a custom Pilate himself initiated, though it is more likely an earlier one he merely decided to continue (John 18:39). Pilate could have abolished a preexisting custom, but given previous conflicts with the people (e.g., Josephus *War* 2.174, 177) and the dangers of popular unrest at festivals (e.g., Josephus *War* 2.224), he probably would not have done so (though its lack of attestation in Josephus may suggest that one of his successors eventually abolished the custom). Politically prudent rulers in the East presumably often continued festival traditions begun by their predecessors (e.g., Alexander in Diodorus Siculus 17.16.3; contrast the imprudent Verres in Cicero *Verr.* 2.2.21.51–52). Doing away with pardons and other civic customs was considered despicable (Cicero *Rosc. Amer.* 1.3), and governors who wished to make a positive impression typically continued as many as possible of the precedents the people liked (Cicero *Att.* 6.1).

---

426 See Brown, *Death,* 793–95. If John knows the passion tradition followed by Mark, however, the value of independent attestation is weakened.

427 E.g., Cohn, *Trial,* 166; Winter, *Trial,* 91; Brown, *Death,* 814–19. Theissen, *Gospels,* 196, links this story with the Caligula crisis when he thinks that more of the populace would have sided with the "bandits" than with Christians (citing Tacitus *Ann.* 12.54.1; Josephus *Ant.* 20.5, 97, 102); but this is hardly the only period in the first century in which that would be the case, and Jesus would be less popular than Barabbas to those prone to revolution and, probably more to the point here, less popular with most of the Jerusalem masses than the priestly authorities were.

428 The comments on the paschal amnesty have been adapted from Keener, *Matthew,* 668–69. One could at least regard the custom's historical existence as "plausible" (as in Culpepper, *John,* 225).

429 Bauer, "Namen."

430 See Ferguson, *Backgrounds,* 50.

431 Ibid. This freedom may call into question the supposed official report cited by Eusebius (*Hist. eccl.* 2.2) and Tertullian (*Apol.* 21:24; cf. 5:2), which may depend on an earlier Christian forgery that the Christians assumed to be accurate (probably as in Justin *1 Apol.* 35, 48; *pace* Stauffer, *Jesus,* 145–46).

432 E.g., P.Oxy. 1668.17–19 (third century C.E., perhaps referring to a political disturbance); cf. Seneca *Controv.* 5.8 (hypothetical); Plutarch *Caesar* 67.4 (the senate).

Romans sometimes deferred to local custom in forgiving an offense (e.g., Plutarch *R.Q.* 83, *Mor.* 283F); they also sometimes freed prisoners en masse on local feasts (Livy 5.13.8),[433] a custom known in various other ancient Near Eastern and Mediterranean cultures.[434] Although the later practice of pardoning criminals at Easter (*Cod. theod.* 9.38.3–4, 8) is probably dependent on the Gospels,[435] sometimes they also released captives because of the people's demands.[436] Romans usually delayed punishments during their own festivals in Rome.[437] Roman law permitted two kinds of amnesty: *abolitio* (acquitting a prisoner before trial—*Codex* 9.42 *(De abolitionibus); Dig.* 48.16) and *indulgentia* (pardoning a convicted criminal, *Codex* 9.43.3).[438] Since Pilate had not yet pronounced sentence against Jesus, an *abolitio* allowed him to easily circumvent the whole matter placed before him. We accept many ancient claims about customs that are attested in only one source, though more pleased when that source is corroborated in part or whole by other sources; the gospel tradition's account is plausible, and given the fact that it could be checked in the earliest period, appears more likely than not.

## 1C. Barabbas, a "Robber" (18:40)

If Pilate wished to grant any prisoner's release for the festival, it was far safer to release Jesus, whom he now supposed a harmless philosopher, than alternatives such as Barabbas, who, like those ultimately executed with Jesus, was a "robber" (18:40), the aristocracy's derisive title (shared by Josephus) for insurrectionists.[439] In the gospel tradition, those who arrested Jesus treated him as if he were a guerilla as well—a natural category in which to place many messianic pretenders, albeit not Jesus (Mark 14:48).[440]

Pilate appears here as one who attempts to be politically shrewd but proves politically inept. He tries to achieve two goals simultaneously: he is willing to honor an earlier custom—which Roman law did not require him to follow—to curry more favor with the people, and at the same time he is willing to release a prisoner he wishes to release in any case. The narrative meanwhile portrays Pilate as politically inept: the "Jews" prefer Barabbas to Jesus, as Pilate should have expected had he better understood the situation. Perhaps Pilate expects the municipal aristocracy to side with Roman values over against a low-class peasant revolutionary; it was such lower-class revolutionaries who, perhaps over

---

[433] Blinzler, *Trial,* 206. During local festivals Romans sought to show particular benevolence to local populations even with respect to executions (Philo *Flaccus* 83). They offered mass amnesties when it proved politically advantageous (Cicero *Phil.* 8.9.32).

[434] Merritt, "Barabbas"; cf. P.Tebt. 5.1–13 (118 B.C.E.); Cornelius Nepos 8 (Thrasybulus), 3.2; a fictitius example in Iamblichus *Bab. St.* 16 (Photius *Bibliotheca* 94.77a).

[435] With Cohn, *Trial,* 167. Blinzler, *Trial,* 207, 218–21, argues for the custom of a paschal release of prisoners in *m. Pesah.* 8:6 (cf. also Schnackenburg, *John,* 3:252); but see Bammel, "Trial," 427, who argues more persuasively that the text merely indicates the special Jewish desire to free prisoners at this time.

[436] P.Florentinus 61.59ff., cited in Deissmann, *Light,* 269; Blinzler, *Trial,* 207; Lane, *Mark,* 553. Roman rulers sometimes handed over convicted persons at the people's request as an act of benevolence (Livy 8.35.1–9); governors might also release prisoners in acceding to terrorist demands (Josephus *Ant.* 20.208–210).

[437] Seneca *Controv.* 5.4; Cicero *Cael.* 1.1; New Year's Day in Suetonius *Tib.* 61.

[438] Blinzler, *Trial,* 207–8.

[439] Commentators typically note its use for insurrectionists in Josephus (Barrett, *John,* 539; Michaels, *John,* 308; cf. Malina, *World,* 77).

[440] Some argue plausibly that Jesus shared the social bandits' "basic goals" while rejecting their violent means; see, e.g., Oakman, "Peasant," 121.

two decades before this Gospel was written, ultimately had slaughtered much of the priestly aristocracy in the temple area (Josephus *War* 4.302–334).

John's presentation of the Jerusalem leaders, however, reveals more explicit irony than his presentation of Pilate. They had handed Jesus over themselves as a political revolutionary; yet they themselves favored the real political revolutionary, and it was following his course, not that of Jesus, that would ultimately lead to Judea's demise before Roman armies (11:48).[441] If Barabbas was a "robber," so were any who were preferred by others to Jesus; the leaders of the "Jews" themselves were "robbers" for not glorifying Jesus as the only way to the Father (10:1, 8).

Judean leaders seem to have developed the technique of large delegations, sometimes with loud demands, as the most appropriate tactic for dealing with potentially recalcitrant Roman officials.[442] Governors whose primary responsibility was public order might ultimately need to negotiate or accede to their demands (Philo *Embassy* 301–302, 305–6). Pilate thus proceeded to scourge Jesus (19:1) in response to (οὖν, 19:1) their demands.

## 2. Abusing the Prisoner (19:1–3)

As was typical in such cases, the soldiers' abuse includes ridicule and some torture. Yet the narrative is deeply ironic: the one whom they mock as king of the Jews really is king of the Jews.[443] Neither the world (1:10) nor his own (1:11) embraced him.

### 2A. The Scourging (19:1)

The scourging is not at all incompatible with Pilate's belief that Jesus was innocent; the procurator Albinus later reportedly flogged Joshua ben Hananiah until his bones showed, for similarly disrupting public order (Josephus *War* 6.304), but afterward released him as harmless (*War* 6.305). And as mentioned before, Roman officials sometimes delivered over even Roman soldiers to maintain public order (*War* 2.231); Pilate would be more concerned about keeping the peace—and his political reputation—than about a non-Roman wandering philosopher of some sort. Still, Pilate was not known for his cooperative spirit (Josephus *Ant.* 18.61–62; *War* 2.176–177) and, in appropriate character, holds out against the priestly wishes as long as he can (19:4–6; cf. Philo *Embassy* 302–303). Ultimately, he will do what political necessity demands: although it may be an internal religious matter, Jesus' innocence is not absolutely clear, so Pilate might feel freer to give way to the crowd's claims, as he had on other occasions (Josephus *War* 2.174; *Ant.* 18.59).[444]

The preliminary scourging here (19:1) is more serious than the maximum thirty-nine lashes allowed by the law (Deut 25:3) and administered by synagogue communities (cf. 2 Cor 11:23–24). Even if its placement in the narrative would suggest to attentive first-century readers a "judicial warning" rather than a preexecution scourging as in Mark 15:15,[445]

---

[441] That Barabbas does not appear in Josephus does not count against his historicity; many such bandits arose, and Josephus mentions even Jesus only briefly (Brown, *Death*, 811).

[442] Stauffer, *Jesus*, 128, cites Acts 24:1; Philo, *Embassy* 300; Josephus *Ant.* 18.273.

[443] The ironies of the soldiers' mockeries were perceived by early students of the Gospels (Cyprian *Good of Patience* 7; Cyril of Jerusalem *Sermon on the Paralytic* 12; Oden and Hall, *Mark*, 226–27).

[444] Brown, *Death*, 722. Philo *Embassy* 302 provides a portrait that combines Pilate's obstinate disagreeability with his reluctance to face political repercussions, as in the Passion Narrative.

[445] E.g., Neyrey, "Shame of Cross," 125.

the beating could be serious; and given their knowledge of Jesus' impending crucifixion, many readers might not have noticed the distnction anyway. Like many other peoples,[446] Romans did not limit the number of lashes, and thus sometimes victims not even sentenced to death died or were disabled under cruel supervisors.[447] Indeed, Josephus had opponents scourged "until their entrails were visible" (*War* 2.612) and reports a procurator laying bare a man's bones, though the man survived (*War* 6.304). This form of scourging also proved more severe than most Roman public corporal disciplines as well (cf. Acts 16:22; 2 Cor 11:25);[448] sometimes this kind of scourging caused death itself.[449] Unlike the lesser *fustigatio* (beating), the severer disciplines of *flagellatio* (flogging) and especially *verberatio* (scourging) accompanied the death sentence,[450] although John's audience and even John himself probably would not have recognized these fine distinctions.[451] Whereas Romans used rods on freepersons and sticks on soldiers, they used scourges on slaves or provincials of equivalent status.[452] In the Synoptic tradition Pilate orders the preliminary scourging that, whether with rods or whips, generally preceded crucifixion and other forms of capital punishment.[453] In John he offers an earlier scourging, but in light of the negative outcome of Pilate's complaint to the Jerusalem aristocracy, it will have served the same purpose.

Probably stripped[454] and tied to a pillar or post,[455] Jesus was beaten with *flagella*—leather whips "whose thongs were knotted and interspersed" with pieces of iron or bone, or a spike;[456] it left skin hanging from the back in bloody strips.[457] Various texts[458] attest the horror with which this punishment was viewed. Soldiers normally executed this task in the provinces.[459] Some felt that the *flagellum* was merciful because it so weakened the prisoner as to hasten his death on the cross.[460] That the Gospels mention but do not describe

---

[446] E.g., P.Hal. 1.188–189, 196–199 (mid-third century B.C.E.; a slave who strikes a free person receives at least one hundred stripes, a penalty known for slaves [Petronius *Sat.* 28] but also at times for freedpersons [P.Hal. 1.203–205] and others [Plato *Laws* 9, 881C]).

[447] Commentators cite *Dig.* 18.19.8.3; Cicero *Verr.* 2.4.39.85; Philo *Flaccus* 75 (see Blinzler, *Trial*, 222–23). I have borrowed most of the information on scourging from Keener, *Matthew*, 672–73.

[448] T. Jos. 2:3; *Dig.* 47.21.2. For *coercitio* as part of preliminary examinations, cf. Lake and Cadbury, *Commentary*, 282–83. Josephus adapts such discipline (*Life* 335).

[449] Bruce, *Commentary*, 445; cf., e.g., Cicero *Pis.* 34.84.

[450] Brown, *John*, 2:874.

[451] Brown, *Death*, 851.

[452] *Dig.* 48.19.10; 68.28.2; Blinzler, *Trial*, 222.

[453] E.g., Josephus *War* 2.306–308; 5.449; Livy 2.5.8; 9.24.15; 10.1.3; 26.40.13; 41.11.8; Appian *R.H.* 3.9.3; Polybius 11.30.2; Dionysius of Halicarnassus *R.A.* 3.40.3; 5.43.2; 7.69.1; 9.40.3–4; 12.6.7; 20.16.2; 20.17.2; Arrian *Alex.* 3.30.5; Cicero *Verr.* 5.62.162; Klausner, *Jesus*, 350; cf. Lucian *Dead to Life/Fishermen* 2.

[454] Stripping before execution was standard (e.g., Polybius 11.30.1–2; Dionysius of Halicarnassus *R.A.* 7.69.2; Herodian 8.8.6; Josephus *Ag. Ap.* 1.191; 2.53; *m. Sanh.* 6:3; *b. Sanh.* 45a, bar.), as before public beatings (Longus 2.14; Aulus Gellius 10.3.3; Cicero *Verr.* 2.4.40.86; Herodes *Mime* 5.20).

[455] Plautus *Bacchides* 4.7.25; Artemidorus *Onir.* 1.78, in Blinzler, *Trial*, 222; see also *m. Mak.* 3:12. One could also be scourged, presumably across the breast, while bound to the cross itself (Dio Cassius *R.H.* 49.22.6).

[456] Apuleius *Metam.* 7.30.154; *Cod. theod.* 8.5.2; 9.35.2; Goguel, *Jesus*, 527; Blinzler, *Trial*, 222.

[457] Klausner, *Jesus*, 350; Blinzler, *Trial*, 222.

[458] E.g., Horace *Sat.* 1.3.119; Cicero *Rab. perd.* 5.15–16; Brown, *Death*, 851.

[459] Cf. Suetonius *Calig.* 26; Blinzler, *Trial*, 222.

[460] Wilkinson, *Jerusalem*, 151.

the practice makes them read more like official reports than rhetorical documents with a heavy element of *pathos* at this point;[461] nevertheless, John's audience would undoubtedly understand the basic procedure, for floggings and executions were generally public affairs in the Roman Empire.

The scourging is independently attested by John and the Synoptics, although the sequence differs.[462] Because John's scourging occurs earlier in the narrative's sequence, some scholars argue that John represents a lesser form of scourging than the form that took place in the Synoptics, perhaps as an inquisition rather than the first stage of execution.[463] John's readers might indeed draw this conclusion, but it is likely that whatever the nuances in the various Gospel writers' reports, the same historical event stands behind them; and the distinctions may well have eluded the Gospel writers' original audiences anyway.[464] Accustomed to thinking of the scourging as they probably had heard it in other forms of the passion narrative, or simply from what they expected of public beatings before executions, they would recognize its severity.

Jesus' abuse fits the criterion of embarrassment; public beatings produced shame as well as physical pain.[465] Given abundant ancient attestation for the abuse of prisoners coupled with the known tendency of humans to abuse power, the account is not implausible.[466] Multiple attestation further supports the tradition of Jesus' abuse; not only John and the Synoptics but also Paul seems aware of the tradition of Jesus' abuse (Rom 15:3, citing Ps 69:9).[467] John's sequence is different,[468] but an audience familiar with the tradition of Jesus' final week would have anticipated resequencing from John's temple-cleansing scene forward. John may include the beating here so he can retain as his climax the Jewish leaders' demands for Jesus' execution.

### 2B. The Mocking (19:2–3)

The ridicule of Jesus as "king of the Jews" (19:3) reinforces a title this narrative ironically grants Jesus through the mouth of his pagan enemies (18:33; 19:14, 19);[469] for John, it is not the high priest alone who can unwittingly prophesy (11:51). Even after Jesus' flogging (19:1), physical abuse continues as part of the mockery: that the soldiers "gave" Jesus

---

461 Goguel, *Jesus*, 527.

462 Brown, *Death*, 852.

463 Cf. Bruce, "Trial," 15; Blinzler, *Trial*, 224; Bammel, "Trial," 440–41, though Blinzler and Bammel go too far in separating this from the crucifixion historically. Blinzler (*Trial*, 223) distinguishes forms of scourging thus: "an inquisitional torture (Acts 22:24; probably Josephus *War* 4.304), as a death sentence (*fustuarium*, primarily a military punishment—Horace *Sat.* 1.2.41–42), as an independent police chastisement (P. Flor. 61; Josephus *War* 2.269; cf. *Dig.* 48.2.6; Philo *Flaccus* 75), and as the introductory stage to execution after the sentence of death (*War* 2.306, 308; 5.449; 7.200, 202; Livy 33.36)."

464 Brown, *Death*, 851.

465 Dupont, *Life*, 126–27.

466 Davies and Allison, *Matthew*, 3:600. Public abuse of prisoners, even adorning one as a king and beating him, occurred on other occasions; see comment below.

467 Johnson, *Real Jesus*, 120.

468 Winter, *Trial*, 101, argues that John 19:2–3 simply modifies the timing of Mark 15:16–20.

469 Malina and Rohrbaugh, *John*, 249, point to "formal elements" of a royal coronation in 19:1–22: (1) crowning and homage (19:1–3); (2) proclamation (19:4–5); (3) acclamation (19:6–7); (4) enthronement on the judgment seat (19:13–16, assuming Jesus seated there); (5) naming and title (19:19–22); and (6) royal burial; of these, I would regard only 1–3 and 5 as persuasive, all ironic.

"blows" (19:3) connects them with Jesus' Jewish captors (18:22), reminding the reader that Jesus faced rejection from both his own nation and the larger "world" (1:10–11).[470] The imperfect verb ἐδίδοσαν probably suggests repeated blows.[471]

Some soldiers guarding the Temple Mount seem to have converted to Judaism,[472] but those who abused Jesus (19:2), whether from the Antonia garrison or (perhaps more likely) the addition troops Pilate had brought in for Passover, were certainly of the majority who remained Gentile (19:3). (Although one would expect to find a larger contingent of soldiers in the Fortress Antonia,[473] Pilate brought soldiers with him at Passover and would keep his own temporary residence heavily guarded.)

That soldiers would take the opportunity to taunt a captive for entertainment should not surprise us; although one cannot prove that they did so in this case, evidence suggests that such events were not unusual.[474] Public abuse of prisoners, even adorning one as a king and beating him, occurred on other occasions.[475] Games of mockery included the game of king,[476] and theatrical mimes were common as well.[477] Most daily entertainment was less dramatic. Soldiers usually had to entertain themselves by games such as tossing coins, stones, or dice;[478] tossing knuckle bones seems to have been a common game.[479]

The Gospels reveal Jesus' status as a servant-king in part by revealing how unlike a king the world thought him to be: Syrian or other Eastern auxiliaries,[480] but also Romans stationed in Palestine, might be happy to ridicule the notion of a Jewish king—thereby also ridiculing the people among whom they were stationed.[481] Anti-Judaism was common in parts of the Greek East, especially Greek-speaking Egypt;[482] it also appeared in

---

[470] Possibly, though not certainly, John contrasts the world's "giving" here with God's gracious gift (e.g., 3:16; 4:10).

[471] With, e.g., Michaels, *John*, 308.

[472] Bamberger, *Proselytism*, 232–33.

[473] Anderson, *Mark*, 335.

[474] See Brown, *Death*, 877.

[475] Commentators cite Philo *Flaccus* 36–39; *CPJ* 154, 158; Plutarch *Pompey* 24; Dio Cassius 15.20–21; cf. also Winter, *Trial*, 102–3; cf. Josephus's mock funeral (*Life* 323); the occasions of abuse in Alexandria were especially to be expected (cf. Herodian 4.9.2–3). Robbins, *Jesus*, xxvi, 189 helpfully supplies another parallel from Persian behavior at the Sacian festival (Dio Chrysostom *Or.* 4.67–70), though he lays too much emphasis on this to the exclusion of other parallels.

[476] Livy 36.14.4; Cornelius Nepos 14 (Datames), 3.1–4; some commentators cite Pollux *Onomasticon* 9.110; cf. also Herodotus *Hist.* 1.114; Horace *Carm.* 1.4.18.

[477] For a full survey of games of mockery, see Brown, *Death*, 874–77.

[478] Cary and Haarhoff, *Life*, 149; cf. in general Martial *Epigr.* 4.14; 5.84; 11.6.2; 14.14–17; Ps.-Callisthenes *Alex.* 1.39; Philostratus *Hrk.* 20.2; 33.3; Carcopino, *Life*, 250–53, esp. 251; Grant, *Christianity*, 82–83; Stamps, "Children," 198; it appears naughty (or frivolous) in Anacharsis *Ep.* 3.6; Aelius Aristides *Defense of Oratory* 380, §§126D–127D; certainly childish in Maximus of Tyre *Or.* 12.10. Some people gambled on dice and similar instruments (Xenophon *Hell.* 6.3.16; Athenaeus *Deipn.* 15.666E–668B), sometimes leading to tragic results (Xenophon *Hell.* 6.3.16; Alciphron *Parasites* 6 [Rhagostrangisus to Stemphylodaemon], 3.42; 18 [Chytroleictes to Patellocharon], 3.54; Philostratus *Hrk.* 22.3). Archaeology confirms that Roman soldiers probably played such games in the Fortress Antonia (see Finegan, *Archeology*, 161).

[479] Martial *Epig.* 14.14–17; Diogenes Laertes 9.1.3; Callimachus frg. 676; Plutarch *Alc.* 2.2; *Lysander* 8.4; Maximus of Tyre *Or.* 3.5–6; 12.10; 36.5; Philostratus *Hrk.* 45.4.

[480] E.g., France, *Matthew*, 393.

[481] Malina and Rohrbaugh, *Commentary*, 163.

[482] E.g., *CPJ* 1:24–25; 2:36–55, §153; 3:119–21, §520; Philo *Flaccus* 1, 47, 85; Josephus *Ag. Ap.* 2; *Sib. Or.* 3.271–372.

Rome, especially in response to Jewish successes in attracting Roman converts.[483] The abuse of Jesus' captivity to disdain the Jerusalemites strikes a note of irony that might recall John's audience to 11:48: whereas the aristocratic priests want Jesus executed to preserve their nation's status with Rome, Rome's agents ridicule Jesus precisely because they already despise Judea.

The crown of thorns (probably woven from the branches of an available shrub such as acanthus) was probably an instrument of mockery rather than one of torture.[484] The crown recalls the garlands worn by Hellenistic vassal princes, as generally only the highest ruler wore a diadem with white wool.[485] The long thorns may thus have turned outward to imitate contemporary crowns rather than inward to draw blood, and the soldiers probably removed it along with the other mocking regalia before leading him to crucifixion.[486] Mark (15:17) and John (19:2) apparently independently describe the robe as "purple,"[487] reflecting the color of garments worn by Hellenistic princes (e.g., Polybius 10.26.1). Some well-to-do Romans added a cape, "fastened at the neck," to their tunic and outer garment. Soldiers wore a sort of purple cape over the shoulders in warm weather but "wrapped around the body like a heavy shawl when necessary for warmth."[488] Genuine purple dye was quite expensive;[489] Matthew has a "scarlet" robe, suggesting that a faded red soldier's cloak had sufficed for the ridicule (Matt 27:28).[490]

Those in the East who worshiped Caesar or Hellenistic rulers would kneel and cry *Ave* or "Hail, Caesar!";[491] the soldiers here offer the same to Christ. One scholar points out that Jesus is claimed as king by various groups the way a new emperor might be acclaimed by the military (cf. 19:1–3), the people (19:4–7), and a representative of the senate (19:8–12);[492] although "the people" here are mainly the Jewish aristocracy and Pilate's role

---

[483] Horace *Sat.* 1.5.100–101; Juvenal *Sat.* 14.96–106; Quintilian 3.7.21; Tacitus *Hist.* 5.1–5; Persius *Sat.* 5.179–184; for more general Roman xenophobia, cf., e.g., *Rhet. ad Herenn.* 3.3.4; Cicero *Leg.* 2.10.25. For more detail, see Whittaker, *Jews and Christians,* 85–91; Sevenster, *Anti-Semitism;* Daniel, "Anti-Semitism"; Meagher, "Twig"; and esp. Gager, *Anti-Semitism.*

[484] Blinzler, *Trial,* 227; Haenchen, *John,* 2:181. Some suggest thorns from date palms, also turned outward, matching the source of fronds in 12:13 (Whitacre, *John,* 447, following Hart, "Crown"); John's audience would probably not know the source of thorns, in any case.

[485] See, e.g., Blinzler, *Trial,* 226–27; Jeremias, *Theology,* 78; Lane, *Mark,* 559; Anderson, *Mark,* 339; Hill, *Prophecy,* 52; Carson, "Matthew," 573; Brown, *Death,* 866; cf. 1 Macc 11:58; 14:43–44. Some refused a diadem in 1 Macc 8:14, but cf. the gold crown in 10:20.

[486] Blinzler, *Trial,* 244–45; Gundry, *Matthew,* 567.

[487] "Purple" could mean scarlet (e.g., Rev 17:4; 18:16; Appian *C.W.* 2.21.150; cited in Brown, *Death,* 866; cf. Dupont, *Life,* 260), though the Gospel tradition probably preserves it for its symbolic value, both to the soldiers and to Jesus' later followers. Egyptian gentry in nome capitals purchased green, red, and especially blue outer apparel (Lewis, *Life,* 52–53).

[488] Jeffers, *World,* 43.

[489] For its association with wealth, see, e.g., Lucretius *Nat.* 5.1423; Horace *Carm.* 1.35.12, 2.18.7–8; Cicero *Sen.* 17.59; Athenaeus *Deipn.* 4.159d; Diogenes Laertius 8.2.73; 1 Macc 10:20, 62, 64, 14:43–44; 1QapGen 20.31; *Sib. Or.* 3.389, 658–659; 8.74; Petronius *Sat.* 38, 54; Epictetus frg. 11; Martial *Epigr.* 5.8.5; 8.10; Juvenal *Sat.* 1.106; 4.31; Apuleius *Metam.* 10.20; Chariton 3.2.17; *Pesiq. Rab Kah.* 2:7, 15:3; *T. Ab.* 4:2A; *Jos. Asen.* 2:2/3, 8/14–15; 5:5/6. Some writers complained about its extravagance (Seneca *Dial.* 12.11.2; Plutarch *T.T.* 3.1.2, *Mor.* 646B; *1 En.* 98:2 MSS).

[490] Cf. Brown, *John,* 2:875. Derrett, "Ruber," suggests that the red alludes to Isa 1:18 and (somewhat less unlikely) 63:1–2; Luke's white robe in Luke 23:11 characterized Jewish kings as well (Hill, *Prophecy,* 52).

[491] Blinzler, *Trial,* 227; Brown, *John,* 2:875.

[492] Tilborg, *Ephesus,* 213–15.

as a representative for the senate might not be the first feature of his office to resonate with John's audience, John surely does count on his audience's appreciation of an image of mock acclamation. The irony of the narrative is that it inverts their own irony: he is genuinely the person whom they sarcastically claim him to be.

### 3. Rejecting God's Son (19:4–7)

Pilate initially (and somewhat in character with our other sources) refuses to cooperate in Jesus' condemnation, repeating his earlier invitation to Jerusalem's elite to deal with Jesus themselves if they want him dead (19:6; cf. 18:31). This underlines the primary responsibility of the leaders of Jesus', and John's audience's, own people. The greatest irony, however, is the claim that the law demands Jesus' execution for claiming to be God's Son (19:7) when in fact the rest of the Gospel demonstrates that Jesus provided ample evidence that he was God's Son (10:34–38) and that the law supported his claims against theirs (e.g., 5:45–47).

### 3A. "Behold the Man" (19:4–5)

Whether or not one accepts a proposed chiastic structure for this section,[493] these two presentations of Jesus by Pilate to "the Jews" are closely parallel, with Pilate offering titles for Jesus and with "the Jews" responding (19:4–7, 13–16; cf. 18:39).[494] Some suggest that "man" (19:5) is a messianic title;[495] the late Samaritan text *Memar Marqah* applies the title frequently to Moses, the Samaritan messianic prototype.[496] But the title is too rare for us to infer that it was probably known both to John and to his audience; "man" was also an occasional euphemism for "God,"[497] but it is unlikely that John alludes to that usage here. Nevertheless, in the context of the soldiers' mockery (19:2–3), "Behold the man!" probably parallels 19:14 and functions as a mock royal acclamation; Jesus stands before them in royal apparel (not explicitly removed as in Mark 15:20), and Pilate mocks the ceremony of acclamation *(acclamatio)*.[498] Some sources use "That is he!" as an acclamation;[499] here John may well expect the more biblically literate members of his audience to recall Samuel's acclamation of Israel's first king with identical words: "ἰδοὺ ὁ ἄνθρωπος" (1 Sam 9:17 LXX).[500]

In the final analysis, however, John is less interested in the mocking significance of Pilate's title in his tradition than in Jesus' opponents speaking unwitting and ironic truth. Thus, in the context of the Fourth Gospel, the title "man" epitomizes Jesus' enfleshment:[501] Jesus revealed God's glory in his mortality, especially in the ultimate expression of that

---

[493] See Nicholson, *Death*, 54.

[494] Meeks, *Prophet-King*, 69 (who considers Pilate's titles throne names).

[495] See Suggit, "Man."

[496] Meeks, *Prophet-King*, 255, citing *Memar Marqah* 4.3, 4; 5.2, 3; 6.6 and Deut 33:1.

[497] E.g., Ezekiel *Exagoge* 70; *Eccl. Rab.* 2:21, §1; 8:1, §1; *Pesiq. Rab.* 14:10; cf. 1QM 12.10.

[498] Flusser, *Judaism*, 600 (cf. Suggit, "Man"); Flusser argues (*Judaism*, 602) that on the historical level it is perfectly in character to suppose that Pilate joined in the ridicule of Jesus. Cf. Smith, *John*, 346.

[499] Flusser, *Judaism*, 601, citing Lucian *Somn.* 11; Persius *Sat.* 1.28.

[500] Böhler, "Zitat."

[501] For the emphasis on Jesus' humanity here, see also Sevenster, "Humanity"; Koester, *Symbolism*, 187; Smith, *John*, 346. Schwank, "Ecce Homo," finds an answer to Pilate's own question in 18:38; but the connection, while possible, is unclear.

mortality, his death (see comment on 1:14).[502] In the same manner, Jesus will appear as "king" here (19:14) in the context of ridicule, rejection, and ultimately death (19:19). In the logic of the story, Pilate appeals not to the crowd's compassion but to their sense in recognizing that Jesus remains no threat—a serious miscalculation concerning mob psychology on his part.[503] Jesus' very mortality provokes their desire that he be executed (19:6)—but the informed reader recognizes that this constitutes an ultimate rejection of the God who had made himself vulnerable to his people (3:16).

Four acclamations frame Jesus' public ministry: two announcements of Jesus as God's lamb by John the Baptist at the beginning (1:29, 36) and two announcements, one of Jesus' humanity and one of his kingship, by Rome's representative at the end. John surely wanted to parallel these acclamations, whatever Pilate's own intentions may have been.[504]

### 3B. The Law and God's Son (19:6–7)

Pilate's response that the Judean leaders should crucify Jesus themselves (19:6) develops the earlier recognition that it is they who want Jesus dead and they are merely using Pilate to accomplish their purposes (18:31)—although this ultimately and unwittingly accomplishes God's (18:32). Pilate might have looked the other way in the case of an illegal execution, but the point is ironic both in the story world and in John's theology: it underlines the responsibility of the Judean leaders.

In Mark the Jewish crowd twice cries out, "Crucify him!" (Mark 15:13–14); here, however, the crowd who cries out for Jesus' crucifixion (twice in 19:6 and again in 19:15) is equivalent to the Jerusalem elite. Whereas in Mark the chief priests incite the crowds who are present (Mark 15:11), the chief priests and officers (19:6; cf. 18:3) here bear full responsibility, though they are called "the Jews" in 19:7. Earlier we expressed doubt that John increased Roman involvement in the arrest of Jesus as much as some commentators think; here, however, we note that his emphasis on the Judean elite reduces his emphasis on the behavior of the people as a whole (cf. 7:12, 26, 31, 41). As we have repeatedly suggested, John is undoubtedly familiar with the more popular passion tradition, but here he focuses on the theological significance of Jesus' condemnation by the crowds: it is their elite who led Israel astray. This portrait has important implications for the identity of "the Jews" in this Gospel and the question of the Jewish commitment of John's own ideal audience.

The crowd (equivalent in John, as we have noted, to the Jerusalem elite) now explains why Jesus' execution is so urgent (19:7). Instead of regarding Jesus as no threat (19:5), the crowd responds that their law sentenced Jesus to death for making himself God's Son (19:7).[505] The response bristles with Johannine irony: Jesus' very identification with humanity (19:5) opened him to the charge of "making himself" God's Son (10:33, 36). Further, those who cry out that the law condemns Jesus have never answered Nicodemus's objection that the law does not condemn one unless he has first been heard (7:51). Yet the

---

[502] John elsewhere juxtaposes announcements of Jesus' humanity with his messianic identity (4:29; cf. 5:27) though more often those who do not recognize Jesus' fuller identity call him "human" (5:12; 7:46, 51; 9:16, 24; 10:33; 11:47, 50; 18:17, 29); he may link his humanity and mortality in 3:14; 6:53; 8:40; 12:23, 34; 13:31.

[503] Blinzler, *Trial*, 228–29; cf. Haenchen, *John*, 2:181; Brown, *Death*, 828.

[504] Brownlee, "Whence," 174.

[505] A familiar accusation; they may allude in part to Jesus' claims to authority to revise the Sabbath law (5:18; cf. Wead, "Law"); but cf. esp. 10:33. Less probably, Barrett, *John*, 541, thinks the law of blasphemy is particularly in view.

informed reader knows that the Father, rather than Jesus himself, has chosen this title for Jesus; and perhaps most dramatically of all, the law to which they appealed was the very word now enfleshed they sought to execute (1:1–18). The law required Jesus' death—but that he might save the world and, by their lifting him up, fulfill his mission as God's Son (8:28; 12:32–33; cf. υἱὸν τοῦ ἀνθρώπου in 3:14).

## 4. True Authority (19:8–11)

Jesus truly is God's Son (19:7) and king of the Jews (19:14), but he has come in obedience to his Father's mission. In submitting to his Father's authority, he therefore acknowledges the delegated authority God provided Rome's representatives—which underlines all the more his rejection of the Jerusalem hierarchy's authority, likely viewing them as usurpers of Israel's rightful leadership roles (19:11).

### 4A. Pilate's Question and Demand (19:8–10)

That Jesus claimed to be God's "son" (19:7) could fit an occasional self-understanding of philosophers (cf. comment on 18:36–38)[506] or, more dangerously, that of rivals to the emperor.[507] But Pilate's actions in the narrative suggest that he entertains this charge on a more religious level, hence his fear (19:8). As a Roman, he would have known many stories of deities appearing in human form and of judgment coming on the mortals who rejected them.[508] Naturally, a polytheist would be more open to multiple claims of divine sonship than a monotheist, but on the level of Johannine theology as a whole, this feature of the account likewise exudes irony: the agent of Rome proves more ready to believe something divine about God's son than his own people do (cf. 1:11; Mark 15:39).

Because Pilate demands Jesus' origin (19:9) after hearing that he claimed to be God's "son" (19:7), his question may imply an understanding of origin language that Jesus' Jewish interlocutors had earlier misapprehended: he refers to ultimate rather than geographical origin (cf. 1:46; 7:41–42, 52),[509] and Jesus is from God. Jesus is "from heaven" (3:13, 31; 6:32–33, 38, 41–42, 51), "from above" (8:23; cf. 3:3; 17:14, 16), "from God" (3:2; 7:28; 8:42; 13:3). Jesus' unwillingness to answer at this point (19:9) may exemplify the ancient theme of "divine" philosophers refusing to answer worldly judges[510] but is broader than that, reminiscent of the Maccabean martyr tradition (see comment on the Passion Narrative) or anyone defying authorities for a higher cause. In this case, Jesus' silence here (although he earlier speaks more than in the Synoptics—18:36–37) fits the Markan line of tradition (Mark 15:5).

Pilate responds to Jesus' silence with hostility (19:10). Roman law did not interpret silence as a confession of guilt,[511] but failure to respond to charges could leave a case one-sided and hasten conviction;[512] if a defendant failed to offer a defense, the judge would

---

[506] E.g., Epictetus *Diatr.* 1.9.6; cf. Diogenes Laertius 6.2.77, of Diogenes.

[507] See comments on "Son of God" Christology, pp. 291–94.

[508] With Blinzler, *Trial*, 231. See, e.g., Homer *Od.* 17.484–487; Ovid *Metam.* 5.451–461; 8.618–724.

[509] Noted also by others, e.g., Whitacre, *John*, 450, citing also Calvin.

[510] See most usefully Zeller, "Philosophen." Boring et al., *Commentary*, 304, cite Maximus of Tyre *Lectures* 3; Philostratus *Vit. Apoll.* 8.2; for Socrates, see also Xenophon *Mem.* 4.8.4.

[511] Bammel, "Trial," 422, citing Sallust *Catil.* 52.

[512] E.g., Appian *R.H.* 11.7.41.

normally ask about the charge three times before the defendant would be convicted by default.[513] Neither legal custom is at issue here: as noted above, Pilate is not bound by the *ordo* and can act at his own discretion.[514] Rather, he seems simply exasperated that Jesus fails to recognize both his office and his attempts to act on Jesus' behalf (cf. the amazement in 4 Macc 17:16). It was appropriate to express confidence in the jurors' or judge's integrity, to secure their favor (Lysias *Or.* 9.21, §116; Isaeus *Estate of Astyphilus* 35; Cicero *Verr.* 2.1.7.18; *Pro rege Deiotaro* 15.43; *Quinct.* 2.1, 10; 9.34; *Rosc. com.* 3.7). Sometimes a legal debater might also appeal to the judge's interests; for example, the defendant is said to have slandered the judge (Cicero *Verr.* 2.4.40.86–41.90; 2.4.42.90).

If Pilate had wished to free Jesus, he might view Jesus' failure to cooperate in terms of the sort of philosophers (see comment on 18:37–38) who regarded death as unimportant (beginning with the Socratic tradition)—the sort of passive, harmless philosophers whose martyrdom merely multiplied them.[515] Whether he sees Jesus as a deluded philosopher, a divine man, or some sort of philosophical divine man (see introduction, pp. 268–72), he is plainly irritated by Jesus' unwillingness to cooperate with the one person who might pose a barrier to his crucifixion. Philosophers without worldly means regularly disdained the masses,[516] and Brown may be correct that Pilate "understands that by not answering Jesus is somehow looking down on him."[517]

Pilate's claim to hold authority to execute Jesus (19:10) reaffirms the earlier portrait of Rome's capital jurisdiction (18:31–32) and is not repudiated here (19:11).[518] Jewish Christians suffering at the hands of pagan Roman governors might do so respectfully (though cf. Rev 13); it was the leaders of their own people, who unexpectedly misrepresented God's will, whom they would criticize most harshly. Earlier prophets, such as Jeremiah, had also been viewed as unpatriotic (cf. Jer. 26:8, 11) for seeing God's hand behind Israel's oppressors (Jer 21:9; 29:7; 38:2) while harshly criticizing the leaders of their own people, for whom God demanded a higher standard (Jer 2:8, 26; 4:9; 5:31; 10:21; 12:10; 13:13; 23:1–2; 25:34–36; 32:32). Still, Pilate's claim to authority to crucify Jesus (19:10) contrasts with Jesus' authority not only to lay down his own life (10:18) but to rule over all humanity (17:2; cf. 3:35; 13:3).

## 4B. Divinely Delegated Authority (19:11)

Jesus responds that Pilate's authority comes "from above" and hence the one who delivered Jesus over to Pilate has a greater sin (19:11). This text makes explicit the distribution of responsibility the rest of the passage implies: Pilate is responsible, but not as responsible as the Judean elite. It would not be impossible to read Rome, the source of Pilate's authority, as the one who delivered Jesus over;[519] but such an interpretation would

---

[513] Brown, *John,* 2:853, following Sherwin-White, "Trial," 105.

[514] See, e.g., Ferguson, *Backgrounds,* 50–51; Dodd, *Tradition,* 105; Brown, *John,* 2:885.

[515] Some philosophers were even known to end their own lives, sometimes following an Indian tradition (Cicero *Div.* 1.23.47; Arrian *Alex.* 7.3.1–6; Lucian *Dialogues of the Dead* 416–417; *Peregr.* 36–38; *Greek Anth.* 7.123).

[516] E.g., Epictetus *Diatr.* 1.18.10; Diogenes the Cynic in Diogenes Laertius 6 passim.

[517] Brown, *Death,* 841. Neyrey, "Shame of Cross," 128–29, argues that Jesus' silence challenges Pilate's honor, but Jesus in 19:11 acknowledges the honor of Pilate's office, securing more of his favor (19:12).

[518] Pilate held legal authority to both condemn and acquit (Justinian *Digest* 50.17.37; Whitacre, *John,* 451).

[519] Or Satan (cf. perhaps *b. Tamid* 32a).

ignore John's use of language elsewhere. Clearly "from above" in the Fourth Gospel means "from God" (3:3, 7, 31; 8:23), as it normally would in early Jewish literature (see comment on 3:3); even in the story world, Pilate should understand, for Greeks and Romans also recognized the importance of favor from heavenly deities.[520] Jewish people normally believed that God had authorized various angels to rule the different nations (Dan 10:13)[521] but that ultimately the authority derived from God (Dan 4:32).[522] John, like other early Christian writers, recognized that God in some sense authorized even the Roman government (Rom 13:1–4; probably 1 Pet 2:13–15; cf. Jer 29:7; 38:2).[523] The Roman government's authority was permitted by God, Johannine Christians recognized, even when it became demonic (Rev 17:17; cf. Prov 21:1). Jesus thus surrendered himself willingly, not so much to Pilate as to his own Father's plan (10:18; 18:11).[524]

Those who "delivered" Jesus directly to Pilate were the Jewish leaders (18:30, 35),[525] though Judas (18:2, 5, 36) and Pilate himself (19:16) provide other links in the same chain of guilt and in the end it is Jesus himself who "delivers" over his life (19:30). By declaring that those who handed Jesus to Pilate are guiltier because (διὰ τοῦτο) his authority comes from "above," that is, from God, the text clearly implies that the high priests' authority did not come from that source. This probably represents an allusion to the Roman interference in the appointment of high priests and perhaps also to Caiaphas's participation in what appeared to many of his contemporaries unscrupulous politics (see comment on 11:49). Pilate's predecessor Valerius Gratus (15–26 C.E.) had appointed Caiaphas as a priest with whom Rome could work, and Pilate had retained him.[526]

Jesus' answer reflects his willingness to face death, regularly associated with courage and virtue in ancient Mediterranean texts[527]—for instance, the Spartan boy who allegedly let a fox eat its way through his abdomen to prevent capture during training exercises.[528] Yet Jesus' allusion to authority "from above" may remind John's audience of the one whose authorization from above is beyond that of all others (3:27, 31, 35).

## 5. Handing Over the Jewish King (19:12–16)

Pilate may have some interest in justice, but he exhibits greater interest in protecting himself politically (19:12). After a final repudiation of Jesus' rulership (19:14–15), he delivers Jesus "to them" (19:16). On the literal level, this handing over of Jesus means simply "handing him over to their will" (Roman soldiers remain in charge of the execution in 19:23); but on the symbolic level, John again reinforces that it was the machinations of the Judean aristocracy, not the specific hostility of Rome, that would bring about Jesus' execution (18:31–32; 19:6).

---

[520] Cf. Achilles Tatius 5.2.2; Seneca *Dial.* 12.8.5.

[521] E.g., *Jub.* 15:31–32; 35:17; 1QM 14.15; 15.13–14; *Mek. Šir.* 2.112–116.

[522] E.g., *Jub.* 49:2–4; *3 En.* 26:12; 30:2; *Sipre Deut.* 315.2.1. Cf. further references in Keener, *Paul,* 41, 64–65.

[523] Most commentators recognize God as the source of Pilate's authority here, e.g., Johnston, *Spirit-Paraclete,* 15; Pancaro, *Law,* 323.

[524] Cf. accounts of Socrates' martyrdom (e.g., Maximus of Tyre *Or.* 3.2) and Jewish martyr stories.

[525] As generally acknowledged, e.g., Goppelt, *Jesus, Paul, and Judaism,* 88.

[526] E.g., Reicke, *Era,* 175.

[527] E.g., Musonius Rufus 3, p. 42.1–2; cf. comment on 12:25–26.

[528] Plutarch *S.S.,* anonymous 35, *Mor.* 234AB.

### 5A. Pilate's Political Dilemma (19:12)

Pilate's response to Jesus' words is striking: he seeks all the more to release him (19:12). Again the narrative seems to imply that Pilate was taking Jesus' words seriously; but John recognizes that it is possible even to believe Jesus' words yet fail to affirm them because one loves human honor more than God's (12:42–43). Provincial governors were generally politically ambitious men of senatorial rank aspiring to yet higher offices;[529] bad reports could mar one's political ambitions. Pilate, who was of lower rank by birth but had gained his office through the graces of the anti-Jewish Sejanus (Tiberius's immediate agent of government), was more politically vulnerable than most.[530] Further, more is at stake now than merely political advancement; governors who abused their power could be tried,[531] but the greatest crime for Romans, even worse than murdering one's father, was treason.[532] To release a self-proclaimed king (19:12) was to accommodate treason, hence to warrant execution oneself![533]

"Friend of the king" was a special designation for those close to the ruler.[534] Roman emperors conferred "friendship" on trusted associates, from whom they drew their primary advisors.[535] As a client of Sejanus, Pilate may literally have been enrolled among the "friends of Caesar" (cf. Tacitus *Ann.* 6.8).[536] (Despite good citizens' loyalty to Caesar, however, many readers would respect a person of integrity who refused to compromise principle for the sake of friendship with a ruler.[537] Pilate's role in the narrative is not, however, fully respectable.) The threat of denunciation as unfaithful to the wishes of Caesar had made Pilate back down before, even in his most brutal stage of governorship. When he had wished to set up votive shields in Herod's palace in Jerusalem, the leaders of the people (i.e., the sort of priests he now confronted) reportedly asked if he had letters from Tiberius requesting this behavior. They implied that if he did not, he lacked authority for the act; and if he claimed to have such authority, they would appeal the matter directly to Tiberius. Fearful of trouble, Pilate quickly backed away from part of his plan (Philo *Embassy* 301–302). Nor was Pilate simply paranoid; when the Jewish leaders considered his response inadequate and did appeal to Tiberius, Pilate was reportedly humiliated by the emperor (Philo *Embassy* 304–305), undoubtedly providing him grounds for more caution by this point. Indeed, a later complaint ultimately led to "his recall, his exile in Gaul and perhaps his forced suicide."[538] Roman governors exercised considerable freedom but could suffer if charged in Rome with abusing their position.[539] The faith (e.g., 3:16) to which the Fourth Gospel calls is not mere consideration of the truth of Jesus' claims (19:12a) but act-

---

[529] E.g., Reicke, *Era,* 138.

[530] E.g., Schnackenburg, *John,* 3:262.

[531] See Jones, *History,* 192–95, citing Pliny *Ep.* 2.11 (on executions of innocent people, especially Roman citizens). This may also help explain Pilate's reluctance to prosecute Jesus if he thought the prosecution might yield complaints.

[532] Dionysius of Halicarnassus *R.A.* 8.80.1.

[533] Cf. Smallwood, *Jews,* 169; Blinzler, *Trial,* 236.

[534] E.g., Diodorus Siculus 17.31.6. See other texts cited under John 15:13–15.

[535] Judge, *Pattern,* 33–34; see in more detail various texts cited under John 15:13–15. The term also applied to alliances with peoples (e.g., Strabo *Geog.* 8.5.5).

[536] This is pointed out by Brown (*Death,* 843), but he warns that the connection with Sejanus is here uncertain (p. 844).

[537] Iamblichus *V.P.* 31.194.

[538] Benoit, *Jesus,* 1:142.

[539] E.g., Cicero *Verr.* 2.3.3.6

ing in a manner consistent with faith in those claims, even if the price is disgrace or death (12:24–26). Pilate prefers friendship with Caesar to friendship with Christ (19:12), but the informed audience of the Gospel recognizes how misinformed a choice this is (15:15).

## 5B. The Judgment Seat (19:13)

Pilate apparently responded to such threats by bringing Jesus out to the will of the people (19:13–15); he would leave the responsibility of conviction with them, unwilling to pay the price of acknowledging his own responsibility for justice. For some time scholars thought that the "pavement" referred to here was one that has been excavated at the Fortress Antonia on the Temple Mount, easily accessible to the high priests who lived and worked in the vicinity.[540] But that stone pavement now appears to be Hadrianic. Further, Pilate had been interrogating Jesus inside the procurator's Jerusalem residence, the old palace of Herod the Great,[541] and brought him to the judgment seat outside that residence.[542] This was naturally somewhat further from the temple than the Antonia (Josephus *War* 1.401–402) but better suits our evidence for the site of Jesus' conviction, as most recent commentators and some earlier ones recognize.[543] On the use of a Semitic term with a translation, see the introduction (esp. pp. 158–59).

Some suppose that Pilate seated Jesus in the judgment seat as part of the mockery (19:13);[544] but this act would have breached Roman protocol so thoroughly that it is inconceivable that Pilate would have done it.[545] One might argue that John left the Greek wording ambiguous to permit this interpretation theologically,[546] but while Jesus truly is the judge in this narrative, Pilate is afraid of Jesus, not mocking him, by this point in the narrative. Instead Pilate sits in the judgment seat himself because the time has arrived for him to render the judgment. A governor would issue a formal condemnation in a capital case (as opposed to other kinds of cases) only *pro tribunali,* from the judgment seat (19:13).[547] Pilate need not have adopted the sentence of the Sanhedrin, but as prefect he was free to do so.[548]

## 5C. The Timing (19:14a)

The announcement of both the "day of preparation for Passover" and the "sixth hour" (19:14) is significant for developing a Johannine hermeneutic consistent with the specific character of the Fourth Gospel's intrinsic genre. This announcement signals to us that the Fourth Gospel's passion chronology differs from that of the Synoptic tradition, probably already popular in John's day (Mark 15:25). We could read John's "sixth hour" in terms of the rare reckoning of civil days from midnight, so that Jesus' condemnation would be

---

540 E.g., Thompson, *Archaeology,* 278; Yamauchi, *Stones,* 108, following Albright. Cf. Josephus *War* 2.328–231.

541 Pilate's residence in Philo *Embassy* 299; that of Florus in Josephus *War* 2.301, 328.

542 See Josephus *War* 2.175–176, 301, 308.

543 See Wilkinson, *Jerusalem,* 141; Brown, *Death,* 705–10; Strachan, *Gospel,* 212; Blinzler, *Trial,* 173–76; Reicke, *Era,* 140; Benoit, *Jesus,* 1:167–88; Benoit, "Reconstitution."

544 E.g., tentatively, MacRae, *Invitation,* 210. Manns, "Encore," thinks he seated him "toward" (εἰς) the "pavement" of the old temple; but cf. comment on "pavement" above.

545 Bruce, "Trial," 17.

546 Trebolle Barrera, "Substrato," citing evidence from the Hebrew Bible.

547 Blinzler, *Trial,* 240; Sherwin-White, *Society,* 47.

548 Sherwin-White, *Society,* 47.

at 6 a.m.;[549] but this reckoning also contradicts the Synoptics, allows too little time from sunrise (near 18:28) for the events preceding the condemnation, relies on a rare calculation of time that would have been in no way obvious to most ancient readers, and confuses the other references to specific hours in the Gospel. Others have tried to harmonize Mark and John by claiming that Mark's "third hour" refers to the quarter day from ca. 9 a.m. to noon whereas John's "sixth hour" means "about" noon;[550] but such "approximations" invite us to suppose a margin of factual error so great as to render the approximations effectively worthless.

Brown thus notes that one may regard either Mark (9 a.m.) or John (noon) as theological symbolism but one cannot reconcile them both as literally accurate chronologically.[551] Given John's literary method elsewhere, we incline toward reading John symbolically rather than Mark.[552] Members of John's audience familiar with the traditional passion story presumably behind the Synoptics and Paul would have already noticed the difference at 18:28, a difference linking Jesus more directly with Passover. No longer do the symbolic bread and wine of the Last Supper represent Passover, but the death of Jesus itself does so directly (6:51–58). Biographies could exercise a degree of chronological freedom (see introduction, ch. 1), and John may adapt the chronology to infuse it with his symbolic message. In this Gospel Jesus is delivered over for crucifixion on the day the Passover lambs are being slaughtered (18:28). Many scholars also explain the "sixth hour" in light of Passover, though the case, while intriguing, is difficult to prove.

Passover lambs for families and other groups were slaughtered during the day, but the most significant specific times remembered, if any, might be those of the daily lamb offerings in the temple, the morning and evening offerings. In the Markan tradition, Jesus died ca. 3 p.m. (Mark 15:34), roughly the time the daily evening offering was being slaughtered (ca. 2:30) and offered (ca. 3:30).[553] But if later tradition is accurate (it may not be), it appears that on the eve of the Passover (19:14) the lamb is slaughtered an hour earlier, and an hour earlier still on a Passover eve that is also the eve of a Sabbath (19:31; m. Pesah. 5:1). Thus, in John, Jesus appears to be sentenced around noon and perhaps crucified within an hour afterward, close to the time of the evening offering.

Even if our information concerning the time of the paschal sacrifice is correct, however, it was probably not widely known to John's audience; even those who had gone as pilgrims had undoubtedly simply gotten their own lambs slaughtered when they could; to accommodate the massive number of pilgrims, priests reportedly supervised the slaughter of lambs for pilgrims from ca. 4 to ca. 6 p.m.,[554] and few would think about the hour of a "national" paschal lamb. Some begin the slaughter of lambs more helpfully

---

[549] Westcott, John, 282. Michaels, John, 309, entertains but ultimately rejects this view.

[550] Morris, John, 801; Miller, "Time." Cf. Augustine Tract. Ev. Jo. 117.1 (cited in Whitacre, John, 455).

[551] Brown, Death, 958–59. Theodore of Mopsuestia (239.9–17) claimed that the Gospels could be harmonized on this point, but allowed that it would not be very problematic if they could not be (Wiles, Gospel, 19). The association of 1:39 and 19:14 with a Johannine community's festival calendar (Hanhart, "Tenth Hour," 345) seems less likely.

[552] Yee, Feasts, 68. Some have, however, found secondary schematization in Mark's account because of the three-hour intervals (cf., e.g., Hurtado, Mark, 262).

[553] M. Pesah. 5:1; cf. Sanders, Jesus to Mishnah, 74.

[554] Sanders, Judaism, 135, cites Josephus War 6.423. Yet even with Josephus's exaggerated numbers of pilgrims, the number of priests that could fit in the sanctuary might suggest instead a slaughtering of lambs from sunrise on.

around noon, providing a more specific parallel to John here.[555] Many scholars have argued, as one puts it, that "the paschal lamb of the N.T. dies, according to the Johannine chronology, just when the paschal lambs of the Jews are being slaughtered in the temple, and none of his bones are broken."[556] Certainly John does link Jesus' death with the slaughter of Passover lambs in the temple; this is, however, a link of the day rather than of the hour, for he does not specify the precise time of Jesus' death. Further, other scholars suggest that the slaughter begins at 3 p.m.,[557] and ultimately the matter is not easily decided; the rabbinic description of the sacrifices is idealized and impractical and may afford us few clues concerning actual priestly practice in Jerusalem's temple before 70 or views about it in Roman Asia by the 90s.

Yet in the context of the Fourth Gospel, the informed reader might catch another allusion more immediately: the sixth hour was about noon, the heat of day when many country people preferred to find shade, the same time Jesus' human mortality had been revealed in 4:6 ("weary"). Jesus' "hour" had come (2:4; 7:30; 8:20; 12:23, 27; 13:1; 16:21; 17:1), the "hour" for the inbreaking of God's new era (4:21, 23; 5:25, 28).

5D. "Behold Your King" (19:14b–15)

Most significant in 19:14–15 are Pilate's presentations of Jesus to the people as their king;[558] they respond, however, that they have no king but Caesar (19:15). Within the logic of the story, they continue to claim loyalty to Rome,[559] the pretense on which Jesus as "king" should be executed (18:29–33; 19:12); their preference for the λῃστής Barabbas, however, has demonstrated the insincerity of that loyalty (18:40). Nevertheless, John's description would undoubtedly evoke among his audience more-sinister thoughts concerning the speakers' meaning; the Fourth Gospel is full of ironic statements not intended by the speakers (e.g., 11:49, 50–52; 12:19). Judaism warned against any act that would profane the divine name among Gentiles[560]—which in Johannine terms is precisely what these leaders do. The same set of benedictions that cursed the *minim* (see introduction, pp. 207–14) included a prayer for the coming of Messiah, acknowledging daily the hope for a Messiah's coming;[561] more to the point, Israel's ultimate king was God (Judg 8:23; 1 Sam 8:7).[562] While it is difficult to ascertain the antiquity of most of the Passover haggadah,

---

[555] Stauffer, *Jesus,* 138; Wilkinson, *Jerusalem,* 154; Ellis, *Genius,* 265–66; Beasley-Murray, *John,* 341; Yee, *Feasts,* 68. Schnackenburg, *John,* 3:265, claims that preparation for slaughtering the lambs began at this hour.

[556] Schnackenburg, *John,* 1:299; cf. Jaubert, "Calendar," 63; Morris, *John,* 785; Wilkinson, *Jerusalem,* 125. For John's heavy use of Passover imagery in 19:16–37, see Badiola Sáenz de Ugarte, "Tipología."

[557] Safrai, "Temple," 892. Admittedly it is difficult to envision pilgrims completing the sacrifices by sundown if the slaughter begins this late.

[558] Pilate's question is not merely rhetorical (cf. 18:39), but speakers were accustomed to asking at least rhetorical questions of crowds, though not expecting answers contrary to their views (note *anakoinōsis* and *aporia* in Anderson, *Glossary,* 18, 24; Rowe, "Style," 140–41).

[559] Cf. the Greek epigraphic proclamation of Roman propaganda about Roman benefaction, reacting against Hellenistic kings (Erskine, "Benefactors").

[560] Disobeying God's will or misrepresenting it through false teaching profanes it (e.g., *m. ʾAbot* 1:11; *Num. Rab.* 7:5; 8:4; *Pesiq. Rab.* 22:2); one must never profane God's name before Gentiles (CD 12.6–8; *t. B. Meṣiʿa* 5:18; *Gen. Rab.* 39:7). Everything is forgiveable, said some teachers, except profaning the Name (*Sipre Deut.* 328.1.5).

[561] Schnackenburg, *John,* 3:266.

[562] Barrett, *John,* 546.

John's paschal context and the similarity of language do suggest an allusion to the hymn sung at the end of the Greater Hallel in the Passover haggadah:

> From everlasting to everlasting thou art God;
> Beside thee we have no king, redeemer, or savior, . . .
> We have no king but thee.[563]

The deliberate contrast underlines again the association of the opponents of John's audience with Rome's agendas: those who effectively may hand the Jewish Christians over to Roman discipline by denying their fidelity to Judaism function as Rome's instruments the way the chief priests of Jesus' day did, leaving the Jewish Christians the faithful remnant true to the religious heritage of Israel. (For the demands of the imperial cult in John's setting, see introduction, pp. 178–79.) As Dahl observes concerning John's portrayal of the "Jews" in this narrative, "They end up representing the world even in putting Caesar at the place of God, whereas they deny the fundamentals of their own faith and forfeit the history of Israel."[564]

Because Jesus' primary support in the Fourth Gospel was Galilean and because Judean crowds were divided (7:12; 9:16), John appears to play less on the crowds' fickleness than the Synoptics do.[565] Because he speaks of the crowds as simply "Jews," in fact, he makes no distinction between the crowds who now demand Jesus' execution and the authorities who delivered him to Pilate. One could argue that John views all ethnic Jews or, more reasonably, Judeans through the prism of the Jerusalem elite. But given John's Jewishness, that of his audience, and the smaller number of positive or divided Judeans in this Gospel, it is more probable that John instead lays the behavior of the passion tradition's crowds at the feet of his "Jews," who represent primarily the elite of Jesus' day viewed through the prism of those of John's own (see more fully our introduction, pp. 214–28).

## 5E. Handing Jesus Over (19:16)

In delivering Jesus over (19:16), the prefect would have declared, *Ibis in crucem* ("You will mount the cross") or a phrase much like it.[566] That he "delivered" Jesus to be crucified implicates Pilate in the chain of responsibility (18:2, 5, 30, 35–36; 19:11); he would bear the political responsibility for it, in any case (Tacitus *Ann.* 15.44.3). But John's ominous αὐτοῖς, "to them," reverses the direction of their delivering Jesus to him (18:30, 35), confirming Jesus' evaluation: it is the priestly aristocracy who should have perfomed God's will but instead delivered Jesus to Pilate, whose sin is greater (19:11). Historically Pilate handed Jesus over to the soldiers, as John recognizes (19:23–25); in this context, he hands him over to the will of the Judean leaders.

---

[563] Meeks, *Prophet-King,* 77, citing *b. Pesaḥ.* 118a.

[564] Dahl, "History," 135; cf. also Strachan, *Gospel,* 216; Schnackenburg, *John,* 3:266; Barrett, *John,* 546; Meeks, "Agent," 58.

[565] Ancient literature is replete with examples of masses being easily swayed by leaders (e.g., Cornelius Nepos 3 [Aristides], 1.4), including these priests (Josephus *War* 2.237–238, 316–317, 321–325; cf. 2.406), and being fickle in the populist favor they bestowed on various figures (Livy 31.34.3; Tacitus *Ann.* 2.41; *Hist.* 1.32, 45; 3.85; Lucan *C.W.* 3.52–56; Cornelius Nepos 10 [Dion], 10.2; 13 [Timotheus], 4.1; Ps.-Phoc. 95–96; Philo *Embassy* 120; Josephus *Life* 87, 97, 143–144, 313–317, 333; 1 Sam 18:16; 25:10; 2 Sam 3:36). This was always a negative trait (often used by Romans to characterize other peoples, e.g., Sallust *Jug.* 56.5; Cicero *Pro Flacco* 11.24; Caesar *Gall. W.* 4.5).

[566] Blinzler, *Trial,* 238, cites Petronius *Sat.* 137; Plautus *Mostellaria* 3.2.63, §850.

Though the implied subject of the third-person plural verb παρέλαβον (19:16b) from the context might again be these Judean leaders, John's audience would have to know that Roman soldiers would have to carry out the execution, even if they did not know the passion tradition attested in the Synoptics (which is unlikely), and any ambiguity in this regard is cleared up by 19:23–25. But John may allow this ambiguity of language as another of his wordplays: for all practical purposes, the Judean leaders may as well have crucified Jesus themselves (as Pilate ironically invited them to do in 19:6), just as, by accusing disciples to the Roman government, they were de facto killing them themselves (16:2).

## Jesus' Crucifixion (19:17–37)

Finally Jesus is "lifted up" as he had predicted (12:32–33, a saying recalled in 18:31–32). But perhaps in deliberate contrast to the passion tradition preserved for us in the Markan, Synoptic line of tradition, the crucifixion in John is Jesus' triumph. Granted, it is an agony he would prefer to have foregone (12:27); but here, in contrast to the Synoptics, he carries his own cross, closes his life's words with an announcement of completion, and (perhaps in conjunction with extant tradition) offers up his own spirit in death. No one takes Jesus' life from him; he offers it up freely (10:18).

### 1. The Crucifixion (19:17–18)

There is no real question that Jesus was crucified, executed at the order of Roman authorities.[567] In the Gospels, however, the event of the crucifixion itself is depicted quickly. That Jesus ἐξῆλθεν, "went out" (19:17), is clearly historical reminiscence. Both Jewish people[568] and Romans[569] performed executions outside a town.[570] Soldiers would march the prisoner through crowds of spectators;[571] crowds normally gathered to watch executions, especially if near the city.[572] If, as most scholars today conclude, Herod's old palace was the site of Jesus' trial, the route from there to Golgotha "led through the upper part of the city and probably out through the garden gate, which was located near the Hippicus tower."[573]

### 1A. Carrying His Own Cross (19:17a)

More significantly from the standpoint of Johannine theology, John is emphatic that Jesus carried ἑαυτῷ, "his own," cross (19:17); again he may be adapting previously circulated images of the passion tradition to make his point.[574] Just as Jesus gave the sop (John

---

[567] Sanders, *Jesus and Judaism*, 11. It is not the sort of fate one would invent for one's leader.

[568] Lev 24:14; Num 15:35–36; Deut 17:5; 1 Kgs 21:13; Josephus *War* 4.360; *Ant.* 4.264.

[569] Artemidorus *Onir.* 2.53; Plautus *Soldier* 2.4.6–7, §359–360.

[570] Blinzler, *Trial*, 251; Lane, *Hebrews*, 2:541. In this case, a proposed site for the execution is only about a thousand feet north to northeast of Herod's palace, where Pilate pronounced the sentence (Reicke, *Era*, 185).

[571] E.g., Reicke, *Era*, 185.

[572] Morris, *John*, 807; Whitacre, *John*, 460.

[573] Gnilka, *Jesus*, 309. This would contradict the traditional route.

[574] Also Brown, *Death*, 917; Lightfoot, *Gospel*, 315; Wilkinson, *Jerusalem*, 150. Some find Isaac typology (cf. Gen 22:6; Ellis, *Genius*, 268; many church fathers), but in the absence of clearer contextual allusions, the normal procedure for crucifixion obviates the need for this view.

13:26) rather than mentioned that one had dipped "with him" (Mark 14:20), just as Jesus "laid down his life" (10:18) and "delivered up" his spirit (19:30), just as Jesus rather than his disciples "finds" the donkey (John 12:14; cf. Mark 11:2), so here he remains in control in the narrative. A condemned criminal normally carried his own *patibulum,* or transverse beam of the cross, to the site of the execution, where soldiers would fix the *patibulum* to the upright stake *(palus, stipes, staticulum)* that they regularly reused for executions.[575] (Prisoners were also often scourged on the way, a practice probably foregone in Jesus' case because he had been scourged so brutally beforehand.)[576]

In the Synoptic tradition and probably the broader passion tradition, Jesus is too weak to carry his cross, and it is carried by Simon of Cyrene.[577] Given the unlikehilood that the soldiers would simply show mercy to a condemned prisoner, scholars are probably correct to suppose that Jesus was too weak to carry the cross and that his executioners preferred to have him alive on the cross than dead on the way.[578] Since crucifixion sometimes lasted days (Josephus *Life* 420–421), the quickness of Jesus' death (multiply attested, Mark 15:44; John 19:31) reinforces the notion that Jesus was already quite weak.[579] In such circumstances, that the soldiers would have drafted a bystander is not improbable;[580] one would not expect them to carry the beam themselves if they could "impress" another into service.[581]

That the Synoptic report is undoubtedly historical does not render impossible a historical basis for John's account: it is in fact most likely that the soldiers would have sought to make Jesus carry his own cross at the beginning, following standard custom, until it became clear that he could not continue to do so. But merely reporting (or inferring) those initial steps is hardly John's point; by emphasizing Jesus' carrying his own cross, he emphasizes Jesus' continuing control of his passion. Just as condemned criminals must bear their own instrument of death, Jesus chose and controlled his death.[582] As Drury puts it, in John Jesus bears his own cross "as befits the one who alone can bear the sin of the world" (1:29).[583]

### 1B. Golgotha (19:17b)

Golgotha (19:17) was undoubtedly near the site of the Holy Sepulchre; that traditional location was outside the city walls but only roughly a thousand feet north-northeast

---

[575] Artemidorus *Onir.* 2.56; Plutarch *D.V.* 9, *Mor.* 554AB; Chariton 4.2.7; 4.3.10; also Brown, *Death,* 913.

[576] E.g., Blinzler, *Trial,* 244, citing Valerius Maximus 1.7.4; Dionysius of Halicarnassus *R.A.* 7.69.

[577] Some second-century gnostics had Simon die in Jesus' place (Talbert, *John,* 242, who sees antidocetic polemic here, cites Irenaeus *Haer.* 1.24.3–6; *Second Treatise of the Great Seth* 7.56); but that view is probably too late to have provoked Johannine polemic here (Carson, *John,* 609).

[578] Cf. Goguel, *Jesus,* 530–31; Lane, *Mark,* 562; Davies, *Matthew,* 197; Brown, *Death,* 914–15.

[579] Klausner, *Jesus,* 353.

[580] Most scholars agree that Simon of Cyrene is a historical figure (Brown, *Death,* 913; see Sanders, "Simon," 56–57).

[581] Brown, *Death,* 914, questions whether the Romans would force someone when Josephus says they did not force subjects to break their own laws (*Ag. Ap.* 2.73), but this objection lays too much weight on Josephus's propaganda; Josephus employs legal precedents apologetically (cf. Rajak, "Charter").

[582] Crosses also became a natural metaphor for sufferings (e.g., Apuleius *Metam.* 7.16, *cruciatibus;* 10.9; cf. Seneca *Dial.* 7.19.3) or the pain of grief (Apuleius *Metam.* 9.31) or anxiety (9.23); for other nonliteral usages, cf. Epictetus *Diatr.* 3.26.22. John employs βαστάζω in a fairly common figurative sense in 16:12, albeit more literally in 10:31; 12:6; 20:15.

[583] Drury, *Design,* 113. The different term may simply represent literary variation, though αἴρων may better connote complete removal.

of Herod's palace, where Pilate was staying.[584] The traditional Protestant "Garden Tomb" is a substantially later site and cannot represent the site of Jesus' burial;[585] by contrast, the Catholic Holy Sepulcher and tombs in its vicinity date to the right period.[586] The tradition of the latter vicinity is as early as the second century (when Hadrian erected a pagan temple there; he defiled many Jewish holy sites in this manner)[587] and probably earlier. Good evidence exists, in fact, that this site dates to within the first two decades after the resurrection. This is because (1) Christian tradition is unanimous that Jesus was buried outside the city walls and no one would make up a site inside (cf. Heb 13:12; John 19:41); (2) Jewish custom made it common knowledge that burials would be outside the city walls;[588] (3) the traditional vicinity of the Holy Sepulchre is *inside* Jerusalem's walls; (4) Agrippa I expanded the walls of Jerusalem sometime in the 40s C.E.[589]

The "place of a skull" (19:17) may have gotten its name from the shape of the terrain,[590] but more likely from the executions carried out there. (In any event, the current terrain of the traditional Protestant Golgotha did not exist in Jesus' day.)

## 1C. Crucifixion (19:18)

The Gospel writers require little description of crucifixion (19:18), which was well known in their world. Jesus' crucifixion by the Romans outside Jerusalem is an "almost indisputable" historical fact;[591] early Christians would not have invented the crucifixion. The full horror of that mode of execution (e.g., Apuleius *Metam.* 3.9; 6.32; Chariton 3.3.12) remained vivid enough in the first century that all four evangelists hurry by the event itself quickly, Matthew, for example, "disposing of it in a participial clause."[592] (It was established rhetorical practice to hurry most quickly over points that might disturb the audience, Theon *Progymn.* 5.52–56.)

Although some features of crucifixions remained common, executioners could perform them in a variety of manners, limited only by the extent of their sadistic creativity.[593]

---

[588] Reicke, *Era*, 185.

[589] Tomb architecture changed radically after Jerusalem's fall (Goodenough, *Symbols*, 1:84–89; Brown, *Death*, 938–39).

[586] On the latter, see Brown, *John*, 2:899; idem, *Death*, 1279–83; cf. Blinzler, *Trial*, 251–52; Smith, "Tomb"; Ross, "Church"; Riesner, "Golgotha."

[587] Cf. Finegan, *Archeology*, 164.

[588] *4 Bar.* 7:13; Wilkinson, *Jerusalem*, 146.

[589] See, e.g., Brown, *Death*, 1281–82; cf. Blinzler, *Trial*, 251–52; for archaeological data, see the notes in Cornfeld, *Josephus*, 338–40, on Josephus *War* 5.148–155.

[590] Cf. the kind of cup traditionally called a κρανίον, or skull, perhaps due to its shape (Athenaeus *Deipn.* 11.479–480).

[591] Sanders, *Jesus and Judaism*, 11. We have borrowed much of the material from Keener, *Matthew*, 678–79.

[592] Bruce, "Matthew," 328.

[593] Hengel, *Crucifixion*, 25. Thus, e.g., one man is bound to a fig tree and anointed with honey so that the ants devour him, but this, too, is called a cross *(cruciatum)*; Apuleius *Metam.* 8.22; cf. Prometheus's fetters (Martial *Epigr.* 7; Lucian *Prometheus* 2). Positions varied, but for evidence for one probably common position, see Tzaferis, "Crucifixion," 52–53. Before the Roman conquest, following Hellenistic (e.g., Josephus *Ant.* 12.256) and Persian (Esth 9:25; De Vaux, *Israel*, 159) practice, Jewish executions had also adopted hanging by crucifixion (e.g., Josephus *War* 1.97; *Ant.* 13.380; 4QpNah 1.7–8; *Sipre Deut.* 221.1.1; *p. Sanh.* 6:6, §2; cf. 11QT 64); though read back into earlier times (*L.A.B.* 55:3), Israelites originally hanged corpses posthumously (cf. Gen 40:19) only till nightfall, limiting the shame (Deut 21:23; *m. Sanh.* 6:4).

Executioners usually tied victims to the cross with ropes but in some cases hastened their death by also nailing their wrists (20:25).[594] The nails were typically five to seven inches long, enough to penetrate both the wrist and well into the wood of the cross.[595] One being executed on the cross could not swat flies from one's wounds nor withhold one's bodily wastes from coming out while hanging naked for hours and sometimes days.[596] The upright stakes were normally ten feet at the highest, more often closer to six or seven feet so that the man hung barely above the ground, with a seat *(sedile)* in the middle;[597] animals sometimes assaulted the feet of the crucified. Romans could employ high crosses to increase visibility for significant public executions (Suetonius *Galba* 9.1), and given the branch here (19:29; cf. Mark 15:36), Jesus may have been slightly higher than usual.[598]

That Jesus was crucified with two others is not surprising,[599] given the propaganda value of public executions during festivals, when Jerusalem's crowds were the highest.[600] The later mishnaic rule against executing two persons on a day contradicted earlier practices by those in power (*m. Sanh.* 6:4) and would have had no effect on the Romans, in any case.[601]

## 2. The Titulus (19:19–22)

The charge posted above Jesus' head (19:19–22)[602] reveals the irony of the situation: Jesus is executed for being king of Israel, though the leaders of his own people reject his kingship. They might have preferred the charge of λῃστής, a social bandit or revolutionary (which he applied to them, 10:8–10), but they themselves had supplied the wording for the treason charge "king of the Jews" (18:33–35), and now they cannot dismiss it.[603] Yet for all the charge's irony, it is historically quite probable.[604] Jesus' triumphal entry (12:13) marked

---

[594] See Artemidorus *Onir.* 2.56; Plautus *Mostellaria* 2.1.12–13; *m. Šabb.* 6.10; Lane, *Mark,* 564; cf. Luke 24:39; for ropes alone, see, e.g., Xenophon *Eph.* 4.2 (though this is convenient for the story). Cf. Diodorus Siculus 25.5.2 (if προσηλόω here means "nailed," as it often does); also the skeleton recovered at Givat ha-Mivtar (Bruce, "Trial," 18), though original reports about the ankle nail(s) re-been revised (Stanton, *Gospels,* 148; Kuhn, "Gekreuzigten"); on the wrists, see Yamauchi, "Crucifixion," 2; Tzaferis, "Crucifixion," 52.

[595] Whitacre, *John,* 457.

[596] Klausner, *Jesus,* 350; cf. also Malina and Rohrbaugh, *John,* 264 ("bodily distortions, loss of bodily control, and enlargement of the penis").

[597] Blinzler, *Trial,* 249; Reicke, *Era,* 186.

[598] Blinzler, *Trial,* 249; Brown, *Death,* 948–49 guesses seven feet.

[599] The proposed typological allusion to Exod 17:12 LXX (Glasson, *Moses,* 41) is fanciful, given the natural tenor of the language and the robbers in the Synoptic passion tradition. Jesus in the "midst" (19:18) could parallel 1:26; 20:19, 26 (cf. Rev 1:13; 2:1; 5:6; 7:17; Luke 24:36), though the idea clearly stems from tradition (Mark 15:27).

[600] Brown, *Death,* 1026–27. The Jewish leaders may have also preferred executions then, for their deterrent value; see Jeremias, *Theology,* 78; Hill, *Prophecy,* 52; Stauffer, *Jesus,* 209; *m. Sanh.* 11:4.

[601] Blinzler, *Trial,* 253.

[602] The location of the charge identifies the shape of the cross as in Christian tradition, rather than the T- or X-shaped crosses also used; mass executions sometimes simply employed scaffolds (on various forms of crucifixion, Brown, *Death,* 948 cites, e.g., Seneca *Consol.* 20.3; Josephus *War* 5.451; on the four-armed cross, the *crux immissa,* Irenaeus *Haer.* 2.24.4; Tertullian *Ad nationes* 1.12.7).

[603] Cf. also Bultmann, *John,* 670. On the distinction, see, e.g., Bammel, "Titulus," 357.

[604] So even Winter, *Trial,* 108–9. Boring et al., *Commentary,* 151–52, compares *Acta Appiani* 33 (second or third century C.E.), in which the martyr receives the mark of distinction "he claims, even if only mockingly." Whereas many details of martyr stories may be relevant, however, this one is not; in view of the many acts of martyrs with which Jesus' passion could be compared, a minor parallel involving such ridicule is easily enough coincidental.

him as a royal aspirant; the priestly aristocracy would arrest, and the Romans execute, anyone who offered the slightest grounds for suspicion of treason against Rome. The title is not a traditional Christian confession, and Romans crucified many self-proclaimed kings and their followers under the *Lex Iulia de maiestate* (Josephus *Ant.* 17.285, 295).[605] Other Jewish rebels apparently hoped for kingship (Josephus *War* 2.443–444; *Ant.* 17.285),[606] but unless they desired repression, Christians would have hardly invented the claim that Jesus was crucified on these grounds (cf. Acts 17:7).[607]

A further datum supports the plausibility of the posted charge: on other known occasions, a member of the execution squad would carry in front of or beside the condemned a small tablet *(tabula)* declaring the charge *(titulus)*, the cause of execution *(causa poenae)*, which at times he might later post on the cross.[608] That Matthew and Luke (perhaps Q; "this is") and Matthew and John ("Jesus") share some common elements against Mark suggests the prominence of this memory in the common passion tradition. That 19:19 uses the Greek τίτλος, transliterating the Latin *titulus*, probably suggests earlier tradition as well.[609]

John's distinctive elements are the three languages, the high priests' rejection of the posted charge, and Pilate's ironic insistence on "its irrevocability."[610] The three languages suggest the universality of Jesus' reign;[611] these very languages all coexist on Roman Jewish burial inscriptions.[612] Many scholars take these as the major languages of the first-century Mediterranean world[613] (interpreting Hebrew as Aramaic, which may be reasonable),[614] hence Jesus' rightful reign even over the Gentiles. On the cross, he draws all people to himself (12:32–33). One could also read them as the three major languages of Mediterranean Jewry. Some later rabbis felt that God made Torah available from Sinai in four languages (Hebrew, Latin, Arabic, and Aramaic)[615] or that four languages (Greek, Latin, Aramaic, and Hebrew) were appropriate to various occasions,[616] although only Hebrew was the divine language.[617] (John himself often offers a Semitic term with a Greek translation, as in 1:38, 41–42; 4:25; 9:7; 19:13, 17; 20:16.) One's interpretation of the significance here will probably accord with whether one

---

[605] Brown, *Death,* 968.

[606] Harvey, *History,* 13 n. 12.

[607] Ibid., 13–14; Stanton, *Gospel Truth,* 173.

[608] Cullmann, *State,* 42–43; Blinzler, *Trial,* 251; Winter, *Trial,* 109; Reicke, *Era,* 186; Brown, *Death,* 963, cite Suetonius *Calig.* 32.2; *Dom.* 10.1; Dio Cassius 54.3.7; 54.8; Tertullian *Apol.* 2.20; Eusebius *Hist. eccl.* 5.1.44; cf. the herald in *b. Sanh.* 43a. The posting of the accusation on the cross is not well attested, either because those describing crucifixion had already mentioned it being carried (Bammel, *"Titulus,"* 353) or because the practice was not in fact standard although, given the variations among executions, in no way improbable (Harvey, *History,* 13); wearing tablets around the neck was not unusual in the broader culture (students in Philostratus *Vit. soph.* 2.1.557). Blinzler, *Trial,* 254, thinks the tablets included "black or red letters on a white ground."

[609] So Geiger, "Titulus Crucis," despite the more problematic three languages.

[610] Meeks, *Prophet-King,* 80.

[611] Allen, "Church," 88; Bultmann, *John,* 669.

[612] Cf. Blinzler, *Trial,* 255.

[613] E.g., Allen, "Church," 88.

[614] Epigraphic data suggest that Aramaic probably predominated in Galilee (Horsley, *Galilee,* 247–49) despite Hebrew's use as a holy language and the ideal of its use (*pace* Safrai, "Literary Languages"; idem, "Spoken Languages"; *Let. Aris.* 11, 30, 38; *Sipre Deut.* 46.1.2).

[615] One among several interpretations of Deut 33 in *Sipre Deut.* 343.3.1.

[616] *P. Meg.* 1:9, §2.

[617] E.g., *Jub.* 12:25–27; *p. Meg.* 1:9, §1; hence its use in the Mishnah, many DSS, and the Bar Kokhba materials (cf. Carmon, *Inscriptions,* 73).

reads "Greeks" in John as Gentiles or as Diaspora Jews (see comment on 7:35; 12:20); because we have favored the former, we concur with most scholars that this passage suggests the universality of Jesus' rule. He is a king of Israel, but paradoxically for all humanity (cf. 4:42).

Brown argues that while multilingual inscriptions were common, especially in multicultural civil proclamations,[618] soldiers would not have taken the time to have recorded all three on Jesus' *titulus*.[619] An exception would have been had Pilate so ordered, perhaps as part of his revenge on being forced to capitulate to the leaders (a surrender Pilate rarely offered willingly; Philo *Embassy* 303). Perhaps even the soldiers might have been happy to supply it as mockery; if any of the soldiers were Syrian recruits, they would probably know Aramaic. But regardless of one's view on the historical merits of John's tradition on this point, his theology is clear: Jesus died for the "world" (3:16).

The finality of Pilate's claim about "what I have written" (19:22; cf. esp. γεγραμμένον in 19:19–20) may remind the reader of every other use of "written" to this point in the Gospel—every other use refers to Scripture (2:17; 6:31, 45; 8:17; 10:34; 12:14, 16; 15:25), which cannot be broken (10:35). Thus John may ironically suggest that Pilate, as God's unwitting agent (19:11), may carry out God's will in the Scriptures.

## 3. Dividing Jesus' Property (19:23–24)

Confiscation of goods was a common penalty attending execution or other sentences of judgment,[620] but Jesus has few goods on him to confiscate. The removal of clothing (19:23–24) fits what we know of typical ancient executions;[621] Romans crucified their victims naked.[622] Although some later rabbis, explaining the proper way to carry out theoretical executions, allowed men a loincloth,[623] it is unlikely that Pilate's soldiers would have accommodated their sensitivities;[624] further, other tradition indicates that most Jewish teachers allowed men to be executed naked.[625] Public nakedness could cause shame in other settings,[626] and Romans stripped those they would punish to degrade them,[627] but it was especially shaming for Palestinian Jews.[628]

---

[618] Brown, *Death*, 965; he also cites the five languages (Greek, Latin, Persian, Hebrew, and Egyptian) at Gordian III's tomb. Talbert, *John*, 243, cites these plus the Greek and Latin warnings in the temple (Josephus *War* 5.194).

[619] Brown, *Death*, 965.

[620] Tob 1:20; Sallust *Catil.* 51.43; 52.14; *CPJ* 2:251–52, §445; 2:255–57, §448; *BGU* 5.16.51–5.17.52; P.Oxy. 513; Dionysius of Halicarnassus *R.A.* 4.5.3; 4.15.6; Appian *C.W.* 4.5.31; Cornelius Nepos 7 (Alcibiades), 4.5; Herodian 7.3.2; Josephus *Life* 370–371; Heb 10:34.

[621] E.g., Polybius 11.30.1–2; also in illegal lynchings (e.g., Herodian 8.8.6); also in beatings (Longus 2.14); see comment on scourging, above.

[622] Artemidorus *Onir.* 2.61; Brown, *Death*, 870, adds Dionysius of Halicarnassus *R.A.* 7.69.2; Valerius Maximus 1.7.4; Josephus *Ant.* 19.270.

[623] *M. Sanh.* 6:3; Blinzler, *Trial*, 253.

[624] Brown, *Death*, 870, thinks the Gospels might "reflect a local concession," noting that Josephus *War* 2.246 and *Ant.* 20.136 do not mention Celer's disrobing; but this would be an argument from silence. (Brown, citing Melito of Sardis *On the Pasch* 97 in favor of nakedness and *Acts of Pilate* 10.1 in favor of a loincloth, ultimately doubts that we can know either way [p. 953].) Nakedness was probably the rule of thumb (in public Roman punishments, e.g., Dionysius of Halicarnassus *R.A.* 7.69.2; in non-Roman executions, e.g., Josephus *Ag. Ap.* 1.191; 2.53).

[625] *M. Sanh.* 6:3; *Soṭah* 3:8; *b. Sanh.* 45a, bar.

[626] E.g., Juvenal *Sat.* 1.71; Phaedrus 4.16.5–6; Plutarch *R.Q.* 40, *Mor.* 274A; Diogenes Laertius 2.73; but contrast Plato *Rep.* 5.452C; Dio Chrysostom *Or.* 13.24.

[627] See Rapske, *Custody*, 297–98.

The specific mention of divided clothing (19:23–24) explicitly recalls Ps 22:18 (21:19 LXX),[629] which plays a prominent role in the Gospels' passion traditions.[630] Although one can read the two lines of the verse as parallel, John exegetes from them as much as is possible, like Matthew in Matt 21:5.[631] (Their contemporaries also read more into texts than they required when it suited their purposes to do so.)[632] John also clearly provides fulfillment quotations in his Passion Narrative (19:24, 28, 36–37) for apologetic purposes; even details of Jesus' death, which was scandalous in the ancient Mediterranean, fulfilled the divine plan. In addition to his apologetic purpose, John seeks to bring out the symbolic spiritual significance of Jesus' death.[633]

Nevertheless, the Gospels' reports of divided clothing can scarcely represent a mere accommodation to the psalm without historical substance,[634] even if pre-Christian Jewish interpreters typically understood the psalm messianically in this period[635] (which is unlikely). Roman law allowed the execution squad to seize the few possessions the condemned might have on his person *(Digest* 48.20.6;[636] against the Jewish custom, e.g., *b. Sanh.* 48b, *bar.);* it is doubtful that soldiers would have observed later restrictions.[637] The Roman army's basic unit was a *contubernium,* eight men who shared a tent; normally half of such a unit would be dispatched for a work detail such as a crucifixion,[638] thus the four soldiers in 19:23. The casting of lots (19:24) may involve the guessing of another's hidden fingers,[639] but the bored soldiers may have as easily brought dice to entertain themselves.[640]

---

[628] E.g., Gen 3:7, 10–11; *Jub.* 3:21–22, 30–31; 7:8–10, 20; 1QS 7.12; *t. Ber.* 2:14; *Sipre Deut.* 320.5.2.

[629] Often recognized even in gospels where the psalm is not cited (e.g., Cope, *Scribe,* 103). Dodd, *Tradition,* 122, thinks John found the *testimonium* in a non-Markan stream of tradition. There is probably no symbolic allusion to the custom of a wearer rending garments for mourning (Plutarch *Cicero* 31.1; 1 Macc 2:14; 4:39–40; 5:14; Keener, *Matthew,* 651–52).

[630] See Brown, *Death,* 1455–64.

[631] Soares Prabhu, *Quotations,* 158–59; Freed, *Quotations,* 102.

[632] Cope, *Scribe,* 87; Goulder, *Midrash,* 22–23; cf., e.g., *3 En.* 18:24; *p. Meg.* 1:11, §4; *Gen. Rab.* 51:8; *Pesiq. Rab.* 5:3; Gal 3:16.

[633] See Garland, "Quotations."

[634] Cf. Freed, *Quotations,* 101.

[635] Edersheim, *Life,* 608, citing *Yal. Isa.* 60; cf. also *Pesiq. Rab.* 36:2; 37:1. Whether this interpretation existed before the time of Jesus is unclear (Longenecker, *Exegesis,* 156, notes its use five times in 1QH to suggest that it may be messianic, but this is not absolutely clear), and certainly other interpretations existed (e.g., *Midr. Pss.* 22:6 applies to Esther—Bowman, *Gospel,* 136); in any case, though many parallels with Ps 22 in the Passion Narrative are noteworthy, they also correspond with what we genuinely know of crucifixion.

[636] With Dibelius, *Tradition,* 188; Sherwin-White, *Society,* 46; also recognized in *b. Sanh.* 48b, *bar.* This practice stemmed from the custom of plundering the slain on the battlefield (cf., e.g., 1 Sam 31:8; Joel 3:2–3; 2 Macc 8:27; Virgil *Aen.* 11.193–194; Polybius 9.26; Dionysius of Halicarnassus *R.A.* 3.40.3; 3.56.4; 6.29.4–5; Livy 41.11.8; Appian *R.H.* 4.2; Philostratus *Hrk.* 35.3; and throughout ancient literature).

[637] Brown, *Death,* 955, notes that the law itself exempts the clothing the condemned is wearing, but acknowledges that such rules may not have been followed in the first century. We would add doubts that anyone would have restrained provincial soldiers from such seizure (especially given the abuses of requisitioning from persons not condemned).

[638] Jones, "Army," 193–94.

[639] Brown, *Death,* 955, reporting the suggestion of De Waal.

[640] Cf. Cary and Haarhoff, *Life,* 149. On the use of dice, see, e.g., Martial *Epigr.* 4.14; 14.15–16; cf. 11.6.2; for knucklebones, see Martial *Epigr.* 14.14; Diogenes Laertius 9.1.3; see further the comment on 19:2–3.

The "outer garments" would represent the rectangular cloth draped around the body in inclement weather; the tunic was normally "a long, tight-fitting shirt made of two pieces of cloth sewn together," typically sleeveless, whether of "wool, linen or leather." A seamless tunic, which would fit the neck more closely and generally have short sleeves, was of special value.[641] That Jesus' tunic was "seamless" might recall the high priest's garment,[642] as may the failure to tear his garments (Lev 21:10).[643] The term ὑφαντός appears especially in conjunction with the high-priestly raiment in the LXX (Exod 28:6; 39:3, 5, 8, 22, 27 [36:10, 12, 15, 29, 34 LXX]), though also with other furniture of the tabernacle (Exod 26:31; 35:35; 38:23 [37:21 LXX]). In that case, the narrative would reveal Jesus as high priest while undermining the role of the official high priest (11:49–51; 18:13–24), another case of Johannine irony.[644] But the allusion remains far from certain; for example, the LXX of Exodus does not depict any of the priest's garments with ἱμάτιον, the standard language for an outer cloak; it does use χιτών (Exod 28:4, 39, 40; 29:5, 8; 35:19; 39:27 [36:34 LXX]; 40:14), but that term, like ἱμάτιον, was the usual term.[645] More significantly, John seems to lack the sort of explicit priestly emphasis one finds in Hebrews (2:17; 3:1; 4:14–5:10; 6:20–8:4; 9:11, 25; 10:21; 13:11).[646]

Allegorizing the tunic's seamlessness as the unity of the church (cf. 17:11; 9:16)[647] fails at the least because Jesus is deprived of the tunic and perhaps also because John speaks of a tunic and not a robe.[648] Mention of the tunic's seamlessness may simply signify that it is woven rather than knitted, and hence more expensive.[649] In the context of the whole Gospel, John may emphasize simply that Jesus divests himself of all earthly possessions at the cross, as he earlier laid aside his garments to take on the role of a servant (13:4).[650] If so, the text reminds disciples of the suffering they may also need to embrace to serve one another (13:14–16). Or John may mention its seamlessness primarily to explain why soldiers had to draw lots for it, so fulfilling Ps 22:18 literalistically.[651]

John's most central implication at this point, however, is the fulfillment of Scripture. His οὖν at the end of v. 24 ("*this is why* the soldiers did these things") reinforces the point: the soldiers may have acted according to custom and may have acted according to evil desires, but they ultimately were unwittingly fulfilling God's unbreakable word (13:18; 15:25; cf., e.g., Gen 50:20; 1 Kgs 22:30, 34–35, 38).

## 4. The Women at the Cross (19:25–27)

Women play significant roles in the Gospel, sometimes shaming the male disciples by the women's positive contrast with them. Thus the Samaritan woman's witness provides

---

[641] See Jeffers, *World*, 43–44; Watkins, *John*, 388. John leaves unstated the irony of a soldier afterward wearing (or perhaps selling) the very tunic Jesus had worn.

[642] Stauffer, *Jesus*, 60; Watkins, *John*, 388; cf. Josephus *Ant.* 3.161. Dunstan, "Clothing," prefers an allusion to the new temple by contrast with the rending of the veil (Mark 15:38), which John omits; but this seems overly subtle (cf. Mark 15:24).

[643] Ellis, *Genius*, 270; cf. Mark 14:63.

[644] Heil, "High Priest."

[645] Liefeld, "Preacher," 181, finds no special garb here (vs. the philosopher's *pallium*).

[646] Schnackenburg, *John*, 3:274.

[647] Based on Philo *Flight* 110–112.

[648] Schnackenburg, *John*, 3:274; Beasley-Murray, *John*, 347. An allegorical application of ἄνωθεν as a play on the tradition (Mark 15:38) or more likely on John's vertical dualism (3:3, 7, 31; 19:11) is plausible but difficult to make sense of.

[649] See Primentas, "Χιτώνας."

[650] Schnackenburg, *John*, 3:274.

[651] Whitacre, *John*, 459.

opportunity for Jesus' male disciples to reap (4:37–39), Mary's lavish devotion contrasts starkly with Judas (12:3–7), and now women disciples appear at the cross when, with the exception of the beloved disciple (19:26–27, 35), the male disciples appear to have scattered (16:32) and Peter has denied Jesus (18:25–27). Because human gender was most often noticed when it was feminine, in Greek thought some women could be understood as bringing shame on their entire gender;[652] John's positive portrayal of these women may thus speak favorably of women, countering negative perceptions. At the same time, women's courage (see comment below) could be used to shame or encourage men,[653] so these women also likely function paradigmatically for genuine disciples in general.

### 4A. Women Bystanders (19:25)

On the literary level, Jesus' women supporters form a contrast to the soldiers just described (note the μέν . . . δέ construction in 19:24–25); but their presence is historically likely as well as theologically suggestive (cf. Mark 15:40–41). It is not unlikely that the soldiers would have permitted women followers to remain among the bystanders.[654] First, they might not have recognized who among the crowds constituted Jesus' followers. Many people would be present merely to watch the execution;[655] the onlookers could not be immediately beside the cross, of course, but could be within hearing range. Within John's story world, if anyone pondered the details, more men might be in the temple preparing the paschal lambs, yielding a crowd with more women present; on the more historically likely Synoptic chronology, at least much of the crowd would remain women.

But second, soldiers would be less likely to punish women present for mourning; those supposed to be relatives might be allowed near an execution.[656] Ancient Mediterranean society in general allowed women more latitude in mourning,[657] and women were far less frequently executed than men, though there were plenty of exceptions.[658] The Synoptic ἀπὸ μακρόθεν must allow a range within eyesight, yet it remains unclear how distant; the Synoptic language might echo Ps 38:11 (37:12 LXX: ἀπὸ μακρόθεν), in which friends and neighbors remain distant from the righteous psalmist's suffering.[659] Such factors might render John's account more historically precise in this instance.[660] But in any event, John's language (παρά), if pressed literally (whatever symbolic double entendre John may intend to evoke), requires only hearing distance, and that only for the exchange of 19:26–27.

---

652 E.g., Homer *Od.* 11.432–434, 436–439 (even though Clytemnestra also slew Cassandra in 11.422); Euripides *Orest.* 1153–1154. (The subtext of the *Iliad* was that male warriors were fighting because of women, such as Helen and Briseis; cf. esp. *Il.* 9.339–342.)

653 E.g., Virgil *Aen.* 11.734; Ovid *Metam.* 8.380–389, 392, 401–402; cf. Plutarch *Cam.* 8.3.

654 *Pace* Barrett, *John*, 551. Women relatives were typically allowed, e.g, to visit a man in prison (e.g., Lysias *Or.* 13.39–40, §133).

655 On crowds present, see, e.g., Morris, *John*, 807.

656 E.g., Witherington, *Women*, 94, 187 n. 103.

657 See, e.g., Josephus *Ant.* 4.320 (Israelite society); Homer *Il.* 18.30–31, 50–51; 19.284–285; Sophocles *Ajax* 580; Euripides *Herc. fur.* 536; Thucydides 2.34.4; Cicero *Fam.* 5.16.6; Diodorus Siculus 17.37.3; Dionysius of Halicarnassus *R.A.* 7.67.2; 8.39.1; Livy 26.9.7; Valerius Maximus 2.6.13; Pomeroy, *Women*, 44; Dupont, *Life*, 115. Ancients did, however, expect both parents of a crucified person to mourn (*Sipre Deut.* 308.2.1).

658 Cf., e.g., Valerius Maximus 5.4.7 (cited in Rapske, *Custody*, 247); 9.2.1; Polybius 5.56.15 (mob action); Josephus *Ag. Ap.* 2.267 (on Athenian execution of women); Ovid *Metam.* 13.497 (among captives; cf. Polybius 5.111.6, in a camp).

659 The other LXX uses are irrelevant (Ezra 3:13; Neh 12:43; Ps 138:6 [137:6 LXX]; 139:2 [138:2 LXX]).

660 Witherington, *Women*, 120.

Only historical tradition would seem to account for Jesus' "mother's sister" and probably for "Mary wife of Clopas" (though cf. a Mary in Mark 15:40, 47; 16:1). (Mary Magdalene also appears here without introduction, as if known to John's audience from other accounts.)[661] The named women present could be four in number;[662] if Jesus' mother and brothers are for some reason unnamed, it makes sense that his aunt would be for the same reason. It is also possible (though less probable) that "Mary wife of Clopas" could be Jesus' mother's sister, despite the overlap with the name of Jesus' mother in the tradition; in some Roman homes, for example, a father might give two sisters the same name.[663] It is unlikely that John simply accidentally names Jesus' mother's sister Mary through disagreement with, or ignorance of, Jesus' mother's traditional name. Although John sometimes puts a different twist on other traditions available to us in the Synoptics, these twists appear particularly in the passion tradition, where Jesus' mother does not appear in the Synoptics; nor can we surmise why he would wish to correct the Synoptics regarding the name of Jesus' mother.[664] It is otherwise difficult to believe that John does not know the name of Jesus' mother, which appears frequently in the traditions, including Mark (Mark 6:3) and specifically Matthean (e.g., Matt 1:16, 18) and Lukan (e.g., Luke 2:5; Acts 1:14) traditions.

Although John alone among the canonical gospels includes the presence of a male disciple at the cross (19:26–27), he agrees with the Synoptics in emphasizing the presence of women after the male disciples had fled (16:32), although the departure of the disciples in this Gospel also reflects Jesus' plan (18:8–9). Given general perspectives on women's courage, however, this emphasis probably shames Jesus' male disciples, calling for greater courage in the future. Women were normally viewed as unequal to men in internal fortitude[665] and hence unfit for activities that required courage, such as war.[666] Granted, ancient texts regularly praise women's courage when it appears, but usually remark on how unusual it is[667] or depict it as "manliness";[668] conversely, cowardly men were taunted as "women."[669]

---

[661] E.g., Blomberg, *Reliability*, 260.

[662] Morris, *John*, 810.

[663] Ilan, *Women*, 53, following Hallett, *Fathers*, 77–81. "Mary" (and variations) was "easily the most popular woman's name in 1st-century Palestine" (Williams, "Personal Names," 90–91, 107). If one sister had two names, perhaps she came to use the shared name after marriage removed her from her original home?

[664] One could argue that one Mary in Mark 15:40 is Jesus' mother (Mark 6:3; cf. Matt 13:55; 27:56), but if Jesus was the eldest (or even if he was not), one would expect "mother of Jesus" there unless the passion had somehow terminated that relationship (certainly not Luke's view, Luke 24:10; Acts 1:14).

[665] E.g., Phaedrus 4.17.6.

[666] E.g., Homer *Il.* 20.251–255.

[667] 4 Macc 15:30; Aristotle *Pol.* 3.2.10, 1277b; Dionysius of Halicarnassus *R.A.* 4.82.3; 6.92.6; Diodorus Siculus 5.32.2; 10.24.2; Livy 2.13.6; 28.19.13; Appian *R.H.* 2.5.3; 7.5.29; Iamblichus *V.P.* 31.194. Some philosophers held that women were capable of courage (Musonius Rufus 4, p. 48.8) and that philosophy improved women's courage (3, p. 40.33–35).

[668] 2 Macc 7:21; 4 Macc 15:23; 16:14; Diodorus Siculus 17.77.1; 32.10.9; Apuleius *Metam.* 5.22. "Courage" is literally "manliness" (e.g., 1 Macc 2:64; Aristotle *E.E.* 3.1.2–4, 1228ab; Dio Cassius 58.4.6; Diodorus Siculus 17.45.6; 40.3.6; Theon *Progymn.* 9.22; Crates *Ep.* 19; Chariton 7.1.8).

[669] E.g., Homer *Il.* 7.96; 8.163; 11.389; 16.7–8; Virgil *Aen.* 9.617; 12.52–53; Dionysius of Halicarnassus *R.A.* 9.7.2; 10.28.3; Diodorus Siculus 12.16.1; 34/35.2.22; Aulus Gellius 17.21.33; Ps.-Callisthenes *Alex.* 1.46; cf. an unarmed man in Homer *Il.* 22.124–125; an effeminate man in Aristophanes *Lys.* 98.

4B. Jesus' Mother (19:26a)

The presence of Jesus' mother is not mentioned in the Synoptic line of tradition but is plausible and consistent with her reported presence in Jerusalem a short time later (Acts 1:14). Some suggest she merely came later to reclaim the body; returning Galilean pilgrims could have brought back word of Jesus' death, requiring her to go to Jerusalem to claim the corpse, before she received word of the resurrection.[670] It is no less likely, however, that she and Jesus' brothers were already in Jerusalem for the Passover (7:10; Luke 2:41–42); and if she was present, she would surely have heard of Jesus' crucifixion several hours before he died. If she knew of her son's execution, it is almost certain that she would have been present to mourn.[671] The beloved disciple's presence is theologically significant and proves an exception to the dispersion promised in 16:32 (fulfilled in 18:8–9).[672]

The historical evidence may not settle the historical question, but John surely has an interest in reporting Mary's presence that both Mark and the pre-Markan passion narrative may not have had. Scholars have offered various theological proposals as to what that interest was. Some have suggested that Jesus' mother, sometimes along with other women in the Gospel, represents a new Eve and, like the mother of Rev 12:1–3, the mother of the spiritual community of Israel.[673] Intriguingly but less than convincingly, some even connect Jesus' title "man" (19:5) with a new Adam, and his mother's title, "woman," here with a new Eve.[674] In this case, the new mother of the beloved disciple (who may represent ideal discipleship, as we have mentioned elsewhere) could function as the mother of believers.[675] (Or conversely, the beloved disciple represents the authoritative interpreter, to whose care Jesus entrusts the believing community.)[676] The best argument for such a view is 16:21, as understood in light of Rev 12.[677] But had John intended such an allegorical allusion, one would have expected stronger clues in the narrative, particularly more telling parallels with Eve or with Israel (or at least the term for "garden" used in Genesis LXX in John 18:1, 26; 19:41).

It therefore appears more likely that John expects the readers to draw lessons the way they normally did from straightforward narratives: to learn from and with the character of Jesus' mother. It was Jesus' answer to his mother's request, close to the opening of the Gospel narrative, that began Jesus' journey toward his "hour" (2:4); now he makes final preparations for his mother after his departure (19:26–27). When one takes the two passages together, the closing passage completes the issue introduced in the earlier one; Jesus can ultimately care for his mother's needs only in his "hour," where he not only cares for her physically but provides for her as savior. His role as her and the world's savior must take

---

670 Cf. Malina, *World*, 99.

671 Mothers (Homer *Il.* 22.79–90, 405–407; Euripides *Suppl.* 1114–1164) mourned sons; see especially a mother's mourning the death of the son who would have solaced her in old age (e.g., Virgil *Aen.* 9.481–484; Luke 7:12–13).

672 It may support an identification with the disciple of 18:15–16. The disciple perhaps departs in 19:27, "to his own" (Michaels, *John*, 319).

673 Hoskyns, "Genesis," 211–13; Ellis, *Genius*, 271; cf. Peretto, "María." The specific meaning in Rev 12 is clearer, but even there the mariological reading is unclear unless one resorts to subsequent tradition; cf., e.g., Keener, *Revelation*, 313–14, 325–27.

674 Barosse, "Days," 516.

675 Cf. Moloney, "Mary." Boguslawski, "Mother," sees this new "eschatological family" confirmed by the coming of the Spirit in 19:30.

676 Malina and Rohrbaugh, *John*, 270.

677 Hoskyns, "Genesis," 211–12.

precedence over his role as her son and material provider. Jesus' mother "learns that she is to be a mother as a disciple, not a mother and also a disciple. Discipleship must be the larger context in which her role as mother is delimited and defined."[678]

## 4C. Entrusting His Mother to His Disciple (19:26b–27)

Care for aged parents was part of honoring them, a requirement of piety;[679] both Luke (Acts 1:14) and John may uphold Jesus' honor by "guarding the shame of Mary by locating her in a new family, an honorable household, the church."[680] Jesus' γύναι may create an aura of distance (see comment on 2:4), but Jesus cares for his mother. What we know of Jewish customs suggests that they invited a dying man, including one who was crucified, to settle the legal status of the women for whom he was responsible;[681] a crucified man could make his testament even from the cross.[682] (The soldiers would have confiscated whatever property he had with him, on the treason charge; they would not, however, have taken time to investigate and seize any minimal property he might still have had in Galilee.)

By taking over Jesus' own role of caring for his mother, normally passed on to a younger brother, the "beloved disciple" models how true disciples adopt the concerns of Jesus as their own and follow in his steps (cf. 1 John 2:6). Adoptive ties held significant legal force in Roman culture, but intimate friendships could also create functional kinship ties; in a famous Roman epic, a friend promises that if Euryalus dies, the friend will make Euryalus's mother a mother to himself just like his very own.[683] In one novel popular in late antiquity, Darius entrusted his mother to Alexander's care "as though she were your mother."[684] A childless man facing death might also adopt a son to tend to his last days and burial and to carry on after him;[685] and given the relation between teachers and disciples, a prized disciple might do (cf. comment on 13:33; Mark 6:29; Iamblichus V.P. 30.184; 35.252). Thus an ancient audience could readily recognize the intimate bonds between individuals such as Jesus and the beloved disciple that would lead the latter to readily adopt Jesus' mother. Perhaps the passage also provides a model for caring for widows in the community (cf. Acts 6:1–3; 1 Tim 5:5–10) who have been cut off from family support because of their faith in Jesus,[686] although this proposal would be at best a guess.

---

[678] Witherington, *Women*, 95. Cf. Jesus' mother as an example of discipleship also in Seckel, "Mère."

[679] For care of parents in their old age, see P.Enteux. 26 (220 B.C.E.); Hierocles *Parents* 4.25.53; Diogenes Laertius 1.37; Quintilian 7.6.5; Sir 3:16; *Gen. Rab.* 100:2. Some texts view such care as "repayment" of parents (Homer *Il.* 4.477–478; 17.302; 1 Tim 5:4; possibly Christian interpolation in *Sib. Or.* 2.273–275). More generally on honor of parents, see comment on 2:4.

[680] Malina and Neyrey, "Shame," 64. Mother-son bonds may have been even closer than sibling bonds (Malina and Rohrbaugh, *John*, 272–73, based on knowledge of Mediterranean societies).

[681] Dalman, *Jesus-Jeshua*, 201.

[682] Stauffer, *Jesus*, 138; Witherington, *Women*, 95–96; Beasley-Murray, *John*, 349. Cf. esp. Seneca *Controv.* 7.7.12 (unless this means he simply wants them to hurry away because he is embarrassed by their presence, 7.7.20; but this interpretation is less likely). In earliest Rome, soldiers would name their heirs in front of witnesses before a battle (Plutarch *Cor.* 9.2); one might bequeath possessions as one lay dying (cf. Philostratus *Hrk.* 28.1).

[683] Virgil *Aen.* 9.297.

[684] Ps.-Callisthenes *Alex.* 2.20 (trans. Dowden, 701).

[685] E.g., Isaeus *Estate of Menecles* 10, 25, 46; *Estate of Astyphilus* 4, 7; cf. Philostratus *Vit. soph.* 2.1.565 (instructions for his freedmen, but his fellow citizens buried him honorably like a father).

[686] Stauffer, *Jesus*, 138, wrongly assumes that her allegiance to Jesus at the cross would cut her off from support from his brothers; 7:5 refers to unbelief, but does not imply overt hostility.

John appears concerned about discipleship creating familial alienation (7:5), but this passage might address primarily familial reconciliation (cf. 2:4). It may also suggest the simplicity of Jesus' earthly lifestyle (cf. 4:31–34); his only earthly inheritance to his disciples is his responsibility to care for his mother.[687] (If 19:30 implies the gift of his spirit, that larger spiritual legacy appears a few verses after this one.) Most important, because Jesus' brothers did not believe (7:5), Jesus entrusted his believing mother to a disciple (19:26–27). Later chuch tradition suggests that Jesus' siblings were older, children of Joseph by a marriage before his marriage to Mary; but 19:27 simply suggests that Jesus was responsible for his mother because he was the eldest son; other references to "the Lord's brothers" (1 Cor 9:5) suggest a direct relationship,[688] and literary cues in this Gospel link Jesus' mother and brothers (see comment on 7:4–5). A father might admonish a son to always care for the son's mother, going to great pains to honor her as she went to great pains to bear him (Tob 4:3–4); one might expect an elder brother to pass similar responsibility to younger family members. (A younger woman might be expected to remarry or return to her father's household, but Jesus' mother would be older and have greater independence than either of those alternatives.)[689]

The theological import of Jesus' entrusting his mother to a disciple rather than to unbelieving siblings comports well with extant Jesus tradition. This model suggests that the ties of the believing community must be stronger than natural familial bonds, a moral amply illustrated by the Jesus tradition (Mark 3:33–35; 13:12). Others also described a disciple's virtue in terms of caring for the teacher's family.[690]

## 5. Jesus' Thirst and Death (19:28–30)

Jesus' thirst is a visible symbol of his mortality, embracing the death his Father planned for him. Once he has died, his mission is complete.

### 5A. Jesus Drinks Sour Wine (19:28–29)

"After this" (19:28) is a customary Johannine transition (cf. 5:1; 19:38); Jesus' knowledge of his mission fits a more theological Johannine motif (13:1; cf. 2:24–25).

Jesus' statement of "thirst" (19:28) is a central affirmation at Jesus' death, framed as it is by the announcements that Jesus' work is now complete (19:28a, 30b).[691] Jesus' "thirst" is the language of mortality, emphasizing his humanity as in 4:6–7, where he requests a drink;[692] yet shortly after 4:7, Jesus promised an unending supply of living water to others

---

[687] Cf. the "similar bequest" of Eudamidas in Lucian's *Toxaris,* cited by MacGregor, *John,* 347.

[688] Martin, *James,* xxxii.

[689] Tilborg, *Love,* 13, suggests that Jesus frees her from dependence on a male patron here, rightly recognizing the nature of guardianship; but surely her genetic sons would have deferred to her not much less than a guardian.

[690] E.g., Socratics *Ep.* 21 (Aeschines to Xanthippe, Socrates' widow, concerning her children). Cross-gender bonds (father to daughter, mother to son) were often viewed as the strongest (Plutarch *Bride* 36, *Mor.* 143B).

[691] Cf. Brown, *Death,* 1077. Τελέω appears in this Gospel only in 19:28, 30, but its cognate τελειόω is more frequent (4:34; 5:36; 17:4, 23; 19:28). Luke also emphasizes Jesus completing his work (Luke 12:50; 13:32; 18:31; 22:37); for Jesus' agents, see Rev 11:7 (for eschatological prerequisites, see Rev 10:7; 15:1; 16:17; cf. 6:11).

[692] John limits this weakness by the priority of Jesus' devotion to the Father's will in 4:34.

(4:14).[693] Whereas the Samaritan woman enters into conversation with Jesus, bystanders respond differently to Jesus' request for drink in 19:29. Jesus was less interested in food or drink than in "finishing" the Father's will (4:34); now that the Father's will is "finished," he expresses his thirst (19:28).[694] Most significantly, shortly after Jesus thirsts (19:28) and is given only sour wine to drink (19:29), he provides living water for all humanity (19:34).[695]

Who are the bystanders who give Jesus drink in 19:29? Because John's audience probably knew the basic story of the passion in a form similar to the Synoptic passion narratives, they may have assumed that those who offered Jesus the drink did so in mockery (Mark 15:36). It is also grammatically possible—though hardly historically conceivable, given the soldiers at the cross—that John allows his audience to think of the disciple and Jesus' mother as the subjects of the verb (John 19:26–27), in which case they seek to care for Jesus' need.[696] But on the theological as well as the historical level, John apparently expects his audience to presuppose the hostility of those providing the drink, for they fulfill the role of persecutors in the psalm to which John here alludes.

Whether the scriptural allusion is to Ps 22 or to Ps 69,[697] both place the righteous sufferer's thirst in the context of persecution. The probably widespread passion tradition followed in Mark (Mark 15:23) was understood by Matthew as a reference to Ps 69:21 (68:22 LXX): they gave me "gall" (Matt 27:34).[698] The other line of this verse in the psalm indicates that the psalmist's persecutors gave him vinegar for his thirst.[699] Likewise, the popular passion tradition included a citation from Ps 22:1 (Mark 15:34); because Jewish traditions could allude to a larger context by citing only a small sampling, John may suspect (reasonably) that Jesus recited more of the psalm, including its cry of thirst (Ps 22:15 [21:16 LXX]).[700] That John intends an allusion to one of these verses is clear in his observation that Jesus declared his thirst so "Scripture might be fulfilled" (19:28).[701]

Most significantly, those already familiar with the passion tradition would recognize once more that Jesus himself remains in control of the events surrounding his death, consciously fulfilling Scripture (10:18; 13:26). In the popular passion tradition, the sour wine lifted to Jesus' mouth is part of the ridicule heaped against him (conjoined with the skepticism that Elijah would rescue him; Mark 15:36); here, however, Jesus deliberately invites

---

[693] If γύναι in 4:21 connects the Samaritan woman with Jesus' mother in 2:4 and 19:26 (the expression is not incongruous for a stranger), the appearance of Jesus' mother in the context of 19:28 (19:26–27) may be significant.

[694] Cf. Lightfoot, *Gospel,* 318.

[695] Also others, e.g., Glasson, *Moses,* 53–54 (following E. A. Abbott).

[696] Cf. the mourning women of Luke 23:27, who may have provided a merciful narcotic (*b. Sanh.* 43a; Stauffer, *Jesus,* 135; Blinzler, *Trial,* 252–53). Some used pennyroyal or mint stored in vinegar to revive those who had fainted (Pliny *Nat.* 20.54.152); but these were probably not available. People could also use wine to deaden pain (Prov 31:6–7; Tibullus 1.2.1–4; 1.7.39–42; Ovid *Her.* 14.42; Silius Italicus 13.273–275).

[697] Augustine *Tract. Ev. Jo.* 17.15.2 favors Ps 69:21 (68:22 LXX). Less likely, Witkamp, "Woorden," suggests spiritual thirst in Ps 42:2–3; 63:1–2; in any case, others applied psalms in somewhat analogous manners (Ps 37:23–26 applies to the Teacher of Righteousness in 4Q171 frg. 1–2, col. 3, lines 14–19). The righteous sufferer of Ps 69 may portray Israel in exile (69:33, 35).

[698] See Freed, *Quotations,* 106.

[699] The ὄξος (Mark 15:36; Luke 23:36; John 19:29–30) and χολή (Matt 27:34) are linked together in Jewish Christian tradition in *Gk. Apoc. Ezra* 2:25.

[700] Stauffer, *Jesus,* 140–41.

[701] Some (e.g., van der Waal, "Gospel," 39) apply it more generally to Israel's rejection of Jesus (1:11), but the Jewish identity of the torturer is not clear here, nor is this act the Gospel's most decisive or climactic act of repudiation.

the sour wine to fulfill Scripture (19:28–29). In light of this moment, the informed reader might encounter Jesus' miracle at Cana in a new way: Jesus began the road to the cross when he turned water into wine (2:3–4, 9–10). Now he receives sour wine (19:29–30) before giving forth water (19:34). Only when he has fulfilled this final scripture does he hand over his spirit (19:30).

The "wine vinegar" (19:29) was probably "*poska,* wine vinegar diluted with water, the usual refreshing drink of laborers and soldiers";[702] there should thus have been plenty on hand. Scholars have debated the force of John's ὑσσώπῳ, "hyssop."[703] Some have conjecturally emended the text to read ὑσσῷ, that is, a soldier's javelin (*pilum,* lance), but "hyssop," as the more difficult reading, remains the more likely one.[704] Others have identified hyssop "with the *Origanum Maru L.,* which has a woody stem over a yard long";[705] but the most likely meaning of "hyssop" (which lacks a stalk) prohibits the image of such a long reed.[706] A low cross[707] would not require a long reed, however; Mark may call the instrument by the specific term "reed" (καλάμῳ, Mark 15:36) to recall Jesus' earlier beating and ridicule (Mark 15:19). Likewise, John may envision the stalk of a plant that he calls "hyssop" to draw a parallel with the Passover ritual, in which hyssop played a prominent role (Exod 12:22);[708] John elsewhere portrays Jesus' death as a new Passover (18:28; 19:36; cf. 1 Cor 5:7; 1 Pet 1:19).[709] The very implausibility of the literal portrait reinforces the probability that John intended his audience to envision the symbolic allusion to Passover; perhaps John plays on the similar sound of "javelin" for a literal meaning but uses "hyssop" to convey his symbolic sense (cf. comment on double entendres in 3:3, 6).

### 5B. It Is Finished (19:30a)

Mark reports that Jesus uttered a loud, perhaps inarticulate cry (Mark 15:37); in John that note is a cry of triumph: "It has been completed!" (19:30).[710] The perfect tense most likely connotes action finished in the past with continuing effects in the present.[711] If, as we think likely, John's audience knew the basic form of the passion tradition known to us in Mark, they may have noticed the striking contrast between the final recorded words of Jesus in John (perhaps revealing the content of the loud cry, as we have suggested) and those in Mark.

This portrayal of Jesus' triumph in death fits John's emphasis on Jesus' glorification through death and the events his death introduces (e.g., 12:23–24). The Jewish martyr tradition emphasized courageous defiance, but Mark emphasizes Jesus' brokenness at his

---

702 Blinzler, *Trial,* 255, citing both Jewish and Greco-Roman texts; cf. Brown, *John,* 2:909.

703 Also a Semitic term (Smith, *Parallels,* 8).

704 "Javelin" appears in miniscule 476, probably accidentally; see Sanders, *John,* 409; Blinzler, *Trial,* 256 n. 38. Less probably, Schwarz, "Johannes 19.29," suggests instead the misreading of the Aramaic *'ēz* as *'ēzôb,* "switch" as "hyssop."

705 Blinzler, *Trial,* 256 n. 38.

706 Cf., e.g., Harrison, "Hyssop"; Hepper, *Plants,* 70–71.

707 For the low cross here, see Hepper, *Plants,* 71; Blinzler, *Trial,* 249; Brown, *Death,* 948–49.

708 E.g., Lightfoot, *Gospel,* 318; Sanders, *John,* 409; Barrett, *John,* 553; Brown, *Death,* 1076. For hyssop in other sacrificial rituals, see Lev 14:4, 6, 29, 51–52; Num 19:6, 18. Cf. *m. Parah* 11:8–9; for detail, Beetham and Beetham, "Note."

709 Clearly some Diaspora Jews applied the Passover to figurative or spiritual principles (Philo *Sacrifices* 63). Jewish people expected a new exodus (see comment on 1:23), which probably implied a new Passover of some sort (later, *Exod. Rab.* 19:6; *Pesiq. Rab.* 52:8).

710 The contrast is often observed, e.g., Goguel, *Jesus,* 172; Stendahl, *Paul,* 74; Brown, *Death,* 34.

711 See Blass, Debrunner, and Funk, *Grammar,* 175–76.

death; John is closer to the martyr tradition here, emphasizing Jesus' commitment to his mission.[712] John of course differs from the martyr tradition as well (see pp. 1068–69 in our introduction to the Passion Narrative); his Jesus is not merely a righteous martyr but deity in the flesh. Nor is this picture of Jesus' triumph docetic, as if he were less human in the Fourth Gospel (cf. 1:14); a Jewish martyr story in the philosophic tradition could go much further in praising triumph in death, even working from an explicit dualism, without ever adopting a fully docetic understanding. Thus, for example, Eleazar in 4 Maccabees treated his torture as if it were a dream (4 Macc 6:5) and maintained the dignity of his reasoning even though his body could no longer withstand the pain (4 Macc 6:7). For all his emphasis on Jesus' deity, John's Christology appears less docetic than this Hellenistic Jewish work's anthropology, which itself cannot be properly considered docetic.

Jesus had earlier in this Gospel emphasized that he had come to "finish" the Father's work (4:34); his ministry had "finished" that work (17:4), and his death crowned his ministry as its completed act. John elsewhere discusses this completion of his work in the context of God's creative work continued even on the Sabbath (5:36). It is possible that John's audience, especially on encountering 19:31, might recall the pivotal biblical support for the Sabbath, perhaps already used in many Jewish blessings for the Sabbath:[713] God finished his creative work, and then the Sabbath began. Jesus declares, "It has been finished!" (19:30), and John reminds his audience that the Sabbath began at sundown that evening (19:31). (John does not invent this Sabbath tradition—cf. Mark 15:42—but may make theological use of it.)[714] Or Jesus may have "finished" "preparing" dwelling places for believers (14:2–3); or "finished" may signify the fulfillment of Scripture (19:28) and Jesus' word (18:32).[715]

## 5C. Handing Over His Spirit (19:30b)

Jesus bows his head, perhaps as a matter of mortal weakness (cf. 4:6) but, on the Johannine level, perhaps as an authoritative nod of approval.[716] What invites more comment is what follows: Jesus "gave his spirit."

John probably intends "finish" to include the work of redemption (cf. 1:29). One suggestion that might support this probability is the appearance of John's verb for the surrender of Jesus' spirit, παραδίδωμι, twice in the LXX of Isa 53:12 (παρεδόθη).[717] By itself, such an observation would remain insignificant; the verb is frequent elsewhere. But John elsewhere portrays Jesus' death in servant language, especially "glorified" and "lifted up" (Isa 52:13 LXX), and his proclivity toward double entendres commends for us the possibility that he reads the "betrayals" of the Passion Narrative in light of Isaiah. In Isaiah LXX as elsewhere in the Passion Narrative, the "handing over" is in the passive voice; here Jesus takes the lead in his death, consistent with John's Christology and view of Jesus' "hour" and submission to the Father's will.

---

[712] Cf. Boring et al., *Commentary,* 157, 159–60.

[713] So Stauffer, *Jesus,* 141. Later midrash could view "finished" in Gen 2:1 in terms of dedication (Exod 39:32).

[714] Given the multiple attestation that it was the day of preparation for the Sabbath, most commentators concur that Jesus was crucified on a Friday (see Brown, *Death,* 1350–51).

[715] On Scripture and Jesus' word here, see Bergmeier, "ΤΕΤΕΛΕΣΤΑΙ."

[716] Malina and Rohrbaugh, *John,* 271, suggest that kings nodded approval (citing *Hom. Hymn,* Hymn to Aphrodite 222, where Zeus does this; we might add Zeus in Maximus of Tyre *Or.* 4.8; 41.2; Callimachus *Hymns* 3 [to Artemis], lines 39–40; Athena in Callimachus *Hymn* 5 [on Pallas's Bath], lines 131–136).

[717] Noted by various commentators, e.g., Bernard, *John,* 2:641; Brown, *John,* 2:910.

Although the departure (often breathing out) of one's spirit appears frequently in ancient texts as a euphemism for death,[718] that Jesus gave up his spirit (19:30) is theologically significant. In Mark's tradition, Jesus breathed his final "breath" (ἐξέπνευσεν, Mark 15:37); here he hands over his "spirit" (πνεῦμα, John 19:30), suggesting a Johannine twist on a more familiar tradition. (What John would add to Mark may also stem from tradition; see Luke 23:46, where Jesus "commits" his "spirit" to God before "breathing" his last breath.) The text does not clarify to whom Jesus hands over his spirit; probably the term for "hand over" here is employed for its symbolic value (see below; cf. 18:2, 30; 19:16) rather than with an indirect object in view, but if an indirect object is implied, it must be the Father (Luke 23:46). This image of handing over his spirit to his Father could evoke the Roman custom in which the nearest kin would receive in the mouth the dying person's final breath to ensure the survival of that person's spirit *(spiritum)*.[719] But the custom seems to have been a local Italian one largely removed from John's eastern Mediterranean audience,[720] and in any case, a more typical Johannine image is likely.

Jesus gives up his πνεῦμα so that now his πνεῦμα may be multiplied and available to his followers as he had promised (7:39).[721] If 19:30 reflects the more popular tradition of Jesus breathing his last (Mark 15:37), it links "spirit" and "breath" in a Johannine way (cf. 3:8) that climaxes in 20:22, when the glorified Jesus who gave up his spirit/breath on the cross now imparts it to his disciples. This is not to deny the distinguishability of the Spirit and Jesus,[722] which is clear in the Fourth Gospel (14:16, 26; 15:26), but to suggest that John, ever quick to offer double entendres, provides symbolic import in the events of the cross.[723]

Again the narrative emphasizes Jesus' control over his situation. Jesus' final words, in contrast to the last recorded words in Mark (Mark 15:34), announce the completion of his mission (John 19:30), though Mark also recognizes a theophany in Jesus' death (Mark 15:38–39). John's term παραδίδωμι ("hand over," "deliver," "betray") in 19:30 connects Judas (18:2, 5, 36), the chief priests (18:30, 35; 19:11), and Pilate (19:16) in a chain of guilt but here reminds the informed reader that Jesus ultimately embraced his own death (10:18).[724] The departure of the spirit was a common enough Jewish expression for death; Jesus' *surrender* of his spirit, however, is rare language, and probably underlines the point that Jesus died voluntarily.[725] As Tertullian emphasizes (*Apol.* 21), Jesus dismissed his spirit with a word, by his own will.

---

[718] E.g., Ovid *Metam.* 10.43 *(exhalata anima)*; Ps.-Callisthenes *Alex.* 1.14; *T. Ab.* 17A; *L.A.E.* 45:3 ("gave up the spirit," *OTP* 2:286); *2 En.* 70:16; cf. Jas 2:26. One also breathed out (e.g., Homer *Il.* 13.654, ἀποπνείων; Euripides *Phoen.* 1454, ἐξέπνευσαν; *Heracl.* 566, ἐκπνεῦσαι) one's life, or "breathed" *(exanimatus est)* one's last (Cornelius Nepos 15 [Epaminondas], 9.3).

[719] Quintilian pref.12 (and LCL 2:378 n. 1); Virgil *Aen.* 4.684–685; Ovid *Metam.* 7.861. The soul normally escaped through the mouth unless a mortal puncture created another opening (Seneca *Ep. Lucil.* 76.33; *Nat.* 3.pref.16; cf. Aune, *Revelation,* 894, for some non-Roman sources).

[720] The mouth seems to have been a typical organ for the spirit's departure at death, however *(L.A.E.* 27:1).

[721] Also, e.g., Lightfoot, *Gospel,* 319; Lindars, *Apologetic,* 58; Smith, *John* (1999), 361–62. Some find two gifts of the Spirit (19:30; 20:22) linked with Jesus' passion and resurrection respectively (Swetnam, "Bestowal"; Létourneau, "Don").

[722] Even less would John embrace a docetic distinction between Jesus and the Christ-Spirit (Irenaeus *Haer.* 1.26.1; cf. 1 John 2:22).

[723] On the symbolic (rather than actual) import, see Burge, *Community,* 134.

[724] Brown, *John,* 2:910, also cites 19:16.

[725] E.g., Morris, *John,* 816. Stoics accepted death when Nature demanded back one's breath *(spiritum)*, and also suicide for appropriate occasions (Seneca *Dial.* 7.20.5), but Jesus' acceptance of death here is at others' hands and so would not technically represent suicide.

## 6. Breaking Bones (19:31–37)

The Roman execution squad breaks the bones of those crucified with Jesus, but not his because, in God's sovereign plan revealed in Scripture, Jesus has already died. God confirms Jesus' prior promise of the Spirit at his glorification (7:37–39) with water flowing from his wound (19:34), which provides a context for the meaning of Jesus "handing over his Spirit" (19:30).

Talbert suggests that this section parallels the activity of the previous section: (a) Jewish authorities act and request Pilate, or request Pilate that they may act (19:31; cf. 19:17–22); (b) the soldiers act (19:32–34; cf. 19:23–25a); (c) the beloved disciple's presence (19:35–37; cf. 19:25–27); (d) those who love Jesus act (19:38–40; cf. 19:28–29); (e) Jesus' death (19:30) and burial (19:41–42).[726] By reinforcing the activities of various characters through repetition, John highlights the division in humanity (cf. 15:18–25).

### 6A. The Soldiers Break Bones (19:31–33)

That the soldiers act out the designs of the Judean authorities ("the Jews") again reinforces John's emphasis on the Judean leaders' primary responsibility for the events that take place—which makes their unwitting fulfilment of Scripture all the more noteworthy.

Because it was widely known that crucifixion victims often took several days to die (Josephus *Life* 420–421), Jesus' death in a matter of hours in the passion tradition invited some explanation. Those bound with cords instead of nails probably survived longer,[727] but this seems not the whole explanation. Here the explanation is that Jesus chose to die when he had completed his mission (19:30) and that he needed to do so before his bones could be broken (19:36). That his bones were in danger of being broken likely reflects the genuine historical practice of some crucifixions, but John also derives theological mileage from this as from other traditions he employs.

The breaking of bones in this context derives from the piety of the Judean authorities, who were scrupulous about Sabbath observance (see comment on 5:9–12) and Passover (18:28) but whose piety John views negatively.[728] Romans normally allowed corpses to rot on crosses; Deut 21:23, however, warned that this practice defiled the land.[729] Undoubtedly, in practice, Judean authorities' sensitivities did invite some concessions from the Romans, especially during local festival times, when Romans sought to show particular benevolence to local populations even with respect to executions (Philo *Flaccus* 83).[730] Even during nonfestal times, Romans appear to have normally deferred to Jewish sensitivities in the matter, for Josephus writes as if they were normally able to bury crucifixion victims before sunset (Josephus *War* 4.317).

Although some later rabbis could argue that the religious duty of executing a murderer overrides the Sabbath, others responded that courts should not even go into session on the Sabbath.[731] As a Sabbath during the festival time, this Sabbath was a particularly sa-

---

[726] Talbert, *John,* 242.

[727] Blinzler, *Trial,* 250; Brown, *Death,* 1222.

[728] "Preparation" here refers to the Sabbath, not to the Passover (Brown, *John,* 2:933; cf. Mark 15:42; Reicke, *Era,* 178), despite John's paschal emphasis.

[729] E.g., Hunter, *John,* 181; Reicke, *Era,* 187. On the emphasis on rapid burial in this period, see Meyers and Strange, *Archaeology,* 97.

[730] See Michaels, *John,* 321.

[731] R. Simeon b. Laqish and R. La in R. Yannai's name, in *p. Sanh.* 4:6, §2.

cred one; by John's chronology, it would be the first day of the Passover festival (the second day by the Synoptic chronology).[732] Leaving the bodies hanging on any day would have violated Jewish custom; leaving them up on a Sabbath was worse; leaving them up on a festal Sabbath was unconscionable. The Judean leaders wish to safeguard the holiness of the day. Yet the passage again drips with Johannine irony, underlining a matter of serious religious incongruity (as in 18:28): those who have falsely convicted Jesus and secured his execution now express piety concerning Sabbath observance.

Early Christian sources note that on other occasions soldiers would also beat a crucified person's limbs to hasten death, sometimes with an iron club *(crurifragium)*.[733] Roman sources, such as Cicero, also attest the use of *crurifragium* in breaking both legs to complete a crucifixion.[734] For some time, scholars have illustrated this practice by means of a skeleton of one Jehohanan, found in an ossuary in 1968; examiners thought that the young man had been nailed to a cross through both wrists and ankles and that his legs had been broken through the *crurifragium*.[735] More recent investigation allows that his legs may have been broken during burial,[736] so we are again dependent mainly on literary sources for secure attestation of the practice. Nevertheless, Dodd is probably correct to think that John preserves historical tradition here.[737] John applies the description, however, for theological purposes (see comment on 19:36).

## 6B. Water from Jesus' Side (19:34)

Brown notes that execution squads sometimes pierced victims on the cross (19:34), perhaps to be sure that they were dead.[738] Certainly soldiers would have such weapons on hand; they carried both a short sword and a lance, or *pilum*, which was roughly "three and one-half feet long with an iron point on a long stem joined to a shaft of light wood."[739] Dodd regards the lance thrust as genuine historical tradition rather than

---

[732] The second day was also very important (see Carson, "Matthew," 532). But "great day" here (19:31) recalls Jesus' announcement of living waters in 7:37–39 on a "great day."

[733] Blinzler, *Trial*, 250–51, citing Origen *Comm. Matt.* 140; *Gos. Pet.* 4:14; cf. Schnackenburg, *John*, 3:288. Some regard this practice as merciful because it hastened death (e.g., Hunter, *John*, 181), but John's Judean authorities have other motives (19:31), and breaking legs was sometimes part of fatal torture (Polybius 1.80.13).

[734] Harrison, "Cicero."

[735] Tzaferis, "Tombs"; Haas, "Remains"; Brown, *John*, 2:934; Meyers and Strange, *Archaeology*, 97; Bruce, "Trial," 18.

[736] Stanton, *Gospel Truth*, 119; Brown, *Death*, 950–51. Such breakage would have been accidental; according to the most likely Jewish custom from this period (given that the rabbis, where we can check them, often preserved more widespread early Jewish burial customs), those who buried the dead sought to keep from bending their limbs (so *m. Naz.* 9:3 as understood in the Gemaras; Safrai, "Home," 780–81).

[737] Dodd, *Tradition*, 133. Breaking Jesus' bones could provide a plausible explanation for why Jesus died so quickly in the tradition, but John insists that they did not break his bones.

[738] Brown, *Death*, 1177, citing Quintilian *Declamationes maiores* 6.9. But could this "piercing" refer to those fastened to the cross with nails? Jewish tradition also required proof of death before treating one as dead (*Semahot* 1; *m. Šabb.* 23:5; Safrai, "Home," 773); sometimes one died as the spear was withdrawn (Valerius Maximus 3.2.ext.5). The later tradition that the piercing soldier's name was Longinus was a midrashic extrapolation from λόγχη, "spear" (as also recognized by Calvin, *John*, 2:239, on John 19:34).

[739] Ferguson, *Backgrounds*, 40.

Johannine theology,[740] and indeed, the emphatic claim to eyewitness testimony in 19:35 suggests that John reports what he believes to be an eyewitness account, not merely a symbolic event.[741] Insufficient historical evidence exists otherwise to prove or disprove the likelihood of historical tradition in this instance, but Dodd is surely mistaken on at least one count: the account of the lance thrust is clearly Johannine theology. John is interested in interpreting, not merely reporting, his tradition.

Some think that John responds to a docetic-type heresy in this passage, underlining the reality of Jesus' death,[742] but while this proposal is possible (especially in conjunction with the possible use of the image in 1 John 5:6),[743] it hardly fits the primary emphases of the Gospel as a whole.[744] Indeed, one could have argued in a somewhat different direction: Greeks might recall that wounded deities "bled" a sort of immortal ("ambrosiac") blood called ichor,[745] a transparent substance that could appear like water. In one legend, Alexander, though deemed a god by others, observed that what flowed from his wound was blood, not ichor, signifying his mortality.[746] If one reads this passage outside its Johannine and early Jewish context, one could portray Jesus as a Greek demigod or hero; but this is not the most natural way to understand the Gospel as a whole.[747] Even a very hellenized Jewish reader speaking of ichor alongside blood might use it at most metaphorically for the divine nobility of a faithful (and quite mortal) martyr (4 Macc 9:20, ἰχώρων).[748] One could also argue that the pouring forth of another substance in addition to blood would be

---

[740] Dodd, *Tradition*, 133.

[741] Ibid., 135. Descriptions of grotesque emissions from those violently slain can indeed serve a purely physical purpose in their narratives (e.g., Homer *Il.* 17.297–298).

[742] Nunn, *Authorship*, 13; Allen, "Church," 92; Talbert, *John*, 246 (citing Irenaeus *Haer.* 3.22.2); cf. Wilkinson, "Blood."

[743] Docetism appealed to the Greek worldview even before its developed Christian varieties (see Hippolytus *Haer.* 8.3–4); Greeks could praise rulers as "seeming" (δοκεῖν) human but really being from God (Menander Rhetor 2.1–2, 370.21–26). The docetic idea of a wraith as substituted for Jesus on the cross (critiqued in Irenaeus *Haer.* 1.24.4), followed in the Qur'an (cf. Cook, *Muhammad*, 79), derives from Hellenistic mythology, e.g., in Homer *Il.* 5.449–453; Helen in Euripides *Helen* (following the *Recantation of Stesichorus*) and Apollodorus *Epitome* 3.5; Iphigeneia in Lycophron *Alex.* 190–191 and Apollodorus *Epitome* 3.22; Ovid *Fasti* 3.701–702 (allowing Caesar's being snatched up to heaven despite his apparent death, 3.703–704); Ixion's cloud in Apollodorus *Epitome* 1.20; cf. the angel arrested in Moses' place in *p. Ber.* 9:1, §8 (third century C.E.).

[744] Against this position is also the greater likelihood of the symbolic position articulated below (see Hunter, *John*, 181).

[745] Homer *Il.* 5.339–342, 855–859, 870 (Diomedes at Athene's command; cf. 5.130–132, 335–339, 829–830); Apollonius of Rhodes 3.853; Apollodorus *Epitome* 4.2; Apollodorus 1.7.1; (metaphorically) Athenaeus *Deipn.* 9.399E; immortality from imbibing nectar and ambrosia (e.g., Pindar *Pyth.* 9.63). The bronze giant Talos, who lost all his ichor, died (Apollonius of Rhodes 4.1679–1680; Apollodorus 1.9.26); Chiron had to trade away his immortality so he could die rather than endure the pain of his wound (Apollodorus 2.5.4); cf. perhaps Polyphemus in Euripides *Cycl.* 231, 321 (Kovacs, "Introduction," 55); on the mortality of some ancient Near Eastern deities, see, e.g., *ANET* 139–40; *UT* 19.1816; Albright, *Yahweh*, 125–27; Gordon, "Psalm 82," 130–31. Such "divine" mortality was rejected by Stoics (e.g., Seneca *Ep. Lucil.* 95.49–50).

[746] Plutarch *Alex.* 28.2 (quoting Homer *Il.* 5.340).

[747] With or without such background, the blood would fit antidocetic polemic (some see such polemic here, e.g., Brown, *Essays*, 132–33); the ichor, however, would fit a demigod rather than incarnation.

[748] Various scholars find here possible allusions to martyr language as in 4 Macc 9 (e.g., Perkins, "John," 982, though, like us, she finds its special meaning in its Johannine context, citing 7:39).

understood by ancients as a portent of impending doom;[749] but this is not likely John's point, as he omits the very evidences that might serve that function in the wider passion tradition (Mark 15:38; Matt 27:51–54).

Others suggest more plausibly that the mingled blood alludes, like the hyssop and bones (19:29, 36), to Passover tradition.[750] An allusion to Passover is plausible and possible but fails to explain the entire point of 19:34. Granted, tradition specifies that paschal lambs were hung up on iron hooks in the wall and pillars to be flayed (*m. Pesah.* 5:9), which might recall the crucifixion for early Jewish Christians who had been Passover pilgrims three decades before. More significantly, the paschal lamb was also "pierced," with a piece of pomegranate wood running through its mouth and buttocks, to roast it (*m. Pesah.* 7:1).[751] Further, as would be fitting for most sacrifices, the blood of slaughtered paschal lambs was collected and sprinkled on the altar.[752] The Synoptics can speak of shedding "blood" as a metaphor for violent death (Mark 14:24; Matt 23:30, 35; 27:4, 6), but John here provides explicit testimony of literal blood at Jesus' cross, making further sense of Jesus' language in 6:53–56.[753] While blood in the Fourth Gospel might allude to the paschal lamb, however (cf. 6:53–56), the primary emphasis in this passage is on the anomaly of water.

The theological significance of the water from Jesus' side is clear enough in the context of the entire Gospel. Given John's water motif (1:31, 33; 2:6; 3:5; 4:14; 5:2; 9:7; 13:5) and especially its primary theological exposition (7:37–39), the water has immense symbolic value. Granted, a substance that appears like water could flow from the pericardial sac around the heart along with blood,[754] and this could explain the source of John's tradition. But he specifically records the event for theological reasons (cf. 20:30–31; 21:25), reasons clarified in his water motif, which climaxes here.[755] Now that Jesus has been glorified (7:39), the water of the Spirit of life flows from him as the foundation stone of God's eschatological temple (see comment on 7:37–38). Just as Revelation speaks of a river of water flowing from the throne of God and of the lamb in the world to come (Rev 22:1), a Johannine Christian who emphasized the realized aspect of early Christian eschatology could drink freely from that river in the present (Rev 22:17). As Jesus was enthroned by humans as "king of the Jews" (John 19:19–22) and crowned with thorns (19:2, 5), the river of the Spirit began to flow in a symbolic sense from his throne.

As in 7:37–39, this passage may suggest secondary allusions to the rock in the wilderness (cf. 1 Cor 10:4), as frequently in early Christian exegesis.[756] Rabbinic tradition mentions that when Moses struck the rock twice, first blood and then water flowed from it;[757]

---

[749] As in Lucan *C.W.* 1.614–615.

[750] Ford, "Blood."

[751] The tradition seems to predate John's day; R. Jose and R. Akiba merely debate the position of the legs and entrails in this mishnah.

[752] See Bowman, *Gospel,* 315. Malina and Rohrbaugh, *John,* 274, suggest that the blood spurting out (because the death is fresh) reveals that an animal remains kosher (citing *m. Hul.* 2:6), comparing εὐθύς.

[753] One could speak graphically of a cross still wet with blood (Cicero *Verr.* 2.4.11.26), perhaps contemplating the effects of nails in the wrists in cases where that was practiced.

[754] Wilkinson, "Blood."

[755] Association with the gift of the Spirit (whether or not proleptic) and 7:37–39 is the most common scholarly view; see Vellanickal, "Blood"; McPolin, *John,* 249; Brown, *Death,* 1178–82; Koester, *Symbolism,* 181.

[756] Glasson, *Moses,* 52–53, cites Cyprian *Epistles* 63.8 (who uses Isa 48:21); Aphraates and Ephrem; Origen *Hom. Exod.* 11.2; Gregory of Nyssa *Life of Moses* 2.270.

[757] Glasson, *Moses,* 54, cites *Exod. Rab.* 122a (citing Ps 78:20) and the Palestinian Targum on Num 20:11.

but the tradition is of uncertain date and may reflect the water-blood tradition from the plagues in Egypt (Exod 7:15–21; cf. Rev 8:8; 11:6; 16:3–6). Although we have expressed some skepticism concerning the degree to which John's audience would have connected the particular time of Jesus' death to the Passover sacrifice in the temple, it may be significant that in early popular tradition the water libation for the festival of Tabernacles was poured out at the time of the daily offering.[758]

Hoskyns suggests that the water of life flows from Jesus' side to recall Adam's side as the origin for Eve's life (Gen 2:21–22), which he connects to his portrayal of Jesus' mother (John 19:26–27) as a new Eve.[759] Yet as widely used as the Genesis creation account was,[760] one would hope for clearer clues than this if John intended such an allusion, and we have already expressed some skepticism concerning the proposal that Jesus' mother appears as a new Eve in 19:26–27.

## 6C. The Witness of the Disciple and Scripture (19:35–37)

The beloved disciple (19:26–27) offers eyewitness testimony of water and blood from Jesus' pierced side (19:35); Scripture provides the meaning for that event (19:36–37). Early readers of the Gospel noted and discussed reasons for the eyewitness claim at this point; Theodore of Mopsuestia suggested that it referred to personal revelation seen only by John; John Chrysostom felt that such a degrading experience for the Lord demanded particularly documented testimony.[761] Of the two opinions, Chrysostom would be nearer the truth; but most likely John underlines the eyewitness claim here to emphasize its veracity for the sake of the symbolism he will draw from it.

The narrator[762] claims that his source, presumably the beloved disciple (19:26), is an eyewitness (19:35). Eyewitnesses, particularly participants, were considered the most reliable sources.[763] Some have argued that the use of the third person here requires a distinction between the beloved disciple (the eyewitness source of the tradition) and the narrator or author.[764] Such a distinction of language makes sense and is possible (cf. the first-person testimony in Rev 22:8) but, given John's style, is not a necessary inference from the text; Jesus speaks of himself both in the first (3:11–12; 5:24, 30–47; 12:44–50; 17:4–26) and the third person (3:13–18; 5:19–23, 25–29; 12:35–36; 17:1–3). Further, narrator-authors often described themselves in the third person (see comment on 13:23).[765] More important, the

---

[758] *T. Sukkah* 3:16 (the tradition appears to be early and populist; but the event is more secure than its interpretation—Josephus *Ant.* 13.372; *m. Sukkah* 4:9).

[759] Hoskyns, "Genesis," 213.

[760] It is the most natural LXX allusion, even though another text spoke of pierced sides (2 Sam 2:16) and a new temple allusion (Ezek 41:5, 7–9) might be possible if more language in the text supported it; none of the texts conjoined πλευρά with νύσσω.

[761] Theodore of Mopsuestia 242.27–34; John Chrysostom *Hom. Jo.* 85.3 (noted in Wiles, *Gospel*, 9). Contrast *Apocrit.* 2.12–15, which takes John's claim (unmentioned by the Synoptics) as deliberate deception, inferring from its emphatic nature the opposite of what such a claim was meant to imply.

[762] Because the narrator is nowhere clearly distinguished from the implied author, I believe that the burden of proof rests with those seeking to differentiate the two here; but I retain the title "narrator" because it is most relevant here.

[763] E.g., Josephus *War* 1.2–3; *Ant.* 20.266; *Ag. Ap.* 1.45–49; *Life* 357. Even in fiction they carried special weight in the story world (Euripides *Iph. aul.* 1607).

[764] E.g., Witherington, *Wisdom,* 17; see pp. 81–139, esp. 111–12.

[765] E.g., Xenophon *Anab.* 2.5.41; 3.1.4–6; Thucydides 1.1.1; 2.103.2; 5.26.1; Caesar *C.W.* 1.1; *Gall. W.* 7.17; Josephus *War* 3.171–175, 190–206, 222–226, 234, 240, 258, 262, 271, 350–408; see further the comment on 13:23. Whenever Eunapius inserts himself in the narrative (normally in the

distinction may fail to account for some of the verse's language. The disciple's "witness" is in the perfect tense in 19:35, suggesting completed past action with continuing effects in the present; this could be used, however, even of a present speaker about a completed witness (1:34; cf. 3:26; 5:33).[766] Yet the present tense of λέγει probably suggests that the subject of the verb is the narrator (as in 21:24). One could argue that the witness of the beloved disciple continues to speak because inspired by the Paraclete (16:7–15), like that of John the Baptist (historical present in 1:15); but usually the Baptist's completed witness appears in the aorist (1:7–8, 32) or perfect (1:34; 3:26; 5:33) tense. One need not read λέγει as the voice of the narrator, but it seems the most natural way to take the verb here.

We argued in the introduction that the narrator appears identical with the beloved disciple (the witness in 21:24 is said to be the writer), although dispute on the matter will surely continue (especially among those skeptical concerning the testimony of 21:24, which most regard as an addendum or an addendum to an addendum). In any case, the beloved disciple is likely the witness in this text. He appears primarily in the narrative concerning the night and day of the eve of Passover and after the resurrection (13:23; 20:2–10; 21:7, 20–23, 24); most significantly, he is the only "disciple" so designated to appear in this scene (19:26–27), which supports the likelihood of his presence here.[767]

John declares that Jesus had to die before the soldiers could break his legs (19:31–33) to fulfill the Scripture about none of his bones being broken (19:36); blood and water flowed from his side (19:34) to fulfill the Scripture about looking on the one whom they pierced (19:37). Once Jesus died, the Father spared his body this final indignity.

That Jesus' bones remained unbroken to fulfill Scripture (19:36) invites the informed reader to consider which text or texts John intends. Daube contends that Jesus' unbroken bones stem from pre-Johannine (but not necessarily eyewitness) tradition. He argues that the claim that Jesus' bones were not broken was essential to early Jewish Christian apologetic, since their adversaries, the Pharisees, believed that one was resurrected in the same state in which one died.[768] The Pharisees and Jewish Christians probably did not clash as much in the earliest period as Daube here assumes,[769] but this provides no fatal flaw to his case; this understanding of the resurrection body seems to have been widespread (*2 Bar.* 50:2–4). More important, however, one might ask why early Christians would concern themselves specifically with Jesus' bones in the resurrection body when other wounds that might also be thought to restrict mobility were not considered problematic (20:20, 25, 27; Luke 24:40).[770] Whatever John's tradition, his own emphasis lies in his assimilation of Jesus to the paschal lamb, as in the text he probably cites (see comment below), an assimilation Daube also recognizes.[771]

---

third person, "this writer") it is based on his own presence, intended to point out his direct knowledge of the events or reports (e.g., Eunapius *Lives* 494).

766 The perfect form οἶδα is likewise inconclusive, as those familiar with it will immediately recognize; it regularly bears the present sense, but occurs only in this perfect form (68 times in John, including 21:24; 263 times in the NT), never in a present form.

767 See Smalley, *John,* 75 (who finds 1:41 and 18:15–16 doubtful).

768 Daube, "Gospels," 343.

769 See Josephus *Ant.* 20.200–201; cf. *War* 2.162; *Life* 191; Acts 23:9; Theissen, *Gospels,* 230–31; discussion in Keener, *Matthew,* 351–52.

770 Hunter, *John,* 182, thinks that John may specify the Jewish method of burial (19:40) to prevent suspicion of the body's mutilation (as in Egyptian custom), but the text addresses only the wrapping custom.

771 Daube, "Gospels," 343.

That Jesus' bones would not be broken may well allude to God's promise to the righteous sufferer in Ps 34:19–20 (33:20–21 LXX). That text declares concerning τὰ ὀστᾶ αὐτῶν (his bones) that ἓν ἐξ αὐτῶν οὐ συντριβήσεται (Ps 34:20 [33:21 LXX]), which corresponds well with John's ὀστοῦν οὐ συντριβήσεται αὐτοῦ (cf. the similar paraphrase of 13:10's negation in 13:11).[772] Were another source not more likely, one might have supposed this John's primary basis for the citation. John's use of the same form of the verb (third singular future passive indicative) may suggest a secondary allusion to this text, perhaps midrashically blended with another allusion to which we now turn.[773]

In a paschal context, John's predominant allusion would seem to be the prohibition in Exodus and Numbers against breaking the bones of the Passover lamb about to be eaten. The verb appears in a different form, but this allusion is otherwise closer than the language of the psalm: ὀστοῦν οὐ συντρίψετε ἀπ᾽ αὐτοῦ (Exod 12:46); ὀστοῦν οὐ συντρίψουσιν ἀπ᾽ αὐτοῦ (Num 9:12). John's citation is virtually the same, apart from the different form of the same verb and the use or omission of the preposition. The former difference may be a midrashic adaptation based on Ps 34[774] or may be meant to avoid citing the Exodus or Numbers text as a command (hence implying the obedience of Israel's leaders rather than the fulfillment by Jesus);[775] the latter may be a stylistic variation. Early Judaism carefully continued to observe this prohibition against breaking the lamb's bones (Jub. 49:13); one who broke a Passover lamb's bones could incur the public discipline of forty lashes.[776] Scholars frequently recognize John's allusion to the paschal lamb in this verse.[777]

In 19:37 John uses familiar Jewish language when he declares that "Scripture says,"[778] implying an appeal to Scripture's authority even though expressing it in a manner different from its expression in 19:36. He cites Zech 12:10, which some later rabbis expounded messianically[779] but which in its context refers to the wounding of God himself by his people—a matter of no small significance given John's Christology. The verse in Zechariah also speaks of God pouring out the Spirit to turn his people to him; this fits the Johannine context (19:30, 34).[780] If John understands the text eschatologically as in Rev 1:7 (which also universalizes the text's audience; cf. Zech 12:12–14), it could mean that those who wounded him will recognize him by his marks at the day of judgment. Even if John interprets this text eschatologically, however, it is more likely, given his emphasis on realized eschatology, that he suggests that Jesus' side was pierced so that the soldiers and Jewish

---

[772] Dodd, *Tradition*, 43, thinks this psalm the more likely source for John.

[773] Others also recognize a possible blending of texts here (e.g., Barrett, "Old Testament," 157; Higgins, "Eucharist," 208). Combining biblical texts was not uncommon in this period (e.g., 4Q266, 270, in Baumgarten, "Citation"; Matt 2:23).

[774] Schuchard, *Scripture*, 133–40, thinks that John refers to Exod 12:10 or 12:46 or both but that the verb form may recall the psalm. Grayston, *Gospel*, 164, sees both Ps 34:20 and Exod 12:46; Num 9:12 here.

[775] Nevertheless, the Judean leaders (19:31) appear again as "the indirect and unconscious cause of the fulfilment of scripture" (Lightfoot, *Gospel*, 319).

[776] *M. Mak.* 3:3; *Pesaḥ.* 7:11; *t. Pisha* 6:8; cf. *t. Pisha* 5:2; 6:7–9.

[777] Meeks, *Prophet-King*, 77; Pancaro, *Law*, 350. On John's Passover typology, see also comment on 18:28.

[778] Cf. Rom 4:3; 9:17; 10:11; *3 En.* 48A:7; *Sipre Deut.* 45.1.3.

[779] Edersheim, *Life*, 616, cites *b. Sukkah* 52a. The form of citation may represent a standard early Christian translation (Menken, "Form").

[780] Malina and Rohrbaugh, *John*, 275, also citing Zech 13:1 (from the immediate context) for John 19:34.

leaders who handed Jesus over to them would look at him on the day of his death rather than at his second coming.

## Jesus' Burial (19:38–42)

This pericope reveals Jesus' secret allies—who, though at first lacking appropriate faith (12:42–43), now show more fidelity to Jesus than those who have just celebrated their third Passover (in this Gospel's framework) with Jesus. Their role suggests that ultimate perseverance matters more than the prior duration of perseverance, and provides another invitation to secret listeners to the Christian message still in the synagogues.[781] That Joseph had remained a "secret" disciple "for fear of the Jews" (19:38) may remind the attentive first-time reader of crowds in 7:13 but will quickly provide a stark contrast with the disciples, who *after* Jesus' death became secret disciples "for fear of the Jews" until Jesus' appearance to them (20:19). (John uses διὰ τὸν φόβον τῶν Ἰουδαίων in all three of these texts.) The parenthetical reminder that Nicodemus had come "by night" (19:39) also underlines that he had been a secret disciple with inadequate courage (3:2) who had now come out into the open.[782] This time, coming before sundown (when the festival begins and work is forbidden, 19:31, 42), Nicodemus necessarily comes by day. He may not expect reward from the now deceased teacher, but he now values honoring God above his own honor (12:43).

### 1. Historical Likelihood of the Burial

That Jewish officials would permit, and that some pious Jewish leader might aid in, Jesus' burial is historically reasonable. As already mentioned, the Romans normally preferred the bodies of condemned criminals to rot on crosses,[783] but Jewish custom prohibited this final indignity, demanding burial by sunset (Deut 21:23; Josephus *War* 4.317).[784] If a Jewish court, rather than a Roman one, rendered the verdict,[785] Jewish people may have usually buried condemned criminals in a common grave reserved for that purpose (cf. *m. Sanh.* 6:5; *t. Sanh.* 9:8),[786] a purposely shameful burial. Because the punishment was in Pilate's hands (and Jewish courts could not execute capital sentences; see comment on 18:31), Jewish authorities would not supervise the burial, but it is unlikely that Pilate would be unaware of the Jewish concern for burial. Jewish law required burial even for foreigners passing through their territory (Josephus *Ag. Ap.* 2.211), and even the most dishonorable burial for executed, including crucified, transgressors, was burial nonetheless

---

[781] In more detailed reconstructions, perhaps still reciting a curse against schismatics even though they do not believe it themselves.

[782] It is possible that John includes it merely to remind a first-time reader of Nicodemus's identity, but after two previous mentions, he is not easily forgotten; cf. similarly Polybius 1.23.4, whose mention of Hannibal's earlier, probably humiliating night escape provides a foil for his current confidence.

[783] Petronius *Sat.* 112; Brown, *Death,* 962, 1208, cites also Phaedrus *Fables of Aesop,* Perotti's Appendix 15.9; Horace *Ep.* 1.16.48. Llewelyn, *New Documents,* 8:1–3, §1, cites a slave left to hang so animals could eat him.

[784] See further Safrai, "Home," 774.

[785] Cf. Josephus *Ant.* 5.44; *b. Sanh.* 47b.

[786] Daube, *Judaism,* 311; Daube, "Gospels," 342. Other places, such as Sparta, reserved special areas for burying criminals (Cornelius Nepos 4 [Pausanias], 5.5).

(Josephus *Ant.* 4.202, 264–265).[787] If he accommodated a demand for execution, he might also accommodate local sensitivities concerning disposal of the corpse.

Even such dishonorable burials probably did not allow authorities to lose track of the particular bodies, which would be handed over to their families a year later; if one objects that the handing-over custom is late,[788] one might suppose the same for the regular use of common graves for the executed.[789] That Jesus was buried is also attested in pre-Pauline tradition known to Paul's readers in his own and other congregations (Rom 6:4; 1 Cor 15:4). That Jesus was buried thus fits the culture as well as pre-Pauline tradition (1 Cor 15:4).[790]

## 2. Joseph and Nicodemus (19:38–39)

Yet it is likely that Jesus was not only buried but buried in an honorable, distinguishable grave; the Joseph story has much to commend it.[791]

### 2A. Joseph and History

Apart from specifying his discipleship, John provides such little introduction to Joseph of Arimathea that it sounds as if his audience is already familiar with this character,[792] probably from the early passion traditions. John and Mark independently attest Joseph's historical role: given early Christian experiences with, and feelings toward, the Sanhedrin, the invention of a Sanhedrist acting piously toward Jesus (Mark 15:43) is not likely.[793] Neither Mark nor his tradition invents many names; despite its bias against the Jewish authorities, early Christian tradition preserves burial by them (Acts 13:29; contrast *Mart. Pol.* 17.2);

---

[787] Honorable burials were, however, important to most people (e.g., Cornelius Nepos 10 [Dion], 10.3; Aulus Gellius 15.10.2).

[788] A Sadducean aristocracy might have cared little for the protestations of the powerless, regardless of Pharisaic concerns for popular justice.

[789] If the Mishnah reflects general first-century Jewish practice here (which is uncertain), Jewish courts granted criminals obscure burials in a common place but then expected the gathering of the bones to the place of one's ancestors a year later (*m. Sanh.* 6:6), meaning that the bones were kept track of even in the "common" grave, not scattered (Brown, *Death,* 1209–11; cf. Stauffer, *Jesus,* 209).

[790] We would therefore question the view attributed to J. D. Crossan by Ostling, "Jesus" (as cited in Craig, "Rise?" 142), namely, that Jesus' corpse was merely covered with a little dirt and probably eaten by wild dogs (being eaten by birds or dogs was the normal fate of the unburied, e.g., Homer *Il.* 11.395; Aeschylus *Suppl.* 751–752, 801–802; other sources in Keener, *Matthew,* 582, 695). But this view seems unduly skeptical that Pilate would have accommodated Jewish burial practices, especially if he did not insist on Jesus' guilt. (Even among Greeks, it could seem unthinkable that one would not have at least provided mass graves to enemies slain in battle, e.g., Pausanias 1.32.5.)

[791] See also Green, "Burial." On Joseph rescuing Jesus' body from a common burial, cf. also Bammel, "Trial," 444, though a Jewish execution is improbable. Change of opinion could transform a dishonorable to an honorable burial (Cornelius Nepos 10 [Dion], 10.2–3).

[792] That John intends a connection with Jesus' reputed father (1:45; 6:42) or Jacob's son (4:5) is unlikely; the name was a common one (see *CPJ* 3:182–83).

[793] Brown, *Death,* 1240; Davies and Allison, *Matthew,* 3:647. Although others might appreciate certain benevolent rich persons (e.g., Homer *Il.* 6.12–19) and early Christians had some well-to-do patrons, one wonders whether early Christians would fabricate benevolence from establishment insiders such as Joseph or Nicodemus (Jas 2:6–7, though cf. Jas 2:3).

burial was part of the earliest passion tradition (1 Cor 15:4).[794] The narrative is plausible for other reasons; Brown is certain that pious Jews, given their views of burial, would not have allowed Jesus to go unburied.[795] "The only surprise," Davies and Allison note, is that Joseph buries Jesus in a family tomb rather than a criminals' burial plot.[796]

That even Jesus' enemies in the Sanhedrin would have wanted him buried is clear enough; to prevent his burial would be in open defiance of Scripture (Deut 21:23), and Josephus additionally testifies to this practice (*War* 4.317). Although reports existed of cultures that did not bury (Sextus Empiricus *Pyr.* 3.226–228; Silius Italicus 13.486–487), burial was an essential duty both in Jewish[797] and in broader Mediterranean culture.[798] In Greco-Roman culture, burial societies ensured that even poor people would receive proper burial,[799] whereas the rich and well-known had elaborate public funerals[800] and other honors.[801] Like most of their contemporaries,[802] Jewish culture regarded lack of burial as a horrible fate,[803] and later rabbis demanded that even the most insignificant citizens be mourned by someone.[804] Roman authorities did withhold burial under some circumstances, however, so the most critical point in favor of arguing that Jesus' enemies would have granted his burial is the demand of Scripture, which the Jerusalem leaders would have wished to uphold. Whether Pilate would have granted the body burial (see below), it seems unlikely that any of the Jewish leaders would have opposed its burial, even if they would have expected a less honorable burial than Joseph secures for Jesus' body.

Although Brown is convinced that Jesus was buried and believes that Joseph played a role in this, he doubts that Joseph was a disciple, supposing that this is why the women did not cooperate with him in the burial;[805] but we may well question to what degree the women would have trusted a Sanhedrist they did not know at that point in any case. The preservation of his name and other details may suggest that Joseph either followed Jesus at this time (as we think more likely) or, as Brown thinks,[806] became a disciple later.

---

[794] Davies and Allison, *Matthew*, 3:647. Acts 13:29 can be construed as burial by his enemies among the rulers (13:27) who also sought his execution (13:28), but it is summary language; Luke also knows of Joseph as righteous (Luke 23:50–53).

[795] Brown, *Death*, 1240.

[796] Davies and Allison, *Matthew*, 3:648.

[797] E.g., Gen 23:3–20; 50:12–14, 25–26; Sir 38:16–17; Tob 1:17–20; 2:7–10; 4:3–4; 6:14; 1QM 7.2; Acts 8:2; Josephus *Ag. Ap.* 2.205, 211; *T. Job* 39:10/7. According to later rabbis, failure to honorably bury a righteous person invited judgment (*p. Yoma* 1:1, §6).

[798] Sophocles *Ant.* 43–48; Diodorus Siculus 20.84.3; Plutarch *Nicias* 6.5–6; Diogenes Laertius 6.2.52; Pausanias 1.32.5; Chariton 4.1.3; Philostratus *Hrk.* 33.33; cf. Plutarch *Solon* 21.1.

[799] E.g., *ILS* 7360a; Sherk, *Empire*, 234; Cary and Haarhoff, *Life*, 151–52; for slaves, cf. Buckland, *Slavery*, 74.

[800] E.g., Polybius 6.53; Dionysius of Halicarnassus *R.A.* 6.96.1; Apuleius *Metam.* 2.27; Herodian 4.2.2; Philostratus *Hrk.* 51.13; 1 Macc 2:70; Josephus *Ant.* 9.166; 13.406; *Mart. Pol.* 17.

[801] Theon *Progymn.* 9.4–5; cf. Josephus *Ant.* 4.320; *b. Šabb.* 153a; *Gen. Rab.* 100:2; *Eccl. Rab.* 7:12, §1; 9:10, §3.

[802] E.g., Homer *Il.* 23.65–71; *Od.* 11.71–76; 21.363–364; 22.476; Euripides *Heracl.* 588–590; *Hec.* 47–50; *Phoen.* 1447–1450; *Suppl.* passim; Diodorus Siculus 15.35.1; Philostratus *Hrk.* 19.7; it was necessary to enter the netherworld (Homer *Il.* 23.71; Virgil *Aen.* 6.365–366; Heliodorus *Aeth.* 6.15). Many Greek philosophers constituted notable exceptions (Seneca *Ep. Lucil.* 92.35; Epictetus *Diatr.* 4.7.31; Diogenes Laertius 6.2.79; Stowers, *Letter Writing*, 142–43), though even their own disciples often disobeyed their instructions (Socratics *Ep.* 14; Diogenes Laertius 6.2.78).

[803] Eccl 6:3; *Jub.* 23:23; Josephus *War* 5.514; *Sib. Or.* 3.643; *Eccl. Rab.* 3:2, §2.

[804] E.g., *m. Ketub.* 4:4 (two flutists and one wailing woman); *Gen. Rab.* 100:4.

[805] Brown, *Death*, 1218.

[806] Ibid., 1230.

## 2B. Joseph as a Model

Attested in all four gospels (19:38; Mark 15:43; Matt 27:57; Luke 23:51), Joseph's role is secure in pre-Johannine tradition. Yet even where it is clearest that John rests on prior tradition, he also preaches through that tradition. John mentions Joseph's discipleship, which probably accurately reflects the passion tradition (Matt 27:57), but places his special mark on it: Joseph was a secret disciple "for fear of the Jews" (John 19:38). Thus he, like Nicodemus, was among those of inadequate faith in 12:42–43 but now, with Nicodemus, becomes a more public disciple. That Joseph has more reason to fear "the Jews"—the Judean authorities—than the Romans undoubtedly reflects the ironic situation of the Johannine Christians; those most committed to their demise appear to be their Jewish siblings who accuse them rather than the Romans who punish them (see comment on 16:2).

The narrative also presents Joseph's current act as a positive model for discipleship, for, in coming forward to seek Jesus' body, Joseph ceases to be merely a "secret" disciple.[807] Joseph's coming forward is significant in securing Jesus' burial. In the case of a particularly heinous crime (or personal enmity), many sought to prohibit or prevent burial[808] or even public mourning.[809] Most important, Roman custom in this period officially prohibited burying the executed (Tacitus *Ann.* 6.29).[810] Nevertheless, a long history of Mediterranean tradition emphasized the need for burial, as noted above; refusal to allow burial was normally viewed as impiety,[811] and for centuries most persons in power, even those considered morally reprehensible, permitted burials even of their enemies.[812] Significantly, the Romans sometimes surrendered the corpse to friends or relatives who sought permission

---

[807] Requesting an official for a burial place, because the official controls the land (*4 Bar.* 7:14), is not an adequate analogy.

[808] E.g., Homer *Il.* 17.126–127, 255, 272; Sophocles *Ant.* 21–30, 697; Euripides *Phoen.* 1627–1630, 1650; Virgil *Aen.* 9.485; Diodorus Siculus 16.16.4; 18.67.6; Dionysius of Halicarnassus *R.A.* 3.21.8; 4.40.5–6; 6.9.4; 20.16.2; Appian *R.H.* 12.8.52; 12.16.107; *C.W.* 1.8.73; Lucan *C.W.* 2.166–168; 7.825–835; Lysias *Or.* 19.7, §152; Thucydides 1.138.6; Seneca *Controv.* 1.7.2; 8.4.intr.; Suetonius *Aug.* 13; Valerius Maximus 1.4.2; *Apoll. K. Tyre* 50; Iamblichus *V.P.* 35.252; Philostratus *Hrk.* 21.6; Herodian 1.13.6; 8.8.7; Chariton 1.5.25; *1 En.* 98:13; 2 Macc 13:7; for executions in Rome, see sources in Rapske, *Custody,* 14. Sometimes the prohibition of honorable burial by free persons did not exclude burial altogether (carried out by slaves; Cornelius Nepos 19 [Phocion], 4.4).

[809] Euripides *Phoen.* 1631–1634; *m. Sanh.* 6:6; cf. Josephus *Ant.* 9.104. Jewish aristocrats apparently felt that even relatives should withhold mourning when those destroyed were wicked (Josephus *Ant.* 4.53); but it was normally considered heartless to forbid mourning (Cicero *Pis.* 8.18), and to die unmourned was a cruel fate (Ovid *Tristia* 3.3.45–46). Contrast public mourning for heroes (e.g., Lysias *Or.* 2.66, §196; Philostratus *Vit. soph.* 2.1.565) and expenses lavished for an official or person of wealth (Cicero *Fam.* 4.12.3; Statius *Silvae* 2.1.157–162; *Alex. K. Tyre* 26; disapproved in Iamblichus *V.P.* 27.122–123).

[810] Cf. Petronius *Sat.* 112. Daube, "Gospels," 342, thinks that Jewish custom also usually withheld anointing from corpses of the executed. Bammel, "Trial," 444, thinks that requests for the body usually preceded the execution (as in *Gos. Pet.* 2:3ff.).

[811] E.g., Homer *Il.* 24.22–137; Sophocles *Ajax* 1326–1369; *Ant.* 278–279, 450–455, 692–695, 1348–1353; Euripides *Suppl.* 19; Cicero *Verr.* 2.1.3.7; Lucan *C.W.* 7.809–811; Valerius Maximus 5.3.ext.3c; Philostratus *Hrk.* 33.32.

[812] E.g., Homer *Il.* 7.79, 84, 409–410; Virgil *Aen.* 11.100–107; Livy 38.2.14; Appian *R.H.* 12.9.60; Cornelius Nepos 18 (Eumenes), 13.4; Silius Italicus 10.518–520; 12.473–478; Valerius Maximus 5.1.11; 5.1.ext.6; Ps.-Callisthenes *Alex.* 1.14, 41; 2 Sam 2:5; 21:12–14; 2 Macc 4:49; Josephus *Ant.* 4.264–265; cf. Ps.-Phoc. 99–101.

to bury them.[813] While Pilate would not likely hand over the corpse if he admits the charge of *maiestas*,[814] Pilate does not seem to take that charge seriously.[815]

But Joseph could not know how Pilate would feel until he approached him, and unless he already held special favor before Pilate (cf. Josephus *Life* 420–421), which for an individual Jewish aristocrat would be unlikely, only a courageous ally would identify himself before the governor as "friend" or patron of one condemned for conspiracy against Rome (19:38; cf. 19:12).[816] Mere association with one condemned for treason could lead to a person's execution under paranoid rulers;[817] granted, Pilate hardly viewed Jesus as a threat, but Joseph could not be sure of this. Although Joseph's social status might have afforded him some measure of protection, the general aristocratic view in the ancient Mediterranean (although particularly severe under Pilate's patron Sejanus in Rome) was that the prominent were the most notorious targets[818] and that prominence often aroused envy, hence hostility, from others.[819] Even detention on criminal charges involved great shame, which created severe social pressure on people of status to abandon ties with the prisoner.[820] Burying the dead despite prohibitions against this practice,[821] or in the face of other dangers,[822] functions as a model of courage in ancient texts, and disciples could elsewhere perform this function (Mark 6:29; Iamblichus *V.P.* 30.184; 35.252). Thus the tradition prefers Joseph's devotion at this point to that of the long-term disciples,[823] though perhaps Joseph's status (like the women's gender, 19:25) would render him less vulnerable to retaliation.

### 2C. Nicodemus

But whereas tradition strongly urged some comment about Joseph, John's distinctive interest is in Nicodemus.[824] Both texts that mention Nicodemus after the first occasion explicitly recall the reader to the first occasion (7:50; 19:39). Nicodemus had come to Jesus "by night" (3:2; 19:39) but, as a ruler of the Jews (3:1; 7:48), had subtly defended him

---

[813] Philo *Flaccus* 83–84; Taylor, *Mark*, 600; Gnilka, *Jesus*, 314; Lane, *Mark*, 578, cites also Cicero *Phil.* 2.7.17; Plutarch *Antonius* 2.

[814] Brown, *Death*, 1207–8, shows that Justinian *Dig.* 48.24 reports Roman law as early as Augustus allowing relatives to bury the corpse but refusing it for *maiestas* (treason); but he rightly observes that magistrates made these decisions themselves in the provinces (cf. Cicero *Verr.* 2.5.45, §119; Philo *Flaccus* 83–84).

[815] Brown, *Death*, 1208–9; whether a crime was truly against the *maiestas* of the state was sometimes debatable (e.g., Seneca *Controv.* 9.2.13; cf. the wordplay in Cicero *Fam.* 3.11.2). The Jewish officials would surely not object to the burial, however, and without opposition Pilate was free to act as he pleased. He had settled matters adequately for the chief priests.

[816] Also Brown, *Death*, 1217 (citing Cicero *Phil.* 1.9, §23; Suetonius *Tib.* 58).

[817] E.g., Herodian 1.13.4–6; 3.5.6; 4.6.1. Continued ties with a prisoner could be dangerous; this concern reduced Apollonius's disciples by more than three-quarters (Rapske, *Custody*, 388, citing Philostratus *Vit. Apoll.* 4.37).

[818] E.g., Cornelius Nepos 1 (Miltiades), 7.5–6; 2 (Themistocles), 8.1–7; 3 (Aristides), 1.1–5; 7 (Alcibiades), 4.1–2; Babrius 4.6–8; 31.23–24; 64.10–11; Phaedrus 1.21.1–2; 2.7.14–15; 3.5.1; 4.6.11–13.

[819] E.g., Cornelius Nepos 5 (Cimon), 3.1; 8 (Thrasybulus), 4.1–2; 12 (Chabrias), 3.3; 14 (Datames), 5.2; 15 (Epaminondas), 7.1; 18 (Eumenes), 7.2; 10.2; 19 (Phocion), 4.3; 23 (Hannibal), 1.2; Herodian 3.2.3; Plutarch *Demosthenes* 26.5.

[820] See Rapske, *Custody*, 288–97, esp. 293, and 388–90.

[821] Euripides *Suppl.* passim; Demosthenes *Or.* 60, *Funeral Speech* 8; Tob 1:17–20; 2:8; 4:3–4.

[822] Dio Cassius *R.H.* 57.18.1.

[823] John Chrysostom *Hom. Matt.* 88 also takes Joseph of Arimathea as a model of courage, risking enmity and death.

[824] Suggit, "Nicodemus," 100.

(7:50–52); now he openly risks his reputation and security to honor him. Nicodemus becomes a paradigm for the secret believers among the "Jews" (12:42–43): John invites them to go public with their confession of faith in Jesus.[825]

Yet both Joseph, here said to be a "secret" disciple of Jesus (19:38), and Nicodemus, who came "by night" (19:39), now render a service to Jesus that is potentially dangerous—a service the long-term disciples were unwilling to offer (cf. 20:19).[826] Given the nature of true discipleship, the other disciples' unwillingness to follow Jesus to this extent—their attempt, by contrast, to, in a sense, become secret disciples as best they could—was an act of temporary apostasy (see 12:25–26).

### 3. Burial Preparations (19:39–40, 42)

Not only because few gathered to mourn but because the Sabbath would begin soon (19:42), Jesus' burial activities were incomplete. In the Synoptic chronology, Jesus died ca. 3 p.m.; after Joseph stopped to seek Pilate's permission, perhaps only an hour remained before sundown and the prohibition of work. John's chronology (which does not specify the length of the crucifixion) allows perhaps two additional hours but still does not permit full preparation for burial, hence perhaps the importance of Jesus' preliminary anointing (though note the difference between 12:7 and Mark 14:8; the former may mean that the full anointing was kept for the day of Jesus' burial).

Although anointing (19:39) and washing the corpse were permissible even on the Sabbath (*m. Šabb.* 23:5),[827] some other elements of the burial[828] could be conducted only in the most preliminary manner for the moment, though undoubtedly hastened considerably through the agency of Joseph's servants. One could not move the corpse or its members on the Sabbath (*m. Šabb.* 23:5). The Sabbath interrupted various activities, which could be resumed after its completion (e.g., 2 Macc 8:27–28).

In a Jewish setting, linen shrouds were part of honorable burial (19:40),[829] specifically for the righteous.[830] Although the plural form of linen strips in John 19:40; 20:7[831] could tell against the authenticity of the traditional shroud,[832] others have argued that the evidence fits the shroud[833] and that the shroud could be included among the grave clothes or

---

[825] Cf. Jonge, *Jesus,* 29.

[826] *Pace* Goulder, "Nicodemus," Nicodemus is not negative throughout the Gospel; he grows closer to a disciple and further from the Jerusalem leaders (Dschulnigg, "Nikodemus").

[827] Washing the corpse was standard preburial practice in Mediterranean antiquity (e.g., Homer *Il.* 18.345, 350; 24.582; Euripides *Phoen.* 1667; Virgil *Aen.* 6.219; 9.487; Ovid *Metam.* 13.531–532; Apuleius *Metam.* 9.30; Acts 9:37), and anointing appears to be frequent as well (e.g., Homer *Il.* 18.350–351; 24.582; Virgil *Aen.* 6.219; Martial *Epigr.* 3.12; *T. Ab.* 20:11A); for ointments in embalming, e.g., Herodian 4.2.8; Hagner, *Matthew,* 758, cites P.Oxy. 736.13; Artemidorus 1.5; Gen 50:2 LXX. For the practice in other cultures, see Mbiti, *Religions,* 329.

[828] See Safrai, "Home," 776–77, for samples of these.

[829] Finegan, *Archeology,* 213. For information on wrapping in shrouds, see Safrai, "Home," 777.

[830] *T. Ab.* 20:10A; *L.A.E.* 48.1; *Apoc. Mos.* 40.1–3; *b. Ber.* 18b; cf. white wrappings in *L.A.B.* 64:6; *Gen. Rab.* 96:5.

[831] Probably "bandages" as opposed to the Synoptic σινδών (Mark 15:46; Matt 27:59; Luke 23:53), which indicates a shroud (Morris, *John,* 826 n. 110).

[832] So Brown, *John,* 2:941–42.

[833] E.g., Babinet, "Sindon." Although the radiocarbon dating seems against it (Stanton, *Gospel Truth,* 119–20, noting the three independent carbon 14 tests, each claiming 95 percent certainty) and the colors are known from medieval artists' pigments (cf. Thompson, *Debate,* 238–43, who sur-

the plural could be idiomatic for "grave clothes."[834] (For further discussion of linen and white garments, see comment on 20:12.) They "bound" Jesus' body (19:40), but in contrast to Lazarus at his resuscitation (11:44), Jesus would require no one to loose him at his resurrection (20:6–7).

When spices were used (19:40),[835] they were important, not to preserve the corpse[836] but to diminish the stench and, in practice, to pay final respects to the deceased.[837] (Jewish burials in this period did not seek to preserve the corpse; rather, they expected the flesh to rot off the bones for one year, after which the person responsible would inter the corpse in an ossuary.)[838] Against the traditional Markan account of women coming to anoint the body after the Sabbath (Mark 16:1), some doubt that women would seek to anoint a corpse decomposing that long;[839] but Mark's account is quite credible, as William Lane Craig points out: "In point of fact, Jerusalem, being 700 meters above sea level, can be quite cool in April" (cf. also John 18:18); the body remained in the tomb only a day and two nights, and "a rock-hewn tomb in a cliff side would stay naturally cool."[840] If we accept the Johannine account, Nicodemus had already left some aromatic spices with the body at its hasty deposition in the tomb before the Sabbath.

But the amount of spices mentioned in 19:39 is extraordinary. The Roman pound was about twelve ounces by modern standards, and hence the figure probably represents about seventy-five pounds;[841] some have proposed that if one takes the amount as a measure of volume equivalent to the biblical *log*, one might find an abundant but hardly impossible amount close to seventy fluid ounces.[842] In the Synoptics, no one was completely prepared for Jesus' burial; the lavish amount of spices here, however, are "as befits a king."[843]

This extravagance matches the devotion that some bestow on Jesus (12:3) and that Jesus bestows on his followers (2:6; 6:11–13; 21:11); some therefore take it symbolically for messianic abundance.[844] Whether one takes the amount literally or not, its meaning is clear enough: Nicodemus honored Jesus lavishly, as had the woman in 12:3; but if her gift had been worth 300 denarii (12:5), Nicodemus's was perhaps worth 30,000, a gift befitting

---

veys both sides), traces of Palestinian plant fibers and early-first-century Judean burial customs suggest elements of accurate portrayal in the Shroud of Turin. For a thorough and well-documented survey of scientific data for the latter, as well as scientific evaluations on the contamination of the radiocarbon sample, see Borkan, "Authenticity." If the Shroud dates from 1260 to 1390 as the radiocarbon tests suggest, it displays remarkable technology.

[834] Thompson, *Debate*, 240; Ducatillon, "Linceul." In *Death*, 1264–65, Brown argues that the Synoptics probably think of a single cloth whereas John has multiple wrappings.

[835] E.g., Virgil *Aen.* 6.224–225; Ovid *Metam.* 2.626. Aloe is a Semitic word used of perfume in the OT (Ps 45:8 [45:7 MT]; Prov 7:17; Song 4:14). Probably these came from the *Aloe vera* of southwestern Arabia (Hepper, "Aloes").

[836] Unlike the immortals' ambrosia in Greek myth (Homer *Il.* 19.37–39; 23.184–187; another temporary expedient in 23.188–191).

[837] Spices would diminish the stench and could be sprinkled on the bier or burned during the funeral procession (Meyers and Strange, *Archaeology,* 97–98), but were not used as preservatives. For the use of spices at funerals, see Josephus *Ant.* 17.199; *War* 1.673; *m. Ber.* 8:6; Safrai, "Home," 776.

[838] Cf. *m. Sanh.* 6:6; *m. Pesaḥ.* 8:8; *Mo˒ed Qaṭ.* 1:5; Meyers and Strange, *Archaeology,* 28. For a possible contrast between ossuaries and Christian reliquaries, see McCane, "Bones."

[839] Weeden, *Mark,* 104.

[840] Craig, "Tomb," 184.

[841] Brown, *John,* 2:941.

[842] Cf. Kruijf, "Hundredweight."

[843] Longenecker, *Wine,* 122.

[844] Brown, *Death,* 1260; idem, 2:941.

"a ruler of the Jews" (3:1). Such honors were not unheard of: another story reports that a proselyte burned eighty pounds of spices to honor Gamaliel I at his death.[845] Five hundred servants carried the spices for Herod's burial (Josephus *War* 1.673; *Ant.* 17.199).[846] But the lavish sacrifice here illustrates particularly how even those whom John reproved as secret believers could emerge as disciples committed to Jesus, sometimes even more committed than those who had long followed him openly when they were not literally threatened with death (despite expectations of fidelity in 11:16; 13:37). In a setting where Jesus has been condemned for treason as a messianic claimant, Nicodemus lavishes gifts on him as a true king in his death.

## 4. The Tomb (19:41)

The historical tradition and probably even the site of Jesus' tomb remained known to the writer of this Gospel. John may emphasize the honorable nature of Jesus' burial, the genuine nature of his physical death, and that Jesus' disciples knew the site where he was buried. (Although John does not narrate the presence of others besides Joseph and Nicodemus in 19:38–42, he clearly supposes that element of the passion tradition in 20:1–11.)

### 4A. A New Tomb in a Garden

Only Matthew explicitly notes the use of Joseph's own family tomb (Matt 27:60), fulfilling Isa 53:12, but the tradition behind Mark 15:46 probably presupposes it;[847] how else would Joseph acquire a tomb so quickly? (Most burial sites were private, the property of individual families.)[848] Further, archaeological evidence for the tombs in this area may suggest that the tomb belonged to a person of some material substance.[849] The "newness" of the tomb (John 19:41) may suggest that wealth had come into his family only in his own generation or that rising prominence had led him to move closer to Jerusalem from another home.[850]

The dead were often buried in fields and gardens, so a tomb in a garden area (19:41; cf. 20:15) is not unlikely.[851] Some read the garden symbolically, as a reversal of humanity's expulsion from God's garden (Gen 3:22).[852] Those who connect Jesus' mother with the new Eve (see comment on 19:26–27) could therefore find a new Adam motif in the context. If this were the case, however, it would be surprising that John's term for garden (κῆπος) differs from the common LXX rendering for the Genesis garden (see comment on 18:1, 26). More likely, if John has any symbolic meaning in view, he recalls Jesus' arrest in a garden, underlining the injustice of his execution; in the former garden, Jesus was "bound" by hos-

---

[845] Hunter, *John,* 182. That John specifically responds to this story is possible but not likely.

[846] See Brown, *Death,* 1260–61, who also provides other texts.

[847] *Pace* ibid., 1252. To bury Jesus in his own tomb fits the situation of haste and location but also suggests a special love normally reserved for family members or those equally esteemed (1 Kgs 13:30–31; cf. Gen 23).

[848] Safrai, "Home," 779–80.

[849] Craig, "Rise?" 148.

[850] For rabbinic regulations for new tombs, see *b. Sanh.* 47b. Καινός can often indicate "unused" (Barclay, "Man," 76).

[851] Brown, *Death,* 1268–70. See also Josephus *Ant.* 9.227; 10.46, following 2 Kgs 21:18, 26 (κῆπος).

[852] Bowman, *Jews,* 314.

tile officers (18:12), whereas here he is "bound" by allies determined to honor him posthumously (19:40).[853] By recalling the earlier section, John may heighten the irony: gardens were normally pleasant places (e.g., Eccl 2:5; Song 4:12, 15–16; 6:2, 11), but there Jesus was unjustly arrested, and after his unjust execution he was deposited in one. They were appropriate places to be buried (2 Kgs 21:18, 26, LXX), but the connection with the arrest may be in the background.

Most Judean burial sites were private family tombs scattered around Jerusalem and elsewhere.[854] Often these were caves with an opening covered by a large stone rolled in a groove (20:1); such stones could not be removed from within.[855] Indeed, such stones would be cumbersome to move from the outside; people generally moved them only for reburials or new burials.[856] Because Joseph was well-to-do, he probably owned a more ornate tomb, whose disk-shaped stone would be too large (a yard in diameter) for a single man to move even from outside.[857] The practice of secondary burial—in which the corpse rots in an antechamber in the tomb for a year,[858] then the bones are gathered in a box that will be slid into a niche in the wall—is a largely first-century custom.[859] Despite some relevant pagan models, among Jews ossuaries are not yet attested outside Palestine.[860] (The story is certainly not a later Diaspora invention.) Such burial involved no shoveling of dirt as today, and often no coffin.[861]

## 4B. The Site of the Tomb

As noted above (see comment on 19:17b), all available historical evidence favors the premise that the earliest Christians preserved the accurate site of the tomb. That Jesus' followers would forget the site of the tomb (or that officials who held the body would not

---

853 Ellis, *Genius*, 247.

854 Safrai, "Home," 779–80.

855 Reicke, *Era*, 187; Yamauchi, *Stones*, 112; Anderson, *Mark*, 351; cf. *m. ʿErub.* 1:7; *Naz.* 7:3; *ʾOhal.* 2:4. So commonly did Judeans use caves that Jewish immigrants in Rome probably adapted this idea in carving their subterranean catacombs (Leon, *Jews*, 54–55). That John can mention the stone in 20:1 without prior introduction may suggest his audience's familiarity with the resurrection story (Blomberg, *Reliability*, 260); but it was also common on at least Judean tombs, though it might be less familiar in urban Asia Minor.

856 Thompson, *Archaeology*, 318; cf. examples in Cornfeld, *Josephus*, 283, 393. The use of heavy stones to cover an opening was ancient (Gen 29:8, 10).

857 Thompson, *Archaeology*, 318–19; Lane, *Mark*, 581.

858 Some later rabbis opined that this decomposition effected atonement (*b. Sanh.* 47b). The "year" period for mourning also appears in some probably unrelated cultures (Mbiti, *Religions*, 197–98).

859 Hachlili, "Necropolis," 239; idem, "Art and Architecture," 127; Hachlili and Killebrew, "Customs," suggest a window perhaps as narrow as 10–70 C.E. (cf. this older custom mentioned in *p. Moʾed Qaṭ.* 1:5, §§4–5). It is rare outside the Herodian and, irrelevant here, Chalcolithic periods (Silberman, "Ossuary"; Carmon, *Inscriptions*, 121); a major change occurred after the fall of Jerusalem (Goodenough, *Symbols*, 1:84–89; Safrai, "Home," 780). But some evidence suggests a less significant use for more than a century later (Goodenough, *Symbols*, 1:114; cf. Rahmani, "Customs"; idem, "Remarks"). Palestinian Judaism in the Hasmonean period may have already borrowed the custom of ossuaries from Roman secondary burial (of ashes in urns or boxes; Levine, *Hellenism*, 67; McCane, "Burial Practices," 174). For Jewish loculi in Rome, cf. Leon, *Jews*, 59; for a broader sweep of archaeological data on Jewish burial customs, cf. Puech, "Nécropoles"; Goodenough, *Symbols*, 12:22–39.

860 McCane, "Burial Practices," 174.

861 Meyers and Strange, *Archaeology*, 98; Safrai, "Home," 780–81, 786; Carmon, *Inscriptions*, 121.

think it worth the trouble to produce it after the postresurrection Jesus movement arose) is extremely improbable. James and the Jerusalem church could have easily preserved the tradition of the site in following decades,[862] especially given Middle Eastern traditions of pilgrimage to holy sites.[863] As noted in our comment on 19:17, the traditional Protestant "Garden Tomb" is a much later site and cannot represent the site of Jesus' burial;[864] by contrast, the Catholic Holy Sepulcher and tombs in its vicinity date to the right period.[865]

If Joseph of Arimathea owned the ground in which he buried Jesus (Mark 15:46; more explicit in Matt 27:60),[866] the Jerusalem Christians could well have maintained the site, at least until 70, and it apparently remained known by Judeans in the early second century[867] and preserved afterward.[868] Whether the specific tomb is the precise one, the area is certainly right and the tombs from the correct period. An early-eighth-century description of a pilgrim's report of the tomb contended,

> It was a vaulted chamber, hollowed out of rock. Its height was such that a person standing in the middle could touch the summit with his hand. Its entrance faced east, and the great stone about which the gospel tells us was placed over it. To the right as one enters was the place that was specially prepared as a resting place for the Lord's body, seven feet in length, about two feet above the rest of the floor. The opening was not made like that of ordinary sepulchers, from above, but entirely from the side, from which the body could be placed inside.[869]

We can probably reconstruct some other details about the tomb as well, given details in 20:5–7 and what we know of various kinds of first-century tombs; see comment on 20:5–7.

---

[862] Brown, *Death*, 1280–81.

[863] Admittedly evidence for early veneration there is lacking, perhaps because the body was not there (Craig, "Rise?" 148–49, 152).

[864] Tomb architecture changed radically after Jerusalem's fall (Goodenough, *Symbols*, 1:84–89), and the skull shape of the Protestant tomb is later than the first century (Brown, *Death*, 938–39).

[865] See the full argument in comment on 19:17.

[866] See further Keener, *Matthew*, 694; patrons would normally bury only members of their *familia* in their tombs, though this included their freedpersons (Jeffers, *World*, 45). John is the least clear of the Gospels on the tomb belonging to Joseph (19:41–42).

[867] For Eusebius's report (believable in most of its details) that this was among the Judean holy sites desecrated by Hadrian (for whom Jewish and Christian holy sites were probably indistinguishable), see Finegan, *Archeology*, 164.

[868] Talbert, *John*, 246, cites Eusebius *Life of Constantine* 3.26; Bordeaux Pilgrim; Cyril of Alexandria *Catechetical Lectures* 13.39; 14.5, 22; 18.

[869] Bede *Homilies on the Gospels* 2.10 (trans. Oden and Hall, *Mark*, 243)

# JESUS' RESURRECTION

## 20:1–29

The NARRATIVES OF DISCIPLES coming to faith in Jesus' resurrection toward the close of this Gospel may serve the same function as the stories of people coming to faith in his messiahship, including those near the beginning of the Gospel.[1] These narratives include both personal discovery and witness. Parallel confessions unite the resurrection narratives: "I have seen the Lord" (20:18 in 20:11–18); "We have seen the Lord" (20:25 summarizing 20:19–23); "My Lord and my God!" (20:28 in 20:24–29); the epilogue follows the same pattern in 21:1–14, where the beloved disciple is permitted the final confession, "It is the Lord" (21:7).[2]

The chapter also unites various responses to Jesus, illustrating the diverse ways people can become believers in the resurrection: the beloved disciple believes when he sees Jesus' grave clothes (20:1–10); Mary believes when Jesus calls her name (20:11–18); the disciples believe when they see him (20:19–23); Thomas, more skeptical, believes when called to probe (20:24–29); and finally, the Gospel praises most highly those who believe without seeing (20:29).[3]

## Historical Questions

Although literary analysis may be more fruitful in discerning the Gospel's message (the purpose most relevant for its many readers today who wish to translate that message for fresh cultural situations), historical questions remain important for students of early Christian history. The Fourth Gospel's genre invites us to investigate the reliability of its historical claims, to whatever degree such an investigation is possible. Although external corroboration for most details may no longer remain extant, strong evidence appears to favor the substantial picture of resurrection appearances.[4]

### 1. The Traditions

Probably John's resurrection narratives represent discrete units of tradition woven by the evangelist into a seamless whole.[5] The empty tomb account resembles Mark and Matthew, the remainder of his account being closer to Luke; but as many scholars recognize,

---

[1] Niccacci, "Fede," emphasizes parallels between 1:19–51 and 20:1–29, including in the four units of each section (some others make the parallels with the epilogue, ch. 21—e.g., Breck, "Conclusion"; Ellis, "Authenticity").

[2] Cf. Sabugal, "Resurrección."

[3] See Brown, "Resurrection."

[4] Here we have used material especially from Keener, *Matthew*, 697–712.

[5] Dodd, *Tradition*, 148.

John probably used "traditions which lie behind the Synoptic Gospels, and not the Gospels themselves."[6]

Various non-Markan material recurs in two of the other gospels (e.g., Matt 28:6; cf. Luke 24:6), suggesting access to non-Markan resurrection traditions or perhaps material in a now lost ending of Mark,[7] if indeed the ending we have in Mark 16:8 was not the original one (a disputable premise).[8] It is, in fact, difficult to doubt that such other traditions would have existed, given the large number of reported witnesses to the resurrection (cf. 1 Cor 15:5–7).

Some scholars are convinced that one can completely harmonize the stories of the women at the tomb if we grant that the Gospel writers only reported data essential to their distinctive accounts;[9] on the other end of the spectrum, some, while acknowledging that the conviction of the resurrection is early, doubt that our current Easter stories belong to the earliest stratum of tradition.[10] Although harmonization approaches become strained when they misunderstand the liberties literary historians sometimes applied on details (see our introduction, ch. 1), they do exhibit the merit of working harder than more skeptical approaches to make the best possible sense of the data we have. On any account, two matters are plain and a third likely follows: (1) the differences in accounts demonstrate that the Gospel writers were aware of a variety of independent traditions. The likely diversity and number of such traditions precisely here (more so than at many other points in extant gospel tradition) suggest a variety of initial reports, not merely later divergences in an originally single tradition. Sanders may be right to argue that "a calculated deception should have produced greater unanimity. Instead, there seem to have been *competitors:* 'I saw him first!' 'No! I did.'"[11] Eyewitness reports often varied on such details (e.g., Thucydides 1.22.3). (2) The divergent details suggest independent traditions, thereby underlining the likelihood of details the accounts share in common.[12] Yet these divergent traditions overlap significantly and hence independently corroborate the basic outlines of the story. (3) Given the likely variety of initial reports, explaining the similarities and differences in terms of multiple witnesses surrounding a core historical event appears plausible and indeed probable. (One might compare eyewitnesses' different accounts of Callisthenes' death, which nevertheless agree that he was indicted, publicly scorned, and died.)[13]

---

[6] See Lindars, "Composition," 147. He believes that John utilized his material creatively (Lindars, *Behind,* 76).

[7] Wenham, "Narratives"; Gundry, *Matthew,* 590–91.

[8] The sudden ending in Mark 16:8 fits some ancient narration patterns; though in some cases, e.g., *L.A.B.,* the ending may be lost, one may compare also abrupt original endings, e.g., in some of Plutarch's speeches (*Fame of Athenians* 8, *Mor.* 351B; *Fort. Alex.* 2.13, *Mor.* 345B; *Fort. Rom.* 13, *Mor.* 326C; *Uned. R.* 7, *Mor.* 782F); Isocrates *Demon.* 52, *Or.* 1; Demetrius 5.304; Lucan *C.W.* 10.542–546; Herodian 8.8.8. See esp. Magness, *Sense,* for more ancient literary parallels; for consistency with Markan style, especially a final γάρ, cf. Boomershine and Bartholomew, "Technique." An abbreviated conclusion allows Mark to retain the centrality of the cross without actually playing down the resurrection (cf. also Thompson, *Debate,* 225), because he points to resurrection appearances beyond his narrative (e.g., Anderson, *Mark,* 353; Rhoads and Michie, *Mark,* 42; Hooker, *Mark,* 120). Farmer, *Verses,* even makes a noteworthy case on external (pp. 3–75) and internal (79–103) grounds that Mark 16:9–20 has more support for being the original ending than usually accepted.

[9] E.g., Hodges, "Tomb."

[10] E.g., Dibelius, *Jesus,* 139.

[11] Sanders, *Figure,* 280.

[12] E.g., Boyd, *Sage,* 277–78.

[13] Arrian *Alex.* 4.14.3.

The various resurrection narratives vary considerably in length, focus, and detail. If Q included a resurrection narrative (a thesis that would probably be greeted with skepticism, since most of it is held to be sayings, but for which we lack concrete evidence either way), most of the Gospel writers treated it as one among many; given the many witnesses of the risen Christ (1 Cor 15:6), it is hardly surprising that numerous accounts would exist and different Gospel writers would draw on different accounts. The four gospels differ in detail, but in all four the women become the first witnesses, and Mary Magdalene is explicitly named as one witness among them (also *Gos. Pet.* 12:50–13:57).[14]

The variation in length of the Gospels' resurrection narratives (Luke 24 is long though recapitulated briefly in Acts 1; Mark 16:1–8 and Matt 28 are quite brief; John includes both Judean and Galilean appearances) may represent the desire to make optimum use of the scroll length instead of leaving a blank space at the end (as sometimes happened, Diogenes Laertius 6.2.38). Josephus seems once caught unexpectedly by the end of his scroll (Josephus *Ag. Ap.* 1.320); Matthew, approaching the length limit of his standardized scroll (see introduction, p. 7), may hasten to his conclusion; Luke may have sufficient space remaining to provide further detail before his closing. John's "second" conclusion (ch. 21) fits the Gospel if John employed a scroll of standardized length, but by early in ch. 20 it would be clear to either the Fourth Gospel's author or a later disciple how much space would remain at ch. 20's completion.

## 2. Pagan Origins for the Christian Resurrection Doctrine?

Supposed pagan parallels to the resurrection stories are weak; Aune even declares that "no parallel to them is found in Graeco-Roman biography."[15] Whether any "parallels" exist depends on what we mean by a "parallel"; but plainly none of the alleged parallels involves a resurrected person, probably in part because resurrection in its strict sense was an almost exclusively Jewish belief. Most pagans would have preferred to play down a savior's human death (cf. Philostratus *Vit. Apoll.* 7.14).[16] Ancients commonly reported apparitions of deceased persons (e.g., Apuleius *Metam.* 8.8; 9.31; *'Abot R. Nat.* 40A)[17] or deities, and hence occasionally those of persons who had become immortal (e.g., Plutarch's reports of Romulus more than half a millennium earlier),[18] but these are not *resurrection* appearances.

Even the appearance of Apollonius of Tyana, which exhibits some parallels with the Gospel accounts (Philostratus *Vit. Apoll.* 8.31),[19] is not an exception. This story appears in

---

[14] Ancient sources more often than not left women unnamed (see Ilan, "Distribution"), but Mary is abundantly dcoumented in the resurrection traditions (Mark 16:1; Matt 28:1; Luke 24:10).

[15] See Aune, "Problem," 48.

[16] See Boring et al., *Commentary*, 151.

[17] One supposed divine apparition turned out to be a conjured ghost of a gladiator (one of low class; Eunapius *Lives* 473). Likewise, although the biblical tradition reported only apparitions of angels in dreams, both pagan (e.g., Homer *Il.* 23.65, 83–85; Euripides *Hec.* 30–34, 703–706; Virgil *Aen.* 1.353–354; 2.268–297, 772–794; 4.351–352; 5.721–723; Ovid *Metam.* 11.586–588, 635, 650–673; Apuleius *Metam.* 8.8; 9.31; Plutarch *Bravery of Women, Mor.* 252F) and Jewish (*'Abot R. Nat.* 40A; *Pesiq. Rab Kah.* 11:23; *p. Ḥag.* 2:2, §5; *Ketub.* 12:3, §7; *Sanh.* 6:6, §2; cf. *Acts Paul* 11.6) dreams often included apparitions of deceased persons.

[18] In Talbert, *Gospel*, 41; cf. Plutarch *Camillus* 33.7. Boring et al., *Commentary*, 163–64, cites Romulus's apotheosis appearance to Proculus Julius in Livy 1.16.2–8; Plutarch *Romulus* 28; *Numa* 11.3; Ovid *Fasti* 2.500–509 and notes that Justin *1 Apol.* 21 made an apologetic comparison between Jesus' resurrection appearances and pagan understanding of imperial apotheosis.

[19] Sanders, *Jesus and Judaism*, 320.

a third-century source, after Christian teaching on the resurrection had become widely disseminated; further and more to our present point, Apollonius proves that he has not died, not that he has risen.[20] In another third-century C.E. work by the same author, the hero Protesilaos appears to people and lives on; he is said to have "come back to life," though he refuses to explain the nature of this claim (*Hrk.* 58.2). But whatever else his "return" from death might claim, it does not involve bodily resurrection: his body remains buried (9.1).[21] Even claims like this made for Protesilaos do not predate the rise and spread of Christianity.[22]

Nor do stories about magical resuscitation of corpses have much in common—for example, when a witch drills holes in the corpse to pour in hot blood, dog froth, and so forth.[23] Ancient readers never supposed that bodily immortality followed such resuscitations, because they did not connect them with any doctrine like the Jewish notion of eschatological resurrection. Celsus, a second-century critic of Christians, was fully able to distinguish bodily resurrection from "old myths of returning from the Underworld" and hence argued instead that Jesus' resurrection was merely staged, as commonly in novels.[24]

Most cultures believe in some form of life after death, and such cultures frequently accept some form of contact with the spirits of the dead or some of the dead. Such phenomena may help explain how ancient Mediterranean hearers may have conceived of Jesus' resurrection appearances; but to cite them as "parallels" to those appearances, as if they define the latter, stretches the category of parallel too far to be useful. If Jesus rose again, how would the disciples know it and proclaim it if he failed to appear to them?

## 2A. Mystery Cults as Background?

Some have offered parallels between dying-and-rising deities, especially in the Mysteries, and the early Christian teaching of the resurrection. We must therefore address the alleged parallels first and then turn to what proves a far closer background for the early Christian teaching of the resurrection and the first articulations of it offered even in a Greco-Roman setting (see 1 Cor 15).

The Mysteries apparently influenced some Palestinian Jewish thought in late antiquity, though the exact date is unclear. Numismatic evidence indicates some presence of the Mysteries in Palestine;[25] the influence of a third-century C.E. Mithraeum in Caesarea[26] is unclear, since Caesarea was of mixed population and the date is much later than our

---

[20] Blackburn, "ΑΝΔΡΕΣ," 193.

[21] He visits both Hades and the world of the living (Philostratus *Hrk.* 11.7) but visits his wife only in Hades (11.8). Others returned from Hades without immortality (e.g., Antonius Diogenes *Thule* 109ab).

[22] See Bowersock, *Fiction as History,* 108–13; even his mid-first-century parallel does not indicate a bodily resurrection (it may simply mean "a brief tryst with his wife," 112, as in earlier sources; see Petronius *Sat.* 129.1).

[23] Lucan *C.W.* 6.667–775; cf. Antonius Diogenes *Thule* 110b. Resuscitation stories are common (see our introduction to John 11), but most simply claim apparent deaths (Bowersock, *Fiction as History,* 99–100, 104–8; more convincing are OT parallels), which often invite suspense on behalf of characters with whom readers have begun to identify; see, e.g., Xenophon *Eph.* 3.5–7; *Apoll. K. Tyre* 25–26; Iamblichus *Bab. St.* 3–6 (Photius *Bibliotheca* 94.74b–75a).

[24] Bowersock, *Fiction as History,* 117–18.

[25] Avi-Yonah, "Sources," 60; Flusser, "Paganism."

[26] On the Mithraeum, see Bull, "Medallion"; Lease, "Mithraeum"; Flusser, "Paganism," 1099.

period.[27] Mystery language may have infiltrated some forms of Judaism,[28] but the use of such language is hardly evidence for widespread influence.[29] Pagan accusations that confused Judaism and the Mysteries[30] do not constitute good evidence that Judaism as a whole made that confusion; Reitzenstein's claim that "even in Trajan's time the Roman Jewish community still . . . either altogether or in large part worshiped the *Zeus Hupsistos Ouranios* and the Phrygian Attis together with Yahweh"[31] have been refuted by subsequent research into Roman Judaism.[32]

The language of the Mysteries clearly infiltrated Christian writers of the second century and later. Tertullian claims that Christianity has the true Mysteries, of which others are poorer and later copies (*Apol.* 47.14). Such language becomes much more prevalent in the third and fourth centuries C.E.[33] Yet it is in fact possible that some features of the Mysteries by this period derive from Christianity. As they began to lose devotees to Christians in a later period, the Mysteries could have adopted some features of Christianity; many of the "parallels" in the Mysteries are known only from the later period.[34] (The proposed similarities between Mithraism and Christianity[35] also come from the later period in which both had become popular.)[36] That the Fathers understood the Mysteries as "imitation demoniaque du Christianisme"[37] may suggest that they, like many early modern students of these cults, read them through the grid of their own Christian background, and the ready-to-hand explanation of demonic imitation may have led them to heighten rather than play down the similarities between the two.

Much of the most specifically mystery vocabulary is lacking in earliest Christianity: Metzger, following Nock, lists such terms as *mystēs, mystikos, mystagōgos, katharmos, katharsia, katharsis, teletē,* and so on.[38] What is perhaps more significant is the different perspective on the events described by both kinds of religions. As Metzger points out:[39]

> The Mysteries differ from Christianity's interpretation of history. The speculative myths of the cults lack entirely that reference to the spiritual and moral meaning of history which is inextricably involved in the experiences and triumph of Jesus Christ.[40]

---

[27] Cf. Charlesworth, *Pseudepigrapha and NT,* 82.

[28] Cf. arguments in Philonenko, "Initiation"; idem, "Mystère," 65–70; Petuchowski, "Mystery."

[29] Willoughby, *Initiation,* 225–62, tries to compare Philonic language with the conversion language of the Mysteries but, like Godwin, *Mystery Religions,* 78–83, tends to generalize too much. More nuanced is the approach of Wolfson, *Philo,* 1:27–36 (and cf. 1:101; Philo adapts their language but denounces them as religious alternatives).

[30] Russell, "Mysteries," 338; cf. Reitzenstein, *Religions,* 174–84.

[31] Reitzenstein, *Religions,* 125.

[32] On Roman Judaism, see more fully Leon, *Jews.*

[33] Eliade, *Rites,* 120.

[34] Metzger, "Consideration," 10–11; Eliade, *Rites,* 115.

[35] Cf. Gervers, "Iconography," though qualifying on p. 598; cf. Gager, *Kingdom,* 132–34; note the contrast stressed by Mattingly, *Christianity,* 5.

[36] Some others may be coincidence; Deman, "Mithras," e.g., notes the later link between the twelve apostles and the twelve signs of the zodiac; yet the twelve apostles in earliest Christian tradition stem from the twelve tribes (though Judaism had already linked the tribes with the zodiac in that period). The closest true parallels address only later Gentile Christianity as it assimilated into a broader Roman cultural context.

[37] Benoit, "Mystères," 79–81.

[38] Metzger, "Consideration," 11.

[39] Ibid., 20.

[40] Manson, *Paul and John,* 64–65, stresses the moral contrast between the Mysteries (where moral ideals were irrelevant) and Christianity (cf. Carcopino, *Life,* 138–39).

In the apostolic and subapostolic literature,[41]

> in all strata of Christian testimony concerning the resurrection of Jesus Christ, "everything is made to turn upon a dated experience with a historical Person," [citing Nock] whereas nothing in the Mysteries points to any attempt to undergird belief with historical evidence of the god's resurrection.

To notice this is perhaps to notice the different cultural matrixes in which these religions took root; it would be difficult indeed for a cult rooted in Israelite biblical piety to have ignored a *heilsgeschichtliche* perspective on history. In this perspective, God's acts might be celebrated annually in cultic ritual, but they were viewed as unique events secured by the testimony of witnesses and grounded in corporate piety.[42]

Nock points out that while many of Paul's hearers may have understood him in terms of the Mysteries, most of the early Jewish-Christian missionaries, like Paul, had probably had little firsthand exposure to the Mysteries and reflected instead a broader milieu of which the Mysteries were only a part.[43]

## 2B. Dying-and-Rising Deities?

One area of special comparison between the Mysteries and Christianity, especially in early-twentieth-century literature, involves the matter of salvation and of dying and rising gods. The motif of dying and rising gods certainly predates the time of Jesus. Just as fertility fled the earth during Demeter's search for Persephone in the Eleusinian myth,[44] so it flees during the absence of the Hittite deity Telepinus (*ANET* 126–28), the Canaanite Baal (*ANET* 129–42),[45] and perhaps the man Aqhat (*ANET* 149–55).[46] The same theme appears in the late-second-millennium B.C.E. story of Ishtar's descent to the netherworld (*ANET* 108, lines 76–79; cf. reverse, lines 34, 38–49). It seems likely that a much older story line or lines stand behind all the regional variations.

Descent to the underworld in such texts need not be permanent. In the "Epic of Gilgamesh" (6.97–99 [*ANET* 84]), Ishtar forces Anu to comply with her demands by threatening to smash the doors of the netherworld and to raise up the dead so that they outnumber the living, and similarly addresses the gatekeeper of that world in the tale of her descent there ("Descent of Ishtar to the Nether World," lines 12–20 [*ANET* 107]). In a tale perhaps dating to the first half of the second millennium B.C.E. or earlier, Inanna is put to death (though she is a goddess), but after three days and nights, she is restored as the food and water of life are sprinkled sixty times on her corpse (*ANET* 52–57,

---

[41] Metzger, "Consideration," 15.

[42] Cf. Nock, "Vocabulary," 136, for Christianity's "Oriental" nature but lack of "Oriental" trappings. This is not to suggest that many other Greco-Roman cults could not be distinguished from one another but, rather, to point out that the originating cultural matrix of Christianity was different enough, and earliest Christianity's monotheism rigorous enough, to disallow the degree of assimilation that could characterize most of the cults.

[43] Cf. Nock, *Christianity*, 31; Cadbury, *Acts in History*, 28; Meyer, "Mysteries," 724.

[44] Burkert argues that Persephone's connection with the nature cycle must go back to pre-Greek, perhaps Neolithic times because the real facts of Mediterranean vegetation suggest an interpretation earlier than the one the Greeks themselves held (*Religion*, 160). Whether or not his argument is accepted as persuasive, it is clear that Persephone's return from the underworld precedes the apostolic proclamation of Christ's resurrection by many centuries.

[45] Bright, *History*, 118.

[46] Esp. Ginsberg's note, *ANET* 155.

esp. 55).[47] Greeks seem to have been most familiar with Egyptian accounts of dying and rising deities.[48]

But the significance of such parallels remains problematic. Although there is widespread pre-Christian evidence for the account of Osiris's resuscitation (cf. also Plutarch *Isis* 35, *Mor.* 364F), he is magically revivified, not transformed into an eschatological new creation; his corpse is awakened through the same potencies as exist in procreation, and he remains in the netherworld, still needing protection by vigilant gods and replacement on earth by his heir.[49] Adonis's death was mourned annually (e.g., Plutarch *Nicias* 13.7), but his rising is not documented before the middle of the second century C.E.[50] (Some sources suggest seasonal revivification,[51] which, as we argue below, differs greatly from early Jewish and Christian notions and origins of the resurrection.) Attis, too, was mourned as dead, but there is no possible evidence for his resurrection before the third century C.E., and aside from the testimony of the Christian writer Firmicus Maternus, no clear evidence exists before the sixth century C.E.[52]

Dionysus's return from death[53] is clear enough but perhaps in the same category as Heracles' apotheosis or the wounding of Ares in the *Iliad*; mortals could be deified and deities could suffer harm;[54] some also understood him as returning annually for his holy days in the spring.[55] And even Persephone was taken down to the underworld alive, as Orpheus descended alive to rescue his beloved Eurydice.[56] Frazer's scheme of the "dying and rising god" has thus come under heavy criticism in recent times.[57]

Many Christian writers have asserted, again perhaps through the grid of their own religious understanding, that the Mysteries must have provided salvation through union with dying-and-rising gods.[58] While there may be some truth in the idea that a god not subject to death could grant immortality, Burkert cautions, "This multiplicity of images

---

[47] Some have likewise claimed that Marduk died and rose again in some sense (Klausner, *Paul*, 103, though I have not noticed this in *Enuma Elish* in Heidel, *Genesis*, 18–60).

[48] E.g., Maximus of Tyre *Or.* 2.5; cf. also Plutarch *Isis* passim.

[49] Wagner, *Baptism*, 119; on Nile water, see 127–35. The patching together of his parts either reflected or produced a more widespread story line (e.g., Ovid *Metam.* 6.401–411); Greeks also told of severed divine genitals creating life (Uranus's form the Furies, Apollodorus 1.1.4). Some Greeks treated Osiris and Isis as genuine historical characters (Manetho *Aegyptiaca* frg. 1.1, in [Armenian version] Eusebius *Chronicon* 1.p. 93).

[50] Wagner, *Baptism*, 171–207, esp. 195. The Adonis tradition itself was Semitic and imported into Greek religion from an early period (Burkert, *Religion*, 176–77, thinks perhaps as early as the sixth century B.C.E.). Cf. Ovid *Metam.* 10.710–739; Callimachus *Iambi* 3.193.37; Philostratus *Hrk.* 45.6; in the Greek bucolic poets, e.g., *Women at the Adonis Festival* (third century B.C.E.), a lament for Adonis perhaps by Bion, and *The Dead Adonis* (*Greek Bucolic Poets*, LCL 176–95, 386–95, 480–83).

[51] Apollodorus 3.14.4, where Persephone and Aphrodite originally had a time-share agreement about Adonis (probably derived from the Persephone myth about the custody battle between Hades and Demeter, e.g., Apollodorus 1.5.3); cf. Iamblichus *Myst.* 1.11.

[52] Wagner, *Baptism*, 219, 229; for the typical story, see Vermaseren, *Cybele*, 91.

[53] Cf. Otto, *Dionysus*, 79–80, 103–19.

[54] E.g., Homer *Il.* 5.339–342, 382–404, 855–859, 870; on the death of Pan in Plutarch *Mor.* 419.17, see Borgeaud, "Death."

[55] Fragments of dithyrambic poetry (ca. 1 B.C.E.) in *Sel. Pap.* 3:390–93.

[56] E.g., Apollodorus 1.5.3; cf. Guthrie, *Orpheus*, 31.

[57] See documentation in Gasparro, *Soteriology*, 30 n. 16.

[58] E.g., Conzelmann, *Theology*, 11; cf. Case, *Origins*, 111; Bultmann, *Christianity*, 158–59; Ridderbos, *Paul*, 22–29.

can hardly be reduced to a one-dimensional hypothesis, one ritual with one dogmatic meaning: death and rebirth of 'the' god and the initiand."[59] Much of the evidence is late[60] or specifically Christian (e.g., Firmicus Maternus *De errore profanarum religionum* 22).[61] More recent writers are therefore generally more cautious about connecting spiritual salvation (when it appears in the Mysteries) with the dying-deity motif.[62]

In the Eleusinian rites, the *mystēs* received the promise of a happy afterlife, but by being pledged to the goddess rather than being reborn or by dying and rising with the deity.[63] The cult of Cybele also does not support the common conclusion, as Gasparro notes.[64] The main problem with the view that many members of the old *Religionsgeschichte* school, eager to produce "parallels" to primitive Christianity, adduced, is that most of the people who turned to the Mysteries already believed in some afterlife in the netherworld anyway; it was merely a happier afterlife in that world that the gods could guarantee.

Those, like Bousset, who drew such connections[65] did not take adequate account of the vegetative, cyclical, and seasonal nature of most of the resuscitation rituals.[66] This is a far cry from the earliest Christian picture of Christ's bodily resurrection, rooted in explicit Jewish eschatological hopes—a perspective on the resurrection that Paul affirms is guaranteed by hundreds of eyewitnesses, including himself, and that he argues, despite his Hellenistic audience, is a necessary understanding of resurrection for a true follower of Jesus (1 Cor 15). One would not think that earlier Palestinian Christianity held a less rigorously Jewish perspective than Paul did.[67]

While the third day is used for resurrection in the later ritual for Attis and perhaps for Adonis, these may be based on Christian precedents.[68] (Some Greeks may have also thought of "three days" in terms of some burial traditions.)[69] The third day in the cult of Osiris is most significant, but the traditional Jewish view about the corpse, the use of a "third day" for an interval between two events in close succession in the Hebrew Bible, and the inherent likelihood of some coincidence between a brief period in early Christian tradition and one in the Mysteries qualify its significance considerably. Some other Jewish traditions may also shed light on this idea, but appeal to them must remain tentative because of their uncertain date or because they were not widely enough recognized to have

---

[59] Burkert, *Cults*, 100.

[60] E.g., Apuleius, whom Dunand, "Mystères," 58, interprets thus.

[61] In Grant, *Religions*, 146.

[62] E.g., Davies, *Paul*, 91.

[63] Wagner, *Baptism*, 87. Thus Heracles sought initiation so he could capture Cerberus in Hades (Apollodorus 2.5.12).

[64] Gasparro, *Soteriology*, 82.

[65] Bousset, *Kyrios Christos*, 57.

[66] For the vegetative association see, e.g., Ovid *Metam.* 5.564–571; Gasparro, *Soteriology*, 29, 43–49; Ruck, "Mystery," 44–45; Guthrie, *Orpheus*, 55–56.

[67] Cf. Metzger, "Consideration," 19–20; Ring, "Resurrection," 228.

[68] Bousset's Hellenistic parallels (*Kyrios Christos*, 58) are unconvincing (cf. Nock, *Christianity*, 105–6; Jeremias, *Theology*, 304; Fuller, *Formation*, 25). Many think that the LXX is a more likely source (Hos 6:2; Jonah 1:17; cf. 1 Cor 15:4; Nock, *Christianity*, 108), though it is unlikely that the early Christians would have noticed elements favoring it had the "third day" not been their initial experience. (Rabbis associated Hos 6:2 with the resurrection of the dead; see *p. Sanh.* 11:6, §1; cf. McArthur, "Day," 83–84.)

[69] Cf. Thucydides 2.34.2 for honoring Athenian war dead.

been obvious without explicit qualification.[70] The fixing of the third day in the pre-Pauline formula in 1 Cor 15:3, however, weights the case in favor of a Palestinian Jewish-Christian tradition for Jesus' resurrection prior to any exposure to the cult of Osiris in the Hellenistic world.[71] And while gods could often die in the Mysteries, their deaths were not portrayed as triumphant or meaningful as in many strands of early Christian tradition. Further, the Gospel narratives suggest that to whatever the early Christians might have adapted the language of three days, they historically intended only parts of three days.[72]

## 2C. Jewish Doctrine of the Resurrection

The Jewish doctrine of the resurrection was not simply an assertion of immortality. Because Greek religion in general, like many religions in the world,[73] addressed the survival of the soul after death,[74] it should not surprise us that the Eleusis cult promised a happy life in the underworld,[75] that Isis promised patronage and protection,[76] and that the Dionysiac Mysteries may have indicated a happy afterlife.[77] But there is little evidence for any future hopes in the cult of Cybele, and certainly none linked with Attis.[78] When the early Christian picture of bodily resurrection plainly derives directly from Jewish eschatological teaching, one casts the net rather widely to make all human hopes for afterlife parallel to it.[79]

Mack makes Jesus' resurrection purely mythical[80] by wrongly equating immortality in Wisdom of Solomon with "resurrection" in 2 Maccabees, by wrongly interpreting eschatological *narratives* about Christ's resurrection as if they were eschatological allegory, and by wrongly taking the Spirit in a purely Hellenistic sense instead of its Jewish usage, easily

---

[70] Some later traditions suggest the retention of the soul for three days after death (until the soul sees the body begin to decompose; *Gen. Rab.* 100:7; *Lev. Rab.* 18:1; though cf. Dola, "Interpretacja") or required three days of purgatory before preparation to appear before God (*3 En.* 28:10; cf. *Apoc. Zeph.* 4:7) or that one confirm the actuality of the person's death within three days (Safrai, "Home," 784–85). This might possibly fit a broader idea expressed in three days of mourning (Apollonius of Rhodes 2.837).

[71] Metzger, "Consideration," 18–19.

[72] E.g., Ign. *Trall.* 9; Augustine *On the Trinity* 4.6, 10 (Oden and Hall, *Mark,* 238). The third day can mean "after three days," as in *L.A.B.* 11:1–3, or *parts* of each of three days (Scott, *Customs,* 260; *p. Kil.* 2:2, §1, on *t. Kil.* 1:16); in either case, it means "soon" (Gen 40:12–13, 18–19; Exod 3:18).

[73] Some utterly unrelated cultures also supply examples of resurrection legends (e.g., the Sonjo myth in Mbiti, *Religions,* 251), although without the historical attestation surrounding the case of Jesus. But given the transcultural interest in life after death, one need not suppose an organic connection among all such accounts except when they are geographically close and the story line is substantially similar.

[74] E.g., Herodotus *Hist.* 2.123; Plato *Phaedo* 64CD, 80DE. For further references, see comment on John 3:6.

[75] Burkert, *Cults,* 21; Grant, *Hellenism,* 11–12; Mylonas, *Eleusis,* 268–69; Wagner, *Baptism,* 87.

[76] Wagner, *Baptism,* 112.

[77] Burkert, *Religion,* 293–95; idem, *Cults,* 21–22.

[78] Gasparro, *Soteriology,* 84–106, 125; Wagner, *Baptism,* 255–56.

[79] Cumont's view of astral immortality (Cumont, *After Life,* 91–109; cf. Reitzenstein, *Religions,* 64–65; Dahl, *Paul,* 17; Avi-Yonah, *Hellenism,* 40–41) is much broader than the Mysteries and thus should not be directly linked to them (Gasparro, *Soteriology,* 98). The doctrine of bodily resurrection apparently also appears in the Hebrew Bible earlier than it is attested in Persian texts (Yamauchi, *Persia,* 456–57, 461; cf. 409; for immortality, however, cf. Olmstead, *History,* 40, 100–101).

[80] Mack, *Myth,* 112–13.

demonstrable in early Christianity.[81] Pagan afterlife notions and myths of risen deities did provide Gentiles a handle for apprehending aspects of early Christian teaching about the resurrection,[82] but the Christian teaching remains distinctly Jewish in its origin. The teaching appears in some OT texts (Isa 26:19; Dan 12:2)[83] and probably has early antecedents in Israel's history, though personalized eschatology appears in texts only after the exile.[84]

Not all streams of early Judaism clearly articulate a doctrine of bodily resurrection. The Sadducees denied it (Josephus *Ant.* 18.16–17; *War* 2.165);[85] rabbinic texts, which here probably represent the populist Pharisaic consensus, complain about the offensiveness of such a denial.[86] The evidence we do have from Qumran supports the likelihood that the Qumran community accepted it, though we lack concrete evidence.[87] Clearly the Pharisees and their probable successors in the rabbinic movement[88] affirmed the doctrine of the bodily resurrection,[89] almost equating belief in it with belief in the afterlife.[90] But the Pharisees were the most popular "sect," according to Josephus, and popular views of the afterlife might be expected to follow an optimistic rather than a pessimistic line of thought, though history does afford exceptions.

In any case, widepread attestation indicates that the doctrine was much more widely held than among the Pharisees, representing common Judaism (e.g., *Pss. Sol.* 3:12; 15:12–13; *1 En.* 22:13).[91] Indeed, the widespread use of Daniel (especially in the LXX) would almost require this (Dan 12:2). The Second Benediction of the *Amidah* undoubtedly was recited beyond Pharisaic circles. The use of ossuaries for secondary burial in the

---

[81] On the last point, see Keener, *Spirit*, 6–48; Turner, *Spirit*, 1–18.

[82] Cf. Lewis, *Life*, 100.

[83] See Ferguson, *Backgrounds*, 439.

[84] Cf. Wifall, "Status."

[85] Osborne, "Resurrection," 932, cites also some Hellenistic works (4 Macc; Wis 2:23–24; 3:1–4; Philo *Creation* 135; *Giants* 14; perhaps also *1 En.* 103:4); and, as denying even immortality, Sirach (17:27–28; 30:17; 37:26; 39:9; 44:8–15; 46:19).

[86] Rabbinic texts often emphasize that the Sadducees, unlike Pharisees, denied the teaching and hence held no place in the coming world (e.g., *m. Sanh.* 10:1; ʾ*Abot R. Nat.* 5A; 10, §26B; cf. *b. Sanh.* 90b). The doctrine of the resurrection was particularly relevant in the context of martyrdom (2 Macc 7:9, 11; 14:46); those inclined to defend the honor of martyrs hence took serious offense at the denial (rabbinic texts also suggest moral consequences for denying resurrection and judgment, which they viewed together).

[87] See Puech, *Croyance*; Sanders, *Judaism*, 370; cf. Ulrichsen, "Troen." The supposed resurrection of the Teacher of Righteousness is based on inference from a reconstructed text (cf. 4QpPs 37 frg. 2.2–4, in Dupont-Sommer, *Writings*, 272), which other scholars have reconstructed quite differently.

[88] E.g., Stemberger, "Auferstehungslehre"; in the Targumim, see, e.g., *Tg. Hos.* 14:8; McNamara, *Targum*, 136.

[89] This is true though Josephus, adapting his depiction of Jewish "sects" to Greek schools such as the Pythagoreans and middle Platonists, depicts the Pharisaic confidence in more acceptable Hellenistic terms suggesting reincarnation (Josephus *Ant.* 18.14; *War* 2.163; 3.374; *Ag. Ap.* 2.218).

[90] They condemned a few others for its denial besides explicit Sadducees, e.g., *p. Sanh.* 10:2, §11. Other texts regularly defend the resurrection long after the Sadducees themselves had ceased to be an issue (e.g., *Lev. Rab.* 27:4; *Lam. Rab.* 3:23, §8), but that the rabbis would engage in "textbook apologetics" (not uncommon in some more traditional religious circles today) would not be surprising, given the variety of hypothetical legal situations they also surveyed.

[91] Also 2 Macc 7:9, 14, 23, 29; *2 Bar.* 30:1; *L.A.B.* 3:10; *T. Ab.* 7:16B; cf. *T. Jud.* 25:1–4; *Zeb.* 10:2; *Apocr. Ezek.* introduction. See more fully Osborne, "Resurrection," 933 (who adds to those above *1 En.* 46:6; 51:1–2; *Ps. Sol.* 13:9–11; 14:4–10; 4 Ezra 4:41–43; 7:32–38; *2 Bar.* 49:2–51:12; 85:13).

first century may also support the widespread character of belief in the bodily resurrection.[92] (Compare also the graffito in Greek at Beth She'arim: "Good fortune in your resurrection.")[93] Sanders is probably right that nearly everyone but the Sadducees affirmed the doctrine.[94]

The belief was probably less widely held initially in the Diaspora, though some evidence for it exists.[95] Some Hellenistic Jewish writers, while accommodating the idea to Hellenistic notions of immortality (e.g., Ps.-Phoc. 105) and the language of deification (104), also allude to the doctrine of bodily resurrection (102–104). Perhaps after rabbinic Judaism consolidated its influence, the doctrine of a literal, bodily resurrection also became standard in much of the Diaspora.[96] Paul's contention with the Corinthian Christians might reflect not only pagan Greek but also first-century Hellenistic Jewish aversion to discussion about the resurrection;[97] although many Diaspora Jews would affirm the resurrection and most would know about the doctrine, in the first century it was probably most widespread in Palestine, to the east, and among the least hellenized communities. But the Christian idea of resurrection was not simply adopted wholesale from Judaism without an adaptation: traditional Jewish expectation was a collective, future resurrection.[98] The notion of an individual's bodily resurrection fulfilled in history would therefore not arise without more factors (many of us would argue the experience of the disciples) to explain it.

## 3. Conclusion: Historicity of the Resurrection Tradition?

All our early Christian sources unanimously affirm the doctrine of the bodily resurrection of Jesus,[99] although 1 Cor 15 attests that Paul had to deal with Gentiles who could assimilate the Palestinian Jewish doctrine only with difficulty and did not wish to accept it beyond the case of Jesus. Within earliest Christianity, however, there remains no debate about the received tradition that Jesus himself rose bodily, unless one is inclined to count inferences by some modern scholars without explicit supporting evidence. By some point in the second century, however, gnostics and others who found the notion of a bodily resurrection of any sort incompatible with Platonic metaphysics sought to interpret the early Christian tradition differently (cf., e.g., in Irenaeus *Haer.* 2.29). Orthodox Jewish scholar Pinhas Lapide, although doubting that the resurrection proves Jesus' messianic or divine

---

[92] Rahmani, "Glwsqmwt"; cf. Goodenough, *Symbols*, 1:164–77. Ossuaries belong especially to the Roman imperial period and the pre-Israelite Chalcolithic period (see Silberman, "Ossuary"). But Levine, *Hellenism*, 65–67, argues that ossuaries are irrelevant to belief in the resurrection (they could have adapted instead the Roman custom of secondary burial of cremated ashes).

[93] Finegan, *Archeology*, 208.

[94] Sanders, *Jesus and Judaism*, 237; cf. Wright, *People of God*, 320–34; Schuller, "Resurrection."

[95] Some evidence exists in contemporary Egyptian Judaism, but Philo himself never mentions the doctrine (Wolfson, *Philo*, 1:404). The Samaritans may well have accepted it, though our evidence here is late (see MacDonald, *Samaritans*, 376). For Rome ca. 100 C.E., Boring et al., *Commentary*, 289, cites *CIJ* 1.348–350.

[96] See Garte, "Resurrection."

[97] One might think that more factitity stands behind Paul's assertion in Acts 23:6 than the narrative otherwise supports, but see also Acts 24:15.

[98] Collins, "Apotheosis," 97.

[99] One cannot, however, cite the widespread use of crosses on early ossuaries, which probably are simply markings for the placement of the lids (Smith, "Cross Marks"). Is Gustafsson, "Graffiti," more helpful?

identity (connected though this has traditionally been to the resurrection),[100] nevertheless finds the evidence for his resurrection compelling.[101] Many scholars doubt the resurrection on philosophical or other grounds, but Ladd is generally correct that "those scholars who are unable to believe in an actual resurrection of Jesus admit that the disciples believed it."[102]

# Mary at the Tomb (20:1–18)

The faithfulness of Mary Magdalene frames, hence unites, the first two paragraphs of the resurrection narrative (20:1–2, 11–18), emphasizing the important roles played by women in this narrative—whose behavior again shames the supposedly bolder men (see comment on 19:25).[103] Eastern Christianity later called Mary "isapostolos," "equal to the apostles."[104] Some early medieval commentators found in women's initial resurrection announcement a reversal of Eve's role at the fall.[105] As in the earliest tradition, Mary is the first to find the tomb empty and the first to see Jesus risen from the dead.

## 1. The Empty Tomb (20:1–10)

Mary comes to the tomb first (20:1), and because she remains at the tomb after the male disciples leave (20:10–11), she also receives the first resurrection appearance in 20:15–16.

### 1A. Mary's Discovery (20:1–2)

Although the narrative focuses on Mary (perhaps for purposes of reader identification, esp. at 20:16, after she returns to the tomb), John undoubtedly knows the tradition that several women came to the tomb together, of whom Mary was one (Mark 16:1; Luke 23:55–24:1). This is evident both from the plural οἴδαμεν in 20:2 and the unlikelihood of the disciples' allowing a woman to travel alone (especially when she was not from the area).[106] The focus on Mary may permit the focus on personal relationship the narrative seems to develop (compare 20:16 with 10:3), and fits John's characteristic "staging" technique of often focusing on individuals (e.g., 3:1–9; 4:7–26; 5:1–9; 9:1–7; 11:20–37).

That it was yet dark (20:1) could symbolize Mary coming from darkness to the light (cf. 3:21); but in contrast to Nicodemus, Mary appears so positively here that other explanations are more likely. Because the Synoptics mention only that it was early but John that it was "dark" (cf. also 13:30), John may play on his light-and-darkness symbolism a different way; the light of the world was about to be revealed in its darkness.[107] The darkness may indicate Mary's fear (cf. 3:2) or may emphasize her devotion (cf. 20:16–17) in coming as soon as possible after the Sabbath and the night that followed it. Other accounts show

---

[100] See Rivkin, "Meaning," 398.

[101] See the review in Kennedy, "Resurrection."

[102] Ladd, *Theology,* 320.

[103] On Mary's positive role in discipleship here, see Evenson, "Mary"; Grassi, "Leadership Roles"; on women in this Gospel in general, see comment on 4:28–30.

[104] Davies and Allison, *Matthew,* 3:637.

[105] Bede *Commentary on Acts* 12.13; *Homilies on the Gospels* (Oden and Hall, *Mark,* 247).

[106] Blomberg, *Reliability,* 259. Matthew also abbreviates (two women, Matt 28:1).

[107] Cf. Whitacre, *John,* 471–72.

mourners coming at the moment of dawn to show their affection for someone they loved dearly.[108] Thus, perhaps as the priests were eager to dispense with Jesus as "early" as possible (18:28), she is unable to sleep and eager to demonstrate her devotion as early as possible.

As in John 20:1 (cf. 20:19, 26), all the Gospel narratives agree that the revelation of Christ's resurrection began on the first day of the week, after the Sabbath (Matt 28:1; Mark 16:1; Luke 24:1). Especially in Mark and Matthew, this language makes it clear that the earliest Christians regarded Sunday as a special day celebrating the resurrection (cf. Acts 20:7; 1 Cor 16:2),[109] perhaps even "the Lord's day" (cf. Rev 1:10; *Did.* 14.1),[110] though not as a new Sabbath (this developed in the second century and later; cf. Ign. *Magn.* 9.1; *Barn.* 15.8–9),[111] which among the earliest Jewish Christians remained on the last day of the week.[112] The tradition is too early to be influenced by Mithraism,[113] which did not spread widely in the Roman world until the next century;[114] this simply was the day Jesus' followers found the empty tomb, the day after the Sabbath. Sunday became the Lord's Day because of the discovery of the empty tomb rather than the reverse.

When Mary sees the stone removed from the tomb entrance (20:1; contrast the need in 11:38–41), her inference that Jesus' body was removed (20:2) was a natural one (Chariton 3.3.1). Stones in front of tombs were not easily moved (see comment on 19:41), so it would not be missing without a purpose. Yet John's audience, by this point accustomed to this Gospel's irony, might recognize some truth in her words: God had taken away their Lord, and they did not yet know where he was (13:33, 36). Her title for Jesus is significant and may reflect John's theology of the resurrection proclamation (even though Mary, within the story world, does not yet suspect that he has risen). Jesus is comparatively rarely called "Lord" in this Gospel (by the postresurrection narrator: 4:1; 6:23; 11:2; cf. 13:13–14), except in the vocative (the force of which can be ambiguous), until his resurrection, after which not only the narrator (20:20) but also the disciples (20:2, 13, 18, 25; 21:7, 12; cf. 20:28) recognize his Lordship.[115]

---

[108] E.g., Chariton 3.3.1 (though Chaereas intends suicide). The most intense days of the Jewish mourning period would still be in effect, but one close to the deceased might go to the tomb to weep there (John 11:31).

[109] Cf. more certainly Justin *1 Apol.* 67; Irenaeus frg. 7. In Qumran imagery possibly related to a new creation, the dove returned with the olive leaf, and the earth was completely dry, on Sunday (4Q252 frg. 1, col. 1, line 17; col. 2, line 2, on Gen 8:14).

[110] Vanni, "Giorno"; but note Strand, "Day"; Lewis, "Ignatius."

[111] Chadwick, *Church,* 128; Bacchiocchi, *Sabbath;* Hinson, "Worshiping," 20; later, Athanasius *Homilies* (in Oden and Hall, *Mark,* 240); cf. discussion in Keener, *Revelation,* 87.

[112] As early as *L.A.E.* 51:2, an emphasis on the seventh-day resurrection may polemicize against the Christian eighth-day tradition.

[113] *Pace* Cary and Haarhoff, *Life,* 344.

[114] Grant, *Gods,* 40–41. It already existed in other areas, such as the northern coast of the Black Sea (Blawatsky and Kochelenko, *Culte*) or farther to the east (cf. Cumont, "Mithraeum"; Francis, "Graffiti"); it later spread widely in the Roman army (Daniels, "Army"; Gager, *Kingdom,* 134; Serban and Baluta, "Mithraism"; Koester, *Introduction,* 1:372–74; Burkert, *Cults,* 7, 42) but even then remained limited to particular parts of the empire (Frank, *Aspects,* 49–50; Nock, "Mithraism," 113; Daniels, "Army," 273; Bianchi, "Epilegomena," 879).

[115] Manns, "Christologie johannique," thinks the sevenfold repetition of "Lord" in 20:1–29 provides an *inclusio* with the seven christological titles in 1:19–51; this is possible, but one wonders how many readers (and especially hearers) would have counted. Bousset's proposal that John omits the title because Christ's followers are not his servants in the Johannine community (15:15; *Kyrios Christos,* 212) is utterly inadequate (cf. 15:20), especially in view of the abundant postresurrection use.

## 1B. The Missing Body (20:1–7)

Because Paul explicitly reports only resurrection appearances, some suppose that the empty-tomb tradition was a myth.[116] Weeden, for instance, is among those who doubt that the empty-tomb tradition precedes Mark; his claim that there is no "hard evidence that the early church ever knew of Jesus' grave's being empty"[117] suggests that it did not occur to him that anyone would have checked the tomb—an omission of investigation as unlikely in Roman antiquity as today. Yet Boyd rightly questions whether Mark could have been inventing 16:1–8 as apologetic—aside from pre-Markan Semitic expressions in the passage, its conclusion with the women's fear and silence is hardly apologetic, and it lacks mention of corroborating attestation from Joseph of Arimathea or others.[118] The variant versions of the tomb discoveries in the other gospels suggest multiple and pre-Markan empty-tomb traditions. That Paul does not mention it does not mean that he did not believe in it. First, witnesses of the risen Jesus counted as much stronger evidence (an empty tomb does not reveal what happened to the body), so there was no need for Paul to recount the empty tomb in his brief narration of eyewitness evidence. Further, Paul believed that Jesus was "buried" (1 Cor 15:4; cf. Rom 6:4; Col 2:12), and must therefore have assumed that the risen Jesus left the tomb; as noted above, Palestinian Jewish doctrine of resurrection meant transformation of whatever remained of the body. For the same reason, the thesis that Palestinian Jewish disciples and authorities would have simply ignored the tomb after the resurrection appearances strains all credulity. Indeed, the disciples might well have examined the tomb immediately after the Sabbath (hence before most of the appearances), given the need to show respect to their teacher's body.

Nor is there historical merit to the old "swoon" theory (that Jesus was not yet dead and hence managed to revive sufficiently to act "resurrected" but then died somewhere unknown). Crucified persons simply did not revive: Josephus had three friends taken from crosses, and despite medical attention, two died (Josephus *Life* 420–421).[119] Further, if one could revive, one would still be trapped within the tomb, which would lead to death (Chariton 1.4.11–12; 1.8).

Those inventing an empty-tomb tradition would hardly have included women as the first witnesses (see comment on 20:1–2), and "Jesus' resurrection could hardly have been proclaimed in Jerusalem if people knew of a tomb still containing Jesus' body."[120]

Failure to find the body (20:1–2) may reflect an ancient motif (see esp. 2 Kgs 2:16–17; Gen 5:24 LXX)[121] but need not be fictitious; such a narration is appropriate to the belief

---

[116] Cf. Dibelius, *Tradition*, 191, though he admits that, on Jewish presuppositions, a resurrection meant "that the body of Jesus had not remained in the grave," and hence does not claim that Paul did not believe the tomb was empty.

[117] Weeden, *Mark*, 102.

[118] Boyd, *Sage*, 275.

[119] Cf. death a month after a beating, due to swelled intestines (Philostratus *Vit. soph.* 2.10.588). Apuleius *Metam.* 10.11 cites a drug to simulate death (cf. also Diogenes Laertius 8.2.61), but his novel is full of magic herbs that can do almost anything, here accommodating the story line (cf. the similar plot device in Achilles Tatius 3.15–21; 5.18.2; 7.6.2).

[120] Schweizer, *Jesus*, 48. For a fuller defense of the empty-tomb traditions, see Craig, "Tomb"; idem, "Historicity"; idem, "Rise?" 146–52; Ladd, "Resurrection"; on the bodily character of the resurrection, see Craig, "Resurrection," 47–74.

[121] See Boring et al., *Commentary*, 162–63; Robbins, *Jesus*, 192.

that the hero was still (or newly) alive, and in the case of the Gospels is attested for the recent, eyewitness past rather than the distant, legendary past as in most pagan parallels. Admitting historical evidence favoring Jesus' resurrection is not purely the domain of Christian apologetic; for example, without addressing Jesus' resurrection appearances, Vermes, a Jewish scholar closely acquainted with the primary evidence, opines that "the only conclusion acceptable to the historian" must be that the women actually found the tomb empty.[122]

Mary may believe that the owners of the site have removed a body not legally deposited there (20:15), but might also fear the more horrifying possibility of tomb robbers (20:2, 13).[123] Whereas tomb robbers normally carried off wealth, carrying off the body was so rare that it would shock those who heard of it (Chariton 3.3, which also emphasizes the tragedy of a missing corpse).[124] It is not impossible that someone would steal a body, and at least some opponents of the apostolic testimony suggested that this was in fact the fate of Jesus' corpse (Matt 28:13–15).[125] Corpses were used for magic,[126] and people suspected that witches sometimes stole bodies for magic.[127] Indeed, corpses that died violent deaths were considered particularly potent for magic.[128] Nevertheless, one would not expect disciples guilty of its theft to maintain the truth of their claim in the face of death, nor others to withhold the body when bringing it forward in the situation of the emerging Jesus movement could have secured substantial reward. If the disciples did not protect Jesus while he was alive, surely they would not have risked their lives to rob his tomb after his death.[129] Other factors also militate against supposing that the disciples stole the body. Vermes notes, "From the psychological point of view, they would have been too depressed and shaken to be capable of such a dangerous undertaking. But above all, since neither they nor anyone else expected a resurrection, there would have been no purpose in faking one."[130]

---

[122] Vermes, *Jesus the Jew*, 41.

[123] Many scholars think that tomb robberies were common enough to warrant the fear (Kysar, *John,* 296; Beasley-Murray, *John,* 371); cf. Iamblichus *Bab. St.* 7 (Photius *Bibliotheca* 94.75a). Many tomb inscriptions threatened curses on tomb violators (Jeffers, *World,* 45); Cyrus's tomb reportedly bore the warning not to rob it, for it held little wealth (Plutarch *Alex.* 69.2). For the sanctity of tombs, see, e.g., Seneca *Controv.* 4.4 excerpts, introduction; Diodorus Siculus 17.17.3; Dionysius of Halicarnassus *R.A.* 8.24.6; 11.10.1; Appian *R.H.* 8.12.89; Josephus *Ag. Ap.* 2.58.

[124] Cf. also Xenophon *Eph.* 3.8–9; perhaps *Apoll. K. Tyre* 32 (though cf. 44).

[125] Stauffer, *Jesus,* 144–45, who suspects the question also stands behind John 20:15 (where it is not clear), points out that the theory continued to circulate in later times (Justin *Dial.* 108; Tertullian *Spec.* 30).

[126] Lewis, *Life,* 96.

[127] E.g., Apollonius of Rhodes 4.51–53; Lucan *C.W.* 6.538–568, 626; Ovid *Her.* 6.90; see especially the tale of Telephron in Apuleius *Metam.* 2.30; in other cultures, e.g., Mbiti, *Religions,* 261.

[128] *PGM* 1.248–249; 2.49–50; 4.342–343, 1390–1395, 1402–1403, 2211–2217; 57.5–6; 58.5–9; 67.21; 101.1–3; these ghosts were more malevolent (Plutarch *Cimon* 1.6; 6.5–6). If Jesus' enemies considered him a magician (Matt 12:24), some Jewish leaders may have even anticipated the theft of the body as in Matt 27:64. In less severe cases, tombs generally settled for divine threats against robbers (e.g., *IG* 3.1417, in Grant, *Religions,* 9). Both tying rope from a cross (Pliny *Nat.* 28.11.46) and iron pounded through the hands (Lucan *C.W.* 6.547) were used in witchcraft (as a superstitious cure in *m. Šabb.* 6:10; *p. Šabb.* 6:9, §2).

[129] Grave robbing was not only impious (e.g., Plutarch *Mor.* 173B) but a capital offense (e.g., SEG 8.13, in Sherk, *Empire,* 52, §27).

[130] Vermes, *Jesus the Jew,* 40. On Matthew's guards, see Keener, *Matthew,* 696–97, 713–15.

## 1C. The Wrappings (20:5–7)

John is emphatic that only the linen wrappings were κείμενα in the tomb (20:5–7); the body of Jesus no longer ἔκειτο there (20:12).[131] The description of Jesus' wrappings and separate face-cloth (σουδάριον) links Jesus' resurrection with the sign of Lazarus (11:44).[132] Whereas Lazarus needs help to be fully released, however (11:44), Jesus had left his shrouds and face-cloth behind.[133] Hunter suggests that Jesus' face-cloth was "'twirled up' like a turban, just as it had been wrapped around his head,"[134] but this is not a necessary sense of ἐντυλίσσω. More to the point is his observation that the scene was not that of disarray left by thieves acting in haste;[135] Jesus had folded the face-cloth as a sign of his triumph. Most clearly, the fact that the grave clothes remained behind at all testified that the body had not been taken by tomb robbers or anyone else, who would not have taken the body yet left its wrappings. By process of elimination, the missing body but remaining clothes should suggest to the disciples that Jesus' promise about reclaiming his life was literal (10:17–18).

The description of the clothes may also comment on the nature of the resurrection or the supremacy of Christ; it contrasts with the view of many later teachers that people were resurrected in the same shrouds in which they were buried.[136] Another proposal concerning the face-cloth is intriguing in view of our conclusions regarding 1:14–18: Moses' veil represented the partial revelation available under the old covenant, but the "veil" is now left behind because the new covenant revelation is without limit (1:18; 2 Cor 3:7–18).[137] Nevertheless, we cannot be sure that John intended this allusion or that most of his first audience would have grasped it; it is not the term used in 2 Cor 3, and John could have made such an allusion more obvious by employing the LXX term κάλυμμα (Exod 34:33–35), which he does not.[138]

Given the stooping of 20:5, the tomb probably

> had a low entrance and a step down into the central, rectangular pit, with shelves cut into the rock around the pit. . . . If Jesus had been laid on the shelf either to the right or left of the entrance, then only part of the grave clothes would be visible from the entrance. If he had been positioned with his head toward the entrance wall, this would explain why the cloth for Jesus' head was not noticed until they actually entered the tomb.[139]

---

[131] The term κεῖται was common for lying in a tomb; to merely sample some Roman Jewish inscriptions, see, e.g., *CIJ* 1:8, §4; 1:12, §§6–7; 1:14, §§10–11; 1:15, §§12–13; 1:16, §§14–15; 1:17, §17; 1:19, §20; 1:21, §23; 1:23, §28; 1:24, §30; 1:26, §35; 1:30, §42; 1:31, §45; 1:32, §§46–47; 1:35, §§51–52; 1:36, §53; 1:37, §§55–56; 1:38, §58; 1:39, §§62–63; 1:49, §78; 1:52, §79; 1:56, §81; 1:60, §86; 1:62, §88; 1:66, §93; 1:69, §97; 1:70, §§99–100; 1:74, §105.

[132] Winandy, "Vestiges," suggests this connection helps explain the beloved disciple's faith (20:8).

[133] Marsh, *John*, 634; Beasley-Murray, *John*, 372; cf. Osborne, "Napkin," who suggests that Lazarus was still subject to death (cf. the "veil" of Isa 25:7 in light of 25:8 and later rabbinic tradition) but Jesus was not.

[134] Hunter, *John*, 184, arguing (undoubtedly correctly—cf. 20:19—but for the wrong reason) that Jesus' transformed body passed through his grave clothes (cf. also Salvoni, "Proof").

[135] Hunter, *John*, 184. Sanders, *John*, 420, argues that the point is that they are "laid out in an orderly manner," not that Jesus' body passed directly through the clothes.

[136] E.g., *Gen. Rab.* 100:2 (though R. Judah disagrees). Cf. 1 Cor 15:35–38, 53–54.

[137] Schneiders, "Veil," 96. Robert, "Suaire," makes a similar argument from the Aramaic Targumim; but such an argument could at most address John's traditions, not his present Greek text.

[138] Σουδάριον is not specifically technical, appearing among "toilet articles" listed in a dowry (Deissmann, *Studies*, 223), but appears nowhere in the LXX.

[139] Whitacre, *John*, 473. For a description of the tomb in the early Middle Ages by a pilgrim reported in Bede *Homilies on the Gospels* 2.10, see comment on 19:38–42.

1D. The Beloved Disciple, Peter, and Scripture (20:2–10)

Responding to Mary's testimony, Peter and the beloved disciple hurry to the tomb. Some suggest that the lack of contact between men and women disciples at the site of the tomb indicates the joining of separate narratives;[140] although this proposal is possible, it is no less natural to assume that John simply follows his usual staging technique of including only two or three primary characters on stage at one time.[141] (This could also help explain why Mary speaks alone rather than in company with the other women, though John just as easily could have presented them as a composite character, like a chorus, as he sometimes does with Jesus' enemies.)[142] Further, those who rejected the testimony of women or of just one man would accept the testimony of two men as legally valid (Deut 19:15).[143]

That Peter immediately ran to the tomb and, unlike the beloved disciple, charged into it fits what we know of Peter's character from the Synoptic tradition; this can count in favor of historical tradition here,[144] although by itself it need not do so.[145] In this case, however, it is also directly verified in the tradition of Luke 24:12. Peter's witness was too established in the widespread passion tradition (1 Cor 15:5; cf. Luke 24:12) to be omitted (20:6–7),[146] but the Fourth Gospel frames it in the context of the beloved disciple seeing the grave clothes first (20:5; not even claimed for Mary in 20:1–2) and being the first to believe (20:8).[147] The tradition, in any case, reports Peter's testimony in conjunction with a resurrection appearance, not the empty tomb (1 Cor 15:5); the beloved disciple is the first here said to believe.[148]

That the beloved disciple outruns Peter may be significant;[149] it is one of several comparisons of the two figures in the Gospel (13:22–25; 21:7, 20). Argument by comparison was a standard rhetorical technique,[150] and rhetorical principles suggested that narrative employ comparison of characters in ways useful to the point. A narrative extolling a

---

[140] Sloyan, *John*, 222.

[141] Cf. Koester, *Symbolism*, 36; Ellis, *Genius*, 8.

[142] The plural in her claim in 20:2 may reflect a plural in John's source (Kysar, *John*, 296, comparing Mark 16:1).

[143] Beasley-Murray, *John*, 372.

[144] Bruce, *John*, 385.

[145] Historians often reconstructed what was most probable on the basis of information they did have, including a person's characteristic behavior. But it is noteworthy that the later apocryphal gospels usually fit the Synoptic tradition less well.

[146] Early tradition stresses Peter's priority at least in resurrection appearances (1 Cor 15:5; cf. Luke 24:34; John 21:7; Haenchen, *John*, 2:208; Dunn, *Jesus and Spirit*, 126), which Farmer and Kereszty, *Peter and Paul*, 46, regard as a pro-Petrine tradition.

[147] That Peter and John appear together early in the Acts narratives (Acts 1:13; 3:1–11; 4:13, 19; 8:14), as well as in the Synoptics (Mark 5:37; 9:2; 13:3; 14:33) and other early Christian tradition (Gal 2:9), may support our hypothesis that the beloved disciple represents John son of Zebedee here (see introduction, ch. 3).

[148] Borse, "Glaube," recognizes that Peter believes here when he sees Jesus, but thinks John "corrects" the Synoptic tradition of the disciples' unbelief (Luke 24:1–11).

[149] Barrett, *John*, 563, thinks ἀκολουθῶν may subordinate Peter to the beloved disciple, given the term's Johannine significance (cf. 21:22). Swiftness of foot is a benefit in epic literature, albeit not always sufficient for survival (2 Sam 2:18; Homer *Il.* 10.372–375; 16.186; 20.411–418).

[150] E.g., Plato *Sophist* 221D; Aristotle *Rhet.* 2.20.4, 1393b; Cicero *Brutus* 93.321–322; see more fully Anderson, *Glossary,* 110–11, 121; the comment on 13:23–24. Comparing different authors provided a way to locate their strongest and weakest points (Dionysius of Halicarnassus *Letter to Gnaeus Pompeius* 1–2), so one could offer the best examples (*Letter to Gnaeus Pompeius* 6); one might even compare a single writer's best and worst speeches (Dionysius of Halicarnassus *Thucyd.* 35, end).

person could include a statement of his physical prowess (e.g., Josephus outswimming others, *Life* 15) as part of the praise.[151] The beloved disciple becomes the first, hence a paradigmatic, believer (20:8), for he believes before a resurrection appearance, merely on the less substantial basis of the empty tomb (cf. 20:29–31).[152] Yet if the γάρ of 20:9 retains its customary force, this verse may be claiming that although the beloved disciple's faith is a paradigm, it is still signs-faith, faith based on seeing (20:8), not the ultimate level of faith (cf. 2:23; 6:30). Better would have been faith in advance that Jesus must rise, based on understanding the word in Scripture (20:9; cf. 2:22). Scripture remains the necessary means for interpreting the event or witness, just as Nathanael understood Jesus' identity both in light of Jesus' revelation and Philip's earlier appeal to scriptural categories (cf. 1:45, 48).[153]

The Scripture to which John refers is unclear here; none of the other explicit references to "Scripture" in this Gospel (7:42; 10:35; 13:18; 17:12; 19:24, 28, 36–37) speak of a resurrection, though some may be taken to imply it and could be recalled after his resurrection (2:22; 7:38).[154] Granted, many Pharisaic exegetical defenses of the resurrection, ingenious though they are, were hardly obvious by themselves,[155] but at least they usually provided their texts. Instead of first appealing primarily to texts supporting the general resurrection, early Christian apologists made significant use of what their contemporaries would accept as specifically Davidic material in Ps 2:7 (Acts 13:33), Ps 16:10 (Acts 2:25–28; 13:35), Ps 110 (Acts 2:34–35), and, by means of *gezerah sheva* (linking together texts on the basis of common key terms),[156] probably material about the Davidic covenant, as in Isa 55:3 (Acts 13:34). But they seem to have often drawn from a broader base of texts than these alone (e.g., Luke 24:44–47).

Just as John's Passion Narrative concurs with early Christian tradition in regarding Jesus as the righteous sufferer (13:18; 19:24), so early Christian apologetic found traits of Jesus in various righteous characters in Scripture (e.g., Acts 7:25), especially where explicit connections could be made (e.g., Acts 7:37; Heb 5:6). A recurrent principle in the biblical narratives is that the righteous suffer but often (e.g., in the case of Joseph) God ultimately vindicates and exalts them to fulfill his call. Early Christians could then argue by means of an implicit *qal vaomer* (a "how-much-more" argument)[157] that this principle of exalta-

---

[151] E.g., Philostratus *Hrk.* 27.1–13; cf. Xenophon *Eph.* 1.1. These did not necessarily denigrate the other (see, e.g., Menander Rhetor 2.10, 417.10–11 [citing Homer *Il.* 22.158]; Philostratus *Hrk.* 13.3–4). Running for a good reason could be praiseworthy; e.g., running to hear Torah does not desecrate even the Sabbath (*b. Ber.* 6b), and one might run to greet a king (*b. Ber.* 58a) or to greet a loved one presumed possibly lost (Livy 4.40.3; Appian *R.H.* 2.5.3; Tob 11:9–10; Luke 15:20; other examples in Hock, "Novel," 140) or because otherwise impelled by sudden news of a loved one (*Apoll. K. Tyre* 25). On physical prowess, see comments on 21:7, 11.

[152] See also Byrne, "Faith"; Talbert, *John*, 250; cf. 1 Pet 1:8. Faith here refers to faith in the resurrection (20:25, 27, 29; Hoskyns, *Gospel*, 540).

[153] The need to understand Scripture after the resurrection also fits the gospel tradition in Luke 24:25–27, 32, 44–47 (Beasley-Murray, *John*, 373).

[154] Westcott, *John*, 290, favors Ps 16:10, but no clues allow us to narrow down the range of possible verses. John 2:22 could refer to Ps 69:9 in John 2:17, but that is likely only if the entire psalm is in view.

[155] See, e.g., *Sipre Deut.* 306.28.3; 329.2.1; *b. Pesaḥ.* 68a; *Sanh.* 90b; *Gen. Rab.* 20:10.

[156] A frequent rabbinic interpretive method, e.g., *Mek. Nez.* 10.15–16, 26, 38; 17.17; *Pisha* 5.103; *b. Ber.* 9a; 35a; *B. Qam.* 25b; *Giṭ.* 49a; *Ker.* 5a; *Qidd.* 15a; 35b; *Menaḥ.* 76a; *Naz.* 48a; *Nid.* 22b–23a; *Roš Haš.* 3b; 34a; *Sanh.* 40b; 51b; 52a; *Šabb.* 64a; *Tem.* 16a; *Zebaḥ.* 18a; 49b–50b; *Exod. Rab.* 1:20; cf. CD 7.15–20; Chernick, "Application."

[157] Typical in Jewish sources (e.g., *t. ʿEd.* 3:4; *Sipre Num.* 1.4.1; see much fuller documentation in comment on 7:23).

tion should be applied even more naturally to the ultimate righteous one, who will be exalted most highly as supreme king under God. Indeed, they could argue, he would be exalted first, before his other enemies would be subdued (Ps 110:1); those who accepted the resurrection as the bodily experience of the eschatological hope and believed that the Messiah would reign eternally (e.g., Isa 9:7; cf. Dan 2:44; 7:14) could argue that Jesus' resurrection would commence his reign even before his full conquest of other enemies. In any case, Scripture had to be fulfilled (10:35), and Jesus "had" to rise from the dead.[158]

## 2. Appearance to Mary (20:11–18)

Mary was not only the first to notice the tomb empty (or to at least infer this from the missing stone, 20:1–2) but the first to see her risen Lord (20:11–18). The text may imply a connection with her fidelity; though ancient custom expected women to express lamentation more freely than men[159] (of whom they also generally expected it to some extent), it may be noteworthy that when the male disciples leave (20:10), Mary remains (20:11).[160] Mary remains not out of faith in the resurrection but out of love and desire to perform the final acts available for those already dead (20:13, 15). Yet the narrative emphasizes by repetition that she need not weep; both an angel and Jesus confront her weeping (20:11, 13, 15) not because her weeping is wrong (cf. 11:31, 33) but because it is about to become joy, as Jesus promised his disciples (16:20).

### 2A. Resurrection Appearances (20:15–29)

The resurrection appearances in John 20 become paradigmatic for all believers' encounters with Jesus, which give way to believers' relationship with Jesus (14:21–23; 20:19–23). Because of her devotion to Jesus, Mary functions as one of the more positive paradigms for witness in this section, as well as the first one.[161] She was the first agent Jesus commissioned with the message of his resurrection and of believers as God's children.[162]

Witnesses who said that they had seen Jesus alive from the dead (e.g., 1 Cor 15:1–8; virtually all the narrative accounts also suggest significant conversation with him rather than fleeting appearances) were so convinced of the veracity of their claims that many devoted their lives to proclaiming what they had seen, and some died for it; clearly their testimony was not fabricated.[163] Ancients also recognized that the willingness of people to die for their convictions verified at least the sincerity of their motives, arguing against fabrication.[164]

---

[158] Throughout this Gospel, δεῖ usually stands for divine necessity (e.g., 3:14, 30; 10:16).

[159] E.g., Euripides *Medea* 928; Diodorus Siculus 17.37.3; Dionysius of Halicarnassus *R.A.* 7.67.2; 8.39.1; Josephus *Ant.* 4.320.

[160] Their going out in 20:10 may be simply "to them" (cf. 7:50) rather than to their homes (NRSV; NASB); in 20:19 they are all together.

[161] Cf. Schneiders, "Encounter," who argues that John presents Mary as the official witness of the resurrection, symbolic for the Johannine community (though her allusions to Song of Songs may be more dubious).

[162] Okure, "Commission." Mary's testimony may or may not (cf. Maccini, *Testimony*, 240–52) teach specifically about women's testimony, but it prefigures Christian testimony in general, which implies the participation of women in that witness.

[163] Sanders, *Figure*, 280.

[164] Dio Cassius 58.4.5–6; 63.11.2–12.1. Josephus cites Jews' willingness to die for the law (*Ag. Ap.* 1.42–43).

As noted above, some scholars deny the empty-tomb tradition; most, however, affirm that the disciples believed they had seen Jesus alive. Yet some scholars even find ways to deny the historical value of the resurrection appearances; Mack, for example, suggests that before the Gospels we have only Paul's account of "visions."[165] But although the language Paul employs is general enough that it *could* include visionary experiences, he is reporting earlier Palestinian tradition in 1 Cor 15:3–7[166] and Palestinian Jews did not speak of nonbodily resurrections (see discussion of the Jewish resurrection belief above). Nor would anyone have persecuted them for simply affirming that they had seen someone who had been dead; apart from the bodily character of the resurrection—the sort that would leave an empty tomb—people would merely assume they claimed to see a ghost, a noncontroversial phenomenon.[167] Ghosts were "phantasms" that appeared especially at night (Plutarch *Brutus* 36; *Caesar* 69.5, 8; *Cimon* 6.5), but this is not what the resurrection narratives report (Luke 24:40).[168] Further, Jesus "appeared" to his followers in Acts 1:3 but there provided concrete proofs of his physicality (cf. Luke 24:39–40).[169] Finally, Paul himself distinguishes between the Easter appearances and mere visions (cf. 1 Cor 9:1; 15:8; 2 Cor 12:1–4).[170]

Deities periodically "manifested" themselves to mortals in Greek tradition, sometimes in sleep and sometimes as apparitions.[171] Paul's language in 1 Cor 15 applied, in the LXX, especially to revelations of God or angels (cf. Bar 3:37; *Sib. Or.* 1.200).[172] From the late Hellenistic age, "epiphanies" of Greek gods usually meant the activity of a deity rather than its appearance;[173] it is primarily these which witnesses attest,[174] though appearances in personal dreams and visions occur (e.g., *PDM* 14.74–91, 95, 98–102, 169). Appearances of deities visible to large numbers of people normally belonged to an era many centuries earlier than the writings.[175]

---

[165] Mack, *Myth*, 308. Likewise, against the unanimous witness of extant evidence, from earliest to latest, he supposes that the resurrection was a late myth originated by Christians not in Jewish Palestine but in northern Syria and Asia (*Lost Gospel*, 2). Evidence for early tradition for the site of the tomb, the largely Palestinian evidence for Jewish belief in the resurrection, the extreme unlikelihood of a Diaspora movement becoming more Palestinian or Judaized in the anti-Judaism of parts of the Greek East, etc., render his suggestion incredible.

[166] See, e.g., Dibelius, *Tradition*, 18–20; Gerhardsson, *Memory*, 299–300; Barrett, *Jesus*, 1–2; Conzelmann, *Corinthians*, 251; Hunter, *Predecessors*, 15–17; Fuller, *Formation*, 10–11; Webber, "Note"; Fee, *Corinthians*, 722.

[167] E.g., Dio Cassius 42.11.2–3; Lucan *C.W.* 1.11; Plutarch *Cimon* 1.6; 6.6; Achilles Tatius 5.16.1–2; cf. Thom, "*Akousmata*," 104–5, for the Pythagorean view. Deities also sent phantom images made only of cloud (e.g., Apollodorus *Epitome* 1.20; 3.5).

[168] Sanders, *Figure*, 278. Some contended that the particular identity of ghosts was difficult to distinguish, since they interchanged their appearances (Philostratus *Hrk.* 21.1).

[169] Although the second-century date makes the work's value here questionable, we may also note postresurrection conversations of Jesus in the antignostic *Epistula apostolorum*.

[170] Goppelt, *Times*, 18–19

[171] E.g., Euripides *Bacch.* 42, 53–54; Plutarch *Cicero* 14.3; Aelius Aristides *Or.* 48.41; Apuleius *Metam.* 11.3; Achilles Tatius 7.12.4; Chariton 2.2.5; 2.3.5; Philostratus *Hrk.* 2.8; 18.1–2 (see further Maclean and Aitken, *Heroikos*, xxvi); reports in Grant, *Religions*, 9–13, 123; in unrelated cultures, see Wolf, "Virgin"; Mbiti, *Religions*, 105–12 passim; for more concrete effects of angelic manifestations in Hellenistic Jewish tradition, see Tob 12:19, 22; 2 Macc 3:24–26 (cf. God in 2 Macc 3:30).

[172] See further Bartsch, "Inhalt."

[173] Nilsson, *Piety*, 106; Diodorus Siculus 5.62.4; 11.14.3–4; Dionysius of Halicarnassus *R.A.* 8.56.1–3.

[174] Cf. Grant, *Gods*, 66, 54–55, 64–65.

[175] So, e.g., Plutarch *Cor.* 3.4 (writing of the time of Tarquin, 3.1); or, less dramatically, the appearance of the Dioscuri's stars (Plutarch *Lysander* 12.1; 18.1).

Further, very little evidence suggests the plausibility of successive and mass, corporate visions (see esp. 1 Cor 15:5–7).[176] Conditions in first-century Judea and Galilee were not those that produced the seventeenth-century messiah Sabbetai Zevi, many of whose followers failed to be deterred by his apostasy,[177] and some even by his death.[178] Aside from different social conditions, knowledge of the Christian belief in Jesus' resurrection and redefinition of messiahship could provide later messianic movements a model for redefining the messianic mission in a manner that did not exist before Jesus.

Some less-than-persuasive parallels could be adduced. Josephus *War* 6.297–299 reports that people saw heavenly chariots moving through the clouds and surrounding cities (cf. 2 Kgs 6:17; 2 Macc 3:24–26; 4 Macc 4:10–11; *Sib. Or.* 3.805–808) and priests heard voices in the temple; Horsley and Hanson regard these as collective fantasies,[179] but they could also be (1) true (which we regard as extremely unlikely but which a post-Enlightenment perspective need not simply dismiss); (2) the sun playing tricks on eyes at dusk; (3) propaganda to justify Jerusalem's fall after the event, which Josephus has accepted;[180] or (4) Josephus's own propaganda (he is the only extant witness concerning witnesses apart from sources dependent on him).[181]

In fact, Josephus may be following a standard sort of report of such events as portents of destruction.[182] Some poetic writers engaged in poetic license in such reports,[183] such as a giant Fury stalking the city and shaking the snakes in her hair;[184] others were more sober historians citing reports for particular years. Portents included events we might regard as natural phenomena today, such as physical deformities at birth, lightning striking temples, comets, and so forth,[185] but also included visions of celestial figures or armies.[186] The armies were sometimes heard rather than seen;[187] sights that were seen were often acknowledged as divine illusions rather than objects physically present;[188] and the apparitions of armies did not draw near anyone.[189] Such reports were normally not verified by citing witnesses, and the historians who report them sometimes express skepticism concerning their value, at times allowing for imagination in their production[190] and at times pointing out that such reports fed on each other among the gullible.[191] In any case, this phenomenon is

---

[176] E.g., Schweizer, *Jesus,* 48–49.

[177] Grayzel, *History,* 516; Bamberger, *Story,* 240.

[178] Scholem, *Sabbatai Sevi,* 920; Greenstone, *Messiah,* 225–30.

[179] Horsley and Hanson, *Bandits,* 182–84.

[180] Somewhat similarly, Saulnier, "Josèphe," suggests that Josephus borrows the tradition from Flavian propaganda.

[181] Tacitus *Hist.* 5.13.2–7 likely depends on Josephus *War* 6.288–315.

[182] E.g., Aulus Gellius 4.6.2.

[183] E.g., Lucan *C.W.* 1.526–557; most obviously, who reported on Charybdis (1.547–548)?

[184] Lucan *C.W.* 1.572–573.

[185] E.g., many of the portents listed in Livy 21.62.5; 24.10.7–10; 25.7.7–8; 26.23.4–5; 27.4.11–14; 27.11.2–5; 29.37.1–5; 29.14.3; 32.1.10–12; 33.26.7–8; 34.45.6–7; 35.9.2–3; 35.21.3–6; 36.37.2–3; 40.45.1–4; 41.21.12–13; 43.13.3–6; 45.16.5; Lucan *C.W.* 1.562–563.

[186] E.g., Livy 21.62.4–5; 24.10.10; 42.2.4; Plutarch *Themistocles* 15.1; Herodian 8.3.8–9.

[187] Appian *C.W.* 4.1.4 (43 B.C.E.); one of the portents in Livy 24.44.8 (213 B.C.E.); Caesar *C.W.* 3.105; Philostratus *Hrk.* 56.2.

[188] E.g., Livy 24.10.11; 24.44.8. If I correctly interpret Livy's summaries, in some cases some reported seeing figures at another location when those present at that location could not confirm them.

[189] Livy 21.62.5.

[190] E.g., Livy 21.62.1; Herodian 8.3.8 (though he concludes that it is credible, 8.3.9).

[191] Livy 21.62.1; 24.10.6; 27.37.2; 29.14.2.

quite different from meeting again and talking with a person one has personally known, which the Gospel accounts stress.

But the difference again concerns the resurrection. To most ancient Mediterranean peoples, the concept of corporal resurrection was barely intelligible; to Jewish people, it was strictly eschatological. Yet once one grants, from a neutral starting point, the possibility of a bodily resurrection of Jesus within past history, the appearances would follow such an event naturally with or without parallels. In a Jewish framework, Jesus' resurrection within history must also signify the arrival of the eschatological era in some sense (e.g., Acts 1:3–6; "from among the dead ones," Rom 1:4; 1 Cor 15:20; Gal 1:4; Heb 6:5).

### 2B. The Angelic Testimony (20:11–13)

The angels were at the head and feet of where Jesus had been, marking the holiness of the site of the resurrection.[192] Mary probably did not recognize, but probably should have, that the figures before her in 20:12 were angels, partly because of their garb. To be sure, white clothes could allude to a variety of nonangelic functions. Mediterranean religion often employed white for the worship of heavenly deities;[193] priests generally wore linen, including Egyptian priests,[194] those at the temple of Artemis (*Acts John* 38), and Jewish priests (Josephus *War* 5.229).[195] Worshipers wore white or linen in other worship settings,[196] including in the Jerusalem temple (Josephus *War* 2.1; *Ant.* 11.327)[197] and the Therapeutae during worship (Philo *Contempl. Life* 66). Some schools of philosophers such as Pythagoras and his sect might wear white (Iamblichus *V.P.* 28.153, 155; whether linen, as in *V.P.* 21.100; 28.149, or wool, replaced in later times with linen, as in Diogenes Laertius 8.1.19). Perhaps because white could signify good and black, evil (Diogenes Laertius 8.1.34)[198]—which in turn probably reflects associations with day and night[199]—converts might wear linen (*Jos. Asen.* 14:12/13).[200]

---

[192] Simenel, "Jean 20," compares the position of the cherubim on the mercy seat, hence the tomb with the ark of the covenant; this is possible but may be overreaching; after all, Jesus' presence was gone from the site.

[193] E.g., Euripides *Bacch.* 112; Livy 27.37.11–12. Cf. the temple of Jupiter (Livy 40.51.3).

[194] Plutarch *Isis* 3–4, *Mor.* 352C; Appian *C.W.* 4.6.47; Apuleius *Metam.* 11.10, 23; Lewis, *Life,* 92; other worshipers of Io (apparently Isis) in Ovid *Metam.* 1.747.

[195] Also *p. Yoma* 7:2 (paralleling heavenly priests); *Pesiq. Rab.* 33:10; Yadin, *War Scroll,* 219; cf. Exod 39:27–29; Lev 6:10; 16:4, 32.

[196] Pausanias 2.35.5; 6.20.3; Pythagoras in Diodorus Siculus 10.9.6; Diogenes Laertius 8.1.33; Hipponax frg. 65; Ovid *Her.* 4.71 (Eleusinian rituals); Athenaeus *Deipn.* 4.149d; SEG 11.923, in Sherk, *Empire,* 58; Ramsay, *Letters,* 386; cf. the change of garments in Olmstead, *History,* 511. Cf. Rev 3:4–5, 18; 4:4; 6:11; 7:9, 13. Linen was not limited to worship settings, however (e.g., Indians in Arrian *Ind.* 16.1–2).

[197] Naturally, Archelaus in Josephus *War* 2.1 could afford a special garment; one doubts that all comers (despite *Ant.* 11.327) had the same opportunity.

[198] Cf. Homer *Il.* 1.103; Ovid *Metam.* 2.832; *Ex Ponto* 2.5.37–38; 4Q183, 2.4–8 (possibly also 4Q185 frg. 1–2, col. 2, lines 6–7); 4Q544, 1.10–14; 2.3–5 (both depicting the ruler of darkness); 4Q548, lines 10–15; Silius Italicus 11.548; Dupont, *Life,* 260. Black functions negatively in Aeschylus *Sept.* 832–833 (a terrible, "black curse"); Ovid *Fasti* 1.58 (inauspicious); Marcus Aurelius 4.28. Athenians used white ballots for acquittal, black for a death sentence (Plutarch *Alc.* 22.2).

[199] Cf. Hesiod *Op.* 154–155; Aeschylus *Eumenides* 745 (the Furies spring from Night); Ovid *Amores* 1.8.3–8 (night as the time for witchcraft); Philostratus *Hrk.* 33.6 (white associated with the sun god); Lucan *C.W.* 6.624; Philo thinks black the absence of light and white (*Creation* 29; *Abraham* 10). Ephraim Isaac, an Ethiopian translator of *1 Enoch,* points out that in *1 En.* 87:2 white suggests the image of purity in Ethiopic (*OTP* 1:63 n.) Against some modern assumptions, these

But in paganism, pagan deities could appear in white garments;[201] more important, Jewish angels likewise appeared in linen (*L.A.B.* 9:10; Rev 15:6) or white (e.g., *1 En.* 71:1)[202] garments or clothed in glory (3 Macc 6:18).[203] In John 20:12, the angelic or theophanic functions are paramount. Because black garb typically symbolized mourning or death[204] and white, joy,[205] their garb also signified that the departure of the body represented good news, ending the mourning appropriate for a death. The white also probably fits John's "light/darkness" motif, though the mention of white makes sense, as we have noted, even had he omitted the light/darkness motif.

### 2C. Recognizing Jesus (20:14–16)

Mary's encounter with Jesus in 20:14–16 is one of several "recognition scenes" in the Gospel, reflecting a dramatic-type scene in ancient literature.[206] Mary turns because Jesus initially appears "behind" her (20:14; cf. Rev 1:10). That Mary at first does not recognize Jesus (20:14) reflects early tradition that Jesus was not immediately recognized by all who saw him after the resurrection (21:4–7; Luke 24:16, 31; though we may note that she was also weeping). This tradition may also imply something about the character of the resurrection body, analogous to the early Jewish belief that angels could appear in different forms. According to Greek folklore, deities assumed various familiar shapes to communicate with people or to disguise themselves or escape,[207] or concealed or transformed the appearance of their favorite mortals,[208] but in Jewish terms, one would think especially of

---

associations with color derive from day/night divisions, not human pigment. White is associated positively with the spirit world in various traditional African societies (Mbiti, *Religions*, 73, 277; Isichei, *History*, 64).

[200] In early Christianity, cf. Rev 3:4–5; 4:4; 19:8, 14.

[201] E.g., *PGM* 4.637–638, 698–699; also an inscription in Grant, *Religions*, 16.

[202] Also *1 En.* 87:2; 90:31–33; 2 Macc 3:26; 11:8; Jannes and Jambres fragments in P.Beatty 16; cf. the exception in late *Pesiq. Rab.* 20:4.

[203] Also *1 En.* 71:1; cf. Adam in *Gen. Rab.* 20:12. For angels' beauty, see also *Liv. Pro.* 16.2 (Malachi) (Greek §23: ed. Schermann, 73).

[204] *Jos. Asen.* 10:8–9/10; 14:12; Isaeus *Estate of Nicostratus* 7; Lysias *Or.* 13.40, §133; Euripides *Alc.* 216, 427; Aristophanes *Frogs* 1337; Ovid *Metam.* 8.777–778; Valerius Maximus 1.7.7; Seneca *Controv.* 10.1.1, 4; Plutarch *Alex.* 49.3; Apollodorus *Epitome* 1.7, 10; Silius Italicus 11.257–258; Valerius Maximus 2.4.5; Philostratus *Hrk.* 31.9; 53.9, 11, 17; Herodian 4.2.3; Dupont, *Life*, 260; death is regularly dark (e.g., Homer *Il.* 5.22, 47, 310; cf. Homer *Od.* 11.32–33; death as "black" in Statius *Thebaid* 4.528; the Styx in Lycophron *Alex.* 705; see further the comment on 1:4–5).

[205] E.g., *p. Roš Haš.* 1:3, §27; Ovid *Tristia* 5.5.8; hence the burial clothes of the righteous (*L.A.B.* 64:6; cf. *T. Ab.* 20:10A; *L.A.E.* 48.1; *Apoc. Mos.* 40.1–3; *b. Ber.* 18b; cf. Plutarch *R.Q.* 26, *Mor.* 270DE). Gregory the Great *Homilies* 21 opined that the angel came in white because of joy (Oden and Hall, *Mark*, 243). But people might prefer either white or dark wool (Seneca *Nat.* 3.25.4).

[206] Culpepper, *John*, 85 (on the scenes in ancient literature, see 72–77; in John's Gospel, 77–86).

[207] Homer *Il.* 4.86–87, 121–124; 5.127–128, 177, 183, 191, 461–462; 5.604, 784–785; 7.58–59; 13.43–45, 69, 215–216, 356–357; 14.136; 16.715–720, 788–789; 17.71–73, 322–326, 551–555, 582–583; 20.79–81; 21.284–286, 599–611; *Od.* 1.420; 2.267–268, 382–387, 399–401; 4.417–18; 6.21–22; 7.19–20; 8.8, 193–194; Virgil *Aen.* 1.314–315, 402–406, 657–660; 5.618–620, 645–652; 7.415–416; 9.646–652, 657–658; 12.784–785; *Georg.* 4.405–414, 440–442; Ovid *Metam.* 1.676; 11.241–246, 633–643; 14.765–771; Pausanias 3.16.2–3; Achilles Tatius 2.15.4; Apollodorus 2.4.8; 3.8.2; 3.10.7; 3.12.6; 3.13.5; Silius Italicus 7.422–425, 435; Eunapius *Lives* 468; for ghosts, cf. Philostratus *Hrk.* 21.1 (the closest parallel to John 20:14–16 is *Hrk.* 21.5–6, it but may be derivative). They could also disguise the appearance of mortals (e.g., Homer *Od.* 13.397–399) and become invisible (Homer *Il.* 5.845).

[208] E.g., Homer *Od.* 13.189–193; see more fully the comment on 8:59.

the disguises of angels.[209] Tobias could not recognize that Raphael, who claimed to be son of one Anania known to Tobias's father (Tob 5:12), was an angel (Tob 5:4–6; 9:1–5); he explains the "vision" in Tob 12:19. In the Hebrew Bible, God himself sometimes came unrecognized at first (Gen 18:9–13), especially through the angel of the Lord (Judg 6:22; 13:20–23).

Pseudo-Philo's *Biblical Antiquities,* possibly dating from the first century C.E., shows how common the motif of God disguising his people became in some later Jewish traditions. Moses, having been glorified on the mountain, was unrecognizable to the Israelites, just as Joseph was unrecognized by his brothers when they came to Egypt (*L.A.B.* 12:1). Perhaps to explain why Saul failed to recognize David in 1 Sam 17:55–56 (cf. 1 Sam 16:19–23), *L.A.B.* 61:9 declares that the angel of the Lord changed David's appearance so no one recognized him. The witch of Endor did not recognize Saul because his appearance was changed (*L.A.B.* 64:4).[210]

That Mary thought Jesus a "gardener" (20:15) fits the story: the tomb was, after all, in a "garden" (19:41).[211] Gardeners tended to belong to the poorest class (Apuleius *Metam.* 9.31; Philostratus *Hrk.* 4.11). But John may suggest an ironic allusion to the joint work of Father and Son; just as the Father was a γεωργός, a vinedresser (15:1; cf. 1 Cor 3:9), Jesus was a κηπουρός, watching his garden.[212] But without a clearer verbal connection, the allusion seems tenuous; certainly Jesus does not "prune" Mary here but affirms her. That Mary offers to carry Jesus away (20:15) if the present burial site was inappropriate suggests great devotion; to protect his body from the dishonor of an unmarked or unmourned grave (see above), she is willing to exert what, for Mary by herself, would have likely involved tremendous physical effort.[213] Mary is willing to take away, αἴρειν, the body of Jesus; in his death, however, Jesus αἴρει the sins of the world (1:29).

Asking Mary whom she seeks (20:15) will prove to be a rhetorical question leading to an invitation, as in 1:38;[214] her response will prove positive, in contrast to the response to 18:4, 7.[215] Mary's supposition that her dialogue partner has "carried" Jesus away might be another example of John's irony: Jesus indeed had laid down his life and taken it again (10:17–18); but the irony, if present, is subtle and may be merely our expectation as readers too accustomed to the author's irony.

To reveal his identity to Mary, Jesus need only reveal her name to her: "Mary" (20:16).[216] This fits Jesus' prior teaching: his own sheep would recognize his voice, espe-

---

[209] See Gen 18; Tob 5:4–6, 12; 9:1–5; Philo *Abraham* 114; *Sipre Deut.* 38.1.4; *p. Pe'ah* 3:8, §3; Heb 13:2; cf. Luke 24:16, 31. Also Satan in *T. Job* 6:4; 17:2/1; 23:1; cf. *Pesiq. Rab Kah.* 26:2.

[210] *Sipre Deut.* 47.2.8 speaks of the righteous as sometimes unseen but not in the sense of disguised (maybe intended corporately).

[211] One need not regard him as a custodian (Brown, *John,* 2:990). Suggit, "Gardener," finds here Jesus as a new Adam; but in this Gospel he is likelier Adam's life giver instead (cf. 20:22).

[212] The term is a NT and LXX hapax legomenon, but the cognate κῆπος appears in 18:1, 26; 19:41; Luke 13:19; and thirty-one times in the LXX; the use of κῆπος in 19:41 dictates the use of κηπουρός here. Cf. the sacred gardener of Philostratus *Hrk.* 4.11–12 (though it is third century C.E.).

[213] Strachan, *Gospel,* 225, argues this on the basis of the term βαστάζω (cf. 19:17; but cf. also 10:31), but John uses αἴρω for Mary's offer, which need not connote heaviness (2:16; 5:8). It is, however, intrinsically likely given the usual relative weight of men and women.

[214] Stibbe, *Gospel,* 1, presses the parallel too far in calling it an *inclusio.*

[215] The parallels should not, however, be pressed as if John expected his audience to catch all of them; to some extent, "Whom/What do you seek?" is merely language characteristic of the author (4:27).

[216] Derrett's attempt to parallel her with the earlier Miriam who watched over Moses' infant body (Exod 2:3–8; "Miriam") is farfetched.

cially when he called them by name (10:3–5).[217] In Scripture and in other early Jewish sources, God often secured his people's attention by calling them by name,[218] often a double name.[219] When she turns to him,[220] her immediate response is, "my teacher," a more personalized and perhaps intimate form than in 1:38, 49 (elsewhere in the NT only at Mark 10:51); because of this, the first and last uses of the "Rabbi" title in this Gospel are the ones interpreted for readers unfamiliar with the terms (1:38; 20:16). Like John the Baptist (3:26), Jesus is often called "Rabbi," both by his disciples (1:38, 49; 4:31; 9:2; 11:8) and by others who recognize respectfully his office (3:2; 6:25).

## 2D. Mary's Testimony (20:17–18)

Mary calls Jesus her "teacher" (20:16), and Jesus responds by commissioning Mary as his agent—although first-century Palestinian Jews rarely appear to have used women as agents—to his "brothers" (20:17). Although his physical brothers had traveled with him and his disciples at least on occasion at first (2:12), his physical brothers did not believe him (7:5); but because Jesus had returned from above and a birth from above (3:3) was now available to others, those who believed in him were now his "brothers" as well (cf. earlier in Jesus' public ministry in Mark 3:34). This became a familiar title for believers among one another (e.g., Acts 10:23; 11:1, 12, 29; Rom 1:13; 7:1, 4; Phil 2:25),[221] including in Johannine circles (21:23; 1 John 2:9–11; 3:10–17; 4:20–21; 5:16; 3 John 3, 5, 10; Rev 1:9; 6:11; 12:10; 19:10; 22:9); such fictive kinship language was common among both ethnic and religious groups, so that one might thus address fellow Israelites (Acts 2:29; 3:22; 9:17).[222] (Sibling terminology also extended to fellow rabbis or fellow disciples,[223] coinitiates into mysteries,[224] alliances,[225] friendships,[226] and other commonalities.)[227] "My God and your God" was also a way of emphasizing a common bond.[228]

That Jesus after his resurrection first revealed himself to women (here Mary Magdalene, 20:11–18)[229] belongs to the earliest stage of tradition, appearing in all four canonical gospels. John includes this tradition even though he omits the reason given elsewhere in the tradition, namely, that the women came to anoint the body.[230] Joseph or his agents had

---

[217] Most commentators note the parallel here (e.g., Kysar, *John*, 300; Quast, *Reading*, 133).

[218] E.g., to Abraham in Gen 22:1; *Jub.* 18:1, 14.

[219] Gen 22:11; 46:2; Exod 3:4; 1 Sam 3:10; Luke 10:41; 22:31; Acts 9:4; *4 Ezra* 14:1; *2 Bar.* 22:2; *Apoc. Mos.* 41:1; *Jos. Asen.* 14:4; *T. Ab.* 14:14; 15:1A; *T. Job* 3:1; 24:1; 25:9. Such doubling provided rhetorical emphasis (Demetrius 5.267; *Pesiq. Rab Kah.* 16:4) or endearment (*t. Ber.* 1:14; *Sipra VDDen. par.* 1.1.4.3–4).

[220] Because she had already turned in 20:14, Schneiders, "Encounter," 162–63, thinks the turning of 20:16 symbolizes conversion (*shuv;* assuming John did not forget what he wrote in 20:14).

[221] Over one hundred uses in Pauline literature alone.

[222] E.g., Tob 5:10; 6:10; 7:3; 2 Macc 1:1.

[223] *Sipre Deut.* 34.5.3 (cf. 34.3.1–3); *b. ʿAbod. Zar.* 18a, bar; cf. Matt 23:8.

[224] Burkert, *Cults*, 45.

[225] E.g., 1 Macc 10:18; 12:6, 10, 21; 14:40; cf. Curty, "Propos."

[226] Euripides *Iph. taur.* 497–498; Plutarch *Many Friends* 2, *Mor.* 93E; Marcus Aurelius 1.14; Ahiqar 49 (col. 4). Cf. fictive parental language, e.g., Diodorus Siculus 17.37.6.

[227] E.g., *CPJ* 3:41, §479; Diodorus Siculus 1.1.3. Cf. its use in a conspicuous display of hospitality to a stranger (*T. Ab.* 2:5B).

[228] E.g., Abraham's words to Isaac in *Jub.* 21:25.

[229] *Gos. Pet.* 12:50–13:57 mentions women (plural) but begins with and names only Mary Magdalene.

[230] This is not because it would be physically impossible, as some have argued; Jerusalem can be cool in April (18:18), and a rock-hewn tomb would remain cool (Craig, "Tomb," 184).

purchased the linen before the Sabbath (Mark 15:46), but the women either purchased or prepared the spices only after the Sabbath (Mark 16:1; Luke 23:56; 24:1).[231] Women were expected to mourn more freely than men (Dionysius of Halicarnassus *R.A.* 7.67.2) and accordingly given more latitude;[232] although without guarantee of ingress, it was safer for the women than for the men to be found near the tomb.

It is unlikely that the early Christians would have invented the testimony of women: not all testimony was regarded as being of equal merit, and the trustworthiness of witnesses was considered essential (CD 9.21–22; 10:1).[233] Most of Jesus' Jewish contemporaries held little esteem for the testimony of women;[234] this reflects a broader Mediterranean limited trust of women's testimony and speech, also enshrined in Roman law.[235] Some, though not all, Jewish writers condemned listening to women more generally (e.g., Josephus *Ant.* 18.255; *Syr. Men.* 118–121, 336–339).[236] Indeed, even the disciples in the late tradition in Mark 16:11 did not believe the women—a tradition that may reflect historical reality at this point (Luke 24:11).[237] For the early Christians, neither the empty tomb nor the testimony of the women was adequate evidence by itself (cf. Luke 24:22–24); they further depended on the testimony of men for the public forum (1 Cor 15:5–8).[238] No one had apologetic reason to invent the testimony of these women, but the gospel writers may have a profound theological purpose in preserving it, perhaps related to the gospel's power to transcend gender restrictions.[239] For the account's theological function in context, see the comment on 20:18.

## 2E. The Ascension (20:17)

Such a moment of revelation would evoke intense emotion in an ancient setting, as it would be today.[240] That she would embrace Jesus (implied in 20:17) would not be surprising whether or not mentioned; a woman might be expected to embrace a loved one she

---

[231] Dalman, *Jesus-Jeshua,* 101. Taylor thinks the Markan chronology confirms the Johannine tradition here (*Mark,* 601); Jeremias observes that one could buy necessary food for Passover even on the Sabbath but pay later (Jeremias, *Eucharistic Words,* 77; *m. Šabb.* 23:1).

[232] E.g., Pomeroy, *Goddesses,* 44; see comment above.

[233] Discrediting opposing witnesses was a standard tactic (e.g., Cicero *Pro Scauro* 13.29; 17.38).

[234] See, e.g., Josephus *Ant.* 4.219; *m. Yebam.* 15:1, 8–10; 16:7; *Ketub.* 1:6–9; *t. Yebam.* 14:10; *Sipra VDDeho. pq.* 7.45.1.1; cf. Luke 24:11; Keener, *Paul,* 162–63; Baumgarten, "Testimony"; Hooker, *Mark,* 119. Ilan, *Women,* 227, thinks that in practice the non-Pharisaic legal system "often" required women's witness; even if this is overstated, women could testify concerning various matters, and some views of 1QSa 1.10–11 suggest that Qumran was more open to the practice than Pharisees were (Ilan, *Women,* 163–66).

[235] Hesiod *Op.* 375; Avianus *Fables* 15–16; Babrius 16.10; Justinian *Inst.* 2.10.6 (though contrast the earlier Gaius *Inst.* 2.105); Plutarch *Publicola* 8.4; Phaedrus 4.15; Gardner, *Women,* 165; Kee, *Origins,* 89. Many men regarded women as gullible (cf. Philo *Good Person* 117; Juvenal *Sat.* 1.38–39), and classical Athenians rejected adoptions or changes of will made under women's influence (e.g., Isaeus *Estate of Menecles* 1, 19; *Estate of Philoctemon* 29–30).

[236] Cf. also Maccini, *Testimony,* 63–97, who argues that their witness was usually proscribed in legal contexts but sometimes accepted and sometimes rejected in nonlegal contexts.

[237] Vermes, *Jesus the Jew,* 40–41. Cf. *L.A.B.* 9:10: Miriam's parents wrongly disbelieved Miriam's prophetic dream (Miriam was a biblical prophetess).

[238] Cf. Stauffer, *Jesus,* 151; Dunn, *Jesus and Spirit,* 126.

[239] Thompson, *Debate,* 233.

[240] E.g., Euripides *El.* 569–581 (after the expectation of 274–281).

had wrongly assumed dead.[241] In the context, "touch" probably refers to "embrace"; it is difficult to envision Mary, under such circumstances, merely poking a suspicious finger at Jesus' arm (cf. 20:25) or grabbing his right hand for an ancient promise of fidelity.

Scholars have offered various proposals to explain the prohibition of "touching" Jesus—for example, an allusion to a biblical prohibition against touching the sacred during theophanies (Exod 19:12–13; but contrast 20:27).[242] Some have suggested that Jesus' warning in 20:17 that Mary not "touch" him before his ascension implies an ascension before the appearance in which Jesus invites Thomas's touch (20:25–27).[243] In such a case, the prohibition may recall the concept that elsewhere appears in the *Apocalypse of Moses,* where touching Adam's body in a particular state endangers not only Eve but Adam (*Apoc. Mos.* 31:3–4);[244] the value of this parallel, even if viewed as close, must presuppose that the account in the *Apocalypse of Moses* does not depend on an interpretation of Johannine tradition here; moreover, Adam refers to his corpse, and the idea or nature of danger is not clearly articulated.

But this suggestion about the nature of Jesus' resurrection body and ascension is unlikely for two reasons. First, it is grammatically unnecessary; Jesus' prohibition here is a present imperative with μή, which most often would be read as, "Stop touching me," or perhaps, "Stop attempting to touch me," rather than simply, "Do not touch me."[245] Because of the context, the command probably means here (as the verb sometimes means elsewhere) not merely "Stop touching me"[246] but "Stop holding on to me,"[247] suggesting a persistent clinging that fits the emotional character of the encounter (cf. Matt 28:9–10). (Although the terminology differs in the two passages, John might link Mary's embrace with Thomas's touch by way of contrast—the first a response of mature faith, the latter a demand of signs-faith.)

Second, it invites some clues to theological reasons for such an intermediate ascension and why Mary could not touch Jesus in this state, yet the Fourth Gospel provides no such clues.[248] More than likely Jesus simply places a temporal limitation on Mary's embrace or wish to embrace: soon Jesus must ascend, so the postresurrection rendezvous Jesus promised (14:19–20; 16:16, 21–22) must be carried out urgently.[249] Or because he has not yet

---

[241] Sophocles *El.* 1226; *Apoll. K. Tyre* 45. Given the difference in status relationship (e.g., Orestes was Electra's brother), Mary may have grasped Jesus by the feet, as the women did in Matt 28:9; but this is unclear. Cf. Philostratus *Hrk.* 11.2 (a deceased hero not fleeing like a phantom); 51.13 (embracing the deceased's tomb; the same term clearly applies to an "embrace" in 54.8).

[242] Antoniotti, "L'apparition," intriguingly even if not fully persuasively.

[243] E.g., Smith, *John* (1999), 378. Haenchen, *John,* 2:210 even suggests a demythologized tradition in which Jesus had returned as a spirit but still awaited an earthly body.

[244] See D'Angelo, "Note."

[245] As frequently noted, e.g., Barrett, *John,* 565–66; Holwerda, *Spirit,* 22; Michaels, *John,* 328; Whitacre, *John,* 476; see Blass, Debrunner, and Funk, *Grammar,* 172–73; Carson, *John,* 644.

[246] Fowler, "Meaning," prefers "touch," arguing that Jesus warns Mary that the nature of their relationship must be different now. Derrett, *Law,* 440, suggests a Nazirite vow in Mark 14:25, so that Jesus' resurrection body must not be defiled by one who recently touched his corpse (Num 6:6–7; 19:16).

[247] Schnackenburg, *John,* 3:318; Brown, *John,* 2:992; McPolin, *John,* 255; Morris, *John,* 841; Bruce, *John,* 389; Carson, *John,* 644; Whitacre, *John,* 476; Smith, *John* (1999), 377.

[248] One could try to distinguish the prohibition for Mary from the invitation to Thomas by suggesting that Mary as a woman might be impure (Lev 15:19–30), but apart from lacking clues in the text, this position would violate Johannine thought about purity as well as about gender (e.g., 2:6; 4:9).

[249] One might sever the first imperative grammatically from the following statement if one could take 20:17's γάρ as anticipatory ("since," for the following clause) rather than causal (for the preceding; McGehee, "Reading"), but Johannine style makes that suggestion less likely.

ascended, he will still be available once she has delivered the message to his "brothers" (20:17).[250] Perhaps Jesus is also warning Mary not to become excessively attached to his physical presence (the flesh profits nothing, 6:63); his Spirit would remain with her and her fellow disciples (20:22).[251] In any case, Mary seems to understand Jesus' message correctly, for she devotes herself immediately to bearing his message (20:18).

To what "ascension" does 20:17 refer? (The reference in 6:62 is not very helpful in answering this question; by itself, that passage may be even more obscure than 20:17.) In the context of the rest of the Gospel, one might think John refers to the lifting of Jesus to the Father by way of the cross (3:13–15), but this view is problematic on the usual way of reading the verse: 20:17 occurs only after the crucifixion. Therefore, if Jesus refers to this ascension, we must take his words as an ironic question, "Am I not yet ascended?"—implying that he has ascended and been glorified.[252] This proposal is grammatically and logically plausible, but it is not the most natural way for Jesus to have made the point (an emphatic statement that he had ascended would be far less ambiguous) and, in light of other early Christian ascension traditions, may not be our best alternative.

We should remember that whereas John strongly emphasizes realized eschatology, he does not thereby abandon all future eschatology (e.g., 5:28–29; 6:39, 40, 44, 54; 12:48; 21:22–23). That Jesus was no longer physically present with the Johannine community was obvious, and the Lukan tradition of an ascension was the most obvious spatial solution to the current fact (Luke 24:50; Acts 1:9–11; cf. Mark 16:19; Rom 8:34; Eph 1:20; Col 3:1–2; Heb 1:3). Matthew, Mark, and John close before the point where the event would be described (Mark even before resurrection appearances), but the ascension is presupposed by Jesus' Parousia from heaven, a teaching found in Paul's earliest letters (e.g., Phil 3:20; 1 Thess 4:16; 2 Thess 1:7).[253] It appears multiply attested outside the Gospels, at least on a theological level (Eph 4:8–10; 1 Tim 3:16; Heb 4:14; 7:26; 8:1; 9:24; 1 Pet 3:22). That the Spirit came as another advocate, standing in for Jesus, suggests that John also understood that Jesus would be absent from the community, while not "in spirit," yet in body (cf. 1 John 2:1).[254] Jesus would not only go to the Father and return to give them the Spirit; though it is not John's emphasis, he also implies that Jesus would remain with the Father until the "last day," when those in the tombs would arise.

It is also clear that ancient writers could predict events never recounted in their narratives but that the reader would understand to be fulfilled in the story world; the Greek East's favorite work, the *Iliad,* could predict, without recounting, the fall of Troy, which was already known to the *Iliad*'s tradition and which it reinforced through both subtle allusions and explicit statements in the story.[255] The book ends with Hector's burial, but because the book emphasized that Hector was Troy's last adequate defender,[256] this conclusion certainly implies the tragic demise of Troy. The *Odyssey* predicts but does not nar-

---

[250] Bruce, *John,* 389; Carson, *John,* 644.

[251] Cf. McPolin, *John,* 255.

[252] Schneiders, "Encounter," 165.

[253] Witherington, *Acts,* 112–13.

[254] This real presence was, however, stronger than the mere epistolary presence that such language conventions as "absent in body, present in spirit" could imply (1 Cor 5:3; Col 2:5; 1 Thess 2:17; Isocrates *Nic.* 51–52, *Or.* 3.37; Seneca *Ep. Lucil.* 32.1; Achilles Tatius 5.20.5; Stowers, *Letter Writing,* 60; Funk, "*Parousia,*" 264; cf. Diogenes Laertius 7.1.24; contrast Diogenes *Ep.* 17).

[255] E.g., Homer *Il.* 12.15. The *Iliad* regularly predicts (e.g., *Il.* 21.110; 23.80–81) but does not narrate Achilles' death.

[256] Homer *Il.* 6.403; 22.506–507.

rate Odysseus's final trial,[257] but in view of the other fulfillments in the story, the reader or hearer is not left with discomfort. The *Argonautica* will not directly address Medea's unpleasant slaying of Pelias yet hints at that tradition.[258] Likewise, that Mark probably ends without resurrection appearances (Mark 16:8) hardly means that Mark wanted his readers to doubt that they occurred (cf. Mark 14:28)! John probably assumes the tradition of the ascension more widely held by his audience, just as he has probably assumed their knowledge of a more widely circulated passion tradition in earlier narratives.

Ascension was a recognized-enough category in ancient traditions to require little explanation, although Jesus' ascension was qualitatively different in specific respects from most comparable stories. Ancients could depict the soul rising to heaven (e.g., *T. Ab.* 20:12A; 7:13; 14:7B), told stories of newly divinized immortals ascending to heaven,[259] and handed on traditions about Enoch, Elijah, Ezra, and others thought to have escaped death (e.g., 1 Macc 2:58; *1 En.* 39:3)[260] and, on a more regular basis, about angels (e.g., Tob 12:20–22).[261] But whereas Greeks were comfortable with the notion of bodily or nonbodily ascensions,[262] the central Christian concept of Jesus' bodily resurrection, which the Christian ascension tradition presupposes, was utterly foreign to them.

That John accepts an ascension and future eschatology does not mean that his Gospel emphasizes it frequently. To the contrary, as we have already noted, the "ascending to the Father" to which he normally refers is Jesus' ascension by means of the cross that he might now impart the Spirit. John does not narrate an ascension precisely because, through the Spirit's coming (20:22; cf. 14:16–26), he wishes to emphasize the continuing presence and activity of Jesus (21:12–14). But for John in a theological sense, the passion, resurrection, and imparting of the Spirit (fulfilled in 20:22) are all of one piece. Thus it is not surprising that "ascends" is (in Jesus' message for the disciples) in the present tense (20:17). The present tense could denote the "certainty" involved[263] but may be another Johannine double entendre: in Johannine terms, Jesus' ascent, his "lifting up," began with the cross and may be completed only with the giving of the Spirit.

## 2F. Women's Witness (20:18)

Whereas Mary first announced to the leading disciples that someone had carried off the body (20:2), she now announces that she has seen the Lord and that he told her "these matters" (20:18)—presumably, that his ascension is coming and therefore his revelations

---

[257] E.g., Homer *Od.* 23.266–284.

[258] Apollonius of Rhodes 3.64, 75, 1135; 4.241–245. Writing after Euripides, this must be expected.

[259] E.g., Ovid *Metam.* 14.824–828; Diogenes Laertius 8.2.68; Phaedrus 4.12.3; cf. Euripides *Iph. aul.* 1608, 1614, 1622. See more fully Talbert, "Immortals."

[260] See also *2 En.* 67:1–3; *Gk. Apoc. Ezra* 5:7; more fully, Palatty, "Ascension"; Luke, "Ascension"; Tabor, "Divinity"; Begg, "Disappearance."

[261] See also *Jos. Asen.* 17:8, MSS; *T. Ab.* 4:5; 8:1; 15:11; 20:12A; 4:4; 8:1; 10:2B; cf. *Jub.* 32:20–21.

[262] Because of Heracles' apotheosis, people searched only vainly for his corpse (Diodorus Siculus 4.38.3–5); Romulus "vanished" (Plutarch *Camillus* 33.7); other deified persons, such as Aeneas, also "disappeared" (ἠφανίσθη, Diodorus Siculus 7.5.2; the term applies to Heracles in Lysias *Or.* 2.11, §191), as did Moses in Josephus *Ant.* 4.326. Boring et al., *Commentary*, 163–64, also compare the first-century B.C.E. traditions of Romulus's ascension (Livy 1.16.2–8; Ovid *Metam.* 14.805–851; *Vir. illustr.* 2.13; Plutarch *Numa* 11.2–3), even by horses and carriage (Ovid *Fasti* 2.475–510; cf. 2 Kgs 2:11–18), and Job's children in *T. Job* 39:8–40:4.

[263] Morris, *John,* 841.

to them are urgent (20:17). Mary announces her personal-eyewitness experience even though she must be aware of the prejudice against women's testimony in her culture;[264] she could offer it in defiance of such prejudice but most likely offers it simply because it is necessary and because she has nothing else to offer; she trusts the one who sent her to make it adequate (cf. 12:7).

John's primary purpose in emphasizing her witness is undoubtedly less apologetic (cf. 1 Cor 15:5–8) than didactic. The faith of Jesus' mother births his public ministry in 2:3–5; more critically as a parallel here, the Samaritan woman's testimony brings her whole town to meet Jesus for themselves (4:39–42). This sort of testimony and invitation is the same method of witness John recommends for male disciples (1:46). Further, Mary's message (20:18) is precisely that of the male disciples after her (20:25), the sort of witness on which the Spirit would summon subsequent generations to faith (20:30–31).

## Appearances to the Disciples (20:19–29)

Jesus' first appearance to the disciples (20:19–23) provides the pneumatological climax to the Gospel, the fulfillment of the Paraclete sayings and much of the rest of the final discourse; here Jesus "comes again" to them. But Jesus' second appearance (20:24–29) demonstrates the futility of discipleship without the requisite Christology; Thomas's skepticism illustrates what disciples would be like without hope in the resurrection. This second appearance to the gathered disciples provides the central climax for the Gospel because it climaxes John's Christology and his faith motif, defining the basis for sufficient, persevering faith; the Gospel's primary conclusion, 20:30–31, flows directly out of 20:24–29.

### 1. Appearance to the Ten (20:19–23)

The two major aspects of John's pneumatology (rebirth and prophetic empowerment)[265] are fulfilled together in Jesus' "return" to give the disciples the Holy Spirit. One may also note the recurrent context of persecution; although the closed door may allow John to communicate something about the resurrection body (see below and in 20:26), its most explicit function in 20:19 is to indicate that the disciples were afraid of persecution until Jesus came to them, just as John's audience experiences persecution and requires the empowerment of the Paraclete for boldness to confess Christ. They require an adequate Christology as a foundation for boldness, and boldness to maintain such an offensive Christology.

### 1A. A Johannine Pentecost?

Views on the relation between this passage and a later impartation of the Spirit, such as Acts 2 depicts, vary.[266] Some would argue that John retains a distinction between Easter and a later Pentecost, perhaps by John 20:22 symbolically pointing forward to the histori-

---

[264] See, e.g., Josephus *Ant.* 4.219; *m. Yebam.* 15:1, 8–10; 16:7; *Ketub.* 1:6–9; *t. Yebam.* 14:10; *Sipra VDDeho. pq.* 7.45.1.1; cf. Hesiod *Op.* 375; Livy 6.34.6–7; Babrius 16.10; Phaedrus 4.15; Avianus *Fables* 15–16; Justinian *Inst.* 2.10.6.

[265] See Keener, "Pneumatology," 58–114; and Keener, *Spirit*, 8–26.

[266] For one useful summary, see Burge, *Community*, 119–23.

cal Pentecost.[267] Whatever its historical plausibility, however, the view that Jesus merely symbolically promises the Spirit here does not pull together an adequate narrative climax on the literary-theological level of John's earlier promises of the Spirit. Certainly the verb for Jesus breathing on the disciples means more than mere exhalation.[268] Whether John might use Jesus' breathing symbolically, however, is a different question than whether Jesus is portrayed as acting merely symbolically in the story world.

Granted, Luke and John may employ their language for "receiving the Spirit" in different manners,[269] and both experiences are historically compatible, the historical core adapted by John being either a symbolic or a less substantial impartation.[270] But some scholars argue too much in contending that, because John does not describe the Spirit's *activity* beginning in this passage, the disciples have not yet received the Spirit as Paraclete, although they may have received the Spirit in some sense here.[271] Whatever truth this contention may represent in terms of pre-Johannine tradition, suggesting that John intends to communicate a lesser impartation ignores the nature of his narrative. This passage is not the appropriate place to demonstrate the new Paraclete's activity (persecution is present, but so is Jesus) but to introduce him; John can assume that those familiar with his discourses will expect the fulfillment of all long-range promises related to the Paraclete's activity, on the basis of short-range fulfillments implied in the text, the same way readers of Mark can anticipate resurrection appearances even if none are narrated in the Gospel itself (on the assumption of the shorter ending).

Others show that John 20:19–23 fulfills specific promises of the final discourse, especially the promise of the Spirit (14:16–17, 27) and Jesus' promise that after he went away, he would return to them (14:18–19, 22).[272] Other allusions include the fulfillment of "peace" (14:27; 20:19, 21) and "rejoicing" (16:20–24; 20:20),[273] and the language of rebirth or re-creation in Jesus breathing on them also recalls earlier Johannine pneumatological motifs (3:3, 8; 20:22).[274] Empowerment for mission (20:21, 23; cf. Acts 1:8) fits Jesus' earlier promises (15:26–27; 16:7–11). Jesus' glorification began at the cross, so it is logical in the narrative for Jesus to make available the Spirit at this point (7:39), although this by itself would not exclude a continuing or further impartation later.[275] The present passage

---

[267] E.g., Holwerda, *Spirit*, 133 (who sees this as a distinctly apostolic gift, voiding the narrative of its prescriptive function); Carson, *John*, 648–55; Rossum, "Pentecost." Acts separates the resurrection, exaltation, and outpouring of the Spirit temporally but not theologically (Acts 2:33; cf. Robinson, *Studies*, 166).

[268] Turner, *Spirit*, 90–92, arguing that the verb cannot mean "exhale" and that Carson's view of the symbolic promise revives the view of Theodore of Mopsuestia, condemned at the Council of Constantinople (553 C.E.).

[269] With Turner, "Spirit"; see also others, including Keener, *Questions*, 17–78; idem, *Giver*, 137–69.

[270] See Chrysostom *Hom. Jo.* 86; Origen *Cels.* 7.51; Menoud, "Pentecôte"; Horton, *Spirit*, 127–33; cf. Ladd, *Theology*, 297. On the symbolic view, see Burge, *Community*, 117–18, who notes, however, that it does not work on the level of Johannine theology. Barrett, *Acts*, 74, doubts Origen's view on quantity because "the Spirit is personal," but this may read later Trinitarian theology (or even too much of John's Paraclete) into passages that are more functional than ontological in description.

[271] Turner, "Spirit," 28–34, esp. 34.

[272] See Bartlett, "Coming," 73; Beare, "Spirit," 96.

[273] Cf., e.g., Beare, "Spirit," 96; Lightfoot, *Gospel*, 335.

[274] Hatina, "Context," also employs *Tg. Onq.* and *Tg. Neof.* on Gen 2:7 to argue for genuine rather than merely symbolic eschatological fulfillment here.

[275] Because I doubt that the ascension-glorification is actually complete in 20:25 (cf. comment on 20:17; this is a primary objection of Turner, *Spirit*, 94), the text allows a subsequent

merely confirms the link between Jesus' return after the resurrection and the impartation of the Spirit already implied in the final discourse;[276] the fulfillment is nearly as clear as that between Luke 24:49 and Acts 2:4.[277] Thus some write that this passage and Acts 2 ultimately represent the same event.[278]

After summarizing arguments for identifying 20:22 with Pentecost, Turner offers several reasoned arguments distinguishing the two events, to each of which I will respond in turn.[279] First, Turner states that the glorification (a prerequisite for the Spirit's coming, 7:39) is not complete by 20:22 because the ascension remains future (20:17).[280] I agree that the ascension remains future (see my comment on 20:17), but would argue that for the purposes of John's theological point, Jesus was already "lifted up" sufficiently on the cross for the Spirit to be "given" proleptically (and symbolically) in 19:30. Second, Turner argues that Jesus will not be present when he provides the Spirit, since 16:7 says he will "send" the Spirit to them after his departure. In view of the larger narrative, I would contend that this argument reads too much into the particular words, which if pressed would undercut Turner's argument as well; Jesus "goes" at his death and returns at the resurrection (16:16–22), so sending the Spirit in his absence should technically place the Spirit's coming *before* the resurrection. The language of "sending" deliberately parallels the Father sending the Son, without necessary reference to distinction in location; it simply involves delegated authority and mission (as in 20:21, 23).

Third, Turner argues that the Paraclete is a substitute or replacement for Jesus' presence (14:16–17) yet Jesus continues appearing to the disciples after 20:22 (20:26–29; 21:1). Again, I would respond that this weights the meaning of replacement too heavily; after all, the Spirit also replaces Jesus' presence in Acts (Acts 1:8–11), but this does not preclude a very rare subsequent resurrection appearance (Acts 9:3–4). We might expect overlap even more in John, for whom the cross and exaltation are theologically a single event, than for Luke, whose scheme of salvation history is more chronological. Turner adds here that no empowerment of the disciples convinces Thomas. But Thomas, like Nathanael and the Samaritans, "comes and sees" (1:46; 4:29; cf. 1:39)—now, however, in the midst of the community. Fourth, Turner points out that the disciples remain behind locked doors in 20:26 and still do not understand in 21:15–17, and argues that these experiences appear too anticlimactic to fulfill the glorious promises of John 14–16. In my opinion, this is a stronger argument, pointing at least to a strand of dissonance in John's narrative, created by the historical experience of a later Pentecost that his narrative must stop before recounting. It does not, however, negate the fact that in this short encounter (20:19–23) nearly every promise associated with the Spirit's coming appears at least proleptically.[281]

Part of the conflict between views here may be semantic: are we speaking of the historical events behind John's Gospel or of the theological points he is emphasizing by the arrangement of the elements in his narrative? Some of Turner's observations may suggest

---

impartation—but I do not believe that the text by itself requires it; Jesus has already "gone away" and returned (14:18–20; 16:7, 16–22).

[276] See further Jonge, *Jesus,* 174.

[277] With Ashton, *Understanding,* 425.

[278] E.g., Chevallier, "Pentecôtes."

[279] Turner, *Spirit,* 92–94, summarizes Brown's and other arguments for identifying the two.

[280] One could also note that the disciples, by abandoning Jesus, have not yet met the condition of 14:15; but one could respond that their remaining together (20:19) fulfilled part of the command (cf. 13:34; 1 John 2:19; Acts 2:1).

[281] Turner, *Spirit,* 94–97.

legitimate complexities or incongruities in John's language. These in turn may suggest that John is aware of a subsequent Pentecost event and lays emphasis on an earlier event that also provided an encounter with the Spirit.[282] On the level of Johannine theology, however, this event ties together diverse elements of Jesus' promise of the Spirit, fulfilling a function theologically analogous to Pentecost in Acts: the promised Spirit has come, so the church must live in the empowerment provided. (Even in Acts, on the theological level, the gift of the Spirit is of a piece with Jesus' resurrection and exaltation; as in Acts 2:32–33 [even though they are chronologically distinct; Acts 1:3–5].)

The question whether John intends 20:19–23 as an equivalent to Luke's Pentecost presupposes the question whether he knows about Luke's version of Pentecost. Although other early Christian writers attest the Spirit empowerment of early Christianity (e.g., Rom 5:5; Tit 3:5), they do not comment on the time at which it occurred. Still, an association with Pentecost probably precedes the writing of Luke-Acts. Early Judaism connected Pentecost with covenant renewal[283] and, especially prominent in the rabbis, the giving of Torah.[284] Some have therefore concluded that Luke connects the outpouring with specific aspects of that festival.[285] Intriguing as such a connection would prove, however, it appears tenuous; possible as it was in pre-Lukan tradition, it receives little emphasis in Acts 2,[286] which suggests that Luke already had tradition of an outpouring of the Spirit on the church on its first Pentecost.

Given the connections I believe existed among early Christian communities (see introduction, esp. pp. 41–42), I do think it likely that John knew of a story of Pentecost such as appears in Acts, whether through pre-Lukan tradition or tradition stemming from Acts. Even if Luke's tradition were widespread in the early church, however, and even if it were therefore likely that John and his audience knew the tradition of Pentecost, it would not be necessary to assume that John is directly adapting or reacting against the Pentecost tradition. John completes his Gospel in ch. 21; if he is to narrate any fulfillment of his Paraclete promises that provide continuity between the missions of Jesus and his followers, he must do so here. Further, John's theology necessitates a close connection between the passion/resurrection and the giving of the Spirit (7:39); indeed, he may report a proleptic "giving of the Spirit" at both Jesus' death (19:30) and his resurrection appearance (20:22).[287] Even if the giving of the Spirit in the tradition behind 20:22 represents merely a symbolic or partial impartation, it must bear in John's narrative the full theological weight equivalent to Luke's Pentecost.[288]

But if its narrative function (in terms of its full theological weight) is in some sense symbolic of an outpouring of the Spirit, one need not seek a chronological harmonization with Acts 2.[289] As Burge emphasizes, Luke-Acts itself provides a similar chronological

---

[282] Turner (ibid., 100–102) thinks John sees the Spirit as a single "gift" that arrived in "two chronological stages," yet denies that these need be paradigmatic for subsequent Christian experience. I see the possibility of subsequent experiences in Acts (esp. Acts 8:14–17; treated in Keener, *Questions*, 54–59, revised in idem, *Giver*, 157–68) but also doubt that John speaks to the question directly.

[283] *Jub.* 6:17; Noack, "Pentecost," 89; Le Déaut, "ŠăvŰʿōt."

[284] E.g., Weinfeld, "Pentecost"; Delcor, "Bundesfest"; cf. Charnov, "Shavuot"; Potin, "Fête."

[285] E.g., Williams, *Acts*, 40.

[286] See comments in Keener, *Spirit*, 193.

[287] Cf. Swetnam, "Bestowal."

[288] Cf., e.g., Strachan, *Gospel*, 228; Bultmann, *John*, 692; Michaels, *John*, 335. See more fully the evidence in Burge, *Community*, 123–31.

[289] E.g., Dunn, "Spirit," 704.

situation: because Luke must end his Gospel where he does, he describes the ascension as if it occurs on Easter (Luke 24:51) even though he will soon inform or remind his readers that it occurred only forty days afterward (Acts 1:3, 9). Likewise, "knowing his Gospel would have no sequel," the Fourth Evangelist theologically compressed "the appearances, ascension, and Pentecost into Easter. Yet for him, this is not simply a matter of literary convenience.... John weaves these events into 'the hour' with explicit theological intentions."[290]

### 1B. The Setting (20:19)

By announcing that it was evening on the first day of the week (20:19), John informs the reader that the first revelation to the gathered disciples occurred shortly after the resurrection appearances began. Although some question the timing,[291] it certainly appears consistent with the gospel tradition (1 Cor 15:5).[292] Luke in particular indicates that Jesus left two Judean disciples about sundown (Luke 24:29, 31) and the disciples hurried immediately to Jerusalem (Luke 24:33), where Jesus greeted all the disciples together (Luke 24:36). Mark's Galilean emphasis makes sense of why Jesus promises an appearance to the disciples in Galilee (Mark 14:28; 16:7), which John does not treat as incompatible with a prior Judean appearance such as in Luke (John 21:1). The disciples would also be continuing in their most intense mourning period at this time; later rabbinic traditions suggest that such mourning included sitting without shoes on the ground, abstaining from working, washing, anointing, and even study of Torah.[293]

John may mention the time of day particularly to connect the events of this paragraph closely with the one that preceded.[294] There Jesus surprised Mary, who did not recognize him, and commissioned her to tell his other followers the remaining detail of his mission (20:17), which she carried out (20:18). Now he commissions the disciples to carry his message to those who are not yet his disciples (20:21–23); the story world presumes that they, too, would prove obedient to their commission (17:20).

The disciples have reason to be fearful of "the Jews" within the story world. These authorities (see introduction, pp. 214–28) engineered the execution of their teacher, and the authorities' Roman allies normally sought to stamp out followers of leaders regarded as treasonous.[295] But their fears do not take into account Jesus' promise to return to them (which they do not at this point believe); they act like the secret believers John has so often condemned for acting "on account of fear of the 'Jews'" (7:13; 19:38; cf. 12:42). But whereas some secret believers became more public with their faith under persecution (19:38), those who had been faithful to Jesus in happier times now have abandoned and denied him (16:31–32; 18:25, 27). If the first disciples had reasons to fear, John's audience

---

[290] Burge, *Community*, 148.

[291] Fuller, "Jn 20," finds a historical nucleus behind 20:19–23 but doubts that it occurred on Easter Sunday evening. It is nevertheless interesting that early tradition in Asia Minor claimed that the apostle John celebrated Easter on 14 Nisan (as done probably earlier in Judea) regardless of whether it fell on a Sunday, in contrast to Western churches (Irvin and Sunquist, *Movement*, 79).

[292] Black, *Approach*, 124, regards the peculiar "use of cardinals for ordinals" as a Semitism, which might (though need not) also indicate antiquity; but it may simply be acceptable in eastern Mediterranean Greek in this period.

[293] See Safrai, "Home," 782.

[294] Also Schnackenburg, *John*, 3:322.

[295] Freyne, *Galilee*, 195. He attributes the lack of early Roman persecution of Jesus' followers to Galilean-Judean differences (p. 196), but is it not possible that they simply did not view Jesus' disciples as a threat (18:36–38)?

probably has similar reasons to fear the successors of the Judean authorities in their own day and therefore will learn from the model of assurance Jesus provides in this passage.

Although John informs his audience only that the doors were "shut," this itself is sufficient, given the circumstances for which they were shut (20:19), to imply that they were secured shut, that is, locked or bolted (cf., e.g., Matt 25:10). Normal residences had doors with bolts and locks,[296] which one might especially secure if expecting hostility (*T. Job* 5:3). Those familiar with the passion tradition might envision a spacious room in well-to-do upper-city Jerusalem (Mark 14:15; Luke 22:12; Acts 1:13), where such features would also be likely to be assumed.

John may record that the doors were locked for two reasons. First, he may wish to underline the nature of the resurrection body[297]—corporeal (20:20) but capable of acting as if incorporeal (20:19),[298] though presumably not like the "phantoms" of Greek thought that could pass through the thong of a bolt in a door[299] (which would contradict the image of 20:20). Some have argued that Jesus' body was not yet glorified, on the basis of 20:20 (some cite also Luke 24:39–43); they suggest that John merely neglects to mention that the disciples opened the doors for him. But the repetition of the closed doors in 20:26, again as the context of Jesus' sudden appearance among them, is emphatic; John wishes to underline that Jesus appeared despite closed doors and to the disciples' astonishment.[300] As Witherington notes, "The one who could pass through the grave clothes and leave a neat pile behind would not find locked doors any obstacle."[301] Second, through the locked doors, John underlines the fear of the disciples before Jesus' coming, a deliberate contrast to the boldness implied for their mission to the world after he has imparted his presence to them (20:21–23).[302]

### 1C. Jesus' Appearance (20:19d–21a)

Jesus stood in their midst (20:19, 26), which appears to be the appropriate place for revelations (Rev 1:13; 2:1; 5:6; 7:17), undoubtedly because it is the most visible location (and hence could function as in dramatic staging or any planned appearance). More relevantly, Jesus announces to his fearful disciples, "Peace be with you" (20:19). Although the greeting is customary,[303] one would not think such blessings to lack force (cf. 2 John 10–11; Matt 10:12),[304] especially in view of Jesus' promise of peace due at this point (14:27) and the blessing's repetition in 20:19, 21, 26. Wish-prayers are known in various societies[305] and were certainly common in early Judaism. Jesus intends to communicate

---

[296] Safrai, "Home," 734; cf. Aristophanes *Wasps* 154–155.

[297] Cf. different views on the nature of the resurrection body in early Judaism (Ferguson, *Backgrounds*, 439–40).

[298] Cook, "Exegesis," 4.

[299] E.g., Homer *Od.* 4.795–803, 838–839; Boring et al., *Commentary*, 306, cites *Hom. Hymn*, Hymn to Hermes 145–146. Laurin, *John*, 258, speculates on "molecular displacement," an image not likely to have crossed the minds of John's audience.

[300] Cf. Tholuck, *John*, 452–53.

[301] Witherington, *Wisdom*, 342.

[302] Cook, "Exegesis," 4.

[303] E.g., *Jub.* 12:29; 18:16; 19:29; 21:25; *Gen. Rab.* 100:7. It appears commonly in tomb inscriptions as well (Goodenough, *Symbols*, 2:108).

[304] For situation-appropriate words of "peace," see, e.g., Tob 12:17 (at an angelophany). On the efficacy of such words, cf. 1QS 2.9

[305] Mbiti, *Religions*, 85.

not merely formal greetings but actual peace to his disciples on an occasion where they need it,[306] and this functions as an encouragement to John's audience, who also face opposition.

Jesus showing his wounds (20:20) undoubtedly serves as evidence. Some showed wounds to stir judges or juries against the accused—that is, for the emotive value of *pathos* (e.g., Quintilian 6.1.30);[307] others similarly revealed war wounds to stir emotion and demonstrate one's commitment to the nation.[308] But Jesus here undoubtedly shows his wounds as evidence that he is in fact the same Jesus who was crucified and that he has therefore been raised bodily. Scars could be used to identify a person.[309] Moreover, in a significant stream of Jewish tradition, a person would be resurrected in the same form in which he or she died before being healed.[310] (One may also compare the Greco-Roman view that wounds remained with people who died violently.[311] But because this tradition addresses especially shades in Hades and dreams, it is of only secondary importance to understanding the early Jewish and Johannine perspectives.) Some soldiers also reportedly pleaded to their general that their wounds revealed their mortality and so he should quit pressing them beyond measure.[312] Mortality is not an issue in this instance, but humanity could be. Lest anyone misinterpret 17:5, the resurrection did not cancel the incarnation; Jesus retained a resurrection *body* (an idea naturally uncomfortable for many later gnostics).[313]

The wounds in the "hands" means wounds in the forearms; "hand" can carry this sense and very likely carries the sense here, since crucifixion nails had to be driven higher up the arm than the hand unless ropes were also used; otherwise a person's weight would tear the hands rather than allow the nails to suspend one on a cross.[314] Whether or not John knows the tradition about Jesus showing his feet as well as hands (Luke 24:39–40),[315] he mentions only the hands and the side; the side recalls the source of living water (John 19:34) he has now come to give (20:22; 7:37–39).

That the disciples rejoice when they see him is to be expected; one need not seek parallels in mystery religions. Granted, worshipers of Isis rehearsing the recovery of Osiris might

---

[306] So also others, e.g., Lightfoot, *Gospel*, 335; Haenchen, *John*, 2:210; Cook, "Exegesis," 5.

[307] Also Cicero *Verr.* 2.5.1.3; Seneca *Controv.* 1.4.2. Likewise, wounds could be displayed in corpses to stir indignation (Ovid *Fasti* 2.849; Plutarch *Caesar* 68.1).

[308] E.g., Ovid *Metam.* 13.262–267; *Fasti* 2.696–699 (in this case deceptively); Plutarch *Alex.* 50.6; Arrian *Alex.* 7.10.1–3; Dionysius of Halicarnassus *R.A.* 7.62.3; Livy 45.39.17; Valerius Maximus 7.7.1; cf. Sallust *Letter of Gnaeus Pompeius* 1–2; Caesar *C.W.* 1.72; Silius Italicus 9.350–351; Valerius Maximus 3.2.24; or citing dangers one had faced, e.g., Aeschines *False Embassy* 168–169; Cicero *Cat.* 4.1.2; 1 Cor 15:30. Cf. also bruises as marks of athletic exertion (Maximus of Tyre *Or.* 3.4).

[309] E.g., Homer *Od.* 19.467–473; P.Ryl. 174.6–7; P.Lond. 334.6; P.Oxy. 494.31; Philostratus *Hrk.* 12.4.

[310] E.g., *2 Bar.* 50:2–4; *Gen. Rab.* 95:1; *Eccl. Rab.* 1:4, §2; for very literalistic understandings of the resurrection, Osborne, "Resurrection," 933, cites 2 Macc 7:10–11; 14:46; *Sib. Or.* 4.176–82. This idea probably is assumed in Matt 5:29 but appears less probable in 1 Cor 15:35–44, 50.

[311] Hilhorst, "Wounds." See Virgil *Aen.* 2.270–279; 6.446, 494–499; Silius Italicus 13.825; cf. also Philostratus *Hrk.* 10.2 (where a spirit appears the same age as when he died). Thus one might amputate a corpse's extremities so its ghost could not exact vengeance (Aeschylus *Cho.* 439).

[312] Plutarch *Caesar* 37.3.

[313] Tertullian *Against Marcion* 4.40, used Jesus promising his body as bread against the docetic view of Jesus' body as a phantom; cf. Luke 24:39.

[314] E.g., Yamauchi, "Crucifixion," 2.

[315] Yohanan's skeleton from Givat ha-Mivtar confirms that legs were occasionally nailed in this period, as in early Athens (Stanton, *Gospel Truth*, 119; Brown, *John*, 2:1022; Brown, *Death*, 950–51; cf. Ps 22:16); piercing of feet was shameful even for a corpse (Homer *Il.* 22.396–397).

cry, "We have found him; let us rejoice!"[316] But joy is the natural response to finding what was lost in general (Luke 15:6, 9, 32), characterized arrival speeches,[317] and was certainly a natural response to receiving their teacher back from the dead. Johannine literature often refers to joy (15:11; 16:20, 22, 24; 17:13; 1 John 4; 2 John 12; 3 John 4) but derives it from more commonplace images than dying-and-rising mystery deities (3:29; 4:36; 16:21). If one need seek parallels, joy was sometimes eschatological in early Judaism[318]—as was the resurrection; perhaps less revealing, some later texts also associate joy with the Torah,[319] and Jesus is the Word (1:1–18). Given the circumstances in the story, it is hard to imagine the disciples failing to rejoice, but John mentions it specifically because it fulfills Jesus' promise in 16:20–24.

### 1D. The Commissioning (20:21)

Comparing Jesus' final commissions in Matthew and Luke-Acts (which also reflect characteristics of OT commissions),[320] it is clear that John preserves substantial elements of his commission from the tradition.[321] More important, however, are the ways John adapts both traditional and distinctive elements to climax a commissioning hinted throughout his Gospel. Both John (1:19–36) and the first disciples (1:41–42, 45–46; 4:39) are prototypical witnesses; Jesus himself functions as the narrative model for the activity of the Spirit-Paraclete, who empowers disciples after Jesus' resurrection to continue his mission (14:16–17, 26; 15:26; 16:7–11); the announcements concerning the risen Jesus also serve as narrative illustrations of this proclamation (20:18, 25, 28).

Early Jewish interpreters often assumed that disciples of prophets received the Spirit to carry on the prophetic mission.[322] In the Fourth Gospel as in the Synoptics, the disciples are partly foils for Jesus, always falling far short when compared with his majesty; their very ordinariness, however, makes them approachable models for readers of the Gospels, who can pattern themselves after them.

That Jesus begins the commission with a second mention of peace indicates that the commission is an assurance oracle rather than a frightful task.[323] Some try to distinguish the two terms for "send" here,[324] but they are used interchangeably throughout the Gospel.[325] Believers can do the work because God has worked for them: the Father sent the Son and empowered believers by the Spirit imparted through the Son (20:22; cf. 15:26–27).[326]

---

[316] E.g., Seneca *Apocol.* 13, applied to Claudius's arrival in the realm of Hades because he favored Eastern cults.

[317] Menander Rhetor 2.3, 385.7–8 (i.e., the rhetor greeting a city in which he arrives or an official arriving there).

[318] E.g., 1QM 17.7; Tob 13:10, 13–14; *Jub.* 23:30; *1 En.* 5:7; 25:6; 47:4; 103:3; *Pss. Sol.* 11:3; *Sib. Or.* 3.619; *2 Bar.* 14:13; see comment on John 3:29.

[319] E.g., *b. Yoma* 4b; *Lev. Rab.* 16:4 (purportedly from Ben Azzai); *Pesiq. Rab.* 21:2/3; 51:4; Urbach, *Sages,* 1:390–92; see comment on John 15:11.

[320] See Hubbard, *Redaction.*

[321] On the agreement of diverse sources concerning the sending and mission, cf. Guillet, "Récits." That John substitutes a Gentile mission for an earlier Jewish one is nowhere implied (see Martyn, "Mission").

[322] See, e.g., *Mek. Pisha* 1.150–153; on the Spirit and succession, see more fully the comment on 14:16.

[323] Lenski, *John,* 1368–69, suggests that they will dispense Christ's peace.

[324] E.g., Laurin, *John,* 261; Bengel, *Gnomen,* 491.

[325] See our introduction, pp. 310–17; cf. also Barrett, *John,* 569.

[326] Stott, "Commission," 5, borrows the anachronistic language of "a trinitarian framework" but accurately captures the relationships in their Johannine framework.

Whereas the sending of the Son is the heart of the Fourth Gospel's plot, its conclusion is open-ended, spilling into the story of the disciples.[327] Thus the church's mission is, for John's theology, to carry on Jesus' mission (14:12; 17:18).[328] Because Jesus was sending "just as" (καθώς) the Father sent him (20:21), the disciples would carry on Jesus' mission, including not only signs pointing to Jesus (14:12) but also witness (15:27) through which the Spirit would continue Jesus' presence and work (16:7–11). The idea of agents passing on a gift to others as one had received it from Jesus is familiar from elsewhere in the Jesus tradition (Matt 10:8).[329]

## 1E. Empowerment for the Mission (20:22)

The breathing alludes back to the wind of 3:8, linking it with the image of regeneration by the Spirit in that context (3:3–6). Even if the punctiliar force of the aorist were pressed, it would not imply that the gift was solely for the apostles present, although the gift may be unrepeatable, but, rather, that the gift was imparted on this occasion once for all to be available hereafter to the rest of the church.[330] The imperative may, however, connote that although the gift is freely offered to all, it must be embraced by those who would accept the offer.[331]

This passage combines two of the central aspects of the Spirit's work that appear elsewhere in John and various early Jewish sources,[332] both purification or rebirth (Gen 2:7) and empowerment. Most scholars concur that when Jesus breathes on the disciples, John is alluding to the creative, life-imparting act of God in Gen 2:7;[333] Jesus is creating a new humanity, a new creation.[334] Although the verb for "breathe" here is a rare one, it occurs in Gen 2:7 and Ezek 37:9 as well as quotes of it in Philo and Wis 15:11.[335] Similar images appear elsewhere in early Jewish texts, but many depend on Genesis (such as Wis 15:11; 4 Ezra 3:5–7)[336] or simply reflect common language in the milieu (cf. perhaps 2 Kgs 4:34).[337]

---

[327] Stibbe, "Return," employing actantial analysis.

[328] Cf. Kallarangatt, "Mission."

[329] Some taught that God commissioned Torah teachers to offer Torah freely as he did (b. Bek. 29a; Derek Ereṣ 2.4; Dalman, Jesus-Jeshua, 226; Lachs, Commentary, 180; cf. m. ʾAbot 1:3; Sipre Deut. 48.2.7; p. Ned. 4:4); in secular contexts, see, e.g., Xenophon Cyr. 8.3.3 (royal gifts).

[330] Cf. Westcott, John, 294. On the usual punctiliar force of aorist imperatives, see Blass, Debrunner, and Funk, Grammar, 172–73, §§335–337.

[331] See Hawthorne, Presence, 236.

[332] See Keener, Spirit, 8–13.

[333] Haenchen, John, 2:211; Sanders, John, 433; Dunn, "Spirit," 703; Ellis, Genius, 293; Wojciechowski, "Don" (though reading too much from the Targumim, which is then used to connect John 20 with Pentecost); O'Day, "John," 846; du Rand, "Ellips."

[334] Cook, "Exegesis," 8; Meier, "John 20:19–23." On the Spirit and creation, some suggest also Wis 1:7; 12:1. Stauffer, "ἐμφυσάω," 536–37, notes the association of the Spirit and creation in Ps 104:30 [103:30 LXX].

[335] Turner, Spirit, 90–92, who also notes (p. 92) that Wis 15:11 and Philo on Gen 2:7 show God breathing his own Spirit at the creative event of Gen 2:7, suggesting new creation here (3:3, 5).

[336] Also Philo Creation 139. The Spirit of God creates or builds creatures in Jdt 16:14; cf. God's gift of truth by God's breath (Odes Sol. 18:15), etc. Witherington, Wisdom, 343, helpfully compares Jesus with Wisdom here (Wis 7:22–23).

[337] Derrett, "Blow," suggests an allusion to the Asian custom of catching the dying person's last breath (attested at times in India and farther east). One might add Roman examples (see Quintilian pref.12; Virgil Aen. 4.684–685; Ovid Metam. 7.861; comment on 19:30), but Jesus is clearly not dying here and the biblical allusion would be far more obvious, especially in view of the rest of the Gospel (cf. 3:8).

In some manuscripts of *Joseph and Aseneth,* Joseph imparts the spirit of life with a kiss to Aseneth, who is now converting (*Jos. Asen.* 19:11).[338] But despite the value of these other images to suggest language that was "in the air," such sources shared with John, his audience, and early Judaism in general a thorough knowledge of the language of Genesis in Greek. (A specifically Philonic interpretation of Gen 2:7 on the earthly versus the heavenly man is probably too remote to prove particularly helpful here.)[339]

Genesis 2:7 was naturally connected with Ezek 37:9 in later midrash and Jewish artwork,[340] and Ezek 37:9 was explicitly understood to refer to the resurrection of the dead.[341] Given John's earlier treatment of rebirth imagery (3:3–5) and his linking of water (3:6) and wind (3:8) images for the Spirit (cf. Ezek 36–37), it is likely that he recalls here the regenerating aspect of the Spirit of purification. Jesus had promised that his return to them alive would bring them new life as well (14:19).

Jesus as the giver of the Spirit is a recurrent theme in the Gospel, starting in 1:33 and climaxing here (e.g., 3:5; 7:37–39; 19:30, 34). This emphasis serves an important christological function (cf. 3:34) because, as the giver of God's Spirit, Jesus himself is divine (especially here, where his action evokes God's creative work of breathing life into Adam). In biblical imagery, only God would baptize in his Spirit (as in 1:33; 3:5) or pour out his Spirit (Isa 42:1; 44:3; 61:1; 63:11; Ezek 36:27; 37:14; 39:29; Joel 2:28–29; Hag 2:5; Zech 4:6; 12:10).

Although the purification aspect of the Spirit is important here, the other main aspect of the Spirit, as prophetic anointing to declare God's message, is explicit in this text.[342] Immediately before Jesus commands them to receive the "Holy Spirit" (the phrase connects the Spirit of purification in 1:33 and the Spirit of prophecy in 14:26), he commissions them to carry on his own mission from the Father (20:21). (This phrase appears only three times in the Gospel, including its first [1:33] and final [20:22] uses. Just as the Gospel proper concludes with Thomas's confession of Jesus' deity, forming a christological *inclusio* with the prologue, this passage closes a slightly smaller pneumatological *inclusio*.) These relate to the prophetic mission of his disciples. John 20:19–23 binds together the two main pneumatological motifs in the Fourth Gospel, showing that only those who are purified or regenerated by the Spirit will be empowered by him to experience and proclaim the risen Christ.

For John, all those who believe are to "receive" the Spirit after Jesus' glorification (7:39), so the experience depicted here for the disciples functions proleptically for the

---

[338] Perhaps the writer wanted to avoid the impression that Joseph could have kissed her for less sacred reasons at this point? The breath of life in magical papyri (*PGM* 12.237, in Grant, *Religions,* 46) may be influenced by Jewish sources or common ancient Near Eastern roots; cf. *Orphic Hymns* 30.8. Greek deities could breathe strength into wounded heroes (Homer *Il.* 15.60—ἐμπνεύσῃσι; 19.159—πνεύσῃ).

[339] Philo *Alleg. Interp.* 1.31–32; more relevant for 1 Cor 15:45–49. For Philonic exegesis of Gen. 2:7, applying it especially to the soul's immortality, see esp. Pearson, *Terminology* (he addresses the gnostic exegesis in pp. 51–81); for later rabbinic exegesis with the two impulses, see, e.g., Hirsch, *Pentateuch,* 1:56–57.

[340] *Gen. Rab.* 14:8; Grassi, "Ezekiel," 164. Wojciechowski, "Don," also notes that God's breath in the Targumim on Gen 2:7 brings the word, enabling Adam to speak, suggesting relevance for John 20:22 and Acts 2:4; cf. perhaps also *1 En.* 84:1.

[341] E.g., *Sipre Deut.* 306.28.3; *p. Šeqal.* 3:3; *Exod. Rab.* 48:4. Rabbis also assumed that the Spirit implied resurrection in some other texts (e.g., *p. Sanh.* 10:3, §1; *Gen. Rab.* 26:6; cf. *1 En.* 71:11). Philonenko, "Qoumrân," parallels 4Q385 and the Dura Europos mural of Ezek 37:1–14.

[342] If the traditions they preserve are early enough (which is uncertain), it may be relevant that *Tg. Ps.-J.* on Gen 2:7 and *Tg. Neof.* on Gen 2:7 both attribute Adam's gift of speech to divine insufflation.

whole church. The language of "receiving the Spirit" (also 14:17; cf. 1 John 2:27) accords with early Christian tradition, normally for the experience of new relationship (Rom 8:15; 1 Cor 2:12; 2 Cor 11:4; Gal 3:2, 14) or empowerment for mission (Acts 1:8) temporally at (Acts 10:47), or theologically implicit in (Acts 2:33; 19:2), conversion, although in the early church's experience it may have applied to a postconversion experience in some cases (Acts 8:15, 17).[343] That John uses λαμβάνω rather than δέχομαι here (20:22) does not merit more than passing interest, although the former term could sometimes bear stronger force. In the whole Gospel, John employs the latter term only once (4:45, and nowhere in the Epistles; probably interchangeably with λαμβάνω; cf. 4:44; 1:11) and the former forty-six times (plus six times in the Epistles). The imperative may, however, connote that although the gift is freely offered to all, it must be embraced by those who would accept the offer.[344] "Receiving" the Spirit here also refers to the beginning of an indwelling (14:17, 23) and hence implies a fuller inspiration than that reported among the biblical prophets.[345]

### 1F. Authority for Forgiveness (20:23)

Immediately after breathing on them and announcing the Spirit, Jesus grants them the authority of representative forgiveness.[346] It is anachronistic to read into this passage the later Catholic doctrine of penance or others' views about admission to baptism;[347] it is likewise anachronistic to read into it Protestant polemic against the Catholic interpretation of the passage. Read on its own terms, the passage makes good sense as it stands.

Because the Spirit would continue among them (20:22), they would be able to carry on Jesus' work (cf. 16:7–11);[348] given the backdrop of 16:7–11, which explains the meaning of the Spirit's coming here, the disciples announce both righteousness and judgment based on people's response to Christ (cf. 14:6).[349] Although the promise is given directly to those present at the time (20:19), it will no more exclude later generations of Christians (such as John's audience, 17:20–22) than it would Thomas once he believes (20:24). If the Spirit is for later Johannine Christians as well as for the first ones (3:5; 1 John 2:20, 27), then they, too, will bear witness (15:26–27) and be recipients of the Spirit (16:7), who prosecutes the world concerning sin, righteousness, and judgment (16:8–11).[350]

The passive is a divine passive; forgiveness comes from God; further, in John's perspective, only Jesus' sacrifice takes away sin (1:29). In the perspective of Johannine

---

[343] See my discussion in Keener, *Questions,* 46–61; idem, *Giver,* 157–68.

[344] See Hawthorne, *Presence,* 236.

[345] Cf. Johnston, *Spirit-Paraclete,* 49–50; Ezek 36:27; though cf. 1 Pet 1:11; Gen 41:38; Num 27:38; Dan 4:8–9, 18; 5:11–14; corporately, Isa 63:11; Hag 2:5.

[346] In 4QNab 1.4 an exorcist "forgives" sins; but this may only mean that he *pronounced* forgiveness, a prerogative Sanders, *Judaism,* 240, associates with the priesthood in the pre-70 period; the idea of being mediators of God's forgiveness appears with regard to conversion and disciple making in rabbinic texts (e.g., *b. Sanh.* 107b; cf. *b. Yoma* 86b–87a). Here it is associated with the bearers of the divine word.

[347] Quast, *Reading,* 137.

[348] With, e.g., Cook, "Exegesis," 7–8.

[349] Cf. Isaacs, "Spirit," 405. Differently, Tholuck thinks the Spirit provides discernment of who is truly repentant (*John,* 454–55).

[350] Most commentators acknowledge that all believers are in view from the standpoint of John's theology (e.g., Beare, "Spirit"; Smith, "John 16," 60; Lenski, *John,* 1389; Wheldon, *Spirit,* 283–84). "Disciples" (20:19) certainly includes the Twelve (20:24–25), but its Johannine usage is broader; cf. also Morris, *John,* 844.

Christians, however, believers can play a role in other believers' forgiveness, at least by prayer (1 John 5:16–17);[351] the present passage speaks of believers' ministry to nonbelievers, mediating God's forgiveness through the word they bring (20:21; 16:8–11).[352] (We mean "word" in its Johannine sense; by proclaiming the message of Jesus, to whom the Spirit testifies, believers proclaim Jesus the word himself, who is revealed by the Spirit to unbelievers.) In the Synoptics, the disciples had already exercised such discretion based on evidence of repentance (Mark 6:11; Matt 10:14; Luke 9:5); John has, however, omitted that preresurrection ministry of the disciples, probably to avoid playing down the full role of Christ before the resurrection and the full role of the Spirit and believers after 20:19–23.[353]

Some take the perfect tense as meaning that "the apostolic sentence is forthwith confirmed—is effective as soon as spoken."[354] Others suggest that the perfect tense here, like the future perfect in Matt 16:19; 18:18, may be intended literally, that is, that those who pronounce forgiveness are merely confirming what has already taken place from God's perspective.[355]

The Qumran community recognized some individuals who were to control entrance to the community. Later rabbinic literature also testifies to the authority of interpreters to apply biblical legislation and hence, by implication, of judges to exclude and admit on behalf of the community.[356] One might also think of strategies: later rabbis portrayed Shammai as driving away prospective converts but Hillel intentionally welcoming them.[357] Less relevant but helping Western interpreters better grasp the broader milieu, some scholars point out that in some Middle Eastern communities today, particular individuals are held to be able to exercise the wisdom necessary to resolve conflicts in the community.[358]

Some scholars argue that the saying differs significantly from Johannine style, which may suggest its pre-Johannine origin.[359] While the case against Johannine style is overstated—ἀφίημι may not appear elsewhere in this Gospel for forgiveness, but the conception is certainly not foreign to it (1:29; 3:15–17; 16:9)[360]—other features may imply a pre-Johannine origin. Some propose an Aramaic source for this saying, possibly linking it with a similar saying in Matthew 16:19; 18:18[361] (though the linkage alone would not guarantee its authenticity).[362] The Jewish Aramaic, together with the Syriac שׁרא, "means,

---

351 See Brown, *John*, 2:1044.

352 E.g., Fuller, *Formation*, 141, applies it to "the granting or withholding of baptism on acceptance or rejection of the kerygma"; Beare, "Spirit," 99, applies it to both baptismal authority and church discipline.

353 Cf. Ladd, *Theology*, 118.

354 E.g., Beare, "Spirit," 99; cf. Westcott, *John*, 295.

355 So Mantey, "Translations"; idem, "Evidence." Metzger, *Commentary*, 255, regards the present and future tenses for ἀφίημι as possible "scribal simplifications."

356 See Keener, *Matthew*, 454–55. Bernard, *John*, 2:680, notes that John lacks the rabbinic "bind" and "loose."

357 See ²*Abot R. Nat.* 15A; *b. Šabb.* 31a; Daube, *Judaism*, 336–41. Longenecker, *Paul* 207, is, however, correct that Paul's strategy (1 Cor 9:19) resembles Jesus more than tradition about Hillel.

358 Derrett, "Binding."

359 Beare, "Spirit," 97, on Bauer. Some accept its early character yet attribute it to early Christian prophecy (e.g., Fuller, *Formation*, 141).

360 Elsewhere in Johannine literature, see 1 John 1:9–2:2; 2:12.

361 E.g., Emerton, "Binding"; McNamara, *Targum*, 129–30; Dodd, *Interpretation*, 348. The term κρατῆτε is not normal Greek, but neither has it been satisfactorily explained as a Semitism (Emerton, "Binding," 327).

362 E.g., Claudel, "Parallèles," affirms the relationship of the sayings but doubts their authenticity.

not only 'to untie, loose,' but also 'to forgive, absolve'" and sometimes is used interchangeably with an Aramaic term more likely behind the Matthean saying.[363] That John and Matthew ultimately reflect the same saying is by no means clear,[364] but at the very least they reflect analogous concepts.[365]

## 2. Appearance to Thomas (20:24–29)

Thomas's unwillingness to believe without seeing reflects a thread that runs throughout the Gospel: many respond to signs with faith (1:50; 10:38; 11:15, 40; 14:11) and refuse faith without signs (4:48; 6:30), but unless this faith matures into discipleship, it must prove inadequate in the end (8:30–31). (Signs were inadequate, not negative, however; unbelief even in the face of signs was particularly hardened unbelief—12:37.) A good rhetorical strategist gradually building a case might save an especially irrefutable, clinching argument for the conclusion of the speech.[366] This paragraph will therefore set the stage for the conclusion of the Gospel proper (preceding the epilogue in John 20): John's generation believes the signs available to it because the Spirit confirms for it the testimony of the eyewitness who testifies these things (20:30–31; cf. 15:26–27; 16:7–15).

### 2A. Thomas's Skepticism (20:24–25)

Jesus has lost none except Judas (17:12), and "the Twelve" remain a defined group even without Judas (20:24).[367] Thus Jesus must appear once more while Thomas is present; this happens after eight days (20:26) to suggest the following Sunday, perhaps to emphasize the worship experience of early Christians as the context for Jesus' revelations (cf. Rev 1:10). Thomas may suppose that his fellow disciples had seen merely a ghost[368] if in fact they had seen anything at all; but ghost stories were not resurrections (see comments above), and Thomas is unwilling to believe.

Because Thomas plays no significant individual role in other extant first-century traditions (i.e., the Synoptics), some scholars have proposed special reasons for Thomas being the particular disciple to fill this role here, proposing a specific Thomas tradition existing in this period. One approach connects Thomas with the beloved disciple, thereby affecting how readers encounter that disciple as a model for faith.[369] Yet it appears difficult to reconcile the anonymous disciple with Thomas.[370] Another approach takes Thomas's appearances in this Gospel as instances of polemic against the Thomas tradition that stood

---

[363] Emerton, "Binding," 328, 330.

[364] Ibid., 326. Feuillet, *Studies,* 24, suggests the same idea in less strictly Jewish language.

[365] This would not be the case if one reads κρατέω here as "overpowering" sins where mere release proved ineffective (Seitz, "Bemerkungen"), but this interpretation is less likely (see Weidemann, "Joh 20, 23").

[366] E.g., Cicero *Quinct.* 25.78–80. Although 20:30–31 is technically John's concluding summation, sometimes a closing argument or summation could be a proposal that was one's strongest argument for the case (Isaeus *Estate of Hagnias* 50). A good rhetor should announce the topic beforehand, then sum up at the end (Cicero *Or. Brut.* 40.137), which John does in a sense in 1:1, 18; 20:28.

[367] A group could retain its numerical label even if not numerically accurate, such as classical Athens's "so-called Five Thousand" (Plutarch *Alc.* 26.2, LCL 4:75) or more contemporary Roman "centuries" consisting of about eighty soldiers (Jones, "Army," 194).

[368] A widespread belief, e.g., Lucan *C.W.* 1.11; see further above.

[369] See Charlesworth, *Disciple.*

[370] See introduction, chapter 3, on authorship.

behind the *Gospel of Thomas* and its community.[371] If we nuance this view to allow for traditions that later became the *Gospel of Thomas* rather than that work itself, this approach is possible and plausible. It is not, however, by any means certain. Synoptic tradition recognizes that the disciples responded with skepticism, and some more than others (Matt 28:17; Luke 24:11, 24, 38, 41); it is not impossible that John simply preserves a more detailed tradition where a notably skeptical disciple is named, one who was eager to follow Jesus (11:16; 14:5) though too devastated by Jesus' death to accept the apostolic witness of his colleagues (20:25). That a tradition that later became the *Gospel of Thomas* adapted some ideas once related to Thomas is possible, but it is also possible that it merely exploited his name.

That some disciples disbelieved (cf. Mark 16:11, 13–14)—some even after seeing (Matt 28:17; Luke 24:37, 41)—fits other historical traditions about Jesus' resurrection appearances. That John draws on genuine historical tradition need not deter us, however, from asking what theological capital his first audience might have drawn from his narrative. One might naturally protest something unbelievable, that one could believe only if one saw it for oneself.[372] In some ancient stories, deities appeared to and healed doubters in spite of their unbelief[373] (though in some others, a deity enraged with mortals' unbelief might turn them into bats!).[374] Thomas's unbelief need not strike an ancient audience as dramatically anticlimactic; rather, it prepares for a higher climax (in this case, a further resurrection appearance). For example, at the climactic moment of Orestes' self-revelation in Aeschylus, his sister Electra initially fails to believe that it is he.[375] In some ancient Jewish stories, people were punished for unbelief. One student believed R. Johanan only after seeing, whereupon R. Johanan concluded that he scoffed at the words of the sages, and turned him into a pile of bones.[376] A later tradition contends that fire fell from heaven and consumed Haran because he refused to commit himself before he saw whether Abram would defeat Nimrod's fiery furnace.[377] In the biblical exodus narrative, God put up with Israel's unbelief for a long time but finally grew angry with their unwillingness to believe after seeing a number of signs (Num 14:11, 22). When Thomas is skeptical because he has only the word (20:25), he has available what most of the Johannine Christians have (20:31).[378]

## 2B. Jesus' Wounds (20:26–27)

Jesus comes under the same circumstances (closed doors) and with the same greeting of peace as before (20:19, 26). The eighth day held special significance in some early Christian

---

[371] DeConick, *Mystics*, 77–85 (with Thomas replacing Judas as the fool; some later traditions may have linked them, 74–76; but that may be based on this passage). *Gospel of Thomas* 59 supports vision mysticism (pp. 86–108), but John emphasizes instead a *faith* mysticism (109–32), which "replaces the visionary experience with one of faith" (127).

[372] So, e.g., Moses about Israel's calf in *Exod. Rab.* 46:1. Epideictic rhetoric could also be thought exaggerated and disbelieved "on account of envy" (Thucydides 2.35.2).

[373] Epid. inscr. 3, 4, in Grant, *Religions*, 56–57.

[374] Ovid *Metam.* 4.272–273, 402–415; see documentation concerning ancient skepticism in the section of our introduction about signs. Xenophon *Cyr.* 7.2.17 opines that Apollo's oracle led Croesus to ruin precisely because he tested it, so demonstrating unbelief.

[375] Aeschylus *Cho.* 219–20.

[376] *B. B. Bat.* 75a; *Pesiq. Rab Kah.* 18:5 (here the interlocutor is a *min*); *Pesiq. Rab.* 32:3/4. Some rabbis claimed that Moses and Abraham never doubted God (*Sipra Sh. M.D.* 99.5.13).

[377] *Tg. Ps.-J.* on Gen 11:28.

[378] Haenchen, *John*, 2:211.

thought (cf. *Barn.* 15.8–9),[379] but here may simply indicate that Jesus came to them again on the first day of the week (20:19), that is, a day when later Christians frequently met (Acts 20:7; 1 Cor 16:2). This would suggest that the disciples not only stayed for the whole of the Feast of Unleavened Bread[380] but also somewhat longer, perhaps in anticipation of Pentecost. The parallel between the two paragraphs suggests that something remains incomplete until Thomas's confession of Jesus with its high Christology (20:28).

Crucifixion victims often had wounds, and those who had been wounded often showed their wounds to make a point (see comment on 20:20); that Jesus did so stems from pre-Johannine tradition (Luke 24:39–40, though 24:40 is textually uncertain). Soldiers who carried out crucifixions often used rope[381] but also used nails through the wrists,[382] which seem to have been used for Jesus (20:25, 27). Dibelius, noting that Matthew and Mark omit the piercing of hands and/or feet, which appears only as hints in the Easter narratives of Luke (24:39) and John (20:20, 25, 27), thinks the hints of piercing stem from Ps 22:17 rather than historical recollection.[383] But Dibelius's skepticism on this point is unwarranted for several reasons: all four extant first-century gospels omit it in descriptions of the crucifixion (as well as many other explicit details, such as the height of the cross, shape of the cross, and other variables we must reconstruct secondhand); Mark and Matthew include the briefest resurrection narratives, Mark without any appearances, so one would not expect them to recount it there; and finally, Luke and John probably supply independent attestation of a tradition that predates both of them, yet neither allude clearly to Ps 22:17.[384]

Putting hands into Jesus' wounds would convince Thomas that this was the same Jesus (see comment on 20:20); no trickery would be possible.[385] John omits another tradition in which Jesus confirms his bodily resurrection by eating with the disciples (Luke 24:41–43), preferring the stronger proof of his corporal resurrection.[386] In the third-century *Vita Apollonii* by Philostratus, Apollonius invites two of his disciples to grasp him to confirm that he has not, in fact, been executed;[387] but the Christian resurrection narratives were widespread in the Roman Empire by the time Philostratus dictated his stories.[388]

## 2C. The Climactic Christological Confession (20:28–29)

Ancient writers often used characterization to communicate points about "kinds" of people. Nicodemus was slow to believe (3:2; cf. 7:50) but eventually proved a faithful dis-

---

[379] Probably adapted from the seven ages in some Jewish thought, climaxing with the seventh Sabbath age (*L.A.E.* 51:1–2; *Apoc. Mos.* 43:2–3; cf. *T. Ab.* 19:7A; 7:16B; *Mek. Šabb.* 1.38–43; perhaps also *Jub.* 50:9, but probably not).

[380] Marsh, *John,* 648.

[381] Brown, *Death,* 949, cites Pliny *Nat.* 28.11.46; Livy *Hist.* 1.26.6.

[382] Brown, *Death,* 949, cites Philo *Posterity* 61; Lucan *C.W.* 6.547 (the cross appears in 6.545); Plautus *Mostellaria* 2.1, §360; *m. Šabb.* 6:10; Seneca *De vita beata* 19.3.

[383] Dibelius, *Tradition,* 188–89.

[384] Brown, *Death,* 949–50. *Gos. Pet.* 6:21; Ign. *Smyrn.* 1.2 also mention the nails.

[385] Stauffer, *Jesus,* 152, cites Jewish accusations against Jesus of practicing magical resurrections, this also being a trick.

[386] Apparent eating was sometimes visionary (Tob 12:19); for the strange nature of a demigod's eating, cf. Philostratus *Hrk.* 11.9.

[387] Blackburn, "ΑΝΔΡΕΣ," 193, emphasizes the distinction between Apollonius proving he has not yet died and Jesus proving that he has risen bodily.

[388] The same factor may account for Jesus' appearance here after a week, and Philostratus's report that Protesilaos appeared roughly that often (*Hrk.* 11.3), though there it is to provide regular gardening instructions.

ciple (19:38–42). Likewise, Thomas had missed the first corporate resurrection appearance, which convinced most of his fellow disciples; given the problem with secessionists in some Johannine communities (1 John 2:19), his missing might provide a warning to continue in fellowship with fellow believers (to whatever extent Thomas's fellow disciples had already been disciples and believers when Jesus first appeared at that point!) Nevertheless, Thomas becomes the chief spokesman for full christological faith here (20:28–29)—and the foil by which John calls his readers to a faith deeper than the initial resurrection faith of any of the twelve disciples (20:29).

Thomas's very skepticism makes him the ideal proponent of a high Christology by indicating the greatness of the revelation by which he was convinced.[389] Thomas has spoken for the disciples in this Gospel before (11:16),[390] and his revelation elicits the Gospel's climactic christological confession, "My Lord and my God" (20:28), which forms an *inclusio* with the prologue (1:1, 18).[391] (Poetic works often repeated refrains; in a manner analogous with climactic refrains in some such works, however, the christological confessions in John's narrative build toward a crescendo.)[392] In this case, as in the prologue, the confession of Jesus' deity is unmistakeable (cf. Rev 4:11).[393] It cannot simply represent an acclamation to the Father, since John explicitly claims that the words are addressed to Jesus (αὐτῷ).[394]

The linkage of "Lord" and "God" may derive ultimately from the LXX, where the two terms recur together consistently, translating יהוה and אלהים, respectively;[395] the two titles of God continued together in early Judaism.[396] One passage in the LXX even promises at Israel's eschatological repentance the confession "You are the Lord my God" (Hos 2:25 LXX [2:23 MT]), although it is not certain that John alludes to this passage in particular;[397] Ps 35:23 (34:23 LXX: ὁ θεός μου καὶ ὁ κύριός μου) has also been suggested.[398] By the time of the Fourth Gospel, however, the term might have become more familiar in another setting to Christians in the Eastern empire. Eastern cults also conjoined the titles together,[399] and these may have affected the rhetoric of Domitian, who called himself "Lord God" in

---

[389] For arguments that Thomas's faith is a positive model here, see Charlesworth, *Disciple*, 301, 307–8, 312–13.

[390] See Xavier, "Thomas," citing also 14:5.

[391] Also Cullmann, *Christology*, 308; Fenton, *John*, 206; Harris, *Jesus as God*, 127–28. A slightly smaller pneumatological *inclusio* appears in 1:33 with 20:22.

[392] For refrains, e.g., one in Catullus 61.4–5, 39–40, 49–50, 59–60; and others cited in our introduction to the prologue (p. 338). One repeated throughout Catullus 64 (e.g., 64.333, 356) appears in slightly fuller and more explicit form in 64.327. In the case of an incredible report, one should also save it for a climax, first establishing credibility along the way (*Rhet. Alex.* 30, 1438b.4–10).

[393] See Harris, *Jesus as God*, 105–29.

[394] Hoskyns, *Gospel*, 548, with most of early Christianity, against Theodore of Mopsuestia. The conjunction of "Lord" and "God" and lack of vocative indicates far more than Thomas's vocative address of 14:5 (cf. 13:25, 36–37; 14:8, 22; over thirty times in the Gospel).

[395] Ellis, *Genius*, 296; cf. Deissmann, *Light*, 361; Hoskyns, *Gospel*, 548. See esp. "my God" and "my Lord," Ps 35:23 (LXX 34:23)

[396] E.g., *1 En.* 84:5. Bury, *Logos-Doctrine*, 77, cites the distinction between "God" and "Lord" in Philo *Dreams* 1.163; but the joint use in Philo *Sobriety* 55 may be more to the point.

[397] Among those who see allusions to Hos 2:23 here are Hoskyns, *Gospel*, 548; Brown, *John*, 2:1048. An allusion would explain the use of the nominative κύριος rather than the vocative κύριε; the nominative has been otherwise explained as a Semitism here and in Rev 4:11 (Foerster, "Κύριος," 1086; cf. Blass, Debrunner, and Funk, *Grammar*, 81–82).

[398] Brown, *Christology*, 188–89.

[399] Deissmann, *Light*, 361, citing a North African inscription.

imperial edicts and expected to be called "Lord God" (Suetonius *Dom.* 13).[400] As noted in the introduction, the increased civic demands of the imperial cult in Asia, in addition to pressures within the synagogues, would have created a hostile situation for the early Christians. This situation could have tempted them to either tone down their Christology (for the synagogues) or to compromise its uniqueness (allowing also participation in the civic or imperial cults). Instead John exhorts the Christians to respond by affirming their full Christology: Jesus alone is Lord and God.

Most disciples in the Gospel had begun to "believe" Jesus before the resurrection, often with minimal signs (cf. 1:49); they become paradigmatic for believers after Jesus' ascension.[401] Like the disciples before the resurrection appearances, John's own audience comprised entirely, or almost entirely, believers through the word of others (17:20), who had not seen Christ for themselves (cf. 1 Pet 1:8);[402] through Jesus' words to Thomas, John exhorts his own audience to believe despite having to depend on the eyewitnesses. The Spirit, after all, presented the real Jesus through the witnesses' testimony (John 16:7–11).

Signs-faith is not rejected here; Thomas's faith is a start. But signs are not always available, and signs do not in themselves guarantee faith (6:26; 11:45–47). Thus Jesus provides a beatitude (see comment on 13:17) for those who believe without signs, on the testimony of others about signs Jesus already worked (20:30–31). The argument that those who had not seen yet believed were more blessed (20:29) would have been intelligible in terms of Jewish logic about rewards.[403] But as Thomas's confession demonstrates, the true, resurrection faith requires more than commitment to Jesus (cf. 11:16); it requires in addition the recognition of Jesus' divine role.

---

[400] As often noted, e.g., Deissmann, *Light,* 361; Caird, *Age,* 19; Fenton, *John,* 206; Brown, *Christology,* 189. Cf. probable allusions in Martial *Epigr.* 9.66.3 *(dominoque deoque);* 10.72.3 *(dominum deumque);* already in 41 C.E. Eastern cities called the emperor τοῦ θεοῦ ἡμῶν (P.Lond. 1912.9; see further our introduction, pp. 178–79, 292–93).

[401] See more fully Gloer, "Disciples," 301.

[402] Stressed, e.g., by Strachan, *Gospel,* 16.

[403] Thus, e.g., in one tradition a proselyte is more praiseworthy than one born a Jew because he converted without the signs at Sinai (Vermes, *Religion,* 132 n. 13, citing *Tanḥ. Lekh-Lekha* 6, 63).

# CONCLUSION

## 20:30–31

**M**ANY REGARD THE CONCLUSION of 20:30–31 as the end of the Gospel, viewing ch. 21 as a later addition; others view 20:30–31 as the summary only of the resurrection chapter.[1] Because 20:30–31 pulls together John's themes of witness, faith, and signs so fully, it is best to regard this conclusion as a conclusion to the book. We will argue that ch. 21 is a legitimate part of the Fourth Gospel; ancient writers did not need to stop writing after a conclusion even if it adequately summarized what had preceded (cf., e.g., Phil 3:1; 4:8), and writers were perfectly capable of composing their own anticlimactic epilogues without needing redactors to add such appendices for them (see comment on John 21). But 20:30–31 functions not only as the close of the resurrection narratives but as the close of the body of the Gospel itself, to be followed by its epilogue.

Ancient writers and speakers often closed with clear conclusions, often even summarizing or recapitulating their argument from the start.[2] John does not recapitulate his argument here (cf. perhaps 12:44–50), but he does sum it up. As noted, such a conclusion here need not exclude ch. 21 from the original plan of the document; sometimes such closing summations appear before the very end.[3] (E.g., after offering his concluding summation, Aeschines finishes with an illustration, reserved for the end to augment pathos.)[4]

As Thomas came to full christological faith (20:28) but would have been better to have done so without signs (20:29), the call to faith in 20:30–31 is a summons to full christological faith on the testimony of others backed by the Paraclete. John likely summons his audience to persevere or, in some cases of a more peripheral audience listening in, to come out of secrecy to become publicly identified with other followers of Jesus.

---

[1] E.g., Ellis, *Genius,* 297–98; Minear, "Functions." The "signs" include the resurrection chapter (esp. 20:27, 29) but also the rest of the "signs" in this Gospel (with, e.g., Lightfoot, *Gospel,* 336).

[2] E.g., Aeschines *Timarchus* 196; Cicero *Fin.* 5.32.95–96; *Or. Brut.* 40.137; Polybius 39.8.3; Dionysius of Halicarnassus *Demosth.* 32; *Thucyd.* 55; Musonius Rufus 6, pp. 54.26–56.11 (esp. 54.26; 56.7–11); Aelius Aristides *Fifth Leuctrian Oration* 43–44; *Rhet. Alex.* 36, 1443b.15–16; 1444b.21–35; 37, 1445b.21–23; Hippolytus *Haer.* 10.1; Anderson, *Rhetorical Theory,* 181–82; less fully, cf. Matt 28:18–20; Rom 16:17–19. Of course, open or abrupt endings also appear, as in Mark 16:8 (see our comments on Mark 16:9–20 above, on the resurrection tradition).

[3] E.g., Isaeus *Estate of Cleonymus* 48, out of fifty-one paragraphs. Often they come at the conclusion of the proofs, though this might be near the work's end (Cicero *Quinct.* 28.85–29.90), possibly relevant here; they could also conclude a section (Xenophon *Hell.* 3.5.25, ending book 3; 4.8.19, ending only some events; Polybius 2.71.7–10, esp. 2.71.7–8; Cicero *Fin.* 3.9.31; *Quinct.* 19.60).

[4] Aeschines *Timarchus* 177. After his closing summary (Polybius 39.8.4–6), Polybius adds only closing comments (39.8.7–8).

## Many Other Signs

That John notes that he provides merely a sample of Jesus' signs (20:30; 21:25) is not surprising. (John's words here naturally provided an "open invitation" to later apocryphal writers.)[5] Ancient writers sometimes reported that more stories were available about their protagonists than they could possibly record.[6] Diogenes Laertius complains of Diogenes the Cynic that it would take long to list all the other sayings attributed to him (Diogenes Laertius 6.2.69); he recounts stories about Hipparchia and adds that people tell "innumerable other ones" (literally ἄλλα μυρία, undoubtedly hyperbolically!) about her (Diogenes Laertius 6.7.98). Phaedrus reports that Aesop left so much material that Phaedrus could employ only a small portion, leaving much for others to write.[7] Aristotle notes that a plot derives unity from addressing a single action or theme;[8] thus Homer did not include everything that happened to Odysseus (focusing instead on his travels) or the entirety of the Trojan War.[9] Diodorus Siculus claims that stories about the feats of Heracles were by his time so many and so incredible that a writer must either omit the greatest ones, thus diminishing the god's honor, or recount all of them, so making the narrative "difficult to believe" (ἀπιστουμένην, Diodorus Siculus 4.8.2). Writing essays on Alexander and Caesar, Plutarch warns that their deeds were too many for him to offer more than a sampling (*Alex.* 1.1), "For it is not Histories that I am writing, but Lives" (*Alex.* 1.2; LCL 7:225). He thus promises to focus on the deeds that are σημεῖα, signs, revealing their inner character (*Alex.* 1.3). Although John uses σημεῖα in a different sense, the choice of the same term remains interesting. John or (in other views) the redactor employs more hyperbolic rhetoric to underline this point in 21:25 (for other ancient parallels, see comment there).

Similar statements appeared in more rhetorical essays and speeches as well as narratives, revealing how widespread this rhetorical convention was. Thus Dionysius of Halicarnassus emphasizes that he could offer numerous examples but stops with those he has used lest his treatise become too long; those he has offered, he says, are adequate to demonstrate his claims.[10] Cicero likewise charges that a person or group was so evil that time permitted him only to sample their crimes (hence insinuating further guilt).[11] Other rhetoricians employed the same technique: Lysias, for example, complains that his only problem in prosecuting Eratosthenes is to know when to stop reciting his crimes.[12] He warns that even if they executed Ergocles many times, they would not have avenged all the

---

[5] Achtemeier, "Miracle Workers," 176. Even if redactional, Homer's claim that Aeneas would rule the Trojans (*Il.* 20.303–308) is pre-Virgil and virtually invited the sort of development one finds in Virgil *Aeneid.*

[6] E.g., Valerius Maximus 2.7.5; 3.8.ext.1; Musonius Rufus 10, p. 78.22. Epideictic bards might also complain that time provided the only limit on their praises (Pindar *Nem.* 4.33–34; *Ol.* 2.95; *Pyth.* 4.247–248; cf. Heb 11:32). In many oral genres, one should limit one's examples (Menander Rhetor 2.4, 393.25–30).

[7] Phaedrus 3, *Epil.* 6–7.

[8] Aristotle *Poet.* 8.1–4, 1451a.

[9] Aristotle *Poet.* 8.1.3, 1451a.

[10] Dionysius of Halicarnassus *Thucyd.* 55; *Isaeus* 19–20; *Demosth.* 42, 46, 58; *Lit. Comp.* 11. More detailed discussion might await another occasion, but he needed to use most wisely the space that he had (*Demosthenes* 32; *Isaeus* 14); he wanted to avoid wasting the reader's time (*Demosthenes* 40).

[11] Cicero *Verr.* 2.2.47.118; 2.2.48.118; 2.4.26.57; 2.4.46.102; 2.4.47.105; *Pro Flaccus* 5.12. Likewise, Isocrates *Antidosis* 140, 310, 320, *Or.* 15, feigned inability to complete all his thoughts on a matter within the required time.

[12] Lysias *Or.* 12.1, §120.

wrongs he had done.[13] Aeschines also declares that recounting all his opponent's crimes from one year would consume his entire court day.[14]

Rhetoricians also employed such language for praise: for example, one doubts that anyone could recount all the great deeds of those who died for Athens in battle.[15] A rhetorical biographer would not recount further civil honors of Rufus of Perinthus because such honors cannot compare with Rufus's "skill and learning."[16] Most rhetoricians provided the examples they did include as models for imitation (see introduction, pp. 14–16, 19, 46). Jewish writers could speak of God's deeds and expect them to elicit a response.[17]

John could have written other signs but provides a basic sample for a specific purpose, namely to elicit adequate faith (20:31). In this Gospel, signs are inadequate to guarantee solid faith (cf. 2:23; 4:48; 6:2, 30), but they can provoke one to begin on that journey (e.g., 2:11; 6:26; 7:31; 9:16; 12:37). John had "written" these things (20:31), and as in 19:22, he uses the perfect tense, signifying the continuing impact of what he has written.[18] In John's (and often early Christian) style, however, "written" in the perfect most often refers to Scripture (2:17; 6:31, 45; 8:17; 10:34; 12:14, 16; 15:25).[19] Because he is inspired by the Paraclete (see pp. 115–22, 979–81), the author of the Fourth Gospel may quietly suggest that his work belongs in the same category with the Scriptures of old.[20]

## Purpose of the Conclusion

Surely this conclusion (20:30–31) emphasizes the purpose of the Gospel, which should imply something about the sort of audience the Gospel originally addressed.[21] Because John says, "that you may believe," many think that the purpose of the Gospel is evangelistic.[22] The issue is difficult to settle textually: the aorist subjunctive has the broader geographical support and makes more sense in a summons to initial faith; the present subjunctive depends on the earliest manuscripts and makes more sense in a summons to persevere.[23] But the matter can hardly be settled purely by appeal to the divided textual witness; if this is a conclusion, it should end where the rest of the Gospel's evidence points. Thus many scholars would concur with Luke Timothy Johnson: "The present tense seems

---

[13] Lysias *Or.* 28.1, §179.

[14] Aeschines *Timarchus* 109.

[15] Lysias *Or.* 2.2, §190; 2.54, §195.

[16] Philostratus *Vit. soph.* 2.17.597 (LCL 249).

[17] E.g., 4Q185 frg. 1–2, col. 1, lines 14–15; Ps 66:5–6; Rev 15:1–3.

[18] Morris, *John*, 855.

[19] Analogous phrases appear often enough in the Scrolls (1QS 5.15, 17; 8.14; CD 1.13; 5.1; 7.10–11; 11.18, 20) and in later rabbis (*m. Giṭ.* 9:10; *Sanh.* 10:1; *Mek. Pisha* 1.76–77; *Sipre Deut.* 56.1.2; *p. Meg.* 1:5, §1; *Sukkah* 2:10, §1; 3:5, §1; *Taʿan.* 3:11, §5; *Gen. Rab.* 1:4; cf. *3 En.* 2:4; 5:14; 18:7, 18, 24; 28:4, 9–10; 31:2). Deissmann, *Bible Studies*, 249–50, cites its legal use in Hellenistic papyri.

[20] Apocalyptic revelations could be "written" with analogous authority (Rev 1:3; 5:1; 22:18–19); the uses in 1 John (2:13–14, 21, 26; 5:13) bear such force only if it is imported from the Gospel. For this Gospel possibly functioning as Scripture for Johannine Christians, see Smith, "Gospels," 12–19.

[21] Cf. Reinhartz, *Word*, 9, who argues for a more open definition of implied readers. But the length of time it took the Gospel to spread may also imply its smaller initial audience. For opening or closing explanations for one's manner of presentation, see, e.g., Quintilian *Inst. Or.* 9.2.17 (Anderson, *Glossary*, 104–5).

[22] E.g., Robinson, "Destination," 130; Carson, "Purpose"; Carson, Moo, and Morris, *Introduction*, 170–71; Carson, *John*, 87–95.

[23] Riesenfeld, "*hina*-Sätzen," preferring the present subjunctive here.

the more likely reading, and the whole tenor of the Gospel suggests less a document for proselytism than one of propaganda for the converted."[24]

Undoubtedly John would like to invite faith from his opponents; certainly he wants the closet believers among them to go public with their faith (12:42–43; 19:38–40). But by what means would John get the Gospel into the hands of unbelievers except through the preaching of believers? From the perspective of marketing strategies, the intrinsic probabilities favor a primary audience of believers.

But the Gospel itself suggests the same. Throughout the Gospel, many people become initial believers, but their initial faith proves insufficient without perseverance (2:23–25; 8:30, 59). John's goal is not simply initial faith but persevering faith, discipleship (8:30–32; 15:4–7).[25] John's purpose is to address believers at a lesser stage of discipleship and to invite them to persevere as true disciples.

The immediate context of Thomas provides the climax immediately preceding the conclusion and offers a paradigm for the sort of faith John seeks to elicit. Thomas had been a disciple; he was prepared to die for Jesus (11:16) and to follow where he led (14:5); but his faith was insufficient (20:29). Only when Thomas embraced the full testimony of the resurrection and offered the climactic christological confession that Jesus was Lord and God (20:28) had he become a developed model of faith for John's audience. John is calling his audience to a full confession of resurrection faith: Jesus is God in the flesh, and therefore his claims cannot be compromised, for synagogue or for Caesar. John will settle for no faith less secure than this. Further, while Thomas's faith by sight is accepted, the faith without sight expected of John's audience is greater (20:29; cf. 2 Cor 5:6–7; 1 Pet 1:8). It is grounded in the beloved disciple's testimony sampled in the Gospel (20:30–31), confirmed to hearers by the Paraclete (15:26–16:15).

---

[24] Johnson, *Writings*, 472. Many prefer the present tense and believers here (Brown, *Essays*, 133); Smith, *John* (1999), 386–87, is probably right to regard this as the majority view (though noting that some think the Gospel originally evangelistic and later modified for Christians).

[25] Cf. also others, e.g., Stibbe, *Gospel*, 62.

# 21:1–25

# EPILOGUE

If read as an integral part of the work, John's epilogue provides a model for the disciples' continuing experience of Jesus beyond the resurrection; subsequent disciples would experience this presence of Jesus through the Paraclete (16:8–15; 20:22), but because John emphasizes Jesus' continuing presence, he will close his Gospel with a resurrection encounter rather than with the announced ascension (20:17).

Here the general commission of the disciples in 20:21 becomes a more specific call regarding Peter and the beloved disciple; the former must carry on Jesus' mission as a shepherd yet as also one of his sheep; he will also be able to die for Jesus as he promised in 13:37 but failed to do in 18:25–27. The latter will remain alive, albeit not until Jesus' return. The clarification suggests that Peter was the accepted spiritual leader of the original apostolic circle until his death, and that the beloved disciple became prominent (at least in his own circle) during the period (on our reading, as much as three decades) that followed. It also suggests that some expected Jesus to return before the final original member of the apostolic circle (or, in other readings, circle of eyewitnesses) died and, further, that by the time the Gospel is published, that member has died or expects death in the imminent future and Jesus has not yet returned (except in the realized eschatological sense already fulfilled in 20:19–23).

# THE FUNCTION OF JOHN 21

M ANY REGARD JOHN 21 as a later addition to the Gospel from a different hand; those who regard it as from the same author as the rest of the Gospel usually also regard it as an appendix, recognizing its anticlimactic nature following the conclusion of 20:30–31. Many question the historical veracity of its contents.

## A Later Addition?

Many scholars regard the entirety of ch. 21 as an addition to the original Gospel. Johannine scholarship has traditionally regarded John 21 as an addition distinct from the original Gospel, often for stylistic reasons and nearly always (even by those who believe it was added later by the same author) because the chapter is anticlimactic following the conclusion of 20:30–31.[1] This chapter is a literary unit,[2] and undeniably it is anticlimactic to the primary narrative of the Gospel. Nor would 20:30–31 (or even 20:29) constitute too abrupt a conclusion for the Gospel; ancient books often had abrupt endings.[3]

Yet apart from the special vocabulary needed for the matters at hand (such as fishing), the vocabulary does not differ significantly from that of analogous portions of the Gospel.[4] Various features reveal Johannine style; for example, "the variation of synonyms (verses 15–17), the double 'Amen' (verse 18), the construction 'This he said, indicating . . .' (verse 19; cf. 12:33)"; only in this Gospel is the lake called the "Sea of Tiberias" (21:1; 6:1).[5] Smalley rightly notes that "its general flavour is characteristically Johannine" and that John 21 ties up loose ends previously introduced in the Gospel.[6] Westcott, who regarded the chapter as an appendix, nevertheless insisted that it stemmed from the author of the Gospel, noting its "style and the general character of the language"; he also observed that

---

[1] E.g., Bultmann, *John*, 700; Schnackenburg, *John*, 3:350; Smith, *Johannine Christianity*, 18–19; Schulz, *Evangelium*, 249; Kysar, *John*, 311; Barrett, *Essays*, 160; Beasley-Murray, *John*, 395–96. Ancients also used stylistic criteria (e.g., Dionysius of Halicarnassus *Lysias* 11–12). For inner development of Johannine theology in light of John 21 and beloved-disciple texts, see Thyen, "Entwicklungen."

[2] For its internal unity, see Wiarda, "Unity."

[3] E.g., Isocrates *Demon.* 52, *Or.* 1; Demetrius 5.304; Lucan *C.W.* 10.542–546; Herodian 8.8.8; and further citations above. Cf. Thucydides 8.109.1 (though Thucydides may have added book 8 some time after completing the more adequate break of 7.87.6; he never included speeches in book 8).

[4] There are twenty-eight terms that appear nowhere else in John, but similar figures may obtain for terms in some of the other chapters. E.g., nearly 20 percent of the words in John 11:2 apply only or almost only to the Lazarus narrative, two or three times higher than the percentage in John 21.

[5] Bruce, *John*, 398.

[6] Smalley, *John*, 96. Also Minear, "Functions," who regards ch. 21 as the conclusion to the Gospel and (probably wrongly) 20:30–31 merely as the conclusion to ch. 20.

we lack any textual evidence that the Gospel ever circulated without this "appendix."[7] The "appendix" itself notes the beloved disciple's presence (21:7), which, if taken at face value, allows for the same source as the rest of the Gospel.

Most scholars today acknowledge the weakness of the stylistic argument against authenticity. D. Moody Smith regards the chapter as "unquestionably a later addition, whether by the original author or a later hand";[8] nevertheless he acknowledges that it does not show "a divergent style or vocabulary," that it remains debated whether the theological perspective differs from the rest of the Gospel, and therefore that it may stem from within the community.[9] Margaret Davies thinks that this chapter was added after the completion of the body of the Gospel, but notes that this view is not clear on stylistic grounds; the style and most of the vocabulary and themes fit the rest of the Gospel.[10] "Whether by the same author or another," she concludes, John 21 "provides a fitting conclusion."[11]

Fuller admits, "There is nothing in the style of John 21 to suggest a different hand," but he doubts that it derives from the same author as the rest of the Gospel, because John does not prepare the reader for this section with cross-references, as he has prepared the reader for other sections.[12] But the many connections between John 21 and the rest of the Gospel (see commentary below) call into question Fuller's approach. The Gospel provides few explicit announcements of narratives in the Gospel apart from ch. 20 (e.g., about a chapter on eating Jesus' flesh, John 6); but similar themes connect the material, and ch. 21 is no exception. As even Bultmann admits, no manuscript evidence, vocabulary, or stylistic evidence shows that the chapter is secondary; further, it is not clear that the thematic conclusion of 20:30–31 must close the Gospel, and one could argue that John 21's ecclesial focus is a necessary supplement to the conclusions of John 20.[13] Some use the repetition of the colophon in 21:30–31 and 21:24–25 to suggest that this is a later appendix.[14] But the *inclusio* could constitute a mark of original literary composition as easily as one of redaction (cf. 1:1, 18; 20:28; Matt 5:3, 10; Luke 15:24, 32).

The anticlimactic character of the chapter cannot count against authenticity if the style does not. Granted, John 20 may be "a complete presentation" of the resurrection appearances,[15] but John 21's focus is not confirming the resurrection but tying up the Gospel's loose ends concerning the continuing call of the church (cf. 20:21–23). Some complain that the author of ch. 21 "could manage the Johannine style reasonably well" but his interests lie "outside the main scope of the Gospel";[16] unless one thinks of the author's interest in fishing, however, this objection is debatable. The matter of call has been stressed throughout the Gospel, and images such as sheep, spiritual food, demonstrating love by obedience, and the witness of the beloved disciple hardly appear here for this first time.

---

[7] Westcott, *John*, 299; cf. similarly (especially on authorship of the chapter) Robinson, *Trust*, 83; Hunter, *John*, 191; Morris, *John*, 858; Michaels, *John*, xxii; Feuillet, *Studies*, 25; Trudinger, "John 21."

[8] Smith, "Learned," 227.

[9] Ibid., 227–28.

[10] Davies, *Rhetoric*, 263, following Ruckstuhl, *Einheit*, 218, on the style.

[11] Davies, *Rhetoric*, 263.

[12] Fuller, *Formation*, 146; he believes that Luke 5:1–11 was transposed to a resurrection appearance here (pp. 151, 160–61). Many who doubt that it was original to the Gospel nevertheless affirm (e.g., Trudinger, "Ironies"; cf. Witherington, *Wisdom*, 352) or allow that it stems from the same author.

[13] Cf. O'Day, "John," 854–55, summarizing Hoskyns.

[14] Smith, *John* (1999), 27.

[15] Beasley-Murray, *John*, 395.

[16] Grayston, *Gospel*, 172.

John 21 provides a different kind of closure than the conclusion of 20:30–31, showing that the story will continue after the Gospel's completion.[17]

This ending is anticlimactic, but other works could close the main body of the work yet include a substantial epilogue.[18] Indeed, 1 John continues seven verses after its conclusion in 1 John 5:13.[19] Whitacre, who thinks this chapter may be "the intended conclusion and not an epilogue," also points to other "summary conclusions" appearing "before the actual end of the material" in Johannine texts (12:36–37; Rev 22:5).[20] Most significantly, the most widely read work in the Greek East was the *Iliad,* which would therefore provide a standard literary model.[21] Yet the closing book of the *Iliad* (book 24), recounting Priam's rescue of Hector's body, is completely anticlimactic to the action of the plot; its importance is for characterization, not for action. To reject as secondary any endings that are anticlimactic is to ignore the primary literary model of Mediterranean antiquity.[22]

Ancient editors sometimes did add endings that spoiled a book's cohesive unity, but when we have clear examples, they are clear because they reverse the author's views.[23] John's epilogue does not reverse the ideas of the Gospel's body. Literary connections tie this epilogue to the rest of John,[24] though these do not demonstrate unity conclusively. For example, it includes a confession parallel to those of the resurrection narratives of ch. 20 (20:18, 25, 28; 21:7).[25] Others connect the call stories of the first chapter with the themes of John 21.[26] If one reads the Gospel as a whole, 20:30–21:25 can function as a final farewell scene (in which case, 20:30–31 and 21:24–25 function as a rather obvious *inclusio*).[27] Such connections, however, could be explained either as the work of the original author or as the work of an editor steeped in his Gospel. One could argue, against the originality of such connections, the pneumatological inclusion at 1:33 and 20:22 ("Holy Spirit," elsewhere in John only at 14:26) and the larger christological *inclusio* at 1:1–18 and 20:28;[28] but this argument would appeal to a sense of perfect symmetry that is not characteristic of most of John's literary design. Many scholars understandably believe the burden of proof rests with those who challenge scholarly consensus; I am more inclined to leave the burden with those who challenge the simplest explanation, which is usually unity. In the absence of

---

[17] See Gaventa, "Archive," 249.

[18] See Jackson, "Conventions," on postscripts.

[19] Hunter, *John,* 191. He also notes (pp. 191–92) that Matthew and Luke conclude not with initial resurrection appearances but with a commissioning, which he finds in ch. 21 (but which one could just as easily argue, on the other side, is provided sufficiently in 20:21–23).

[20] Whitacre, *John,* 489.

[21] In addition to manuscript evidence and the readily available quotations in antiquity, some people of antiquity acted out details of the *Iliad* in their own day (Herodian 4.8.4–5).

[22] One could argue that even the end of the *Iliad* is secondary, but this would not help the case against authenticity; the point is that the *Iliad* in its accepted first-century form had an anticlimactic ending that was not believed secondary. Cf. also Homer *Od.* 23–24, though it may constitute a necessary wrap-up to allow Penelope to recognize Odysseus.

[23] E.g., Xenophon *Cyr.* 8.8.

[24] Cf., e.g., Breck, "Conclusion" (who regards it as authentic); Neirynck, "John 21." Cf. Spencer, "Narrative Echoes," though he reads the connections as results of the later author's intertextual relationship with the Gospel (which would be how we would need to take them if other grounds persuaded us that John 21 is later).

[25] Cf. Sabugal, "Resurrección."

[26] E.g., Franzmann and Klinger, "Stories."

[27] On the coherency of 20:30–21:25 if one wishes to read the Gospel as a whole, see Segovia, "Farewell."

[28] By contrast, Carson, *John,* 665–68, favors John 21 as an epilogue that balances that prologue.

evidence to the contrary (and being anticlimactic is not evidence, as we have noted), it is normally better to view a work as a unity.[29]

# Historical Questions

Regardless of questions of unity with the rest of the Gospel and of authorship, scholars also question the historical likelihood of the passage's contents, an issue more difficult to evaluate given the relative paucity of extant historical data.

## 1. Both Galilean and Judean Revelations?

Some regard this chapter as an appendix so that the writer could add a Galilean revelation to the Judean revelations in John 20.[30] Some have thought these revelations incompatible; Marxsen thinks that Mark emphasized a parousia in Galilee (Mark 14:28; 16:7) and was followed by later traditions in Matt 28 and John 21, whereas Luke and John had Judean appearances.[31] But both kinds of appearances appear early in the tradition; it made little sense to invent Galilean appearances despite Mark's favoritism toward Galilee, and it is difficult to account for Luke's certitude in Acts without a Judean apostolate, despite his theological use of Jerusalem. Sanders may be right that when Luke's Jerusalem center for Luke-Acts is taken into account, the most plausible scenario is that the disciples "fled to Galilee and then returned to Jerusalem,"[32] where Galileans often traveled.

## 2. Pre- or Postresurrection Tradition?

Many think that John 21 recycles the same tradition as behind Luke 5:1–11.[33] One could view John 21 as an allusion to Peter's first encounter with Jesus, but given the form of that encounter only in Luke, this proposal may expect too much knowledge of Lukan tradition from John's audience. In any case, a direct literary relationship between Luke 5:1–11 and John 21:5–8 is improbable; the only two significant words shared by both are ἰχθύς and δίκτυον.[34] Redaction in the chapter need not, of course, deny the possibility of genuine historical tradition here;[35] one could even argue that the similarities point merely to consistency in the tradition rather than to two distinct events. But as throughout the Gospel, historical tradition is difficult to test in the absence of material parallel with the Synoptics.

---

[29] Talbert, *John*, 63–64, points out that we have this chapter in the final, canonical form of the text, which is the available object for literary inquiry.

[30] Sandmel, *Judaism*, 389. Philostratus's third-century C.E. *Heroikos* distributes Protesilaos's appearances over a wide geographic range (*Hrk.* 11.7–8; Maclean and Aitken, *Heroikos*, xxvi–xxvii), but this may be too late and peripheral to prove relevant.

[31] Marxsen, *Mark*, 82–83.

[32] Sanders, *Figure*, 278.

[33] Meier, *Marginal Jew*, 2:896–904; Quast, *Reading*, 141; cf. Fuller, *Formation*, 151. Perhaps less likely is the view that Luke uses a resurrection appearance account in a pre-Easter context (Fuller, *Formation*, 160–61), making John more helpful for historical reconstruction here (Brown, *Essays*, 269–70).

[34] Blomberg, "Miracles as Parables," 345. Many who find a parallel doubt "a direct literary relationship" (see Smith, *John* [1999], 390–91).

[35] Cf. Osborne, "John 21."

Fish symbols were common in Diaspora Judaism and contemporary paganism,[36] but such symbolism is improbable here. Others also think that OT imagery stands behind the Gospel accounts of the calling of fishermen or (more commonly) at least behind Jesus' Markan summons to become "fishers of people" (Mark 1:17; Hab 1:15; Jer 16:16; cf. Ezek 47:10).[37] But the OT use is a judgment metaphor (*Jos. Asen.* 21:21 MSS would be closer), so the image is questionable unless Jesus provocatively pictured those who should "trap" people for the kingdom[38] or intended the allusion by way of contrast.[39] Derrett, who thinks Ezek 47 stands behind both the Synoptic fishing calls and John 21:5–6, appeals to the early Jewish use of fish symbolism to represent individual salvation,[40] but John 21, at least, provides no clues that support this interpretation. Jesus more likely called them to be "fishers of men" primarily because fishing was their prior profession, as the text indicates.[41]

That Jesus called some fishermen as disciples was probably widely known (cf. Mark 1:16–17) and is historically likely.[42] Although the primary occupation even on the Lake of Galilee was agricultural,[43] fishing remained a major industry there,[44] and fish was a primary staple in Mediterranean antiquity.[45] Fishermen were "among the more economically mobile of the village culture,"[46] even if later educated urban readers might regard their occupation as a humble one.[47] Clues in other gospels suggest that Jesus' fishermen disciples may have often had adequate income: Zebedee's family had hired servants (Mark 1:20)[48]

---

[36] See Goodenough, *Symbols,* 5:3–30.

[37] Later, CD 4.15–17; 1QH 5.7–8; *L.A.B.* 3:11; Matt 13:47; Strauss, "Quellen." For proposals on this background, see Jeremias, *Theology,* 132–33; Fenton, *Matthew,* 73; Gundry, *Matthew,* 62; Lane, *Mark,* 67–68; MacLaurin, "Fishermen."

[38] As suggested by Davies and Allison, *Matthew,* 1:398.

[39] Cf. Vermes, *Religion,* 102 n. 27.

[40] Derrett, "Fishermen."

[41] A bilingual milieu may also help explain Jesus' use of the figure, since "catch" (Heb. *tzud,* Aram. *tzadë*) could apply to both physical catching and to winning others by deception or debate (Lachs, *Commentary,* 58–59); that image also appears in Greek (Boring et al., *Commentary,* 55).

[42] See Keener, *Matthew,* 148–49; Davies and Allison, *Matthew,* 393–94; Witherington, *Christology,* 129–30.

[43] Horsley, *Galilee,* 194.

[44] Safrai, "Home," 747. Cf. fishing implements found in Bethsaida (Arav, "Bethsaida") and the Galilean fishing boat that was uncovered (Stone, "Boat"). Cf. also the abundance of small boats available for crossing the sea from one town to another (Josephus *Life* 163–164).

[45] Pliny *Nat.* 22.68.138; Horsley, *Documents,* 5:99; Lewis, *Life,* 68. Among the poor, smoked fish could rank "the most popular item" in a general market's sales for a day (P.Oxy. 520; Lewis, *Life,* 136). Rarer, luxury fish (Dupont, *Life,* 277) and the complex market system in second-century Roman legislation cited by Malina and Rohrbaugh, *Commentary,* 44–45, are probably less relevant to the towns of lakeside Galilee (excepting urban Sepphoris and Tiberias), where the market was not far from the industry. A custom of eating fish on the Sabbath (Safrai, "Home," 747) may have obtained this early, though Galileans near the lake surely ate fish much more regularly.

[46] Freyne, *Galilee,* 241; cf. ILS 7486; Wilkinson, *Jerusalem,* 29–30; Hengel, *Property,* 27; on systems of commercial fishing, see Malina and Rohrbaugh, *John,* 289; urban fishing guilds in Horsley, *Documents,* 5:101–7 (though these systems may not have obtained in Galilee).

[47] E.g., Augustine *Tract. Ev. Jo.* 7.17.3 (citing 1 Cor 1:27). In parts of the Mediterranean world, poverty could even drive fishermen toward the desperation of piracy (Alciphron *Fishermen* 8 [Eucolymbus to Glaucê], 1.2–3, 8).

[48] Cf. Hengel, *Property,* 27. Still, such hired workers could be contract fishermen, lured away easily by better wages to the first employer's detriment (Alciphron *Fishermen* 2 [Galenaeus to Cyrton], 1.2, par. 2 and 4; 5 [Naubates to Rhothius], 1.5, par. 1).

and may have formed a fishing cooperative with Simon and Andrew (Luke 5:7).[49] Such professional background had not provided much help that night, however (21:3).

D. Moody Smith's observations are of interest here. He suggests that the appearance narrative of 21:1–14 "is exactly the one that Mark's Gospel leads us to expect, even to the extent that Peter plays a leading role" (cf. Mark 16:7). Perhaps this narrative "may well be the earliest account of Jesus' appearance to his disciples that we possess."[50] Whether or not the narrative may be the earliest, there is no reason to doubt that John depends here on prior tradition (or, in our view, an eyewitness account).

---

[49] Cf. Stambaugh and Balch, *Environment,* 69; Applebaum, "Life," 685. Business partners normally shared profits somehow (Cicero *Verr.* 2.3.20.50), though sometimes relationships soured (Cicero *Quinct.* 4.15; 5.22).

[50] Smith, "Problem," 266, who notes that Bultmann, *John,* 705, accepts the strong possibility that the story in John 21 was in the original ending of Mark.

# THE FISH SIGN

## 21:1–14

O THER SOURCES MAY SUGGEST that Jesus revealed himself on a regular basis to the disciples immediately after the resurrection; Luke seems most emphatic about this point (Acts 1:3), though he omits the Galilean appearances and may therefore refer to a state after the disciples had returned to Jerusalem (reading Luke, one would not know that they had left Jerusalem). In any case, John is emphatic that this is the disciples' third revelation (21:14); that Jesus manifested himself to them also frames this sign narrative (21:1, 14), underlining the significance of this appearance. When John counts, it may be primarily to tie events together (compare 2:1, 19; 2:11 with 4:54); this event takes the previous resurrection appearances to a fuller level, though Thomas's christological confession was climactic.

What is John's point? In the light of the rest of the Gospel, Jesus again provides food for his people (6:10–11; cf. Rev 7:16–17; 12:6); the emphasis here will be spiritual food (4:32–34; 6:35; 10:9; see 21:15–17). Given the following dialogue, the point of the narrative seems to be to define more specifically the character of Jesus' call in 20:21, especially for church leaders: loving Jesus requires Jesus' servants to love Jesus' followers.

### The Setting: Failing at Fishing (21:1–3)

These verses provide examples of typical Johannine language in the nontheological vocabulary when one would least expect it from a later hand: for example, "after these things" (21:1; see 3:22; 5:1, 14; 6:1; 7:1). Likewise, only this Gospel calls the lake "the sea of Tiberias" (6:1) or mentions Tiberias at all (6:23). In the very incomplete list of Jesus' followers here,[1] the two named characters besides Peter (who is necessary to the following story) are distinctly Johannine: only in this Gospel does Thomas appear outside lists of names (11:16; 14:5; 20:24–28) and is he called Didymus, meaning "Twin" (11:16; 20:24);[2] and only in this Gospel do Nathanael and Cana appear (1:45–49; 2:1, 11; 4:46).[3] The "sons

---

[1] Fuller lists for the Twelve include Matt 10:2–4; Mark 3:16–19; Luke 6:14–16; Acts 1:13. Lists of those who did exploits constitutes a common form (e.g., 2 Sam 23:8–39; 1 Chr 25:1–7; Homer *Il.* 3.161–242; Apollonius of Rhodes 1.23–228; cf. Philostratus *Hrk.* 6.3, expanding on Homer *Il.* 2.484–760), though lists of officeholders and other forms may be equally relevant, especially lists of disciples (Iamblichus *V.P.* 23.104; 35.251; see further Davies and Allison, *Matthew,* 2:150, citing *m. Ab.* 2:8; Diogenes Laertius 8.46).

[2] Twins were typically closer in affection than other brothers (Cicero *Quint. fratr.* 1.3.3); one could apply the term figuratively to those who shared the same character (Cicero *Phil.* 11.1.2); Seneca *Benef.* 7.1.3 doubts that one can fathom the reasons for twins' existence. "Thomas" bears the same sense ("twin") and may be a nickname (Williams, "Personal Names," 103); for "Didymus" or "Didymas," see, e.g., "Arius Didymus"; P.Oxy. 115.

[3] The connection between Nathanael and Cana is nowhere stated earlier in the Gospel and seems a curious piece of information to simply be invented by a later redactor.

of Zebedee" admittedly weigh against the thesis that this epilogue stems from the same author or source, since the rest of the Gospel reflects a studied, probably deliberate avoidance of mentioning them; but it is noteworthy that even here they are not individually named. The mention of Thomas (21:2) provides a connection with the previous narrative (20:24–29),[4] demonstrating that he did persevere.

That Jesus "manifested himself" to the disciples (21:1; this provides an *inclusio* with 21:14) is also Johannine language (1:31; 2:11; 3:21; 7:4; 9:3; 17:6) and, on a theological level, reflects the expectation in 14:21–23 of postresurrection encounters with Christ (albeit normally in the Spirit after the first encounter of 20:19–23). Jesus was, literally, "on the sea" (21:1); this is acceptable language for "beside the sea" (Mark 4:1; 5:21; cf. John 21:4, 9–10). It might recall Jesus' theophany *on* the sea (6:19; cf. Mark 6:47–49); but this is probably overexegesis (see 6:16). When John concludes the narrative by reminding the reader that this is the "third" time Jesus was revealed to the disciples (21:14), he includes in this count only the two appearances in the upper room (20:19–23, 24–29). Like John's other counts (2:1, 11; 4:46, despite the plural "signs" in 3:2), however, his language may indicate only the third time in the narrative, not the third appearance altogether.[5] That John 21 does not enumerate all the gospels' resurrection appearances but counts only those in this Gospel seems to me a further piece of evidence favoring Johannine authorship of this chapter.[6]

This passage reflects knowledge of the tradition that Peter and at least some of his colleagues (21:3)—here presumably the sons of Zebedee (21:2)—were fishermen, a tradition undoubtedly widely known in the early church (cf. Mark 1:16–20).[7] It has often been argued as well that the passage reflects knowledge of the same tradition as appears in Luke 5:1–10; although the argument depends, to some degree, on the relative paucity of extant traditions available for our modern perusal, it is probably correct.

Peter acts in character, taking the lead in 21:3 (13:24; 18:10, 15; cf. Mark 14:31, 37), as some students in ancient schools were known to do.[8] He also displays for Jesus his physical prowess in 21:7 and 21:11; this might appeal to heroic or masculine ideals in the ancient Mediterranean world—perhaps acceptable provided it was used to demonstrate loyalty to his Lord (as it was in 21:7, 11).[9] This might also be in character; at least some ancient people viewed fishermen as "tough," inured to the labors of their trade.[10]

At night (21:3), fish were more apt to be in deep water, when the circular throwing net (typically about fifteen feet in diameter) used for shallow water would be useless and a large

---

[4] Beasley-Murray, *John*, 398.

[5] It is the fourth revelation, but the third "to the disciples" (21:14), not including the appearance to Mary alone (Smith, *John*, 389). There is no reason to associate it specifically with Peter's three denials (13:38), though both may express a preference for narrative triplets in the passion tradition (cf. 21:15–17).

[6] Cf., e.g., Calvin, *John*, 2:287, who claims seven appearances but argues that this is the third distinct day (so harmonizing them).

[7] In defense of the authenticity of this tradition, see Davies and Allison, *Matthew*, 2:393–94; Witherington, *Christology*, 129–30.

[8] E.g., Seneca *Controv.* 1.pref.24; LCL 1:25 n. 4 cites Quintilian 1.2.24 as an example of competition in Roman schools.

[9] He compensates for the other's prowess in 20:4. Ephesus, like other cities of the Greek East, demonstrated their appreciation for physical strength by providing gymnasia (on gymnasia, see Harrill, "Asia Minor," 131), though gymnasia also served nonathletic functions.

[10] In Alciphron *Fishermen* 15 (Nausibius to Prymnaeus), 1.12, par. 2–3, they normally reclined on bare wooden decks, whereas a rich passenger might need shade (par. 2; but they were pleased that he paid cash, par. 5).

dragnet between two boats would be more useful.[11] Such a dragnet and second boat may have been unavailable here. Still, fishermen worked in the night as well as in the day, at night using torchlight with their nets.[12] Night fishing is said to be more profitable on the Lake of Galilee than day fishing (cf. Luke 5:5); those who fished at night could also sell their fish in the morning, getting a jump on most of their competition.[13] They nevertheless caught nothing (οὐδέν) all night (21:3); probably John illustrates the principle that apart from Jesus they could do οὐδέν, "nothing" (15:5),[14] for only at his intervention (21:6) and after their own admission of inability (21:5; cf. 2:3; 5:6–7; 6:5–9) are they able to obtain fish.

## Jesus Provides Fish (21:4–6)

Fish miracles appear elsewhere in ancient sources,[15] as should be expected in a world where fishers were common and peoples looked to deities for help with nature. (It is the modern industrial and postindustrial secular mind-set that is unusual from the standpoint of the broader scope of human history.) One Amphimnestus vowed a tenth of his catch of fish to Asclepius; when he failed to fulfill his vow, Asclepius caused fish to attack him in punishment.[16] In a widely told Jewish story, a fish jumps from the River Euphrates to devour Tobias, but with Raphael's help Tobias gets special medicine from the fish.[17] God could also provide abundance as a reward for faithful behavior; cooking, preparing, and sharing fish with others (cf. 21:9–12) was considered generous behavior warranting God's repayment in one's catching more fish (*T. Zeb.* 6:5–6).

Many commentators view the disciples' fishing (21:3) as apostasy from the work of the kingdom, from which Jesus must call them again to ministry (21:15–22). But this view does not comport well with any sense of realism in the story world. The disciples made use of free time,[18] and as Beasley-Murray complains, "Even though Jesus be crucified and risen from the dead, the disciples must still *eat!*"[19] As in other passages in the Gospel (e.g., 2:1–11; 5:6–8; 6:5–12), Jesus does care about "mundane" needs and provides for others through their obedience to his commands (e.g., 2:7; 5:8–9; 6:10–12).[20]

---

[11] Jeffers, *World*, 22.

[12] Alciphron *Fishermen* 2 (Galenaeus to Cyrton), 1.2, par. 1.

[13] Brown, *John*, 2:1069; MacGregor, *John*, 370; Milne, *Message*, 310; Talbert, *John*, 259. Carson, *John*, 670, acknowledges this but also appeals to Johannine symbolism as at 13:30.

[14] In its various forms, οὐδείς appears fifty-three times in the Gospel; but more than any other, 15:5 seems to provide the rationale for the usage here. The other uses of πιάζω (7:30, 32, 44; 8:20; 10:39; 11:57), however, are clearly irrelevant.

[15] E.g., Iamblichus *V.P.* 8.36; Protesilaos resurrecting a dead fish (Herodotus *Hist.* 9.120.1–2; Philostratus *Hrk.* 9.5).

[16] Epid. inscr. 47, in Theissen, *Stories*, 110. Priests also used the types of fish gathering in a sacred pool to divine the future (Athenaeus *Deipn.* 8.333de).

[17] Tob 6:2–5. Following an old Greek story, some Jewish stories of uncertain date speak of God blessing pious people by having them find precious objects in fish (e.g., Matt 17:27; *b. Šabb.* 119a; Bultmann, *Tradition*, 238; Jeremias, *Theology*, 87); ancients thought such occasional fortune plausible (e.g., Alciphron *Fishermen* 5 [Naubates to Rhothius], 1.5, par. 1; Valerius Maximus 4.1.ext.7).

[18] Bruce, *John*, 399.

[19] Beasley-Murray, *John*, 399.

[20] Cf. Protesilaos's participation in farming in Philostratus *Hrk.* 4.10; 11.4; neither work reflects a gnostic antipathy toward creation.

MacGregor appeals to the use of παιδία ("lads," 21:5) to suggest simply men at work,[21] but in Johannine literature the term appears interchangeably with τεκνία (the former in 1 John 2:14, 18; the latter in 1 John 2:1, 12, 28; 3:7, 18; 4:4; 5:21), which Jesus elsewhere applies to the disciples (John 13:33). Jesus' question follows the appropriate Greek idiom to inquire whether fishers or hunters had experienced success but is framed to anticipate a negative response.[22] As before Jesus miraculously provided bread and fish in 6:11, here he asks the disciples if they have sufficient resources on their own (6:5–6; 21:5), forcing them to recognize afresh that "without him they can do nothing" (15:5).

Jesus gives seemingly nonsensical instructions (21:6), underlining the principle that obedience to one wiser than oneself is more prudent than depending on one's own wisdom (cf., e.g., Prov 3:5). It has been argued that because the steering oar would be on the right side, nets would normally be cast on the left, making Jesus' command unusual;[23] such an image would fit the emphasis of the narrative well. Scholars often suggest that the net in view here is a large seine net (cf. Matt 13:47–50), which normally would have floats on top and weights on the bottom; one end would be attached to the shore or to another boat, allowing the boat to which the other end was attached to surround and catch fish.[24] Since Jesus tells them to cast it from the boat, however, the net envisioned here may be different, although undoubtedly large.

The story at this point communicates a moral lesson rather than an allegory; that the disciples obey the master indicates the obedience involved in discipleship.[25] This is especially the case if casting from the right side of the boat was unusual. That they remain as yet unaware of his identity—or at least uncertain—may suggest the ambiguity of initial revelation (cf. 1 Cor 13:12), which one must obey to receive fuller revelation (cf. John 14:15–16, 21). More likely, however, John provides a moral based on what the audience knows, even though the disciples do not.

## Recognizing and Approaching Jesus (21:7–8)

Although the disciples did not immediately recognize Jesus, as in 20:14 (on his temporary unrecognizability, see comment there), the miracle revealed him at least to the beloved disciple. The world did not know Jesus (1:10), but his own recognized him when he called them by name (20:16) or they heard his voice (10:3; 21:5–7).

The beloved disciple here, as in 20:4–8, proves quicker to believe than Peter (see comment there on the significance of such comparisons); some sort of competition, albeit on a collegial level, seems to continue in the background here (21:20). If the disciple whom Jesus loved is assumed to be one of the disciples of 21:2 (which is almost certainly understood to be the case), he could be Thomas or Nathanael if willing to name himself; otherwise he is one of Zebedee's sons (as church tradition holds) or one of the two anonymous

---

[21] MacGregor, John, 370. Whitacre, John, 491, notes that the usage "lads" stems from modern Greek, unattested in ancient usage.

[22] Brown, John, 2:1070.

[23] Selms, "Fishing," 310. Fishermen normally used nets (e.g., Ovid Metam. 13.922; Babrius 4.1–5; 9.6; Valerius Maximus 4.1.ext.7; Mark 1:19; Matt 13:47) except for personal subsistence fishing by the poor (e.g., Ovid Metam. 13.923; Babrius 6.1–4; cf. Matt 17:27); on traditional fishing in the Lake of Galilee, see Nun, "Net."

[24] Rasmussen, "Net," 524.

[25] Cf. Kysar, John, 313–14.

disciples (protecting still more fully his anonymity, more in accordance with most contemporary scholarly views).[26]

Once Peter recognized Jesus, however, he immediately came to him (21:7); this suggests his zealous love for Jesus (cf. 10:4; 21:15–17).[27] The narrative of Peter's coming to Jesus for the breakfast prepared on shore illustrates another principle the Gospel previously articulated: those who come to him will not hunger (6:35).

While one could read 21:7 as claiming that Peter was working completely naked (a frequent use of γυμνός and one not unexpected for work),[28] this might not fit as well what we know about Palestinian Judaism or about the sort of conservative Diaspora Jewish communities from which most early Christians came.[29] Further, he had been laboring during the night (21:3), and it was only now daybreak (21:4), so the air may have been cooler than during the day. The term "naked" also applied to having little clothing or being less than fully clothed;[30] it could apply even to being without armor or shield.[31] Possibly, Peter had removed his outer garment for work[32] but now clothed himself more appropriately out of respect for the teacher.[33] Perhaps Peter was wearing one of his garments loosely, since normally one would not simply don a garment before hurling into water; then, as today, people recognized that it was much easier to swim naked![34]

It seems most likely that Peter already had a garment on, whether his tunic (undergarment) alone, his outer garment, or both. Whether or not he had his outer garment loosely on, he now wrapped it around his waist, tucking up the lower part of it to avoid restricting his legs.[35] The verb form διεζώσατο is the third singular aorist middle of διαζώννυμι, which is used for girding oneself around, as with a belt. Cognates of this term for "gird" are frequent, and though they can function more generally, in the NT they usually indicate

---

[26] For the beloved disciple as one of the two anonymous eyewitnesses present, see, e.g., Boismard, "Disciple."

[27] Peter's quickness to act fits his character elsewhere in this Gospel and the gospel tradition as a whole (see, e.g., Blomberg, *Reliability*, 275).

[28] See Whitacre, *John*, 492, following Nun, "Wearing," 20–23, 37; certainly Greeks in this period stripped for strenuous activities (e.g., Dionysius of Halicarnassus *R.A.* 7.72.2–3; see further references below). Citing art and texts, Nun, "Wearing," argues that cast-net fishermen were typically naked. Even Marcus Cato stripped to work alongside his servants (Plutarch *Marcus Cato* 3.2), but here γυμνός probably means "stripped to the waist" (LCL).

[29] On early Judaism's antipathy toward nakedness, see, e.g., Gen 3:7, 10–11; *Jub.* 3:21–22, 30–31; 7:8–10, 20; 1QS 7.12–14; *t. Ber.* 2:14; *Sipre Deut.* 320.5.2; *Targum Rishon to Esther* 1:11; cf. Moon, "Nudity." Some Gentiles (especially in some periods) also found nudity embarrassing (Juvenal *Sat.* 1.71; Plutarch *R.Q.* 40, *Mor.* 274A; Diogenes Laertius 2.73; cf. the "buffoon" who lifts his shirt in front of freeborn women, Theophrastus *Char.* 11.2), but even outside athletic activities, many did not (Plato *Rep.* 5.452C; Dio Chrysostom *Or.* 13.24; Arrian *Ind.* 11.7).

[30] E.g., Euripides *El.* 308; Livy 45.39.17 (*nudasse*); Epictetus *Diatr.* 3.22.45 (having one cloak); 2 Cor 11:27; probably Tob 1:16–17; 4:16; Rom 8:35.

[31] E.g., Homer *Il.* 21.50; 22.124; Herodian 2.13.8, 10; Philostratus *Hrk.* 23.24–25.

[32] On Greeks stripping for exercise or strenuous activity, see, e.g., Homer *Il.* 21.50–52; Apollonius of Rhodes 1.364; Dionysius of Halicarnassus *R.A.* 7.72.2–3; Diogenes *Ep.* 37. It is not clear if this practice would have appealed to Galilean fishermen.

[33] See in more detail Soards, "Ἐπενδύτην"; cf. also Morris, *John*, 864–65. Peter had not been at the cross to witness Jesus' nakedness (19:23–24).

[34] E.g., Longus 1.30. If a Greek with servants (unlike Peter) needed to swim from a boat, he might remove even his short tunic (χιτωνίσκον) and give it to a servant to hold (Theophrastus *Char.* 25.2).

[35] Bruce, *John*, 400; Carson, *John*, 671; Quast, *Reading*, 142; Watkins, *John*, 411. Laborers often wore loincloths around the hips (Jeffers, *World*, 43–44), but it is doubtful Peter would have one available.

girding about the waist or breast;[36] the LXX usually employs the cognate ζώννυμι for gird-ing on like a belt.[37] The particular term appears elsewhere in the NT and the LXX only in John 13:4–5. Perhaps Peter did not want to leave his cloak in the boat, but given the greater inconvenience of having it wet, the action is more likely symbolic, recalling Jesus' action of service in John 13: Peter now comes to serve Jesus.[38] Unknown to Peter, this show of devo-tion may prefigure his martyrdom (cf. the girding in 21:18–19).[39]

A description of swimming prowess, like other kinds of athletic prowess, can function epideictically as praise for the protagonist,[40] though here, in contrast to 20:4, there is no suggestion of competition with the beloved disciple. Peter has apparently donned or failed to remove his outer tunic despite its impediment to swimming, yet he may beat the boat to land (21:8). He is eager to prove his devotion to Jesus and demonstrates his commitment by physical exertion (undoubtedly as a "young man" who can devote his strength to God's glory; cf. 1 John 2:14).

## Jesus Feeds His Sheep (21:9–14)

That fish were already being cooked before they hauled in their own catch (21:9) rein-forces their conviction that Jesus has complete control over nature. Perhaps as in 4:27, the disciples do not need to say anything (21:12); here, in fact, they did not "dare" to do so, probably recalling Jesus' recent responses to their questions and affirmations in 13:36 and 14:5, 8, experiences probably also recalled in 16:19, 23, 30.

### 1. The Banquet

Jesus invites the disciples to have "breakfast" (ἀριστήσατε, 21:12); the ἄριστον was typically a morning meal,[41] a sense dictated here by the context (21:4). Well-to-do Romans in particular ate three times a day, breakfast being a light fare of bread and cheese.[42] Earlier Greeks typically ate ἄριστον near midday and δεῖπνον nearer sundown.[43] The earlier meal was so important that an army might insist on having it before marching or facing battle.[44] But it was also held that in earlier times Greeks ate around dawn.[45] Whenever the disciples customarily ate, they would undoubtedly be prepared for this early meal (21:4) after an arduous night of work (21:3). The early hour may also recall the first resurrection appearances (20:1; cf. also Jesus' condemnation, 18:28).

---

[36] Eph 6:14; 1 Pet 1:13; Rev 1:13; 15:6; probably Luke 12:37; cf. Acts 12:8.

[37] Exod 29:9; 1 Sam 17:39; 25:13; 2 Kgs 4:29; 9:1; Job 38:3; 40:7; Isa 11:5; but not in 1 Kgs 21:27 (sackcloth) or 2 Macc 10:25.

[38] In this case, the water of John 21 may also recall the water of John 13, which may recall the salvific-water motif in earlier narratives; but both connections might be coincidental.

[39] Quast, Reading, 142, notes this view without endorsing it.

[40] E.g., Josephus Life 15; Homer Od. 5.388–389, 399, 438–441; 7.276–277, 280–281; 23.23–38. Earlier Jewish references are rarer because ancient Israel engaged in maritime activity more rarely than Greeks.

[41] So Westcott, John, 302, on the usual technical sense when opposed to δεῖπνον; but this is not its exclusive sense in Koine (cf. Luke 11:37–38; Gen 43:25; probably Matt 22:4).

[42] Jeffers, World, 39.

[43] Walter Miller, comment on Xenophon Cyropaedia (LCL 1:19 n. 1).

[44] Xenophon Hell. 4.5.3; Anab. 5.4.22, 30; 6.5.21; Polybius 3.71.11–3.72.6; cf. also Xenophon Anab. 4.3.9–10; Cyr. 1.2.11.

[45] Dionysius of Halicarnassus Lit. Comp. 3.

John omits the Last Supper but presents Jesus at a wedding banquet (2:1–11) and here feeding his disciples (21:12–13); the use of bread and fish (21:13) plainly recalls Jesus' provision of food in 6:11, probably emphasizing that as Jesus acted the part of host before the passion, he remains the host after the resurrection.[46] Thus Jesus' public ministry begins at a wedding feast where he provides wine (2:1–11), and closes with a meal for his disciples here. Some find in this passage a messianic meal[47] or a deliberate allusion to the Eucharist;[48] but the presence of the fish provide no clear eucharistic overtones, and this passage lacks mention of breaking bread, drinking, or giving of thanks.[49] Our comments about the Eucharist in ch. 6 should obtain here as well, where one finds far less potentially eucharistic language than in ch. 6. Rather, it provides the setting for Peter's commission; just as Jesus has now fed his followers, so Peter must tend Jesus' sheep (21:15–17), which would particularly entail grazing, and hence feeding, them. Given our interpretation of ch. 6, this would mean not merely serving the Eucharist but providing them the living bread through proclaiming the message that mediates Jesus' presence (16:7–11; cf. Rev 3:20).

## 2. The Abundance of Fish (21:11)

By pulling the heavy net to shore (21:11), Peter uses his physical prowess to demonstrate the same devotion as he did by swimming to shore in 21:7.[50] In the context of the preceding passion narratives, he presumably wishes to demonstrate his devotion to Jesus despite his earlier denials, which demonstrated lack of faith. The counting of fish (21:11) suggests the great abundance of Jesus' miracle; as in the case of the fish already cooking (21:9), it suggests the unlimited supply available from Jesus (cf. also 6:12–13). Scholars have struggled long over the meaning of 153. Some solve it by the Jewish hermeneutical practice gematria;[51] although mainly known to us in rabbinic texts, it has earlier antecedents.[52] Thus some suggest, for example, that 153 is the numerical value of בני אלהים, "children of God," those whom the fishers would gather in.[53] This proposal assumes that Peter's gathering of fish stands for (rather than is replaced by) his call to shepherd,[54] importing a ministry image from Mark 1:17 that John never explicitly mentions (though he undoubtedly knew of it). Others suggest a gematria allusion to the names of fishing villages in Ezek 47:10, to which some think John's fish image alludes.[55] One scholar suggests "Nathanael

---

[46] It may be significant that "Sea of Tiberias" in 21:1 probably recalls 6:1, its only other occurrence in the NT.

[47] E.g., Bowman, *Gospel*, 330, albeit contrasting John's messianic meal with the eating of Leviathan in later Jewish sources.

[48] E.g., Brown, *Essays*, 104–5 (admitting the lack of wine and the dominance of fish over bread but citing 6:11, which he believes is sacramental).

[49] Witherington, *Wisdom*, 354; cf. Feuillet, *Studies*, 27.

[50] See also comment on 21:7. Fishermen were known to be inured to the hardships of their profession, particularly the hot sun (Alciphron *Fishermen* 15 [Nausibius to Prymnaeus], 1.12, par. 2–3).

[51] See, e.g., Russell, "Arithmetic"; Cohen, "Taryag." Cf., e.g., *Pesiq. Rab Kah.* 2:8; Rev 13:18; Irenaeus *Haer.* 1.3.2; 1.14–15; *Sib. Or.* 1.141–146; 3.24–26; 5:14–42; 11:29–30, 91–92, 114, 141–142, 190, 208, 256, 274; book 12 passim; *Treat. Shem* 3:1–2. Many texts use gematria on the 318 in Gen 14:14 (*b. Ned.* 32a; *Gen. Rab.* 43:2; *Lev. Rab.* 28:4; *Num. Rab.* 18:21; *Pesiq. Rab.* 18:3; *Barn.* 9.8).

[52] Cf. the practice in Assyrian cuneiform texts (Lieberman, "Hermeneutics"; cf. proposed Babylonian influences on Jewish hermeneutics in Cavigneaux, "Sources") and Greek commentaries (Sambursky, "Gematria"). Greeks and Romans also counted letters in names as numbers (Lucian *Alex.* 11).

[53] Romeo, "Gematria."

[54] Romeo rightly parallels sheep and fish and notes that the sheep stand for God's people (ibid., 264).

[55] Barrett, *John*, 581–82; Grigsby, "Gematria"; Trudinger, "Fishes."

gamma" (for the third appearance to Nathanael) or "alpha Maria" (one Mary, for the unified church); "For allegorists," he contends, "the same word or object may symbolize several different things at the same time, and this may be the case here."[56] One wonders whether John could have expected any members of his original audience to catch another suggested view, an allusion to Mount Pisgah that might compare to Moses' departure Jesus' passing on the mission to Peter.[57]

Most forced of all, to arrive at IXΘ, short for Ἰχθύς and an acronym for Ἰησοῦς Χριστὸς Θεός, one scholar suggests revising the numerical value of letters by counting the original (rather than Koine) Greek alphabet backward as if it were Hebrew![58] Another scholar argues that, including the fish on the fire in 21:9, 154 fish are in view, suggesting by gematria the word "day" (ἡμέρα), which was an early title for Jesus.[59] Yet this view seems unlikely not only for its less than obvious gematria but also because John specifically numbers only the 153.

But all such appeals to gematria require too much complexity for a reader to discover without already knowing the proposed "answer," and their very abundance demonstrates the extreme subjectivity with which their examination is blighted.[60] Ultimately any suggestion of gematria must meet the same fate in this passage; an appeal to reconstruct a Hebrew original without explicit clues pointing to it must have eluded John's audience. (Revelation 13:18, by contrast, explicitly invites the use of gematria.)

Some note Jerome's claim that there were held to be 153 kinds of fish;[61] this computation would make the 153 fish in this passage symbolic for Jesus' lordship over all kinds of fish. It is not impossible that this is true; such symbolism would not violate John's style, and Jerome's commentary on Ezek 47:9–12 mentions that both Latin and Greek biologists (including a particular poet) classified 153 kinds of fish. This intriguing proposal, however, appears to falter for lack of extant evidence;[62] none of Jerome's reputed sources survive, and it is possible that the ones he had (especially the one he clearly named) were influenced by this passage in John.[63] Certainly 153 was not the only count of fish species circulating in his day; thus, for all Pliny the Elder's comments on fish,[64] the one place he numbers them yields 74 species of fish, plus 30 more with a hard covering.[65]

The number 153 is also a triangular number, the sum of numbers from 1 to 17;[66] triangular numbers represent the number of blocks from which one could build a triangle with none left over. This is the sort of observation that would have interested neo-

---

[56] Bury, *Logos-Doctrine*, 80.

[57] The view articulated in Owen, "Fishes"; it is roundly refuted by Ross, "Fishes."

[58] McEleney, "Fishes."

[59] Cardwell, "Fish."

[60] Dodd, *More Studies*, 109 n. 1, also expresses his skepticism toward the value of "fantastic applications of *gematria*"; cf. also Ross, "Fishes."

[61] E.g., Strachan, *Gospel*, 235; Hoskyns, *Gospel*, 554; Dodd, *More Studies*, 109 n. 1; Lightfoot, *Gospel*, 342–43.

[62] Sanders, *John*, 447; Morris, *John*, 866; Talbert, *John*, 260; it is missing from extant texts of Oppianus Cilix, though he may have written much more than remains. Hunter, *John*, 194, calls it "the best of a bad lot of guesses."

[63] Michaels, *John*, 343.

[64] Pliny *Nat.* 9.16.43–9.45.84.

[65] Pliny *Nat.* 9.16.43.

[66] Augustine *Tr. Ev. Jo.* 122.8 (also explaining 17: 10 for the law plus 7 for the Spirit); Hoskyns, *Gospel*, 553. Cf. Wojciechowski, "Aspects," who suggests this significance or 9 (3 x 3) x 17 (7 + 10). The suggestion of an allusion to the five loaves and two baskets (ultimately yielding 17) of 6:9, like

Pythagorean interpreters in antiquity.[67] But while there is only one chance in nine that a random number would be a triangular number, if one asks the odds of finding a number that was triangular or square or a prime number or a multiple of 7, 12, or 50, the "coincidence" decreases somewhat; nothing in advance leads us to predict a triangular number here, and with many randomly selected numbers it is possible to retroactively observe peculiar features not found elsewhere. Further, it is difficult to see what bearing a triangular number has on interpreting the passage[68] unless perhaps to say that John simply chose a number of recognized importance to represent a large or perfect catch of fish.[69]

More likely the number stresses an important feature of the miracle analogous to many other ancient miracle accounts: the abundance of the fish underlines the miraculous character of the provision (cf. 6:13).[70] In this case, the number could simply stem from an accurate memory of a careful count on the occasion, because fish had to be counted to be divided among fishermen; 153 is too exact for a round number (such as 150).[71] As Hunter puts it, the 153 fish may turn out to be "no more symbolical than the hundred yards that Peter swam. It is the remembered number of a 'bumper' catch."[72] It also underlines the miracle of the net not being torn despite the vast number of fish (even more dramatic if the audience is at all familiar with the tradition in Luke 5:1–11, esp. 5:6).[73]

The narrator's perspective remains with the boat in 21:8–9 instead of following Peter's swimming (21:7, 11), though the latter is the center of action; this may support the suggestion that the beloved disciple remains the narrative's source here (21:7).[74] The boat pulled the net as it approached the shore (21:8–9), but it was Peter, in obedience to the Lord's word (21:10), who pulled the net, suspended from the side of the boat, to Jesus on the land (21:11).[75] Although it was easier to pull a full net from shallow water to land rather than through deep water, pulling such a large net of fish (21:11) suggests considerable physical strength.[76] As in 21:7, this was a way that a laborer could express his devotion to his Lord; compare the beloved disciple's speed in 20:4.

---

some other details of these explanations, requires more mathematical training than is likely for John's (at least predominantly) non-Pythagorean audience (though interestingly 666 in Rev 13:18, also a Johannine text, is the thirty-sixth triangular number; see Bauckham, *Climax*, 393).

[67] Pythagoreanism exerted the greatest influence on the symbolic use of numbers in the ancient Mediterranean (Laroche, "Numbers"); on ancient theories on symbolic numbers, see Menken, *Techniques*, 27–29.

[68] Lightfoot, *Gospel*, 343; Sanders, *John*, 447; Morris, *John*, 866–67.

[69] Hoskyns, *Gospel*, 556.

[70] Theissen, *Stories*, 67. This fits large numbers stressing abundance in John (2:6; 6:10–13; Brown, *John*, 2:1076).

[71] Westcott, *John*, 301; Bernard, *John*, 2:699; Morris, *John*, 867.

[72] Hunter, *John*, 194–95, following Calvin. Koester, *Symbolism*, 268, compares the thirty-eight years (5:5) and five thousand with five loaves and two fish (6:9–10).

[73] Carson, *John*, 673; Koester, *Symbolism*, 268; Smith, *John* (1999), 393. This tearing of nets was apparently not uncommon (Alciphron *Fishermen* 13 [Evagrus to Philotherus], 3.3, par. 1; 17 [Encymon to Halictypus], 1.14; 18 [Halictypus to Encymon], 1.15), though sometimes they might survive even great weights (if intending to be other than humorous, Alciphron *Fishermen* 20 [Eusagenus to Limenarchus], 1.17, par. 1–2).

[74] Carson, *John*, 671.

[75] Cf. Larsen, "Boat." Selms, "Fishing," 310, suggests that the net was caught on some rocks. Gee, "Spring," thinks Peter dove into the water to avoid Jesus because of guilt yet obeyed his command in 21:10; but this overpsychologizes the narrative and creates needless inconsistency between the two acts.

[76] Bruce, *John*, 401.

# THE CALL

## 21:15–23

Some signs in the Fourth Gospel yield to explanatory discourses (5:6–9 with 5:19–47; 6:11–13 with 6:32–70; 9:6–7 with 9:39–10:18), and 21:1–14 follows this pattern. After Jesus provides fish for his followers, he summons their leader to continue to provide for his followers; as in Markan tradition, Jesus calls Peter to fish for people, so here he plays on Peter's fishing from a different angle. Peter's call ultimately involves following his Lord in martyrdom (21:18–19).

The beloved disciple's call was different from Peter's and might not involve martyrdom (21:21–22). Barrett helpfully suggests that Peter's role is pastoral whereas the beloved disciple's is as a witness;[1] in this case, the Gospel may be framed by John the Baptist (1:19–36) and the beloved disciple (21:20–24) as narrative models of witness. The shift to the beloved disciple then provides the transition for closing the Gospel on the note about that disciple's testimony (21:24–25).

## Feed My Sheep (21:15–17)

Just as Jesus fed his disciples here (21:9–14), so Peter is to feed them after Jesus departs. This involves not so much physical nourishment as the bread of life (6:26–27). It is, however, noteworthy that Jesus invites Peter to feed others only after Peter has himself first eaten (21:15); just as Peter had to accept Jesus' washing before he could serve the Lord (13:8–10), he had to eat his meal.

### 1. Peter's Role

Brown suggests that this passage, being redactional, allows Peter a more pastoral role than elsewhere in the Gospel.[2] Yet the portrait of Peter's pastoral role here is hardly incompatible with the rest of the Gospel; it can either add to it or complete it. Thus one's view on Peter's role here may depend on one's prior assumptions concerning whether the chapter is a later addition from a different hand; it cannot be used as evidence in making that decision.

It is true that Peter's calling receives little emphasis elsewhere in the Gospel; but if one does not start with the assumption that John 21 belongs to a different hand than the rest of the Gospel, this apparent difference stems from an argument based on silence. Explicit mention of Peter's special call (as opposed to merely his special prominence as an outspoken disciple or his intimacy as one of the three closest disciples) is rare in the Syn-

---

[1] Barrett, *Essays*, 165–66; cf. Hartin, "Peter".
[2] Brown, *Community*, 162.

optics except for Matt 16:18 and Luke 22:32, both of which discuss it in the same context as Peter's failure.

Peter certainly remains one of the most prominent disciples throughout the Fourth Gospel, as in the other gospels. Given the model for gospel genre found in Matthew and Luke, one most naturally expects report of a commission at the end of the Gospel (which could be and is, to a significant degree, fulfilled in 20:21 but which could also be developed further). Even here Jesus is correcting as well as encouraging Peter (especially if the three questions recall the three denials, 13:38).[3] The passage is consistent with, but develops, the role of Peter found earlier in the Gospel. It also may provide a model for other church leaders (cf. 1 Pet 5:1–2).

## 2. The Demand of Love

Loving Jesus demands fulfilling his commands (14:15), particularly the command to love one another as Jesus did (13:34); in Peter's case, this general call includes a specific command to care for Jesus' sheep, for whom Jesus cares. The appointed undershepherds of the old covenant scattered when they saw a wolf coming (10:12–13), but Peter was to care for the sheep as Jesus did, ultimately to the point of offering his life (21:18–19, 22), as he had once promised he would (13:36–37). As noted above, Peter is given three opportunities to affirm his love for Jesus (21:15–17)—possibly three in number to balance Peter's three denials (13:38).

Peter was "grieved" by the Lord's questions (21:17)—a strong term John elsewhere uses of the disciples' sorrow over Jesus' death (16:20). He still felt loyalty for Jesus; but Jesus demands a love that is demonstrated by obedience (14:15), which Peter's recent behavior failed to demonstrate (18:25–27). Peter is certain that he remains faithful to Jesus—despite his recent lapse in such readily promised fidelity (13:37–38)—and that Jesus must know this, for he knows "all things" (21:17; cf. 16:30; 18:4). That Jesus' knowledge has already led him to refuse to trust untrustworthy believers (2:23–25) might lead the first-time reader—and perhaps Peter—to doubt whether Peter will do any better on this commitment than he did in his first assurance that he would die for Jesus (13:37). Yet Jesus was merely testing and confirming him, for, as Jesus accurately predicted Peter's betrayal (13:38), he also predicts here that Peter will eventually die for Jesus (21:18).

Some writers have pointed to the use of both ἀγαπάω and φιλέω in 21:15–17, arguing that ἀγαπάω here refers to a deeper kind of love than φιλέω entails.[4] The shift between the terms in the first two examples does seem to provide a discordant note, which might lend credence to this view if one did not approach this text in the context of the rest of the Gospel that has preceded it. Some nineteenth-century scholars wrongly even regarded ἀγάπη as an example of "biblical" Greek, as if it were nonexistent in secular Greek.[5] Secular Greek did not, to be sure, use it frequently, but it had already entered the LXX with reference to God's love[6] and appears in the gospel tradition for normal human relations (Matt 5:46;

---

[3] As suggested, e.g., by Augustine *Tr. Ev. Jo.* 123.5; Westcott, *John,* 303; Sandmel, *Judaism,* 389. Threefold repetition of a basic question with a threefold answer also appears in Ps.-Callisthenes *Alex.* 1.16 (with the third answer the most honest), though that work's earliest possible date is a generation after John.

[4] Hunter, *John,* 196, regards the distinction as "possible."

[5] Refuted in Deissmann, *Studies,* 198–200.

[6] Héring, *Corinthians,* 135 n. 4 (though wrongly differentiating it too much from φιλία; it obviously differs from ἔρως).

Luke 6:32) and in other examples that do not fit the "divine love" paradigm (Matt 6:24; Luke 7:5; 11:43; 16:13; John 3:19; 12:43).

Rhetorically skilled writers regularly employed synonyms for the sake of rhetorical variation,[7] and the Fourth Gospel uses ἀγαπάω and φιλέω interchangeably (see analysis in the introduction, pp. 324–25). As Painter puts it, "Both Greek verbs . . . are used of the Father's love for the Son, indicating that no difference of meaning can be attributed to these verbs in John."[8] Bruce compares the interchangeability of other terms in the passage, such as ἀρνία and προβάτια, οἶδα and γινώσκω, and (in our view less certainly) βόσκω and ποιμαίνω.[9] Talbert notes three terms for departure in 16:5–10; three more for sorrow in 16:20–22; two terms for "ear" in 18:10, 26; and two for "guarding" in 17:12.[10] Thus most scholars today recognize that the interchange of verbs between Jesus and Peter is not of much significance[11]—unless one wishes to say that Peter finally brings Jesus down to Peter's level, reducing Jesus' demand for love! Because the demonstration of love remains the same the whole way through, however, it is difficult to imagine that Jesus here makes a concession to Peter's weakness.[12] Partially excepting Origen, most Greek commentators (e.g., John Chrysostom and Cyril of Alexandria), as well as other commentators, saw no real distinction between the sense of the terms until the arguments of nineteenth-century British scholars Trench, Westcott, and Plummer.[13]

To love Jesus more "than these" may refer to loving him more than the fellow disciples,[14] but probably refers to loving him more than the fish. In Mark, Jesus calls Peter to be a fisher of people; here he calls him to abandon fishing and be a shepherd. (It might also suggest that devotion to Christ must take priority over earthly food, as in the bread-of-life image in John 6; cf. Rev 12:6; 13:17.) Although the shepherd image is natural for leadership, in any case (see comment on 10:1–5), it may appear particularly appropriate in a Gospel that compares the disciples with Moses beholding God's glory (1:14–18). Whether "these" refers to fellow disciples or to the fish, Jesus' demand for greater love requires still greater love in the context of Peter's role in this Gospel. Earlier Peter had promised to follow Jesus to the death (13:37) but loved his own life too much to give it up (cf. 12:25); one day he will have another opportunity to demonstrate his love by martyrdom (21:18–19).

## 3. Tending the Flock

Peter the fisherman of this context (21:1–14) and of his Synoptic calling (Mark 1:17) here becomes Peter the shepherd (21:15–17), a role also implied in other early Christian tradition (1 Pet 5:1–2; cf. Acts 20:28; Eph 4:11). The two verbs for Peter's pastoral duties, while synonymous, in a general sense might express different nuances of his role. The term

---

[7] E.g., *Rhet. ad Herenn.* 4.28.38; Aulus Gellius 1.4; 2.5.1.

[8] Painter, *John*, 62.

[9] Bruce, *John*, 404.

[10] Talbert, *John*, 261. The two terms for "ear" are distinct diminutive forms of one term, almost certainly neither retaining diminutive force.

[11] E.g., Lightfoot, *Gospel*, 343; Thiselton, "Semantics," 93; Culpepper, *John*, 248; Ridderbos, *John*, 665–66; cf. Smith, *John* (1999), 218 (on 11:3, 5).

[12] See Painter, *John*, 92.

[13] Brown, *John*, 2:1102.

[14] Hunter, *John*, 196, noting that Peter claimed his loyalty greater than theirs (13:37); but "these" is in the genitive, not the nominative.

βόσκε (21:15, 17) focuses on feeding the animals,[15] whereas ποίμαινε (21:16) includes all the duties of the shepherd.[16] "Lambs" functions as a general synonym for "sheep" here (the two terms for "love" and "tend" in the context express the writer's appreciation for variety) but may increase the measure of attention required for the animal, recalling the "little ones" of the Synoptic tradition (e.g., Matt 18:3–14).

Clearly Peter is an undershepherd, but he is to reflect Jesus' concern for his sheep more than a mere "hireling" would (10:12–13). The point of the passage has nothing to do with a supposed difference between two Greek terms for love here but everything to do with the way love for Jesus is expressed in this Gospel: obeying him (14:15, 21), in this case by caring for his flock the way he does, which implies utter self-sacrifice and potentially death (10:11, 15; 21:18–19).

## The Price of Tending Sheep (21:18–19)

As a shepherd, Peter must face death (21:18–19), as his good shepherd had (10:11, 15, 17–18); as one of the sheep,[17] Peter must "follow" Jesus (21:19; 10:4–5, 27)—even to death (13:36–37).[18] Peter would not always have the vigor that he had devoted to Jesus that morning (cf. 21:7, 10–11; 1 John 2:14). Other ancient texts also present powerlessness in terms of dependence;[19] Diogenes the Cynic reportedly told a man whose servant was putting on his shoes that he would ultimately have to depend on the man to wipe his nose as well (Diogenes Laertius 6.2.44). A third-century Palestinian Amora opined that God might punish a person by withdrawing the person's control over his members so that another would have power to do that person harm (*Gen. Rab.* 67:3). The description of dependence here could apply simply to old age,[20] which could sometimes incline judges and observers toward mercy;[21] but the language of "stretching out the hands" probably suggests more than merely the dependence of old age. Usually it indicates the image of supplication,[22] but here it may refer to voluntarily submitting one's hands to binding, which preceded execution.[23] In view of 21:19, Jesus is explaining that when Peter is old and dependent, he will suffer execution. Second Peter 1:14, probably independently of John, suggests the tradition that Jesus showed Peter that he would die. Early Christian tradition reports that Peter died by

---

[15] It appears for pasturing a flock in Gen 29:7; 37:12, 16; it applies to pasturing God's flock in Jer 31:10; Ezek 34:2–3, 8, 10–16; elsewhere the term can function figuratively for feeding someone without their toil (Philostratus *Hrk.* 1.5).

[16] See more fully Brown, *John*, 2:1105.

[17] One could likewise view Moses and Aaron as sheep from the flock (*1 En.* 89:18). Begg, "Sheep," thinks the three sheep of *1 En.* 89:72 refer to Zerubbabel and Joshua, plus either Ezra or (more likely) Nehemiah.

[18] Smalley, *John*, 91, also connects 21:16 and John 10 via the images of feeding the flock and following Jesus.

[19] Slaves and prisoners of war regularly had to act at others' bidding, e.g., Homer *Il.* 6.455–458.

[20] That the dependence of old age is at least partly in view is frequently noted, e.g., Hunter, *John*, 196.

[21] E.g., Sophocles *Oed. tyr.* 402–403, 1153; Dionysius of Halicarnassus *R.A.* 10.29.1; Cornelius Nepos 19 (Phocion), 4.1; Herodian 2.5.8; *Dig.* 47.21.2; 2 Macc 6:21–22; *Mart. Pol.* 9.2.

[22] Lam 1:17; Virgil *Aen.* 1.487; 11.414; 12.930; Ovid *Metam.* 3.723; 5.215; 6.358–359; Seneca *Controv.* 1.7.10; Apuleius *Metam.* 3.7.

[23] E.g., Livy 1.26.7, 11; Ovid *Amores* 1.2.19–20. Many regarded it as shameful to die at another's hand (e.g., Cornelius Nepos 23 [Hannibal], 12.5).

crucifixion,[24] probably upside down,[25] finally "following" (21:19) Jesus fully (13:36); early Christian texts applied "stretching out one's hands" to crucifixion.[26]

Many commentators thus see crucifixion implied here.[27] Whether the specific picture of crucifixion is present here or not (it probably is), Peter's martyrdom certainly follows Jesus. Jesus explained here by what sort of death Peter would glorify God (21:19), just as he had earlier explained by what sort of death (12:33, also using σημαίνων) he himself would glorify God (12:23; 13:31–33; just as Lazarus's death glorified Jesus by allowing him to raise Lazarus, 11:4). Jewish hearers might express little surprise that Jesus would predict the manner of Peter's death for him.[28] That Peter understands that Jesus refers to his death is likely; this is why he wants to know the beloved disciple's fate, but Jesus refuses to comment on that disciple's death (21:21–23). Peter had earlier volunteered to "follow" Jesus to the cross (13:37), but Peter had failed to do so (13:38); now Jesus explains to him that he will in fact be able to "follow" Jesus to the cross later, as he had told him more ambiguously before (13:36).[29]

## The Beloved Disciple's Future (21:20–23)

Peter's question about the beloved disciple reflects some continuing (albeit not hostile) competition between the two figures (21:21; cf. 20:4).[30] That Jesus may respond harshly ("What is that to you?" 21:22; cf. 2:4) also would send a message to early Christians divided in devotion to different Christian leaders, a problem that had existed decades earlier in the urban house-churches of the East (1 Cor 1:10–13; cf. the principle in Rom 14:4, 10).

In supposing that the beloved disciple would remain alive until Jesus' eschatological return, the other disciples misunderstood what Jesus was saying. In other words, even disciples were continuing to take Jesus too literally at times, just as many people had misunderstood Jesus throughout the Gospel. Certainly, the return of which Jesus speaks cannot be the coming to which he had previously referred in 14:18 (and 14:3), which was fulfilled in the resurrection appearances of ch. 20, especially in 20:19–23; nor may it refer to Christ's "coming" for a believer at death (cf. 13:36), unless John intends a tautology applicable to all believers.[31] Instead it must refer to an eschatological coming, as in 1 John 2:28;

---

[24] Tertullian *Scorpiace* 15 (including his binding, though this could reflect John 21:18); Eusebius *Hist. eccl.* 2.25.5–8; see Bruce, *History,* 403; on Peter's martyrdom, see *1 Clem.* 5. Other evidence also supports his stay in Rome, e.g., Ign. *Rom.* 4.3; perhaps Falasca, "Bones."

[25] *Acts of Peter;* Origen according to Eusebius *Hist. eccl.* 3.1 (for crucifixion in this posture, see also Seneca *Consolation to Marcia* 20; references from Talbert, *John,* 262; Culpepper, *John,* 249).

[26] Talbert, *John,* 262, cites early Christian comments on Isa 65:2 (*Barn.* 12.4; Justin *1 Apol.* 35; Irenaeus *Demonstration of the Apostolic Preaching* 79) and Exod 17:12 (*Barn.* 12.2; Justin *Dial.* 90–91) and notes the analogy in Epictetus *Diatr.* 3.26.22. Cf. also Plautus *Miles gloriosus* 2.6–7 (in Gnilka, *Jesus,* 309); others cite Hippolytus *Apostolic Tradition* 4–6.

[27] E.g., Glasson, *Moses,* 44; Hunter, *John,* 196.

[28] Cf. the story in which R. Eliezer ben Hyrcanus, on his deathbed, foretells the manner of Akiba's death (*'Abot R. Nat.* 25A). Gentiles also accepted deathbed predictions of others' deaths (Homer *Il.* 16.853–854, 859; 22.359–360), which might be relevant though Jesus departs rather than dies here.

[29] Cf. similarly Lightfoot, *Gospel,* 343.

[30] Smith, *John* (1999), 397, comments here on the realism and verisimilitude of the way John's "characters react to one another," including in 21:17, 20.

[31] Bernard, *John,* 2:711. Johannine Christians could use Jesus' "coming" as a figure for judgments before the end (Rev 2:5, 16).

rare though this idea is earlier in the Gospel,[32] it is not absent (5:28–29; 6:39). John may have avoided much emphasis on future eschatology, which could have distracted from his emphasis on the coming in ch. 20, but now that this coming has taken place, he may indulge more freely in future eschatology.

Perhaps John implied in this promise a subtle double entendre, playing on the usual sense of μένω in his Gospel,[33] although one would hope for more explicit clarification to that effect, since the misunderstanding appears to have already caused some problems for John's audience. Most likely, John emphasizes ἐὰν θέλω, "if I will"; Jesus was not telling Peter that the beloved disciple would live until Jesus' return but that it was not Peter's business to know the beloved disciple's fate.[34] This seems the most logical way to take τί πρὸς σέ, "What is it to you?" (21:22); precisely the same question appears with the same force when Epictetus declares that another's death is not one's own business (Epictetus *Diatr.* 3.18.2).

---

[32] To some this contrast argues against the authenticity of ch. 21 (Lightfoot, *Gospel*, 343).

[33] Culpepper, *Anatomy*, 161.

[34] With, e.g., Bernard, *John*, 2:711. It is merely a possibility (Barrett, *John*, 586). Those who knew the future were thought sometimes not free to divulge it (e.g., Eunapius *Lives* 469).

# THE CLOSE OF THE GOSPEL

## 21:24–25

M ANY SCHOLARS THINK THAT the emphasis on the conditional nature of the questions (21:22–23) suggests that disappointment with the beloved disciple's death existed in the early church.[1] That is, Jesus apparently said something about some disciples remaining until he returned, which the Synoptics already apply to the transfiguration (Mark 9:1–2; Matt 16:28–17:2; Luke 9:27–29); the death of the last disciple could well provoke some confusion about the meaning of such a saying. In such a case, 21:24–25 would likely constitute a later addition to the text (especially if one accepts the rest of ch. 21 as part of the Gospel), which is the view of most scholars. It can read like a miniature letter of recommendation (cf. Rom 16:2; 1 Cor 4:17; 16:10; Phil 2:19; Col 4:7; Phlm 17; 3 John 12).[2]

At the same time, the disciple himself could issue the same sort of warning as he was recognizing his age and impending death; the Lord might well not return in his lifetime. If the disciple remains alive at the time of the Gospel's completion, this could help explain the present tense of μαρτυρῶν in 21:24,[3] although one could also interpret 21:24 otherwise (e.g., the disciple's witness continues to live even if the disciple does not; see comment on 19:35). The community ("we") may second the verdict of the singular voice in 19:35, which commends the truth of the beloved disciple's witness, unless this represents an editorial "we,"[4] which many argue, on the basis of Johannine style in general, seems less likely.[5]

The concluding verse (21:25) harks back to 20:30,[6] suggesting that it stems either from the author or from those close enough to the author to understand and articulate his

---

[1] Cf., e.g., Hunter, *John*, 197; Minear, "Audience," 348; Blomberg, *Reliability*, 37–39. "Siblings" here refers to believers, at least (though not necessarily exclusively) in the Johannine circle of believers (cf. Brown, *John*, 2:1110).

[2] For letters of recommendation, cf. also, e.g., P.Grenf. 2.77.34–38; P.Lond. 1912.105–108; P.Oxy. 32; 292; Socratics *Ep.* 28; 1 Esd 4:61; *p. Moʾed Qaṭ.* 3:1, §2; Acts 9:2; 18:27; 22:5; 1 Cor 16:3; 2 Cor 3:1; see further Kim, *Letter*, 37–42.

[3] Early Christians usually regarded 21:24 "as John's own seal of authority" (Wiles, *Gospel*, 9; cf. 1 Cor 16:21; Gal 6:11; Col 4:18; 2 Thess 3:17).

[4] Carson, *John*, 684, though allowing that it may refer to the elders of the Ephesian church; Köstenberger, *John*, 195. Cf. 3:11; the apostolic circle in 1:14; 1 John 1:2, 4 (though church tradition makes John its final survivor).

[5] See Charlesworth, *Disciple*, 28; Whitacre, *John*, 500. Paul often uses the rhetorical first person plural in letters where he opens with plural authors or intends his apostolic circle (e.g., 1 Cor 1:23; 2 Cor 3:1; 4:7); but he frequently also employs it inclusively with his readers (e.g., Rom 1:5; 2:2).

[6] As frequently noted, e.g., Bultmann, *John*, 718. Theodore of Mopsuestia thought that 21:25 was a later editorial addition, but there is no textual evidence for this view (Sinaiticus's first hand omits and then corrects the verse; Birdsall, "Source").

mind. At least the plural in 21:24, however, would seem to represent others,[7] perhaps the Johannine circle of disciples,[8] confirming the veracity of the beloved disciple's witness.[9] Ancient Mediterranean legal documents typically listed witnesses at the end of the document,[10] just as the book (perhaps of life?) in Revelation is sealed with seven attesting seals.[11] Nonlegal documents could also follow the legal pattern and cite a past figure's saying as if citing a closing legal testimony (Seneca *Nat.* 5.18.16).

Some take 21:25's comments about many possible books as a reference to the proliferation of other gospels, possibly including one or more of the Synoptics.[12] While this proposal is certainly possible (we know on other grounds that they did proliferate), 21:25 can be explained easily enough without recourse to it. Epideictic biographies sometimes ended with summary praise; after recounting Alexander's death, for example, Arrian eulogizes him, both praising him and excusing the faults Arrian has recorded.[13] The concluding announcement that the writer has provided only a sample of the subject's works was common in hyperbolic praise of one's subject.[14] Although John's Christology (cf. 1:1–3) may diminish the element of hyperbole here,[15] the text probably speaks of Jesus' incarnate signs (cf. 20:30), not works in creation (1:3). Homer complains hyperbolically that no mortal could recount all the evils that the Achaian leaders suffered, then (slightly less hyperbolically) adds that five or six years would not be enough to recount their sufferings.[16] Similarly, Diodorus Siculus (16.95.5) observes that it will be difficult, but promises to attempt to include Alexander's entire career in one book (book 17). Philo points out that Genesis deals with creation but also with ten thousand other matters (*Abraham* 1);[17] he closes his final volume of *Special Laws* by noting that human longevity is inadequate to provide an exhaustive treatment of justice (*Spec. Laws* 4.238; cf. *Moses* 1.213; *Dreams* 2.63). Plutarch complains that it would require many books (βιβλίων) to fully criticize all of Herodotus's

---

[7] This is the only verse in John that Robinson, *Trust*, 83, thinks must be an addition. Morris, *John*, 879; but his secondary appeal to the transition from plural to singular in 1 Thess 2:18 may recall Silvanus and Timothy (1 Thess 1:1).

[8] Cullmann, *Circle*, 2. This might be the "elders of the Ephesian church" (Hunter, *John*, 198), though we think Smyrna somewhat more likely.

[9] The final verses establish the beloved disciple's authority, but not necessarily against Peter (Kysar, *John*, 321). Smith, *John* (1999), 400, thinks 21:24 attests that probably "the Beloved Disciple's witness authorized the Gospel," though he doubts that he actually wrote it down.

[10] E.g., P.Eleph. 1.16–18; 2.17–18; P.Lond. 1727.68–72; P.Tebt. 104.34–35; P.Col. 270.1.25–28; *BGU* 1273.36–40; P.Cair.Zen. 59001.48–52; the Aramaic *git* from Wadi Murabba'at ca. 72 C.E. (Carmon, *Inscriptions*, 90–91, 200–201); Cicero *Quinct.* 6.25; cf. further comments in Epictetus (LCL 1:136–37 n. 1). Prof. Dale Martin, then of Duke University, first pointed out this correspondence with legal documents to me (January 23, 1990).

[11] The genuineness of witnesses' seals could be tested (P.Oxy. 494.31–43); such seals were broken when a document was opened (e.g., *BGU* 326.21; Euripides *Hipp.* 864–865; Chariton 4.5.8; *3 En.* 27:2; Rev 5:2).

[12] Smith, "Gospels," 13, 19; idem, *John* (1999), 372; cf. Luke 1:1.

[13] Arrian *Alex.* 7.28.1–7.30.3.

[14] E.g., Fenton, *John*, 212; Bultmann, *John*, 718.

[15] Historians liked to claim the uniqueness of their own subjects (e.g., Polybius 1.4.5; 39.8.7; Dionysius of Halicarnassus *Thucydides* critiques Thucydides for this claim), but John's Christology invites a greater claim of uniqueness, despite its rooting in earlier salvific history.

[16] Homer *Od.* 3.113–117.

[17] A familiar number in hyperbole, both regarding more stories than one could publish (Iamblichus *V.P.* 28.135) and in general (Philo *Abr.* 64; Euripides *Medea* 965; 1 Cor 14:19; Justin *Dial.* 115), though greater exaggerations were possible (Catullus 48.3).

lies (Plutarch *Malice of Herodotus* 1, *Mor.* 854F); Lysias, that even all time would be inadequate for all humanity to declare all the exploits of Athens's deceased war heroes (Lysias *Or.* 2.1, §190).[18] Second Maccabees notes that many possible things could be said but the author abridges them for the sake of readability (2 Macc 2:24–25).[19]

First Maccabees claims that the exploits of the Maccabees were simply too numerous to record them all (1 Macc 9:22); some later rabbis declared that no one had tried to write all the teachings of the scribes because there would have been no end to the books needing to be written.[20] A probably later tradition, purportedly stemming from the late first century, claims that though all the seas were ink and the earth scrolls, R. Eliezer and R. Joshua, teachers of R. Akiba, believed it would not be enough to record all the Torah that they had learned, and they had understood at most a drop of what there was to understand about Torah.[21] The number of books actually available in John's day would have been limited in any case, but estimates remained hyberbolic. One widespread Jewish story offers an estimate on the number of books then in circulation; Demetrius of Phalerum reportedly sought to collect for Ptolemy all the books in the world (*Let. Aris.* 9), which came to over 200,000, reaching for 500,000 (*Let. Aris.* 10).

The point is that the author provided only a small selection of Jesus' works;[22] Jesus is further praised by what the author must leave unsaid (cf. Heb 11:32). What John does include, however, is sufficient to summon his audience to deeper faith and was selected for that purpose (20:30–31).

---

[18] Ovid *Tristia* 2.324 claims that Caesar spread his exploits everywhere *(omnia)*; for similar hyperboles, see, e.g., Cicero *Verr.* 2.5.72.189; Eunapius *Lives* 493; Mark 13:19. See further relevant sources in Boring et al., *Commentary,* 308 (Aelius Aristides *Or.* 45; Valerius Alexandria of Harpocration *On the Powers of Nature* [end of vine essay]; Porphyry *V.P.* 29).

[19] Cf. similarly Iamblichus *V.P.* 27.128; 28.135; and the passages we cited for 20:30, including Diogenes Laertius 6.2.69; 6.7.98.

[20] *Pesiq. Rab.* 3:2, citing Eccl 12:12. Nor could the world contain Israel's eschatological reward (*Exod. Rab.* 30:24) or an adequate depiction of God's greatness (Marmorstein, *Names,* 163). The Samaritan book of Joshua claims that the world could not contain Israel's wealth in Samson's day (Bowman, *Documents,* 76).

[21] *Song Rab.* 1:3, §1.

[22] Cf. *The Life* of Josephus, who summarizes and skips over details recounted in the *Jewish War* (*Life* 412), then adds material not in the *War* (*Life* 413).

# BIBLIOGRAPHY

## ANCIENT SOURCES

Achilles Tatius. *Clitophon and Leucippe.* Translated by S. Gaselee. LCL. London: Heinemann, 1917.

*Acts of John.* Translated by K. Schäferdiek. Pages 188–259 in vol. 2 of *New Testament Apocrypha.* Edited by Edgar Hennecke, William Schneemelcher, and R. McL. Wilson. 2 vols. Philadelphia: Westminster, 1963–1965.

Aelian. *On the Characteristics of Animals.* Translated by A. F. Scholfield. 3 vols. LCL. Cambridge: Harvard University Press, 1958–1959.

*Aelius Aristides.* Translated by C. A. Behr. 4 vols. LCL. Cambridge: Harvard University Press, 1973.

Aeschines. *The Speeches of Aeschines.* Translated by Charles Darwin Adams. LCL. Cambridge: Harvard University Press, 1919.

*Aeschylus.* Translated by Herbert Weir Smyth. 2 vols. LCL. Cambridge: Harvard University Press, 1922, 1926.

*Ahiqar.* Translated by J. M. Lindenberger. *OTP* 2:494–507. *See also Words of Ahiqar,* below.

Alciphron, Aelian, and Philostratus. *The Letters of Alciphron, Aelian, and Philostratus.* Translated by Allen Rogers Bonner and Francis H. Forbes. LCL. Cambridge: Harvard University Press, 1949.

"The Amarna Letters." Translated by W. F. Albright. *ANET* 483–90.

*Ancient Near Eastern Texts Relating to the Old Testament.* Edited by James B. Pritchard. 2d ed. Princeton: Princeton University Press, 1955.

*The Ante-Nicene Fathers: Translations of the Writings of the Fathers down to A. D. 325.* Edited by Alexander Roberts and James Donaldson. Revised by A. Cleveland Coxe. 10 vols. Grand Rapids: Eerdmans, 1975.

Antonius Diogenes. "The Wonders beyond Thule." Introduction and translation by Gerald N. Sandy. Pages 775–82 in *Collected Ancient Greek Novels.* Edited by B. P. Reardon. Berkeley: University of California Press, 1989.

*Apocalypse of Abraham.* Introduction and translation by R. Rubinkiewicz. *OTP* 1:681–705.

*Apocalypse of Elijah.* Translated by Orval S. Wintermute. *OTP* 1:735–53.

*Apocalypse of Zephaniah.* Introduction and translation by Orval S. Wintermute. *OTP.* 1:497–515.

*Apocalypsis Esdrae, Apocalypsis Sedrach, Visio beati Esdrae.* Edited by O. Wahl. Pseudepigrapha Veteris Testamenti Graece 4. Leiden: Brill, 1977.

*Apocryphon of Ezekiel.* Introduction and translation by J. R. Mueller and S. E. Robinson. *OTP* 1:487–95.

*Apocryphon of John.* Translated by Frederick Wisse. Pages 98–116 in *NHL.*

Apollodorus. *Library* and *Epitome.* Translated by Sir James George Frazer. 2 vols. LCL. Cambridge: Harvard University Press, 1921.

Apollonius Rhodius. *The Argonautica.* Translated by R. C. Seaton. LCL. Cambridge: Harvard University Press, 1912.

*The Apostolic Fathers: Greek Texts and English Translations of Their Writings.* 2d ed. Translated by J. B. Lightfoot and J. R. Harmer. Edited and revised by Michael W. Holmes. Grand Rapids: Baker, 1992.

Appian. *Historia Romana.* Translated by Horace White. 4 vols. LCL. Cambridge: Harvard University Press, 1912–1913.

Apuleius. *The Golden Ass.* Translated by W. Adlington. Revised by S. Gaselee. LCL. Cambridge: Harvard University Press, 1915.

Aratus. *Phaenomena.* Translated by G. R. Mair. In volume on Callimachus, Lycophron and Aratus. LCL. Rev. ed. Cambridge: Harvard University Press, 1955.

*Aristeas to Philocrates: Letter of Aristeas.* Edited and translated by Moses Hadas. New York: Harper & Brothers, for the Dropsie College for Hebrew and Cognate Learning, 1951.

Aristobulus. "Fragments." Introduction and translation by A. Yarbro Collins. *OTP* 2:831–42.

*Aristophanes.* Translated by Benjamin Bickley Rogers. 3 vols. LCL. Cambridge: Harvard University Press, 1924.

*Aristotle.* Translated by G. Cyril Armstrong et al. 23 vols. LCL. Cambridge: Harvard University Press, 1926–1970.

Arrian. *Anabasis Alexandri* and *Indica.* Translated by P. A. Brunt. 2 vols. LCL. Cambridge: Harvard University Press, 1976–1983.

Artapanus. Introduction and translation by J. J. Collins. *OTP* 2:889–903.

Artemidorus Daldianus. *The Interpretation of Dreams (Oneirocritica).* Translated with commentary by Robert J. White. Noyes Classical Studies. Park Ridge, N.J.: Noyes Press, 1975.

Artemidorus Daldianus. *Onirocriticon Libri V.* Bibliotheca Scriptorum Graecorum et Romanorum Teubneriana. Leipzig: Tuebner, 1963.

"Assyrian Oracles and Prophecies." Translated by Robert H. Pfeiffer. *ANET* 449–450.

Athenaeus. *The Deipnosophists.* Translated by Charles Burton Gulick. 7 vols. LCL. London: Heinemann, 1927–1941.

Augustine. *Tractates on the Gospel of John 1–112.* Translated by John W. Rettig. Fathers of the Church 78–79, 88, 90, 92. Washington, D.C.: Catholic University of America Press, 1988–1995.

Aulus Gellius. *The Attic Nights.* Translated by John C. Rolfe. 3 vols. Rev. ed. LCL. Cambridge: Harvard University Press, 1927–1952.

*Babrius and Phaedrus.* Translated by Ben Edwin Perry. LCL. Cambridge: Harvard University Press, 1965.

"Babylonian and Assyrian Historical Texts." Translated by A. Leo Oppenheim. *ANET* 265–317.

*The Babylonian Talmud.* Edited by Isidore Epstein. London: Soncino, 1948.

*2 Baruch.* Translated by A. F. J. Klijn. *OTP* 1:615–52.

*3 Baruch.* Translated by H. E. Gaylord Jr. *OTP* 1:653–79.

*4 Baruch.* Translated by S. E. Robinson. *OTP* 2:418–25. *See also Paraleipomena Jeremiou.*

*The Book of the Dead or Going Forth by Day: Ideas of the Ancient Egyptians Concerning the Hereafter as Expressed in Their Own Terms.* Translated by Thomas George Allen. Prepared for publication by Elizabeth Blaisdell Hauser. Oriental Institute of the University of Chicago Studies in Ancient Oriental Civilization 37. Chicago: University of Chicago Press, 1974.

Caesar. *Alexandrian, African, and Spanish Wars.* Translated by A. G. Way. LCL. Cambridge: Harvard University Press, 1955.

Caesar, *The Civil Wars.* Translated by A. G. Peskett. LCL. Cambridge: Harvard University Press, 1914.

Caesar. *The Gallic War.* Translated by H. J. Edwards. LCL. Cambridge: Harvard University Pres, 1917.

Callimachus. *Aetia, Iambi, Lyric Poems, Hecale, Minor Epic and Elegiac Poems, and other Fragments.* Translated by C. A. Trypanis. LCL. Cambridge: Harvard University Press, 1958.

Callimachus. *Hymns and Epigrams.* Translated by A. W. Mair. Rev. ed. LCL. Cambridge: Harvard University Press, 1955.

*Catullus.* Translated by Francis Warre Cornish. Revised by G. P. Goold. 2d ed. LCL. Cambridge: Harvard University Press, 1988.

Chariton. *Aphrodisiensis: De Chaerea et Callirhoe amatoriarum narrationum libri octo.* Oxford: Clarendon; London: Humphrey Milford, 1938.

Chariton. *Chaereas and Callirhoe.* Translated by Warren E. Blake. Ann Arbor: University of Michigan Press, 1939.

*Cicero.* Translated by Harry Caplan et al. 28 vols. LCL. Cambridge: Harvard University Press, 1913–1972.

Columella. *De re rustica* and *De arboribus.* Translated by Harrison Boyd Ash, E. S. Forster, and Edward H. Heffner. 3 vols. LCL. Cambridge: Harvard University Press, 1941–1955.

*Cornelius Nepos.* Translated by John C. Rolfe. New ed. LCL. Cambridge: Harvard University Press, 1984.

*Corpus of the Aramaic Incantation Bowls.* Edited and translated by Charles D. Isbell. SBLDS 17. Missoula, Mont.: Scholars Press, 1975.

*Corpus Inscriptionum Iudaicarum: Recueil des inscriptions juives qui vont du IIIe siècle de notre ère.* Edited by P. Jean-Baptiste Frey. 3 vols. Rome: Pontificio Istituto di Archeologa Cristiana, 1936–1952.

*Corpus Papyrorum Judaicarum.* Vol. 1 edited by Victor A. Tcherikover, with Alexander Fuks. Vol. 2 edited by Victor A. Tcherikover and Alexander Fuks.Vol. 3 edited by Victor A. Tcherikover, Alexander Fuks, and Menahem Stern, with David M. Lewis. 3 vols. Cambridge: Harvard University Press for the Magnes Press, Hebrew University, 1957–1964.

*The Cynic Epistles: A Study Edition.* Edited by Abraham J. Malherbe. SBLSBS 12. Missoula, Mont.: Scholars Press, 1977.

Dead Sea Scrolls. *Die Texte aus Qumran.* Edited by Eduard Lohse. Munich: Kösel, 1971.

*The Dead Sea Scrolls: A New Translation.* Wise, Michael, Martin Abegg Jr., and Edward Cook. San Francisco: Harper San Francisco, 1999.

*The Dead Sea Scrolls in English.* Edited by Geza Vermes. 2d ed. New York: Penguin, 1981.

Demetrius. *On Style.* Translated by W. Rhys Roberts. Pages 255–487 in Aristotle, *Poetics.* Rev. ed. LCL Cambridge: Harvard University Press, 1932.

Demetrius the Chronographer. Introduction and translation by J. Hanson. *OTP* 2:843–47 (introduction), 848–54 (translation).

*Demosthenes.* Translated by J. H. Vince, C. A. Vince, A. T. Murray, N. W. DeWitt, and N. J. DeWitt. 7 vols. LCL. Cambridge: Harvard University Press, 1926–1949.

Dio Cassius. *Roman History.* Translated by Earnest Cary. 9 vols. LCL. Cambridge: Harvard University Press, 1914–1922.

*Dio Chrysostom.* Translated by J. W. Cohoon and H. Lamar Crosby. 5 vols. LCL. Cambridge: Harvard University Press, 1932–1951.

Diodorus Siculus. *The Library of History.* Translated by C. H. Oldfather, Charles L. Sherman, C. Bradford Welles, Russel M. Geer, and Francis R. Walton. 12 vols. LCL. Cambridge: Harvard University Press, 1933–1967.

Diogenes Laertius. *Lives of Eminent Philosophers.* Translated by R. D. Hicks. 2 vols. LCL. Cambridge: Harvard University Press, 1925.

Dionysius of Halicarnassus. *Critical Essays.* Translated by Stephen Usher. 2 vols. LCL. Cambridge: Harvard University Press, 1974.

Dionysius of Halicarnassus. *The Roman Antiquities.* Translated by Earnest Cary, following Edward Spelman. 7 vols. LCL. Cambridge: Harvard University Press, 1937–1945.

"The Divine Nomination of an Ethiopian King." Translated by John A. Wilson. *ANET* 447–448.

"The Divine Nomination of Thut-Mose III." Translated by John A. Wilson. *ANET* 446–447.

*1 Enoch (Ethiopic Apocalypse).* Translated by E. Isaac. *OTP* 1:5–89. *See also Ethiopic Book of Enoch.*

*2 Enoch.* Translated by F. I. Anderson. *OTP* 1:91–221.

*3 Enoch (Hebrew Apocalypse).* Translated by P. Alexander. *OTP* 1:223–315.

Epictetus. *The Discourses as Reported by Arrian, the Manual, and Fragments.* Translated by W. A. Oldfather. 2 vols. LCL. Cambridege: Harvard University Press, 1926–1928.

*The Ethiopic Book of Enoch: A New Edition in the Light of the Aramaic Dead Sea Fragments.* Edited by Michael A. Knibb, in consultation with Edward Ullendorff. 2 vols. Oxford: Clarendon, 1978.

Eunapius. *See* Philostratus and Eunapius.

*Euripides.* Translated by A. S. Way. 4 vols. LCL. Cambridge: Harvard University Press, 1912.

*Euripides.* Translated by David Kovacs. 2 vols. LCL new series. Cambridge: Harvard University Press, 1994–1995.

Eusebius. *Ecclesiastical History.* Translated by C. F. Cruse. Grand Rapids: Baker, 1955.

*The Fathers according to Rabbi Nathan.* Translated by Judah Goldin. Yale Judaica Series 10. New Haven: Yale University Press, 1955.

*The Fathers according to Rabbi Nathan (Abot de Rabbi Nathan) Version B.* Translation and commentary by Anthony J. Saldarini. Studies in Judaism in Late Antiquity 11. Leiden: Brill, 1975.

"Fragments of Pseudo-Greek Poets." Introduction and translation by H. Attridge. *OTP* 2:821–30.

Gaius. *The Institutes of Gaius.* Translation and introduction by W. M. Gordon and O. F. Robinson, with the Latin text of Seckel and Kuebler. Texts in Roman Law. Ithaca, N.Y.: Cornell University Press, 1988.

Galen. *On the Natural Faculties.* Translated by Arthur John Brock. LCL. London: Heinemann, 1916.

*The Gospel according to Philip.* Translated by C. J. De Catanzaro. *JTS* NS 13, no. 1 (1962): 35–71.

*The Gospel of the Egyptians.* Translated by Böhlig and F. Wisse. Pages 195–205 in *NHL.*

*The Gospel of Philip.* Translated by W. W. Isenberg. Pages 131–51 in *NHL.*

*The Greek Anthology.* Translated by W. R. Paton. 5 vols. LCL. Cambridge: Harvard University Press, 1916–1917.

*The Greek Bucolic Poets.* Translated by J. M. Edmonds. LCL. Cambridge: Harvard University Press, 1912.

*The Greek Magical Papyri in Translation Including the Demotic Spells.* Edited by Hans Dieter Betz. 2d ed. Chicago: University of Chicago Press, 1992.

*The Greek Version of the Testaments of the Twelve Patriarchs, Edited from Nine MSS. together with the Variants of the Armenian and Slavonic Versions and Some Hebrew Fragments.* Edited by R. H. Charles. Oxford: Clarendon, 1908.

Heliodorus. *Ethiopian Story.* Translated by Sir Walter Lamb. Everyman's Library 276. New York: Dutton, 1961.

*Hermogenes, On Issues: Strategies of Argument in Later Greek Rhetoric.* Translated with commentary by Malcolm Heath. Oxford: Clarendon, 1995.

*Herodes, Cercidas, and the Greek Choliambic Poets.* Translated by A. D. Knox. LCL. Cambridge: Harvard University Press, 1961.

Herodian. *History.* Translated by C. R. Whittaker. 2 vols. LCL. Cambridge: Harvard University Press, 1969.

Herodotus. *History.* Translated by A. D. Godley. 4 vols. LCL. Cambridge: Harvard University Press, 1920–1925.

*Hesiod, the Homeric Hymns, and Homerica.* Translated by Hugh G. Evelyn-White. Rev. ed. LCL. Cambridge: Harvard University Press, 1936.

*Hippocrates.* Translated by W. H. S. Jones, E. T. Withington, Wesley D. Smith, and Paul Potter. 8 vols. LCL. Cambridge: Harvard University Press, 1923–1995.

*History of Joseph.* Introduction and translation by G. T. Zervos. *OTP* 2:467–75.

Homer. *The Iliad.* Translated by A. T. Murray. 2 vols. LCL. Cambridge: Harvard University Press, 1924.

Homer. *The Odyssey.* Translated by A. T. Murray. 2d ed. Revised by George E. Dimock. 2 vols. LCL. Cambridge: Harvard University Press, 1995.

Horace. *The Odes and Epodes.* Translated by C. E. Bennett. LCL. Cambridge: Harvard University Press, 1914.

Horace. *Satires, Epistles, and Ars poetica.* Translated by H. Rushton Fairclough. LCL. London: Heinemann, 1926.

"A Hymn to Amon-Re." Translated by J. A. Wilson. *ANET* 365–367.

Iamblichus. "A Babylonian Story." Introduction and translation by Gerald N. Sandy. Pages 783–97 in *Collected Ancient Greek Novels.* Edited by B. P. Reardon. Berkeley: University of California Press, 1989.

Iamblichus. *On the Mysteries of the Egyptians, Chaldeans, and Assyrians.* Translated by Thomas Taylor. 3d ed. London: Stuart & Watkins, 1968.

Iamblichus. *On the Pythagorean Way of Life: Text, Translation, and Notes.* By John Dillon and Jackson Hershbell. SBL Texts and Translations 29, Graeco-Roman Religion Series 11. Atlanta: Scholars Press, 1991.

*Die Inschriften von Ephesos.* Edited by Hermann Wankel et al. 8 vols. Inschriften Griechischer Städte aus Kleinasien 11. Bonn: Rudolf Habelt, 1979–1984.

"The Instruction for King Meri-Ka-Re." Translated by John A. Wilson. *ANET* 414–418.

"Instructions for Palace Personnel to Insure the King's Purity." Translated by Albrecht Goetze. *ANET* 207.

"Instructions for Temple Officials." Translated by Albrecht Goetze. *ANET* 207–10.

*Isaeus.* Translated by Edward Seymour Forster. LCL. Cambridge: Harvard University Press, 1927.

Isocrates. *Orations.* Translated by George Norlin and Larue van Hook. 3 vols. LCL. London: Heinemann, 1928–1961.

John Chrysostom. *Commentary on Saint John the Apostle and Evangelist, Homilies 1–47.* Translated by Sister Thomas Aquinas Goggin. The Fathers of the Church 33. New York: Fathers of the Church, 1957.

*Joseph and Asenath.* Translated by C. Burchard. *OTP* 2:177–247.

*Joseph et Aséneth: Introduction, texte critique, traduction, et notes.* Edited by Marc Philonenko. StPB 13. Leiden: Brill, 1968.

*Josephus.* Translated by H. St. J. Thackeray, Ralph Marcus, Allen Wikgren, and Louis H. Feldman. 10 vols. LCL. Cambridge: Harvard University Press, 1926–1965.

*Josephus. The Jewish War.* Edited by Gaalya Cornfeld with Benjamin Mazar and Paul L. Maier. Grand Rapids: Zondervan, 1982.

*Jubilees.* Translated by Orval S. Wintermute. *OTP* 2:35–142.

Justinian. *Institutes.* Translation and introduction by Peter Birks and Grant McLeod, with the Latin text of Paul Krueger. Ithaca, N.Y.: Cornell University Press, 1987.

Juvenal. *Satires.* Translated by G. G. Ramsay. Rev. ed. LCL. Cambridge: Harvard University Press, 1940.

*The Ladder of Jacob.* Introduction and translation by H. G. Lunt. *OTP* 2:401–11.

*The Legend of King Keret.* Translated by H. L. Ginsberg. *ANET* 142–49.

*Liber antiquitatum biblicarum. See* Pseudo-Philo, below.

*Life of Adam and Eve.* Translated by M. D. Johnson. *OTP* 2:249–95.

*Life of Adam and Eve.* Greek text of the *Vita* of Adam and Eve, and the *Apocalypse of Moses.* Pages 1–23 in *Apocalypses Apocryphae.* Edited by Konstantin von Tischendorf. Hildesheim: Georg Olms, 1966.

*Lives of the Prophets.* Introduction and translation by D. R. A. Hare. *OTP* 2:379–99. Greek text in *Propheten und Apostellegenden nebst Jüngerkatalogen,* edited by Theodor Schermann.

Livy. *Ab urbe condita.* Translated by B. O. Foster, Frank Gardner, Evan T. Sage, and A. C. Schlesinger. 14 vols. LCL. Cambridge: Harvard University Press, 1919–1959.

Longinus. *On the Sublime.* Translated by W. Hamilton Fyfe. Pages 119–254 in Aristotle, *Poetics.* Rev. ed. LCL. Cambridge: Harvard University Press, 1932.

Longus. *Daphnis and Chloe.* Translated by George Thornley. Revised by J. M. Edmunds. With Parthenius, *Love Romances* and *Fragments; The Alexandrian Erotic Fragment; The Ninus Romance.* Translated by S. Gaselee. LCL. Cambridge: Harvard University Press, 1916.

Lucan. *The Civil War.* Translated by J. D. Duff. LCL. Cambridge: Harvard University Press, 1928.

Lucian. Translated by A. M. Harmon, K. Kilburn, and M. D. Macleod. 8 vols. LCL. Cambridge: Harvard University Press, 1913–1967.

Lucretius. *De rerum natura.* Translated by W. H. D. Rouse. 3d rev. ed. LCL. Cambridge: Harvard University Press, 1937.

Lycophron. *Alexandra.* Translated by A. W. Mair. LCL. Cambridge: Harvard University Press, 1955.

*Lysias.* Translated by W. R. M. Lamb. LCL. Cambridge: Harvard University Press, 1930.

*3 Maccabees.* Introduction and translation by H. Anderson. *OTP* 2:509–29.

*4 Maccabees.* Introduction and translation by H. Anderson. *OTP* 2:531–64.

*Manetho.* Translated by W. G. Waddell. LCL. Cambridge: Harvard University Press, 1940.

Marcus Aurelius. *The Communings with Himself.* Edited and translated by C. R. Haines. LCL. Cambridge: Harvard University Press, 1916.

Martial. *Epigrams.* Translated by Walter C. A. Ker. 2 vols. LCL. London: Heinemann, 1920.

*The Martyrdom and Ascension of Isaiah.* Translated by M. A. Knibb. *OTP* 2:143–76.

Maximus of Tyre. *The Philosophical Orations.* Translated by M. B. Trapp. Oxford: Clarendon, 1997.

*Mekilta de-Rabbi Ishmael.* Translated by Jacob Z. Lauterbach. 3 vols. Philadelphia: The Jewish Publication Society of America, 1933–1935.

*Menander Rhetor.* Translated with commentary by D. A. Russell and N. G. Wilson. Oxford: Clarendon, 1981.

*The Midrash on Psalms.* Translated by William G. Braude. 2 vols. Yale Judaica Series 13. Edited by Leon Neomy. New Haven: Yale University Press, 1959.

*The Midrash Rabbah.* Edited by Harry Freedman and Maurice Simon. Foreword by I. Epstein. 5 vols. London: Soncino, 1977.

*Minor Latin Poets.* Translated by J. Wight Duff and Arnold M. Duff. 2 vols. Rev. ed. LCL. Cambridge: Harvard University Press, 1935.

*The Mishnah.* Translated by Herbert Danby. London: Oxford University Press, 1933.

*The Mishnah.* Pointed Hebrew text, introductions, translations, notes, and supplements by Philip Blackman. 7 vols. New York: Judaica Press, 1963.

Musaeus. *Hero and Leander.* Translated by Cedric Whitman. Introduction by Thomas Gelzer. LCL. Cambridge: Harvard University Press, 1975.

"Musonius Rufus: The Roman Socrates." Translated by Cora E. Lutz. *Yale Classical Studies* 10 (1947): 3–147.

*The Nag Hammadi Library in English.* Edited by James M. Robinson. San Francisco: Harper & Row, 1977.

*New Testament Apocrypha.* Edited by Edgar Hennecke, William Schneemelcher, and R. McL. Wilson. 2 vols. Philadelphia: Westminster, 1963–1965.

*The Odes of Solomon.* Translated by James H. Charlesworth. *OTP* 2:725–71.

*The Odes of Solomon.* Translated by James H. Charlesworth. Oxford: Clarendon, 1973.

*Die Oracula sibyllina.* Edited by Johannes Geffcken. Die griechische christliche Schriftsteller der ersten drei Jahrhunderte 8. Leipzig: Hinrichs, 1902. *See also Sibylline Oracles,* below.

Origen. *Commentary on the Gospel according to John, Books 1–32.* Translated by Ronald E. Heine. The Fathers of the Church 80, 89. Washington, D.C.: Catholic University of America Press, 1989, 1993.

*On the Origin of the World.* Introduction by Hans-Gebhard Bethge. Translated by Hans-Gebhard Bethge and Orval S. Wintermute. Pages 161–179 in *NHL.*

*The Orphic Hymns: Text, Translation, and Notes.* Translated by Apostolos N. Athanassakis. Society of Biblical Literature Texts and Translations 12. Graeco-Roman Religion Series 4. Missoula, Mont.: Scholars Press, 1977.

*Orphica.* Introduction and translation by M. LaFargue. *OTP* 2:795–801.

Ovid. *Fasti.* Translated by Sir James George Frazer. LCL. Cambridge: Harvard University Press, 1931.

Ovid. *Heroides* and *Amores.* Translated by Grant Showerman. LCL. Cambridge: Harvard University Press, 1914.

Ovid. *Metamorphoses.* Translated by Frank Justus Miller. 2 vols. 2d ed. LCL. Cambridge: Harvard University Press, 1916–1921.

Ovid. *Tristia* and *Ex Ponto.* Translated by Arthur Leslie Wheeler. LCL. Cambridge: Harvard University Press, 1924.

*Paraleipomena Jeremiou.* Edited and translated by Robert A. Kraft and Ann-Elizabeth Purintun. Texts and Translations 1, Pseudepigrapha Series 1. Missoula, Mont.: Society of Biblical Literature, 1972.

Pausanias. *Description of Greece.* Translated by W. H. S. Jones and H. A. Ormerod. Index by R. E. Wycherley. 5 vols. LCL. Cambridge: Harvard University Press, 1918–1935.

Persius. In *Juvenal and Perseus.* Translated by G. G. Ramsay. Rev. ed. LCL. Cambridge: Harvard University Press, 1940.

*Pervigilium Veneris.* Translated by J. W. Mackail. 2d ed., revised by G. P. Goold. LCL. Cambridge: Harvard University Press, 1988.

*Pesikta de-Rab Kahana: R. Kahana's Compilation of Discourses for Sabbaths and Festival Days.* Translated by William G. Braude and Israel J. Kapstein. Philadelphia: The Jewish Publication Society of America, 1975.

*Pesikta Rabbati.* Translated by William G. Braude. 2 vols. Yale Judaica Series 18. New Haven: Yale University Press, 1968.

Petronius. *Satyricon, Fragments, and Poems.* Translated by W. H. D. Rouse. LCL. London: Heinemann, 1913.

Phaedrus. *See Babrius and Phaedrus.*

Philo. Translated by F. H. Colson, G. H. Whitaker, and R. Marcus. 12 vols. LCL, 1929–1962.

Philostratus, Flavius. *Heroikos.* Translated and edited by Jennifer K. Berenson Maclean and Ellen Bradshaw Aitken. Prologue by Gregory Nagy, xi–xxxv. Epilogue by Hemut Koester, 257–64. SBL Writings from the Greco-Roman World 1. Atlanta: Society of Biblical Literature, 2001.

Philostratus, Flavius. *The Life of Apollonius of Tyana.* Translated by F. C. Conybeare. 2 vols. LCL. Cambridge: Harvard University Press, 1912.

Philostratus, Flavius, and Eunapius. *The Lives of the Sophists.* Translated by Wilmer Cave Wright. LCL. Cambridge: Harvard University Press, 1921.

Pindar. *Odes.* Translated by William H. Race. 2 vols. LCL. Cambridge: Harvard University Press, 1997.

*Plato.* Translated by Harold North Fowler et al. 12 vols. LCL. Cambridge: Harvard University Press, 1914–1926.

Pliny. *Letters and Panegyricus.* Translated by Betty Radice. 2 vols. LCL. Cambridge: Harvard University Press, 1969.

Pliny. *Natural History.* Translated by H. Rackham, W. H. S. Jones, and D. E. Eichholz. 10 vols. LCL. Cambridge: Harvard University Press, 1938–1962.

Plotinus. Translated by A. H. Armstrong. 6 vols. LCL. Cambridge: Harvard University Press, 1966–.

Plutarch. *Lives.* Translated by Bernadotte Perrin et al. 11 vols. LCL. Cambridge: Harvard University Press, 1914–; London: Wm. Heinemann, 1914–.

Plutarch. *Moralia.* Translated by Frank Cole Babbitt et al. 15 vols. LCL. London: Heinemann, 1927–1969.

Polybius. *The Histories.* Translated by W. R. Paton. 6 vols. LCL. Cambridge: Harvard University Press, 1922–1927.

Porphyry. *Against the Christians: The Literary Remains.* Edited and translated by R. Joseph Hoffman. Amherst, N.Y.: Prometheus, 1994.

Porphyry. *On Aristotle's Categories.* Translated by Steven K. Strange. Ithaca, N.Y.: Cornell University Press, 1992.

Porphyry the Philosopher. *To Marcella.* Text and translation with introduction and notes by Kathleen O'Brien Wicker. Index of words by Lee E. Klosinski. SBL Texts and Translations 28, Graeco-Roman Religion Series 10. Atlanta: Scholars Press, 1987.

*Prayer of Joseph.* Introduction and translation by Jonathan Z. Smith. *OTP* 2:699–714.

Propertius. *The Elegies.* Translated by H. E. Butler. LCL. Cambridge: Harvard University Press, 1912.

*Propheten und Apostellegenden nebst Jüngerkatalogen.* Edited by Theodor Schermann. Texte und Untersuchungen 31, n.s. 16, 3. Leipzig: Hinrichs, 1907.

*Psalms of Solomon.* Translated by R. B. Wright. *OTP* 2:651–670. Greek text, pages 471–89 in vol. 2 of *Septuaginta.* Edited by Alfred Rahlfs. Stuttgart: Deutsche Bibelgesellschaft, 1979.

Pseudo-Callisthenes. "Alexander Romance." Introduction and translation by Ken Dowden. Pages 650–735 in *Collected Ancient Greek Novels.* Edited by B. P. Reardon. Berkeley: University of California Press, 1989.

*Pseudo-Eupolemus.* Introduction and translation by R. Doran. *OTP* 2:873–82.

*Pseudo-Philo.* Translated by D. J. Harrington. *OTP* 2:297–377.

*Pseudo-Philo. Liber antiquitatum biblicarum.* (Latin text.) Edited by Guido Kisch. Publications in Mediaeval Studies, The University of Notre Dame. Notre Dame, Ind.: University of Notre Dame, 1949.

*Pseudo-Phocylides.* Translated by P. W. van der Horst. *OTP* 2:565–82. *See also* Theognis.

Ptolemy. *Tetrabiblos.* Edited and translated by F. E. Robbins. LCL. Cambridge: Harvard University Press, 1940.

*Publilius Syrus.* Translated by J. Wight Duff and Arnold M. Duff. Pages 14–111 in *Minor Latin Poets.* Rev. ed. LCL. Cambridge: Harvard University Press, 1935.

Quintilian. *The Institutio oratoria.* Translated by H. E. Butler. 4 vols. LCL. London: Heinemann, 1969.

"The Repulsing of the Dragon and the Creation." Translated by J. A. Wilson. *ANET* 6–7.

*Rhetorica ad Alexandrum. See* Aristotle.

*Rhetorica ad Herennium. See* Cicero.

Sallust. Translated by J. C. Rolfe. LCL. Cambridge: Harvard University Press, 1931.

*Select Papyri.* Vol. 1: *Non-literary Papyri: Private Affairs.* Vol. 2: *Non-literary Papyri: Public Documents.* Translated by A. S. Hunt and C. C. Edgar. Vol. 3: *Literary Papyri, Poetry.* Translated by D. L. Page. LCL. Cambridge: Harvard University Press, 1932–1941.

Seneca. Translated by John W. Basore et al. 10 vols. LCL. Cambridge: Harvard University Press, 1920–1970.

Seneca the Elder. *Controversiae* and *Suasoriae.* Translated by M. Winterbottom. 2 vols. LCL. Cambridge: Harvard University Press, 1974.

*The Sentences of Sextus.* Edited and translated by Richard A. Edwards and Robert A. Wild. Society of Biblical Literature Texts and Translations 22. Early Christian Literature Series 5. Chico, Calif.: Scholars Press, 1981.

*Sentences of the Syriac Menander.* Translated by T. Baarda. *OTP* 2:583–606.

*Septuaginta id est Vetus Testamentum Graece.* Edited by Alfred Rahlfs. 2 vols. Stuttgart: Deutsche Bibelgesellschaft, 1979.

*Sextus Empiricus.* Translated by R. G. Bury. 4 vols. LCL. Cambridge: Harvard University Press, 1933–1949.

*Sibylline Oracles.* Translated by J. J. Collins. *OTP* 1:317–472. *See also Oracula sibyllina,* above.

*Sifra: An Analytical Translation.* Translated by Jacob Neusner. 3 vols. Brown Judaic Studies 138–140. Atlanta: Scholars Press, 1988.

*Sifre to Deuteronomy: An Analytical Translation.* Translated by Jacob Neusner. 2 vols. Brown Judaic studies 98, 101. Atlanta: Scholars Press, 1987.

*Sifré to Numbers: An American Translation and Explanation.* Translated by Jacob Neusner. 2 vols. Brown Judaic Studies 118–119. Atlanta: Scholars Press, 1986.

Silius Italicus. *Punica.* Translated by J. D. Duff. 2 vols. LCL. Cambridge: Harvard University Press, 1927–1934.

*Sophocles.* Translated by Hugh Lloyd-Jones. 2 vols. LCL. Cambridge: Harvard University Press, 1994.

Statius. *Silvae, Thebaid, Achilleid.* Vol. 1. Translated by J. H. Mozley. 2 vols. Rev. ed. LCL. Cambridge: Harvard University Press, 1928.

"The Story of Apollonius King of Tyre." Introduction and translation by Gerald N. Sandy. Pages 736–72 in *Collected Ancient Greek Novels.* Edited by B. P. Reardon. Berkeley: University of California Press, 1989.

Strabo. *Geography.* Translated by Horace Leonard Jones and John Robert Sitlington Sterrett. 8 vols. LCL. Cambridge: Harvard University Press, 1917–1932.

Suetonius. *The Twelve Caesars.* Translated by Robert Graves. Baltimore: Penguin, 1957.

Tacitus. *The Complete Works of Tacitus.* Translated by Alfred John Church and William Jackson Brodribb. New York: The Modern Library, 1942.

"The Tale of Aqhat." Translated by H. L. Ginsberg. *ANET* 149–55.

*Talmud of the Land of Israel: A Preliminary Translation and Explanation.* Translated by Jacob Neusner et al. 34 vols. Chicago: University of Chicago Press, 1982–1993.

*Targumim. The Aramaic Bible: The Targums.* Translated by Martin McNamara et al. 19 vols. Collegeville, Minn.: Liturgical Press, 1987–1994.

*Terence.* Translated by John Sargeaunt. 2 vols. LCL. Cambridge: Harvard University Press, 1912.

Tertullian. *Apology; De spectaculis.* Translated by T. R. Glover. LCL. Cambridge: Harvard University Press, 1931.

*Testament of Abraham.* Translated by E. P. Sanders. *OTP* 1:882–902.

*The Testament of Abraham: The Greek Recensions.* Translated by Michael E. Stone. Society of Biblical Literature Texts and Translations 2. Pseudepigrapha Series 2. Missoula, Mont.: Society of Biblical Literature, 1972.

*Testament of Adam.* Translated by S. E. Robinson. *OTP* 1:993–95.

*Testament of Job.* Translated by R. P. Spittler. *OTP* 1:839–68.

*The Testament of Job according to the SV Text.* Edited by Robert A. Kraft with Harold Attridge, Russell Spittler, and Janet Timbie. Society of Biblical Literature Texts and Translations 5. Pseudepigrapha Series 4. Missoula, Mont.: Scholars Press, 1974.

*Testament of Solomon.* Introduction and translated by D. C. Duling. *OTP* 1:935–87.

*The Testament of Solomon.* (Greek text.) Edited by Chester Charlton McCown. Leipzig: Hinrichs, 1922.

*Testaments of the Twelve Patriarchs.* Translated by Howard Clark Kee. *OTP* 1:775–828. *See also The Greek Version of the Testaments of the Twelve Patriarchs.*

*The Testimony of Truth.* Translated by Birger A. Pearson and Søren Giverson. Pages 406–16 in *NHL.*

Theodotus. Translated by F. Fallon. *OTP* 2:790–93.

*Theognis, Ps.-Pythagoras, Ps.-Phocylides, Chares, Anonymi Aulodia, Fragmentum Teliambicum.* Edited by Douglas Young. Bibliotheca Scriptorum Graecorum et Romanorum Teubneriana. Leipzig: Teubner, 1971.

"The Theology of Memphis." Translated by John A. Wilson. *ANET* 4–6.

Theon. *The Progymnasmata of Theon: A New Text with Translation and Commentary.* By James R. Butts. Ann Arbor, Mich.: University Microfilms International, 1989.

Theophrastus. *Characters.* Translated by J. M. Edmonds. LCL. Cambridge: Harvard University Press, 1929.

Theophrastus. *De causis plantarum.* Translated by Benedict Einarson and George K. K. Link. 3 vols. LCL. Cambridge: Harvard University Press, 1976–1990.

Thucydides. *History of the Peloponnesian War.* Translated by Charles Forster Smith. 4 vols. Rev. ed. LCL. Cambridge: Harvard University Press, 1921–1930.

Tibullus. Translated by J. P. Postgate. In *Catullus, Tibullus, Pervigilium Veneris.* Revised by G. P. Goold. 2d ed., rev. LCL. Cambridge: Harvard University Press, 1988.

*The Tosefta.* Translated by Jacob Neusner et al. 6 vols. New York: Ktav, 1977–1986.

*Treatise of Shem.* Translated by J. H. Charlesworth. *OTP* 1:481–86.

Valerius Flaccus. *Argonautica.* Translated by J. H. Mozley. Rev. ed. LCL. Cambridge: Harvard University Press, 1936.

Valerius Maximus. *Memorable Deeds and Sayings.* Translation and commentary by D. Wardle. Oxford: Clarendon Press, 1998.

Valerius Maximus. *Memorable Deeds and Sayings.* Edited and translated by D. R. Shackleton Bailey. 2 vols. LCL. Cambridge: Harvard University Press, 2000.

Varro. *On the Latin Language.* Translated by Roland G. Kent. 2 vols. LCL. Cambridge: Harvard University Press, 1938.

*Virgil.* Translated by H. Rushton Fairclough. 2 vols. Rev. ed. LCL. Cambridge: Harvard University Press, 1934–1935.

"Words of Ahiqar." Translated by H. L. Ginsberg. *ANET* 427–30.

Xenophon. *Cyropaedia.* Translated by Walter Miller. 2 vols. LCL. Cambridge: Harvard University Press, 1914.

Xenophon. *Hellenica* and *Anabasis.* Translated by Carleton L. Brownson. 3 vols. LCL. Cambridge: Harvard University Press, 1918–1922.

Xenophon. *Memorabilia* and *Oeconomicus.* Translated by E. C. Marchant. LCL. London, Heineman, 1923.

Xenophon. *Scripta minora.* Translated by E. C. Marchant. LCL. London: Heineman, 1925.

Xenophon. *Symposium* and *Apology.* Translated by O. J. Todd. LCL. London: Heineman, 1922.

Xenophon of Ephesus. "An Ephesian Tale." Introduction and translation by Graham Anderson. Pages 125–69 in *Collected Ancient Greek Novels.* Edited by B. P. Reardon. Berkeley: University of California Press, 1989.

# MODERN SOURCES

Abecassis, "Miracle"     Abecassis, A. "The Jewish Miracle." *Sidic* 21, no. 2 (1988): 4–8.

Abegg, "Calendars"     Abegg, Martin G. Jr. "Calendars, Jewish." Pages 180–83 in *Dictionary of New Testament Background.* Edited by Craig A. Evans and Stanley E. Porter. Downers Grove, Ill.: InterVarsity, 2000.

Abegg, "Hope"     Abegg, Martin G. "Messianic Hope and 4Q285: A Reassessment." *JBL* 113 (1994): 81–91.

Abegg, "Introduction to 4Q285"     Abegg, Martin. Introduction to 4Q285. Pages 291–92 in *The Dead Sea Scrolls: A New Translation,* by Michael Wise, Martin Abegg Jr., and Edward Cook. San Francisco: Harper San Francisco, 1999.

Abegg, "Introduction to 4Q369"     Abegg, Martin. Introduction to 4Q369. Pages 328–29 in *The Dead Sea Scrolls: A New Translation,* by Michael Wise, Martin Abegg Jr., and Edward Cook. San Francisco: Harper San Francisco, 1999.

Abegg, "Liturgy"     Abegg, Martin G., Jr. "Liturgy: Qumran." Pages 648–50 in *Dictionary of New Testament Background.* Edited by Craig A. Evans and Stanley E. Porter. Downers Grove, Ill.: InterVarsity, 2000.

Abegg, "Messiah"     Abegg, Martin G. "The Messiah at Qumran: Are We Still Seeing Double?" *DSD* 2 (1995): 125–44.

Abelson, *Immanence*     Abelson, Joshua. *The Immanence of God in Rabbinical Literature.* 2d ed. New York: Hermon, 1969.

Aberbach, "Ḥzqyhw"     Aberbach, Moses. "Ḥzqyhw mlk yhwdh wrby yhwdh hšnyʾ: hqšrym mšyḥyym [Hezekiah King of Judah and Rabbi Judah the Patriarch—Messianic Aspects]." *Tarbiz* 53 (1984): 353–71.

Aberle, "Zweck"     Aberle, M. von. "Über den Zweck des Johannesevangelium." *Theologische Quartalschrift* 42 (1861): 37–94.

Abogunrin, "Debate"     Abogunrin, Samuel O. "The Synoptic Gospel Debate: A Re-examination in the African Context." *African Journal of Biblical Studies* 2 (1987): 25–51.

Abogunrin, "Search"    Abogunrin, Samuel O. "The Modern Search of the Historical Jesus in Relation to Christianity in Africa." *Africa Theological Journal* 9 (1980): 18–29.

Abrahams, *Studies* 1    Abrahams, I. *Studies in Pharisaism and the Gospels.* 1st series. Prolegomenon by Morton S. Enslin. Library of Biblical Studies. 1917. Repr., New York: Ktav, 1967.

Abrahams, *Studies* 2    Abrahams, I. *Studies in Pharisaism and the Gospels.* 2d series. Cambridge: Cambridge University Press, 1924.

Abrahamsen, "Reliefs"    Abrahamsen, Valerie Ann. "The Rock Reliefs and the Cult of Diana at Philippi." Th.D. diss., Harvard University, 1986. Ann Arbor: University Microfilms International, 1986.

Abrahamsen, "Women"    Abrahamsen, Valerie Ann. "Women at Philippi: The Pagan and Christian Evidence." *Journal of Feminist Studies in Religion* 3 (1987): 17–30.

Abramowski, "Memoirs"    Abramowski, Luise. "The 'Memoirs of the Apostles' in Justin." Pages 323–35 in *The Gospel and the Gospels.* Edited by P. Stuhlmacher. Grand Rapids: Eerdmans, 1991.

Abrams, "Boundaries"    Abrams, Daniel. "The Boundaries of Divine Ontology: The Inclusion and Exclusion of Metatron in the Godhead." *HTR* 87 (1994): 291–321.

Achtemeier, "Miracle Workers"    Achtemeier, Paul J. "Jesus and the Disciples as Miracle Workers in the Apocryphal New Testament." In *Aspects of Religious Propaganda in Judaism and Early Christianity.* Pages 149–86. Edited by Elisabeth Schüssler Fiorenza. University of Notre Dame Center for the Study of Judaism and Christianity in Antiquity 2. Notre Dame, Ind.: University of Notre Dame Press, 1976.

Ackerman, "Psalm 82"    Ackerman, James S. "The Rabbinic Interpretation of Psalm 82 and the Gospel of John: John 10:34." *HTR* 59 (1966): 186–91.

Adan, "Siloam"    Adan, David. "The 'Fountain of Siloam' and 'Solomon's Pool' in First-Century C.E. Jerusalem." *IEJ* 29 (1979): 92–100.

Adan-Bayewitz and Perlman, "Trade"    Adan-Bayewitz, David, and Perlman, Isadore. "The Local Trade of Sepphoris in the Roman Period." *IEJ* 40 (1990): 153–72.

Adinolfi, "L'invio"    Adinolfi, Marco. "L'invio del Figlio in *Rom* 8,3." *RivB* 33 (1985): 291–317.

Adinolfi, "Lago"    Adinolfi, Marco. "Il lago di Tiberiade e le sue città nella letteratura greco-romana." *Studii biblici franciscani liber annuus* 44 (1994): 375–80.

Adler, "Rosh Hashanah"    Adler, R. J. "The Rabbinic Development of Rosh Hashanah." *Conservative Judaism* 41, no. 2 (winter 1989): 34–41.

Ådna, "Herrens"    Ådna, Jostein. "Herrens tjener i Jesaja 53 skildret som triumferende Messias: Profettargumens gjengivelse og tolkning av Jes 52,13–53,12." *Tidsskrift for Teologi og Kirke* 63 (1992): 81–94.

Agouridis, "Son of Man"    Agouridis, S. "The Son of Man in Enoch." *Deltion biblikōn meletōn* 2 (1973): 130–47.

Agus, "Gnosticism"    Agus, Aharon. "Some Early Rabbinic Thinking on Gnosticism." *JQR* 71 (1980–1981): 18–30.

Alarcón Sainz, "Vocables"    Alarcón Sainz, Juan J. "Vocables griegos y latinos en los *Proemios (Pētîḥôt) de Lamentaciones Rabbah.*" *Sefarad* 49 (1989): 3–10.

Albright, "Discoveries"    Albright, William Foxwell. "Recent Discoveries in Palestine and the Gospel of St John." Pages 153–71 in *The Background of the New Testament and Its Eschatology: Essays in Honour of Charles Harold Dodd.* Edited by W. D. Davies and D. Daube. Cambridge: Cambridge University Press, 1964.

Albright, "Logos"    Albright, William Foxwell. "The Supposed Babylonian Derivation of the Logos." *JBL* 39 (1920): 143–51.

Albright, *Period*    Albright, William Foxwell. *The Biblical Period from Abraham to Ezra.* New York: Harper, 1963.

Albright, *Stone Age*    Albright, William Foxwell. *From the Stone Age to Christianity: Monotheism and the Historical Process.* Baltimore: Johns Hopkins Press, 1946.

Albright, "Wisdom"    Albright, William Foxwell. "Some Canaanite-Phoenician Sources of Hebrew Wisdom." Pages 1–15 in *Wisdom in Israel and in the Ancient Near East: Presented to Professor Harold Henry Rowley for His 65th Birthday.* Edited by M. Noth and D. Winton Thomas. Supplements to Vetus Testamentum 3. Leiden: Brill, 1955.

Albright, *Yahweh*    Albright, William Foxwell. *Yahweh and the Gods of Canaan.* Jordan Lectures 1965. Garden City, N.Y.: Doubleday, 1968.

Albright and Mann, *Matthew*  Albright, W. F., and C. S. Mann. *Matthew*. AB 26. Garden City, N.Y.: Doubleday, 1971.

Alexander, "3 Enoch"  Alexander, P. Introduction to "3 (Hebrew Apocalypse of) Enoch." *OTP* 1:223–253.

Alexander, "Imago Mundi"  Alexander, Philip S. "Notes on the 'Imago Mundi' of the Book of Jubilees." *JJS* 33 (1982): 197–213.

Alexander, "Ipse Dixit"  Alexander, Loveday. "Ipse Dixit: Citation of Authority in Paul and in the Jewish and Hellenistic Schools." Pages 103–27 in *Paul beyond the Judaism/Hellenism Divide*. Ed. Troels Engberg-Pedersen. Louisville: Westminster John Knox, 2001.

Alexander, "Logos"  Alexander, Archibald B. D. "The Johannine Doctrine of the Logos." *ExpTim* 36 (1924–1925): 394–99, 467–72.

Alexander, *Possession*  Alexander, William Menzies. *Demonic Possession in the New Testament: Its Historical, Medical, and Theological Aspects*. 1902. Repr., Grand Rapids: Baker, 1980.

Alexander, "Preface"  Alexander, Loveday. "Luke's Preface in the Context of Greek Preface-Writing." *NovT* 28 (1986): 48–74.

Alexander, "Production"  Alexander, Loveday. "Ancient Book Production and the Circulation of the Gospels." Pages 71–112 in *The Gospels for All Christians: Rethinking the Gospel Audiences*. Edited by Richard Bauckham. Grand Rapids: Eerdmans, 1998.

Allegro, "History"  Allegro, John M. "Further Light on the History of the Qumran Sect." *JBL* 75 (1956): 89–95.

Allegro, "References"  Allegro, John M. "Further Messianic References in Qumran Literature." *JBL* 75 (1956): 174–87.

Allegro, *Scrolls*  Allegro, John M. *The Dead Sea Scrolls*. Baltimore: Penguin Books, 1959.

Allen, "Church"  Allen, E. L. "The Jewish Christian Church in the Fourth Gospel." *JBL* 94 (1955): 88–92.

Allen, "John vii.37, 38"  Allen, Willoughby C. "St. John vii.37, 38." *ExpTim* 34 (1922–1923): 329–30.

Allen, *Philosophy*  Allen, Reginald E., ed. and trans. *Greek Philosophy: Thales to Aristotle*. Readings in the History of Philosophy. New York: Free Press, 1966.

Allison, "Baptism"  Allison, Dale C., Jr. "The Baptism of Jesus and a New Dead Sea Scroll." *BAR* 18, no. 2 (March/April 1992): 58–60.

Allison, "Elijah"  Allison, Dale C., Jr. "Elijah Must Come First." *JBL* 103 (1984): 256–58.

Allison, "Eye"  Allison, Dale C., Jr. "The Eye Is the Lamp of the Body [Matthew 6.22–23–Luke 11.34–36]." *NTS* 33 (1987): 61–83.

Allison, "Land"  Allison, Dale C., Jr. "Land in Early Christianity." Pages 642–44 in *Dictionary of the Later New Testament and Its Developments*. Edited by Ralph P. Martin and Peter H. Davids. Downers Grove, Ill.: InterVarsity, 1997.

Allison, "Jesus and Moses"  Allison, Dale C., Jr. "Jesus and Moses (Mt 5:1–2)." *ExpTim* 98 (1986–1987): 203–5.

Allison, *Moses*  Allison, Dale C., Jr. *The New Moses: A Matthean Typology*. Minneapolis: Fortress, 1993.

Allison, "Plea"  Allison, Dale C., Jr. "A Plea for Thoroughgoing Eschatology." *JBL* 113 (1994): 651–68.

Allison, "Water"  Allison, Dale C., Jr. "The Living Water (John 4:10–14; 6:35c; 7:37–39)." *St. Vladimir's Theological Quarterly* 30 (1986): 143–57.

Alsup, "Pronouncement Story"  Alsup, John E. "Type, Placement, and Function of the Pronouncement Story in Plutarch's *Moralia*." *Semeia* 20 (1981): 15–27.

Alter, *Art*  Alter, Robert. *The Art of Biblical Narrative*. New York: Basic Books, 1981.

Amaru, "Prophets"  Amaru, Betsy Halpern. "The Killing of the Prophets: Unraveling a Midrash." *HUCA* 54 (1983): 153–80.

Amaru, "Theology"  Amaru, Betsy Halpern. "Land Theology in Josephus' *Jewish Antiquities*." *JQR* 71 (1980–1981): 201–29.

Amaru, "Women"  Amaru, Betsy Halpern. "Portraits of Biblical Women in Josephus' Antiquities." *JJS* 39 (1988): 143–70.

Amir, "Philo"  Amir, Y. "Philo and the Bible." *Studia philonica* 2 (1973): 1–8.

Anderson, "3 Maccabees"  Anderson, Hugh. Introduction to "'3 Maccabees.'" *OTP* 2:509–516.

Anderson, "4 Maccabees"  Anderson, Hugh. Introduction to "'4 Maccabees.'" *OTP* 2:531–43.

Anderson, *Christology*   Anderson, Paul N. *The Christology of the Fourth Gospel: Its Unity and Disunity in the Light of John 6.* Wissenschaftliche Untersuchungen zum Neuen Testament, Second Series 78. Tübingen:. Mohr, 1996.

Anderson, *Glossary*   Anderson, R. Dean, Jr. *Glossary of Greek Rhetorical Terms Connected to Methods of Argumentation, Figures, and Tropes from Anaximenes to Quintilian.* Leuven: Peeters, 2000.

Anderson, "Interpretation"   Anderson, Gary. "The Interpretation of Genesis 1:1 in the Targums." *CBQ* 52 (1990): 21–24.

Anderson, "Joy"   Anderson, Gary. "The Expression of Joy as a Halakhic Problem in Rabbinic Sources." *JQR* 80 (1989–1990): 221–52.

Anderson, *Mark*   Anderson, Hugh. *The Gospel of Mark.* New Century Bible. London: Oliphants (Marshall, Morgan & Scott), 1976.

Anderson, "Matthew"   Anderson, Janice Capel. "Matthew: Sermon and Story." Pages 233–250 in *Treasures New and Old: Recent Contributions to Matthean Studies.* Edited by David R. Bauer and Mark Allan Powell. SBLSymS 1. Atlanta: Scholars Press, 1996.

Anderson, *Rhetorical Theory*   Anderson, R. Dean, Jr. *Ancient Rhetorical Theory and Paul.* Rev. ed. Contributions to Biblical Exegesis and Theology 18. Leuven: Peeters, 1999.

Anderson, "Samaritan Literature"   Anderson, Robert T. "Samaritan Literature." Pages 1052–56 in *Dictionary of New Testament Background.* Edited by Craig A. Evans and Stanley E. Porter. Downers Grove, Ill.: InterVarsity, 2000.

Anderson, "Temple"   Anderson, Robert T. "The Elusive Samaritan Temple." *BA* 54 (1991): 104–7.

Anderson, "Xenophon"   Anderson, Graham. Introduction to Xenophon of Ephesus, *An Ephesian Tale.* Pages 125–28 in *Collected Ancient Greek Novels.* Edited by B. P. Reardon. Berkeley: University of California Press, 1989.

Andiñach, "Barca"   Andiñach, Pablo. "Una antigua barca del Mar de Galilea." *Rivista Bíblica* 52 (1990): 178–84.

Angus, *Religions*   Angus, S. *The Mystery-Religions and Christianity.* New York: Scribner, 1928.

Antonaccio, "Hero Cult"   Antonaccio, Carla M. "Contesting the Past: Hero Cult, Tomb Cult, and Epic in Early Greece." *American Journal of Archaeology* 98 (1994): 389–410.

Antoniotti, "L'apparition"   Antoniotti, L.-M. "L'apparition de Jésus à Marie de Magdala." *Revue thomiste* 96 (1996): 302–11.

Applebaum, *Cyrene*   Applebaum, Shim'on. *Jews and Greeks in Ancient Cyrene.* Studies in Judaism in Late Antiquity 28. Leiden: Brill, 1979.

Applebaum, "Life"   Applebaum, Shim'on. "Economic Life in Palestine." Pages 631–700 in Safrai and Stern, *Jewish People.*

Applebaum, "Status"   Applebaum, Shim'on. "The Legal Status of the Jewish Community in the Diaspora." Pages 420–63 in Safrai and Stern, *Jewish People.*

Appold, *Motif*   Appold, Mark L. *The Oneness Motif in the Fourth Gospel: Motif Analysis and Exegetical Probe into the Theology of John.* Tübingen: Mohr, 1976.

Arav, "Bethsaida"   Arav, Rami. "Bethsaida, 1989." *IEJ* 41 (1991): 184–85.

Arav and Rousseau, "Bethsaïde"   Arav, Rami, and J. Rousseau. "Bethsaïde, ville perdue et retrouvée." *RB* 100 (1993): 415–28.

Arbel, "Liturgy"   Arbel, Daphna V. "Liturgy: Rabbinic." Pages 650–52 in *Dictionary of New Testament Background.* Edited by Craig A. Evans and Stanley E. Porter. Downers Grove, Ill.: InterVarsity, 2000.

Argyle, "Greek"   Argyle, A. W. "Greek among the Jews of Palestine in New Testament Times." *NTS* 20 (1973–1974): 87–89.

Argyle, "Incarnation"   Argyle, A. W. "The New Testament Doctrine of the Incarnation." *ExpTim* 60 (1948–1949): 135–38.

Argyle, "Logos"   Argyle, A. W. "The Logos of Philo: Personal or Impersonal?" *ExpTim* 66 (1954–1955): 13–14.

Argyle, *Matthew*   Argyle, A. W. *The Gospel according to Matthew.* Cambridge: Cambridge University Press, 1963.

Argyle, "Philo"   Argyle, A. W. "Philo and the Fourth Gospel." *ExpTim* 63 (1951–1952): 385–86.

Argyle, "Semitism"   Argyle, A. W. "An Alleged Semitism." *ExpTim* 67 (1955–1956): 247.

Armenti, "Galileans"   Armenti, Joseph R. "On the Use of the Term 'Galileans' in the Writings of Josephus Flavius: A Brief Note." *JQR* 72 (1981–1982): 45–49.

Armstrong, "Platonism"   Armstrong, H. Hilary. "The Self-Definition of Christianity in Relation to Later Platonism." Pages 74–99 in vol. 1 of Meyer and Sanders, *Self-Definition.*

Arnéra, "Rocher"   Arnéra, G. "Du rocher d'Esaïe aux douze montagnes d'Hermas." *Études théologiques et religieuses* 59 (1984): 215–20.

Arnold, *Ephesians*   Arnold, Clinton E. *Ephesians—Power and Magic: The Concept of Power in Ephesians in Light of Its Historical Setting.* SNTSMS 63. Cambridge: Cambridge University Press, 1989.

Arntz, "Hirt"   Arntz, Klaus. "Der gute Hirt. Ein Programm Kritischer selbstevangelisierung." *Geist und Leben* 73, no. 3 (2000): 217–24.

Aron-Schnapper and Hanet, "Archives"   Aron-Schnapper, Dominique, and Daniele Hanet. "Archives orales et histoire de institutions sociales." *Revue francaise de sociologie* 19 (1978): 261–275.

Arowele, "Signs"   Arowele, P. J. "This Generation Seeks Signs: The Miracles of Jesus with Reference to the African Situation." *Africa Theological Journal* 10/3 (1981): 17–28.

Arrington, *Theology*   Arrington, French L. *Paul's Aeon Theology in 1 Corinthians.* Washington, D.C.: University Press of America, 1978.

Asen, "Faith"   Asen, Bernard Arthur. "Amos' Faith: A Structural-Developmental Approach." Ph.D. diss., St. Louis University, 1980.

Ashby, "Lamb"   Ashby, G. "The Lamb of God—II." *Journal of Theology for Southern Africa* 25 (December 1978): 62–65.

Ashton, "Ioudaioi"   Ashton, John. "The Identity and Function of the *Ioudaioi* in the Fourth Gospel." *NovT* 27 (1985): 40–75.

Ashton, *Studying*   Ashton, John. *Studying John: Approaches to the Fourth Gospel.* Oxford: Clarendon, 1994.

Ashton, *Understanding*   Ashton, John. *Understanding the Fourth Gospel.* Oxford: Clarendon, 1991.

Ashton, "Wisdom"   Ashton, John. "The Transformation of Wisdom: A Study of the Prologue of John's Gospel." *NTS* 32 (1986): 161–86.

Astour, "Names"   Astour, Michael C. "Greek Names in the Semitic World and Semitic Names in the Greek World." *Journal of Near Eastern Studies* 23 (1964): 193–201.

Asurmendi, "Torno"   Asurmendi, Jesús. "En torno a la serpeinte de bronce." *EstBib* 46 (1988): 283–94.

Attridge, "Development"   Attridge, Harold W. "Thematic Development and Source Elaboration in John 7:1–36." *CBQ* 42 (1980): 160–70.

Attridge, "Historiography"   Attridge, Harold W. "Jewish Historiography." Pages 311–43 in *Early Judaism and Its Modern Interpreters.* Edited by Robert A. Kraft and George W. E. Nickelsburg. SBLBMI 2. Atlanta: Scholars Press, 1986.

Aune, "Biography"   Aune, David Edward. "Greco-Roman Biography." In *Greco-Roman Literature and the New Testament: Selected Forms and Genres.* Pages 107–26. Edited by David E. Aune. SBLSBS 21. Atlanta: Scholars Press, 1988.

Aune, *Environment*   Aune, David Edward. *The New Testament in Its Literary Environment.* LEC 8. Philadelphia: Westminster, 1987.

Aune, *Eschatology*   Aune, David Edward. *The Cultic Setting of Realized Eschatology in Early Christianity.* NovTSup 28. Leiden: Brill, 1972.

Aune, "Magic"   Aune, David Edward. "Magic in Early Christianity." *ANRW* 23.1:1505–57. Part 2, *Principat,* 23.1. Edited by H. Temporini and W. Haase. New York: de Gruyter, 1980.

Aune, "Matrix"   Aune, David Edward. "The Social Matrix of the Apocalypse of John." *Biblical Research* 26 (1981): 16–32.

Aune, "Problem"   Aune, David Edward. "The Problem of the Genre of the Gospels: A Critique of C. H. Talbert's *What Is a Gospel?*" Pages 9–60 in S*tudies of History and Tradition in the Four Gospels.* Vol. 2 of *Gospel Perspectives.* Edited by R. T. France and David Wenham. Sheffield: JSOT Press, 1981.

Aune, *Prophecy*   Aune, David Edward. *Prophecy in Early Christianity and the Ancient Mediterranean World.* Grand Rapids: Eerdmans, 1983.

Aune, "Religion"   Aune, David Edward. "Religion, Greco-Roman." Pages 917–26 in *Dictionary of New Testament Background.* Edited by Craig A. Evans and Stanley E. Porter. Downers Grove, Ill.: InterVarsity, 2000.

Aune, "Response"   Aune, David Edward. "Orthodoxy in First Century Judaism? A Response to N. J. McEleney." *JSJ* 7 (1976): 1–10.

Aune, *Revelation*    Aune, David E. *Revelation.* 3 vols. WBC 52. Dallas: Word, 1997.

Auwers, "Nuit"    Auwers, Jean-Marie. "La nuit de Nicodème (Jean 3,2; 19,39) ou l'ombre du langage." *RB* 97 (1990): 481–503.

Avery-Peck, "Argumentation"    Avery-Peck, Alan J. "Rhetorical Argumentation in Early Rabbinic Pronouncement Stories." *Semeia* 64 (1993): 49–71.

Avigad, "Burnt House"    Avigad, Nahman. "The Burnt House Captures a Moment in Time." *BAR* 9, no. 6 (November/December 1983): 66–72.

Avigad, "Flourishing"    Avigad, Nahman. "Jerusalem Flourishing—a Craft Center for Stone, Pottery, and Glass." *BAR* 9, no. 6 (November/December 1983): 48–65.

Avigad, *Jerusalem*    Avigad, Nahman. *Discovering Jerusalem.* Nashville: Nelson, 1980.

Avigad, "Wealthy"    Avigad, Nahman. "How the Wealthy Lived in Herodian Jerusalem." *BAR* 2, no. 4 (December 1976): 1, 23–35.

Avi–Yonah, "Geography"    Avi–Yonah, Michael. "Historical Geography of Palestine." Pages 78–116 in Safrai and Stern, *Jewish People.*

Avi–Yonah, *Hellenism*    Avi–Yonah, Michael. *Hellenism and the East: Contacts and Interrelations from Alexander to the Roman Conquest.* Jerusalem: Institute of Languages, Literature and the Arts, Hebrew University; University Microfilms International, 1978.

Avi–Yonah, "Sources"    Avi–Yonah, Michael. "Archaeological Sources." Pages 46–62 in Safrai and Stern, *Jewish People.*

Ayali, "Apostasie"    Ayali, Meir. "Die Apostasie des Elischa ben Abuya." *Kairos* 30–31 (1988–1989): 31–40.

Ayali, "Gottes"    Ayali, Meir. "Gottes und Israels Trauer über die Zerstörung des Temples." *Kairos* 23 (1981): 215–31.

Baarda, "John 1, 17b"    Baarda, T. "John 1, 17b: The Origin of a Peshitta Reading." *Ephemerides theologicae lovanienses* 77, no. 1 (2001): 153–62.

Baarda, "Siloam"    Baarda, T. "'Siloam' in John 5, 2? Ephraem's Commentary on the Diatessaron." *Ephemerides theologicae lovanienses* 76, no. 1 (2000): 136–48.

Babinet, "Sindon"    Babinet, Robert. "Le Sindon et la découverte du tombeau vide en Jean *20*,3–10." *Esprit et vie* 98 (1988): 330–36.

Bacchiocchi, "John 5:17"    Bacchiocchi, Samuele. "John 5:17: Negation or Clarification of the Sabbath?" *Andrews University Seminary Studies* 19 (1981): 3–19.

Bacchiocchi, *Sabbath*    Bacchiocchi, Samuele. *From Sabbath to Sunday: A Historical Investigation of the Rise of Sunday Observance in Early Christianity.* Rome: Gregorian University Press, 1977.

Bacchiocchi, "Typologies"    Bacchiocchi, Samuele. "Sabbatical Typologies of Messianic Redemption." *JSJ* 17 (1986): 153–76.

Backhaus, "Beziehungen"    Backhaus, Knut. "Praeparatio Evangelii: Die religionsgeschichtlichen Beziehungen zwischen Täufer- und Jesus-Bewegung im Spiegel der sog. Semeia-Quelle des vierten Evangeliums." *Theologie und Glaube* 81 (1991): 202–15.

Backhaus, "Täuferkreise"    Backhaus, Knut. "Täuferkreise als Gegenspieler jenseits des Textes: Erwägungen zu einer kriteriologischen Verlegenheit am Beispiel der Joh-Forschung." *Theologie und Glaube* 81 (1991): 279–301.

Bacon, "Comforter"    Bacon, Benjamin Wisner. "The 'Other' Comforter." *The Expositor,* 8th series 14 (1917): 274–82.

Bacon, "Displacement"    Bacon, Benjamin Wisner. "The Displacement of John xiv." *JBL* 13 (1894): 64–76.

Bacon, "House"    Bacon, Benjamin Wisner. "'In My Father's House Are Many Mansions' (Jn xiv.2)." *ExpTim* 43 (1931–1932): 477–78.

Badiola Sáenz de Ugarte, "Tipología"    Badiola Sáenz de Ugarte, José Antonio. "Tipología pascual en el relato joánico de la muerto de Jesús." *Scriptorium victoriense* 47, nos. 1–2 (2000): 5–19.

Baer, *Categories*    Baer, Richard A., Jr., *Philo's Use of the Categories Male and Female.* Arbeiten zur Literatur und Geschichte des Hellenistichen Judentums 3. Leiden: Brill, 1970.

Bagatti, *Church*    Bagatti, Bellarmino. *The Church from the Circumcision.* Jerusalem: Franciscan Printing Press, 1971.

Bagatti, "Dove"    Bagatti, Bellarmino. "Dove avvenne la moltiplicazione dei pani?" *Salmanticensis* 28 (1981): 293–98.

Baggott, *Approach*    Baggott, L. J. *A New Approach to Colossians.* London: A. R. Mowbray, 1961.

Bailey, *Peasant Eyes*    Bailey, Kenneth Ewing. *Through Peasant Eyes: More Lucan Parables, Their Culture and Style*. Grand Rapids: Eerdmans, 1980.

Bailey, *Poet*    Bailey, Kenneth Ewing. *Poet and Peasant: A Literary Cultural Approach to the Parables in Luke*. Grand Rapids: Eerdmans, 1976.

Bailey, "Shepherd Poems"    Bailey, Kenneth E. "The Shepherd Poems of John 10: Their Culture and Style." *Near East School of Theology Theological Review* 14 (1993): 3–21.

Bailey, "Tradition"    Bailey, Kenneth Ewing. "Informal Controlled Oral Tradition and the Synoptic Gospels." *Asia Journal of Theology* 5 (1991): 34–54.

Baines, "Square"    Baines, William. "The Rotas-Sator Square: A New Investigation." *NTS* 33 (1987): 469–76.

Balch, "Encomia"    Balch, David L. "Two Apologetic Encomia: Dionysius on Rome and Josephus on the Jews." *JSJ* 13 (1982): 102–22.

Balch, "Friendship"    Balch, David L. "Political Friendship in the Historian Dionysius of Halicarnassus, *Roman Antiquities*." Pages 123–44 in *Greco-Roman Perspectives on Friendship*. Edited by John T. Fitzgerald. SBLRBS 34. Atlanta: Scholars Press, 1997.

Balch, *Wives*    Balch, David L. *Let Wives Be Submissive: The Domestic Code in 1 Peter*. SBLMS 26. Chico, Calif.: Scholars Press for the Society of Biblical Literature, 1981.

Balfour, "Jewishness"    Balfour, Glenn. "The Jewishness of John's Use of the Scriptures in John 6:31 and 7:37–38." *Tyndale Bulletin* 46 (1995): 357–80.

Ball, *I Am*    Ball, David Mark. *'I Am' in John's Gospel: Literary Function, Background, and Theological Implications*. JSNTSup 124. Sheffield: Sheffield Academic Press, 1996.

Bamberger, "Philo"    Bamberger, Bernard J. "Philo and the Aggadah." *HUCA* 48 (1977): 153–85.

Bamberger, "Prophet"    Bamberger, Bernard J. "The Changing Image of the Prophet in Jewish Thought." Pages 301–23 in *Interpreting the Prophetic Tradition: The Goldman Lectures, 1955–1966*. Edited by Harry M. Orlinski. Cincinnatti: Hebrew Union College Press, 1969; New York: Ktav, 1969.

Bamberger, *Proselytism*    Bamberger, Bernard J. *Proselytism in the Talmudic Period*. 2d ed. Foreword by Julian Morgenstern. New York: Ktav, 1968.

Bamberger, *Story*    Bamberger, Bernard J. *The Story of Judaism*. New York: Union of American Hebrew Congregations, 1962.

Bammel, "Discourse"    Bammel, C. P. "The Farewell Discourse in Patristic Exegesis." *Neotestamentica* 25 (1991): 193–207.

Bammel, "Feeding"    Bammel, Ernst. "The Feeding of the Multitude." Pages 211–40 in *Jesus and the Politics of His Day*. Edited by Ernst Bammel and C. F. D. Moule. Cambridge: Cambridge University Press, 1984.

Bammel, "Name"    Bammel, Ernst. "What Is Thy Name?" *NovT* 12 (1970): 223–28.

Bammel, "Paraklet"    Bammel, Ernst. "Jesus und der Paraklet im Johannes 16." Pages 199–217 in *Christ and Spirit in the NT: In Honour of Charles Francis Digby Moule*. Edited by Barnabas Lindars and Stephen S. Smalley. Cambridge: Cambridge University Press, 1973.

Bammel, "Poor"    Bammel, Ernst. "The Poor and the Zealots." Pages 109–28 in *Jesus and the Politics of His Day*. Edited by Ernst Bammel and C. F. D. Moule. Cambridge: Cambridge University Press, 1984.

Bammel, "*Titulus*"    Bammel, Ernst. "The *Titulus*." Pages 353–64 in *Jesus and the Politics of His Day*. Edited by Ernst Bammel and C. F. D. Moule. Cambridge: Cambridge University Press, 1984.

Bammel, "Trial"    Bammel, Ernst. "The Trial before Pilate." Pages 415–51 in *Jesus and the Politics of His Day*. Edited by Ernst Bammel and C. F. D. Moule. Cambridge: Cambridge University Press, 1984.

Bampfylde, "Light"    Bampfylde, Gillian. "More Light on John XII 34." *JSNT* 17 (1983): 87–89.

Bampfylde, "Prince"    Bampfylde, Gillian. "The Prince of the Host in the Book of Daniel and the Dead Sea Scrolls." *JSJ* 14 (1983): 129–34.

Bandstra, "Errorists"    Bandstra, Andrew J. "Did the Colossian Errorists Need a Mediator?" Pages 329–343 in *New Dimensions in New Testament Study*. Edited by Richard N. Longenecker and Merrill C. Tenney. Grand Rapids: Zondervan, 1974.

Banks, *Community*    Banks, Robert. *Paul's Idea of Community: The Early House Churches in Their Historical Setting*. Grand Rapids: Eerdmans, 1980.

Barag, "Castle"    Barag, Dan. "King Herod's Royal Castle at Samaria-Sebaste." *PEQ* 125 (1993): 3–18.

Barc, "Taille"   Barc, B. "La taille cosmique d'Adam sans la littérature juive rabbinique des trois premiers siècles après J.-C." *RevScRel* 49 (1975): 173–85.

Barclay, "Man"   Barclay, William. "The One, New Man." Pages 73–81 in *Unity and Diversity in New Testament Theology: Essays in Honor of George E. Ladd.* Edited by Robert A. Guelich. Grand Rapids: Eerdmans, 1978.

Barclay, "Themes"   Barclay, William. "Great Themes of the New Testament, II: John i.1–14." *ExpTim* 70 (1958-1959): 78–82, 114–17.

Bardtke, "Erwägungen"   Bardtke, Hans. "Einige Erwägungen zum Problem 'Qumran und Karaismus.'" *Henoch* 10 (1988): 259–75.

Barkhuizen, "Lazarus"   Barkhuizen, J. H. "Lazarus of Bethany—Suspended Animation or Final Death? Some Aspects of Patristic and Modern Exegesis." *Hervormde Teologiese Studies* 51 (1995): 167–74.

Barnard, "Judaism"   Barnard, L. W. "The Old Testament and Judaism in the Writings of Justin Martyr." *VT* 14 (1964): 395–406.

Barnard, *Justin*   Barnard, L. W. *Justin Martyr: His Life and Thought.* Cambridge: Cambridge University Press, 1967.

Barnard, "Logos Theology"   Barnard, L. W. "The Logos Theology of St Justin Martyr." *DRev* 89 (1971): 132–41.

Barnard, "Matt. III"   Barnard, L. W. "Matt. III.ll//Luke III.16." *JTS* NS 8 (1957): 107.

Barnard, "Study"   Barnard, L. W. "Justin Martyr in Recent Study." *SJT* 22 (1969): 152–64.

Barnett, "Feeding"   Barnett, Paul W. "The Feeding of the Multitude in Mark 6/John 6." Pages 273–93 in *The Miracles of Jesus.* Edited by David Wenham and Craig Blomberg. Vol. 6 of *Gospel Perspectives.* Edited by R. T. France and David Wenham. Sheffield: JSOT Press, 1986.

Barnett, "Parallelism"   Barnett, Paul. "Polemical Parallelism: Some Further Reflections on the Apocalypse." *JSNT* 35 (1989): 111–20.

Barnett, "Prophets"   Barnett, Paul W. "The Jewish Sign Prophets—A.D. 40–70—Their Intentions and Origin." *NTS* 27 (1980–1981): 679–97.

Barnett, *Reliable*   Barnett, Paul. *Is the New Testament Reliable? A Look at the Historical Evidence.* Downers Grove, Ill.: InterVarsity, 1986.

Baron, "Progression"   Baron, M. "La progression des confessions de foi dans les dialogues de saint Jean." *Bible et vie chrétienne* 82 (1968): 32–44.

Barosse, "Days"   Barosse, Thomas. "The Seven Days of the New Creation in St. John's Gospel." *CBQ* 21 (1959): 507–16.

Barr and Wentling, "Conventions"   Barr, David L., and Judith L. Wentling. "The Conventions of Classical Biography and the Genre of Luke-Acts: A Preliminary Study." Pages 63–88 in *Luke-Acts: New Perspectives from the Society of Biblical Literature Seminar.* Edited by Charles H. Talbert. New York: Crossroad, 1984.

Barrett, *Acts*   Barrett, C. K. *A Critical and Exegetical Commentary on the Acts of the Apostles.* 2 vols. Edinburgh: T&T Clark, 1994–1998.

Barrett, *Adam*   Barrett, C. K. *From First Adam to Last.* New York: Scribner, 1962.

Barrett, "Anecdotes"   Barrett, D. S. "'One-Up' Anecdotes in Jewish Literature of the Hellenistic-Roman Era." *Prudentia* 13 (1981): 119–126.

Barrett, *Background*   Barrett, C. K. *The New Testament Background: Selected Documents.* New York: Harper & Row, 1961; London: SPCK, 1956.

Barrett, *Essays*   Barrett, C. K. *Essays on John.* Philadelphia: Westminster, 1982.

Barrett, *Jesus*   Barrett, C. K. *Jesus and the Gospel Tradition.* London: SPCK, 1967.

Barrett, *John*   Barrett, C. K. *The Gospel according to St. John: An Introduction with Commentary and Notes on the Greek Text.* 2d ed. Philadelphia: Westminster, 1978.

Barrett, *John and Judaism*   Barrett, C. K. *The Gospel of John and Judaism.* Translated from the German by D. Moody Smith. Philadelphia: Fortress, 1975.

Barrett, "John and Judaism"   Barrett, C. K. "John and Judaism." Pages 401–17 in *Anti-Judaism and the Fourth Gospel: Papers of the Leuven Colloquium, 2000.* Edited by R. Bieringer, D. Pollefeyt, and F. Vandecasteele-Vanneuville. Assen: Royal Van Gorcum, 2001.

Barrett, "Katelaben"   Barrett, C. K. "Katelaben in John i.5." *ExpTim* 53 (1941–1942): 297.

Barrett, "Lamb"   Barrett, C. K. "The Lamb of God." *NTS* 1 (1954–1955): 210–18.

Barrett, "Old Testament"    Barrett, C. K. "The Old Testament in the Fourth Gospel." *JTS* 48/191–92 (July 1947): 155–69.

Barrett, "Parallels"    Barrett, C. K. "The Parallels between Acts and John." Pages 163–78 in *Exploring the Gospel of John: In Honor of D. Moody Smith*. Edited by R. Alan Culpepper and C. Clifton Black. Louisville, Ky.: Westminster John Knox, 1996.

Barrett, *Spirit*    Barrett, C. K. *The Holy Spirit and the Gospel Tradition*. London: SPCK, 1966.

Barrett, "Spirit"    Barrett, C. K. "The Holy Spirit in the Fourth Gospel." *JTS* NS 1 (1950): 1–15.

Barrett, "Synoptic Gospels"    Barrett, C. K. "John and the Synoptic Gospels." *ExpTim* 85 (1973–1974): 228–33.

Barrett, "Vocabulary"    Barrett, C. K. "The Theological Vocabulary of the Fourth Gospel and the Gospel of Truth." Pages 210–23 in *Current Issues in NT Interpretation: Essays in Honor of Otto A. Piper*. Edited by William Klassen and Graydon F. Snyder. New York: Harper & Row, 1962.

Barry, "Aristocrats"    Barry, W. D. "Aristocrats, Orators, and the 'Mob': Dio Chrysostom and the World of the Alexandrians." *Historia* 42 (1993): 82–103.

Barth, *Ephesians*    Barth, Markus. *Ephesians*. 2 vols. AB 34, 34A. Garden City, N.Y.: Doubleday, 1974.

Barth, *Justification*    Barth, Markus. *Justification: Pauline Texts Interpreted in the Light of the Old and New Testaments*. Translated by A. M. Woodruff III. Grand Rapids: Eerdmans, 1971.

Barth, "Law"    Barth, Gerhard. "Matthew's Understanding of the Law." Pages 58–164 in *Tradition and Interpretation in Matthew*. Edited by Günther Bornkamm, Gerhard Barth, and Heinz Joachim Held. Philadelphia: Westminster, 1963; London: SCM, 1963.

Barth, *People of God*    Barth, Markus. *The People of God*. JSNTSup 5. Sheffield: JSOT Press, 1983.

Barth, *Witness*    Barth, Karl. *Witness to the Word—a Commentary on John 1: Lectures at Münster in 1925 and at Bonn in 1933*. Edited by Walther Fürst. Translated by Geoffrey W. Bromiley. Grand Rapids: Eerdmans, 1986.

Bartlett, "Coming"    Bartlett, W. "The Coming of the Holy Ghost according to the Fourth Gospel." *ExpTim* 37 (1925–1926): 72–75.

Bartlett, *Jews*    Bartlett, John R. *Jews in the Hellenistic World: Josephus, Aristeas, The Sibylline Oracles, Eupolemus*. Cambridge Commentaries on Writings of the Jewish and Christian World 200 BC to AD 200, vol. 1, part 1. Cambridge: Cambridge University Press, 1985.

Bartnicki, "Zapowiedzi "    Bartnicki, Roman. "Ewangeliczne zapowiedzi meki, smierci, i zmartwychwstania w swietle kryteriow autentyeznosci logiow Jezusa [The Evangelical Annoucements of the Passion, Death, and Resurrection in the Light of the Criteria for Distinguishing the Authentic Words of Jesus]." *Collectanea theologica* 51, no. 2 (1981): 53–64.

Barton, "Audiences"    Barton, Stephen C. "Can We Identify the Gospel Audiences?" Pages 173–94 in *The Gospels for All Christians: Rethinking the Gospel Audiences*. Edited by Richard Bauckham. Grand Rapids: Eerdmans, 1998.

Bartsch, "Inhalt"    Bartsch, Hans W. "Inhalt und Funktion des urchristlichen Osterglaubens." *NTS* 26 (1979–1980): 180–96.

Basser, *Allusions*    Basser, Herbert W. *Allusions to Christian and Gnostic Practices in Talmudic Tradition*. New York: Jewish Theological Seminary of America, 1965.

Basser, "Attempt"    Basser, Herbert W. "The Rabbinic Attempt to Democratize Salvation and Revelation." *SR* 12 (1983): 27–33.

Basser, "Interpretations"    Basser, Herbert W. "Superstitious Interpretations of Jewish Laws." *JSJ* 8 (1977): 127–38.

Basser, "Practices"    Basser, Herbert W. "Allusions to Christian and Gnostic Practices in Talmudic Tradition." *JSJ* 12 (1981): 87–105.

Basser, "Priests"    Basser, Herbert W. "Priests and Priesthood, Jewish." Pages 824–27 in *Dictionary of New Testament Background*. Edited by Craig A. Evans and Stanley E. Porter. Downers Grove, Ill.: InterVarsity, 2000.

Bassler, "Cain"    Bassler, Jouette M. "Cain and Abel in the Palestinian Targums. A Brief Note on an Old Controversy." *JSJ* 17 (1986): 56–64.

Bassler, "Galileans"    Bassler, Jouette M. "The Galileans: A Neglected Factor in Johannine Community Research." *CBQ* 43 (1981): 243–57.

Bates, "Born"    Bates, William H. "Born of Water." *BSac* 85 (1928): 230–36.

Batey, *Imagery*    Batey, Richard A. *New Testament Nuptial Imagery*. Leiden: Brill, 1971.

Batey, "Sepphoris"   Batey, Richard A. "Sepphoris: An Urban Portrait of Jesus." *BAR* 18, no. 3 (May/June 1992): 50–62.

Bauckham, *"Acts of Paul"*   Bauckham, Richard J. "The *Acts of Paul* as a Sequel to Acts." Pages 105–52 in *The Book of Acts in Its Ancient Literary Setting.* Edited by Bruce W. Winter and Andrew D. Clarke Vol. 1 of *The Book of Acts in Its First Century Setting.* Edited by Bruce W. Winter. Grand Rapids: Eerdmans, 1993.

Bauckham, "Apocalypse"   Bauckham, Richard. "Synoptic Parousia Parables and the Apocalypse." *NTS* 23 (1976–1977): 162–76.

Bauckham, "Author"   Bauckham, Richard. "The Beloved Disciple as Ideal Author." *JSNT* 49 (1993): 21–44.

Bauckham, *Climax*   Bauckham, Richard. *The Climax of Prophecy: Studies on the Book of Revelation.* Edinburgh: T&T Clark, 1993.

Bauckham, *God Crucified*   Bauckham, Richard. *God Crucified: Monotheism and Christology in the New Testament.* Grand Rapids: Eerdmans, 1998.

Bauckham, "Gospels"   Bauckham, Richard. "For Whom Were the Gospels Written?" Pages 9–48 in *The Gospels for All Christians: Rethinking the Gospel Audiences.* Edited by Richard Bauckham. Grand Rapids: Eerdmans, 1998.

Bauckham, *Gospels for Christians*   Bauckham, Richard, ed. *The Gospels for All Christians: Rethinking the Gospel Audiences.* Grand Rapids: Eerdmans, 1998.

Bauckham, "Gurion Family"   Bauckham, Richard J. "Nicodemus and the Gurion Family." *JTS* 47 (1996): 1–37.

Bauckham, "John"   Bauckham, Richard. "John for Readers of Mark." Pages 147–72 in *The Gospels for All Christians: Rethinking the Gospel Audiences.* Edited by Richard Bauckham. Grand Rapids: Eerdmans, 1998.

Bauckham, *Jude*   Bauckham, Richard J. *Jude, 2 Peter.* WBC 50. Waco, Tex.: Word, 1983.

Bauckham, "'Midrash'"   Bauckham, Richard J. "The Liber antiquitatum biblicarum of Pseudo-Philo and the Gospels as 'Midrash.'" Pages 33–76 in *Studies in Midrash and Historiography.* Vol. 3 of *Gospel Perspectives.* Edited by R. T. France and David Wenham. Sheffield: JSOT Press, 1983.

Bauckham, "Papias"   Bauckham, Richard. "Papias and Polycrates on the Origen of the Fourth Gospel." *JTS* NS 44 (1993): 24–69.

Bauckham, "Parables"   Bauckham, Richard J. "Synoptic Parousia Parables Again." *NTS* 29 (1983): 129–34.

Bauckham and Porter, "Apocryphal Gospels"   Bauckham, Richard J., and Stanley E. Porter. "Apocryphal Gospels." Pages 71–79 in *Dictionary of New Testament Background.* Edited by Craig A. Evans and Stanley E. Porter. Downers Grove, Ill.: InterVarsity, 2000.

Baudry, "Péché"   Baudry, Gerard-Henry. "Le péché originel dans les pseudépigraphes de l'Ancien Testament." *Mélanges de science religieuse* 49 (1992): 163–92.

Bauer, "Function"   Bauer, David R. "The Literary and Theological Function of the Genealogy in Matthew's Gospel." Pages 129–59 in *Treasures New and Old: Recent Contributions to Matthean Studies.* Edited by David R. Bauer and Mark Allan Powell. SBLSymS 1. Atlanta: Scholars Press, 1996.

Bauer, *Lexicon*   Bauer, Walter, W. F. Arndt, F. Wilbur Gingrich, and Frederick W. Danker. *Greek-English Lexicon of the New Testament and Other Early Christian Literature.* 2d ed. Chicago: University of Chicago, 1979.

Bauer, "Namen"   Bauer, Johannes B. "'Literarische' Namen und 'literarische' Bräuche (zu Joh 2,10 und 18,39)." *BZ* 26 (1982): 258–64.

Bauer, *Orthodoxy*   Bauer, Walter. *Orthodoxy and Heresy in Earliest Christianity.* Edited by Robert A. Kraft and Gerhard Krodel. Philadelphia: Fortress, 1971.

Bauer, *Verbi*   Bauer, Johannes Baptist, ed. *Sacramentum Verbi: An Encyclopedia of Biblical Theology.* 3 vols. New York: Herder and Herder, 1970.

Bauer, Gingrich, and Danker, *Lexicon*   Bauer, Walter. *A Greek-English Lexicon of the New Testament and Other Early Christian Literature.* 2d ed. Revised by F. Wilbur Gingrich and Frederick W. Danker. Chicago: University of Chicago Press, 1977.

Bauernfeind and Michel, "Eleazarreden"   Bauernfeind, Otto, and Otto Michel. "Die beiden Eleazarreden in Jos. bell. 7, 323–336; 7, 341–388." *ZNW* 58 (1967): 267–72.

Baum, *Jews*   Baum, Gregory. *The Jews and the Gospel: A Re-examination of the New Testament.* London: Bloomsbury, 1961.

Baumbach, "Sadducees"   Baumbach, Günther. "The Sadducees in Josephus." Pages 173–95 in *Josephus, the Bible, and History.* Edited by Louis H. Feldman and Gohei Hata. Detroit: Wayne State University Press, 1989.

Baumbach, "Sadduzäerverständnis"   Baumbach, Günther. "Das Sadduzäerverständnis bei Josephus Flavius und im Neuen Testament." *Kairos* 13 (1971): 17–37.

Baumgarten, "Beginning"   Baumgarten, Joseph M. "The Beginning of the Day in the Calendar of Jubilees." *JBL* 77 (1958): 355–60.

Baumgarten, "Citation"   Baumgarten, Joseph M. "A 'Scriptural' Citation in 4Q Fragments of the Damascus Document." *JJS* 43 (1992): 95–98.

Baumgarten, "Miracles"   Baumgarten, Albert I. "Miracles and Halakah in Rabbinic Judaism." *JQR* 73 (1982–1983): 238–53.

Baumgarten, "Source"   Baumgarten, Albert I. "Rabbinic Literature as a Source for the History of Jewish Sectarianism in the Second Temple Period." *DSD* 2 (1995): 14–57.

Baumgarten, "Testimony"   Baumgarten, Joseph M. "On the Testimony of Women in 1QSa." *JBL* 76 (1957): 266–69.

Baumgarten, "Unwritten Law"   Baumgarten, Joseph M. "The Unwritten Law in the Pre-rabbinic Period." *JSJ* 3 (1972): 7–29.

Baumgarten, "Vineyard"   Baumgarten, Joseph M. "4Q500 and the Ancient Conception of the Lord's Vineyard." *JJS* 40 (1989): 1–6.

Baumgarten and Mansoor, "Studies"   Baumgarten, Joseph, and Menahem Mansoor. "Studies in the New *Hodayot* (Thanksgiving Hymns), II." *JBL* 74 (1955): 188–95.

Baylis, "Adultery"   Baylis, Charles P. "The Woman Caught in Adultery: A Test of Jesus as the Greater Prophet." *BSac* 146 (1989): 171–84.

Beale, "Daniel"   Beale, G. K. "The Use of Daniel in the Synoptic Eschatological Discourse and in the Book of Revelation." Pages 129–53 in *The Jesus Tradition outside the Gospels.* Edited by David Wenham. Vol. 5 of *Gospel Perspectives.* Edited by R. T. France and David Wenham. Sheffield: JSOT Press, 1985.

Beale, *Revelation*   Beale, Gregory K. *The Book of Revelation: A Commentary on the Greek Text.* Grand Rapids: Eerdmans, 1999.

Beare, *Matthew*   Beare, Francis Wright. *The Gospel according to Matthew.* San Francisco: Harper & Row, 1981.

Beare, *Philippians*   Beare, Francis Wright. *A Commentary on the Epistle to the Philippians.* 2d ed. London: A&C Black, 1969.

Beare, "Spirit"   Beare, Francis Wright. "The Risen Jesus Bestows the Spirit: A Study of John 20:19–23." *Canadian Journal of Theology* 4 (1958): 95–100.

Beasley-Murray, *Baptism*   Beasley-Murray, G. R. *Baptism in the New Testament.* Grand Rapids: Eerdmans, 1962.

Beasley-Murray, "Colossians"   Beasley-Murray, Paul. "Colossians 1:15–20: An Early Christian Hymn Celebrating the Lordship of Christ." Pages 169–183 in *Pauline Studies: Essays Presented to Professor F. F. Bruce on His 70th Birthday.* Edited by Donald A. Hagner and Murray J. Harris. Exeter: Paternoster Press; Grand Rapids: Eerdmans, 1980.

Beasley-Murray, *John*   Beasley-Murray, George R. *John.* WBC 36. Waco, Tex.: Word, 1987.

Beasley-Murray, *Revelation*   Beasley-Murray, G. R. *The Book of Revelation.* New Century Bible. Greenwood, S.C.: Attic Press, 1974.

Beasley-Murray, "Spirit"   Beasley-Murray, G. R. "The Holy Spirit, Baptism, and the Body of Christ." *Review and Expositor* 63 (1966): 177–85.

Beattie, "Discipleship of Love"   Beattie, T. "A Discipleship of Love: Mary of Bethany and the Ministry of Women." *Month* 30, no. 5 (1997): 171–75.

Beavis, "Trial"   Beavis, Mary Ann L. "The Trial before the Sanhedrin (Mark 14:53–65): Reader Response and Greco-Roman Readers." *CBQ* 49 (1987): 581–96.

Beck, "Anonymity"   Beck, David R. "The Narrative Function of Anonymity in Fourth Gospel Characterization." *Semeia* 63 (1993): 143–58.

Beck, *Paradigm*   Beck, David R. *The Discipleship Paradigm: Readers and Anonymous Characters in the Fourth Gospel.* Leiden: Brill, 1997.

Becker, "Abschiedsreden"   Becker, Jürgen. "Die Abschiedsreden Jesu im Johannesevangelium." *ZNW* 61 (1970): 215–46.

Becker, "Auferstehung"   Becker, Jürgen. "Ich bin die Auferstehung und das Leben: Eine Skizze der johanneischen Christologie." *Theologische Zeitschrift* 39 (1983): 138–51.

Becker, *Evangelium*   Becker, Jürgen. *Das Evangelium nach Johannes.* 2 vols. Ökumenischer Taschenbuchkommentar zum Neuen Testament 4. Würzburg: Gütersloher Verlagshaus, 1981.

Becker, "Frohbotschaft "   Becker, Jürgen. "Jesu Frohbotschaft und Freudenmahl für die Armen." *Bibel und Kirche* 33 (1978): 43–47.

Beckwith, "Daniel 9"   Beckwith, Roger T. "Daniel 9 and the Date of Messiah's Coming in Essene, Hellenistic, Pharisaic, Zealot, and Early Christian Computation." *RevQ* 10 (1979–1981): 521–42.

Beer, "lykwdm"   Beer, Moshe. "ʿl lykwdm hḥbrty šl ḥzʾl [On Solidarity among the Sages]." *Zion* 53 (1988): 149–66.

Beetham and Beetham, "Note"   Beetham, F. G., and P. A. Beetham. "A Note on John 19:29." *JTS* NS 44 (1993): 163–69.

Begg, "Ahab"   Begg, Christopher. "The Death of King Ahab according to Josephus." *Antonianum* 64 (1989): 225–45.

Begg, "Amaziah"   Begg, Christopher. "Amaziah of Judah according to Josephus (*Ant.* 9.186–204)." *Antonianum* 70 (1995): 3–30.

Begg, "Blanks"   Begg, Christopher T. "Filling in the Blanks: Josephus' Version of the Campaign of the Three Kings, 2 Kings 3." *HUCA* 64 (1993): 89–109.

Begg, "Disappearance"   Begg, Christopher. "'Josephus's Portrayal of the Disappearances of Enoch, Elijah, and Moses': Some Observations." *JBL* 109 (1990): 691–93.

Begg, "Doves"   Begg, Christopher. "Doves and Treaty-Making: Another Possible Reference." *BN* 48 (1989): 8–11.

Begg, "Fall"   Begg, Christopher. "Ahaziah's Fall (2 Kings 1): The Version of Josephus." *Sefarad* 55 (1995): 25–40.

Begg, "Gedaliah"   Begg, Christopher. "The Gedaliah Episode and Its Sequels in Josephus." *JSP* 12 (1994): 21–46.

Begg, "Illness"   Begg, Christopher. "Hezekiah's Illness and Visit according to Josephus." *EstBib* 53 (1995): 365–85.

Begg, "Jehoahaz"   Begg, Christopher. "Jehoahaz, King of Israel, according to Josephus." *Sefarad* 55 (1995): 227–37.

Begg, "Jehoshaphat"   Begg, Christopher. "Jehoshaphat at Mid-Career according to *AJ* 9,1–17." *RB* 102 (1995): 379–402.

Begg, "Josiah"   Begg, Christopher. "The Death of Josiah: Josephus and the Bible." *Ephemerides theologicae lovanienses* 64 (1988): 157–63.

Begg, "Jotham"   Begg, Christopher. "Jotham and Amon: Two Minor Kings of Judah according to Josephus." *Bulletin for Biblical Research* 6 (1996): 1–13.

Begg, "Nahum"   Begg, Christopher. "Josephus and Nahum Revisited." *Revue des études juives* 154 (1995): 5–22.

Begg, "Portrait"   Begg, Christopher. "Josephus' Portrait of Jehoshaphat Compared with the Biblical and Rabbinic Portrayals." *BN* 78 (1995): 39–48.

Begg, "Putsch"   Begg, Christopher. "Josephus's Version of Jehu's Putsch (2 Kgs 8,25–10,36)." *Antonianum* 68 (1993): 450–84.

Begg, "Sheep"   Begg, Christopher. "The Identity of the Three Building Sheep in 1 Enoch 89,72–73." *Ephemerides theologicae lovanienses* 64 (1988): 152–56.

Begg, "Uzziah"   Begg, Christopher. "Uzziah (Azariah) of Judah according to Josephus." *EstBib* 53 (1995): 5–24.

Begg, "Zedekiah"   Begg, Christopher. "Josephus's Zedekiah." *Ephemerides theologicae lovanienses* 65 (1989): 96–104.

Belkin, *Philo*   Belkin, Samuel. *Philo and the Oral Law: The Philonic Interpretation of Biblical Law in Relation to the Palestinian Halakah.* Harvard Semitic Series 11. Cambridge: Harvard University Press, 1940.

Bell, "Pliny"   Bell, A. A. "Pliny the Younger: The Kinder, Gentler Roman." *Classical Bulletin* 66 (1990): 37–41.

Belleville, "Born"    Belleville, Linda L. "'Born of Water and Spirit': John 3:5." *Trinity Journal* NS 1 (1980): 125–41.

Ben-Amos and Mintz, *Baal Shem Tov*    Ben-Amos, Dan, and Jerome R. Mintz, trans. and eds. *In Praise of the Baal Shem Tov [Shivhei ha-Besht]: The Earliest Collection of Legends about the Founder of Hasidism*. Bloomington: Indiana University Press, 1970. Repr., New York: Schocken, 1984.

Bengel, *Gnomon*    Bengel, John Albert. *Gnomon of the New Testament*. Edited by Andrew R. Fausset. 5 vols. Edinburgh: T&T Clark, 1878.

Benko, "Claudius"    Benko, Stephen. "The Edict of Claudius of A.D. 49 and the Instigator Chrestus." *Theologische Zeitschrift* 25 (1969): 406–18.

Benoit, *Jesus*    Benoit, Pierre. *Jesus and the Gospel*. Translated by Benet Weatherhead. 2 vols. Vol. 1: New York: Herder & Herder; London: Darton, Longman & Todd, 1973. Vol. 2: New York: Seabury (Crossroad), 1974.

Benoit, "Mystères"    Benoit, A. "Les mysteres paiens et le christianisme." Pages 73–92 in *Mystères et syncrétismes* by Françoise Dunand et al. Études d'histoire des religions 2. Paris: Librairie Orientaliste Paul Geuthner, 1975.

Benoit, "'Plerôma'"    Benoit, Pierre. "The 'plerôma' in the Epistles to the Colossians and the Ephesians." *Svensk exegetisk årsbok* 49 (1984): 136–58.

Benoit, "Reconstitution"    Benoit, Pierre. "La reconstitution archéologique de la forteresse Antonia." *Australian Journal of Biblical Archaeology* 2 (1973): 16–22.

Berg, "Pneumatology"    Berg, Robert Alan. "Pneumatology and the History of the Johannine Community: Insights from the Farewell Discourses and the First Epistle." Ph.D. diss., Graduate School of Drew University, 1988. Ann Arbor, Mich.: University Microfilms International, 1989.

Berger, "Bedeutung"    Berger, Klaus. "Die Bedeutung der wiederentdeckten Weisheitsschrift aus der Kairoer Geniza für das Neue Testament." *NTS* 36 (1990): 415–30.

Berger, "Themes"    Berger, David. "Three Typological Themes in Early Jewish Messianism: Messiah Son of Joseph, Rabbinic Calculations, and the Figure of Armilus." *Association for Jewish Studies Review* 10 (1985): 141–64.

Berger and Wyschogrod, "*Jewish Christianity*"    Berger, David, and Michael Wyschogrod. *Jews and "Jewish Christianity."* New York: Ktav, 1978.

Bergmeier, "Beobachtungen"    Bergmeier, Roland. "Beobachtungen zu 4Q521 f 2, II, 1–13." *Zeitschrift der Deutschen Morgenländischen Gesellschaft* 145 (1995): 38–48.

Bergmeier, "Erfüllung"    Bergmeier, Roland. "Erfüllung der Gnadenzusagen an David." *ZNW* 86 (1995): 277–86.

Bergmeier, "Frühdatierung"    Bergmeier, Roland. "Zur Frühdatierung samaritanischer Theologoumena." *JSJ* 5 (1974): 121–53.

Bergmeier, "ΤΕΤΕΛΕΣΤΑΙ"    Bergmeier, Roland. "ΤΕΤΕΛΕΣΤΑΙ Joh 19:30." *ZNW* 79 (1988): 282–90.

Bernabe Ubieta, "Mujer"    Bernabe Ubieta, Carmen. "La mujer en el evangelio de Juan: La revelación, el discipulado, y la misión." *Ephemerides mariologicae* 43 (1993): 395–416.

Bernal, *Athena*    Bernal, Martin. *Black Athena: The Afroasiatic Roots of Classical Civilization*. Vol. 1: *The Fabrication of Ancient Greece, 1785–1985*. London: Free Association Books, 1987. Vol. 2: *The Archaeological and Documentary Evidence*. New Brunswick, N.J.: Rutgers University Press, 1991.

Bernard, *John*    Bernard, J. H. *A Critical and Exegetical Commentary on the Gospel according to St. John*. 2 vols. International Critical Commentary. Edinburgh: T&T Clark, 1928.

Berrouard, "Paraclet"    Berrouard, M.-F. "Le Paraclet, defenseur du Christ devant la conscience du croyant (Jo. XVI, 8–11)." *Revue des sciences philosophiques et théologiques* 33 (1949): 361–89.

Berry and Heath, "Declamation"    Berry, D. H., and Malcolm Heath. "Oratory and Declamation." Pages 393–420 in *Handbook of Classical Rhetoric in the Hellenistic Period, 330 B.C.–A.D. 400*. Edited by Stanley E. Porter. Leiden: Brill, 1997.

Best, *Mark*    Best, Ernest. *Mark: The Gospel as Story*. Studies of the New Testament and Its World. Edinburgh: T&T Clark, 1983.

Best, *Peter*    Best, Ernest. *1 Peter*. New Century Bible. London: Marshall, Morgan & Scott, 1971.

Best, *Thessalonians*    Best, Ernest. *A Commentary on the First and Second Epistles to the Thessalonians*. Black's New Testament Commentaries. London: A&C Black, 1977.

Betz, "Gospel"   Betz, Otto. "Jesus' Gospel of the Kingdom." Pages 53–74 in *The Gospel and the Gospels*. Edited by Peter Stuhlmacher. Grand Rapids: Eerdmans, 1991.

Betz, "Hermetic Interpretation"   Betz, Hans Dieter. "The Delphic Maxim *GNŌTHI SAUTON* in Hermetic Interpretation." *HTR* 63 (1970): 465–84.

Betz, *Jesus*   Betz, Otto. *What Do We Know about Jesus?* Philadelphia: Westminster, 1968.

Betz, "John"   Betz, Otto. "Was John the Baptist an Essene?" *Bible Review* 6 no. 6 (December 1990): 18–25.

Betz, "Maxim in Papyri"   Betz, Hans Dieter. "The Delphic Maxim 'Know Yourself' in the Greek Magical Papyri." *History of Religions* 21 (1981): 156–71.

Betz, "Miracles"   Betz, Otto. "Miracles in the Writings of Flavius Josephus." Pags 212–35 in *Josephus, Judaism, and Christianity*. Edited by Louis H. Feldman and Gohei Hata. Detroit: Wayne State University Press, 1987.

Betz, *Papyri*   Betz, Hans Dieter, ed. *The Greek Magical Papyri in Translation Including the Demotic Spells*. 2d ed. Chicago: University of Chicago Press, 1992.

Betz, "φωνή"   Betz, Otto. "φωνή." *TDNT* 9:278–309.

Betz, *Paraklet*   Betz, Otto. *Der Paraklet Fürsprecher im häretischen Spätjudentum, im Johannes-Evangelium, und in neu gefundenen gnosticischen Schriften*. Arbeiten zur Geschichte des Spätjudentums und Urchristentums 2. Leiden and Cologne: Brill, 1963.

Betz, "Trial"   Betz, Otto. "The Temple Scroll and the Trial of Jesus." *Southwestern Journal of Theology* 30, no. 3 (summer 1988): 5–8.

Betz and Smith, "De E"   Betz, H. D., and Edgar W. Smith Jr. "De E apud Delphos (Moralia 384–394C)." Pages 85–102 in *Plutarch's Theological Writings and Early Christian Literature*. Edited by Hans Dieter Betz. Studia ad Corpus Hellenisticum Novi Testamenti 3. Leiden: Brill, 1975.

Betz and Smith, "De Iside"   Betz, H. D., and Edgar W. Smith Jr. "De Iside et Osiride (Moralia 351C–384C)." Pages 36–84 in *Plutarch's Theological Writings and Early Christian Literature*. Edited by Hans Dieter Betz. Studia ad Corpus Hellenisticum Novi Testamenti 3. Leiden: Brill, 1975.

Beutler, "Greeks"   Beutler, Johannes. "Greeks Come to See Jesus (John 12,20f)." *Biblica* 71 (1990): 333–47.

Beutler, "Identity"   Beutler, Johannes. "The Identity of the 'Jews' for the Readers of John." Pages 229–38 in *Anti-Judaism and the Fourth Gospel: Papers of the Leuven Colloquium, 2000*. Edited by R. Bieringer, D. Pollefeyt, and F. Vandecasteele-Vanneuville. Assen: Royal Van Gorcum, 2001.

Beutler, "Scripture"   Beutler, Johannes. "The Use of 'Scripture' in the Gospel of John." Pages 147–62 in *Exploring the Gospel of John: In Honor of D. Moody Smith*. Edited by R. Alan Culpepper and C. Clifton Black. Louisville, Ky.: Westminster John Knox, 1996.

Beutler, "Struktur"   Beutler, Johannes. "Zur Struktur von Johannes 6." *Studien zum Neuen Testament und seiner Umwelt* 16 (1991): 89–104.

Bianchi, "Epilegomena"   Bianchi, Ugo. "Epilegomena." Pages 873–79 in *Mysteria Mithrae*. Edited by Ugo Bianchi. Études préliminaires aux religions orientales dans l'empire romain 80. Leiden: Brill, 1979.

"Bible's Psalm"   "Bible's Psalm 20 Adapted for Pagan Use." *BAR* 11, no. 1 (January/February 1985): 20–23.

Bienaimé, "L'annonce"   Bienaimé, Germain. "L'annonce des fleuves d'eau vive en Jean 7,37–39." *Revue théologique de Louvain* 21 (1990): 281–310, 417–54.

Bieringer, Pollefeyt, and Vandecasteele-Vanneuville, "Framework"   Bieringer, R., D. Pollefeyt, and F. Vandecasteele-Vanneuville. "Wrestling with Johannine Anti-Judaism: A Hermeneutical Framework for the Analysis of the Current Debate." Pages 3–44 in *Anti-Judaism and the Fourth Gospel: Papers of the Leuven Colloquium, 2000*. Edited by R. Bieringer, D. Pollefeyt, and F. Vandecasteele-Vanneuville. Assen: Royal Van Gorcum, 2001.

Bietenhard, "ὄνομα"   Bietenhard, Hans. "ὄνομα, κτλ." *TDNT* 5:242–83.

Bilde, "Galilaea"   Bilde, Per. "Galilaea og galilaeerne på Jesu tid." *Dansk teologisk tidsskrift* 43 (1980): 113–35.

Bilezikian, *Liberated Gospel*   Bilezikian, Gilbert G. *The Liberated Gospel: A Comparison of the Gospel of Mark and Greek Tragedy*. Baker Biblical Monograph Series. Grand Rapids: Baker, 1977.

Bilezikian, "Tragedy"    Bilezikian, Gilbert G. "The Gospel of Mark and Greek Tragedy." *Gordon Review* 5 (1959): 79–86.

Billerbeck, *Kommentar*    Strack, H. L., and P. Billerbeck. *Kommentar zum Neuen Testament aus Talmud und Midrasch.* 6 vols. Munich: Beck, 1922–1961.

Bindemann, "Johannesprolog"    Bindemann, Walter. "Der Johannesprolog: Ein Versuch, ihn zu verstehen." *NovT* 37 (1995): 330–54.

Binyamin, "*Birkath*"    Binyamin, Ben-Zion. "*Birkath ha-Minim* and the Ein Gedi Inscription." *Immanuel* 21 (1987): 68–79.

Birdsall, "Source"    Birdsall, J. Neville. "The Source of Catena Comments on John 21:25." *NovT* 36 (1994): 271–79.

Bishop, *Apostles*    Bishop, Eric Francis Fox. *Apostles of Palestine: The Local Background to the New Testament Church.* London: Lutterworth, 1958.

Bishop, "Bread"    Bishop, E. F. "'He That Eateth Bread with Me Hath Lifted Up His Heel against Me.'—Jn xiii.18 (Ps xli.9)." *ExpTim* 70 (1958–1959): 331–33.

Black, *Approach*    Black, Matthew. *An Aramaic Approach to the Gospels and Acts.* 3d ed. Oxford: Clarendon Press, 1967.

Black, "Form"    Black, C. Clifton. "The Rhetorical Form of the Hellenistic Jewish and Early Christian Sermon: A Response to Lawrence Wills." *HTR* 81 (1988): 1–18.

Black, "Messiah"    Black, Matthew. "The Messiah in the Testament of Levi XVIII." *ExpTim* 60 (1948–1949): 321–22.

Black, "Oration at Olivet"    Black, C. Clifton. "An Oration at Olivet: Some Rhetorical Dimensions of Mark 13." Pages 66–92 in *Persuasive Artistry: Studies in New Testament Rhetoric in Honor of George A. Kennedy.* Edited by Duane F. Watson. JSNTSup 50. Sheffield: Sheffield Academic Press, 1991.

Black, "Recovery"    Black, Matthew. "The Recovery of the Language of Jesus." *NTS* 3 (1956–1957): 305–313.

Black, *Scrolls*    Black, Matthew. *The Scrolls and Christian Origins.* London: Nelson, 1961.

Black, "Tradition"    Black, Matthew. "Does an Aramaic Tradition Underlie John 1, 16?" *JTS* 42/165–66 (January–April 1941): 69–70.

Black, "Words"    Black, C. Clifton. "'The Words That You Gave to Me I Have Given to Them': The Grandeur of Johannine Rhetoric." Pages 220–39 in *Exploring the Gospel of John: In Honor of D. Moody Smith.* Edited by R. Alan Culpepper and C. Clifton Black. Louisville, Ky.: Westminster John Knox, 1996.

Blackburn, "ANDRES"    Blackburn, Barry L. "'Miracle Working THEIOI ANDRES' in Hellenism (and Hellenistic Judaism)." Pages 185–218 in *The Miracles of Jesus.* Edited by David Wenham and Craig Blomberg. Vol. 6 of *Gospel Perspectives.* Edited by R. T. France and David Wenham. Sheffield: JSOT Press, 1986.

Blackman, "Purification"    Blackman, Aylward M. "Purification (Egyptian)." Pages 476–82 in vol. 10 of *The Encyclopedia of Religion and Ethics.* Edited by James Hastings. 12 vols. Edinburgh: T&T Clark, 1908–1926.

Blaiklock, "Acts"    Blaiklock, E. M. "The Acts of the Apostles as a Document of First Century History." Pages 41–54 in *Apostolic History and the Gospel: Biblical and Historical Essays Presented to F. F. Bruce on His 60th Birthday.* Edited by W. Ward Gasque and Ralph P. Martin. Grand Rapids: Eerdmans, 1970.

Blank, "Irrlehrer"    Blank, Josef. "Die Irrlehrer des ersten Johannesbriefes." *Kairos* 26 (1984): 166–93.

Blasi, *Sociology*    Blasi, Anthony J. *A Sociology of Johannine Christianity.* Texts and Studies in Religion 69. Lewiston, N.Y.: Mellen, 1996.

Blass, Debrunner, and Funk, *Grammar*    Blass, F., A. Debrunner, and R. W. Funk. *A Greek Grammar of the New Testament and Other Early Christian Literature.* Chicago: University of Chicago Press, 1961.

Blau and Kohler, "Angelology"    Blau, Ludwig, and Kaufmann Kohler. "Angelology." Pages 583–97 in vol. 1 of *The Jewish Encyclopedia.* Edited by Isidore Singer. 12 vols. New York: Funk & Wagnalls, 1901–1906.

Blawatsky and Kochelenko, *Culte*    Blawatsky, W., and G. Kochelenko. *Le culte de Mithra sur la côte septentrionale de la mer Noire.* Études préliminaires aux religions orientales dans l'empire romain, tome 8. Leiden: Brill, 1966.

Bleeker, *Festivals*    Bleeker, C. J. *Egyptian Festivals: Enactments of Religious Renewal.* Numen Supplements 13. Leiden: Brill, 1967.

Blenkinsopp, "Note"    Blenkinsopp, Joseph. "John VII.37–9: Another Note on a Notorious Crux." *NTS* 6 (1959–1960): 95–98.

Blenkinsopp, "Prophecy"    Blenkinsopp, Joseph. "Prophecy and Priesthood in Josephus." *JJS* 25 (1974): 239–62.

Blenkinsopp, "Quenching"    Blenkinsopp, Joseph. "The Quenching of Thirst: Reflections on the Utterance in the Temple, John 7:37–9." *Scripture* 12 (18, 1960): 39–48.

Blenkinsopp, "Reproach"    Blenkinsopp, Joseph. "The Prophetic Reproach." *JBL* 90 (1971): 267–78.

Bligh, "Blind"    Bligh, John. "Four Studies in St John, I: The Man Born Blind." *Heythrop Journal* 7 (1966): 129–44.

Bligh, "Logos"    Bligh, John. "The Origin and Meaning of Logos in the Prologue of St. John." *The Clergy Review* 40 (1955): 393–405.

Blinzler, *Trial*    Blinzler, Josef. *The Trial of Jesus: The Jewish and Roman Proceedings against Jesus Christ Described and Assessed from the Oldest Accounts.* Translated by Isabel and Florence McHugh. Westminster, Md.: Newman, 1959.

Bliss and Dickie, *Excavations*    Bliss, Frederick Jones, and Dickie, Archibald Campbell. *Excavations at Jerusalem, 1894–1897.* London: Committee of the Palestine Exploration Fund, 1898.

Blomberg, *Matthew*    Blomberg, Craig L. *Matthew.* New American Commentary 22. Nashville: Broadman, 1992.

Blomberg, "Miracles as Parables"    Blomberg, Craig L. "The Miracles as Parables." Pages 327–59 in *The Miracles of Jesus.* Edited by David Wenham and Craig Blomberg. Vol. 6 of *Gospel Perspectives.* Edited by R. T. France and David Wenham. Sheffield: JSOT Press, 1986.

Blomberg, *Poverty*    Blomberg, Craig L. *Neither Poverty Nor Riches: A Biblical Theology of Material Possessions.* Grand Rapids: Eerdmans, 1999.

Blomberg, "Reflections"    Blomberg, Craig L. "Concluding Reflections on Miracles and Gospel Perspectives." Pages 443–457 in *The Miracles of Jesus.* Edited by David Wenham and Craig Blomberg. Vol. 6 of *Gospel Perspectives.* Edited by R. T. France and David Wenham. Sheffield: JSOT Press, 1986.

Blomberg, *Reliability*    Blomberg, Craig L. *The Historical Reliability of John's Gospel: Issues and Commentary.* Downers Grove, Ill.: InterVarsity, 2001.

Blomberg, "Reliable"    Blomberg, Craig L. "To What Extent Is John Historically Reliable?" Pages 27–56 in *Perspectives on John: Method and Interpretation in the Fourth Gospel.* National Association of the Baptist Professors of Religion Special Studies Series 11. Edited by Robert B. Sloan and Mikeal C. Parsons. Lewiston, N.Y.: Mellen, 1993.

Blomberg, "Thomas"    Blomberg, Craig L. "Tradition and Redaction in the Parables of the Gospel of Thomas." Pages 177–205 in *The Jesus Tradition outside the Gospels.* Edited by David Wenham. Vol. 5 of *Gospel Perspectives.* Edited by R. T. France and David Wenham. Sheffield: JSOT Press, 1984.

Blomberg, "Where"    Blomberg, Craig L. "Where Do We Start Studying Jesus?" Pages 17–50 in *Jesus under Fire.* Edited by Michael J. Wilkins and J. P. Moreland. Grand Rapids: Zondervan, 1995.

Blumenthal, "Χάρις"    Blumenthal, C. "Χάρις ἀντὶ χάριτος (Joh 1, 16)." *ZNW* 92, nos. 3–4 (2001): 290–94.

Boatwright, "Theaters"    Boatwright, Mary T. "Theaters in the Roman Empire." *BA* 53 (1990): 184–92.

Boccaccini, *Judaism*    Boccaccini, Gabriele. *Middle Judaism: Jewish Thought, 300 B.C.E. to 200 C.E.* Foreword by James H. Charlesworth. Minneapolis: Fortress, 1991.

Boccaccini, "Judaisms"    Boccaccini, Gabriele. "Multiple Judaisms." *Bible Review* 11, no. 1 (February 1995): 38–41, 46.

Böcher, "Johanneisches"    Böcher, Otto. "Johanneisches in der Apokalypse des Johannes." *NTS* 27 (1980–1981): 310–21.

Bock, "Words"    Bock, Darrell L. "The Words of Jesus in the Gospels: Love, Jive, or Memorex?" Pages 73–99 in *Jesus under Fire.* Edited by Michael J. Wilkins and J. P. Moreland. Grand Rapids: Zondervan, 1995.

Bockmuehl, "Messiah"    Bockmuehl, Markus. "A 'Slain Messiah' in 4Q Serekh Milhamah (4Q285)?" *Tyndale Bulletin* 43 (1992): 155–69.

Bockmuehl, *Theology*    Bockmuehl, Klaus. *The Unreal God of Modern Theology—Bultmann, Barth, and the Theology of Atheism: A Call to Recovering the Truth of God's Reality.* Translated by Geoffrey W. Bromiley. Colorado Springs, Colo.: Helmers & Howard, 1988.

Boelter, "Sepphoris"    Boelter, F. W. "Sepphoris—Seat of the Galilean Sanhedrin." *Explor* 3 (1977): 36–43.

Boer, *Morality*    Boer, W. Den. *Private Morality in Greece and Rome: Some Historical Aspects.* Leiden: Brill, 1979.

Boers, *Mountain*    Boers, Hendrikus. *Neither on This Mountain nor in Jerusalem: A Study of John 4.* SBLMS 35. Atlanta: Scholars Press, 1988.

Boettner, "Postmillenialism"    Boettner, Loraine. "Postmillenialism." Pages 117–42 in *The Meaning of the Millennium: Four Views.* Edited by Robert G. Clouse. Downers Grove, Ill.: InterVarsity, 1977.

Bogdasavich, "*Pleroma*"    Bogdasavich, M. "The Idea of *Pleroma* in the Epistles to the Colossians and Ephesians." *DRev* 83 (1965): 118–30.

Boguslawski, "Mother"    Boguslawski, S. "Jesus' Mother and the Bestowal of the Spirit." *Irish Biblical Studies* 14 (1992): 106–29.

Böhl, "Verhältnis"    Böhl, Felix. "Über das Verhältnis von Shetija-Stein und Nabel der Welt in der Kosmogonie der Rabbinen." *Zeitschrift der Deutschen Morgenländischen Gesellschaft* 124 (1974): 253–70.

Böhler, "Zitat"    Böhler, Dieter. "'Ecce Homo!' (Joh 19, 5) ein Zitat aus dem Alten Testament." *BZ* 39 (1995): 104–8.

Boice, *Witness*    Boice, James Montgomery. *Witness and Revelation in the Gospel of John.* Grand Rapids: Zondervan, 1970.

Boismard, "Aenon"    Boismard, Marie-Emile. "Aenon, près de Salem (*Jean,* III, 23)." *RB* 80 (1973): 218–29.

Boismard, "Bethzatha ou Siloé?"    Boismard, Marie-Émile. "Bethzatha ou Siloé?" *RB* 106, no. 2 (1999): 206–18.

Boismard, "Disciple"    Boismard, Marie-Émile. "Le disciple que Jésus aimait d'après Jn 21,1ss et 1,35ss." *RB* 105 (1998): 76–80.

Boismard, "Epistle"    Boismard, Marie-Émile. "The First Epistle of John and the Writings of Qumran." Pages 156–65 in *John and Qumran.* Edited by James H. Charlesworth. London: Geoffrey Chapman, 1972.

Boismard, *Moïse*    Boismard, Marie-Émile. *Moïse ou Jésus: Essai de christologie johannique.* BETL 84. Leuven: Leuven University Press/Peeters, 1988.

Boismard, *Prologue*    Boismard, Marie-Émile. *St. John's Prologue.* Translated by Carisbrooke Dominicans. London: Blackfriars, 1957.

Boismard, "Review"    Boismard, Marie-Émile. Review of A. Kragerund, *Die Lieblingsjünger im Johannesevangelium. RB* 67 (1960): 405–10.

Boismard and Lamouille, *Actes*    Boismard, Marie-Émile, and Arnaud Lamouille. *Les actes des deux apôtres.* 3 vols. Études bibliques, n.s. 12. Paris: Librairie Lecoffre, 1990.

Bokser, "Passover"    Bokser, Baruch M. "Changing Views of Passover and the Meaning of Redemption according to the Palestinian Talmud." *AJSR* 10 (1985): 1–18.

Bokser, "Wonder-Working"    Bokser, Baruch M. "Wonder-Working and the Rabbinic Tradition: The Case of Hanina ben Dosa." *JSJ* 16 (1985): 42–92.

Boman, "Thought-Forms"    Boman, Thorleif. "Hebraic and Greek Thought-Forms in the New Testament." Pages 1–22 in *Current Issues in New Testament Interpretation: Essays in Honor of Otto A. Piper.* Edited by William Klassen and Graydon F. Snyder. New York: Harper & Row, 1962.

Bondi, "Abraham"    Bondi, Richard A. "John 8:39–47: Children of Abraham or of the Devil?" *Journal of Ecumenical Studies* 34 (1997): 473–98.

Bonnard, "Épître"    Bonnard, Pierre. "La première épître de Jean est-elle johannique?" Pages 301–5 in *L'évangile de Jean: Sources, rédaction, théologie.* Edited by Marinus de Jonge. BETL 45. Gembloux: J. Duculot; Leuven: Leuven University Press, 1977.

Bonneau, "Woman"    Bonneau, Norman R. "The Woman at the Well—John 4 and Genesis 24." *The Bible Today* 67 (October 1973): 1252–59.

Bons, "Psaume 2"    Bons, Eberhard. "Psaume 2: Bilan de recherche et essai de réinterprétation." *RevScRel* 69 (1995): 147–71.

Bonsirven, *Judaism*   Bonsirven, Joseph. *Palestinian Judaism in the Time of Jesus Christ.* New York: Holt, Rinehart & Winston, 1964.

Bonz, "Approaches"   Bonz, Marianne Palmer. "Differing Approaches to Religious Benefaction: The Late Third-century Acquisition of the Sardis Synagogue." *HTR* 86 (1993): 139–54.

Boomershine and Bartholomew, "Technique"   Boomershine, Thomas E., and Gilbert L. Bartholomew. "The Narrative Technique of Mark 16:8." *JBL* 100 (1981): 213–23.

Borchert, "Gnosticism"   Borchert, Gerald L. "Is Bultmann's Theology a New Gnosticism?" *EvQ* 36 (1964): 22–28.

Borchert, *John*   Borchert, Gerald L. *John 1–11.* New American Commentary 25A. N.p.: Broadman & Holman, 1996.

Borchert, "Passover"   Borchert, Gerald L. "The Passover and the Narrative Cycles in John." Pages 303–16 in *Perspectives on John: Method and Interpretation in the Fourth Gospel.* National Association of the Baptist Professors of Religion Special Studies Series 11. Edited by Robert B. Sloan and Mikeal C. Parsons. Lewiston, N.Y.: Mellen, 1993.

Borg, *Conflict*   Borg, Marcus J. *Conflict, Holiness, and Politics in the Teachings of Jesus.* Studies in the Bible and Early Christianity 5. New York: Mellen, 1984.

Borg, *Vision*   Borg, Marcus J. *Jesus: A New Vision (Spirit, Culture, and the Life of Discipleship).* San Francisco: Harper & Row, 1987.

Borgeaud, "Death"   Borgeaud, Philippe. "The Death of the Great Pan: The Problem of Interpretation." *History of Religions* 22 (1983): 254–83.

Borgen, "Agent"   Borgen, Peder. "God's Agent in the Fourth Gospel." Pages 137–148 in *Religions in Antiquity: Essays in Memory of Erwin Ramsdell Goodenough.* Edited by Jacob Neusner. Studies in the History of Religions, Supplements to Numen 14. Leiden: Brill, 1968.

Borgen, *Bread*   Borgen, Peder. *Bread from Heaven: An Exegetical Study of the Concept of Manna in the Gospel of John and the Writings of Philo.* Leiden: Brill, 1965.

Borgen, "Hellenism"   Borgen, Peder. "The Gospel of John and Hellenism: Some Observations." Pages 98–123 in *Exploring the Gospel of John: In Honor of D. Moody Smith.* Edited by R. Alan Culpepper and C. Clifton Black. Louisville, Ky.: Westminster John Knox, 1996.

Borgen, "Logos"   Borgen, Peder. "Logos Was the True Light: Contributions to the Interpretation of the Prologue of John." *NovT* 14 (1972): 115–30.

Borgen, "Observations"   Borgen, Peder. "Observations on the Midrashic Character of John 6." *ZNW* 54 (1963): 232–40.

Borgen, "Passion Narrative"   Borgen, Peder. "John and the Synoptics in the Passion Narrative." *NTS* 5 (1958–1959): 246–59.

Borgen, "Traditions"   Borgen, Peder. "Some Jewish Exegetical Traditions as Background for Son of Man Sayings in John's Gospel (Jn 3,13–14 and Context)." Pages 243–58 in *L'évangile de Jean: Sources, rédaction, théologie.* Edited by Marinus De Jonge. BETL 45. Gembloux: J. Duculot; Leuven: Leuven University Press, 1977.

Borgen, "Unity"   Borgen, Peder. "The Unity of the Discourse in John 6." *ZNW* 50 (1959): 277–78.

Borig, *Weinstock*   Borig, Rainer. *Der wahre Weinstock, Untersuchungen zu Jo 15.1–10.* Studien zum alten und neuen Testament 16. Munich: Kösel, 1967.

Boring, "Prophecy"   Boring, M. Eugene. "The Influence of Christian Prophecy on the Johannine Portrayal of the Paraclete and Jesus." *NTS* 25 (1978–1979): 113–23.

Boring, *Sayings*   Boring, M. Eugene. *Sayings of the Risen Jesus: Christian Prophecy in the Synoptic Tradition.* SNTSMS 46. Cambridge: Cambridge University Press, 1982.

Boring et al., *Commentary*   Boring, M. Eugene, Klaus Berger, and Carsten Colpe, eds. *Hellenistic Commentary to the New Testament.* Nashville: Abingdon, 1995.

Borkan, "Authenticity"   Borkan, Mark. "Ecce Homo? Science and the Authenticity of the Turin Shroud." *Vertices: The Duke University Magazine of Science, Technology, and Medicine* 10 (1995): 18–51.

Bornkamm, *Experience*   Bornkamm, Günther. *Early Christian Experience.* New York: Harper & Row, 1969.

Bornkamm, "Heresy"   Bornkamm, Günther. "The Heresy of Colossians." Pages 123–45 in *Conflict at Colossae: A Problem in the Interpretation of Early Christianity Illustrated by Selected Modern Studies.* Edited and translated by Fred O. Francis and Wayne A. Meeks. Sources for Biblical Study 4. Missoula, Mont.: Society of Biblical Literature, 1973.

Bornkamm, "Interpretation"    Bornkamm, G. "Towards the Interpretation of John's Gospel: A Discussion of *The Testament of Jesus* by Ernst Käsemann (1968)." Pages 79–98 in *The Interpretation of John*. Edited by John Ashton. Issues in Religion and Theology 9. Philadelphia: Fortress; London: SPCK, 1986.

Bornkamm, "Paraklet"    Bornkamm, Günther. "Der Paraklet im Johannesevangelium." Pages 12–35 in *Festschrift Rudolf Bultmann zum 65. Geburstag Überreicht*. Stuttgart: Kohlhammer, 1949.

Borowitz, *Christologies*    Borowitz, Eugene B. *Contemporary Christologies: A Jewish Response*. New York: Paulist Press, 1980.

Borsch, "Exemplars"    Borsch, Frederick H. "Jesus and Women Exemplars." Pages 29–40 in *Christ and His Community: Essays in Honor of Reginald H. Fuller*. Edited by Arland J. Hultgren and Barbara Hall. Anglican Theological Review Supplementary Series 11. Evanston, Ill.: Anglican Theological Review, 1990.

Borse, "Glaube"    Borse, Udo. "Joh 20,8: österlicher oder vorösterlicher Glaube." *Studien zum Neuen Testament und seiner Umwelt* 14 (1989): 151–60.

Bostock, "Elisha"    Bostock, D. Gerald. "Jesus as the New Elisha." *ExpTim* 92 (1980–1981): 39–41.

Botermann, "Die Synagoge"    Botermann, Helga. "Die Synagoge von Sardes: Eine Synagoge aus dem 4. Jahrhundert?" *ZNW* 81 (1990): 103–21.

Botha, "*Ebaptisa*"    Botha, F. J. "*Ebaptisa* in Mark i. 8." *ExpTim* 64 (1952–1953): 268.

Botha, "Literacy"    Botha, Pieter J. J. "Greco-Roman Literacy as Setting for NT Writings." *Neotestamentica* 26 (1992): 195–215.

Botha, "Prayer"    Botha, F. J. "Recent Research on the Lord's Prayer." *Neotestamentica* 1 (1967): 42–50.

Botha, "Voice"    Botha, Pieter J. J. "Living Voice and Lifeless Letters: Reserve towards Writing in the Graeco-Roman World." *Hervormde teologiese studies* 49 (1993): 742–59.

Bourgeois, "Spittle"    Bourgeois, Sarah L. "Mark 8:22–26: Jesus and the Use of Spittle in a Two-Stage Healing." Th.M. thesis, Dallas Theological Seminary, 1999.

Bousset, *Kyrios Christos*    Bousset, William. *Kyrios Christos: A History of the Belief in Christ from the Beginnings of Christianity to Irenaeus*. Translated by John E. Steely. Nashville: Abingdon, 1970.

Bowers, "Paul"    Bowers, Paul. "Paul and Religious Propaganda in the First Century." *NovT* 22 (1980): 316–23.

Bowersock, *Fiction as History*    Bowersock, G. W. *Fiction as History: Nero to Julian*. Berkeley: University of California Press, 1994.

Bowker, "Origin"    Bowker, J. W. "The Origin and Purpose of St. John's Gospel." *NTS* 11 (1964–1965): 398–408.

Bowker, *Pharisees*    Bowker, John. *Jesus and the Pharisees*. Cambridge: Cambridge University Press, 1973.

Bowker, "Visions"    Bowker, J. W. "'Merkabah' Visions and the Visions of Paul." *Journal of Semitic Studies* 16 (1971): 157–73.

Bowley, "Pax Romana"    Bowley, James E. "Pax Romana." Pages 771–75 in *Dictionary of New Testament Background*. Edited by Craig A. Evans and Stanley E. Porter. Downers Grove, Ill.: InterVarsity, 2000.

Bowman, *Documents*    Bowman, John, trans. and ed. *Samaritan Documents Relating to Their History, Religion, and Life*. Pittsburgh Original Texts and Translations Series 2. Pittsburgh: Pickwick, 1977.

Bowman, *Drama*    Bowman, John Wick. *The First Christian Drama: The Book of Revelation*. Philadelphia: Westminster, 1968.

Bowman, *Gospel*    Bowman, John. *The Fourth Gospel and the Jews: A Study in R. Akiba, Esther, and the Gospel of John*. Pittsburgh Theological Monograph Series 8. Pittsburgh: Pickwick, 1975.

Bowman, "Prophets"    Bowman, John. "Prophets and Prophecy in Talmud and Midrash." *EvQ* 22 (1950): 107–114, 205–220, 255–275.

Bowman, "Studies"    Bowman, John. "Samaritan Studies." *Bulletin of the John Rylands Library* 40 (1957–1958): 298–327.

Bowman, "Thought-Forms"    Bowman, Thorleif. "Hebraic and Greek Thought-Forms in the New Testament." Pages 1–22 in *Current Issues in New Testament Interpretation: Essays in Honor of Otto A. Piper*. Edited by William Klassen and Graydon F. Snyder. New York: Harper & Row, 1962.

Box, "Intermediation"  Box, G. H. "The Idea of Intermediation in Jewish Theology." *JQR* 23 (1932–1933): 103–19.

Boyarin, "Binitarianism"  Boyarin, Daniel. "The Gospel of the *Memra:* Jewish Binitarianism and the Prologue to John." *HTR* 94, no. 3 (2001): 243–84.

Boyd, "Ascension"  Boyd, W. J. Peter. "Ascension according to St John: Chapters 14–17 Not Pre-passion but Post-resurrection." *Theology* 70 (1967): 207–11.

Boyd, *Sage*  Boyd, Gregory A. *Cynic Sage or Son of God?* Wheaton, Ill.: BridgePoint, 1995.

Boyer, "Étude"  Boyer, C. "Une étude sur le texte de l'épître aux Philippiens 2,6–11." *Doctor Communis* 32 (1979): 5–14.

Boyle, "Discourse"  Boyle, John L. "The Last Discourse (Jn 13,31–16,33) and Prayer (Jn 17): Some Observations on Their Unity and Development." *Biblica* 56 (1975): 210–22.

Boyle, "Lawsuit"  Boyle, Marjorie O'Rourke. "The Covenant Lawsuit of the Prophet Amos: III 1–IV 13." *VT* 21 (1971): 338–62.

Braine, "Jewishness"  Braine, David D. C. "The Inner Jewishness of St. John's Gospel as the Clue to the Inner Jewishness of Jesus." *Studien zum Neuen Testament und seiner Umwelt* 13 (1988): 101–55.

Brakke, "Plain Speech"  Brakke, David. "Parables and Plain Speech in the Fourth Gospel and the *Apocryphon of James.*" *Journal of Early Christian Studies* 7 (1999): 187–218.

Brändle, "Vida"  Brändle, Francisco. "La fe que se hace vida: La fe en el evangelio du Juan y la experiencìa del místico." *Revista de Espiritualidad* 54/217 (1995): 523–43.

Branham, "Humor"  Branham, R. Bracht. "Authorizing Humor: Lucian's *Demonax* and Cynic Rhetoric." *Semeia* 64 (1993): 33–48.

Brant, "Husband Hunting"  Brant, Jo-Ann A. "Husband Hunting: Characterization and Narrative Art in the Gospel of John." *Biblical Interpretation* 4 (1996): 205–23.

Bratcher, "Glory"  Bratcher, Robert G. "What Does 'Glory' Mean in Relation to Jesus? Translating *doxa* and *doxazo* in John." *Bible Translator* 42 (1991): 401–8.

Bratcher, "Jews"  Bratcher, Robert G. "'The Jews' in the Gospel of John." *Bible Translator* 26 (1975): 401–9.

Braun, "Arrière-fond"  Braun, François-M. "L'arrière-fond judaïque du quatrième évangile et la communauté de l'alliance." *RB* 62 (1955): 5–44.

Braun, "Beobachtungen"  Braun, Herbert. "Beobachtungen zur Tora-Vershärfung im häretischen Spätjudentum." *Theologische Literaturzeitung* 79 (1954): 347–52.

Braun, "Hermetisme"  Braun, François-M. "Hermetisme et johannisme." *Revue thomiste* 55 (1955): 259–99.

Braun, *Jean*  Braun, François-M. *Jean le théologien et son évangile dans l'église ancienne.* Études bibliques. Paris: Librairie Lecoffre, 1959.

Braun, "Prophet"  Braun, M. "The Prophet Who Became a Historian." *Listener* 56 (1956): 53–57.

Braun, "Sacrifice"  Braun, François-M. "Le sacrifice d'Isaac dans le quatrième Évangile d'après le Targum." *Nouvelle revue théologique* 101 (1979): 481–97.

Braun, "Vie"  Braun, François-M. "La vie d'en haut." *Revue des sciences philosophiques et théologiques* 40 (1956): 3–24.

Brawley, *Jews*  Brawley, Robert L. *Luke–Acts and the Jews: Conflict, Apology, and Conciliation.* SBLMS 33. Atlanta: Scholars Press, 1987.

Brayer, "Psychosomatics"  Brayer, Menahem M. "Psychosomatics, Hermetic Medicine, and Dream Interpretation in the Qumran Literature (Psychological and Exegetical Considerations)." *JQR* 60 (1969–1970): 112–27, 213–30.

Breck, "Conclusion"  Breck, John. "John 21: Appendix, Epilogue, or Conclusion?" *St. Vladimir's Theological Quarterly* 36 (1992): 27–49.

Bremmer, "Prophets"  Bremmer, Jan N. "Prophets, Seers, and Politics in Greece, Israel, and Early Modern Europe." *Numen* 40 (1993): 150–83.

Bretherton, "Lazarus"  Bretherton, Donald J. "Lazarus of Bethany: Resurrection or Resuscitation?" *ExpTim* 104 (1992–1993): 169–73.

Bricker, "Ways"  Bricker, Daniel P. "The Doctrine of the 'Two Ways' in Proverbs." *JETS* 38 (1995): 501–17.

Bridges, "Aphorisms"  Bridges, Linda McKinnish. "Flashes of Light in the Night: Reading the Aphorisms of Jesus in the Fourth Gospel." Pages 103–20 in *Perspectives on John: Method and Inter-*

*pretation in the Fourth Gospel.* National Association of the Baptist Professors of Religion Special Studies Series 11. Edited by Robert B. Sloan and Mikeal C. Parsons. Lewiston, N.Y.: Mellen, 1993.

Bright, *History*   Bright, John. *A History of Israel.* 3d ed. Philadelphia: Westminster, 1981.

Brin, "Prophets"   Brin, Gershon. "The Laws of the Prophets in the Sect of the Judaean Desert: Studies in 4Q375." *JSP* 10 (1992): 19–51.

Brin, "Scroll"   Brin, Gershon. "Concerning Some of the Uses of the Bible in the Temple Scroll." *RevQ* 12 (1985–1987): 519–28.

Brodie, "Elisha"   Brodie, Thomas L. "Jesus as the New Elisha: Cracking the Code." *ExpTim* 93 (1981–1982): 39–42.

Brodie, *Gospel*   Brodie, Thomas L. *The Gospel according to John: A Literary and Theological Commentary.* New York: Oxford University Press, 1993.

Brodie, *Quest*   Brodie, Thomas L. *The Quest for the Origin of John's Gospel: A Source-Oriented Approach.* New York: Oxford University Press, 1993.

Brodie, "Unravelling"   Brodie, Thomas L. "Towards Unravelling Luke's Use of the OT: Luke 7.11–17 as an *Imitatio* of 1 Kings 17.17–24." *NTS* 32 (1986): 247–67.

Broer, "Einmal"   Broer, Ingo. "Noch einmal: Zur religionsgeschichtlichen 'Ableitung' von Jo 2,1–11." *Studien zum Neuen Testament und seiner Umwelt* 8 (1983): 103–23.

Bromiley, "Faith"   Bromiley, G. W. "Faith." Pages 270–73 in vol. 2 of *The International Standard Bible Encyclopedia.* Edited by Geoffrey W. Bromiley. 4 vols. Grand Rapids: Eerdmans, 1979–1988.

Broneer, "Corinth"   Broneer, Oscar. "Corinth: Center of Paul's Missionary Work in Greece." *BA* 14 (1951): 78–96.

Brooke, "Beatitudes"   Brooke, George. "The Wisdom of Matthew's Beatitudes (4QBeat and Mt. 5:3–12)." *Scripture Bulletin* 19 (1989): 35–41.

Brooks, "Design"   Brooks, Oscar S. "Matthew xxviii 16–20 and the Design of the First Gospel." *JSNT* 10 (1981): 2–18.

Brooten, *Leaders*   Brooten, Bernadette J. *Women Leaders in the Ancient Synagogue: Inscriptional Evidence and Background Issues.* Chico, Calif.: Scholars Press, 1982.

Broshi, "Dimensions"   Broshi, Magen. "The Gigantic Dimensions of the Visionary Temple in the Temple Scroll." *BAR* 13, no. 6 (November/December 1987): 36–37.

Broshi, "Jérusalem"   Broshi, Magen. "La population de l'ancienne Jérusalem." *RB* 82 (1975): 5–14.

Broshi, "Population"   Broshi, Magen. "Estimating the Population of Ancient Jerusalem." *BAR* 4, no. 2 (June 1978): 10–15.

Brown, Colin, ed. *New International Dictionary of New Testament Theology.* 4 vols. Grand Rapids: Zondervan, 1975–1978.

Brown, "Burney"   Brown, Schuyler. "From Burney to Black: The Fourth Gospel and the Aramaic Question." *CBQ* 26 (1964): 323–39.

Brown, *Christology*   Brown, Raymond E. *An Introduction to New Testament Christology.* Mahwah, N.J.: Paulist Press, 1994.

Brown, *Community*   Brown, Raymond E. *The Community of the Beloved Disciple.* New York: Paulist Press, 1979.

Brown, *Death*   Brown, Raymond E. *The Death of the Messiah—from Gethsemane to Grave: A Commentary on the Passion Narratives in the Four Gospels.* 2 vols. New York: Doubleday, 1994.

Brown, "Deliverance"   Brown, Schuyler. "Deliverance from the Crucible: Some Further Reflexions on 1QH iii.1–18." *NTS* 14 (1967–1968): 247–59.

Brown, "Elements"   Brown, John Pairman. "Yahweh, Zeus, Jupiter: The High God and the Elements." *ZAW* 106 (1994): 175–97.

Brown, *Epistles*   Brown, Raymond E. *The Epistles of John.* AB 30. Garden City, N.Y.: Doubleday, 1982.

Brown, *Essays*   Brown, Raymond E. *New Testament Essays.* Garden City, N.Y.: Doubleday, 1968.

Brown, *Healer*   Brown, Michael L. *Israel's Divine Healer.* Studies in Old Testament Biblical Theology. Grand Rapids: Zondervan, 1995.

Brown, *John*   Brown, Raymond E. *The Gospel according to John.* 2 vols. AB 29, 29A. Garden City, N.Y.: Doubleday, 1966–1970.

Brown, "Kingship"   Brown, John Pairman. "From Divine Kingship to Dispersal of Power in the Mediterranean City-State." *ZAW* 105 (1993): 62–86.

Brown, "Know"    Brown, Raymond E. "Did Jesus Know He Was God?" *Biblical Theology Bulletin* 15 (1985): 74–79.

Brown, "Messianism"    Brown, Raymond E. "The Messianism of Qumran." *CBQ* 19 (1957): 53–82.

Brown, "Mother"    Brown, Raymond E. "The 'Mother of Jesus' in the Fourth Gospel." Pages 307–10 in *L'évangile de Jean: Sources, rédaction, théologie.* Edited by Marinus De Jonge. BETL 45. Gembloux: J. Duculot; Leuven: Leuven University Press, 1977.

Brown, "Paraclete"    Brown, Raymond E. "The Paraclete in the Fourth Gospel." *NTS* 13 (1966–1967): 113–32.

Brown, "Prologue"    Brown, Raymond Bryan. "The Prologue of the Gospel of John: John 1:1–18." *Review and Expositor* 62 (1965): 429–39.

Brown, "Resurrection"    Brown, Raymond E. "The Resurrection in John 20—a Series of Diverse Reactions." *Worship* 64 (1990): 194–206.

Brown, "Rock"    Brown, Colin. "Rock," section c. *NIDNTT* 3:385–88.

Brown, "Scrolls"    Brown, Raymond E. "The Dead Sea Scrolls and the New Testament." Pages 1–8 in *John and Qumran.* Edited by James H. Charlesworth. London: Geoffrey Chapman, 1972.

Brown, "Theory"    Brown, Raymond E. "J. Starcky's Theory of Qumran Messianic Development." *CBQ* 28 (1966): 51–57.

Brown, "Thomas"    Brown, Raymond E. "The Gospel of Thomas and St John's Gospel." *NTS* 9 (1962–1963): 155–77.

Brown, Donfried, and Reumann, *Peter*    Brown, Raymond E., Karl P. Donfried, and John Reumann, eds. *Peter in the New Testament.* Minneapolis: Augsburg, 1973.

Brown, Driver, Briggs, *Lexicon*    Brown, Francis, S. R. Driver, and Charles A. Briggs. *A Hebrew and English Lexicon of the Old Testament.* London: Oxford University Press, 1972.

Brownlee, "Comparison"    Brownlee, William H. "A Comparison of the Covenanters of the Dead Sea Scrolls with Pre-Christian Jewish Sects." *BA* 13 (1950): 50–72.

Brownlee, "Jubilees"    Brownlee, William H. "Light on the Manual of Discipline (DSD) from the Book of Jubilees." *BASOR* 123 (October 1951): 30–32.

Brownlee, "Motifs, I"    Brownlee, William H. "Messianic Motifs of Qumran and the New Testament." *NTS* 3 (1956–1957): 12–30.

Brownlee, "Motifs, II"    Brownlee, William H. "Messianic Motifs of Qumran and the New Testament, II." *NTS* 3 (1956–1957): 195–210.

Brownlee, "Servant"    Brownlee, William H. "The Servant of the Lord in the Qumran Scrolls, I." *BASOR* 132 (December 1953): 8–15.

Brownlee, "Whence"    Brownlee, William H. "Whence the Gospel according to John?" Pages 166–194 in *John and Qumran.* Edited by James H. Charlesworth. London: Geoffrey Chapman, 1972.

Brownson, "Introduction"    Brownson, Carleton L. Introduction. Pages vii–xi in vol. 1 of Xenophon, *Hellenica.* Translated by Carleton L. Brownson. 2 vols. LCL. Cambridge: Harvard University Press, 1918–1921.

Bruce, *Acts: Greek*    Bruce, F. F. *The Acts of the Apostles: The Greek Text with Introduction and Commentary.* Grand Rapids: Eerdmans, 1951.

Bruce, "Apocalypse"    Bruce, F. F. "The Spirit in the Apocalypse." Pages 333–44 in *Christ and Spirit in the NT: Studies in Honour of C. F. D. Moule.* Edited by Barnabas Lindars and Stephen S. Smalley. Cambridge: Cambridge University Press, 1973.

Bruce, *Books*    Bruce, F. F. *The Books and the Parchments.* Old Tappan, N.J.: Revell, 1963.

Bruce, "Classical Studies"    Bruce, F. F. "The New Testament and Classical Studies." *NTS* 22 (1975–1976): 229–42.

Bruce, *Commentary*    Bruce, F. F. *Commentary on the Book of the Acts: The English Text with Introduction, Exposition, and Notes.* New International Commentary on the New Testament. Grand Rapids: Eerdmans, 1977.

Bruce, *Corinthians*    Bruce, F. F. *1 and 2 Corinthians.* New Century Bible 38. Greenwood, S.C.: Attic Press, 1971.

Bruce, *Documents*    Bruce, F. F. *The New Testament Documents: Are They Reliable?* 5th rev. ed. Grand Rapids: Eerdmans, 1981.

Bruce, *History*    Bruce, F. F. *New Testament History.* Garden City, N.Y.: Doubleday, 1972.

Bruce, "History"   Bruce, F. F. "The History of New Testament Study." Pages 21–59 in *New Testament Interpretation: Essays on Principles and Methods*. Edited by I. Howard Marshall. Grand Rapids: Eerdmans, 1977.

Bruce, "Jesus"   Bruce, F. F. "Jesus and the Gospels in the Light of the Scrolls." Pages 70–82 in *The Scrolls and Christianity: Historical and Theological Significance*. Edited by Matthew Black. London: SPCK, 1969.

Bruce, *John*   Bruce, F. F. *The Gospel of John: Introduction, Exposition, and Notes*. Grand Rapids: Eerdmans, 1983.

Bruce, "Matthew"   Bruce, Alexander Balmain. "Matthew." Pages 61–340 in vol. 1 of *The Expositor's Greek Testament*. Edited by W. Robertson Nicoll. 5 vols. 1897–1910. Repr., Grand Rapids: Eerdmans, 1979.

Bruce, *Message*   Bruce, F. F. *The Message of the New Testament*. Grand Rapids: Eerdmans, 1981.

Bruce, "Myth"   Bruce, F. F. "Myth and History." Pages 79–99 in *History, Criticism, and Faith*. Edited by Colin Brown. Downers Grove, Ill.: InterVarsity, 1976.

Bruce, *Paul*   Bruce, F. F. *Paul: Apostle of the Heart Set Free*. Grand Rapids: Eerdmans, 1977.

Bruce, *Peter*   Bruce, F. F. *Peter, Stephen, James, and John: Studies in Early Non-Pauline Christianity*. Grand Rapids: Eerdmans, 1979.

Bruce, "Qumrân"   Bruce, F. F. "Qumrân and Early Christianity." *NTS* 2 (1955–1956): 176–90.

Bruce, "Spirit"   Bruce, F. F. "Holy Spirit in the Qumran Texts." *The Annual of Leeds University Oriental Society* 6 (1966): 49–55.

Bruce, *Thessalonians*   Bruce, F. F. *1 and 2 Thessalonians*. WBC 45. Waco, Tex.: Word, 1982.

Bruce, *Thoughts*   Bruce, F. F. *Second Thoughts on the Dead Sea Scrolls*. Grand Rapids: Eerdmans, 1956.

Bruce, *Time*   Bruce, F. F. *The Time Is Fulfilled*. Grand Rapids: Eerdmans, 1978.

Bruce, "Trial"   Bruce, F. F. "The Trial of Jesus in the Fourth Gospel." Pages 7–20 in *Studies of History and Tradition in the Four Gospels*. Vol. 1 of *Gospel Perspectives*. Edited by R. T. France and David Wenham. Sheffield: JSOT Press, 1980.

Bruns, "Ananda"   Bruns, J. Edgar. "Ananda: The Fourth Evangelist's Model for 'the Disciple Whom Jesus Loved'?" *Studies in Religion* 3 (1973–1974): 236–43.

Bruns, *Art*   Bruns, J. Edgar. *The Art and Thought of John*. New York: Herder & Herder, 1969.

Bruns, *Buddhism*   Bruns, J. Edgar. *The Christian Buddhism of St. John*. Foreword by Gregory Baum. New York: Paulist Press, 1971.

Bruns, "Shepherd"   Bruns, J. Edgar. "The Discourse on the God Shepherd and the Rite of Ordination." *American Ecclesiastical Review* 149 (1963): 386–91.

Bruns, "Time"   Bruns, J. Edgar. "The Use of Time in the Fourth Gospel." *NTS* 13 (1966–1967): 285–290.

Bryan, "Hallel"   Bryan, Christopher. "Shall We Sing Hallel in the Days of the Messiah? A Glance at John 2:1–3:21." *Saint Luke's Journal of Theology* 29 (1985): 25–36.

Buchanan, "Age"   Buchanan, George Wesley. "The Age of Jesus." *NTS* 41 (1995): 297.

Buchanan, *Consequences*   Buchanan, George Wesley. *The Consequences of the Covenant*. NovTSup 20. Leiden: Brill, 1970.

Buchanan, *Hebrews*   Buchanan, George Wesley. *To the Hebrews*. AB 36. Garden City, N.Y.: Doubleday, 1972.

Buchanan, "Samaritan Origin"   Buchanan, George Wesley. "The Samaritan Origin of the Gospel of John." Pages 149–75 in *Religions in Antiquity: Essays in Memory of Erwin Ramsdell Goodenough*. Edited by Jacob Neusner. Studies in the History of Religions, Supplements to Numen 14. Leiden: Brill, 1968.

Buchanan, "Teacher"   Buchanan, George Wesley. "The Office of Teacher of Righteousness." *RevQ* 9 (1977–1978): 241–43.

Buchanan, "Use"   Buchanan, George Wesley. "The Use of Rabbinic Literature for New Testament Research." *Biblical Theology Bulletin* 7 (1977): 110–22.

Büchler, *Conditions*   Büchler, Adolf. *The Economic Conditions of Judaea after the Destruction of the Second Temple*. London: Jews' College, 1912.

Büchsel, *Geist*   Büchsel, D. Friedrich. *Der Geist Gottes im Neuen Testament*. Gütersloh: Bertlesmann, 1926.

Buckland, *Slavery*   Buckland, W. W. *The Roman Law of Slavery: The Condition of the Slave in Private Law from Augustus to Justinian*. Cambridge: Cambridge University Press, 1908.

Buckwalter, "Saviour"   Buckwalter, H. Douglas. "The Divine Saviour." Pages 107–24 in *Witness to the Gospel: The Theology of Acts*. Edited by I. Howard Marshall and David Peterson. Grand Rapids: Eerdmans, 1998.

Buetubela, "L'Esprit"   Buetubela, B. "Jn 3,8: L'Esprit-Saint ou le vent naturel?" *Revue africaine de théologie* 4 (1980): 55–64.

Bull, "Context"   Bull, Robert J. "An Archaeological Context for Understanding John 4:20." *BA* 38 (1975): 54–59.

Bull, "Medallion"   Bull, R. "A Mithraic Medallion from Caesarea." *IEJ* 24 (1974): 187–90.

Bull, "Report XII"   Bull, Robert J. "Field Report XII." *BASOR* 180 (December 1965): 37–41.

Bull and Wright, "Temples"   Bull, Robert J., and G. Ernest Wright. "Newly Discovered Temples on Mt. Gerizim in Jordan." *HTR* 58 (1965): 234–37.

Bulman, "Son"   Bulman, James M. "The Only Begotten Son." *Calvin Theological Journal* 16 (1981): 56–79.

Bultmann, "Background"   Bultmann, Rudolf. "The History of Religions Background of the Prologue to the Gospel of John (1923)." Pages 18–35 in *The Interpretation of John*. Edited by John Ashton. Issues in Religion and Theology 9. Philadelphia: Fortress; London: SPCK, 1986.

Bultmann, "Bedeutung"   Bultmann, Rudolf. "Die Bedeutung der neuerschlossenen mandäischen und manichäischen Quellen für das Verständnis des Johannesevangeliums." *ZNW* 24 (1925): 100–46.

Bultmann, "Between Times"   Bultmann, Rudolf. "Man between the Times according to the New Testament." Pages 248–266 in *Existence and Faith: Shorter Writings of Rudolf Bultmann*. Edited by Schubert Ogden. New York: Meridian Books, 1960.

Bultmann, *Christianity*   Bultmann, Rudolf. *Primitive Christianity in Its Contemporary Setting*. Translated by Reginald H. Fuller. New York: Meridian Books, 1956.

Bultmann, *Corinthians*   Bultmann, Rudolf. *The Second Letter to the Corinthians*. Translated by Roy A. Harrisville. Minneapolis: Augsburg, 1985.

Bultmann, "Demythologizing"   Bultmann, Rudolf. "On the Problem of Demythologizing (1952)." Pages 95–130 in *New Testament Mythology and Other Basic Writings*. Edited by Schubert Ogden. Philadelphia: Fortress, 1984.

Bultmann, *Epistles*   Bultmann, Rudolf. *The Johannine Epistles*. Translated by R. Philip O'Hara with Lane C. McGaughy and Robert W. Funk. Edited by Robert W. Funk. Hermeneia. Philadelphia: Fortress, 1973.

Bultmann, "Eschatology"   Bultmann, Rudolf. "History and Eschatology in the New Testament." *NTS* 1 (1954–1955): 5–16.

Bultmann, "Exegesis"   Bultmann, Rudolf. "Is Exegesis without Presuppositions Possible?" Pages 145–53 in *New Testament Mythology and Other Basic Writings*. Edited by Schubert Ogden. Philadelphia: Fortress, 1984.

Bultmann, "γινώσκω"   Bultmann, Rudolf. "γινώσκω, κτλ." *TDNT* 1:689–719.

Bultmann, *John*   Bultmann, Rudolf. *The Gospel of John: A Commentary*. Translated by G. R. Beasley-Murray, R. W. N. Hoare, and J. K. Riches. Philadelphia: Westminster, 1971.

Bultmann, "Man and Faith"   Bultmann, Rudolf. "The Historicity of Man and Faith." Pages 92–100 in *Existence and Faith: Shorter Writings of Rudolf Bultmann*. Edited by Schubert Ogden. New York: Meridian Books, 1960.

Bultmann, *Mythology*   Bultmann, Rudolf. *Jesus Christ and Mythology*. New York: Scribner, 1958.

Bultmann, "Mythology"   Bultmann, Rudolf. "New Testament and Mythology." Pages 1–43 in *New Testament and Mythology and Other Basic Writings*. Edited by Schubert Ogden. Philadelphia: Fortress, 1984.

Bultmann, *Theology*   Bultmann, Rudolf. *Theology of the New Testament*. Translated by Kendrick Grobel. 2 vols. New York: Scribner, 1951.

Bultmann, *Tradition*   Bultmann, Rudolf. *The History of the Synoptic Tradition*. 2d ed. Translated by John Marsh. Oxford: Blackwell, 1968.

Bultmann, *Word*   Bultmann, Rudolf. *Jesus and the Word*. Translated by Louise Smith and Erminie Lantero. New York: Scribner, 1958.

Bünker, "Disposition"   Bünker, Michael. "Die rhetorische Disposition der Eleazarreden (Josephus, Bell. 7, 323–388)." *Kairos* 23 (1981): 100–107.

Burchard, "Supper"  Burchard, Christopher. "The Importance of Joseph and Aseneth for the Study of the New Testament: A General Survey and a Fresh Look at the Lord's Supper." *NTS* 33 (1987): 102–34.

Burdick, "Οἶδα"  Burdick, Donald W. "Οἶδα and γινώσκω in the Pauline Epistles." Pages 344–56 in *New Dimensions in New Testament Study*. Edited by Richard N. Longenecker and Merrill C. Tenney. Grand Rapids: Zondervan, 1974.

Burge, *Community*  Burge, Gary M. *The Anointed Community: The Holy Spirit in the Johannine Tradition*. Grand Rapids: Eerdmans, 1987.

Burge, *John*  Burge, Gary M. *John*. NIV Application Commentary. Grand Rapids: Zondervan, 2000.

Burge, "Problem"  Burge, Gary M. "A Specific Problem in the New Testament Text and Canon: The Woman Caught in Adultery (John 7:53–8:11)." *JETS* 27 (1984): 141–48.

Burkert, "Craft"  Burkert, Walter. "Craft versus Sect: The Problem of Orphics and Pythagoreans." Pages 1–22 in vol. 3 of Meyer and Sanders, *Self-Definition*.

Burkert, *Cults*  Burkert, Walter. *Ancient Mystery Cults*. Carl Newell Jackson Lectures. Cambridge: Harvard University Press, 1987.

Burkert, *Religion*  Burkert, Walter. *Greek Religion*. Translated by John Raffan. Cambridge: Harvard University Press, 1985.

Burkhardt, "Inspirationslehre"  Burkhardt, Helmut. "Inspiration der Schrift durch weisheitliche Personalinspiration: Zur Inspirationslehre Philos von Alexandrien." *Theologische Zeitschrift* 47 (1991): 214–25.

Burkill, *Light*  Burkill, T. A. *New Light on the Earliest Gospel: Seven Markan Studies*. Ithaca, N.Y.: Cornell University Press, 1972.

Burkitt, *Gnosis*  Burkitt, F. Crawford. *The Church and Gnosis: A Study of Christian Thought and Speculation in the Second Century*. Morse Lectures for 1931. Cambridge: Cambridge University Press, 1932.

Burkitt, *History*  Burkitt, F. Crawford. *The Gospel History and Its Transmission*. Edinburgh: T&T Clark, 1907.

Burkitt, *Sources*  Burkitt, F. Crawford. *The Earliest Sources for the Life of Jesus*. Boston and New York: Houghton Mifflin, 1910.

Burnett, "Immortality"  Burnett, Fred W. "Philo on Immortality: A Thematic Study of Philo's Concept of *palingenesia*." *CBQ* 46 (1984): 447–70.

Burney, "Equivalent"  Burney, C. F. "The Aramaic Equivalent of ἐκ τῆς κοιλίας in Jn. VII 38." *JTS*, first series 24 (1922–1923): 79–80.

Burney, *Origin*  Burney, C. F. *The Aramaic Origin of the Fourth Gospel*. Oxford: Clarendon Press, 1922.

Burrell, Gleason, and Netzer, "Palace"  Burrell, Barbara, Kathryn Gleason, and Ehud Netzer. "Uncovering Herod's Seaside Palace." *BAR* 19, no. 3 (May/June 1993): 50–57, 76.

Burridge, "Biography"  Burridge, Richard A. "Biography." Pages 371–91 in *Handbook of Classical Rhetoric in the Hellenistic Period, 330 B.C.–A.D. 400*. Edited by Stanley E. Porter. Leiden: Brill, 1997.

Burridge, "Biography, Ancient"  Burridge, Richard A. "Biography, Ancient." Pages 167–70 in *Dictionary of New Testament Background*. Edited by Craig A. Evans and Stanley E. Porter. Downers Grove, Ill.: InterVarsity, 2000.

Burridge, *Gospels*  Burridge, Richard A. *What Are the Gospels? A Comparison with Graeco-Roman Biography*. SNTSMS 70. Cambridge: Cambridge University Press, 1992.

Burridge, "Gospels and Acts"  Burridge, Richard A. "The Gospels and Acts." Pages 507–32 in *Handbook of Classical Rhetoric in the Hellenistic Period, 330 B.C.–A.D. 400*. Edited by Stanley E. Porter. Leiden: Brill, 1997.

Burridge, *One Jesus*  Burridge, Richard A. *Four Gospels, One Jesus?* Grand Rapids: Eerdmans, 1994.

Burridge, "People"  Burridge, Richard A. "About People, by People, for People: Gospel Genre and Audiences." Pages 113–46 in *The Gospels for All Christians: Rethinking the Gospel Audiences*. Edited by Richard Bauckham. Grand Rapids: Eerdmans, 1998.

Burrows, *More Light*  Burrows, Millar. *More Light on the Dead Sea Scrolls*. New York: Viking, 1958.

Burrows, "Prologue"  Burrows, Millar. "The Johannine Prologue as Aramaic Verse." *JBL* 45 (1926): 57–69.

Burrows, *Theology*    Burrows, Millar. *An Outline of Biblical Theology*. Philadelphia: Westminster, 1946.

Burton, "Plan"    Burton, Ernest D. "The Purpose and Plan of the Gospel of John: The Readers of the Gospel, and Its Purpose." *The Biblical World* 13 (1899): 36–41.

Bury, *Logos-Doctrine*    Bury, R. G. *The Fourth Gospel and the Logos-Doctrine*. Cambridge: W. Heffer & Sons, 1940.

Busada, "Calendar"    Busada, Charles. "Calendar and Theology: An Investigation into a Possible Mutable Calendric System in the Fourth Gospel." Ph.D. dissertation, Southeastern Baptist Theological Seminary, 2003.

Busto Saiz, "Sabiduría"    Busto Saiz, José Ramón. "Sabiduría y Torá en Jesús ben Sira." *EstBib* 52 (1994): 229–39.

Buzzard, "John 1:1"    Buzzard, Anthony. "John 1:1: *Caveat Lector* (Reader Beware)." *Journal from the Radical Reformation* 10, no. 1 (2001): 4–19.

Byatt, "Numbers"    Byatt, Anthony. "Josephus and Population Numbers in First Century Palestine." *PEQ* 105 (1973): 51–60.

Byrne, "Faith"    Byrne, Brendan. "The Faith of the Beloved Disciple and the Community in John 20." *JSNT* 23 (1985): 83–97.

Byron, "Bethany"    Byron, Brian Francis. "Bethany across the Jordan or Simply: Across the Jordan." *ABR* 46 (1998): 36–54.

Byron, "Passover"    Byron, Brian. "The Last Supper a Passover? The Theological Response." *Australasian Catholic Record* 70 (1993): 233–39.

Cachia, "Servant"    Cachia, Nicholas. "The Servant in a Fellowship of Suffering and Life with the Lord: An Exegesis of John 12,26." *Melita theologica* 43 (1992): 39–60.

Cadbury, *Acts in History*    Cadbury, Henry J. *The Book of Acts in History*. London: A&C Black, 1955.

Cadbury, "Features"    Cadbury, Henry J. "Four Features of Lucan Style." Pags 87–102 in *Studies in Luke–Acts: Essays in Honor of Paul Schubert*. Nashville: Abingdon, 1966.

Cadbury, *Making*    Cadbury, Henry J. *The Making of Luke–Acts*. London: SPCK, 1968.

Cadbury, Foakes-Jackson, and Lake, "Traditions"    Cadbury, Henry J., F. J. Foakes-Jackson, and Kirsopp Lake. "The Greek and Jewish Traditions of Writing History." Pages 7–29 in vol. 2 of Foakes-Jackson and Lake, *Beginnings*.

Cadman, *Heaven*    Cadman, W. H. *The Open Heaven: The Revelation of God in the Johannine Sayings of Jesus*. Edited by G. B. Caird. New York: Herder & Herder, 1969.

Caird, *Age*    Caird, George B. *The Apostolic Age*. London: Duckworth, 1955.

Caird, "Glory"    Caird, G. B. "The Glory of God in the Fourth Gospel: An Exercise in Biblical Semantics." *NTS* 15 (1968–1969): 265–77.

Caird, *Revelation*    Caird, G. B. *A Commentary on the Revelation of Saint John the Divine*. Harper's New Testament Commentaries. New York: Harper & Row, 1966.

Calvin, *John*    Calvin, John. *Commentary on the Gospel according to John*. Translated by William Pringle. 2 vols. Edinburgh: Calvin Translation Society, 1847.

Cancik, "Historiography"    Cancik, Hubert. "The History of Culture, Religion, and Institutions in Ancient Historiography: Philological Observations Concerning Luke's History." *JBL* 116 (1997): 673–95.

Canevet, "Genre"    Canevet, Mariette. "Remarques sur l'utilisation du genre littéraire historique par Philon d'Alexandrie dans la *Vita Moysis* ou Moïse général en chef-prophète." *RevScRel* 60 (1986): 189–206.

Cangh, "Miracles"    Cangh, Jean-Marie van. "Miracles de rabbins et miracles de Jésus: La tradition sur Honi et Hanina." *Revue théologique de Louvain* 15 (1984): 28–53.

Cangh and Esbroek, "Primauté"    Van Cangh, Jean-Marie van, and Michel van Esbroek. "La primauté de Pierre (Mt 16,16–19) et son contexte judaïque." *Revue théologique de Louvain* 11 (1980): 310–24.

Capper, "Monks"    Capper, Brian J. "'With the Oldest Monks . . .': Light from Essene History on the Career of the Beloved Disciple?" *JTS* NS 49 (1998): 1–55.

Caquot, "Secte"    Caquot, André. "La secte de Qoumrân et le temple (essai de synthèse)." *Revue d'histoire et de philosophie religieuses* 72 (1992): 3–14.

Caragounis, "Journey to Feast"    Caragounis, Chrys C. "Jesus, His Brothers, and the Journey to the Feast (John 7:8–10)." *Svensk exegetisk årsbok* 63 (1998): 177–87.

Caragounis, "Vineyard"    Caragounis, Chrys C. "Vine, Vineyard, Israel, and Jesus." *Svensk exegetisk årsbok* 65 (2000): 201–4.

Carcopino, *Life*    Carcopino, Jérôme. *Daily Life in Ancient Rome: The People and the City at the Height of the Empire.* Edited by Henry T. Rowell. Translated by E. O. Lorimer. New Haven: Yale University Press, 1940.

Cardwell, "Fish"    Cardwell, Kennth. "The Fish on the Fire: Jn 21:9." *ExpTim* 102 (1990–1991): 12–14.

Carey, "Lamb"    Carey, George L. "The Lamb of God and Atonement Theories." *Tyndale Bulletin* 32 (1981): 97–122.

Carlebach, "References"    Carlebach, A. "Rabbinic References to Fiscus Judaicus." *JQR* 66 (1975–1976): 57–61.

Carmignac, "Pré-pascal"    Carmignac, Jean. "Pré-pascal et post-pascal: Sens et valeur de ces expressions." *Esprit et vie* 90 (28, 1980): 411–15.

Carmon, *Inscriptions*    Carmon, Efrat, ed. *Inscriptions Reveal: Documents from the Time of the Bible, the Mishna and the Talmud.* Translated by R. Grafman. Jerusalem: Israel Museum, 1973.

Caron, "Dimension"    Caron, Gérald. "Exploring a Religious Dimension: The Johannine Jews." *Studies in Religion* 24 (1995): 159–71.

Carr, *Angels*    Carr, Wesley. *Angels and Principalities.* Cambridge: Cambridge University Press, 1981.

Carriera das Neves, "Pronome"    Carriera das Neves, Joaquim. "O pronome pessoal ἡμεῖς como chave hermenêutica do IV Evangelho." *Didaskalia* 20 (1990): 43–65.

Carroll, "Eschatology"    Carroll, John T. "Present and Future in Fourth Gospel 'Eschatology.'" *Biblical Theology Bulletin* 19 (1989): 63–69.

Carroll, "Exclusion"    Carroll, Kenneth L. "The Fourth Gospel and the Exclusion of Christians from the Synagogues." *Bulletin of the John Rylands Library* 40 (1957–1958): 19–32.

Carroll, "Peter"    Carroll, Kenneth L. "'Thou Art Peter.'" *NovT* 6 (1963): 268–76.

Carson, *Discourse*    Carson, D. A. *The Farewell Discourse and Final Prayer of Jesus.* Grand Rapids: Baker, 1980.

Carson, *Fallacies*    Carson, D. A. *Exegetical Fallacies.* Grand Rapids: Baker, 1984.

Carson, *John*    Carson, D. A. *The Gospel according to John.* Grand Rapids: Eerdmans, 1991.

Carson, "Matthew"    Carson, D. A. "Matthew." Pages 3–599 in vol. 8 of *The Expositor's Bible Commentary.* Edited by Frank Gaebelein. Grand Rapids: Zondervan, 1984.

Carson, "Paraclete"    Carson, D. A. "The Function of the Paraclete in John 16:7–11." *JBL* 98 (1979): 547–66.

Carson, "Purpose"    Carson, D. A. "The Purpose of the Fourth Gospel: John 20:31 Reconsidered." *JBL* 106 (1987): 639–51.

Carson, "Responsibility"    Carson, D. A. "Divine Sovereignty and Human Responsibility in Philo: Analysis and Method." *NovT* 23 (1981): 148–64.

Carson, "Source Criticism"    Carson, D. A. "Current Source Criticism of the Fourth Gospel: Some Methodological Questions." *JBL* 97 (1978): 411–29.

Carson, *Sovereignty*    Carson, D. A. *Divine Sovereignty and Human Responsibility: Biblical Perspectives in Tension.* New Foundations Theological Library. Atlanta: John Knox, 1981.

Carson, "Tradition"    Carson, D. A. "Historical Tradition in the Fourth Gospel: After Dodd, What?" Pages 83–145 in *Studies of History and Tradition in the Four Gospels.* Vol. 2 of *Gospel Perspectives.* Edited by R. T. France and David Wenham. Sheffield: JSOT Press, 1981.

Carson, *Triumphalism*    Carson, D. A. *From Triumphalism to Maturity: An Exposition of 2 Corinthians 10–13.* Grand Rapids: Baker, 1984.

Carson, Moo, and Morris, *Introduction*    Carson, D. A., Douglas J. Moo, and Leon Morris. *An Introduction to the New Testament.* Grand Rapids: Zondervan, 1992.

Cary and Haarhoff, *Life*    Cary, M., and T. J. Haarhoff. *Life and Thought in the Greek and Roman World.* 4th ed. London: Methuen, 1946.

Casciaro Ramirez, "'Himnos'"    Casciaro Ramirez, J. M. "Los 'himnos' de Qumrán y el 'misterio' paulino." *Scripta theologica* 8 (1976): 9–56.

Case, *Origins*    Case, Shirley Jackson. *The Social Origins of Christianity.* 1923. Repr., New York: Cooper Square, 1975.

Casey, "Gnosis"    Casey, R. P. "Gnosis, Gnosticism, and the New Testament." Pages 52–80 in *The Background of the New Testament and Its Eschatology: Essays in Honor of Charles Harold Dodd.* Edited by W. D. Davies and David Daube. Cambridge: Cambridge University Press, 1964.

Casey, "Μάρτυς"   Casey, Robert P. "Μάρτυς." Pages 30–37 in vol. 5 of *The Beginnings of Christianity.*

Casey, "Simon"   Casey, Robert P. "Simon Magus." Pages 151–64 in vol. 5 of *The Beginnings of Christianity.*

Casey, "Son of Man"   Casey, Maurice. "The Use of Term 'Son of Man' in the Similitudes of Enoch." *JSJ* 7 (1976): 11–29.

Casselli, "Torah"   Casselli, Stephen J. "Jesus as Eschatological Torah." *Trinity Journal* NS 18 (1997): 15–41.

Casson, *Travel*   Casson, Lionel. *Travel in the Ancient World.* London: Allen & Unwin, 1974.

Cassuto, *Exodus*   Cassuto, Umberto. *A Commentary on the Book of Exodus.* Translated by Israel Abrahams. Jerusalem: Magnes, 1967.

Casurella, *Paraclete*   Casurella, Anthony. *The Johannine Paraclete in the Church Fathers: A Study in the History of Exegesis.* Beiträge zur Geschichte der biblischen Exegese 25. Tübingen: Mohr, 1983.

Catchpole, "Beginning"   Catchpole, David R. "The Beginning of Q: A Proposal." *NTS* 38 (1992): 205–21.

Catchpole, "Entry"   Catchpole, David R. "The Triumphal Entry." Pages 319–34 in *Jesus and the Politics of His Day.* Edited by Ernst Bammel and C. F. D. Moule. Cambridge: Cambridge University Press, 1984.

Catchpole, *Quest*   Catchpole, David R. *The Quest for Q.* Edinburgh: T&T Clark, 1993.

Catchpole, "Tradition History"   Catchpole, David R. "Tradition History." Pages 165–180 in *New Testament Interpretation: Essays in Principles and Methods.* Edited by I. Howard Marshall. Grand Rapids: Eerdmans, 1977.

Catchpole, *Trial*   Catchpole, David R. *The Trial of Jesus: A Study in the Gospels and Jewish Historiography from 1770 to the Present Day.* StPB 18. Leiden: Brill, 1971.

Cavigneaux, "Sources"   Cavigneaux, A. "Aux sources du Midrash: L'herméneutique babylonienne." *Aula orientalis* 5 (1987): 243–55.

Cerfaux, *Paul*   Cerfaux, L. *The Church in the Theology of St. Paul.* Translated by Geoffrey Webb and Adrian Walker. New York: Herder & Herder, 1959.

Chadwick, *Church*   Chadwick, Henry. *The Early Church.* New York: Penguin, 1967.

Chadwick, "Defence"   Chadwick, Henry. "Justin Martyr's Defence of Christianity." *Bulletin of the John Rylands Library* 47 (1964): 275–97.

Chadwick, *Reformation*   Chadwick, Owen. *The Reformation.* Pelican History of the Church 3. Baltimore: Penguin, 1964.

Chamberlain, "Functions"   Chamberlain, John V. "The Functions of God as Messianic Titles in the Complete Qumran Isaiah Scroll." *VT* 5 (1955): 366–72.

Chance, "Fiction"   Chance, J. Bradley. "Fiction in Ancient Biography: An Approach to a Sensitive Issue in Gospel Interpretation." *Perspectives in Religious Studies* 18, no. 2 (1991): 125–42.

Charles, *Jubilees*   Charles, R. H. *The Book of Jubilees or The Little Genesis.* London: A&C Black, 1902.

Charles, *Pseudepigrapha*   Charles, R. H., ed. *The Apocrypha and Pseudepigrapha of the Old Testament in English.* 2 vols. Oxford: Clarendon, 1913.

Charles, "Witness"   Charles, J. Daryl. " 'Will the Court Please Call in the Prime Witness?' John 1:29–34 and the 'Witness'-Motif." *Trinity Journal* NS 10 (1989): 71–83.

Charlesworth, James H. Introduction to "Odes of Solomon." *OTP* 2:725–34.

Charlesworth, James H., ed. *The Old Testament Pseudepigrapha.* 2 vols. Garden City, N.Y.: Doubleday, 1983–1985.

Charlesworth, "Comparison"   Charlesworth, James H. "A Critical Comparison of the Dualism in IQS III,13–IV,26 and the 'Dualism' Contained in the Fourth Gospel." *NTS* 15 (1968–1969): 389–418.

Charlesworth, *Disciple*   Charlesworth, James H. *The Beloved Disciple: Whose Witness Validates the Gospel of John?* Valley Forge, Pa.: Trinity Press International, 1995.

Charlesworth, "Exclusivism"   Charlesworth, James H. "The Gospel of John: Exclusivism Caused by a Social Setting Different from That of Jesus (John 11:54 and 14:6)." Pages 479–513 in *Anti-Judaism and the Fourth Gospel: Papers of the Leuven Colloquium, 2000.* Edited by R. Bieringer, D. Pollefeyt, and F. Vandecasteele-Vanneuville. Assen: Royal Van Gorcum, 2001.

Charlesworth, "Introduction"    Charlesworth, James H., with J. A. Sanders. Introduction to "More Psalms of David." *OTP* 2:609–11.

Charlesworth, "Judeo-Hellenistic Works"    Charlesworth, James H. "Editor's Introduction to Fragments of Lost Judeo-Hellenistic Works." *OTP* 2:775–76.

Charlesworth, *Pseudepigrapha and* NT    Charlesworth, James H. *OTP and the New Testament: Prolegomena for the Study of Christian Origins.* SNTSMS 54. Cambridge: Cambridge University Press, 1985.

Charlesworth, "Qumran and Odes"    Charlesworth, James H. "Qumran, John, and the Odes of Solomon." Pages 107–36 in *John and Qumran.* Edited by James H. Charlesworth. London: Geoffrey Chapman, 1972.

Charlesworth, "Reinterpreting"    Charlesworth, James H. "Reinterpreting John: How the Dead Sea Scrolls Have Revolutionized Our Understanding of the Gospel of John." *Bible Review* 9, no. 1 (February 1993): 18–25, 54.

Charlesworth, *Routes*    Charlesworth, M. P. *Trade Routes and Commerce of the Roman Empire.* 2d rev. ed. New York: Cooper Square, 1970.

Charlesworth, "Scrolls and Gospel"    Charlesworth, James H. "The Dead Sea Scrolls and the Gospel according to John." Pages 65–97 in *Exploring the Gospel of John: In Honor of D. Moody Smith.* Edited by R. Alan Culpepper and C. Clifton Black. Louisville, Ky.: Westminster John Knox, 1996.

Charlesworth, "Voice"    Charlesworth, James H. "The Jewish Roots of Christology: The Discovery of the Hypostatic Voice." *SJT* 39 (1986): 19–41.

Charlier, "L'exégèse"    Charlier, Jean-Pierre. "L'exégèse johannique d'un précepte légal: Jean VIII 17." *RB* 67 (1960): 503–15.

Charlier, "Notion"    Charlier, Jean-Pierre. "La notion de signe (semeion) dans le IVe évangile." *Revue des sciences philosophiques et théologiques* 43 (1959): 434–48.

Charnov, "Shavuot"    Charnov, Bruce H. "Shavuot, 'Matan Torah,' and the Triennial Cycle." *Judaism* 23 (1974): 332–36.

Chennattu, "Women in Mission"    Chennattu, Rekha. "Women in the Mission of the Church: An Interpretation of John 4." *Vidyajyoti* 65 (10, 2001): 760–73.

Chernick, "Application"    Chernick, Michael. "Internal Restraints on *Gezerah Shawah's* Application." *JQR* 80 (1989–1990): 253–82.

Chernick, "Responses"    Chernick, Michael. "Some Talmudic Responses to Christianity, Third and Fourth Centuries." *Journal of Ecumenical Studies* 17 (1980): 393–406.

Chernus, "Individual"    Chernus, Ira. "Individual and Community in the Redaction of the Hekhalot Literature." *HUCA* 52 (1981): 253–74.

Chernus, "Visions"    Chernus, Ira. "Visions of God in Merkabah Mysticism." *JSJ* 13 (1982): 123–46.

Cheung, "Women"    Cheung, L. "Women in the Gospel of John." (In Chinese.) *CGST Journal* 18 (1995): 89–124.

Chevallier, *L'Esprit*    Chevallier, Max–Alain. *L'Esprit et le Messie dans le bas-judaïsme et le Nouveau Testament.* Études d'histoire et de philosophie religieuses 49. Paris: Presses Universitaires de France, 1958.

Chevallier, "Filioque"    Chevallier, Max–Alain. "L'évangile de Jean et le 'filioque.'" *RevScRel* 57 (1983): 93–111.

Chevallier, "Pentecôtes"    Chevallier, Max–Alain. "'Pentecôtes' lucaniennes et 'Pentecôtes' johanniques." *Recherches de science religieuse* 69 (April 1981): 301–13.

Chevallier, "Pierre"    Chevallier, Max–Alain. "'Tu es Pierre, tu es le nouvel Abraham' (Mt 16/18)." *Études théologiques et religieuses* 57 (1982): 375–87.

Chevallier, *Souffle*    Chevallier, Max–Alain. *Souffle de Dieu: Le Saint-Esprit dans le Nouveau Testament.* Vol. 1: *Ancien Testament, hellénisme et judaïsme, la tradition synoptique, l'oeuvre de Luc.* Le point théologique 26. Paris: Éditions Beauchesne, 1978.

Chilton, "Announcement"    Chilton, Bruce. "Announcement in Nazara: An Analysis of Luke 4:16–21." Pages 147–172 in *Studies of History and Tradition in the Four Gospels.* Vol. 2 of *Gospel Perspectives.* Edited by R. T. France and David Wenham. Sheffield: JSOT Press, 1981.

Chilton, *Approaches*    Chilton, Bruce. *Judaic Approaches to the Gospels.* University of South Florida International Studies in Formative Christianity and Judaism 2. Atlanta: Scholars Press, 1994.

Chilton, "Development"   Chilton, Bruce. "A Comparative Study of Synoptic Development: The Dispute between Cain and Abel in the Palestinian Targums and the Beelzebul Controversy in the Gospels." *JBL* 101 (1982): 553–62.

Chilton, "Exorcism"   Chilton, Bruce. "Exorcism and History: Mark 1:21–28." Pages 253–271 in *The Miracles of Jesus*. Edited by David Wenham and Craig Blomberg. Vol. 6 of *Gospel Perspectives*. Edited by R. T. France and David Wenham. Sheffield: JSOT Press, 1986.

Chilton, "John xii34"   Chilton, Bruce. "John xii34 and Targum Isaiah lii13." *NovT* 22 (1980): 176–78.

Chilton, "Midrash"   Chilton, Bruce. "Varieties and Tendencies of Midrash: Rabbinic Interpretations of Isaiah 24.23." Pages 9–32 in *Studies in Midrash and Historiography*. Vol. 3 of *Gospel Perspectives*. Edited by R. T. France and David Wenham. Sheffield: JSOT Press, 1983.

Chilton, "Thomas"   Chilton, Bruce. "The Gospel according to Thomas as a Source of Jesus' Teaching." Pages 155–175 in *The Jesus Tradition outside the Gospels*. Edited by David Wenham. Vol. 5 of *Gospel Perspectives*. Edited by R. T. France and David Wenham. Sheffield: JSOT Press, 1985.

Chilton, "Transmission"   Chilton, Bruce. "Targumic Transmission and Dominical Tradition." Pages 21–45 in *Studies of History and Tradition in the Four Gospels*. Vol. 1 of *Gospel Perspectives*. Edited by R. T. France and David Wenham. Sheffield: JSOT Press, 1980.

Chilton and Yamauchi, "Synagogues"   Chilton, Bruce, and Edwin M. Yamauchi. "Synagogues." Pages 1145–53 in *Dictionary of New Testament Background*. Edited by Craig A. Evans and Stanley E. Porter. Downers Grove, Ill.: InterVarsity, 2000.

Cholin, "Prologue"   Cholin, Marc. "Le prologue de l'évangile selon Jean: Structure et formation." *Science et esprit* 41 (1989): 189–205, 343–62.

Chow, "Applications"   Chow, Peter K. "Analogical Applications of Information Theory to Semantic Problems." *Bible Translator* 31 (1980): 310–18.

Chroust, "Comments"   Chroust, A.-H. "Some Comments on Philo of Alexandria, *De aeternitate mundi*." *Laval théologique et philosophique* 31 (1974–1975): 135–45.

Chroust, "Fragment"   Chroust, A.-H. "A Fragment of Aristotle's *On Philosophy* in Philo of Alexandria, *De opificio mundi* I, 7." *Divus Thomas* 77 (1974): 224–35.

Cidrac, "Ponctuation"   Cidrac, Charles de. "Une ponctuation de Jn 1.3–4." *Semiotique et Bible* 82 (1997): 16–29.

Clark, "Criticism"   Clark, Kenneth W. "The Effect of Recent Textual Criticism upon New Testament Studies." Pages 27–51 in *The Background of the New Testament and Its Eschatology: Studies in Honour of Charles Harold Dodd*. Edited by W. D. Davies and D. Daube. Cambridge: Cambridge University Press, 1964.

Clark, *Logos*   Clark, Gordon Haddon. *The Johannine Logos*. International Library of Philosophy and Theology. Nutley, N.J.: Presbyterian and Reformed Publishing Company, 1972.

Clark, "Miracles"   Clark, David K. "Miracles in the World Religions." Pages 199–213 in *In Defense of Miracles: A Comprehensive Case for God's Action in History*. Edited by R. Douglas Geivett and Gary R. Habermas. Downers Grove, Ill.: InterVarsity, 1997.

Clark, "Signs"   Clark, Douglas K. "Signs in Wisdom and John." *CBQ* 45 (1983): 201–9.

Clark, "Worship"   Clark, Kenneth W. "Worship in the Jerusalem Temple after A.D. 70." *NTS* 6 (1959–1960): 269–80.

Clarke, "Dream"   Clarke, E. G. "Jacob's Dream at Bethel as Interpreted in the Targums and the New Testament." *Studies in Religion* 4 (1974–1975): 367–377.

Clarke, "Italy"   Clarke, Andrew D. "Rome and Italy." Pages 455–81 in *The Book of Acts in Its Graeco-Roman Setting*. Edited by David W. J. Gill and Conrad Gempf. Vol. 2 of *The Book of Acts in Its First Century Setting*. Edited by Bruce W. Winter. Grand Rapids: Eerdmans, 1994.

Claudel, "Parallèles"   Claudel, Gérard. "Jean 20,23 et ses parallèles matthéens." *RevScRel* 69 (1995): 71–86.

Clements, *Prophecy*   Clements, R. E. *Prophecy and Tradition*. Atlanta: John Knox, 1975.

Clifford, "Tent"   Clifford, Richard J. "Tent of El and Israelite Tent of Meeting." *CBQ* 33 (1971): 221–27.

Coakley, "Anointing"   Coakley, J. F. "The Anointing at Bethany and the Priority of John." *JBL* 107 (1988): 241–56.

Cocchini, "Evoluzione"   Cocchini, F. "L'evoluzione storico-religiosa della festa di Pentecoste." *RivB* 25 (1977): 297–326.

Cody, "Paraclete"   Cody, Z. T. "The Work of the Paraclete." *Review and Expositor* 16 (1919): 164–80.

Coetzee, "Life"   Coetzee, J. C. "Life (Eternal Life) in St. John's Writings and the Qumran Scrolls." *Neotestamentica* 6 (1972): 48–66.

Coggins, *Samaritans*   Coggins, R. J. *Samaritans and Jews: The Origins of Samaritanism Reconsidered.* Atlanta: John Knox, 1975.

Coggins, "Samaritans"   Coggins, R. J. "The Samaritans in Josephus." Pages 257–73 in *Josephus, Judaism, and Christianity.* Edited by Louis H. Feldman and Gohei Hata. Detroit: Wayne State University Press, 1987.

Cohee, "1.3–4"   Cohee, Peter. "John 1.3–4." *NTS* 41 (1995): 470–77.

Cohen, "Analysis"   Cohen, N. J. "Analysis of an Exegetic Tradition in the *Mekhilta de-Rabbi Ishmael:* The Meaning of '*Amanah* in the Second and Third Centuries." *AJSR* 9 (1984): 1–25.

Cohen, "Ceremony"   Cohen, Shaye J. D. "The Rabbinic Conversion Ceremony." *JJS* 41 (1990): 177–203.

Cohen, "Conversion"   Cohen, Shaye J. D. "Conversion to Judaism in Historical Perspective: From Biblical Israel to Postbiblical Judaism." *Conservative Judaism* 36, no. 4 (summer 1983): 31–45.

Cohen, "Evidence"   Cohen, Shaye J. D. "Pagan and Christian Evidence on the Ancient Synagogue." Pages 159–81 in *The Synagogue in Late Antiquity.* Edited by Lee I. Levine. Philadelphia: American Schools of Oriental Research, 1986.

Cohen, "Fathers"   Cohen, Shaye J. D. "Can Converts to Judaism Say 'God of Our Fathers'? *Judaism* 40 (1991): 419–28.

Cohen, *Law*   Cohen, Boaz. *Jewish and Roman Law: A Comparative Study.* 2 vols. New York: Jewish Theological Seminary of America, 1966.

Cohen, *Maccabees*   Cohen, Shaye J. D. *From the Maccabees to the Mishnah.* LEC 7. Philadelphia: Westminster, 1987.

Cohen, "Masada"   Cohen, Shaye J. D. "What Really Happened at Masada?" *Moment* 13, no. 5 (1988): 28–35.

Cohen, "Names"   Cohen, Naomi G. "The Names of the Translators in the Letter of Aristeas: A Study in the Dynamics of Cultural Transition." *JSJ* 15 (1984): 32–64.

Cohen, "Respect"   Cohen, Shaye J. D. "Respect for Judaism by Gentiles according to Josephus." *HTR* 80 (1987): 409–30.

Cohen, "Shekhinta"   Cohen, Norman J. "Shekhinta ba-Galuta: A Midrashic Response to Destruction and Persecution." *JSJ* 13 (1982): 147–59.

Cohen, "Taryag"   Cohen, Naomi G. "Taryag and the Noahide Commandments." *JJS* 43 (1992): 46–57.

Cohen, "Viticulture"   Cohen, Dan. "On Viticulture and Wine—in Israel and the Ancient World." (In Hebrew.) *Beth Mikra* 37 (1991–92): 59–69.

Cohn, *Trial*   Cohn, Haim. *The Trial and Death of Jesus.* New York: Ktav, 1977.

Cohn-Sherbok, "Mandaeans"   Cohn-Sherbok, D. "The Mandaeans and Heterodox Judaism." *HUCA* 54 (1983): 147–51.

Cole, *Theoi*   Cole, Susan Guettel. *Theoi Megaloi: The Cult of the Great Gods at Samothrace.* Études préliminaires aux religions orientales dans l'Empire romain 96. Leiden: Brill, 1984.

Collins, "Apotheosis"   Collins, Adela Yarbro. "Apotheosis and Resurrection." Pages 88–100 in *The New Testament and Hellenistic Judaism.* Edited by Peder Borgen and Søren Giversen. Peabody, Mass.: Hendrickson, 1997.

Collins, "Artapanus"   Collins, John J. Introduction to "Artapanus." *OTP* 2:889–96.

Collins, "Cana"   Collins, Raymond F. "Cana (Jn. 2:1–12)—the First of His Signs or the Key to His Signs?" *Irish Theological Quarterly* 47, no. 2 (1980): 79–95.

Collins, "Commentary"   Collins, Raymond F. "The Oldest Commentary on the Fourth Gospel." *The Bible Today* 98 (November 1978): 1769–75.

Collins, *Divorce*   Collins, Raymond F. *Divorce in the New Testament.* Good News Studies 38. Collegeville, Minn.: Liturgical Press, 1992.

Collins, "*Doxa*"   Collins, Matthew S. "The Question of *Doxa:* A Socioliterary Reading of the Wedding at Cana." *Biblical Theology Bulletin* 25 (1995): 100–109.

Collins, *Oracles*   Collins, John J. *The Sibylline Oracles of Egyptian Judaism.* SBLDS 13. Missoula, Mont.: Society of Biblical Literature, 1972.

Collins, "Servant"    Collins, John J. "The Suffering Servant at Qumran?" *Bible Review* 9, no. 6 (December 1993): 25–27, 63.

Collins, "Son of God"    Collins, John J. "A Pre-Christian 'Son of God' among the Dead Sea Scrolls." *Bible Review* 9, no. 3 (June 1993): 34–38, 57.

Collins, "Son of Man"    Collins, John J. "The Son of Man in First-Century Judaism." *NTS* 38 (1992): 448–66.

Collins, "Speaking of Jews"    Collins, Raymond F. "Speaking of the Jews: 'Jews' in the Discourse Material of the Fourth Gospel." Pages 281–300 in *Anti-Judaism and the Fourth Gospel: Papers of the Leuven Colloquium, 2000.* Edited by R. Bieringer, D. Pollefeyt, and F. Vandecasteele-Vanneuville. Assen: Royal Van Gorcum, 2001.

Collins, "Spirit"    Collins, C. John. "John 4:23–24, 'In Spirit and Truth': An Idiomatic Proposal." *Presbyterion* 21, no. 2 (1995): 118–21.

Collins, "Testamentary Literature"    Collins, John J. "The Testamentary Literature in Recent Scholarship." Pages 268–85 in *Early Judaism and Its Modern Interpreters.* Edited by Robert A. Kraft and George W. E. Nickelsburg. SBLBMI 2. Atlanta: Scholars Press, 1986.

Collins, "Twelve"    Collins, Raymond F. "The Twelve, Another Perspective: John 6,67–71." *Melita theologica* 40, no. 2 (1989): 95–109.

Collins, "Vessels"    Collins, M. F. "The Hidden Vessels in Samaritan Traditions." *JSJ* 3 (1972): 97–116.

Collins, *Witness*    Collins, Raymond F. *John and His Witness.* Zacchaeus Studies: New Testament. Collegeville, Minn.: Liturgical Press, 1991.

Collins, *Written*    Collins, Raymond F. *These Things Have Been Written: Studies on the Fourth Gospel.* Louvain Theological & Pastoral Monographs 2. Louvain: Peeters; Grand Rapids: Eerdmans, 1990.

Coloe, "Structure"    Coloe, Mary. "The Structure of the Johannine Prologue and Genesis 1." *ABR* 45 (1997): 40–55.

Coloe, *Temple Symbolism*    Coloe, Mary L. *God Dwells with Us: Temple Symbolism in the Fourth Gospel.* Collegeville, Minn.: Liturgical Press, a Michael Glazier Book, 2001.

Colwell and Titus, *Spirit*    Colwell, Ernest Cadman, and Eric Lane Titus. *The Gospel of the Spirit: A Study in the Fourth Gospel.* New York: Harper & Brothers, 1953.

Comfort, "Pericope"    Comfort, Philip. "The Pericope of the Adulteress." *Bible Translator* 40 (1989): 145–47.

Conzelmann, "Areopagus"    Conzelmann, Hans. "The Address of Paul on the Areopagus." Pages 217–230 in *Studies in Luke–Acts: Essays in Honor of Paul Schubert.* Edited by Leander E. Keck and J. Louis Martyn. Nashville: Abingdon Press, 1966.

Conzelmann, *Corinthians*    Conzelmann, Hans. *1 Corinthians: A Commentary on the First Epistle to the Corinthians.* Translated by James W. Leitch. Bibliography and references by James W. Dunkly. Edited by George W. MacRae. Hermeneia. Philadelphia: Fortress, 1975.

Conzelmann, *Theology*    Conzelmann, Hans. *An Outline of the Theology of the New Testament.* Translated by John Bowden. New York: Harper & Row, 1969.

Cook, "4Q246"    Cook, E. M. "4Q246." *Bulletin of Biblical Research* 5 (1995): 43–66.

Cook, *Dogma*    Cook, Michael. *Early Muslim Dogma: A Source-Critical Study.* Cambridge: Cambridge University Press, 1981.

Cook, "Exegesis"    Cook, James I. "John 20:19–23—an Exegesis." *Reformed Review* 21, no. 2 (December 1967): 2–10.

Cook, "Introduction to Secrets"    Cook, Edward. Introduction to the "Book of Secrets." Pages 174–75 in *The Dead Sea Scrolls: A New Translation.* By Michael Wise, Martin Abegg Jr., and Edward Cook. San Francisco: Harper San Francisco, 1999.

Cook, *Muhammad*    Cook, Michael. *Muhammad.* Past Masters Series. General editor Keith Thomas. New York: Oxford University Press, 1983.

Cook, "Zenon Papyri"    Cook, Rosalie R. E. "Zenon Papyri." Pages 1300–3 in *Dictionary of New Testament Background.* Edited by Craig A. Evans and Stanley E. Porter. Downers Grove, Ill.: InterVarsity, 2000.

Cooper, "Wine"    Cooper, Karl T. "The Best Wine: John 2:1–11." *Westminster Theological Journal* 41 (1978–1979): 364–80.

Coote, *Amos*   Coote, Robert B. *Amos among the Prophets: Composition and Theology.* Philadelphia: Fortress, 1981.

Cope, *Scribe*   Cope, O. Lamar. *Matthew: A Scribe Trained for the Kingdom of Heaven.* CBQ Monograph 5. Washington, D.C.: Catholic Biblical Association of America, 1976.

Copeland, "Nomos"   Copeland, E. Luther. "Nomos as a Medium of Revelation—Paralleling Logos—in Ante-Nicene Christianity." *Studia theologica* 27 (1973): 51–61.

Coppens, "Don"   Coppens, J. "Le don de l'Esprit d'après les textes de Qumrân et le quatrième évangile." Pages 209–23 in *L'évangile de Jean: Études et problèmes.* Recherches bibliques 3. Louvain: Desclée de Brouwer, 1958.

Coppens, "Logia"   Coppens, J. "Les logia johanniques du fils de l'homme." Pages 311–15 in *L'évangile de Jean: Sources, rédaction, théologie.* Edited by Marinus De Jonge. BETL 45. Gembloux: J. Duculot; Leuven: Leuven University Press, 1977.

Corley, "Trial"   Corley, B. "Trial of Jesus." Pages 841–54 in *Dictionary of Jesus and the Gospels.* Edited by Joel B. Green, Scot McKnight, and I. Howard Marshall. Downers Grove, Ill.: InterVarsity, 1992.

Cornfeld, *Josephus*   Cornfeld, Gaalya, ed., with Benjamin Mazar and Paul L. Maier. *The Jewish War* by Josephus. Grand Rapids: Zondervan, 1982.

Corsini, *Apocalypse*   Corsini, Eugenio. *The Apocalypse: The Perennial Revelation of Jesus Christ.* Translated and edited by Francis J. Moloney. Good News Studies 5. Wilmington, Del.: Glazier, 1983.

Cortés, "Look"   Cortés, Juan B. "Yet Another Look at Jn 7,37–38." *CBQ* 29 (1967): 75–86.

Cosgrove, "Place"   Cosgrove, Charles H. "The Place Where Jesus Is: Allusions to Baptism and the Eucharist in the Fourth Gospel." *NTS* 35 (1989): 522–39.

Cothenet, "Communautés"   Cothenet, Edouard. "Les communautés johanniques." *Esprit et vie* 107 (1997): 433–40.

Cothenet, "Témoignage"   Cothenet, Edouard. "Le témoignage selon saint Jean." *Esprit et vie* 101 (28, 1991): 401–7.

Cotton and Geiger, "Yyn"   Cotton, Hannah M., and Joseph Geiger. "Yyn lhwrdws hmlk [Wine for Herod]." *Cathedra* 53 (1989): 3–12.

Coulot, "Quelqu'un"   Coulot, Claude. "'Si quelqu'un me sert, qu'il me suive!' (Jn 12,26a)." *RevScRel* 69 (1995): 47–57.

Countryman, *Crossing*   Countryman, L. William. *The Mystical Way in the Fourth Gospel: Crossing Over into God.* Philadelphia: Fortress, 1987.

Couturier, "Baptisé"   Couturier, Guy. "Jésus baptisé à Béthanie?" *Parabole* 22, no 4 (2000): 16.

Cox, "Tragedy"   Cox, Roger L. "Tragedy and the Gospel Narratives." Pages 298–317 in *The Bible in Its Literary Milieu.* Edited by Vincent L. Tollers and John R. Maier. Grand Rapids: Eerdmans, 1979.

Craghan, "Mari"   Craghan, John F. "Mari and Its Prophets: The Contributions of Mari to the Understanding of Biblical Prophecy." *Biblical Theology Bulletin* 5 (1975): 32–55.

Craig, "Historicity"   Craig, William Lane. "The Historicity of the Empty Tomb of Jesus." *NTS* 31 (1985): 39–67.

Craig, "Miracles"   Craig, William Lane. "The Problem of Miracles: A Historical and Philosophical Perspective." Pages 9–48 in *The Miracles of Jesus.* Edited by David Wenham and Craig Blomberg. Vol. 6 of *Gospel Perspectives.* Edited by R. T. France and David Wenham. Sheffield: JSOT Press, 1986.

Craig, "Resurrection"   Craig, William Lane. "The Bodily Resurrection of Jesus." Pages 47–74 in *Studies of History and Tradition in the Four Gospels.* Vol. 1 of *Gospel Perspectives.* Edited by R. T. France and David Wenham. Sheffield: JSOT Press, 1980.

Craig, "Rise?"   Craig, William Lane. "Did Jesus Rise from the Dead?" Pages 141–76 in *Jesus under Fire.* Edited by Michael J. Wilkins and J. P. Moreland. Grand Rapids: Zondervan, 1995.

Craig, "Tomb"   Craig, William Lane. "The Empty Tomb of Jesus." Pages 173–200 in *Studies of History and Tradition in the Four Gospels.* Vol. 2 of *Gospel Perspectives.* Edited by R. T. France and David Wenham. Sheffield: JSOT Press, University of Sheffield, 1981.

Craigie, *Ugarit*   Craigie, Peter C. *Ugarit and the Old Testament.* Grand Rapids: Eerdmans, 1983.

Crane, *Spirit*   Crane, Louis Burton. *The Teachings of Jesus Concerning the Holy Spirit.* New York: American Tract Society, 1905.

Cranfield, "Baptism"   Cranfield, C. E. B. "The Baptism of our Lord—a Study of St. Mark 1.9–11." *SJT* 8 (1955): 53–63.

Cranfield, "'Became'"   Cranfield, C. E. B. "John 1:14: 'Became.'" *ExpTim* 93 (1981–1982): 215.

Cranfield, *Romans*   Cranfield, C. E. B. *A Critical and Exegetical Commentary on the Epistle to the Romans.* 2 vols. International Critical Commentary. Edinburgh: T&T Clark, 1975.

Cranfield, "Romans 1.18"   Cranfield, C. E. B. "Romans 1.18." *SJT* 21 (1968): 330–35.

Cribbs, "Agreements"   Cribbs, F. Lamar. "The Agreements That Exist between John and Acts." Pages 40–61 in *Perspectives on Luke-Acts.* Edited by Charles H. Talbert. Danville, Va.: Association of Baptist Professors of Religion; Edinburgh: T&T Clark, 1978.

Cribbs, "Reassessment"   Cribbs, F. Lamar. "A Reassessment of the Date of Origin and the Destination of the Gospel of John." *JBL* 89 (1970): 38–55.

Crocker, "Bethsaida"   Crocker, P. T. "Where Is Bethsaida?" *Buried History* 25, no. 3 (1989): 78–81.

Crocker, "Priests"   Crocker, P. T. "Corrupt Priests—a Common Phenomenon." *Buried History* 26 (1990): 36–43.

Crocker, "Sepphoris"   Crocker, P. T. "Sepphoris: Past History and Present Discoveries." *Buried History* 23, no. 4 (1987): 64–76.

Cross, "Genres"   Cross, Anthony R. "Genres of the New Testament." Pages 402–11 in *Dictionary of New Testament Background.* Edited by Craig A. Evans and Stanley E. Porter. Downers Grove, Ill.: InterVarsity, 2000.

Cross, *Library*   Cross, Frank Moore. *The Ancient Library of Qumran and Modern Biblical Studies.* Rev. ed. Garden City, N.Y.: Doubleday, 1961. Repr.,Grand Rapids: Baker, 1980.

Cross, *Myth*   Cross, Frank Moore. *Canaanite Myth and Hebrew Epic.* Cambridge: Harvard University Press, 1973.

Crossan, "Anti-Semitism"   Crossan, Dominic M. "Anti-Semitism and the Gospel." *Theological Studies* 26 (1965): 189–214.

Crossan, "Cynic"   Crossan, John Dominic. "Open Healing and Open Eating: Jesus as a Jewish Cynic." *Biblical Research* 36 (1991): 6–18.

Crossan, *Jesus*   Crossan, John Dominic. *The Historical Jesus: The Life of a Mediterranean Jewish Peasant.* San Francisco: Harper, 1991.

Crossan, "Tomb"   Crossan, John Dominic. "Empty Tomb and Absent Lord (Mark 16:1–8)." Pages 135–52 in *The Passion in Mark: Studies in Mark 14–16.* Edited by Werner H. Kelber. Philadelphia: Fortress, 1976.

Crown, "Schism"   Crown, Alan D. "Redating the Schism between the Judaeans and the Samaritans." *JQR* 82 (1991–1992): 17–50.

Croy, "Neo-Pythagoreanism"   Croy, N. Clayton. "Neo-Pythagoreanism." Pages 739–42 in *Dictionary of New Testament Background.* Edited by Craig A. Evans and Stanley E. Porter. Downers Grove, Ill.: InterVarsity, 2000.

Croy, "Religion"   Croy, N. Clayton. "Religion, Personal." Pages 926–31 in *Dictionary of New Testament Background.* Edited by Craig A. Evans and Stanley E. Porter. Downers Grove, Ill.: InterVarsity, 2000.

Cryer, "Prologue"   Cryer, Cecil. "The Prologue of the Fourth Gospel." *ExpTim* 32 (1920–1921): 440–43.

Culham, "Archives"   Culham, Phyllis. "Archives and Alternatives in Republican Rome." *Classical Philology* 84 (1989): 100–115.

Cullmann, "Approach"   Cullmann, Oscar. "A New Approach to the Interpretation of the Fourth Gospel." *ExpTim* 71 (1959–1960): 8–12, 39–43.

Cullmann, *Christology*   Cullmann, Oscar. *The Christology of the New Testament.* Philadelphia: Westminster, 1959.

Cullmann, *Church*   Cullmann, Oscar. *The Early Church.* Edited by A. J. B. Higgins. London: SCM, 1956.

Cullmann, *Circle*   Cullmann, Oscar. *The Johannine Circle.* Translated by John Bowden. Philadelphia: Westminster, 1976.

Cullmann, *Peter*   Cullmann, Oscar. *Peter: Disciple–Apostle–Martyr.* Philadelphia: Westminster, 1953.

Cullmann, "Πέτρα"   Cullmann, Oscar. "Πέτρα." *TDNT* 6:95–99.

Cullmann, "Πέτρος, Κηφᾶς"   Cullmann, Oscar. "Πέτρος, Κηφᾶς," *TDNT* 6:100–12.

Cullmann, "Qumran Texts"   Cullmann, Oscar. "The Significance of the Qumran Texts for Research into the Beginnings of Christianity." *JBL* 74 (1955): 213–26.

Cullmann, *State*   Cullmann, Oscar. *The State in the New Testament.* New York: Scribner, 1956.

Cullmann, *Time*   Cullmann, Oscar. *Christ and Time.* Translated by Floyd V. Filson. Philadelphia: Westminster, 1950.

Cullmann, *Worship*   Cullmann, Oscar. *Early Christian Worship.* Philadelphia: Westminster, 1953.

Culpepper, *Anatomy*   Culpepper, R. Alan. *Anatomy of the Fourth Gospel: A Study in Literary Design.* Philadelphia: Fortress, 1983.

Culpepper, "Culture"   Culpepper, R. Alan. "The Gospel of John as a Document of Faith in a Pluralistic Culture." Pages 107–27 in *"What Is John?" Readers and Reading of the Fourth Gospel.* Edited by Fernando F. Segovia. SBLSymS 3. Atlanta: Scholars Press, 1996.

Culpepper, "*Hypodeigma*"   Culpepper, R. Alan. "The Johannine *Hypodeigma:* A Reading of John 13." *Semeia* 53 (1991): 133–52.

Culpepper, "Irony"   Culpepper, R. Alan. "Reading Johannine Irony." Pages 193–207 in *Exploring the Gospel of John: In Honor of D. Moody Smith.* Edited by R. Alan Culpepper and C. Clifton Black. Louisville, Ky.: Westminster John Knox, 1996.

Culpepper, "Jews"   Culpepper, R. Alan. "The Gospel of John and the Jews." *Review and Expositor* 84 (1987): 273–88.

Culpepper, *John*   Culpepper, R. Alan. *The Gospel and Letters of John.* Interpreting Biblical Texts. Nashville: Abingdon, 1998.

Culpepper, "Pivot"   Culpepper, R. Alan. "The Pivot of John's Prologue." *NTS* 27 (1980–1981): 1–31.

Culpepper, "Plot"   Culpepper, R. Alan. "The Plot of John's Story of Jesus." *Interpretation* 49 (1995): 347–58.

Culpepper, "Problem for Interpreters"   Culpepper, R. Alan. "Anti-Judaism in the Fourth Gospel as a Theological Problem for Christian Interpreters." Pages 68–91 in *Anti-Judaism and the Fourth Gospel: Papers of the Leuven Colloquium, 2000.* Edited by R. Bieringer, D. Pollefeyt, and F. Vandecasteele-Vanneuville. Assen: Royal Van Gorcum, 2001.

Culpepper, "Sayings"   Culpepper, R. Alan. "The AMHN, AMHN Sayings in the Gospel of John." Pages 57–101 in *Perspectives on John: Method and Interpretation in the Fourth Gospel.* National Association of the Baptist Professors of Religion Special Studies Series 11. Edited by Robert B. Sloan and Mikeal C. Parsons. Lewiston, N.Y.: Mellen, 1993.

Culpepper, *School*   Culpepper, R. Alan. *The Johannine School: An Evaluation of the Johannine-School Hypothesis Based on an Investigation of the Nature of Ancient Schools.* SBLDS 26. Missoula, Mont.: Scholars Press, 1975.

Cuming, "*Epotisthēmen*"   Cuming, G. J. "*Epotisthēmen* (I Corinthians 12. 13)." *NTS* 27 (1980–1981): 283–85.

Cuming, "Jews"   Cuming, G. J. "The Jews in the Fourth Gospel." *ExpTim* 60 (1948–1949): 290–92.

Cumont, *After Life*   Cumont, Franz. *After Life in Roman Paganism: Lectures Delivered at Yale Unversity on the Silliman Foundation.* New Haven: Yale University Press, 1922.

Cumont, "Mithraeum"   Cumont, Franz. "The Dura Mithraeum." Paages 151–214 in vol. 1 of *Mithraic Studies: Proceedings of the First International Congress of Mithraic Studies.* Edited by John R. Hinnells. 2 vols. Manchester: Manchester University Press, 1975.

Cunningham and Bock, "Midrash"   Cunningham, Scott, and Darrell L. Bock. "Is Matthew Midrash?" *BSac* 144 (1987): 157–80.

Curchin, "Literacy"   Curchin, Leonard A. "Literacy in the Roman Provinces: Qualitative and Quantitative Data from Central Spain." *American Journal of Philology* 116 (1995): 461–76.

Currid, *Ancient Egypt*   Currid, John D. *Ancient Egypt and the Old Testament.* Foreword by Kenneth A. Kitchen. Grand Rapids: Baker, 1997.

Curty, "Propos"   Curty, Olivier. "À propos de la parenté entre Juifs et Spartiates." *Historia* 41 (1992): 246–48.

Dahl, "Abraham"   Dahl, Nils Alstrup. "The Story of Abraham in Luke–Acts." Pages 139–58 in *Studies in Luke–Acts: Essays in Honor of Paul Schubert.* Edited by Leander E. Keck and J. Louis Martyn. Nashville: Abingdon, 1966.

Dahl, "History"   Dahl, Nils Alstrup. "The Johannine Church and History." Pages 124–42 in *Current Issues in New Testament Interpretation: Essays in Honor of Otto A. Piper.* Edited by William Klassen and Graydon F. Snyder. New York: Harper & Row, 1962.

Dahl, "Kristus"  Dahl, Nils Alstrup. "Kristus, jødene og verden etter Johannesevangelist." *Norsk Teologisk Tidsskrift* 60 (1959):189–203.

Dahl, "Manndraperen"  Dahl, Nils Alstrup. "Manndraperen og hans far (Joh 8:44)." *Norsk Teologisk Tidsskrift* 64 (1963): 129–62. (NTA 9:204).

Dahl, *Paul*  Dahl, Nils Alstrup. *Studies in Paul: Theology for the Early Christian Mission*. Minneapolis: Augsburg, 1977.

Dahl and Segal, "Name"  Dahl, Nils Alstrup, and Segal, Alan F. "Philo and the Rabbis on the Name of God." *JSJ* 9 (1978): 1–28.

Dahms, "Monogenēs"  Dahms, John V. "The Johannine Use of monogenēs Reconsidered." *NTS* 29 (1983): 222–32.

Dahood, "Ebla"  Dahood. Mitchell. "Ebla, Genesis, and John." *Christian Century* 98 (1981): 418–21.

Dahood, *Psalms*  Dahood. Mitchell. *Psalms 1: Psalms 1–50*. AB 16. Garden City, N.Y.: Doubleday, 1966.

Dalman, *Arbeit*  Dalman, Gustaf. *Arbeit und Sitte in Palästina*. 7 vols. Hildesheim: Georg Olms, 1964.

Dalman, *Jesus in Talmud*  Dalman, Gustaf. *Jesus Christ in the Talmud, Midrash, Zohar, and the Liturgy of the Synagogue*. 1893. Repr., New York: Arno Press, 1973.

Dalman, *Jesus-Jeshua*  Dalman, Gustaf. *Jesus-Jeshua: Studies in the Gospels*. New York: Macmillan, 1929.

Daly-Denton, "Shades of David"  Daly-Denton, M. "Shades of David in the Johannine Presentation of Jesus." *Proceedings of the Irish Biblical Association* 19 (1996): 9–47.

Dana and Mantey, *Grammar*  Dana, H. E., and Julius R. Mantey. *A Manual Grammar of the Greek New Testament*. Toronto: Macmillan, 1955.

Danby, *Mishnah*  Danby, Herbert. *The Mishnah*. London: Oxford University Press, 1933.

D'Angelo, "Note"  D'Angelo, Mary Rose. "A Critical Note: John 20:17 and *Apocalypse of Moses* 31." *JTS* NS 41 (1990): 529–36.

Daniel, "Prophètes"  Daniel, Constantin. "'Faux prophètes': Surnom des esséniens dans le sermon sur la montagne." *RevQ* 7 (1969–1971): 45–79.

Daniel, "Anti-Semitism"  Daniel, Jerry. "Anti-Semitism in the Hellenistic-Roman Period." *JBL* 98 (1979): 45–65.

Daniélou, "Symbolisme"  Daniélou, J. "Le symbolisme eschatologique de la fête de Tabernacles." *Irénikon* 31 (1958): 19–40.

Daniélou, *Theology*  Daniélou, Jean. *The Theology of Jewish Christianity*. Translated and edited by John A. Baker. Development of Christian Doctrine before the Council of Nicaea 1. London: Darton, Longman & Todd, 1964.

Daniels, Boyd L., and M. Jack Suggs, eds. *Studies in the History and Text of the New Testament, in Honor of Kenneth Willis Clark*. Studies and Documents 29. Salt Lake City: University of Utah Press, 1967.

Daniels, "Army"  Daniels, C. M. "The Role of the Roman Army in the Spread and Practice of Mithraism." Pages 249–74 in vol. 2 of *Mithraic Studies: Proceedings of the First International Congress of Mithraic Studies*. Edited by John R. Hinnells. 2 vols. Manchester: Manchester University Press, 1975.

Danker, *Age*  Danker, Frederick W. *Jesus and the New Age: According to St. Luke*. St. Louis: Clayton, 1972.

Danker, *Benefactor*  Danker, Frederick W. *Benefactor: Epigraphic Study of a Greco-Roman and New Testament Semantic Field*. St. Louis: Clayton, 1982.

Danker, "God with Us"  Danker, Frederick W. "God with Us: Hellenistic Christological Perspectives in Matthew." *Currents in Theology and Mission* 19 (1992): 433–39.

Danna, "John 4:29"  Danna, Elizabeth. "A Note on John 4:29." *RB* 106, no. 2 (1999): 219–23.

Dar, "*Menorot*"  Dar, S. "Three *Menorot* from Western Samaria." *IEJ* 34 (1984): 177–79, plate 20BC.

Dar and Kokkinos, "Inscriptions"  Dar, Shimon, and Nikos Kokkinos. "The Greek Inscriptions from Senaim on Mount Hermon." *PEQ* 124 (1992): 9–25.

Daube, "Enfant"  Daube, David. "Enfant Terrible." *HTR* 68 (1975): 371–76.

Daube, "Gospels"  Daube, David. "The Gospels and the Rabbis." *The Listener* 56 (1956): 342–46.

Daube, *Judaism*    Daube, David. *The New Testament and Rabbinic Judaism*. London: University of London, 1956. Repr., Peabody, Mass.: Hendrickson, n.d.

Daube, "Limitations"    Daube, David. "Limitations on Self-Sacrifice in Jewish Law and Tradition." *Theology* 72 (1969): 291–304.

Daube, "Notes"    Daube, David. "Three Notes Having to Do with Johanan ben Zaccai." *JTS* NS 11 (1960): 53–62.

Daube, *Pattern*    Daube, David. *The Exodus Pattern in the Bible*. All Souls Studies 2. London: Faber & Faber, 1963.

Daube, "Witnesses"    Daube, David. "The Law of Witnesses in Transferred Operation." *Journal of the Ancient Near Eastern Society of Columbia University* 5 (1973): 91–93.

David, "Eloquentia"    David, J. M. "Eloquentia popularis et urbanitis: Les oratoeurs originaires des villes italiennes à Rome à la fin de la republic." *Actes de la recherche en sciences sociales* 60 (November 1965): 68–71.

Davids, *James*    Davids, Peter H. *The Epistle of James: A Commentary on the Greek Text*. New International Greek Testament Commentary. Grand Rapids: Eerdmans, 1982.

Davids, "Tradition"    Davids, Peter H. "The Gospels and Jewish Tradition: Twenty Years after Gerhardsson." Pages 75–99 in *Studies of History and Tradition in the Four Gospels*. Vol. 1 of *Gospel Perspectives*. Edited by R. T. France and David Wenham. Sheffield: JSOT Press, 1980.

Davies, "Aboth"    Davies, W. D. "Reflexions on Tradition: The Aboth Revisited." Pages 129–37 in *Christian History and Interpretation: Studies Presented to John Knox*. Edited by W. R. Farmer, C. F. D. Moule, and R. R. Niebuhr. Cambridge: Cambridge University Press, 1967.

Davies, "Aspects"    Davies, W. D. "Reflections on Aspects of the Jewish Background of the Gospel of John." Pages 43–64 in *Exploring the Gospel of John: In Honor of D. Moody Smith*. Edited by R. Alan Culpepper and C. Clifton Black. Louisville, Ky.: Westminster John Knox, 1996.

Davies, *Invitation*    Davies, W. D. *Invitation to the New Testament: A Guide to Its Main Witnesses*. Garden City, N.Y.: Doubleday, 1966.

Davies, *Land*    Davies, W. D. *The Gospel and the Land: Early Christianity and Jewish Territorial Doctrine*. Berkeley: University of California Press, 1974.

Davies, *Matthew*    Davies, Margaret. *Matthew*. Readings: A New Biblical Commentary. Sheffield: JSOT Press, 1993.

Davies, "Mekilta"    Davies, W. D. "Reflections on the Spirit in the Mekilta: A Suggestion." *Journal of the Ancient Near Eastern Society of Columbia University* 5 (1973): 95–105.

Davies, "Parakleitos"    Davies, J. G. "The Primary Meaning of Parakleitos." *JTS* NS 4 (1953): 35–38.

Davies, *Paul*    Davies, W. D. *Paul and Rabbinic Judaism: Some Rabbinic Elements in Pauline Theology*. 4th ed. Philadelphia: Fortress, 1980.

Davies, *Rhetoric*    Davies, Margaret. *Rhetoric and Reference in the Fourth Gospel*. JSNTSup 69. Sheffield: Sheffield Academic Press, 1992.

Davies, *Sermon*    Davies, W. D. *The Sermon on the Mount*. Cambridge: Cambridge University Press, 1966.

Davies, *Setting*    Davies, W. D. *The Setting of the Sermon on the Mount*. Cambridge: Cambridge University Press, 1964.

Davies, "Tabernacle"    Davies, G. Henton. "Tabernacle." Pages 498–506 in vol. 4 of *The Interpreter's Dictionary of the Bible*. Edited by G. A. Buttrick. Nashville: Abingdon, 1962.

Davies, *Torah*    Davies, W. D. *Torah in the Messianic Age and/or the Age to Come*. SBLMS 7. Philadelphia: Society of Biblical Literature, 1952.

Davies and Allison, *Matthew*    Davies, W. D., and Dale C. Allison. *A Critical and Exegetical Commentary on the Gospel according to Saint Matthew*. International Critical Commentary. 3 vols. Edinburgh: T&T Clark, 1988–1997.

Davis, "Cana"    Davis, Stephen T. "The Miracle at Cana: A Philosopher's Perspective." Pages 419–42 in *The Miracles of Jesus*. Edited by David Wenham and Craig Blomberg. Vol. 6 of *Gospel Perspectives*. Edited by R. T. France and David Wenham. Sheffield: JSOT Press, 1986.

De Boer, *Fatherhood*    De Boer, P. A. H. *Fatherhood and Motherhood in Israelite and Judean Piety*. Leiden: Brill, 1974.

De Boer, "Jews"    De Boer, M. C. "The Depiction of 'the Jews' in John's Gospel: Matters of Behavior and Identity." Pages 260–80 in *Anti-Judaism and the Fourth Gospel: Papers of the Leuven Collo-*

*quium, 2000.* Edited by R. Bieringer, D. Pollefeyt, and F. Vandecasteele-Vanneuville. Assen: Royal Van Gorcum, 2001.

Decharneux, "Interdits"    Decharneux, B. "Interdits sexuels dans l'oeuvre de Philon d'Alexandrie dit 'Le Juif.'" *Problèmes d'histoire des religions* 1 (1990): 17–31.

Decock, "Understanding"    Decock, P. B. "The Understanding of Isaiah 53:7–8 in Acts 8:32–33." *Neotestamentica* 14 (1981): 111–33.

DeConick, *Mystics*    DeConick, April O. *Voices of the Mystics: Early Christian Discourse in the Gospels of John and Thomas and Other Ancient Christian Literature.* JSNTSup 157. Sheffield: Sheffield Academic Press, 2001.

Deeks, "Prologue"    Deeks, David. "The Prologue of St. John's Gospel." *Biblical Theology Bulletin* 6 (1976): 62–78.

Deissmann, *Light*    Deissmann, G. Adolf. *Light from the Ancient East.* Reprinted. Grand Rapids: Baker, 1978.

Deissmann, *Paul*    Deissmann, G. Adolf. *Paul: A Study in Social and Religious History.* 2d ed. New York: Harper & Brothers, 1927. Repr., New York, Harper & Brothers, 1957.

Deissmann, *Studies*    Deissmann, G. Adolf. *Bible Studies: Contributions Chiefly from Papyri and Inscriptions to the History of the Language, the Literature, and the Religion of Hellenistic Judaism and Primitive Christianity.* Translated by Alexander Grieve. Edinburgh: T&T Clark, 1923. Repr., Winona Lake, Ind.: Alpha Publications, 1979.

Delaney, "Seeds"    Delaney, Carol. "Seeds of Honor, Fields of Shame." Pages 35–48 in *Honor and Shame and the Unity of the Mediterranean.* Edited by David D. Gilmore. American Anthropological Association 22. Washington, D.C.: American Anthropological Association, 1987.

Delaygue, "Grecs"    Delaygue, M.-P. "Les Grecs connaissaient-ils les religions de l'Inde à l'époque hellénistique?" *Bulletin de l'Association Guillaume Budé* 54 (1995): 152–72.

Delcor, "Bundesfest"    Delcor, Mathias. "Das Bundesfest in Qumran und das Pfingstfest." *Bibel und Leben* 4 (1963): 188–204.

Delcor, "Guerre"    Delcor, M. "La guerre des fils de lumière contre les fils de ténèbres." *Nouvelle revue théologique* 77, no. 4 (April 1955): 372–99.

Delebecque, "Contemporain"    Delebecque, Edouard. "Jésus contemporain d'Abraham selon Jean 8,57." *RB* 93 (1986): 85–92.

Delmore, "Pratique"    Delmore, J. "La pratique du baptême dans le judaïsme contemporain des origines chrétiennes." *Lumière et vie* 26 (1956): 165–204.

Delobel, "Papyri"    Delobel, J. "The Bodmer Papyri of John." Pages 317–323 in *L'évangile de Jean: Sources, rédaction, théologie.* Edited by Marinus De Jonge. BETL 45. Gembloux: J. Duculot; Leuven: Leuven University Press, 1977.

Deman, "Mithras"    Deman, A. "Mithras and Christ: Some Iconographical Similarities." Pages 507–17 in vol. 2 of *Mithraic Studies: Proceedings of the First International Congress of Mithraic Studies.* Edited by John R. Hinnells. 2 vols. Manchester: Manchester University Press, 1975.

De Maria, "Regno"    De Maria, Antonio. "Il mio regno non è di questo mondo: Breve analisi del commento patristico a Gv 18, 36." *Laós* 5, no. 2 (1998): 11–18.

Dembski, *Design*    Dembski, William A. *Intelligent Design: The Bridge between Science and Theology.* Foreword by Michael Behe. Downers Grove, Ill.: InterVarsity, 1999.

Dembski, *Inference*    Dembski, William A. *The Design Inference.* Cambridge: Cambridge University Press, 1998.

De Nazareth, "Maison"    De Nazareth, M. "La maison de saint Joseph à Nazareth." *Cahiers de Joséphologie* 4 (1956): 243–72.

Dentan, *Knowledge*    Dentan, Robert C. *The Knowledge of God in Ancient Israel.* New York: Seabury, 1968.

Dequeker, "Saints"    Dequeker, L. "The 'Saints of the Most High' in Qumran and Daniel." *Oudtestamentische Studiën* 18 (1973): 108–87.

Dequeker, "Zodiaque"    Dequeker, Luc. "Le zodiaque de la synagogue de Beth Alpha et le midrash." *Bijdragen* 47 (1986): 2–30.

Derickson, "Viticulture"    Derickson, Gary W. "Viticulture and John 15:1–6." *BibSac* 153 (Jan. 1996): 34–52.

De Ridder, *Discipling*    De Ridder, Richard R. *Discipling the Nations.* Grand Rapids: Baker, 1971.

De Ridder, *Dispersion*    De Ridder, Richard R. *The Dispersion of the People of God: The Covenant Basis of Matthew 28:18–20 against the Background of Jewish, Pre-Christian Proselyting and Diaspora, and the Apostleship of Jesus Christ.* Kampen: J. H. Kok, 1971.

De Roo, "4Q525"    De Roo, Jacqueline C. R. "Beatitudes Text (4Q525)." Pages 151–53 in *Dictionary of New Testament Background.* Edited by Craig A. Evans and Stanley E. Porter. Downers Grove, Ill.: InterVarsity, 2000.

Derrett, "Advocacy"    Derrett, J. D. M. "Advocacy at John 16:8–11." *ExpTim* 110, no. 6 (1999): 181–82.

Derrett, "Ἄρχοντες"    Derrett, J. D. M. "Ἄρχοντες, ἀρχαί: A Wider Background to the Passion Narratives." *Filologia Neotestamentaria* 2 (1989): 173–85.

Derrett, *Audience*    Derrett, J. D. M. *Jesus's Audience: The Social and Psychological Environment in Which He Worked.* New York: Seabury, 1973.

Derrett, "Binding"    Derrett, J. D. M. "Binding and Loosing (Matt 16:19; 18:18; John 20:23)." *JBL* 102 (1983): 112–17.

Derrett, "Blow"    Derrett, J. D. M. "Why Did Jesus Blow on the Disciples? (John 20,22)." *Bibbia e oriente* 40 (1999): 235–46.

Derrett, "Cursing"    Derrett, J. D. M. "Cursing Jesus (I Cor. XII.3): The Jews as Religious 'Persecutors.'" *NTS* 21 (1974–1975): 544–54.

Derrett, "Domine"    Derrett, J. D. M. "'Domine, tu mihi lavas pedes?' (studio su Giovanni 13,1–30)." *Bibbia e oriente* 21 (1979): 13–42.

Derrett, "Ἐργάζῃ"    Derrett, J. D. M. "Τί ἐργάζῃ; (Jn 6:30): An Unrecognized Allusion to Is 45,9." *ZNW* 84 (1993): 142–44.

Derrett, "Fishermen"    Derrett, J. D. M. "Āsan gar halieis (Mk. I.16): Jesus's Fishermen and the Parable of the Net." *NovT* 22 (1980): 108–37.

Derrett, "Iscariot"    Derrett, J. D. M. "The Iscariot, *Mesira,* and the Redemption." *JSNT* 8 (1980): 2–23.

Derrett, "John 8, 32–36"    Derrett, J. D. M. "Oriental Sources for John 8, 32–36?" *Bibbia e oriente* 43, no. 1 (2001): 29–32.

Derrett, "John's Jesus and Buddha"    Derrett, J. D. M. "St. John's Jesus and the Buddha." *Journal of Higher Criticism* 6, no. 2 (1999): 161–74.

Derrett, *Law*    Derrett, J. D. M. *Law in the New Testament.* London: Darton, Longman, & Todd, 1970.

Derrett, "Lazarus"    Derrett, J. D. M. "Lazarus, the Body, and Water (John 11,44; Isaiah 58,11; Numbers 20,9–11)." *Bibbia e oriente* 39 (1997): 169–82.

Derrett, "Miriam"    Derrett, J. D. M. "Miriam and the Resurrection (John 20,16)." *Bibbia e oriente* 33 (1991): 211–19.

Derrett, "Purity"    Derrett, J. D. M. "The Samaritan Woman's Purity (John 4:4–52)." *EvQ* 60 (1988): 291–98.

Derrett, "Ruber"    Derrett, J. D. M. "Ecce Homo Ruber (John 19.5 with Isaiah 1:18; 63:1–2)." *Bibbia et Oriente* 32 (1990): 215–29.

Derrett, "Seeing"    Derrett, J. D. M. "Not Seeing and Later Seeing (John 16:16)." *ExpTim* 109 (1997–1998): 208–9.

Derrett, "Shepherd"    Derrett, J. D. M. "The Good Shepherd: St. John's Use of Jewish Halakah and Haggadah." *Studia theologica* 27 (1973): 25–50.

Derrett, "Sword"    Derrett, J. D. M. "Peter's Sword and Biblical Methodology." *Bibbia e oriente* 32 (1990): 180–92.

Derrett, "Teach"    Derrett, J. D. M. "'Dost Thou Teach Us?' (John 9:34c)." *DRev* 116 (1998): 183–94.

Derrett, "Walked"    Derrett, J. D. M. "Why and How Jesus Walked on the Sea." *NovT* 23 (1981): 330–48.

Derrett, "Woman"    Derrett, J. D. M. "The Samaritan Woman in India c. A. D. 200." *Zeitschrift für Religions und Geistesgeschichte* 39, no. 4 (1987): 328–36.

DeSilva, *Honor*    DeSilva, David A. *Honor, Patronage, Kinship, and Purity: Unlocking New Testament Culture.* Downers Grove, Ill.: InterVarsity, 2000.

DeSilva, "Honor and Shame"    DeSilva, David A. "Honor and Shame." Pages 519–21 in *Dictionary of New Testament Background.* Edited by Craig A. Evans and Stanley E. Porter. Downers Grove, Ill.: InterVarsity, 2000.

DeSilva, "Patronage"    DeSilva, David A. "Patronage." Pages 766–71 in *Dictionary of New Testament Background.* Edited by Craig A. Evans and Stanley E. Porter. Downers Grove, Ill.: InterVarsity, 2000.

DeSilva, "Wisdom of Solomon"  DeSilva, David A. "Wisdom of Solomon." Pages 1268–76 in *Dictionary of New Testament Background.* Edited by Craig A. Evans and Stanley E. Porter. Downers Grove, Ill.: InterVarsity, 2000.

Desprez, "Groups"  Desprez, Vincent. "Jewish Ascetical Groups at the Time of Christ: Qumran and the Therapeuts." *American Benedictine Review* 41 (1990): 291–311.

Deutsch, "Wisdom"  Deutsch, Celia. "Wisdom in Matthew: Transformation of a Symbol." *NovT* 32 (1990): 13–47.

De Vaux, *Israel*  De Vaux, Roland. *Ancient Israel: Its Life and Institutions.* Translated by John MacHugh. New York: McGraw-Hill, 1961.

Devillers, "Exégèse"  Devillers, Luc. "Exégèse et théologie de Jean I,18." *Revue thomiste* 89 (1989): 181–217.

Devillers, "Piscine"  Devillers, Luc. "Une piscine peut en cacher une autre: À propos de Jean 5,1–9a." *RB* 106 (1999): 175–205.

De Waard, "Quotation"  De Waard, Jan. "The Quotation from Deuteronomy in Acts 3,22.23 and the Palestinian Text: Additional Arguments." *Biblica* 52 (1971): 537–40.

De Wet, "Unity"  De Wet, B. W. "Unity in John 17 and in 1QS I–IX: A Comparative Study." *Skrif en kerk* 18 (1997): 34–51.

Dewey, "Curse"  Dewey, Kim E. "Peter's Curse and Cursed Peter (Mark 14:53–54, 66–72)." Pages 96–114 in *The Passion in Mark: Studies in Mark 14–16.* Edited by Werner H. Kelber. Philadelphia: Fortress, 1976.

Dewey, "Oral-Aural Event"  Dewey, Joanna. "The Gospel of Mark as an Oral-Aural Event: Implications for Interpretation." Pages 145–63 in *The New Literary Criticism and the New Testament.* Edited by Edgar V. McKnight and Elizabeth Struthers Malbon. Valley Forge, Pa.: Trinity Press International, 1994; Sheffield: JSOT Press, 1994.

Dexinger, "Limits"  Dexinger, Ferdinand. "Limits of Tolerance in Judaism: The Samaritan Example." Pages 88–114 in vol. 2 of Meyer and Sanders, *Self-Definition.*

Dexinger, "Taheb-Vorstellung"  Dexinger, Ferdinand. "Die Taheb-Vorstellung als politische Utopie." *Numen* 37 (1990): 1–23.

Dey, *World*  Dey, Lala Kalyan Kumar. *The Intermediary World and Patterns of Perfection in Philo and Hebrews.* SBLDS 25. Missoula, Mont.: Society of Biblical Literature, 1975.

De Zwaan, "Language"  De Zwaan, J. "The Use of the Greek Language in Acts." Pages 30–65 in vol. 2 of *The Beginnings of Christianity.*

Dibelius, "Initiation"  Dibelius, Martin. "The Isis Initiation in Apuleius and Related Initiatory Rites." Pages 61–121 in *Conflict at Colossae: A Problem in the Interpretation of Early Christianity Illustrated by Selected Modern Studies.* Edited and translated by Fred O. Francis and Wayne A. Meeks. SBLSBS 4. Missoula, Mont.: Society of Biblical Literature, 1973.

Dibelius, *James*  Dibelius, Martin. *James: A Commentary on the Epistle of James.* Revised by Heinrich Greeven. Translated by Michael A. Williams. Edited by Helmut Koester. Hermeneia. Philadelphia: Fortress, 1976.

Dibelius, *Jesus*  Dibelius, Martin. *Jesus.* Translated by Charles B. Hedrick and Frederick C. Grant. Philadelphia: Westminster, 1949.

Dibelius, *Paul*  Dibelius, Martin. *Paul.* Edited and completed by Werner Georg Kümmel. Philadelphia: Westminster, 1953.

Dibelius, *Studies*  Dibelius, Martin. *Studies in the Acts of the Apostles.* Edited by Heinrich Greeven. London: SCM, 1956.

Dibelius, *Tradition*  Dibelius, Martin. *From Tradition to Gospel.* Translated from the 2d German ed. by Bertram Lee Woolf. Greenwood, S.C.: Attic Press, 1971.

Dibelius and Conzelmanm, *Epistles*  Dibelius, Martin, and Conzelmann, Hans. *The Pastoral Epistles: A Commentary on the Pastoral Epistles.* Translated by Philip Buttolph and Adela Yarbro. Edited by Helmut Koester. Hermeneia. Philadelphia: Fortress, 1972.

Diel and Solotareff, *Symbolism*  Diel, Paul, and Jeannine Solotareff. *Symbolism in the Gospel of John.* Translated by Nelly Marans. San Francisco: Harper & Row, 1988.

Dietzfelbinger, "Paraklet"  Dietzfelbinger, Christian. "Paraklet und theologischer Anspruch im Johannesevangelium." *Zeitschrift für Theologie und Kirche* 82 (1985): 389–408.

Dietzfelbinger, "Werke"  Dietzfelbinger, Christian. "Die grösseren Werke (Joh 14.12f.)." *NTS* 35 (1989): 27–47.

Díez Merino, "Sintagma"   Díez Merino, Luís. "El sintagma *nš* '*ynm* en la tradición aramea." *Aula orientalis* 2 (1984): 23–41.

Dihle, "Biography"   Dihle, Albrecht. "The Gospels and Greek Biography." Pages 361–86 in *The Gospel and the Gospels.* Edited by Peter Stuhlmacher. Grand Rapids: Eerdmans, 1991.

Dihle, "Fête"   Dihle, Albrecht. "La fête chrétienne." *Revue des études augustiniennes* 38 (1992): 323–35.

Di Lella, "Holy Ones"   Di Lella, Alexander A. "The One in Human Likeness and the Holy Ones of the Most High in Daniel 7." *CBQ* 39 (1977): 1–19.

Dillon, "Ganymede"   Dillon, John. "Ganymede as the Logos: Traces of a Forgotten Allegorization in Philo?" *Classical Quarterly* 31 (1981): 183–85.

Dillon, "Logos"   Dillon, John. "Ganymede as the Logos: Traces of a Forgotten Allegorization in Philo." *Studia philonica* 6 (1979–1980): 37–40.

Dillon, "Philosophy"   Dillon, John M. "Philosophy." Pages 793–96 in *Dictionary of New Testament Background.* Edited by Craig A. Evans and Stanley E. Porter. Downers Grove, Ill.: InterVarsity, 2000.

Dillon, *Platonists*   Dillon, John. *The Middle Platonists: 80 B.C. to A.D. 220.* Ithaca, N.Y.: Cornell University Press, 1977.

Dillon, "Transcendence"   Dillon, John. "The Transcendence of God in Philo: Some Possible Sources." Pages 1–8 in *The Transcendence of God in Philo: Some Possible Sources.* Edited by John Dillon. Colloquy—The Center for Hermeneutical Studies in Hellenistic and Modern Culture 16. Berkeley: Center for Hermeneutical Studies in Hellenistic and Modern Culture, 1975.

Dillon and Hershbell, "Introduction"   Dillon, John, and Jackson Hershbell. Introduction. Pages 1–29 in Iamblichus, *On the Pythagorean Way of Life: Text, Translation, and Notes.* SBL Texts and Translations 29, Graeco-Roman Religion Series 11. Atlanta: Scholars Press, 1991.

Dimant and Strugnell, "Vision"   Dimant, Devorah, and John Strugnell. "The Merkabah Vision in Second Ezekiel (4Q385 4)." *RevQ* 14 (1989–1990): 331–48.

Dimock, "Introduction"   Dimock, G. E. Introduction. Pages 1–5 in vol. 1 of Homer, *The Odyssey.* 2d ed. Translated A. T. Murray. Revised by George E. Dimock. 2 vols. LCL. Cambridge: Harvard University Press, 1995.

Dion, "Paraclet"   Dion, Hyacinthe-M. "L'origine du titre de 'Paraclet': À propos d'un livre récent." *Sciences ecclesiastiques* 17 (1965): 143–49.

Dion and Pummer, "Note"   Dion, Paul E., and Reinhard Pummer. "A Note on the 'Samaritan-Christian Synagogue' in Ramat-Aviv." *JSJ* 11 (1980): 217–22.

Di Segni, "Inscription"   Di Segni, Leah. "A Fragmentary Greek Inscription from the Giv'at Seled Burial Cave." *ʾAtiqot* 20 (1991): 164–65.

Di Segni, "Toponym"   Di Segni, Leah. "A New Toponym in Southern Samaria." *Studii biblici franciscani liber annuus* 44 (1994): 579–84.

Dix, *Ministry*   Dix, Gregory. *The Apostolic Ministry.* Edited by Kenneth E. Kirk. London: Hodder & Stoughton, 1947.

Dix, "Wisdom"   Dix, G. H. "The Heavenly Wisdom and the Divine Logos in Jewish Apocalyptic." *JTS* 26/101 (October 1924): 1–12.

Dixon, *Mother*   Dixon, Suzanne. *The Roman Mother.* Norman, Okla.: Oklahoma University Press, 1988.

Dockx, "Compagnon"   Dockx, S. "Luc a-t-il été le compagnon d'apostolat de Paul?" *Nouvelle revue théologique* 103, no. 3 (1981): 385–400.

Dodd, "L'arrière-plan"   Dodd, C. H. "À l'arrière-plan d'un dialogue johannique." *Revue d'histoire et de philosophie religieuses* 37 (1957): 5–17.

Dodd, "Background"   Dodd, C. H. "The Background of the Fourth Gospel." *Bulletin of the John Rylands Library* 19 (1935): 329–43.

Dodd, *Bible*   Dodd, C. H. *The Bible and the Greeks.* London: Hodder & Stoughton, 1935.

Dodd, *Epistles*   Dodd, C. H. *The Johannine Epistles.* Moffatt New Testament Commentary. London: Hodder & Stoughton, 1946.

Dodd, *Founder*   Dodd, C. H. *The Founder of Christianity.* New York: Macmillan, 1970.

Dodd, "'Herrenworte'"   Dodd, C. H. "Some Johannine 'Herrenworte' with Parallels in the Synoptic Gospels." *NTS* 2 (1955–1956): 75–86.

Dodd, *Interpretation*    Dodd, C. H. *The Interpretation of the Fourth Gospel.* Cambridge: Cambridge University Press, 1965.

Dodd, *More Studies*    Dodd, C. H. *More New Testament Studies.* Grand Rapids: Eerdmans, 1968.

Dodd, *Parables*    Dodd, C. H. *The Parables of the Kingdom.* London: Nisbet, 1936.

Dodd, "Portrait"    Dodd, C. H. "The Portrait of Jesus in John and in the Synoptics." Pages 183–98 in *Christian History and Interpretation: Studies Presented to John Knox.* Edited by W. R. Farmer, C. F. D. Moule, and R. R. Niebuhr. Cambridge: Cambridge University Press, 1967.

Dodd, *Preaching*    Dodd, C. H. *The Apostolic Preaching and Its Developments.* London: Hodder & Stoughton, 1936.Repr., Grand Rapids: Baker, 1980;.

Dodd, "Prologue"    Dodd, C. H. "The Prologue to the Fourth Gospel and Christian Worship." Pages 9–22 in *Studies in the Fourth Gospel.* Edited by F. L. Cross. London: Mowbray, 1957.

Dodd, *Studies*    Dodd, C. H. *New Testament Studies.* Manchester: Manchester University Press, 1967.

Dodd, *Tradition*    Dodd, C. H. *Historical Tradition in the Fourth Gospel.* Cambridge: Cambridge University Press, 1965.

Dods, "John"    Dods, Marcus. "John." Pages 655–872 in vol. 1 of *The Expositor's Greek Testament.* Edited by W. Robertson Nicoll. 5 vols. 1897–1910. Repr., Grand Rapids: Eerdmans, 1979.

Doeve, *Hermeneutics*    Doeve, J. W. *Jewish Hermeneutics in the Synoptic Gospels and Acts.* Assen: Van Gorcum, 1954.

Doh, "Paroimiai"    Doh, H. "Paroimiai in the Fourth Gospel." *Asia Adventist Seminary Studies* 3 (2000): 25–34.

Dola, "Interpretacja"    Dola, Tadeusz. "Antropologiczna interpretacja formuly 'zmartwychwstal dnia trzeciego' (Die anthropologische Interpretation der Formel 'auferweckt am dritten Tag nach der Schrift')." *Collectanea theologica* 53 (1983): 37–52.

Domeris, "Confession"    Domeris, William R. "The Confession of Peter according to John 6:69." *Tyndale Bulletin* 44 (1993): 155–67.

Domeris, "Drama"    Domeris, William R. "The Johannine Drama." *Journal of Theology for Southern Africa* 42 (March 1983): 29–35.

Donahue, *Christ*    Donahue, John R. *Are You the Christ? The Trial Narrative in the Gospel of Mark.* SBLDS 10. Missoula, Mont.: Society of Biblical Literature, 1973.

Donahue, "*Hauptstrasse?*"    Donahue, John R. "Redaction Criticism: Has the *Hauptstrasse* Become a *Sackgasse?*" Pages 27–57 in *The New Literary Criticism and the New Testament.* Edited by Edgar V. McKnight and Elizabeth Struthers Malbon. Valley Forge, Pa.: Trinity Press International, 1994; Sheffield: JSOT Press, 1994.

Donahue, "Temple"    Donahue, John R. "Temple, Trial, and Royal Christology (Mark 14:53–65)." Pages 61–79 in *The Passion in Mark: Studies in Mark 14–16.* Edited by Werner H. Kelber. Philadelphia: Fortress, 1976.

Donaldson, *Paul and Gentiles*    Donaldson, Terence L. *Paul and the Gentiles: Remapping the Apostle's Convictional World.* Minneapolis: Fortress, 1997.

Donaldson, "Typology"    Donaldson, Terry L. "Moses Typology and the Sectarian Nature of Early Christian Anti-Judaism: A Study in Acts 7." *JSNT* 12 (1981): 27–52.

Doriani, "Review"    Doriani, Daniel M. Review of Craig Keener, *A Commentary on the Gospel of Matthew. Presbyterion* 26 (2000): 34–35.

Dowd, "Theology"    Dowd, Sharyn E. "Toward a Johannine Theology of Prayer." Pages 317–35 in *Perspectives on John: Method and Interpretation in the Fourth Gospel.* National Association of the Baptist Professors of Religion Special Studies Series 11. Edited by Robert B. Sloan and Mikeal C. Parsons. Lewiston, N.Y.: Mellen, 1993.

Dowden, "Apuleius"    Dowden, K. "Apuleius and the Art of Narration." *Classical Quarterly* 32 (1982): 419–35.

Dowden, "Callisthenes"    Dowden, Ken. Introduction to "Pseudo-Callisthenes: The Alexander Romance." Pages 650–54 in *Collected Ancient Greek Novels.* Edited by B. P. Reardon. Berkeley: University of California Press, 1989.

Dowell, "Conflict"    Dowell, Thomas M. "Jews and Christians in Conflict: Why the Fourth Gospel Changed the Synoptic Tradition." *Louvain Studies* 15 (1990): 19–37.

Downing, "Actuality"    Downing, F. Gerald. "Actuality versus Abstraction: The Synoptic Gospel Model." *Continuum* 1 (1991): 104–20.

Downing, "Conventions"   Downing, F. Gerald. "Compositional Conventions and the Synoptic Problem." *JBL* 107 (1988): 69–85.

Downing, "Like Q"   Downing, F. Gerald. "Quite Like Q: A Genre for 'Q'—the 'Lives' of Cynic Philosophers." *Biblica* 69 (1988): 196–225.

Downing, "Literature"   Downing, F. Gerald. "A bas les aristos: The Relevance of Higher Literature for the Understanding of the Earliest Christian Writings." *NovT* 30 (1988): 212–30.

Downing, "Prosecutions"   Downing, F. Gerald. "Pliny's Prosecutions of Christians: Revelation and 1 Peter." *JSNT* 34 (1988): 105–23.

Downing, "Redaction Criticism"   Downing, F. Gerald. "Redaction Criticism: Josephus' Antiquities and the Synoptic Gospels (I)." *JSNT* 8 (1980): 46–65.

Dozeman, "*Sperma*"   Dozeman, Thomas B. "*Sperma Abraam* in John 8 and Related Literature." *CBQ* 42 (1980): 342–58.

Drane, "Background"   Drane, John W. "The Religious Background." Pages 117–25 in *New Testament Interpretation: Essays on Principles and Methods*. Edited by I. Howard Marshall. Grand Rapids: Eerdmans, 1977.

Draper, "Didache"   Draper, Jonathan. "The Jesus Tradition in the Didache." Pages 269–287 in *The Jesus Tradition outside the Gospels*. Edited by David Wenham. Vol. 5 of *Gospel Perspectives*. Edited by R. T. France and David Wenham. Sheffield: JSOT Press, 1984.

Draper, "Greek"   Draper, H. Mudie. "Did Jesus Speak Greek?" *ExpTim* 67 (1955–1956): 317.

Driver, *Scrolls*   Driver, G. R. *The Judaean Scrolls: The Problem and a Solution*. Oxford: Blackwell, 1965.

Droge, "Peter"   Droge, Arthur J. "The Status of Peter in the Fourth Gospel: A Note on John 18:10–11." *JBL* 109 (1990): 307–11.

Drower, *Mandaeans*   Drower, E. S. *The Mandaeans of Iraq and Iran: Their Cults, Customs, Magic, Legends, and Folklore*. Leiden: Brill, 1962.

Drummond, "Genesis"   Drummond, Robert J. "Genesis 1 and John 1:1–14." *ExpTim* 49 (1937–1938): 568.

Drury, *Design*   Drury, John. *Tradition and Design in Luke's Gospel: A Study in Early Christian Historiography*. London: Darton, Longman & Todd, 1976.

Dschulnigg, "Berufung"   Dschulnigg, Peter. "Die Berufung der Jünger: Joh 1,35–51 im Rahmen des vierten Evangeliums." *Freiburger Zeitschrift für Philosophie und Theologie* 36 (1989): 427–47.

Dschulnigg, "Gleichnis"   Dschulnigg, Peter. "Gleichnis vom Kind, das zum Vater flieht (JosAs 12,8)." *ZNW* 80 (1989): 269–71.

Dschulnigg, "Hirt"   Dschulnigg, Peter. "Der Hirt und die Schafe (Joh 10,1–18)." *Studien zum Neuen Testament und seiner Umwelt* 14 (1989): 5–23.

Dschulnigg, "Nikodemus"   Dschulnigg, Peter. "Nikodemus im Johannesevangelium." *Studien zum Neuen Testament und seiner Umwelt* 24 (1999): 103–18.

Dschulnigg, "Überlegungen"   Dschulnigg, Peter. "Überlegungen zum Hintergrund der Mahlformel in Jos As: Ein Versuch." *ZNW* 80 (1989): 272–75.

Dubois, "Postérité"   Dubois, Jean-Daniel. "La postérité du quatrième évangile au deuxième siècle." *Lumière et vie* 29 (149, 1980): 31–48.

Ducatillon, "Linceul"   Ducatillon, Jeanne. "Le linceul de Jésus d'après saint Jean." *Revue thomiste* 91 (1991): 421–24.

Dudley, "Speeches"   Dudley, Merle B. "The Speeches in Acts." *EvQ* 50 (1978): 147–55.

Duff, "Introduction"   Duff, J. D. Introduction. Pages ix–xv in Lucan, *The Civil War*. Translated by J. D. Duff. LCL. Cambridge: Harvard University Press, 1928.

Duhaime, "Dualisme"   Duhaime, Jean. "Le dualisme de Qumrân et le littérature de sagesse vétérotestamentaire." *Église et théologie* 19 (1988): 401–22.

Duke, *Irony*   Duke, Paul D. *Irony in the Fourth Gospel*. Atlanta: John Knox, 1985.

Dumbrell, "Law"   Dumbrell, W. J. "Law and Grace: The Nature of the Contrast in John 1:17." *EvQ* 58 (1986): 25–37.

Dunand, "Mystères"   Dunand, Françoise. "Les mystères égyptiens." Pages 11–62 in *Mystères et syncrétismes* by Françoise Dunand et al. Études d'histoire des religions 2. Paris: Librairie Orientaliste Paul Geuthner, 1975.

Dunand, *Religion en Égypte*    Dunand, Françoise. *Religion populaire en Égypte romaine.* ÉPROER 77. Leiden: Brill, 1979.

Duncan, "Logos"    Duncan, Robert L. "The Logos: From Sophocles to the Gospel of John." *Christian Scholar's Review* 9 (1979–1980): 121–30.

Dunkerley, "Lazarus"    Dunkerley, R. "Lazarus." *NTS* 5 (1958–1959): 321–27.

Dunn, *Acts*    Dunn, James D. G. *The Acts of the Apostles.* Narrative Commentaries. Valley Forge, Pa.: Trinity Press International, 1996.

Dunn, *Baptism*    Dunn, James D. G. *Baptism in the Holy Spirit: A Re-examination of the New Testament Teaching on the Gift of the Spirit in relation to Pentecostalism Today.* SBT. Second Series 15. London: SCM, 1970.

Dunn, "Demythologizing"    Dunn, James D. G. "Demythologizing—the Problem of Myth in the New Testament." Pages 285–307 in *New Testament Interpretation: Essays on Principles and Methods.* Edited by I. Howard Marshall. Grand Rapids: Eerdmans, 1977.

Dunn, "Discourse"    Dunn, James D. G. "John VI—a Eucharistic Discourse?" *NTS* 17 (1970–1971): 328–38.

Dunn, "Embarrassment"    Dunn, James D. G. "The Embarrassment of History: Reflections on the Problem of 'Anti-Judaism' in the Fourth Gospel." Pages 47–67 in *Anti-Judaism and the Fourth Gospel: Papers of the Leuven Colloquium, 2000.* Edited by R. Bieringer, D. Pollefeyt, and F. Vandecasteele-Vanneuville. Assen: Royal Van Gorcum, 2001.

Dunn, "Incident"    Dunn, James D. G. "The Incident at Antioch (Gal. 2:11–12)." *JSNT* 18 (1983): 3–57.

Dunn, *Jesus and Spirit*    Dunn, James D. G. *Jesus and the Spirit: A Study of the Religious and Charismatic Experience of Jesus and the First Christians as Reflected in the New Testament.* London: SCM, 1975.

Dunn, "Jesus Tradition"    Dunn, James D. G. "Prophetic 'I'-Sayings and the Jesus Tradition: The Importance of Testing Prophetic Utterances within Early Christianity." *NTS* 24 (1977–1978): 175–98.

Dunn, "John"    Dunn, James D. G. "Let John Be John: A Gospel for Its Time." Pages 293–322 in *The Gospel and the Gospels.* Edited by Peter Stuhlmacher. Grand Rapids: Eerdmans, 1991.

Dunn, *Partings*    Dunn, James D. G. *The Partings of the Ways: Between Christianity and Judaism and Their Significance for the Character of Christianity.* Philadelphia: Trinity Press International, 1991.

Dunn, "Question"    Dunn, James D. G. "John and the Synoptics as a Theological Question." Pages 301–13 in *Exploring the Gospel of John: In Honor of D. Moody Smith.* Edited by R. Alan Culpepper and C. Clifton Black. Louisville, Ky.: Westminster John Knox, 1996.

Dunn, "Spirit"    Dunn, James D. G. "Spirit: NT." *NIDNTT* 3:693–707.

Dunn, *Theology of Paul*    Dunn, James D. G. *The Theology of Paul the Apostle.* Grand Rapids: Eerdmans, 1998.

Dunstan, "Clothing"    Dunstan, G. J. O. "The Clothing of the Passion: Symbolism in the Passion Narrative of St. John." *Search* 22, no. 1 (1999): 26–33.

Du Plessis, "'Only Begotten'"    Du Plessis, I. J. "Christ as the 'Only Begotten.'" *Neotestamentica* 2 (1968): 22–31.

Dupont, *Life*    Dupont, Florence. *Daily Life in Ancient Rome.* Translated by Christopher Woodall. Oxford: Blackwell, 1992.

Dupont, *Salvation*    Dupont, Jacques. *The Salvation of the Gentiles: Essays on the Acts of the Apostles.* Translated by John R. Keating. New York: Paulist Press, 1979.

Dupont, *Sources*    Dupont, Jacques. *The Sources of Acts: The Present Position.* Translated by Kathleen Pond. London: Darton, Longman & Todd, 1964.

Dupont-Sommer, *Writings*    Dupont-Sommer, A. *The Essene Writings from Qumran.* Translated by G. Vermes. Gloucester, Mass.: Peter Smith, 1973.

Du Rand, "Ellips"    Du Rand, Jan A. "'n Ellips skeppingsgebeure in die Evangelieverhaal volgens Johannes." *Skrif en kerk* 21, no. 2 (2000): 243–59.

Du Rand, "John 7:49"    Du Rand, J. "Does ὁ ὄχλος Refer to the 'Am Ha'Ares in John 7:49?" *Ekklesiastikos pharos* 77 (1995): 32–38.

Dutheil, "Aimeras"    Dutheil, J. "Tu aimeras ton prochain comme toi-même." *Chronique* 2 (1993): 31–32.

Dvorak, "Relationship"    Dvorak, James D. "The Relationship between John and the Synoptic Gospels." *JETS* 41 (1998): 201–13.

Dyer, "Light"    Dyer, Jacob A. "The Unappreciated Light." *JBL* 79 (1960): 170–71.

Eddy, "Diogenes"    Eddy, Paul Rhodes. "Jesus as Diogenes? Reflections on the Cynic Jesus Thesis." *JBL* 115 (1996): 449–69.

Edelstein, "Villa"    Edelstein, Gershon. "What's a Roman Villa Doing outside Jerusalem?" *BAR* 16, no. 6 (November/December 1990): 32–42.

Edersheim, *Life*    Edersheim, Alfred. *The Life and Times of Jesus the Messiah.* 1883. Repr., Peabody, Mass.: Hendrickson, n.d.

Edwards, *Concordance*    Edwards, R. A. *A Concordance to Q.* SBLSBS 7. Missoula, Mont.: Society of Biblical Literature and Scholars Press, 1975.

Edwards, "Fifty"    Edwards, M. J. "'Not Yet Fifty Years Old': John 8.57." *NTS* 40 (1994): 449–54.

Edwards, "Grace"    Edwards, R. B. "Χάριν ἀντὶ χάριτος (John 1.16). Grace and Law in the Johannine Prologue." *JSNT* 32 (1988): 3–15.

Edwards, *Theology of Q*    Edwards, R. A. *A Theology of Q: Eschatology, Prophecy, and Wisdom.* Philadelphia: Fortress, 1975.

Efferin, "Paraclete"    Efferin, Henry. "The Paraclete in John 14–16." *Stulos Theological Journal* 1 (1993): 149–56.

Efroymson, "Connection"    Efroymson, David P. "The Patristic Connection." Pages 98–117 in *Antisemitism and the Foundations of Christianity.* Edited by Alan T. Davies. New York: Paulist Press, 1979.

Ehrhardt, *Acts*    Ehrhardt, Arnold. *The Acts of the Apostles.* Manchester: Manchester University Press, 1969.

Ehrhardt, *Ministry*    Ehrhardt, Arnold. *The Apostolic Ministry.* Scottish Journal of Theology Occasional Papers 7. Edinburgh: Oliver Boyd, 1958.

Ehrlich, "Tora"    Ehrlich, Ernst Ludwig. "Tora im Judentum." *Evangelische Theologie* 37 (1977): 536–49.

Ehrman, Fee, and Holmes, *Text*    Ehrman, Bart D., Gordon D. Fee, and Michael W. Holmes. *The Text of the Fourth Gospel in the Writings of Origen.* Vol. 1. Society of Biblical Literature The New Testament in the Greek Fathers 3. Atlanta: Scholars Press, 1992.

Eickelman, *Middle East*    Eickelman, Dale F. *The Middle East: An Anthropological Approach.* 2d ed. Englewood Cliffs, N.J.: Prentice Hall, 1989.

Eisenman, *Maccabees*    Eisenman, Robert. *Maccabees, Zadokites, Christians, and Qumran: A New Hypothesis of Qumran Origins.* StPB 34. Leiden: Brill, 1983.

Eisman, "Dio and Josephus"    Eisman, M. M. "Dio and Josephus: Parallel Analyses." *Latomus* 36 (1977): 657–73.

Elgvin, "Devil"    Elgvin, Torleif. "Belial, Beliar, Devil, Satan." Pages 153–57 in *Dictionary of New Testament Background.* Edited by Craig A. Evans and Stanley E. Porter. Downers Grove, Ill.: InterVarsity, 2000.

Elgvin, "Section"    Elgvin, Torleif. "The Genesis Section of 4Q422 (4Q ParaGenExod)." *DSD* 1 (1994): 180–96.

Eliade, *Rites*    Eliade, Mircea. *Rites and Symbols of Initiation: The Mysteries of Birth and Rebirth.* Translated by Willard R. Trask. New York: Harper & Row, 1958.

Eller, *Disciple*    Eller, Vernard. *The Beloved Disciple—His Name, His Story, His Thought: Two Studies from the Gospel of John.* Grand Rapids: Eerdmans, 1987.

Ellis, "Authenticity"    Ellis, Peter F. "The Authenticity of John 21." *St. Vladimir's Theological Quarterly* 36 (1992): 17–25.

Ellis, "Christ and Spirit"    Ellis, E. Earle. "Christ and Spirit in 1 Corinthians." Pages 269–77 in *Christ and Spirit in the New Testament: Studies in Honor of C. F. D. Moule.* Edited by Barnabas Lindars and Stephen S. Smalley. Cambridge: Cambridge University Press, 1973.

Ellis, "Christology"    Ellis, E. Earle. "Background and Christology of John's Gospel." Pages 1–25 in *Perspectives on John: Method and Interpretation in the Fourth Gospel.* National Association of the Baptist Professors of Religion Special Studies Series 11. Edited by Robert B. Sloan and Mikeal C. Parsons. Lewiston, N.Y.: Mellen, 1993.

Ellis, "Composition"    Ellis, E. Earle. "The Composition of Luke 9 and the Sources of Its Christology." Pages 121–127 in *Current Issues in Biblical and Patristic Interpretation: Studies in Honor of*

Merrill C. Tenney Presented by His Former Students. Edited by Gerald F. Hawthorne. Grand Rapids: Eerdmans, 1975.

Ellis, "Criticism"   Ellis, E. Earle. "Gospels Criticism: A Perspective on the State of the Art." Pages 26–52 in *The Gospel and the Gospels.* Edited by Peter Stuhlmacher. Grand Rapids: Eerdmans, 1991.

Ellis, *Genius*   Ellis, Peter F. *The Genius of John: A Composition-Critical Commentary on the Fourth Gospel.* Collegeville, Minn.: Liturgical Press, 1984.

Ellis, "Inclusion, Chiasm"   Ellis, Peter F. "Inclusion, Chiasm, and the Division of the Fourth Gospel." *St. Vladimir's Theological Quarterly* 42, nos. 3–4 (1999): 269–338.

Ellis, *Matthew*   Ellis, Peter F. *Matthew: His Mind and His Message.* Collegeville, Minn.: Liturgical Press, 1974.

Ellis, *Paul*   Ellis, E. Earle. *Paul and His Recent Interpreters.* Grand Rapids: Eerdmans, 1961.

Ellis, "Uses"   Ellis, E. Earle. "How the New Testament Uses the Old." Pages 199–219 in *New Testament Interpretation: Essays on Principles and Methods.* Edited by I. Howard Marshall. Grand Rapids: Eerdmans, 1977.

Ellis, *World*   Ellis, E. Earle. *The World of St. John.* New York: Abingdon, 1965.

Ellul, *Apocalypse*   Ellul, Jacques. *Apocalypse: The Book of Revelation.* Translated by George W. Schreiner. New York: Seabury, 1977.

Ellul, "Targum"   Ellul, Danielle. "Le Targum du Pseudo-Jonathan sur Genèse 3 à la lumière de quelques traditions haggadiques." *Foi et vie* 80, no. 6 (1981): 12–25.

Elman, "Suffering"   Elman, Yaakov. "The Suffering of the Righteous in Palestinian and Babylonian Sources." *JQR* 80 (1989–1990): 315–39.

Emerton, "Binding"   Emerton, John A. "Binding and Loosing—Forgiving and Retaining." *JTS* NS 13 (1962): 325–31.

Endres, *Interpretation*   Endres, John C. *Biblical Interpretation in the Book of Jubilees.* Catholic Biblical Quarterly Monograph 18. Washington, D.C.: Catholic Biblical Association of America, 1987.

Engberg-Pedersen, *Divide*   Engberg-Pedersen, Troels, ed. *Paul beyond the Judaism/Hellenism Divide.* Louisville, Ky.: Westminster John Knox, 2001.

Engberg-Pedersen, *Paul and Stoics*   Engberg-Pedersen, Troels. *Paul and the Stoics.* Louisville, Ky.: Westminster John Knox; Edinburgh: T&T Clark, 2000.

Engle, "Amphorisk"   Engle, Anita. "An Amphorisk of the Second Temple Period." *PEQ* 109 (1977): 117–22.

English, "Miracle"   English, E. Schuyler. "A Neglected Miracle." *BSac* 126 (1969): 300–5.

Ensley, "Eternity"   Ensley, Eugene C. "Eternity Is Now: A Sermon on John 14:1–11." *Interpretation* 19 (1965): 295–98.

Ensor, "John 4.35."   Ensor, Peter W. "The Authenticity of John 4.35." *EvQ* 72, no. 1 (2000): 13–21.

Enz, "Dualism"   Enz, Jacob J. "Origin of the Dualism Expressed by 'Sons of Light' and 'Sons of Darkness.'" *Biblical Research* 21 (1976): 15–18.

Enz, "Exodus"   Enz, Jacob J. "The Book of Exodus as a Literary Type for the Gospel of John." *JBL* 76 (1957): 208–15.

Epp, "Wisdom"   Epp, Eldon Jay. "Wisdom, Torah, Word: The Johannine Prologue and the Purpose of the Fourth Gospel." Pages 128–46 in *Current Issues in Biblical and Patristic Interpretation: Studies in Honor of Merrill C. Tenney Presented by His Former Students.* Edited by Gerald F. Hawthorne. Grand Rapids: Eerdmans, 1975.

Eppstein, "Historicity"   Eppstein, Victor. "The Historicity of the Gospel Account of the Cleansing of the Temple." *ZNW* 55 (1964): 42–58.

Ernst, "Mystik"   Ernst, Jozef. "Das Johannesevangelium—ein frühes Beispiel christlicher Mystik." *Theologie und Glaube* 81 (1991): 323–38.

Erskine, "Benefactors"   Erskine, Andrew. "The Romans as Common Benefactors." *Historia* 43 (1994): 70–87.

Evans, "Action"   Evans, Craig A. "Jesus' Action in the Temple: Cleansing or Portent of Destruction?" *CBQ* 51 (1989): 237–70.

Evans, "Ἀγαπᾶν"   Evans, Ernest. "The Verb ἀγαπᾶν in the Fourth Gospel." Pages 64–71 in *Studies in the Fourth Gospel.* Edited by F. L. Cross. London: Mowbray, 1957.

Evans, "Apollonius"    Evans, Craig A. "Apollonius of Tyana." Pages 80–81 in *Dictionary of New Testament Background*. Edited by Craig A. Evans and Stanley E. Porter. Downers Grove, Ill.: InterVarsity, 2000.

Evans, "Caiaphas Ossuary"    Evans, Craig A. "Caiaphas Ossuary." Pages 179–80 in *Dictionary of New Testament Background*. Edited by Craig A. Evans and Stanley E. Porter. Downers Grove, Ill.: InterVarsity, 2000.

Evans, "Friendship"    Evans, Katherine G. "Friendship in Greek Documentary Papyri and Inscriptions: A Survey." Pages 181–202 in *Greco-Roman Perspectives on Friendship*. Edited by John T. Fitzgerald. SBLRBS 34. Atlanta: Scholars Press, 1997.

Evans, "Isaiah 6:9–10"    Evans, Craig A. "Isaiah 6:9–10 in Rabbinic and Patristic Writings." *Vigiliae christianae* 36 (1982): 275–81.

Evans, "Jesus"    Evans, Craig A. "What Did Jesus Do?" Pages 101–15 in *Jesus under Fire*. Edited by Michael J. Wilkins and J. P. Moreland. Grand Rapids: Zondervan, 1995.

Evans, "Jesus ben Ananias"    Evans, Craig A. "Jesus ben Ananias." Pages 561–62 in *Dictionary of New Testament Background*. Edited by Craig A. Evans and Stanley E. Porter. Downers Grove, Ill.: InterVarsity, 2000.

Evans, *John*    Evans, Owen E. *The Gospel according to St John*. Epworth Preacher's Commentaries. London: Epworth, 1965.

Evans, "Messianism"    Evans, Craig A. "Messianism." Pages 698–707 in *Dictionary of New Testament Background*. Edited by Craig A. Evans and Stanley E. Porter. Downers Grove, Ill.: InterVarsity, 2000.

Evans, "Note"    Evans, Craig A. "A Note on the Function of Isaiah, VI." *Revista biblica* 88 (1981): 234–35.

Evans, "Passion"    Evans, Craig A. "The Passion of Jesus: History Remembered or Prophecy Historicized?" *Bulletin for Biblical Research* 6 (1996): 159–65.

Evans, "Pilate Inscription"    Evans, Craig A. "Pilate Inscription." Pages 803–4 in *Dictionary of New Testament Background*. Edited by Craig A. Evans and Stanley E. Porter. Downers Grove, Ill.: InterVarsity, 2000.

Evans, "Prayer of Enosh"    Evans, Craig A. "Prayer of Enosh (4Q369 + 4Q458)." Pages 820–21 in *Dictionary of New Testament Background*. Edited by Craig A. Evans and Stanley E. Porter. Downers Grove, Ill.: InterVarsity, 2000.

Evans, "Prologue"    Evans, Craig A. "On the Prologue of John and the *Trimorphic Protennoia*." *NTS* 27 (1980–1981): 395–401.

Evans, "Son"    Evans, Craig A. "A Note on the 'First-Born Son' of 4Q369." *DSD* 2 (1995): 185–201.

Evans, "Warming"    Evans, Craig A. "'Peter Warming Himself': The Problem of an Editorial 'Seam.'" *JBL* 101 (1982): 245–49.

Evans, Craig A., and Stanley Porter, eds. *Dictionary of New Testament Background*. Downers Grove, Ill.: InterVarsity, 2000.

Evenson, "Mary"    Evenson, Ardy. "Mary of Magdala." *The Bible Today* 27 (1989): 219–24.

Fabry, "Texte"    Fabry, Heinz-Josef. "Neue Texte aus Qumran." *Bibel und Kirche* 48 (1993): 24–27.

Fahy, "Note"    Fahy, Thomas. "A Note on Romans 9:1–18." *Irish Theological Quarterly* 32 (1965): 261–62.

Faierstein, "Elijah"    Faierstein, Morris M. "Why Do the Scribes Say That Elijah Must Come First?" *JBL* 100 (1981): 75–86.

Falasca, "Bones"    Falasca, Stefania. "Where Are Peter's Bones?" *30 Days* 3, no. 2 (1990): 38–45.

Falconer, "Prologue"    Falconer, R. A. "The Prologue to the Gospel of John." *The Expositor*, Fifth Series 5 (1897): 222–34.

Falk, "4Q542"    Falk, Daniel K. "Testament of Qahat (4Q542)." Pages 1199–1200 in *Dictionary of New Testament Background*. Edited by Craig A. Evans and Stanley E. Porter. Downers Grove, Ill.: InterVarsity, 2000.

Falk, "Confession"    Falk, Daniel. "4Q393: A Communal Confession." *JJS* 45 (1994): 184–207.

Falk, *Jesus*    Falk, Harvey. *Jesus the Pharisee: A New Look at the Jewishness of Jesus*. New York: Paulist Press, 1985.

Fallaize, "Purification"    Fallaize, E. N. "Purification: Introductory and Primitive." Pages 455–66 in vol. 10 of *Encyclopedia of Religion and Ethics*. Edited by James Hastings. 13 vols. Edinburgh: T&T Clark, 1918.

Fallon, "Law"   Fallon, Francis T. "The Law in Philo and Ptolemy: A Note on the Letter to Flora." *Vigiliae christianae* 30 (1976): 45–51.

Fallon, "Theodotus"   Fallon, F. Introduction to "Theodotus." *OTP* 2:785–89.

Farmer, *Problem*   Farmer, William R. *The Synoptic Problem: A Critical Analysis.* New York: Macmillan, 1964.

Farmer, "Samaritan Woman"   Farmer, Craig S. "Changing Images of the Samaritan Woman in Early Reformed Commentaries on John." *Church History* 65 (1996): 365–75.

Farmer, *Verses*   Farmer, William R. *The Last Twelve Verses of Mark.* SNTSMS 25. Cambridge: Cambridge University Press, 1974.

Farmer and Kereszty, *Peter and Paul*   Farmer, William R., and Roch Kereszty. *Peter and Paul in the Church of Rome: The Ecumenical Potential of a Forgotten Perspective.* Studies in Contemporary Biblical and Theological Problems. Mahwah, N.J.: Paulist Press, 1990.

Farrer, "Q"   Farrer, Austin. "Q." *Theology* 59 (1956): 247–48.

Fascher, "Jesus"   Fascher, E. "Jesus der Lehrer." *Theologische Literaturzeitung* 79 (1954): 325–42.

Fass, "Angels"   Fass, David E. "How the Angels Do Serve." *Judaism* 40 (1991): 281–89.

Fauth, "Metatron"   Fauth, Wolfgang. "Tatrosjah-Totrosjah und Metatron in der judischen Merkabah-Mystik." *JSJ* 22 (1991): 40–87.

Fears, "Rome"   Fears, J. Rufus. "Rome: The Ideology of Imperial Power." *Thought* 55 (216, 1980): 98–109. (NTA 24:284).

Fee, *Corinthians*   Fee, Gordon D. *The First Epistle to the Corinthians.* New International Commentary on the New Testament. Grand Rapids: Eerdmans, 1987.

Fee, "Inauthenticity"   Fee, Gordon D. "On the Inauthenticity of John 5:3b–4." *EvQ* 54 (1982): 207–18.

Fee, "Once More"   Fee, Gordon D. "Once More—John 7:37–39." *ExpTim* 89 (1977–1978): 116–18.

Fee, *Presence*   Fee, Gordon D. *God's Empowering Presence: The Holy Spirit in the Letters of Paul.* Peabody, Mass.: Hendrickson, 1994.

Fee, *Spirit*   Fee, Gordon D. *Paul, the Spirit, and the People of God.* Peabody, Mass.: Hendrickson, 1996.

Fehribach, *Bridegroom*   Fehribach, Adeline. *The Women in the Life of the Bridegroom: A Feminist Historical-Literary Analysis of the Female Characters in the Fourth Gospel.* Collegeville, Minn.: Liturgical Press, 1998.

Feinberg, "Meaning"   Feinberg, Paul D. "The Meaning of Inerrancy." Pages 267–306 in *Inerrancy.* Edited by Norman L. Geisler. Grand Rapids: Zondervan, 1979.

Feldman, "Ahab"   Feldman, Louis H. "Josephus' Portrait of Ahab." *Ephemerides theologicae lovanienses* 68 (1992): 368–84.

Feldman, "Ahasuerus"   Feldman, Louis H. "Josephus' Portrait of Ahasuerus." *ABR* 42 (1994): 17–38.

Feldman, "Antiquities"   Feldman, Louis H. "Josephus' *Jewish Antiquities* and Pseudo-Philo's *Biblical* Antiquities." Pages 59–80 in *Josephus, the Bible, and History.* Edited by Louis H. Feldman and Gohei Hata. Detroit: Wayne State University Press, 1989.

Feldman, "'Aqedah"   Feldman, Louis H. "Josephus as a Biblical Interpreter: The *'Aqedah." JQR* 75 (1984–1985): 212–52.

Feldman, "Asa"   Feldman, Louis H. "Josephus' Portrait of Asa." *Bulletin for Biblical Research* 4 (1994): 41–59.

Feldman, "Daniel"   Feldman, Louis H. "Josephus' Portrait of Daniel." *Henoch* 14 (1992): 37–96.

Feldman, "David"   Feldman, Louis H. "Josephus' Portrait of David." *HUCA* 60 (1989): 129–74.

Feldman, "Elijah"   Feldman, Louis H. "Josephus' Portrait of Elijah." *Scandinavian Journal of the Old Testament* 8 (1994): 61–86.

Feldman, "Ezra"   Feldman, Louis H. "Josephus' Portrait of Ezra." *VT* 43 (1993): 190–214.

Feldman, "God-Fearers"   Feldman, Louis H. "The Omnipresence of the God-Fearers." *BAR* 12, no. 5 (September/October 1986): 58–69.

Feldman, "Hellenism"   Feldman, Louis H. "How Much Hellenism in Jewish Palestine?" *HUCA* 57 (1986): 83–111.

Feldman, "Hellenizations"   Feldman, Louis H. "Hellenizations in Josephus' *Jewish Antiquities:* The Portrait of Abraham." Pages 133–53 in *Josephus, Judaism, and Christianity.* Edited by Louis H. Feldman and Gohei Hata. Detroit: Wayne State University Press, 1987.

Feldman, "Hezekiah"    Feldman, Louis H. "Josephus's Portrait of Hezekiah." *JBL* 111 (1992): 597–610.

Feldman, "Intimations"    Feldman, Louis H. "Pro-Jewish Intimations in Anti-Jewish Remarks Cited in Josephus' *Against Apion*." *JQR* 78 (1987–1988): 187–251.

Feldman, "Introduction"    Feldman, Louis H. Introduction. Pages 17–49 in *Josephus, the Bible, and History*. Edited by Louis H. Feldman and Gohei Hata. Detroit: Wayne State University Press, 1989.

Feldman, "Isaac"    Feldman, Louis H. "Josephus' Portrait of Isaac." *Rivista di storia e letteratura religiosa* 29 (1993): 3–33.

Feldman, "Jacob"    Feldman, Louis H. "Josephus' Portrait of Jacob." *JQR* 79 (1988–1989): 101–51.

Feldman, "Jehoram"    Feldman, Louis H. "Josephus's Portrait of Jehoram, King of Israel." *Bulletin of the John Rylands University Library* 76 (1994): 3–20.

Feldman, "Jehoshaphat"    Feldman, Louis H. "Josephus' Portrait of Jehoshaphat." *Scripta classica israelica* 12 (1993): 159–75.

Feldman, "Jeroboam"    Feldman, Louis H. "Josephus' Portrait of Jeroboam." *Andrews University Seminary Studies* 31 (1993): 29–51.

Feldman, "Jonah"    Feldman, Louis H. "Josephus' Interpretation of Jonah." *Association for Jewish Studies Review* 17 (1992): 1–29.

Feldman, "Joseph"    Feldman, Louis H. "Josephus' Portrait of Joseph." *RB* 99 (1992): 397–417, 504–28.

Feldman, "Joshua"    Feldman, Louis H. "Josephus's Portrait of Joshua." *HTR* 82 (1989): 351–76.

Feldman, "Josiah"    Feldman, Louis H. "Josephus' Portrait of Josiah." *Louvain Studies* 18 (1993): 110–30.

Feldman, "Manasseh"    Feldman, Louis H. "Josephus' Portrait of Manasseh." *JSP* 9 (1991): 3–20.

Feldman, "Methods and Tendencies"    Feldman, Louis H. "Josephus: Interpretive Methods and Tendencies." Pages 590–96 in *Dictionary of New Testament Background*. Edited by Craig A. Evans and Stanley E. Porter. Downers Grove, Ill.: InterVarsity, 2000.

Feldman, "Moses"    Feldman, Louis H. "Josephus' Portrait of Moses." *JQR* 82 (1991–1992): 285–328; 83 (1992–1993): 7–50.

Feldman, "Nehemiah"    Feldman, Louis H. "Josephus' Portrait of Nehemiah." *JJS* 43 (1992): 187–202.

Feldman, "Noah"    Feldman, Louis H. "Josephus' Portrait of Noah and Its Parallels in Philo, Pseudo-Philo's *Biblical Antiquities*, and Rabbinic Midrashim." *Proceedings of the American Academy of Jewish Research* 55 (1988): 31–57.

Feldman, "Palestine"    Feldman, Louis H. "Some Observations on the Name of Palestine." *HUCA* 61 (1990): 1–23.

Feldman, "Pharaohs"    Feldman, Louis H. "Josephus' Portraits of the Pharaohs." *Syllecta Classica* 4 (1993): 49–63.

Feldman, "Samson"    Feldman, Louis H. "Josephus' Version of Samson." *JSJ* 19 (1988): 171–214.

Feldman, "Samuel"    Feldman, Louis H. "Josephus' Portrait of Samuel." *Abr-Nahrain* 30 (1992): 103–45.

Feldman, "Saul"    Feldman, Louis H. "Josephus' Portrait of Saul." *HUCA* 53 (1982): 45–99.

Feldman, "Sympathizers"    Feldman, Louis H. "Proselytes and 'Sympathizers' in the Light of the New Inscriptions from Aphrodisias." *Revue des études juives* 148 (1989): 265–305.

Feldmeier, "Excursus"    Feldmeier, Reinhold. "Excursus: The Portrayal of Peter in the Synoptic Gospels." Pages 59–63 in *Studies in the Gospel of Mark*. By Martin Hengel. Translated by John Bowden. Philadelphia: Fortress, 1985.

Feldmeier, "Peter"    Feldmeier, Reinhard. "The Portrayal of Peter in the Synoptic Gospels." Pages 252–56 in *The Gospel and the Gospels*. Edited by Peter Stuhlmacher. Grand Rapids: Eerdmans, 1991.

Fennema, "Only Son"    Fennema, D. A. "John 1.18: 'God the Only Son.'" *NTS* 31 (1985): 124–35.

Fensham, "Hand"    Fensham, F. Charles. "Judas' Hand in the Bowl and Qumran." *RevQ* 5 (1964–1966): 259–61.

Fensham, "Love"    Fensham, F. Charles. "Love in the Writings of Qumrân and John." *Neotestamentica* 6 (1972): 67–77.

Fenske, "Feigenbaum"   Fenske, Wolfgang. "Unter dem Feigenbaum sah ich dich (Joh 1,48): Die Bedeutung der Nathanaelperikope für die Gesamtrezeption des Johannesevangeliums." *Theologische Zeitschrift* 54 (1998): 210–27.

Fenton, *John*   Fenton, J. C. *The Gospel according to John in the Revised Standard Version.* New Clarendon Bible. London: Oxford University Press, 1970.

Fenton, *Matthew*   Fenton, J. C. *Saint Matthew.* Philadelphia: Westminster, 1977.

Ferch, "Aeons"   Ferch, Arthur J. "The Two Aeons and the Messiah in Pseudo-Philo, 4 Ezra, and 2 Baruch." *Andrews University Seminary Studies* 15, no. 2 (1977): 135–51.

Ferguson, *Backgrounds*   Ferguson, Everett. *Backgrounds of Early Christianity.* 2d ed. Grand Rapids: Eerdmans, 1993.

Ferrando, "Filosofía"   Ferrando, Miguel A. "Filosofía y evangelio de Juan." *Teología y vida* 33 (1992): 27–34.

Ferraro, "Pneuma"   Ferraro, Giuseppe. "'Pneuma' in Giov. 13,21." *RivB* 28 (1980): 185–211.

Feuillet, *Apocalypse*   Feuillet, André. *The Apocalypse.* Translated by Thomas E. Crane. Staten Island, N.Y.: Alba House, 1965.

Feuillet, *Studies*   Feuillet, André. *Johannine Studies.* Translated by Thomas E. Crane. Staten Island, N.Y.: Alba House, 1964.

Fiensy, "Composition"   Fiensy, David A. "The Composition of the Jerusalem Church." Pages 213–36 in *The Book of Acts in Its Palestinian Setting.* Edited by Richard Bauckham. Vol. 4 of *The Book of Acts in Its First Century Setting.* Edited by Bruce W. Winter. Grand Rapids: Eerdmans, 1995.

Filson, "Ephesus"   Filson, Floyd V. "Ephesus and the New Testament." *BA* 8 (1945): 73–80.

Filson, *History*   Filson, Floyd V. *A New Testament History.* Philadelphia: Westminster, 1964.

Filson, "Life"   Filson, Floyd V. "The Gospel of Life, A Study of the Gospel of John." Pages 111–23 in *Current Issues in New Testament Interpretation: Essays in Honor of Otto A. Piper.* Edited by William Klassen and Graydon F. Snyder. New York: Harper & Row, 1962.

Finegan, *Archeology*   Finegan, Jack. *The Archeology of the New Testament.* Princeton, N.J.: Princeton University Press, 1969.

Finegan, *Records*   Finegan, Jack. *Hidden Records of the Life of Jesus.* Philadelphia: Pilgrim Press, 1969.

Finegan, *Religions*   Finegan, Jack. *The Archeology of World Religions.* Princeton, N.J.: Princeton University Press, 1952.

Finkel, "Liturgy"   Finkel, Asher. "Yavneh's Liturgy and Early Christianity." *Journal of Ecumenical Studies* 18 (1981): 231–50.

Finkelstein, "Core"   Finkelstein, Louis. "The Core of the Sifra: A Temple Textbook for Priests." *JQR* 80 (1989–1990): 15–34.

Finkelstein, "Documents"   Finkelstein, Louis. "Pre-Maccabean Documents in the Passover Haggadah." *HTR* 35 (1942): 291–332; 36 (1943): 1–38.

Finkelstein, *Making*   Finkelstein, Louis. *Pharisaism in the Making: Selected Essays.* New York: Ktav, 1972.

Finkelstein, *Pharisees*   Finkelstein, Louis. *The Pharisees: The Sociological Background of Their Faith.* 2 vols. 3d ed. Philadelphia: Jewish Publication Society of America, 1962.

Finley, *Economy*   Finley, M. I. *The Ancient Economy.* Sather Classical Lectures 43. Berkeley: University of California Press, 1973.

Finn, "God-Fearers"   Finn, Thomas M. "The God-Fearers Reconsidered." *CBQ* 47 (1985): 75–84.

Fiore, "Theory"   Fiore, Benjamin. "The Theory and Practice of Friendship in Cicero." Pages 59–76 in *Greco-Roman Perspectives on Friendship.* Edited by John T. Fitzgerald. SBLRBS 34. Atlanta: Scholars Press, 1997.

Fiorenza, "Apocalyptic"   Fiorenza, Elisabeth Schüssler. "Apocalyptic and Gnosis in the Book of Revelation." *JBL* 92 (1973): 565–81.

Fiorenza, *Revelation*   Fiorenza, Elisabeth Schüssler. *The Book of Revelation: Justice and Judgment.* Philadelphia: Fortress, 1985.

Fischel, "Gnosticism"   Fischel, H. A. "Jewish Gnosticism in the Fourth Gospel." *JBL* 65 (1946): 157–74.

Fischer, "Christus"   Fischer, Karl Martin. "Der johanneische Christus und der gnostiche Erlöser." Pages 245–67 in *Gnosis und Neues Testament: Studien aus Religionswissenschaft und Theologie.* Edited by Karl-Wolfgang Tröger. Berlin: Gerd Mohn, 1973.

Fischer and Stein, "Marble"   Fischer, Moshe L., and Alla Stein. "Josephus on the Use of Marble in Building Projects of Herod the Great." *JJS* 45 (1994): 79–85.

Fisher, "Polemic"   Fisher, Eugene J. "From Polemic to Objectivity? A Short History of the Use and Abuse of Hebrew Sources by Recent Christian New Testament Scholarship." *Hebrew Studies* 20–21 (1979–1980): 199–207.

Fishwick, "Caesar"   Fishwick, Duncan. "The Temple of Caesar at Alexandria." *American Journal of Ancient History* 9, no. 2 (1984): 131–34.

Fishwick, "Caesareum"   Fishwick, Duncan. "The Caesareum at Alexandria Again." *American Journal of Ancient History* 12, no. 1 (1995): 62–72.

Fishwick, "Ovid"   Fishwick, Duncan. "Ovid and Divus Augustus." *Classical Philology* 86 (1991): 36–41.

Fishwick, "Pliny"   Fishwick, Duncan. "Pliny and the Christians: The Rites *ad imaginem principis*." *American Journal of Ancient History* 9, no. 2 (1984): 123–30.

Fisk, "Bible"   Fisk, Bruce N. "Rewritten Bible in Pseudepigrapha and Qumran." Pages 947–53 in *Dictionary of New Testament Background*. Edited by Craig A. Evans and Stanley E. Porter. Downers Grove, Ill.: InterVarsity, 2000.

Fitzgerald, "Aristotle"   Fitzgerald, John T. "Friendship in the Greek World Prior to Aristotle." Pages 13–34 in *Greco-Roman Perspectives on Friendship*. Edited by John T. Fitzgerald. SBLRBS 34. Atlanta: Scholars Press, 1997.

Fitzgerald, *Cracks*   Fitzgerald, John T. *Cracks in an Earthen Vessel: An Examination of the Catalogues of Hardships in the Corinthian Correspondence*. SBLDS 99. Atlanta: Scholars Press, 1988.

Fitzgerald, *Friendship*   Fitzgerald, John T., ed. *Greco-Roman Perspectives on Friendship*. SBLRBS 34. Atlanta: Scholars Press, 1997.

Fitzgerald, "Introduction"   Fitzgerald, John T. Introduction. 1–11 in *Greco-Roman Perspectives on Friendship*. Edited by John T. Fitzgerald. SBLRBS 34. Atlanta: Scholars Press, 1997.

Fitzmyer, "4Q246"   Fitzmyer, Joseph A. "4Q246: The 'Son of God' Document from Qumran." *Biblica* 74 (1993): 153–74.

Fitzmyer, *Apocryphon*   Fitzmyer, Joseph A. *The Genesis Apocryphon of Qumran Cave 1: A Commentary*. 2d rev. ed. Biblia et Orientalia 18A. Rome: Biblical Institute Press, 1971.

Fitzmyer, "Christianity"   Fitzmyer, Joseph A. "Jewish Christianity in Acts in Light of the Qumran Scrolls." Pages 233–57 in *Studies in Luke–Acts: Essays in Honor of Paul Schubert*. Edited by Leander E. Keck and J. Louis Martyn. Nashville: Abingdon, 1966.

Fitzmyer, "Elijah"   Fitzmyer, Joseph A. "More about Elijah Coming First." *JBL* 104 (1985): 295–96.

Fitzmyer, *Essays*   Fitzmyer, Joseph A. *Essays on the Semitic Background of the New Testament*. 2d ed. SBLSBS 5. Missoula, Mont.: Scholars Press, 1974.

Fitzmyer, "Quotations"   Fitzmyer, Joseph A. "The Use of Explicit Old Testament Quotations in Qumran Literature and in the New Testament." *NTS* 7 (1960–1961): 297–333.

Fitzmyer, *Scrolls*   Fitzmyer, Joseph A. *The Dead Sea Scrolls: Major Publications and Tools for Study*. SBLSBS 8. Missoula, Mont.: Scholars Press, 1977.

Flanagan, "Women"   Flanagan, Neal M. "The Position of Women in the Writings of St. Luke." *Marianum* 40 (1978): 288–304.

Flannery, *Anguish*   Flannery, Edward H. *The Anguish of the Jews: Twenty-Three Centuries of Anti-Semitism*. New York: Macmillan, 1965.

Fleddermann, "Flight"   Fleddermann, Harry. "The Flight of a Naked Young Man (Mark 14:51–52)." *CBQ* 41 (1979): 412–18.

Fletcher, "Women"   Fletcher, Mary-Elsie C. "The Role of Women in the Book of John." *Evangelical Journal* 12 (1994): 41–48.

Floor, "Spirit"   Floor, L. "The Lord and the Holy Spirit in the Fourth Gospel." *Neotestamentica* 2 (1968): 122–30.

Flory, "Women"   Flory, M. B. "Where Women Precede Men: Factors Influencing the Order of Names in Roman Epitaphs." *Classical Journal* 79 (1983–1984): 216–24.

Flowers, "Pneumati"   Flowers, H. J. "En pneumati hagiō kai puri." *ExpTim* 64 (1952–1953): 155–56.

Flusser, "Gnosticism"   Flusser, David. "Gnosticism." Pages 637–38 in vol. 7 of *Encyclopaedia judaica*. 16 vols. Jerusalem: Keter, 1972.

Flusser, "Goddess"   Flusser, David. "The Great Goddess of Samaria." *IEJ* 25 (1975): 13–20.

Flusser, *Judaism*    Flusser, David. *Judaism and the Origins of Christianity.* Jerusalem: Magnes Press, Hebrew University, 1988.

Flusser, "Mastema"    Flusser, David. "Mastema." Columns 1119–20 in vol. 11 of *Encyclopaedia judaica.* 16 vols. Jerusalem: Keter, 1972.

Flusser, "Mqst"    Flusser, David. "'Mqst mᶜśy htwrh' wbrkt hmynym. ['Some of the Precepts of the Torah' from Qumran (4QMMT) and the Benediction against the Heretics]." *Tarbiz* 61 (1992): 333–74.

Flusser, "Paganism"    Flusser, David. "Paganism in Palestine." Pages 1065–1100 in Safrai and Stern, *Jewish People.*

Flusser and Safrai, "Hypostasis"    Flusser, David, and Shmuel Safrai. "The Essene Doctrine of Hypostasis and Rabbi Meir." *Immanuel* 14 (1982): 47–57.

Foakes-Jackson and Lake, "Beginnings"    Foakes-Jackson, F. J., and Kirsopp Lake, eds. *The Beginnings of Christianity.* 5 vols. 1920–1933. Repr., Grand Rapids: Baker, 1979.

Foakes-Jackson and Lake, "Development"    Foakes-Jackson, F. J., and Kirsopp Lake. "The Development of Thought on the Spirit, the Church, and Baptism." Pages 321–44 in vol. 1 of *The Beginnings of Christianity.*

Foakes-Jackson and Lake, "Dispersion"    Foakes-Jackson, F. J., and Kirsopp Lake. "The Dispersion." Pages 137–168 in vol. 1 of *The Beginnings of Christianity.*

Foakes-Jackson and Lake, "Evidence"    Foakes-Jackson, F. J., and Kirsopp Lake. "The Internal Evidence of Acts." Pages 121–204 in vol. 2 of *The Beginnings of Christianity.*

Foerster, "Geist"    Foerster, Werner. "Der Heilige Geist im Spätjudentum." *NTS* 8 (1961–1962): 117–34.

Foerster, "κύριος"    Foerster, Werner. "κύριος, κτλ. E" *TDNT* 3:1086–95.

Foerster, "Reliefs"    Foerster, G. "Some Menorah Reliefs from Galilee." *Israel Exploration Journal* 24, nos. 3–4 (1974): 191–96.

Forbes, *Prophecy*    Forbes, Christopher. *Prophecy and Inspired Speech in Early Christianity and Its Hellenistic Environment.* Tübingen: Mohr, 1995. Repr., Peabody, Mass.: Hendrickson, 1997.

Ford, *Abomination*    Ford, Desmond. *The Abomination of Desolation in Biblical Eschatology.* Washington, D.C.: University Press of America, 1979.

Ford, "Abraham"    Ford, J. Massyngberde. "'Thou Art 'Abraham' and upon This Rock . . . .'" *Heythrop Journal* 6 (1965): 289–301.

Ford, "Blood"    Ford, J. Massyngberde. "'Mingled Blood' from the Side of Christ (John XIX.34)." *NTS* 15 (1968–1969): 337–38.

Ford, "Influence"    Ford, J. Massyngberde. "Can We Exclude Samaritan Influence from Qumran?" *RevQ* 6 (1967–1969): 109–29.

Ford, *Revelation*    Ford, J. Massyngberde. *Revelation.* AB 38. Garden City, N.Y.: Doubleday, 1975.

Ford, "Shalom"    Ford, J. Massyngberde. "Shalom in the Johannine Corpus." *Horizons in Biblical Theology* 6, no. 2 (December 1984): 67–89.

Forestell, "Paraclete"    Forestell, J. T. "Jesus and the Paraclete in the Gospel of John." Pages 151–97 in *Word and Spirit: Essays in Honor of David Michael Stanley, S. J., on His 60th Birthday.* Edited by Joseph Plevnik. Willowdale, Ont: Regis College, 1975.

Fornara, *Nature of History*    Fornara, Charles William. *The Nature of History in Ancient Greece and Rome.* Berkeley: University of California Press, 1983.

Fortna, "Christology"    Fortna, Robert T. "Christology in the Fourth Gospel: Redaction-Critical Perspectives." *NTS* 21 (1974–1975): 489–504.

Fortna, "Locale"    Fortna, Robert T. "Theological Use of Locale in the Fourth Gospel." Pages 58–95 in *Gospel Studies in Honor of Sherman Elbridge Johnson.* Edited by Massey H. Shepherd and Edward C. Hobbs. Anglican Theological Review Supplement 3. Evanston, Ill.: Anglican Theological Review, 1974.

Fortna, *Predecessor*    Fortna, Robert Tomson. *The Fourth Gospel and Its Predecessor: From Narrative Source to Present Gospel.* Philadelphia: Fortress, 1988.

Fossum, "Gen"    Fossum, Jarl. "Gen. 1,26 and 2,7 in Judaism, Samaritanism, and Gnosticism." *JSJ* 16 (1985): 202–39.

Foster, "Introduction"    Foster, B. O. Introduction. Pages ix–xxxv in vol. 1 of Livy, *Ab urbe condita.* Translated by B. O. Foster, Frank Gardner, Evan T. Sage, A. C. Schlesinger. 14 vols. LCL. Cambridge: Harvard University Press, 1919–1959.

Foucart, *Associations religieuses*   Foucart, P. *Des associations religieuses chez les Grecs: Thiases, Éranes, Orgéons*. Paris: Chez Klincksieck, 1873. Repr., New York: Arno Press, 1975.

Fowler, "Meaning"   Fowler, David C. "The Meaning of 'Touch Me Not' in John 20:17." *EvQ* 47 (1975): 16–25.

France, "Authenticity"   France, R. T. "The Authenticity of the Sayings of Jesus." Pages 101–43 in *History, Criticism, and Faith*. Edited by Colin Brown. Downers Grove, Ill.: InterVarsity, 1976.

France, *Evangelist*   France, R. T. *Matthew: Evangelist and Teacher*. Grand Rapids: Zondervan, 1989.

France, "Exegesis"   France, R. T. "Exegesis in Practice: Two Examples." Pages 252–81 in *New Testament Interpretation: Essays on Principles and Methods*. Edited by I. Howard Marshall. Grand Rapids: Eerdmans, 1977.

France, "Historiography"   France, R. T. "Jewish Historiography, Midrash, and the Gospels." Pages 99–127 in *Studies in Midrash and Historiography*. Vol. 3 of *Gospel Perspectives*. Edited by R. T. France and David Wenham. Sheffield: JSOT Press, 1983.

France, *Matthew*   France, R. T. *Matthew*. Tyndale New Testament Commentaries. Grand Rapids: Eerdmans, 1985.

Francis, "Graffiti"   Francis, E. D. "Mithraic Graffiti from Dura-Europos." Pages 424–45 in vol. 2 of *Mithraic Studies: Proceedings of the First International Congress of Mithraic Studies*. Edited by John R. Hinnells. 2 vols. Manchester: Manchester University Press, 1975.

Francis, "Humility"   Francis, Fred O. "Humility and Angelic Worship in Col 2:18." Pages 163–95 in *Conflict at Colossae: A Problem in the Interpretation of Early Christianity Illustrated by Selected Modern Studies*. Edited and translated by Fred O. Francis and Wayne A. Meeks. SBLSBS 4. Missoula, Mont.: Society of Biblical Literature, 1973.

Franck, *Revelation*   Franck, Eskil. *Revelation Taught: The Paraclete in the Gospel of John*. Coniectanea biblica, New Testament series 14. Lund: Gleerup, 1985.

Frank, *Aspects*   Frank, Tenney. *Aspects of Social Behavior in Ancient Rome*. Cambridge: Harvard University Press, 1932.

Frankfurter, "City"   Frankfurter, David. "Lest Egypt's City Be Deserted: Religion and Ideology in the Egyptian Response to the Jewish Revolt (116–117 C.E.)." *JJS* 43 (1992): 203–20.

Frankfurter, *Religion in Egypt*   Frankfurter, David. *Religion in Roman Egypt: Assimilation and Resistance*. Princeton, N.J.: Princeton University Press, 1998.

Franzmann and Klinger, "Stories"   Franzmann, M., and M. Klinger. "The Call Stories of John 1 and John 21." *St. Vladimir's Theological Quarterly* 36 (1992): 7–15.

Fredriksen, *Christ*   Fredriksen, Paula. *From Jesus to Christ: The Origins of the New Testament Images of Jesus*. New Haven: Yale University Press, 1988.

Freed, "*Egō Eimi*"   Freed, Edwin D. "*Egō Eimi* in John 1:20 and 4:25." *CBQ* 41 (1979): 288–91.

Freed, "Influences"   Freed, Edwin D. "Some Old Testament Influences on the Prologue of John." Pages 145–161 in *A Light unto My Path: Old Testament Studies in Honor of Jacob M. Myers*. Edited by Howard N. Bream, Ralph D. Heim, and Carey A. Moore. Gettysburg Theological Studies 4. Philadelphia: Temple University Press, 1974.

Freed, "Prelude"   Freed, Edwin D. "Theological Prelude to the Prologue of John's Gospel." *SJT* 32 (1979): 257–69.

Freed, *Quotations*   Freed, Edwin D. *Old Testament Quotations in the Gospel of John*. NovTSup 11. Leiden: Brill, 1965.

Freed, "Samaritan Converts"   Freed, Edwin D. "Did John Write His Gospel Partly to Win Samaritan Converts?" *NovT* 12 (1970): 241–56.

Freed, "Samaritan Influence"   Freed, Edwin D. "Samaritan Influence in the Gospel of John." *CBQ* 30 (1968): 580–87.

Freedman and Simon, *Midrash Rabbah*   Freedman, H., and M. Simon. *The Midrash Rabbah*. 5 vols. London: Soncino, 1977.

Frei, "Apologetics"   Frei, Hans. "Apologetics, Criticism, and the Loss of Narrative Interpretation." Pages 45–64 in *Why Narrative? Readings in Narrative Theology*. Edited by Stanley Hauerwas and L. Gregory Jones. Grand Rapids: Eerdmans, 1989.

Frenschkowski, "Indizien"   Frenschkowski, M. "Τὰ βαΐα τῶν φοινίκων (Joh 12, 13) und andere Indizien für einen ägyptischen Ursprung des Johannesevangeliums." *ZNW* 91, nos. 3–4 (2000): 212–29.

Freund, "Deception"  Freund, Richard A. "Lying and Deception in the Biblical and Post-biblical Judaic Tradition." *Scandanavian Journal of the Old Testament* 5 (1991): 45–61.

Freyne, "Disciples"  Freyne, Sean. "The Disciples in Mark and the *maskilim* in Daniel: A Comparison." *JSNT* 16 (1982): 7–23.

Freyne, "Ethos"  Freyne, Sean. "The Ethos of First-Century Galilee." *Proceedings of the Irish Biblical Association* 17 (1994): 69–79.

Freyne, "Galileans"  Freyne, Sean. "The Galileans in the Light of Josephus' *Vita*." *NTS* 26 (1979–1980): 397–413.

Freyne, *Galilee*  Freyne, Sean. *Galilee, Jesus, and the Gospels: Literary Approaches and Historical Investigations.* Philadelphia: Fortress, 1988.

Freyne, "Relations"  Freyne, Sean. "Galilee-Jerusalem Relations according to Josephus' *Life*." *NTS* 33 (1987): 600–609.

Freyne, "Religion"  Freyne, Sean. "Galilean Religion of the First Century C.E. against Its Social Background." *Proceedings of the Irish Biblical Association* 5 (1981): 98–114.

Frickenschmidt, *Evangelium als Biographie*  Frickenschmidt, Dirk. *Evangelium als Biographie: Die vier Evangelien im Rahmen antiker Erzählkunst.* Texte und Arbeiten zum neutestamentlichen Zeitalter 22. Tübingen: Francke, 1997.

Friedländer, *Life*  Friedländer, Ludwig. *Roman Life and Manners under the Early Empire.* Translated from the 7th rev. ed. by Leonard A. Magnus, J. H. Freese, and A. B. Gough. 4 vols. Vols. 1 and 4: New York: Barnes & Noble, 1907, 1965. Vols. 2 and 3: New York: Dutton, 1908–1913.

Friedman, "Features"  Friedman, Theodore. "Some Unexplained Features of Ancient Synagogues." *Conservative Judaism* 36, no. 3 (spring 1983): 35–42.

Friend, "Agency"  Friend, Howard S. "Like Father, Like Son: A Discussion of the Concept of Agency in Halakah and John." *Ashland Theological Journal* 21 (1990): 18–28.

Frier, "Annuities"  Frier, Bruce W. "Subsistence Annuities and per Capita Income in the Early Roman Empire." *Classical Philology* 88 (1993): 222–30.

Fritsch, "Angelos"  Fritsch, I. "' . . . videbitis . . . angelos Dei ascendentes et descendentes super Filium hominis [Io. 1,51]." *Verbum Domini* 37 (1959): 3–11.

Fritsch, *Community*  Fritsch, Charles T. *The Qumran Community: Its History and Scrolls.* New York: Macmillan, 1956.

Fritz, "Midrash"  Fritz, Maureena. "A Midrash: The Self-Limitation of God." *Journal of Ecumenical Studies* 22 (1985): 703–14.

Fry et al., *Religions*  Fry, C. George, James R. King, Eugene R. Swanger, and Herbert C. Wolf. *Great Asian Religions.* Grand Rapids: Baker, 1984.

Frymer-Kensky, "Relationships"  Frymer-Kensky, Tikva. "Patriarchal Family Relationships and Near Eastern Law." *BA* 44 (1981): 209–14.

Fujita, "Plant"  Fujita, S. "The Metaphor of Plant in Jewish Literature of the Intertestamental Period." *JSJ* 7 (1976): 30–45.

Fuks, "Freedmen"  Fuks, Gideon. "Where Have All the Freedmen Gone? On an Anomaly in the Jewish Grave-Inscriptions from Rome." *JJS* 36 (1985): 25–32.

Fuller, *Formation*  Fuller, Reginald H. *The Formation of the Resurrection Narratives.* New York: Macmillan, 1971.

Fuller, *Gospel*  Fuller, Daniel P. *Gospel and Law: Contrast or Continuum?* Grand Rapids: Eerdmans, 1980.

Fuller, "'Jews'"  Fuller, Reginald H. "The 'Jews' in the Fourth Gospel." *Dialog* 16 (1977): 31–37.

Fuller, "Jn 20"  Fuller, Reginald H. "John 20:19–23." *Interpretation* 32 (1978): 180–84.

Funk, *Gospels*  Funk, Robert W., Roy W. Hoover, and the Jesus Seminar. *The Five Gospels: The Search for the Authentic Words of Jesus.* New York: Macmillan, 1993.

Funk, "*Parousia*"  Funk, Robert W. "The Apostolic *Parousia*: Form and Significance." Pages 249–68 in *Christian History and Interpretation: Studies Presented to John Knox.* Edited by W. R. Farmer, C. F. D. Moule, and R. R. Niebuhr. Cambridge: Cambridge University Press, 1967.

Furness, "Hymn"  Furness, J. M. "Behind the Philippian Hymn." *ExpTim* 79 (1967–1968): 178–82.

Fusco, "Sezioni-noi"  Fusco, Vittorio. "Le sezioni-noi degli Atti nella discussione recente." *Bibbia e oriente* 25 (1983): 73–86.

Gabriel, "Faith"  Gabriel, A. "Faith and Rebirth in the Fourth Gospel." *Biblebhashyam* 16, no. 4 (1990): 205–15.

Gafni, "Josephus"  Gafni, Isaiah M. "Josephus and 1 Maccabees." Pages 116–31 in *Josephus, the Bible, and History*. Edited by Louis H. Feldman and Gohei Hata. Detroit: Wayne State University Press, 1989.

Gager, *Anti-Semitism*  Gager, John G. *The Origins of Anti-Semitism: Attitudes toward Judaism in Pagan and Christian Antiquity*. New York: Oxford University Press, 1983.

Gager, "Judaism"  Gager, John G. "Judaism as Seen by Outsiders." Pages 99–116 in *Early Judaism and Its Modern Interpreters*. Edited by Robert A. Kraft and George W. E. Nickelsburg. SBLBMI 2. Atlanta: Scholars Press, 1986.

Gager, *Kingdom*  Gager, John G. *Kingdom and Community: The Social World of Early Christianity*. Englewood Cliffs, N.J.: Prentice-Hall, 1975.

Gager, "Magician"  Gager, John G. "Moses the Magician: Hero of an Ancient Counter-culture?" *Helios* 21 (1994): 179–88.

Gager, *Moses*  Gager, John G. *Moses in Greco-Roman Paganism*. SBLMS 16. Nashville: Abingdon Press, for the Society of Biblical Literature, 1972.

Gager, "Synagogues"  Gager, John G. "Jews, Gentiles, and Synagogues in the Book of Acts." *HTR* 79 (1986): 91–99.

Gal, "T'syyt"  Gal, Zvi. "T'syyt kly 'bn bglyl hthtwn." *'Atiqot* 20 (1991): 25–26.

Gallagher, "Conversion"  Gallagher, Eugene V. "Conversion and Community in Late Antiquity." *Journal of Religion* 73 (1993): 1–15.

Gallagher, *Divine Man*  Gallagher, Eugene V. *Divine Man or Magician? Celsus and Origen on Jesus*. SBLDS 64. Chico, Calif.: Scholars Press, 1982.

Gamble, "Canonical Formation"  Gamble, Harry Y. "Canonical Formation of the New Testament." Pages 183–94 in *Dictionary of New Testament Background*. Edited by Craig A. Evans and Stanley E. Porter. Downers Grove, Ill.: InterVarsity, 2000.

Gamble, "Literacy"  Gamble, Harry Y. "Literacy and Book Culture." Pages 644–48 in *Dictionary of New Testament Background*. Edited by Craig A. Evans and Stanley E. Porter. Downers Grove, Ill.: InterVarsity, 2000.

Gamble, "Philosophy"  Gamble, J. "The Philosophy of the Fourth Gospel." *The Expositor*, Ninth Series 4 (1925): 50–59.

Gammie, "Dualism"  Gammie, John G. "Spatial and Ethical Dualism in Jewish Wisdom and Apocalyptic Literature." *JBL* 93 (1974): 356–85.

Garber, "Sheep"  Garber, P. L. "Sheep; Shepherd." Pages 462–65 in vol. 4 of *The International Standard Bible Encyclopedia*. Edited by Geoffrey W. Bromiley. 4 vols. Grand Rapids: Eerdmans, 1979–1988.

Garcia, "Lazare"  Garcia, Hugues. "Lazare, du mort vivant au disciple bien-aimé: Le cycle trajectoire narrative de Lazare dans le quatrième évangile." *RevScRel* 73, no. 3 (1999): 259–92.

García de la Fuente, "Búsqueda"  García de la Fuente, O. "La búsqueda de Dios en los escritos de Qumrán." *EstBib* 32 (1973): 25–42.

García Martínez, "Textos"  García Martínez, Florentino. "Nuevos textos mesiánicos de Qumrán y el mesías del Nuevo Testamento." *Communio* 26 (1993): 3–31.

Gard, *Method*  Gard, Donald H. *The Exegetical Method of the Greek Translator of the Book of Job*. SBLMS 8. Philadelphia: Society of Biblical Literature, 1952.

Gardner, "Mqbym"  Gardner, A. E. "Mqbym g' wmqbym d' whmšbr bymy hmqbym." *Zion* 53 (1988): 291–301.

Gardner, *Women*  Gardner, Jane F. *Women in Roman Law and Society*. Bloomington: Indiana University Press, 1986.

Gardner-Smith, *Gospels*  Gardner-Smith, Percival. *Saint John and the Synoptic Gospels*. Cambridge: Cambridge University Press, 1938.

Garland, *Matthew*  Garland, David E. *Reading Matthew: A Literary and Theological Commentary on the First Gospel*. New York: Crossroad, 1993.

Garland, "Quotations"  Garland, David E. "The Fulfillment Quotations in John's Account of the Crucifixion." Pages 229–50 in *Perspectives on John: Method and Interpretation in the Fourth Gospel*. Edited by Robert B. Sloan and Mikeal C. Parsons. National Association of the Baptist Professors of Religion Special Studies Series 11. Lewiston, N.Y.: Mellen, 1993.

Garner, "Synagogue"  Garner, G. G. "The Synagogue at Capernaum." *Buried History* 20, no. 3 (1984): 49–52.

Garner, "Temples"   Garner, G. G. "The Temples of Mt. Gerizim: Tell er Ras—Probable Site of the Samaritan Temple." *Buried History* 11, no. 1 (1975): 33–42.

Garnet, "Baptism"   Garnet, Paul. "The Baptism of Jesus and the Son of Man Idea." *JSNT* 9 (1980): 49–65.

Garnet, "Soteriology"   Garnet, Paul. "Qumran Light on Pauline Soteriology." Pages 19–32 in *Pauline Studies: Essays Presented to Professor F. F. Bruce on His 70th Birthday.* Edited by Donald A. Hagner and Murray J. Harris. Grand Rapids: Eerdmans, 1980.

Garnsey and Saller, *Empire*   Garnsey, Peter, and Richard Saller. *The Roman Empire: Economy, Society, and Culture.* Berkeley: University of California Press, 1987.

Garte, "Resurrection"   Garte, Edna. "The Theme of Resurrection in the Dura-Europos Synagogue Paintings." *JQR* 64 (1973–1974): 1–15.

Gärtner, "Know"   Gärtner, Bertril E. "The Pauline and Johannine Idea of 'to Know God' against the Hellenistic Background." *NTS* 14 (1967–1968): 209–31.

Gärtner, *Temple*   Gärtner, Bertril. *The Temple and the Community in Qumran and the New Testament: A Comparative Study in the Temple Symbolism of the Qumran Texts and the New Testament.* Cambridge: Cambridge University Press, 1965.

Garvie, "Prologue"   Garvie, Alfred E. "The Prologue to the Fourth Gospel and the Evangelist's Theological Reflexions." *The Expositor,* Eighth Series 10 (1915): 163–72.

Gasparro, *Soteriology*   Gasparro, Giulia Sfameni. *Soteriology and Mystic Aspects in the Cult of Cybele and Attis.* Études préliminaires aux religions orientales dans l'empire romain 103. Leiden: Brill, 1985.

Gasque, *History*   Gasque, W. Ward. *A History of the Criticism of the Acts of the Apostles.* Grand Rapids: Eerdmans.

Gasque, "Speeches"   Gasque, W. Ward. "The Speeches of Acts: Dibelius Reconsidered." Pages 232–50 in *New Dimensions in New Testament Study.* Edited by Richard N. Longenecker and Merrill C. Tenney. Grand Rapids: Zondervan, 1974.

Gaster, *Scriptures*   Gaster, Theodor H. *The Dead Sea Scriptures.* Garden City, N.Y.: Doubleday, 1976.

Gaston, *Stone*   Gaston, Lloyd. *No Stone on Another: Studies in the Significance of the Fall of Jerusalem in the Synoptic Gospels.* NovTSup 23. Leiden: Brill, 1970.

Gaster, *Studies*   Gaster, Moses. *Studies and Texts in Folklore, Magic, Mediaeval Romance, Hebrew Apocrypha, and Samaritan Archaeology.* 3 vols. New York: Ktav, 1971.

Gaustad, *History*   Gaustad, Edwin S., ed. *A Documentary History of Religion in Americas since 1965.* Grand Rapids: Eerdmans, 1983.

Gaventa, "Archive"   Gaventa, Beverly Roberts. "The Archive of Excess: John 21 and the Problem of Narrative Closure." Pages 240–52 in *Exploring the Gospel of John: In Honor of D. Moody Smith.* Edited by R. Alan Culpepper and C. Clifton Black. Louisville, Ky.: Westminster John Knox, 1996.

Gee, "Spring"   Gee, D. H. "Why Did Peter Spring into the Sea? (John 21:7)." *JTS* NS 40 (1989): 481–89.

Geiger, "ᵓpyqwrws"   Geiger, Joseph. "ltwldwt hmynh 'ᵓpyqwrws' [To the History of the Term Apikoros]." *Tarbiz* 42, nos. 3–4 (1973): 499–500.

Geiger, "Titulus Crucis"   Geiger, Joseph. "Titulus Crucis." *Scripta Classica Israelica* 15 (1996): 202–7.

Geivett and Habermas, *Miracles*   Geivett, R. Douglas, and Gary R. Habermas. *In Defense of Miracles: A Comprehensive Case for God's Action in History.* Downers Grove, Ill.: InterVarsity, 1997.

Geldenhuys, *Luke*   Geldenhuys, Norval. *The Gospel of Luke.* London: Marshall, Morgan & Scott, 1950; Grand Rapids: Eerdmans, 1951.

Gelfand, "Disorders"   Gelfand, Michael. "Psychiatric Disorders as Recognized by the Shona." Pages 156–73 in *Magic, Faith, and Healing: Studies in Primitive Psychiatry Today.* Edited by Ari Kiev. Foreword by Jerome D. Frank. New York: Free Press, Macmillan, 1964.

Gempf, "Speaking"   Gempf, Conrad. "Public Speaking and Published Accounts." Pages 259–303 in *The Book of Acts in Its Ancient Literary Setting.* Edited by Bruce W. Winter and Andrew D. Clarke. Vol. 1 of *The Book of Acts in Its First Century Setting.* Edited by Bruce W. Winter. Grand Rapids: Eerdmans, 1993.

Gemser, "Controversy-Pattern"   Gemser, B. "The *Rîb-* or Controversy-Pattern in Hebrew Mental-ity." Pages 120–37 in *Wisdom in Israel and in the Ancient Near East: Presented to Professor Harold Henry Rowley for His 65th Birthday*. Edited by Martin Noth and D. Winton Thomas. Vetus Testamentum Supplements 3. Leiden: Brill, 1960.

Gemünden, "Palmensymbolik"   Gemünden, P. von. "Palmensymbolik in Joh 12,13." *Zeitschrift des Deutschen Palästina-Vereins* 114 (1998): 39–70.

Georgi, *Opponents*   Georgi, Dieter. *The Opponents of Paul in Second Corinthians*. Philadelphia: Fortress, 1986.

Georgi, "Reasons"   Georgi, Dieter. "Socioeconomic Reasons for the 'Divine Man' as a Propagan-distic Pattern." Pages 27–42 in *Aspects of Religious Propaganda in Judaism and Early Christian-ity*. Edited by Elisabeth Schüssler Fiorenza. University of Notre Dame Center for the Study of Judaism and Christianity in Antiquity 2. Notre Dame, Ind.: University of Notre Dame Press, 1976.

Gerhardsson, *Memory*   Gerhardsson, Birger. *Memory and Manuscript: Oral Tradition and Written Transmission in Rabbinic Judaism and Early Christianity*. Acta seminarii neotestamentici upsaliensis 22. Uppsala: Gleerup, 1961. Reprinted as *Memory and Manuscript: Oral Tradition and Written Transmission in Rabbinic Judaism and Early Christianity* (1961) with *Tradition and Transmission in Early Christianity* (1964). Grand Rapids: Eerdmans, 1998.

Gerhardsson, *Origins*   Gerhardsson, Birger. *The Origins of the Gospel Traditions*. Philadelphia: For-tress, 1979.

Gerhardsson, "Path"   Gerhardsson, Birger. "The Path of the Gospel Tradition." Pages 75–96 in *The Gospel and the Gospels*. Edited by Peter Stuhlmacher. Grand Rapids: Eerdmans, 1991.

Gericke, "*Logos*-Philosophy"   Gericke, J. D. "Dimensions of the *Logos*: From *Logos*-Philosophy to *Logos*-Theology." *Acta patristica et byzantina* 11 (2000): 93–116.

Gero, "Messiah"   Gero, Stephen. "'My Son the Messiah': A Note on 4 Esr 7:28–29." *ZNW* 66 (1975): 264–67.

Gero, "Polemic"   Gero, Stephen. "Jewish Polemic in the Martyrium Pionii and a 'Jesus' Passage from the Talmud." *JJS* 29 (1978): 164–68.

Geroussis, *Delphi*   Geroussis, Panayotis. *Guide to Delphi*. 2d ed. n.p.: 1967.

Gershenzon and Slomovic. "Debate"   Gershenzon, Rosalie, and Elieser Slomovic. "A Second-Century Jewish-Gnostic Debate: Rabbi Jose ben Halafta and the Matron." *JSJ* 16 (1985): 1–41.

Gersht, "Reader"   Gersht, Rivka. "The Reader of the Scroll from Caesarea Maritima." *Tel Aviv* 13–14 (1986–87): 67–70, plate 4.

Gervers, "Iconography"   Gervers, Michael. "The Iconography of the Cave in Christian and Mith-raic Tradition." Pages 579–99 in *Mysteria Mithrae*. Edited by Ugo Bianchi. Études préliminaires aux religions orientales dans l'empire romain 80. Leiden: Brill, 1979.

Geyser, "Israel"   Geyser, Albert S. "Israel in the Fourth Gospel." *Neotestamentica* 20 (1986): 13–20.

Geyser, "Semeion"   Geyser, A. "The Semeion at Cana of the Galilee." Pages 12–21 in *Studies in John: Presented to Professor Dr. J. N. Sevenster on the Occasion of His Seventieth Birthday*. Edited by W. C. van Unnik. NovTSup 24. Leiden: Brill, 1970.

Gibbs, *Creation*   Gibbs, John G. *Creation and Redemption: A Study in Pauline Theology*. NovTSup 26. Leiden: Brill, 1971.

Gibert, "L'invention"   Gibert, Pierre. "L'invention d'un genre littéraire." *Lumière et vie* 30 (153–54, 1981): 19–33.

Giblet, "Développements"   Giblet, J. "Développements dans la théologue johannique." Pages 45–72 in *L'évangile de Jean: Sources, rédaction, théologie*. Edited by Marinus De Jonge. BETL 45. Gembloux: J. Duculot; Leuven: Leuven University Press, 1977.

Giblin, "Suggestion"   Giblin, C. H. "Suggestion, Negative Response, and Positive Action in St. John's Portrayal of Jesus (2:1–11; 4:46–54; 7:2–14; 11:1–44)." *NTS* 26 (1979–1980): 197–211.

Giesen, "Ermutigung"   Giesen, Heinz. "Ermutigung zur Glaubenstreue in schwerer Zeit: Zum Zweck der Johannesoffenbarung." *Trierer theologische Zeitschrift* 105 (1996): 61–76.

Gilbert, "Convert"   Gilbert, Gary. "The Making of a Jew: 'God-Fearer' or Convert in the Story of Izates." *Union Seminary Quarterly Review* 44 (1990–1991): 299–313.

Gilbert, "Notes"   Gilbert, George H. "Exegetical Notes: John, Chapter I." *The Biblical World* 13 (1899): 42–46.

Ginsberg, "Scrolls"    Ginsberg, H. L. "The Cave Scrolls and the Jewish Sects: New Light on a Scholarly Mystery." *Commentary* 16 (1953): 77–81.

Ginsburg, *Essenes*/Ginsburg, *Kabbalah*    Ginsburg, Christian D. *The Essenes: Their History and Doctrines* (1864); *The Kabbalah: Its Doctrines, Development, and Literature* (1863). Repr., London: Routledge & Kegan Paul, 1955.

Ginzberg, "Cabala"    Ginzberg, Louis. "Cabala." Pages 459–79 in vol. 3 of *The Jewish Encyclopedia*. Edited by Isidore Singer. 12 vols. New York: Funk & Wagnalls, 1901–1906.

Girard, "Composition"    Girard, Marc. "La composition structurelle des sept 'signes' dans le quatrième évangile." *SR* 9 (1980): 315–24.

Gispert-Sauch, "Upanisad"    Gispert-Sauch, G. "Brhadaranyaka Upanisad 1.3.28 in Greek Literature?" *Vidyajyoti* 40 (1976): 177–80.

Gitler, "Amulets"    Gitler, Haim. "Four Magical and Christian Amulets." *Studii biblici franciscani liber annuus* 40 (1990): 365–74.

Glasson, *Advent*    Glasson, T. Francis. *The Second Advent: The Origin of the New Testament Doctrine.* 3d rev. ed. London: Epworth, 1963.

Glasson, "Anecdote"    Glasson, T. Francis. "The Place of the Anecdote: A Note on Form Criticism." *JTS* NS 32 (1981): 142–250.

Glasson, "Colossians"    Glasson, T. Francis. "Colossians I 18, 15 and Sirach XXIV." *NovT* 11 (1969): 154–56.

Glasson, "John 1 9"    Glasson, T. Francis. "John 1 9 and a Rabbinic Tradition." *ZNW* 46 (1958): 288–90.

Glasson, "Logos Doctrine"    Glasson, T. Francis. "Heraclitus' Alleged Logos Doctrine." *JTS* NS 3 (1952): 231–38.

Glasson, *Moses*    Glasson, T. Francis. *Moses in the Fourth Gospel.* SBT 40. Naperville, Ill.: Allenson, 1963.

Glasson, "Notes"    Glasson, T. Francis. "Two Notes on the Philippians Hymn (II.6–11)." *NTS* 21 (1974–1975): 133–39.

Glatzer, "Prophecy"    Glatzer, Nahum Norbert. "A Study of the Talmudic Interpretation of Prophecy." *The Review of Religion* 10 (1945–1946): 115–37.

Glaze, "Emphases"    Glaze, R. E. "Evangelistic Emphases in the Gospel of John." *Theological Educator* 57 (1998): 11–21.

Gloer, "Disciples"    Gloer, W. Hulitt. "'Come and See': Disciples and Discipleship in the Fourth Gospel." In *Perspectives on John: Method and Interpretation in the Fourth Gospel.* Pages 269–301. National Association of the Baptist Professors of Religion Special Studies 11. Edited by Robert B. Sloan and Mikeal A. Parsons. Lewiston, N.Y.: Mellen, 1993.

Gnilka, *Jesus*    Gnilka, Joachim. *Jesus of Nazareth: Message and History.* Translated by Siegfried S. Schatzmann. Peabody, Mass.: Hendrickson, 1997.

Godet, *Gospel*    Godet, F. *Commentary on the Gospel of St. John.* Edinburgh: T&T Clark, 1900.

Godwin, *Mystery Religions*    Godwin, Joscelyn. *Mystery Religions in the Ancient World.* San Francisco: Harper & Row, 1981.

Goergen, *Mission*    Goergen, D. J. *The Mission and Ministry of Jesus.* Wilmington, Del.: Glazier, 1986.

Goetz and Blomberg, "Burden of Proof"    Goetz, Stewart C., and Craig L. Blomberg, "The Burden of Proof." *JSNT* 11 (1981): 39–63.

Goguel, *Jesus*    Goguel, Maurice. *The Life of Jesus.* Translated by Olive Wyon. New York: Macmillan, 1948.

Goldenberg, "*Antiquities* iv"    Goldenberg, David M. "*Antiquities* iv,277 and 288, Compared with Early Rabbinic Law." Pages 198–211 in *Josephus, Judaism, and Christianity.* Edited by Louis H. Feldman and Gohei Hata. Detroit: Wayne State University Press, 1987.

Goldenberg, "Axis"    Goldenberg, Robert. "The Broken Axis: Rabbinic Judaism and the Fall of Jerusalem." *Journal of the American Academy of Religion* 45, no. 3 Sup. (September 1977): 869–82.

Goldenberg, "Explanations"    Goldenberg, Robert. "Early Rabbinic Explanations of the Destruction of Jerusalem." *JJS* 33 (1982): 517–25.

Goldenberg, "Halakha"    Goldenberg, David. "The Halakha in Josephus and in Tannaitic Literature: A Comparative Study." *JQR* 67 (1976–1977): 30–34.

Goldenson, *Behavior*   Goldenson, Robert M. *The Encyclopedia of Human Behavior: Psychology, Psychiatry, and Mental Health*. 2 vols. Garden City, N.Y.: Doubleday, 1970.

Goldin, "Magic"   Goldin, Judah. "The Magic of Magic and Superstition." Pages 115–47 in *Aspects of Religious Propaganda in Judaism and Early Christianity*. Edited by Elisabeth Schüssler Fiorenza. University of Notre Dame Center for the Study of Judaism and Christianity in Antiquity 2. Notre Dame, Ind.: University of Notre Dame Press, 1976.

Goldstein, "Acceptance"   Goldstein, Jonathan A. "Jewish Acceptance and Rejection of Hellenism." Pages 64–87 in vol. 2 of Meyer and Sanders, *Self-Definition*.

Goldstein, "Composition"   Goldstein, Jonathan A. "The Central Composition of the West Wall of the Synagogue of Dura-Europos." *Journal of the Ancient Near Eastern Society* 16–17 (1984–1985): 99–142.

Goldstein, "Creation"   Goldstein, Jonathan A. "Creation ex Nihilo: Recantations and Restatements." *JJS* 38 (1987): 187–94.

Goldstein, "Origins"   Goldstein, Jonathan A. "The Origins of the Doctrine of Creatio ex Nihilo." *JJS* 35 (1984): 127–35.

Good, *King*   Good, Deirdre J. *Jesus the Meek King*. Harrisburg, Pa.: Trinity Press International, 1999.

Goodblatt, "Suicide"   Goodblatt, David. "Suicide in the Sanctuary: Traditions on Priestly Martyrdom." *JJS* 46 (1995): 10–29.

Goodenough, *Church*   Goodenough, Erwin R. *The Church in the Roman Empire*. New York: Cooper Square, 1970.

Goodenough, *Philo*   Goodenough, Erwin R. *An Introduction to Philo Judaeus*. 2d ed. Oxford: Blackwell, 1962.

Goodenough, "Stamp"   Goodenough, Erwin R. "An Early Christian Bread Stamp." *HTR* 57 (1964): 133–37.

Goodenough, *Symbols*   Goodenough, Erwin R. *Jewish Symbols in the Greco-Roman Period*. 13 vols. Bollingen Series 37. Vols. 1–12: New York: Pantheon Books, for Bollingen Foundation, 1953–1965. Vol. 13: Princeton, N.J.: Princeton University Press, for Bollingen Foundation, 1968.

Goodman, *Demons*   Goodman, Felicitas D. *How about Demons? Possession and Exorcism in the Modern World*. Bloomington: Indiana University Press, 1988.

Goodman, "Essenes"   Goodman, Martin. "A Note on the Qumran Sectarians, the Essenes, and Josephus." *JJS* 46 (1995): 161–66.

Goodman, "Identity"   Goodman, Martin. "Identity and Authority in Ancient Judaism." *Judaism* 39 (1990): 192–201.

Goodman, "Nerva"   Goodman, Martin. "Nerva, the *Fiscus judaicus*, and Jewish Identity." *Journal of Roman Studies* 79 (1989): 40–44.

Goodman, *State*   Goodman, Martin. *State and Society in Roman Galilee, A. D. 132–212*. Oxford Centre for Postgraduate Hebrew Studies. Totowa, N.J.: Rowman & Allanheld, 1983.

Goodman, Henney, and Pressel, *Trance*   Goodman, Felicitas D., Jeannette H. Henney, and Esther Pressel. *Trance, Healing, and Hallucination: Three Field Studies in Religious Experience*. New York: John Wiley & Sons, 1974.

Goppelt, "Church in History"   Goppelt, Leonhard. "The Existence of the Church in History according to Apostolic and Early Catholic Thought." Pages 193–209 in *Current Issues in New Testament Interpretation: Essays in Honor of Otto A. Piper*. Edited by William Klassen and Graydon F. Snyder. New York: Harper & Row, 1962.

Goppelt, *Jesus, Paul, and Judaism*   Goppelt, Leonhard. *Jesus, Paul, and Judaism*. Translated by Edward Schroeder. New York: Nelson, 1964.

Goppelt, *Theology*   Goppelt, Leonhard. *Theology of the New Testament*. Translated by John E. Alsup. Edited by Jürgen Roloff. 2 vols. Grand Rapids: Eerdmans, 1981–1982.

Goppelt, *Times*   Goppelt, Leonhard. *Apostolic and Post-apostolic Times*. Translated by Robert Guelich. Grand Rapids: Baker, 1980.

Gordis, "Messiah"   Gordis, Robert. "The 'Begotten' Messiah in the Qumran Scrolls." *VT* 7 (1957): 191–94.

Gordon, *Civilizations*   Gordon, Cyrus H. *The Common Background of Greek and Hebrew Civilizations*. New York: W. W. Norton, 1965.

Gordon, *East*   Gordon, Cyrus H. *The Ancient Near East.* New York: W. W. Norton, 1965.

Gordon, "Prayer"   Gordon, Ernest. "Our Lord's Priestly Prayer." *Homiletic and Pastoral Review* 92, no. 2 (1992): 17–21.

Gordon, "Psalm 82"   Gordon, Cyrus H. "History of Religion in Psalm 82." Pages 129–31 in *Biblical and Near Eastern Studies: Essays in Honor of William Sanford LaSor.* Edited by Gary A. Tuttle. Grand Rapids: Eerdmans, 1978.

Görg, "Beckenhausen"   Görg, Manfred. "Betesda: 'Beckenhausen.'" *Bibische Notizen* 49 (1989): 7–10.

Görg, "Wehen"   Görg, Manfred. "Vom Wehen des Pneuma." *BN* 66 (1993): 5–9.

Goshen Gottstein, "Body"   Goshen Gottstein, Alon. "The Body as Image of God in Rabbinic Literature." *HTR* 87 (1994): 171–95.

Goshen Gottstein, "Love"   Goshen Gottstein, Alon. "Love as a Hermeneutic Principle in Rabbinic Literature." *Literature and Theology* 8 (1994): 247–67.

Goshen Gottstein, "Testaments"   Goshen Gottstein, Alon. "Testaments in Rabbinic Literature: Transformations of a Genre." *JSJ* 25 (1994): 222–51.

Gottlieb, "Abot"   Gottlieb, Isaac B. "Pirqe Abot and Biblical Wisdom." *VT* 40, no. 2 (1990): 152–64.

Gould, *Ethics*   Gould, John. *The Development of Plato's Ethics.* Cambridge: Cambridge University Press, 1955.

Gould, *Love*   Gould, Thomas. *Platonic Love.* London: Routledge & Kegan Paul, 1963.

Goulder, *Acts*   Goulder, Michael Douglas. *Type and History in Acts.* London: SPCK, 1964.

Goulder, "Friend"   Goulder, Michael. "An Old Friend Incognito." *SJT* 45 (1992): 487–513.

Goulder, *Midrash*   Goulder, Michael Douglas. *Midrash and Lection in Matthew.* Speaker's Lectures in Biblical Studies 1969–71. London: SPCK, 1974.

Goulder, "Ministry"   Goulder, Michael Douglas. "From Ministry to Passion in John and Luke." *NTS* 29 (1983): 561–68.

Goulder, "Nicodemus"   Goulder, M. "Nicodemus." *SJT* 44 (1991): 153–68.

Goulder, "Q"   Goulder, Michael Douglas. "On Putting Q to the Test." *NTS* 24 (1977–1978): 218–34.

Gourgues, "Mots"   Gourgues, Michel. "'Moi non plus je ne te condamne pas': Les mots et la théologie de Luc en Jean 8,1–11 (la femme adultère)." *SR* 19 (1990): 305–18.

Grässer, "Polemic"   Grässer, Erich. "Die antijüdische Polemik im Johannesevangelium." *NTS* 11 (1964–1965): 74–90.

Grabbe, *Etymology*   Grabbe, Lester L. *Etymology in Early Jewish Interpretation: The Hebrew Names in Philo.* Brown Judaic Studies 115. Atlanta: Scholars Press, 1988.

Graf, "Initiation"   Graf, Fritz. "The Magician's Initiation." *Helios* 21 (1994): 161–77.

Grant, "Ambiguity"   Grant, Colleen C. "Ambiguity in an Ambiguous Gospel." *Journal of Theology* 103 (1999): 1–15.

Grant, *Christianity*   Grant, Robert M. *Early Christianity and Society: Seven Studies.* San Francisco: Harper & Row, 1977.

Grant, "Church"   Grant, Robert M. "The Fourth Gospel and the Church." *HTR* 35 (1942): 95–116.

Grant, "Clock"   Grant, Frederick C. "Turning Back the Clock." *Interpretation* 19 (1965): 352–354.

Grant, "Feedings"   Grant, Robert M. "The Problem of Miraculous Feedings in the Graeco-Roman Period." *Center for Hermeneutical Studies Protocol* 42 (1982): 1–15.

Grant, *Gnosticism*   Grant, Robert M. *Gnosticism and Early Christianity.* 2d ed. New York: Columbia University Press, 1966.

Grant, *Gods*   Grant, Robert M. *Gods and the One God.* LEC 1. Philadelphia: Westminster, 1986.

Grant, *Gospel*   Grant, Frederick C. *The Earliest Gospel.* New York: Abingdon-Cokesbury, 1943.

Grant, *Hellenism*   Grant, Frederick C. *Roman Hellenism and the New Testament.* New York: Scribner, 1962.

Grant, *Judaism*   Grant, Frederick C. *Ancient Judaism and the New Testament.* New York: Macmillan, 1959.

Grant, *Paul*   Grant, Robert M. *Paul in the Roman World: The Conflict at Corinth.* Louisville, Ky.: Westminster John Knox, 2001.

Grant, *Religions*   Grant, Frederick C., ed. *Hellenistic Religions: The Age of Syncretism.* Library of Liberal Arts. Indianapolis: Bobbs-Merrill Company, Liberal Arts Press, 1953.

Grant, "Review"   Grant, Frederick. Review of A. N. Sherwin-White, *Roman Society and Roman Law in the New Testament. JTS* NS 15 (1964): 352–58.

Grappe, "Essai"   Grappe, Christian. "Essai sur l'arrière-plan pascal des récrits de la dernière nuit de Jésus." *Revue d'histoire et de philosophie religieuses* 65 (1985): 105–25.

Grassi, "Ezekiel"   Grassi, Joseph A. "Ezekiel xxxvii.1–14 and the New Testament." *NTS* 11 (1964–1965): 162–64.

Grassi, "Leadership Roles"   Grassi, Joseph A. "Women's Leadership Roles in John's Gospel." *The Bible Today* 35 (1997): 312–17.

Grassi, "Wedding"   Grassi, Joseph A. "The Wedding at Cana (John II.1–11): A Pentecostal Meditation?" *NovT* 14 (1972): 131–36.

Grassi, *World*   Grassi, Joseph A. *A World to Win: The Missionary Methods of Paul the Apostle.* Maryknoll, N.Y.: Maryknoll Publications, 1965.

Grayston, *Epistles*   Grayston, Kenneth. *The Johannine Epistles.* New Century Bible Commentary. Grand Rapids: Eerdmans, 1984.

Grayston, *Gospel*   Grayston, Kenneth. *The Gospel of John.* Philadelphia: Trinity Press International, 1990.

Grayston, "Misunderstandings"   Grayston, Kenneth. "Who Misunderstands the Johannine Misunderstandings?" *Scripture Bulletin* 20 (1989): 9–15.

Grayston, "ΠΑΡΑΚΛΗΤΟΣ"   Grayston, Kenneth. "The Meaning of ΠΑΡΑΚΛΗΤΟΣ." *JSNT* 13 (October 1981): 67–82.

Grayzel, *History*   Grayzel, Solomon. *A History of the Jews.* Philadelphia: Jewish Publication Society of America, 1961.

Green, "Burial"   Green, Joel B. "Burial of Jesus." Pages 88–92 in *Dictionary of Jesus and the Gospels.* Edited by Joel B. Green, Scot McKnight, and I. Howard Marshall. Downers Grove, Ill.: InterVarsity, 1992.

Green, "Gethsemane"   Green, Joel B. "Gethsemane." Pages 265–68 in *Dictionary of Jesus and the Gospels.* Edited by Joel B. Green, Scot McKnight, and I. Howard Marshall. Downers Grove, Ill.: InterVarsity, 1992.

Green, *Matthew*   Green, H. B. *The Gospel according to Matthew.* Oxford: Clarendon Press, 1975.

Green, "Prologue"   Green, Humphrey C. "The Composition of St. John's Prologue." *ExpTim* 66 (1954–1955): 291–94.

Greenhut, "Cave"   Greenhut, Zvi. "Burial Cave of the Caiaphas Family." *BAR* 18, no. 5 (September/October 1992): 28–36, 76.

Greenhut, "Tomb"   Greenhut, Zvi. "Discovery of the Caiaphas Family Tomb." *Jerusalem Perspective* 4, nos. 4–5 (1991): 6–12.

Greenspahn, "Prophecy"   Greenspahn, Frederick E. "Why Prophecy Ceased." *JBL* 108 (1989): 37–49.

Greenspoon, "Pronouncement Story"   Greenspoon, Leonard. "The Pronouncement Story in Philo and Josephus." *Semeia* 20 (1981): 73–80.

Greenstone, *Messiah*   Greenstone, Julius H. *The Messiah Idea in Jewish History.* Philadelphia: Jewish Publication Society of America, 1906.

Grelot, "Rocher"   Grelot, Pierre. "Jean. vii,38: Eau du rocher ou source du temple?" *RB* 70 (1963): 43–51.

Grese, "Born Again"   Grese, William C. "'Unless One Is Born Again': The Use of a Heavenly Journey in John 3." *JBL* 107 (1988): 677–93.

Griffiths, "Deutero-Isaiah"   Griffiths, David R. "Deutero-Isaiah and the Fourth Gospel: Some Points of Comparison." *ExpTim* 65 (1953–1954): 355–60.

Griffiths, "Isis"   Griffiths, J. Gwyn. "Isis and *Agapē.*" *Classical Philology* 80 (1985): 139–41.

Griffiths, "Predicate"   Griffiths, J. Gwyn. "A Note on the Anarthrous Predicate in Hellenistic Greek." *ExpTim* 62 (1950–1951): 314–16.

Grigsby, "Cross"   Grigsby, Bruce H. "The Cross as an Expiatory Sacrifice in the Fourth Gospel." *JSNT* 15 (1982): 51–80.

Grigsby, "Gematria"   Grigsby, Bruce. "Gematria and John 21:11—Another Look at Ezekiel 47:10." *ExpTim* 95 (1983–1984): 177–78.

Grigsby, "Reworking"   Grigsby, Bruce. "The Reworking of the Lake-Walking Account in the Johannine Tradition." *ExpTim* 100 (1988–1989): 295–97.

Grigsby, "Siloam"    Grigsby, Bruce. "Washing in the Pool of Siloam—a Thematic Anticipation of the Johannine Cross." *NovT* 27 (1985): 227–35.

Grigsby, "Thirsts"    Grigsby, Bruce H. "'If Any Man Thirsts . . .': Observations on the Rabbinic Background of John 7,37–39." *Biblica* 67 (1986): 100–108.

Grintz, "Jubilees"    Grintz, Yehoshua M. "Jubilees, Book of." Columns 324–26 in vol. 10 of *Encyclopaedia judaica*. 16 vols. Jerusalem: Keter, 1972.

Grob, "Explication"    Grob, Francis. "'Vous me cherchez, non parce que vous avez vu des signes . . .': Essai d'explication cohérente de Jean 6.26." *Revue d'histoire et de philosophie religieuses* 60 (1980): 429–39.

Grobel, "After Me"    Grobel, K. "He That Cometh after Me." *JBL* 60 (1941): 397–401.

Groh, "Jews and Christians"    Groh, Dennis E. "Jews and Christians in Late Roman Palestine: Towards a New Chronology." *BA* 51 (1988): 80–96.

Grossfeld, "Torah"    Grossfeld, Bernard. "Torah." Pages 1241–45 in *Dictionary of New Testament Background*. Edited by Craig A. Evans and Stanley E. Porter. Downers Grove, Ill.: InterVarsity, 2000.

Grudem, *Prophecy*    Grudem, Wayne A. *The Gift of Prophecy in 1 Corinthians*. Lanham, Md.: University Press of America, 1982.

Gruenler, *Trinity*    Gruenler, Royce Gordon. *The Trinity in the Gospel of John: A Thematic Commentary on the Fourth Gospel*. Grand Rapids: Baker, 1986.

Grummond, "Pax Augusta"    Grummond, Nancy T. de. "Pax Augusta and the Horae on the Ara Pacis Augustae." *American Journal of Archaeology* 94 (1990): 663–77.

Grundmann, "Decision"    Grundmann, Walter. "The Decision of the Supreme Court to Put Jesus to Death (John 11:47–57) in Its Context: Tradition and Redaction in the Gospel of John." Pages 295–318 in *Jesus and the Politics of His Day*. Edited by Ernst Bammel and C. F. D. Moule. Cambridge: Cambridge University Press, 1984.

Gryglewicz, "Geist"    Gryglewicz, Feliks. "Die Aussagen über den Heiligen Geist im vierten Evangelium: Überlieferung und Redaktion." *Studien zum Neuen Testament und seiner Umwelt* 4 (1979): 45–53.

Gryglewicz, "Pharisäer"    Gryglewicz, Feliks. "Die Pharisäer und die Johanneskirche." Pages 144–158 in *Probleme der Forschung*. Edited by Albert Fuchs. Studien Zum Neuen Testament und Seiner Umwelt A-3. Munich: Herold Wien, 1978.

Guelich, "Genre"    Guelich, Robert. "The Gospel Genre." Pages 173–208 in *The Gospel and the Gospels*. Edited by Peter Stuhlmacher. Grand Rapids: Eerdmans, 1991.

Guenther, "Greek"    Guenther, Heinz O. "Greek: Home of Primitive Christianity." *Toronto Journal of Theology* 5 (1989): 247–79.

Guilding, *Worship*    Guilding, Aileen. *The Fourth Gospel and Jewish Worship*. Oxford: Clarendon Press, 1960.

Guillaume, *Islam*    Guillaume, Alfred. *Islam*. New York: Penguin, 1956.

Guillaume, "Midrash"    Guillaume, Alfred. "The Midrash in the Gospels." *ExpTim* 37 (1925–1926): 392–98.

Guillet, "Récits"    Guillet, Jacques. "Les récits évangeliques de la résurrection." *Quatres fleuves* 15–16 (1982): 7–21.

Gundry, "Framework"    Gundry, Robert H. "The Narrative Framework of Matthew xvi 17–19: A Critique of Professor Cullmann's Hypothesis." *NovT* 7 (1964): 1–9.

Gundry, "Genre"    Gundry, Robert H. "Recent Investigations into the Literary Genre 'Gospel.'" Pages 97–114 in *New Dimensions in New Testament Study*. Edited by Richard N. Longenecker and Merrill C. Tenney. Grand Rapids: Zondervan, 1974.

Gundry, "House"    Gundry, Robert H. "'In My Father's House Are Many Monai' (Joh 14:2)." *ZNW* 58 (1967): 68–72.

Gundry, *Matthew*    Gundry, Robert H. *Matthew: A Commentary on His Literary and Theological Art*. Grand Rapids: Eerdmans, 1982.

Gundry, *Tribulation*    Gundry, Robert H. *The Church and the Tribulation*. Grand Rapids: Zondervan, 1973.

Gundry, *Use*    Gundry, Robert H. *The Use of the Old Testament in St. Matthew's Gospel: With Special Reference to the Messianic Hope*. NovTSup 18. Leiden: Brill, 1975.

Gundry and Howell, "Syntax"    Gundry, Robert H., and Russell W. Howell. "The Sense and Syntax of John 3:14–17 with Special Reference to the Use of οὕτως . . . ὥστε in John 3:16." *NovT* 41 (1999): 24–39.

Gundry-Volf, "Spirit"    Gundry-Volf, Judith. "Spirit, Mercy, and the Other." *Theology Today* 51 (1994–1995): 508–23.

Gündüz, "Problems"    Gündüz, Sinasi. "The Problems of the Nature and Date of Mandaean Sources." *JSNT* 53 (1994): 87–97.

Gunther, "Gospel"    Gunther, John J. "The Alexandrian Gospel and Letters of John." *CBQ* 41 (1979): 581–603.

Gunther, "Relation"    Gunther, John J. "The Relation of the Beloved Disciple to the Twelve." *Theologische Zeitschrift* 37 (1981): 129–48.

Gurney, *Aspects*    Gurney, O. R. *Some Aspects of Hittite Religion.* Oxford: Oxford University Press, 1977.

Gustafsson, "Graffiti"    Gustafsson, Berndt. "The Oldest Graffiti in the History of the Church?" *NTS* 3 (1956–1957): 65–69.

Guthrie, *Introduction*    Guthrie, Donald. *New Testament Introduction.* 4th ed. Downers Grove, Ill.: InterVarsity, 1990.

Guthrie, *Orpheus*    Guthrie, W. K. C. *Orpheus and Greek Religion: A Study of the Orphic Movement.* 2d ed. New York: W. W. Norton, 1966.

Guttmann, "Miracles"    Guttmann, Alexander. "The Significance of Miracles for Talmudic Judaism." *HUCA* 20 (1947): 363–406.

Gwynne, "Invisible Father"    Gwynne, Paul. "YHWH and the Invisible Father." *Australasian Catholic Record* 77, no. 3 (2000): 278–91.

Haas, "Remains"    Haas, N. "Anthropological Observations on the Skeletal Remains from Givʾat ha-Mivtar." *IEJ* 20 (1970): 38–59.

Habermas, "Miracles"    Habermas, Gary R. "Did Jesus Perform Miracles?" Pages 117–40 in *Jesus under Fire.* Edited by Michael J. Wilkins and J. P. Moreland. Grand Rapids: Zondervan, 1995.

Hachlili, "Art and Architecture"    Hachlili, Rachel. "Art and Architecture: Jewish." Pages 125–29 in *Dictionary of New Testament Background.* Edited by Craig A. Evans and Stanley E. Porter. Downers Grove, Ill.: InterVarsity, 2000.

Hachlili, "Necropolis"    Hachlili, Rachel. "A Second Temple Period Jewish Necropolis in Jericho." *BA* 43 (1980): 235–40.

Hachlili, "Zodiac"    Hachlili, Rachel. "The Zodiac in Ancient Jewish Art: Representation and Significance." *BASOR* 228 (December 1977): 61–77.

Hachlili and Killebrew, "Byt glyt"    Hachlili, Rachel, and Ann Killebrew. "Byt glyt—mšpḥh byryḥw bmʾh hʾ lsh-n [The House of 'Goliath'—a Family at Jericho in the First Century C.E.]." *Qadmoniot* 14 (1981): 118–22.

Hachlili and Killebrew, "Customs"    Hachlili, Rachel, and Ann Killebrew. "Jewish Funerary Customs during the Second Temple Period, in the Light of the Excavations at the Jericho Necropolis." *PEQ* 115 (1983): 109–39.

Hachlili and Killebrew, "Saga"    Hachlili, Rachel, and Ann Killebrew. "The Saga of the Goliath Family." *BAR* 9, no. 1 (January/February 1983): 44–53.

Hadas, *Aristeas*    Hadas, Moses, ed. and trans. *Aristeas to Philocrates: Letter of Aristeas.* New York: Harper & Brothers, for the Dropsie College for Hebrew and Cognate Learning, 1951.

Hadas and Smith, *Heroes*    Hadas, Moses, and Morton Smith. *Heroes and Gods: Spiritual Biographies in Antiquity.* Religious Perspectives 13. New York: Harper & Row, 1965.

Hadidian, "Philonism"    Hadidian, Yervant H. "Philonism in the Fourth Gospel." Pages 211–22 in *The MacDonald Presentation Volume: A Tribute to Duncan Black MacDonald, Consisting of Articles by Former Students, Presented to Him on His Seventieth Birthday, April 9, 1933.* Princeton, N.J.: Princeton University Press, 1933.

Haenchen, *Acts*    Haenchen, Ernst. *The Acts of the Apostles: A Commentary.* Philadelphia: Westminster, 1971.

Haenchen, *John*    Haenchen, Ernst. *A Commentary on the Gospel of John.* Translated by Robert W. Funk. Edited by Robert W. Funk with Ulrich Busse. 2 vols. Hermeneia. Philadelphia: Fortress, 1984.

Hafemann, "Moses"  Hafemann, Scott J. "Moses in the Apocrypha and Pseudepigrapha: A Survey." *JSP* 7 (1990): 79–104.

Hagner, *Matthew*  Hagner, Donald A. *Matthew*. 2 vols. WBC 33. Dallas: Word, 1993–1995.

Hagner, "Sayings"  Hagner, Donald A. "The Sayings of Jesus in the Apostolic Fathers and Justin Martyr." Pages 233–68 in *The Jesus Tradition outside the Gospels*. Edited by David Wenham. Vol. 5 of *Gospel Perspectives*. Edited by R. T. France and David Wenham. 6 vols. Sheffield: JSOT Press, 1980–1986.

Hagner, "*Sitz*"  Hagner, Donald A. "The *Sitz im Leben* of the Gospel of Matthew." Pages 27–68 in *Treasures New and Old: Recent Contributions to Matthean Studies*. Edited by David R. Bauer and Mark Allan Powell. SBLSymS 1. Atlanta: Scholars Press, 1996.

Hagner, "Vision"  Hagner, Donald A. "The Vision of God in Philo and John: A Comparative Study." *JETS* 14 (1971): 81–93.

Hahn, "Verständnis"  Hahn, Ferdinand. "Das biblische Verständnis des Heiligen Geistes. Soteriologische Funktion und 'Personalität' des Heiligen Geistes." Pages 131–47 in *Erfahrung und Theologie des Heiligen Geistes*. Edited by Claus Heitmann and Heribert Mühlen. Hamburg: Agentur des Rauhen Hauses, 1974.

Hall, "History"  Hall, Robert Givin. "Revealed History: A Jewish and Christian Technique of Interpreting the Past." Ph.D. diss., Duke University, 1986.

Hall, *Revealed Histories*  Hall, Robert G. *Revealed Histories: Techniques from Ancient Jewish and Christian Historiography*. Journal for the Study of the Pseudepigrapha Supplement 6. Sheffield: JSOT Press, 1991.

Hall, *Scripture*  Hall, Christopher A. *Reading Scripture with the Church Fathers*. Downers Grove, Ill.: InterVarsity, 1998.

Hallett, *Fathers*  Hallett, Judith P. *Fathers and Daughters in Roman Society: Women and the Elite Family*. Princeton, N.J.: Princeton University Press, 1984.

Halperin, "Invasion"  Halperin, David J. "Ascension or Invasion: Implications of the Heavenly Journey in Ancient Judaism." *Religion* 18 (1988): 47–67.

Halperin, "Midrash"  Halperin, David J. "Merkabah Midrash in the Septuagint." *JBL* 101 (1982): 351–363.

Hambly, "Creation"  Hambly, W. F. "Creation and Gospel: A Brief Comparison of Genesis 1,1–2, 4 and John 1,1–2, 12." *Studia Evangelica* 5 (1968): 69–74.

Hamel, "Argo"  Hamel, Gildas. "Taking the Argo to Nineveh: Jonah and Jason in a Mediterranean Context." *Judaism* 44 (1995): 341–59.

Hamerton-Kelly, *Pre-existence*  Hamerton-Kelly, R. G. *Pre-existence, Wisdom, and the Son: A Study of the Idea of Pre-existence in the New Testament*. Cambridge: Cambridge University Press, 1973.

Hamid-Khani, *Revelation and Concealment*  Hamid-Khani, Saeed. *Revelation and Concealment of Christ: A Theological Inquiry into the Elusive Language of the Fourth Gospel*. WUNT 2d series, 120. Tübingen: Mohr Siebeck, 2000.

Hamilton, *Spirit*  Hamilton, Neill Q. *The Holy Spirit and Eschatology in Paul*. Scottish Journal of Theology Occasional Papers 6. Edinburgh: Oliver & Boyd, 1957.

Hammond, "Settlement"  Hammond, Philip C. "Nabataean Settlement Patterns Inside Petra." *Ancient History Bulletin* 5 (1991): 36–46.

Hanfmann, "Campaign"  Hanfmann, George M. A. "The Tenth Campaign at Sardis." *BASOR* 191 (October 1968): 2–41.

Hanfmann, *Sardis*  Hanfmann, George M. A., assisted by William E. Mierse. *Sardis from Prehistoric to Roman Times: Results of the Archaeological Exploration of Sardis, 1958–1975*. Cambridge: Harvard University Press, 1983.

Hanhart, "Structure"  Hanhart, K. "The Structure of John i 35–iv 54." Pages 22–46 in *Studies in John: Presented to Professor Dr. J. N. Sevenster on the Occasion of His Seventieth Birthday*. Edited by W. C. van Unnik. NovTSup 24. Leiden: Brill, 1970.

Hanhart, "Tenth Hour"  Hanhart, K. "'About the Tenth Hour' . . . on Nisan 15 (Jn 1,35–40)." Pages 335–47 in *L'évangile de Jean: Sources, rédaction, théologie*. Edited by Marinus De Jonge. BETL 45. Gembloux: J. Duculot; Leuven: Leuven University Press, 1977.

Hanson, "Comparison"  Hanson, A. T. "Hodayoth xv and John 17: A Comparison of Content and Form." *Hermathena* 118 (1974): 48–58.

Hanson, "Etymologies"   Hanson, A. "Philo's Etymologies." *JTS* NS 18 (1967): 128–39.

Hanson, "Exodus"   Hanson, Anthony. "John I.14–18 and Exodus XXXIV." *NTS* 23 (1976–1977): 90–101.

Hanson, *Gospel*   Hanson, Anthony Tyrrell. *The Prophetic Gospel: A Study of John and the Old Testament.* Edinburgh: T&T Clark, 1991.

Hanson, "Midrash"   Hanson, A. T. "The Midrash in II Corinthians 3: A Reconsideration." *JSNT* 9 (1980): 2–28.

Hanson, *Unity*   Hanson, Stig. *The Unity of the Church in the New Testament: Colossians and Ephesians.* Lexington, Ky.: American Theological Library Association, 1963.

Hanson and Oakman, *Palestine*   Hanson, K. C., and Douglas E. Oakman. *Palestine in the Time of Jesus: Social Structures and Social Conflicts.* Minneapolis: Fortress, 1998.

Haran, "Image"   Haran, Menahem. "The Priestly Image of the Tabernacle." *HUCA* 36 (1965): 191–226.

Harding, "Prayer"   Harding, Mark. "A Hebrew Congregational Prayer from Egypt." Pages 145–47 in *A Review of the Greek Inscriptions and Papyri Published 1984–85.* Vol. 8 of *New Documents Illustrating Early Christianity.* Edited by S. R. Llewelyn. Grand Rapids: Eerdmans, 1998.

Hare, *Persecution*   Hare, Douglas R. A. *The Theme of Jewish Persecution of Christians in the Gospel according to St. Matthew.* Cambridge: Cambridge University Press, 1967.

Hare, "Rejection"   Hare, Douglas R. A. "The Rejection of the Jews in the Synoptic Gospels and Acts." Pages 27–47 in *Antisemitism and the Foundations of Christianity.* Edited by Alan T. Davies. New York: Paulist Press, 1979.

Hargreaves, "Westcott, India"   Hargreaves, Cecil. "Westcott, India, and 'John.'" *ExpT* 112, no. 10 (2001): 333–35.

Harms, "Tradition"   Harms, Robert. "Oral Tradition and Ethnicity." *Journal of Interdisciplinary History* 10 (1979–1980): 61–85.

Harner, *Analysis*   Harner, Philip B. *Relation Analysis of the Fourth Gospel: A Study in Reader-Response Criticism.* Lewiston, N.Y.: Mellen, 1993.

Harner, *I Am*   Harner, Philip B. *The "I Am" of the Fourth Gospel: A Study in Johannine Usage and Thought.* Facet Books Biblical Series 26. Philadelphia: Fortress, 1970.

Harner, "Nouns"   Harner, Philip B. "Qualitative Anarthrous Predicate Nouns: Mark 15:39 and John 1:1." *JBL* 92 (1973): 75–87.

Harrell, *Divorce*   Harrell, Pat Edwin. *Divorce and Remarriage in the Early Church: A History of Divorce and Remarriage in the Ante-Nicene Church.* Austin, Tex.: R. B. Sweet, 1967.

Harrell, *Possible*   Harrell, David Edwin , Jr. *All Things Are Possible: The Healing and Charismatic Revivals in Modern America.* Bloomington: Indiana University Press, 1975.

Harrelson, *Cult*   Harrelson, Walter. *From Fertility Cult to Worship.* Garden City, N.Y.: Doubleday, 1969.

Harrill, "Asia Minor"   Harrill, J. Albert. "Asia Minor." Pages 130–36 in *Dictionary of New Testament Background.* Edited by Craig A. Evans and Stanley E. Porter. Downers Grove, Ill.: InterVarsity, 2000.

Harrington, "Abraham Traditions"   Harrington, D. J. "Abraham Traditions in the Testament of Abraham and in the 'Rewritten Bible' of the Intertestamental Period." Pages 165–172 in *Studies on the Testament of Abraham.* Edited by George W. E. Nickelsburg Jr. Society of Biblical Literature Septuagint and Cognate Studies 6. Missoula, Mont.: Scholars Press, 1976.

Harrington, "Bible"   Harrington, D. J. "The Bible Rewritten (Narratives)." Pages 239–47 in *Early Judaism and Its Modern Interpreters.* Edited by Robert A. Kraft and George W. E. Nickelsburg. SBLBMI 2. Atlanta: Scholars Press, 1986.

Harrington, "Jews"   Harrington, D. J. "'The Jews' in John's Gospel." *The Bible Today* 27 (1989): 203–9.

Harrington, *People*   Harrington, D. J. *God's People in Christ.* Philadelphia: Fortress, 1980.

Harrington, "Problem"   Harrington, Daniel J. "The Problem of 'The Jews' in John's Gospel." *Explorations* 8 (1994): 3–4.

Harris, "Athena"   Harris, J. Rendel. "Athena, Sophia, and the Logos." *Bulletin of the John Rylands Library* 7 (1922–1923): 56–72.

Harris, "Dead"   Harris, Murray J. "'The Dead Are Restored to Life': Miracles of Revivification in the Gospels." Pages 295–326 in *The Miracles of Jesus.* Edited by David Wenham and Craig

Blomberg. Vol. 6 of *Gospel Perspectives*. Edited by R. T. France and David Wenham. Sheffield: JSOT Press, 1986.

Harris, "Deity"   Harris, Murray J. "Titus 2:13 and the Deity of Christ." Pages 262–77 in *Pauline Studies: Essays Presented to Professor F. F. Bruce on His 70th Birthday*. Edited by Donald A. Hagner and Murray J. Harris. Grand Rapids: Eerdmans, 1980.

Harris, *Jesus as God*   Harris, Murray J. *Jesus as God: The New Testament Use of Theos in Reference to Jesus*. Grand Rapids: Baker, 1992.

Harris, "Origin"   Harris, J. Rendel. "The Origin of the Prologue to St. John's Gospel." *The Expositor*, Eighth Series 12 (1916): 147–60, 161–70, 314–20, 388–400, 415–26.

Harris, *Prologue*   Harris, J. Rendel. *The Origin of the Prologue to St. John's Gospel*. Cambridge: Cambridge University Press, 1917.

Harris, "References"   Harris, Murray J. "References to Jesus in Early Classical Authors." Pages 343–68 in *The Jesus Tradition outside the Gospels*. Edited by David Wenham. Vol. 5 of *Gospel Perspectives*. Edited by R. T. France and David Wenham. Sheffield: JSOT Press, 1984.

Harrison, "Cicero"   Harrison, S. J. "Cicero and 'crurifragium.'" *Classical Quarterly* 33 (1983): 453–55.

Harrison, "Garden"   Harrison, R. K. "Garden." Pages 399–400 in vol. 2 of *The International Standard Bible Encyclopedia*. Edited by Geoffrey W. Bromiley. 4 vols. Grand Rapids: Eerdmans, 1979–1988.

Harrison, "Hyssop"   Harrison, R. K. "Hyssop." Page 790 in vol. 2 of *The International Standard Bible Encyclopedia*. Edited by Geoffrey W. Bromiley. 4 vols. Grand Rapids: Eerdmans, 1979–1988.

Harrison, "John 1:14"   Harrison, Everett F. "A Study of John 1:14." Pages 23–36 in *Unity and Diversity in NT Theology: Essays in Honor of G. E. Ladd*. Edited by Robert A. Guelich. Grand Rapids: Eerdmans, 1978.

Harrison, "Ministry"   Harrison, Cyril. "The Ministry of the Spirit." *The Modern Churchman* 15 (1971–1972): 191–95.

Harrison, "Myrrh"   Harrison, R. K. "Myrrh." Pages 450–51 in vol. 3 of *The International Standard Bible Encyclopedia*. Edited by Geoffrey W. Bromiley. 4 vols. Grand Rapids: Eerdmans, 1979–1988.

Harrison, "Rites"   Harrison, R. K. "The Rites and Customs of the Qumran Sect." Pages 26–36 in *The Scrolls and Christianity: Historical and Theological Significance*. Edited by Matthew Black. London: SPCK, 1969.

Harrison, "Vine"   Harrison, R. K. "Vine." Pages 986–87 in vol. 4 of *The International Standard Bible Encyclopedia*. Edited by Geoffrey W. Bromiley. 4 vols. Grand Rapids: Eerdmans, 1979–1988.

Hart, "Crown"   Hart, H. St. J. "The Crown of Thorns in John 19.2–5." *Journal of Theological Studies* NS 3 (1952): 66–75.

Hartin, "Peter"   Hartin, P. J. "The Role of Peter in the Fourth Gospel." *Neotestamentica* 24 (1990): 49–61.

Hartman, "Temple"   Hartman, Lars. "'He Spoke of the Temple of His Body' (Jn 2:13–22)." *Svensk exegetisk årsbok* 54 (1989): 70–79.

Harvey, *History*   Harvey, A. E. *Jesus and the Constraints of History*. Philadelphia: Westminster, 1982.

Harvey, *Listening to the Text*   Harvey, John D. *Listening to the Text: Oral Patterning in Paul's Letters*. Grand Rapids: Baker; Leicester: Apollos, 1998.

Harvey, "Torah"   Harvey, Warren. "Torah." Columns 1239–46 in vol. 5 of *Encyclopaedia judaica*. 16 vols. Jerusalem: Keter, 1972.

Harvey, *Trial*   Harvey, A. E. *Jesus on Trial: A Study in the Fourth Gospel*. London: SPCK, 1976.

Hasel, *Remnant*   Hasel, Gerhard F. *The Remnant: The History and Theology of the Remnant Idea from Genesis to Isaiah*. 3d ed. Berrien Springs, Mich.: Andrews University Press, 1980.

Hasel, "Saints"   Hasel, Gerhard F. "The Identity of 'The Saints of the Most High' in Daniel 7." *Biblica* 56 (1975): 173–92.

Hasel, *Theology*   Hasel, Gerhard F. *New Testament Theology: Basic Issues in the Current Debate*. Grand Rapids: Eerdmans, 1978.

Hasitschka, "Anmerkungen"   Hasitschka, Marin. "Sozialgeschichtliche Anmerkungen zum Johannesevangelium." *Protokolle zur Bibel* 1 (1992): 59–67.

Hasitschka, "Parakletworte"   Hasitschka, Marin. "Die Parakletworte im Johannesevangelium: Versuch einer Auslegung in synchroner Textbetrachtung." *Studien zum Neuen Testament und seiner Umwelt* 18 (1993): 97–112.

Hata, "Moses"   Hata, Gohei. "The Story of Moses Interpreted within the Context of Anti-Semitism." Pages 180–97 in *Josephus, Judaism, and Christianity*. Edited by Louis H. Feldman and Gohei Hata. Detroit: Wayne State University Press, 1987.

Hata, "Version"   Hata, Gohei. "Is the Greek Version of Josephus' *Jewish War* a Translation or a Rewriting of the First Version?" *JQR* 66 (1975–1976): 89–108.

Hatch, "Meaning"   Hatch, W. H. P. "The Meaning of John XVI,8–11." *HTR* 14 (1921): 103–5.

Hatina, "Context"   Hatina, Thomas R. "John 20,22 in Its Eschatological Context: Promise or Fulfillment?" *Biblica* 74 (1993): 196–219.

Hauptman, "Sugya"   Hauptman, Judith. "Development of the Talmudic Sugya by Amoraic and Post-Amoraic Amplification of a Tannaitic Proto-Sugya." *HUCA* 58 (1987): 227–50.

Hawthorne, *Presence*   Hawthorne, Gerald F. *The Presence and the Power: The Significance of the Holy Spirit in the Life and Ministry of Jesus*. Dallas: Word, 1991.

Hawthorne, "Translation"   Hawthorne, Gerald F. "A New English Translation of Melito's Paschal Homily." Pages 147–75 in *Current Issues in Biblical and Patristic Interpretation: Studies in Honor of Merrill C. Tenney Presented by His Former Students*. Edited by Gerald F. Hawthorne. Grand Rapids: Eerdmans, 1975.

Hayes, "Oracles"   Hayes, John H. "The Usage of Oracles against Foreign Nations in Ancient Israel." *JBL* 87 (1968): 81–92.

Hayman, "Magician"   Hayman, Peter. "Was God a Magician? Sefer Yesira and Jewish Magic." *JJS* 40 (1989): 225–37.

Hayman, "Monotheism"   Hayman, Peter. "Monotheism—a Misused Word in Jewish Studies." *JJS* 42 (1991): 1–15.

Hayman, "Observations"   Hayman, Peter. "Some Observations on Sefer Yesira: (2) The Temple at the Centre of the Universe." *JJS* 37 (1986): 176–82.

Hays, *Vision*   Hays, Richard B. *The Moral Vision of the New Testament: A Contemporary Introduction to New Testament Ethics*. San Francisco: Harper San Francisco, 1996.

Hayward, *Name*   Hayward, C. T. Robert. *Divine Name and Presence: The Memra*. Oxford Centre for Postgraduate Hebrew Studies. Totowa, N.J.: Allanheld, Osmun & Co., 1981.

Hayward, "Name"   Hayward, C. T. Robert. "The Holy Name of the God of Moses and the Prologue of St John's Gospel." *NTS* 25 (1978–1979): 16–32.

Hayward, "Memra and Shekhina"   Hayward, C. T. Robert. "Memra and Shekhina: A Short Note." *JJS* 31 (1980): 210–13.

Hayward, "Memra in Neofiti"   Hayward, C. T. Robert. "The Memra of YHWH and the Development of Its Use in Targum Neofiti." *JJS* 25 (1974): 412–18.

Hayward, "Sacrifice"   Hayward, C. T. Robert. "The Sacrifice of Isaac and Jewish Polemic against Christianity." *CBQ* 52 (1990): 292–306.

Heath, *Hermogenes*   Heath, Malcolm, trans. and commentator. *Hermogenes, On Issues: Strategies of Argument in Later Greek Rhetoric*. Oxford: Clarendon, 1995.

Heath, "Invention"   Heath, Malcolm. "Invention." Pages 89–119 in *Handbook of Classical Rhetoric in the Hellenistic Period, 330 B.C.–A.D. 400*. Edited by Stanley E. Porter. Leiden: Brill, 1997.

Hedrick, "Unreliable Narration"   Hedrick, Charles W. "Unreliable Narration: John on the Story of Jesus; the Chronicler on the History of Israel." Pages 121–43 in *Perspectives on John: Method and Interpretation in the Fourth Gospel*. Edited by Robert B. Sloan and Mikeal C. Parsons. National Association of the Baptist Professors of Religion Special Studies Series 11. Lewiston, N.Y.: Mellen, 1993.

Hegstad, "Hellige"   Hegstad, Harald. "Den Hellige Ånd som veileder til 'den fulle sannhet' (Joh 16,13)—prinsippteologisk belyst." *Tidsskrift for Teologi og Kirke* 64 (1993): 95–109.

Heidel, *Genesis*   Heidel, Alexander. *The Babylonian Genesis*. 2d ed. Chicago: University of Chicago Press, 1951.

Heil, "High Priest"   Heil, John Paul. "Jesus as the Unique High Priest in the Gospel of John." *CBQ* 57 (1995): 729–45.

Heil, "Rejoinder"   Heil, John Paul. "A Rejoinder to 'Reconsidering "The Story of Jesus and the Adulteress Reconsidered."'" *Église et théologie* 25 (1994): 361–66.

Heil, "Story"   Heil, John Paul. "The Story of Jesus and the Adulteress (John 7,53–8,11) Reconsidered." *Biblica* 72 (1991): 182–91.

Heinemann, *Prayer*   Heinemann, Joseph. *Prayer in the Talmud*. Berlin: de Gruyter, 1977.

Heinen, "Grundlagen"   Heinen, Heinz. "Ägyptische Grundlagen des antiken Antijudaismus: Zum Judenexkurs des Tacitus, Historien V 2–13." *Trierer theologische Zeitschrift* 101 (1992): 124–49.

Helfmeyer, "Gott"   Helfmeyer, Franz Josef. "'Gott nachfolgen' in den Qumrantexten." *RevQ* 7 (1969–1971): 81–104.

Helmbold, "Hymns"   Helmbold, Andrew K. "Redeemer-Hymns—Gnostic and Christian." Pages 71–78 in *New Dimensions in New Testament Study.* Edited by Richard N. Longenecker and Merrill C. Tenney. Grand Rapids: Zondervan, 1974.

Hemer, *Acts*   Hemer, Colin J. *The Book of Acts in the Setting of Hellenistic History.* Edited by Conrad H. Gempf. Wissenschaftliche Untersuchungen zum Neuen Testament 49. Tübingen: Mohr, 1989.

Hemer, *Letters*   Hemer, Colin J. *The Letters to the Seven Churches of Asia in Their Local Setting.* JSNTSup 11. Sheffield: JSOT Press, 1986.

Hemer, "*Ostraka*"   Hemer, Colin J. "The Edfu *Ostraka* and the Jewish Tax." *PEQ* 105 (1973): 6–12.

Hengel, *Acts*   Hengel, Martin. *Acts and the History of Earliest Christianity.* Translated by John Bowden. Philadelphia: Fortress, 1980.

Hengel, *Atonement*   Hengel, Martin. *The Atonement: The Origins of the Doctrine in the New Testament.* Translated by John Bowden. Philadelphia: Fortress, 1981.

Hengel, *Crucifixion*   Hengel, Martin. *Crucifixion in the Ancient World and the Folly of the Message of the Cross.* Philadelphia: Fortress, 1977.

Hengel, "Geography"   Hengel, Martin. "The Geography of Palestine in Acts." Pages 27–78 in *The Book of Acts in Its Palestinian Setting.* Edited by Richard Bauckham. Vol. 4 of *The Book of Acts in Its First Century Setting.* Edited by Bruce W. Winter. Grand Rapids: Eerdmans, 1995.

Hengel, *Judaism*   Hengel, Martin. *Judaism and Hellenism: Studies in Their encounter in Palestine during the Early Hellenistic period.* Translated by John Bowden. 2 vols. Philadelphia: Fortress, 1974.

Hengel, *Leader*   Hengel, Martin. *The Charismatic Leader and His Followers.* Edited by John Riches. Translated by James Greig. New York: Crossroad, 1981.

Hengel, "OT"   Hengel, Martin. "The Old Testament in the Fourth Gospel." *Horizons in Biblical Theology* 12 (1990): 19–41.

Hengel, "Problems"   Hengel, Martin. "Literary, Theological, and Historical Problems in the Gospel of Mark." Pages 209–51 in *The Gospel and the Gospels.* Edited by Peter Stuhlmacher. Grand Rapids: Eerdmans, 1991.

Hengel, *Property*   Hengel, Martin. *Property and Riches in the Early Church: Aspects of Social History of Early Christianity.* Philadelphia: Fortress, 1974.

Hengel, *Question*   Hengel, Martin. *The Johannine Question.* Translated by John Bowden. Philadelphia: Trinity Press International, 1989.

Hengel, *Son*   Hengel, Martin. *Son of God.* Translated by John Bowden. Philadelphia: Fortress, 1976.

Hengel, *Studies in Mark*   Hengel, Martin. *Studies in the Gospel of Mark.* Translated by John Bowden. Philadelphia: Fortress, 1985.

Hengel, "Throngemeinschaft"   Hengel, Martin. "Die Throngemeinschaft des Lammes mit Gott in der Johannesapokalypse." *Theologische Beiträge* 27 (1996): 159–75.

Hennecke, *Apocrypha*   Hennecke, Edgar, Wilhelm Schneemelcher, and R. McL. Wilson, eds. *New Testament Apocrypha.* 2 vols. Philadelphia: Westminster, 1963–1965.

Hepper, "Aloes"   Hepper, F. Nigel. "The Identity and Origin of Classical Bitter Aloes (Aloe)." *PEQ* 120 (1988): 146–48.

Hepper, *Plants*   Hepper, F. Nigel. *Baker Encyclopedia of Bible Plants.* Grand Rapids: Baker, 1992.

Herbert, "Orientation"   Herbert, Sharon C. "The Orientation of Greek Temples." *PEQ* 116 (1984): 31–34.

Herford, *Christianity*   Herford, R. Travers. *Christianity in Talmud and Midrash.* Library of Philosophical and Religious Thought. 1903. Repr., Clifton, N.J.: Reference Book Publishers, 1966.

Hergesel, "Aretalogia"   Hergesel, Thomas. "Aretalogia starozytna: Szkic genologiczny [Aretalogie, Versuch einer näheren Gattungsbestimmung]." *Roczniki teologiczno-kanoniczne* 26, no. 1 (1979): 35–41.

Héring, *1 Corinthians*   Héring, Jean. *The First Epistle of Saint Paul to the Corinthians.* Translated by A. W. Heathcote and P. J. Allcock. London: Epworth, 1962.

Herlong, "Covenant"   Herlong, T. H. "The Covenant in John." *Emmanuel* 95 (1989): 394–400.

Herr, "Calendar"  Herr, M. D. "The Calendar." Pages 834–64 in Safrai and Stern, *Jewish People.*

Herzfeld, "Hospitality"  Herzfeld, Michael. "'As in Your Own House': Hospitality, Ethnography, and the Stereotype of Mediterranean Society." Pages 75–89 in *Honor and Shame and the Unity of the Mediterranean.* American Anthropological Association 22. Washington, D.C.: American Anthropological Association, 1987.

Hes, "*Mori*"  Hes, Jozef Ph. "The Changing Social Role of the Yemenite *Mori.*" Pages 364–83 in *Magic, Faith, and Healing: Studies in Primitive Psychiatry Today.* Edited by Ari Kiev. Foreword by Jerome D. Frank. New York: Free Press, Macmillan, 1964.

Heschel, "Anti-Semitism"  Heschel, Susannah. "Redemptive Anti-Semitism: The De-Judaization of the New Testament in the Third Reich." Pages 235–63 in *Literary Studies in Luke–Acts: Essays in Honor of Joseph B. Tyson.* Edited by Richard P. Thompson and Thomas E. Phillips. Macon, Ga.: Mercer University Press, 1998.

Hester, *Inheritance*  Hester, James D. *Paul's Concept of Inheritance: A Contribution to the Understanding of Heilsgeschichte.* Scottish Journal of Theology Occasional Papers 14. Edinburgh: Oliver & Boyd, 1968.

Hickling, "Attitudes"  Hickling, C. J. A. "Attitudes to Judaism in the Fourth Gospel." Pages 347–55 in *L'évangile de Jean: Sources, rédaction, théologie.* Edited by Marinus de Jonge. BETL 45. Gembloux: J. Duculot; Leuven: Leuven University Press, 1977.

Higgins, "Belief"  Higgins, A. J. B. "Jewish Messianic Belief in Justin Martyr's *Dialogue with Trypho.*" *NovT* 9 (1967): 298–305.

Higgins, "Eucharist"  Higgins, A. J. B. "The Origins of the Eucharist." *NTS* 1 (1954–1955): 200–9.

Higgins, *Historicity*  Higgins, A. J. B. *The Historicity of the Fourth Gospel.* London: Lutterworth, 1960.

Higgins, "Messiah"  Higgins, A. J. B. "The Priestly Messiah." *NTS* 13 (1966–1967): 211–39.

Higgins, "Priest"  Higgins, A. J. B. "Priest and Mesiah." *VT* 3, no. 4 (October 1953): 321–36.

Higgins, *Son of Man*  Higgins, A. J. B. *Jesus and the Son of Man.* Philadelphia: Fortress, 1964.

Hilhorst, "Wounds"  Hilhorst, A. "The Wounds of the Risen Jesus." *EstBib* 41 (1983): 165–67.

Hill, "Βαΐα"  Hill, John S. "Τὰ βαΐα τῶν φοινίκων (John 12:13): Pleonasm or Prolepsis?" *JBL* 101 (1982): 133–35.

Hill, *Matthew*  Hill, David. *The Gospel of Matthew.* New Century Bible. Grand Rapids: Eerdmans, 1972.

Hill, "Nathanael"  Hill, C. E. "The Identity of John's Nathanael." *JSNT* 67 (1997): 45–61.

Hill, *Prophecy*  Hill, David. *New Testament Prophecy.* New Foundations Theological Library. Atlanta: John Knox, 1979.

Hill, "Prophets"  Hill, David. "On the Evidence for the Creative Role of Christian Prophets." *NTS* 20 (1973–1974): 262–74.

Hill, "Sanhedrin"  Hill, David. "Jesus before the Sanhedrin—on What Charge?" *Irish Biblical Studies* 7 (1985): 174–86.

Hill, "Son"  Hill, David. "Son and Servant: An essay on Matthean Christology." *JSNT* 6 (1980): 2–16.

Hillard, Nobbs, and Winter, "Acts"  Hillard, T., A. Nobbs, and B. W. Winter. "Acts and the Pauline Corpus, I: Ancient Literary Parallels." Pages 183–213 in *The Book of Acts in Its Ancient Literary Setting.* Edited by Bruce W. Winter and Andrew D. Clarke. Vol. 1 of *The Book of Acts in Its First Century Setting.* Edited by Bruce W. Winter. Grand Rapids: Eerdmans, 1993.

Hillman, "Statements"  Hillman, T. P. "Authorial Statements, Narrative, and Character in Plutarch's *Agesilaus-Pompeius.*" *Greek, Roman and Byzantine Studies* 35 (1994): 255–80.

Hillyer, "Lamb"  Hillyer, N. "'The Lamb' in the Apocalypse." *EvQ* 39 (1967): 228–36.

Hilton and Marshall, *Gospels and Judaism*  Hilton, Michael, with Gordian Marshall. *The Gospels and Rabbinic Judaism: A Study Guide.* Hoboken, N.J.: Ktav, 1988.

Himmelfarb, "Ascent"  Himmelfarb, Martha. "Heavenly Ascent and the Relationship of the Apocalypse and the *Hekhalot* Literature." *HUCA* 59 (1988): 73–100.

Hinson, "Worshiping"  Hinson, E. Glenn. "Worshiping Like Pagans?" *Christian History* 37 (1993): 16–20.

Hirsch, *Interpretation*  Hirsch, E. D., Jr. *Validity in Interpretation.* New Haven: Yale University Press, 1967.

Hirsch, *Pentateuch*    Hirsch, Samson Raphael. *The Pentateuch.* Translated by Isaac Levy. 5 vols. London: Isaac Levy, 1956.

Hirschfeld, "Tiberias"    Hirschfeld, Yizhar. "Tiberias: Preview of Coming Attractions." *Bibical Archaeology Review* 17, no. 2 (1991): 44–51.

Hirschfeld, "Town-Plan"    Hirschfeld, Yizhar. "The History and Town-Plan of Ancient *Hammat Gädër.*" *Zeitschrift des Deutschen Palästina-Vereins* 103 (1987): 101–16 and plates 12–14.

Hirschfeld and Solar, "Baths"    Hirschfeld, Yizhar, and Giora Solar. "Sumptuous Roman Baths Uncovered near Sea of Galilee." *BAR* 10, no. 6 (November/December 1984): 22–40.

Hirschfeld and Solar, "Hmrhs'wt"    Hirschfeld, Yizhar, and Giora Solar. "Hmrhs'wt hrwmyym šl hmt-gdr—šlwš ʿwnwt-hpyrh [The Roman Thermae at Hammath-Gader—Three Seasons of Excavations]." *Qadmoniot* 13 (1980): 66–70.

Hirschman, "Units"    Hirschman, Marc. "Polemic Literary Units in the Classical Midrashim and Justin Martyr's *Dialogue with Trypho.*" *JQR* 83 (1992–1993): 369–84.

Hock, *Context*    Hock, Ronald F. *The Social Context of Paul's Ministry: Tentmaking and Apostleship.* Philadelphia: Fortress, 1980.

Hock, "Friend"    Hock, Ronald F. "An Extraordinary Friend in Chariton's *Callirhoe*: The Importance of Friendship in the Greek Romances." Pages 145–62 in *Greco-Roman Perspectives on Friendship.* Edited by John T. Fitzgerald. SBLRBS 34. Atlanta: Scholars Press, 1997.

Hock, "Novel"    Hock, Ronald F. "The Greek Novel." In *Greco-Roman Literature and the New Testament: Selected Forms and Genres.* Pages 127–46. Edited by David E. Aune. SBLSBS 21. Atlanta: Scholars Press, 1988.

Hodges, "Adultery"    Hodges, Zane C. "Problem Passages in the Gospel of John, Part 8: The Woman Taken in Adultery (John 7:53–8:11): The Text." *BSac* 136 (1979): 318–32.

Hodges, "Angel"    Hodges, Zane C. "Problem Passages in the Gospel of John, Part 5: The Angel at Bethesda—John 5:4." *BSac* 136 (1979): 25–39.

Hodges, "Rivers"    Hodges, Zane C. "Problem Passages in the Gospel of John, Part 7: Rivers of Living Water—John 7:37–39" *BSac* 136 (1979): 239–48.

Hodges, "Tomb"    Hodges, Zane C. "The Women and the Empty Tomb." *BSac* 123 (1966): 301–9.

Hodges, "Water"    Hodges, Zane C. "Problem Passages in the Gospel of John, Part 3: Water and Spirit—John 3:5." *BSac* 135 (1978): 206–220.

Hodgson, "Valerius Maximus"    Hodgson, Robert. "Valerius Maximus and Gospel Criticism." *CBQ* 51 (1989): 502–10.

Hoehner, *Antipas*    Hoehner, Harold W. *Herod Antipas.* SNTSMS 17. Cambridge: Cambridge University Press, 1972.

Hoehner, "Significance"    Hoehner, Harold W. "The Significance of the Year of our Lord's Crucifixion for New Testament Interpretation." In *New Dimensions in New Testament Study.* Pages 115–26. Edited by Richard N. Longenecker and Merrill C. Tenney. Grand Rapids: Zondervan, 1974.

Hoenig, "Conversion"    Hoenig, Sidney B. "Conversion during the Talmudic Period." Pages 33–66 in *Conversion to Judaism.* Edited by D. M. Eichhorn. New York: Ktav, 1965.

Hoenig, "Fantasies"    Hoenig, Sidney B. "Qumran Fantasies: A Rejoinder to Dr. Driver's 'Mythology of Qumran.'" *JQR* 63 (1972–1973): 292–316.

Hoenig, "Kinds of Labor"    Hoenig, Sidney B. "The Designated Number of Kinds of Labor Prohibited on the Sabbath." *JQR* 68 (1977–1978): 193–208.

Hoeree and Hoogbergen, "History"    Hoeree, Joris, and Wim Hoogbergen. "Oral History and Archival Data Combined: The Removal of the Saramakan Granman Kofi Bosuman as an Epistemological Problem." *Communication and Cognition* 17 nos. 2–3 (1984): 245–89.

Hofius, "Geist ohne Mass"    Hofius, Otfried. "'Er gibt den Geist ohne Mass' Joh 3,34b." *ZNW* 90, nos. 1–2 (1999): 131–34.

Hofius, "Sayings"    Hofius, Otfried. "Unknown Sayings of Jesus." Pages 336–60 in *The Gospel and the Gospels.* Edited by Peter Stuhlmacher. Grand Rapids: Eerdmans, 1991.

Hofius, "Schoss"    Hofius, Otfried. "'Der in des Vaters Schoss ist' Joh 1,18." *ZNW* 80 (1989): 163–71.

Hoheisel, "Seelenwanderung"    Hoheisel, Karl. "Das frühe Christentum und die Seelenwanderung." *Jahrbuch für Antike und Christentum* 27–28 (1984–1985): 24–46.

Holladay, "Statecraft"    Holladay, John S. "Assyrian Statecraft and the Prophets of Israel." *HTR* 63 (1970): 29–51.

Holladay, *Theios Aner*    Holladay, Carl R. *Theios Aner in Hellenistic Judaism: A Critique of the Use of This Category in New Testament Christology.* SBLDS 40. Missoula, Mont.: Scholars Press, 1977.

Hollenbach, "Irony"    Hollenbach, Bruce. "Lest They Should Turn and Be Forgiven: Irony." *Bible Translator* 34 (1983): 312–21.

Hollenweger, *Pentecostals*    Hollenweger, Walter J. *The Pentecostals.* London, SCM, 1972. Repr., Peabody, Mass.: Hendrickson, 1988.

Hollis, "Pun"    Hollis, H. "The Root of the Johannine Pun—ΥΨΩΘΗΝΑΙ." *NTS* 35 (1989): 475–78.

Holmberg, *Sociology and New Testament*    Holmberg, Bengt. *Sociology and the New Testament: An Appraisal.* Minneapolis: Fortress, 1990.

Holst, "One Anointing"    Holst, Robert. "The One Anointing of Jesus: Another Application of the Form-Critical Method." *JBL* 95 (1976): 435–46.

Holte, "Logos"    Holte, Ragnar. "Logos Spermatikos: Christianity and Ancient Philosophy according to St. Justin's Apologies." *Studia theologica* 12 (1958): 109–68.

Holwerda, *Spirit*    Holwerda, David Earl. *The Holy Spirit and Eschatology in the Gospel of John: A Critique of Rudolf Bultmann's Present Eschatology.* Kampen: Kok, 1959.

Homcy, "Gods"    Homcy, Stephen L. "'You Are Gods'? Spirituality and a Difficult Text." *JETS* 32 (1989): 485–91.

Hooke, "Spirit"    Hooke, S. H. "'The Spirit Was Not Yet.'" *NTS* 9 (1962–1963): 372–80.

Hooker, "Baptist"    Hooker, Morna D. "John the Baptist and the Johannine Prologue." *NTS* 16 (1969–1970): 354–58.

Hooker, *Message*    Hooker, Morna D. *The Message of Mark.* London: Epworth, 1983.

Hooker, *Preface*    Hooker, Morna D. *A Preface to Paul.* New York: Oxford University Press, 1980.

Hooker, *Servant*    Hooker, Morna D. *Jesus and the Servant.* London: SPCK, 1959.

Hoppe, "Synagogue"    Hoppe, Leslie J. "Synagogue and Church in Palestine." *The Bible Today* 27 (1989): 278–84.

Horbury, "Benediction"    Horbury, William. "The Benediction of the *Minim* and Early Jewish-Christian Controversy." *JTS* NS 33 (1982): 19–61.

Horbury, "Brigand"    Horbury, William. "Christ as Brigand in Ancient Anti-Christian Polemic." Pages 183–95 in *Jesus and the Politics of His Day.* Edited by Ernst Bammel and C. F. D. Moule. Cambridge: Cambridge University, 1984.

Horbury, "Extirpation"    Horbury, William. "Extirpation and Excommunication." *VT* 35 (January 1985): 13–38.

Horbury, "Ossuaries"    Horbury, William. "The 'Caiaphas' Ossuaries and Joseph Caiaphas." *PEQ* 126 (1994): 32–48.

Horsley, "Change"    Horsley, G. H. R. "Name Change as an Indication of Religious Conversion in Antiquity." *Numen* 34 (1987): 1–17.

Horsley, *Documents,* 1    Horsley, G. H. R., ed. *New Documents Illustrating Early Christianity.* Vol. 1: *A Review of the Greek Inscriptions and Papyri Published in 1976.* North Ryde, N.S.W.: Ancient History Documentary Research Centre, Macquarie University, 1981.

Horsley, *Documents,* 2    Horsley, G. H. R., ed. *New Documents Illustrating Early Christianity.* Vol. 2: *A Review of the Greek Inscriptions and Papyri Published in 1977.* North Ryde, N.S.W.: Ancient History Documentary Research Centre, Macquarie University, 1982.

Horsley, *Documents* 3    Horsley, G. H. R, ed. *New Documents Illustrating Early Christianity.* Vol. 3: *A Review of the Greek Inscriptions and Papyri Published in 1978.* North Ryde, N.S.W.: Ancient History Documentary Research Centre, Macquarie University, 1983.

Horsley, *Documents,* 4    Horsley, G. H. R., ed. *New Documents Illustrating Early Christianity.* Vol. 4: *A Review of the Greek Inscriptions and Papyri Published in 1979.* North Ryde, N.S.W.: Ancient History Documentary Research Centre, Macquarie University, 1987.

Horsley, *Documents,* 5    Horsley, G. H. R., ed. *New Documents Illustrating Early Christianity.* Vol. 5: *Linguistic Essays.* North Ryde, N.S.W.: Ancient History Documentary Research Centre, Macquarie University, 1989.

Horsley, "Formula"    Horsley, Richard A. "The Background of the Confessional Formula in 1Kor 8:6." *ZNW* 69 (1978): 130–35.

Horsley, *Galilee*   Horsley, Richard A. *Galilee: History, Politics, People.* Valley Forge, Pa.: Trinity Press International, 1995.

Horsley, "Groups"   Horsley, Richard. "Palestinian Jewish Groups and Their Messiahs in Late Second Temple Times." *Concilium*, no. 1 (1993): 14–29.

Horsley, "High Priests"   Horsley, Richard A. "High Priests and the Politics of Roman Palestine: Contextual Analysis of the Evidence in Josephus." *JSJ* 17 (1986): 23–55.

Horsley, "Inscriptions"   Horsley, G. H. R. "The Inscriptions of Ephesos and the New Testament." *NovT* 34 (1992): 105–68.

Horsley, "Law of Nature"   Horsley, Richard A. "The Law of Nature in Philo and Cicero." *HTR* 71 (1978): 35–59.

Horsley, "Prophets"   Horsley, Richard A. " 'Like One of the Prophets of Old': Two Types of Popular Prophets at the Time of Jesus." *CBQ* 47 (1985): 435–63.

Horsley, "Speeches"   Horsley, G. H. R. "Speeches and Dialogue in Acts." *NTS* 32 (1986): 609–14.

Horsley and Hanson, *Bandits*   Horsley, Richard A., and John S. Hanson. *Bandits, Prophets, and Messiahs: Popular Movements in the Time of Jesus.* Minneapolis: A Seabury Book, Winston Press, 1985.

Hoskyns, "Genesis"   Hoskyns, Edwyn Clement. "Genesis I-III and St. John's Gospel." *JTS* 21/83 (April 1919): 210–18.

Hoskyns, *Gospel*   Hoskyns, Edwyn Clement. *The Fourth Gospel.* Edited and completed by Francis Noel Davey. 2d rev. ed. London: Faber & Faber, 1947.

Horton, *Spirit*   Horton, Stanley M. *What the Bible Says about the Holy Spirit.* Springfield, Mo.: Gospel Publishing House, 1976.

Houlden, *Epistles*   Houlden, James Leslie. *A Commentary on the Johannine Epistles.* Harper's New Testament Commentaries. New York: Harper & Row, 1973.

Howard, "Beginnings"   Howard, George. "The Beginnings of Christianity in Rome: A Note on Suetonius, Life of Claudius XXV.4." *Restoration Quarterly* 24 (1981): 175–77.

Howard, *Gospel*   Howard, Wilbert Francis. *The Fourth Gospel in Recent Criticism and Interpretation.* 3d ed. London: Epworth, 1945.

Howard, "Tetragram"   Howard, George. "The Tetragram and the NT." *JBL* 96 (1977): 63–83.

Howton, "Son"   Howton, Dom John. " 'Son of God' in the Fourth Gospel." *NTS* 10 (1963–1964): 227–37.

Hoynacki, "Flesh"   Hoynacki, George J. " 'And the Word Was Made Flesh'—Incarnations in Religious Traditions." *Asia Journal of Theology* 7 (1993): 12–34.

Hruby, "Torah"   Hruby, K. "La Torah identifée à la sagesse et l'activité du 'sage' dans la tradition rabbinique." *Bible et vie chrétienne* 76 (1967): 65–78.

Hubbard, *Redaction*   Hubbard, Benjamin Jerome. *The Matthean Redaction of a Primitive Apostolic Commissioning: An Exegesis of Matthew 28:16–20.* SBLDS 19. Missoula, Mont.: Society of Biblical Literature, 1974.

Huffmon, "Background"   Huffmon, Herbert B. "The Treaty Background of Hebrew *Yada*." *BASOR* 181 (February 1966): 31–37.

Hughes, *Hebrews*   Hughes, Graham. *Hebrews and Hermeneutics: The Epistle to the Hebrews as a New Testament Example of Biblical Interpretation.* SNTSMS 36. Cambridge: Cambridge University Press, 1979.

Hultgren, "Footwashing"   Hultgren, Arland J. "The Johannine Footwashing (13.1–11) as Symbol of Eschatological Hospitality." *NTS* 28 (1982): 539–46.

Hume, "Miracles"   Hume, David. "Of Miracles." Pages 29–44 in *In Defense of Miracles: A Comprehensive Case for God's Action in History.* Edited by R. Douglas Geivett and Gary R. Habermas. Downers Grove, Ill.: InterVarsity, 1997.

Hunt, "Paraclete"   Hunt, Dwight. "Jesus' Teaching Concerning the Paraclete in the Upper Room Discourse." Master of Theology thesis, Western Conservative Baptist Seminary, April 1981.

Hunter, *John*   Hunter, Archibald M. *The Gospel according to John.* Cambridge Bible Commentary. Cambridge: Cambridge University Press, 1965.

Hunter, "John 11:41b–42"   Hunter, W. Bingham. "Contextual and Genre Implications for the Historicity of John 11:41b–42." *JETS* 28 (1985): 53–70.

Hunter, *Message*   Hunter, Archibald M. *The Message of the New Testament.* Philadelphia: Westminster, 1944.

Hunter, *Paul*    Hunter, Archibald M. *The Gospel according to St. Paul*. Philadelphia: Westminster, 1966.

Hunter, *Predecessors*    Hunter, Archibald M. *Paul and His Predecessors*. Rev. ed. Philadelphia: Westminster, 1961.

Hunter, *Romans*    Hunter, Archibald M. *The Epistle to the Romans*. London: SCM, 1955.

Hunter, "Trends"    Hunter, Archibald M. "Recent Trends in Johannine Studies." *ExpTim* 71 (1959–1960): 164–67.

Hunter, "Trends (Continued)"    Hunter, Archibald M. "Recent Trends in Johannine Studies (Continued)." *ExpTim* 71 (1959–1960): 219–22.

Huntingford, "Axum"    Huntingford, G. W. B. "The Kingdom of Axum." Pages 22–29 in *The Dawn of African History*. Edited by Roland Oliver. London: Oxford University Press, 1961.

Hurtado, *Mark*    Hurtado, Larry W. *Mark*. Good News Commentary. San Francisco: Harper & Row, 1983.

Hurtado, *One God*    Hurtado, Larry. *One God, One Lord: Early Christian Devotion and Ancient Jewish Monotheism*. Philadelphia: Fortress, 1988.

Hyldahl, "Kvinde"    Hyldahl, Niels. "Samtalen med den samaritanske kvinde." *Dansk teologisk tidsskrift* 56 (1993): 153–65.

Iglesias, "Reflexoes"    Iglesias, Esther. "Reflexoes sobre o quefazer da historia oral no mundo rural." *Dados* 27 (1984): 59–70.

Ilan, "Attraction"    Ilan, Tal. "The Attraction of Aristocratic Women to Pharisaism during the Second Temple Period." *HTR* 88 (1995): 1–33.

Ilan, "Cohabitation"    Ilan, Tal. "Premarital Cohabitation in Ancient Judea: The Evidence of the Babatha Archive and the Mishnah (*Ketubbot* 1.4)." *HTR* 86 (1993): 247–64.

Ilan, "Distribution"    Ilan, Tal. "Notes on the Distribution of Jewish Women's Names in Palestine in the Second Temple and Mishnaic Periods." *JJS* 40 (1989): 186–200.

Ilan, "Lhbdly"    Ilan, Tal. "Lhbdly ktyb šl šmwt btqwpt byt šny." *Leshonenu* 52 (1987): 3–7.

Ilan, *Women*    Ilan, Tal. *Jewish Women in Greco-Roman Palestine*. Peabody, Mass.: Hendrickson, 1996.

Infante, "L'amico"    Infante, Lorenzo. "L'amico dello sposo, figura de ministero di Giovanni Battista nel quarto vangelo." *RivB* 31 (1983): 3–19.

Infante, "Samaritana"    Infante, R. "Gesù, la samaritana, e la Samaria (Gv 4)." *Vetera Christianorum* 36, no. 1 (1999): 39–59.

Ingelaere, "Tradition"    Ingelaere, Jean-Claude. "La tradition des *logia* de Jésus dans l'évangile de Jean: Introduction à la problématique." *RevScRel* 69 (1995): 3–11.

Ingram, "Women"    Ingram, K. J. "Good News for Modern Women: The Gospel of John." *Spirituality Today* 41 (1989): 305–18.

Irsai, "'ny mkzb hw'"    Irsai, O. "ʾmr r. ʾbhw: ʾm yʾmr lk ʾdm ʾl ʾny mkzb hwʾ [R. Abbahu Said: 'If a Man Should Say to You "I am God"—He Is a Liar']." *Zion* 47 (1982): 173–77.

Irvin and Sunquist, *Movement*    Irvin, Dale T., and Scott W. Sunquist. *History of the World Christian Movement*. Vol. 1: *Earliest Christianity to 1453*. Maryknoll, N.Y.: Orbis, 2001.

Isaacs, *Spirit*    Isaacs, Marie E. *The Concept of Spirit: A Study of Pneuma in Hellenistic Judaism and Its Bearing on the New Testament*. Heythrop Monographs 1. London: Heythrop College, 1976.

Isaacs, "Spirit"    Isaacs, Marie E. "The Prophetic Spirit in the Fourth Gospel." *Heythrop Journal* 24 (1983): 391–407.

Isbell, *Bowls*    Isbell, Charles D. *Corpus of the Aramaic Incantation Bowls*. SBLDS 17. Missoula, Mont.: Scholars Press, 1975.

Isbell, "Story"    Isbell, Charles D. "The Story of the Aramaic Magical Incantation Bowls." *BA* 41 (1978): 5–16.

Isichei, *History*    Isichei, Elizabeth. *A History of Christianity in Africa from Antiquity to the Present*. Grand Rapids: Eerdmans, 1995.

Issar, "Evolution"    Issar, Arie. "The Evolution of the Ancient Water System in the Region of Jerusalem." *IEJ* 26 (1976): 130–36.

Isser, "Chronicles"    Isser, Stanley. "Jesus in the Samaritan Chronicles." *JJS* 32 (1981): 166–94.

Jackson, "Conventions"    Jackson, Howard M. "Ancient Self-Referential Conventions and Their Implications for the Authorship and Integrity of the Gospel of John." *JTS* NS 50 (1999): 1–34.

Jacobs, *Exegesis*    Jacobs, Louis. *Jewish Biblical Exegesis*. New York: Behrman House, 1973.

Jacobs, "Love"  Jacobs, Louis. "Greater Love Hath No Man . . . : The Jewish Point of View of Self-Sacrifice." *Judaism* 6 (winter 1957): 41–47.

Jacobson, "Q"  Jacobson, Arland D. "The Literary Unity of Q." *JBL* 101 (1982): 365–89.

Jacobson, "Serpent"  Jacobson, Howard. "Ezekiel the Tragedian and the Primeval Serpent." *American Journal of Philology* 102 (1981): 316–20.

Jacobson, "Tammuz"  Jacobson, Howard. "The *Liber antiquitatum biblicarum* and Tammuz." *JSP* 8 (1991): 63–65.

Jacobson, "Vision"  Jacobson, Howard. "Samuel's Vision in Pseudo-Philo's *Liber antiquitatum biblicarum*." *JBL* 112 (1993): 310–11.

Jacobson, "Visions"  Jacobson, Howard. "Visions of the Past: Jews and Greeks." *Judaism* 35 (1986): 467–82.

James, "Adulteress"  James, Stephen A. "The Adulteress and the Death Penalty." *JETS* 22 (1979): 45–53.

Jannière, "Problèmes"  Jannière, A. "'En arkhê ên o logos': Notes sur des problèmes de traduction." *Recherches de science religieuse* 83 (1995): 241–47.

Janssens, "Source gnostique"  Janssens, Yvonne. "Une source gnostique du prologue?" Pages 355–58 in *L'évangile de Jean: Sources, rédaction, théologie*. Edited by M. de Jonge. BETL 45. Gembloux: J. Duculot; Leuven: Leuven University Press, 1977.

Jastrow, *Dictionary*  Jastrow, Marcus. *A Dictionary of the Targumim, the Talmud Babli and Yerushalmi, and the Midrashic Literature*. New York: Judaica Press, 1985.

Jathanna, "Religious"  Jathanna, Origen Vasantha. "On Being Religious: A Meditation on John 7:1–14." *Asia Journal of Theology* 11, no. 2 (1997): 398–401.

Jaubert, "Calendar"  Jaubert, A. "The Calendar of Qumran and the Passion Narrative in John." Pages 62–75 in *John and Qumran*. Edited by James H. Charlesworth. London: Geoffrey Chapman, 1972.

Jaubert, *Date*  Jaubert, Annie. *The Date of the Last Supper*. Staten Island, N.Y.: Alba House, 1965.

Jeffers, *World*  Jeffers, James S. *The Greco-Roman World of the New Testament Era: Exploring the Background of Early Christianity*. Downers Grove, Ill.: InterVarsity, 1999.

Jenkins, *Next Christendom*  Jenkins, Philip. *The Next Christendom: The Coming of Global Christianity*. New York: Oxford University Press, 2002.

Jensen, "Binding"  Jensen, Robin M. "The Binding or Sacrifice of Isaac: How Jews and Christians See Differently." *Bible Review* 9, no. 5 (October 1993): 42–51.

Jepsen, "אמן"  Jepsen, Alfred. "אמן." Pages 292–323 in vol. 1 of *Theological Dictionary of the Old Testament*. Rev. ed. Edited by G. Johannes Botterweck and Helmer Ringgren. Translated by John T. Willis. Grand Rapids: Eerdmans, 1977–.

Jeremias, "ἀμνός"  Jeremias, Joachim. "ἀμνός, ἀρήν, ἀρνίον." *TDNT* 1:338–41.

Jeremias, *Eucharistic Words*  Jeremias, Joachim. *The Eucharistic Words of Jesus*. Translated by Norman Perrin. Philadelphia: Fortress, 1966.

Jeremias, *Jerusalem*  Jeremias, Joachim. *Jerusalem in the Time of Jesus*. London: SCM, 1969. Repr., Philadelphia: Fortress, 1975.

Jeremias, "Logos-Problem"  Jeremias, Joachim. "Zum Logos-Problem." *ZNW* 59 (1968): 82–85.

Jeremias, *Message*  Jeremias, Joachim. *The Central Message of the New Testament*. New York: Scribner, 1965.

Jeremias, *Parables*  Jeremias, Joachim. *The Parables of Jesus*. 2d rev. ed. New York: Scribner, 1972.

Jeremias, *Prayers*  Jeremias, Joachim. *The Prayers of Jesus*. Philadelphia: Fortress, 1964.

Jeremias, *Promise*  Jeremias, Joachim. *Jesus' Promise to the Nations*. Translated by S. H. Hooke. SBT 24. London: SCM, 1958.

Jeremias, "Qumran Texts"  Jeremias, Joachim. "The Qumran Texts and the New Testament." *ExpTim* 70 (1958–1959): 68–69.

Jeremias, *Sayings*  Jeremias, Joachim. *Unknown Sayings of Jesus*. 2d English ed. Translated by Reginald H. Fuller. London: SPCK, 1964.

Jeremias, *Theology*  Jeremias, Joachim. *New Testament Theology*. Translated by John Bowden. New York: Scribner, 1971.

Jervell, *Luke*  Jervell, Jacob. *Luke and the People of God: A New Look at Luke–Acts*. Foreword by Nils Dahl. Minneapolis: Augsburg, 1972.

Jervell, *Paul*  Jervell, Jacob. *The Unknown Paul: Essays on Luke-Acts and Early Christian History*. Translated by Roy A. Harrisville. Minneapolis: Augsburg, 1984.

Jewett, *Chronology*   Jewett, Robert. *A Chronology of Paul's Life.* Philadelphia: Fortress, 1979.

Jobling, "Dominion"   Jobling, David. "'And Have Dominion . . .': The Interpretation of Genesis 1,28 in Philo Judaeus." *JSJ* 8 (1977): 50–82.

Jochim, *Religions*   Jochim, Christian. *Chinese Religions: A Cultural Perspective.* Prentice-Hall Series in World Religions. Englewood Cliffs, N.J.: Prentice-Hall, 1986.

Jocz, *People*   Jocz, Jakob. *The Jewish People and Jesus Christ: The Relationship between Church and Synagogue.* 3d ed. London: SPCK, 1962. Repr., Grand Rapids: Baker, 1979.

Jóczwiak, "Mesjanizm"   Jóczwiak, F. "Mesjanizm w literaturze z Qumran (Le messianisme dans les textes de Qumran)." *Roczniki teologiczno-kanoniczne* 10, no. 1 (1963): 35–42.

Johansson, *Parakletoi*   Johansson, Nils. *Parakletoi: Vorstellungen von Fürsprechern für die Menschen vor Gott in der alttestamentlichen Religion, im Spätjudentum und Urchristentum.* Lund: Gleerup, 1940.

Johns and Miller, "Signs"   Johns, Loren L., and Douglas B. Miller. "The Signs as Witnesses in the Fourth Gospel: Reexamining the Evidence." *CBQ* 56 (1994): 519–35.

Johnson, *Acts*   Johnson, Luke Timothy. *The Acts of the Apostles.* Sacra pagina 5. Collegeville, Minn.: Liturgical Press, 1992.

Johnson, "Adam"   Johnson, M. D. Introduction to "Life of Adam and Eve." *OTP* 2:249–57.

Johnson, "*Delatorum*"   Johnson, Gary J. "*De conspiratione delatorum:* Pliny and the Christians Revisited." *Latomus* 47 (1988): 417–22.

Johnson, *Genealogies*   Johnson, Marshall D. *The Purpose of the Biblical Genealogies: With Special reference to the Setting of the Genealogies of Jesus.* 2d ed. SNTSMS 8. Cambridge: Cambridge University Press, 1988.

Johnson, *Possessions*   Johnson, Luke Timothy. *Sharing Possessions: Mandate and Symbol of Faith.* Philadelphia: Fortress, 1981.

Johnson, *Prayer*   Johnson, Norman B. *Prayer in the Apocrypha and Pseudepigrapha.* SBLMS 2. Philadelphia: Society of Biblical Literature and Exegesis, 1948.

Johnson, *Real Jesus*   Johnson, Luke Timothy. *The Real Jesus: The Misguided Quest for the Historical Jesus and the Truth of the Traditional Gospels.* San Francisco: Harper San Francisco, 1996.

Johnson, "Slander"   Johnson, Luke Timothy. "The New Testament's Anti-Jewish Slander and Conventions of Ancient Rhetoric." *JBL* 108 (1989): 419–41.

Johnson, *Writings*   Johnson, Luke Timothy. *The Writings of the New Testament: An Interpretation.* Philadelphia: Fortress, 1986.

Johnston, *Ephesians*   Johnston, George. *Ephesians, Philippians, Colossians, and Philemon.* Century Bible. Greenwood, S.C.: Attic Press, 1967.

Johnston, *Parables*   Johnston, Robert M. "Parabolic Interpretations Attributed to Tannaim." Ph.D. diss., Hartford Seminary Foundation, 1977. Ann Arbor, Mich.: University Microfilms International, 1978.

Johnston, "Sabbath"   Johnston, Robert M. "The Eschatological Sabbath in John's Apocalypse: A Reconsideration." *Andrews University Seminary Studies* 25 (1987): 39–50.

Johnston, *Spirit-Paraclete*   Johnston, George. *The Spirit-Paraclete in the Gospel of John.* SNTSMS 12. Cambridge: Cambridge University Press, 1970.

Johnston, "Version"   Johnston, Edwin D. "The Johannine Version of the Feeding of the Five Thousand—an Independent Tradition?" *NTS* 8 (1961–1962): 151–54.

Johnstone, "Paraclete"   Johnstone, G. Patrick. "The Promise of the Paraclete." *BSac* 127 (1970): 333–45.

Joly, *Vocabulaire*   Joly, R. *Le vocabulaire chrétien de l'amour, est-il original?* Brussels: Universitaires de Bruxelles, 1968.

Jonas, *Religion*   Jonas, Hans. *The Gnostic Religion: The Message of the Alien God and the Beginnings of Christianity.* 2d rev. ed. Boston: Beacon, 1963.

Jones, "Army"   Jones, James L. "The Roman Army." Pages 187–217 in *The Catacombs and the Colosseum: The Roman Empire as the Setting of Primitive Christianity.* Edited by Stephen Benko and John J. O'Rourke. Valley Forge, Pa.: Judson, 1971.

Jones, *Chrysostom*   Jones, C. P. *The Roman World of Dio Chrysostom.* Cambridge: Harvard University Press, 1978.

Jones, "Epigram"   Jones, C. P. "An Epigram on Apollonius of Tyana." *Journal of Hellenic Studies* 100 (1980): 190–94.

Jones, *History*    Jones, A. M. H. *A History of Rome through the Fifth Century.* Vol. 2: *The Empire.* New York: Walker and Company, 1970.

Jones, "Inscription"    Jones, Richard N. "A New Reading of the Petra Temple Inscription." *BASOR* 275 (August 1989): 41–46.

Jones, "Moïse"    Jones, P. "Moïse et Christ dans Jean 1,17: Opposition ou complémentarité?" *Hokhma* 55 (1994): 3–17.

Jones, *Parables*    Jones, Ivor H. *The Matthean Parables: A Literary and Historical Commentary.* NovTSup 80. Leiden: Brill, 1995.

Jonge, "'Anointed'"    Jonge, Marinus de. "The Use of the Word 'Anointed' in the Time of Jesus." *NovT* 8 (1966): 132–48.

Jonge, *L'évangile*    Jonge, Marinus de, ed. *L'évangile de Jean: Sources, rédaction, théologie.* BETL 45. Gembloux: J. Duculot; Leuven: Leuven University Press, 1977.

Jonge, "Expectations"    Jonge, Marinus de. "Jewish Expectations about the 'Messiah' according to the Fourth Gospel." *NTS* 19 (1972–1973): 246–70.

Jonge, *Jesus*    Jonge, Marinus de. *Jesus: Stranger from Heaven and Son of God.* Edited and translated by John E. Steely. Missoula, Mont.: Scholars Press, 1977.

Jonge, "Jews"    Jonge, Henk Jan de. "The 'Jews' in the Gospel of John." Pages 239–59 in *Anti-Judaism and the Fourth Gospel: Papers of the Leuven Colloquium, 2000.* Edited by R. Bieringer, D. Pollefeyt, and F. Vandecasteele-Vanneuville. Assen: Royal Van Gorcum, 2001.

Jonge, "New Testament"    Jonge, Marinus de. "The New Testament." Pages 37–43 in Safrai and Stern, *Jewish People.*

Jonge, "Psalms of Solomon"    Jonge, Marinus de. "The Expectation of the Future in the Psalms of Solomon." *Neotestamentica* 23 (1989): 93–117.

Jonge and Van Der Woude, "11QMelchizedek"    Jonge, Marinus de, and A. S. Van Der Woude. "11QMelchizedek and the New Testament." *NTS* 12 (1965–1966): 301–26.

Jordan, *Egypt*    Jordan, Paul. *Egypt the Black Land.* New York: Dutton, 1976.

Joubert, "Contention"    Joubert, S. J. "A Bone of Contention in Recent Scholarship: The 'Birkath Ha-minim' and the Separation of Church and Synagogue in the First Century A.D." *Neotestamentica* 27 (1993): 351–63.

Judge, "Community"    Judge, E. A. "The Early Christians as a Scholastic Community." *The Journal of Religious History* 1 (1960–1961): 4–15, 125–37.

Judge, *Pattern*    Judge, E. A. *The Social Pattern of the Christian Groups in the First Century: Some Prolegomena to the Study of New Testament Ideas of Social Obligation.* London: Tyndale, 1960.

Judge, *Rank*    Judge, E. A. *Rank and Status in the World of the Caesars and St Paul.* Broadhead Memorial Lecture 1981. University of Canterbury Publications 29. n.p.: University of Canterbury, 1982.

Judge, "Rhetoric of Inscriptions"    Judge, Edwin A. "The Rhetoric of Inscriptions." Pages 807–28 in *Handbook of Classical Rhetoric in the Hellenistic Period, 330 B.C.–A.D. 400.* Edited by Stanley E. Porter. Leiden: Brill, 1997.

Judge, "Rise"    Judge, E. A. "Judaism and the Rise of Christianity: A Roman Perspective." *Tyndale Bulletin* 45 (1994): 355–68.

Juel, "Dimensions"    Juel, Donald. "Social Dimensions of Exegesis: The Use of Psalm 16 in Acts 2." *CBQ* 42 (1981): 543–56.

Juel, *Messiah*    Juel, Donald. *Messiah and Temple: The Trial of Jesus in the Gospel of Mark.* SBLDS 31. Missoula: Scholars Press, 1977.

Jungkuntz, "John 10:34–36"    Jungkuntz, Richard. "An Approach to the Exegesis of John 10:34–36." *Concordia Theological Monthly* 35 (1964): 556–65.

Kadushin, *Mind*    Kadushin, Max. *The Rabbinic Mind.* 3d ed. New York: Bloch, 1972.

Kahle, "Karaites"    Kahle, P. "The Karaites and the Manuscripts from the Cave." *VT* 3 (January 1953): 82–84.

Kaiser, "Pantheon"    Kaiser, Walter C., Jr. "The Ugaritic Pantheon." Ph.D. diss., Brandeis University, 1973.

Kaiser, *Theology*    Kaiser, Walter C., Jr. *Toward an Old Testament Theology.* Grand Rapids: Zondervan, 1978.

Kalantzis, "Ephesus"    Kalantzis, George. "Ephesus as a Roman, Christian, and Jewish Metropolis in the First and Second Centuries C.E." *Jian Dao* 8 (1997): 103–19.

Kalimi and Purvis, "Hiding"  Kalimi, Isaac, and James D. Purvis. "The Hiding of the Temple Vessels in Jewish and Samaritan Literature." *CBQ* 56 (1994): 679–85.

Kallarangatt, "Mission"  Kallarangatt, Joseph. "Johannine Understanding of Mission." *Third Millennium* 2, no. 4 (1999): 49–58.

Kallas, "Apocalypse"  Kallas, James. "The Apocalypse—an Apocalyptic Book?" *JBL* 86 (1967): 69–80.

Kalmin, "Heretics"  Kalmin, Richard. "Christians and Heretics in Rabbinic Literature of Late Antiquity." *HTR* 87 (1994): 155–69.

Kanagaraj, "Mysticism"  Kanagaraj, Jey J. "Jesus the King, Merkabah Mysticism, and the Gospel of John." *Tyndale Bulletin* 47 (1996): 349–66.

Kanagaraj, *"Mysticism" in John*  Kanagaraj, Jey J. *"Mysticism" in the Gospel of John: An Inquiry into Its Background.* JSNTSS 158. Sheffield: Sheffield Academic Press, 1998.

Kangas, "Father's House"  Kangas, Ron. "'In My Father's House': The Unleavened Truth of John 14." *Affirmation & Critique* 5, no. 2 (2000): 22–36.

Kantowicz, *Rage*  Kantowicz, Edward R. *The Rage of Nations.* Vol. 1 of *The World in the Twentieth Century.* 2 vols. Grand Rapids: Eerdmans, 1999.

Kany, "Bericht"  Kany, R. "Der lukanische Bericht von Tod und Auferstehung Jesu aus der Sicht eines hellenistichen Romanlesers." *NovT* 28 (1986): 75–90.

Kaplan and Johnson, "Meaning"  Kaplan, Bert, and Dale Johnson. "The Social Meaning of Navajo Psychopathology and Psychotherapy." Pages 203–29 in *Magic, Faith, and Healing: Studies in Primitive Psychiatry Today.* Edited by Ari Kiev. Foreword by Jerome D. Frank. New York: Free Press, Macmillan, 1964.

Karris, *Marginalized*  Karris, Robert J. *Jesus and the Marginalized in John's Gospel.* Zacchaeus Studies: New Testament. Collegeville, Minn.: Liturgical Press, a Michael Glazier Book, 1990.

Karwiese, "Church of Mary"  Karwiese, Stefan. "The Church of Mary and the Temple of Hadrian Olympius." Pages 311–19 in *Ephesos—Metropolis of Asia: An Interdisciplinary Approach to Its Archaeology, Religion, and Culture.* Edited by Helmut Koester. Harvard Theological Studies. Valley Forge, Pa.: Trinity Press International, 1995.

Käsemann, *Questions*  Käsemann, Ernst. *New Testament Questions of Today.* Translated by W. J. Montague. Philadelphia: Fortress, 1969.

Käsemann, *Romans*  Käsemann, Ernst. *Commentary on Romans.* Translated and edited by Geoffrey W. Bromiley. Grand Rapids: Eerdmans, 1980.

Käsemann, *Testament*  Käsemann, Ernst. *The Testament of Jesus.* Translated by Gerhard Krodel. Philadelphia: Fortress, 1978.

Kassing, "Weib"  Kassing, A. "Das Weib, das den Mann gebar (Apk 12,13)." *Benediktinische Monatschrift* 34 (1958): 427–33.

Katz, "Separation"  Katz, Steven T. "Issues in the Separation of Judaism and Christianity after 70 C.E.: A Reconsideration." *JBL* 103 (1984): 43–76.

Katzoff, "Suffragium"  Katzoff, Ranon. "Suffragium in Exodus Rabbah 37.2." *Classical Philology* 81 (1986): 235–40.

Kaufman, "Anti-Semitism"  Kaufman, Philip S. "Anti-Semitism in the New Testament: The Witness of the Beloved Disciple." *Worship* 63 (1989): 386–401.

Kaufman, *Disciple*  Kaufman, Philip S. *The Beloved Disciple: Witness against Anti-Semitism.* Collegeville, Minn.: Liturgical Press, 1991.

Kaufmann, "Idea"  Kaufmann, Yehezkel. "The Messianic Idea: The Real and the Hidden Son-of-David." *Jewish Bible Quarterly* 22, no. 3 (1994): 141–50.

Kaye, *Apology*  Kaye, John. *The First Apology of Justin Martyr.* Edinburgh: John Grant, 1912.

Kazui Yagi, "Theology"  Kazui Yagi, Dickson. "Christ for Asia: Yellow Theology for the East." *Review and Expositor* 88 (1991): 357–78.

Keck, "Derivation"  Keck, Leander E. "Derivation as Destiny: 'Of-ness' in Johannine Christology, Anthropology, and Soteriology." Pages 274–88 in *Exploring the Gospel of John: In Honor of D. Moody Smith.* Edited by R. Alan Culpepper and C. Clifton Black. Louisville, Ky.: Westminster John Knox, 1996.

Keck, "Ethos"  Keck, Leander E. "On the Ethos of Early Christians." *Journal of the American Academy of Religion* 42 (1974): 435–52.

Kee, *Community*   Kee, Howard Clark. *Community of the New Age: Studies in Mark's Gospel.* Philadelphia: Westminster, 1977.

Kee, "Isis"   Kee, Howard Clark. "Myth and Miracle: Isis, Wisdom, and the Logos of John." Pages 99–125 in *Myth, Symbol, Reality.* Edited by Alan M. Olson. Notre Dame, Ind.: University of Notre Dame Press, 1980.

Kee, *Miracle*   Kee, Howard Clark. *Miracle in the Early Christian World: A Study in Sociohistorical Method.* New Haven: Yale University Press, 1983.

Kee, *Origins*   Kee, Howard Clark. *Christian Origins in Sociological Perspective: Methods and Resources.* Philadelphia: Westminster, 1980.

Kee, "Self-Definition"   Kee, Howard Clark. "Self-Definition in the Asclepius Cult." Pages 118–36 in vol. 3 of Meyer and Sanders, *Self-Definition.*

Kee, "Tell-Er-Ras"   Kee, Howard Clark. "Tell-Er-Ras and the Samaritan Temple." *NTS* 13 (1966–1967): 401–2.

Keener, "Adultery"   Keener, Craig S. "Adultery, Divorce." Pages 6–16 in *Dictionary of New Testament Background.* Edited by Craig A. Evans and Stanley E. Porter. Downers Grove, Ill.: InterVarsity, 2000.

Keener, *Background Commentary*   Keener, Craig S. *The IVP Bible Background Commentary: New Testament.* Downers Grove, Ill.: InterVarsity, 1993.

Keener, "Court"   Keener, Craig S. "Matthew 5:22 and the Heavenly Court." *ExpTim* 99 (1987–1988): 46.

Keener, "Critique"   Keener, Craig S. Review of *The Lost Gospel: The Book of Q and Christian Origins,* by Burton L. Mack. Paper presented at the 47th National Conference of the Evangelical Theological Society, Philadelphia, Pa., November 16–18, 1995. Theological Research Exchange Network, ETS-4738 [9217]. Microfiche.

Keener, "Family"   Keener, Craig S. "Family and Household." Pages 353–68 in *Dictionary of New Testament Background.* Edited by Craig A. Evans and Stanley E. Porter. Downers Grove, Ill.: InterVarsity, 2000.

Keener, "Friendship"   Keener, Craig S. "Friendship." Pages 380–88 in *Dictionary of New Testament Background.* Edited by Craig A. Evans and Stanley Porter. Downers Grove, Ill.: InterVarsity, 2000.

Keener, *Giver*   Keener, Craig S. *Gift and Giver: The Holy Spirit for Today.* Grand Rapids: Baker, 2001.

Keener, "Head Coverings"   Keener, Craig S. "Head Coverings." Pages 442–47 in *Dictionary of New Testament Background.* Edited by Craig A. Evans and Stanley Porter. Downers Grove, Ill.: InterVarsity, 2000.

Keener, "Husband"   Keener, Craig S. "Husband of One Wife." *The A.M.E. Zion Quarterly Review* 109 (1997): 5–24.

Keener, "Knowledge"   Keener, Craig S. "Studies in the Knowledge of God in the Fourth Gospel in Light of Its Historical Context." M.Div. thesis, Assemblies of God Theological Seminary, 1986.

Keener, "Lamb"   Keener, Craig S. "Lamb." Pages 641–42 in *Dictionary of the Later New Testament and Its Developments.* Edited by Ralph P. Martin and Peter H. Davids. Downers Grove, Ill.: InterVarsity, 1997.

Keener, "Man"   Keener, Craig S. "Woman and Man." Pages 1205–15 in *Dictionary of the Later New Testament and Its Developments.* Edited by Ralph P. Martin and Peter H. Davids. Downers Grove, Ill.: InterVarsity, 1997.

Keener, "Marriage"   Keener, Craig S. "Marriage." Pages 680–93 in *Dictionary of New Testament Background.* Edited by Craig A. Evans and Stanley Porter. Downers Grove, Ill.: InterVarsity, 2000.

Keener, *Marries*   Keener, Craig S. *. . . And Marries Another: Divorce and Remarriage in the Teaching of the New Testament.* Peabody, Mass.: Hendrickson, 1991.

Keener, *Matthew*   Keener, Craig S. *A Commentary on the Gospel of Matthew.* Grand Rapids: Eerdmans, 1999.

Keener, "Mistrial"   Keener, Craig S. "Mistrial of the Millennium." *Christian History* 59 (1998): 38–40.

Keener, *Paul*   Keener, Craig S. *Paul, Women, and Wives: Marriage and Women's Ministry in the Letters of Paul.* Peabody, Mass.: Hendrickson, 1992.

Keener, "Pneumatology"    Keener, Craig S. "The Function of Johannine Pneumatology in the Context of Late First-Century Judaism." Ph.D. diss., Duke University, 1991.

Keener, *Questions*    Keener, Craig S. *Three Crucial Questions about the Holy Spirit.* Grand Rapids: Baker, 1996.

Keener, *Revelation*    Keener, Craig S. *Revelation.* NIV Application Commentary. Grand Rapids: Zondervan, 2000.

Keener, "Review of Beck"    Keener, Craig S. Review of David R. Beck, *Discipleship Paradigm. Faith and Mission* 16 (1998–1999): 118–20.

Keener, "Review of Chilton"    Keener, Craig S. Review of Bruce Chilton, *Judaic Approaches to the Gospels. Ashland Theological Journal* 27 (1995): 149–51.

Keener, "Review of Collins"    Keener, Craig S. Review of Raymond F. Collins, *Divorce in the New Testament. Critical Review of Books in Religion 1993.* Vol. 6. Atlanta: Scholars Press, 1994.

Keener, "Review of Fitzgerald"    Keener, Craig S. Review of John T. Fitzgerald, ed., *Greco-Roman Perspectives on Friendship. JETS* 43, no. 1 (March 2000): 128–29.

Keener, "Shepherd"    Keener, Craig S. "Shepherd, Flock." Pages 1090–93 in *Dictionary of the Later New Testament and Its Developments.* Edited by Ralph P. Martin and Peter H. Davids. Downers Grove, Ill.: InterVarsity, 1997.

Keener, *Spirit*    Keener, Craig S. *The Spirit in the Gospels and Acts.* Peabody, Mass.: Hendrickson, 1997.

Keener, "Subordination"    Keener, Craig S. "Is Subordination within the Trinity Really Heresy? A Study of John 5:18 in Context." *Trinity Journal* NS 20 (1999): 39–51.

Keener, "Woman"    Keener, Craig S. "Man and Woman." Pages 583–92 in *Dictionary of Paul and His Letters.* Edited by Gerald F. Hawthorne, Ralph P. Martin, and Daniel G. Reid. Downers Grove, Ill.: InterVarsity, 1993.

Keener and Usry, *Faith*    Keener, Craig S., and Glenn Usry. *Defending Black Faith.* Downers Grove, Ill.: InterVarsity, 1997.

Kelber, *Gospel*    Kelber, Werner H. *The Oral and the Written Gospel.* Philadelphia: Fortress, 1983.

Kelber, "Metaphysics"    Kelber, Werner H. "Metaphysics and Marginality in John." Pages 129–54 in *"What Is John?" Readers and Reading of the Fourth Gospel.* Edited by Fernando F. Segovia. SBLSymS 3. Atlanta: Scholars Press, 1996.

Kelber, *Story*    Kelber, Werner H. *Mark's Story of Jesus.* Philadelphia: Fortress, 1979.

Kelly, *Peter*    Kelly, J. N. D. *A Commentary on the Epistles of Peter and Jude.* Thornapple Commentaries. Grand Rapids: Baker, 1981.

Kennard, "Assembly"    Kennard, J. Spencer, Jr. "The Jewish Provincial Assembly." *ZNW* 53 (1962): 25–51.

Kennedy, *Art of Rhetoric*    Kennedy, George A. *The Art of Rhetoric in the Roman World: 300 B.C.–A.D. 300.* Princeton, N.J.: Princeton University Press, 1972.

Kennedy, *Classical Rhetoric*    Kennedy, George A. *Classical Rhetoric and Its Christian and Secular Tradition from Ancient to Modern Times.* Chapel Hill, N.C.: University of North Carolina Press, 1980.

Kennedy, "Criticism"    Kennedy, George A. "Classical and Christian Source Criticism." Pages 125–55 in *The Relationship among the Gospels: An Interdisciplinary Dialogue.* Edited by W. W. Walker Jr., et al. Trinity University Monograph Series in Religion 5. San Antonio, Tex.: Trinity University Press, 1978.

Kennedy, *Epistles*    Kennedy, H. A. A. *The Theology of the Epistles.* New York: Scribner, 1920.

Kennedy, *Interpretation*    Kennedy, George A. *New Testament Interpretation through Rhetorical Criticism.* Chapel Hill, N.C.: University of North Carolina Press, 1984.

Kennedy, "Resurrection"    Kennedy, K. A. "The Resurrection of Jesus." *Studies* 74 (1985): 440–54.

Kennedy, "Rhetoric of Gospels"    Kennedy, George A. "An Introduction to the Rhetoric of the Gospels." *Rhetorica* 1, no. 2 (1983): 17–31.

Kennedy, "Survey of Rhetoric"    Kennedy, George A. "Historical Survey of Rhetoric." Pages 3–41 in *Handbook of Classical Rhetoric in the Hellenistic Period, 330 B.C.–A.D. 400.* Edited by Stanley E. Porter. Leiden: Brill, 1997.

Kenney, *John 1:1*    Kenney, Garrett C. *John 1:1 as Prooftext: Trinitarian or Unitarian?* Lanham, Md.: University Press of America, 1999.

Kent, *Jerusalem*    Kent, Homer A. *Jerusalem to Rome: Studies in the Book of Acts.* Grand Rapids: Baker, 1972.

Kern-Ulmer, "Bewertung"    Kern-Ulmer, Brigitte. "Die Bewertung der Proselyten in rabbinischen Schrifttum." *Judaica* 50, no. 1 (1994): 1–17.

Keylock, "Distinctness"    Keylock, Leslie R. "Bultmann's Law of Increasing Distinctness." Pages 193–210 in *Current Issues in Biblical and Patristic Interpretation: Studies in Honor of Merrill C. Tenney Presented by His Former Students.* Edited by Gerald F. Hawthorne. Grand Rapids: Eerdmans, 1975.

Kieffer, "L'arrière-fond juif"    Kieffer, René. "L'arrière-fond juif du lavement des pieds." *RB* 105, no. 4 (1998): 546–55.

Kieffer, "Fottvagningens"    Kieffer, René. "Fottvagningens tolkning mot dess judiska bakgrund." *Svensk exegetisk årsbok* 63 (1998): 217–23.

Kiev, *Magic*    Kiev, Ari, ed. *Magic, Faith, and Healing: Studies in Primitive Psychiatry Today.* Foreword by Jerome D. Frank. New York: Free Press, Macmillan, 1964.

Kiley, "Geography"    Kiley, Mark. "The Geography of Famine: John 6:22–25." *RB* 102 (1995): 226–30.

Kilpatrick, "Background"    Kilpatrick, G. D. "The Religious Background of the Fourth Gospel." Pages 36–44 in *Studies in the Fourth Gospel.* Edited by F. L. Cross. London: Mowbray, 1957.

Kilpatrick, "Punctuation"    Kilpatrick, G. D. "The Punctuation of John VII.37–38." *JTS* NS 11 (1960): 340–42.

Kim, "Invitation"    Kim, Chan-Hie. "The Papyrus Invitation." *JBL* 94 (1975): 391–402.

Kim, *Letter*    Kim, Chan-Hie. *Form and Structure of the Familiar Greek Letter of Recommendation.* SBLDS 4. Missoula, Mont.: Society of Biblical Literature, 1972.

Kim, "Mark"    Kim, Deuk-Joong. "Mark—a Theologian of Resurrection." Ph.D. diss., Drew University Graduate School, 1978.

Kim, *Origin*    Kim, Seyoon. *The Origin of Paul's Gospel.* Tübingen: Mohr, 1981.

Kimbrough, "Sabbath"    Kimbrough, S. T. "The Concept of Sabbath at Qumran." *RevQ* 5 (1964–1966): 483–502.

Kimelman, "'Amidah"    Kimelman, Reuven. "The Daily 'Amidah and the Rhetoric of Redemption." *JQR* 79 (1988–1989): 165–97.

Kimelman, "*Birkath*"    Kimelman, Reuven. "*Birkath Ha-minim* and the Lack of Evidence for an Anti-Christian Jewish Prayer in Late Antiquity." Pages 226–44 in vol. 2 of Meyer and Sanders, *Self-Definition.*

Kimelman, "Note"    Kimelman, Reuven. "A Note on Weinfeld's 'Grace after Meals in Qumran." *JBL* 112 (1993): 695–96.

King, "Brown"    King, J. S. "R. E. Brown on the History of the Johannine Community." *Scripture Bulletin* 13, no. 2 (1983): 26–30.

King, "Sychar"    King, J. S. "Sychar and Calvary: A Neglected Theory in the Interpretation of the Fourth Gospel." *Theology* 77 (1974): 417–22.

Kingsbury, *Christology*    Kingsbury, Jack Dean. *The Christology of Mark's Gospel.* Philadelphia: Fortress, 1983.

Kingsbury, "Conclusion"    Kingsbury, Jack Dean. "Conclusion: Analysis of a Conversation." Pages 259–69 in *Social History of the Matthean Community: Cross-disciplinary Approaches.* Edited by David L. Balch. Minneapolis: Fortress, 1991.

Kingsbury, "Plot"    Kingsbury, Jack Dean. "The Plot of Matthew's Story." *Interpretation* 46 (1992): 347–56.

Kingsbury, *Structure*    Kingsbury, Jack Dean. *Matthew: Structure, Christology, Kingdom.* Philadelphia: Fortress, 1975.

Kinzig, "Non-separation"    Kinzig, Wolfram. "'Non-separation': Closeness and Co-operation between Jews and Christians in the Fourth Century." *Vigiliae christianae* 45 (1991): 27–53.

Kirby, *Ephesians*    Kirby, John C. *Ephesians: Baptism and Pentecost (an Inquiry into the Structure and Purpose of the Epistle to the Ephesians).* Montreal: McGill University Press, 1968.

Kirchhevel, "Children"    Kirchhevel, Gordon D. "The Children of God and the Glory That John 1:14 Saw." *Bulletin of Biblical Research* 6 (1996): 87–93.

Kirk, "Apostleship"    Kirk, J. Andrew. "Apostleship Since Rengstorf: Towards a Synthesis." *NTS* 21 (1974–1975): 249–64.

Kirk, *Vision*   Kirk, Kenneth E. *The Vision of God: The Christian Doctrine of the Summum Bonum.* Bampton Lectures for 1928. Abridged edition. London: Longmans, Green, 1934.

Kirschner, "Imitatio"   Kirschner, Robert. "Imitatio Rabbini." *JSJ* 17 (1986): 70–79.

Kitchen, "Background"   Kitchen, Kenneth A. "Some Egyptian Background to the Old Testament." *Tyndale Bulletin* 5 (1960): 4–18.

Kitchen, *Orient*   Kitchen, Kenneth A. *Ancient Orient and the Old Testament.* Chicago: InterVarsity, 1968.

Kittel, "λέγω, λόγος, κτλ"   Kittel, Gerhard. "λέγω, λόγος, κτλ. C, D." *TDNT* 4:101–143.

Klaiber, "Zeuge"   Klaiber, Walter. "Der irdische und der himmlische Zeuge: Eine Auslegung von Joh 3 22–36." *NTS* 36 (1990): 205–33.

Klassen, "Law"   Klassen, William. "The King as 'Living Law' with Particular Reference to Musonius Rufus." *SR* 14 (1985): 63–71.

Klauck, "Rhetorik"   Klauck, Hans-Josef. "Hellenistische Rhetorik im Diasporajudentum: Das Exordium des vierten Makkabäerbuchs (4 Makk 1.1–12)." *NTS* 35 (1989): 451–65.

Klauck, "Sendschreiben"   Klauck, Hans-Josef. "Das Sendschreiben nach Pergamon und der Kaiserkult in der Johannesoffenbarung." *Biblica* 73 (1992): 153–82.

Klausner, *Jesus*   Klausner, Joseph. *Jesus: His Life, Times, and Teaching.* Translated by Herbert Danby. Foreword by Sidney B. Hoenig. n.p.: Macmillan, 1925. Repr., New York: Menorah, 1979;.

Klausner, *Paul*   Klausner, Joseph. *From Jesus to Paul.* Translated by W. Stinespring. n.p.: Macmillan, 1943. Repr., New York: Menorah, 1979.

Klein, "Messianism"   Klein, Ralph W. "Aspects of Intertestamental Messianism." Pages 191–203 in *The Bible in Its Literary Milieu.* Edited by Vincent L. Tollers and John R. Maier. Grand Rapids: Eerdmans, 1979.

Klijn, "Introduction"   Klijn, A. F. J. "Introduction" to 2 (Syriac Apocalypse of) Baruch. 1:615–20 in *OTP.*

Klinger, "Bethesda"   Klinger, Jerzy. "Bethesda and the Universality of the Logos." Translated by D. Johnson. *St. Vladimir's Theological Quarterly* 27 (1983): 169–85.

Kloner, "Lintel"   Kloner, A. "A Lintel with a Menorah from Horvat Kishor." *IEJ* 24 (1974): 197–200.

Knackstedt, "Brotvermekrungen"   Knackstedt, J. "Die beiden Brotvermerkungen im Evangelium." *NTS* 10 (1963–1964): 309–35.

Knibb, *Esdras*   Knibb, Michael A. *The First and Second Books of Esdras.* Cambridge: Cambridge University Press, 1979.

Knight, "*Aletheia*"   Knight, Thomas E. "The Use of *aletheia* for the 'Truth of Unreason': Plato, the Septuagint, and Philo." *American Journal of Philology* 114 (1993): 581–609.

Knight, "Anti-Semitism"   Knight, George A. F. "Anti-Semitism in the Fourth Gospel." *Reformed Theological Review* 27 (1968): 81–88.

Knowles, "Moses"   Knowles, Michael P. "Moses, the Law, and the Unity of 4 Ezra." *NovT* 31 (1989): 257–74.

Knowling, "Acts"   Knowling, R. J. "The Acts of the Apostles." Pages 1–554 in vol. 2 of *The Expositor's Greek Testament.* Edited by W. Robertson Nicoll. 5 vols. 1897–1910. Repr., Grand Rapids: Eerdmans, 1979.

Knox, *Gentiles*   Knox, Wilfred L. *St. Paul and the Church of the Gentiles.* Cambridge: Cambridge University Press, 1939.

Kobelski, "Melchizedek"   Kobelski, Paul Joseph. "Melchizedek and Melchiresa: The Heavenly Prince of Light and the Prince of Darkness in the Qumran Literature." Diss. Fordham University, 1978.

Koch, "Investigation"   Koch, Glenn Alan. "An Investigation of the Possible Relationship between the Gospel of John and the Sectarian Documents of the Dead Sea Scrolls as Suggested by Certain Recent Authors." M.Th. thesis, Eastern Baptist Theological Seminary, 1959.

Kodell, *Luke*   Kodell, Jerome. *The Gospel according to Luke.* Collegeville Bible Commentary. Collegeville, Minn.: Liturgical Press, 1983.

Koenig, *Hospitality*   Koenig, John. *New Testament Hospitality: Partnership with Strangers as Promise and Mission.* Overtures to Biblical Theology 17. Philadelphia: Fortress, 1985.

Koester, "Being"   Koester, Helmut. "The Divine Human Being." *HTR* 78 (1985): 243–52.

Koester, "Brown and Martyn"   Koester, Craig R. "R. E. Brown and J. L. Martyn: Johannine Studies in Retrospect." *Biblical Theology Bulletin* 21 (1991): 51–55.

Koester, "Ephesos"   Koester, Helmut. "Ephesos in Early Christian Literature." Pages 119–40 in *Ephesos—Metropolis of Asia: An Interdisciplinary Approach to Its Archaeology, Religion, and Culture.* Edited by Helmut Koester. Harvard Theological Studies. Valley Forge, Pa.: Trinity Press International, 1995.

Koester, "Exegesis"   Koester, Craig R. "Messianic Exegesis and the Call of Nathanael (John 1.45–51)." *JSNT* 39 (1990): 23–34.

Koester, "GNOMAI"   Koester, Helmut. "GNOMAI DIAPHORAI: The Origin and Nature of Diversification in the History of Early Christianity." Pages 114–57 in *Trajectories through Early Christianity.* By James M. Robinson and Helmut Koester. Philadelphia: Fortress, 1971.

Koester, *Gospels*   Koester, Helmut. *Ancient Christian Gospels: Their History and Development.* Philadelphia: Trinity Press International, 1990.

Koester, "Gospels"   Koester, Helmut. "Written Gospels or Oral Tradition?" *JBL* 113 (1994): 293–97.

Koester, "Hearing"   Koester, Craig R. "Hearing, Seeing, and Believing in the Gospel of John." *Biblica* 70 (1989): 327–48.

Koester, *Introduction*   Koester, Helmut. *Introduction to the New Testament.* Vol. 1: *History, Culture, and Religion of the Hellenistic Age.* Vol. 2: *History and Literature of Early Christianity.* Hermeneia Foundations and Facets Series. Philadelphia: Fortress, 1982.

Koester, "One Jesus"   Koester, Helmut. "One Jesus and Four Primitive Gospels." Pages 158–204 in *Trajectories through Early Christianity.* By James M. Robinson and Helmut Koester. Philadelphia: Fortress, 1971.

Koester, "Savior"   Koester, Craig R. "'The Savior of the World' (John 4:42)." *JBL* 109 (1990): 665–80.

Koester, "Spectrum"   Koester, Craig R. "The Spectrum of Johannine Readers." Pages 5–19 in *"What Is John?" Readers and Reading of the Fourth Gospel.* Edited by Fernando F. Segovia. SBLSymS 3. Atlanta: Scholars Press, 1996.

Koester, "Supper"   Koester, Craig R. "John Six and the Lord's Supper." *Lutheran Quarterly* 4 (1990): 419–37.

Koester, *Symbolism*   Koester, Craig R. *Symbolism in the Fourth Gospel: Meaning, Mystery, Community.* Minneapolis: Fortress, 1995.

Kohler, *Theology*   Kohler, K. *Jewish Theology.* New York: Macmillan, 1923.

Kokkinos, "Felix"   Kokkinos, Nikos. "A Fresh Look at the *gentilicium* of Felix, Procurator of Judaea." *Latomus* 49 (1990): 126–41.

Kolenkow, "Miracle"   Kolenkow, Anitra Bingham. "Relationships between Miracle and Prophecy in the Greco-Roman World and Early Christianity." *ANRW* 23.2.1470–1506. Part 2, *Principat,* 23.2. Edited by H. Temporini and W. Haase. New York: De Gruyter, 1980.

Kolenkow, "Role"   Kolenkow, Anitra Bingham. "What Is the Role of Testament in the Testament of Abraham?" *HTR* 67 (1974): 182–84.

Kolenkow, "Testament"   Kolenkow, Anitra Bingham. "The Literary Genre 'Testament.'" Pages 259–67 in *Early Judaism and Its Modern Interpreters.* Edited by Robert A. Kraft and George W. E. Nickelsburg. SBLBMI 2. Atlanta: Scholars Press, 1986.

Kollmann, *Kreuzigung*   Kollmann, Hanjo-Christoph. *Die Kreuzigung Jesu nach Joh 19, 16–22: Ein Beitrag zur Kreuzestheologie des Johannes im Vergleich mit den Synoptikern.* Europäische Hochschulschriften, Reihe 23, Theologie 710. Frankfurt: Lang, 2000.

Konstan, "Patrons"   Konstan, David. "Patrons and Friends." *Classical Philology* 90 (1995): 328–42.

Kopas, "Women"   Kopas, Jane. "Jesus and Women in Matthew." *Theology Today* 47 (1990–1991): 13–21.

Kossen, "Greeks"   Kossen, H. B. "Who Were the Greeks of John xii 20?" Pages 97–110 in *Studies in John: Presented to Professor Dr. J. N. Sevenster on the Occasion of His Seventieth Birthday.* Edited by W. C. van Unnik. NovTSup 24. Leiden: Brill, 1970.

Köstenberger, "Frühe Zweifel"   Köstenberger, Andreas J. "Frühe Zweifel an der johanneischen Verfasserschaft des vierten Evangeliums in der modernen Interpretationsgeschichte." *European Journal of Theology* 5 (1996): 37–46.

Köstenberger, *John*   Köstenberger, Andreas J. *Encountering John: The Gospel in Historical, Literary, and Theological Perspective.* Grand Rapids: Baker, 1999.

Kotansky, "Amulet"  Kotansky, Roy. "An Inscribed Copper Amulet from ᶜEvron." ᶜAtiqot 20 (1991): 81–87.

Kotlar, "Mikveh"  Kotlar, David. "Mikveh." Columns 1534–44 in vol. 11 of Encyclopaedia Judaica. 16 vols. Jerusalem: Keter, 1972.

Kovacs, "Introduction"  Kovacs, David. Introduction to "Cyclops." Pages 53–58 in vol. 1 of Euripides. Translated by David Kovacs. 2 vols. LCL new series. Cambridge: Harvard University Press, 1994–1995.

Kraabel, "Diaspora"  Kraabel, Alf Thomas. "The Roman Diaspora: Six Questionable Assumptions." JJS 33 (1982): 445–64.

Kraabel, "Disappearance"  Kraabel, Alf Thomas. "The Disappearance of the 'God-Fearers.'" Numen 28 (1981): 113–26.

Kraabel, "Evidence"  Kraabel, Alf Thomas. "New Evidence of the Samaritan Diaspora Has Been Found on Delos." BA 47 (1984): 44–46.

Kraabel, "Jews"  Kraabel, Alf Thomas. "Greeks, Jews, and Lutherans in the Middle Half of Acts." HTR 79 (1986): 147–57.

Kraabel, "Judaism"  Kraabel, Alf Thomas. "Judaism in Western Asia Minor under the Roman Empire, with a Preliminary Study of the Jewish Community at Sardis, Lydia." Th.D. diss., Harvard Divinity School, 1968.

Kraeling, John  Kraeling, Carl H. John the Baptist. New York: Scribner, 1951.

Kraeling and Mowry, "Music"  Kraeling, Carl, and Lucetta Mowry. "Music in the Bible." Pages 283–312 in Ancient and Oriental Music. Edited by Egon Wellesz. New Oxford History of Music 1. London: Oxford University Press, 1966.

Kraemer, "Ecstasy"  Kraemer, Ross Shepard. "Ecstasy and Possession: The Attraction of Women to the Cult of Dionysus." HTR 72 (1979): 55–80.

Kraemer, "Ecstatics"  Kraemer, Ross Shepard. "Ecstatics and Ascetics: Studies in the Functions of Religious Activities for Women in the Greco-Roman World." Ph.D. diss., Princeton University, 1976.

Kraemer, "Jew"  Kraemer, Ross Shepard. "On the Meaning of the Term 'Jew' in Greco-Roman Inscriptions." HTR 82 (1989): 35–53.

Kraemer, Maenads  Kraemer, Ross Shepard. Maenads, Martyrs, Matrons, Monastics: A Sourcebook on Women's Religions in the Greco-Roman World. Philadelphia: Fortress, 1988.

Kraemer, "Reliability"  Kraemer, David. "On the Reliability of Attributions in the Babylonian Talmud." HUCA 60 (1989): 175–90.

Kragerund, Lieblingsjünger  Kragerund, Alv. Die Lieblingsjünger im Johannesevangelium. Oslo: Osloer Universitätsverlag, 1959.

Kraybill, Cult  Kraybill, J. Nelson. Imperial Cult and Commerce in John's Apocalypse. JSNTSup 132. Sheffield: Sheffield Academic Press, 1996.

Kreitzer, "Apotheosis"  Kreitzer, Larry. "Apotheosis of the Roman Emperor." BA 53 (1990): 210–17.

Kreitzer, John  Kreitzer, Larry. The Gospel according to John. Regent's Study Guides. Oxford: Regent's Park College, 1990.

Kremer, "Verheissung"  Kremer, Jacob. "Jesu Verheissung des Geistes." Pages 247–76 in Die Kirche des Anfangs. Für Heinz Schürmann. Edited by R. Schnackenburg, J. Ernst, and J. Wanke. Freiburg: Herder, 1978.

Krieger, "Hauptquelle"  Krieger, Klaus-Stefan. "Zur Frage nach der Hauptquelle über die Geschichte der Provinz Judäa in den Antiquitates judaicae des Flavius Josephus." BN 63 (1992): 37–41.

Krieger, "Judenfeind"  Krieger, Klaus-Stefan. "Pontius Pilate—ein Judenfeind? Zur Problematik einer Pilatus-biographie." BN 78 (1995): 63–83.

Krieger, "Problematik"  Krieger, Klaus-Stefan. "Die Problematik chronologischer Rekonstruktionen zur Amtszeit des Pilatus." BN 61 (1992): 27–32.

Krieger, "Verwandter"  Krieger, Klaus-Stefan. "War Flavius Josephus ein Verwandter des hasmonäischen Königshauses?" BN 73 (1994): 58–65.

Kruijf, "Glory"  Kruijf, T. C. de. "The Glory of the Only Son (John i 14)." Pages 111–23 in Studies in John: Presented to Professor Dr. J. N. Sevenster on the Occasion of His Seventieth Birthday. Edited by W. C. van Unnik. NovTSup 24. Leiden: Brill, 1970.

Kruijf, "Hundredweight"  Kruijf, T. C. de. "'More than Half a Hundredweight' of Spices (John 19,39 NEB): Abundance and Symbolism in the Gospel of John." *Bijdragen* 43 (1982): 234–39.

Kugel and Greer, *Interpretation*  Kugel, James L., and Rowan A. Greer. *Early Biblical Interpretation.* LEC 3. Philadelphia: Westminster, 1986.

Kugelman, "Pentecost"  Kugelman, Richard. "The Gospel for Pentecost (Jn. 14:23–31)." *CBQ* 6 (1944): 259–75.

Kügler, "König"  Kügler, Joachim. "Der andere König: Religionsgeschichtliche Anmerkungen zum Jesusbild des Johannesevangeliums." *ZNW* 88 (1997): 223–41.

Kügler, "Sohn"  Kügler, Joachim. "Der Sohn im Schoss des Vaters: Eine motivgeschichtliche Notiz zu *Joh 1,18.*" *Biblische Notizen* 89 (1997): 76–87.

Kuhn, "Gekreuzigten"  Kuhn, Heinz W. "Zum Gekreuzigten von Givᶜat ha-Mivtar: Korrektur eines Versehens in der Erstveröffentlichung." *ZNW* 69 (1978): 118–22.

Kuhn, "John vii.37–8"  Kuhn, K. H. "St. John vii.37–8." *NTS* 4 (1957–1958): 63–65.

Kuhn, "Messias"  Kuhn, Heinz-Wolfgang. "Die beiden Messias in den Qumrantexten und die Messiasvorstellung in der rabbinischen Literatur." *ZAW* 70 (1958): 200–208.

Kümmel, *Introduction*  Kümmel, Werner Georg. *Introduction to the New Testament.* Rev. ed. Translated by Howard C. Kee. Nashville: Abingdon, 1975.

Kümmel, *Promise*  Kümmel, Werner Georg. *Promise and Fulfilment: The Eschatological Message of Jesus.* SBT 23. Naperville, Ill.: Allenson, 1957.

Kümmel, *Theology*  Kümmel, Werner Georg. *The Theology of the New Testament according to Its Major Witnesses—Jesus, Paul, John.* Translated by John E. Steely. Nashville: Abingdon, 1973.

Kurz, "Disciple"  Kurz, William S. "The Beloved Disciple and Implied Readers." *Biblical Theology Bulletin* 19 (1989): 100–107.

Kurz, "Luke 22:14–38"  Kurz, William S. "Luke 22:14–38 and Greco-Roman and Biblical Farewell Addresses." *JBL* 104 (1985): 251–68.

Kurz, "Models"  Kurz, William S. "Narrative Models for Imitation in Luke-Acts." Pages 171–89 in *Greeks, Romans, and Christians: Essays in Honor of Abraham J. Malherbe.* Edited by David L. Balch, Everett Ferguson, and Wayne A. Meeks. Minneapolis: Fortress, 1990.

Kurz, *Reading Luke–Acts*  Kurz, William S. *Reading Luke–Acts: Dynamics of Biblical Narrative.* Louisville, Ky.: Westminster John Knox, 1993.

Kuśmirek, "Żydzi"  Kuśmirek, A. "Żydzi w ewangelii Jana (The Jews in the Gospel of John)." *Studia theologica varsaviensia* 30 (1992): 121–35.

Kustas, "Diatribe"  Kustas, George L. "Diatribe in Ancient Rhetorical Theory." *Center for Hermeneutical Studies Protocol* 22 (1976): 1–15.

Kuyper, "Grace"  Kuyper, Lester J. "Grace and Truth: An Old Testament Description of God and Its Use in the Johannine Gospel." *Interpretation* 18 (1964): 3–19.

Kuzenzama, "Préhistoire"  Kuzenzama, K. P. M. "La préhistoire de l'expression 'pain de vie' (Jn 6,35b, 48): Continuité ou émergence?" *Revue africaine de théologie* 4, no. 7 (1980): 65–83.

Kydd, *Gifts*  Kydd, Ronald A. N. *Charismatic Gifts in the Early Church.* Peabody, Mass.: Hendrickson, 1984.

Kysar, "Background"  Kysar, Robert. "The Background of the Prologue of the Fourth Gospel: A Critique of Historical Methods." *Canadian Journal of Theology* 16 (1970): 250–55.

Kysar, "Contributions"  Kysar, Robert. "The Contributions of the Prologue of the Gospel of John to New Testament Christology and Their Historical Setting." *Currents in Theology and Mission* 5, no. 6 (1978): 348–64.

Kysar, *Evangelist*  Kysar, Robert. *The Fourth Evangelist and His Gospel.* Minneapolis: Augsburg, 1975.

Kysar, "Gospel"  Kysar, Robert. "John, the Gospel of." Pages 912–31 in vol 3 of *Anchor Bible Dictionary.* Edited by David Noel Freedman. 6 vols. New York: Doubleday, 1992.

Kysar, *John*  Kysar, Robert. *John.* Augsburg Commentary on the New Testament. Minneapolis: Augsburg, 1986.

Kysar, *Maverick Gospel*  Kysar, Robert. *John, The Maverick Gospel.* Atlanta: John Knox, 1976.

Kysar, "Metaphor"  Kysar, Robert. "The Making of Metaphor: Another Reading of John 3:1–15." Pages 21–41 in *"What Is John?" Readers and Reading of the Fourth Gospel.* Edited by Fernando F. Segovia. SBLSymS 3. Atlanta: Scholars Press, 1996.

Kysar, "Polemic"   Kysar, Robert. "The Gospel of John and Anti-Jewish Polemic." *Explorations* 6, no. 2 (1992): 3–4.

Kysar, "Vectors"   Kysar, Robert. "Community and Gospel: Vectors in Fourth Gospel Criticism." *Interpretation* 31 (1977): 355–66.

Lachs, *Commentary*   Lachs, Samuel Tobias. *A Rabbinic Commentary on the New Testament: The Gospels of Matthew, Mark, and Luke.* Hoboken, N.J.: Ktav, 1987.

Lacomara, "Deuteronomy"   Lacomara, Aelred. "Deuteronomy and the Farewell Discourse (Jn 13:31–16:33)." *CBQ* 36 (1974): 65–84.

Ladd, *Church*   Ladd, George Eldon. *The Young Church.* New York: Abingdon, 1964.

Ladd, *Criticism*   Ladd, George Eldon. *The New Testament and Criticism.* Grand Rapids: Eerdmans, 1967.

Ladd, *Last Things*   Ladd, George Eldon. *The Last Things.* Grand Rapids: Eerdmans, 1978.

Ladd, "Resurrection"   Ladd, George Eldon. "The Resurrection and History." *Religion in Life* 32 (1963): 247–56.

Ladd, *Revelation*   Ladd, George Eldon. *A Commentary on the Revelation of John.* Grand Rapids: Eerdmans, 1972.

Ladd, *Theology*   Ladd, George Eldon. *A Theology of the New Testament.* Grand Rapids: Eerdmans, 1974.

Lake, "Proselytes"   Lake, Kirsopp. "Proselytes and God-Fearers." Pages 74–96 in vol. 5 of *The Beginnings of Christianity.*

Lake, "Spirit"   Lake, Kirsopp. "The Holy Spirit." Pages 96–111 in vol. 5 of *The Beginnings of Christianity.*

Lake, "Twelve"   Lake, Kirsopp. "The Twelve and the Apostles." Pages 37–59 in vol. 5 of *The Beginnings of Christianity.*

Lake and Cadbury, *Commentary*   Lake, Kirsopp, and Henry J. Cadbury. *English Translation and Commentary.* Vol. 4 of *The Beginnings of Christianity.*

LaMarche, "Prologue"   LaMarche, Paul. "The Prologue of John (1964)." Pages 36–52 in *The Interpretation of John.* Edited by John Ashton. Issues in Religion and Theology 9. Philadelphia: Fortress, 1986.

Lampe, *Lexicon*   Lampe, G. W. H., ed. *A Patristic Greek Lexicon.* Oxford: Clarendon, 1961.

Lampe, "Petrusnamen"   Lampe, Peter. "Das Spiel mit dem Petrusnamen—Matt. xvi.18." *NTS* 25 (1978–1979): 227–45.

Lampe, *Seal*   Lampe, G. W. H. *The Seal of the Spirit.* New York: Longmans, Green, 1951.

Lampe, "Zeltmacher"   Lampe, Peter. "Paulus—Zeltmacher." *BZ* 31 (1987): 256–61.

Lampe and Luz, "Overview"   Lampe, Peter, and Ulrich Luz. "Overview of the Discussion." Pages 387–404 in *The Gospel and the Gospels.* Edited by Peter Stuhlmacher. Grand Rapids: Eerdmans, 1991.

Landes, "Tradition"   Landes, George M. "Creation Tradition in Proverbs 8:22–31 and Genesis 1." Pages 279–93 in *A Light unto My Path: Old Testament Studies in Honor of Jacob M. Myers.* Edited by Howard N. Bream, Ralph D. Heim, Carey A. Moore. Gettysburg Theological Studies 4. Philadelphia: Temple University Press, 1974.

Landman, "Aspects"   Landman, Leo. "Some Aspects of Traditions Received from Moses at Sinai. *Halakhah le-Mosheh mi-Sinai.*" *JQR* 67 (1976–1977): 111–28.

Lane, *Hebrews*   Lane, William L. *Hebrews.* 2 vols. WBC 47. Dallas: Word, 1991.

Lane, *Mark*   Lane, William L. *The Gospel according to Mark.* New International Commentary on the New Testament. Grand Rapids: Eerdmans, 1974.

Lane, "Theios Aner"   Lane, William L. "Theios Aner Christology and the Gospel of Mark." Pages 144–161 in *New Dimensions in New Testament Study.* Edited by Richard N. Longenecker and Merrill C. Tenney. Grand Rapids: Zondervan, 1974.

Lapide, *Hebrew*   Lapide, Pinchas E. *Hebrew in the Church: The Foundations of Jewish-Christian Dialogue.* Translated by Erroll F. Rhodes. Grand Rapids: Eerdmans, 1984.

Laroche, "Numbers"   Laroche, Roland A. "Popular Symbolic/Mystical Numbers in Antiquity." *Latomus* 54 (1995): 568–76.

Larsen, "Boat"   Larsen, Iver. "Did Peter Enter the Boat (John 21:11)?" *Notes on Translation* 2, no. 2 (1988): 34–41.

LaSor, *Knew*   LaSor, William Sanford. *Men Who Knew Christ.* Glendale, Calif.: Regal Books, 1971.

LaSor, "Messiahs"   LaSor, William Sanford. "'The Messiahs of Aaron and Israel.'" *VT* 6 (1956): 425–29.

LaSor, "Miqvaʾot"   LaSor, William Sanford. "Discovering What Jewish miqvaʾot Can Tell Us about Christian Baptism." *BAR* 13, no. 1 (January/.February 1987): 52–59.

LaSor, *Scrolls*   LaSor, William Sanford. *The Dead Sea Scrolls and the Christian Faith.* Chicago: Moody Press, 1962.

LaSor, *Scrolls and NT*   LaSor, William Sanford. *The Dead Sea Scrolls and the New Testament.* Grand Rapids: Eerdmans, 1972.

Lataire, "Lap"   Lataire, B. "The Son on the Father's Lap: The Meaning of εἰς τὸν κόλπον in John 1:18." *Studien zum Neuen Testament und seiner Umwelt* 22 (1997): 125–38.

Latourelle, *Miracles*   Latourelle, René. *The Miracles of Jesus and the Theology of Miracles.* New York: Paulist, 1988.

Latourette, *Expansion*   Latourette, Kenneth Scott. *The First Five Centuries.* Vol. 1 of *A History of the Expansion of Christianity.* 5 vols. New York: Harper & Row, 1970.

Lattke, *Einheit*   Lattke, Michael. *Einheit im Wort: Die spezifische Bedeutung von ἀγάπη, ἀγαπᾶν, und φιλεῖν im Johannesevangelium.* Studien zum Alten und Neuen Testament 41. Munich: Kösel, 1975.

Laufer, "Commentary"   Laufer, Catherine E. "The Farewell Discourse in John's Gospel as a Commentary on the Seder Service." *Colloquium* 27, no. 2 (1995): 147–60.

Laughlin, "Capernaum"   Laughlin, John C. H. "Capernaum from Jesus' Time and After." *BAR* 19, no. 5 (September/October 1993): 54–61, 90.

Laurentin, "*Weʾattah*"   Laurentin, A. "*Weʾattah—kai nun:* Formule caractéristique des textes juridiques et liturgiques (à propos de Jean 17,5)." *Biblica* 45 (1964): 168–97, 413–32.

Laurin, *John*   Laurin, Roy L. *John: Life Eternal.* Chicago: Moody, 1972.

Laurin, "Messiahs"   Laurin, Robert B. "The Problem of Two Messiahs in the Qumran Scrolls." *RevQ* 4 (1963–1964): 39–52.

Lavery, "*Lucullus*"   Lavery, Gerard B. "Plutarch's *Lucullus* and the Living Bond of Biography." *Classical Journal* 89 (1993–1994): 261–73.

Laws, *James*   Laws, Sophie. *A Commentary on the Epistle of James.* Harper's New Testament Commentaries. San Francisco: Harper & Row, 1980.

Lea, "Killed"   Lea, Thomas D. "Who Killed the Lord? A Defense against the Charge of Anti-Semitism in John's Gospel." *Criswell Theological Review* 7 (1994): 103–23.

Lea, "Reliability"   Lea, Thomas D. "The Reliability of History in John's Gospel." *JETS* 38 (1995): 387–402.

Leal, "Via"   Leal, J. "Ego sum via et veritas et vita (JN 14:6)." *Verbum Domini* 33 (1955): 336–41.

Leaney, *Luke*   Leaney, A. R. C. *A Commentary on the Gospel according to St. Luke.* London: A&C Black, 1958.

Leaney, "Paraclete"   Leaney, A. R. C. "The Johannine Paraclete and the Qumran Scrolls." Pages 38–61 in *John and Qumran.* Edited by James H. Charlesworth. London: Geoffrey Chapman, 1972.

Lease, "Mithraeum"   Lease, Gary. "The Caesarea Mithraeum: A Preliminary Announcement." *BA* 38 (1975): 2–10.

Lebram, "Review"   Lebram, J. C. H. Review of B. J. Malina, *The Palestinian Manna Tradition. VT* 20 (1970): 124–28.

Le Déaut, "L'intercession"   Le Déaut, Roger. "Aspects de l'intercession dans le judaïsme ancien." *JSJ* 1 (1970): 35–57.

Le Déaut, "Šāvúʿōt"   Le Déaut, Roger. "Šāvúʿōt och den kristna pingsten i NT." *Svensk exegetisk årsbok* 44 (1979): 148–70.

Lee, "Friends"   Lee, G. M. "John XV 14 'Ye Are My Friends.'" *NovT* 15 (1973): 260.

Lee, *Narratives*   Lee, Dorothy A. *The Symbolic Narratives of the Fourth Gospel: The Interplay of Form and Meaning.* JSNTSup 95. Sheffield: Sheffield Academic Press, 1994.

Lee, "Powers"   Lee, Jung Young. "Interpreting the Demonic Powers in Pauline Thought." *NovT* 12 (1970): 54–69.

Lee, *Thought*   Lee, Edwin Kenneth. *The Religious Thought of St. John.* London: SPCK, 1962.

Lee, "Translations of OT"   Lee, A. L. "Translations of the Old Testament: Greek." Pages 775–83 in *Handbook of Classical Rhetoric in the Hellenistic Period, 330 B.C.–A.D. 400.* Edited by Stanley E. Porter. Leiden: Brill, 1997.

Lee, "Unrest"   Lee, Clarence L. "Social Unrest and Primitive Christianity." Pages 121–38 in *The Catacombs and the Colosseum: The Roman Empire as the Setting of Primitive Christianity*. Edited by Stephen J. Benko and John J. O'Rourke. Valley Forge, Pa.: Judson Press, 1971.

Lefèvre, "Cult"   Lefèvre, Eckard. "A Cult without God or the Unfreedom of Freedom in Seneca Tragicus." *Classical Journal* 77 (1981–1982): 32–36.

Lefkowitz, *Africa*   Lefkowitz, Mary. *Not out of Africa: How Afrocentrism Became an Excuse to Teach Myth as History*. New York: Basic Books, HarperCollins, 1996.

Lefkowitz and Fant, *Life*   Lefkowitz, Mary R., and Maureen B. Fant. *Women's Life in Greece and Rome*. Baltimore: Johns Hopkins, 1982.

Légasse, "Baptême"   Légasse, Simon. "Baptême juif des prosélytes et baptême chrétien." *Bulletin de littérature ecclésiastique* 77 (1976): 3–40.

Légasse, "Pain"   Légasse, Simon. "Le pain de la vie." *Bulletin de littérature ecclésiastique* 83 (1982): 243–61.

Légasse, "Retour"   Légasse, Simon. "Le retour du Christ d'après l'évangile de Jean, chapîtres 14 et 16: Une adaptation du motif de la parousie." *Bulletin de littérature ecclésiastique* 81 (1980): 161–74.

Leibig, "Jews"   Leibig, Janis E. "John and 'the Jews': Theological Anti-Semitism in the Fourth Gospel." *Journal of Ecumenical Studies* 20 (1983): 209–234.

Leidig, "Natanael"   Leidig, E. "Natanael, ein Sohn des Tholomäus." *Theologische Zeitschrift* 36 (1980): 374–75.

Leivestad, "Exit"   Leivestad, Ragnar. "Exit the Apocalyptic Son of Man." *NTS* 18 (1971–1972): 243–67.

Lemaire, "Burial Box of James"   Lemaire, André. "Burial Box of James, the Brother of Jesus." *BAR* 28, no. 6 (November 2002): 24–33.

Lemaire, "Scepter"   Lemaire, André. "Probable Head of Priestly Scepter from Solomon's Temple Surfaces in Jerusalem." *BAR* 10, no. 1 (January/February 1984): 24–29.

Lemcio, "Evidence"   Lemcio, Eugene E. "External Evidence for the Structure and Function of Mark iv.1–20, vii.14–23, and viii.14–21." *JTS* NS 29 (1978): 323–38.

Lenski, "Crystallization"   Lenski, Gerhard E. "Status Crystallization: A Non-vertical Dimension of Social Status." *American Sociological Review* 19 (1954): 405–13.

Lenski, *John*   Lenski, R. C. H. *The Interpretation of St. John's Gospel*. Minneapolis: Augsburg, 1943.

Lentzen-Deis, "Motiv"   Lentzen-Deis, Fritzleo. "Das Motiv der 'Himmelsöffnung' in verschiedenen Gattungen der Umweltliteratur des Neuen Testaments." *Biblica* 50 (1969): 301–27.

Leon, *Jews*   Leon, Harry J. *The Jews of Ancient Rome*. Morris Loeb Series. Philadelphia: Jewish Publication Society of America, 1960.

Léonard, "Notule"   Léonard, Jeanne M. "Notule sur l'évangile de Jean: Le disciple que Jésus aimait et Marie." *Études théologiques et religieuses* 58 (1983): 355–57.

Léon-Dufour, "Reading"   Léon-Dufour, Xavier. "Towards a Symbolic Reading of the Fourth Gospel." *NTS* 27 (1980–1981): 439–56.

Lerle, "Reformen"   Lerle, Ernst. "Liturgische Reformen der Synagogengottesdienstes als Antwort auf die judenchristliche Mission des ersten Jahrhunderts." *NovT* 10 (1968): 31–42.

Letis, "Influences"   Letis, Theodore P. "The Gnostic Influences on the Text of the Fourth Gospel: John 1:18 in the Egyptian Manuscripts." *Bulletin of the Institute for Reformation Biblical Studies* 1 (1989): 4–7.

Létourneau, "Don"   Létourneau, Pierre. "Le double don de l'Esprit et la christologie du quatrième évangile." *Science et esprit* 44 (1992): 281–306.

Levey, "Secret"   Levey, Samson H. "The Best Kept Secret of the Rabbinic Tradition." *Judaism* 21 (1972): 454–69.

Levine, *Hellenism*   Levine, Lee I. *Judaism and Hellenism in Antiquity: Conflict or Confluence?* Peabody, Mass.: Hendrickson, 1998.

Levine, "Purification"   Levine, Lee. "R. Simeon b. Yohai and the Purification of Tiberias: History and Tradition." *HUCA* 49 (1978): 143–85.

Levine, "Symbolism"   Levine, Etan. "On the Symbolism of the *pedilavium*." *American Benedictine Review* 33 (1982): 21–29.

Levine, "Synagogue"   Levine, Lee I. "The Second Temple Synagogue: The Formative Years." Pages 7–31 in *The Synagogue in Late Antiquity*. Edited by Lee I. Levine. Philadelphia: American Schools of Oriental Research, 1986.

Levine, "Women"   Levine, Amy-Jill. "Second Temple Judaism, Jesus, and Women." *Biblical Interpretation* 2 (1994): 8–33.

Levinskaya, "Aphrodisias"   Levinskaya, Irina A. "The Inscription from Aphrodisias and the Problem of God-Fearers." *Tyndale Bulletin* 41 (1990): 312–18.

Levinskaya, *Diaspora Setting*   Levinskaya, Irina. *The Book of Acts in Its Diaspora Setting*. Vol. 5 of *The Book of Acts in Its First Century Setting*. Edited by Bruce W. Winter. Grand Rapids: Eerdmans, 1996.

Levison, "Prophecy in Philo"   Levison, John R. "Two Types of Ecstatic Prophecy according to Philo." *Studia philonica Annual* 6 (1994): 83–89.

Levison, "Ruth"   Levison, John R. "Josephus's Version of Ruth." *JSP* 8 (1991): 31–44.

Lévy, "Conversation"   Lévy, C. "La conversation à Rome à la fin de la république: Des pratiques sans théorie?" *Rhetorica* 11, no. 4 (1993): 399–414.

Lewis, *History*   Lewis, Bernard. *History Remembered, Recovered, Invented*. New York: Simon & Schuster, 1975.

Lewis, "Ignatius"   Lewis, R. B. "Ignatius and the 'Lord's Day.'" *Andrews University Seminary Studies* 6 (1968): 46–59.

Lewis, *Life*   Lewis, Naphtali. *Life in Egypt under Roman Rule*. Oxford: Clarendon Press, 1983.

Lewis, *Prophets*   Lewis, Jack P. *The Minor Prophets*. Grand Rapids: Baker, 1966.

Licht, "Town Plan"   Licht, J. "An Ideal Town Plan from Qumran—the Description of the New Jerusalem." *IEJ* 29 (1979): 45–59.

Lichtenberger, "Lebenskraft"   Lichtenberger, Hermann. "Dass du nicht vergisst (Devarim-Dtn 4,9): Von der Lebenskraft der Tora." *Theologische Beiträge* 21 (1990): 196–204.

Liddell and Scott, *Lexicon*   Liddell, Henry George, and Robert Scott. *A Greek-English Lexicon*. Revised by Henry Stuart Jones and Roderick McKenzie. Oxford: Clarendon Press, 1968.

Lieberman, *Hellenism*   Lieberman, Saul. *Hellenism in Jewish Palestine: Studies in the Literary Transmission, Beliefs, and Manners of Palestine in the I Century B.C.E.–IV Century C.E.* 2d ed. Texts and Studies of the Jewish Theological Seminary of America, 18. New York: Jewish Theological Seminary of America, 1962.

Lieberman, "Hermeneutics"   Lieberman, Stephen J. "A Mesopotamian Background for the So-Called *Aggadic* 'Measures' of Biblical Hermeneutics?" *HUCA* 58 (1987): 157–225.

Lieberman, "Scrolls"   Lieberman, Saul. "Light on the Cave Scrolls from Rabbinic Sources." *Proceedings of the American Academy for Jewish Research* 20 (1951): 395–404.

Liefeld, "Preacher"   Liefeld, Walter Lewis. "The Wandering Preacher as a Social Figure in the Roman Empire." Ph.D. diss., Columbia University, 1967.

Lietzmann, "Prozess"   Lietzmann, Heinrich. "Der Prozess Jesu." *Sitzenberichte der Preussischen Akademie der Wissenschaften*, phil.-hist. Klasse 1931, 14 (1934): 310–22.

Lifshitz, "Sympathisants"   Lifshitz, B. "Du nouveau sur les 'sympathisants.'" *JSJ* 1 (1970): 77–84.

Lightfoot, *Colossians*   Lightfoot, J. B. *Saint Paul's Epistles to the Colossians and to Philemon*. n.p.: Macmillan, 1879. Repr., Grand Rapids: Zondervan, 1959.

Lightfoot, *Galatians*   Lightfoot, J. B. *St Paul's Epistle to the Galatians*. 3d ed. London: Macmillan, 1869.

Lightfoot, *Gospel*   Lightfoot, R. H. *St. John's Gospel: A Commentary*. Edited by C. F. Evans. London: Oxford University Press, 1960.

Lightfoot, *Notes*   Lightfoot, J. B. *Notes on the Epistles of St Paul (I and II Thess, I Cor 1–7, Rom 1–7, Eph 1:1–14)*. Winona Lake, Ind.: Alpha Publications, n.d.

Lightfoot, *Talmud*   Lightfoot, John. *A Commentary on the New Testament from the Talmud and Hebraica*, 4 vols. n.p.: Oxford, 1959. Repr., Grand Rapids: Baker, 1979.

Lim, "Alteration   Lim, Timothy H. "Eschatological Orientation and the Alteration of Scripture in the Habakkuk Pesher." *Journal of Near Eastern Studies* 49 (1990): 185–94.

Limbeck, *Ordnung*   Limbeck, M. *Die Ordnung des Heils: Untersuchungen zum Gesetzesversändnis des Frühjudentums*. Kommentare und Beiträge zum Alten und Neuen Testament. Düsseldorf: Patmos, 1971.

Lincoln, *Ephesians*   Lincoln, Andrew T. *Ephesians*. WBC 42. Dallas: Word, 1990.

Lincoln, *Lawsuit Motif*   Lincoln, Andrew T. *Truth on Trial: The Lawsuit Motif in the Fourth Gospel*. Peabody, Mass.: Hendrickson, 2000.

Lincoln, *Paradise*    Lincoln, Andrew T. *Paradise Now and Not Yet: Studies in the Role of the Heavenly Dimension in Paul's Thought with Special Reference to His Eschatology.* SNTSMS 43. Cambridge: Cambridge University Press, 1981.

Lindars, *Apologetic*    Lindars, Barnabas. *New Testament Apologetic.* London: SCM, 1961.

Lindars, *Behind*    Lindars, Barnabas. *Behind the Fourth Gospel: Studies in Creative Criticism.* London: Talbot, 1971.

Lindars, "Composition"    Lindars, Barnabas. "Composition of John XX." *NTS* 7 (1960–1961): 142–47.

Lindars, "Discourse and Tradition"    Lindars, Barnabas. "Discourse and Tradition: The Use of the Sayings of Jesus in the Discourses of the Fourth Gospel." *JSNT* 13 (1981): 83–101.

Lindars, *John*    Lindars, Barnabas. *John.* New Testament Guides. Sheffield: Sheffield Academic Press, 1990.

Lindars, "Rebuking"    Lindars, Barnabas. "Rebuking the Spirit: A New Analysis of the Lazarus Story in John 11." *NTS* 38 (1992): 89–104.

Lindars, "Re-enter"    Lindars, Barnabas. "Re-enter the Apocalyptic Son of Man." *NTS* 22 (1975–1976): 52–72.

Lindars, "Traditions"    Lindars, Barnabas. "Traditions behind the Fourth Gospel." Pages 107–24 in *L'évangile de Jean: Sources, rédaction, théologie.* Edited by M. De Jonge. BETL 45. Gembloux: J. Duculot; Leuven: Leuven University Press, 1977.

Lindemann, "Samaria"    Lindemann, Andreas. "Samaria und Samaritaner im Neuen Testament." *Wort und Dienst* 22 (1993): 51–76.

Lindenberger, "Ahiqar"    Lindenberger, J. M. Introduction to "Ahiqar." *OTP* 2:479–93.

Lindner, "Geschichtsauffassung"    Lindner, Helgo. "Die Geschichtsauffassung des Flavius Josephus im Bellum judaicum: Gleichzeitig ein Beitrag zur Quellenfrage, Diss., Tübingen 1970" (summary). *Theologische Literaturzeitung* 96, no. 12 (1971): 953–954.

Lindner, "Heiligtum"    Lindner, Manfred. "Ein nabatäisches Heiligtum oberhalb der Nischenklamm *(Sidd el-Ma'ägïn)* von Petra (Jordanien)." *Zeitschrift des Deutschen Palästina-Vereins* 106 (1990): 145–54, plates 14–19.

Lindsay, "Truth"    Lindsay, Dennis R. "What Is Truth? Ἀλήθεια in the Gospel of John." *Restoration Quarterly* 35 (1993): 129–45.

Lindsey, *Jesus*    Lindsey, Robert L. *Jesus, Rabbi and Lord: The Hebrew Story of Jesus behind Our Gospels.* Oak Creek, Wis.: Cornerstone, 1990.

Ling, "Stranger"    Ling, R. "A Stranger in Town: Finding the Way in an Ancient City." *Greece and Rome* 37 (1990): 204–14.

Linneman, "Gospel of Q"    Linneman, Eta. "The Gospel of Q—Fact or Fantasy?" *Trinity Journal* NS 17 (1996): 3–18.

Linneman, "Taufer"    Linneman, Eta. "Jesus und der Taufer." Pages 219–36 in *Festschrift für Ernst Fuchs.* Edited by G. Ebeling et al. Tübingen: Mohr, 1973.

Llewelyn, *New Documents*, 8    S. R. Llewelyn, ed. *New Documents Illustrating Early Christianity.* Vol. 8: *A Review of the Greek Inscriptions and Papyri Published 1984–85.* Ancient History Documentary Research Centre, Macquarie University, N.S.W., Australia. Grand Rapids: Eerdmans, 1998.

Loader, "Structure"    Loader, W. R. G. "The Central Structure of Johannine Christology." *NTS* 30 (1984): 188–216.

Locher, "Geist"    Locher, Gottfried W. "Der Geist als Paraklet: Eine exegetische-dogmatische Besinnung." *Evangelische Theologie* 26 (1966): 565–79.

Lock, *Epistles*    Lock, Walter. *A Critical and Exegetical Commentary on the Pastoral Epistles.* International Critical Commentary. Edinburgh: T&T Clark, 1924.

Lodge, *Theory*    Lodge, R. C. *Plato's Theory of Ethics: The Moral Criterion and the Highest Good.* New York: Harcourt, Brace, 1928.

Loffreda, "Scavi"    Loffreda, Stanislao. "Scavi a Kafr Kanna: Rapporto preliminaire." *Studii biblici franciscani liber annuus* 19 (1969): 328–48.

Loffreda, "Tombe"    Loffreda, Stanislao. "Due tombe a Betania presso le Suore della Nigrizia." *Studii biblici franciscani liber annuus* 19 (1969): 349–66.

Lofthouse, "Spirit"    Lofthouse, W. F. "The Holy Spirit in the Acts and the Fourth Gospel." *ExpTim* 52 (1940–1941): 334–36.

Loftus, "Note"   Loftus, Francis. "A Note on *syntagma tón Galilaión* B.J. iv 558." *JQR* 65 (1974–1975): 182–83.

Loftus, "Revolts"   Loftus, Francis. "The Anti-Roman Revolts of the Jews and the Galileans." *JQR* 68 (1977–1978): 78–98.

Lohmeyer, "Überlieferung"   Lohmeyer, E. "Zur Evangelischen Überlieferung von Johannes dem Täufer." *JBL* 61 (1932): 311–17.

Lohse, *Colossians*   Lohse, Eduard. *Colossians and Philemon*. Translated by William R. Poehlmann and Robert J. Karris. Edited by Helmut Koester. Hermeneia. Philadelphia: Fortress, 1971.

Lohse, *Environment*   Lohse, Eduard. *The New Testament Environment*. Translated by John E. Steely. Nashville: Abingdon, 1976.

Lohse, "Synagogue"   Lohse, Eduard. "Synagogue of Satan and Church of God: Jews and Christians in the Book of Revelation." *Svensk exegetisk årsbok* 58 (1993): 105–23.

Lombard and Oliver, "Supper"   Lombard, H. A., and W. H. Oliver. "A Working Supper in Jerusalem: John 13:1–38 Introduces Jesus' Farewell Discourses." *Neotestamentica* 25 (1991): 357–78.

Long, *Philosophy*   Long, A. A. *Hellenistic Philosophy: Stoics, Epicureans, Sceptics*. New York: Scribner, 1974.

Long, "Soul"   Long, A. A. "Soul and Body in Stoicism." *Center for Hermeneutical Studies Protocol* 36 (1980): 1–17.

Longenecker, "Amanuenses"   Longenecker, Richard N. "Ancient Amanuenses and the Pauline Epistles." Pages 281–97 in *New Dimensions in New Testament Study*. Edited by Richard N. Longenecker and Merrill C. Tenney. Grand Rapids: Zondervan, 1974.

Longenecker, *Christology*   Longenecker, Richard N. *The Christology of Early Jewish Christianity*. London: SCM, 1970. Repr., Grand Rapids: Baker, 1981.

Longenecker, *Exegesis*   Longenecker, Richard N. *Biblical Exegesis in the Apostolic Period*. Grand Rapids: Eerdmans, 1975.

Longenecker, "Messiah"   Longenecker, Bruce W. "The Unbroken Messiah: A Johannine Feature and Its Social Functions." *NTS* 41 (1995): 428–41.

Longenecker, *Ministry*   Longenecker, Richard N. *The Ministry and Message of Paul*. Grand Rapids: Zondervan, 1971.

Longenecker, *Paul*   Longenecker, Richard N. *Paul, Apostle of Liberty*. Grand Rapids: Baker, 1976.

Longenecker, *Wine*   Longenecker, Richard N. *New Wine into Fresh Wineskins: Contextualizing the Early Christian Confessions*. Peabody, Mass.: Hendrickson, 1999.

Longstaff, *Conflation*   Longstaff, Thomas R. W. *Evidence of Conflation in Mark? A Study in the Synoptic Problem*. SBLDS 28. Missoula, Mont.: Scholars Press, 1977.

López Barja de Quiroga, "Mobility"   López Barja de Quiroga, P. "Freedmen's Social Mobility in Roman Italy." *Historia* 44, no. 3 (1995): 326–48.

Lord, *Singer*   Lord, Albert B. *The Singer of Tales*. New York: Atheneum, 1965.

Losie, "Entry"   Losie, Lynn A. "Triumphal Entry." Pages 854–59 in *Dictionary of Jesus and the Gospels*. Edited by Joel B. Green, Scot McKnight, and I. Howard Marshall. Downers Grove, Ill.: InterVarsity, 1992.

Losie, "Gospel"   Losie, Lynn A. "Mark, Secret Gospel of." Pages 708–12 in *Dictionary of the Later New Testament and Its Developments*. Edited by Ralph P. Martin and Peter H. Davids. Downers Grove, Ill.: InterVarsity, 1997.

Lourenço, "Targum"   Lourenço, João. "Targum de Is 52,13–53,12: Pressupostos históricos e processos literários." *Didaskalia* 20 (1990): 155–66.

Lowe, "IOUDAIOI"   Lowe, Malcolm. "Who Were the IOUDAIOI?" *NovT* 18 (1976): 101–30.

Lowe and Flusser, "Synoptic Theory"   Lowe, Malcolm, and David Flusser. "Evidence Corroborating a Modified Proto-Matthean Synoptic Theory." *NTS* 29 (1983): 25–47.

Lown, "Miraculous"   Lown, John S. "The Miraculous in the Greco-Roman Historians." *Forum* 2, no. 4 (December 1986): 36–42.

Lucas, "Origin"   Lucas, Ernest C. "The Origin of Daniel's Four Empires Scheme Re-examined." *Tyndale Bulletin* 40 (1989): 185–202.

Lührmann, "Geschichte"   Lührmann, Dieter. "Die Geschichte von einer Sünderin und andere Apokryphe Jesusüberlieferungen bei Didymos von Alexandrien." *NovT* 32 (1990): 289–316.

Luke, "Ascension"   Luke, K. "Enoch's Ascension: The Apocalyptic Tradition." *Indian Theological Studies* 25 (1988): 236–52.

Luke, "Society"  Luke, K. "Society Divided by Religion: The Jewish World of Jesus' Time." *Bible-bhashyam* 1, no. 3 (1975): 195–209.

Lukito, "Christology"  Lukito, Daniel L. "Logos Christology: An Interaction between Early Christian Beliefs and Modern Scholars' Attempts to Relate Them to the Asia Context." *Stulos Theological Journal* 1 (1993): 105–21.

Lull, *Spirit*  Lull, David John. *The Spirit in Galatia: Paul's Interpretation of Pneuma as Divine Power.* SBLDS 49. Chico, Calif.: Scholars Press, 1980.

Lupieri, "Morte"  Lupieri, Edmondo. "La morte di croce: Contributi per un'analisi di *Fil.* 2,6–11." *RivB* 27 (1979): 271–311.

Luther, *John*  Luther, Martin. *Sermons on the Gospel of St. John.* Vols. 22–24 of *Works.* Edited by Jaroslav Pelikan. St. Louis: Concordia, 1957–1961.

Lutkemeyer, "Paraclete"  Lutkemeyer, Lawrence J. "The Role of the Paraclete: Jn 16:7–15." *CBQ* 8 (1946): 220–29.

Lutz, "Musonius"  Lutz, Cora E. "Musonius Rufus: The Roman Socrates." *Yale Classical Studies* 10 (1947): 3–147.

Luwel, "Begrip"  Luwel, Andre. "Het economisch begrip van de techniek in Oudheid en Middeleeuwen." *Tijdschrift voor sociale wetenschappen* 28, no. 2 (April 1983): 148–58.

Luz, "Cynic"  Luz, M. "A Description of the Greek Cynic in the Jerusalem Talmud." *JSJ* 20 (1989): 49–60.

Luz, *Matthew*  Luz, Ulrich. *Matthew 1–7: A Commentary.* Translated by Wilhelm C. Linss. Minneapolis: Augsburg Fortress, 1989.

Luz, "Speech"  Luz, Menahem. "Eleazar's Second Speech on Masada and Its Literary Precedents." *Rheinisches Museum für Philologie* 126 (1983): 25–43.

Luzitu, "Mariological Interpretation"  Luzitu, Jean-Jacques. "Who Is the 'Mother of Jesus' at Cana? A Mariological Interpretation of John 2:1–12." *Hekima Review* 23 (2000): 8–21.

Lyall, "Law"  Lyall, Francis. "Roman Law in the Writings of Paul—Adoption." *JBL* 88 (1969): 458–66.

Lyall, *Slaves*  Lyall, Francis. *Slaves, Citizens, Sons: Legal Metaphors in the Epistles.* Grand Rapids: Zondervan, 1984.

Lyman, "Religion"  Lyman, Mary Ely. "Hermetic Religion and the Religion of the Fourth Gospel." *JBL* 49 (1930): 265–76.

Lyonnet, "Adversaries"  Lyonnet, Stanislas. "Paul's Adversaries in Colossae." Pages 147–161 in *Conflict at Colossae: A Problem in the Interpretation of Early Christianity Illustrated by Selected Modern Studies.* Edited and translated by Fred O. Francis and Wayne A. Meeks. SBLSBS 4. Missoula, Mont.: Society of Biblical Literature, 1973.

Lyons, *Autobiography*  Lyons, George. *Pauline Autobiography: Toward a New Understanding.* SBLDS 73. Atlanta: Scholars Press, 1985.

Maccini, *Testimony*  Maccini, Robert Gordon. *Her Testimony Is True: Women as Witnesses according to John.* JSNTSup 125. Sheffield: Sheffield Academic Press, 1996.

MacDonald, "Mother"  MacDonald, Dennis. "The Mother of Jesus Was There." *The Review of Religion* 47, no. 5 (1988): 755–62.

MacDonald, *Samaritans*  MacDonald, John. *The Theology of the Samaritans.* Philadelphia: Westminster, 1964.

MacGregor, "Eucharist"  MacGregor, G. H. C. "The Eucharist in the Fourth Gospel." *NTS* 9 (1962–1963): 111–19.

MacGregor, *John*  MacGregor, G. H. C. *The Gospel of John.* Moffatt New Testament Commentary. London: Hodder & Stoughton, 1928.

MacGregor, *Pacifism*  MacGregor, G. H. C. *The New Testament Basis of Pacifism and the Relevance of an Impossible Ideal.* Nyack, N.Y.: Fellowship Publications, 1954.

MacGregor, "Principalities"  MacGregor, G. H. C. "Principalities and Powers: The Cosmic Background of Paul's Thought." *NTS* 1 (1954–1955): 17–28.

Mack, "Imitatio"  Mack, Burton L. "Imitatio Mosis: Patterns of Cosmology and Soteriology in the Hellenistic Synagogue." *Studia philonica* 1 (1972): 27–55.

Mack, *Lost Gospel*  Mack, Burton L. *The Lost Gospel: The Book of Q and Christian Origins.* San Francisco: Harper San Francisco, 1993.

Mack, *Myth*    Mack, Burton L. *A Myth of Innocence: Mark and Christian Origins.* Philadelphia: Fortress, 1988.

Mack and Murphy, "Literature"    Mack, Burton L., and Murphy, Roland E. "Wisdom Literature." Pages 371–410 in *Early Judaism and Its Modern Interpreters.* Edited by Robert A. Kraft and George W. E. Nickelsburg. SBLBMI 2. Atlanta: Scholars Press, 1986.

Mack and Robbins, *Patterns*    Mack, Burton L., and Vernon K. Robbins. *Patterns of Persuasion in the Gospels.* Sonoma, Calif.: Polebridge Press, 1989.

Mackowski, "Qanah"    Mackowski, Richard M. "Scholars' Qanah: A Re-examination of the Evidence in Favor of Khirbet-Qanah." *BZ* 23 (1979): 278–84.

MacLaurin, "Fishermen"    MacLaurin, E. C. B. "The Divine Fishermen." *St. Mark's Review* 94 (1978): 26–28.

Maclean and Aitken, *Heroikos*    Maclean, Jennifer K. Berenson, and Ellen Bradshaw Aitken. *Heroikos* by Flavius Philostratus. Prologue by Gregory Nagy, xi–xxxv. Epilogue by Hemut Koester, 257–64. SBL Writings from the Greco-Roman World 1. Atlanta: Society of Biblical Literature, 2001.

MacLennan and Kraabel, "God-Fearers"    MacLennan, Robert S., and A. Thomas Kraabel. "The God-Fearers—a Literary and Theological Invention." *BAR* 12, no. 5 (September/October 1986): 46–53, 64.

MacMullen, "Conversion"    MacMullen, Ramsay. "Conversion: A Historian's View." *Second Century* 5 (1985–1986): 67–81.

MacMullen, *Enemies*    MacMullen, Ramsay. *Enemies of the Roman Order: Treason, Unrest, and Alienation in the Empire.* Cambridge: Harvard University Press, 1966.

MacMullen, *Relations*    MacMullen, Ramsay. *Roman Social Relations: 50 B.C. to A.D. 284.* New Haven: Yale University Press, 1974.

MacMullen, "Women"    MacMullen, Ramsay. "Women in Public in the Roman Empire." *Historia* 29 (1980): 209–18.

MacRae, "Gnosticism"    MacRae, George W. "Gnosticism and New Testament Studies." *The Bible Today* 38 (November 1968): 2623–2630.

MacRae, *Invitation*    MacRae, George W. *Invitation to John: A Commentary on the Gospel of John with Complete Text from the Jerusalem Bible.* Garden City, N.Y.: Doubleday, 1978.

MacRae, "Myth"    MacRae, George W. "The Jewish Background of the Gnostic Sophia Myth." *NovT* 12 (1970): 86–101.

Maddox, *Purpose*    Maddox, Robert. *The Purpose of Luke–Acts.* Edinburgh: T&T Clark, 1982.

Magen, "Bty-knst"    Magen, I. "Bty-knst šwmrynyym [Samaritan Synagogues]." *Qadmoniot* 25 (1992): 66–90.

Magen, "Qʾlʾndyh"    Magen, Y. "Qʾlʾndyh—ḥwwh ḥqlʾyt lgydwl gpnym wlyyṣwr yyn mymy byt šny [Kalandia—a Vineyard Farm and Winery of Second Temple Times]." *Qadmoniot* 17 (1984): 61–71.

Magen, "Yrwšlym"    Magen, Y. "Yrwšlym kmrkz šl tᶜśyyt kly-ʾbn btqwpt hwrdws [Jerusalem as the Center for Stone-Ware Production in Herodian Times]." *Qadmoniot* 17 (1984): 124–27.

Magness, "Observations"    Magness, J. "Some Observations on the Roman Temple at Kadesh." *IEJ* 40 (1990): 173–81.

Magness, *Sense*    Magness, J. Lee. *Sense and Absence: Structure and Suspension in the Ending of Mark's Gospel.* Society of Biblical Literature Semeia Studies. Atlanta: Society of Biblical Literature, 1986.

Magnien, *Mystères*    Magnien, Victor. *Les mystères d'Éleusis: Leurs origines, le rituel de leurs initiations.* 3d ed. Paris: Payot, 1950.

Maher, "Humble"    Maher, Michael. "Humble of Heart: The Virtue of Humility in Rabbinic Literature." *Milltown Studies* 11 (1983): 25–43.

Maier, *Jesus in Überlieferung*    Maier, Johann. *Jesus von Nazareth in der talmudischen Uberlieferung.* Erträge der Forschung 82. Darmstadt: Wissenschaftliche Buchgesellschaft, 1978.

Maier, "Kult"    Maier, Johann. "Zu Kult und Liturgie der Qumrangemeinde." *RevQ* 14 (1989–1990): 543–86.

Maier, *Scroll*    Maier, Johann. *The Temple Scroll: An Introduction, Translation, and Commentary.* Journal for the Study of the Old Testament Supplement 34. Sheffield: JSOT Press, 1985.

Malan, "Apostolate"    Malan, F. S. "The Relationship between Apostolate and Office in the Theology of Paul." *Neotestamentica* 10 (1976): 53–68.

Malatesta, *Interiority*   Malatesta, Edward. *Interiority and Covenant: A Study of einai en and menein en in the First Letter of Saint John.* Analecta biblica 69. Rome: Biblical Institute Press, 1978.

Malatesta, "Spirit/Paraclete"   Malatesta, Edward. "The Spirit/Paraclete in the Fourth Gospel." *Biblica* 54 (1973): 539–50.

Malherbe, *Aspects*   Malherbe, Abraham J. *Social Aspects of Early Christianity.* 2d ed. Philadelphia: Fortress, 1983.

Malherbe, "Corner"   Malherbe, Abraham J. "Not in a Corner: Early Christian Apologetic in Acts 26:26." *Second Century* 5 (1986): 193–210.

Malherbe, "Description"   Malherbe, Abraham J. "A Physical Description of Paul." *HTR* 79 (1986): 170–75.

Malherbe, *Exhortation*   Malherbe, Abraham J. *Moral Exhortation, a Greco-Roman Sourcebook.* LEC 4. Philadelphia: Westminster, 1986.

Malherbe, "Gentle"   Malherbe, Abraham J. "'Gentle as a Nurse': The Cynic Background to I Thess ii." *NovT* 12 (1970): 203–17.

Malherbe, "Life"   Malherbe, Abraham J. "Life in the Graeco-Roman World." Pages 4–36 in *The World of the New Testament.* Edited by Abraham J. Malherbe. Austin, Tex.: R. B. Sweet, 1967.

Malherbe, "Theorists"   Malherbe, Abraham J. "Ancient Epistolary Theorists." *Ohio Journal of Religious Studies* 5, no. 2 (October 1977): 3–77.

Malina, *Manna Tradition*   Malina, Bruce J. *The Palestinian Manna Tradition: The Manna Tradition in the Palestinian Targums and Its Relationship to the New Testament Writings.* Arbeiten zur Geschichte des späteren Judentums und des Urchristentums 7. Leiden: Brill, 1968.

Malina, *Windows*   Malina, Bruce J. *Windows on the World of Jesus: Time Travel to Ancient Judea.* Louisville, Ky.: Westminster John Knox, 1993.

Malina, *World*   Malina, Bruce J. *The New Testament World: Insights from Cultural Anthropology.* Atlanta: John Knox, 1981.

Malina and Neyrey, "Honor and Shame"   Malina, Bruce J., and Jerome H. Neyrey. "Honor and Shame in Luke–Acts: Pivotal Values of the Mediterranean World." Pages 25–65 in *The Social World of Luke–Acts: Models for Interpretation.* Edited by Jerome H. Neyrey. Peabody, Mass.: Hendrickson, 1991.

Malina and Rohrbaugh, *Commentary*   Malina, Bruce J., and Richard L. Rohrbaugh. *Social Science Commentary on the Synoptic Gospels.* Minneapolis: Augsburg Fortress, 1992.

Malina and Rohrbaugh, *John*   Malina, Bruce J., and Richard L. Rohrbaugh. *Social-Science Commentary on the Gospel of John.* Minneapolis: Fortress, 1998.

Malinowski, "Tendencies"   Malinowski, Francis X. "Torah Tendencies in Galilean Judaism according to Flavius Josephus with Gospel Comparisons." *Biblical Theology Bulletin* 10 (1980): 30–36.

Maller, "Hanukkah"   Maller, Allen S. "Hanukkah: Evolution of a Miracle." *Living Light* 25 (1988): 54–58.

Maloney, "Authorship"   Maloney, Elliott C. "Biblical Authorship and the Pastoral Letters." *The Bible Today* 24 (1986): 119–23.

Maly, "Women"   Maly, Eugene H. "Women and the Gospel of Luke." *Biblical Theology Bulletin* 10 (1980): 99–104.

Malzoni, "La résurrection"   Malzoni, Claudio V. "'Moi, je suis la résurrection': Jean 11,25 dans la tradition syriaque ancienne." *RB* 106, no. 3 (1999): 421–40.

Mancini, *Discoveries*   Mancini, Ignazio. *Archaeological Discoveries Relative to the Judaeo-Christians: Historical Survey.* Translated by G. Bushell. Publications of the Studium Biblicum Franciscanum, Collectio minor 10. Jerusalem: Franciscan Printing Press, 1970.

Mandell, "Tax"   Mandell, Sara. "The Jewish Christians and the Temple Tax: *hy'bd kwkbym* and *hkwty* in Mishnah Seqalim 1:5." *Second Century* 7 (1989–1990): 76–84.

Manns, "Altercation"   Manns, Fréderic. "Une altercation doctrinale entre les rabbins et les judéo-chrétiens au début du troisième siècle: *Sifre Dt* 32,1 (§306)." *Vetera Christianorum* 26 (1989): 49–58.

Manns, "Amis"   Manns, Fréderic. "Je vous appelle mes amis." *Bibbia e oriente* 38 (1996): 227–38.

Manns, "Christologie johannique"   Manns, Fréderic. "Elements de christologie johannique." *Bibbia e oriente* 40, no. 3 (1999): 169–92.

Manns, "Encore"   Manns, Fréderic. "Encore une fois le lithostrotos de Jn 19,13." *Antonianum* 70 (1995): 187–97.

Manns, "Entente"   Manns, Fréderic. "Les mots à double entente: Antécédents et fonction herméneutique d'un procédé johannique." *Studii biblici franciscani liber annuus* 38 (1988): 39–57.

Manns, "Evangelio"   Manns, Fréderic. "El evangelio de Juan a la luz del judaísmo." *Teología espiritual* 41 (1997): 351–65.

Manns, "Exégèse"   Manns, Fréderic. "Exégèse rabbinique et exégèse johannique." *RB* 92 (October 1985): 525–38.

Manns, "Fête"   Manns, Fréderic. "La fête des Juifs de Jean 5,1." *Antonianum* 70 (1995): 117–24.

Manns, "Galilée"   Manns, Fréderic. "La Galilée dans le quatrieme évangile." *Antonianum* 72 (1997): 351–64.

Manns, "Halakah"   Manns, Fréderic. "La halakah dans l'évangile de Matthieu: Note sur Mt. 16,16–19." *Bibbia e oriente* 25 (1983): 129–35.

Manns, "Jacob"   Manns, Fréderic. "Jacob, le Min, selon la Tosephta Hulin 2,22–24: Contribution à l'étude du christianisme primitif." *Cristianesimo nella storia* 10 (1989): 449–65.

Manns, "Jour"   Manns, Fréderic. "Le troisième jour il y eut des noces à Cana." *Marianum* 40 (1978):160–63.

Manns, "Lumière"   Manns, Fréderic. "Marc 6,21–29 à la lumière des dernières fouilles du Machéronte." *Studii biblici franciscani liber annuus* 31 (1981): 287–90.

Manns, "Midrash"   Manns, Fréderic. "Col. 1,15–20: Midrash chrétien de Gen. 1,1." *RevScRel* 53 (1979): 100–110.

Manns, "Oeuvres"   Manns, Fréderic. "Les oeuvres de miséricorde dans le quatrième évangile." *Bibbia e oriente* 27, no. 4 (1985): 215–21.

Manns, "Paraclet"   Manns, Fréderic. "Le Paraclet dans l'évangile de Jean." *Studii biblici franciscani liber annuus* 33 (1983): 99–152.

Manns, "Polémique"   Manns, Fréderic. "La polémique contre les judéo-chrétiens en Pesiqta de Rab Kahana 15." *Studii biblici franciscani liber annuus* 40 (1990): 211–26.

Manns, "Réponse"   Manns, Fréderic. "L'évangile de Jean, réponse chrétienne aux décisions de Jabne: Note complémentaire." *Studii biblici franciscani liber annuus* 32 (1982): 85–108.

Manns, "Sagesse"   Manns, Fréderic. "La sagesse nourricière dans l'évangile de Jean." *Bibbia e oriente* 39 (1997): 207–34.

Manns, "Source"   Manns, Fréderic. "Une source de l'aggadah juive: La littérature grecque." *Studii biblici franciscani liber annuus* 29 (1979): 111–44.

Manns, "Symbolisme"   Manns, Fréderic. "Le symbolisme du jardin dans le récit de la passion selon St Jean." *Studii biblici franciscani liber annuus* 37 (1987): 53–80.

Manns, "Traditions"   Manns, Fréderic. "Traditions targumiques en Jean 2,1–11." *Marianum* 45 (1983): 297–305.

Manson, *Hebrews*   Manson, William. *The Epistle to the Hebrews: An Historical and Theological Reconsideration.* Baird Lecture, 1949. London: Hodder & Stoughton, 1951.

Manson, *Paul and John*   Manson, T. W. *On Paul and John: Some Selected Theological Themes.* SBT 38. London: SCM, 1963.

Manson, *Sayings*   Manson, T. W. *The Sayings of Jesus.* London: SCM Press, 1957.Repr., Grand Rapids: Eerdmans, 1979.

Manson, *Servant-Messiah*   Manson, T. W. *The Servant-Messiah.* Cambridge: Cambridge University Press, 1961.

Mantel, "Oral Law"   Mantel, Hugo D. "The Antiquity of the Oral Law." *Annual of the Swedish Theological Institute* 12 (1983): 93–112.

Mantel, *Sanhedrin*   Mantel, Hugo. *Studies in the History of the Sanhedrin.* Harvard Semitic Studies 17. Cambridge: Harvard University Press, 1961.

Mantey, "Evidence"   Mantey, Julius R. "Evidence That the Perfect Tense in John 20:23 and Matthew 16:19 Is Mistranslated." *JETS* 16 (1973): 129–38.

Mantey, "Translations"   Mantey, Julius R. "Distorted Translations in John 20:23; Matthew 16:18–19 and 18:18." *Review and Expositor* 78 (1981): 409–16.

Manus, "Parallels"   Manus, Ukachukwu Chris. "Jn 6:1–15 and Its Synoptic Parallels: An African Approach toward the Solution of a Johannine Critical Problem." *Journal of the Interdenominational Theological Center* 19 (1991–92): 47–71.

Ma'oz. "Synagogues"   Ma'oz, Zvi Uri. "Ancient Synagogues and the Golan." *BA* 51 (1988): 116–28.

Marchant, "Introduction"   Marchant, E. C. Introduction. Pages vii–xxvii in Xenophon, *Memorabilia* and *Oeconomicus*. Translated by E. C. Marchant. LCL. Cambridge: Harvard University Press, 1923.

Marconi, "Struttura di Gv 9, 1–41"   Marconi, Gilberto. "La vista del cieco: Struttura di Gv 9, 1–41." *Gregorianum* 79, no. 4 (1998): 625–43.

Marcus, "Names"   Marcus, Ralph. "Divine Names and Attributes in Hellenistic Jewish Literature." *Proceedings of the American Academy for Jewish Research* 3 (1931–1932): 43–120.

Marcus, "Mebaqqer"   Marcus, Ralph. "Mebaqqer and Rabbim in the Manual of Discipline vi.11–13." *JBL* 75 (1956): 298–302.

Marcus, "Rivers"   Marcus, Joel. "Rivers of Living Water from Jesus' Belly (John 7:38)." *JBL* 117 (1998): 328–30.

Marcus, "Schism"   Marcus, Ralph. "Josephus on the Samaritan Schism." Pages 498–511 in vol. 6 of Josephus, *Works*. 10 vols. LCL. Cambridge: Harvard University Press, 1926–1965.

Marcus, "Scrolls"   Marcus, Ralph. "The Qumran Scrolls and Early Judaism." *Biblical Research* 1 (1956): 9–47.

Marmorstein, "Amidah"   Marmorstein, A. "The Amidah of the Public Fast Days." *JQR* 15 (1924–1925): 409–18.

Marmorstein, *Anthropomorphism*   Marmorstein, A. *The Old Rabbinic Doctrine of God: Essays in Anthropomorphism*. 1937. Repr., New York: Ktav, 1968.

Marmorstein, "Attitude"   Marmorstein, A. "The Attitude of the Jews towards Early Christianity." *The Expositor*, 8th series, 26 (1923): 383–89.

Marmorstein, *Merits*   Marmorstein, A. *The Doctrine of Merits in Old Rabbinical Literature*. New York: Ktav, 1968.

Marmorstein, *Names*   Marmorstein, A. *The Old Rabbinic Doctrine of God: The Names and Attributes of God*. 1927. Repr., New York: Ktav, 1968.

Marrow, *John*   Marrow, Stanley B. *The Gospel of John: A Reading*. New York: Paulist, 1995.

Marsden, *Fundamentalism*   Marsden, George M. *Fundamentalism and American Culture: The Shaping of Twentieth-Century Evangelicalism, 1870–1925*. New York: Oxford University Press, 1980.

Marsh, *John*   Marsh, John. *Saint John*. Westminster Pelican Commentaries. Philadelphia: Westminster, 1968.

Marshall, "Criticism"   Marshall, I. Howard. "Historical Criticism." Pages 126–38 in *New Testament Interpretation: Essays on Principles and Methods*. Edited by I. Howard Marshall. Grand Rapids: Eerdmans, 1977.

Marshall, *Enmity*   Marshall, Peter. *Enmity in Corinth: Social Conventions in Paul's Relations with the Corinthians*. WUNT 2d series, 23. Tübingen: J. C. B. Mohr (Paul Siebeck), 1987.

Marshall, *Interpretation*   Marshall, I. Howard, ed. *New Testament Interpretation: Essays on Principles and Methods*. Grand Rapids: Eerdmans, 1977.

Marshall, *Kept*   Marshall, I. Howard. *Kept by the Power of God: A Study in Perseverance and Falling Away*. London: Epworth, 1969. Repr., Minneapolis: Bethany Fellowship, 1974.

Marshall, *Origins*   Marshall, I. Howard. *The Origins of New Testament Christology*. 2d ed. Downers Grove, Ill.: InterVarsity, 1990.

Marshall, "Son of Man"   Marshall, I. Howard. "The Synoptic Son of Man Sayings in Recent Discussion." *NTS* 12 (1965–1966): 327–51.

Marshall, "Son or Servant"   Marshall, I. Howard. "Son of God or Servant of Yahweh? A Reconsideration of Mark i.11." *NTS* 15 (1968–1969): 326–36.

Marshall, *Thessalonians*   Marshall, I. Howard. *1 and 2 Thessalonians*. New Century Bible. Grand Rapids: Eerdmans, 1983.

Martens, "Law"   Martens, John W. "Unwritten Law in Philo: A Response to Naomi G. Cohen." *JJS* 43 (1992): 38–45.

Martens, "Prologue"   Martens, Ray F. "The Prologue of the Gospel of John: An Examination of Its Origins and Emphases." Doctor of Sacred Theology diss., Lutheran School of Theology at Chicago, 1974.

Martin, *Carmen Christi*   Martin, Ralph P. *Carmen Christi*. Cambridge: Cambridge University Press, 1967.

Martin, *Colossians*   Martin, Ralph P. *Colossians and Philemon*. New Century Bible. Grand Rapids: Eerdmans, 1978.

Martin, "Epithet"    Martin, T. W. "Assessing the Johannine Epithet 'the Mother of Jesus.'" *CBQ* 60 (1998): 63–73.

Martin, "Evidence"    Martin, R. A. "Syntactical Evidence of Aramaic Sources in Acts i-xv." *NTS* 11 (1964–1965): 38–59.

Martin, "Footsteps"    Martin, Ralph P. "Following in the First Christians' Footsteps." *Christian History* 37 (1993): 42–43.

Martin, "Hymn"    Martin, Ralph P. "An Early Christian Hymn (Col 1:15–20)." *EvQ* 36 (1964): 195–205.

Martin, "Ideology"    Martin, Luther H. "The Anti-individualistic Ideology of Hellenistic Culture." *Numen* 41 (1994): 117–40.

Martin, "Interpretation"    Martin, R. A. "The Earliest Messianic Interpretation of Genesis 3:15." *JBL* 84 (1965): 425–27.

Martin, *James*    Martin, Ralph P. *James.* WBC 48. Waco, Tex.: Word, 1988.

Martin, *Mark*    Martin, Ralph P. *Mark: Evangelist and Theologian.* Grand Rapids: Zondervan, 1972.

Martin, "Mithraism"    Martin, Luther H. "Roman Mithraism and Christianity." *Numen* 36 (1989): 2–15.

Martin, "*Morphē*"    Martin, Ralph P. "*Morphē* in Philippians ii.6." *ExpTim* 70 (1958–1959): 183–84.

Martin, "Q"    Martin, W. H. Blyth. "The Indispensability of Q." *Theology* 59 (1956): 182–88.

Martin, *Religions*    Martin, Luther H. *Hellenistic Religions: An Introduction.* New York: Oxford University Press, 1987.

Martin, "Servant"    Martin, Ralph P. "The Pericope of the Healing of the 'Centurion's' Servant/Son (Matt 8:5–13 par. Luke 7:1–10): Some Exegetical Notes." Pages 14–22 in *Unity and Diversity in New Testament Theology: Essays in Honor of George E. Ladd.* Ed. Robert A. Guelich. Grand Rapids: Eerdmans, 1978.

Martin, *Slavery*    Martin, Dale B. *Slavery as Salvation: The Metaphor of Slavery in Pauline Christianity.* New Haven: Yale University Press, 1990.

Martin, *Worship*    Martin, Ralph P. *The Worship of God.* Grand Rapids: Eerdmans, 1982.

Martins Terra, "Milagres"    Martins Terra, J. E. "Os milagres helenísticos." *Revista de cultura bíblica* 4 (15–16, 1980): 229–62.

Martitz, "υἱός"    Martitz, W. von. "υἱός, υἱοθεσία A." *TDNT* 8:335–40.

Martone, "Testo"    Martone, Corrado. "Un testo qumranico che narra la morte del Messia? A propositio del recente dibattito su 4Q285." *RivB* 42 (1994): 329–36.

Martyn, "Glimpses"    Martyn, J. Louis. "Glimpses into the History of the Johannine Community." Pages 149–76 in *L'évangile de Jean: Sources, rédaction, théologie.* Edited by M. De Jonge. BETL 45. Gembloux: J. Duculot; Leuven: Leuven University Press, 1977.

Martyn, "Mission"    Martyn, J. Louis. "A Gentile Mission That Replaced an Earlier Jewish Mission?" Pages 124–44 in *Exploring the Gospel of John: In Honor of D. Moody Smith.* Edited by R. Alan Culpepper and C. Clifton Black. Louisville, Ky.: Westminster John Knox, 1996.

Martyn, "Religionsgeschichte"    Martyn, J. Louis. "Source Criticism and Religionsgeschichte in the Fourth Gospel (1970)." Pages 99–121 in *The Interpretation of John.* Edited by John Ashton. Issues in Religion and Theology 9. Philadelphia: Fortress, 1986.

Martyn, *Theology*    Martyn, J. Louis. *History and Theology in the Fourth Gospel.* Nashville: Abingdon, 1968.

Marx, "Prédestination"    Marx, Alfred. "Y a-t-il une prédestination à Qumran?" *RevQ* 6 (1967–1969): 163–81.

Marxsen, *Mark*    Marxsen, Willi. *Mark the Evangelist: Studies on the Redaction History of the Gospel.* Translated by James Boyce, Donald Juel, and William Poehlmann, with Roy A. Harrisville. Nashville: Abingdon, 1969.

Marzotto, "Targum"    Marzotto, Damiano. "Giovanni 17 e il Targum di Esodo 19–20." *RivB* 25 (1977): 375–88.

Mason, "Chief Priests"    Mason, Steve. "Chief Priests, Sadducees, Pharisees, and Sanhedrin in Acts." Pages 115–78 in *The Book of Acts in Its Palestinian Setting.* Edited by Richard Bauckham. Vol. 4 of *The Book of Acts in Its First Century Setting.* Edited by Bruce W. Winter. Grand Rapids: Eerdmans, 1995.

Mason, "Dominance"    Mason, Steven. "Pharisaic Dominance before 70 C.E. and the Gospels' Hypocrisy Charge (Matt 23:2–3)." *HTR* 83 (1990): 363–81.

Mason, *Josephus and NT*    Mason, Steven. *Josephus and the New Testament*. Peabody, Mass.: Hendrickson, 1992.

Mason, *Pharisees*    Mason, Steven. *Flavius Josephus on the Pharisees*. StPB 39. Leiden: Brill, 1991.

Massa, *Pompeii*    Massa, Aldo. *The World of Pompeii*. Geneva: Minerva, 1972.

Matera, *Kingship*    Matera, Frank J. *The Kingship of Jesus: Composition and Theology in Mark 15*. SBLDS 66. Chico, Calif.: Scholars Press for Society of Biblical Literature, 1982.

Mates, *Logic*    Mates, Benson. *Stoic Logic*. University of California Publications in Philosophy 26. Berkeley: University of California Press, 1953.

Matson, *Dialogue*    Matson, Mark A. *In Dialogue with Another Gospel? The Influence of the Fourth Gospel on the Passion Narrative of the Gospel of Luke*. SBLDS 178. Atlanta: Society of Biblical Literature, 2001.

Matsunaga, "Anti-sacramental"    Matsunaga, Kikuo. "Is John's Gospel Anti-sacramental?—a New Solution in the Light of the Evangelist's Milieu." *NTS* 27 (1980–1981): 516–24.

Matsunaga, "Galileans"    Matsunaga, Kikuo. "The Galileans in the Fourth Gospel." *Annual of the Japanese Biblical Institute* 2 (1976): 139–58.

Matsunaga, "'Theos'"    Matsunaga, Kikuo. "The 'Theos' Christology as the Ultimate Confession of the Fourth Gospel." *Annual of the Japanese Biblical Institute* 7 (1981): 124–45.

Matthiae, "Nabatäer"    Matthiae, Karl. "Die Nabatäer: Ein antikes Handelsvolk in der Wüste." *Das Altertum* 35 (1989): 222–31.

Mattila, "Eschatologies"    Mattila, Sharon Lea. "Two Contrasting Eschatologies at Qumran (4Q246 vs 1QM)." *Biblica* 75 (1994): 518–38.

Mattill, *Last Things*    Mattill, A. J., Jr. *Luke and the Last Things: A Perspective for the Understanding of Lukan Thought*. Dillsboro, N.C.: Western North Carolina Press, 1979.

Mattingly, *Christianity*    Mattingly, Harold. *Christianity in the Roman Empire*. New York: Norton, 1967.

Mauser, *Wilderness*    Mauser, Ulrich. *Christ in the Wilderness*. SBT 39. London: SCM, 1963.

May, *Atlas*    May, Herbert Gordon, ed. *The Oxford Bible Atlas*. London: Oxford University Press, 1962.

May, "Logos"    May, Eric. "The Logos in the Old Testament." *CBQ* 8 (1946): 438–47.

May, "Synagogues"    May, Herbert Gordon. "Synagogues in Palestine." *BA* 7 (1944): 1–20.

Mayer, "Aspekte"    Mayer, Günter. "Aspekte des Abrahambildes in der hellenistisch-jüdischen Literatur." *Evangelische Theologie* 32 (1972): 118–27.

Mayer, "Anfang"    Mayer, Reinhold. "Der Anfang des Evangeliums in Galiläa." *Bibel und Kirche* 36, no. 2 (1981): 213–21.

Mayer, "Elijah"    Mayer, Allan. "Elijah and Elisha in John's Signs Sources." *ExpTim* 99 (1987–1988): 171–73.

Maynard, "Peter"    Maynard, Arthur H. "The Role of Peter in the Fourth Gospel." *NTS* 30 (1984): 531–48.

Mayor, *James*    Mayor, Joseph B. *The Epistle of St. James*. 3d rev. ed. n.p.: MacMillan, 1913. Repr., Minneapolis: Klock & Klock Christian, 1977.

Mazar, "Excavations"    Mazar, Benjamin. "Excavations near Temple Mount Reveal Splendors of Herodian Jerusalem." *BAR* 6, no. 4 (July/August 1980): 44–59.

Mazar, "Josephus"    Mazar, Benjamin. "Josephus Flavius and the Archaeological Excavations in Jerusalem." Pages 325–29 in *Josephus, the Bible, and History*. Edited by Louis H. Feldman and Gohei Hata. Detroit: Wayne State University Press, 1989.

Mbiti, *Religions*    Mbiti, John S. *African Religions and Philosophies*. Garden City, N.Y.: Doubleday, 1970.

McArthur, "Day"    McArthur, Harvey K. "On the Third Day.'" *NTS* 18 (1971–1972): 81–86.

McCabe, "Water and Spirit"    McCabe, Robert V. "The Meaning of 'Born of Water and the Spirit' in John 3:5." *Detroit Baptist Seminary Journal* 4 (1999): 85–107.

McCaffrey, *House*    McCaffrey, James. *The House with Many Rooms: The Temple Theme of Jn 14, 2–3*. Rome: Pontifical Biblical Institute, 1988.

McCane, "Bones"    McCane, Byron R. "Bones of Contention? Ossuaries and Reliquaries in Early Judaism and Christianity." *Second Century* 8 (1991): 235–46.

McCane, "Burial Practices"    McCane, Byron R. "Burial Practices, Jewish." Pages 173–75 in *Dictionary of New Testament Background*. Edited by Craig A. Evans and Stanley E. Porter. Downers Grove, Ill.: InterVarsity, 2000.

McCane, "Dead"   McCane, Byron R. "'Let the Dead Bury Their Own Dead': Secondary Burial and Matt 8:21–22." *HTR* 83 (1990): 31–43.

McCasland, "Way"   McCasland, S. V. "'The Way.'" *JBL* 77 (1958): 222–230.

McClelland, "'Super-apostles'"   McClelland, Scott E. "'Super-apostles, Servants of Christ, Servants of Satan': A Response." *JSNT* 14 (1982): 82–87.

McCown, "Structure"   McCown, Wayne. "The Hymnic Structure of Colossians 1:15–20." *EvQ* 51 (1979): 156–62.

McCoy, "Thucydides"   McCoy, W. J. "In the Shadow of Thucydides." Pages 3–32 in *History, Literature, and Society in the Book of Acts.* Edited by Ben Witherington, III. Cambridge: Cambridge University Press, 1996.

McEleney, "Conversion"   McEleney, Neil J. "Conversion, Circumcision, and the Law." *NTS* 20 (1973–1974): 319–41.

McEleney, "Fishes"   McEleney, Neil J. "153 Great Fishes (John 21,11)—Gematriacal Atbash." *Biblica* 58 (1977): 411–17.

McEleney, "Orthodoxy"   McEleney, Neil J. "Orthodoxy in Judaism of the First Christian Century." *JSJ* 4 (1973): 19–42.

McEleney, "Replies"   McEleney, Neil J. "Orthodoxy in Judaism of the First Christian Century: Replies to David E. Aune and Lester L. Grabbe." *JSJ* 9 (1978): 83–88.

McGehee, "Reading"   McGehee, Michael. "A Less Theological Reading of John 20:17." *JBL* 105 (1986): 299–302.

McGinn, "Taxation"   McGinn, T. A. J. "The Taxation of Roman Prostitutes." *Helios* 16 (1989): 79–110.

McGrath, *Apologetic Christology*   McGrath, James F. *John's Apologetic Christology: Legitimation and Development in Johannine Christology.* SNTSMS 111. Cambridge: Cambridge University Press, 2001.

McGrath, "Rebellious Son"   McGrath, James F. "A Rebellious Son? Hugo Odeberg and the Interpretation of John 5.18." *NTS* 44 (1998): 470–73.

McKenzie, "Know"   McKenzie, John L. "Know, Knowledge." *Dictionary of the Bible.* Milwaukee, Wis: Bruce, 1965.

McKenzie, "Sculpture"   McKenzie, Judith Sheila. "The Development of Nabataean Sculpture at Petra and Khirbet Tannur." *PEQ* 120 (1988): 81–107.

McKnight, "Critic"   McKnight, Scot. "A Loyal Critic: Matthew's Polemic with Judaism in Theological Perspective." Pages 55–79 in *Anti-Semitism and Early Christianity: Issues of Polemic and Faith.* Edited by Craig A. Evans and Donald A. Hagner. Minneapolis: Fortress, 1993.

McKnight, "Jesus"   McKnight, Scot. "Who Is Jesus? An Introduction to Jesus Studies." Pages 51–72 in *Jesus under Fire: Modern Scholarship Reinvents the Historical Jesus.* Edited by Michael J. Wilkins and J. P. Moreland. Grand Rapids: Zondervan.

McKnight, "Prosleytism"   McKnight, Scot. "Proselytism and Godfearers." Pages 835–47 in *Dictionary of New Testament Background.* Edited by Craig A. Evans and Stanley E. Porter. Downers Grove, Ill.: InterVarsity, 2000.

McKnight and Malbon, "Introduction"   McKnight, Edgar V., and Elizabeth Struthers Malbon. Introduction. Pages 15–26 in *The New Literary Criticism and the New Testament.* Edited by Edgar V. McKnight and Elizabeth Struthers Malbon. Valley Forge, Pa.: Trinity Press International, 1994; Sheffield: JSOT Press, 1994.

McNamara, *Judaism*   McNamara, Martin. *Palestinian Judaism and the New Testament.* Good News Studies 4. Wilmington, Del.: Glazier, 1983.

McNamara, "*Logos*"   McNamara, Martin. "*Logos* of the Fourth Gospel and *Memra* of the Palestinian Targum (Ex 12.42)." *ExpTim* 79 (1967–1968): 115–17.

McNamara, "Resting-Place"   McNamara, Martin. "'To Prepare a Resting-Place for You': A Targumic Expression and John 14:2f." *Milltown Studies* 3 (1979): 100–108.

McNamara, *Targum*   McNamara, Martin. *Targum and Testament.* Grand Rapids: Eerdmans, 1972.

McNaugher, "Spirit"   McNaugher, J. "The Witnessing Spirit and the Witnessed Christ." *BSac* 88 (1931): 207–19.

McNeil, "Quotation"   McNeil, Brian. "The Quotation at John XII 34." *NovT* 19 (1977): 22–33.

McNicol, "Temple"   McNicol, Allan J. "The Eschatological Temple in the Qumran Pesher 4QFlorilegium 1:1–7." *Ohio Journal of Religious Studies* 5, no. 2 (1977): 133–41.

McPolin, *John* McPolin, James. *John.* New Testament Message 6. Wilmington, Del.: Glazier, 1979.

McRay, "Archaeology" McRay, John R. "Archaeology and the New Testament." Pages 93–100 in *Dictionary of New Testament Background.* Edited by Craig A. Evans and Stanley E. Porter. Downers Grove, Ill.: InterVarsity, 2000.

McRay, "Tiberias" McRay, John R. "Tiberias." Pages 1235–38 in *Dictionary of New Testament Background.* Edited by Craig A. Evans and Stanley E. Porter. Downers Grove, Ill.: InterVarsity, 2000.

Meadors, "Orthodoxy" Meadors, Edward P. "The Orthodoxy of the 'Q' Sayings of Jesus." *Tyndale Bulletin* 43 (1992): 233–57.

Meagher, "Twig" Meagher, John C. "As the Twig Was Bent." Pages 1–26 in *Antisemitism and the Foundations of Christianity.* Edited by Alan T. Davies. New York: Paulist Press, 1979.

Mealand, "Test" Mealand, David L. "The Dissimilarity Test." *SJT* 31 (1978): 41–50.

Meecham, "θεός" Meecham, H. G. "The Anarthrous θεός in John i.1 and 1 Corinthians iii.16." *ExpTim* 63 (1951–1952): 126.

Meeks, "Agent" Meeks, Wayne A. "The Divine Agent and His Counterfeit in Philo and the Fourth Gospel." Pages 43–67 in *Aspects of Religious Propaganda in Judaism and Early Christianity.* Edited by Elisabeth Schüssler Fiorenza. University of Notre Dame Center for the Study of Judaism and Christianity in Antiquity 2. Notre Dame, Ind.: University of Notre Dame Press, 1976.

Meeks, "Artificial Aliens" Meeks, Wayne A. "Corinthian Christians as Artificial Aliens." Pages 129–38 in *Paul beyond the Judaism/Hellenism Divide.* Ed. Troels Engberg-Pedersen. Louisville, Ky.: Westminster John Knox, 2001.

Meeks, *Christians* Meeks, Wayne A. *The First Urban Christians: The Social World of the Apostle Paul.* New Haven: Yale University Press, 1983.

Meeks, "Ethics" Meeks, Wayne A. "The Ethics of the Fourth Evangelist." Pages 317–26 in *Exploring the Gospel of John: In Honor of D. Moody Smith.* Edited by R. Alan Culpepper and C. Clifton Black. Louisville, Ky.: Westminster John Knox, 1996.

Meeks "Jew" Meeks, Wayne A. "'Am I a Jew?'—Johannine Christianity and Judaism." Pages 163–86 in *New Testament.* Vol. 1 of *Christianity, Judaism, and Other Greco-Roman Cults: Studies for Morton Smith at Sixty.* Edited by Jacob Neusner. 4 vols. Studies in Judaism in Late Antiquity 12. Leiden: Brill, 1975.

Meeks, "Man" Meeks, Wayne A. "The Man from Heaven in Johannine Sectarianism." *JBL* 91 (1972): 44–72.

Meeks, *Moral World* Meeks, Wayne A. *The Moral World of the First Christians.* LEC 6. Philadelphia: Westminster, 1986.

Meeks, *Prophet-King* Meeks, Wayne A. *The Prophet-King: Moses Traditions and the Johannine Christology.* NovTSup 14. Leiden: Brill, 1967.

Meggitt, "Artemidorus" Meggitt, Justin J. "Artemidorus and the Johannine Crucifixion." *Journal of Higher Criticism* 5, no. 2 (1998): 203–8.

Meier, "John" Meier, John P. "John the Baptist in Josephus: Philology and Exegesis." *JBL* 111 (1992): 225–37.

Meier, "John 20:19–23" Meier, J. P. "John 20:19–23." *Mid-Stream* 35 (1996): 395–98.

Meier, *Marginal Jew* Meier, John P. *A Marginal Jew: Rethinking the Historical Jesus.* Vol. 1: *The Roots of the Problem and the Person.* Vol. 2: *Mentor, Message, and Miracles.* Vol. 3: *Companions and Competitors.* Anchor Bible Reference Library. New York: Doubleday, 1991–2001.

Meier, *Matthew* Meier, John P. *Matthew.* New Testament Message: A Biblical-Theological Commentary, 3. Wilmington, Del.: Glazier, 1980.

Meier, "Twelve" Meier, John P. "The Circle of the Twelve: Did It Exist during Jesus' Public Ministry?" *JBL* 116 (1997): 635–72.

Meier, *Vision* Meier, John P. *The Vision of Matthew: Christ, Church, and Morality in the First Gospel.* Theological Inquiries. New York: Paulist Press, 1979.

Ménard, "Self-Definition" Ménard, Jacques E. "Normative Self-Definition in Gnosticism." Pages 134–50 in vol. 1 of Meyer and Sanders, *Self-Definition.*

Mendels, "Empires" Mendels, Doron. "The Five Empires: A Note on a Propagandistic Topos." *American Journal of Philology* 102 (1981): 330–37.

Mendels, "History" Mendels, D. "'Creative History' in the Hellenistic Near East in the Third and Second Centuries B.C.E.: The Jewish Case." *JSP* 2 (1988): 13–20.

Menken, "Eucharist"    Menken, M. J. J. "John 6,51c–58: Eucharist or Christology?" *Biblica* 74 (1993): 1–26.

Menken, "Form"    Menken, M. J. J. "The Textual Form and the Meaning of the Quotation from Zechariah 12:10 in John 19:37." *CBQ* 55 (1993): 494–511.

Menken, "John 6,45"    Menken, M. J. J. "The Old Testament Quotation in John 6,45: Sources and Redaction." *Ephemerides theologicae lovanienses* 64 (1988): 164–72.

Menken, "Origin"    Menken, M. J. J. "The Origin of the Old Testament Quotation in John 7:38." *NovT* 38 (1996): 160–75.

Menken, "Quotation"    Menken, M. J. J. "The Quotation from Isa 40,3 in John 1,23." *Biblica* 66 (1985): 190–205.

Menken, "Redaktion"    Menken, M. J. J. "Die Redaktion des Zitates aus Sach 9,9 in Joh 12,15." *ZNW* 80 (1989): 193–209.

Menken, *Techniques*    Menken, M. J. J. *Numerical Literary Techniques in John: The Fourth Evangelist's Use of Numbers of Words and Syllables.* NovTSup 55. Leiden: Brill, 1985.

Menken, "Translation"    Menken, M. J. J. "The Translation of Psalm 41.10 in John 13.18." *JSNT* 40 (1990): 61–79.

Menken, "Zitates"    Menken, M. J. J. "Die Form des Zitates aus Jes 6,10 in Joh 12,40: Ein Beitrag zum Schriftgebrauch des vierten Evangelisten." *BZ* 32 (1988): 189–209.

Menoud, "Pentecôte"    Menoud, Philippe H. "La Pentecôte lucanienne et l'histoire." *Revue d'histoire et de philosophie religieuses* 42 (1962): 141–47.

Menzies, *Pneumatology*    Menzies, Robert P. *The Development of Early Christian Pneumatology: With special reference to Luke–Acts.* JSNTSup 54. Sheffield: Sheffield Academic Press, 1991.

Mercer, "ΑΠΟΣΤΕΛΛΕΙΝ"    Mercer, Calvin. "ΑΠΟΣΤΕΛΛΕΙΝ and ΠΕΜΠΕΙΝ in John." *NTS* 36 (1990): 619–24.

Mercer, "Apostle"    Mercer, Calvin. "Jesus the Apostle: 'Sending' and the Theology of John." *JETS* 35 (1992): 457–62.

Merritt, "Barabbas"    Merritt, Robert L. "Jesus Barabbas and the Paschal Pardon." *JBL* 104 (1985): 57–68.

Metzger, *Civil Trial*    Metzger, Ernest. *A New Outline of the Roman Civil Trial.* Oxford: Clarendon Press, 1997.

Metzger, *Commentary*    Metzger, Bruce M. *A Textual Commentary on the Greek New Testament.* London and New York: United Bible Societies, 1971.

Metzger, "Consideration"    Metzger, Bruce M. "Considerations of Methodology in the Study of the Mystery Religions and Early Christianity." *HTR* 48 (1955): 1–20.

Metzger, "Papyri"    Metzger, Bruce M. "Recently Published Greek Papyri of the NT." *BA* 10 (1947): 25–44.

Metzger, *Text*    Metzger, Bruce M. *The Text of the New Testament.* New York: Oxford University Press, 1968.

Metzger, "Translation"    Metzger, Bruce M. "On the Translation of John i.1." *ExpTim* 63 (1951–1952): 125–26.

Metzner, "Geheilte"    Metzner, Rainer. "Der Geheilte von Johannes 5—Repräsentant des Unglaubens." *ZNW* 90, nos. 3–4 (1999): 177–93.

Meyer, "Mysteries"    Meyer, Marvin W. "Mysteries." Pages 720–25 in *Dictionary of New Testament Background.* Edited by Craig A. Evans and Stanley E. Porter. Downers Grove, Ill.: InterVarsity, 2000.

Meyer, "Note"    Meyer, Paul W. "A Note on John 10:1–18." *JBL* 75 (1956): 232–35.

Meyer and Sanders, *Self-Definition*    Meyer, Ben F., and E. P. Sanders, eds. *Jewish and Christian Self-Definition.* Vol. 1: *The Shaping of Christianity in the Second and Third Centuries.* Edited by E. P. Sanders. Vol. 2: *Aspects of Judaism in the Graeco-Roman Period.* Edited by E. P. Sanders with A. I.Baumgarten and Alan Mendelson. Vol. 3: *Self-Definition in the Greco-Roman World.* Edited by Ben F. Meyer and E. P. Sanders. Philadelphia: Fortress: 1980–1983.

Meyers, "Hellenism"    Meyers, Eric M. "The Challenge of Hellenism for Early Judaism and Christianity." *BA* 55 (1992): 84–91.

Meyers, "Judaism and Christianity"    Meyers, Eric M. "Early Judaism and Christianity in the Light of Archaeology." *BA* 51 (1988): 69–79.

Meyers, "Regionalism"   Meyers, Eric M. "Galilean Regionalism as a Factor in Historical Reconstruction." *BASOR* 221 (February 1976): 93–101.

Meyers, "Setting"   Meyers, Eric M. "Ancient Synagogues in Galilee: Their Religious and Cultural Setting." *BA* 43 (1980): 97–108.

Meyers, "State"   Meyers, Eric M. "The Current State of Galilean Synagogues Studies." Pages 127–137 in *The Synagogue in Late Antiquity*. Edited by Lee I. Levine. Philadelphia: American Schools of Oriental Research, 1986.

Meyers and Kraabel, "Iconography"   Meyers, Eric M., and A. Thomas Kraabel. "Archaeology, Iconography, and Nonliterary Written Remains." Pages 175–210 in *Early Judaism and Its Modern Interpreters*. Edited by Robert A. Kraft and George W. E. Nickelsburg. SBLBMI 2. Atlanta: Scholars Press, 1986.

Meyers and Meyers, "Stamp"   Meyers, Carol L. and Eric M. "Another Jewish Bread Stamp?" *IEJ* 25 (1975): 154–55.

Meyers, Netzer, and Meyers, "Byt-mydwt"   Meyers, Eric M., Ehud Netzer, and Carol L. Meyers. "Byt-mydwt šnḥšp bʾqrwpwlys šl ṣypwry wbmrkzw psyps mpwʾr [A Mansion in the Sepphoris Acropolis and Its Splendid Mosaic]." *Qadmoniot* 21 (1988): 87–92.

Meyers, Netzer, and Meyers, "Sepphoris"   Meyers, Eric M., Ehud Netzer, and Carol L. Meyers. "Sepphoris 'Ornament of All Galilee.'" *BA* 49 (1986): 4–19.

Meyers and Strange, *Archaeology*   Meyers, Eric M., and James F. Strange. *Archaeology, the Rabbis, and Early Christianity*. Nashville: Abingdon, 1981.

Meyers and White, "Jews and Christians"   Meyers, Eric M., and L. M. White. "Jews and Christians in a Roman World." *Archaeology* 42, no. 2 (March/April 1989): 26–33.

Meyshan, "Coins"   Meyshan, Joseph. "Jewish Coins in Ancient Historiography: The Importance of Numismatics for the History of Israel." *PEQ* 96 (1964): 46–52.

M'Gillivray, "Prologue"   M'Gillivray, Donald. "The Prologue of the Fourth Gospel." *ExpTim* 32 (1920–21): 281–82.

Michael, "Prologue"   Michael, J. Hugh. "Notes on the Johannine Prologue." *ExpTim* 31 (1919–20): 276–79.

Michaelis, "Herkunft"   Michaelis, Wilhelm. "Zur Herkunft des johanneischen Paraklet-Titels." Pages 147–62 in *Coniectanea Neotestamentica 11: Festschrift Antoni Fridrichsen*. Lund: Gleerup; Copenhagen: Munksgaard, 1947.

Michaels, "Anti-Semitism"   Michaels, J. Ramsey. "Alleged Anti-Semitism in the Fourth Gospel." *Gordon Review* 1 (1968): 12–24.

Michaels, "Apocalypse"   Michaels, J. Ramsey. "The Gospel of John as a Kinder, Gentler Apocalypse for the 20th Century." Pages 191–97 in *"What Is John?" Readers and Reading of the Fourth Gospel*. Edited by Fernando F. Segovia. SBLSymS 3. Atlanta: Scholars Press, 1996.

Michaels, "Discourse"   Michaels, J. Ramsey. "The Temple Discourse in John." Pages 200–213 in *New Dimensions in New Testament Study*. Edited by Richard N. Longenecker and Merrill C. Tenney. Grand Rapids: Zondervan, 1974.

Michaels, *John*   Michaels, J. Ramsey. *John*. Good News Commentaries. San Francisco: Harper & Row, 1984.

Michaels, "Nathanael"   Michaels, J. Ramsey. "Nathanael under the Fig Tree." *ExpTim* 78 (1966–1967): 182–83.

Michaels, *Servant*   Michaels, J. Ramsey. *Servant and Son: Jesus in Parable and Gospel*. Atlanta: John Knox, 1981.

Michaels, "Trial"   Michaels, J. Ramsey. "John 18.31 and the 'Trial' of Jesus." *NTS* 36 (1990): 474–79.

Michel, *Abschiedsrede*   Michel, H. J. *Die Abschiedsrede des Paulus an die Kirche Apg 20 17–38*. Studien zum Alten und Neuen Testament 35. Munich: Kösel, 1973.

Michel, "Faith"   Michel, O. "Faith: Πίστις." *NIDNTT* 1:593–605.

Michl, "Bemerkungen"   Michl, Johann. "Bemerkungen zu Joh. 2,4." *Biblica* 36 (1955): 492–509.

Middleton, "Logos"   Middleton, R. D. "Logos and Shekinah in the Fourth Gospel." *JQR* 29 (1938–1939): 101–33.

Mielcarek, "Interpretacja"   Mielcarek, K. "Interpretacja frazy 'bogami jestescie' (J 10, 34) w swietle tradycji Starego Testamentu I literatury miedzytestamentalnej." *Collectanea theologica* 70, no. 1 (2000): 63–85.

Mielgo, "Presencia"    Mielgo, G. S. "Presencia y actuación del Parákletos en la Iglesia (Jn. 14–16)." *Teología espiritual* 24 (1980): 79–117.

Milik, "Écrits"    Milik, J. T. "Écrits préesséniens de Qumrân: D'Hénoch à Amram." Pages 91–106 in *Qumrân: Sa piété, sa théologie, et son milieu.* Edited by M. Delcor. BETL 46. Paris: Gembloux, 1978.

Milik, *Discovery*    Milik, J. T. *Ten Years of Discovery in the Wilderness of Judaea.* London: SCM, 1959.

Milikowsky, "ʾlyhw"    Milikowsky, C. "ʾlyhw whmšyḥ (Elijah and the Messiah)." *Jerusalem Studies in Jewish Thought* 2 (1982–1983): 491–96.

Milikowsky, "Gehenna"    Milikowsky, Chaim. "Which Gehenna? Retribution and Eschatology in the Synoptic Gospels and in Early Jewish Texts." *NTS* 34 (1988): 238–49.

Millar, "World"    Millar, Fergus. "The World of the *Golden Ass.*" *Journal of Roman Studies* 71 (1981): 63–75.

Millard, *Reading*    Millard, Alan. *Reading and Writing in the Time of Jesus.* Sheffield: Sheffield Academic Press, 2000.

Miller, "Christology"    Miller, E. L. "The Christology of John 8:25." *Theologische Zeitschrift* 36 (1980): 257–65.

Miller, "City"    Miller, Stuart S. "Sepphoris, the Well Remembered City." *BA* 55 (1992): 74–83.

Miller, "Introduction"    Miller, Walter. Introduction. Pages vii–xiii in vol. 1 of Xenophon, *Cyropaedia.* Translated by Walter Miller. 2 vols. LCL. Cambridge: Harvard University Press, 1914.

Miller, "*Logos*"    Miller, E. L. "'The *Logos* Was God.'" *EvQ* 53 (1981): 65–77.

Miller, "*Minim*"    Miller, Stuart S. "The *minim* of Sepphoris Reconsidered." *HTR* 86, no. 4 (1993): 377–402.

Miller, "Origins"    Miller, E. L. "The Johannine Origins of the Johannine Logos." *JBL* 112 (1993): 445–57.

Miller, *Salvation-History*    Miller, E. L. *Salvation-History in the Prologue of John: The Significance of John 1:3/4.* NovTSup 60. Leiden: Brill, 1989.

Miller, "Sepphoris"    Miller, Stuart S. "Intercity Relations in Roman Palestine: The Case of Sepphoris and Tiberias." *AJSR* 12 (1987): 1–24.

Miller, "Time"    Miller, Johnny V. "The Time of the Crucifixion." *JETS* 26 (1983): 157–66.

Miller, "Updating"    Miller, Ed. L. "The Logos of Heraclitus: Updating the Report." *HTR* 74 (1981): 161–76.

Milligan, *Thessalonians*    Milligan, George. *St Paul's Epistles to the Thessalonians: The Greek Text with Introduction and Notes.* London: Macmillan, 1908.

Milne, *Message*    Milne, Bruce. *The Message of John.* Downers Grove, Ill.: InterVarsity, 1993.

Minde, "Absonderung"    Minde, Hans-Jürgen van der. "Die Absonderung der Frommen: Die Qumrangemeinschaft als Heiligtum Gottes." *Bibel und Liturgie* 61, no. 3 (1988): 190–97.

Minear, "Audience"    Minear, Paul S. "The Audience of the Fourth Evangelist." *Interpretation* 31 (1977): 339–54.

Minear, "Functions"    Minear, Paul S. "The Original Functions of John 21." *JBL* 102 (1983): 85–98.

Minear, *Images*    Minear, Paul S. *Images of the Church in the New Testament.* Philadelphia: Westminster, 1960.

Minear, *Kingdom*    Minear, Paul S. *The Kingdom and the Power: An Exposition of the New Testament Gospel.* Philadelphia: Westminster, 1950.

Mitchell, "Friends"    Mitchell, Alan C. "'Greet the Friends by Name': New Testament Evidence for the Greco-Roman *topos* on Friendship." Pages 225–62 in *Greco-Roman Perspectives on Friendship.* Edited by John T. Fitzgerald. SBLRBS 34. Atlanta: Scholars Press, 1997.

Mitchell, *Rhetoric of Reconciliation*    Mitchell, Margaret M. *Paul and the Rhetoric of Reconciliation: An Exegetical Investigation of the Language and Composition of 1 Corinthians.* Louisville, Ky.: Westminster John Knox, 1991.

Mitten, "Sardis"    Mitten, David Gordon. "A New Look at Ancient Sardis." *BA* 29 (1966): 38–68.

Mitton, "Provenance"    Mitton, Charles L. "Modern Issues in Biblical Studies: The Provenance of the Fourth Gospel." *ExpTim* 71 (1959–1960): 337–40.

Moeller, "Motifs"    Moeller, Henry R. "Wisdom Motifs and John's Gospel." *Bulletin of the Evangelical Theological Society* 6 (1963): 92–100.

Moffatt, *Corinthians*    Moffatt, James D. *The First Epistle of Paul to the Corinthians.* Moffatt New Testament Commentary. London: Hodder & Stoughton, 1938.

Moffatt, *Hebrews*    Moffatt, James D. *A Critical and Exegetical Commentary on the Epistle to the Hebrews*. International Critical Commentary. Edinburgh: T&T Clark, 1924.

Moffatt, "Revelation"    Moffatt, James D. "Revelation." Pages 279–494 in vol. 5 of *The Expositor's Greek Testament*. Edited by W. Robertson Nicoll. 5 vols. 1897–1910. Repr., Grand Rapids: Eerdmans, 1979.

Moloney, *Belief*    Moloney, Francis J. *Belief in the Word: Reading the Fourth Gospel—John 1–4*. Minneapolis: Fortress, 1993.

Moloney, "Bosom"    Moloney, Francis J. "John 1:18: 'In the Bosom of' or 'Turned towards' the Father?" *ABR* 31 (1983): 63–71.

Moloney, "Cana"    Moloney, Francis J. "From Cana to Cana (Jn 2:1–4:54) and the Fourth Evangelist's Concept of Correct (and Incorrect) Faith." *Salesianum* 40 (1978): 817–43.

Moloney, "Jesus of History"    Moloney, Francis J. "The Fourth Gospel and the Jesus of History." *NTS* 46, no. 1 (2000): 42–58.

Moloney, "Mary"    Moloney, Francis J. "Mary in the Fourth Gospel: Woman and Mother." *Salesianum* 51 (1989): 421–40.

Moloney, "Reading"    Moloney, Francis J. "A Sacramental Reading of John 13:1–38." *CBQ* 53 (1991): 237–56.

Moloney, *Signs*    Moloney, Francis J. *Signs and Shadows: Reading John 5–12*. Minneapolis: Fortress, 1996.

Momigliano, *Historiography*    Momigliano, Arnaldo. *Essays in Ancient and Modern Historiography*. Oxford: Blackwell, 1977.

Mondin, "Esistenza"    Mondin, Battista. "Esistenza, natura, inconoscibilità, e ineffabilità di Dio nel pensiero di Filone Alessandrino." *Scuola cattolica* 95 (1967): 423–47.

Monshouwer, "Reading"    Monshouwer, Dirk. "The Reading of the Bible in the Synagogue in the First Century." *Bijdragen* 51 (1990): 68–84.

Monson et al., *Manual*    Monson, J., et al. *Student Map Manual: Historical Geography of the Bible Lands*. Jerusalem: Pictorial Archive, 1979.

Montefiore, "Father"    Montefiore, Hugh. "God as Father in the Synoptic Gospels." *NTS* 3 (1956–1957): 31–46.

Montefiore, *Gospels*    Montefiore, C. G. *The Synoptic Gospels*. 2 vols. Library of Biblical Studies. 1927. Repr., New York: Ktav, 1968.

Montefiore, *Hebrews*    Montefiore, Hugh. *A Commentary on the Epistle to the Hebrews*. Black's New Testament Commentaries. London: A&C Black, 1964.

Montefiore, "Judaism"    Montefiore, C. G. "The Spirit of Judaism." Pages 35–81 in vol. 1 of *The Beginnings of Christianity*.

Montefiore and Loewe, *Anthology*    Montefiore, C. G., and Herbert Loewe. *A Rabbinic Anthology*. London: Macmillan, 1938. Repr., New York: Schocken, 1974.

Moon, "Nudity"    Moon, Warren G. "Nudity and Narrative: Observations on the Frescoes from the Dura Synagogue." *Journal of the American Academy of Religion* 60, no. 4 (1992): 587–658.

Moore, "Cadaver."    Moore, Stephen D. "How Jesus' Risen Body Became a Cadaver." Pages 269–82 in *The New Literary Criticism and the New Testament*. Edited by Edgar V. McKnight and Elizabeth Struthers Malbon. Valley Forge, Pa.: Trinity Press International, 1994; Sheffield: JSOT Press, 1994.

Moore, "Canon"    Moore, George Foot. "The Definition of the Jewish Canon and the Repudiation of the Christian Scriptures." Pages 99–125 in *Essays in Modern Theology and Related Subjects: Gathered and Published as a Testimonial to Charles Augustus Briggs on the Completion of His Seventieth Year, January 15, 1911*. New York: Scribner, 1911.

Moore, "Intermediaries"    Moore, George Foot. "Intermediaries in Jewish Theology." *HTR* 15 (1922): 41–61.

Moore, *Judaism*    Moore, George Foot. *Judaism in the First Centuries of the Christian Era*. 2 vols. Cambridge: Harvard University Press, 1927. Repr., New York: Schocken Books, 1971.

Moore, "Life"    Moore, Clifford H. "Life in the Roman Empire at the Beginning of the Christian Era." Pages 218–62 in vol. 1 of *The Beginnings of Christianity*.

Moore, "Nazarene"    Moore, George Foot. "Nazarene and Nazareth" (Appendix B). Pages 426–32 in vol. 1 of *The Beginnings of Christianity*.

Mor, "Bibliography"    Mor, Menahem. "More Bibliography on the Samaritans (with Emphasis on Samaritanism and Christianity)." *Henoch* 1 (1979): 99–122.

Moran, "Prophecy"    Moran, William L. "New Evidence from Mari on the History of Prophecy." *Biblica* 50 (1969): 15–56.

Moreno Martínez, "Logos"    Moreno Martínez, José L. "El Logos y la creación: La referencia al Logos en el 'principio' de Gen 1,1, según Filón de Alejandría." *Scripta theologica* 15 (1983): 381–419.

Morgan-Wynne, "Note"    Morgan-Wynne, J. E. "A Note on John 14.17b." *BZ* 23 (1979): 93–96.

Morgen, "Bulletin johannique"    Morgen, Michele. "Bulletin johannique." *Recherches de science religieuse* 89, no. 4 (2001): 561–91.

Morgen, "Perdre"    Morgen, Michele. "'Perdre sa vie', Jn 12,25: Un dit traditionnel?" *RevScRel* 69 (1995): 29–46.

Morgen, "Promesse"    Morgen, Michele. "La promesse de Jésus à Nathanaël (Jn 1,51) éclairée par la hagaddah de Jacob-Israël." *RevScRel* 67, no. 3 (1993): 3–21.

Morgenstern, "Calendar"    Morgenstern, Julian. "The Calendar of the Book of Jubilees, Its Origin and Its Character." *VT* 5 (1955): 34–76.

Moriarty, "Word"    Moriarty, Frederick L. "Word as Power in the Ancient Near East." Pages 345–62 in *A Light unto My Path: Old Testament Studies in Honor of Jacob M. Myers*. Edited by Howard N. Bream, Ralph D. Heim, and Carey A. Moore. Gettysburg Theological Studies 4. Philadelphia: Temple University Press, 1974.

Morrice, "John"    Morrice, W. G. "John the Seer: Narrative Exegesis of the Book of Revelation." *ExpTim* 97 (1985–1986): 43–46.

Morris, *Apocalyptic*    Morris, Leon. *Apocalyptic*. Grand Rapids: Eerdmans, 1972.

Morris, *Cross*    Morris, Leon. *The Apostolic Preaching of the Cross*. 3d ed. Grand Rapids: Eerdmans, 1965.

Morris, "Jesus"    Morris, Leon. "The Jesus of Saint John." Pages 37–53 in *Unity and Diversity in New Testament Theology: Essays in Honor of George E. Ladd*. Edited by Robert A. Guelich. Grand Rapids: Eerdmans, 1978.

Morris, *John*    Morris, Leon. *The Gospel according to John: The English Text with Introduction, Exposition, and Notes*. New International Commentary on the New Testament. Grand Rapids: Eerdmans, 1971.

Morris, *Judgment*    Morris, Leon. *The Biblical Doctrine of Judgment*. Grand Rapids: Eerdmans, 1960.

Morris, *Lectionaries*    Morris, Leon. *The New Testament and the Jewish Lectionaries*. London: Tyndale, 1964.

Morris, *Luke*    Morris, Leon. *The Gospel according to St. Luke*. Grand Rapids: Eerdmans, 1974.

Morris, *Romans*    Morris, Leon. *The Epistle to the Romans*. Grand Rapids: Eerdmans, 1988.

Morris, *Studies*    Morris, Leon. *Studies in the Fourth Gospel*. Grand Rapids: Eerdmans, 1969.

Morris, *Thessalonians*    Morris, Leon. *The First and Second Epistles to the Thessalonians*. New International Commentary on the New Testament. Grand Rapids: Eerdmans, 1959.

Morton and MacGregor, *Structure*    Morton, A. Q., and G. H. C. MacGregor. *The Structure of Luke and Acts*. New York: Harper & Row, 1964.

Moses, *Transfiguration Story*    Moses, A. D. A. *Matthew's Transfiguration Story and Jewish-Christian Controversy*. JSNTSup 122. Sheffield: Sheffield Academic Press, 1996.

Mosley, "Reporting"    Mosley, A. W. "Historical Reporting in the Ancient World." *NTS* 12 (1965–1966): 10–26.

Moss, "Lamp"    Moss, L. W. "A Menorah Lamp from Atripalda." *IEJ* 25 (1975): 156.

Most, "Luke"    Most, William G. "Did St. Luke Imitate the Septuagint?" *JSNT* 15 (1982): 30–41.

Motyer, "Anti-Semitic"    Motyer, Stephen. "Is John's Gospel Anti-Semitic?" *Themelios* 23 (1998): 1–4.

Motyer, *Father the Devil*    Motyer, Stephen. *Your Father the Devil? A New Approach to John and 'The Jews.'* Carlisle: Paternoster, 1997.

Motyer, "Method"    Motyer, Stephen. "Method in Fourth Gospel Studies: A Way out of the Impasse?" *JSNT* 66 (1997): 27–44.

Motyer, "New Start"    Motyer, Stephen. "The Fourth Gospel and the Salvation of Israel: An Appeal for a New Start." Pages 92–110 in *Anti-Judaism and the Fourth Gospel: Papers of the Leuven Col-

*loquium, 2000.* Edited by R. Bieringer, D. Pollefeyt, and F. Vandecasteele-Vanneuville. Assen: Royal Van Gorcum, 2001.

Moulder, "Background"    Moulder, W. J. "The Old Testament Background and the Interpretation of Mark X.45." *NTS* 24 (1977–1978): 120–27.

Moule, *Birth*    Moule, C. F. D. *The Birth of the New Testament.* New York: Harper & Row, 1962.

Moule, "Factor"    Moule, C. F. D. "A Neglected Factor in the Interpretation of Johannine Eschatology." Pages 155–60 in *Studies in John: Presented to Professor Dr. J. N. Sevenster on the Occasion of His Seventieth Birthday.* Edited by W. C. van Unnik. NovTSup 24. Leiden: Brill, 1970.

Moule, "Individualism"    Moule, C. F. D. "The Individualism of the Fourth Gospel." Pages 21–40 in *The Composition of John's Gospel: Selected Studies from Novum Testamentum.* Compiled by David E. Orton. Brill's Readers in Biblical Studies 2. Leiden: Brill, 1999.

Moule, *Mark*    Moule, C. F. D. *The Gospel according to Mark.* Cambridge: Cambridge University Press, 1965.

Moulton and Milligan, *Vocabulary*    Moulton, James Hope, and George Milligan. *The Vocabulary of the Greek New Testament.* Grand Rapids: Eerdmans, 1976.

Mounce, "Eschatology"    Mounce, Robert H. "Pauline Eschatology and the Apocalypse." *EvQ* 46 (1974): 164–66.

Mounce, *Matthew*    Mounce, Robert H. *Matthew.* A Good News Commentary. San Francisco: Harper & Row, 1985.

Mowinckel, "Geist"    Mowinckel, Sigmund. "Die Vorstellung des Spätjudentums vom Heiligen Geist als Fürsprecher und der johanneische Paraklet." *ZNW* 32 (1933): 97–130.

Mowinckel, "Remarks"    Mowinckel, Sigmund. "Some Remarks on Hodayot 39.5–20." *JBL* 75 (1956): 265–76.

Mowry, "Scrolls"    Mowry, Lucetta. "The Dead Sea Scrolls and the Gospel of John." *BA* 17 (1954): 78–97.

Mowvley, "Exodus"    Mowvley, Henry. "John 1.14–18 in the Light of Exodus 33.7–34.35." *ExpTim* 95 (1983–1984): 135–37.

Moxnes, "Relations"    Moxnes, Halvor. "Patron-Client Relations and the New Community in Luke–Acts." Pages 241–68 in *The Social World of Luke–Acts: Models for Interpretation.* Edited by Jerome H. Neyrey. Peabody, Mass: Hendrickson, 1991.

Moyer, "Purity"    Moyer, James. "The Concept of Ritual Purity among the Hittites." Ph.D. diss., Brandeis University, 1969.

Mozley, "Introduction"    Mozley, J. H. Introduction. Pages vii–xx in Valerius Flaccus, *Argonautica.* Translated by J. H. Mozley. Rev. ed. LCL. Cambridge: Harvard University Press, 1936.

Muddiman, "John's Use"    Muddiman, John. "John's Use of Matthew: A British Exponent of the Theory." *Ephemerides theologicae lovanienses* 59 (1983): 333–37.

Müller, "Parakletenvorstellung"    Müller, Ulrich B. "Die Parakletenvorstellung im Johannesevangelium." *Zeitschrift für Theologie und Kirche* 71 (1974):31–78.

Müller, *Traditionsprozess*    Müller, Paul-Gerhard. *Der Traditionsprozess im Neuen Testament: Kommunikationsanalytische Studien zur Versprachlichung des Jesusphänomens.* Freiburg: Herder, 1982.

Munck, *Acts*    Munck, Johannes. *The Acts of the Apostles.* Revised by W. F. Albright and C. S. Mann. AB 31. Garden City, N.Y.: Doubleday, 1967..

Munck, "Gnosticism"    Munck, Johannes. "The New Testament and Gnosticism." Pages 224–38 in *Current Issues in NT Interpretation: Essays in Honor of Otto A. Piper.* Edited by William Klassen and Graydon F. Snyder. New York: Harper & Row, 1962.

Mundkur, "Symbolism"    Mundkur, Balaji. "The Roots of Ophidian Symbolism." *Ethos* 6, no. 3 (fall 1978): 125–58.

Mundkur et al., "Serpent"    Mundkur, Balaji, et al. "The Cult of the Serpent in the Americas: Its Asian Background." *Current Anthropology* 17 (1976): 429–41.

Munn, "Introduction"    Munn, G. Lacoste. "An Introduction to the Gospel of John." *Southwestern Journal of Theology* 31, no. 1 (fall 1988): 7–11.

Muñoz Léon, "Discípulo"    Muñoz Léon, Domingo. "¿Es el apóstol Juan el discípulo amado? Razones en contra y en pro del carácter apostólico de la tradición joánica." *EstBib* 45 (1987): 403–92.

Muñoz Léon, "Juan"   Muñoz Léon, Domingo. "Juan el presbítero y el discípulo amado: Consideraciones críticas sobre la opinión de M. Hengel en sa libro 'La cuestión joánica.'" *EstBib* 48 (1990): 543–63.

Munro, "Pharisee"   Munro, Winsome. "The Pharisee and the Samaritan in John: Polar or Parallel?" *CBQ* 57 (1995): 710–28.

Muraoka, "Hymn"   Muraoka, T. "Sir. 51,13–30: An Erotic Hymn to Wisdom?" *JSJ* 10 (1979): 166–78.

Murphy, "Idolatry"   Murphy, Frederick J. "Retelling the Bible: Idolatry in Pseudo-Philo." *JBL* 107 (1988): 275–87.

Murphy-O'Connor, "God-Fearers"   Murphy-O'Connor, Jerome. "Lots of God-Fearers? *Theosebeis* in the Aphrodisias Inscription." *RB* 99 (1992): 418–24.

Murray, "Conflator"   Murray, A. Gregory. "Mark the Conflator." *DRev* 102 (1984): 157–62.

Murray, "Feasts"   Murray, George "Jesus and the Feasts of the Jews." *DRev* 109 (1991): 217–25.

Murray, "Introduction"   Murray, A. T. Introduction. Pages i–xv in vol. 1 of Homer, *The Iliad.* Translated by A. T. Murray. 2 vols. LCL. Cambridge: Harvard University Press, 1924.

Murray, *Philosophy*   Murray, Gilbert. *The Stoic Philosophy.* New York: Putnam, 1915.

Murray, *Stages*   Murray, Gilbert. *Five Stages of Greek Religion.* New York: Columbia University Press, 1925. Repr., Westport, Conn.: Greenwood Press, 1976.

Mussies, "Vehicle"   Mussies, G. "Greek as the Vehicle of Early Christianity." *NTS* 29 (1983): 356–69.

Mussies, "Greek in Palestine"   Mussies, G. "Greek in Palestine and the Diaspora." Pages 1040–64 in Safrai and Stern, *Jewish People.*

Mussner, "Gleichnis"   Mussner, Franz. "1QHodajoth und das Gleichnis von Senfkorn (Mk 4.30–32 Par.)." *BZ* 4 (1960): 128–30.

Mussner, "Parakletsprüche"   Mussner, Franz. "Die johanneischen Parakletsprüche und die apostolische Tradition." *BZ* 5 (1961): 56–70.

Myllykoski, "Luke and John"   Myllykoski, Matti. "The Material Common to Luke and John: A Sketch." Pages 115–56 in *Luke–Acts: Scandinavian Perspectives.* Edited by Petri Luomanen. Publications of the Finnish Exegetical Society 54. Helsinki: Finnish Exegetical Society; Göttingen: Vandenhoeck & Ruprecht, 1991.

Mylonas, *Eleusis*   Mylonas, George E. *Eleusis and the Eleusinian Mysteries.* Princeton, N.J.: Princeton University Press, 1961.

Myre, "Caractéristiques"   Myre, André. "Les caractéristiques de la loi mosaïque selon Philon d'Alexandrie." *Science et esprit* 27 (1975): 35–69.

Myre, "Loi"   Myre, André. "La loi dans l'ordre cosmique et politique selon Philon d'Alexandrie." *Science et esprit* 24 (1972): 217–47.

Nádor, "Sophismus"   Nádor, Georg. "Sophismus und seine Beurteilung im Talmud." *Sefarad* 55 (1995): 327–33.

Nagy, "Prologue"   Nagy, Gregory. "The Sign of the Hero: A Prologue." Pages xi–xxxv in Flavius Philostratus, *Heroikos.* Translated and edited by Jennifer K. Berenson Maclean and Ellen Bradshaw Aitken. SBL Writings from the Greco-Roman World 1. Atlanta: Society of Biblical Literature, 2001.

Nanan, "Sorcerer"   Nanan, Madame. "The Sorcerer and Pagan Practices." Pages 81–87 in *Our Time Has Come: African Christian Women Address the Issues of Today.* Edited by Judy Mbugua. Grand Rapids: Baker; 1994.

Narkiss, "Elements"   Narkiss, Bezalel. "Pagan, Christian, and Jewish Elements in the Art of Ancient Synagogues." Pages 183–88 in *The Synagogue in Late Antiquity.* Edited by Lee I. Levine. Philadelphia: American Schools of Oriental Research, 1986.

Nebe, "Inschrift"   Nebe, Gerhard-Wilhelm. "Eine spätsabäisch-jüdische Inschrift mit satzeinleitendem doppelten Amen aus dem 4./6. Jahrhundert nach Chr.?" *JSJ* 22 (1991): 235–53.

Negev, "Nabateans"   Negev, Avraham. "Understanding the Nabateans." *BAR* 14, no. 6 (November/December 1988): 26–45.

Negoïtsa, "Essenes"   Negoïtsa, Athanase. "Did the Essenes Survive the 66–71 War?" *RevQ* 6 (1967–1969): 517–30.

Neil, *Thessalonians*   Neil, William. *The Epistle of Paul to the Thessalonians.* Moffatt New Testament Commentary. London: Hodder & Stoughton, 1950.

Neirynck, *Agreements*   Neirynck, Frans., ed. *The Minor Agreements of Matthew and Luke against Mark with a Cumulative List.* BETL 37. Gembloux: J. Duculot, 1974.

Neirynck, "Disciple"   Neirynck, Frans. "The Anonymous Disciple in John 1." *Ephemerides theologicae lovanienses* 66 (1990): 5–37.

Neirynck, "John 21"   Neirynck, Frans. "John 21." *NTS* 36 (1990): 321–36.

Neirynck, "Kritiek"   Neirynck, Frans. "De semeia-bron in het vierde evangelie: Kritiek van een hypothese." *Academiae analecta* 45 (1983): 1–28.

Neirynck, "Moody Smith"   Neirynck, Frans. "The Question of John and the Synoptics: D. Moody Smith, 1992–1999." *Ephemerides theologicae lovanienses* 76, no. 1 (2000): 122–32.

Neirynck, "Recent Commentaries"   Neirynck, Frans. "John and the Synoptics in Recent Commentaries." *Ephemerides theologicae lovanienses* 74, no. 4 (1998): 386–97.

Neirynck, "Synoptics"   Neirynck, Frans. "John and the Synoptics." Pages 73–106 in *L'évangile de Jean: Sources, rédaction, théologie.* Edited by M. De Jonge. BETL 45. Gembloux: J. Duculot; Leuven: Leuven University Press, 1977.

Nepper-Christensen, "Discipel"   Nepper-Christensen, Poul. "Hvem var den discipel, som Jesus elskede?" *Dansk teologisk tidsskrift* 53 (1990): 81–105.

Netzer, "Mqww'wt"   Netzer, Ehud. "Mqww'wt-hthrh mymy byt šny byryhw [Miqvaot of the Second Temple Period at Jericho]." *Qadmoniot* 11 (1978):54–59.

Neudecker, "Neighbor"   Neudecker, Reinhard. "'And You Shall Love Your Neighbor as Yourself—I Am the Lord' (Lev 19,18) in Jewish Interpretation." *Biblica* 73 (1992): 496–517.

Neugebauer, "Textbezüge"   Neugebauer, Johannes. "Die Textbezüge von Joh 4,1–42 und die Geschichte der johannieschen Gruppe." *ZNW* 84 (1993): 135–41.

Neusner, "Attributions"   Neusner, Jacob. "Evaluating the Attributions of Sayings to Named Sages in the Rabbinic Literature." *JSJ* 26 (1995): 93–111.

Neusner, *Beginning*   Neusner, Jacob. *Judaism in the Beginning of Christianity.* Philadelphia: Fortress, 1984.

Neusner, *Biography*   Neusner, Jacob. *In Search of Talmudic Biography: The Problem of the Attributed Saying.* Brown Judaic Studies 70. Chico, Calif.: Scholars Press, 1984.

Neusner, "Cambiavalute"   Neusner, Jacob. "I cambiavalute ne tempio: La spiegazione della Mishnah." *RivB* 35 (1987): 485–89.

Neusner, "Conversion"   Neusner, Jacob. "The Conversion of Adiabene to Judaism." *JBL* 83 (1964): 60–66.

Neusner, *Crisis*   Neusner, Jacob. *First-Century Judaism in Crisis: Yohanan ben Zakkai and the Renaissance of Torah.* Nashville: Abingdon, 1975.

Neusner, "Death-Scenes"   Neusner, Jacob. "Death-Scenes and Farewell Stories: An Aspect of the Master-Disciple Relationship in Mark and in Some Talmudic Tales." *HTR* 79 (1986): 187–96.

Neusner, "Development"   Neusner, Jacob. "The Development of the Merkavah Tradition." *JSJ* 2 (1971): 149–60.

Neusner, "Foreword"   Neusner, Jacob. Pages xxv–xlvi in *Memory and Manuscript: Oral Tradition and Written Transmission in Rabbinic Judaism and Early Christianity,* with *Tradition and Transmission in Early Christianity.* By Birger Gerhardsson. Grand Rapids: Eerdmans, 1998.

Neusner, *Legend*   Neusner, Jacob. *Development of a Legend: Studies on the Traditions Concerning Yohanan ben Zakkai.* StPB 16. Leiden: Brill, 1970.

Neusner, *New Testament*   Neusner, Jacob. *Rabbinic Literature and the New Testament: What We Cannot Show, We Do Not Know.* Valley Forge, Pa.: Trinity Press International, 1994.

Neusner, "Pharisees"   Neusner, Jacob. "Josephus' Pharisees: A Complete Repertoire." Pages 274–92 in *Josephus, Judaism, and Christianity.* Edited by Louis H. Feldman and Gohei Hata. Detroit: Wayne State University Press, 1987.

Neusner, *Purities*   Neusner, Jacob. *A History of the Mishnaic Law of Purities.* 22 vols. Leiden: Brill, 1974–1977.

Neusner, *Sat*   Neusner, Jacob. *There We Sat Down: Talmudic Judaism in the Making.* Nashville: Abingdon, 1972.

Neusner, *Saying*   Neusner, Jacob. *The Peripatetic Saying: The Problem of the Thrice-Told Tale in Talmudic Literature.* Brown Judaic Studies 89. Chico, Calif.: Scholars Press, 1985.

Neusner, *Traditions*   Neusner, Jacob. *The Rabbinic Traditions about the Pharisees before 70.* 3 vols. Leiden: Brill, 1971.

Newell, "Anger"    Newell, K. N. E. "St Paul and the Anger of God." *Irish Biblical Studies* 1 (1979): 99–114.

Newell, "Forms"    Newell, Raymond R. "The Forms and Historical Value of Josephus' Suicide Accounts." Pages 278–94 in *Josephus, the Bible, and History*. Edited by Louis H. Feldman and Gohei Hata. Detroit: Wayne State University Press, 1989.

Newheart, "Reading"    Newheart, Michael Willett. "Toward a Psycho-literary Reading of the Fourth Gospel." Pages 43–58 in *"What Is John?" Readers and Reading of the Fourth Gospel*. Edited by Fernando F. Segovia. SBLSymS 3. Atlanta: Scholars Press, 1996.

Newmyer, "Climate"    Newmyer, Stephen. "Climate and Health: Classical and Talmudic Perspective." *Judaism* 33 (1984): 426–38.

Newmyer, "Medicine"    Newmyer, Stephen. "Talmudic Medicine: A Classicist's Perspective." *Judaism* 29 (1980): 360–67.

Newport, "*Ek*"    Newport, Kenneth G. C. "The Use of *ek* in Revelation: Evidence of Semitic Influence." *Andrews University Seminary Studies* 24 (1986): 223–30.

Newport, "Evidence"    Newport, Kenneth G. C. "Semitic Influence in Revelation: Some Further Evidence." *Andrews University Seminary Studies* 25 (1987): 249–56.

Newport, "Meanings"    Newport, Kenneth G. C. "Some Greek Words with Hebrew Meanings in the Book of Revelation." *Andrews University Seminary Studies* 26 (1988): 25–31.

Newport, "Prepositions"    Newport, Kenneth G. C. "Semitic Influence on the Use of Some Prepositions in the Book of Revelation." *Bible Translator* 37 (1986): 328–34.

Neyrey, "Allusions"    Neyrey, Jerome H. "The Jacob Allusions in John 1:51." *CBQ* 44 (1982): 586–605.

Neyrey, "Debate"    Neyrey, Jerome H. "John III—a Debate over Johannine Epistemology and Christology." *NovT* 23 (1981): 115–17.

Neyrey, "Encomium"    Neyrey, Jerome H. "Josephus' *Vita* and the Encomium: A Native Model of Personality." *JSJ* 25 (1994): 177–206.

Neyrey, "Gods"    Neyrey, Jerome H. "'I Said: You Are Gods': Psalm 82:6 and John 10." *JBL* 108 (1989): 647–63.

Neyrey, "Noble Shepherd"    Neyrey, Jerome H. "The 'Noble Shepherd' in John 10: Cultural and Rhetorical Background." *JBL* 120, no. 2 (2001): 267–91.

Neyrey, "Shame of Cross"    Neyrey, Jerome H. "'Despising the Shame of the Cross': Honor and Shame in the Johannine Passion Narrative." *Semeia* 68 (1994): 113–37.

Neyrey, "Traditions"    Neyrey, Jerome H. "Jacob Traditions and the Interpretation of John 4:10–26." *CBQ* 41 (1979): 419–37.

Neyrey, "Trials and Tribulations"    Neyrey, Jerome H. "The Trials (Forensic) and Tribulations (Honor Challenges) of Jesus: John 7 in Social Science Perspective." *Biblical Theology Bulletin* 26 (1996): 107–24.

Neyrey and Rohrbaugh, "Increase, Decrease"    Neyrey, Jerome H., and Richard L. Rohrbaugh. "'He Must Increase, I Must Decrease' (John 3:30): A Cultural and Social Interpretation." *CBQ* 63, no. 3 (2001): 464–83.

Niccacci, "Fede"    Niccacci, Alviero. "La fede nel Gesù storico et la fede nel Cristo risorto (Gv 1,19–51//20,1–29)." *Antonianum* 53 (1978): 423–42.

Nicholson, *Death*    Nicholson, Godfrey C. *Death as Departure: The Johannine Descent-Ascent Schema*. SBLDS 63. Chico, Calif.: Scholars Press, 1983.

Nickelsburg, "Genre"    Nickelsburg, George W. E., Jr. "The Genre and Function of the Markan Passion Narrative." *HTR* 73 (1980): 153–84.

Nickelsburg, "Structure"    Nickelsburg, George W. E., Jr. "Structure and Message in the Testament of Abraham." Pages 85–94 in *Studies on the Testament of Abraham*. Edited by George W. E. Nickelsburg Jr. Society of Biblical Literature Septuagint and Cognate Studies 6. Missoula, Mont.: Scholars Press, 1972.

Nickle, *Collection*    Nickle, Keith F. *The Collection: A Study in Biblical Theology*. SBT 48. London: SCM, 1966.

Nicol, "Research"    Nicol, W. "The History of Johannine Research during the Past Century." *Neotestamentica* 6 (1972): 8–18.

Nicol, "Washing"    Nicol, George G. "Jesus' Washing the Feet of the Disciples: A Model for Johannine Christology?" *ExpTim* 91 (1979–1980): 20–21.

Niditch, "Adam"   Niditch, Susan. "The Cosmic Adam: Man as Mediator in Rabbinic Literature." *JJS* 34 (1983): 137–46.

Nielsen, "Mødet"   Nielsen, Eduard. "Mødet ved brønden: Nogle betragtninger oder Joh. Ev. Kap. 4." *Dansk teologisk tidsskrift* 53 (1990): 243–59.

Niemand, "Fusswaschung"   Niemand, Christoph. "Was bedeutet die Fusswaschung—Sklavenarbeit oder Liebesdienst? Kulturkundliches als Auslegungshilfe für Joh 13,6–8." *Protokolle zur Bibel* 3 (1994): 115–27.

Niemand, "Taüferpredigt"   Niemand, Christoph. "Spuren der Taüferpredigt in Johannes 15,1–11: Motivgeschichtliches zur Weinstockrede." *Protokolle zur Bibel* 4 (1995): 13–28.

Niklas, "Söhne Kains"   Niklas, Tobias. "'Söhne Kains': Berührungspunkte zwischen Textkritik und Interpretationsgeschichte am Beispiel Joh 8,44 bei Aphrahat." *RB* 108, no. 3 (2001): 349–59.

Niklas and Kraus, "Joh 5,3b–4"   Niklas, Tobias, and Thomas J. Kraus. "Joh 5,3b–4: Ein längst erledigtes textkritisches Problem?" *Annali di storia dell'esegesi* 17, no. 2 (2000): 537–56.

Nilsson, *Cults*   Nilsson, Martin Persson. *Cults, Myths, Oracles, and Politics in Ancient Greece.* Skrifter Utgivna av Svenska Institutet I Athen 8, no. 1. Lund: Gleerup, 1951.

Nilsson, *Piety*   Nilsson, Martin Persson. *Greek Piety.* Translated by Herbert Jennings Rose. Oxford: Clarendon Press, 1948.

Noack, "Pentecost"   Noack, Bent. "The Day of Pentecost in Jubilees, Qumran, and Acts." *Annual of the Swedish Theological Institute* 1 (1962): 73–95.

Noack, "Qumran and Jubilees"   Noack, Bent. "Qumran and the Book of Jubilees." *Svensk exegetisk årsbok* 22–23 (1957–1958): 119–207.

Nock, *Christianity*   Nock, Arthur Darby. *Early Gentile Christianity and Its Hellenistic Background.* New York: Harper & Row, 1964.

Nock, *Conversion*   Nock, Arthur Darby. *Conversion: The Old and the New in Religion from Alexander the Great to Augustine of Hippo.* Oxford: Clarendon Press, 1933.

Nock, "Gnosticism"   Nock, Arthur Darby. "Gnosticism." *HTR* 57 (1964): 255–79.

Nock, "Mithraism"   Nock, Arthur Darby. "The Genius of Mithraism." *Journal of Roman Studies* 27 (1937): 108–13.

Nock, *Paul*   Nock, Arthur Darby. *St. Paul.* 1938. Repr., New York: Harper & Row, 1963.

Nock, "Vocabulary"   Nock, Arthur Darby. "The Vocabulary of the New Testament." *JBL* 52 (1933): 131–39.

Noll, *History*   Noll, Mark A. *A History of Christianity in the United States and Canada.* Grand Rapids: Eerdmans, 1992.

Nolland, "Proselytes"   Nolland, John. "Uncircumcised Proselytes?" *JSJ* 12 (1981): 173–94.

Nortjé, "Doper"   Nortjé, S. J. "Johannes die Doper in Betanië oorkant die Jordaan." *Hervormde teologiese Studies* 45 (1989): 573–85.

Nortjé, "John"   Nortjé, S. J. "John the Baptist and the resurrection traditions in the Gospels." *Neotestamentica* 23 (1989): 349–58.

Nothomb, "Juifs"   Nothomb, Paul. "Nouveau regard sur 'les Juifs' de Jean." *Foi et vie* 71, no. 4 (1972): 65–69.

Nötscher, "Schicksalsglaube"   Nötscher, Friedrich. "Schicksalsglaube in Qumrân und Umwelt (2. Teil)." *BZ* 4 (1960): 98–121.

Nugent, "Write"   Nugent, Andrew. "What Did Jesus Write? (John 7,53–8,11)." *DRev* 108 (1990): 193–98.

Nun, "Net"   Nun, Mendel. "Cast Your Net upon the Waters: Fish and Fishermen in Jesus' Time." *BAR* 19, no. 6 (November/December 1993): 46–56, 70.

Nun, "Wearing"   Nun, Mendel. "What Was Simon Peter Wearing When He Plunged into the Sea?" *Jerusalem Perspective* 52 (1997): 18–23, 37.

Nunn, *Authorship*   Nunn, H. P. V. *The Authorship of the Fourth Gospel.* Windsor: Alden & Blackwell (Eton), 1952.

Oakman, "Peasant"   Oakman, Douglas E. "Was Jesus a Peasant? Implications for Reading the Samaritan Story." *Biblical Theology Bulletin* 22 (1992): 117–25.

O'Brien, *Colossians*   O'Brien, Peter T. *Colossians, Philemon.* WBC 44. Waco, Tex.: Word, 1982.

Ockinga, "Divinity"   Ockinga, Boyo. "Thoughts on the Nature of the Divinity of the Ruler in Ancient Egypt and Imperial Rome." *Prudentia* 26 (1994): 17–34.

O'Day, "Faith"    O'Day, Gail R. "Surprised by Faith: Jesus and the Canaanite Woman." *Listening* 24 (1989): 290–301.

O'Day, "John"    O'Day, Gail R. "The Gospel of John: Introduction, Commentary, and Reflections." Pages 491–865 in vol. 9 of *The New Interpreter's Bible*. Edited by Leander E. Keck. Nashville: 12 vols. Abingdon, 1995.

O'Day, "Misreading"    O'Day, Gail R. "John 7:53–8:11: A Study in Misreading." *JBL* 111 (1992): 631–40.

O'Day, *Revelation*    O'Day, Gail R. *Revelation in the Fourth Gospel: Narrative Mode and Theological Claim*. Philadelphia: Fortress, 1986.

O'Day, "Study"    O'Day, Gail R. "Toward a Narrative-Critical Study of John." *Interpretation* 49 (1995): 341–46.

O'Day, "Theology"    O'Day, Gail R. "Johannine Theology as Sectarian Theology." Pages 199–203 in *"What Is John?" Readers and Reading of the Fourth Gospel*. Edited by Fernando F. Segovia. SBLSymS 3. Atlanta: Scholars Press, 1996.

O'Day, *Word*    O'Day, Gail R. *The Word Disclosed: John's Story and Narrative Preaching*. St. Louis: CBP Press, 1987.

Odeberg, *Gospel*    Odeberg, Hugo. *The Fourth Gospel Interpreted in Its Relation to Contemporaneous Religious Currents in Palestine and the Hellenistic-Oriental World*. Uppsala: Almqvist & Wiksells, 1929. Repr., Chicago: Argonaut, 1968.

Odeberg, *Pharisaism*    Odeberg, Hugo. *Pharisaism and Christianity*. Translated from the 1943 Swedish edition by J. M. Moe. St. Louis: Concordia, 1964.

Oden and Hall, *Mark*    Oden, Thomas C., and Christopher A. Hall, eds. *Mark*. Ancient Christian Commentary on Scripture. Downers Grove, Ill.: InterVarsity, 1998.

Oesterley, *Liturgy*    Oesterley, William Oscar Emil. *The Jewish Background of the Christian Liturgy*. Oxford: Clarendon Press, 1925.

Oesterley, *Proverbs*    Oesterley, William Oscar Emil. *Proverbs*. Westminster Commentaries. London: Methuen, 1929.

O'Grady, "Disciple"    O'Grady, John F. "The Beloved Disciple, His Community, and the Church." *Chicago Studies* 37 (1998): 16–26.

O'Grady, "Human Jesus"    O'Grady, John F. "The Human Jesus in the Fourth Gospel." *Biblical Theology Bulletin* 14 (1984): 63–66.

O'Grady, "Shepherd and Vine"    O'Grady, John F. "The Good Shepherd and the Vine and the Branches." *Biblical Theology Bulletin* 8 (1978): 86–89.

Oke, "Doxology"    Oke, C. Clare. "A Doxology Not to God but Christ." *ExpTim* 67 (1955–1956): 367–68.

Okorie, "Self-Revelation"    Okorie, A. M. "The Self-Revelation of Jesus in the 'I Am' Sayings of John's Gospel." *Currents in Theology and Mission* 28, no. 5 (2001): 486–490.

Okure, "Commission"    Okure, Teresa. "The Significance Today of Jesus' Commission to Mary Magdalene." *International Review of Mission* 81 (1992): 177–88.

Olbricht, "Delivery and Memory"    Olbricht, Thomas H. "Delivery and Memory." Pages 159–67 in *Handbook of Classical Rhetoric in the Hellenistic Period, 330 B.C.–A.D. 400*. Edited by Stanley E. Porter. Leiden: Brill, 1997.

Oldfather, "Introduction"    Oldfather, W. A. Introduction. Pages 1:i–viii in Epictetus, *The Discourses as Reported by Arrian, the Manual, and Fragments*. 2 vols. LCL. Cambridge: Harvard University Press, 1926–1928.

Olmstead, *History*    Olmstead, A. T. *History of the Persian Empire*. Chicago: University of Chicago Press, 1959.

Olsson, *Structure*    Olsson, Birger. *Structure and Meaning in the Fourth Gospel: A Text Linguistic Analysis of John 2:1–11 and 4:1–42*. Translated by Jean Gray. Lund, Gleerup, 1974.

O'Neal, "Delation"    O'Neal, W. J. "Delation in the Early Empire." *Classical Bulletin* 55, no. 2 (1978): 24–28.

O'Neil, "Plutarch on Friendship"    O'Neil, Edward N. "Plutarch on Friendship." Pages 105–22 in *Greco-Roman Perspectives on Friendship*. Edited by John T. Fitzgerald. SBLRBS 34. Atlanta: Scholars Press, 1997.

O'Neill, "Flesh"    O'Neill, J. C. "The Word Did Not 'Become' Flesh." *ZNW* 82 (1991): 125–27.

O'Neill, "Jews"   O'Neill, J. C. "The *Jews* in the Fourth Gospel." *Irish Biblical Studies* 18 (1996): 58–74.

O'Neill, "Prologue"   O'Neill, J. C. "The Prologue to St. John's Gospel." *JTS* NS 20 (1969): 41–52.

Ong, *Orality*   Ong, Walter J. *Orality and Literacy: The Technologizing of the Word.* London: Methuen, 1982.

O'Rourke, "Asides"   O'Rourke, John J. "Asides in the Gospel of John." Pages 205–14 in *The Composition of John's Gospel: Selected Studies from Novum Testamentum.* Compiled by David E. Orton. Brill's Readers in Biblical Studies 2. Leiden: Brill, 1999.

O'Rourke, "Law"   O'Rourke, John J. "Roman Law and the Early Church." Pages 165–86 in *The Catacombs and the Colosseum: The Roman Empire as the Setting of Primitive Christianity.* Ed. Stephen Benko and John J. O'Rourke. Valley Forge, Pa.: Judson, 1971.

Orton, *Scribe*   Orton, David E. *The Understanding Scribe: Matthew and the Apocalyptic Ideal.* JSNTSup 25. Sheffield: Sheffield Academic Press, 1989.

Osborn, *Justin*   Osborn, Eric Francis. *Justin Martyr.* Beiträge zur historischen Theologie 47. Tübingen: Mohr, 1973.

Osborne, "John 21"   Osborne, Grant R. "John 21: Test Case for History and Redaction in the Resurrection Narratives." Pages 293–328 in *Studies of History and Tradition in the Four Gospels.* Vol. 2 of *Gospel Perspectives.* Edited by R. T. France and David Wenham. Sheffield: JSOT Press, 1981.

Osborne, "Napkin"   Osborne, B. "A Folded Napkin in an Empty Tomb: John 11:44 and 20:7 Again." *Heythrop Journal* 14 (1973): 437–40.

Osborne, "Resurrection"   Osborne, Grant R. "Resurrection." Pages 931–36 in *Dictionary of New Testament Background.* Edited by Craig A. Evans and Stanley E. Porter. Downers Grove, Ill.: InterVarsity, 2000.

Osiek, "Community"   Osiek, Carolyn. "The Jewish-Christian Community at Capharnaum." *The Bible Today* 19 (1981): 36–39.

Ostling, "Jesus"   Ostling, Richard N. "Jesus Christ, Plain and Simple." *Time,* January 10, 1994: 32–33.

O'Toole, "Observations"   O'Toole, Robert F. "Some Observations on *anistēmi*, 'I Raise', in Acts 3:22, 26." *Science et esprit* 31 (1979): 85–92.

Otto, *Dionysus*   Otto, Walter F. *Dionysus: Myth and Cult.* Translated by Robert B. Palmer. Bloomington: Indiana University Press, 1965.

Ovadiah, "Pavements"   Ovadiah, Asher. "Mosaic Pavements of the Herodian Period in Israel." *Mediterranean Historical Review* 5 (1990): 207–21.

Overfield, "Pleroma"   Overfield, P. D. "Pleroma: A Study in Content and Context." *NTS* 25 (1978–1979): 384–96.

Overman, "Archaeology"   Overman, John Andrew. "Recent Advances in the Archaeology of the Galilee in the Roman Period." *Currents in Research: Biblical Studies* 1 (1993): 35–57.

Overman, *Community*   Overman, John Andrew. *Church and Community in Crisis: The Gospel according to Matthew.* New Testament in Context. Valley Forge, Pa.: Trinity Press International, 1996.

Overman, "Deciphering"   Overman, John Andrew. "Deciphering the Origins of Christianity" (review of *A Myth of Innocence: Mark and Christian Origins* by Burton L. Mack). *Interpretation* 44 (1990): 193–95.

Overman, "God-Fearers"   Overman, John Andrew. "The God-Fearers: Some Neglected Features." *JSNT* 32 (1988): 17–26.

Overman, *Gospel and Judaism*   Overman, John Andrew. *Matthew's Gospel and Formative Judaism: The Social World of the Matthean Community.* Minneapolis: Fortress, 1990.

Owen, "Fishes"   Owen, O. T. "One Hundred and Fifty Three Fishes." *ExpTim* 100 (1988–1989): 52–54.

Pace, "Stratigraphy"   Pace, Sharon. "The Stratigraphy of the Text of Daniel and the Question of Theological *Tendenz* in the Old Greek." *Bulletin of the International Organization for Septuagint and Cognate Studies* 17 (1984): 15–35.

Page, "Authenticity"   Page, Sydney H. T. "The Authenticity of the Ransom Logion (Mark 10:45b)." Pages 137–61 in *Studies of History and Tradition in the Four Gospels.* Vol. 1 of *Gospel Perspectives.* Edited by R. T. France and David Wenham. Sheffield: JSOT Press, 1980.

Pagels, "Exegesis"   Pagels, Elaine H. "Exegesis of Genesis 1 in the Gospels of Thomas and John." *JBL* 118 (1999): 477–96.

Pagels, *Gospels*   Pagels, Elaine. *The Gnostic Gospels*. New York: Random House, 1979.

Pagels, *Paul*   Pagels, Elaine. *The Gnostic Paul: Gnostic Exegesis of the Pauline Letters*. Philadelphia: Fortress, 1975.

Painter, "Christology"   Painter, John. "Christology and the Fourth Gospel: A Study of the Prologue." *ABR* 31 (1983): 45–62.

Painter, "Church"   Painter, John. "Christ and the Church in John 1,45–51." Pages 359–62 in *L'évangile de Jean: Sources, rédaction, théologie*. Edited by Marinus de Jonge. BETL 45. Gembloux: J. Duculot; Leuven: Leuven University Press, 1977.

Painter, "Discourses"   Painter, John. "The Farewell Discourses and the History of Johannine Christianity." *NTS* 27 (1980–1981): 525–43.

Painter, "Glimpses"   Painter, John. "Glimpses of the Johannine Community in the Farewell Discourses." *ABR* 28 (1980): 21–38.

Painter, "Gnosticism"   Painter, John. "Gnosticism and the Qumran Texts." *ABR* 17 (1969): 1–6.

Painter, "Israel"   Painter, John. "The Church and Israel in the Gospel of John: A Response." *NTS* 25 (1978–1979): 103–12.

Painter, *John*   Painter, John. *John: Witness and Theologian*. Foreword by C. K. Barrett. London: SPCK, 1975.

Painter, "John 9"   Painter, John. "John 9 and the Interpretation of the Fourth Gospel." *JSNT* 28 (1986): 31–61.

Painter, "Opponents"   Painter, John. "The 'Opponents' in 1 John." *NTS* 32 (1986): 48–71.

Painter, "Tradition"   Painter, John. "Tradition and Interpretation in John 6." *NTS* 35 (1989): 421–50.

Palatty, "Ascension"   Palatty, Paul. "The Ascension of Christ in Lk-Acts: A Study of the Texts." *Biblebhashyam* 12, no. 3 (1986): 100–17.

Palatty, "Covenant"   Palatty, Paul. "Discipleship and the Covenant (continued)." *Biblebhashyam* 15, no. 4 (1989): 254–72.

Palatty, "Disciple and Thomas"   Palatty, Paul. "The Beloved Disciple and Apostle Thomas." *Bible Bhashyam* 27, no. 3 (2001): 161–73.

Palmer, "Monograph"   Palmer, Darryl W. "Acts and the Ancient Historical Monograph." Pages 1–29 in *The Book of Acts in Its Ancient Literary Setting*. Edited by Bruce W. Winter and Andrew D. Clarke. Vol. 1 of *The Book of Acts in Its First Century Setting*. Edited by Bruce W. Winter. Grand Rapids: Eerdmans, 1993.

Pamment, "17:20–23"   Pamment, Margaret. "John 17:20–23." *NovT* 24 (1982): 383–84.

Pamment, "Disciple"   Pamment, Margaret. "The Fourth Gospel's Beloved Disciple." *ExpTim* 94 (1982–1983): 363–67.

Pamment, "*Doxa*"   Pamment, Margaret. "The Meaning of *doxa* in the Fourth Gospel." *ZNW* 74 (1983): 12–16.

Pamment, "Samaritan Influence"   Pamment, Margaret. "Is There Convincing Evidence of Samaritan Influence on the Fourth Gospel?" *ZNW* 73 (1982): 221–30.

Pamment, "Son of Man in First Gospel"   Pamment, Margaret. "The Son of Man in the First Gospel." *NTS* 29 (1983): 116–29.

Pamment, "Son of Man in Fourth Gospel"   Pamment, Margaret. "The Son of Man in the Fourth Gospel." *JTS* NS 36 (1985): 56–66.

Pamment, "Water and Spirit"   Pamment, Margaret. "John 3:5: 'Unless One Is Born of Water and the Spirit, He Cannot Enter the Kingdom of God.'" *NovT* 25 (1983): 189–90.

Pancaro, "Israel"   Pancaro, Severino. "The Relationship of the Church to Israel in the Gospel of St John." *NTS* 21 (1974–1975): 396–405.

Pancaro, *Law*   Pancaro, Severino. *The Law in the Fourth Gospel*. Leiden: Brill, 1975.

Pancaro, "People"   Pancaro, Severino. "'People of God' in St. John's Gospel?" *NTS* 16 (1969–1970): 114–29.

Pardini, "Gv 4,29"   Pardini, Alessandro. "Gv 4,29: Una precisazione grammaticale." *Annali di storia dell'esegesi* 17, no. 1 (2000): 217–19.

Parke, *Oracle*   Parke, H. W. *A History of the Delphic Oracle*. Oxford: Blackwell, 1939.

Parke, *Sibyls*    Parke, H. W. *Sibyls and Sibylline Prophecy in Classical Antiquity.* Edited by B. C. McGing. New York: Routledge, 1988.

Parkes, *Conflict*    Parkes, James. *The Conflict of the Church and the Synagogue: A Study in the Origins of Antisemitism.* New York: Atheneum, Temple Books, 1979.

Parkhurst, "Reconsidered"    Parkhurst, L. G. "Matthew 28:16–20 Reconsidered." *ExpTim* 90 (1978–1979): 179–80.

Parratt, "Spirit"    Parratt, J. K. "The Holy Spirit and Baptism." *ExpTim* 82 (1970–1971): 231–35.

Parsons, "Saying"    Parsons, Mikeal C. "A Neglected ΕΓΩ ΕΙΜΙ Saying in the Fourth Gospel? Another Look at John 9:9." Pages 145–80 in *Perspectives on John: Method and Interpretation in the Fourth Gospel.* National Association of the Baptist Professors of Religion Special Studies Series 11. Edited by Robert B. Sloan and Mikeal C. Parsons. Lewiston, N.Y.: Mellen, 1993.

Pass, *Glory*    Pass, H. Leonard. *The Glory of the Father: A Study in S. John XIII–XVII.* London: Mowbray, 1935.

Patte, *Hermeneutic*    Patte, Daniel. *Early Jewish Hermeneutic in Palestine.* SBLDS 22. Missoula, Mont.: Scholars Press, 1975.

Patzia, "Knowledge"    Patzia, Arthur G. "Knowledge." Pages 638–40 in *Dictionary of the Later New Testament and Its Developments.* Edited by Ralph P. Martin and Peter H. Davids. Downers Grove, Ill.: InterVarsity, 1997.

Paul, "Prophets"    Paul, Shalom M. "Prophets and Prophecy (in the Bible)." Columns 1160–64 in vol. 13 of *Encyclopaedia judaica.* 16 vols. Jerusalem: Keter, 1972.

Paul, "Wine"    Paul, Shalom M. "Classifications of Wine in Mesopotamian and Rabbinic Sources." *IEJ* 25 (1975): 42–45.

Payne, *Appearing*    Payne, J. Barton. *The Imminent Appearing of Christ.* Grand Rapids: Eerdmans, 1962.

Payne, "Claim"    Payne, Philip Barton. "Jesus' Implicit Claim to Deity in His Parables." *Trinity Journal* NS 2 (1981): 3–23.

Payne, "Midrash"    Payne, Philip Barton. "Midrash and History in the Gospels with Special Reference to R. H. Gundry's *Matthew.*" Pages 177–215 in *Studies in Midrash and Historiography.* Vol. 3 of *Gospel Perspectives.* Edited by R. T. France and David Wenham. Sheffield: JSOT Press, 1983.

Payne, "Semitisms"    Payne, D. F. "Semitisms in the Book of Acts." Pages 134–50 in *Apostolic History and the Gospel: Biblical and Historical Essays Presented to F. F. Bruce on His 60th Birthday.* Edited by W. Ward Gasque and Ralph P. Martin. Grand Rapids: Eerdmans, 1970.

Pazdan, "Feasts"    Pazdan, Mary Margaret. "Jesus, Disciples, and Jewish Feasts in John." *The Bible Today* 36 (1998): 79–85.

Pazdan, "Nicodemus"    Pazdan, Mary Margaret. "Nicodemus and the Samaritan Woman: Contrasting Models of Discipleship." *Biblical Theology Bulletin* 17 (1987): 145–48.

Peabody, "Tradition"    Peabody, David. "A Pre-Markan Prophetic Sayings Tradition and the Synoptic Problem." *JBL* 97 (1978): 391–409.

Peachey, "Building"    Peachey, Claire. "Model Building in Nautical Archaeology: The Kinneret Boat." *BA* 53 (1990): 46–53.

Pearce, "Raising"    Pearce, Keith. "The Lucan Origins of the Raising of Lazarus." *ExpTim* 96 (1984–1985): 359–61.

Pearcy, "Galen"    Pearcy, Lee T. "Galen and Stoic Rhetoric." *Greek, Roman, and Byzantine Studies* 24 (1983): 259–72.

Pearl, *Theology*    Pearl, Chaim. *Theology in Rabbinic Stories.* Peabody, Mass.: Hendrickson, 1997.

Pearlman, *Zealots*    Pearlman, Moshe. *The Zealots of Masada.* New York: Scribner, 1967.

Pearson, "Hermeticism"    Pearson, Brook W. R. "Hermeticism." Pages 482–85 in *Dictionary of New Testament Background.* Edited by Craig A. Evans and Stanley E. Porter. Downers Grove, Ill.: InterVarsity, 2000.

Pearson, "Origins"    Pearson, Birger A. "Friedländer Revisited: Alexandrian Judaism and Gnostic Origins." *Studia philonica* 2 (1973): 23–39.

Pearson, "Philo"    Pearson, Birger A. "Philo and the Gnostics on Man and Salvation." *Center for Hermeneutical Studies Protocol* 29 (1977): 1–17.

Pearson, *Terminology*    Pearson, Birger A. *The Pneumatikos-Psychikos Terminology in 1 Corinthians: A Study in the Theology of the Corinthian Opponents of Paul and Its Relation to Gnosticism.* SBLDS 12. Missoula, Mont.: Scholars Press, 1973.

Pélaez del Rosal, "Reanimación"   Pélaez del Rosal, Jesús. "'La reanimación de un cadáver': Un problema de fuentes y géneros." *Alfinge* 1 (1983): 151–73.

Pelikan, "Peter"   Pelikan, Jaroslav. "The Two Sees of Peter." Pages 57–73 in vol. 1 of Meyer and Sanders, *Self-Definition.*

Pelling, "Plutarch's Method"   Pelling, C. B. R. "Plutarch's Method of Work in the Roman Lives." *Journal of Hellenic Studies* 99 (1979): 74–96.

Pendrick, "Μονογενής"   Pendrick, Gerard. "Μονογενής." *NTS* 41 (1995): 587–600.

Pereira, "Word"   Pereira, Rufus. "And the Word Was Made Flesh and Dwelt among Us . . . ." *Biblebhashyam* 8, no. 4 (December 1982): 181–88.

Pereyra , "Significado"   Pereyra, R. "El significado de IOUDAIOI en el evangelio de Juan." *Theologika* 3, no. 2 (1988): 116–36.

Perdue, "Sage"   Perdue, Leo G. "The Death of the Sage and Moral Exhortation: From Ancient Near Eastern Instructions to Graeco-Roman Paraenesis." *Semeia* 50 (1990): 81–109.

Peretto, "María"   Peretto, E. "María Donna in Gv 2,3–4; 19,26–27; Ap. 12,1–6: Ipotesi di lettura continuativa in prospettiva ecclesiale." *Ephemerides mariologicae* 39, nos. 3–4 (1989): 427–42.

Pérez, "Freedom"   Pérez, F. "Freedom according to the Freedman Epictetus." (In Japanese.) *Katorikku Kenkyu* 27, no. 53 (1988): 73–97.

Perkin, "Money"   Perkin, H. W. "Money." Pages 402–9 in vol. 3 of *The International Standard Bible Encyclopedia.* Edited by Geoffrey W. Bromiley. 4 vols. Grand Rapids: Eerdmans, 1986.

Perkins, "Christologies"   Perkins, Pheme. "John's Gospel and Gnostic Christologies: The Nag Hammadi Evidence." Pages 68–76 in *Christ and His Community: Essays in Honor of Reginald H. Fuller.* Edited by Arland J. Hultgren and Barbara Hall. Anglican Theological Review Supplementary Series 11. Evanston, Ill.: Anglican Theological Review, 1990.

Perkins, "John"   Perkins, Pheme. "The Gospel according to John." Pages 942–85 in *The New Jerome Biblical Commentary.* Edited by Raymond E. Brown, Joseph A. Fitzmyer, and Roland E. Murphy. Englewood Cliffs, N.J.: Prentice Hall, 1990.

Perkins, *Reading*   Perkins, Pheme. *Reading the New Testament: An Introduction.* 2d ed. New York: Paulist Press, 1988.

Pernot, "Rendez-vous"   Pernot, Laurent. "Un rendez-vous manqué." *Rhetorica* 11, no. 4 (1993): 421–34.

Perrin, *Bultmann*   Perrin, Norman. *The Promise of Bultmann.* Philadelphia: Fortress, 1969.

Perrin, *Kingdom*   Perrin, Norman. *The Kingdom of God in the Teaching of Jesus.* Philadelphia: Westminster, 1963.

Perrin, "Question"   Perrin, Norman. "The High Priest's Question and Jesus' Answer (Mark 14:61–62)." Pages 80–95 in *The Passion in Mark: Studies in Mark 14–16.* Edited by Werner H. Kelber. Philadelphia: Fortress, 1976.

Perry, "Eucharist"   Perry, John M. "The Evolution of the Johannine Eucharist." *NTS* 39 (1993): 22–35.

Perry, *Sources*   Perry, Alfred Morris. *The Sources of Luke's Passion Narrative.* Chicago: University of Chicago Press, 1920.

Pervo, "Friends"   Pervo, Richard I. "With Lucian: Who Needs Friends? Friendship in the *Toxaris.*" Pages 163–80 in *Greco-Roman Perspectives on Friendship.* Edited by John T. Fitzgerald. SBLRBS 34. Atlanta: Scholars Press, 1997.

Pesce and Destro, "Lavanda"   Pesce, Mauro, and Adriana Destro. "La lavanda dei piedi di Gv 13,1–20, il *Romanzo di Esopo,* e I *Saturnalia* di Macrobio." *Biblica* 80 (1999): 240–49.

Pesch, "Jerusalem"   Pesch, Rudolph. "The Gospel in Jerusalem: Mark 14:12–26 as the Oldest Tradition of the Early Church." Pages 106–48 in *The Gospel and the Gospels.* Edited by Peter Stuhlmacher. Grand Rapids: Eerdmans, 1991.

Petersen, *Criticism*   Petersen, Norman R. *Literary Criticism for New Testament Critics.* Philadelphia: Fortress, 1978.

Petersen, *Sociology*   Petersen, Norman R. *The Gospel of John and the Sociology of Light: Language and Characterization in the Fourth Gospel.* Valley Forge, Pa.: Trinity Press International, 1993.

Petit, "Exemplaire"   Petit, M. "À propos d'une traversée exemplaire du désert du Sinaï selon Philon (*Hypothetica* VI, 2–3.8): Texte biblique et apologétique concernant Moïse chez quelques écrivains juifs." *Semitica* 26 (1976): 137–42.

Pétrement, *Dualisme*    Pétrement, Simone. *Le dualisme chez Platon, les gnostiques, et les manichéens.* Paris: Presses Universitaires de France, 1947.

Petrie, "Q"    Petrie, C. Stewart. "'Q' Is Only What You Make It." *NovT* 3 (1959): 28–33.

Petuchowski, "Glaube"    Petuchowski, Jakob J. "Glaube und Werke in der rabbinischen Literatur." *Judaica* 46, no. 1 (1990): 12–21.

Petuchowski, "Mystery"    Petuchowski, Jakob J. "Judaism as 'Mystery'—the Hidden Agenda?" *HUCA* 52 (1981): 141–52.

Petuchowski, "Qol Adonai"    Petuchowski, Jakob J. "Qol Adonai: A Study in Rabbinic Theology." *Zeitschrift für Religions- und Geistesgeschichte* 24 (1972): 13–21.

Pfeiffer, *Scrolls*    Pfeiffer, Charles F. *The Dead Sea Scrolls and the Bible.* Grand Rapids: Baker, 1969.

Pfitzner, "School"    Pfitzner, Victor C. "The School of Jesus: Jesus-Traditions in Pauline Paranesis." *Lutheran Theological Journal* 13, nos. 2–3 (1979): 22–36.

Phillips, "Faith"    Phillips, G. L. "Faith and Vision in the Fourth Gospel." Pages 83–96 in *Studies in the Fourth Gospel.* Edited by F. L. Cross. London: Mowbray, 1957.

Phillips, "Samaritan Woman Meets Derrida"    Phillips, Gary A. "The Ethics of Reading Deconstructively, or Speaking Face-to-Face: The Samaritan Woman Meets Derrida at the Well." Pages 283–325 in *The New Literary Criticism and the New Testament.* Edited by Edgar V. McKnight and Elizabeth Struthers Malbon. Valley Forge, Pa.: Trinity Press International, 1994; Sheffield: JSOT Press, 1994.

Philonenko, "Initiation"    Philonenko, Marc. "Initiation et mystère dans Joseph et Asénath." Pages 147–53 in *Initiation: Contributions to the Theme of the Study-Conference of the International Association for the History of Religions Held at Strasburg, September 17th to 22nd 1964.* Edited by C. J. Bleeker. Studies in the History of Religions, Supplements to Numen 10. Leiden: Brill, 1965.

Philonenko, "Juda"    Philonenko, Marc. "Juda et Héraklès." *Revue d'histoire et de philosophie religieuses* 50 (1970): 61–62.

Philonenko, "Mystère"    Philonenko, Marc. "Un mystère juif?" Pages 65–75 in *Mystères et syncrétismes* by Françoise Dunand et al. Études d'histoire des religions 2. Paris: Librairie Orientaliste Paul Geuthner, 1975.

Philonenko, "Qoumrân"    Philonenko, Marc. "De Qoumrân à Doura-Europos: La vision des ossements desséchés (*Ézéchiel* 37,1–4)." *Revue d'histoire et de philosophie religieuses* 74 (1994): 1–12.

Pilch, "Lying"    Pilch, John J. "Lying and Deceit in the Letters to the Seven Churches." *Biblical Theology Bulletin* 22 (1992): 126–35.

Pilch, "Ribs"    Pilch, John J. "'Beat His Ribs While He Is Young' (Sir 30:12): A Window on the Mediterranean World." *Biblical Theology Bulletin* 23 (1993): 101–13.

Pilch, "Sickness"    Pilch, John J. "Sickness and Healing in Luke–Acts." Pages 181–209 in *The Social World of Luke–Acts: Models for Interpretation.* Edited by Jerome H. Neyrey. Peabody, Mass.: Hendrickson, 1991.

Pilgaard, *"Theios aner"*    Pilgaard, Aage. "The Hellenistic *theios aner*—a Model for Early Christian Christology?" Pages 101–22 in *The New Testament and Hellenistic Judaism.* Edited by Peder Borgen and Søren Giversen. Peabody, Mass.: Hendrickson, 1997.

Piñero, "Inspiration"    Piñero, Antonio. "A Mediterranean View of Prophetic Inspiration: On the Cocnept of Inspiration in the *Liber antiquitatum biblicarum* by Pseudo-Philo." *Mediterranean Historical Review* 6 (1991): 5–34.

Pinto, "Papel"    Pinto, Carlos O. C. "O papel da mulher no evangelho de João." *Vox scripturae* 3 (1993): 193–213.

Piper, *Justification*    Piper, John. *The Justification of God: An Exegetical and Theological Study of Romans 9:1–23.* Grand Rapids: Baker, 1983.

Pippin, "Fear"    Pippin, Tina. "'For Fear of the Jews': Lying and Truth-Telling in Translating the Gospel of John." *Semeia* 76 (1996): 81–97.

Pixner, "Gate"    Pixner, Bargil. "The History of the 'Essene Gate' Area." *Zeitschrift des deutschen Palästina-Vereins* 105 (1989): 96–104, plates 8–16a.

Pixner, Chen, and Margalit, "Zion"    Pixner, Bargil, Doron Chen, and Shlomo Margalit. "Mount Zion: The 'Gate of the Essenes' Reexcavated." *Zeitschrift des deutschen Palästina-Vereins* 105 (1989): 85–95, plates 8–16a.

Plummer, *Epistles*   Plummer, Alfred. *The Epistles of St. John.* Cambridge: Cambridge University Press, 1886. Repr., Grand Rapids: Baker, 1980.

Pöhlmann, "All-Prädikationen"   Pöhlmann, Wolfgang. "Die hymnischen All-Prädikationen in Kol 1:15–20." *ZNW* 64 (1973): 53–74.

Poirier, "Punctuation"   Poirier, John C. "'Day and Night' and the Punctuation of John 9.3." *NTS* 42 (1996): 288–94.

Poland, *Criticism*   Poland, Lynn M. *Literary Criticism and Biblical Hermeneutics.* American Academy of Religion Academy Series 48. Atlanta: Scholars Press, 1985.

Pollard, *Christology*   Pollard, T. E. *Johannine Christology and the Early Church.* London: Cambridge University Press, 1970.

Pollard, "Poems"   Pollard, Edward B. "Two Poems of Beginnings." *The Biblical World* 17 (1901): 107–11.

Pollard, "Relationships"   Pollard, T. E. "The Father-Son and God-Believer Relationships according to St John: A Brief Study of John's Use of Prepositions." Pages 363–70 in *L'évangile de Jean: Sources, rédaction, théologie.* Edited by Marinus de Jonge. BETL 45. Gembloux: J. Duculot; Leuven: Leuven University Press, 1977.

Pomeroy, *Women*   Pomeroy, Sarah B. *Goddesses, Whores, Wives, and Slaves: Women in Classical Antiquity.* New York: Schocken, 1975.

Pope, "Hosanna"   Pope, Marvin H. "Hosanna—What It Really Means." *Bible Review* 4, no. 2 (April 1988): 16–25.

Porsch, "Antijudaismus"   Porsch, Felix. "'Ihr habt den Teufel zum Vater' (Joh 8,44): Antijudaismus im Johannesevangelium?" *Bibel und Kirche* 44, no. 2 (1989): 50–57.

Porsch, *Wort*   Porsch, Felix. *Pneuma und Wort: Ein exegetischer Beitrag zur Pneumatologie des Johannesevangeliums.* Frankfurter theologische Studien 16. Frankfurt: Josef Knecht, 1974.

Porter, "Creeds and Hymns"   Porter, Wendy J. "Creeds and Hymns." Pages 231–38 in *Dictionary of New Testament Background.* Edited by Craig A. Evans and Stanley E. Porter. Downers Grove, Ill.: InterVarsity, 2000.

Porter, "Greek"   Porter, Stanley E. "Did Jesus Ever Teach in Greek?" *Tyndale Bulletin* 44 (1993): 199–235.

Porter, "Paul and Letters"   Porter, Stanley E. "Paul of Tarsus and His Letters." Pages 533–85 in *Handbook of Classical Rhetoric in the Hellenistic Period, 330 B.C.–A.D. 400.* Edited by Stanley E. Porter. Leiden: Brill, 1997.

Porter, *Paul in Acts*   Porter, Stanley E. *Paul in Acts.* Library of Pauline Studies. Peabody, Mass.: Hendrickson, 2001. Reprint of *The Paul of Acts: Essays in Literary Criticism, Rhetoric, and Theology.* WUNT 115. Tübingen: J. C. B. Mohr (Paul Siebeck), 1999.

Porter, "Thucydidean View?"   Porter, Stanley E. "Thucydides 1.22.1 and Speeches in Acts: Is There a Thucydidean View?" *NovT* 32, no. 2 (1990): 121–42.

Porter, "Variation"   Porter, Calvin L. "An Analysis of the Textual Variation between pap75 and Codex Vaticanus in the Text of John." Pages 71–80 in *Studies in the History and Text of the New Testament, in Honor of Kenneth Willis Clark.* Edited by Boyd L. Daniels and M. Jack Suggs. Studies and Documents 29. Salt Lake City: University of Utah Press, 1967.

Porter, "'We' Passages"   Porter, Stanley E. "Excursus: The 'We' Passages." Pages 545–74 in *The Book of Acts in Its Graeco-Roman Setting.* Edited by David W. J. Gill and Conrad Gempf. Vol. 2 of *The Book of Acts in Its First Century Setting.* Edited by Bruce W. Winter. Grand Rapids: Eerdmans, 1994.

Porton, "Diversity"   Porton, Gary G. "Diversity in Postbiblical Judaism." Pages 57–80 in *Early Judaism and Its Modern Interpreters.* Edited by Robert A. Kraft and George W. E. Nickelsburg. SBLBMI 2. Atlanta: Scholars Press, 1986.

Porton, "Pronouncement Story"   Porton, Gary G. "The Pronouncement Story in Tannaitic Literature: A Review of Bultmann's Theory." *Semeia* 20 (1981): 81–99.

Porton, "Sadducees"   Porton, Gary G. "Sadducees." Pages 1050–52 in *Dictionary of New Testament Background.* Edited by Craig A. Evans and Stanley E. Porter. Downers Grove, Ill.: InterVarsity, 2000.

Potin, "Fête"   Potin, J. "Approches de la fête juive de la Pentecôte." *Foi et vie* 80, no. 1 (1981): 91–95.

Potterie, "Demeurer"   Potterie, Ignace de la. "L'emploi du verbe 'demeurer' dans la mystique johannique." *Nouvelle revue théologique* 117, no. 6 (1995): 843–59.

Potterie, "Finale"    Potterie, Ignace de la. "'C'est lui qui a ouvert la voie': La finale du prologue johannique." *Biblica* 69 (1988): 340–70.

Potterie, "Naître"    Potterie, Ignace de la. "'Naître de l'eau et naître de l'Esprit'—le texte baptismal de Jean 3,5." Pages 31–63 in *La vie selon l'esprit: Condition du chrétien.* By Ignace de la Potterie and S. Lyonnet. Paris: Cerf, 1965.

Potterie, "Paraklet"    Potterie, Ignace de la. "Le Paraklet." Pages 85–105 in *La vie selon L'esprit: Condition du chrétien.* By I. de la Potterie and S. Lyonnet. Paris: Cerf, 1965.

Potterie, "Parole"    Potterie, Ignace de la. "Parole et esprit dans S. Jean." Pages 177–201 in *L'évangile de Jean: Sources, rédaction, théologie.* Edited by Marinus De Jonge. BETL 45. Gembloux: J. Duculot; Leuven: Leuven University Press, 1977.

Potterie, "Truth"    Potterie, Ignace de la. "The Truth in Saint John (1963)." Pages 53–66 in *The Interpretation of John.* Edited by John Ashton. Issues in Religion and Theology 9. Philadelphia: Fortress, 1986.

Poulos, "Pronouncement Story"    Poulos, Paula Nassen. "Form and Function of the Pronouncement Story in Diogenes Laertius' *Lives.*" *Semeia* 20 (1981): 53–63.

Poythress, "Holy Ones"    Poythress, Vern S. "The Holy Ones of the Most High in Daniel VII." *VT* 26 (1976): 208–13.

Poythress, "Intersentence Conjunctions"    Poythress, Vern S. "The Use of the Intersentence Conjunctions *de, oun, kai,* and Asyndeton in the Gospel of John." *NovT* 26 (1984): 312–40.

Poythress, "Revelation"    Poythress, Vern S. "Johannine Authorship and the Use of Intersentence Conjunctions in the Book of Revelation." *Westminster Theological Journal* 47 (1985): 329–36.

Poythress, "Testing"    Poythress, Vern S. "Testing for Johannine Authorship by Examining the Use of Conjunctions." *Westminster Theological Journal* 46 (1984): 350–69.

Prest, "Woman"    Prest, Loring A. "The Samaritan Woman." *The Bible Today* 30 (1992): 367–71.

Price, "Enigma"    Price, J. J. "The Enigma of Philip Ben Jakimos." *Historia* 40 (1991): 77–94.

Price, "Qumran"    Price, James L. "Light from Qumran upon Some Aspects of Johannine Theology." Pages 9–37 in *John and Qumran.* Edited by James H. Charlesworth. London: Geoffrey Chapman, 1972.

Priest, "Mebaqqer"    Priest, John F. "Mebaqqer, Paqid, and the Messiah." *JBL* 81 (1962): 55–61.

Priest, "Messiah"    Priest, John F. "The Messiah and the Meal in 1QSa." *JBL* 82 (1963): 95–100.

Primentas, "Χιτώνας"    Primentas, Nikolaos. "Ὁ ἄρραφος χιτώνας: Τεχνολογικὴ καὶ ἑρμηνευτικὴ προσέγγιση [The Tunic without Seam: Technological and Hermeneutical Approach]." *Deltion biblikōn meletōn* 10, no. 2 (1991): 38–50.

Prince, "Psychiatry"    Prince, Raymond. "Indigenous Yoruba Psychiatry." Pages 84–120 in *Magic, Faith, and Healing: Studies in Primitive Psychiatry Today.* Edited by Ari Kiev. Foreword by Jerome D. Frank. New York: Free Press, 1964.

Pritchard, James B., ed. *Ancient Near Eastern Texts Relating to the Old Testament.* 2d ed. Princeton, N.J.: Princeton University Press, 1955.

Pritz, *Nazarene Christianity*    Pritz, Ray A. *Nazarene Jewish Christianity: From the End of the New Testament Period until Its Disappearance in the Fourth Century.* StPB 37. Leiden, Brill, 1988.

Probst, "Jésus"    Probst, A. "Jésus et Yahvé." *Revue réformée* 41 (1990): 44–45.

Pryke, "Eschatology"    Pryke, John. "Eschatology in the Dead Sea Scrolls." Pages 45–57 in *The Scrolls and Christianity: Historical and Theological Significance.* London: SPCK, 1969.

Pryke, "John"    Pryke, John. "John the Baptist and the Qumran Community." *RevQ* 4 (1963–1964): 483–96.

Pryke, *Style*    Pryke, E. J. *Redactional Style in the Marcan Gospel: A Study of Syntax and Vocabulary as Guides to Redaction in Mark.* Cambridge: Cambridge University Press, 1978.

Pryor, "Egerton"    Pryor, John W. "Papyrus Egerton 2 and the Fourth Gospel." *ABR* 37 (1989): 1–13.

Pryor, *John*    Pryor, John W. *John—Evangelist of the Covenant People: The Narrative and Themes of the Fourth Gospel.* Foreword by Graham N. Stanton. Downers Grove, Ill.: InterVarsity, 1992.

Pryor, "Justin Martyr"    Pryor, J. W. "Justin Martyr and the Fourth Gospel." *Second Century* 9 (1992): 153–69.

Pryor, "Relation"    Pryor, John W. "John 3.3, 5: A Study in the Relation of John's Gospel to the Synoptic Tradition." *JSNT* 41 (1991): 71–95.

Pryor, "Thanksgiving"    Pryor, John W. "The Great Thanksgiving and the Fourth Gospel." *BZ* 35 (1991): 157–79.

Przybylski, *Righteousness*    Przybylski, Benno. *Righteousness in Matthew and His World of Thought.* SNTSMS 41. Cambridge: Cambridge University Press, 1980.

Pucci Ben Zeev, "Position"    Pucci Ben Zeev, Miriam. "Did the Jews Enjoy a Privileged Position in the Roman World?" *Revue des études juives* 154 , nos. 1–2 (1995): 23–42.

Pucci Ben Zeev, "Reliability"    Pucci Ben Zeev, M. "The Reliability of Josephus Flavius: The Case of Hecataeus' and Manetho's Accounts of Jews and Judaism—Fifteen Years of Contemporary Research (1974–1990)." *JSJ* 24 (1993): 215–34.

Puech, "Apocalypse"    Puech, Émile. "Une apocalypse messianique *(4Q521).*" *RevQ* 15 (1991–1992): 475–522, plates 1–3.

Puech, *Croyance*    Puech, Émile. *La croyance des Esséniens en la vie future—immortalité, resurrection, vie éternelle? Histoire d'un croyance dans le judaïsme ancien.* Vol. 2: *Les données qumraniennes et classiques.* École biblique 22. Paris: Gabalda, 1993.

Puech, "Manuscrit"    Puech, Émile. "Notes sur le manuscrit de 11QMelchîsédeq." *RevQ* 12 (1985–1987): 483–513.

Puech, "Nécropoles"    Puech, Émile. "Les nécropoles juives palestiniennes au tournant de notre ère." *Quatre fleuves* 15–16 (1982): 35–55.

Pulleyn, "Names"    Pulleyn, Simon. "The Power of Names in Classical Greek Religion." *Classical Quarterly* 44 (1994): 17–25.

Pummer, "Samaritans"    Pummer, Reinhard. "The Samaritans—a Jewish Offshoot or a Pagan Cult?" *Bible Review* 7, no. 5 (October 1991): 22–29, 40.

Purvis, "Samaritans"    Purvis, James D. "The Fourth Gospel and the Samaritans." *NovT* 17 (1975): 161–98.

Purvis, "Samaritans and Judaism"    Purvis, James D. "The Samaritans and Judaism." Pages 81–98 in *Early Judaism and Its Modern Interpreters.* Edited by Robert A. Kraft and George W. E. Nickelsburg. SBLBMI 2. Atlanta: Scholars Press, 1986.

Pusey, "Baptism"    Pusey, Karen. "Jewish Proselyte Baptism." *ExpTim* 95 (1983–1984): 141–45.

Quast, "Community"    Quast, Kevin B. "Reexamining Johannine Community." *Toronto Journal of Theology* 5 (1989): 293–95.

Quast, *Reading*    Quast, Kevin. *Reading the Gospel of John: An Introduction.* New York: Paulist Press, 1991.

Quasten, "Shepherd"    Quasten, John. "Parable of the Good Shepherd: Jn. 10:1–21." *CBQ* 10 (1948): 1–12, 151–69.

Qedar, "Weights"    Qedar, Shraga. "Two Lead Weights of Herod Antipas and Agrippa II and the Early History of Tiberias." *Israel Numismatic Journal* 9 (1986–87): 29–35, plates 4–5.

Quispel, "Qumran"    Quispel, Gilles. "Qumran, John, and Jewish Christianity." Pages 137–55 in *John and Qumran.* Edited by James H. Charlesworth. London: Geoffrey Chapman, 1972.

Rabe, "Prophecy"    Rabe, Virgil W. "Origins of Prophecy." *BASOR* 221 (February 1976): 125–28.

Rabello, "Condition"    Rabello, Alfredo Mordechai. "The Legal Condition of the Jews in the Roman Empire." *ANRW* 10.13.662–762. Part 2, *Principat,* 10.13. Edited by H. Temporini and W. Haase. New York: de Gruyter, 1980.

Rabiej, "Jestem"    Rabiej, Stanislaw. "'Ja jestem' w ewangelii św. Jana znakiem boskiej godności Jezusa ['I am' in the Gospel according to St. John as the Sign of Jesus' Divine Dignity]." *Roczniki teologiczno-kanoniczne* 35, no. 2 (1988): 183–92.

Rabin, "Hebrew"    Rabin, Ch. "Hebrew and Aramaic in the First Century." Pages 1007–39 in Safrai and Stern, *Jewish People.*

Rabinovitch, "Parallels"    Rabinovitch, Nachum L. "Damascus Document IX,17–22 and Rabbinic Parallels." *RevQ* 9 (1977–1978): 113–16.

Race, "Introduction"    Race, William H. Introduction. Pages 1–41 in vol. 1 of Pindar, *Odes.* Translated by William H. Race. 2 vols. LCL. Cambridge: Harvard University Press, 1997.

Rahmani, "Amulet"    Rahmani, L. Y. "A Magic Amulet from Nahariyya." *HTR* 74 (1981): 387–90.

Rahmani, "Cameo"    Rahmani, L. Y. "An Ancient Cast of a Cameo." *IEJ* 28 (1978): 83–85, plate 21B.

Rahmani, "Customs"    Rahmani, L. Y. "Ancient Jerualem's Funerary Customs and Tombs, Part Four." *BA* 45 (1982): 109–19.

Rahmani, "Glwsqmwt"    Rahmani, L. Y. "Glwsqmwt wlyqwṭ ʿsnwt bšlhy tqwpt byt šny [Ossuaries and Bone-Gathering in the Late Second Temple Period]." *Qadmoniot* 11 (1978): 102–12.

Rahmani, "Remarks"    Rahmani, L. Y. "Some Remarks on R. Hachlili's and A. Killebrew's 'Jewish Funerary Customs.'" *PEQ* 118 (1986): 96–100.

Rainbow, "Christology"    Rainbow, P. A. "Logos Christology." Pages 665–67 in *Dictionary of the Later New Testament and Its Developments*. Edited by Ralph P. Martin and Peter H. Davids. Downers Grove, Ill.: InterVarsity, 1997.

Rajak, "Charter"    Rajak, Tessa. "Was There a Roman Charter for the Jews?" *Journal of Roman Studies* 74 (1984): 107–23.

Rajak, *Josephus*    Rajak, Tessa. *Josephus: The Historian and His Society*. London: Duckworth, 1983.

Rajak, "Justus of Tiberias"    Rajak, Tessa. "Josephus and Justus of Tiberias." Pages 81–94 in *Josephus, Judaism, and Christianity*. Edited by Louis H. Feldman and Gohei Hata. Detroit: Wayne State University Press, 1987.

Rajak, "Moses"    Rajak, Tessa. "Moses in Ethiopia: Legend and Literature." *JJS* 29 (1978): 111–22.

Ramsay, *Church*    Ramsay, William M. *The Church in the Roman Empire*. 5th ed. London: Hodder & Stoughton, 1897. Repr., Grand Rapids: Baker, 1979.

Ramsay, *Cities*    Ramsay, William M. *The Cities of St. Paul: Their Influence on His Life and Thought*. London: Hodder & Stoughton, 1907;.Repr., Grand Rapids: Baker, 1979.

Ramsay, *Discovery*    Ramsay, William M. *The Bearing of Recent Discovery on the Trustworthiness of the New Testament*. London: Hodder & Stoughton, 1915. Repr., Grand Rapids: Baker, 1979.

Ramsay, *Letters*    Ramsay, William M. *The Letters to the Seven Churches of Asia*. London: Hodder & Stoughton, 1904. Repr., Grand Rapids: Baker, 1979.

Ramsay, *Luke*    Ramsay, William M. *Luke the Physician and Other Studies in the History of Religion*. London: Hodder & Stoughton, 1908. Repr., Grand Rapids: Baker, 1979.

Ramsay, "Roads"    Ramsay, William M. "Roads and Travel (in NT)." Pages 375–402 in vol. 5 of *Dictionary of the Bible*. Edited by James Hastings. 5 vols. Edinburgh: T&T Clark, 1898–1923.

Ramsay, *Teaching*    Ramsay, William M. *The Teaching of Paul in Terms of the Present Day*. London: Hodder & Stoughton, 1913. Repr., Grand Rapids: Baker, 1979.

Ramsey, "Speech-Forms"    Ramsey, George W. "Speech-Forms in Hebrew Law and Prophetic Oracles." *JBL* 96 (1977): 45–58.

Raphael, "Travail"    Raphael, Freddy. "Le travail de la memoire et les limites de l'histoire orale." *Annales* 35 (1980): 127–45.

Rapske, *Custody*    Rapske, Brian. *The Book of Acts and Paul in Roman Custody*. Vol. 3 of *The Book of Acts in Its First Century Setting*. Edited by Bruce W. Winter. Grand Rapids: Eerdmans, 1994.

Rapske, "Travel"    Rapske, Brian M. "Acts, Travel, and Shipwreck." Pages 1–47 in *Acts in Its Graeco-Roman Setting*. Edited by David W. J. Gill and Conrad Gempf. Vol. 2 of *The Book of Acts in Its First Century Setting*. Edited by Bruce W. Winter. Grand Rapids: Eerdmans, 1994.

Rashidi, "Africans"    Rashidi, Runoko. "Africans in Early Asian Civilizations: A Historical Overview." Pages 15–52 in *African Presence in Early Asia*. Edited by Ivan Van Sertima and Runoko Rashidi. New Brunswick, N.J.: Transaction (Rutgers)/Journal of African Civilizations, 1988.

Rasmussen, "Journey"    Rasmussen, Krud. "A Shaman's Journey to the Sea Spirit." Pages 308–11 in *Reader in Comparative Religion: An Anthropological Approach*. Edited by William A. Lessa and Evon Z. Vogt. 4th ed. New York: Harper & Row, 1979.

Rasmussen, "Net"    Rasmussen, C. G. "Net, Seine." Pages 523–24 in vol. 3 of *The International Standard Bible Encyclopedia*. Edited by Geoffrey W. Bromiley. 4 vols. Grand Rapids: Eerdmans, 1979–1988.

Ratzinger, *Interpretation*    Ratzinger, Joseph. *Biblical Interpretation in Crisis*. Grand Rapids: Eerdmans, 1989.

Rawson, "Family"    Rawson, Beryl. "The Roman Family." Pages 1–57 in *The Family in Ancient Rome: New Perspectives*. Edited by Beryl Rawson. Ithaca, N.Y.: Cornell University Press, 1986.

Raynor, "Moeragenes"    Raynor, D. H. "Moeragenes and Philostratus: Two Views of Apollonius of Tyana." *Classical Quarterly* 34 (1984): 222–26.

Read, "Logos"    Read, Walter Patten. "Logos: A Principle of Mediation between Transcendence and Immanence." Ph.D. diss., Duke University, 1980.

Redditt, "*Nomos*"    Redditt, Paul L. "The Concept of *nomos* in Fourth Maccabees." *CBQ* 45 (1983): 249–70.

Reese, "Paraclete"  Reese, K. D. "The Role of the Paraclete in John 16:7–11." *Theological Educator* 51 (1995): 39–48.

Reese, "Structure"  Reese, James M. "Literary Structure of Jn 13:31–14:31; 16:5–6, 16–33." *CBQ* 34 (1972): 321–31.

Reeves, "Utnapishtim"  Reeves, John G. "Utnapishtim in the Book of Giants?" *JBL* 112 (spring 1993): 110–15.

Regopoulos, "Ἕλληνες"  Regopoulos, Georgios C. "Ὁ Ἰησοῦς καὶ οἱ Ἕλληνες (ἑρμηνευτικὴ προσέγγισις τοῦ Ἰω. 12, 20–26)." *Deltion biblikōn meletōn* 27, no. 1 (1998): 81–101.

Reich, "Hᶜrh"  Reich, Ronny. "Hᶜrh lpsyps hrwmy mmgdl ᵓšr lḥwp ym-kynrt [A Note on the Roman Mosaic from Magdala on the Shore of the Sea of Galilee]." *Qadmoniot* 22 (1989): 43–44.

Reich, "Inscriptions"  Reich, Ronny. "Ossuary Inscriptions from the Caiaphas Tomb." *Jerusalem Perspective* 4, nos. 4–5 (1991): 13–22.

Reich, "Jars"  Reich, Ronny. "6 Stone Water Jars." *Jerusalem Perspective* 48 (1995): 30–33.

Reich, "Miqweh"  Reich, R. "A Miqweh at 'Isawiya near Jerusalem." *IEJ* 34 (1984): 220–23.

Reich, "Mqwwᵓwt"  Reich, Ronny. "Mqwwᵓwt-ṭhrh yhwdyym btl gzr [Jewish Ritual Baths at Tel Gezer]." *Qadmoniot* 15 (1982): 74–76.

Reich, "Name"  Reich, Ronny. "Caiaphas Name Inscribed on Bone Boxes." *BAR* 18, no. 5 (September/October 1992): 38–44.

Reicke, *Era*  Reicke, Bo. *The New Testament Era: The World of the Bible from 500 B.C. to A.D. 100.* Translated by David E. Green. Philadelphia: Fortress, 1974.

Reicke, "Gnosticism"  Reicke, Bo. "Traces of Gnosticism in the Dead Sea Scrolls." *NTS* 1 (1954–1955):137–41.

Reid, "Sacrifice"  Reid, Daniel G. "Sacrifice and Temple Service." Pages 1036–50 in *Dictionary of New Testament Background.* Edited by Craig A. Evans and Stanley E. Porter. Downers Grove, Ill.: InterVarsity, 2000.

Reid, "Trial"  Reid, Barbara. "The Trial of Jesus—or Pilate?" *The Bible Today* 26 (1988): 277–82.

Reider, "MSHTY"  Reider, Joseph. "On MSHTY in the Qumran Scrolls." *BASOR* 134 (April 1954): 27.

Reif, "Review"  Reif, Stefan C. Review of P. Schäfer, *Die Vorstellung vom Heiligen Geist in der rabbinischen Literatur. Journal of Semitic Studies* 18 (1973): 156–62.

Reim, "Gotteskinder/Teufelskinder"  Reim, Günter. "Joh. 8.44—Gotteskinder/Teufelskinder: Wie antijudaistisch ist 'die wohl antijudaistischste Äusserung des NT'?" *NTS* 30 (1984): 619–24.

Reim, "Jesus as God"  Reim, Günter. "Jesus as God in the Fourth Gospel: The Old Testament Background." *NTS* 30 (1984): 158–60.

Reim, *Studien*  Reim, Günter. *Studien zum alttestamentlichen Hintergrund des Johannesevangeliums.* Cambridge: Cambridge University Press, 1974.

Reinhartz, "Jews"  Reinhartz, Adele. "'Jews' and Jews in the Fourth Gospel." Pages 341–56 in *Anti-Judaism and the Fourth Gospel: Papers of the Leuven Colloquium, 2000.* Edited by R. Bieringer, D. Pollefeyt, and F. Vandecasteele-Vanneuville. Assen: Royal Van Gorcum, 2001.

Reinhartz, "Prophet"  Reinhartz, Adele. "Jesus as Prophet: Predictive Prolepses in the Fourth Gospel." *JSNT* 36 (1989): 3–16.

Reinhartz, "Reads"  Reinhartz, Adele. "A Nice Jewish Girl Reads the Gospel of John." *Semeia* 77 (1997): 177–93.

Reinhartz, *Word*  Reinhartz, Adele. *The Word in the World: The Cosmological Tale in the Fourth Gospel.* SBLMS 45. Atlanta: Scholars Press, 1992.

Reinhold, *Diaspora*  Reinhold, Meyer. *Diaspora: The Jews among the Greeks and Romans.* Sarasota and Toronto: Samuel Stevens, 1983.

Reiser, "Erkenne"  Reiser, Marius. "Erkenne dich selbst! Selbsterkenntnis in Antike und Christentum." *Trierer theologische Zeitschrift* 101 (1992): 81–100.

Reitzenstein, *Religions*  Reitzenstein, Richard. *Hellenistic Mystery-Religions: Their Basic Ideas and Significance.* Translated by John E. Steeley. Pittsburgh Theological Monograph Series 15. Pittsburgh: Pickwick, 1978.

Remus, "Magic"  Remus, Harold. "'Magic or Miracle'? Some Second-Century Instances." *Second Century* 2 (1982): 127–56.

Renehan, "Quotations"   Renehan, Robert. "Classical Greek Quotations in the New Testament." Pages 17–46 in *The Heritage of the Early Church: Essays in Honor of the Very Reverend Georges Vasilievich Florovsky.* Edited by David Neiman and Margaret Schatkin. Orientalia christiana analecta 195. Rome: Pontificium Institutum Studiorum Orientalium, 1973.

Rengstorf, *Apostolate*   Rengstorf, Karl Heinrich. *Apostolate and Ministry.* St. Louis: Concordia, 1969.

Rengstorf, "ἀπόστολος"   Rengstorf, Karl Heinrich. "ἀποστέλλω, ἀπόστολος, κτλ." *TDNT* 1:398–447.

Rensberger, *Faith*   Rensberger, David. *Johannine Faith and Liberating Community.* Philadelphia: Westminster, 1988.

Reynolds, "Election"   Reynolds, Stephen M. "The Supreme Importance of the Doctrine of Election to the Eternal Security of the Elect as Taught in the Gospel of John." *Westminster Theological Journal* 28 (1965–1966): 38–41.

Reynolds, "Misunderstanding"   Reynolds, Edwin E. "The Role of Misunderstanding in the Fourth Gospel." *Journal of the Adventist Theological Society* 9, nos. 1–2 (1998): 150–59.

Rhoads and Michie, *Mark*   Rhoads, David, and Donald Michie. *Mark as Story: An Introduction to the Narrative of a Gospel.* Philadelphia: Fortress, 1982.

Richardson, *Israel*   Richardson, Peter. *Israel in the Apostolic Church.* SNTSMS 10. Cambridge: Cambridge University Press, 1969.

Richardson, *Theology*   Richardson, Alan. *An Introduction to the Theology of the New Testament.* New York: Harper & Brothers, 1958.

Richardson and Gooch, "Logia"   Richardson, Peter, and Peter Gooch. "Logia of Jesus in 1 Corinthians." Pages 39–62 in *The Jesus Tradition outside the Gospels.* Edited by David Wenham. Vol. 5 in *Gospel Perspectives.* Edited by R. T. France and David Wenham. Sheffield: JSOT Press, 1985.

Richlin, "Adultery"   Richlin, Amy. "Approaches to the Sources on Adultery at Rome." *Women's Studies* 8 (1981): 225–50.

Ridderbos, *Galatia*   Ridderbos, Herman N. *The Epistle of Paul to the Churches of Galatia.* Translated by Henry Zylstra. Grand Rapids: Eerdmans, 1953.

Ridderbos, *John*   Ridderbos, Herman N. *The Gospel according to John: A Theological Commentary.* Translated by John Vriend. Grand Rapids: Eerdmans, 1997.

Ridderbos, *Paul*   Ridderbos, Herman N. *Paul: An Outline of His Theology.* Translated by John Richard De Witt. Grand Rapids: Eerdmans, 1975.

Ridderbos, *Paul and Jesus*   Ridderbos, Herman N. *Paul and Jesus.* Translated by David H. Freeman. Philadelphia: Presbyterian and Reformed Publishing Company, 1974.

Ridderbos, "Prologue"   Ridderbos, Herman N. "The Structure and Scope of the Prologue to the Gospel of John." *NovT* 8 (1966): 180–201.

Ridderbos, "Speeches"   Ridderbos, Herman N. "The Speeches of Peter in the Acts of the Apostles." Tyndale New Testament Lecture, 1961. Rushden, Northants: Stanley L. Hunts, for Tyndale Press, 1962.

Riesenfeld, "Background"   Riesenfeld, Harald. "The Mythological Background of New Testament Christology." Pages 81–95 in *The Background of the New Testament and Its Eschatology: Essays in Honor of Charles Harold Dodd.* Edited by W. D. Davies and D. Daube. Cambridge: Cambridge University Press, 1964.

Riesenfeld, "ἵνα-Sätzen"   Riesenfeld, Harald. "Zu den johanneischen ἵνα-Sätzen." *Studia theologica* 19 (1965): 213–20.

Riesenfeld, "Paraclete"   Riesenfeld, Harald. "A Probable Background to the Johannine Paraclete." Pages 266–74 in *Ex Orbe Religionum: Studia Geo Widengren oblata.* Edited by C. J. Bleeker et al. Leiden: Brill, 1972.

Riesenfeld, *Tradition*   Riesenfeld, Harald. *The Gospel Tradition.* Philadelphia: Fortress, 1970.

Riesner, "Bethany"   Riesner, Rainer. "Bethany beyond the Jordan (John 1:28): Topography, Theology, and History in the Fourth Gospel." *Tyndale Bulletin* 38 (1987): 29–63.

Riesner, "Education élémentaire"   Riesner, Rainer. "Education élémentaire juive et tradition évangélique." *Hokhma* 21 (1982): 51–64.

Riesner, "Familiengrab"   Riesner, Rainer. "Wurde das Familiengrab des Hohenpriesters Kajaphas entdeckt?" *Bibel und Kirche* 46, no. 2 (1991): 82–84.

Riesner, "Fragen"    Riesner, Rainer. "Fragen im 'Kana in Galiläa.'" *Bibel und Kirche* 43, no. 2 (1988): 69–71.

Riesner, "Gate"    Riesner, Rainer. "Josephus' 'Gate of the Essenes' in Modern Discussion." *Zeitschrift des deutschen Palästina-Vereins* 105 (1989): 105–9, plates 8–16a.

Riesner, "Golgotha"    Riesner, Rainer. "Golgotha und die Archäologie." *Bibel und Kirche* 40 (1985): 21–26.

Riesner, *Jesus*    Riesner, Rainer. *Jesus als Lehrer: Eine Untersuchung zum Ursprung der Evangelien-Überlieferung.* 2d ed. WUNT 2d series, 7. Tübingen: Mohr, 1984.

Riesner, "Machärus"    Riesner, Rainer. "Johannes der Täufer auf Machärus." *Bibel und Kirche* 39 (1984): 176.

Riesner, "Neues"    Riesner, Rainer. "Neues vom See Gennesaret." *Bibel und Kirche* 42, no. 4 (1987): 171–73.

Riesner, "Synagogues"    Riesner, Rainer. "Synagogues in Jerusalem." Pages 179–211 in *The Book of Acts in Its Palestinian Setting.* Edited by Richard Bauckham. Vol. 4 of *The Book of Acts in Its First Century Setting.* Edited by Bruce W. Winter. Grand Rapids: Eerdmans, 1995.

Riga, "Blind"    Riga, Peter J. "The Man Born Blind." *The Bible Today* 22 (1984): 168–73.

Rigato, "Apostolo"    Rigato, Maria-Luisa. "L' 'apostolo ed evangelista Giovanni,' 'sacerdote' levitico." *RivB* 38 (1990): 451–83.

Rigato, "Quale"    Rigato, Maria-Luisa. "'Era festa dei giudei' (Gv 5,1): Quale?" *RivB* 39 (1991): 25–29.

Riley, *Fruits*    Riley, Loretta. *The Best Fruits.* Philadelphia: Riley, 1999.

Ring, "Resurrection"    Ring, George C. "Christ's Resurrection and the Dying and Rising Gods." *CBQ* 6 (1944): 216–29.

Ringe, *Wisdom's Friends*    Ringe, Sharon H. *Wisdom's Friends: Community and Christology in the Fourth Gospel.* Louisville, Ky.: Westminster/John Knox, 1999.

Ringgren, *Faith*    Ringgren, Helmer. *The Faith of Qumran.* Philadelphia: Fortress, 1963.

Ringgren, *Religion*    Ringgren, Helmer. *Israelite Religion.* Translated by David E. Green. Philadelphia: Fortress, 1966.

Ringgren, *Word*    Ringgren, Helmer. *Word and Wisdom: Studies in the Hypostatization of Divine Qualities and Functions in the Ancient Near East.* Lund: Häkan Ohlssons Boktryckeri, 1947.

Rissi, "Logoslieder"    Rissi, Mathias. "Die Logoslieder im Prolog des vierten Evangeliums." *Theologische Zeitschrift* 31 (1975): 321–36.

Rissi, *Time*    Rissi, Mathias. *Time and History: A Study on the Revelation.* Translated by Gordon C. Winsor. Richmond, Va.: John Knox, 1966.

Rissi, "Word"    Rissi, Mathias. "Jn 1:1–18 (the Eternal Word)." *Interpretation* 31 (1977): 394–401.

Rius-Camps, "Origen"    Rius-Camps, Josep. "Origen lucano de la pericopa de la mujer adúltera (Jn 7,53–8,11)." *Filología neotestamentaria* 6 (1993): 149–75.

Rives, "Sacrifice"    Rives, James. "Human Sacrifice among Pagans and Christians." *Journal of Roman Studies* 85 (1995): 65–85.

Rivkin, "Jubilees"    Rivkin, Ellis. "The Book of Jubilees—an Anti-Pharisaic Pseudepigraph?" *Erets-Yisrael* 16 (1982): 193–98.

Rivkin, "Meaning"    Rivkin, Ellis. "The Meaning of Messiah in Jewish Thought." *Union Seminary Quarterly Review* 26 (1970–1971): 383–406.

Rivkin, "Messiah"    Rivkin, Ellis. "The Meaning of Messiah in Jewish Thought." Pages 54–75 in *Evangelicals and Jews in Conversation on Scripture, Theology, and History.* Edited by Marc H. Tanenbaum, Marvin R. Wilson, and James A. Rudin. Grand Rapids: Baker, 1978.

Robbins, "Apocalyptic"    Robbins, Ray Frank. "Apocalyptic." Pages 147–222 in *Revelation: Three Viewpoints.* Edited by David C. George. Nashville: Broadman, 1977.

Robbins, "Chreia"    Robbins, Vernon K. "The Chreia." Pages 1–23 in *Greco-Roman Literature and the New Testament: Selected Forms and Genres.* Edited by David E. Aune. SBLSBS 21. Atlanta: Scholars Press, 1988.

Robbins, "Plutarch and Gospels"    Robbins, Vernon K. "Writing as a Rhetorical Act in Plutarch and the Gospels." Pages 142–68 in *Persuasive Artistry: Studies in New Testament Rhetoric in Honor of George A. Kennedy.* Edited by Duane F. Watson. JSNTSup 50. Sheffield: Sheffield Academic Press, 1991.

Robbins, "Prefaces"    Robbins, Vernon K. "Prefaces in Greco-Roman Biography and Luke–Acts." *Perspectives in Religious Studies* 6, no. 2 (1979): 94–108.

Robbins, "Pronouncement Stories"    Robbins, Vernon K. "Classifying Pronouncement Stories in Plutarch's *Parallel Lives*." *Semeia* 20 (1981): 29–52.

Robbins, *Teacher*    Robbins, Vernon K. *Jesus the Teacher: A Socio-rhetorical Interpretation of Mark.* Minneapolis: Augsburg Fortress, 1992.

Robbins, "Test Case"    Robbins, Vernon K. "Socio-rhetorical Criticism: Mary, Elizabeth, and the Magnificat as a Test Case." Pages 164–209 in *The New Literary Criticism and the New Testament.* Edited by Edgar V. McKnight and Elizabeth Struthers Malbon. Valley Forge, Pa.: Trinity Press International, 1994; Sheffield: JSOT Press, 1994.

Roberge, "Composition"    Roberge, Michel. "La composition de Jean 6,22–59 dans l'exégèse récente." *Laval théologique et philosophique* 40 (1984): 91–123.

Robert, "Malentendu"    Robert, René. "Le malentendu sur le nom divin au chapitre VIII du quatrième évangile." *Revue thomiste* 88 (1988): 278–87.

Robert, "Mot"    Robert, René. "Le mot final du prologue johannique: A propos d'un article récent." *Revue thomiste* 89 (1989): 279–88.

Robert, "Précédent"    Robert, René. "Un précédent platonicien à l'équivoque de Jean I,18." *Revue thomiste* 90 (1990): 634–39.

Robert, "Solution"    Robert, René. "Une solution pour Jean, I, 16: Kai charin anti charitos." *Revue thomiste* 84 (1984): 243–51. (NTA 29:31).

Robert, "Suaire"    Robert, René. "Du suaire de Lazare à celui de Jésus: Jean XI,44 et XX,7." *Revue thomiste* 88 (1988): 410–20.

Roberts, *Fragment*    Roberts, C. H. *An Unpublished Fragment of the Fourth Gospel.* Manchester: Manchester University Press, 1935.

Roberts, "'Only Begotten'"    Roberts, R. L. "The Rendering 'Only Begotten' in John 3:16." *Restoration Quarterly* 16 (1973): 2–22.

Robertson, *Luke*    Robertson, A. T. *Luke the Historian in the Light of Research.* New York: Scribner, 1923.

Robertson and Plummer, *Corinthians*    Robertson, Archibald, and Alfred Plummer. *A Critical and Exegetical Commentary on the First Epistle of St Paul to the Corinthians.* 2d ed. International Critical Commentary. Edinburgh: T&T Clark, 1914.

Robinson, "Adam and Liturgy"    Robinson, S. E. "The Testament of Adam and the Angelic Liturgy." *RevQ* 12 (1985–1987): 105–10.

Robinson, "Baptism"    Robinson, D. W. B. "Born of Water and Spirit: Does John 3:5 Refer to Baptism?" *Reformed Theological Review* 25 (1966): 15–23.

Robinson, *Coming*    Robinson, John A. T. *Jesus and His Coming.* 2d ed. Philadelphia: Westminster, 1979.

Robinson, "Destination"    Robinson, John A. T. "The Destination and Purpose of St. John's Gospel." *NTS* 6 (1959–1960): 117–31.

Robinson, "Discovery"    Robinson, James M. "The Discovery of the Nag Hammadi Codices." *BA* 42 (1979): 206–24.

Robinson, "Dismantling"    Robinson, James M. "Introduction: The Dismantling and Reassembling of Categories of New Testament Scholarship." Pages 8–19 in *Trajectories through Early Christianity.* By James M. Robinson and Helmut Koester. Philadelphia: Fortress, 1971.

Robinson, "Epistles"    Robinson, John A. T. "The Destination and Purpose of the Johannine Epistles." *NTS* 7 (1960–1961): 56–65.

Robinson, *Historical Character*    Robinson, J. Armitage. *The Historical Character of St John's Gospel.* 2d ed. New York: Longmans, Green, 1929.

Robinson, "Introduction"    Robinson, James M. Introduction. Pages 1–25 in *The Nag Hammadi Library in English.* Edited by James M. Robinson. San Francisco: Harper & Row, 1977.

Robinson, "Oracles"    Robinson, Thomas L. "Oracles and Their Society: Social Realities as Reflected in the Oracles of Claros and Didyma." *Semeia* 56 (1991): 59–77.

Robinson, "Parable"    Robinson, John A. T. "The Parable of John 10:1–5." *ZNW* 46 (1955): 233–40.

Robinson, *Priority*    Robinson, John A. T. *The Priority of John.* Edited by J. F. Coakley. London: SCM, 1985.

Robinson, *Problem*   Robinson, James M. *The Problem of History in Mark and Other Marcan Studies.* Philadelphia: Fortress, 1982.

Robinson, "Prologue"   Robinson, John A. T. "The Relation of the Prologue to the Gospel of St John." *NTS* 9 (1962–1963): 120–29.

Robinson, *Redating*   Robinson, John A. T. *Redating the New Testament.* London: SCM, 1976.

Robinson, *Studies*   Robinson, John A. T. *Twelve New Testament Studies.* SBT 34. London: SCM, 1962.

Robinson, "Trajectory"   Robinson, James M. "The Johannine Trajectory." Pages 232–68 in *Trajectories through Early Christianity.* By James M. Robinson and Helmut Koester. Philadelphia: Fortress, 1971.

Robinson, *Trust*   Robinson, John A. T. *Can We Trust the New Testament?* Grand Rapids: Eerdmans, 1977.

Robinson, "Witness"   Robinson, John A. T. "'His Witness Is True': A Test of the Johannine Claim." Pages 453–76 in *Jesus and the Politics of His Day.* Edited by Ernst Bammel and C. F. D. Moule. Cambridge: Cambridge University Press, 1984.

Rochais, "Scénario"   Rochais, Gérard. "Jean 7: Une construction littéraire dramatique, à la manière d'un scénario." *NTS* 39 (1993): 355–78.

Rodd, "Spirit"   Rodd, Cyril S. "Spirit or Finger." *ExpTim* 72 (1960–1961): 157–58.

Rodríguez Ruiz, "Composición"   Rodríguez Ruiz, Miguel. "El lugar de composición del cuarto evangelio: Exposición y valoración de las diversas opiniones." *EstBíb* 57 (1999): 613–41.

Rodríguez Ruiz, "Discurso"   Rodríguez Ruiz, M. "El discurso del Buen Pastor (Jn 10,1–18): Coherencia teológico-literaria e interpretación." *EstBib* 48 (1990): 5–45.

Rogers, "*Epotisthēmen*"   Rogers, E. R. "*Epotisthēmen* Again." *NTS* 29 (1983): 139–42.

Rohrbaugh, "City"   Rohrbaugh, Richard L. "The Pre-industrial City in Luke–Acts: Urban Social Relations." Pages 125–49 in *The Social World of Luke–Acts: Models for Interpretation.* Edited by Jerome H. Neyrey. Peabody, Mass.: Hendrickson , 1991.

Rokeah, "Tacitus"   Rokeah, David. "Tacitus and Ancient Antisemitism." *Revue des études juives* 154, nos. 3–4 (1995): 281–94.

Roloff, "Lieblingsjünger"   Roloff, Jürgen. "Der johanneische 'Leiblingsjünger' und der Lehrer der Gerechtigkeit." *NTS* 15 (1968–1969): 129–51.

Romaniuk, "Jezus"   Romaniuk, Kazimierz. "Jezus i jawnogrzesznica (J 7,53–8,11) [Jesus and the adulteress (Jn 7:53–8:11)]." *Collectanea theologica* 59, no. 4 (1989): 5–14.

Romeo, "Gematria"   Romeo, Joseph A. "Gematria and John 21:11—the Children of God." *JBL* 97 (1978): 263–64.

Rondorf, "Bultmann"   Rondorf, W. "The Theology of Rudolf Bultmann and Second-Century Gnosis." *NTS* 13 (1966–1967): 351–62.

Rook, "Names"   Rook, John. "The Names of the Wives from Adam to Abraham in the Book of Jubilees." *JSP* 7 (1990): 105–17.

Rosenberg, "Messiah"   Rosenberg, Roy A. "The Slain Messiah in the Old Testament." *ZAW* 99 (1987): 259–61.

Roshwald, "Ben Zoma"   Roshwald, Mordecai. "The Teaching of Ben Zoma." *Judaism* 42 (1993): 14–28.

Rosner, "History"   Rosner, Brian S. "Acts and Biblical History." Pages 65–82 in *The Book of Acts in Its Ancient Literary Setting.* Edited by Bruce W. Winter and Andrew D. Clarke. Vol. 1 of *The Book of Acts in Its First Century Setting.* Edited by Bruce W. Winter. Grand Rapids: Eerdmans, 1993.

Ross, "Church"   Ross, J.-P. B. "The Evolution of a Church—Jerusalem's Holy Sepulchre." *BAR* 2, no. 3 (September 1976): 3–8.

Ross, "Fishes"   Ross, J. M. "One Hundred and Fifty-Three Fishes." *ExpTim* 100 (1988–1989): 375.

Ross, "Lament"   Ross, James F. "Job 33:14–30: The Phenomenology of Lament." *JBL* 94 (1975): 38–46.

Ross, "Prophecy"   Ross, James F. "Prophecy in Hamath, Israel, and Mari." *HTR* 63 (January 1970): 1–28.

Ross, "Revelation"   Ross, Jacob Joshua. "Revelation: In Talmudic Literature." Columns 119–22 in vol. 14 of *Encyclopaedia Judaica.* 16 vols. Jerusalem: Keter, 1972.

Ross, "Titles"   Ross, J. M. "Two More Titles of Jesus." *ExpTim* 85 (1973–1974): 281.

Rossum, "Pentecost"    Rossum, Joost van. "The 'Johannine Pentecost': John 20:22 in Modern Exegesis and in Orthodox Theology." *St. Vladimir's Theological Quarterly* 35 (1991): 149–67.

Rost, *Einleitung*    Rost, Leonhard. *Einleitung in die alttestamentlichen Apokryphen und Pseudepigraphen einschlieīlich der groīen Qumran-Handschriften.* Heidelberg: Quelle & Meyer, 1971.

Rost, *Judaism*    Rost, Leonhard. *Judaism outside the Hebrew Canon: An Introduction to the Documents.* Translated by David E. Green. Nashville: Abingdon, 1976.

Roth, "Vessels"    Roth, Wolfgang. "The Six Vessels of John." *The Bible Today* 30 (1992): 241–45.

Rough, "Capitals"    Rough, Robert H. "A New Look at the Corinthian Capitals at Capernaum." *Studii biblici franciscani liber annuus* 39 (1989): 119–28, plates 9–14.

Rowe, "Style"    Rowe, Galen O. "Style." Pages 121–57 in *Handbook of Classical Rhetoric in the Hellenistic Period, 330 B.C.–A.D. 400.* Edited by Stanley E. Porter. Leiden: Brill, 1997.

Rowland, "John 1.51"    Rowland, Christopher. "John 1.51, Jewish Apocalyptic, and Targumic Tradition." *NTS* 30 (1984): 498–507.

Rowland, "Visions"    Rowland, Christopher. "The Visions of God in Apocalyptic Literature." *JSJ* 10 (1979): 137–54.

Rowley, "Baptism"    Rowley, H. H. "Jewish Proselyte Baptism and the Baptism of John." *HUCA* 15 (1940): 313–34.

Ruager, "Nadveren"    Ruager, S. "Johannes 6 og nadveren [John 6 and the Eucharist]." *Tidsskrift for Teologi og Kirke* 50, no. 2 (1979): 81–92.

Rubenstein, "Dwelling"    Rubenstein, Jeffrey. "The *Sukka* as Temporary or Permanent Dwelling: A Study in the Development of Talmudic Thought." *HUCA* 64 (1993): 137–66.

Rubenstein, "Libation"    Rubenstein, Jeffrey. "The Sadducees and the Water Libation." *JQR* 84 (1993–1994): 417–44.

Rubenstein, "*Sukkah*"    Rubenstein, Jeffrey L. "The Symbolism of the *Sukkah*." *Judaism* 43 (1994): 371–87.

Ruck, "Mystery"    Ruck, Carl A. P. "Solving the Eleusinian Mystery." Pages 35–50 in *The Road to Eleusis: Unveiling the Secret of the Mysteries.* By Robert Gordon Wasson, Albert Hofmann, and Carl A. P. Ruck. New York: Harcourt Brace Jovanovich, 1978.

Ruckstuhl, "Einheit"    Ruckstuhl, E. *Die literarische Einheit des Johannesevangelium: Der gegenwärtige Stand der einschlägigen Forschungen.* Studia friburgensia, n.s 3. Freiburg: Herder, 1951.

Ruckstuhl, "Jünger"    Ruckstuhl, E. "Der Jünger, den Jesus liebte." Pages 355–401 in *Jesus im Horizont der Evangelien.* Stuttgarter biblische Aufsatzbände 3. Stuttgart: Katholisches Bibelwerk, 1988.

Rüger, "ΝΑΖΑΡΕΘ"    Rüger, Hans Peter. "ΝΑΖΑΡΕΘ / ΝΑΖΑΡΑ ΝΑΖΑΦΝΟΣ / ΝΑΖΩΡΑΙΟΣ." *ZNW* 72 (1981): 257–63.

Rummel, "Parallels"    Rummel, Stan. "Using Ancient Near Eastern Parallels in Old Testament Study." *BAR* 3, no. 3 (September 1977): 3–11.

Runia, "God"    Runia, David T. "God and Man in Philo of Alexandria." *JTS* NS 39 (1988): 48–75.

Runnalls, "Campaign"    Runnalls, Donna. "Moses' Ethiopian Campaign." *JSJ* 14 (1983): 135–56.

Rupprecht, "House"    Rupprecht, A. "The House of Annas-Caiaphas." *Archaeology in the Biblical World* 1 (1991): 4–17.

Russell, *Apocalyptic*    Russell, D. S. *The Method and Message of Jewish Apocalyptic.* Philadelphia: Westminster, 1964.

Russell, "Arithmetic"    Russell, D. S. "Countdown: Arithmetic and Anagram in Early Biblical Interpretation." *ExpTim* 104 (1992–1993): 109–13.

Russell, "Mysteries"    Russell, Elbert. "Possible Influence of the Mysteries on the Form and Interrelation of the Johannine Writings." *JBL* 51 (1932): 336–51.

Russell and Wilson, *Menander Rhetor*    Russell, D. A., and N. G. Wilson. *Menander Rhetor.* Oxford: Clarendon Press, 1981.

Rutenber, "Imitation"    Rutenber, Culbert Gerow. "The Doctrine of the Imitation of God in Plato." Ph.D. diss., University of Pennsylvania, 1946.

Ryan, "Hymn"    Ryan, William F. "John's Hymn to the Word." *Worship* 37 (1963): 285–92.

Sabourin, *Miracles*    Sabourin, Leopold. *The Divine Miracles Discussed and Defended.* Rome: Catholic Book Agency, 1977.

Sabugal, "Exégesis"    Sabugal, Santos. "La exégesis bíblica de Aristábulo y del seudo-Aristeas." *Revista agustiniana de espiritualidad* 20 (1979): 195–202.

Sabugal, "Resurrección"  Sabugal, Santos. "La resurrección de Jesús en el cuarto evangelio (Jn 20,1–29; 21,1–14)." *Salesianum* 53 (1991): 649–67.

Safrai, "Description"  Safrai, Zeev. "The Description of the Land of Israel in Josephus' Works." Pages 295–324 in *Josephus, the Bible, and History.* Edited by Louis H. Feldman and Gohei Hata. Detroit: Wayne State University Press, 1989.

Safrai, "Education"  Safrai, S. "Education and the Study of the Torah." Pages 945–70 in Safrai and Stern, *Jewish People.*

Safrai, "Home"  Safrai, S. "Home and Family." Pages 728–92 in Safrai and Stern, *Jewish People.*

Safrai, "Literary Languages"  Safrai, S. "Literary Languages in the Time of Jesus." *Jerusalem Perspective* 4 (1991): 3–9.

Safrai, "Literature"  Safrai, S. "Talmudic Literature as an Historical Source for the Second Temple Period." *Mishkan* 17–18 (1992–93): 121–37.

Safrai, *Pilgrimage*  Safrai, S. *The Pilgrimage at the Time of the Second Temple.* Tel Aviv: Am Hassefer, 1965.

Safrai, "Relations"  Safrai, S. "Relations between the Diaspora and the Land of Israel." Pages 184–215 in Safrai and Stern, *Jewish People.*

Safrai, "Religion"  Safrai, S. "Religion in Everyday Life." Pages 793–833 in Safrai and Stern, *Jewish People.*

Safrai, "Self-Government"  Safrai, S. "Jewish Self-Government." Pages 377–419 in Safrai and Stern, *Jewish People.*

Safrai, "Sources"  Safrai, S. "Hebrew and Aramaic Sources." Pages 1–18 in Safrai and Stern, *Jewish People.*

Safrai, "Spoken Languages"  Safrai, Shmuel. "Spoken Languages in the Time of Jesus." *Jerusalem Perspective* 4 (1991): 3–8, 13.

Safrai, "Temple"  Safrai, S. "The Temple." Pages 865–907 in Safrai and Stern, *Jewish People.*

Safrai and Stern, *Jewish People*  Safrai, S., and M. Stern, eds., with D. Flusser and W. C. van Unnik. *The Jewish People in the First Century: Historical Geography, Political History, Social, Cultural, and Religious Life and Institutions.* 2 vols. Compendia rerum iudaricarum ad Novum Testamentum, Section 1. Assen: Van Gorcum, 1974–1976.

Saldarini, *Community*  Saldarini, Anthony J. *Matthew's Christian-Jewish Community.* Chicago Studies in the History of Judaism. Chicago: University of Chicago Press, 1994.

Saldarini, "Deathbed Scenes"  Saldarini, Anthony J. "Last Words and Deathbed Scenes in Rabbinic Literature." *JQR* 68 (1977–1978): 28–45.

Salters, "Psalm 82"  Salters, R. B. "Psalm 82,1 and the Septuagint." *ZAW* 103 (1991): 225–39.

Salvoni, "Hour"  Salvoni, Fausto. "Nevertheless, My Hour Has Not Yet Come (John 2:4)." *Restoration Quarterly* 7 (1963): 236–41.

Salvoni, "Proof"  Salvoni, Fausto. "The So-Called Jesus Resurrection Proof (John 20:7)." *Restoration Quarterly* 22 (1979): 72–76.

Sambursky, "*Gematria*"  Sambursky, Shmuel. "On the Origin and Significance of the Term *Gematria*." *JJS* 29 (1978): 35–38.

Samuel, "Kairos"  Samuel, S. Johnson "The Kairos of the Galilaioi: An Indian Liberationist Reading of John 1–7." *Jeevadhara* 25 (1995): 149–60.

Sánchez Navarro, "Acerca"  Sánchez Navarro, Luis A. "Acerca de 'ΟΡΑΩ in Jn." *Estudios bíblicos* 55 (1997): 263–66.

Sánchez Navarro, "No existe"  Sánchez Navarro, Luis A. "'ΟΡΑΩ no existe en Jn." *Burgense* 37 (1996): 579–81.

Sanday, *Criticism*  Sanday, William. *The Criticism of the Fourth Gospel.* Oxford: Clarendon Press, 1905.

Sanday and Headlam, *Romans*  Sanday, William, and Arthur Headlam. *A Critical and Exegetical Commentary on the Epistle to the Romans.* 5th ed. International Critical Commentary. Edinburgh: T&T Clark, 1902.

Sanders, *Figure*  Sanders, E. P. *The Historical Figure of Jesus.* New York: Penguin, 1993.

Sanders, *Hymns*  Sanders, Jack T. *The New Testament Christological Hymns: Their Historical Religious Background.* Cambridge: Cambridge University Press, 1971.

Sanders, *Jesus and Judaism*  Sanders, E. P. *Jesus and Judaism.* Philadelphia: Fortress, 1985.

Sanders, *Jesus to Mishnah*    Sanders, E. P. *Jewish Law from Jesus to the Mishnah: Five Studies.* London: SCM, 1990.

Sanders, *John*    Sanders, J. N. *A Commentary on the Gospel according to St. John.* Edited and completed by B. A. Mastin. Harper's New Testament Commentaries. New York: Harper & Row, 1968.

Sanders, *Judaism*    Sanders, E. P. *Judaism: Practice and Belief, 63 B.C.E.–66 C.E.*. London: SCM, 1992.

Sanders, *Law*    Sanders, E. P. *Paul, the Law, and the Jewish People.* Philadelphia: Fortress, 1983.

Sanders, "Patmos"    Sanders, J. N. "St John on Patmos." *NTS* 9 (1962–1963): 75–85.

Sanders, *Paul and Judaism*    Sanders, E. P. *Paul and Palestinian Judaism.* Philadelphia: Fortress, 1977.

Sanders, "Simon"    Sanders, Boykin. "In Search of a Face for Simon the Cyrene." Pages 51–63 in *The Recovery of Black Presence: An Interdisciplinary Exploration, Essays in Honor of Dr. Charles B. Copher.* Nashville: Abingdon, 1995.

Sanders, *Tendencies*    Sanders, E. P. *The Tendencies of the Synoptic Tradition.* SNTSMS 9. Cambridge: Cambridge University Press, 1969.

Sanders, "Who"    Sanders, J. N. "Who Was the Disciple Whom Jesus Loved?" Pages 72–82 in *Studies in the Fourth Gospel.* Edited by F. L. Cross. London: Mowbray, 1957.

Sandmel, *Anti-Semitism*    Sandmel, Samuel. *Anti-Semitism in the New Testament?* Philadelphia: Fortress, 1978.

Sandmel, *Genius*    Sandmel, Samuel. *The Genius of Paul.* New York: Farrar, Straus and Cudahy, 1958.

Sandmel, *Judaism*    Sandmel, Samuel. *Judaism and Christian Beginnings.* New York: Oxford University Press, 1978.

Sandmel, "Theory"    Sandmel, Samuel. "Palestinian and Hellenistic Judaism and Christianity: The Question of the Comfortable Theory." *HUCA* 50 (1979): 137–48.

Sandy, "Affirmation"    Sandy, D. Brent. "John the Baptist's 'Lamb of God' Affirmation in Its Canonical and Apocalyptic Milieu." *JETS* 34 (1991): 447–59.

Sänger, "Missionsliteratur"    Sänger, Dieter. "Jüdisch-hellenistische Missionsliteratur und die Weisheit." *Kairos* 23 (1981): 231–42.

Sarna, *Genesis*    Sarna, Nahum M. *Understanding Genesis: The Heritage of Biblical Israel.* New York: Schocken, 1970.

Sasse, "Paraklet"    Sasse, Hermann. "Der Paraklet im Johannesevangelium." *ZNW* 24 (1925): 260–77.

Satake, *Gemeindeordnung*    Satake, Akira. *Die Gemeindeordnung in der Johannesapokalypse.* Wissenschaftliche Monographien zum Alten und Neuen Testament 21. Neukirchen-Vluyn: Neukirchener Verlag, 1966.

Satterthwaite, "Acts"    Satterthwaite, Philip E. "Acts against the Background of Classical Rhetoric." Pages 337–79 in *The Book of Acts in Its Ancient Literary Setting.* Edited by Bruce W. Winter and Andrew D. Clarke. Vol. 1 of *The Book of Acts in Its First Century Setting.* Edited by Bruce W. Winter. Grand Rapids: Eerdmans, 1993.

Saulnier, "Josèphe"    Saulnier, Christiane. "Flavius Josèphe et la propagande flavienne." *RB* 98 (1991): 199–221.

Saunders, "Synagogues"    Saunders, Ernest W. "Christian Synagogues and Jewish-Christianity in Galilee." *Explor* 3 (1977): 70–77.

Schaberg, *Father*    Schaberg, Jane. *The Father, the Son, and the Holy Spirit: The Triadic Phrase in Matthew 28:19b.* SBLDS 61. Chico, Calif.: Scholars Press, 1982.

Schäfer, "Journey"    Schäfer, Peter. "New Testament and Hekhalot Literature: The Journey into Heaven in Paul and in Merkavah Mysticism." *JJS* 35 (1984): 19–35.

Schäfer, "Magic Literature"    Schäfer, Peter. "Jewish Magic Literature in Late Antiquity and Early Middle Ages." *JJS* 41 (1990): 75–91.

Schäfer, "Synode"    Schäfer, Peter. "Die sogenannte Synode von Jabne: Zur Trennung von Juden und Christen in ersten/zweiten Jh. n. Chr." *Judaica* 31, no. 2 (June 1975): 54–64.

Schäfer, "Schöpfung"    Schäfer, Peter. "Tempel und Schöpfung: Zur Interpretation einiger Heiligtumstraditionen in der rabbinischen Literatur." *Kairos* 16 (1974): 122–33.

Schäfer, "Torah"    Schäfer, Peter. "Die Torah der messianischen Zeit." *ZNW* 65 (1974): 27–42.

Schäfer, *Vorstellung*    Schäfer, Peter. *Die Vorstellung vom Heiligen Geist in der Rabbinischen Literatur.* Studien zum Alten und Neuen Testament 28. Munich: Kösel, 1972.

Schatzmann, *Theology*    Schatzmann, Siegfried. *A Pauline Theology of Charismata.* Peabody, Mass.: Hendrickson, 1987.

Schechter, *Theology*    Schechter, Solomon. *Aspects of Rabbinic Theology.* n.p.: Macmillan, 1909. Repr., New York: Schocken, 1961.

Schedl, *History*    Schedl, Claus. *History of the Old Testament.* 5 vols. New York: Alba House, 1973.

Schenke, "Entstehungsgeschichte"    Schenke, Ludger. "Die literarische Entstehungsgeschichte von Joh 1,19–51." *BN* 46 (1989): 24–57.

Schenke, "Rätsel"    Schenke, Ludger. "Das Rätsel von Tür und Hirt: Wer es löst, hat gewonnen!" *Trierer theologische Zeitschrift* 105 (1996): 81–100.

Schenke, "Schisma"    Schenke, Ludger. "Das johanneische Schisma und die 'Zwölf' (Johannes 6.60–71)." *NTS* 38 (1992): 105–21.

Schenke, "Szene"    Schenke, Ludger. "Joh 7–10: Eine dramatische Szene." *ZNW* 80 (1989): 172–92.

Schenkeveld, "Prose"    Schenkeveld, Dirk M. "Philosophical Prose." Pages 195–264 in *Handbook of Classical Rhetoric in the Hellenistic Period, 330 B.C.–A.D. 400.* Edited by Stanley E. Porter. Leiden: Brill, 1997.

Schiffman, "4QMysteries"    Schiffman, Lawrence H. "4QMysteries[b,] a Preliminary Edition." *RevQ* 16 (1993–1995): 203–23.

Schiffman, "Crossroads"    Schiffman, Lawrence H. "At the Crossroads: Tannaitic Perspectives on the Jewish Christian Schism." Pages 115–56 in vol. 2 of Meyer and Sanders, *Self-Definition.*

Schiffman, *Jew*    Schiffman, Lawrence H. *Who Was a Jew? Rabbinic and Halakhic Perspectives on the Jewish Christian Schism.* Hoboken, N.J.: Ktav, 1985.

Schiffman, *Law*    Schiffman, Lawrence H. *Sectarian Law in the Dead Sea Scrolls: Courts, Testimony, and the Penal Code.* Brown Judaic Studies 33. Chico: Scholars Press, 1983.

Schiffman, "Light"    Schiffman, Lawrence H. "New Light on the Pharisees—Insights from the Dead Sea Scrolls." *Bible Review* 8, no. 3 (June 1992): 30–33, 54.

Schiffman, "Paraphrase"    Schiffman, Lawrence H. "The Deuteronomic Paraphrase of the *Temple Scroll.*" *RevQ* 15 (1991–1992): 543–67.

Schiffman, "Scrolls"    Schiffman, Lawrence H. "The Dead Sea Scrolls and the Early History of Jewish Liturgy." Pages 33–48 in *The Synagogue in Late Antiquity.* Edited by Lee I. Levine. Philadelphia: American Schools of Oriental Research, 1986.

Schillebeeckx, *Sacrament*    Schillebeeckx, Edward. *Christ the Sacrament of the Encounter with God.* New York: Sheed & Ward, 1963.

Schineller, "Women"    Schineller, Peter. "Women in the Gospels." *Emmanuel* 98 (1992): 256–61.

Schlatter, "Problem"    Schlatter, Frederic W. "The Problem of Jn 1:3b–4a." *CBQ* 34 (1972): 54–58.

Schlier, "Begriff"    Schlier, Heinrich. "Zum Begriff des Geistes nach dem Johannesevangelium." Pages 264–271 in *Besinnung auf das Neue Testament.* Exegetische Aufsätze und Vorträge II. Freiburg: Herder, 1964.

Schlier, "Geist"    Schlier, Heinrich. "Der Heilige Geist als Interpret nach dem Johannesevangelium." *Internationale katholische Zeitschrift* 2, no. 2 (March 1973): 97–108.

Schmeller, "Weg"    Schmeller, Thomas. "Der Weg der Jesusbotschaft in die Städte." *Bibel und Kirche* 47, no. 1 (1992): 18–24.

Schmidt, "Einweihung"    Schmidt, Victor. "Apuleius *Met.* III 15f: Die Einweihung in die falschen Mysterien (Apuleiana Groningana VII)." *Mnemosyne* 35 (1982): 269–82.

Schmithals, *Apostle*    Schmithals, Walter. *The Office of Apostle in the Early Church.* Translated by John E. Steely. Nashville: Abingdon, 1969.

Schmithals, *Gnosticism*    Schmithals, Walter. *Gnosticism in Corinth: An Investigation of the Letters to the Corinthians.* Translated by John E. Steely. Nashville: Abingdon, 1971.

Schmithals, "Prolog"    Schmithals, Walter. "Der Prolog des Johannesevangeliums." *ZNW* 70 (1979): 16–43.

Schmitt, "Form"    Schmitt, Armin. "Zur dramatischen Form von Weisheit 1,1–6.21." *BZ* 37 (1993): 236–58.

Schmitz, "Γινώσκω"    Schmitz, E. D. "Knowledge, etc.: γινώσκω." *NIDNTT* 2:392–406.

Schmuttermayr, "'Schöpfung'"    Schmuttermayr, G. "'Schöpfung aus dem Nichts' in 2 Makk 7, 28? Zum Verhältnis von Position und Bedeutung." *BZ* 17 (1973): 203–28.

Schnackenburg, "Entwicklung"    Schnackenburg, Rudolf. "Entwicklung und Stand der johanneischen Forschung seit 1955." Pages 19–44 in *L'évangile de Jean: Sources, rédaction, théologie.*

Edited by Marinus De Jonge. BETL 45. Gembloux: J. Duculot; Leuven: Leuven University Press, 1977.

Schnackenburg, *Existence*    Schnackenburg, Rudolf. *Christian Existence in the New Testament.* 2 vols. Notre Dame, Ind.: University of Notre Dame Press, 1969.

Schnackenburg, "Gemeinde"    Schnackenburg, Rudolf. "Die johanneische Gemeinde und ihr Geist-erfahrung." Pages 277–306 in *Die Kirche des Anfangs: Für Heinz Schürmann.* Edited by R. Schnackenburg, J. Ernst, and J. Wanke. Freiburg: Herder, 1978.

Schnackenburg, "Holwerda"    Schnackenburg, Rudolf. Review of D. E. Holwerda, *The Holy Spirit and Eschatology in the Gospel of John. BZ* 7 (1963): 297–302.

Schnackenburg, *John*    Schnackenburg, Rudolf. *The Gospel according to St. John.* 3 vols. Vol. 1: Translated by Kevin Smyth. Edited by J. Massingberd Ford and Kevin Smyth. New York: Herder & Herder, 1968. Vol. 2: New York: Seabury, 1980. Vol. 3: New York: Crossroad, 1982.

Schnackenburg, "Redestücke"    Schnackenburg, Rudolf. "Die 'situationsgelösten' Redestücke in Joh 3." *ZNW* 49 (1958): 88–99.

Schneider, "Charge"    Schneider, Gerhard. "The Political Charge against Jesus (Luke 23:2)." Pages 403–14 in *Jesus and the Politics of His Day.* Edited by Ernst Bammel and C. F. D. Moule. Cambridge: Cambridge University Press, 1984.

Schneider, "Reflections"    Schneider, H. P. "Some Reflections on the Dialogue of Justin Martyr with Trypho." *SJT* 15 (1962): 164–75.

Schneiders, "Encounter"    Schneiders, Sandra M. "John 20:11–18: The Encounter of the Easter Jesus with Mary Magdalene—a Transformative Feminist Reading." Pages 155–68 in *"What Is John?" Readers and Reading of the Fourth Gospel.* Edited by Fernando F. Segovia. SBLSymS 3. Atlanta: Scholars Press, 1996.

Schneiders, "Testimony"    Schneiders, Sandra M. "'Because of the Woman's Testimony . . .': Reexamining the Issue of Authorship in the Fourth Gospel." *NTS* 44 (1998): 513–35.

Schneiders, "Veil"    Schneiders, Sandra M. "The Face Veil: A Johannine Sign (John 20:1–10)." *Biblical Theology Bulletin* 13 (1983): 94–97.

Schnelle, "Blick"    Schnelle, Udo. "Ein neuer Blick: Tendenzen gegenwärtiger Johannesforschung." *Berliner theologische Zeitschrift* 16, no. 1 (1999): 21–40.

Schnelle, *Christology*    Schnelle, Udo. *Antidocetic Christology in the Gospel of John: An Investigation of the Place of the Fourth Gospel in the Johannine School.* Translated by Linda M. Maloney. Minneapolis: Fortress, 1992.

Schnelle, "Recent Views"    Schnelle, Udo. "Recent Views of John's Gospel." *Word and World* 21, no. 4 (2001): 352–59.

Schniedewind, "Criticism"    Schniedewind, William M. "Textual Criticism and Theological Interpretation: The Pro-temple *Tendenz* in the Greek Text of Samuel-Kings." *HTR* 87 (1994): 107–16.

Schniedewind, "King"    Schniedewind, William M. "King and Priest in the Book of Chronicles and the Duality of Qumran Messianism." *JJS* 45 (1994): 71–78.

Schoeps, *Argument*    Schoeps, Hans Joachim. *The Jewish-Christian Argument: A History of Theologies in Conflict.* Translated by David E. Green. New York: Holt, Rinehart & Winston, 1963.

Schoeps, *Christenheit*    Schoeps, Hans Joachim. *Israel und Christenheit*. Munich: Ner Tamid, 1961.

Schoeps, *Paul*    Schoeps, Hans Joachim. *Paul: The Theology of the Apostle in the Light of Jewish Religious History.* Translated by Harold Knight. Philadelphia: Westminster, 1961.

Schoeps, "Prophetenmorde"    Schoeps, Hans Joachim. "Die jüdischen Prophetenmorde." Pages 126–43 in *Aus frühchristlicher Zeit: Religionsgeschichtliche Untersuchungen.* Tübingen: Mohr, 1950.

"Scholars' Corner"    "Scholars' Corner: New Testament Illuminated by Dead Sea Scrolls." *BAR* 8, no. 5 (September/October 1982): 6–8.

Scholem, *Gnosticism*    Scholem, Gershom G. *Jewish Gnosticism, Merkabah Mysticism, and Talmudic Tradition.* New York: Jewish Theological Seminary of America, 1965.

Scholem, *Sabbatai Sevi*    Scholem, Gershom. *Sabbatai Sevi: The Mystical Messiah.* Princeton, N.J.: Princeton University Press, 1973.

Scholem, *Trends*    Scholem, Gershom G. *Major Trends in Jewish Mysticism.* 3d rev. ed. New York: Schocken, 1971.

Scholtissek, "Neue Wege"   Scholtissek, Klaus. "Neue Wege in der Johannesauslegung: Ein Forschungsbericht, I." *Theologie und Glaube* 89, no. 2 (1999): 263–95.

Scholtissek, "Survey of Research"   Scholtissek, Klaus. "Johannine Studies: A Survey of Recent Research with Special Regard to German Contributions." *Currents in Research: Biblical Studies* 6 (1998): 227–59; 9 (2001): 277–305.

Schöndorf, "Schreibt"   Schöndorf, H. "Jesus schreibt mit dem Finger auf die Erde: Joh 8:6b.8." *BZ* 40 (1996): 91–93.

Schoneveld, "Thora"   Schoneveld, Jacobus. "Die Thora in Person: Eine Lekture des Prologs des Johannesevangeliums als Beitrag zu einer Christologie ohne Antisemitismus." *Kirche und Israel* 1 (1991): 40–52.

Schoneveld, "Torah"   Schoneveld, Jacobus. "Torah in the Flesh: A New Reading of the Prologue of the Gospel of John as a Contribution to a Christology without Anti-Judaism." *Immanuel* 24/25 (1990): 77–94.

Schottroff. "Aspects"   Schottroff, Luise. "Important Aspects of the Gospel for the Future." Pages 205–10 in *"What Is John?" Readers and Reading of the Fourth Gospel.* Edited by Fernando F. Segovia. SBLSymS 3. Atlanta: Scholars Press, 1996.

Schottroff, "Wanderprophetinnen"   Schottroff, Luise. "Wanderprophetinnen: Eine feministische Analyse der Logienquelle." *Evangelische Theologie* 51 (1991): 332–44.

Schreiber, "Jüngerberufungsszene"   Schreiber, Stefan. "Die Jüngerberufungsszene Joh 1,43–51 als literarische Einheit." *Studien zum Neuen Testament und seiner Umwelt* 23 (1998): 5–28.

Schroeder, "Friendship"   Schroeder, Frederic M. "Friendship in Aristotle and Some Peripatetic Philosophers." Pages 35–57 in *Greco-Roman Perspectives on Friendship.* Edited by John T. Fitzgerald. SBLRBS 34. Atlanta: Scholars Press, 1997.

Schroer, "Geist"   Schroer, Silvia. "Der Geist, die Weisheit, und die Taube: Feministischkritische Exegese eines neutestamentlichen Symbols auf dem Hintergrund seiner altorientalischen und hellenistich-frühjudischen Traditionsgeschichte." *Freiburger Zeitschrift für Philosophie und Theologie* 33 (1986): 197–225.

Schroer, "Grenzüberschreitungen"   Schroer, Silvia. "Zeit für Grenzüberschreitungen: Die göttliche Weisheit im nachexilischen Monotheismus." *Bibel und Kirche* 49, no. 2 (1994): 103–7.

Schuchard, *Scripture*   Schuchard, Bruce G. *Scripture within Scripture: The Interrelationship of Form and Function in the Explicit Old Testament Citations in the Gospel of John.* SBLDS 133. Atlanta: Scholars Press, 1992.

Schuller, "*4Q372*"   Schuller, Eileen. "*4Q372* 1: A Text about Joseph." *RevQ* 14 (1989–1990): 349–76.

Schuller, "Resurrection"   Schuller, Eileen. "Ideas of Resurrection in Intertestamental Sources." *The Bible Today* 27 (1989): 140–45.

Schürer, *History*   Schürer, Emil. *A History of the Jewish People in the Time of Jesus.* Edited by Nahum N. Glatzer. New York: Schocken, 1961.

Schultz, "Opposition"   Schultz, Joseph P. "Angelic Opposition to the Ascension of Moses and the Revelation of the Law." *JQR* 61 (1970–1971): 282–307.

Schultz, "Patriarchs"   Schultz, Joseph P. "Two Views of the Patriarchs: Noahides and Pre-Sinai Israelites." Pages 43–59 in *Texts and Responses: Studies Presented to Nahum N. Glatzner on the Occasion of His Seventieth Birthday by His Students.* Edited by Michael A. Fishbane and Paul R. Flohr. Leiden: Brill, 1975.

Schulz, *Evangelium*   Schulz, Siegfried. *Das Evangelium nach Johannes.* Das Neue Testament Deutsch 4. Göttingen: Vandenhoeck & Ruprecht, 1975.

Schulze-Kadelbach, "Pneumatologie"   Schulze-Kadelbach, Gerhard. "Zur Pneumatologie des Johannes Evangeliums." *ZNW* 46 (1955): 279–80.

Schütz, "Knowledge"   Schütz, E. "Knowledge, etc.: Ἀισθησις, ἀγνοέω." *NIDNTT* 2:391, 406–40.

Schwab, "Portrayal"   Schwab, Joel. "'Encounter with a Stranger'—'Incredibly Inaccurate Portrayal of Judaism.'" *Liberty* (July 1984): 19–20.

Schwank, "Berg"   Schwank, Benedikt. "Grabungen auf 'diesem Berg' (Joh 4,20–21): Der archäologische Beitrag." *Bibel und Kirche* 47, no. 4 (1992): 220–21.

Schwank, "Ecce Homo"   Schwank, Benedikt. "Ecce Homo." *Erbe und Auftrag* 65 (1989): 199–209.

Schwank, "Erhöht"   Schwank, Benedikt. "Erhöht und verherrlicht." *Erbe und Auftrag* 68 (1992): 137–46.

Schwank, "Grabungen"   Schwank, Benedikt. "Die neuen Grabungen in Sepphoris." *Bibel und Kirche* 42, no. 2 (1987): 75–79.

Schwank, "Wasserkrüge"   Schwank, Benedikt. "'Sechs steinerne Wasserkrüge' (Joh 2,6)." *Erbe und Auftrag* 73 (1997): 314–16.

Schwank, "Weinstock"   Schwank, Benedikt. "'Ich bin der wahre Weinstock' (Joh 15,1)." *Erbe und Auftrag* 74 (1998): 241–43.

Schwartz, "Ben Stada"   Schwartz, Joshua. "Ben Stada and Peter in Lydda." *JSJ* 21 (1990): 1–18.

Schwartz, "Jubilees"   Schwartz, Joshua. "Jubilees, Bethel, and the Temple of Jacob." *HUCA* 56 (1985): 63–85.

Schwartz, "Temples"   Schwartz, Daniel R. "The Three Temples of 4QFlorilegium." *RevQ* 10 (1979–1981): 83–91.

Schwarz, "Gen"   Schwarz, Günther. "Gen 1:1; 2:2a und Joh 1:1a.3a—ein Vergleich." *ZNW* 73 (1982): 136–37.

Schwarz, "*Hyssōpō*"   Schwarz, Günther. "*Hyssōpō perithentes* (Johannes 19.29)." *NTS* 30 (1984): 625–26.

Schwarz, "ΜΕΤΡΗΤΑΣ"   Schwarz, Günther. "ΑΝΑ ΜΕΤΡΗΤΑΣ ΔΥΟ Η ΤΡΕΙΣ? (Joh 2,6)." *BN* 62 (1992): 45.

Schwarz, "Welt"   Schwarz, Günther. "'In der Welt habt ihr Angst?' (Johannes 16,33)." *BN* 63 (1992): 49–51.

Schwarz, "Wind"   Schwarz, Günther. "'Der Wind weht, wo er will'?" *BN* 63 (1992): 47–48.

Schweitzer, *Quest*   Schweitzer, Albert. *The Quest of the Historical Jesus.* Introduction by James M. Robinson. Translated by W. Montgomery from 1906 German edition. New York: Macmillan, 1968.

Schweizer, "Christ in Colossians"   Schweizer, Eduard. "Christ in the Letter to the Colossians." *Review and Expositor* 70 (1973): 451–67.

Schweizer, *Colossians*   Schweizer, Eduard. *The Letter to the Colossians: A Commentary.* Translated by Andrew Chester. Minneapolis: Augsburg, 1982.

Schweizer, *Herkunft*   Schweizer, Eduard. *Ego eimi: Die religionsgeschichtliche Herkunft und theologische Bedeutung der johanneischen Bildreden, zugleich ein Beitrag zur Quellenfrage des vierten Evangeliums.* Forschungen zur Religion und Literatur des Alten und Neuen Testaments 56. Göttingen: Vandenhoeck & Ruprecht, 1939.

Schweizer, *Jesus*   Schweizer, Eduard. *Jesus.* Translated by David E. Green. New Testament Library. London: SCM, 1971.

Schweizer, *Matthew*   Schweizer, Eduard. *The Good News according to Matthew.* Translated by David E. Green. Atlanta: John Knox, 1975.

Schweizer, "Parables"   Schweizer, Eduard. "What about the Johannine 'Parables'?" Pages 208–19 in *Exploring the Gospel of John: In Honor of D. Moody Smith.* Edited by R. Alan Culpepper and C. Clifton Black. Louisville, Ky.: Westminster John Knox, 1996.

Schweizer, "Speeches"   Schweizer, Eduard. "Concerning the Speeches in Acts." Pages 208–16 in *Studies in Luke–Acts: Essays in Honor of Paul Schubert.* Edited by Leander E. Keck and J. Louis Martyn. Nashville: Abingdon, 1966.

Schweizer, *Spirit*   Schweizer, Eduard. *The Holy Spirit.* Translated by Reginald H. and Ilse Fuller. Philadelphia: Fortress, 1980.

Scobie, "John"   Scobie, Charles H. H. "John the Baptist." Pages 58–69 in *The Scrolls and Christianity: Historical and Theological Significance.* Edited by Matthew Black. London: SPCK, 1969.

Scobie, "Origins"   Scobie, Charles H. H. "The Origins and Development of Samaritan Christianity." *NTS* 19 (1972–1973): 390–414.

Scobie, "Tension"   Scobie, Charles H. H. "North and South: Tension and Reconciliation in Biblical History." Pages 87–98 in *Biblical Studies: Essays in Honor of William Barclay.* Edited by J. R. McKay and J. F. Miller. Philadelphia: Westminster, 1976.

Scodel. "Drama and Rhetoric"   Scodel, Ruth. "Drama and Rhetoric." Pages 489–504 in *Handbook of Classical Rhetoric in the Hellenistic Period, 330 B.C.–A.D. 400.* Edited by Stanley E. Porter. Leiden: Brill, 1997.

Scott, "Attitudes"   Scott, David. "Buddhist Attitudes to Hellenism: A Review of the Issue." *SR* 15 (1986): 433–41.

Scott, *Customs*   Scott, Julius J. *Customs and Controversies: Intertestamental Jewish Backgrounds of the New Testament.* Grand Rapids: Baker, 1995.

Scott, *Gospel*   Scott, Ernest F. *The Fourth Gospel: Its Purpose and Theology.* 2d ed. Edinburgh: T&T Clark, 1943.

Scott, "Horizon"   Scott, James M. "Luke's Geographical Horizon." Pages 483–544 in *The Book of Acts in Its Graeco-Roman Setting.* Edited by David W. J. Gill and Conrad Gempf. Vol. 2 of *The Book of Acts in Its First Century Setting.* Edited by Bruce W. Winter. Grand Rapids: Eeridmans, 1994.

Scott, "Intention"   Scott, James W. "Matthew's Intention to Write History." *Westminster Theological Journal* 47 (1985): 68–82.

Scott, *Parable*   Scott, Bernard Brandon. *Hear Then the Parable: A Commentary on the Parables of Jesus.* Minneapolis: Augsburg Fortress, 1989.

Scott, *Sophia*   Scott, Martin. *Sophia and the Johannine Jesus.* JSNTSup 71. Sheffield: Sheffield Academic Press, 1992.

Scott, *Spirit*   Scott, Ernest F. *The Spirit in the New Testament.* London: Hodder & Stoughton, [1923].

Scroggs, "Judaizing"   Scroggs, Robin. "The Judaizing of the New Testament." *Chicago Theological Seminary Register* 76 (1986): 36–45.

Seager, "Synagogue"   Seager, Andrew R. "The Synagogue and the Jewish Community: The Building." Pages 168–77 in *Sardis from Prehistoric to Roman Times: Results of the Archaeological Exploration of Sardis, 1958–1975.* Edited by George M. A. Hanfmann with William E. Mierse. Cambridge: Harvard University Press, 1983.

Seckel, "Mère"   Seckel, Marianne. "La mère de Jésus dans le 4ᵉ évangile: De la lignée des femmes-disciples?" *Foi et vie* 88, no. 5 (1989): 33–41.

Séd, "Traditions secrètes"   Séd, N. "Les traditions secrètes et les disciples de Rabban Yohanan ben Zakkai." *Revue de l'histoire des religions* 184 (1973): 49–66.

Seeley, "Cynics"   Seeley, David. "Jesus and the Cynics Revisited." *JBL* 116 (1997): 704–12.

Seeligmann, "Phōs"   Seeligmann, I. "Deixai autō phōs." (In Hebrew.) *Tarbiz* 27 (1958): 127–41.

Segal, "Death Penalty"   Segal, Peter. "The 'Divine Death Penalty' in the Hatra Inscriptions and the Mishnah." *JJS* 40 (1989): 46–52.

Segal, "Inscription"   Segal, Peretz. "The Penalty of the Warning Inscription from the Temple of Jerusalem." *IEJ* 39 (1989): 79–84.

Segal, "Ruler"   Segal, Alan F. "Ruler of This World: Attitudes about Mediator Figures and the Importance of Sociology for Self-Definition." Pages 245–68 in vol. 2 of Meyer and Sanders, *Self-Definition.*

Segal, "Torah"   Segal, Alan F. "Torah and *nomos* in Recent Scholarly Discussion." *SR* 13 (1984): 19–27.

Segal, "Voice"   Segal, Alan F. "Matthew's Jewish Voice." Pages 3–37 in *Social History of the Matthean Community: Cross-disciplinary Approaches.* Edited by David L. Balch. Minneapolis: Fortress, 1991.

Segalla, "Struttura"   Segalla, Giuseppe. "La complessa struttura letteraria di Giovanni 6." *Teologia* 15 (1990): 68–89.

Segovia, "Conclusion"   Segovia, Fernando F. "Conclusion—Reading Readers of the Fourth Gospel and Their Readings: An Exercise in Intercultural Criticism." Pages 237–277 in *"What Is John?" Readers and Reading of the Fourth Gospel.* Edited by Fernando F. Segovia. SBLSymS 3. Atlanta: Scholars Press, 1996.

Segovia, *Farewell*   Segovia, Fernando F. *The Farewell of the Word: The Johannine Call to Abide.* Minneapolis: Fortress, 1991.

Segovia, "Farewell"   Segovia, Fernando F. "The Final Farewell of Jesus: A Reading of John 20:30–21:25." *Semeia* 53 (1991): 167–90.

Segovia, *Relationships*   Segovia, Fernando F. *Love Relationships in the Johannine Tradition.* SBLDS 58. Chico, Calif.: Scholars Press, 1982.

Segovia, "Structure"   Segovia, Fernando F. "The Structure, *Tendenz,* and *Sitz im Leben* of John 13:31–14:31." *JBL* 104 (1985): 471–93.

Segovia, "Tradition History"   Segovia, Fernando F. "The Tradition History of the Fourth Gospel." Pages 179–89 in *Exploring the Gospel of John: In Honor of D. Moody Smith.* Edited by R. Alan Culpepper and C. Clifton Black. Louisville, Ky.: Westminster John Knox, 1996.

Segovia, "What Is John?"    Segovia, Fernando F., ed. "What Is John?" Readers and Reading of the Fourth Gospel. SBLSymS 3. Atlanta: Scholars Press, 1996.

Seitz, "Bemerkungen"    Seitz, W. E. "Philologische Bemerkungen zu einer problematischen Bibelübersetzung: Joh 20, 22–23." Münchener theologische Zeitschrift 51, no. 1 (2000): 55–61.

Selkin, "Exegesis"    Selkin, Carol Barbara. "Exegesis and Identity: The Hermeneutics of Miqwa'ot in the Greco-Roman Period." Ph.D. diss., Duke University, 1993.

Selms, "Fishing"    Selms, A. van. "Fishing." Pages 309–11 in vol. 2 of The International Standard Bible Encyclopedia. Edited by Geoffrey W. Bromiley. 4 vols. Grand Rapids: Eerdmans, 1979–1988.

Selwyn, Peter    Selwyn, Edward Gordon. The First Epistle of St. Peter: The Greek Text with Introduction, Notes, and Essays. 2d ed. New York: Macmillan, 1947.

Serban and Baluta, "Mithraism"    Serban, Ioan, and Closca L. Baluta. "On Mithraism in the Army of Dacia Superior." Pages 573–78 in Mysteria Mithrae. Edited by Ugo Bianchi. Études préliminaires aux religions orientales dans l'empire romain 80. Leiden: Brill, 1979.

Serrano, "Sheol"    Serrano, A. "El 'Sheol' bíblico y el 'Hades' griego: Anticipo del infierno cristiano?" Biblia y fe 3, no. 7 (1977): 27–42.

Setzer, Responses    Setzer, Claudia J. Jewish Responses to Early Christians: History and Polemics, 30–150 C.E. Minneapolis: Fortress, 1994.

Sevenster, Anti-Semitism    Sevenster, J. N. The Roots of Pagan Anti-Semitism in the Ancient World. NovTSup 41. Leiden: Brill, 1975.

Sevenster, Greek    Sevenster, J. N. Do You Know Greek? How Much Greek Could the First Jewish Christians Have Known? NovTSup 19. Leiden: Brill, 1968.

Sevenster, "Humanity"    Sevenster, G. "Remarks on the Humanity of Jesus in the Gospel and Letters of John." Pages 185–93 in Studies in John: Presented to Professor Dr. J. N. Sevenster on the Occasion of His Seventieth Birthday. Edited by W. C. van Unnik. NovTSup 24. Leiden: Brill, 1970.

Sevenster, Seneca    Sevenster, J. N. Paul and Seneca. NovTSup 4. Leiden: Brill, 1961.

Sevrin, "Nicodemus Enigma"    Sevrin, Jean-Marie. "The Nicodemus Enigma: The Characterization and Function of an Ambiguous Actor of the Fourth Gospel." Pages 357–69 in Anti-Judaism and the Fourth Gospel: Papers of the Leuven Colloquium, 2000. Edited by R. Bieringer, D. Pollefeyt, and F. Vandecasteele-Vanneuville. Assen: Royal Van Gorcum, 2001.

Seynaeve, "Verbes"    Seynaeve, J. "Les verbes ἀποστέλλω et πέμπω." Pages 385–89 in L'évangile de Jean: Sources, rédaction, théologie. Edited by Marinus De Jonge. BETL 45. Gembloux: J. Duculot; Leuven: Leuven University Press, 1977.

Shafaat, "Geber"    Shafaat, Ahmed. "Geber of the Qumran Scrolls and the Spirit-Paraclete of the Gospel of John." NTS 27 (1980–1981): 263–69.

Shaheen, "Tunnel"    Shaheen, Naseeb. "The Siloam End of Hezekiah's Tunnel." PEQ 109 (1977): 107–12.

Shank, Life    Shank, Robert. Life in the Son: A Study of the Doctrine of Perseverance. Springfield, Mo.: Westcott, 1960.

Shanks, "Zodiac"    Shanks, Herschel. "Synagogue Excavation Reveals Stunning Mosaic of Zodiac and Torah Ark." BAR 10, no. 3 (May/June 1984): 32–44.

Shapiro, "Wisdom"    Shapiro, David S. "Wisdom and Knowledge of God in Biblical and Talmudic Thought." Tradition 12, no. 2 (1971): 70–89.

Shea, "Form"    Shea, William H. "The Covenantal Form of the Letters to the Seven Churches." Andrews University Seminary Studies 21 (1983): 71–84.

Shedd, "Meanings"    Shedd, Russell. "Multiple Meanings in the Gospel of John." Pages 247–258 in Current Issues in Biblical and Patristic Interpretation: Studies in Honor of Merrill C. Tenney Presented by His Former Students. Edited by Gerald F. Hawthorne. Grand Rapids: Eerdmans, 1975.

Sheeley, Asides    Sheeley, Steven M. Narrative Asides in Luke-Acts. JSNTSup 72. Sheffield; Sheffield Academic Press, 1992.

Sheldon, Mystery Religions    Sheldon, Henry C. The Mystery Religions and the New Testament. New York: Abingdon, 1918.

Shepherd, "Date"    Shepherd, Massey H. "Are Both the Synoptics and John Correct about the Date of Jesus' Death?" JBL 80 (1961): 123–32.

Shepherd, "Jews"    Shepherd, Massey H., Jr. "The Jews in the Gospel of John: Another Level of Meaning." Pages 95–112 in Gospel Studies in Homnor of Sherman Elbridge Johnson. Edited by

Massey H. Shepherd and Edward C. Hobbs. Anglican Theological Review Supplement 3. Evanston, Ill.: Anglican Theological Review, 1974.

Shepherd, *Liturgy*   Shepherd, Massey H., Jr. *The Paschal Liturgy and the Apocalypse.* Ecumenical Studies in Worship 6. Richmond, Va.: John Knox, 1960.

Sheppard, "Wisdom"   Sheppard, Gerald T. "Wisdom and Torah: The Interpretation of Deuteronomy Underlying Sirach 24:23." Pages 166–76 in *Biblical and Near Eastern Studies: Essays in Honor of William Sanford LaSor.* Edited by Gary A. Tuttle. Grand Rapids: Eerdmans, 1978.

Sherk, *Empire*   Sherk, Robert K., ed. and tr. *The Roman Empire: Augustus to Hadrian.* Translated Documents of Greece and Rome 6. New York: Cambridge University Press, 1988.

Sherwin-White, *Society*   Sherwin-White, A. N. *Roman Society and Roman Law in the New Testament.* Oxford: Oxford University Press, 1963. Repr., Grand Rapids: Baker, 1978.

Sherwin-White, "Trial"   Sherwin-White, A. N. "The Trial of Christ." Pages 97–116 in *Historicity and Chronology in the New Testament* by D. E. Nineham et al. London: SPCK, 1965.

Shogren, "Prophecy"   Shogren, Gary. "Christian Prophecy and Canon in the Second Century: A Response to B. B. Warfield." *JETS* 40, no. 4 (1997): 609–26.

Shotwell, *Exegesis*   Shotwell, Willis A. *The Biblical Exegesis of Justin Martyr.* London: SPCK, 1965.

Shuler, *Genre*   Shuler, Philip L. *A Genre for the Gospels: The Biographical Character of Matthew.* Philadelphia: Fortress, 1982.

Shuler, "Hypothesis"   Shuler, Philip L. "The Griesbach Hypothesis and Gospel Genre." *Perkins Journal* 33 (1980): 41–49.

Shutt, "Concept"   Shutt, R. J. H. "The Concept of God in the Works of Flavius Josephus." *JJS* 31 (1980): 171–89.

Sidebottom, *James*   Sidebottom, E. M. *James, Jude, and 2 Peter.* New Century Bible. Greenwood, S.C.: Attic Press, 1967.

Siegal, "Characters"   Siegal, Jonathan P. "The Employment of Palaeo-Hebrew Characters for the Divine Names at Qumran in the Light of Tannaitic Sources." *HUCA* 42 (1971): 159–172.

Siegal, "Scribes"   Siegal, Jonathan P. "The Scribes of Qumran: Studies in the Early History of Jewish Scribal Customs, with Special Reference to the Qumran Biblical Scrolls and to the Tannaitic Traditions of Massekheth Soferim." Ph.D. Diss., Brandeis University, 1971.

Siegel, "Israel"   Siegel, Seymour. "The Meaning of Israel in Jewish Thought." Pages 98–118 in *Evangelicals and Jews in Conversation on Scripture, Theology, and History.* Edited by Marc H. Tanenbaum, Marvin R. Wilson, and James A. Rudin. Grand Rapids: Baker, 1978.

Siegert, "Gottesfürchtige"   Siegert, Folker. "Gottesfürchtige und Sympathisanten." *JSJ* 4 (1973): 109–64.

Siegert, "Homily"   Siegert, Folker. "Homily and Panegyrical Sermon." Pages 421–43 in *Handbook of Classical Rhetoric in the Hellenistic Period, 330 B.C.–A.D. 400.* Edited by Stanley E. Porter. Leiden: Brill, 1997.

Sievers, "Shekhinah"   Sievers, Joseph. "'Where Two or Three . . .': The Rabbinic Concept of Shekhinah and Matthew 18:20." *Sidic* 17 (1984): 4–10.

Sigal, *Halakah*   Sigal, Phillip. *The Halakah of Jesus of Nazareth according to the Gospel of Matthew.* Lanham, Md.: University Press of America, 1986.

Sikes, "Anti-Semitism"   Sikes, Walter W. "The Anti-Semitism of the Fourth Gospel." *Journal of Religion* 21 (1941): 23–30.

Silberman, "Language"   Silberman, Lou H. "Language and Structure in the Hodayot (1QH 3)." *JBL* 75 (1956): 96–106.

Silberman, "Messiahs"   Silberman, Lou H. "The Two 'Messiahs' of the Manual of Discipline." *VT* 5 (1955): 77–82.

Silberman, "Ossuary"   Silberman, Neil Asher. "Ossuary: A Box for Bones." *BAR* 17, no. 3 (May/June 1991): 73–74.

Silberman, "Use"   Silberman, Lou H. "Anent the Use of Rabbinic Material." *NTS* 24 (1977–1978): 415–17.

Silva Santos, "Autoria"   Silva Santos, Bento. "A autoria do quarto evangelho." *Revista bíblica brasileira* 5, no. 4 (1988): 157–81.

Silver, "Moses"   Silver, Daniel J. "Moses and the Hungry Birds." *JQR* 64 (1973–1974): 123–53.

Simenel, "Jean 20"   Simenel, Philippe. "Les 2 anges de Jean 20/11–12." *Études théologiques et religieuses* 67 (1992): 71–76.

Simon, "Life"   Simon, U. E. "Eternal Life in the Fourth Gospel." Pages 97–109 in *Studies in the Fourth Gospel*. Edited by F. L. Cross. London: Mowbray, 1957.

Simon, *Sects*   Simon, Marcel. *Jewish Sects at the Time of Jesus*. Philadelphia: Fortress, 1967.

Simon, *Stephen*   Simon, Marcel. *St Stephen and the Hellenists in the Primitive Church*. Haskell Lectures, 1956. New York: Longmans, Green, 1958.

Simon, "Synkretismus"   Simon, Marie. "Zum Problem des jüdisch-griechischen Synkretismus." *Kairos* 17 (1975): 89–99.

Simon, "Women"   Simon, S. J. "Women Who Pleaded Causes before the Roman Magistrates." *Classical Bulletin* 66, nos. 3–4 (1990): 79–81.

Simonis, *Hirtenrede*   Simonis, Adrian John. *Die Hirtenrede im Johannes-Evangelium: Versuch einer Analyse von Johannes 10, 1–18 nach Entstehung, Hintergrund, und Inhalt*. Analecta biblica 29. Rome: Pontifical Biblical Institute, 1967.

Sinaiko, *Love*   Sinaiko, Herman L. *Love, Knowledge, and Discourse in Plato: Dialogue and Dialectic in Phaedrus, Republic, Parmenides*. Chicago: University of Chicago Press, 1965.

Sinclair, "*Sententia*"   Sinclair, Patrick. "The *Sententia* in *Rhetorica ad Herennium:* A Study in the Sociology of Rhetoric." *American Journal of Philology* 114 (1993): 561–80.

Sinclair, "Temples"   Sinclair, Patrick. "'These Are MY Temples in Your Hearts' (Tac. *Ann.* 4.38.2)." *Classical Philology* 86 (1991): 333–35.

Sirat and Woog, "Maître"   Sirat, René-Samuel, and Agnès Woog. "Moïse 'notre maître,' prince des prophètes." *Vie spirituelle* 146 (1992): 625–32.

Sisti, "Figura"   Sisti, Adalberto. "La figura del giusto perseguitato in *Sap.* 2,12–20." *Bibbia e oriente* 19 (1977): 129–44.

Ska, "Samaritaine"   Ska, Jean-Louis. "Jésus et la Samaritaine *(Jn 4):* Utilité de l'Ancien Testament." *Nouvelle revue théologique* 118 (1996): 641–52.

Sleeper, "Pentecost"   Sleeper, C. F. "Pentecost and Resurrection." *JBL* 84 (1965): 389–99.

Slingerland, "Jews"   Slingerland, H. Dixon. "'The Jews' in the Pauline Portion of Acts." *Journal of the American Academy of Religion* 54 (1986): 305–21.

Sloan, "Absence"   Sloan, Robert B. "The Absence of Jesus in John." Pages 207–27 in *Perspectives on John: Method and Interpretation in the Fourth Gospel*. Edited by Robert B. Sloan and Mikeal C. Parsons. National Association of the Baptist Professors of Religion Special Studies Series 11. Lewiston, N.Y.: Mellen, 1993.

Sloyan, "Adoption"   Sloyan, G. S. "The Gnostic Adoption of John's Gospel and Its Canonization by the Catholic Church." *Biblical Theology Bulletin* 26 (1996): 125–32.

Sloyan, *John*   Sloyan, Gerald S. *John*. Interpretation: A Bible Commentary for Teaching and Preaching. Atlanta: John Knox, 1988.

Sloyan, *Saying*   Sloyan, Gerald S. *What Are They Saying about John?* New York: Paulist Press, 1991.

Small, "Memory"   Small, J. P. "Artificial Memory and the Writing Habits of the Literate." *Helios* 22 (1995): 159–66.

Smalley, *Epistles*   Smalley, Stephen S. *1, 2, 3 John*. WBC 51. Waco, Tex.: Word, 1984.

Smalley, *John*   Smalley, Stephen S. *John: Evangelist and Interpreter*. Exeter: Paternoster, 1978.

Smalley, "Paraclete"   Smalley, Stephen S. "'The Paraclete': Pneumatology in the Johannine Gospel and Apocalypse." Pages 289–300 in *Exploring the Gospel of John: In Honor of D. Moody Smith*. Edited by R. Alan Culpepper and C. Clifton Black. Louisville, Ky.: Westminster John Knox, 1996.

Smalley, "Recent Studies"   Smalley, Stephen S. "The Johannine Literature: A Sample of Recent Studies in English." *Theology* 103 (2000): 13–28.

Smalley, "Relationship"   Smalley, Stephen S. "The Christ-Christian Relationship in Paul and John." Pages 95–105 in *Pauline Studies: Essays Presented to Professor F. F. Bruce on His 70th Birthday*. Edited by Donald A. Hagner and Murray J. Harris. Exeter: Paternoster, 1980.

Smalley, "Revelation"   Smalley, Stephen S. "John's Revelation and John's Community." *Bulletin of the John Rylands Library* 69 (1986–1987): 549–71.

Smalley, "Sayings"   Smalley, Stephen S. "The Johannine Son of Man Sayings." *NTS* 15 (1968–1969): 278–301.

Smallwood, "Historians"   Smallwood, E. Mary. "Philo and Josephus as Historians of the Same Events." Pages 114–29 in *Josephus, Judaism, and Christianity*. Edited by Louis H. Feldman and Gohei Hata. Detroit: Wayne State University Press, 1987.

Smallwood, *Jews*    Smallwood, E. Mary. *The Jews under Roman Rule: From Pompey to Diocletian*. Studies in Judaism in Late Antiquity 20. Leiden: Brill, 1976.

Smallwood, "Priests"    Smallwood, E. Mary. "High Priests and Politics in Roman Palestine." *JTS* NS 13 (1962): 14–34.

Smith, *Among Gospels*    Smith, D. Moody. *John Among the Gospels*. 2d ed. Columbia: University of South Carolina, 2001.

Smith, "Apocalypse"    Smith, Robert H. "Why John Wrote the Apocalypse (Rev 1:9)." *Currents in Theology and Mission* 22 (1995): 356–61.

Smith, "Baptism"    Smith, Derwood. "Jewish Proselyte Baptism and the Baptism of John." *Restoration Quarterly* 25 (1982): 13–32.

Smith, "Begetting"    Smith, Morton. "'God's Begetting the Messiah' in 1QSa." *NTS* 5 (1958–1959): 218–24.

Smith, "Book of Signs"    Smith, T. C. "The Book of Signs, John 2–12." *Review and Expositor* 62 (1965): 441–57.

Smith, "Christianity"    Smith, D. Moody. "Johannine Christianity: Some Reflections on Its Character and Delineation." *NTS* 21 (1974–1975): 222–48.

Smith, "Chronology of Supper"    Smith, Barry D. "The Chronology of the Last Supper." *WTJ* 53 (1991): 29–45.

Smith, *Composition*    Smith, D. Moody, Jr. *The Composition and Order of the Fourth Gospel: Bultmann's Literary Theory*. Yale Publications in Religion 10. New Haven: Yale University Press, 1965.

Smith, "Cross Marks"    Smith, Robert Houston. "The Cross Marks on Jewish Ossuaries." *PEQ* 106 (1974): 53–66.

Smith, "Gospels"    Smith, D. Moody. "When Did the Gospels Become Scripture?" *JBL* 119 (2000): 3–20.

Smith, *Johannine Christianity*    Smith, D. Moody. *Johannine Christianity: Essays on Its Setting, Sources, and Theology*. Columbia, S.C.: University of South Carolina Press, 1984.

Smith, *John*    Smith, D. Moody. *John*. Proclamation Commentaries. Philadelphia: Fortress, 1976.

Smith, *John* (1999)    Smith, D. Moody. *John*. Abingdon New Testament Commentaries. Nashville: Abingdon, 1999.

Smith, "John 16"    Smith, D. Moody. "John 16:1–15." *Interpretation* 33 (1979): 58–62.

Smith, *John among Gospels*    Smith, D. Moody. *John among the Gospels: The Relationship in Twentieth-Century Research*. Minneapolis: Fortress, 1992.

Smith, "John and Synoptics"    Smith, D. Moody. "John and the Synoptics: Some Dimensions of the Problem." *NTS* 26 (1979–1980): 425–44.

Smith, "Learned"    Smith, D. Moody. "What Have I Learned about the Gospel of John?" Pages 217–35 in *"What Is John?" Readers and Reading of the Fourth Gospel*. Edited by Fernando F. Segovia. SBLSymS 3. Atlanta: Scholars Press, 1996.

Smith, *Magician*    Smith, Morton. *Jesus the Magician*. San Francisco: Harper & Row, 1978.

Smith, "Method"    Smith, Morton. "On the Problem of Method in the Study of Rabbinic Literature." *JBL* 92 (1973): 112–13.

Smith, "Note"    Smith, Morton. "A Note on Some Jewish Assimilationists: The Angels (P. Berlin 5025b, P. Louvre 2391)." *Journal of the Ancient Near Eastern Society* 16–17 (1984–85): 207–12.

Smith, *Parallels*    Smith, Morton. *Tannaitic Parallels to the Gospels*. Philadelphia: Society of Biblical Literature, 1951.

Smith, "Problem"    Smith, D. Moody. "Historical Issues and the Problem of John and the Synoptics." Pages 252–67 in *From Jesus to John: Essays on Jesus and New Testament Christology in Honour of Marinus de Jonge*. Edited by Martinus C. De Boer. JSNTSup 84. Sheffield: Sheffield Academic Press, 1993.

Smith, "Prolegomena"    Smith, D. Moody. "Prolegomena to a Canonical Reading of the Fourth Gospel." Pages 169–82 in *"What Is John?" Readers and Reading of the Fourth Gospel*. Edited by Fernando F. Segovia. SBLSymS 3. Atlanta: Scholars Press, 1996.

Smith, "Sarcophagus"    Smith, Robert Houston. "A Sarcophagus from Pella: New Light on Earliest Christianity." *Archaeology* 26, no. 4 (July/August 1973): 250–56.

Smith, "Staircase"    Smith, Morton. "The Case of the Gilded Staircase." *BAR* 10, no. 5 (September/October 1984): 50–55.

Smith, "Studies since Bultmann"    Smith, D. Moody. "Johannine Studies since Bultmann." *Word and World* 21, no. 4 (2001): 343–51.

Smith, *Theology*    Smith, D. Moody. *The Theology of the Gospel of John.* New Testament Theology Series. Cambridge: Cambridge University Press, 1995.

Smith, "Tomb"    Smith, Robert Houston. "The Tomb of Jesus." *BA* 30 (1967): 74–90.

Smith, "Tradition"    Smith, Morton. "A Comparison of Early Christian and Early Rabbinic Tradition." *JBL* 82 (1963): 169–76.

Smith, "Typology"    Smith, Robert Houston. "Exodus Typology in the Fourth Gospel." *JBL* 81 (1962): 329–42.

Smith, "Variety"    Smith, Morton. "What Is Implied by the Variety of Messianic Figures?" *JBL* 78 (1959): 66–72.

Snaith, *Amos*    Snaith, Norman H. *Amos, Hosea, and Micah.* Epworth Preacher's Commentaries. London: Epworth, 1956.

Snaith, "Paraclete"    Snaith, Norman H. "The Meaning of 'the Paraclete.'" *ExpTim* 57 (1945–1946): 47–50.

Snodgrass, "PNEUMA"    Snodgrass, Klyne R. "That Which Is Born from PNEUMA Is PNEUMA: Rebirth and Spirit in John 3:5–6." Pages 181–205 in *Perspectives on John: Method and Interpretation in the Fourth Gospel.* National Association of the Baptist Professors of Religion Special Studies Series 11. Edited by Robert B. Sloan and Mikeal C. Parsons. Lewiston, N.Y.: Mellen, 1993.

Snodgrass, "Streams"    Snodgrass, Klyne R. "Streams of Tradition Emerging from Isaiah 40:1–5 and Their Adaptation in the New Testament." *JSNT* 8 (1980): 24–45.

Snowden, *Blacks*    Snowden, Frank M., Jr. *Blacks in Antiquity: Ethiopians in the Greco-Roman Experience.* Cambridge: Harvard University Press, 1970.

Soards, "Ἐπενδύτην"    Soards, Marion L. "Τὸν ἐπενδύτην διεζώσατο, ἦν γὰρ γυμνός." *JBL* 102 (1983): 283–84.

Soards, "Passion Narrative"    Soards, Marion L. "Appendix IX: The Question of a Premarcan Passion Narrative." Pages 1492–1524 in *The Death of the Messiah—from Gethsemane to Grave: A Commentary on the Passion Narratives in the Four Gospels.* 2 vols. New York: Doubleday, 1994.

Soards, "Psalter"    Soards, Marion L. "The Psalter in the Text and the Thought of the Fourth Gospel." Pages 251–67 in *Perspectives on John: Method and Interpretation in the Fourth Gospel.* National Association of the Baptist Professors of Religion Special Studies Series 11. Edited by Robert B. Sloan and Mikeal C. Parsons. Lewiston, N.Y.: Mellen, 1993.

Soards, *Speeches*    Soards, Marion L. *The Speeches in Acts: Their Content, Context, and Concerns.* Louisville, Ky.: Westminster John Knox, 1994.

Soares Prabhu, *Quotations*    Soares Prabhu, George M. *The Formula Quotations in the Infancy Narrative of Matthew: An Enquiry into the Tradition History of Mt 1–2.* Rome: Biblical Institute Press, 1976.

Söding, "Feindeshass"    Söding, Thomas. "Feindeshass und Bruderliebe: Beobachtungen zur essenischen Ethik." *RevQ* 16 (1993–1995): 601–19.

Söding, "Kann aus Nazareth"    Söding, Thomas. "'Was kann aus Nazareth schon Gutes kommen?' (Joh 1.46): Die Bedeutung des Judenseins Jesu im Johannesevangelium." *NTS* 46, no. 1 (2000): 21–41.

Soggin, *Introduction*    Soggin, J. Alberto. *Introduction to the Old Testament.* Philadelphia: Westminster, 1980.

Sonne, "Use"    Sonne, Isaiah. "The Use of Rabbinic Literature as Historical Sources." *JQR* 36 (1945–1946): 147–69.

Soramuzza, "Policy"    Soramuzza, Vincent. "The Policy of the Early Roman Emperors towards Judaism." Pages 277–97 in vol. 5 of *The Beginnings of Christianity.*

Spencer, "Narrative Echoes"    Spencer, Patrick E. "Narrative Echoes in John 21: Intertextual Interpretation and Intratextual Connection." *JSNT* 75 (1999): 49–68.

Spencer, *Philip*    Spencer, F. Scott. *The Portrait of Philip in Acts: A Study of Roles and Relations.* JSNTSup 67. Sheffield: Sheffield Academic Press, 1992.

Sperber, "Shi'urim"    Sperber, Daniel. "A Note on Some Shi'urim and Graeco-Roman Measurements." *JJS* 20 (1969): 81–86.

Speyer, "Derjenige"    Speyer, Wolfgang. "'Derjenige, der verwundet hat, wird auch heilen.'" *Jahrbuch für Antike und Christentum* 36 (1993): 46–53.

Spicq, "Trōgein"  Spicq, C. "Trōgein: Est-il synonyme de phagein et d'esthein dans le Noveau Testament?" NTS 26 (1979–1980): 414–19.

Spittler, "Introduction"  Spittler, R. P. Introduction to "Testament of Job." OTP 1:829–38.

Spriggs, "Water"  Spriggs, D. G. "Meaning of 'Water' in John 3:5." ExpTim 85 (1973–1974): 149–50.

St. Clair, "Shrine"  St. Clair, A. "The Torah Shrine at Dura-Europos: A Re-evaluation." Jahrbuch für Antike und Christentum 29 (1986): 109–117, plates 14–15.

Stählin, "πνεῦμα"  Stählin, G. "Τὸ πνεῦμα Ἰησοῦ (Apostelgeschichte 16:7)." Pages 229–52 in Christ and Spirit in the NT: In Honour of Charles Francis Digby Moule. Edited by Barnabas Lindars and Stephen S. Smalley. Cambridge: Cambridge University Press, 1973.

Stählin, "φιλέω"  Stählin, Gustav. "φιλέω, κτλ." TDNT 9:113–71.

Staley, Kiss  Staley, Jeffrey Lloyd. The Print's First Kiss: A Rhetorical Investigation of the Implied Reader in the Fourth Gospel. SBLDS 82. Atlanta: Scholars Press, 1988.

Staley, "Stumbling"  Staley, Jeffrey L. "Stumbling in the Dark, Reaching for the Light: Reading Character in John 5 and 9." Semeia 53 (1991): 55–80.

Stambaugh and Balch, Environment  Stambaugh, John E., and David L. Balch. The New Testament in Its Social Environment. LEC 2. Philadelphia: Westminster, 1986.

Stamps, "Children"  Stamps, Dennis L. "Children in Late Antiquity." Pages 197–201 in Dictionary of New Testament Background. Edited by Craig A. Evans and Stanley E. Porter. Downers Grove, Ill.: InterVarsity, 2000.

Stamps, "Johannine Writings"  Stamps, Dennis L. "The Johannine Writings." Pages 609–32 in Handbook of Classical Rhetoric in the Hellenistic Period, 330 B.C.–A.D. 400. Edited by Stanley E. Porter. Leiden: Brill, 1997.

Stanley, Resurrection  Stanley, David Michael. Christ's Resurrection in Pauline Soteriology. Analecta biblica 13. Rome: Pontifical Biblical Institute, 1961.

Stanton, "Convince"  Stanton, V. H. "Convince or Convict (John xvi.8)." ExpTim 33 (1921–1922): 278–79.

Stanton, Gospels  Stanton, Graham N. The Gospels and Jesus. Oxford Bible Series. Oxford: Oxford University Press, 1989.

Stanton, Gospel Truth  Stanton, Graham N. Gospel Truth? New Light on Jesus and the Gospels. Valley Forge, Pa.: Trinity Press International, 1995.

Stanton, Jesus  Stanton, Graham N. Jesus of Nazareth in New Testament Preaching. Cambridge: Cambridge University Press, 1974.

Stanton, New People  Stanton, Graham N. A Gospel for a New People: Studies in Matthew. Edinburgh: T&T Clark, 1992.

Stanton, "Salvation"  Stanton, Graham N. "Salvation Proclaimed, X: Matthew 11:28–30—Comfortable Words?" ExpTim 94 (1982-1983): 3–9.

Stark, "Empire"  Stark, Rodney. "Christianizing the Urban Empire: An Analysis Based on 22 Greco-Roman Cities." Sociological Analysis 52 (1991): 77–88.

Stasiak, "Man"  Stasiak, Kurt. "The Man Who Came by Night." The Bible Today 20 (1982): 84–89.

Stauffer, "ἐμφυσάω"  Stauffer, Ethelbert. "ἐμφυσάω." TDNT 2:536–37.

Stauffer, Jesus  Stauffer, Ethelbert. Jesus and His Story. Translated by Richard and Clara Winston. New York: Knopf, 1960.

Steck, "Zeugen"  Steck, Odil Hannes. "Die getöten 'Zeugen' und die verfolgten 'Tora-Sucher' in Jub 1,12: Ein Beitrag zur Zeugnis-Terminologie der Jubiläenbuchs, I." ZAW 107 (1995): 445–65.

Stefaniak, "Poglady"  Stefaniak, L. "Poglady mesjanskie czy eschatologiczne sekty z Qumrân? (Les opinions de la secte de Qumrân, sont-elles messinaiques ou eschatologiques?)" Roczniki teologiczno-kanoniczne 9, no. 4 (1962): 59–73.

Stegner, "Baptism"  Stegner, William Richard. "The Baptism of Jesus: A Story Modeled on the Binding of Isaac." Bible Review 1, no. 3 (fall 1985): 36–46.

Stegner, "Homily"  Stegner, William Richard. "The Ancient Jewish Synagogue Homily." Pages 51–69 in Greco-Roman Literature and the New Testament: Selected Forms and Genres. Edited by David E. Aune. SBLSBS 21. Atlanta: Scholars Press, 1988.

Stehly, "Upanishads"  Stehly, R. "Une citation des Upanishads dans Joseph et Aséneth." Revue d'histoire et de philosophie religieuses 55 (1975): 209–13.

Stein, "Agreements"  Stein, Robert H. "The Matthew-Luke Agreements against Mark: Insight from John." CBQ 54 (1992): 482–502.

Stein, "'Criteria'"    Stein, Robert H. "The 'Criteria' for Authenticity." Pages 225–63 in *Studies of History and Tradition in the Four Gospels*. Vol. 1 of *Gospel Perspectives*. Edited by R. T. France and David Wenham. Sheffield: JSOT Press, 1980.

Stein, *Method*    Stein, Robert H. *The Method and Message of Jesus' Teachings*. Philadelphia: Westminster, 1978.

Stemberger, "Auferstehungslehre"    Stemberger, Günter. "Zur Auferstehungslehre in der rabbinischen Literatur." *Kairos* 15 (1973): 238–66.

Stemberger, "Bedeutung"    Stemberger, Günter. "Die Bedeutung des 'Landes Israel' in der rabbinischen Tradition." *Kairos* 25 (1983): 176–99.

Stemberger, "Pesachhaggada"    Stemberger, Günter. "Pesachhaggada und Abendmahlsberichte des Neuen Testaments." *Kairos* 29 (1987): 147–58.

Stemberger, "Synode"    Stemberger, Günter. "Die sogenannte 'Synode von Jabne' und das frühe Christentum." *Kairos* 19 (1977): 14–21.

Stendahl, *Paul*    Stendahl, Krister. *Paul among Jews and Gentiles and Other Essays*. Philadelphia: Fortress, 1976.

Stendahl, *School*    Stendahl, Krister. *The School of St. Matthew and Its Use of the Old Testament*. Philadelphia: Fortress, 1968.

Stenger, "*Dikaiosyne*"    Stenger, Werner. "*Dikaiosyne* in Jo. xvi 8.10." *NovT* 21 (1979): 2–12.

Sterling, "Bond"    Sterling, Gregory E. "The Bond of Humanity: Friendship in Philo of Alexandria." Pages 203–23 in *Greco-Roman Perspectives on Friendship*. Edited by John T. Fitzgerald. SBLRBS 34. Atlanta: Scholars Press, 1997.

Sterling, *Sisters*    Sterling, Dorothy. *We Are Your Sisters: Black Women in the Nineteenth Century*. New York: Norton, 1984.

Stern, "Anthropomorphism"    Stern, David. "*Imitatio Hominis*: Anthropomorphism and the Character(s) of God in Rabbinic Literature." *Prooftexts* 12, no. 2 (1992): 151–74.

Stern, "Aspects"    Stern, Menahem. "Aspects of Jewish Society: The Priesthood and Other Classes." Pages 561–630 in Safrai and Stern, *Jewish People*.

Stern, "Attribution"    Stern, Sacha. "Attribution and Authorship in the Babylonian Talmud." *JJS* 45 (1994): 28–51.

Stern, *Authors*    Stern, Menahem. *Greek and Latin Authors on Jews and Judaism: Edited with Introductions, Translations, and Commentary*. Vol. 1: *From Herodotus to Plutarch*. Vol. 2: *From Tacitus to Simplicius*. Vol. 3: *Appendixes and Indexes*. 3 vols. Jerusalem: Israel Academy of Sciences and Humanities, 1974–1984.

Stern, "Diaspora"    Stern, Menahem. "The Jewish Diaspora." Pages 117–83 in vol. 1 of Safrai and Stern, *Jewish People*.

Stern, *Parables*    Stern, David. *Parables in Midrash: Narrative and Exegesis in Rabbinic Literature*. Cambridge: Harvard University Press, 1991.

Sternberg, *Poetics*    Sternberg, Meir. *The Poetics of Biblical Narrative*. Bloomington: Indiana University Press, 1985.

Stevens, *Theology*    Stevens, George B. *The Johannine Theology: A Study of the Doctrinal Contents of the Gospel and Epistles of the Apostle John*. New York: Scribner, 1894.

Stevenson, "Benefactor"    Stevenson, T. R. "The Ideal Benefactor and the Father Analogy in Greek and Roman Thought." *Classical Quarterly* 42 (1992): 421–36.

Stewart, "Domitian"    Stewart, R. "Domitian and Roman Religion: Juvenal, *Satires* Two and Four." *Transactions of the American Philological Association* 124 (1994): 309–32.

Stewart, "Procedure"    Stewart, Roy A. "Judicial Procedure in NT Times." *EvQ* 47 (1975): 94–109.

Stewart, "Synagogue"    Stewart, Roy A. "The Synagogue." *EvQ* 43 (1971): 36–46.

Stibbe, "Elusive Christ"    Stibbe, Mark W. G. "The Elusive Christ: A New Reading of the Fourth Gospel." *JSNT* 44 (1991): 19–37.

Stibbe, *Gospel*    Stibbe, Mark W. G. *John's Gospel*. New Testament Readings. London: Routledge, 1994.

Stibbe, "Return"    Stibbe, Mark W. G. "'Return to Sender': A Structuralist Approach to John's Gospel." *Biblical Interpretation* 1 (1993): 189–206.

Stock, "Mystery Play"    Stock, Augustine. "Literary Criticism and Mark's Mystery Play." *The Bible Today* 100 (February 1979): 1909–15.

Stock, "Peter"    Stock, Augustine. "Is Matthew's Presentation of Peter Ironic?" *Biblical Theology Bulletin* 17 (1987): 64–69.

Stone, "Boat"    Stone, G. R. "The Galilee Boat—a Fishing Vessel of NT Times." *Buried History* 25, no. 2 (1989): 46–54.

Stone, "*Oedipus*"    Stone, Jerry H. "The Gospel of Mark and *Oedipus the King:* Two Tragic Visions." *Soundings* 67 (1984): 55–69.

Story, "Attitude"    Story, Cullen I. K. "The Mental Attitude of Jesus at Bethany: John 11.33, 38." *NTS* 37 (1991): 51–66.

Story, "Chronology"    Story, Cullen I. K. "The Bearing of Old Testament Terminology on the Johannine Chronology of the Final Passover of Jesus." *NovT* 31 (1989): 316–24.

Story, *Truth*    Story, Cullen I. K. *The Nature of Truth in "The Gospel of Truth" and in the Writings of Justin Martyr: A Study of the Pattern of Orthodoxy in the Middle of the Second Christian Century.* NovTSup 25. Leiden: Brill, 1970.

Stott, "Commission"    Stott, John R. W. "The Great Commission." *Christianity Today,* April 26, 1968: 3–5.

Stowers, *Diatribe*    Stowers, Stanley K. *The Diatribe and Paul's Letter to the Romans.* SBLDS 57. Chico, Calif.: Scholars Press for the Society of Biblical Literature, 1981.

Stowers, "Diatribe"    Stowers, Stanley K. "The Diatribe." Pages 71–83 in *Greco-Roman Literature and the New Testament: Selected Forms and Genres.* Edited by David E. Aune. SBLSBS 21. Atlanta: Scholars Press, 1988.

Stowers, *Letter Writing*    Stowers, Stanley K. *Letter Writing in Greco-Roman Antiquity.* LEC 5. Philadelphia: Westminster, 1986.

Stowers, "Resemble Philosophy?"    Stowers, Stanley K. "Does Pauline Christianity Resemble a Hellenistic Philosophy?" Pages 81–102 in *Paul beyond the Judaism/Hellenism Divide.* Ed. Troels Engberg-Pedersen. Louisville: Westminster John Knox, 2001.

Stowers, "Synagogue"    Stowers, Stanley K. "The Synagogue in the Theology of Acts." *Restoration Quarterly* 17 (1974): 129–43.

Strachan, *Gospel*    Strachan, Robert Harvey. *The Fourth Gospel: Its Significance and Environment.* London: SCM, 1917.

Strachan, "Odes"    Strachan, Robert Harvey. "The Newly Discovered Odes of Solomon, and Their Bearing on the Problem of the Fourth Gospel." *ExpTim* 22 (1910–1911): 7–14.

Strack, *Introduction*    Strack, Hermann L. *Introduction to the Talmud and Midrash.* n.p.: Jewish Publication Society of America, 1931. Repr., New York: Atheneum, 1969.

Strand, "Day"    Strand, Kenneth A. "Another Look at 'Lord's Day' in the Early Church and in Rev. I.10." *NTS* 13 (1966–1967): 174–181.

Strange, "Diversity"    Strange, James F. "Diversity in Early Palestinian Christianty, Some Archaeological Evidences." *Anglican Theological Review* 65 (1983): 14–24.

Strange, "Galilee"    Strange, James F. "Galilee." Pages 391–98 in *Dictionary of New Testament Background.* Edited by Craig A. Evans and Stanley E. Porter. Downers Grove, Ill.: InterVarsity, 2000.

Strange and Shanks, "House"    Strange, James F., and Hershel Shanks. "Has the House Where Jesus Stayed in Capernaum Been Found?" *BAR* 8, no. 6 (November/December 1982): 26–37.

Strange and Shanks, "Synagogue"    Strange, James F., and Hershel Shanks. "Synagogue Where Jesus Preached Found at Capernaum." *BAR* 9, no. 6 (November/December 1983): 25–31.

Strauss, "Quellen"    Strauss, Heinrich. "Jüdische Quellen frühchristlicher Kunst—optische oder literarische Anregung." *ZNW* 64 (1973): 323–24.

Streeter, *Gospels*    Streeter, Burnett Hillman. *The Four Gospels: A Study of Origins.* Rev. ed. London: Macmillan, 1930.

Strombeck, "Grace"    Strombeck, J. F. "Grace and Truth: Studies in the Gospel according to St. John." *BSac* 96 (1939): 88–116, 205–23.

Strombeck, *Rapture*    Strombeck, J. F. *First the Rapture.* Foreword by Warren W. Wiersbe. Eugene, Ore.: Harvest House, 1982.

Stronstad, *Theology*    Stronstad, Roger. *The Charismatic Theology of Saint Luke.* Peabody, Mass.: Hendrickson, 1984.

Stroumsa, "Form(s)"    Stroumsa, Gedaliahu G. "Form(s) of God: Some Notes on Metatron and Christ." *HTR* 76 (1983): 269–88.

Stuart, "Examination"    Stuart, Moses. "Exegetical and Theological Examination of John 1:1–18." *BSac* 7 (1850): 13–54, 281–327.

Stuhlmacher, "Theme"    Stuhlmacher, Peter. "The Theme: The Gospel and the Gospels." Pages 1–25 in *The Gospel and the Gospels*. Edited by Peter Stuhlmacher. Grand Rapids: Eerdmans, 1991.

Sturch, "Parables"    Sturch, Richard L. "Jeremias and John: Parables in the Fourth Gospel." *ExpTim* 89 (1977–1978): 235–38.

Styler, "*Argumentum*"    Styler, G. M. "*Argumentum e silentio*." Pages 101–7 in *Jesus and the Politics of His Day*. Edited by Ernst Bammel and C. F. D. Moule. Cambridge: Cambridge University Press, 1984.

Stylianopoulis, *Justin*    Stylianopoulis, Theodore. *Justin Martyr and the Mosaic Law*. SBLDS 20. Missoula, Mont.: Scholars Press, 1975.

Suggit, "Gardener"    Suggit, J. N. "Jesus the Gardener: The Atonement in the Fourth Gospel as Re-creation." *Neotestamentica* 33, no. 1 (1999): 161–68.

Suggit, "LOGOS"    Suggit, J. "John XVII.17: HO LOGOS HO SOS ALĒTHEIA ESTIN." *JTS* NS 35 (1984): 104–17.

Suggit, "Man"    Suggit, John. "John 19:5: 'Behold the Man.'" *ExpTim* 94 (1982–1983): 333–34.

Suggit, "Nicodemus"    Suggit, J. N. "Nicodemus—the True Jew." *Neotestamentica* 14 (1981): 90–110.

Summers, "Water and Spirit"    Summers, Ray. "Born of Water and Spirit." Pages 117–28 in *The Teacher's Yoke: Studies in Memory of Henry Trantham*. Edited by E. Jerry Vardaman. Waco, Tex.: Baylor University Press, 1964.

Sussman, "Sons"    Sussman, L. A. "Sons and Fathers in the *Major Declamations* Ascribed to Quintilian." *Rhetorica* 13, no. 2 (1995): 179–92.

Sutcliffe, "Baptism"    Sutcliffe, Edmund Felix. "Baptism and Baptismal Rites at Qumran?" *Heythrop Journal* 1 (1960): 179–88.

Sutcliffe, "Review"    Sutcliffe, Edmund Felix. Review of H. Mantel, *Studies in the History of the Sanhedrin*. *Heythrop Journal* 4 (1963): 283–87.

Svensson, "Qumrankalendern"    Svensson, Jan. "Johannespåsken och Qumrankalendern." *Svensk exegetisk årsbok* 62 (1997): 87–110.

Swancutt, "Bread from Heaven"    Swancutt, Diana M. "Hungers Assuaged by the Bread from Heaven: 'Eating Jesus' as Isaian Call to Belief—the Confluence of Isaiah 55 and Psalm 78 (77) in John 6.22–71." Pages 218–51 in *Early Christian Interpretation of the Scriptures of Israel: Investigations and Proposals*. Edited by Craig A. Evans and James A. Sanders. JSNTSup 148. Sheffield: Sheffield Academic Press, 1997.

Swartz, "Ritual"    Swartz, Michael D. "'Like the Ministering Angels': Ritual and Purity in Early Jewish Mysticism and Magic." *AJSR* 19 (1994): 135–67.

Swete, *Discourse*    Swete, Henry Barclay. *The Last Discourse and Prayer of our Lord: A Study of St. John XIV.-XVII.* London: Macmillan, 1913.

Swetnam, "Bestowal"    Swetnam, James. "Bestowal of the Spirit in the Fourth Gospel." *Biblica* 74 (1993): 556–76.

Swetnam, *Isaac*    Swetnam, James. *Jesus and Isaac: A Study in the Epistle to the Hebrews in the Light of the Aqedah*. Analecta biblica 94. Rome: Pontifical Biblical Institute, 1981.

Sylvia Mary, *Mysticism*    Sylvia Mary, Sister. *Pauline and Johannine Mysticism*. London: Darton, Longman & Todd, 1964.

Synan, *Tradition*    Synan, Vinson. *The Holiness-Pentecostal Tradition: Charismatic Movements in the Twentieth Century*. Grand Rapids: Eerdmans, 1997.

Syon, "Gamla"    Syon, Danny. "Gamla: Portrait of a Rebellion." *BAR* 18, no. 1 (January/February 1992): 20–37, 72.

Tabor, "Divinity"    Tabor, James D. "'Returning to the Divinity': Josephus's Portrayal of the Disappearances of Enoch, Elijah, and Moses." *JBL* 108 (1989): 225–38.

Tabor, "Messiah"    Tabor, James D. "A Pierced or Piercing Messiah?—The Verdict Is Still Out." *BAR* 18, no. 6 (November/December 1992): 58–59.

Tabor, "Sons"    Tabor, J. "Paul's Notion of Many 'Sons of God' and Its Hellenistic Contexts." *Helios* 13 (1986): 87–97.

Talbert, "Acts"  Talbert, Charles H. "The Acts of the Apostles: Monograph or *Bios*?" Pages 58–72 in *History, Literature, and Society in the Book of Acts*. Edited by Ben Witherington, III. Cambridge: Cambridge University Press, 1996.

Talbert, *Apocalypse*  Talbert, Charles H. *The Apocalypse: A Reading of the Revelation of John*. Louisville, Ky.: Westminster John Knox, 1994.

Talbert, "Chance"  Talbert, Charles H. "Reading Chance, Moessner, and Parsons." Pages 229–40 in *Cadbury, Knox, and Talbert: American Contributions to the Study of Acts*. Edited by Mikeal C. Parsons and Joseph B. Tyson. Atlanta: Scholars Press, 1992.

Talbert, *Gospel*  Talbert, Charles H. *What Is a Gospel? The Genre of the Canonical Gospels*. Philadelphia: Fortress, 1977.

Talbert, "Immortals"  Talbert, Charles H. "The Concept of Immortals in Mediterranean Antiquity." *JBL* 94 (1975): 419–36.

Talbert, *John*  Talbert, Charles H. *Reading John: A Literary and Theological Commentary on the Fourth Gospel and the Johannine Epistles*. New York: Crossroad, 1992.

Talbert, *Luke*  Talbert, Charles H. *Reading Luke: A Literary and Theological Commentary on the Third Gospel*. New York: Crossroad, 1982.

Talbert, "Myth"  Talbert, Charles H. "The Myth of a Descending-Ascending Redeemer in Mediterranean Antiquity." *NTS* 22 (1975–1976): 418–40.

Talbert, *Patterns*  Talbert, Charles H. *Literary Patterns, Theological Themes, and the Genre of Luke–Acts*. SBLMS 20. Missoula, Mont.: Scholars Press, 1974.

Talbert, "Problem"  Talbert, Charles H. "The Problem of Pre-existence in Philippians 2 6–11." *JBL* 86 (1967): 141–53.

Talbert, "Review"  Talbert, Charles H. Review of Richard A. Burridge, *What Are the Gospels? JBL* 112 (1993): 714–15.

Talbert, "Worship"  Talbert, Charles H. "Worship in the Fourth Gospel and in Its Milieu." Pages 337–56 in *Perspectives on John: Method and Interpretation in the Fourth Gospel*. National Association of the Baptist Professors of Religion Special Studies Series 11. Edited by Robert B. Sloan and Mikeal C. Parsons. Lewiston, N.Y.: Mellen, 1993.

Talmon, "Prayer"  Talmon, Shemaryahu. "The Emergence of Institutionalized Prayer in Israel in the Light of the Qumran Literature." Pages 265–84 in *Qumrân: Sa piété, sa théologie, et son milieu*. Edited by M. Delcor. BETL 46. Paris: Gembloux, Leuven University Press, 1978.

Tannehill, *Acts*  Tannehill, Robert C. *The Acts of the Apostles*. Vol. 2 of *The Narrative Unity of Luke–Acts: A Literary Interpretation*. 2 vols. Minneapolis: Fortress, 1990.

Tannehill, *Luke*  Tannehill, Robert C. *The Gospel according to Luke*. Vol. 1 of *The Narrative Unity of Luke-Acts: A Literary Interpretation*. 2 vols. Philadelphia: Fortress, 1986.

Tannehill, *Sword*  Tannehill, Robert C. *The Sword of His Mouth*. Society of Biblical Literature Semeia Supplements 1. Missoula, Mont.: Scholars Press, 1975.

Tannenbaum, "God-Fearers"  Tannenbaum, Robert F. "Jews and God-Fearers in the Holy City of Aphrodite." *BAR* 12, no. 5 (September/October 1986): 54–57.

Tarn, *Civilisation*  Tarn, W. W. *Hellenistic Civilisation*. Revised by W. W. Tarn and G. T. Griffith. 3d. ed. New York: New American Library, 1974.

Tasker, *John*  Tasker, R. V. G. *The Gospel according to St. John*. Grand Rapids: Eerdmans, 1972.

Taylor, "Artemis"  Taylor, Lily Ross. "Artemis of Ephesus." Pages 251–56 in vol. 5 of *The Beginnings of Christianity*.

Taylor, *Atonement*  Taylor, Vincent. *The Atonement in New Testament Teaching*. London: Epworth, 1945.

Taylor, "Baptism"  Taylor, T. M. "The Beginnings of Jewish Proselyte Baptism." *NTS* 2 (1955–1956): 193–98.

Taylor, "Capernaum"  Taylor, Joan E. "Capernaum and Its 'Jewish-Christians': A Re-examination of the Franciscan Excavations." *Bulletin of the Anglo-Israel Archaeological Society* 9 (1989–90): 7–28.

Taylor, "Cave"  Taylor, Joan E. "The Bethany Cave: A Jewish-Christian Cult Site?" *RB* 97 (1990): 453–65.

Taylor, *Formation*  Taylor, Vincent. *The Formation of the Gospel Tradition*. 2d ed. London: Macmillan, 1935.

Taylor, *Immerser*  Taylor, Joan E. *The Immerser: John the Baptist within Second Temple Judaism.* Grand Rapids: Eerdmans, 1997.

Taylor, "Mandaeans"  Taylor, Vincent. "The Mandaeans and the Fourth Gospel." *Hibbert Journal* 28 (1929–30): 531–46.

Taylor, *Mark*  Taylor, Vincent. *The Gospel according to St. Mark.* London: Macmillan, 1952.

Taylor, *Mysteries*  Taylor, Thomas. *The Eleusinian and Bacchic Mysteries: A Dissertation.* 4th ed. Edited by Alexander Wilder. New York: J. W. Bouton, 1891.

Taylor, *Politics*  Taylor, Lily Ross. *Party Politics in the Age of Caesar.* Berkeley: University of California Press, 1966.

Tcherikover, *Civilization*  Tcherikover, Victor. *Hellenistic Civilization and the Jews.* Translated by S. Applebaum. Philadelphia: Magnes Press, Hebrew University, 1961.

Tcherikover, "Ideology"  Tcherikover, Victor. "The Ideology of the Letter of Aristeas." *HTR* 51 (1958): 59–85.

Tchernia, André. "Italian Wine in Gaul at the end of the Republic." Pages 87–104 in *Trade in the Ancient Economy.* Edited by Peter Garnsey, Keith Hopkins, and C. R. Whittaker. Berkeley: University of California Press, 1983.

Teeple, *Origin*  Teeple, Howard M. *The Literary Origin of the Gospel of John.* Evanston, Ill.: Religion and Ethics Institute, 1974.

Teeple, *Prophet*  Teeple, Howard M. *The Mosaic Eschatological Prophet.* SBLMS 10. Philadelphia: Society of Biblical Literature, 1957.

Teeple, "Qumran"  Teeple, Howard M. "Qumran and the Origin of the Fourth Gospel." *NovT* 4 (1960): 6–25.

Temple, *Core*  Temple, Sydney. *The Core of the Fourth Gospel.* London: Mowbray, 1975.

Tenney, "Footnotes"  Tenney, Merrill C. "The Footnotes of John's Gospel." *Bibliotheca sacra* 117 (1960): 350–64.

Tenney, *John*  Tenney, Merrill C. *John—the Gospel of Belief: An Analytical Study of the Text.* Grand Rapids: Eerdmans, 1948.

Tenney, "Keys"  Tenney, Merrill C. "Literary Keys to the Fourth Gospel, III: The Old Testament and the Fourth Gospel." *BSac* 120 (1963): 300–8.

Tenney, "Parallels"  Tenney, Merrill C. "Some Possible Parallels between 1 Peter and 1 John." Pages 370–77 in *New Dimensions in New Testament Study.* Edited by Richard N. Longenecker and Merrill C. Tenney. Grand Rapids: Zondervan, 1974.

Tenney, *Revelation*  Tenney, Merrill C. *Interpreting Revelation.* Grand Rapids: Eerdmans, 1957.

Thackeray, *Josephus*  Thackeray, H. St. John. *Josephus: The Man and the Historian.* Preface by George Foot Moore. Introduction by Samuel Sandmel. 1929. Repr., New York: Ktav, 1967.

Thapar, *India*  Thapar, Romila. *A History of India.* Baltimore: Penguin, 1966.

Thatcher, "Asides"  Thatcher, T. "A New Look at Asides in the Fourth Gospel." *BSac* 151 (1994): 428–39.

Thatcher, "Pilate"  Thatcher, T. "Philo on Pilate: Rhetoric or Reality?" *Restoration Quarterly* 37 (1995): 215–18.

Thatcher, "Riddles in Gospel"  Thatcher, Thomas. "The Riddles of Jesus in the Fourth Gospel." Ph.D. diss., Southern Baptist Theological Seminary, 1996.

Thatcher, *Riddles in John*  Thatcher, Thomas. *The Riddles of Jesus in John: A Study in Tradition and Folklore.* SBLMS 53. Atlanta: Society of Biblical Literature, 2000.

Thatcher, "Sabbath Trick"  Thatcher, Thomas. "The Sabbath Trick: Unstable Irony in the Fourth Gospel." *JSNT* 76 (1999): 53–77.

Theissen, *Gospels*  Theissen, Gerd. *The Gospels in Context: Social and Political History in the Synoptic Tradition.* Translated by Linda M. Maloney. Minneapolis: Fortress, 1991.

Theissen, *Setting*  Theissen, Gerd. *The Social Setting of Pauline Christianity.* Edited and translated by John H. Schütz. Philadelphia: Fortress, 1982.

Theissen, *Sociology*  Theissen, Gerd. *Sociology of Early Palestinian Christianity.* Translated by John Bowden. Philadelphia: Fortress, 1978.

Theissen, *Stories*  Theissen, Gerd. *The Miracle Stories of the Early Christian Tradition.* Translated by Francis McDonagh. Edited by John Riches. Philadelphia: Fortress, 1983.

Therese Mary, "Shepherd"  Therese Mary. "The Good Shepherd." *The Bible Today* 38 (November 1968): 2657–64.

Thielman, "Style of Fourth Gospel"   Thielman, Frank. "The Style of the Fourth Gospel and Ancient Literary Critical Concepts of Religious Discourse." Pages 169–83 in *Persuasive Artistry: Studies in New Testament Rhetoric in Honor of George A. Kennedy.* Edited by Duane F. Watson. JSNTSup 50. Sheffield: Sheffield Academic Press, 1991.

Thiering, "Cleansing"   Thiering, Barbara E. "Inner and Outer Cleansing at Qumran as a Background to New Testament Baptism." *NTS* 26 (1979–1980): 266–77.

Thiering, *Hypothesis*   Thiering, Barbara E. *The Gospels and Qumran: A New Hypothesis.* Australian and New Zealand Studies in Theology and Religion. Sydney: Theological Explorations, 1981.

Thiering, "Initiation"   Thiering, Barbara E. "Qumran Initiation and New Testament Baptism." *NTS* 27 (1980–1981): 615–31.

Thiessen, "Women"   Thiessen, K. H. "Jesus and Women in the Gospel of John." *Direction* 19, no. 2 (1990): 52–64.

Thiselton, *Horizons*   Thiselton, Anthony C. *The Two Horizons: New Testament Hermeneutics and Philosophical Description.* Grand Rapids: Eerdmans, 1980.

Thiselton, "Semantics"   Thiselton, Anthony C. "Semantics and New Testament Interpretation." Pages 75–104 in *New Testament Interpretation: Essays on Principles and Methods.* Edited by I. Howard Marshall. Grand Rapids: Eerdmans, 1977.

Tholuck, *John*   Tholuck, A. *A Commentary on the Gospel of St. John.* Boston: Perkins & Marvin, 1836.

Thom, "*Akousmata*"   Thom, Johan C. "'Don't Walk on the Highways': The Pythagorean *akousmata* and Early Christian Literature." *JBL* 113 (1994): 93–112.

Thom, "Equality"   Thom, Johan C. "'Harmonious Equality': The *topos* of Friendship in Neopythagorean Writings." Pages 77–103 in *Greco-Roman Perspectives on Friendship.* Edited by John T. Fitzgerald. SBLRBS 34. Atlanta: Scholars Press, 1997.

Thom, "Joodse"   Thom, J. D. "Jesus se verhoor voor die Joodse Raad volgens Joh 18:19–24 [The Trial of Jesus by the Jewish Council according to John 18:19–24]." *Nederduits gereformeerde teologiese tydskrif* 25 (1984): 172–78.

Thoma, "Auswirkungen"   Thoma, Clemens. "Auswirkungen des jüdischen Krieges gegen Rom (66–70/73 n. Chr.) auf das rabbinische Judentum." *BZ* 12 (1968): 39–54, 186–210.

Thoma, "Priesthood"   Thoma, Clemens. "The High Priesthood in the Judgment of Josephus." Pages 196–215 in *Josephus, the Bible, and History.* Edited by Louis H. Feldman and Gohei Hata. Detroit: Wayne State University Press, 1989.

Thoma, "Reaktionen"   Thoma, Clemens. "Rabbinische Reaktionen gegen die Gnosis." *Judaica* 44, no. 1 (1988): 2–14.

Thomas, *Footwashing*   Thomas, John Christopher. *Footwashing in John 13 and the Johannine Community.* JSNTSup 61. Sheffield: Sheffield Academic Press, 1991.

Thomas, "Gospel"   Thomas, John Christopher. "The Fourth Gospel and Rabbinic Judaism." *ZNW* 82 (1991): 159–82.

Thomas, "Menteur"   Thomas, J. "'Menteur et homicide depuis l'origine': Lecture de Jean, 8,44." *Christus* 27 (1980): 225–35.

Thompson, *Advice*   Thompson, William G. *Matthew's Advice to a Divided Community: Mt. 17,22–18,35.* Analecta biblica 44. Rome: Biblical Institute Press, 1970.

Thompson, *Archaeology*   Thompson, J. A. *The Bible and Archaeology.* Grand Rapids: Eerdmans, 1962.

Thompson, *Clothed*   Thompson, Michael. *Clothed with Christ: The Example and Teaching of Jesus in Romans 12.1–15.13.* JSNTSup 59. Sheffield: Sheffield Academic Press, 1991.

Thompson, *Debate*   Thompson, William M. *The Jesus Debate: A Survey and Synthesis.* New York: Paulist Press, 1985.

Thompson, "Historical Jesus"   Thompson, Marianne Meye. "The Historical Jesus and the Johannine Christ." Pages 21–42 in *Exploring the Gospel of John: In Honor of D. Moody Smith.* Edited by R. Alan Culpepper and C. Clifton Black. Louisville, Ky.: Westminster John Knox, 1996.

Thompson, *Humanity*   Thompson, Marianne Meye. *The Humanity of Jesus in the Fourth Gospel.* Philadelphia: Fortress, 1988.

Thompson, "Internet"   Thompson, Michael B. "The Holy Internet: Communication between Churches in the First Christian Generation." Pages 49–70 in *The Gospels for All Christians: Rethinking the Gospel Audiences.* Edited by Richard Bauckham. Grand Rapids: Eerdmans, 1998.

Thompson, "Son of Man"    Thompson, George H. P. "The Son of Man: The Evidence of the Dead Sea Scrolls." *ExpTim* 72 (1960–1961): 125.

Thompson, *Syntax*    Thompson, Steven. *The Apocalypse and Semitic Syntax.* SNTSMS 52. Cambridge: Cambridge University Press, 1985.

Thompson, Wenger, and Bartling, "Recall"    Thompson, C. P., S. K. Wenger, and C. A. Bartling. "How Recall Facilitates Subsequent Recall: A Reappraisal." *Journal of Experimental Psychology: Human Learning and Memory* 4 (1978): 210–21.

Thornton, "Calendar"    Thornton, T. C. G. "The Samaritan Calendar: A Source of Friction in New Testament Times." *JTS* NS 42 (1991): 577–80.

Thrall, "Super-apostles"    Thrall, Margaret E. "Super-apostles, Servants of Christ, and Servants of Satan." *JSNT* 6 (1980): 42–57.

Thurn, "Gärtner"    Thurn, Hans Peter. "Gärtner und Totengraber: Zur Paradigmatik der Kultursoziologie." *Kölner Zeitschrift für Soziologie und Sozialpsychologie* 37, no. 1 (March 1985): 60–74.

Thyen, "Entwicklungen"    Thyen, H. "Entwicklungen innerhalb der johanneischen Theologie und Kirche im Spiegel von Joh 21 und der Lieblingsjüngertexte des Evangeliums." Pages 259–99 in *L'évangile de Jean: Sources, rédaction, théologie.* Edited by Marinus De Jonge. BETL 45. Gembloux: J. Duculot; Leuven: Leuven University Press, 1977.

Tiede, *Figure*    Tiede, David Lenz. *The Charismatic Figure as Miracle Worker.* SBLDS 1. Missoula, Mont.: Society of Biblical Literature, 1972.

Tilborg, *Ephesus*    Tilborg, Sjef van. *Reading John in Ephesus.* NovTSup 83. Leiden: Brill, 1996.

Tilborg, *Leaders*    Tilborg, Sjef van. *The Jewish Leaders in Matthew.* Leiden: Brill, 1972.

Tilborg, *Love*    Tilborg, Sjef van. *Imaginative Love in John.* Biblical Interpretation Series 2. Leiden: Brill, 1993.

Tinh, "Sarapis"    Tinh, Tram Tam. "Sarapis and Isis." Pages 101–17 in vol. 3 of Meyer and Sanders, *Self-Definition.*

Titus, *Message*    Titus, Eric Lane. *The Message of the Fourth Gospel.* New York: Abingdon, 1957.

Tiwald, "Jünger"    Tiwald, M. "Der Jünger, der bleibt bis zum kommen des Herrn: Eine textpragmatische Verortung der 'Johannesichen Schule.'" *Protokolle zur Bibel* 10, no. 1 (2002): 1–32.

Tobin, "Speculation"    Tobin, Thomas H. "The Prologue of John and Hellenistic Jewish Speculation." *CBQ* 52 (1990): 252–69.

Todd, "Introduction to *Symposium*"    Todd, O. J. Introduction. Pages 376–79 in Xenophon, *Symposium.* Translated by O. J. Todd. LCL. Cambridge: Harvard University Press, 1922.

Tödt, *Son of Man*    Tödt, H. E. *The Son of Man in the Synoptic Tradition.* Philadelphia: Westminster, 1965.

Tolmie, *Farewell*    Tolmie, D. F. *Jesus' Farewell to the Disciples: John 13:1–17:26 in Narratological Perspective.* Biblical Interpretation Series 12. Leiden: Brill, 1995.

Tomson, "Israel"    Tomson, Peter J. "The Names Israel and Jew in Ancient Judaism and in the New Testament, I." *Bijdragen* 47 (1986): 120–40.

Tomson, "Jews"    Tomson, Peter J. "'Jews' in the Gospel of John as Compared with the Palestinian Talmud, the Synoptics, and Some New Testament Apocrypha." Pages 301–40 in *Anti-Judaism and the Fourth Gospel: Papers of the Leuven Colloquium, 2000.* Edited by R. Bieringer, D. Pollefeyt, and F. Vandecasteele-Vanneuville. Assen: Royal Van Gorcum, 2001.

Tooley, "Shepherd"    Tooley, Wilfred. "The Shepherd and Sheep Image in the Teaching of Jesus." *NovT* 7 (1964): 15–25.

Toon, *Doctrine*    Toon, Peter. *The Development of Doctrine in the Church.* Grand Rapids: Eerdmans, 1979.

Torrance, "Baptism"    Torrance, T. F. "Proselyte Baptism." *NTS* 1 (1954–1955): 150–54.

Torrance, "Origins"    Torrance, T. F. "The Origins of Baptism." *SJT* 11 (1958): 158–71.

Torrey, *Composition*    Torrey, Charles C. *The Composition and Date of Acts.* Harvard Theological Studies 1. Cambridge: Harvard University Press, 1916. Repr., New York: Kraus Reprint Company, 1969.

Torrey, "Messiah"    Torrey, Charles C. "The Messiah Son of Ephraim." *JBL* 66 (1947): 253–77.

Torrey, "Origin"    Torrey, Charles C. "The Aramaic Origin of the Gospel of John." *HTR* 16 (1923): 305–34.

Toussaint, "Significance"    Toussaint, Stanley D. "The Significance of the First Sign in John's Gospel." *BSac* 134 (1977): 45–51.

Townsend, "Education"    Townsend, John T. "Ancient Education in the Time of the Early Roman Empire." Pages 139–63 in *The Catacombs and the Colosseum: The Roman Empire as the Setting of Primitive Christianity*. Edited by Stephen Benko and John J. O'Rourke. Valley Forge, Pa.: Judson, 1971.

Townsend, "Jews"    Townsend, John T. "The Gospel of John and the Jews: The Story of a Religious Divorce." Pages 72–97 in *Antisemitism and the Foundations of Christianity*. Edited by Alan T. Davies. New York: Paulist Press, 1979.

Townsend, "Speeches"    Townsend, John T. "The Speeches in Acts." *Anglican Theological Review* 42 (1960): 150–59.

Toynbee, *Thought*    Toynbee, Arnold J. *Greek Historical Thought*. New York: New American Library, 1952.

Trapp, *Maximus*    Trapp, M. B., trans. and commentator. *The Philosophical Orations* by Maximus of Tyre. Oxford: Clarendon Press, 1997.

Travis, "Criticism"    Travis, Stephen H. "Form Criticism." Pages 153–64 in *New Testament Interpretation: Essays on Principles and Methods*. Edited by I. Howard Marshall. Grand Rapids: Eerdmans, 1977.

Trebilco, "Asia"    Trebilco, Paul. "Asia." Pages 291–362 in *The Book of Acts in Its Graeco-Roman Setting*. Edited by David W. J. Gill and Conrad Gempf. Vol. 2 of *The Book of Acts in Its First Century Setting*. Edited by Bruce W. Winter. Grand Rapids: Eerdmans, 1994.

Trebilco, *Communities*    Trebilco, Paul R. *Jewish Communities in Asia Minor*. SNTSMS 69. Cambridge: Cambridge University Press, 1991.

Trebolle Barrera, "Substrato"    Trebolle Barrera, Julio. "Posible substrato semitico del uso transitivo o intransitivo del verbo ἐκάθισεν en Jn 19,13." *Filología neotestamentaria* 4, no. 7 (1991): 51–54.

Treggiari, "Jobs"    Treggiari, Susan. "Jobs in the Household of Livia." *Papers of the British School at Rome* 43 (1975): 48–77.

Treves, "War"    Treves, Marco. "The Date of the War of the Sons of Light." *VT* 8 (1958): 419–24.

Tribble, "Work"    Tribble, H. W. "The Convicting Work of the Holy Spirit, John 16:7–11." *Review and Expositor* 32 (1935): 269–80.

Trifon, "Mšmrwt"    Trifon, Dalia. "Hʾm ʿbrw mšmrwt hkwhnym myhwdh lglyl ʾḥry mrd brkwkbʾ? [Did the Priestly Courses (Mishmarot) Transfer from Judaea to Galilee after the Bar Kokhba Revolt?]." *Tarbiz* 59 (1989–90): 77–93.

Trites, "Adultery"    Trites, Allison A. "The Woman Taken in Adultery." *BSac* 131 (1974): 137–46.

Trites, *Witness*    Trites, Allison A. *The New Testament Concept of Witness*. SNTSMS 31. Cambridge: Cambridge University Press, 1977.

Trocmé, *Formation*    Trocmé, Etienne. *The Formation of the Gospel according to Mark*. Translated by Pamela Gaughan. Philadelphia: Westminster, 1975.

Troster, "Quest"    Troster, Lawrence. "Journey to the Center of the Earth: *Birkat Ha-Mazon* and the Quest for Holiness." *Conservative Judaism* 47, no. 2 (winter 1995): 3–16.

Trudinger, "Fishes"    Trudinger, Paul. "The 153 Fishes: A Response and a Further Suggestion." *ExpTim* 102 (1990–1991): 11–12.

Trudinger, "Ironies"    Trudinger, Paul. "Subtle Ironies and Word-plays in John's Gospel and the Problems of Chapter 21." *St Mark's Review* 162 (1995): 20–24.

Trudinger, "Israelite"    Trudinger, L. Paul. "An Israelite in Whom There Is No Guile: An Interpretive Note on John 1:45–51." *EvQ* 54 (1982): 117–20.

Trudinger, "John 3:16"    Trudinger, Paul. "Jesus' 'Comfortable Words' in John 3:16: A Note of Disappointment to Some?" *St Mark's Review* 147 (1991): 30–31.

Trudinger, "John 21"    Trudinger, Paul. "John 21 Revisited Once Again." *DRev* 106 (1988): 145–48.

Trudinger, "Non-deity"    Trudinger, Paul. "John's Gospel as Testimony to the Non-deity of Jesus." *Faith and Freedom* 48 (1995): 106–110.

Trudinger, "Prologue"    Trudinger, L. Paul. "The Prologue of John's Gospel: Its Extent, Content and Intent." *Reformed Theological Review* 33 (1974): 11–17.

Trudinger, "Prophet"    Trudinger, Paul. "A Prophet Like Me (Deut. 18:15): Jesus and Moses in St. John's Gospel, Once Again." *DRev* 113 (1995): 193–95.

Trudinger, "Text"    Trudinger, L. Paul. "Some Observations Concerning the Text of the Old Testament in the Book of Revelation." *JTS* NS 17 (1966): 82–88.

Trudinger, "Women"   Trudinger, Paul. "Of Women, Weddings, Wells, Waterpots, and Wine! Reflections on Johannine Themes (John 2:1–11 and 4:1–42)." *St Mark's Review* 151 (1992): 10–16.

Tsuchido, "Anti-Semitism"   Tsuchido, K. "Is There Anti-Semitism in the Fourth Gospel? An Exegetical Study of John 11:45–54." *Annual of the Japanese Biblical Institute* 21 (1995): 57–72.

Tuckett, *History*   Tuckett, Christopher M. *Q and the History of Early Christianity: Studies on Q*. Peabody, Mass.: Hendrickson, 1996.

Tuckett, "Logia"   Tuckett, Christopher M. "Les logia et le judaïsme." *Foi et vie* 92, no. 5 (1993): 67–88.

Tuckett, "Q"   Tuckett, Christopher M. "A Cynic Q?" *Biblica* 70 (1989): 349–76.

Tuñi, "Teología"   Tuñi, J. O. "Teología judía y cristología joánica." *Revista latinoamericana de teología* 15, no. 44 (1998): 139–61.

Turner, "Atonement"   Turner, Max. "Atonement and the Death of Jesus in John—Some Questions to Bultmann and Forestell." *EvQ* 62 (1990): 99–122.

Turner, "Punctuation"   Turner, C. H. "On the Punctuation of St. John VII 37,38." *JTS* 24, no. 93 (October 1923): 66–70.

Turner, *Spirit*   Turner, Max. *The Holy Spirit and Spiritual Gifts in the New Testament Church and Today*. Rev. ed. Peabody, Mass.: Hendrickson, 1998.

Turner, "Spirit"   Turner, M. M. B. "The Concept of Receiving the Spirit in John's Gospel." *Vox evangelica* 10 (1976): 24–42.

Turner, "Thoughts"   Turner, Nigel. "Second Thoughts, VII: Papyrus Finds." *The Expository Times* 76 (1964): 44–48.

Twelftree, "ΕΚΒΑΛΛΩ"   Twelftree, Graham H. "'ΕΙ ΔΕ . . . ΕΓΩ ΕΚΒΑΛΛΩ ΤΑ ΔΑΙΜΟΝΙΑ . . .'" Pages 361–400 in *The Miracles of Jesus*. Edited by David Wenham and Craig Blomberg. Vol. 6 of *Gospel Perspectives*. Edited by R. T. France and David Wenham. Sheffield: JSOT Press, 1986.

Twelftree, *Exorcist*   Twelftree, Graham H. *Jesus the Exorcist: A Contribution to the Study of the Historical Jesus*. Peabody, Mass.: Hendrickson, 1993.

Twelftree, *Miracle Worker*   Twelftree, Graham H. *Jesus the Miracle Worker: A Historical and Theological Study*. Downers Grove, Ill.: InterVarsity, 1999.

Tyson, *Approaches*   Tyson, Joseph B. *Luke, Judaism, and the Scholars: Critical Approaches to Luke-Acts*. Columbia, S.C.: University of South Carolina, 1999.

Tzaferis, "Crucifixion"   Tzaferis, Vassilios. "Crucifixion—the Archaeological Evidence." *BAR* 11, no. 1 (January/February 1985): 44–53.

Tzaferis, "Tombs"   Tzaferis, Vassilios. "Jewish Tombs at and near Giv'at ha-mivtar." *IEJ* 20 (1970): 18–32.

Ukachukwu Manus, "Woman"   Ukachukwu Manus, C. "The Samaritan Woman (Jn 4:7ff): Reflections on Female Leadership and Nation Building in Modern Africa." *African Christian Studies* 4, no. 4 (1988): 73–84.

Ulrichsen, "Troen"   Ulrichsen, Jarl H. "Troen på et liv etter døden i Qumrantekstene [Belief in a Life after Death in the Qumran Texts]." *Norsk Teologisk Tidsskrift* 78 (1977): 151–63.

Umoh, *Plot to Kill Jesus*   Umoh, Camillus. *The Plot of Kill Jesus: A Contextual Study of John 11.47–53*. European University Studies, Series 23: Theology, 696. Frankfurt: Lang, 2000.

Urbach, *Sages*   Urbach, Ephraim E. *The Sages: Their Concepts and Beliefs*. Translated by Israel Abrahams. 2 vols. 2d ed. Jerusalem: Magnes Press, Hebrew University, 1979.

Urbach, "Self-Isolation"   Urbach, Ephraim E. "Self-Isolation or Self-Affirmation in Judaism in the First Three Centuries: Theory and Practice." Pages 269–98 in vol. 2 of Meyer and Sanders, *Self-Definition*.

Urban and Henry, "Abraham"   Urban, Linwood, and Patrick Henry. "'Before Abraham Was I Am': Does Philo Explain John 8:56–58?" *Studia philonica* 6 (1979–1980): 157–95.

Urman, "House"   Urman, Dan. "The House of the Assembly and the House of Study: Are They One and the Same?" *JJS* 44 (1993): 236–57.

Usher, "Introduction to *Dinarchus*"   Usher, Stephen. "Introduction to *Dinarchus*." Pages 246–49 in vol. 2 of Dionysius of Halicarnassus, *Critical Essays*. Translated by Stephen Usher. 2 vols. LCL. Cambridge: Harvard University Press, 1974.

Uval, "Streams"   Uval, Beth. "Streams of Living Water: The Feast of Tabernacles and the Holy Spirit." *Jerusalem Perspective* 49 (1995): 22–23, 37.

Vaage, "Barking"   Vaage, Leif E. "Like Dogs Barking: Cynic *parrēsia* and Shameless Asceticism." *Semeia* 57 (1992): 25–39.

Vale, "Sources"    Vale, Ruth. "Literary Sources in Archaeological Description: The Case of Galilee, Galilees, and Galileans." *JSJ* 18 (1987): 209–26.

Van Belle, "Faith"    Van Belle, Gilbert. "The Faith of the Galileans: The Parenthesis in Jn 4:44." *Ephemerides theologicae lovanienses* 74 (1998): 27–44.

Van Belle, "Salvation Is from Jews"    Van Belle, Gilbert. "'Salvation Is from the Jews': The Parenthesis in John 4:22b." Pages 370–400 in *Anti-Judaism and the Fourth Gospel: Papers of the Leuven Colloquium, 2000.* Edited by R. Bieringer, D. Pollefeyt, and F. Vandecasteele-Vanneuville. Assen: Royal Van Gorcum, 2001.

Van Belle, *Signs Source*    Van Belle, Gilbert. *The Signs Source in the Fourth Gospel: Historical Survey and Critical Evaluation of the Semeia Hypothesis.* Leuven: Louvain University Press and Peeters, 1994.

Van de Bunt-van den Hoek, "Aristobulos"    Van de Bunt-van den Hoek, Annewies. "Aristobulos, Acts, Theophilus, Clement: Making use of Aratus' Phainomena—a Peregrination." *Bijdragen* 41 (1980): 290–99.

Van den Heever, "Socio-rhetorical Reading"    Van den Heever, Gerhard. "Finding Data in Unexpected Places (or: From Text Linguistics to Socio-rhetoric): Towards a Socio-rhetorical Reading of John's Gospel." *Neotestamentica* 33, no. 2 (1999): 343–64.

Vander Broek, "Sitz"    Vander Broek, Lyle D. "The Markan Sitz im Leben: A Critical Investigation." Ph.D. diss., Drew University, 1983. Ann Arbor, Mich.: University Microfilms International, 1983.

Van der Horst, "Acts"    Van der Horst, Pieter W. "Hellenistic Parallels to the Acts of the Apostles." *JSNT* 25 (1985): 49–60.

Van der Horst, "Aphrodisias"    Van der Horst, Pieter W. "Jews and Christians in Aphrodisias in the Light of Their Relations in Other Cities of Asia Minor." *Nederlands theologisch tijdschrift* 43 (1989): 106–21.

Van der Horst, "Beobachtungen"    Van der Horst, Pieter W. "Einige Beobachtungen zum Thema Frauen im antiken Judentum." *Berliner theologische Zeitschrift* 10 (1993): 77–93.

Van der Horst, "Birkath"    Van der Horst, Pieter W. "The Birkath Ha-minim in Recent Research." *ExpTim* 105 (1993–1994): 363–68.

Van der Horst, "Children"    Van der Horst, Pieter W. "Seven Months' Children in Jewish and Christian Literature from Antiquity." *Ephemerides theologicae lovanienses* 54 (1978): 346–60.

Van der Horst, "Cornutus"    Van der Horst, Pieter W. "Cornutus and the New Testament." *NovT* 23 (1981): 165–172.

Van der Horst, "Diaspora"    Van der Horst, Pieter W. "De Samaritaanse diaspora in de oudheid." *Nederlands theologisch tijdschrift* 42 (1988): 134–44.

Van der Horst, "Emission"    Van der Horst, Pieter W. "Sarah's Seminal Emission: Hebrews 11:11 in the Light of Ancient Embryology." Pages 287–302 in *Greeks, Romans, and Christians.* Ed. D. L. Balch et al. Minneapolis: Fortress. 1990.

Van der Horst, "Hierocles"    Van der Horst, Pieter W. "Hierocles the Stoic and the New Testament." *NovT* 17 (1975): 156–60.

Van der Horst, "Inscriptions"    Van der Horst, Pieter W. "Jewish Funerary Inscriptions: Most Are in Greek." *BAR* 18, no. 5 (September/October 1992): 46–57.

Van der Horst, "Macrobius"    Van der Horst, Pieter W. "Macrobius and the New Testament: A Contribution to the Corpus Hellenisticum." *NovT* 15 (1973): 220–32.

Van der Horst, "Maximus"    Van der Horst, Pieter W. "Maximus van Tyrus over het gebed: Een geannoteerde vertaling van Εἰ δεῖ εὐχεσθαι (Maximus of Tyre on Prayer)." *Nederlands theologisch tijdschrift* 49 (1995): 12–23.

Van der Horst, "Musonius"    Van der Horst, Pieter W. "Musonius Rufus and the New Testament." *NovT* 16 (1974): 306–15.

Van der Horst, "Prayer"    Van der Horst, Pieter W. "Silent Prayer in Antiquity." *Numen* 41 (1994): 1–25.

Van der Horst, "Samaritans"    Van der Horst, Pieter W. "Samaritans and Hellenism." *Studia philonica Annual* 6 (1994): 28–36.

Van der Horst, "Vision"    Van der Horst, Pieter W. "Moses' Throne Vision in Ezekiel the Dramatist." *JJS* 34 (1983): 21–29.

VanderKam, "Author"    VanderKam, James C. "The Putative Author of the Book of Jubilees." *Journal of Semitic Studies* 26 (1981): 209–17.

VanderKam, "Jubilees"   VanderKam, James C. "Jubilees—How It Rewrote the Bible." *Bible Review* 8, no. 6 (December 1992): 32–39, 60, 62.

VanderKam, "Pronouncement Stories"   VanderKam, James C. "Intertestamental Pronouncement Stories." *Semeia* 20 (1981): 65–72.

VanderKam, "Traditions"   VanderKam, James C. "Enoch Traditions in Jubilees and Other Second-Century Sources." Pages 229–51 in vol. 1 of *SBL Seminar Papers, 1978.* 2 vols. Society of Biblical Literature Seminar Papers 13. Missoula, Mont.: Scholars Press, 1978.

Vanderlip, "Similarities"   Vanderlip, Dodava George. "A Comparative Study of Certain Alleged Similarities between the Literature of Qumran and the Fourth Gospel." Ph.D. diss., University of Southern California, 1959.

Van der Waal, "Gospel"   Van der Waal, C. "The Gospel according to John and the Old Testament." *Neotestamentica* 6 (1972): 28–47.

Van der Watt and Voges, "Elemente"   Van der Watt, Jan G., and L. Voges. "Metaforiese elemente in die forensiese taalgebruik van die Johannesevangelie." *Skrif en kerk* 21, no. 2 (2000): 387–405.

Van Henton, "Prolegomena"   Van Henton, Jan Willen. "Einige Prolegomena zum Studien der jüdischen Martyrologie." *Bijdragen* 46 (1985): 381–90.

Vanhoye, "Interrogation"   Vanhoye, Albert. "Interrogation johannique et exégèse de Cana (Jn 2,4)." *Biblica* 55 (1974): 157–67.

Vanhoye, "Livre"   Vanhoye, Albert. "L'utilisation du livre d'Ézéchiel dans l'Apocalypse." *Biblica* 43 (1962): 436–76.

Van Minnen, "Punctuation"   Van Minnen, Peter. "The Punctuation of John 1:3–4." *Filología neotestamentaria* 7, no. 13 (1994): 33–41.

Vanni, "Giorno"   Vanni, U. "Il 'giorno del Signore' in Apoc. 1,10, giorno di purificazione e di discernimento." *RivB* 26 (1978): 187–99.

Van Unnik, "Apocalypse"   Van Unnik, W. C. "Μία γνωμή, Apocalypse of John xvii, 13, 17." Pages 209–20 in *Studies in John: Presented to Professor Dr. J. N. Sevenster on the Occasion of His Seventieth Birthday.* Edited by W. C. van Unnik. NovTSup 24. Leiden: Brill, 1970.

Van Unnik, "Works"   Van Unnik, W. C. "The Teaching of Good Works in I Peter." *NTS* 1 (1954–1955): 92–110.

Van Veldhuizen, "Moses"   Van Veldhuizen, Milo. "Moses: A Model of Hellenistic Philanthropia." *Reformed Review* 38 (1984–1985): 215–24.

Vardaman, "Bethesda"   Vardaman, E. Jerry. "The Pool of Bethesda." *Bible Translator* 14 (1963): 27–29.

Vasholz, "Anti-Semitic"   Vasholz, Robert I. "Is the NT Anti-Semitic?" *Presbyterion* 11 (1985): 118–23.

Vawter, "Ezekiel"   Vawter, Bruce. "Ezekiel and John." *CBQ* 26 (1964): 450–58.

Vellanickal, "Blood"   Vellanickal, Matthew. "Blood and Water." *Jeevadhara* 8 (1978): 218–30.

Vellanickal, *Sonship*   Vellanickal, Matthew. *The Divine Sonship of Christians in the Johannine Writings.* Analecta biblica 72. Rome: Biblical Institute Press, 1977.

Verman and Adler, "Path Jumping"   Verman, Mark, and S. H. Adler. "Path Jumping in the Jewish Magical Tradition." *Jewish Studies Quarterly* 1 (1993–94): 131–48.

Vermaseren, *Cybele*   Vermaseren, Maarten J. *Cybele and Attis: The Myth and the Cult.* Translated by A. H. H. Lemmers. London: Thames & Hudson, 1977.

Vermes, "Forum"   Vermes, Geza. "The Oxford Forum for Qumran Research: Seminar on the Rule of War from Cave 4 (4Q285)." *JJS* 43 (1992): 85–94.

Vermes, "Hanina"   Vermes, Geza. "Hanina ben Dosa: A Controversial Galilean Saint from the First Century of the Christian Era." *JJS* 23 (1972): 28–50; 24 (1973): 51–64.

Vermes, *Jesus and Judaism*   Vermes, Geza. *Jesus and the World of Judaism.* London: SCM, 1983.

Vermes, *Jesus the Jew*   Vermes, Geza. *Jesus the Jew: A Historian's Reading of the Gospels.* Philadelphia: Fortress, 1973.

Vermes, "Messiah Text"   Vermes, Geza. "The 'Pierced Messiah' Text—an Interpretation Evaporates." *BAR* 18, no. 4 (July/August 1992): 80–82.

Vermes, "Notice"   Vermes, Geza. "The Jesus Notice of Josephus Re-examined." *JJS* 38 (1987): 1–10.

Vermes, *Religion*   Vermes, Geza. *The Religion of Jesus the Jew.* Minneapolis: Augsburg Fortress, 1993.

Vermes, *Scrolls*   Vermes, Geza, ed. *The Dead Sea Scrolls in English.* 2d ed. New York: Penguin, 1981.

Vermes, "Worship"    Vermes, Geza. "Pre-mishnaic Jewish Worship and the Phylacteries from the Dead Sea." *VT* 9 (1959): 65–72.

Versteeg, *Adam*    Versteeg, J. P. *Is Adam a "Teaching Model" in the New Testament? An Examination of One of the Central Points in the Views of H. M. Kuitert and Others.* Nutley, N.J.: Presbyterian and Reformed Publishing Company, 1977.

Via, *Kerygma*    Via, Dan O. *Kerygma and Comedy in the New Testament: A Structuralist Approach to Hermeneutic.* Philadelphia: Fortress, 1975.

Vicent Cernuda, "Desvaído"    Vicent Cernuda, Antonio. "El desvaído Lázaro y el deslumbrador discípulo amado." *EstBib* 52 (1994): 453–516.

Villalón, "Sources"    Villalón, José R. "Sources vétéro-testamentaires de la doctrine qumrânienne des deux Messies." *RevQ* 8 (1972–1975): 53–63.

Villescas, "Jars"    Villescas, J. "John 2.6: The Capacity of the Six Jars." *Bible Translator* 28 (1977): 447.

Villiers, "Messiah"    Villiers, P. G. R. "The Messiah and Messiahs in Jewish Apocalyptic." *Neotestamentica* 12 (1978): 75–100.

Vinson, "Enthymemes"    Vinson, Richard B. "A Comparative Study of the Use of Enthymemes in the Synoptic Gospels." Pages 119–41 in *Persuasive Artistry: Studies in New Testament Rhetoric in Honor of George A. Kennedy.* Edited by Duane F. Watson. JSNTSup 50. Sheffield: Sheffield Academic Press, 1991.

Visotzky, "Cruxes"    Visotzky, Burton L. "Three Syriac Cruxes." *JJS* 42 (1991): 167–75.

Visotzky, "Polemic"    Visotzky, Burton L. "Anti-Christian Polemic in Leviticus Rabbah." *American Academy for Jewish Research* 56 (1990): 83–100.

Visotzky, "Prolegomenon"    Visotzky, Burton L. "Prolegomenon to the Study of Jewish-Christianities in Rabbinic Literature." *AJSR* 14 (1989): 47–70.

Viviano, "Beatitudes"    Viviano, Benedict T. "Beatitudes Found among Dead Sea Scrolls." *BAR* 18, no. 6 (November/December 1992): 53–55, 66.

Viviano, "Matthew"    Viviano, Benedict T. "Where Was the Gospel according to St. Matthew Written?" *CBQ* 41 (1979): 533–546.

Viviano, "Publication"    Viviano, Benedict T. "Eight Beatitudes at Qumran and in Matthew? A New Publication from Cave Four." *Svensk exegetisk årsbok* 58 (1993): 71–84.

Viviano, "Qumran"    Viviano, Benedict T. "Eight Beatitudes from Qumran." *The Bible Today* 31 (1993): 219–24.

Vogler, "Johannes als Kritiker"    Vogler, W. "Johannes als Kritiker der synoptischen Tradition." *Berliner theologische Zeitschrift* 16, no. 1 (1999): 41–58.

Von der Osten-Sacken, "Geist"    Osten-Sacken, Peter von der. "Geist im Buchstaben: Vom Glanz des Mose und des Paulus." *Evangelische Theologie* 41 (1981): 230–35.

Von Rad, *Theology*    Von Rad, Gerhard. *The Theology of Israel's Prophetic Traditions.* Vol. 2 of *Old Testament Theology.* Translated by D. M. G. Stalker. 2 vols. New York: Harper & Row, 1965.

Von Wahlde, "Apocalyptic Polemic"    Von Wahlde, Urban C. "'You Are of Your Father the Devil' in Its Context: Stereotyped Apocalyptic Polemic in John 8:38–47." Pages 418–44 in *Anti-Judaism and the Fourth Gospel: Papers of the Leuven Colloquium, 2000.* Edited by R. Bieringer, D. Pollefeyt, and F. Vandecasteele-Vanneuville. Assen: Royal Van Gorcum, 2001.

Von Wahlde, "Faith"    Von Wahlde, Urban C. "Faith and Works in John vi 28–29: Exegesis or Eisegesis?" *NovT* 22 (1980): 304–15.

Von Wahlde, "Structure"    Von Wahlde, Urban C. "Literary Structure and Theological Argument in Three Discourses with the Jews in the Fourth Gospel." *JBL* 103 (1984): 575–84.

Von Wahlde, "Survey"    Von Wahlde, Urban C. "The Johannine 'Jews': A Critical Survey." *NTS* 28 (1982): 33–60.

Von Wahlde, "Terms"    Von Wahlde, Urban C. "The Terms for Religious Authorities in the Fourth Gospel: A Key to Literary Strata?" *JBL* 98 (1979): 231–53.

Von Wahlde, *Version*    Von Wahlde, Urban C. *The Earliest Version of John's Gospel: Recovering the Gospel of Signs.* Wilmington, Del.: Glazier, 1989.

Vorster, "Blessedness"    Vorster, Willem S. "Stoics and Early Christians on Blessedness." Pages 38–51 in *Greeks, Romans, and Christians: Essays in Honor of Abraham J. Malherbe.* Edited by David L. Balch, Everett Ferguson, and Wayne A. Meeks. Minneapolis: Fortress, 1990.

Vos, "Range"    Vos, Geerhardus. "The Range of the Logos-Title in the Prologue of the Fourth Gospel." *Princeton Theological Review* 11 (1913): 365–419; 557–602.

Vouga, "Antijudaismus"   Vouga, Francois. "Antijudaismus im Johannesevangelium?" *Theologie und Glaube* 83 (1993): 81–89.

Wacholder, "Reply"   Wacholder, Ben Zion. "A Reply." *JBL* 92 (1973): 114–15.

Wachsmann, "Boat"   Wachsmann, Shelley. "The Galilee Boat: 2,000-Year-Old Hull Recovered Intact." *BAR* 14, no. 5 (September/October 1988): 18–33.

Wächter, "Astrologie"   Wächter, Ludwig. "Astrologie und Schicksalsglaube im rabbinischen Judentum." *Kairos* 11 (1969): 181–200.

Wächter, "Messianismus"   Wächter, Ludwig. "Jüdischer und christlichen Messianismus." *Kairos* 18 (1976): 119–34.

Wagner, *Baptism*   Wagner, Günter. *Pauline Baptism and the Pagan Mysteries: The Problem of the Pauline Doctrine of Baptism in Romans VI.1–11, in Light of Its Religio-historical "Parallels."* Translated by J. P. Smith. Edinburgh: Oliver & Boyd, 1967.

Wagner and Lotfi, "Learning"   Wagner, Daniel A., and Abdelhamid Lotfi. "Learning to Read by 'Rote.'" *International Journal of the Sociology of Language* 42 (1983): 111–21.

Wainwright, "Sophia"   Wainwright, Elaine. "Jesus Sophia." *Bible Today* 36 (1998): 92–97.

Waldstein, "Sendung"   Waldstein, Michael. "Die Sendung Jesu und der Jünger im Johannesevangelium." *Internationale katholische Zeitschrift/Communio* 19 (1990): 203–21.

Walker, "Hours"   Walker, Norman. "The Reckoning of Hours in the Fourth Gospel." *NovT* 4 (1960): 69–73.

Walker, "Prayer"   Walker, William O., Jr. "The Lord's Prayer in Matthew and in John." *NTS* 28 (1982): 237–56.

Wallace, "Date"   Wallace, Daniel B. "John 5,2 and the Date of the Fourth Gospel." *Biblica* 71 (1990): 177–205.

Wallace, "Reconsidering"   Wallace, Daniel B. "Reconsidering 'The Story of Jesus and the Adulteress Reconsidered.'" *NTS* 39 (1993): 290–96.

Walters, "Religions"   Walters, James C. "Egyptian Religions in Ephesos." Pages 281–309 in *Ephesos—Metropolis of Asia: An Interdisciplinary Approach to Its Archaeology, Religion, and Culture.* Edited by Helmut Koester. Harvard Theological Studies. Valley Forge, Pa.: Trinity Press International, 1995.

Wanamaker, "Agent"   Wanamaker, Charles A. "Christ as Divine Agent in Paul." *SJT* 39 (1986): 517–28.

Wanamaker, "Philippians"   Wanamaker, Charles A. "Philippians 2.6–11: Son of God or Adamic Christology?" *NTS* 33 (1987): 179–93.

Wansbrough, *Studies*   Wansbrough, John. *Quranic Studies: Sources and Methods of Scriptural Interpretation.* London Oriental Series 31. Oxford: Oxford University Press, 1977.

Wansink, "Law"   Wansink, Craig S. "Roman Law and Legal System." Pages 984–91 in *Dictionary of New Testament Background.* Edited by Craig A. Evans and Stanley E. Porter. Downers Grove, Ill.: InterVarsity, 2000.

Ward, "Hosea"   Ward, James M. "The Message of the Prophet Hosea." *Interpretation* 23 (1969): 387–407.

Ward, "Women"   Ward, Roy Bowen. "Women in Roman Baths." *HTR* 85 (1992): 125–47.

Wardle, D. comments on Valerius Maximus. See Valerius Maximus in Bibliography 1.

Wasson, Hofmann, Ruck, *Eleusis*   Wasson, Robert Gordon, Albert Hofmann, and Carl A. Ruck. *The Road to Eleusis: Unveiling the Secret of the Mysteries.* New York: Harcourt Brace Jovanovich, 1978.

Waterman, "Sources"   Waterman, G. Henry. "The Sources of Paul's Teaching on the 2nd Coming of Christ in 1 and 2 Thessalonians." *JETS* 18 (1975): 105–13.

Watkins, *John*   Watkins, H. W. *The Gospel according to John.* Edited by Charles John Ellicott. 2d ed. Grand Rapids: Zondervan, 1957.

Watson, "Adulteress"   Watson, A. "Jesus and the Adulteress." *Biblica* 80 (1999): 100–8.

Watson, "Education"   Watson, Duane F. "Education: Jewish and Greco-Roman." Pages 308–13 in *Dictionary of New Testament Background.* Edited by Craig A. Evans and Stanley E. Porter. Downers Grove, Ill.: InterVarsity, 2000.

Watson, "Natural Law"   Watson, Gerard. "The Natural Law and Stoicism." Pages 216–38 in *Problems in Stoicism.* Edited by A. A. Long. London: University of London, Athlone Press, 1971.

Watson, "Reading"   Watson, Francis. "Toward a Literal Reading of the Gospels." Pages 195–217 in *The Gospels for All Christians: Rethinking the Gospel Audiences.* Edited by Richard Bauckham. Grand Rapids: Eerdmans, 1998.

Watson, "Speech to Elders"   Watson, Duane F. "Paul's Speech to the Ephesian Elders (Acts 20:17–38): Epideictic Rhetoric of Farewell." Pages 184–208 in *Persuasive Artistry: Studies in New Testament Rhetoric in Honor of George A. Kennedy.* Edited by Duane F. Watson. JSNTSup 50. Sheffield: Sheffield Academic Press, 1991.

Watt, "Lam"   Watt, Jan G. van der. "'Daar is die lam van God . . .': Plaasvervangende offertradisies in die Johannesevangelie." *Skrif en kerk* 16 (1995): 142–58.

Watts, *Wisdom*   Watts, Alan. *The Wisdom of Insecurity.* New York: Vintage Books, 1951.

Watty, "Anonymity"   Watty, William W. "The Significance of Anonymity in the Fourth Gospel." *ExpTim* 90 (1978–1979): 209–12.

Way, "Introduction"   Way, A. S. Introduction. Pages vii–xiii in Euripides, *Works.* Translated by A. S. Way. 4 vols. LCL, old series. Cambridge: Harvard University Press, 1912.

Wcela, "Messiah(s)"   Wcela, Emil A. "The Messiah(s) of Qumrân." *CBQ* 26 (1964): 340–49.

Wead, "Law"   Wead, David W. "We have a Law." *NovT* 11 (1969): 185–89.

Webber, "Note"   Webber, Randall C. "A Note on 1 Corinthians 15:3–5." *JETS* 26 (1983): 265–69.

Weber, "Notes"   Weber, J.-J. "Notes exégétiques sur le texte 'Tu es Petrus.'" *Ami du clergé* 72 (February 22, 1962): 113–21.

Weber, "Petrus"   Weber, J.-J. "Notes exégétiques sur le texte 'Tu es Petrus.'" *Bulletin ecclésiastique du diocèse de Strasbourg* 80 (October 1–15, 1961): 541–60.

Weder, "Raum"   Weder, Hans. "Der Raum der Lieder: Zur Hermeneutik des Hymnischen im Neuen Testament." *Evangelische Theologie* 53 (1993): 328–41.

Weeden, *Mark*   Weeden, Theodore J., Sr. *Mark—Traditions in Conflict.* Philadelphia: Fortress, 1971.

Wegenast, "Teach"   Wegenast, Klaus. "Teach, etc." *NIDNTT* 3:759–65.

Wegner, *Women*   Wegner, Judith Romney. *Chattel or Person? The Status of Women in the Mishnah.* New York: Oxford University Press, 1988.

Weidemann, "Joh 20, 23"   Weidemann, Hans-Ulrich. "Nochmals Joh 20,23: Weitere philologische und exegetische Bemerkungen zu einer problematischen Bibelübersetzung." *Münchener theologische Zeitschrift* 51, no. 2 (2001): 121–27.

Weidmann, *Polycarp*   Weidmann, Frederick. *Polycarp and John: The Harris Fragments and Their Challenge to the Literary Traditions.* Christianity and Judaism in Antiquity 12. University of Notre Dame Press, 1999.

Weinfeld, "Grace"   Weinfeld, Moshe. "Grace after Meals in Qumran." *JBL* 111 (1992): 427–40.

Weinfeld, "Patterns"   Weinfeld, Moshe. "Ancient Near Eastern Patterns in Prophetic Literature." *VT* 27 (April 1977): 178–95.

Weinfeld, "Pentecost"   Weinfeld, Moshe. "Pentecost as a Festival of the Giving of the Law." *Immanuel* 8 (1978): 7–18.

Weiss, "Foot Washing"   Weiss, H. "Foot Washing in the Johannine Community." *NovT* 21 (1979): 298–325.

Weiss, "Sabbath"   Weiss, Herold. "The Sabbath among the Samaritans." *JSJ* 25 (1994): 252–73.

Weiss and Netzer, "Šty"   Weiss, Zeev, and Ehud Netzer. "Šty ʿwnwt-ḥpyrh bṣypwry [Two Excavation Seasons at Sepphoris]." *Qadmoniot* 24 (1991): 113–21.

Wengst, *Gemeinde*   Wengst, Klaus. *Bedrängte Gemeinde und verherrlichter Christus: Der historische Ort des Johannesevangeliums als Schlüssel zu seiner Interpretation.* Biblisch-theologische Studien 5. Neukirchen-Vluyn: Neukirchener Verlag, 1981.

Wenham, "Apocalypse"   Wenham, David. "Paul and the Synoptic Apocalypse." Pages 345–375 in *Studies of History and Tradition in the Four Gospels.* Vol. 2 of *Gospel Perspectives.* Edited by R. T. France and David Wenham. Sheffield: JSOT Press, 1981.

Wenham, *Bible*   Wenham, John W. *Christ and the Bible.* Downers Grove, Ill.: InterVarsity, 1977.

Wenham, *Discourse*   Wenham, David. *The Rediscovery of Jesus' Eschatological Discourse.* Vol. 4 of *Gospel Perspectives.* Edited by R. T. France and David Wenham. Sheffield: JSOT Press, University of Sheffield, 1984.

Wenham, "Enigma"   Wenham, David. "The Enigma of the Fourth Gospel: Another Look." *Tyndale Bulletin* 48 (1997): 149–78.

Wenham, "Gospel Origins"   Wenham, John W. "Gospel Origins." *Trinity Journal* 7 (1978): 112–34.

Wenham, "Narratives"   Wenham, David. "The Resurrection Narratives in Matthew's Gospel." *Tyndale Bulletin* 24 (1973): 21–54.

Wenham, "Note"   Wenham, David. "A Note on Mark 9:33–42/Matt. 18:1–6/Luke 9:46–50." *JSNT* 14 (1982): 113–18.

Wenham, "Parable"   Wenham, David. "The Interpretation of the Parable of the Sower." *NTS* 20 (1973–1974): 299–319.

Wenham, "View"   Wenham, David. "A Historical View of John's Gospel." *Themelios* 23 (1998): 5–21.

Wessel, "Männer"   Wessel, Friedhelm. "Die fünf Männer der Samaritanerin. Jesus und die Tora nach Joh 4,16–19." *BN* 68 (1993): 26–34.

Wessel, "Mensch"   Wessel, Friedhelm. "'Der Mensch' in der Verteidigungsrede des Nikodemus Joh 7,51 und das 'Ecce homo.'" *Studien zum Neuen Testament und seiner Umwelt* 17 (1992): 195–214.

Westcott, *Epistles*   Westcott, Brooke Foss. *The Epistles of John: The Greek Text with Notes and Essays.* London: Macmillan, 1905. Repr., Grand Rapids: Eerdmans, 1966.

Westcott, *John*   Westcott, Brooke Foss. *The Gospel according to St. John: The Authorized Version with Introduction and Notes.* 1881. Repr., Grand Rapids: Eerdmans, 1950.

Westerholm and Evans, "Sabbath"   Westerholm, Stephen, and Craig A. Evans. "Sabbath." Pages 1031–35 in *Dictionary of New Testament Background.* Edited by Craig A. Evans and Stanley E. Porter. Downers Grove, Ill.: InterVarsity, 2000.

Westermann, *John*   Westermann, Claus. *The Gospel of John in the Light of the Old Testament.* Translated by Siegfried S. Schatzmann. Peabody, Mass.: Hendrickson, 1998.

Wewers, "Wissen"   Wewers, Gerd A. "Wissen in rabbinischen Traditionem." *Zeitschrift für Religions- und Geistesgeschichte* 36 (1984): 141–55.

Wheeler, *Beyond Frontiers*   Wheeler, Sir Mortimer. *Rome beyond the Imperial Frontiers.* London: G. Bell & Sons, 1954. Repr., Westport, Conn.: Greenwood Press, 1971.

Wheeler, "Problems"   Wheeler, Gerald. "The Problems I Enumerated Were Real." *Liberty* (July 1984): 21.

Wheldon, *Spirit*   Wheldon, T. J. *The Holy Spirit: Studies in the Fourth Gospel.* London: W. H. Roberts, c. 1899.

Whisson, "Disorders"   Whisson, Michael G. "Some Aspects of Functional Disorders among the Kenyan Luo." Pages 283–304 in *Magic, Faith, and Healing: Studies in Primitive Psychiatry Today.* Edited by Ari Kiev. Foreword by Jerome D. Frank. New York: Free Press, Macmillan, 1964.

Whitacre, *John*   Whitacre, Rodney A. *John.* IVP New Testament Commentary. Downers Grove, Ill.: InterVarsity, 1999.

Whitacre, *Polemic*   Whitacre, Rodney A. *Johannine Polemic: The Role of Tradition and Theology.* SBLDS 67. Chico, Calif.: Scholars Press, 1982.

White, "Development"   White, L. Michael. "Urban Development and Social Change in Imperial Ephesos." Pages 27–79 in *Ephesos—Metropolis of Asia: An Interdisciplinary Approach to Its Archaeology, Religion, and Culture.* Edited by Helmut Koester. Harvard Theological Studies. Valley Forge, Pa.: Trinity Press International, 1995.

White, "Finances"   White, William, Jr. "Finances." Pages 218–36 in *The Catacombs and the Colosseum: The Roman Empire as the Setting of Primitive Christianity.* Edited by Stephen Benko and John J. O'Rourke. Valley Forge, Pa.: Judson Press, 1971.

White, *Initiation*   White, R. E. O. *The Biblical Doctrine of Initiation.* Grand Rapids: Eerdmans, 1960.

White, "Jews"   White, Martin Christopher. "The Identity and Function of the Jews and Related Terms in the Fourth Gospel." Ph.D. diss., Emory Graduate School, 1972.

White, "No One Comes"   White, R. E. O. "'No One Comes to the Father but by Me.'" *ExpTim* 113, no. 4 (2002): 116–17.

Whittaker, "Introduction"   Whittaker, C. R. Introduction. Pages ix–lxxxvii in vol. 1 of Herodian, *History.* Translated by C. R. Whittaker. 2 vols. LCL. Cambridge: Harvard University Press, 1969.

Whittaker, *Jews and Christians*   Whittaker, Molly. *Jews and Christians: Graeco-Roman Views.* Cambridge Commentaries on Writings of the Jewish and Christian World 200 BC to AD 200, 6. Cambridge: Cambridge University Press, 1984.

Whitters, "Profiles"   Whitters, Mark F. "Discipleship in John: Four Profiles." *Word and World* 18, no. 4 (1998): 422–27.

Wiarda, "Unity"   Wiarda, Timothy. "John 21.1–23: Narrative Unity and Its Implications." *JSNT* 46 (1992): 53–71.

Wicker, "Defectu"   Wicker, Kathleen O'Brien. "De defectu oraculorum (Moralia 409E–438E)." Pages 131–180 in *Plutarch's Theological Writings and Early Christian Literature.* Edited by Hans Dieter Betz. Studia ad corpus hellenisticum Novi Testamenti 3. Leiden: Brill, 1975.

Wieand, "Bethesda"   Wieand, D. J. "John V.2 and the Pool of Bethesda." *NTS* 12 (1965–1966): 392–404.

Wieder, "Exegesis"   Wieder, N. "The Dead Sea Scrolls Type of Biblical Exegesis among the Karaites." Pages 75–105 in *Between East and West.* London: East and West Library, 1958.

Wieder, "Messiahs"   Wieder, N. "The Doctrine of the Two Messiahs among the Karaites." *JJS* 6 (1953–1954): 14–23.

Wieder, "Sectaries"   Wieder, N. "The Qumran Sectaries and the Karaites." *JQR* 47 (1956–1957): 269–92.

Wiersma, "Novel"   Wiersma, S. "The Ancient Greek Novel and Its Heroines: A Female Paradox." *Mnemosyne* 43 (1990): 109–23.

Wifall, "Status"   Wifall, Walter R. "The Status of 'Man' as Resurrection." *ZAW* 90 (1978): 382–94.

Wightman, "*Baris*"   Wightman, Greg J. "Temple Fortresses in Jerusalem, II: The Hasmonean *baris* and Herodian Antonia." *Bulletin of the Anglo-Israel Archaeological Society* 10 (1990–1991): 7–35.

Wikenhauser, *Mysticism*   Wikenhauser, Alfred. *Pauline Mysticism: Christ in the Mystical Teaching of St. Paul.* New York: Herder & Herder, 1960.

Wilckens, "Paraclete"   Wilckens, Ulrich. "Der Paraclete und die Kirche." Pages 184–203 in *Kirche: Festschrift für Günther Bornkamm zum 75 Geburstag.* Edited by Dieter Lührmann and Georg Strecker. Tübingen: Mohr, 1980.

Wilcox, "Dualism"   Wilcox, Max. "Dualism, Gnosticism, and Other Elements in the Pre-Pauline Tradition." Pages 83–96 in *The Scrolls and Christianity: Historical and Theological Significance.* Edited by Matthew Black. London: SPCK, 1969.

Wilcox, "God-Fearers"   Wilcox, Max. "The 'God-Fearers' in Acts—a Reconsideration." *JSNT* 13 (1981): 102–22.

Wilcox, "Tree"   Wilcox, Max. "'Upon the Tree'—Deut 21:22–23 in the New Testament." *JBL* 96 (1977): 85–99.

Wild, *Water*   Wild, Robert A. *Water in the Cultic Worship of Isis and Sarapis.* Études préliminaires aux religions orientales dans l'empire romain 87. Leiden: Brill, 1981.

Wiles, *Gospel*   Wiles, Maurice F. *The Spiritual Gospel: The Interpretation of the Fourth Gospel in the Early Church.* Cambridge: Cambridge University Press, 1960.

Wilken, "Christians"   Wilken, Robert. "The Christians as the Romans (and Greeks) Saw Them." Pages 100–125 in vol. 1 of Meyer and Sanders, *Self-Definition.*

Wilken, "Collegia"   Wilken, Robert. "Collegia, Philosophical Schools, and Theology." Pages 268–91 in *The Catacombs and the Colosseum: The Roman Empire as the Setting of Primitive Christianity.* Edited by Stephen Benko and John J. O'Rourke. Valley Forge, Pa.: Judson Press, 1971.

Wilken, "Interpretation"   Wilken, Robert. "Toward a Social Interpretation of Early Christian Apologetics." *Church History* 39 (1970): 437–58.

Wilkins, *Discipleship*   Wilkins, Michael J. *Discipleship in the Ancient World and Matthew's Gospel.* 2d ed. Grand Rapids: Baker, 1995.

Wilkinson, "Blood"   Wilkinson, John. "The Incident of the Blood and Water in John 19.34." *SJT* 28 (1975): 149–72.

Wilkinson, *Jerusalem*   Wilkinson, John. *Jerusalem as Jesus Knew It.* London: Thames & Hudson, 1978.

Wilkinson, "Orientation"   Wilkinson, John. "Orientation, Jewish and Christian." *PEQ* 116 (1984): 16–30.

Wilkinson, "Water Supply"   Wilkinson, John. "Ancient Jerusalem: Its Water Supply and Population." *PEQ* 106 (1974): 33–51.

Williams, *Acts*   Williams, R. R. *Acts of the Apostles.* London: SCM, 1965.

Williams, "Corycus"   Williams, M. H. "The Jews of Corycus—a Neglected Diaspora Community from Roman Times." *JSJ* 25 (1994): 274–86.

Williams, *Death*   Williams, Sam K. *Jesus' Death as a Saving Event: The Background and Origin of a Concept.* Harvard Dissertations in Religion 2. Missoula, Mont.: Scholars Press, 1975.

Williams, "Domitian"   Williams, M. H. "Domitian, the Jews, and the 'Judaizers'—a Simple Matter of *cupiditas* and *maiestas*?" *Historia* 39 (1990): 196–211.

Williams, *I Am He*   Williams, Catrin H. *I Am He: The Interpretation of 'Anî Hû' in Jewish and Early Christian Literature.* WUNT 2d series, 113. Tübingen: Mohr/Siebeck, 2000.

Williams, "Ioudaios in Inscriptions"   Williams, M. H. "The Meaning and Function of Ioudaios in Graeco-Roman Inscriptions." *Zeitschrift für Papyrologie und Epigraphik* 116 (1997): 251–52.

Williams, *Justin*   Williams, A. Lukyn. *Justin Martyr: The Dialogue with Trypho (Translation, Introduction, and Notes).* Translations of Christian Literature Series I—Greek Texts. New York: Macmillan, 1930.

Williams, "Mother"   Williams, Ritva H. "The Mother of Jesus at Cana: A Social-Science Interpretation of John 2:1–12." *CBQ* 59 (1997): 679–92.

Williams, "Personal Names"   Williams, Margaret H. "Palestinian Jewish Personal Names in Acts." Pages 79–113 in *The Book of Acts in Its Palestinian Setting.* Edited by Richard Bauckham. Vol. 4 in *The Book of Acts in Its First Century Setting.* Edited by Bruce W. Winter. Grand Rapids: Eerdmans, 1995.

Williams, "Smith"   Williams, David S. "Morton Smith on the Pharisees in Josephus." *JQR* 84 (1993–1994): 29–41.

Williams, "Theology"   Williams, Donald L. "The Theology of Amos." *Review and Expositor* 63 (1966): 393–403.

Williamson, *Chronicles*   Williamson, H. G. M. *1 and 2 Chronicles.* New Century Bible Commentary. Grand Rapids: Eerdmans, 1982.

Williamson, "Philo"   Williamson, R. "Philo and NT Christology." *ExpTim* 90 (1978–1979): 361–65.

Willis, "Banquets"   Willis, Wendell L. "Banquets." Pages 143–46 in *Dictionary of New Testament Background.* Edited by Craig A. Evans and Stanley E. Porter. Downers Grove, Ill.: InterVarsity, 2000.

Willis, *Meat*   Willis, Wendell Lee. *Idol Meat in Corinth: The Pauline Argument in 1 Corinthians 8 and 10.* SBLDS 68. Chico, Calif.: Scholars Press, 1985.

Wills, "Form"   Wills, Lawrence. "The Form of the Sermon in Hellenistic Judaism and Early Christianity." *HTR* 77 (1984): 277–99.

Wills, *Quest*   Wills, Lawrence M. *The Quest of the Historical Gospel: Mark, John, and the Origins of the Gospel Genre.* London: Routledge, 1997.

Willoughby, *Initiation*   Willoughby, Harold R. *Pagan Initiation: A Study of Mystery Initiations in the Graeco-Roman World.* Chicago: University of Chicago Press, 1929.

Wilson, "Anti-Judaism"   Wilson, S. "Anti-Judaism in the Fourth Gospel?" *Irish Biblical Studies* 1 (1979): 28–50.

Wilson, *Gentiles*   Wilson, Stephen G. *The Gentiles and the Gentile Mission in Luke–Acts.* SNTSMS 23. Cambridge: Cambridge University Press, 1973.

Wilson, *Gnosis*   Wilson, R. McL. *Gnosis and the New Testament.* Philadelphia: Fortess, 1968.

Wilson, *Gnostic Problem*   Wilson, R. McL. *The Gnostic Problem.* London: Mowbray, 1958.

Wilson, *Luke and Pastoral Epistles*   Wilson, Stephen G. *Luke and the Pastoral Epistles.* London: SPCK, 1979.

Wilson, "Nag Hammadi"   Wilson, R. McL. "Nag Hammadi and the New Testament." *NTS* 28 (1982): 289–302.

Wilson, "Philo"   Wilson, R. McL. "Philo and the Fourth Gospel." *ExpTim* 65 (1953–1954): 47–49.

Wilson, "Prophecy"   Wilson, Robert R. "Early Israelite Prophecy." *Interpretation* 32 (1978): 3–16.

Wilson, "Spirit"   Wilson, R. McL. "The Spirit in Gnostic Literature." Pages 345–55 in *Christ and Spirit in the New Testament: Studies in Honour of C. F. D. Moule.* Edited by Barnabas Lindars and Stephen S. Smalley. Cambridge: Cambridge University Press, 1973.

Wilson, "Studies"   Wilson, R. McL. "Some Recent Studies in Gnosticism." *NTS* 6 (1959–1960): 32–44.

Wilson, "Thought"   Wilson, R. McL. "The Fourth Gospel and Hellenistic Thought." *NovT* 1 (1956): 225–27.

Winandy, "Disciple"   Winandy, Jacques. "Le disciple que Jésus aimait: Pour une vision élargie du problème." *RB* 105 (1998): 70–75.

Winandy, "Vestiges"   Winandy, Jacques. "Les vestiges laissés dans le tombeau et la foi du disciple (*Jn 20*, 1–9)." *Nouvelle revue théologique* 110, no. 2 (1988): 212–19.

Wind, "Destination"   Wind, A. "Destination and Purpose of the Gospel of John." *NovT* 14 (1972): 26–69.

Windisch, *Spirit-Paraclete*   Windisch, Hans. *The Spirit-Paraclete in the Fourth Gospel.* Translated by James W. Cox. Facet Books Biblical Series 20. Philadelphia: Fortress, 1968.

Wink, *John*   Wink, Walter. *John the Baptist in the Gospel Tradition.* Cambridge: Cambridge University Press, 1968.

Winkle, "Model"   Winkle, Ross E. "The Jeremiah Model for Jesus in the Temple." *Andrews University Seminary Studies* 24 (1986): 155–72.

Winslow, "Religion"   Winslow, Donald. "Religion and the Early Roman Empire." Pages 237–54 in *The Catacombs and the Colosseum: The Roman Empire as the Setting of Primitive Christianity.* Edited by Stephen Benko and John J. O'Rourke. Valley Forge, Pa.: Judson Press, 1971.

Winston, "Cosmogony"   Winston, David. "The Book of Wisdom's Theory of Cosmogony." *History of Religions* 11 (1971–1972): 185–202.

Winston, "Creation"   Winston, David. "Creation ex Nihilo Revisited: A Reply to Jonathan Goldstein." *JJS* 37 (1986): 88–91.

Winston, "Determinism"   Winston, David S. "Freedom and Determinism in Greek Philosophy and Jewish Hellenistic Wisdom." *Studia philonica* 2 (1973): 40–50.

Winston, "Freedom"   Winston, David S. "Freedom and Determinism in Philo of Alexandria." *Studia philonica* 3 (1974–1975): 47–70.

Winston, *Wisdom*   Winston, David. *The Wisdom of Solomon: A New Translation with Introduction and Commentary.* AB 43. Garden City, N.Y.: Doubleday, 1979.

Winter, *Paul Left Corinth*   Winter, Bruce W. *After Paul Left Corinth: The Influence of Secular Ethics and Social Change.* Grand Rapids and Cambridge: Eerdmans, 2001.

Winter, *Philo and Paul*   Winter, Bruce W. *Philo and Paul among the Sophists.* SNTSMS 96. Cambridge: Cambridge University Press, 1997.

Winter, *Trial*   Winter, Paul. *On the Trial of Jesus.* Studia judaica: Forschungen zur Wissenschaft des Judentums 1. Berlin: de Gruyter, 1961.

Winter, "Trial"   Winter, Paul. "The Trial of Jesus and the Competence of the Sanhedrin." *NTS* 10 (1963–1964): 494–99.

Winter, *Welfare*   Winter, Bruce W. *Seek the Welfare of the City: Christians as Benefactors and Citizens.* First-Century Christians in the Graeco-Roman World. Grand Rapids: Eerdmans, 1994.

Wintermute, "Jubilees"   Wintermute, Orval S. Introduction to "Jubilees." *OTP* 2:35–50.

Wirgin, *Jubilees*   Wirgin, Wolf. *The Book of Jubilees and the Maccabaean Era of Shmittah Cycles.* Leeds University Oriental Society Monograph 7. n.p.: Leeds University, 1965.

Wise, "General Introduction"   Wise, Michael O. "Dead Sea Scrolls: General Introduction." Pages 252–66 in *Dictionary of New Testament Background.* Edited by Craig A. Evans and Stanley E. Porter. Downers Grove, Ill.: InterVarsity, 2000.

Wise, "Introduction to 3Q15"   Wise, Michael O. Introduction to 3Q15. Pages 188–91 in *The Dead Sea Scrolls: A New Translation.* By Michael Wise, Martin Abegg Jr., and Edward Cook. San Francisco: Harper SanFrancisco, 1999.

Wise, "Introduction to 4Q158"   Wise, Michael O. Introduction to 4Q158. Pages 199–200 in *The Dead Sea Scrolls: A New Translation.* By Michael Wise, Martin Abegg Jr., and Edward Cook. San Francisco: Harper San Francisco, 1999.

Wise, *Scrolls*   Wise, Michael, Martin Abegg Jr., and Edward Cook. *The Dead Sea Scrolls: A New Translation.* San Francisco: Harper San Francisco, 1999.

Wise, "Vision"   Wise, Michael O. "The Eschatological Vision of the Temple Scroll." *Journal of Near Eastern Studies* 49 (1990): 155–72.

Witherington, Ben, III, ed. *History, Literature, and Society in the Book of Acts.* Cambridge: Cambridge University Press, 1996.

Witherington, *Acts*   Witherington, Ben, III. *The Acts of the Apostles: A Socio-rhetorical Commentary.* Grand Rapids: Eerdmans, 1998.

Witherington, *Christology*   Witherington, Ben, III. *The Christology of Jesus.* Minneapolis: Augsburg Fortress, 1990.

Witherington, *Corinthians*   Witherington, Ben, III. *Conflict and Community in Corinth: A Social-Rhetorical Commentary on 1 & 2 Corinthians.* Grand Rapids: Eerdmans, 1995.

Witherington, *End*   Witherington, Ben, III. *Jesus, Paul, and the End of the World.* Downers Grove, Ill.: InterVarsity, 1992.

Witherington, *History*   Witherington, Ben, III, ed. *History, Literature, and Society in the Book of Acts.* Cambridge: Cambridge University Press, 1996.

Witherington, *Quest*   Witherington, Ben, III. *The Jesus Quest: The Third Search for the Jew of Nazareth.* Downers Grove, Ill.: InterVarsity, 1995.

Witherington, *Sage*   Witherington, Ben, III. *Jesus the Sage: The Pilgrimage of Wisdom.* Minneapolis: Fortress, 1994.

Witherington, "Waters"   Witherington, Ben, III. "The Waters of Birth: John 3.5 and 1 John 5.6–8." *NTS* 35 (1989): 155–60.

Witherington, *Wisdom*   Witherington, Ben, III. *John's Wisdom: A Commentary on the Fourth Gospel.* Louisville, Ky.: Westminster John Knox 1995.

Witherington, *Women*   Witherington, Ben, III. *Women in the Ministry of Jesus: A Study of Jesus' Attitudes to Women and Their Roles as Reflected in His Earthly Life.* SNTSMS 51. Cambridge: Cambridge University Press, 1984.

Witkamp, "Woorden"   Witkamp, L. T. "Jezus' laatste woorden volgens Johannes 19:28–30." *Nederlands theologisch tijdschrift* 43 (1989): 11–20.

Wittlieb, "Bedeutung"   Wittlieb, Marian. "Die theologische Bedeutung der Erwähnung von 'Masîah/Christos' in den Pseudepigraphen des Alten Testaments palästinischen Ursprungs." *BN* 50 (1989): 26–33.

Wojciechowski, "Aspects"   Wojciechowski, Michal. "Certains aspects algébriques de quelques nombres symboliques de la Bible (Gen 5; Gen 14.14; Jn 21.11)." *BN* 23 (1984): 29–31.

Wojciechowski, "Don"   Wojciechowski, Michal. "Le don de L'Esprit Saint dans Jean 20.22 selon Tg. Gn. 2.7." *NTS* 33 (1987): 289–92.

Wolf, "Virgin"   Wolf, Eric. "The Virgin of Guadalupe: A Mexican National Symbol." *Journal of American Folklore* 71 (1958): 34–39.

Wolfson, *Philo*   Wolfson, Harry Austryn. *Philo: Foundations of Religious Philosophy in Judaism, Christianity, and Islam.* 2 vols. 4th rev. ed. Cambridge: Harvard University Press, 1968.

Woll, *Conflict*   Woll, D. Bruce. *Johannine Christianity in Conflict: Authority, Rank, and Succession in the First Farewell Discourse.* SBLDS 60. Chico, Calif.: Scholars Press, 1981.

Wolmarans, "Peter"   Wolmarans, J. L. P. "Peter in the Gospel of John: A Study of Character." *Ekklesiastikos pharos* 77 (1995): 22–31.

Wolters, "Copper Scroll"   Wolters, Al. "Copper Scroll (3Q15)." Page 227 in *Dictionary of New Testament Background.* Edited by Craig A. Evans and Stanley E. Porter. Downers Grove, Ill.: InterVarsity, 2000.

Wood, "Dip"   Wood, Bryant G. "To Dip or Sprinkle? The Qumran Cisterns in Perspective." *BASOR* 256 (fall 1984): 45–60.

Wood, "Interpreting"   Wood, H. G. "Interpreting This Time." *NTS* 2 (1955–1956): 262–66.

Wood, "Typology"   Wood, J. Edwin. "Isaac Typology in the New Testament." *NTS* 14 (1967–1968): 583–89.

Worden, "Feast"   Worden, T. "The Marriage Feast at Cana (John 2.1–11)." *Scripture* 20, no. 52 (October 1968): 97–106.

Wotherspoon, "Paraclete"   Wotherspoon, Arthur. "Concerning the Name 'Paraclete.'" *ExpTim* 34 (1922–1923): 43–44.

Wrede, *Origin*   Wrede, William. *The Origin of the New Testament.* Translated by James S. Hill. New York: Harper & Brothers, 1909.

Wrede, *Secret*   Wrede, William. *The Messianic Secret.* Translated by J. C. G. Greig. Cambridge: James Clarke, 1971.

Wright, "Apocryphal Gospels"   Wright, David F. "Apocryphal Gospels: The 'Unknown Gospel' (Pap. Egerton 2) and the *Gospel of Peter*." Pages 207–32 in *The Jesus Tradition outside the Gospels.* Edited by David Wenham. Vol. 5 of *Gospel Perspectives.* Edited by R. T. France and David Wenham. Sheffield: JSOT Press, 1985.

Wright, "Apologetic"   Wright, David F. "Apologetic and Apocalyptic: The Miraculous in the *Gospel of Peter*." Pages 401–18 in *The Miracles of Jesus.* Edited by David Wenham and Craig Blomberg.

Vol. 6 of *Gospel Perspectives*. Edited by R. T. France and David Wenham. Sheffield: JSOT Press, 1986.

Wright, *Archaeology*   Wright, G. Ernest. *Biblical Archaeology*. Philadelphia: Westminster, 1962.

Wright, "Faith"   Wright, David F. "Christian Faith in the Greek World: Justin Martyr's Testimony." *EvQ* 54 (1982): 77–87.

Wright, *Paul*   Wright, N. T. *What Saint Paul Really Said: Was Paul of Tarsus the Real Founder of Christianity?* Grand Rapids: Eerdmans, 1997.

Wright, *People of God*   Wright, N. T. *The New Testament and the People of God*. Vol. 1 of *Christian Origins and the Question of God*. 2 vols. Minneapolis: Fortress, 1992.

Wuellner, "Arrangement"   Wuellner, Wilhelm. "Arrangement." Pages 51–87 in *Handbook of Classical Rhetoric in the Hellenistic Period, 330 B.C.–A.D. 400*. Edited by Stanley E. Porter. Leiden: Brill, 1997.

Wyatt, "Gardener"   Wyatt, Nicolas. "'Supposing Him to Be the Gardener' (John 20,15): A Study of the Paradise Motif in John." *ZNW* 81 (1990): 21–38.

Xavier, "Andrew"   Xavier, Aloysius. "Andrew in the Fourth Gospel: First Disciple of Jesus." *Indian Theological Studies* 33 (1996): 139–46.

Xavier, "Thomas"   Xavier, Aloysius. "Thomas in the Fourth Gospel." *Indian Theological Studies* 30 (1993): 18–28.

Yadin, "Commentaries"   Yadin, Yigael. "Commentaries on Genesis xlix and Isaiah, from Qumran Cave 4." *IEJ* 7 (1957): 66–68.

Yadin, *Masada*   Yadin, Yigael. *Masada: Herod's Fortress and the Zealots' Last Stand*. New York: Random House, 1966.

Yadin, "Scroll"   Yadin, Yigael. "The Temple Scroll." *BAR* 10, no. 5 (September/October 1984): 32–49.

Yadin, *War Scroll*   Yadin, Yigael. *The Scroll of the War of the Sons of Light against the Sons of Darkness*. Translated by Batya and Chaim Rabin. Oxford: Oxford University Press, 1962.

Yamauchi, *Archaeology*   Yamauchi, Edwin. *The Archaeology of New Testament Cities in Western Asia Minor*. Grand Rapids: Baker, 1980.

Yamauchi, "Colosse"   Yamauchi, Edwin. "Qumran and Colosse." *BSac* 121 (1964): 141–52.

Yamauchi, "Concord"   Yamauchi, Edwin. "Concord, Conflict, and Community: Jewish and Evangelical Views of Scripture." Pages 154–96 in *Evangelicals and Jews in Conversation on Scripture, Theology and History*. Edited by Marc H. Tannenbaum, Marvin R. Wilson, and James A. Rudin. Grand Rapids: Baker, 1978.

Yamauchi, "Crucifixion"   Yamauchi, Edwin. "The Crucifixion and Docetic Christology." *Concordia Theological Quarterly* 46 (1982): 1–20.

Yamauchi, *Gnosticism*   Yamauchi, Edwin. *Pre-Christian Gnosticism: A Survey of the Proposed Evidences*. Grand Rapids: Eerdmans, 1973.

Yamauchi, "Gnosticism"   Yamauchi, Edwin M. "Gnosticism." Pages 414–18 in *Dictionary of New Testament Background*. Edited by Craig A. Evans and Stanley E. Porter. Downers Grove, Ill.: InterVarsity, 2000.

Yamauchi, "Magic"   Yamauchi, Edwin. "Magic or Miracle? Diseases, Demons and Exorcisms." Pages 89–183 in *The Miracles of Jesus*. Edited by David Wenham and Craig Blomberg. Vol. 6 of *Gospel Perspectives*. Edited by R. T. France and David Wenham. Sheffield: JSOT Press, 1986.

Yamauchi, "Mandaean Studies"   Yamauchi, Edwin. "The Present Status of Mandaean Studies." *Journal of Near Eastern Studies* 25 (1966): 88–96.

Yamauchi, "Motif"   Yamauchi, Edwin M. "The 'Daily Bread' Motif in Antiquity." *Westminster Theological Journal* 28 (1965–1966): 145–56.

Yamauchi, *Persia*   Yamauchi, Edwin M. *Persia and the Bible*. Foreword by Donald J. Wiseman. Grand Rapids: Baker , 1990.

Yamauchi, *Stones*   Yamauchi, Edwin M. *The Stones and the Scriptures: An Introduction to Biblical Archaeology*. Grand Rapids: Baker, 1972.

Yates, "Worship"   Yates, Roy. "'The Worship of Angels' (Col 2:18)." *ExpTim* 97 (1985–1986): 12–15.

Yavetz, "Judeophobia"   Yavetz, Zvi. "Judeophobia in Classical Antiquity: A Different Approach." *JJS* 44 (1993): 1–22.

Yee, *Feasts*    Yee, Gale A. *Jewish Feasts and the Gospel of John.* Zacchaeus Studies: New Testament. Wilmington, Del.: Glazier, 1989.

Yee. "Sabbath"    Yee, Gale A. "The Day Was the Sabbath." *The Bible Today* 28 (1990): 203–6.

Yegül, "Complex"    Yegül, F. Kret K. "The Bath-Gymnasium Complex." Pages 148–61 in *Sardis from Prehistoric to Roman Times: Results of the Archaeological Exploration of Sardis, 1958–1975.* Edited by George M. A. Hanfmann, assisted by William E. Mierse. Cambridge: Harvard University Press, 1983.

Young, "Cult"    Young, Frances M. "Temple Cult and Law in Early Christianity." *NTS* 19 (1972–1973): 325–38.

Young, "Isaiah"    Young, Franklin W. "A Study of the Relation of Isaiah to the Fourth Gospel." *ZNW* 46 (1955): 215–33.

Young, "Motif"    Young, Brad H. "The Ascension Motif of 2 Corinthians 12 in Jewish, Christian, and Gnostic Texts." *Grace Theological Journal* 9 (1988): 73–103.

Young, *Parables*    Young, Brad H. *Jesus and His Jewish Parables: Rediscovering the Roots of Jesus' Teaching.* New York: Paulist Press, 1989.

Young, *Theologian*    Young, Brad H. *Jesus the Jewish Theologian.* Forewords by Marvin R. Wilson and Rabbi David Wolpe. Peabody, Mass.: Hendrickson, 1995.

Zalcman, "*Noserim*"    Zalcman, Lawrence. "Christians, *noserim,* and Nebuchadnezzar's Daughter." *JQR* 81 (1990–1991): 411–26.

Zehnle, *Discourse*    Zehnle, Richard F. *Peter's Pentecost Discourse: Tradition and Lukan Reinterpretation in Peter's Speeches of Acts 2 and 3.* SBLMS 15. Nashville: Abingdon, for the Society of Biblical Literature, 1971.

Zeitlin, "Character"    Zeitlin, Solomon. "The Book of Jubilees, Its Character and Its Significance." *JQR* 30 (1939–1940): 1–31.

Zeitlin, "Galileans"    Zeitlin, Solomon. "Who Were the Galileans? New Light on Josephus' Activities in Galilee." *JQR* 64 (1973–1974): 189–203.

Zeitlin, "'Jubilees'"    Zeitlin, Solomon. "The Book of 'Jubilees' and the Pentateuch." *JQR* 48 (1957–1958): 218–35.

Zeitlin, "Plague"    Zeitlin, Solomon. "The Plague of Pseudo-rabbinic Scholarship." *JQR* 63 (1972–1973): 187–203.

Zeitlin, "Trial"    Zeitlin, Solomon. "The Trial of Jesus." *JQR* 53 (1962–1963): 85–88.

Zeller, "Elija"    Zeller, Dieter. "Elija und Elischa im Frühjudentum." *Bibel und Kirche* 41, no. 4 (1986): 154–60.

Zeller, "Philosophen"    Zeller, Dieter. "Jesus und die Philosophen vor dem Richter (zu Joh 19.8–11)." *BZ* 37 (1993): 88–92.

Zerwick, "Wirken"    Zerwick, Max. "Vom Wirken des Heiligen Geistes in uns: Meditationsgedanken zu Jo 16,5–15." *Geist und Leben* 38 (1965): 224–30.

Zias, "Remains"    Zias, Joseph. "Human Skeletal Remains from the Mount Scopus Tomb." *'Atiqot* 21 (1992): 97–103.

Zimmerli and Jeremias, *Servant*    Zimmerli, W., and J. Jeremias. *The Servant of God.* SBT 20. Naperville, Ill.: Allenson, 1957.

Zimmermann, "Brautwerbung"    Zimmermann, Mirjam, and Ruben Zimmermann. "Brautwerbung in Samarien? Von der moralischen zur metaphorischen Interpretation von Joh 4." *Zeitschrift für Neues Testament* 1, no. 2 (1998): 40–51.

Zimmermann, "Freund"    Zimmermann, Mirjam, and Ruben Zimmermann. "Der Freund des Bräutigams (Joh 3,29): Deflorations—oder Christuszeuge?" *ZNW* 90 (1999): 123–30.

Zlotnick, "Memory"    Zlotnick, Dov. "Memory and the Integrity of the Oral Tradition." *Journal of the Ancient Near Eastern Society* 85, nos. 16–17 (1984–1985): 229–41.

Zon, "Droga"    Zon, A. "Droga w Regule Wspolnoty. 1QS 9.18 [On the Concept of Life in the Qumran Rule]." *Ruch biblijny i liturgiczny* 16 (1963): 187–96.

Zumstein, "Antioche"    Zumstein, Jean. "Antioche sur l'Oronte et l'évangile selon Matthieu." *Studien zum Neuen Testament und seiner Umwelt* 5 (1980): 122–38.

Zumstein, "Croix"    Zumstein, Jean. "De Cana à la croix." *Christus* 183 (1999): 297–305.

Zuntz, *Persephone*    Zuntz, Günther. *Persephone: Three Essays on Religion and Thought in Magna Graecia.* Oxford: Clarendon Press, 1971.

# Index of Modern Authors

Abbott, E. A., 1146
Abecassis, A., 822
Abegg, M. G., 191, 209, 287, 288, 296, 1102
Abelson, J., 136, 168, 349, 384, 385, 409, 410, 412, 414, 936, 962
Aberbach, M., 285
Aberle, M. von, 196
Abogunrin, S. O., 31, 266
Abramowski, L., 5
Abrahams, I., 135, 199, 306, 328, 358, 441, 445, 447, 459, 522, 523, 552, 579, 642, 652, 736, 738, 750, 777, 778, 793, 1086, 1108
Abrahamsen, V. A., 254, 845
Abrams, D., 300, 351
Achtemeier, P. J., 1214
Ackerman, J. S., 421, 829
Adan, D., 781
Adan-Bayewitz, D., 484
Adinolfi, M., 311, 481
Adler, R. J., 635
Adler, S. H., 674
Ådna, J., 566
Agouridis, S., 303
Agus, A., 198
Aitken, E. B., xxvi, 21, 28, 39, 55, 66, 70, 262, 508, 546, 559, 672, 709, 725, 957, 994, 1015, 1186, 1222
Aker, B., xxxi
Alarcón Sainz, J. J., 155
Albright, W. F., 44, 68, 90, 163, 169, 293, 295, 300, 306, 346, 347, 348, 349, 378, 418, 445, 453, 477, 574, 576, 609, 638, 678, 829, 919, 970, 1037, 1084, 1129, 1152
Alexander, A. B. D., 344
Alexander, L., 7, 140, 299, 333, 679
Alexander, P. S., 168, 300, 729, 879, 935
Alexander, W. M., 260, 599, 676, 777
Allegro, J. M., 172, 241, 286
Allen, E. L., 196, 493, 701, 794, 1137, 1152
Allen, R. E., 235, 236, 341, 342, 376, 377, 440
Allen, T. G., 442
Allen, W. C., 729
Allison, D. C., 4, 185, 213, 215, 267, 289, 304, 312, 321, 359, 382, 436, 460, 476, 482, 600, 604, 613, 629, 664, 729, 777, 840, 876, 1069, 1077, 1120, 1158, 1159, 1178, 1223, 1225, 1226
Alsup, J. E., 63
Alter, R., 598
Amaru, B. H., 15, 613, 629
Amir, Y., 808
Anderson, G., 366, 581, 1004
Anderson, Graham, 800
Anderson, H., 8, 29, 313, 439, 444, 445, 449, 453, 457, 464, 900, 1078, 1086, 1121, 1122, 1165, 1168
Anderson, J. C., 153
Anderson, P. N., 663, 665, 687, 689
Anderson, R. D., 15, 49, 69, 128, 129, 162, 221, 223, 251, 282, 325, 337, 361, 364, 386, 395, 419, 435, 455, 529, 531, 537, 539, 552, 579, 585, 610, 616, 657, 680, 682, 684, 686, 687, 691, 693, 694, 695, 697, 706, 709, 710, 713, 717, 729, 744, 758, 778, 782, 784, 787, 788, 789, 791, 795, 797, 827, 873, 887, 910, 916, 946, 979, 1005, 1030, 1058, 1131, 1183, 1213, 1215
Anderson, R. T., 598, 612
Andiñach, P., 672
Andrews, H. T., 336
Angus, S., 299, 443, 540
Antonaccio, C. M., 291
Antoniotti, L.-M., 1193
Applebaum, S., 101, 176, 231, 397, 467, 484, 1224
Appold, M. L., 41, 305, 370, 436, 619, 673, 729, 797, 826, 1051, 1062
Arav, R., 481, 1223
Arbel, D. V., 209
Argyle, A. W., 78, 305, 344, 345, 383, 401, 406, 437, 440, 445, 453, 564, 673, 767, 1086
Armenti, J. R., 230
Armstrong, H. H., 67
Arndt, W. F., 956, 962
Arnéra, G., 479
Arnold, C. E., 256, 416, 880
Arntz, K., 812
Aron-Schnapper, D., 55

Xavier, A., 87, 475, 1211

Yadin, Y., 27, 122, 241, 438, 443, 510, 512, 526, 604, 667, 761, 977, 1188
Yamauchi, E. M., 131, 162, 164, 165, 166, 168, 169, 172, 178, 215, 225, 241, 257, 288, 375, 416, 453, 484, 523, 591, 636, 637, 667, 692, 715, 780, 799, 838, 1062, 1076, 1099, 1129, 1136, 1165, 1175, 1202
Yates, R., 308
Yavetz, Z., 219
Yee, G. A., 41, 211, 635, 636, 718, 736, 739, 784, 1100, 1130, 1131
Yegül, F. K. K., 229
Young, B. H., 29, 31, 64, 470, 504, 538
Young, F. M., 213

Young, F. W., 173, 620, 660, 664, 884, 1040

Zalcman, L., 211
Zehnle, R. F., 74, 306, 497
Zeitlin, S., 192, 197, 230, 1084, 1085, 1102
Zeller, D., 435, 1125
Zerwick, M., 1023, 1030, 1036
Zias, J., 853
Zimmerli, W., 452, 453
Zimmermann, M., 580, 598, 608
Zimmermann, R., 580, 598, 608
Zlotnick, D., 58
Zon, A., 942
Zumstein, J., 40, 501
Zuntz, G., 909

# INDEX OF SUBJECTS

This index is more detailed in the introduction than the main commentary, although it includes both. Some minor items (like a number of the possible analogies with rhetorical devices, where their mention in ancient sources is documented) are indexed for the sake of readers who may focus on these approaches; theological themes or social context discussions that informed readers can locate merely with a concordance or basic knowledge of the Gospel are much more rarely indexed.

# INDEX OF SCRIPTURE AND OLD TESTAMENT APOCRYPHA

Although the book's "count" of "extrabiblical" references includes the Apocrypha, we include works commonly listed in the Apocrypha, listed alphabetically, in the Scripture index.

## OLD TESTAMENT

Where MT and LXX enumeration systems differ, we list references according to the conventional versification of English translations.

# NEW TESTAMENT

## Matthew

# INDEX OF OTHER ANCIENT SOURCES

2.241   401, 877
2.244–46   371
2.245   370
2.255   688
2.257   156
2.263   156
2.267   1141
2.275   371
2.277   355
2.279   368
2.282   358
2.283   783
2.284   358
2.288   368
2.289   762
2.290   658
2.292   574, 912

**Antiquities**
  6, 27, 34, 70, 71, 1075
1.5   7
1.7   78, 102
1.23   182
1.38–39   730
1.39   662
1.41   761
1.46   71
1.52–59   761
1.53   799
1.70   378
1.74   751
1.107   721
1.108   263
1.156   650
1.200   758
1.222   157, 415
1.285   598
1.288   598
2.217–37   192
2.243–53   26
2.257   586
2.276   400, 771
2.312   454
2.348   263
2.349   987
3.18   940
3.19–20   749
3.21   773
3.26   1052
3.32   680
3.36   727
3.38   727
3.47   545, 905
3.53   1052
3.67   764
3.80   877

3.81   263
3.85–87   653
3.95–99   25
3.161   1140
3.180   269
3.184   877
3.186   698
3.192   952
3.208   528, 875
3.212   906
3.261   600
3.262   842, 850
3.318–19   872
3.322   263, 755
4.25–34   71
4.25   71
4.26–28   705
4.34   705
4.40   849, 1052
4.41   532
4.46   1024, 1031
4.51   847
4.53   1160
4.58   705
4.104   390
4.126–30   390
4.133   751
4.134–38   71
4.157   390
4.158   263
4.177–93   1016
4.179   1047
4.189   1047
4.194   1044
4.196   25
4.202   772, 1158
4.203   872
4.206   594
4.207   25, 523
4.214–15   184
4.214   25, 1075
4.218   111, 431
4.219   25, 32, 599, 623, 656,
   740, 750, 763, 1088, 1192,
   1196
4.223   732
4.238   749, 787, 1095
4.244–45   594
4.244   608
4.245   593
4.248   787, 1095
4.264–65   1158, 1160
4.264   1133
4.287   184
4.318   567
4.320   1141, 1159, 1185

4.321   848
4.322   528, 875
4.326   1195
4.327   670
4.328   661
4.329   315, 653
6.20–21   71
6.21   650
6.36   732
6.86   749
6.126–27   528, 875
6.166   460
6.203   28
6.235   443
6.337   843
7.130–31   25
7.131–46   25
7.202–3   848
7.203   847
8.100   635, 703
8.111   654
8.114   409
8.220–21   314, 653
8.225   703
8.231   28, 944
8.280   366
8.318–19   723
8.343–46   260
8.419   855
9.1–17   15
9.7   869
9.28   435
9.29–43   18
9.104   1160
9.166   1159
9.182   257
9.227   1164
9.288   606
9.291   602
10.24–35   15
10.38   629
10.46   1164
10.80   857
10.98–90   1072
10.118   589
10.180   373
11   24
11.84   599
11.114   599
11.277–78   983
11.327   857, 1188
11.333–34   857
11.340–41   602
12.2   528, 648
12.125   147
12.156   599

**4Q181**
329
1.1–2   777
1.3–4   828

**4Q183**
2.4–8   383, 1188

**4Q185**
1–2.1.8–12   469
1–2.1.14–15   1215
1–2.2.1–2   943
1–2.2.1–4   874
1–2.2.6–8   383
1–2.2.6–7   1188
1.2.7–8   709

**4Q186**
1.1.5–6   709
2.1.3–4   709

**4Q213**
1.1.8   1052

**4Q216**
393

**4Q242**
2.1–2   296

**4Q246**
287, 296, 652
1.5–9   296
2.1   296
2.2–3   296

**4Q251**
1   644

**4Q252**
287
1.1.17   1179
1.2.2   1179
1.3.6–9   415
1.5.1–4   172, 284
1.5.1   287
1.5.3–5   645
1.5.3–4   286
1.5.3   287

**4Q254**
Frg. 4   287

**4Q265**
1.1–2   208
2.2.3   716

**4Q266**
1156
11.2.4–5   679
12   995
18.3.12   286
18.4–5   208
18.5.9–10   900
18.5.13   801

**4Q268**
1.3   983, 1040
1.8   983, 1040

**4Q270**
1156
6   995

**4Q279**
1.6   543

**4Q284a**
208

**4Q285**
287
5.4   288

**4Q286**
2.1   489
2.5   489
2.6   489
2.10   489
5.8   489
7.1.7   489

**4Q287**
5.11   489

**4Q289**
1.2   489
2.4   489

**4Q292**
1   384

**4Q298**
1.1.1   882

**4Q299**
2.2.10–11   532
5.1–4   536, 920

**4Q300**
133
1 2.1–4   70, 797

**4Q301**
1.2   70, 797

**4Q302a**
797

**4Q369**
296
1.2.6–7   296

**4Q371**
1   612
8   612
11   612

**4Q372**
1   602
1.11–12   599
1.12   612

**4Q375**
1.1.1–4   436, 711
1.1.4–5   711

**4Q376**
711
1.1.1   288

**4Q377**
2.2.5   288
2.2.6–7   1012

**4Q378**
22.2   449
26.1   238

**4Q381**
1.1   353
15.7   286
69.4   977

**4Q382**
1   436
3   436
9   436
16.2   286
31   436

**4Q385**
1205
2.7–8   557
4   538

**Oxford Geniza Text**

# TANNAITIC COLLECTIONS

**Mekilta of R. Ishmael**
Citations formatted by Exodus reference

Citations formatted by section

*'Am.*

*Bah.*

*Bes.*

*Nez.*

*Kaspa*

*Pisha*

[1] We include in this list even those portions of Pirke 'Abot which are not in the Mishnah.

8:1   499
8:6   1117
8:8   446, 848, 1163
9:3   479, 526, 868
9:11   920
10   454
10:1   901, 920
10:4   1015
10:5-7   479, 526
10:7   868

*Qidd.*
2:1   311
4:1   907
4:3   598
4:5   484
4:14   200, 357, 368, 758

*Rosh Hash.*
1:2   724
1:7   656
2:5   717, 1044
2:6   656
2:9   1102
3:1   656, 880
3:8   538, 564
4:5   400, 755

*Sanh.*
1:5   433
1:6   1074
3:5   579
4:1   1087, 1088
4:2   1093
4:4   905
4:5   203, 301, 379, 647
5:1-4   789, 1088
6:2   790, 856
6:3   1119, 1138
6:4   1135
6:5   1157
6:6   848, 1158, 1160, 1163
7:2   1108
7:4   737
7:5   400, 647, 771
7:11   256, 715
8:7   1026
9:6   528, 1027
10:1   199, 201, 679, 755, 1002,
   1176, 1215
11:1-2   880
11:1   737
11:2   1088
11:4   356, 1087, 1136

*Sabb.*
1:3   642
1:4-5   430

1:4   786
2:5   715
6:4   1078
6:10   1136, 1181, 1210
7:2   641, 786
9:1   59
10:5   641
11:1   641
16:8   642
18:3   716, 717, 1044
19:1-2   716
22:6   786
23:1   1192
23:5   850, 865, 1151, 1162
24:3   786

*Seb.*
2:1   625
8:10   600

*Seqal.*
1:3   522
1:5   209
4:2   523
5:1-2   443
6:1-2   526, 611
8:1   614, 780

*Sotah*
   736
1:5   863
1:6   750
2:3   488
3:4   787
3:8   1138
5:2-3   430
7:6   400
9:14   155
9:15   273, 286, 402, 435, 436,
   650, 878, 952, 1045

*Sukkah*
2:9   934
3:9-10   868
3:10   479
4:1   868
4:5   771
4:6   727
4:8   479, 868
4:9   722, 726, 1154
5:1   703, 723
5:3-4   739

*Ta'an.*
1:1   724
1:3   624, 823
3:8   260, 274, 723, 787

*Tamid*
5:1   209
7   432

*Tehar.*
4:5   200
5:8   598, 600
5:9   656
8:3   200
8:5   200
8:9   444, 512

*Tem.*
1:1   787, 1095

*Ter.*
3:9   599
5:6   510
8:12   396, 855

*Yad.*
1:1-2:4   909
4:1-4   430
4:4   478
4:7   216, 645

*Yebam.*
6:6   606
15:1   623, 763, 1192, 1196
15:8-10   623, 763, 1192, 1196
16:3   841, 848
16:7   623, 763, 1192, 1196

*Yoma*
3:8   399, 949
5:2   526
8:6   642, 786
8:8-9   644
8:8   135
8:9   552

**Semahot**
1   850, 1151
12   843
12:10   850

***Sipra***
   xxix
Lev 25:23   306

*A.M.*
Par. 6.187.1.1   612
Par. 8.193.1.7   725
Pq. 11.191.1.3   725
Pq. 13.194.2.15   396

*Behor*
Par. 5.255.1.10   641

81b    485
85b    435, 490, 750, 788, 1027
86a    192, 274, 1027
86b    308, 958
89b    485
90a    485
91b    485
92ab   485
93b    816
94a    562
95b    485
96b    485
105b   485
108b   485
109ab  485
113ab  485
114a   485
115b   788, 1095

*B. Qam.*
15ab   472
17a    441, 724
17b    472
18ab   472
19a    472
20b    472
22ab   472
23b    472
24b    472
25b    305, 1184
28a    472
30ab   472
31a    472
37a    472
38b, bar.   599
47b    472
48a    472
52b    472
65a    472
68a    472
69b    501, 502
82a    441, 724
83a    155, 409, 936
85b    472
86b    472
91a    472
92b    482
94b    472
95ab   472
96ab   472
97b    472
101a   472
102ab  314
108a   472
109b   472
114ab  472

114b   803
116b   804
117a   255, 837, 849
119b   472

*'Erub.*
7a     356
11a    485
15ab   485
16ab   485
18b    536
19a    471, 755
21a    357
21b    64, 356, 368
22b    485
30a    485
35b    511–12
36b–37a  600
37b    485
43ab, bar.   436
43b    435
45b    485
52a    485
53b    229, 596
54a    471
54b    458, 876
63a    694
65a    536
70b    485
101a   67, 198

*Git.*
5a     485
12ab   485
15a    485
16a    510
20b    485
23a    311, 313, 580
28b    485
29a    485
33b    485
36b    485
38b    485
41b    485
42ab   485
42b    435
43a    485
44a    485
45b    202
47ab   485
48a    485
49a    305, 1184
49b    485
50ab   485
51a    485
54a    485
56a    221

56b–57a   256, 462, 1002
62b    485
63ab   485
68ab   947
68a    256, 400, 1027
68b–70  256
68b    744
82a    485
85b    485

*Hag.*
3a     849
3b     386, 802
6a     356
9b     435
12a    380, 383, 384, 756
12b–13a  459
12b    384, 407
13a–14b  77
13a    167, 458
13a, bar.   1094
13b    957, 1031
14a    191, 197, 203, 351, 769
14b    129, 167, 901, 912
14b, bar.   743, 1094
15a    167, 378, 460, 788
15a, bar.   1094
15b    201, 1002
16a, bar.   744
17b    485
25a    589
27a    755

*Hor.*
2a     485
3b     485
4b     485
5b     485
6b     485
10a    256
10b, bar.   912
11a    202
13a    485
13b, bar.   457, 905

*Hul.*
4b     716
8a     485
9b     485
10a    512
13a    202
16b    485
25b    510
27b    485
28ab   485
29a    485
31a    485, 512

| | | | | | | | |
|---|---|---|---|---|---|---|---|
| 17:5 | 355 | 39:14 | 397 | 60:16 | 410 |
| 17:8 | 760 | 39:16 | 910 | 61:3 | 473 |
| 18:1 | 498 | 41:1 | 479, 869 | 61:7 | 201, 828 |
| 18:3 | 580 | 41:9 | 441, 724 | 62:2 | 486, 494, 841 |
| 19:7 | 410 | 42:3 | 383, 384 | 63:5 | 646 |
| 19:8 | 192 | 43:2 | 135, 1231 | 63:8 | 366, 547 |
| 20:2 | 984 | 43:3 | 28, 386 | 63:14 | 307 |
| 20:4 | 759 | 43:6 | 681 | 64:4 | 769, 1027 |
| 20:10 | 1184 | 44:5 | 1069 | 64:9 | 688 |
| 20:12 | 1189 | 44:10 | 751 | 64:10 | 613 |
| 21:3 | 756 | 44:12 | 544, 767 | 65:10 | 423, 1012 |
| 21:5 | 760, 765 | 44:15 | 768 | 65:20 | 390 |
| 21:7 | 959 | 44:16 | 755 | 65:23 | 525 |
| 21:9 | 767 | 44:17 | 355 | 67:3 | 1237 |
| 22:2 | 408, 911 | 44:21 | 479 | 67:8 | 532 |
| 23:6 | 673, 761 | 44:22 | 768 | 68:4 | 646 |
| 24:2 | 756, 767 | 46:1 | 758, 769 | 68:12 | 490, 491, 614, 1042 |
| 24:6 | 759, 761 | 47:6 | 167 | 69:2 | 1012 |
| 24:7 | 925 | 47:10 | 397 | 69:3 | 167 |
| 25:1 | 192 | 48:6 | 544 | 69:4 | 209, 210 |
| 26:1 | 192, 398 | 48:8 | 397, 755 | 69:5 | 441, 724 |
| 26:6 | 192, 551, 959, 1205 | 48:9 | 146, 627, 758 | 69:7 | 768 |
| 26:7 | 385 | 48:12 | 682, 755 | 70:5 | 681 |
| 27:4 | 163 | 48:18 | 982 | 70:8–9 | 441, 724 |
| 28:2 | 379 | 49:2 | 1027 | 70:8 | 724, 755, 1075 |
| 28:8 | 192 | 49:9 | 1034 | 71:6 | 778 |
| 29:1 | 192 | 49:11 | 755 | 71:8 | 441 |
| 29:3 | 192 | 50:4 | 146, 627, 758 | 71:9 | 435 |
| 30:8 | 758, 768, 769 | 50:9 | 1042 | 73:3 | 297, 959 |
| 30:10 | 384 | 51:3 | 539 | 73:4 | 723 |
| 31:5 | 355 | 51:8 | 494, 1139 | 74:1 | 614 |
| 31:13 | 192 | 53:3 | 992 | 74:7 | 536 |
| 32:3 | 380 | 53:5 | 777 | 74:12 | 673, 754, 755, 758 |
| 32:8 | 677 | 53:9 | 758 | 74:15 | 1075 |
| 32:10 | 590, 612 | 53:14 | 255 | 75:3 | 804 |
| 33:1 | 387, 1064 | 54:1 | 441, 681, 724 | 75:6 | 870 |
| 33:3 | 297, 435, 569, 904, 959 | 54:3 | 803 | 76:5 | 482, 673, 754 |
| 33:6 | 612 | 55:4 | 958, 1032 | 77:3 | 984 |
| 34:9 | 356, 1006 | 55:7 | 415, 729 | 78:1 | 308, 958 |
| 34:10 | 197 | 55:8 | 380, 673, 754 | 78:2 | 1042 |
| 34:14 | 192, 398 | 56:1 | 497 | 78:8 | 758, 959 |
| 34:15 | 484, 1062 | 56:2 | 612 | 78:11 | 1095 |
| 35:2 | 755 | 56:6 | 65, 192 | 79:1 | 764 |
| 35:3 | 635, 704, 821 | 56:10 | 768 | 79:6 | 676, 786 |
| 36:1 | 192 | 56:11 | 251 | 79:8 | 778 |
| 36:3 | 192 | 58:8 | 756 | 80:2 | 804 |
| 36:6 | 614 | 58:9 | 569 | 80:4 | 778 |
| 38:6 | 163, 539, 982 | 59:1 | 386 | 80:7 | 396, 568 |
| 38:7 | 958, 985, 1032 | 59:5 | 384, 802 | 80:9 | 717 |
| 38:9 | 163, 561 | 59:9 | 414 | 81:2 | 678, 943 |
| 38:13 | 758, 769 | 59:11 | 631, 674 | 81:3 | 590, 612 |
| 39:3 | 755 | 60:1 | 740 | 81:4 | 902 |
| 39:6 | 959 | 60:2 | 755 | 81:5 | 155 |
| 39:7 | 652, 1131 | 60:5 | 604 | 82:2 | 490 |
| 39:8 | 614, 758 | 60:8 | 600, 904 | 82:6 | 167 |
| 39:11 | 256 | 60:13 | 793 | 82:14 | 758 |

4:17, §1   136, 488, 510
5:10, §2   136, 488
5:11, §2   486
5:11, §5   1027
5:15, §1   462
5:17, §1   681
6:6–7, §1   553
6:10, §1   301
7:8, §1   397
7:12, §1   458, 876, 1159
7:13, §1   381
7:14, §3   724, 727
7:23, §4   788
7:27, §1   962
8:1, §1   408, 959, 1123
8:1, §2   498
8:15, §1   681
9:4, §1   670
9:5, §1   652, 766
9:7, §1   1069
9:8, §1   900
9:10, §3   1159
9:15, §7   136, 488
9:18, §2   136, 488
10:8, §1   599, 637, 676, 786
10:11, §1   539
10:19, §1   501
11:1, §1   396
11:6, §1   473
11:7, §1   384, 385
11:8, §1   359
12:1, §1   136, 488, 542
12:7, §1   136, 488, 774
12:12, §1   201
30:9   67

*Song Rab.*

1:1, §5   786, 1002
1:1, §9   952
1:2, §2   64, 316, 351, 356
1:2, §3   441, 542, 724, 755
1:2, §5   64, 356, 829
1:3, §1   1242
1:3, §2   64, 356, 384
1:3, §3   146, 384, 404, 627, 758
1:9, §2   416, 874
1:10, §2   385
1:11, §11   381
1:12, §1   136, 488
1:15, §2   998, 1069
1:15, §4   384
2:1, §1   414

2:1, §3   414, 984, 1032
2:4, §1   308, 958
2:7, §1   1056
2:9, §3   439, 718, 774
2:9, §4   530
2:13, §4   199, 284, 286, 288, 435, 439
2:14, §§1–2   459
2:14, §2   414
2:14, §5   713
2:16, §1   402, 992
2:17, §1   959
3:6, §1   438
3:7, §5   192, 637, 756
3:10, §1   409
3:10, §2   359
3:11, §2   409, 414, 1027
4:1, §2   384, 998, 1069
4:4, §4   673, 754
4:4, §5   612
4:5, §2   410, 682, 728
4:11, §1   1004
4:12, §5   436
5:1, §1   410
5:7, §1   400
5:11, §4   381
5:11, §6   385
5:16, §1   769
5:16, §3   351, 386, 414
6:9, §3   1002
6:10, §1   308, 494, 958
6:11, §1   542, 551
6:12, §1   749
7:1, §1   381
7:2, §2   723, 724
7:2, §3   256, 445
7:3, §1   1075
7:3, §3   201
7:5, §3   136, 488, 615
7:6, §1   410, 755
7:11, §1   878
7:13, §1   992
8:2, §1   542
8:5, §1   400
8:6, §1   751
8:7, §1   568
8:8, §1   984, 1032
8:9, §2   359
8:9, §3   210, 435, 458, 791, 876, 952, 960
8:11, §2   359
8:14, §1   359, 984

*Lam. Rab.*

Proem 2   64, 357, 390, 397, 402, 876
Proem 23   402, 876
Proem 24   959, 1032
Proem 25   410, 774
Proem 31   155
Proem 33   525, 742
1:1, §§12–13   67
1:1, §14   599
1:1, §19   597
1:3, §28   600
1:5, §31   530, 535
1:5, §32   409, 471
1:7, §34   496
1:11–12, §40   1002
1:16, §50   136, 458, 488, 876
1:16, §51   955
1:17, §52   402, 802, 816
2:1, §2   490
2:4, §8   1075
3:1, §1   398
3:20, §7   402
3:23, §8   308, 958, 1176
3:39, §9   684
3:64, §9   729
4:15, §18   155

*Midrash Tannaim*

15:9   306

**Palestinian Talmud (Talmud Yerushalmi)**[2]

*'Abod. Zar.*

2:1, §1   381, 613
2:2, §3   275
2:3, §1   597
2:7, §3   64, 356
2:8, §5   613
3:1, §2   210, 458, 897, 905, 952
3:1, §3   880
4:7, §2   542
5:4, §3   510, 600, 612
5:11, §1   510
5:11, §2   600

*Ber.*

1:1, §8   1052
1:3   356
1:3, §4   876
1:4   201
1:5   102

[2]Cited by mishnaic sections and the enumeration of sections within them in Neusner's translation.

6:8, §3   613
7:1, §6   500

*Nid.*
1:4, §2   58, 504, 926
3:4, §3   188

*Pe'a*
1:1   357, 711
1:1, §8   908
1:1, §13   863
1:1, §15   498, 869, 876
2:5   625
2:6, §3   356
3:8, §3   1190
8:9   796

*Pesah.*
2:5   380
4:4   716
6:1   483
10:1   580
10:6   929

*Qidd.*
1:1, §8   594
1:2, §24   449
1:5, §8   77
1:7, §6   386, 565
1:9, §2   958
3:12, §8   445, 446, 594
4:1, §§2–3   442
4:1, §2   453

*Rosh Hash.*
1:3, §24   357
1:3, §27   1189
1:3, §28   880, 958
1:3, §§39–42   532
1:3, §42   416
1:3, §43   722, 724, 727, 727
1:3, §§45–46   724
2:6, §9   457, 905
3:1, §17   880
3:2, §6   957
3:8, §1   256, 715
3:9, §§1–6   564
3:9, §§1–3   782
4:3, §3   716, 717
4:6, §1   229

*Sabb.*
1:4   216
2:6, §2   384
6:3   642
6:9, §2   1181
6:9, §3   203, 294, 666
7:2, §15   716
10:5, §1   510

14:1, §2   642
14:3   512
14:4, §3   260, 780, 786
19:3, §3   716

*Sanh.*
1:1, §3   1108
1:1, §4   418, 582, 652, 943, 1027
1:2, §10   432, 613
1:2, §13   457, 905
2:1, §2   432, 1073, 1095
2:1, §3   720
2:4, §2   760
3:5, §2   400, 665, 1056
4:6, §2   1101, 1150
5:1, §3   484
6:1, §1   66
6:6, §2   274, 462, 531, 605, 906, 1002, 1135, 1169
6:7, §2   442
7:2, §3   1108
7:2, §4   58, 926
7:13, §2   256
8:8, §1   410, 774, 813
10:1, §1   562
10:1, §6   755
10:1, §7   67, 198
10:1, §8   201
10:1, §9   451, 802
10:2, §7   958, 1032
10:2, §8   390, 402, 878
10:2, §11   1176
10:3, §1   694, 1205
11:4, §1   64, 270, 274, 356, 451
11:5, §1   1027
11:6, §1   1174

*Seb.*
6:1, §8   694
6:1, §12   444, 446, 600
9:1, §13   599, 676, 837

*Sebu.*
1:6, §5   696, 856
1:6, §6   1069
2:1, §6   444
8:2, §7   642

*Seqal.*
2:5   58
3:2   482
3:3   382, 435, 1205
5:1   816

*Sotah*
1:1, §7   597
5:4, §1   802

5:5, §2   756, 787
5:5, §4   448, 985
5:6, §3   662
7:1, §4   78
7:5, §1   397
7:5, §5   458, 876
9:13, §2   22, 478, 906
9:16, §2   210, 458, 897, 952

*Sukkah*
2:5, §1   498, 580
2:10, §1   679, 934, 1215
3:4, §3   830, 1060
3:5, §1   679, 1215
4:3, §5   299
4:6, §1   722
5   581
5:1, §3   724
5:1, §7   284, 385
5:2, §2   288, 542

*Ta'an.*
1:1, §§1–10   724
1:1, §2   260, 547, 723
1:1, §8   673, 754
1:1, §10   409
1:2   793
1:4, §1   260, 723
2:1, §1   959
2:1, §6   359
2:1, §8   781
2:2, §2   210
2:2, §6   210
2:2, §7   256
3:8, §2   273, 947
3:9, §3   274
3:9, §4   384
3:9, §§6–8   260
3:9, §§6–7   723
3:10, §1   294
3:10, §§61–63   273
3:11, §4   260, 274, 432, 596, 723
3:11, §5   679, 1215
4:1, §14   755, 907, 992
4:2, §§8–9   457, 905
4:2, §8   386, 897, 906
4:2, §9   905, 906
4:2, §12   457, 905
4:2, §13   380
4:5, §1   512, 661
4:5, §10   390, 458, 599
4:5, §13   512, 521, 525

*Ter.*
1:1   396, 973
1:6   435, 668

[3] Categories such as "Jewish" and "Christian" were not airtight, though we have grouped known Jewish-Christian works under the latter heading. Some later documents (such as *T. Levi*) include Christian interpolations, editing, or (especially with much later works like Gr. *Apocalypse of Ezra*) could be Christian compositions incorporating earlier Jewish materials.

2:4–5   532
4:1   923
5:3–5   287
8:2   287

*T. Reuben*
1:3   923
2:1   970
2:3–4   970
3:1   841
3:3   594
3:9   572
4:6   594
4:7   693
4:8   910
4:9   256
5:5–6   192
5:6   759
6:1–2   597
6:1   910
6:5–12   287
6:8   287

*T. Simeon*
2:5   553
2:7   919, 984
3:1   970
3:4   751
4:4   933
4:8   553
5:5   287

*T. Zebulon*
1:5–7   28
5:2   532
6:5–6   1227
8:2   933
9:7   552, 1053
9:8   384, 397, 542
10:1–2   847
10:2   1176
10:6   841

**Toledoth Yeshu**
575

**Treatise of Shem**
3:1–2   1231
6:1   804
7:15   594
7:20   804
9:9   594
10:16   594

**Zohar**
409

**EARLY CHRISTIAN AND GNOSTIC LITERATURE**[4]

*Acts John*
127, 148, 219
27   299
38   134, 1188
43   1052
47   837
52   837
53–64   9
55   148
73–80   9, 837
94   215, 564, 762
94.1–2   351

*Acts Paul*
9, 34, 709
3.1   414, 698
3.3   709
3.24   532
11.6   1169

*Acts of Peter*
1238
11   95
28   837

**Acts of Pilate**
2.3   759
10.1   1138

**Ambrose**

*Sacraments*
3.15   781

**Andreas Caesariensis**
375

**Aphrahat**

*Demonstratio*
1153
16.8   761

*Ap. Jas.*
7.1–6   1047

**Apocalypse of Peter/*Apoc. Pet.***
5–12   462, 1002

*Apocr. Jn*/Apocryphon of Jn
375

*Apos. Con.*
7.26.4   667
7.36.1–7   643
7.46   96
8.6.6   544

**Athenagoras**

*Plea*
3   688
4   378
5–6   157
10   413
13   401
20–22   371
24   298
26   192, 761
27   401

**Athanasius**

*Homilies*
1179

*De Incarnatione*
54.3   299

**Augustine**

*Conf.*
8.12   857

*Cons.*
2.67   518
21.51   13

*Ep.*
126.7   796
196.6   386
243   506

*On Virginity*
3   506

*Serm.*
191.19.5   49

[4] In some cases the distinction between early Christian and other early Jewish texts is debatable; some texts in the "early Jewish" category include Christian interpolations, redaction, or may be Jewish-Christian works. When in doubt, the work has generally been classed among "Jewish" works, but the distinction between these categories is certainly anachronistic in John's era.

*Epistula Apostolorum*
482, 1186

**Eusebius**

*Chronicon*
1.p. 93   1173

*Hist. Eccl.*
96–99
2.2   1116
2.23.12–19   810
2.25.5–8   1238
3.1   1238
3.5.3   815
3.17   179
3.19   305
3.20   730
3.20.1–6   305
3.23.6–19   147
3.28   97
3.31.3–4   102, 144
3.31.3   85
3.32.3–6   305
3.39   5, 13, 96, 97, 976
3.39.4   476
3.39.17   736
5.1.44   1137
5.16   34
5.20.5–6   98
5.24.2–3   147
5.24.2   102, 144
5.24.3   85
6.14.7   99
7.25   97

*On Isaiah*
18:1   311

*Life of Constantine*
3.26   1166

*Praep. ev.*
4.11   617
4.12–13   617
8.9.38–8.10.17   408
8.11.2   925
9.10.14   66
9.17.9   27
9.27   26
9.27.3   156
9.27.7   28
9.27.10   445
9.27.24–26   1082
9.27.36   876
9.27.37   709
9.29.16   28
9.33   734

13.12.1–2   66
13.12.9–16   642
13.12.11   646
13.13.3–8   66, 408
13.13.5   26, 299, 423, 562

**Ginza** (Mandean)
R. 5.2179.22–27   383

*Gospel of Philip*
70–71   962

*Gospel of the Ebionites*
Frg. 6   307

*Gospel of the Egyptians*
375

*Gospel of the Hebrews*
736

*Gospel of the Nazarenes*
35

*Gos. Pet.*
34, 36, 219, 1070
2.3ff.   1160
4.14   1151
6.21   1210
12.50–13.57   1169, 1191

*Gos. Thom.*
19, 35–36, 43, 164, 384, 940,
1208–9
12   381
22.1–2   534
31   629
59   1209

*Gospel of Truth*
416, 418, 420, 1037

**Gregory the Great**

*Homilies*
21   1189

**Gregory of Nazianzus**

*Or.*
3   386
28.30   796

**Gregory of Nyssa**

*Life of Moses*
2.270   1153

**Herm.**
173

*Mand.*
1.10   354
2.4   354, 546
3.4   970
9   950
11.2–9   968, 1039

*Sim.*
8   992
8.3.2   362
9.12   352, 546
9.12.2   381

*Vis.*
2.4   381
3.2   526, 1002
3.3   551
3.5–6   526
3.6   546
3.9   526
3.10   546

**Hermetica**

*Poimandres*
167, 340, 383, 940

*Corp. herm.*
1.5   383
1.6   383
1.12   383
1.21   383
4.4   541
10.8   751
13.1   541
13.7–9   383
13.18   383

**Hippolytus**

*Apostolic Tradition*
4–6   1238

*Haer.*
1.7   342
1.15   236
1.16   423
1.23   376
5.5   376
5.8.10   540
5.8.23   540
5.8.40–41   540

## INSCRIPTIONS, PAPYRI AND OTHER COLLECTIONS

[5] Cited by page from 1955 ed.

## OTHER ANCIENT MEDITERRANEAN AND NEAR EASTERN TEXTS

Pseudonymous authors like Ps-Cicero normally appear under their alleged author. Page numbers following books rather than specific citations are passim or to the document as a whole.

[6]We cite here only those entries not cited under other collections.

54.8　1137
54.16.2　594
55.24.2　824
56.46.1　178
56.47.2　677
57.4.5–6　1107, 1111
57.9.2　1107, 1111
57.18.1　1161
57.18.5　205
57.18.6　709
57.19.1　1107, 1111
57.23.1–2　1107, 1111
58.4.5–6　1185
58.4.6　1142
59.11.6　1107
60.4.5–6　178
62.11.3–4　21
62.18.4　856
62.18.5　677
63.11.2–63.12.1　1185
65.7.2　177, 615
65.8　273, 632
66.6.3　874
67.13.4　179
67.14.1–2　179
77.16.5　595
Frg. 1.6.3　423

**Dio Chrys.**

*Or.*
1.14　721
1.62–63　688
2　63
2.75　136, 488
3.30　672
3.99–100　1006
4.67–70　1121
7.9–10　804
8.5　1030
8.33　688
9.12　721
11.154　688
12.11　721
12.27–28　721, 808
13.24　1138, 1229
14.18　748
18　748
21　66
30　847
31.9–10　223
31.20　721
32.26　179
32.35　721
32.95　292
36.43　721

37.32–33　711, 764
47.6　629
57.3–9　656
60.8　688
61　66
64.13　752
66　63, 885
67　66
68　235
77/78.37–45　657

*Troikos*
11　262
54　262
70　262

**Diodorus Siculus**
1.1.3　1191
1.1.4　922
1.3.1–2　40
1.6.2　20
1.9.2　20
1.11.6　527, 999
1.12.1　401, 878
1.12.6　730
1.14.1　688
1.15.6　782
1.15.8　991
1.17.5　991
1.36.4　625
1.37.4　18
1.37.6　18
1.70.6　417
1.76.1–2　957
1.77.2　1088
1.84.1　687, 688
2.1.10　1104
2.6.10　743
2.19.2　743
2.47.3　616
2.58.6　922
3.64.6　782
4.1.1　20
4.3.4　500
4.4.1–5　22
4.4.6　500
4.8.2　1214
4.8.3–5　20
4.8.5　1024
4.10.1　564
4.10.3–4　314, 653
4.11.5–6　564
4.38.3–5　1195
4.47.3–4　263
4.56.7–8　24
4.64.1　607

4.69.5　1002
5.32.2　1142
5.62.4　1186
7.5.2　1195
8.4.1　607
9.9.1　574, 912
9.10.2　236
10.4.4–6　1005
10.5.1　57
10.6.1　539
10.7.3　572, 732
10.9.4　751
10.9.6　1188
10.24.2　1142
10.34.8　749
11.14.3–4　1186
12.12.2　1088
12.12.3　596
12.14.1　596
12.16.1　1142
12.20.2　377, 658
12.21.2　594
12.24.3–4　595
13.111.1　1074
14.1.1–2　1020
14.17.12　823
14.29.4　1052
14.30.4　1007
14.56.2　1007
14.63.1–2　523
14.69.4　523
14.76.3　523
15.1.1　15
15.35.1　1159
15.54.3　595
15.58.3　732
15.73.4　823
15.74.2　500
15.74.3–4　508
16.16.4　1160
16.45.4–5　743
16.65.5–6　760
16.91.2–3　856
16.91.4　499
16.92.1　499
16.95.1　299
16.95.5　1241
17　1241
17.13.6　705
17.16.3　1116
17.17.3　1181
17.31.6　1006, 1128
17.37.3　1141, 1185
17.37.6　924, 1009, 1191
17.39.1　1007
17.39.2　1006

**Horace**

*Carm.*

## Musaeus

*Hero*
1   115

## Musonius Rufus (Lutz ed.)
50

*Fragments from other enumerations*

## Nicolaus

*Progymnasmata*
4.17–18   65

## Ninus Romance/Nin. Rom.
Frg. 1.A.4   957

## Nonius Marcellus
s.v. Nundinae   642

## *Orph. H.*
4.1   401, 878

5.564–71   1174
5.599–641   39
5.621–24   773
5.626–27   816
6.1–5   451
6.26–27   407, 659
6.148–50   451
6.261–62   1052
6.340–41   597
6.343–65   597
6.358–59   1237
6.366–81   597
6.366   623
6.401–11   1173
6.527–28   816
7.192   536
7.861   1149, 1204
8.380–89   1141
8.392   1141
8.401–2   1141
8.618–724   1125
8.621–29   659
8.626–721   561
8.626–27   407
8.679–80   667
8.723–24   291
8.777–78   1189
8.851–54   773
8.872–74   773
9.16–17   291
9.225   22
9.245   878
9.271   371, 878
9.292–304   1044
9.675–84   607
9.702–3   1052
9.704–13   607
9.715   710
10.43   1149
10.54   386
10.126–29   592
10.155–219   371
10.168   729
10.224   145, 627
10.225–28   913
10.710–39   1173
11.100–5   950
11.122   603
11.131   1052
11.139–43   781
11.165   710
11.241–46   163, 1189
11.250–64   163
11.366–75   814
11.586–88   1169
11.633–43   1189

11.633–38   163
11.635   1169
11.638–43   163
11.650–73   1169
12.32–34   773
12.598–99   773
13.92   732
13.137   732
13.262–67   1202
13.382–83   732
13.410–11   1052
13.497   1141
13.531–32   1162
13.673–74   459
13.789   607, 710
13.852–53   532
13.922   1228
13.923   1228
14.129–53   950
14.136–44   328
14.414–15   605
14.765–71   371, 407, 1189
14.778   810
14.805–51   1195
14.807   878
14.816   371
14.824–28   1195
15.62–64   248
15.538–39   773
15.630–31   729
15.659–60   564
15.669–70   564
15.745–50   178
15.758–59   880
15.823–24   856
15.843–51   178
15.859–60   880
15.877–79   865

*Tristia*
1.2.4–5   371
1.10.43   454
1.10.44   454
2.324   1242
3.3.45–46   1160
4.1.11–12   806
4.4.13   921
5.5.8   1189

**Parthenius**

*L.R.*
6.6   877
11.1–3   22
14.5   22
26.4   556, 718
29.2   777

**Pausanias**
1.23.2   55
1.32.5   1158, 1159
1.40.1   299
1.40.3   627
2.1.1   229
2.2.8   744
2.3.5   229, 637
2.5.3   730
2.5.5   22
2.10.2   637
2.20.6   627
2.26.1   637
2.26.3–7   22
2.26.4   607
2.26.5   837
2.27.2   564
2.27.3   253
2.27.4   837
2.27.6   637
2.29.8   723
2.32.2   773
2.35.5   1188
3.11.5   178, 299
3.12.4   160
3.16.2–3   659, 1189
3.23.4   523
4.34.6   627
5.22.5   877
5.24.9   877
6.11.9   298
6.20.3   1188
8.9.6–8   298
8.23.7   773
8.29.1   877
8.31.2   627
8.48.5–6   922
8.51.7   922
9.17.1–2   743
9.22.7   298
9.25.1   743
9.25.10   523
9.26.8   627
9.31.7   20, 22
9.33.6   5239.39.5–7   604
9.39.8   604
10.9.11   877
10.16.3   730

**Persius**

*Sat.*
1.28   1123
2.69–75   617
5.179–84   219, 1122

*Rep.*
2.364BC   715
2.372D   900, 901
2.376A   808
5.452C   1138, 1229
5.472   1114
474BC   424
6.484BD   796
6.484B   572
6.490AB   328
6.508E   406
7.527E   418
10.611BC   553
10.611DE   299, 554
10.621D   137

*Sophist*
   223
221D   967, 1183
227D   910
230D   910

*Statesman*
270DE   541

*Symp.*
   896
200–2   324
217–18   917
222E–223A   915

*Theaet.*
175A   721
191D   582

*Tim.*
   377
28C   237
29A–30   377
29E   377
30B–34B   527
31   414

**Plautus**

*Bacchides*
4.7.25   1119

*Captives*
1.147   414
1.150   414

*Miles gloriosus*
2.6–7   1238

*Mostell.*
2.1.12–13   1136
2.1.360   1210
3.2.63, §850   1132

*Soldier*
2.4.6–7, §§359–60   1133

**Pliny the Elder**

*N.H.*
2.5.17   371
2.18.82   877
2.95.208   637
5.15.70   218, 869
5.15.71   637
5.15.72   577, 637
6.84–85   160
7.49   404
7.124   837
9.16.43–9.45.84   1232
9.16.43   1232
14.4.20–14.5.52   989
14.6.53–14.22.118   501
14.23.119   989
17.35.156–87   989
17.35.190   994
17.35.191   994
17.35.192   994
20.54.152   1146
22.68.138   1223
24.102   902
27.75   780
28.4.6   256
28.5   780
28.11.46   1181, 1210
28.48   780
28.61   780
28.77   780
29.12   780
29.32   780
32.39   780

**Pliny the Younger**

*Ep.*
2.1.10–11   847
2.6.2   1008
2.6.3–4   907
2.11   1105, 1128
3.21.1–6   847
7.3.2   1008
9.13.2   179
10.18.190–91   310
10.65.3   178
10.96–97   179, 1027, 1077
10.96   199, 202, 696, 1027
10.97   852, 1103

*Pan.*
11.1   178
29.1–5   676

**Plotinus**

*On Virtues*
1.2.7   291, 299, 554
1.4   235
1.5.3   553
1.6   248
1.6.9   248
1.8   375, 552
2.1.1   376
2.4   375, 552
2.9   168
2.9.8   375
3.1   573
3.2   377
3.6   375, 552
3.6.6–7   375
4.7–8   553

**Plutarch**
   9, 10, 13, 18, 24, 33, 70, 639,
   967

*Advice about Keeping Well, Mor.
122B–137E*
   256

*Aemilius Paulus*
1.1   17
11.3   706

*Agesilaus*
   859, 1069
10.3   721
21.4–5   63
23.6   1007

*Alc.*
   917
2.2   1121
3.1   18
4.1   997
7.3   926
16.1   669
20.5   1078
21.2–4   1020
22.2   1188
26.2   1208
34.1   496
39.1–2   896

*Alex.*
1.1–3   12
1.1–2   12
1.1   1214
1.2   1214
1.3   251, 1214
2.2–3.2   292
12.3   504

---

⁷ After *Mor.* 919E in LCL, but preserved only in Latin.

## Varro

*Agriculture*

*Lat. Lang.*

## *Vendidad* (Persian source)

## Virgil

*Aen.*